THE CAMBRIDGE HISTORY OF
RUSSIA

This first volume of the Cambridge History of Russia covers the
period from early ('Kievan') Rus' to the start of Peter the Great's
reign in 1689. It surveys the development of Russia through the
Mongol invasions to the expansion of the Muscovite state in
the sixteenth and seventeenth centuries and deals with political,
social, economic and cultural issues under the Riurikid and early
Romanov rulers. The volume is organised on a primarily chronological basis, but a number of general themes are also addressed,
including the bases of political legitimacy; law and society; the inter-
actions of Russians and non-Russians; and the relationship of the
state with the Orthodox Church. The international team of authors
incorporates the latest Russian and Western scholarship and offers
an authoritative new account of the formative 'pre-Petrine' period
of Russian history, before the process of Europeanisation had made
a significant impact on society and culture.

MAUREEN PERRIE is Emeritus Professor of Russian History at
the University of Birmingham. She has published extensively on
Russian history from the sixteenth to the twentieth century. Her
publications include *Pretenders and Popular Monarchism in Early
Modern Russia: The False Tsars of the Time of Troubles* (1995) and
The Cult of Ivan the Terrible in Stalin's Russia (2001).

THE CAMBRIDGE
HISTORY OF
RUSSIA

⋆

VOLUME I
From Early Rus' to 1689

⋆

Edited by
MAUREEN PERRIE
University of Birmingham

CAMBRIDGE
UNIVERSITY PRESS

CAMBRIDGE
UNIVERSITY PRESS

University Printing House, Cambridge CB2 8BS, United Kingdom

Cambridge University Press is part of the University of Cambridge.

It furthers the University's mission by disseminating knowledge in the pursuit of education, learning and research at the highest international levels of excellence.

www.cambridge.org
Information on this title: www.cambridge.org/9781107639423

© Cambridge University Press 2006

First published 2006
Reprinted 2010
First paperback edition 2015

A catalogue record for this publication is available from the British Library

ISBN 978-0-521-81227-6 Hardback
ISBN 978-1-107-63942-3 Paperback

Contents

Contents

PART II

THE EXPANSION, CONSOLIDATION AND CRISIS
OF MUSCOVY (1462–1613)

Contents

Plates

Maps

Figures

Genealogical tables

Notes on contributors

SERGEI BOGATYREV is Lecturer in Early Russian History in the School of Slavonic and East European Studies (University College London) and Docent of Early Russian Culture at the University of Helsinki. He is the author of *The Sovereign and His Counsellors: Ritualised Consultations in Muscovite Political Culture, 1350s–1570s* (2000), and the editor and co-author of *Russia Takes Shape. Patterns of Integration from the Middle Ages to the Present* (2004).

ROBERT O. CRUMMEY is Emeritus Professor of History at the University of California, Davis, and author of *The Old Believers and the World of Antichrist: The Vyg Community and the Russian State, 1694–1855* (1970), *Aristocrats and Servitors: The Boyar Elite in Russia, 1613–1689* (1983) and *The Formation of Muscovy, 1304–1613* (1987).

BRIAN DAVIES is Associate Professor of History at the University of Texas at San Antonio and the author of *State Power and Community in Early Modern Russia: The Case of Kozlov, 1635–1649* (2004).

MARTIN DIMNIK is Senior Fellow and President Emeritus, Pontifical Institute of Mediaeval Studies, Toronto, and Professor of Medieval History, University of Toronto. He is the author of *Mikhail, Prince of Chernigov and Grand Prince of Kiev, 1224–1246* (1981), *The Dynasty of Chernigov, 1054–1146* (1994), and *The Dynasty of Chernigov, 1146–1246* (2003).

MICHAEL S. FLIER is Oleksandr Potebnja Professor of Ukrainian Philology at Harvard University. He is co-editor with Henrik Birnbaum of *Medieval Russian Culture* (1984); with Daniel Rowland of *Medieval Russian Culture*, II (1994); and with Henning Andersen of Francis J. Whitfield's *Old Church Slavic Reader* (2004).

SIMON FRANKLIN is Professor of Slavonic Studies at the University of Cambridge and author of *The Emergence of Rus 750–1200* (with Jonathan Shepard, 1996) and *Writing, Society and Culture in Early Rus c. 950–1300* (2002).

RICHARD HELLIE is Thomas E. Donnelly Professor of Russian History, The University of Chicago, and the author of *Enserfment and Military Change in Muscovy* (1971), *Slavery in Russia 1450–1725* (1982) and *The Economy and Material Culture of Russia 1600–1725* (1999).

LINDSEY HUGHES is Professor of Russian History in the School of Slavonic and East European Studies, University College London, and the author of *Sophia Regent of Russia 1657–1704* (1990), *Russia in the Age of Peter the Great* (1998) and *Peter the Great: A Biography* (2002).

V. L. IANIN is an Academician of the Russian Academy of Sciences, and the author of *Novgorod i Litva. Pogranichnye situatsii XIII–XV vekov* [*Novgorod and Lithuania. Frontier Situations in the 13th–15th centuries*] (1998), *U istokov novgorodskoi gosudarstvennosti* [*The Origins of Novgorod's Statehood*] (2001) and *Novgorodskie posadniki* [*The Governors of Novgorod*] (2nd edn, 2003).

MICHAEL KHODARKOVSKY is a Professor of History at Loyola University, Chicago. He is the author of *Where Two Worlds Met: The Russian State and the Kalmyk Nomads, 1600–1771* (1992) and of *Russia's Steppe Frontier: The Making of a Colonial Empire, 1500–1800* (2002); and the editor, with Robert Geraci, of *Of Religion and Empire: Missions, Conversion, and Tolerance in Tsarist Russia* (2001).

NANCY SHIELDS KOLLMANN is William H. Bonsall Professor in History at Stanford University and the author of *Kinship and Politics. The Making of the Muscovite Political System, 1345–1547* (1987) and *By Honor Bound. State and Society in Early Modern Russia* (1999).

JANET MARTIN is Professor of History at the University of Miami and author of *Treasure of the Land of Darkness: The Fur Trade and its Significance for Medieval Russia* (1986, pb 2004) and *Medieval Russia 980–1584* (1995).

DAVID B. MILLER is Emeritus Professor of Russian History at Roosevelt University, Chicago, and the author of *The Velikie Minei Chetii and the Stepennaia Kniga of Metropolitan Makarii and the Origins of Russian National Consciousness* (1979) and numerous articles on the history of Muscovite and Kievan Russia.

DONALD OSTROWSKI is Research Adviser in the Social Sciences and Lecturer in Extension Studies at Harvard University. He is the author of *Muscovy and the Mongols: Cross-Cultural Influences on the Steppe Frontier, 1304–1589* (1998) and the editor and compiler of *The Povest' vremennykh let: an Interlinear Collation and Paradosis* (2003).

A. P. PAVLOV is Senior Research Fellow in the Institute of History of the Russian Academy of Sciences, St Petersburg, and the author of *Gosudarev dvor i politicheskaia bor'ba pri Borise Godunove (1584–1605 gg.)* [*The Sovereign's Court and Political Conflict under Boris Godunov, 1584–1605*] (1992) and, with Maureen Perrie, *Ivan the Terrible* (2003).

MAUREEN PERRIE is Emeritus Professor of Russian History at the University of Birmingham and the author of *Pretenders and Popular Monarchism in Early Modern Russia: The False Tsars of the Time of Troubles* (1995) and, with Andrei Pavlov, *Ivan the Terrible* (2003).

MARSHALL POE writes for *The Atlantic Monthly*. He is the author of '*A People Born to Slavery': Russia in Early Modern European Ethnography, 1476–1748* (2000), *The Russian Moment in World History* (2003), and *The Russian Elite in the Seventeenth Century* (2 vols., 2004).

DENIS J. B. SHAW is Reader in Russian Geography at the University of Birmingham. He is the author of *Russia in the Modern World* (1999), of *Landscape and Settlement in Romanov Russia, 1613–1917* (with Judith Pallot, 1990) and of articles and chapters on the historical geography of early modern Russia.

JONATHAN SHEPARD was formerly University Lecturer in Russian History at the University of Cambridge and is co-author (with Simon Franklin) of *The Emergence of Rus 750–1200* (1996), and editor of *The Cambridge History of the Byzantine Empire* (2006, forthcoming).

Acknowledgements

I should like to thank all those individuals who have provided me with help and support in the preparation of this volume. I am particularly grateful to Simon Franklin for his advice on the earliest centuries, and for his comments on my draft translation of V. L. Ianin's chapter on Novgorod. Denis Shaw was always willing to lend a sympathetic ear to my editorial grumblings about contributors who were less punctual and conscientious than he was.

The University of Birmingham has provided invaluable back-up throughout the project. I am especially indebted to Marea Arries and Tricia Carr of the Centre for Russian and East European Studies for secretarial assistance; and to Geoff Goode and Hugh Jenkins of the School of Social Sciences for IT support. Nigel Hardware of the Alexander Baykov Library has been unfailingly helpful. Thanks also to Anne Ankcorn and Kevin Burkhill of the School of Geography, Earth and Environmental Sciences for drawing the maps for Chapters 2 and 25.

Note on dates and transliteration

The volume uses the simplified form of the Library of Congress system of transliteration; old orthography has been modernised. Some proper names have been anglicised rather than transliterated, especially in the case of rulers whose names are best known to non-specialists in this form, for example Tsars Michael, Alexis and Peter (rather than Mikhail, Aleksei and Petr) in the seventeenth century. Most Tatar and other Turkic names are given in anglicised (rather than Russified) forms.

Dates follow the Old Style (Julian) calendar. Years began on 1 September: where the month is not known, they are given in the form 1598/9.

Chronology

1157	Death of Iurii Dolgorukii
1159	Rostislav Mstislavich becomes prince of Kiev
1167	Death of Rostislav; Mstislav Iziaslavich becomes prince of Kiev
1169	Andrei Bogoliubskii attacks Kiev
1176	Sviatoslav Vsevolodovich becomes prince of Kiev
1177	Vsevolod 'Big Nest' becomes prince of Vladimir
1185	Prince Igor' is defeated by the Polovtsy
1194	Death of Sviatoslav; Riurik Rostislavich becomes prince of Kiev
1203	Riurik sacks Kiev in course of dynastic conflict
1208	Death of Riurik; Vsevolod Chermnyi ('the Red') becomes prince of Kiev
1212	Deaths of Vsevolod Big Nest and Vsevolod the Red; Mstislav Romanovich becomes prince of Kiev
1223	Tatars defeat princes of Rus' at Battle of Kalka; Mstislav is killed and Vladimir Riurikovich becomes prince of Kiev
1237	Mikhail Vsevolodovich of Chernigov becomes prince of Kiev; Tatar invasion begins
1240	Tatars capture Kiev; Aleksandr Nevskii defeats Swedes on River Neva
1242	Aleksandr Nevskii defeats Teutonic Knights at Lake Chud'
1243	Khan Baty appoints Iaroslav Vsevolodovich of Vladimir as prince of Kiev in place of Mikhail
1246	Baty executes Mikhail; Iaroslav dies
1247	Sviatoslav Vsevolodovich becomes prince of Vladimir
1249	Andrei Iaroslavich becomes prince of Vladimir
1252	Aleksandr Nevskii becomes prince of Vladimir
1263	Death of Aleksandr Nevskii; Iaroslav Iaroslavich becomes prince of Vladimir
1271/2	Death of Iaroslav
1272	Vasilii Iaroslavich becomes prince of Vladimir
1277	Death of Vasilii; Dmitrii Aleksandrovich becomes prince of Vladimir
1294	Death of Dmitrii; Andrei Aleksandrovich becomes prince of Vladimir
1299	Metropolitan Maksim moves from Kiev to Vladimir
1304	Death of Andrei; Mikhail Iaroslavich of Tver' becomes prince of Vladimir
1318	Mikhail executed by Khan Uzbek; Iurii Daniilovich of Moscow becomes prince of Vladimir
1322	Dmitrii Mikhailovich of Tver' becomes prince of Vladimir

1325	Dmitrii executed by Uzbek; Aleksandr Mikhailovich of Tver' becomes prince of Vladimir
1331	Ivan Daniilovich of Moscow (Ivan I Kalita) becomes sole grand prince of Vladimir
1341	Death of Ivan Kalita; Semen Ivanovich becomes grand prince of Vladimir
1353	Death of Semen; Ivan II Ivanovich becomes grand prince of Vladimir
1359	Death of Ivan II
1362	Dmitrii Ivanovich of Moscow (Dmitrii Donskoi) becomes grand prince of Vladimir
1380	Battle of Kulikovo
1389	Death of Dmitrii Donskoi; Vasilii I Dmitr'evich becomes grand prince of Vladimir
1425	Death of Vasilii I; Vasilii II Vasil'evich becomes grand prince of Vladimir
1437–9	Council of Ferrara-Florence: proclaims reunion of Orthodox and Catholic Churches
1441	Vasilii II rejects union with Rome, and deposes Metropolitan Isidor
1448	Russian bishops elect Bishop Iona of Riazan' as metropolitan
1453	Constantinople falls to the Turks
1456	Treaty of Iazhelbitsii with Novgorod
1462	Death of Vasilii II; Ivan III Vasil'evich becomes grand prince of Muscovy
1472	Sophia Palaeologa becomes second wife of Ivan III
1478	Ivan III annexes Novgorod
1480	Encounter with Great Horde on River Ugra
1485	Ivan III annexes Tver'
1497	Law Code (*sudebnik*) issued
1498	Ivan III has his grandson Dmitrii Ivanovich crowned as co-ruler and heir
1502	Ivan III arrests Dmitrii Ivanovich
1503	Church Council meets
1504	Heretics are condemned by a Church Council
1505	Death of Ivan III; Vasilii III Ivanovich becomes grand prince
1510	Vasilii III annexes Pskov
1514	Vasilii III annexes Smolensk
1521	Vasilii III annexes Riazan'
1521	Crimean Tatars attack Moscow

1525	Vasilii III divorces his first wife, Solomoniia
1526	Vasilii III marries Elena Glinskaia
1533	Death of Vasilii III; Ivan IV Vasil'evich becomes grand prince
1538	Death of Ivan's mother, the regent Elena Glinskaia
1542	Makarii becomes metropolitan
1547	Ivan IV is crowned with the title of 'tsar'
1550	New Law Code issued
1551	*Stoglav* Church Council meets
1552	Conquest of Kazan'
1556	Conquest of Astrakhan'
1558–83	Livonian war
1563	Death of Metropolitan Makarii
1565–72	*oprichnina*
1566	First 'Assembly of the Land'
1569	Ottoman–Crimean expedition against Astrakhan'
1570	*oprichniki* sack Novgorod
1571	Crimean Tatars burn Moscow
1572	Crimean Tatars defeated at Battle of Molodi
1575–6	Ivan installs Simeon Bekbulatovich as grand prince of Moscow
1581	Ivan kills his son and heir, Tsarevich Ivan Ivanovich
1582	Ermak defeats Siberian khan
1584	Death of Ivan IV; Fedor Ivanovich becomes tsar
1589	Russian patriarchate established
1591	Death of Tsarevich Dmitrii Ivanovich of Uglich
1597	Legislation on peasants and slaves
1598	Death of Tsar Fedor; election of Boris Godunov as tsar
1601–3	Famine
c.1603–13	'Time of Troubles'
1603	Appearance of First False Dmitrii in Poland
1604	First False Dmitrii invades Russia
1605	Death of Boris Godunov, murder of his son Fedor; First False Dmitrii becomes tsar
1606	Overthrow and murder of First False Dmitrii; Vasilii Shuiskii becomes tsar
1606–7	Bolotnikov revolt
1607–10	Second False Dmitrii challenges Shuiskii
1609	Swedes intervene to support Shuiskii; Poles besiege Smolensk
1610	Shuiskii is deposed; throne is offered to Prince Władysław of Poland; Poles occupy Moscow; Second False Dmitrii is murdered

1611	First national militia attempts to liberate Moscow
1612	Second national militia, led by Minin and Pozharskii, succeeds in liberating Moscow
1613	Michael Romanov is elected tsar
1617	Treaty of Stolbovo with Sweden
1618	Treaty of Deulino with Poland
1619	Filaret Romanov becomes patriarch
1632–4	Smolensk war
1633	Death of Patriarch Filaret
1634	Peace of Polianovka with Poland
1637	Don cossacks capture Azov
1645	Death of Michael; Alexis becomes tsar
1648	Popular uprising in Moscow
1648	Bohdan Khmel'nyts'kyi leads revolt against Poland in Ukraine
1649	Conciliar Law Code (*Ulozhenie*) issued
1652	Nikon becomes patriarch
1654	Pereiaslav Treaty
1654–67	Thirteen Years War
1662	'Copper riot' in Moscow
1666	Nikon is deposed as patriarch
1666–7	Church councils confirm new rites
1668–76	Siege of Solovetskii monastery
1670–71	Sten'ka Razin's revolt
1676	Death of Alexis; Fedor Alekseevich becomes tsar
1676–81	Russo-Turkish war
1682	Death of Fedor; Ivan V and Peter I become co-tsars, under the regency of their sister, Sophia
1689	Overthrow of Regent Sophia

List of abbreviations

AAE	*Akty, sobrannye v bibliotekakh i arkhivakh Rossiiskoi imperii Arkheograficheskoiu ekspeditsieiu Imperatorskoi Akademii nauk*
AI	*Akty Istoricheskie, sobrannye i izdannye Arkheograficheskoiu Kommissieiu*
AN SSSR	Akademiia nauk SSSR
CASS	*Canadian-American Slavic Studies*
ChOIDR	*Chteniia v Imperatorskom Obshchestve Istorii i Drevnostei Rossii pri Moskovskom Universitete*
DopAI	*Dopolneniia k Aktam Istoricheskim, sobrannye i izdannye Arkheograficheskoiu Kommissieiu*
FOG	*Forschungen zur osteuropäischen Geschichte*
HUS	*Harvard Ukrainian Studies*
IZ	*Istoricheskie Zapiski*
JGO	*Jahrbücher für Geschichte Osteuropas*
Kritika	*Kritika: Explorations in Russian and Eurasian History* (new series)
LGU	Leningradskii Gosudarstvennyi Universitet
MERSH	*Modern Encyclopedia of Russian and Soviet History*
MGU	Moskovskii Gosudarstvennyi Universitet
PRP	*Pamiatniki russkogo prava*
PSRL	*Polnoe sobranie russkikh letopisei*
RAN	Rossiiskaia Akademiia Nauk
RH	*Russian History / Histoire Russe*
RR	*Russian Review*
RZ	*Rossiiskoe zakonodatel'stvo X–XX vekov*
SEER	*Slavonic and East European Review*
SGGD	*Sobranie Gosudarstvennykh Gramot i Dokumentov, khraniashchikhsia v Gosudarstvennoi kollegii inostrannykh del*
SR	*Slavic Review*
TODRL	*Trudy Otdela drevnerusskoi literatury*
VI	*Voprosy istorii*

I

Introduction

MAUREEN PERRIE

This first volume of the three-volume *Cambridge History of Russia* deals with
the period before the reign of Peter the Great. The concept of the 'pre-
Petrine' period has a profound resonance in Russian intellectual and cultural
history. Although Russia had not been entirely immune from Western influences before Peter's reign, the speed and scale of Europeanisation increased
greatly from the beginning of the eighteenth century. This process was deeply
divisive, and its significance and effects were debated in the nineteenth century by 'Westerniser' intellectuals, who favoured modernisation, and their
'Slavophile' opponents, who idealised the Muscovite past. In the post-Soviet
period, as Russians attempt to reconstruct their national identity after the
experience of seven decades of state socialism, aspects of this debate have been
revived. The pre-Petrine period has come to be seen in some neo-Slavophile
circles as the repository of indigenous Russian values, uncontaminated by the
Western influences which were to lead eventually to the disastrous Communist
experiment. For many contemporary Westernisers, by contrast, the origins
of the Stalinist dictatorship lay not so much in the dogmas of Marxism as
in old Muscovite traditions of autocracy and despotism. Such views, which
have found an echo in much Western journalistic commentary and in some
popular English-language histories of Russia, tend to be based on outdated
and ill-informed studies. The present volume, which brings together the most
recent interpretations of serious scholars in order to provide an authoritative
and reliable new account of pre-Petrine Russia, is designed to advance the
knowledge and understanding of the period in the anglophone world.

The scope of the volume: what and where is pre-Petrine Russia?

Defining the space to be covered in a history of pre-Petrine Russia poses a particular problem in the post-Soviet period, when the legacy of early ('Kievan')

I

Rus' is claimed by the newly independent Ukrainian and Belarusian states as well as by the Russian Federation. Instead of projecting present-day political and ethnic/national identities into the past, I have chosen to use the dynastic-political criteria which operated in the period itself: thus, the volume focuses on the territories ruled by the Riurikid dynasty (the descendants of the semi-legendary figure of Riurik the Viking) from the tenth to the sixteenth centuries, and by their successors the Romanovs in the seventeenth. The south-western lands of Rus' are largely excluded from consideration in the period when they formed part of Poland-Lithuania (medieval Novgorod is, however, included). This approach acknowledges the existence of a degree of political continuity between early Rus' and Muscovy, without rejecting the claims of present-day Ukraine and Belarus (or the other post-Soviet states) to national histories of their own which are separate and distinct from that of Russia.

Since 'Russia' throughout this period has been identified as that territory which was ruled by the Riurikid grand princes and tsars to 1598, and by their successors thereafter, it occupies a shifting space with constantly changing boundaries. Many of the south-western lands of early Rus' were incorporated into Poland-Lithuania from the fourteenth century, and were annexed by Muscovy only from the mid-seventeenth. By this time the Muscovite state had expanded far beyond the boundaries of the principalities of the north-east that it had absorbed before the reign of Ivan IV. The conquest of the Tatar khanates of Kazan' and Astrakhan', in the 1550s, opened the way to expansion beyond the Volga, into the North Caucasus and Siberia. Expansion westward proved to be more difficult, however, and important cities such as Smolensk and (more briefly) Novgorod were lost as a result of the 'Time of Troubles' of the early seventeenth century.

The geographical space within these shifting and expanding boundaries both shaped, and was shaped by, the institutions of pre-Petrine Russia. The trade routes along the river systems between the Baltic Sea in the north and the Black and Caspian Seas to the south were important for the development of early Rus'. The soils of the forest zones of the north-east afforded low yields for agriculture, and although arable farming was supplemented by produce from the forests and rivers, Russia's rulers in the Muscovite period faced the problems of marshalling scarce resources. Territorial expansion southwards into the forest-steppe and steppe provided access to potentially more productive resources and profitable trade routes; but the great distances involved, together with poor means of communication, posed major challenges for political control and administrative integration.

The organisation and structure of the volume

Striking the appropriate balance between thematic and chronological organisation is a perennial problem for historians. A purely thematic structure would
have posed particular problems for a volume such as this, which spans a period
of several centuries. My preference has been for a primarily chronological
approach, in the hope that this will provide a coherent narrative framework
for the non-specialist reader who uses the volume as a work of reference.
Within this framework, a number of thematic chapters have been commissioned, which are proportionally more prominent for the later centuries.

The period covered by this first volume of the three-volume set begins at the
origins of Rus', about AD 900 (the *Primary Chronicle* dates the activity of Riurik
to the ninth century). The volume ends around 1689 – a choice of date which
may require some explanation. After the death of Tsar Fedor Alekseevich in
1682 his sister, Tsarevna Sophia, acted as regent for her two younger brothers,
the co-tsars Ivan and Peter. Ivan, the elder tsar and Sophia's full brother, was
mentally incompetent, and although he lived until 1696, the year 1689, when
Sophia was overthrown as regent, is conventionally regarded as the beginning
of independent rule by her half-brother, Peter (subsequently to be known as
'the Great'). The year 1689 may therefore be considered to mark the end of
the 'pre-Petrine' era, and the start of the transition to the St Petersburg or
imperial period of Russian history. This latter period, which was to last until
1917, comprises the subject-matter of the second volume of the *Cambridge
History of Russia*.

I have divided pre-Petrine Russia into three main sub-periods: (1) early Rus'
and the rise of Muscovy (c.900–1462); (2) the expansion, consolidation and crisis
of Muscovy (1462–1613); and (3) the early Romanov tsardom (1613–89). Just as
political-dynastic criteria have been applied in order to define the territorial
scope of the volume, its chronological subdivision, too, employs dynastic
criteria. Thus the accession of Grand Prince Ivan III in 1462 has been chosen as
the watershed between the first two sub-periods (rather than the 'stand on the
River Ugra' in 1480, for example – which is sometimes regarded as marking
the end of Mongol overlordship). Rather more arbitrarily, I have chosen as the
starting point of the third sub-period the election of the first Romanov tsar
in 1613, rather than the end of the old (Riurikid) dynasty in 1598, which was
followed by the upheaval of the 'Time of Troubles' (c.1603–13).

The later centuries have been dealt with in the greatest detail, in conformity
with the broader allocation of space within the three-volume *Cambridge History
of Russia* (which allows one volume each for the tenth to seventeenth centuries;

the eighteenth and nineteenth centuries; and the twentieth century). Thus in this volume the 'short' seventeenth century has been allocated roughly the same amount of space as the 'long' sixteenth, and each of these has rather more space than the entire pre-1462 period.

The volume begins with two prefatory chapters. This Introduction sets the agenda by outlining the main themes of the volume; it also deals with some historiographical issues. It is followed by a contextualising 'historical geography' chapter, exploring the natural environment within which pre-Petrine Russia evolved, and its implications for economic, social and political development.

The main body of the text is divided into three Parts, corresponding to the sub-periods identified above. In Part I the principle of subdivision is chronological, with the exception of Chapter 8, which covers the history of medieval Novgorod across the entire period (and slightly beyond), from its origins to its annexation by Moscow. In Part II (the 'long' sixteenth century), four predominantly political-historical chapters, organised on a chronological basis, are supplemented by six thematic chapters dealing with aspects of the period as a whole. In the third and final Part (the 'short' seventeenth century) a purely thematic organisation has been adopted, in view of the degree of political continuity within the period.

The sub-period covered in Part I is the longest in duration and the most territorially diverse, encompassing early ('Kievan') Rus' as well as the north-eastern principalities during the period of Mongol suzerainty. The primarily chronological division of the Part into chapters follows the same political-dynastic criteria as the broader subdivision of the volume. Thus Chapter 3 covers the period to the death of Vladimir Sviatoslavich (1015), Chapter 4 ends with the death of Vladimir Monomakh (1125) and Chapter 5 with that of Mikhail of Chernigov in 1246, the year in which Iaroslav of Vladimir also died. Chapter 6 is devoted to the reigns of the princes of Vladimir and Moscow to the death of Ivan II in 1359; and Chapter 7 concludes with the death of Vasilii II in 1462. In terms of alternative approaches to periodisation, Chapters 3–5 roughly correlate with the Kievan or pre-Mongol period of the history of Rus', while Chapters 6–7 deal with the centuries of Mongol suzerainty (sometimes described as the 'apanage period' or the 'period of feudal fragmentation').

In Part II the subdivision into the four 'chronological' chapters is again political-dynastic. The first of these (Chapter 9) covers the reigns of Grand Princes Ivan III (1462–1505) and Vasilii III (1505–33) – a period which witnessed the process sometimes known as the 'gathering of the lands of Rus'' (the territorial expansion of Moscow to include the other north-eastern principalities).

Chapter 10 is devoted to the reign of Ivan IV ('the Terrible'), who oversaw the formation of what Soviet historians described as 'the centralised multinational state' (the administrative integration of the Tatar khanates of Kazan' and Astrakhan', conquered in the 1550s) as well as the Livonian war (1558–83) and the reign of terror associated with the creation of the *oprichnina* (1565–72). Chapter 11 deals not only with the reign of Tsar Fedor Ivanovich (1584–98), whose death marked the end of the Riurikid dynasty, but also with that of his successor, Boris Godunov (1598–1605). The Time of Troubles, here defined chronologically as spanning the period from 1603 (the appearance of the First False Dmitrii in Poland-Lithuania) to Michael Romanov's election as tsar in 1613, is the subject of Chapter 18, which is placed at the end of the Part in order to provide a 'bridge' to Part III.

Topics to which thematic chapters are devoted in both Parts II and III are: the rural and urban economy and society (Chapters 12, 13, 23, 25); Russian relations with non-Christians and non-Russians (Chapters 14 and 22); the Orthodox Church (Chapters 15 and 27); and the law (Chapters 16 and 24). Part II also includes a chapter on political ideas and rituals (Chapter 17), while Part III has chapters on popular revolts (Chapter 26) and on cultural and intellectual life (Chapter 28). Three 'core' political themes addressed in the 'chronological' chapters of Part II (Chapters 9–11 and 18) are dealt with separately in Part III: central government and its institutions (Chapter 19); local government and administration (Chapter 20); and foreign relations, territorial expansion and warfare (Chapter 21). Most of these topics are of course also dealt with (albeit more briefly) in the 'chronological' chapters of Part I.

Themes of pre-Petrine history

In addition to the issues which are addressed in the 'thematic' chapters in Parts II and III, a number of general topics are traced throughout the volume, in both the 'chronological' and 'thematic' chapters. It may be helpful to the reader if I outline these themes briefly here, and signpost the chapters in which they are discussed.

The external environment and its impact

The first set of themes relates to the fact that pre-Petrine Russia in general, and Muscovy in particular, was a rapidly expanding state which almost continuously acquired territory and population at the expense of its neighbours, so that the external enemies of one century often became part of the internal 'nationalities problem' of the next. The Russian rulers had to adopt a range of strategies in order to acquire, incorporate and defend their new territories, and military requirements profoundly influenced the development of state and society.

Over the period, Russia's rulers faced a succession of enemies who threatened their lands. As demonstrated in Part I, the princes of Rus' had to do battle with many nomadic steppe peoples before the Mongols invaded in the thirteenth century. Muscovy's position within the Eurasian land mass gave rise to the danger of simultaneous warfare in the south and the west, and presented the diplomatic challenge of avoiding war on two fronts: the Russians' main adversaries in the sixteenth and seventeenth centuries were the Livonian knights, Poland-Lithuania and Sweden in the west, and the Crimean Tatars and Ottoman Turks in the south. The wars conducted by the Muscovite rulers in the sixteenth century are described in Part II in Chapters 9–11, 14 and 18; while Chapter 21 in Part III is devoted to foreign relations and warfare in the seventeenth century. Moscow's territorial expansion through its annexation of the other principalities of north-eastern Russia is described in Chapters 7 and 9; Chapter 14 covers the conquest of Kazan', Astrakhan' and Siberia in the sixteenth century; and Chapter 21 pays particular attention to the important period in which the Ukrainian lands of the Polish-Lithuanian Commonwealth were annexed by Muscovy in the seventeenth.

The Slavic inhabitants of early Rus' had to coexist with the non-Slav nomads of the steppes; and from the sixteenth century, with the conquest of the Tatar khanates of Kazan' and Astrakhan' and subsequent expansion into Siberia, Muscovy acquired an increasingly multinational (multiethnic) character. Michael Khodarkovsky's chapters in Parts II and III consider the ways in which the Russian rulers incorporated non-Russians (most of whom before the sixteenth century were also non-Christians) into their realm.

Russian territorial expansion did not always involve the annexation of lands with an existing settled population. From the late sixteenth century, Muscovy acquired an open steppe frontier to the south and east, which gave rise to processes of colonisation both 'from above' (state-sponsored settlement) and 'from below' (spontaneous peasant migration). These processes are outlined in Chapter 2, while Chapters 11 and 18 in Part II describe the building of defensive lines of new towns in the south, the growth of the cossack hosts and their relationship with the state both before and during the Time of Troubles. Moscow's relations with the Don and Zaporozhian cossacks in the seventeenth century, and the fortification of the south-west frontier, are described in Chapter 21 of Part III.

The requirements of military defence had important implications for Russia's internal political, economic and social development. The military retainers of the princes of Kievan Rus' also acted as his political advisers. The obligation of noble landowners to provide military service to the state laid the basis of the Muscovite political system, as Donald Ostrowski explains in Chapter 9 and, as the frontier moved further south into the steppe, the military servitors' demands for control of peasant labour on their estates led to the legal imposition of serfdom in the mid-seventeenth century (see Chapter 23). The military reforms of the seventeenth century which were necessitated by competition with the 'new formation' regiments of Poland-Lithuania and Sweden are described in Chapter 21; and it may have been the requirements of military efficiency, as Marshall Poe suggests in Chapter 19, that led to the political reforms of Tsar Alexis's reign which involved the promotion of 'new men'.

Internal developments

The main focus of this volume is on the development of the Russian state and society, and much attention is paid to political, economic and social issues, including the law, the Orthodox Church and intellectual and cultural life. Political history provides the main organising framework of the volume, and issues of dynastic succession and political legitimacy constitute a major theme of the 'chronological' chapters in Parts I and II as well as of the 'thematic' political chapters in Part III.

In both early Rus' and Muscovy the political legitimacy of rulers was derived from succession systems whose ambiguities often gave rise to conflicts and civil wars. The complex combination of vertical and lateral (or collateral) principles of succession which operated in Kievan Rus' were modified by regional allocations of territory within the dynasty and sometimes by naked power struggles. The legitimacy of the succession was often challenged, whether in relation to the title of grand prince of Kiev or later to that of grand prince of Vladimir. After the Mongol invasion the principles of succession to the grand-princely throne of Vladimir initially continued to operate on a similar basis to those to the Kievan throne. In the fourteenth century, however, as Janet Martin explains (Chapters 6, 7), the descendants of Daniil Aleksandrovich of Moscow acquired the title of grand prince with the support of the Mongol khans, although Daniil himself had not served as grand prince, and the descendants of his cousin Mikhail of Tver' had a stronger claim on the basis of the traditional criterion that 'a prince sits on the throne of his father'. After a series of dynastic wars, the Daniilovich branch of the Riurikid dynasty retained their hold on the grand-princely title against rivals with apparently stronger claims.

They owed their victory largely to the backing of the khans, and also to support from the leaders of the Orthodox Church.

In fifteenth-century Muscovy there was a shift from collateral to linear (vertical) succession, but this change too was not unchallenged; after the death of Vasilii I in 1425, for example, the late grand prince's younger brother Iurii contested the succession of his son, Vasilii II. From the mid-sixteenth century, when the Muscovite rulers boosted their status by adopting the title of 'tsar' (khan, emperor), the ritual of coronation provided an additional source of legitimation, through the sacralisation of the ruler: the tsars were 'divinely crowned' and later also 'divinely anointed'. Semi-legendary tales tracing the ancestry of the dynasty back not only to early Rus', but even to ancient Rome, also served to promote the status of the dynasty. Subsequently, when it suited their purpose the Muscovite rulers also claimed to be the legitimate successors of the Mongol khans.

The end of the Riurikid dynasty in 1598 created a major crisis of political legitimacy. The introduction of the elective principle contributed to the upheaval of the Time of Troubles, when the accession of Tsars Boris Godunov and Vasilii Shuiskii was challenged by a series of pretenders (royal impostors) claiming to be scions of the old dynasty. The election of Michael Romanov by an Assembly of the Land in 1613 restored stability, although the new dynasty still found it necessary to supplement its elective legitimacy by emphasising continuity with the Riurikids (Michael was the great-nephew of Anastasiia Romanovna, the first wife of Ivan IV), and claiming that the young Romanov tsar was chosen by God. Fears of new pretenders continued to preoccupy the Romanov rulers throughout the seventeenth century, when rituals and ceremonies were developed further in order to buttress the legitimacy of the dynasty.

In addition to these central issues of political legitimacy, the 'chronological' chapters in Parts I and II examine the relationships of the grand princes and tsars with their elite servitors and advisers. They consider the nature and extent of formal and informal constraints on the power of the ruler, including the role of the prince's *druzhina* (retinue) in Kievan Rus', the *veche* (city assembly) in medieval Novgorod, and the 'boyar duma (council)' and the *zemskii sobor* (Assembly of the Land) in Muscovy. These themes, together with transformations in the composition of the 'ruling elite', are discussed in more detail in Marshall Poe's chapter (19) in Part III, on central government and its institutions in the seventeenth century.

The shifting balance of responsibility between local and central government is an important theme throughout the volume, and especially in relation to sixteenth- and seventeenth-century Muscovy. There were major reforms of local government in the mid-sixteenth century, when centrally appointed provincial officials were partially replaced by elected institutions of local self-government. Sergei Bogatyrev argues in Chapter 10 that, while accommodating local identities, these reforms also served the political needs of the state. From the late sixteenth century, and especially in the seventeenth century after the Time of Troubles, as Brian Davies describes in Chapter 20, the functions of the locally elected bodies were progressively replaced by governors appointed by Moscow, as part of a broader pattern of increased state control of the localities. Additional mechanisms were necessary, however, in order to prevent the governors from acquiring too many powers of their own at the expense of the centre.

The absence of legal limitations on the power of the ruler is often regarded as a distinguishing feature of Russian autocracy, but both early Rus' and Muscovy possessed well-developed legal systems. The volume examines the development of the law codes, from the eleventh-century *Russkaia pravda* through the *sudebniki* of 1497 and 1550 to the *Ulozhenie* of 1649. Richard Hellie in his chapter on sixteenth-century law emphasises the function of the law as a means of state centralisation and mobilisation, while Nancy Kollmann draws attention to the diversity which still persisted in the seventeenth.

From the conversion of Vladimir Sviatoslavich in 988 the Orthodox Church was associated with the Riurikid dynasty and provided its princes with legitimacy. Together with the dynasty itself, the Church constituted a major element of continuity between Kievan and Muscovite Rus', with the transfer of the metropolitanate from Kiev to Vladimir and subsequently to Moscow; and the metropolitans played an important role in establishing the legitimacy of the Daniilovich branch of the dynasty as grand princes of Vladimir in the fourteenth century. The role of the Orthodox Church as a unifying factor in the Rus'ian lands, and as a source of national identity, was particularly important when the state was weak, as it was after the Mongol invasion, and during the Time of Troubles. The relationship of Church and state is considered throughout the volume. David Miller's chapter on the sixteenth century devotes particular attention to 'popular' as well as 'official' religious practices, while Robert Crummey's contribution on the seventeenth century explains the origins and consequences of the schism of the 1660s.

Until the seventeenth century, Russian cultural and intellectual life was heavily influenced by the Orthodox Church; from the mid-seventeenth century, however, it is possible to speak of elements of secularisation. Even in the seventeenth century, however, as Lindsey Hughes points out in Chapter 28, there was little abstract political thought: ideas about power were still conveyed primarily by non-verbal means, through works of art and architecture, and through rituals and ceremonies of the kind described by Michael Flier in Chapter 17.

Russia remained a predominantly agrarian country well into the twentieth century. In the pre-Petrine period, peasant farming was the basis of the economy, with overlords (both secular and monastic) extracting agricultural surpluses by means which became increasingly coercive in the sixteenth and seventeenth centuries. In Chapters 12 and 23 Richard Hellie – developing some of the themes first raised in Chapter 2 by Denis Shaw – describes the challenges faced by Muscovite peasants in terms of climate and soil, and the effects of these on their diet and housing.

Other economic themes which are addressed in all Parts of the volume include the nature and extent of market relations; the growth of commerce, both domestic and international; and the construction of towns. The development of early Rus' was very much tied up with the trade routes along the river systems which linked the Baltic with the Black Sea ('the route from the Varangians to the Greeks') and the Caspian. Its chief towns were important commercial centres. Novgorod, in particular, derived its great wealth from trade along both the north–south and east–west routes, exporting furs, fish, wax and honey, and importing silver (see Chapter 8). As Janet Martin explains in Chapter 6, trade continued during the period of Mongol suzerainty, when the Rus' principalities acquired access to the Great Silk Route to China.

In the sixteenth century, Muscovy briefly obtained a Baltic port, with the capture of Narva during the Livonian war; the importance of the White Sea trade route, which was developed by the English Muscovy Company from 1553, was recognised when the port of Archangel was constructed in 1583–4. The White Sea route was the most important trade route in the seventeenth century, with its exports increasingly comprising agricultural produce, such as flax and hemp, rather than forest products (see Chapters 13, 25).

The development of towns was largely but not exclusively connected with the growth of trade. As Denis Shaw demonstrates in his chapters in Parts II and III, Muscovite towns were multi-functional: not only were they commercial and manufacturing centres, but they also played important administrative and religious roles. Frontier towns, of course, had a vital military-defensive function. From the perspective of purely commercial development, Russian towns were backward by comparison with their Western European counterparts; but Shaw argues that they played an important role in state-building from the sixteenth century, not only by co-ordinating commerce, but also by integrating administrative and military functions.

As already noted, the chapters on political development pay considerable attention to the political elites and their changing social composition over the period. Military servitors and courtiers in Muscovy were ranked in an elaborate hierarchy, in which landed wealth roughly corresponded to political status and eminent birth. In the seventeenth century a growing bureaucracy of professional administrative personnel, at both central and local government levels, provided an additional hierarchy of officialdom. The great majority of Russians in the sixteenth and seventeenth century, however, were peasants, whose status was gradually reduced to that of serfs by the mid-seventeenth century: their situation, and that of slaves – another significant social group – is discussed in Chapters 12 and 23. The social structure of the towns was much more complex than that of the countryside, as Denis Shaw demonstrates: he describes the various categories of merchants and traders, as well as several kinds of military servitors and clergy who were urban dwellers (Chapters 13, 25). In the middle of the seventeenth century the mobility of townsmen was restricted in a similar manner to that of peasants, leading, as Richard Hellie explains in Chapter 23, to a much more rigidly stratified society.

A final theme of the volume is that of coercion and conflict. Pre-Petrine Russia was not the organic and harmonious society which was imagined by so many nineteenth-century Slavophiles. Before the sixteenth century the most violent internal disruptions took the form of dynastic civil wars. The sixteenth century, however, witnessed an episode of unprecedented state violence, in the form of the reign of terror imposed on his subjects by Ivan IV in the period of the *oprichnina*. The complex events of the Time of Troubles included not only foreign invasion and domestic civil war, but also significant episodes of social conflict, involving attacks on the elites by subaltern groups such as peasants, slaves, cossacks and the urban poor. The later episodes of social and political strife which led the seventeenth century to be described as the 'rebellious age' are described by Maureen Perrie in Chapter 26.

The present state of pre-Petrine Russia

The most significant development in the recent historiography of the pre-Petrine period of Russian history – as of later periods, too – was of course the collapse of the Soviet Union in 1991, which brought to an end the official privileging of ideologically driven Marxist approaches to the study of history, imposed and enforced by censorship and other forms of control. Old habits die hard, however, and many Russian historians, especially those trained in the Soviet period, have continued to research and write in much the same way as before. Fortunately, this means that many of the stronger features of Soviet-era historiography, such as the detailed study of sources and their publication in high-quality scholarly editions, have survived the events of 1991. To the disillusionment of many, moreover, not all of the new developments resulting from the end of the USSR turned out to be positive ones: the economic crisis of the early 1990s adversely affected the pay, conditions and employment opportunities of archivists, librarians and academic historians; and the immediate aftermath of the abolition of censorship and control witnessed a vogue for all kinds of eccentric theories about the past, and the publication of many popular histories and biographies that focused primarily on the sensational and lurid. After the worst effects of the immediate post-Soviet economic crisis were overcome, however, the situation in Russian history-publishing became very lively and exciting. As well as interesting new monographs by Russian scholars, many 'classic' pre-revolutionary historians were republished, and there have been valuable reprints of essential sources for medievalists, such as the chronicles. Many important Western works have also appeared in Russian translation.

The end of the USSR did not have such a dramatic effect on the study of pre-Petrine history as it did on research into the Soviet period, where the opening of the archives created exciting opportunities for both Russian and Western scholars. But new possibilities have opened up for Russian historians of all periods to travel to the West, and to enjoy more frequent contacts and greater co-operation and collaboration with their Western colleagues, whether at conferences or through joint projects and publications. Russian historians have been freed from the ideological constraints of the Soviet period, and many of them, particularly those of the younger generation, have been quick to embrace the newest and most fashionable trends in Western historiography. To that extent, one can justifiably speak of a degree of convergence between Russian and Western historiography of the pre-Petrine period since the 1990s.[1] The traffic in new ideas and approaches has not been all one way, however: in the last decades of the Soviet Union the work of the 'Moscow–Tartu school' of semiotics was highly influential in the West, where

1 For overviews of recent work, in essays commissioned for the tenth anniversary of the collapse of the Soviet Union, see: Nancy Shields Kollmann, 'Convergence, Expansion and Experimentation: Current Trends in Muscovite History-Writing', *Kritika* 2 (2001): 233–40; Simon Franklin, 'Pre-Mongol Rus': New Sources, New Perspectives', *RR* 60 (2001): 465–73; and Robert O. Crummey, 'The Latest from Muscovy', *RR* 60 (2001): 474–86.

the impact of scholars such as B. A. Uspenskii extended far beyond specialists in Russian history, as did that of Mikhail Bakhtin and A. Ia. Gurevich.[2] Nevertheless, varieties of Western post-modernism have provided the most prominent new influences on both Russian and Western historians in the past decade.[3]

Along with new approaches, new themes have flourished. Some topics, such as religion, which were previously obstructed by ideological constraints, have subsequently attracted considerable attention in post-Soviet Russia. But in general the newest themes which have appealed to historians of Russia, both East and West, are not so different from those which have inspired historians of other parts of the world. Women's history and gender history have thrived, particularly in the West:[4] and much interesting work has been done on ritual and ceremony.[5] Witchcraft and magic, however, which have attracted so much attention in the West in recent decades, have been relatively neglected by historians of Russia, perhaps because the phenomena themselves were less in evidence there (although that in itself is the subject of some debate).[6]

At the same time, it must be noted that the problematic nature of the sources for much of the pre-Petrine period, especially compared with the

2 English translations include: Mikhail Bakhtin, *Rabelais and his World*, trans. Hélène Iswolsky (Cambridge, Mass.: MIT Press, 1968); Ju. M. Lotman and B. A. Uspenskij, *The Semiotics of Russian Culture*, ed. Ann Shukman (Ann Arbor: Department of Slavic Languages and Literatures, University of Michigan, 1984); *The Semiotics of Russian Cultural History. Essays by Iurii M. Lotman, Lidiia Ia. Ginsburg, Boris A. Uspenskii*, ed. Alexander D. Nakhimovsky and Alice Stone Nakhimovsky (Ithaca, N. Y., and London: Cornell University Press, 1985); A. Ia. Gurevich, *Categories of Medieval Culture*, trans. G. L. Campbell (London: Routledge and Kegan Paul, 1985).

3 See e.g. Aleksandr I. Filiushkin, 'Post-modernism and the Study of the Russian Middle Ages', *Kritika* 3 (2002): 89–109.

4 See e.g. Eve Levin, *Sex and Society in the World of the Orthodox Slavs, 900–1700* (Ithaca, N.Y.: Cornell University Press, 1989); N. L. Pushkareva, *Zhenshchiny drevnei Rusi* (Moscow: Mysl', 1989); N. L. Pushkareva, *Zhenshchiny Rossii i Evropy na poroge novogo vremeni* (Moscow: Institut etnologii i antropologii RAN, 1996); N. L. Pushkareva, *Women in Russian History from the Tenth to the Twentieth Century*, ed. Eve Levin (Armonk, N.Y.: M. E. Sharpe, 1997; and Stroud: Sutton, 1999); Nada Boškovska, *Die russische Frau im 17. Jahrhundert* (Cologne, Weimar and Vienna: Böhlau Verlag, 1998); Nada Boškovska, 'Muscovite Women during the Seventeenth Century: at the Peak of the Deprivation of their Rights or on the Road Towards New Freedom?', *FOG* 56 (2000): 47–62; Isolde Thyrêt, *Between God and Tsar: Religious Symbolism and the Royal Women of Muscovite Russia* (DeKalb: Northern Illinois University Press, 2001).

5 See the works cited in Michael Flier's chapter in this volume.

6 See e.g. W. F. Ryan, 'The Witchcraft Hysteria in Early Modern Europe: Was Russia an Exception?', *SEER* 76 (1998): 49–84; W. F. Ryan, *The Bathhouse at Midnight: An Historical Survey of Magic and Divination in Russia* (University Park, Pa.: Pennsylvania State University Press; and Stroud: Sutton, 1999); Valerie A. Kivelson, 'Male Witches and Gendered Categories in Seventeenth-Century Russia', *Comparative Studies in Society and History*, 45 (2003): 606–31.

range of sources available for most of Western Europe, constitutes a major
constraint on the types of history which can be written, the approaches which
can be employed, and the questions which can be answered. The relatively late
development of printing in Russia meant that written sources for the period
exist primarily in manuscript form. Many of these survive only in late copies,
and the inevitable problems involved in dating the presumed originals have
given rise to notorious debates about the authenticity of some evidence long
regarded as genuine and significant.[7] Written sources are, however, diverse and
informative even for the earliest part of our period. There is a rich tradition of
chronicle-writing from the eleventh century, and the earliest law codes (which
provide valuable evidence about social hierarchy) also date from the eleventh
century.[8] The famous birch-bark documents from Novgorod, and the more
recently discovered 'Psalter' on waxed tablets, provide fascinating evidence of
the early history of that city.[9]

The relative paucity of written evidence for the earlier part of the period
covered by this volume, in particular, has obliged historians to place greater
reliance on non-written sources, such as archaeological evidence. Coins and
seals also provide important material, especially for the earlier centuries. But
even for the later centuries, when written sources are more plentiful, non-
written evidence, including art and architecture, has been increasingly used by
scholars in order to acquire new understanding of symbolic cultural systems.
In view of the limitations of native sources, and the degree of official control
over them, written accounts by foreign visitors provide a valuable supplement.
Like all sources, of course, they have to be handled with care, but they often
provide uniquely interesting evidence of ethnographic phenomena which,
because they were simply taken for granted by Russians, are not described in
native sources.[10] Foreigners' descriptions and drawings of public ceremonies

7 Edward L. Keenan, *The Kurbskii–Groznyi Apocrypha. The Seventeenth-Century Genesis of
the 'Correspondence' Attributed to Prince A. M. Kurbskii and Tsar Ivan IV* (Cambridge, Mass.:
Harvard University Press, 1971); Edward L. Keenan, 'Putting Kurbskii in his Place, or:
Observations and Suggestions Concerning the Place of the *History of the Grand Prince
of Muscovy* in the History of Muscovite Literary Culture', *FOG* 24 (1978): 131–61. For a
summary of more recent developments in the controversy, see: C. J. Halperin, 'Edward
Keenan and the Kurbskii–Groznyi Correspondence in Hindsight', *JGO* 46 (1998): 376–
403; and Edward L. Keenan, 'Response to Halperin, "Edward Keenan and the Kurbskii–
Groznyi Correspondence in Hindsight"', *JGO* 46 (1998): 404–15. A more recent work of
source scepticism is Edward L. Keenan, *Josef Dobrovsky and the Origins of the Igor' Tale*
(Cambridge, Mass.: Harvard University Press, 2004).
8 See Simon Franklin, *Writing, Society and Culture in Early Rus, c.950–1300* (Cambridge:
Cambridge University Press, 2002).
9 See V. L. Ianin's chapter in this volume.
10 See e.g. Marshall Poe, *'A People Born to Slavery': Russia in Early Modern European Ethnography*
(Ithaca, N.Y., and London: Cornell University Press, 2000).

and rituals, for example, such as the Palm Sunday and Epiphany processions, have provided valuable source material for innovative studies of political and cultural imagery and symbolism.[11] Finally, accounts written by Russian 'defectors' abroad, such as Prince Andrei Kurbskii in the sixteenth century and Grigorii Kotoshikhin in the seventeenth,[12] contain useful written evidence of a kind which is not found in internally generated native sources.

As well as new themes, perennial controversies continue to fascinate historians of both East and West. Some older debates have, however, lost much of their relevance since the end of the USSR. Western critiques of dogmatic Soviet Marxist approaches are now largely in abeyance, as are Russian attacks on the distortions and falsifications of 'bourgeois' historiography. Other long-running debates, such as that between the 'Normanists' and their opponents concerning the role of the Vikings in the formation of the early Rus' state, seem to have run into the sand. Psychiatrised explanations of the behaviour of Ivan the Terrible, and the associated debates about whether he was 'mad or bad', have mostly been superseded by cultural and semiotic approaches to his reign. But some older controversies which had long been considered moribund have unexpectedly sparked back into life. Debate about the nature and extent of Mongol influence on Muscovite institutions was revived by Donald Ostrowski's book on the subject, published in 1998.[13] And arguments about the nature of the Muscovite state in the sixteenth and seventeenth centuries have been revitalised by Marshall Poe, with his attack on the 'Harvard school' of historians for downplaying the despotic and coercive features of the autocratic political system, and for stressing instead its cohesiveness and the existence of informal modes of consultation between the ruler and the elites.[14]

---

11 See Chapter 17 of this volume.

12 J. L. I. Fennell (ed. and trans.), *Prince A. M. Kurbsky's History of Ivan IV* (Cambridge: Cambridge University Press, 1965); Grigorij Kotošixin, *O Rossii v carstvovanie Alekseja Mixajloviča. Text and Commentary*, ed. A. E. Pennington (Oxford: Clarendon Press, 1980).

13 Donald Ostrowski, *Muscovy and the Mongols. Cross-Cultural Influences on the Steppe Frontier, 1304–1598* (Cambridge: Cambridge University Press, 1998). See also the subsequent debate: Charles J. Halperin, 'Muscovite Political Institutions in the 14th Century', *Kritika* 1 (2000), 237–57; David Goldfrank, '*Muscovy and the Mongols*: What's What and What's Maybe', *Kritika* 1 (2000): 259–66; and Donald Ostrowski, 'Muscovite Adaptation of Steppe Political Institutions: A Reply to Halperin's Objections', *Kritika* 1 (2000): 267–304.

14 Marshall Poe, 'The Truth about Muscovy', *Kritika* 3 (2002): 473–86; and responses: Valerie A. Kivelson, 'On Words, Sources and Historical Method: Which Truth about Muscovy?', *Kritika* 3 (2002), 487–99; Charles J. Halperin, 'Muscovy as a Hypertrophic State; a Critique', *Kritika* 3 (2002), 501–7. Poe identifies the following historians as members of the 'Harvard school': Edward L. Keenan, Nancy Shields Kollmann, Daniel Rowland, George G. Weickhardt, Valerie A. Kivelson and Donald Ostrowski. Kivelson, while accepting Poe's classification of her earlier work as falling within the parameters of the 'Harvard school', has recently made an ingenious attempt to reconcile the 'hard' and 'soft'

The debate over the nature of the Muscovite political system also raises the issue of comparative perspectives. While some historians have argued for the uniqueness of pre-Petrine Russia, others have found it to have many features in common with other European and Asian societies.

Soviet historiography, which of course adhered to a Marxist framework, explicitly placed Russian development within the same parameters as that of Western European states, adopting terminology derived from the West: 'feudalism', 'absolutism', 'estates' (*sosloviia*), 'estate-representative monarchy', 'urban corporations', etc. For Soviet historians, both Kievan Rus' and Muscovy were feudal societies, and although they debated issues such as the origins, nature and extent of feudalisation in early Rus',[15] their basic model was still the one which Marx had based on the experience of Western Europe.

Many Western historians, too, see Western Europe as the appropriate comparator for Russia. Hans-Joachim Torke and Robert Crummey argued that Western influences and Western military competition led to the creation in Russia of a variety of European absolutism, at least from the mid-seventeenth century.[16] Some representatives of the 'Harvard school' also favour the model of Western absolutism, albeit in more recent versions which depict it as less 'absolute' in practice than it was in theory.[17] Other historians have preferred to adopt a variant of the absolutist model by describing Muscovy as a 'fiscal-military' state.[18]

The main alternative model which has been suggested is that of Asian societies. Marx's own concept of the 'Asian mode of production', as an Eastern alternative path of development to Western feudalism, was used only rarely by Soviet historians. Western scholars have long debated whether the impact of the Mongol conquest made Muscovy more of an oriental or Asiatic despotism than a Byzantine polity. Karl Wittfogel's application of the term 'oriental

---

interpretations: see her 'Muscovite "Citizenship": Rights without Freedom', *Journal of Modern History* 74 (2002): 465–89.

15 For a summary of this debate in the late Soviet period, see Takeo Kuryuzawa, 'The Debate on the Genesis of Russian Feudalism in Recent Soviet Historiography', in *Facing up to the Past. Soviet Historiography under Perestroika*, ed. Takayuki Ito (Sapporo, Japan: Slavic Research Center, Hokkaido University, 1989), pp. 111–47.

16 Hans-Joachim Torke, *Die staatsbedingte Gesellschaft im Moskauer Reich: Zar und Zemlja in der altrussischen Herrschaftsverfassung, 1613–1689* (Leiden: E. J. Brill, 1974); Robert O. Crummey, 'Seventeenth-Century Russia: Theories and Models', *FOG* 56 (2000): 113–31.

17 See, in particular, Nancy Shields Kollmann, *By Honor Bound: State and Society in Early Modern Russia* (Ithaca, N.Y., and London: Cornell University Press, 1999).

18 For example: Chester S. L. Dunning, *Russia's First Civil War. The Time of Troubles and the Founding of the Romanov Dynasty* (University Park, Pa.: Pennsylvania State University Press, 2001), pp. 19–21, 462–3; and Sergei Bogatyrev's chapter in this volume.

despotism' to Russia enjoyed a certain vogue in the West in the 1960s;[19] and although Donald Ostrowski, in his more recent work, rejects the term itself, he advances the broader case that the Mongols influenced the military and the civil administration of Muscovy.[20]

Another influential model is Max Weber's concept of 'patrimonialism', which he applied to polities in which the ruler owns all the land in his realm. For Weber, examples of such polities could be found at various times and places; the best-known application of the concept to Russia is that of Richard Pipes, who found the closest parallel to Russia in the Hellenistic states of the ancient world.[21] According to Pipes, north-eastern Russia was patrimonial even before the Mongol invasions, and Russia remained a patrimonial state throughout the Muscovite period.[22]

By contrast, a group of Western historians sees Russia's development as *sui generis*. Marshall Poe's recent insistence that Muscovy was a despotism has much in common with Richard Hellie's use of terminology such as the 'garrison', 'service' or 'hypertrophic' state.[23]

* * *

The contributors to this volume include members of all 'schools' (and of none), and exemplify a range of approaches to the period. While I, as editor, bear responsibility for the choice of themes, which I have attempted to make as comprehensive and as coherent as possible, I have not attempted to impose any kind of common interpretation on the contributors. On the contrary, I believe that an important function of this volume is to provide readers with a showcase of examples of the work of some of the most interesting and

19 Karl A. Wittfogel, *Oriental Despotism: A Comparative Study of Total Power* (New Haven: Yale University Press, 1957); Karl A. Wittfogel, 'Russia and the East: A Comparison and Contrast', *SR* 22 (1963): 627–43; Nicholas Riasanovsky, ' "Oriental Despotism" and Russia', *SR* 22 (1963): 644–9; Bertold Spuler, 'Russia and Islam', *SR* 22 (1963): 650–5; and Karl A. Wittfogel, 'Reply', *SR* 22 (1963): 656–62.
20 Ostrowski, *Muscovy and the Mongols*.
21 Richard Pipes, *Russia under the Old Regime* (Harmondsworth: Penguin Books, 1977), pp. 22–4, 112.
22 Ibid., pp. 40–8, 58–111. For a more recent exchange on the topic, see: George G. Weickhardt, 'The Pre-Petrine Law of Property', *SR* 52 (1993): 663–9; Richard Pipes, 'Was there Private Property in Muscovite Russia?', *SR* 53 (1994): 524–30; and George G. Weickhardt, 'Response', *SR* 53 (1994): 531–8.
23 Poe, 'The Truth about Muscovy'; Richard Hellie, 'The Structure of Modern Russian History: Toward a Dynamic Model', *RH* 4 (1977): 1–22, and critiques: Ann Kleimola, 'Muscovy Redux', *RH* 4 (1977): 23–30; James Cracraft, 'Soft Spots in the Hard Line', *RH* 4 (1977): 31–8; and Richard Wortman, 'Remarks on the Service State Interpretation', *RH* 4 (1977): 39–41. See also Richard Hellie, *Enserfment and Military Change in Muscovy* (Chicago: University of Chicago Press, 1971); and his chapters in this volume.

authoritative scholars who are researching pre-Petrine history today from a wide variety of perspectives.

Mainly for practical reasons, the authors are drawn predominantly from the anglophone world, with the largest single number coming from North America, and especially from the United States. All Western historians of Russia owe an enormous debt to the work of their Russian colleagues, past and present, including not only the giants of pre-revolutionary scholarship, but also those historians who kept their legacy alive throughout the Soviet period, often under very difficult conditions. Although the contributors include only a few Russians, the achievements of Russian-language historiography of the pre-Petrine period are reflected throughout the volume.

2

Russia's geographical environment

DENIS J. B. SHAW

Any attempt to discuss Russia's environment over the long period covered by this book immediately faces a problem: what is the geographical extent of the territory which is our focus? For whereas the 'Rus'' of the ninth century AD wandered through the forests of the East European plain between the Baltic and the middle Volga, the vast Muscovite state (soon to become the Russian Empire) of the late seventeenth century stretched almost from the Baltic across Eurasia to the Pacific, and from the Arctic Ocean in the north down towards the Black Sea steppe in the south – a territory which very nearly corresponds with that of the Russian Federation today. Clearly both the geography, and what might be understood as 'Russia', had changed profoundly over the intervening centuries. Any discussion of Russia's geographical environment must take such considerable changes into account.

A partial answer to our problem of defining territory might be suggested by the work of the Berkeley cultural geographer, Carl Sauer.[1] In an essay of 1925, Sauer asserted that the focus of any geographical study should be the 'cultural landscape', which is that territory 'fashioned from a natural landscape by a culture group'. 'Culture is the agent, the natural area is the medium, the cultural landscape the result.' In accordance with Sauer, then, this chapter should focus on the Russian 'cultural landscape', that portion of the earth's natural landscape which was modified by Russian settlement, economic activity and ways of life over the period in question. The obvious objection is that humankind cannot be subdivided into cultural units as easily as the anthropologically inclined Sauer imagined. The 'Rus'' of the early medieval period, for example, were by no means the forerunners of the Russians only. The Ukrainians and Belarusians also descended from them, while there is much to be said for the view that the first 'Rus'' were in fact Scandinavians rather than

---

1 Carl Sauer, 'The Morphology of Landscape', in John Leighly (ed.), *Land and Life: A Selection from the Writings of Carl Ortwin Sauer* (Berkeley and Los Angeles: University of California Press, 1963), pp. 315–50.

Slavs.[2] Furthermore many non-Slavs lived alongside and among the Rus', and this was even more the case among the later Russians.

An alternative and perhaps simpler approach to the definition of our territory would be to assert that it is that region that was occupied by the Russian state – particularly, perhaps, towards the end of our period when it reached its greatest geographical extent. Again this definition is not entirely satisfactory. 'The Land of Rus'' of the period before the thirteenth century, for example, was only in part the predecessor to the Muscovite state (and ultimately the Russian Empire) of later centuries and their geographical co-ordinates by no means corresponded. Parts of what had been Rus' lay outside Russia even in the late seventeenth century, and by no means all 'Russians' lived in Russia. Once again, therefore, the extent of our study is unclear.

In the light of such perplexities, this chapter will adopt a broad, catholic and perhaps even escapist approach, defining 'Russia's geographical environment' as the entire territory with which the remaining chapters of this book are concerned. The intention is to provide a territorial and environmental framework for the ensuing discussions. Two other general points are worth making by way of introduction. One is to state that this chapter does not treat the natural environment as if it were merely a neutral stage upon which the drama of history is played out. Human society can never be divorced from the natural milieu in which it exists, and to attempt to do so is to introduce a level of abstraction and unreality which inevitably militate against understanding. Following Sauer, we understand the natural environment or physical landscape (including its spatial qualities) as a 'habitat complex' which is innate to the life of society. What is important, wrote Sauer, 'is the modification of the area by man and its appropriation to his uses'.[3] Human society, in other words, changes along with the natural environment within which it exists. The second point, to quote Sauer again, is to suggest that 'there are no general laws of society, but only cultural assents'.[4] To be concerned with the natural environment and its historical significance, in other words, is not to be guilty of some kind of environmental determinism, any more than the student of economic history would necessarily be guilty of economic determinism. The natural environment touches human development at many points, indeed is part of that development. But it does not determine it. 'Geography as environmentalism', wrote Sauer, 'represents a dogma – a new evangel for the age

---

2 Simon Franklin and Jonathan Shepard, *The Emergence of Rus, 750–1200* (London: Longman, 1996), pp. xvii–xviii.
3 Sauer, 'Morphology', p. 333.
4 Carl Sauer, 'Foreword to Historical Geography', in Leighly (ed.), *Land and Life*, p. 378.

of reason.' He rejected such a 'narrow, rationalistic thesis' in favour of the humanistic study of cultures for which he was so celebrated.[5] It is in that spirit that we approach the present topic.

Peasant environments

During the period covered by this book the great majority of Russians were peasants, tilling the soil and engaged in a variety of other agrarian pursuits. To talk of 'peasant environments' is therefore to consider the natural environments which confronted most Russians on a day-to-day basis and from which they were obliged to wrest their subsistence. Across the vast East European plain on which most Russians lived there is considerable environmental variation, as shall be seen below, and the means which peasants employed to ensure their subsistence also varied. The different ways in which peasant communities have adapted to utilise the varying sets of resources presented by the physical environment have been analysed by the theory of 'peasant ecotypes'.[6] This chapter can only consider such ecotypes against the broad background of the major zonal differences which existed in the Russian environment rather than discussing the great variety of ecotypes which were found in reality. But the significant point is that, following Sauer, such social differences should be seen as different responses to environmental possibilities rather than as themselves determined by the environment.

Towards the end of the nineteenth century the great Russian soil scientist V. V. Dokuchaev and his followers began to describe the great soil belts which cross the East European plain in a west–east direction and which he ascribed not to geological variations but to the differential effects of climate, vegetation, hydrology, erosional processes and other factors acting over a lengthy period of time. Eventually Russian scientists defined the concept of 'natural' or 'geographical' zonation according to which not only soils but also climate, flora, fauna, hydrology, relief and other factors vary zonally and in an interdependent way, not in Russia only but also at a global scale.[7] Russian territory,

---

5 Sauer, 'Morphology', p. 346ff.
6 E. R. Wolf, *Peasants* (Englewood Cliffs,N. J.: Prentice Hall, 1966); J. Langton, 'Habitat, Society and Economy Revisited: Peasant Ecotypes and Economic Development in Sweden', *Cambria* 12 (1985): 5–24.
7 V. V. Dokuchaev, *Russkii chernozem* (Moscow: Gosudarstvennoe izdatel'stvo sel'skokhoziaistvennoi literatury, 1952); V. V. Dokuchaev, 'K ucheniiu o zonakh prirody', in his *Izbrannye trudy*, vol. III (Moscow: Gosudarstvennoe izdatel'stvo sel'skokhoziaistvennoi literatury, 1949), pp. 317–29; L. S. Berg, *Geograficheskie zony Sovetskogo Soiuza* (Moscow: OGIZ, 1947).

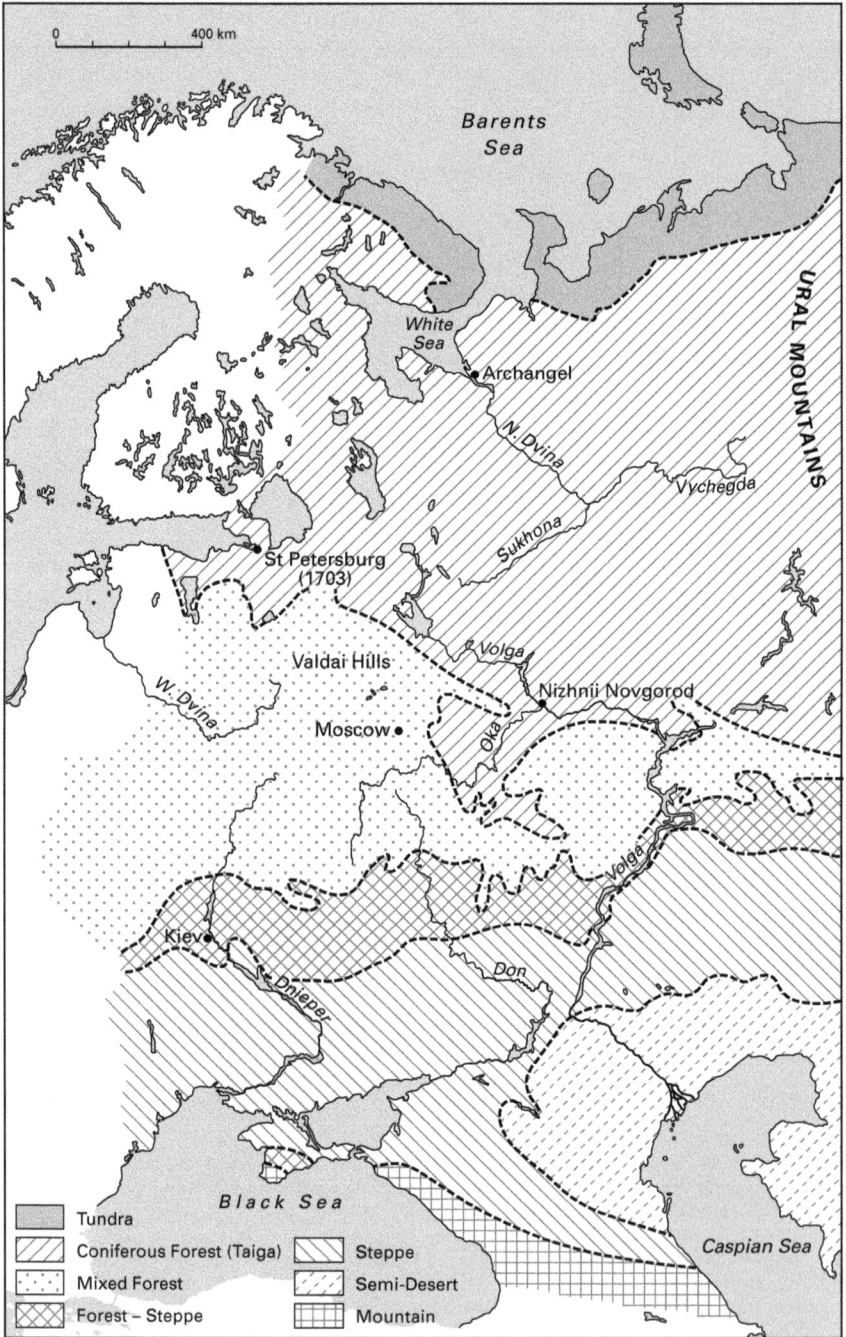

Map 2.1. The East European plain at the close of the medieval period

Legend:

- Tundra
- Coniferous Forest (Taiga)
- Mixed Forest
- Forest – Steppe
- Steppe
- Semi-Desert
- Mountain

Labels on map:

0   400 km

Barents Sea

URAL MOUNTAINS

White Sea

Archangel

N. Dvina

Vychegda

Sukhona

St Petersburg (1703)

R. Volga

Valdai Hills

Nizhnii Novgorod

W. Dvina

Moscow

Oka

Volga

Kiev

Dnieper

Don

Black Sea

Caspian Sea

as defined for the late seventeenth century, can be divided into four major zones according to this approach; from north to south they are: tundra, forest (subdivided into boreal forest and mixed forest), forest-steppe and steppe (see Map 2.1). This chapter will consider them roughly in the order in which they were encountered by the Russian peasants of our period: mixed forest, boreal forest, tundra, forest-steppe and steppe.

The Eastern Slavs who moved on to the East European plain in the early centuries AD, and the Rus' who moved down from the north-west, gradually intermingled with Finno-Ugrian, Baltic and other peoples who lived in the mixed forest zone of the central part of the plain. The mixed forest zone is a region of roughly triangular shape with its base to the west against the Baltic and the western frontier of the former Russian Empire (thus including the territory of present-day Belarus and north-west Ukraine), and its apex pointing towards the Urals in the east. The northern boundary runs approximately south-eastwards from St Petersburg and Novgorod towards Iaroslavl' and Nizhnii Novgorod; the southern runs north-eastwards from Kiev towards Briansk, Kaluga, Riazan' and so to Nizhnii Novgorod where the mixed forest practically disappears between the boreal forest to the north and the forest-steppe to the south. It then continues in a narrow strip eastwards to the Urals, but not beyond. According to one estimate the zone embraced about 12 per cent of the territory of European Russia at the end of the seventeenth century, and at the time of the first revision (census) in 1719 contained about 42.5 per cent of that territory's registered population.[8]

The mixed forest zone's triangular shape reflects environmental conditions on the East European plain. The degree of continentality increases as one moves east away from the Baltic and Central Europe and the zone is gradually squeezed between the moisture-abundant regions of the boreal forest to the north and the moisture-deficit regions of the forest-steppe and steppe to the south. A west–east axis through the zone also defines a line of diminishing agricultural potential, with gradually reducing precipitation levels and longer and more severe winters as one moves towards the east. The zone formed the heartland for Russian agricultural settlement and activity throughout the period embraced by this book. As its name suggests, the mixed forest is a transitional region containing both coniferous forests, which predominate towards the north, and deciduous woodlands, which become more common as one moves south. Common conifers include fir, spruce and pine on sandy soils while oak, elm, birch, lime, ash, maple and hornbeam are deciduous

8 A. V. Dulov, *Geograficheskaia sreda i istoriia Rossii* (Moscow: Nauka, 1983), pp. 12, 39.

varieties. The predominant soils are turfy podzols, which are usually rather acidic, and the relatively fertile grey forest soils, which become more common towards the south.

For many centuries the mixed forest zone, despite its indifferent soils and rather severe continental climate, thus formed the agricultural heartland of the Russian realm. Within the region conditions for settlement and agriculture varied greatly, however. To the north-west, in the region of the Valdai Hills and in areas further west and north, is a landscape greatly affected by recent glacial and fluvio-glacial deposition in which morainic deposits have interfered with the natural drainage and the many lakes, boulders, marshes and morainic features formed a serious barrier to agricultural settlement. Only in some more favoured regions like the area stretching south-west from Lake Il'men' with loamy soils did cultivation prove possible. Soils are generally podzolised. Further south lies the uneven region of terminal moraines known as the Moscow–Smolensk upland, providing better drainage and better prospects for peasant settlement, whilst south again, fringed by the south-western spurs of the central Russian upland, is the Dnieper lowland. Although rather poorly drained historically, this area, with its turfy podzols and grey forest soils developed on loess, and with pine together with broadleaved forests of beech, hornbeam and oak, provided numerous opportunities for peasant farmers.

North-east of the Dnieper lowland, on the interfluve between the Volga and the Oka (the district forming the heartland of the Muscovite state), agricultural settlement was greatly influenced by a detailed topography which reflected the effects of underlying geology, glacial deposition and fluvial action. This was and is a complex landscape of forest, marsh, meadow, pasture and glade which is difficult to summarise and whose patterns of soil and vegetation vary in accordance with local relief, drainage and other factors. Forest cover increases towards the east and north, and, especially beyond the Volga to the north, glacial deposits restricted drainage and acted as hindrances to settlement. To the south, and particularly beyond the Oka, drainage improves and soil fertility increases, and this region fringing on the forest-steppe eventually proved very favourable for agriculture. On the interfluve itself the well-favoured districts where fertile forest-steppe-like soils lie like islands within the mixed forest (like the famous Vladimir Opol'e) contrast with the sandy, ill-drained Meshchera Lowland south-east of Moscow, a mixed territory of pine and spruce forests and marsh.

Finally, beyond the Volga to the east and stretching away towards the Urals, natural conditions were affected by the greater continentality and it was only towards the end of our period that the mixed forest began to be subject to agricultural colonisation.

The mixed forest environment provided peasants with a variety of resources for their subsistence. It may be that initial settlement followed valleys where there was easy access to rivers and streams for water and transport, to meadowlands and to woodland. The better-drained places, such as river terraces, were favoured. Broadleaved tree species were usually not difficult to clear for cultivation. Later, as technology improved and it became feasible to dig deeper wells, watersheds could be settled also. Scholars have discussed how relatively simple agricultural landscapes (like cultivation in patches in the forest perhaps using temporary slash-and-burn techniques) gradually evolved into permanent landscapes with more intensive forms of agriculture, albeit with temporary patches still frequently scattered through the forest.[9] Rye, barley and oats were the principal food crops grown. The hayfields, which might include water meadows, pastures and once again even remote glades in the forest, provided feed for the peasants' limited livestock. Livestock farming involved the necessity of stall-feeding during the long winter months. Woodland provided the peasants with many necessities: timber (for building), wood (logs, poles, rods, brushwood, bark for many purposes including fences, implements, utensils, furniture, fuel, making potash, resin, tar, pitch), food (berries, nuts, fruit, fungi, game, honey) and additional pasturing for animals. Rivers provided fish. Like all pre-industrial societies, traditional Russia made use of a wide variety of plant and animal products for textiles, clothing, foods, flavourings, medicines, tanning, dyeing, preserving, building and other purposes.

From the medieval period Russian peasants began to move north into a very different environment from the one they had experienced in the mixed forest. This region, dubbed by Dokuchaev and others the boreal forest (*taiga*), is clothed by the great belt of conifers which crosses the entire span of northern Eurasia from northern Scandinavia in the west across to the Pacific coast in the east and then, leaping the Bering Strait, continues across Alaska and northern Canada. According to Dulov, at the end of the seventeenth century this region accounted for nearly half of the territory of European Russia but in

---

9 N. Rozhkov, *Sel'skoe khoziaistvo Moskovskoi Rusi v XVI veke* (Moscow: Universitetskaia tipografiia, 1899); M. A. D'iakonov, *Ocherki iz istorii sel'skogo naseleniia v Moskovskom gosudarstve XVI–XVII vv.* (St Petersburg: Tipografiia I. N. Skorokhodova, 1898); G. E. Kochin, *Sel'skoe khoziaistvo na Rusi v period obrazovaniia Russkogo tsentralizovannogo gosudarstva, konets XIII–nachalo XVI v.* (Moscow and Leningrad: Nauka, 1965); A. L. Shapiro, *Agrarnaia istoriia severo-zapada Rossii, vtoraia polovina XV–nachalo XVI v.* (Leningrad: Nauka, 1971); R. E. F. Smith, *Peasant Farming in Muscovy* (Cambridge: Cambridge University Press, 1977).

1719 contained only about 12 per cent of the registered Russian population.[10] As these figures suggest, this is a harsh land whose endless coniferous forests (spruce, pine, fir, birch with greater admixtures of larch and cedar as one moves eastwards into Siberia) are interspersed with vast expanses of swamp. The short summers, long winters and predominantly low temperatures (though climatic conditions vary in detail throughout the region) mean that the boreal forest is an area characterised by excess moisture conditions. Soils are generally low in fertility, leached of the most significant plant minerals by water made acidic by a surface detritus of needles from the coniferous trees. The resulting podzols are frequently characterised by a topsoil of silica and little or no humus, and often have an iron hardpan some half a metre below the surface which further impedes drainage. In the far north of European Russia and across much of northern, central and eastern Siberia the swampy conditions are exacerbated by permafrost. Thus the poor, infertile soils, generally swampy conditions, short summers (ameliorated to some degree by long daylight hours) and low average temperatures mean that agriculture has always been restricted to the most favourable regions. In much of the zone these favoured regions tend to correspond to river valleys which were the most usual sites for settlement. Settlement tended to avoid the watersheds which were often swampy, remote and forested.

Again, the detailed geography varies considerably. In European Russia towards the south of the zone drainage conditions are better than elsewhere, soils are less podzolised in many places and agriculture becomes possible in river valleys and on some watersheds. Better soils include glacial clay loams, Permian marls and alluvial clays. Agricultural settlement proved possible along the valleys of the Sukhona and Vychegda, near Beloe Ozero, on the watershed between the Sukhona and the Volga, and in certain other favoured regions, albeit often in rather isolated pockets. In many places slash and burn was long practised. Natural meadowland on the alluvial soils of river valleys, and pastures elsewhere, probably enhanced the significance of livestock farming in this area, a feature which certainly became more apparent from the eighteenth century. As in the mixed forest zone the coniferous forests provided many resources for subsistence, even though their productivity was hindered by the harsh environment. For many peasants in the north non-agricultural activities loomed large. Thus on coasts, lakes and rivers, fishing proved a most important activity. Both freshwater bodies and the sea were rich in stocks of fish. Favoured species included salmon, sturgeon, pike, cod, herring, sole and

---

10 Dulov, *Geograficheskaia sreda*, pp. 12, 39.

other varieties. Peasants and others also sought for game and, where possible, fur-bearing animals in the forests. The latter included sable, marten, fox, hare, ermine, beaver, squirrel and others. Also hunted in the northern forests were elk, reindeer, roebuck and bear. For yet other northern peasants the salt industry provided an important means of subsistence towards the end of the period.[11]

Only in the late sixteenth century did the Russians begin to penetrate Siberia to any extent and to the end of our period their activities were largely confined to the boreal forest zone (in Siberia's case that zone covers most of the territory). Peasant economies and ways of life bore much similarity to those found in the boreal forests to the west. By the seventeenth century agriculture was being encouraged in some of the most favoured areas in the south-west of Siberia, accompanied by peasant settlement. This was in an attempt to overcome the severe problem of provisioning in this vast region.[12] But both agriculture and Russian peasant settlement remained of minimal importance in Siberia to the end of the period.

Few were the Russian settlers who encountered the tundra lands of the far north before the end of the seventeenth century. The tundra, which is the region of swamp, moss, peat, lichen, scrub and perennial grassland to the north of the tree-line, stretches from the Kola peninsula in the west across the far north of European Russia and northern Siberia to the far north-east of the Eurasian mainland. In certain parts of northern and north-eastern Siberia tundra conditions penetrate further south as a result of mountainous relief. The major Russian subsistence activities in these territories consisted of hunting and fishing. Fowl, reindeer, walruses, seals and whales were among the species sought in the European far north.

To the south of the mixed forest zone of European Russia the landscape gradually merges into the forest-steppe and ultimately into the steppe, regions which today are largely devoted to arable farming but which in the past were covered for the most part by natural grassland. In south-western Siberia, where the mixed forest zone does not exist, the boreal forest merges directly southwards into the forest-steppe. In the European area the forest-steppe forms a zone varying in width between 250 and 500 kilometres running roughly west-south-west to east-north-east from the western parts of present-day Ukraine

---

11 *Istoriia severnogo krest'ianstva*, vol. I: *Krest'ianstvo Evropeiskogo severa v period feodalizma* (Arkhangel'sk: Severo-Zapadnoe knizhnoe izdatel'stvo, 1984).

12 V. I. Shunkov, *Voprosy agrarnoi istorii Rossii* (Moscow: Nauka, 1974), pp. 95ff; V. I. Shunkov, *Ocherki po istorii kolonizatsii Sibiri v XVII–nachale XVIII vekov* (Moscow and Leningrad: AN SSSR, 1946).

and the northern and central parts of Moldova across central Ukraine and on towards the Urals. Beyond the Urals it continues across the southern part of west Siberia until interrupted by the western slopes of the Altai Mountains. The forest-steppe's northern boundary in the European territory has been described above. The southern boundary runs from Chisinau in Moldova to Khar'kov in Ukraine and then to the south of Voronezh to Samara on the Volga and on to Ufa. According to one estimate, the forest-steppe occupied about 21 per cent of the territory of European Russia in the late seventeenth century and accounted for about 43 per cent of the territory's registered population at the time of the first revision.[13]

Although the Eastern Slavs planted settlements in the western part of the forest-steppe in the early centuries of their existence on the East European plain, their activities in the region were subsequently curtailed by various warlike nomadic groups who migrated from the east. The Tatars, who appeared in the European forest-steppe and steppe in the thirteenth century, and the Kalmyks, who made their debut some four centuries later, were the last of these. Only from the middle of the sixteenth century did Russians begin to settle in the area in significant numbers, by which time the Muscovite state had organised sufficient military power to provide some measure of protection against the nomadic raiders. As the name 'forest-steppe' suggests, the zone is a transitional region between the forest to the north and the steppe to the south. Declining moisture levels mean that tree growth is progressively restricted as one moves south, and the predominant natural vegetation gradually becomes grassland. The better-watered river valleys carry the vegetation of the mixed forest zone down to the south. However areas of woodland and forest may also be found on watersheds depending on local climatic, hydrological and soil conditions, and perhaps other factors like frequency of fires. The underlying soils of tree-covered areas are often similar to those found in the southern parts of the mixed forest – grey forest soils, degraded *chernozems* and others. Species of tree are predominantly deciduous: oaks predominate in the European region and birch in Siberia. Other species include ash, lime, aspen, elm and maple, mainly in the European part and depending upon local conditions. Pine groves may be found in sandy regions. It is, however, in the grassland areas in particular where the region's most outstanding characteristic becomes apparent – the black earth or *chernozem* soil, highly fertile and rich in humus, the product of a balance between precipitation and evaporation with ample heat resources. These soils supported a grassland community

13 Dulov, *Geograficheskaia sreda*, pp. 12, 39.

of varied species but declining richness and variety as one moves south into the steppe.

Within the wooded parts of the forest steppe it proved possible for peasants to pursue many of the same agricultural activities as characterised the mixed forest. Initial settlement was typically along river valleys where there was ample water, woods could be cleared for agriculture or exploited in other ways, water meadows and other areas provided hay or grazing, and other productive environments could be utilised. As greater use began to be made of the grasslands with their rich soils, however, other measures became necessary including long fallow (*perelog*) and shifting cultivation (*zalezh*). On many watersheds, settlement was initially difficult because of lack of available water and sometimes because of the difficulties of ploughing the tough steppe grasses. However, in the early days the steppe environment provided an abundance of wildlife. Metropolitan Pimen, who travelled through the European steppe in the fourteenth century, for example, reported seeing a multitude of beasts, including wild goats, elk, wolves, foxes, otters, bears, beavers and birdlife – eagles, geese, swans, cranes and others.[14] In addition to the species typically found in the wooded areas of the forest-steppe – bears, elk, roe deer, squirrel, marten and others – were those which characterised the steppe – marmot, jerboa, bobac. In the early days of settlement various 'hunting lands' were demarcated and rented out to different individuals or monasteries.[15] Later, once the nomadic problem had been contained but before significant settlement, the grasslands were often used for grazing.

During the centuries considered by this book, the above environments were gradually modified by their human inhabitants. Thus forests were cleared for settlement and agriculture, soils were eroded, steppe grasses were burnt, territories were hunted over for their valuable fauna (and sometimes entirely denuded of their resources, especially in consequence of the fur trade), rivers and streams were fished and occasionally dammed, and numerous other inroads on nature were made. The impacts of human activity (and of associated activities like that of domestic livestock) on hydrology, soils, flora and fauna were sometimes profound, and not always reversible. Of course such impacts pale by comparison with what came later under industrialisation and the Communist attempts to transform nature, but should not be ignored. They were inherent to the process whereby Russians adapted and appropriated the

---

14 *PSRL*, vol. XI (St Petersburg: Tipografiia I. N. Skorokhodova, 1897), p. 96.
15 See e.g. L. B. Veinberg and A. A. Poltoratskaia, *Materialy dlia istorii Voronezhskoi i sosednikh gubernii*, vol. II (Voronezh, 1891), pp. 139–41.

natural environment to their needs, and thus gradually made a 'cultural land-scape' out of a natural one.[16]

Location and space

The term 'peasant environments', as noted above, implies the environments which Russian peasants experienced in the course of their daily lives. These were therefore local environments for the most part. But environments can also be significant at broader scales – at the scale of the region, the state and even the international scale. Environments considered at these scales may impinge on the daily lives of the peasant, but they also have ramifications beyond the level of daily experience. This section considers some of the ways in which Russian society, and what eventually became the Muscovite state, were influenced by the fact of their location across an ever-expanding segment of the Eurasian land mass, the problems that such a location entailed and how Russians coped with the sheer fact of space.

We know relatively little about the detailed circumstances which attended the early Russian migrations across the mixed forest and the forest-steppe in the centuries before the Mongol conquest. What is clear is that these regions were not lacking in people and that, as they migrated and settled, Russians intermingled and to some degree merged with their Finno-Ugrian, Baltic and other predecessors. What also seems clear is that the Russians encountered limited organised resistance to their movements in this early period. What resistance there was came largely from the steppe whose nomadic inhabitants proved more than a match for the Russian agriculturalists. Later the threat coming from this direction grew with the arrival of more warlike peoples from the east, notably the Pechenegs, *Polovtsy*, and Tatars. As is well known, the Russians were thus prevented from settling the steppe for many centuries, as well as occasionally having to pay court to, and defend themselves against, their nomadic neighbours and their polities. Penetration of the steppe east of the Urals was likewise long hindered by the nomads.

As in the mixed forest, Russian penetration and settlement of the northlands also proceeded without much organised resistance. To the east, however, the movement of colonisation was hindered until the khanate of Kazan' was finally conquered by Ivan the Terrible in 1552. Thereafter the Russian conquest of Siberia took place remarkably quickly, and the first Russian settlement on the Pacific was planted in 1649. Only when the Russians encountered the

16 Sauer, 'Morphology'.

Chinese during the course of their seventeenth-century expansion did their growing ambitions in the Far East meet with a check. Even then, however, there was plenty of scope for continued expansion towards the Bering Strait and, eventually, on the continent of North America.[17]

To the west of the Russian realm a series of organised states and polities steadily competed with the Russians for the control of territory. These included both relatively ephemeral organisations like the Teutonic knights and organised states like Sweden, Poland, Hungary and Lithuania. In these regions, therefore, the geopolitical situation was much more European, with organised states in competition with one another and challenging territorial expansion by any one of them. Only in the seventeenth century did the Russian state prove powerful enough to make major territorial gains in this direction.

Russia's situation on the Eurasian land mass therefore proved crucial to its long-term development, with the state eventually expanding in virtually every direction from the small core which Muscovy had occupied in the early fourteenth century. Nowhere else in Europe did state expansion on such a scale prove possible – those West European states which began to found empires from the fifteenth century onwards could only do so overseas. Russia as a state on the eastern frontier of Europe was uniquely placed to found an empire across Eurasia.

Historians have long debated over the causes and nature of the colonisation processes which helped to build the Russian Empire. Some have emphasised the leading and stimulating role of the state in its quest for power and resources. Others have placed more emphasis on the spontaneous and opportunistic decisions of the ordinary Russian peasants and others as they sought to resist threats or to make the most of opportunities as they arose. In the nineteenth century, for example, the Ukrainian nationalistic historian of the steppe frontier, D. I. Bagalei, argued that Russian colonisation of the forest-steppe and steppe in the sixteenth and seventeenth centuries largely took place under the aegis of the state, contrasting this with the Ukrainian cossack settlement of the same territories which, Bagalei argued, was free.[18] Alternatively, many Soviet historians with their class-based view of history preferred to emphasise spontaneous peasant migration and settlement as part of the class struggle against the pretensions of the feudal state. Referring to the spontaneous internal colonisation of the mixed forest by the peasants, R. E. F. Smith has written: 'peasant flight

17 James R. Gibson, *Imperial Russia in Frontier America* (New York: Oxford University Press, 1976).
18 D. I. Bagalei, *Ocherki iz istorii kolonizatsii i byta stepnoi okrainy Moskovskogo gosudarstva* (Moscow, 1887), pp. 131–2.

and resistance seems to demonstrate that most peasants preferred life without the state. Their struggle with nature was hard, at times brutal, but they often evidently felt it was not as hard as the exactions and injustices imposed on them by the state.'[19] True as this observation no doubt is, the situation for the period covered by this book undoubtedly varied on different frontiers and at different points in time: sometimes the peasants took the initiative, sometimes the state, the lords or whoever. It is dangerous to attempt to generalise about a colonisation process which existed on such a scale and over such a long period of time as that contemplated here.

The question of how and with what degree of ease people were able to move across the vast distances of Russia naturally arises. Rivers were clearly crucial. As Franklin and Shepard have pointed out: 'When the compilers of the *Primary Chronicle* tried to explain where in the world their land lay, they conceived of it largely in terms of rivers and riverways. Tribes and peoples are named in connection with them, and great thoroughfares are described, together with journeys of famous men.'[20] Rivers thus seem to have been central to the identity of the early Russians. They were important to the peasants as providers of significant resources, as we have seen. And they were major routeways. Across the often featureless East European plain the broad and placid rivers provided relatively easy means of communication, and ones which usually ensured that the traveller did not become lost. Alternatively they often proved major barriers to those journeying by land. Chroniclers and others demonstrated an intimate knowledge of river systems and their interconnecting portages from an early period. As one writer has said of Siberian maps of the seventeenth century: 'One can learn little of Siberia except as a river-crossed land and a coast uniting the mouths of the great rivers.'[21] Little wonder that the key geographical descriptions, like the celebrated 'Book of the Great Map', compiled around 1627, were composed around the river network.[22]

There is no doubt, then, that the river network eased the passage of the Russians across their plain and eventually helped tie the far-flung Russian dominions together. In the era before powered transport, movement by water was generally cheaper and more efficient than that overland because of the reduction in the 'friction of space'. According to one estimate, the same force which can propel a load of 1.6 tons at a speed of one metre per second along

19 Smith, *Peasant Farming*, p. 221.
20 Franklin and Shepard, *The Emergence*, p. 3.
21 Henry R. Huttenbach, 'Hydrography and the origins of Russian cartography', in *Five Hundred Years of Nautical Science* (London: National Maritime Museum, 1981), pp. 142–52.
22 K. N. Serbina, *Kniga bol'shomu chertezhu* (Moscow and Leningrad: AN SSSR, 1950).

a smooth, horizontal road can move 60–100 tons at the same speed over motionless water.[23] Adam Olearius in his journey from Moscow to Astrakhan' down the Volga in the late 1630s reported seeing flat-bottomed boats with up to 400–500 lasts[24] of freight (primarily salt, caviar and salt fish) and with up to 200 workmen on board being hauled upstream in the opposite direction. Olearius left Moscow on 30 June and arrived at his destination, after numerous stops, on 15 September.[25] According to one estimate, average speed by river craft designed to carry passengers in the seventeenth century varied from 44 to 85 kilometres per twenty-four hours travelling downstream (Olearius achieved 144 kilometres in one twenty-four-hour period), and 25 to 46 travelling upstream.[26] At the same time, journeys by water encountered many difficulties and were frequently hazardous. Thus the navigation season was limited and it was often necessary to store cargo over the winter, increasing the possibility that it might perish or be stolen. In addition to the winter freeze, spring floods and summer drought might interfere with navigation. Many rivers suffered from rapids or waterfalls, making portages around the obstruction necessary or increasing the hazards of being wrecked. Shallows, shoals and sandbanks were other problems, with the added difficulty that they frequently moved around on the river bed. Travelling upstream was invariably slow and difficult. Teams of haulers (burlaki) began to be organised on the Volga from the sixteenth century to aid craft travelling in an upstream direction. Sailing across Russia's many lakes had many advantages, including enhanced possibilities for making use of sail, but there was an increased risk of being shipwrecked in storms.

On his journey down the Volga, Olearius encountered many of the hazards expected of a river expedition across the steppe in the seventeenth century. He was shot at by a party of Tatars from the river bank, threatened by cossack brigands, grounded on several occasions, lost an anchor on a drowned tree, encountered ice, faced problems from strong headwinds, was driven against the river bank and slowed up by the wind, suffered from the stale bread and dried fish his party ate, ran out of beer and faced both very hot and also stormy and inclement weather, which further impeded their passage.

---

23 Dulov, *Geograficheskaia sreda*, p. 109.
24 The seventeenth-century German Last appears to have varied in its significance as a unit of weight both regionally and by cargo. It therefore appears difficult to be certain what measure Olearius was using in this case.
25 A. Olearius, *The Travels of Olearius in Seventeenth-Century Russia*, trans. and ed. Samuel H. Baron (Stanford, Calif.: Stanford University Press, 1967), pp. 287, 296, 324.
26 Dulov, *Geograficheskaia sreda*, p. 121. But Olearius (*Travels*, p. 297) estimates no more than about 5 kilometres a day.

All told, it was a trip crowded with incident, but not perhaps unusually so for the period.[27]

In winter when rivers were frozen, or on routes where rivers were of little help, roads came into their own. Amongst the most notable of the latter were the traditional Tatar tracks (*shliakhi*) which followed the watersheds from the southern steppe and up towards the heart of Muscovy and which were used by parties of Tatars on their many raiding expeditions into Russia. For their part the Russians made only limited use of them since they had their own network of roads in the region. They were, however, a strategic threat and were thus the subject of defensive measures, as shown by the elaborate detail of the section of the 'Book of the Great Map' which describes the military map of the southern frontier, composed in the 1620s.[28] Other significant highways included the one running from Moscow to Iaroslavl', on to Vologda and thence either by road and/or river to Archangel, or via the Sukhona and Northern Dvina rivers to the same port. This was a route much frequented by Russian and foreign traders and by foreign ambassadors in the sixteenth and seventeenth centuries. North-west from Moscow ran the Novgorod road which had been used by Olearius on his journey from Western Europe, whilst westwards across the Moscow–Smolensk ridge ran the route via Viaz'ma, Dorogobuzh, Smolensk and into Lithuania. One of the most significant routes from the late sixteenth century was the combined river-and-road route to Siberia. To the end of the sixteenth century this route went from Velikii Ustiug on the River Sukhona in the north (see above) to Sol'vychegodsk, Lal'sk, Cherdyn' and Solikamsk and then via Lozvinsk across to Tavda and Tobol in Siberia. In 1595 it was decided to change this route to a more direct one which crossed the Urals at Verkhotur'e. From here the road ran via Tura and Tobol to Turinsk, Tiumen' and Tobol'sk. From the middle of the seventeenth century a new route was inaugurated from Moscow to Solikamsk via Viatka, whilst at the end of that century the section between Verkhotur'e and Tobol'sk was diverted once again to include the lively trading centre at Irbit. From Tobol'sk it was possible to proceed by river and road to the Enisei and thus into eastern Siberia. The flows of furs and other goods passing along these routes were controlled by a network of government customs posts located at strategic points.[29]

---

27 Olearius, *Travels*, pp. 287–324.
28 Serbina, *Kniga*; A. V. Postnikov, *Razvitie krupnomasshtabnoi kartografii v Rossii* (Moscow: Nauka, 1989), pp. 20–1.
29 *Kratkii istoricheskii ocherk razvitiia vodianykh i sukhoputnykh soobshchenii i torgovykh portov v Rossii* (St Petersburg: Kushnerev, 1900).

Travel by road in medieval Russia involved its own peculiar set of difficulties. The winter freeze allowed the use of the sledge, which had some of the advantages in terms of efficiency of travel by water, providing temperatures were not too low. In favourable circumstances speeds might be increased by 30–50 per cent compared with overland transport in summer.[30] As against that there was always the danger of losing one's way in the unmarked snow, of perishing as one attempted to cross a frozen river, of winter storms and of dying from exposure. Russian roads were not well maintained, neither were they generally furnished with the inns and other comforts which travellers in Western Europe could generally expect by the sixteenth century. Travellers usually had to seek overnight accommodation in private dwellings by the highway and, in a slightly populated land, such dwellings were few and far between. In the season of bad roads (*rasputitsa*) in spring and autumn roads were frequently impassable. Bridges and fords across rivers were a general hazard, floods were common and highways were often blocked by careless locals. Wild animals and wild people (robbers, brigands) added to the discomfort and dangers of travel by road.

As the Russian state unified and expanded it became necessary to devote additional resources to overcoming 'the friction of space'. Attempts were made to improve the upkeep of major highways, to regularise their construction and maintenance and to build and maintain bridges. From the sixteenth century a government postal service (*iamskaia gon'ba*) began to be organised along major routes connecting the capital with provincial centres and strategic points like Archangel. Along these routes relay stations were established at regular intervals at which designated servicemen (*iamshchiki*) were required to maintain teams of horses for the use of couriers carrying the government mails. Those travelling officially on government business might thus travel at speeds well above the norm. Summer journeys by couriers on the Moscow–Novgorod road, for example, might take six to seven days; those on the Moscow–Vologda route about five days. This suggests a speed of 80–100 kilometres per day.[31] Normal journeys were much slower.

Attempts to improve communication occurred alongside other policies to enhance the unity of the expanding state, including the reorganisation of provincial administration and military control, more careful attention paid to demarcation and defence of frontiers, attempts to impose a uniform system of weights and measures, a common currency and common laws. All this

---

30 Dulov, *Geograficheskaia sreda*, p. 116.
31 A. S. Kudriavtsev, *Ocherki istorii dorozhnogo stroitel'stva v SSSR* (Moscow, 1951), pt. I, p. 97.

was accompanied by new mechanisms to improve information-gathering on such matters as landholding, military dispositions, sources of income and wealth, communications and settlement. The sixteenth century witnessed the first attempts to map the realm. State-building, therefore, was much to do with improving government surveillance, pacification and exploitation of its territories and this meant enhancing its control over space. But such were the distances to be covered and the limited nature of the resources available to the state in pursuing its task that the process of state-building was both protracted and partial. In many ways Russia remained a weakly integrated realm down to the end of our period.

In expanding across the vast space of Eurasia Russians thus encountered many natural obstacles but also numerous opportunities. Space posed many challenges but was by no means an entirely negative phenomenon. It meant the possibility of new resources and also new horizons for those seeking to find new ways of life or to escape the restrictions of the old. The state could use space as a way of ridding itself of its internal enemies through exile, and as a means of defence against its external foes. The conquest of space also brought Russians into contact with the outside world.

Russia's particular location on the eastern edge of Europe and its expansion across Eurasia brought it into contact with a wide variety of peoples and cultures. As noted already, even in their initial colonisation of the European mixed forest the Rus' were not alone but were rather preceded by different Finno-Ugrian and Baltic peoples with whom they intermingled and to some degree merged. In this sense Russia was a multicultural realm from the very beginning, although what this meant in terms of cultural interchange is often lost in the mists of time. The Russians' location in the mixed forest zone, a region without definite boundaries and without obvious barriers against the outside world, also meant that they were in ready contact with others. The significance of the steppe, for example, should not be underestimated. Despite the differences in way of life and outlook on the world of the Russian agriculturalists on the one hand and the various steppe nomad peoples on the other, there was much trading and cultural interchange which were, of course, enhanced during the centuries of Mongol domination. What the long-term effects of such contacts were for the Russians have been much debated and there is little agreement among scholars. Relatively little is known of the wider cultural linkages which might have connected Russians to a broader Asian cultural realm beyond the immediate steppe. What is clear, however, is that geography brought the Russians into close contact with Asia in one form or another and that this fact must have had an important influence on their development. Russian expansion across Siberia towards the end of our period served to enhance and multiply such eastern linkages.

From the tenth century AD Russia entered Christendom in the form of Eastern Orthodoxy, bringing it into the cultural realm of Byzantium. Long-standing linkages between the Rus' and the Greek world across the steppe and via the Black Sea are no doubt implicated, as are the more immediate links with the Slavic peoples of the Balkans. Christianity brought the Rus' into a European cultural world, but unfortunately access to much of that cultural heritage was long denied by linguistic and other barriers. Russians thus remained ignorant of many of the cultural underpinnings to Christianity until quite a late stage. Only in the seventeenth century with increased contacts with the West did this situation begin to change significantly.

Russia's Orthodox culture created a barrier with Catholic Europe to the west which was long exacerbated by problems of securing easy access to the sea and to suitable overland routes. Competition with Poland-Lithuania, Sweden and other states compounded these difficulties. Thus, although Novgorod and Pskov had significant trading links with the Baltic and overland links with Central Europe also existed, contacts with Western Europe long remained distant. Russia remained on the edge of many European developments and was unable to participate in the expanding world of European and transatlantic commerce until quite late. The arrival of the English and the Dutch via the White Sea in the late sixteenth century signalled the beginnings of closer contacts and trade relations, after which Russians began to take a greater interest in European affairs, including its technological and cultural achievements. But only with the reign of Peter the Great and the securing of Russia's 'window' on the West at St Petersburg on the Baltic can a 'Europeanisation' of Russian culture be said to have begun.

Resources for subsistence and development

Russia, as we have seen, was hindered by geography as well as by political factors from participating in the expanding commerce which began to assume greater importance in Western Europe from about the fifteenth century. Geography also hindered commercial development in Russia itself. The difficulties of road and river communications which have been commented on above, the huge distances involved, low population densities, and the generally small size and widely spaced character of the towns, all hindered commercial relations. One of the essential differences between Russia and Western Europe was (and is) their geographies, in other words their basic spatial relationships. This essential difference explains much (though not everything) in their differing development trajectories.

Because Russian governments were unable to rely on the fruits of commerce to raise the revenue they required, great emphasis had to be placed on marshalling the country's internal resources. Thus from the sixteenth century at least, landholders found themselves obliged to render service to the state in exchange for their rights to the land. For their part the peasants found themselves tied to their estates and obliged to serve their masters. Their final enserfment occurred in the middle of the seventeenth century. The state regulated landholding and raised its revenues through taxation. It also took great interest in the possibilities of gaining access to new sources of wealth such as new land. A number of scholars have emphasised the importance for European economic development of the greatly enhanced access to a whole range of new and expanded resources which resulted from European overseas expansion.[32] This augmented access was referred to by one scholar as 'the Great Frontier', by another as a once-for-all 'ecological windfall'.[33] Russia too experienced something of a windfall as a result of its territorial expansion, albeit one that was very much more restricted than that experienced in Western Europe. Russia's major acquisitions during our period were the north and Siberia which had considerable resources of many kinds but with a harsh climate and restricted opportunities for settlement and agriculture. It was only towards the end of the period that the Russians began to settle the fertile soils of the forest-steppe and steppe. And of course Russian expansion failed to bring it direct access to the tropical products which were to play such an important role in European commercial expansion.

Agricultural resources remained basic to the Russian economy throughout the period covered by this book. Something has been said already of the conditions under which agriculture was practised and of the difficulties it faced. The available evidence seems to suggest that agriculture under Russian conditions was much less productive than it was in Western Europe. To some degree this can be put down to social factors like the fact that Russian agricultural practices were generally much less intensive than those found further west. But the natural environment was also a significant problem. The long, harsh winters and the restricted growing season (a frost-free period of about 130 days around Moscow), the possibility of late frost in spring and early frosts in the autumn, the low fertility of many soils and lack of manure were among

---

32 W. P. Webb, *The Great Frontier* (Boston: Houghton Mifflin, 1952); E. L. Jones, *The European Miracle* (Cambridge: Cambridge University Press, 1981), pp. 70–84.
33 Jones, *The European Miracle*, p. 84.

the most important difficulties. Yields seem to have been quite low for most crops. Thus a yield of threefold for winter rye seems to have been normal for various parts of the mixed forest zone in the sixteenth century.[34] Yields were apparently little better in the more fertile forest-steppe to the south, perhaps because agricultural practices there were even more extensive.[35] Low soil fertility in the mixed forest zone seems often to have been connected to a lack of manure, and here the difficulties of maintaining livestock are implicated. The long period during which farm animals had to be stall fed (200 days or more) because of the severe winters was made more difficult by a lack of hay in many instances. Hay-lands were not especially productive, again a reflection of the severe climate, and hay had to be taken wherever it could be found, supplemented by whatever feed of other kinds was available. Altogether, the average peasant farm probably found it quite hard to survive. As one study of production and consumption on the peasant farm put it: 'the peasant farm unit could provide enough grain for the humans, especially in those periods of the family's life when the burden of children relative to working adults was not too great, but – the livestock sector was likely to be in part, sometimes in large part, dependent on supplies from the forest.'[36]

Agriculture therefore provided a relatively small surplus, although that surplus may well have been greater where estates were better organised, as was the case for some of the great monasteries.[37] Agricultural products, like flax and hemp and their derivatives, leather, tallow, hides and even some grain entered into trade, including the export trade. Such products seem to have been predominant in Russian exports around 1600.[38] Also important, however, were the products of what Jones called 'the boreal woods'.[39] Firstly, there were the furs for which Muscovy became particularly famous in the sixteenth century, even though the fur trade had been going on for many centuries. Sable, ermine, marten, fox and squirrel from the Russian forests were delivered to 'all ends of the earth'.[40] Forest products like furs, wax and

34 Smith, *Peasant Farming*, pp. 86–7.
35 I. N. Miklashevskii, *K istorii khoziaistvennogo byta Moskovskogo gosudarstva*, vol. 1: *Zaselenie i sel'skoe khoziaistvo iuzhnoi okrainy v XVII veke* (Moscow: D. I. Inozemtsev, 1894), p. 230; L. B. Veinberg, *Ocherk sel'skokhoziaistvennoi promyshlennosti Voronezhskoi gubernii* (Voronezh, 1891), p. 54.
36 Smith, *Peasant Farming*, p. 94.
37 Ibid., pp. 24–32.
38 Paul Bushkovitch, *The Merchants of Moscow, 1580–1650* (Cambridge: Cambridge University Press, 1980), p. 102.
39 Jones, *The European Miracle*, p. 81.
40 Janet Martin, *Treasure of the Land of Darkness* (Cambridge: Cambridge University Press, 1986), p. 167.

honey seem to have predominated in the Russian export trade around 1500.[41] Other boreal and northern resources which entered into trade included skins and hides as well as fish, train oil and other products. In the eighteenth century the export of naval stores (timber, pitch, resin, tar, turpentine as well as hemp) became significant. The relevance of forest resources to the peasant economy was discussed earlier in this chapter. Of course products like timber and wood fuel were important at many levels, as were other items like potash.

The Russian state and economy were dependent on many other natural resources in our period.[42] These were exploited wherever conditions allowed. There is space to mention only two, both important because of their roles in trade and commerce and also in the household economy. One is iron ore or limonite, mined in various swampy parts of the East European plain but in relatively small quantities. Before Peter the Great's development of the Urals iron industry, local ores provided a major source for the Tula iron industry from the first half of the seventeenth century. Iron was, of course, necessary for weaponry and many kinds of equipment; some better-quality iron was imported. The other significant item was salt. The earliest industry may have been concentrated on the shores of the White Sea where salt was initially evaporated from sea water. Later this technique was largely replaced by drilling for brine. Exploitation of surface or underground brine also took place at various points in north and central European Russia, notably at Staraia Rusa near Novgorod, in the Vychegda and Sukhona valleys (Sol' Vychegda, Iarensk, Tot'ma), at various locations in central Russia, and later on the upper Kama (Sol' Kama). Other sources of salt, which came into greater prominence in the seventeenth century, were on the middle Volga near Samara, and near Astrakhan' (Elton, Baskunchak). Some salt also came from the upper Irtysh in Siberia.[43]

Environmental risks and uncertainties

The natural environment is in constant process of change. Some of the changes are, as we have seen, long term, whether human-induced or natural. Others are short term. Some are cyclical, others erratic. This final section is concerned

---

41 Bushkovitch, *The Merchants*, p. 102.
42 See e.g. Richard Hellie, *The Economy and Material Culture of Russia, 1600–1725* (Chicago: University of Chicago Press, 1999).
43 R. E. F. Smith and David Christian, *Bread and Salt: A Social and Economic History of Food and Drink in Russia* (Cambridge: Cambridge University Press, 1984), pp. 27–73.

with events which made life for Russians risky and more uncertain than it might seem to have been when looked at only in a long-term perspective.

That Russia was a disordered and sometimes chaotic society has been noted already. Part of this, as we have seen, was related to the difficulty of controlling space, to the problem of surveillance and pacification over such a huge, sparsely populated territory. Another part related to the problem of securing the frontiers of the state. All pre-modern states had difficulties in this regard, but where frontiers were 'open', as they were across much of southern and eastern Russia during our period, those difficulties were particularly intractable. The steppe frontier to the south was open to the raiding tactics of the nomads, among whom the Crimean Tatars and their allies the Nogais proved especially troublesome over the last two centuries of the period. Raiding for booty and especially slaves was a constant menace, particularly in times when Russia found itself in conflict with the Ottomans, allied perhaps with the Poles or others. In 1571 and 1591, for example, the Tatars attacked Moscow itself. There were serious problems during the Time of Troubles, and again in the 1630s and 1640s. By this time the government had proceeded to the building of the Belgorod defensive line which eventually helped to keep the Tatar raiding parties at bay.[44] But serious raids along and to the south of the line continued, as at Usman' in 1652 and Voronezh district in 1659.[45] Losses of population (through fighting and capture) and of property were considerable, but all estimates are necessarily conjectural. To add to these problems were raids by the Kalmyks, as in 1674,[46] and constant difficulties with cossack groups. The latter reached their climax in the mass uprisings under Ivan Bolotnikov (1606–7) and Sten'ka Razin (1667–71).

One of the many unfortunate by-products of social disorder was destruction of people and property by fire, as at Voronezh in 1590 when a group of Ukrainian cossacks set fire to the wooden town with considerable loss of life.[47] Fire was in fact a constant menace to virtually all Russian towns in view of their closely packed, mainly wooden buildings. According to Sytin, for example, Moscow suffered around thirty big fires between the twelfth and sixteenth centuries, including fires in 1501, 1508, 1531, three times in 1547, 1560–2, 1564–5, 1571 and 1591

---

44 V. P. Zagorovskii, *Belgorodskaia cherta* (Voronezh: Izdatel'stvo Voronezhskogo Gosudarstvennogo Universiteta, 1969).

45 L. B. Veinberg, *Materialy po istorii Voronezhskoi i sosednikh gubernii. Drevnie akty XVII stoletiia* (16 vols., Voronezh, 1885–90), vol. I, no. 54, vol. II, nos. 23, 133, 144, 145.

46 M. De-Pule, *Materialy po istorii Voronezhskoi i sosednikh gubernii. Orlovskie akty XVII–XVIII stoletii* (Voronezh, 1861), pp. 350–4.

47 V. P. Zagorovskii, *Voronezh: istoricheskaia khronika* (Voronezh: Tsentral'no-Chernozemnoe knizhnoe izdatel'stvo, 1989), p. 16.

(years of Tatar attacks) and 1595.[48] It was after the big fire of May 1626, which consumed the Kremlin and much of the Kitai gorod, that the tsar ordered the old 'Great Map' of the state to be renewed.[49] But the new maps, together with the old one, were subsequently lost, possibly as a result of further fires which continued to visit damage and death on the capital and in fact on all Russian towns to the end of the period. It is a notable fact that it was the fear of fire which helped induce the first attempts at building control (and hence at planning) in Russian towns well before the time of Peter the Great and led to the organisation of the first fire patrols.[50]

The vagaries of the weather were, as we know, productive of much suffering in addition to their undoubted contribution to fire outbreaks. Their effects may have been exacerbated by the deterioration in climate which is believed to have occurred in the fifteenth century.[51] Since Russian towns and villages were often located on river banks, for instance, flooding was a constant risk. A flood on the Voronezh River in spring 1616, for example, ruined the wooden buildings of the Assumption monastery standing on the river bank and many adjacent homes.[52] This was only the first of many such floods in subsequent years. The prospect of harvest failure and famine was also constant, either at national scale or locally. The famines of 1601–4, for example, were said by one unreliable report to have killed over half a million people in Moscow alone.[53] That of 1704–5 swept across central Russia after a particularly severe winter which killed the winter crop.[54] Local food shortages were much more common, as at Valuiki in 1667–9 and 1674, and at Orlov in 1677 and 1680–1. Local governors (voevody) were instructed to establish grain stores in case of such eventualities. But the problems of doing so in what was evidently a situation of minimal grain surpluses were evidently considerable.

A greater immediate risk in the everyday lives of Russians was poor health and disease, exacerbated among other things by poor diet. Russians were prey to numerous diseases throughout their usually short lives, ranging from deficiency diseases to ergotism and other fungi-produced diseases, to debilitating illnesses like malaria, tuberculosis and scurvy, and to epidemics of plague,

48 P. V. Sytin, *Istoriia planirovki i zastroiki Moskvy. Materialy i issledovaniia*, vol. I: 1147–1762 (Moscow: Trudy Muzeia Istorii i Rekonstruktsii Moskvy, vyp. 1, 1950), pp. 53, 56, 59.
49 Postnikov, *Razvitie*, p. 26.
50 Sytin, *Istoriia*, pp. 83ff.
51 Dulov, *Geograficheskaia sreda*, pp. 14–18; I. E. Buchinskii, *O klimate proshlogo Russkoi ravniny* (Leningrad, 1958).
52 Zagorovskii, *Voronezh*, p. 20.
53 Smith and Christian, *Bread and Salt*, pp. 109–10.
54 Ibid., p. 189.

smallpox, influenza and typhoid fever. Urban environments were particularly susceptible to the epidemics. The plague of 1654, for example, was reputed to have killed up to 80 per cent of Moscow's inhabitants.[55] That of 1709–13 ravaged the newly conquered Baltic lands, Novgorod, Pskov and some parts of Ukraine. Urban populations suffered particularly.[56] Disease of domesticated animals and crops was also a major problem.[57]

Scholars are generally agreed that medieval Russia was a risky environment for human endeavour, but are less unanimous about how those risks compared with those, say, in Western Europe in the period. This is a topic which awaits further research.

Conclusion

The story of medieval Russia is a story of how Russians adapted to, and also moulded to their needs, a series of rather different natural environments. Whilst Russians first encountered and adapted to the various habitats they found in the mixed forest belt, they were subsequently attracted by the range of resource opportunities available in other natural zones. This, of course, was also true of other societies, and particularly of the West European ones which embarked upon their great overseas ventures from the fifteenth century onwards. Yet Russia was unique in that its expansion took place upon contiguous but hardly uniform territory. Over this territory its peasant communities gradually spread, in the suggestive words of one scholar, 'like biological cells' into the available space.[58] The absence of an intervening ocean, as well as the particular quality of the environments which Russians colonised, may tell us much about that particular society and its evolution. This chapter is written in the belief that Russia's geographical environment is integral to what we understand by Russia.

---

55 *Istoriia Moskvy*, vol. I: *Period feodalizma, XII–XVII vv.* (Moscow: AN SSSR, 1952), p. 453.
56 A. Kahan, *The Plow, the Hammer and the Knout: An Economic History of Eighteenth-Century Russia* (Chicago: Chicago University Press, 1985), p. 15.
57 Dulov, *Geograficheskaia sreda*, pp. 22–4.
58 Smith, *Peasant Farming*, p. 9.

PART I

EARLY RUS' AND THE RISE OF MUSCOVY (*c.*900–1462)

3

The origins of Rus' (*c*.900–1015)

JONATHAN SHEPARD

The Rus' *Primary Chronicle*'s quest for the origins of Rus'

The question of the origins of Rus', how a 'land' of that name came into being and from what, has been asked almost since record-keeping began in the middle Dnieper region. The problem is formulated in virtually these terms at the beginning of the Rus' *Primary Chronicle*. The chronicle supposes a political hierarchy to have formed at a stroke, through a covenant between locals and outsiders. The Slavs, Finns and other natives of a land mass criss-crossed by great rivers agreed jointly to call in a ruler from overseas. Turning to 'the Varangians, to the Rus'' they said 'our land is vast and abundant, but there is no order in it. Come and reign as princes and have authority over us!'[1] The response, in the form of the arrival of three princely brothers with 'their kin' and 'all the Rus'', is dated to around 862. The younger brothers soon died and the survivor, Riurik, joined their possessions to his own and assigned his men to the various 'towns' (*grady*). There were already 'aboriginal inhabitants' in them, 'in Novgorod, the Slovenes; in Polotsk, the Krivichi; in Beloozero, the Ves . . . And Riurik ruled over them all.' Before long a move was made southwards to the middle Dnieper by non-princely 'Varangians', Askold and Dir. They are said to have come upon a small town called Kiev and took charge, having learnt that the inhabitants paid tribute to the Khazars. Later a certain Oleg arrived, not, apparently, a prince himself, but acting on behalf of Riurik's infant son, Igor'. Denouncing Askold and Dir as 'neither princes, nor of princely stock', Oleg brought forth the child with the words 'Behold the son of Riurik!' and the two unlicensed venturers were put to death. The

---

1 *Povest' vremennykh let* (hereafter *PVL*), ed. V. P. Adrianova-Peretts and D. S. Likhachev with revisions by M. B. Sverdlov, 2nd edn (St Petersburg: Nauka, 1996), p. 13. 'Varangians' overseas can, in this context, only have meant Scandinavians.

installation of princely rule in Kiev is dated around 882, with Oleg acting as Igor''s military commander.[2]

This sequence of tableaux was still being incorporated in works such as the chronicle of Nikon in the sixteenth century. They form the framework to any 'political' survey of the areas that would come to form part of Muscovy and, eventually, Russia. The *Primary Chronicle*'s focus on princes can readily be dismissed as an oversimplification, a variant of European foundation myths involving two or three brothers. And the chronology sets developments both too early and too late. In reality, some sort of hegemonial structure already existed in the second quarter of the ninth century, perhaps earlier still, whereas the middle Dnieper only became a significant princely centre a generation or more after 882. Other qualifications could be made to the chronicle's picture, which is very much a product of the time when it neared completion, the opening years of the twelfth century, and also of the place – the Kievan Caves monastery. By then, the routes leading southwards along such rivers as the Volkhov and the Western Dvina to converge at the Dnieper and run down to the sea – 'the way from the Varangians to the Greeks' – formed an axis of obvious (though not unassailable) primacy. The chroniclers' wishful assumption that power was from the first vested at points such as Novgorod and Kiev is understandable. They had little time for alternatives, such as routes from northerly regions to the Khazars based on the lower Volga and to the Islamic world. They note that people's rituals and customs across this 'vast' land had been variegated,[3] but there are only occasional hints that princely authority itself might have been strung across several political centres through the ninth and most of the tenth centuries.

The vicissitudes of one leading family are treated as virtually synonymous with the emergence and extent of the land of Rus'. And yet in addressing the questions posed at the beginning of the chronicle – 'Whence came the land of Rus', who first began to rule as prince in Kiev . . .?'[4] – the chroniclers did not play fast and loose with facts. Some places mentioned as centres of the 'Varangian' newcomers have been shown by excavations to have had Scandinavian occupants and visitors from the outset, for example Staraia Ladoga, while archaeology is uncovering important settlements started by 'aboriginal inhabitants' before the arrival of Scandinavians, for example, at Murom, Sarskoe and Pskov and a fortified settlement on the site of Izborsk. Other aspects of the chronicle's tableaux likewise gain corroboration from independent

2 *PVL*, p. 14.

3 The whereabouts and languages of different tribal groupings are described: *PVL*, pp. 10–11.

4 *PVL*, p. 7.

evidence. The princely line traced back in the chronicle was the most resilient and effective of whichever other ruling kin groups may have existed among the early Rus' (for the known descendants of Riurik, see Table 3.1). The name of the leading brother points clearly to an Old Norse original, *HrǿrīkR*, a form philologically plausible for the ninth century, when Riurik is supposed to have lived.[5] His son Igor' – the Slavic form of whose name harks back to Old Norse *Inghari* – is an unquestionably historical figure. And for the final decade or so of the ninth century there is archaeological evidence of the establishment at Kiev of persons from much further north. Thus the *Primary Chronicle* registers actual political change and population movement under way in the late ninth century. But its composers drew from an exiguous database, spreading it thinly across gaps in their knowledge. Riurik is depicted as a commanding figure in the mid-ninth century, yet his son was active in the mid-tenth.[6] To gain an inkling of antecedents, one has to glance back to sources written far away and without first-hand knowledge, and to the oft equivocal findings of archaeology.

The beginnings of political formations

First signs of an organised power in the forest zone and of long-distance trading between the Muslim and Baltic worlds

There had been a political hierarchy somewhere north of the middle Dnieper long before the turn of the ninth century, but it is hard to reconstruct the barest outlines. One firm fact is that by 838 there existed the ruler of a 'people' known to the Byzantines as *Rhōs* and answering to that, or a very similar, name. Some *Rhōs* accompanied a Byzantine embassy to the court of Louis the Pious, who was requested to assist them back to their 'homeland'.[7] The contemporary Frankish court annal relating this is carefully worded. It shows that the *Rhōs* were well enough organised under a 'king' to send a mission to the Byzantine emperor, with sufficient resources for long-range embassies. The annal provides further clues about the strangers, clues at once suggestive and confusing. They described their own ruler as a *chaganus*, and when Louis investigated 'more diligently' he discovered that they 'belonged to the people

---

5 G. Schramm, *Altrusslands Anfang. Historische Schlüsse aus Namen, Wörtern und Texten zum 9. und 10. Jahrhundert* (Freiburg im Breisgau: Rombach, 2002), pp. 265–6. Names preceded by asterisks are the hypothetical Scandinavian forms from which the Slavonic names derive.

6 *PVL*, pp. 13, 22–7.

7 *Annales Bertiniani*, ed. F. Grat, J. Vielliard and S. Clémencet (Société de l'histoire de France 470) (Paris: C. Klincksieck, 1964), pp. 30–1.

Table 3.1. *Prince Riurik's known descendants*

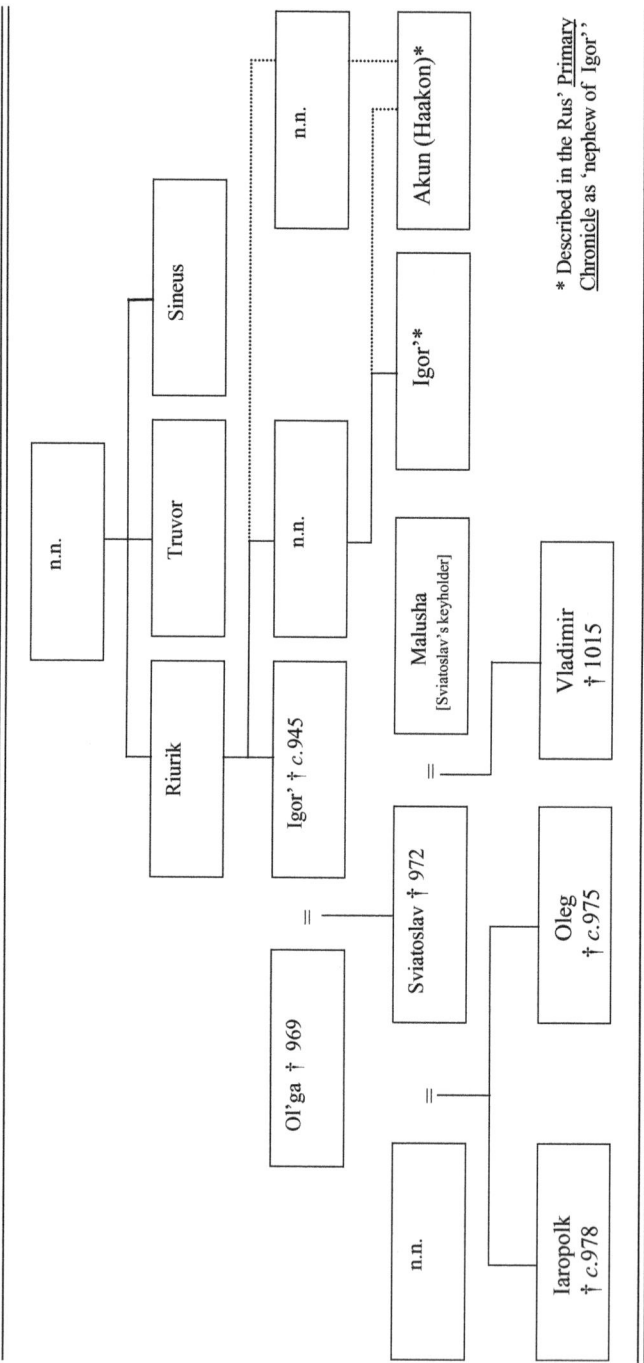

* Described in the Rus' Primary Chronicle as 'nephew of Igor'

of the Swedes'. Fearing they might be spies, he detained them for further questioning. Thus their ruler bore a title akin to that of the ruler of the Khazars, the khagan, while their characteristics suggested those of 'Swedes'.

Countless historical interpretations revolve around this annalistic entry. There is no matrix against which to judge the inherent plausibility of one reconstruction against another. Much depends on assumptions about overall conditions between the Gulf of Finland and the Khazar-dominated Don and Volga steppes. But coexistence of a Scandinavian-led polity to the north with a Khazar power collecting tribute as far west as the Dnieper is the scenario implied in the *Primary Chronicle*. Objections can, of course, be raised: for example, to the discrepancy between the annal's intimation of a polity in 838 and the *Primary Chronicle*'s chronology, and the sheer unlikelihood of a supposedly Swedish potentate assuming a Khazar title. There is, however, suggestive evidence of other Khazar and Turkic nomad traits in some of the Rus' elite's status symbols – for example the sporting of belts studded with metal mounts and of bridles with elaborate sets of ornaments (see also below). Moreover, ambitious Scandinavian warlords in the British Isles were apt to take on local customs and Christian kingly attributes to bolster their regimes.

There are several reasons why Khazar styles of rulership and titles would have resonated among the inhabitants of major river basins north of the Black Sea steppes. This semi-nomadic people showed formidable organisational powers, regularly extracting resources from its neighbours, while the *pax khazarica* in the steppes between the Crimea and north-east of the Caspian Sea beckoned to traffickers along the 'Silk Roads' from the Far East, Caucasian markets and the core lands of the Abbasid caliphate. The abatement of Arab attempts to submit the Khazars and other steppe-dwellers to Islam, followed by the Abbasids' issue of huge quantities of silver dirhams from the mid-eighth century onwards, gave a fillip to trade nexuses of long standing. The dynamics of these exchanges are unknown to us and they fluctuated according to circumstances. But the predisposition of populations to cluster around lakes and along riverways provided staging posts and potential emporia for longer-distance traders. Great lakes such as Il'men' and Ladoga performed a dual function. Their resources and the fertile lakeside soils sustained sizeable concentrations of persons engaged in hunting, fishing and agriculture with iron ploughs. But they also acted as communications hubs, drawing in miscellaneous groups and individuals and enabling them to practise craftsmanship and trade. The nexuses between fur-yielding northern regions, the peoples of the steppes and Sasanian Persian and Byzantine markets attested in the sixth and earlier seventh centuries were probably not obliterated by the first century of Arab conquests. Their persistence would account for the speed with which silver coins from Abbasid mints reached the Gulf of Finland. At the small trading-post of Staraia Ladoga, Abbasid coins occur in almost the earliest 'micro-horizon'; so does a set of smith's tools analogous to kits found in Scandinavia. Workshops welded knives by an apparently Scandinavian technique, produced nails and boat rivets and by the beginning of the ninth century, if not earlier, glass beads were being worked up. One of the earliest hoards of dirhams uncovered in Russia was deposited early in the ninth century beside the Gulf of Finland, just west of modern St Petersburg. On some, Scandinavian-type runes and Arabic characters are scratched while the name of 'Zacharias' is scratched in Greek on one dirham and others have Turkic runes, such as might have been acquired en route through the Khazar dominions.[8] These markings serve as a paradigm of the types of outsider then active in the fur trade. And it can hardly be coincidental that dirhams feature among grave goods in central Sweden from the end of the eighth century. The region of Sweden facing the Åland islands was known in medieval Swedish law codes as 'Rodhen' or 'Rodhs'. The Baltic Finns' designation for persons hailing from there, *Rōtsi*, probably became attached to all Scandinavians whom they encountered. So did the version subsequently borrowed by the Slavs, *Rus'*. These *Rōtsi* probably traded in smallish groups on their own account, but emporia east of the Baltic facilitated travel and exchange, while an overarching symbol of authority would have encouraged order. An overlord sporting the same title as the Khazar ruler's – through whose dominions the dirhams, mentioned above, passed – fitted the bill. There is thus some congruence between the Frankish annals' indication of a Scandinavian 'people' headed by a khagan and the chronicle's tale of the native peoples' covenant with 'Varangians'.

Signs of turbulence c.860–c.871

The location of the principal base of the 'khagan of the Northmen' (as a Byzantine imperial letter of 871 termed him)[9] is controversial, but may well have looked onto Lake Il'men', just south of the later Novgorod. Fortified from the start and with outlying settlements dating from the beginning of the ninth century or earlier, this large settlement-cum-emporium dominated communications northwards to Ladoga, eastwards towards the Volga's headwaters, and south towards the Western Dvina. The island-like site of what is

8 E. A. Mel'nikova, *Skandinavskie runicheskie nadpisi. Novye nakhodki i interpretatsii* (Moscow: Vostochnaia Literatura, 2001), pp. 107, 115–19.
9 'chaganum...Northmannorum': Louis II, *Epistola ad Basilium I.*, Monumenta Germaniae Historica, Epistolae Karolini Aevi, V (Berlin: Weidmann, 1928), p. 388.

now called Riurikovo Gorodishche could well be the inspiration for Arabic descriptions of a huge boggy 'island', three days' journey wide, where 'the *khāqān* of the Rūs' resided.[10] This is presumably where a Byzantine religious mission headed for in the earlier 860s. The mission was requested by the Rus' soon after a great fleet had sailed to Constantinople, looting the suburbs but apparently coming to grief in a storm on the way back. This Viking-style raid had at least the co-operation of the Rus' leadership and our main Byzantine source for the subsequent mission intimates that its purpose was to convert the ruler and notables responsible.[11] Many participants in the 860 expedition are likely to have been newcomers to the lands east of the Baltic and a fresh influx of fortune-seeking war-bands could well account for the disorder and political discontinuity evident for the final third of the century. Staraia Ladoga seems to have been razed to the ground between *c*.863 and *c*.871; around the same time there was a conflagration at Gorodishche and other settlements in the Volkhov basin suffered devastating fires in the second half of the ninth century.

One cannot be sure whether the archaeological evidence registers one wave of turbulence or recurrent bouts. But the damage done to two outstanding emporia cannot have been without political implications, and there was probably at least one change of princely regime. The Byzantine mission could well have been dislodged by such upheavals: there is no further trace of a prelate among the Rus' for a hundred years. The violence did not put paid to commercial vitality and may actually have been prompted by it, in that accumulation of silver and other treasure could be used to win followers and spectacularly raise one's status, while one of the main 'products' exchanged for dirhams was slaves, a trade involving at least the threat of duress. But incessant free-for-all violence was deleterious to so intricate a network, consisting of clusters of settlements around major emporia, towards which countless outlying 'feeders' contributed the most important product of all, furs. So it would not be surprising if a rather tighter political order emerged after a period of instability. One hint is the construction at Staraia Ladoga of what was apparently a citadel, surrounded by limestone slabs. Across the river from the expanding settlement, at Plakun, warriors armed in Scandinavian mode began to fill a separate burial ground. In the mid-890s a 'great hall' was built, partly from dismantled ship's timbers, and this could well have been where a prince or governor lived. The

---

10 Ibn Rusta, *Kitāb al-A'lāk an-nafīsa*, ed. T. Lewicki, *Źródła arabskie do dziejów słowiańszczyzny*, vol. II.2 (Wrocław, Warsaw, Cracow, and Gdansk: Polska Akademia Nauk, 1977), pp. 38–41.
11 *Theophanes Continuatus*, ed. I. Bekker (Corpus scriptorum historiae byzantinae) (Bonn: E. Weber, 1838), pp. 196, 342–3.

ensemble may register an attempt to guard the western approaches of Rus'
against further marauders or conquerors from the Scandinavian world.

At the other end of the Volkhov, Gorodishche likewise recovered from
physical destruction. By the end of the ninth century structures were being
raised on boggier ground below the original hill-fortress. Workshops turned
out Scandinavian-style brooches for women, weaponry and other metalwork
for men. Silver, glass beads and other semi- de luxe items from eastern markets
were dealt in, hoarded or worn as ornaments and, as at other centres of
the trading nexus, pottery was beginning to be turned on the wheel rather
than moulded by hand. Grandees, full-time warriors and wealthy wives were
probably of Scandinavian stock, like the princely family presumed to have
presided over them. But the majority of those choosing to work bone, wood
and clay at Gorodishche were Slavs and Finns, some having travelled great
distances to do so. Finds of their products attest this. The composition of the
populations of other centres such as Pskov varied according to circumstances,
but a constant is the presence of wealthy, armed, Scandinavians.

In the later ninth century a number of settlements, some quite sizeable
and accommodating new arrivals from the Åland isles, appeared near the
largely Finnish settlements flanking major lakes and rivers connected with the
upper Volga. Their inhabitants, like many of the locals, engaged in the fur
trade and it was probably prospects of self-enrichment as well as the fertile
soils around Lake Nero and Lake Pleshcheevo that attracted them. The area
offered good hunting and trapping, and connections between centres such as
Sarskoe and fur-yielding regions much further north were long established.
The newcomers' boatmanship provided means of reaching lucrative markets
by water. Towards the end of the ninth century a new political structure
formed on the middle Volga, under the auspices of the khagan of the Bulgars;
the Bulgars themselves amassed huge quantities of furs from the north through
barter and tribute collection. Two or three weeks' river journey to the Volga
mouth brought one to the Khazar capital, Itil, while caravan routes led overland
to the Samanid realm in Transoxiana. From the end of the ninth century the
Samanids issued immense quantities of dirhams to stimulate trade. The Bulgar
khagan took from them his first silver coins' designs, and soon the Bulgar elite
was Muslim, with mosques and schools. The Rus' newcomers to the upper
Volga fully exploited their relative proximity to ample supplies of silver. Tenth-
century Samanid dirhams form easily the largest group of Islamic coins found
in what is now Russia and a high proportion of those found in the Baltic
world. These exchanges did not, however, require a particularly high level of
regular co-ordination or armed protection. So although the Volga Rus' and

their collaborators made up a kind of polity, perhaps for a while distinct from that in the north-west, they did not create a tight politico-military structure. Silver in the north-east was too easily obtainable and shared out too widely; the routes to northernmost furs were too multifarious. In so far as order needed to be maintained along the middle and lower reaches of the Volga, the Bulgars and Khazars were already there in force.

The installation of northerners on the middle Dnieper towards the end of the ninth century may be viewed against this background. Their cultural characteristics – including language – were still preponderantly Scandinavian and they will have been deemed *Rhōs*, much as the envoys to Byzantium in 838/9 had been. But in so far as status in the burgeoning 'urban' networks was attainable by wealth, advance was open to a wider range of individuals and outriders willing to adopt the elite's working practices. Besides, a likely by-product of the trade in nubile slave girls was children of mixed origins. The newcomers from the north used building techniques characteristic of settlements such as Staraia Ladoga rather than the middle Dnieper region. Log cabins were built on the damp soil beside the river at Kiev in the 890s, judging by dendrochronological analysis, and many structures served as workshops or warehouses. The riverside took on a new importance in the economy of what was still a small town. Kiev had been of significance as an emporium in antiquity, a convenient point for bartering forest produce for products of the steppes and southern civilisations. And it may well have been a staging post for Radhanite Jewish traders shuttling between Western Europe, Itil and China. But only around the end of the ninth century did the Dnieper gain primary importance as a waterway. Kiev became the trading base of navigators capable of negotiating the fearsome Rapids downstream and then, from the Dnieper's mouth, raising masts and setting sail for markets across the sea. It was essentially for this purpose that northerners installed themselves in force at Kiev, Chernigov and nearby Shestovitsa.

Within a few years emissaries were negotiating with the Byzantine emperor and gaining the right for Rus' to trade toll-free in Constantinople itself, entering the city in groups of fifty 'through [only] one gate, without their weapons'. Provided that they brought merchandise, free board and lodgings were theirs for six months as well as 'food, anchors, ropes and sails and whatever is needed' for the return journey.[12] An initial charter of privileges was soon followed by a bilateral treaty laying down procedures to settle likely disputes between individual Rus' and Byzantines, and also regulations for shipwrecks and due

---

12 *PVL*, p. 17.

restitution of cargo. The emissaries' provenance is uncertain, but all five of those named as responsible for the first agreement recur among the fourteen listed for the September 911 treaty. Such continuity and regard for law and order implies a political structure, while the emissaries' names have a Nordic ring: Karl, Rulav, Stemid.

The northerners' move to Kiev might initially have been an attempt at secession from the other Rus' strongpoints, reminiscent of the tale of Askold and Dir. But these traders could scarcely have stood alone for very long, seeing that the finest furs originated far to the north. The 911 treaty, if not its precursor, most probably involved northern-based princes, as well as magnates newly installed on the middle Dnieper. By contrast with Kiev a centre such as Gorodishche was huge and populous, and the military potential of its ruling elite correspondingly formidable. In the early tenth century as earlier, this elite had a paramount leader. An Arab envoy to the Bulgars, who observed Rus' traders on the middle Volga in 922, evoked the court of the Rus' ruler. Residing on a huge throne together with forty slave girls, he mounts his horse without ever touching the ground; 400 'bravest companions' live in his 'palace', 'men who die with him and kill themselves for him'. A lieutenant commands troops and fights his battles.[13] The Rus' debt to Khazar political culture is clear from this and other evidence, including the style of dual rulership, the title of khagan and use of variants of his trident-like authority symbol. It may well be that their sacral ruler was ensconced in the north, at Gorodishche, as late as the 920s. The Rus' on the middle Dnieper, while affiliated to this polity, may also have paid tribute to the Khazars. In the mid-tenth century a Khazar ruler still regarded the Severians, Slavs near the middle Dnieper, as owing him tribute, while Kiev had an alternative, apparently Khazar, name, Sambatas.[14]

Princes of Kiev and the 'Byzantine connection': challenge and response

The earliest firm evidence of Rus' paramount rulership based in the region of Kiev is for the son of Riurik, Igor', and he is only clearly attested there c.940. It is

13 Ibn Fadlan, *Risāla*, ed. T. Lewicki, *Źródła arabskie do dziejów słówiańszczyzny*, vol. III (Wrocław, Warsaw, Cracow, Gdansk, and Łodz: Polska Akademia Nauk, 1985), pp. 75–6. See also J. E. Montgomery, 'Ibn Fadlān and the Rūsiyyah', *Journal of Arabic and Islamic Studies* 3 (2000): 21–2.

14 P. K. Kokovtsov, *Evreisko-khazarskaia perepiska v X veke* (Leningrad: AN SSSR, 1932), p. 98 and n. 4; Constantine VII, *De administrando imperio*, ed. and trans. G. Moravcsik and R. J. H. Jenkins (Corpus fontium historiae byzantinae 1) (Washington: Dumbarton Oaks, 2nd edn., 1967), ch. 9, pp. 56–7.

significant that the politico-military locus of Rus' shifted south little more than a generation after northerners first arrived in force on the middle Dnieper. This registers the rapid development and allure of the 'Byzantine connection', in terms of trading and the wealth it could yield. But it also reflects a unique state of affairs. Demand in Byzantium was particularly strong for slaves and this was of practical convenience to the Rus' because, unlike inanimate goods, slaves could disembark and walk their way round the most hazardous of the Rapids. Other perils, including steppe nomads and shipwreck, tipped the Rus' self-interest in favour of an agreed command structure for voyages in convoy and regular dealings with the Byzantine authorities. So did the need to ensure a steady influx of slaves and confront the relatively well-organised and well-armed Slav groupings in the region of the middle Dnieper. Possessing towns and led by 'princes', they could resist tribute demands deemed excessive. Perhaps most important of all, the Rus' leadership needed to deal diplomatically or otherwise with the Khazar realm, whose resilience is easily overlooked. Events from *c.*940, the first in Rus' relatable with any degree of confidence, tend to bear this out.

Around that time a Rus' leader was impelled by the Byzantine government 'with great presents' to seize the Khazar fortress guarding the Straits of Kerch. Subsequently the Rus' were dislodged and their leader, named by our Khazar source as 'H-l-g-w', was overpowered and obliged to attack Byzantium. Reluctantly he complied and the Rus' expedition lasted four months, but the Byzantines were 'victorious by virtue of Fire'.[15] The latter details concur with our data for the well-attested Rus' attack on Constantinople of 941, the one serious mismatch being that its leader was Igor'. But the name H-l-g-w could well register the Nordic 'Helgi', and the earliest extant precursor of the *Primary Chronicle* actually names Igor' and Oleg (the Slavic form of Helgi) as jointly organising a raid against Byzantium.[16] The slight discrepancies in our sources could well reflect a joint arrangement, reminiscent of the dual rulership mooted by Ibn Fadlan and the chronicle itself. The debacle recounted by our Khazar source also implies the precariousness of the Rus' hold on the middle Dnieper, while the importance of privileged access to Byzantine markets would be demonstrated a few years later. Igor' apparently lacked the wherewithal to satisfy his retainers and was put to death while trying to raise additional tribute from the Derevlians. Their prince sought the hand of Igor''s

15 N. Golb and O. Pritsak, *Khazarian Hebrew Documents of the Tenth Century* (Ithaca, N.Y.: Cornell University Press, 1982), pp. 118–19.
16 *Novgorodskaia pervaia letopis' starshego i mladshego izvodov*, ed. A. N. Nasonov (Moscow and Leningrad: AN SSSR, 1950), pp. 107–8.

widow, Ol'ga, albeit unsuccessfully. By this time, however, a new treaty had
been negotiated with the Byzantines and commerce resumed. Princess Ol'ga,
acting as regent, took measures to regularise the payment of tribute and set up
hunting lodges where birds – probably of prey – could be caught for shipping
to Byzantium together with furs, wax, honey and slaves. Ol'ga herself sailed
to Constantinople, partly to confirm or improve the terms of the foresaid
treaty. She was received at court 'with princesses who were her own relatives
and her ladies-in-waiting' as well as 'emissaries of the princes of *Rhōsia* and
traders'.[17] During her stay Ol'ga was baptised and took the Christian name of
the emperor's wife, Helena. However, no bishop accompanied Ol'ga-Helena
back to Rus', and by autumn 959 she was asking Otto of Saxony for a full religious mission. Eventually a bishop, Adalbert, was sent but he soon returned
together with his followers, describing the venture as futile.[18]

Evaluation of these events is difficult. Even the date of Ol'ga's visit to the
emperor is controversial. The year 946 is one possibility but the main alternative, 957, has its merits, not least in more or less reconciling chronological
pointers in the Rus' and Byzantine sources. What is certain is that Ol'ga made
her journey against a background of economic boom and competent organisation. Constantine VII himself describes the marshalling of convoys at Kiev
every spring. Slaves, together with the tribute collected over the winter by
'their princes (*archontes*) with all the *Rhōs*', were loaded aboard for a voyage
tailed by opportunistic nomads: if a boat was wrecked in the Black Sea, 'they
all put in to land, in order to present a united front against the Pechenegs'.[19]
The underlying stability of the princely regime is suggested by its survival
through major setbacks and challenges in the 940s, although this owed something to Ol'ga's personality. A concentration of wealth and weaponry in the
middle Dnieper region is also suggested by the finds of chamber graves at Kiev
and Shestovitsa. Their occupants were equipped for the next world with arms
and riding gear – sometimes horses or slave girls, too – while their dealings
in trade are signalled by the weights and balances accompanying them (see
Plate 1). Most were probably the retainers of the princes and other leading
notables. The number of chamber graves on the middle Dnieper is not vast,
but this tallies with Constantine VII's indication that Rus' military manpower
was finite, further grounds for self-discipline.

---

17 Constantine VII, *De cerimoniis aulae byzantinae*, II.15, ed. J. J. Reiske, vol. 1 (Corpus scriptorum historiae byzantinae) (Bonn: E. Weber, 1829), pp. 594–5.

18 Adalbert, *Continuatio Reginonis*, ed. A. Bauer and R. Rau, in *Quellen zur Geschichte der
sächsischen Kaiserzeit* (reprinted Darmstadt: Wissenschaftliche Buchgesellschaft, 2002),
pp. 214–19.

19 Constantine VII, *De administrando imperio*, ch. 9, pp. 62–3.

The risks did not throttle trading along the waterway to Byzantium, and its range and vigour are registered at the site of modern Smolensk's precursor. Now called Gnezdovo, this was located near the outflow into the Dnieper of a river accessible via portages from many northern waterways, including the Western Dvina and Lovat. Its *raison d'être* was as emporium and service station for boats hauled over lengthy portages and in need of repair or replacement. From the mid-tenth century the settled area expanded drastically to cover approximately 15 hectares by the century's end and it is from this period that the largest, most lavishly furnished, barrows date. Ten or so contain traces of boat-burnings and while finds of a few iron rivets need not denote the burning of entire boats, their symbolic value is none the less eloquent – of Scandinavian-style funerary rites and the status attaching to trade and boats. Pairs of tortoiseshell brooches attest the burial of well-to-do Scandinavian women and some chamber graves contain Byzantine silks, the single most valuable luxury obtained from 'the Greeks'. Many persons were drawn to Gnezdovo, whether to drag boats or make a living in smithies and other workshops. A pot with a Slavic graffito from the first half of the tenth century denotes, probably, a literate Slav resident. Comparable expansion was under way at Gorodishche, whose overspill began to take up the nearby site of Novgorod. The influx of Muslim dirhams, which had so long driven its economic growth, continued but Western markets were also involved in the networks of exchange. Silks of probable Byzantine manufacture played some part, as witness finds in the burial ground at Birka and, occasionally, still further west, in Scandinavian-dominated parts of the British Isles where dirhams of the later ninth and earlier tenth centuries have also come to light.

The pattern of finds of luxury goods is loosely congruent with that of chamber graves. Chamber graves have been excavated at Birka, Hedeby and elsewhere in Denmark, a kind of 'social register' of the well-to-do. Their occupants had not necessarily belonged to ruling elites, and war-bands could cause serious disorder, especially when legitimate authority was in dispute. However, the direct involvement of many retainers in trading gave them an underlying interest in stability. The distribution pattern of the chamber graves in Rus' charts princely strongpoints and the most regulated trading nodes from the end of the ninth century onwards: from Staraia Ladoga, Gorodishche and Pskov down to Gnezdovo and the middle Dnieper, with a cluster at Timerevo on the upper Volga. Membership of war-bands and trading companies was not closed to talent, and costumes, riding gear and ornament designs were adopted from both host populations and more exotic cultures. But their breeding- and, frequently, homing-ground was the Scandinavian world, long-range travel being a mark of membership.

Christianising impulses reached the Rus' in several ways – from individual warriors and traders frequenting Swedish and Danish kingly courts and emporia; from those who journeyed to Byzantium and back; and through missionary efforts by Byzantine emperors and churchmen. These impulses can hardly have failed to affect the sacral aspects of rulership, whatever its precise complexion at that time, and by 946 baptised Rus' were being paraded at receptions in the Great Palace. Whether to impress her Christian notables or out of personal belief, Ol'ga proceeded to associate herself sacramentally with the ruling family in Byzantium. The Byzantines' apparent reluctance to send a mission is understandable in light of Bishop Adalbert's experiences. After his mission was abandoned, several members were killed and Adalbert claimed that he had only narrowly escaped himself. Ol'ga maintained a priest in her entourage until she died in 969 and the presence of other priests and a church in Kiev would not be surprising, given that a number of leading Rus' were Christian. Yet powerful Rus' were opposed to Christianisation. Their stance is epitomised by the *Primary Chronicle*'s tale of Ol'ga's attempts to convert her son, Sviatoslav. He responded: 'My retainers will laugh at this.'[20] This image of Sviatoslav as swashbuckler, consciously reacting against his mother's new-found eirenic disposition, accords with an eyewitness description. Sviatoslav's head was shorn save for one long strand of hair, a mark of nobility among Turkic peoples. Members of the Rus' elite were no strangers to artefacts evoking myths and customs of steppe dwellers. The mounting on a drinking-horn depicts a scene of men and predators in combat which may evoke Khazar concepts of sacral kingship. The horn, one of a pair, was buried in the barrow of a Chernigov magnate in the 960s, as was a statuette of Thor.

Sviatoslav: the last migration

Sometime in the mid-960s Sviatoslav forged an alliance with a group of nomads, the Oghuz, and launched a joint attack on the Khazars. Sviatoslav's aggression was reportedly triggered by his discovery that the Viatichi were paying tribute in 'shillings' to the Khazars.[21] This vignette illustrates the lucrative involvement of the Slavs with the trading nexus; the long reach of the Khazars;

20 *PVL*, p. 30.
21 *PVL*, p. 31.

and, more generally, the many compass-bearings of the Rus'. In laying waste
to the Khazar capital of Itil, Sviatoslav destroyed a rival power intruding into
his own sphere, and in attacking the Volga Bulgars and the Burtas he was
perhaps seeking unhindered access to the Samanid realm, the main source
of Rus' silver. Sviatoslav did not, however, try and base himself on the lower
Volga or at the Straits of Kerch, where his forces sacked the Khazar fortress of
S-m-k-r-ts. In fact the influx of silver from Samanid mints began to falter from
around this time. Instead he opted for Pereiaslavets on the lower Danube.
This, he determined, would be 'the centre of my land, for there all good things
flow: gold from the Greeks, precious cloths, wines and fruit of many kinds;
silver and horses from the Czechs and Hungarians; and from the Rus' furs,
wax, honey and slaves'.[22] The immediate reason for Sviatoslav's intervention
in the Balkans in 968 was fortuitous. The Byzantine emperor, Nicephorus II,
incited him to raid Bulgaria, offering gold as an inducement. Byzantine sources
portray the Rus' as marvelling at the fertility of the region, and the emissary
delivering the gold is said to have urged Sviatoslav to stay there, furthering
his own ambitions for the imperial throne. But Sviatoslav probably needed
little prompting to stay on in the south. He had already shown impatience
with the status quo in shattering the Khazar hegemony and, as stressed above,
the Rus' on the middle Dnieper were hemmed in by many constraints. The
Pechenegs were incited by the emperor to attack Kiev, once Sviatoslav showed
signs of overstepping his brief, and the town came close to surrendering. But
Sviatoslav proved able to come to terms with the nomads and many Pechenegs accompanied him back to the Balkans in, probably, the autumn of 969.
Hungarians, too, joined in and with their help Sviatoslav ranged as far south
as Arcadiopolis, impaling prisoners en masse. The atrocities were not entirely
random. Sviatoslav seems to have envisaged a commonwealth spanning several cultures and climate zones: his young sons Iaropolk, Oleg and Vladimir
were respectively assigned to Kiev, the Derevlian land and Novgorod, while
Sviatoslav ensconced himself near the Danube's mouth. The Bulgarian Tsar
Boris was left in his capital, Preslav. Rus' garrisons were installed there and
in Danubian towns. Sviatoslav's underlying aim was probably to foster trade
along and between major riverways, employing nomads to police the steppes
and keep the peace. His base had the advantage of proximity to the markets
of both 'the Greeks' and Central Europe, where Saxon silver was beginning
to be mined. Sviatoslav was not the first Rus' leader to have a keen eye for
commercial openings.

22 *PVL*, p. 32.

Sviatoslav overestimated the Byzantines' willingness to accept him as a new neighbour. In April 971 Nicephorus' successor, John I Tzimisces, led a surprise offensive through the Haemus mountain passes and soon Sviatoslav was holed up at Dorostolon. Retreat down the Danube was barred by the imperial fleet, while most of the nomads were won over by imperial bribery. In late July, after ferocious fighting, a deal was struck. The Rus' received grain, safe-conduct and confirmation of the right to trade at Constantinople in return for Sviatoslav's written oath never again to attack imperial territory or Bulgaria. His ambitions had canniness. While reputedly adopting the nomads' lifestyle, with a saddle for pillow,[23] Sviatoslav seems to have determined that the best prospects for commercial growth lay with Byzantine and Western European markets rather than – as traditionally – the East. Had Byzantine forces not then been in peak condition, a Danubian Rus' might have formed. As it was, the outcome of the campaigning was uncertain only days before Sviatoslav proposed terms: he did not actually surrender nor does he seem to have given up his captives or his loot. These spoils and putative slaves were his undoing. Concern for shipping them back to Rus' slowed down withdrawal, and Sviatoslav and his men were ambushed by Pechenegs at the Dnieper Rapids early in 972. Few escaped and Sviatoslav's own skull became a plated drinking cup, a use to which steppe peoples put the heads of enemies.

972–c.978 Fragmentation

Sviatoslav's demise brought instability to the princely dynasty and allowed outsiders to set themselves up near the 'way from the Varangians to the Greeks'. His two eldest sons, Iaropolk and Oleg, fell out after a clash between hunting parties which cost Liut, the son of Iaropolk's military commander, his life. Iaropolk then attacked and defeated his brother, and Oleg perished in the crush of fugitives. Vladimir fled 'beyond the sea'. The *Primary Chronicle*'s account is laconic, a tale of the commander's vengeance for Liut. Nonetheless its intimations of quarrels over resources involving princely retainers may not be sheer fiction. There had been problems with satisfying retainers after Igor''s disastrous expedition to Byzantium; on that occasion the Derevlians themselves had been involved. Both episodes imply reduced princely circumstances after defeat by the Byzantines and probable dislocation of trade. There are hints that Iaropolk attempted a rapprochement with Emperor Otto I, in that Rus' envoys were among those at Otto's court in March 973. An attempt to step

23 *PVL*, p. 31.

up exports of furs and slaves to silver-rich Central European markets through amity with their chief protector would be quite understandable, a substitute for Byzantine and oriental outlets. Taking advantage of the political disarray, figures with Scandinavian names such as Rogvolod (*Ragnvaldr in Old Norse) and Tury reportedly set themselves up at, respectively, Polotsk and Turov. These strongholds could give access to the West but lay near 'the way from the Varangians to the Greeks'. This route had not lost its magnetism and drew Vladimir Sviatoslavich back. Having lodged at some Scandinavian court or courts, he mustered a company of retainers and led them to Rus'. He enjoyed advantages over other power holders or seekers, being a son of Sviatoslav and acquainted with leading figures of Gorodishche-Novgorod. Dobrynia, his mother's brother, had in effect been his guardian there and was probably still with him. Vladimir was thus better able to enlist many citizens, Finns as well as 'Slovenes', and although they may have been inexpert fighters, their numbers together with the 'Varangians' proved more than a match for Rogvolod. Vladimir's personal qualities also gave him a head start. Ruthless and shrewd, he put to death Rogvolod, reportedly a 'prince',[24] and also Rogvolod's sons. But he took Rogvolod's daughter to wife and led his Novgorodians and retainers to Kiev. There he suborned the commander of Iaropolk's defence force and invited his half-brother to parley in their father's old stone hall. As Iaropolk entered, 'two Varangians stabbed him in the chest with their swords'.[25] Thus Vladimir gained the throne city of Kiev around 978.

Vladimir's force, his legitimacy deficit and turning to the gods

Vladimir suffered the handicap of lacking reputable ties with local elites or populations on the middle Dnieper. He was of princely stock, but his mother had been Sviatoslav's key-holder and of unfree status. Vladimir had spent his youth far away and lacked a longstanding retinue, once he had dispatched his 'Varangian' retainers to Byzantium. He sent them off after declining to pay them in precious metal and then reneging on a promised payment in martenskins. This episode demonstrates the high running costs of war-bands and also Vladimir's political nous. He was anxious not to antagonise the better-off inhabitants of Kiev through over-taxation. As at Novgorod, the active co-operation of the citizenry was needed to underpin his regime: at least one

24 *PVL*, p. 36.
25 *PVL*, p. 37.

prominent supporter of his murdered half-brother had fled to the Pechenegs and 'often' took part in their raids.[26]

Lack of material resources partly explains the tempo of Vladimir's early years in power. He needed to reimpose and extend tribute collection so as to feed the markets of Kiev and secure means for rewarding his followers. He led campaigns to the west and campaigned repeatedly against the redoubtable Viatichi, so as to reimpose tribute on them. Besides restoring the exchange nexuses, war-leadership could bond Vladimir with contingents of warriors of his choosing and strengthen his power base. This, however, presupposed victories and the public cult he instituted was designed to induce them, besides appealing to the heterogeneous population of the middle Dnieper region. The 'pantheon' of wooden idols set up outside his hall in Kiev was headed by Perun, the Slavic god of lightning and power. This is our first evidence of a prince's attempt to organise public worship and to associate his rule with a medley of gods, some quite local, others (like Perun) with a widespread following. Vladimir presumably hoped to bolster his legitimacy through such measures, and to win further victories. After subjugating the Iatviagians in the west, he ordered sacrifices in thanksgiving to the idols outside his hall. We know of this only because the father of a boy chosen by lot for sacrifice happened to be Christian, a Varangian who had come from 'the Greeks' to reside in Kiev and who refused to give up his son, at the cost of his own life. Vladimir's command-cult thus gave rise to 'martyrs'. But judging by the coffins and contents of several graves in Kiev's main burial ground, Christians and part-Christians lived peaceably with pagans, and were buried near them. The incessant circulation of travellers between the Baltic and Byzantium prompted individual Rus' to be baptised and Christianity was quite well known to inhabitants of the urban network, but this did not oblige their prince to follow suit.

Vladimir's campaigns brought mastery of the towns between the San and the Western Bug. Among these were Cherven and Peremyshl' (modern Przemyśl in Poland), population centres astride routes to Western markets. The run of victories abated when Vladimir suffered a setback at the hands of the most sophisticated power adjoining Rus', the Volga Bulgars. He had presumably hoped to subjugate their markets, too, but on his uncle's advice came to terms. Dobrynia is supposed to have pointed out that these enemies wore boots: 'Let us go and look for wearers of bast-shoes!'[27] His implication that Vladimir should seek tribute from simpler folk was demeaning, setting

---

26 *PVL*, p. 37.
27 *PVL*, p. 39.

limits to the resources he could bring under his sway. To that extent, Perun and his fellow gods had failed to 'deliver', and a quest for a better guarantor of victory would be understandable. It may be no accident that the *Primary Chronicle*'s next entry after Vladimir's reverse on the Volga is the arrival of a Bulgar mission to convert him to Islam, in the mid-980s. This serves as the preliminary to a lengthy account sometimes termed Vladimir's 'Investigation of the Faiths'. Most – though not all – of the material in the 'Investigation' is stylised doctrinal exegesis. But its image of Vladimir investigating four brands of monotheism – Eastern and Western Christianity besides Islam and Judaism – encapsulates what the immediately preceding chronicle entries and the general historical context lead one to expect. Rus' rulers since Ol'ga had been considering alternative sacral sources of authority. The cult of an all-powerful God had its attractions for a prince pre-eminent, yet light on legitimisation, as Vladimir was. One might consider Vladimir's eventual choice of Byzantine Christianity inevitable, given the exposure of so many of his notables to its wealth and majesty. But Vladimir could have obtained a mission from the Germans, following his grandmother's precedent, had the government during Otto III's minority been better placed to further mission work. And there is evidence that Vladimir sent emissaries to Khorezm and obtained an instructor to teach 'the religious laws of Islam'. This demarche by a Rus' 'king' is recounted by a late eleventh-century Persian writer and it is compatible with the *Primary Chronicle*'s tale of the dispatch of enquirers to the Muslims, Germans and Byzantines.[28] Seeking a mission from the Orient was nothing untoward, even if commercial ties with Central Asia were set to slacken.

An unusual conjuncture of events caused Vladimir to settle for a religious mission, marriage alliance and treaty with the senior Byzantine emperor, Basil II. The outlines are clear: by early 988 Basil was beleaguered in his capital by rebel armies encamped across the Bosporus, while a Bulgarian uprising against Byzantine rule in the Balkans was in full flame. Basil came to terms with Vladimir, sending his sister as bride in exchange for military aid; Vladimir's baptism was the inevitable corollary of this. Vladimir sent an army – 6,000-strong by one account – and they caught the rebels off-guard at Chrysopolis in the opening months of 989, at latest. This turned the tide. Within a couple of years the military rebellion ended and Anna Porphyrogenita settled in Kiev with her spouse, who took the Christian name 'Basil', in honour of his

---

28 V. Minorsky, *Sharaf al-Zamān Tāhir Marvazī on China, the Turks and India* (James G. Forlong Fund 22) (London: Royal Asiatic Society, 1942), p. 36; *PVL*, pp. 48–9.

brother-in-law. These outlines convey the essence, that Basil II's domestic interests momentarily converged with those of Vladimir. The Rus' ruler could supply desperately needed troops and in return received generous concessions, such as had not been vouchsafed to Ol'ga.

The exact course and significance of events is harder to reconstruct, especially the expedition of Vladimir to Cherson. The *Primary Chronicle's* account draws on disparate sources, and our near-contemporaneous foreign sources are sketchy. Various explanations for Vladimir's expedition are feasible. This could have been a 'first strike', akin to his seizure of Cherven and other towns to the west. Cherson had prospered greatly in the tenth century and the town's built-up area expanded. Vladimir may have exploited Basil II's preoccupation with rebellions to grab the Crimea's richest town, reckoning that he could either mulct its revenues or use it as a bargaining counter. As part of an ensuing treaty, he may have sent Basil military aid. Alternatively, Vladimir may have seized Cherson in retaliation for Basil's slowness to honour an initial agreement on similar lines, forcing him to abide by it. Or the capture of Cherson could even have been carried out as a form of assistance to Basil if, as has been suggested, the townsfolk had sided with the rebellious generals.[29] What is not in doubt is that Vladimir exploited Byzantine disarray in order to secure his own authority, underwritten by Almighty God.

Vladimir-Basil, 'new Constantine' and patriarch

Vladimir was acclaimed by later churchmen as an 'apostle among rulers' who had saved them from the devil's wiles.[30] The devil bemoaned expulsion from where he had thought to make his home. Such imagery was fostered by the spectaculars staged in the wake of Vladimir's own baptism, and in the second half of the eleventh century a Kievan monk could still recall 'the baptism of the land of Rus".[31] Kiev's citizens were ordered into the Dnieper for mass baptism. The idol of Perun was dragged by a horse's tail and thrashed with rods, then tossed in the river and kept moving as far as the Rapids, clear of Rus'. Vladimir ordered 'wood to be cut and churches put up on the sites where idols had stood'; 'the idols were smashed and icons of saints were installed.'[32]

---

29 See A. Poppe, 'The Political Background to the Baptism of Rus', *Dumbarton Oaks Papers* 30 (1976), 197-244; reprinted in his *The Rise of Christian Russia* (London: Variorum Reprints, 1982), no. 2.

30 Ilarion, 'Slovo o zakone i blagodati', in D. S. Likhachev et al. (eds.), *Biblioteka literatury drevnei Rusi*, vol. 1 (St Petersburg: Nauka, 1997), p. 52; *PVL*, p. 58.

31 *PVL*, p. 81.

32 *PVL*, p. 53; Ilarion, 'Slovo o zakone i blagodati', p. 44.

This scenario of purification and transformation must be qualified. A fair proportion of the Rus' elite were probably more or less Christian just before the conversion: there had been baptised Rus' in the 940s. Conversely, the extent and nature of the 'Christianisation' of ordinary folk, especially those living outside towns and the immediate sway of princely agents, is very uncertain. Even the chronicle merely has Vladimir getting people *baptised* 'in all the towns and villages'. Priests were assigned to towns, rather than villages. It was pagan idols, sanctuaries and communal rituals – alternative focuses of loyalties and expectation – that were swept away.

The churchmen's portrayal of Vladimir's achievement is not, however, sheer make-believe. The initiatives taken by Vladimir were intended to associate his regime indissolubly with the Christian God and His saints, making promotion of the Church a function of princely rule. And he succeeded in embedding a version of Christianity in the political culture of Rus'. No aspiring prince in Rus' mounted a pagan revival, unlike some usurpers in Scandinavia. Vladimir's Christian leadership predicated victories and the vein of triumphalism in the *Primary Chronicle*'s depiction of Vladimir's activities at Cherson probably relays his own propaganda. But he also exploited his new-found ties with a court renowned among the Rus' for God-given wealth. Anna Porphyrogenita would eventually be laid to rest in a marble sarcophagus beside Vladimir's own, a symbol of parity of status as well as conjugal bonds. Anna probably lived in the halls built on the Starokievskaia Hill and graced the feasts held there every Sunday, presumably after religious services in the church of the Mother of God which the halls flanked. These stone and brick buildings were the work of 'masters' from Byzantium and were embellished with wall-paintings and marble furnishings. The church's design seems to have followed that of the main church in the emperor's palace complex, the church of the Pharos, and they shared a dedicatee, the Mother of God. Vladimir was inviting comparisons between his own residence and that of the emperor. The message that he could match the Greeks was underlined when he placed a certain Anastasius in charge of his palace church. Reputedly, Anastasius had betrayed Cherson to Vladimir by revealing where the pipes supplying its water ran; once these were cut, the thirst-stricken Chersonites surrendered.[33] A number of other priests from Cherson were assigned to the church, which became known as the 'Tithe church' (*Desiatinnaia*) because of the tenth of revenues allocated to it. The relics of St Clement brought back from Cherson had a prominent position, while looted antique statuary was displayed outside. Thus the show church

33 *PVL*, pp. 49–50.

served as a kind of victory monument to Vladimir's role in the conversion of his people.

The middle Dnieper is the region where Rus' churchmen's rhetoric concerning 'new Christian people, the elect of God' rings most true. In order to protect his cult centre, Vladimir established new settlements far into the steppe, taking advantage of the black earth's fertility. Kiev itself was enlarged to enclose some 10 hectares within a formidable earthen rampart and ramparts of similar technique were raised to the south of the town. The construction of barriers and strongholds along the main tributaries of the Dnieper brought a new edge to Rus' relations with the nomads. Although never unproblematic, these had hitherto involved constant trading and had more often than not been peaceable. There was now, according to the *Primary Chronicle*, 'great and unremitting strife'[34] and although Kiev was secure, even the largest of the fortified towns shielding it came under pressure from the Pechenegs. Belgorod, south-west of Kiev, underwent a prolonged siege. It did not, however, fall and this owed something to the layers of unfired bricks forming the core of the ramparts, which still stand between five and six metres high. They enclosed some 105 hectares, and a very high level of organisation was needed to supply the inhabitants. The princely authorities adapted techniques from the Byzantine world, not only brick- and glass-making but also plans for large cisterns and a beacon system perhaps fuelled by naphtha. Few new towns matched Belgorod or Pereiaslavl' in size and many settlements lacked ramparts, the nearby forts serving as places of refuge. But the grain and other produce grown by the farmers fed the cavalrymen and horses stationed in the forts, sickles and ploughshares were manufactured in the smithies, and nexuses of trade burgeoned. Finds of glazed tableware and, in substantial quantities, amphorae and glass bracelets attest the prosperity of the settlements' defenders. The risks of voyages to Byzantium were mitigated – though never dispelled – by ramparts beside the Dnieper and a large fortified harbour near the River Sula's confluence with the Dnieper, at Voin. Cavalry could escort boats to the Rapids, and from the late tenth century the Byzantine government let the Rus' establish a trading settlement in the Dnieper estuary.

The middle Dnieper region had not been densely populated before Vladimir's reign. He is represented by the *Primary Chronicle* as rounding up 'the best men' from among the Slav and Finnish inhabitants of the forest zone and installing them in his settlements.[35] The newcomers to the hundred

34 *PVL*, p. 56.
35 *PVL*, p. 54.

or more forts and settlements in the great arc protecting Kiev were prime targets for evangelisers, as well as raiders. Divine intervention supporting princely leadership was in constant demand, and one of the few bishoprics quite firmly attributable to Vladimir's reign is that of Belgorod. At Vasil'ev Vladimir founded a church and held a great feast in thanksgiving, after hiding under its bridge from pursuing Pechenegs. The apparent intensity of pastoral care and the deracination of most of the population from northern habitats made inculcation of Christian observances the more effective. Judging by the funerary rituals in the burial grounds of these settlements, few flagrantly pagan practices persisted. Barrows were not heaped over graves in cemeteries within a 250-kilometre radius of Kiev, or in regions such as the Cherven towns where Christianity was already well established. Elsewhere barrows were much more common, although heaped over plain Christian burials. The small circular barrows often contained pottery, ashes and food symbolising – if not left over from – funeral feasts, occasions of which the Church disapproved.

The regions and key points where Vladimir's conversion transformed the landscape, physically as well as figuratively, were finite but the number of persons affected was considerable. New Christian communities were instituted in the middle Dnieper region and existing ones in the trading network massively reinforced, especially in the northern towns frequented by Christians from the Scandinavian world. Novgorod was made an episcopal see. Churches were most probably built and priests appointed in Smolensk and Polotsk, albeit without resident bishops. Even in north-eastern outposts, Christianity became the cult of retainers and other princely agents, and it appealed to locals trafficking with them and aspiring to raise their own status. At Uglich on the upper Volga (as at Smolensk, Pskov and Kiev itself) the pagan burial grounds were destroyed in the wake of Vladimir's conversion and in the first quarter of the eleventh century a church dedicated to Christ the Saviour was built. Soon members of the elite began to fill St Saviour's graveyard in strict accordance with Church canons. Vladimir's tribute collectors and other itinerant agents did not just owe allegiance in return for treasure such as his new-fangled silver coins, share-outs of tribute and sumptuous feasts featuring silver spoons, important as these were (for examples of Vladimir's silver coins, see Plate 2). They had religious affiliations with him: greed, ambition and concern for individual survival in life and after death fused with loyalty to the prince. Vladimir probably saw the advantages of instilling the faith into the next generation. There is no particular reason to doubt that the children of 'notable families' were taken off to be instructed in 'book learning' while their mothers, 'still not strong in the faith . . . wept for them as if they were dead'.[36]

The wording of the *Primary Chronicle* seems to treat book learning as more or less synonymous with studying the Scriptures and the new religion, and Vladimir stood to gain moral stature from enlightening his notables' children. One should not, however, suppose that the literacy which boys – maybe also girls – of his elite obtained was of much application to everyday governance. The administrative and ideological underpinnings of princely rule were still quite rudimentary, even if Vladimir loved his 'retainers and consulted them about the ordering of the land, about wars and about the law of the land'.[37] The 'land of Rus'' was an archipelago of largely self-regulating communities. Extensive groupings in the north were still considered tribes, most notoriously the Viatichi. It was mainly in Vladimir's new fortresses and settlements in the middle Dnieper region that princely commanders, town governors and agents were numerous enough to intervene in the affairs of ordinary people; the standing alert against the nomads required as much. But even there the officials seem to have had little occasion to issue deeds or written judgements. Nor do they seem to have played a commanding role in adjudicating disputes or enforcing laws. There had long been some sense of due legal process among the Rus'. Procedures for making amends for insults, injuries, thefts and killings inform the tenth-century treaties with the Byzantines. However, practical measures for conflict resolution of mutually inimical parties fell far short of upholding an inherently ethical code, of punishing upon Christian principle actions deemed sinful. A hint of attitudes towards justice as a non-negotiable quality is offered by a passage in the *Primary Chronicle*, perhaps first set down before Vladimir's reign passed from living memory. Vladimir's bishops urged punitive action against robbers, for 'you have been appointed by God to punish evil-doers'. Vladimir gave up exacting fines in compensation for offences (*viry*) but later he reverted to 'the ways of his father and grandfather'.[38] The story shows awareness in Church circles that Rus''s 'new Constantine'[39] had only limited conceptions concerning his authority.

Vladimir's regime rested less on elaborate institutional frameworks or jus-tifications in law than on well-oiled patronage mechanisms and the aura with which his paternal ancestry invested him. The blood of a murdered half-brother on one's hands could be offset by imposing a well-ordered public cult. In every

36 *PVL*, p. 53.
37 *PVL*, p. 56.
38 *PVL*, p. 56.
39 *PVL*, p. 58.

other way, family blood and concomitant bonds were assets that Vladimir exploited to the full. His maternal uncle, Dobrynia, seems to have been a mainstay and there is no sign of the multiplicity of 'princes' or magnates attested for the middle Dnieper in the mid-tenth century. The losses incurred during Sviatoslav's campaigns and his sons' internecine strife may have cleared what was always a hazardous deck. In any case, Vladimir quite soon came to rely on his own sons in what was probably a new variant of collective, family, leadership. He was not the first Rus' prince to assign sons to distant seats of authority, but he seems to have carried this out on a wider scale than his predecessors. Twelve sons are named and associated with seats by the *Primary Chronicle*, a likely evocation of the twelve Apostles. The actual number of sons assigned to towns may well have been greater, since the distinction between those born in wedlock rather than to a concubine was not sharply drawn. That Vladimir was the father was what mattered: they could deputise for him in a variety of places. If it is unsurprising that a son was installed in Novgorod, the failure to grace Pskov – the town of Vladimir's grandmother and probably a longstanding seat of authority – with a prince of its own is noteworthy. So is the assignment of sons to towns which, though of fairly recent origin, had proved to be potential power bases, Polotsk and Turov. When Iziaslav, Vladimir's first assignee to Polotsk, died in 1001, his son was permitted to take his place and, in effect, put down the roots of a hereditary branch of princes there; Iziaslav's mother had been Rogneda, daughter of Rogvolod. Presumably Vladimir calculated that so strongly rooted a regime would block any future bids for Polotsk by outsiders. Princes were also sent to locales whose ties with the urban network had not been specifically 'political'. For example, Rostov was only developed into a large town in the 980s or 990s, when the local inhabitants were mainly the Finnic Mer. The newly fortified town was dignified with a resident prince, Iaroslav, and an oaken church was subsequently built. Some places of strategic importance but lacking recent princely associations were not assigned a prince. It was a governor who had to cope with Viking-type raids on Staraia Ladoga and the town suffered conflagrations, at the hands of Erik Haakonson in 997 and of Sveinn Haakonson early in 1015.

Sveinn raided down 'the East Way' at a time when the shortcomings of Vladimir's regime were becoming plain. Ties between father and sons could hold together for a generation of peace, but they were not immune from jockeying for prominence and ultimate succession. By around 1013 Vladimir's relations with one leading son, Sviatopolk, were so fraught that he was removed from his seat in Turov and imprisoned. And, ominously, Vladimir's relations with the occupant of the most important seat after Kiev itself deteriorated drastically. In 1014 Iaroslav, now prince of Novgorod, held back the annual payment due from that city to Kiev and Vladimir began detailed preparations for the march north. The fact that Vladimir was on such bad terms with two of his foremost sons suggests that thoughts about the succession were in the air. Iaroslav 'sent overseas and brought over Varangians' for what promised to be outright war.[40] However, Vladimir fell ill, putting off the expedition, and on 15 July 1015 he died.

Essentially, the vast 'land of Rus'' was a family unit, with all the affinities and tensions germane to that term, and there were no effective ritual or legal mechanisms making for a generally accepted succession. Once the family 'patriarch' died, these uncertainties could only be resolved by a virtual free-for-all between the more or less eligible sons of Vladimir. The coming of Christianity fostered economic well-being, fuller settlement of the Black Earth region and cultural advance, while a kind of 'cult of personality' now invested Vladimir, accentuating the aura of princely blood. Over the centuries there would scarcely ever be a question of persons who were not his descendants seizing thrones for themselves in Rus'. This was partly due to force of custom and princely retinues' *force majeure*. But there was also symbiosis amounting to consensus across diverse populations and urban centres with a positive interest in the status quo – and in the profits to be had from long-distance trading. For these members of Rus', the tale of the summoning of Riurik from overseas had resonance. The regime fashioned by Vladimir could maintain order of a sort. There was no other overriding authority, no well-connected senior churchmen to knock princely heads together. But given the remarkable make-up of Christian Rus', how could it have been otherwise?

40 *PVL*, p. 58.

4

Kievan Rus' (1015–1125)

SIMON FRANKLIN

The period from 1015 to 1125, from the death of Vladimir Sviatoslavich to the death of his great-grandson Vladimir Vsevolodovich (known as Vladimir Monomakh), has long been regarded as the Golden Age of early Rus': as an age of relatively coherent political authority exercised by the prince of Kiev over a relatively coherent and unified land enjoying relatively unbroken economic prosperity and military security along with the first and best flowerings of a new native Christian culture.[1]

One reason for the power of the impression lies in the nature of the native sources. This is the age in which early Rus', so to speak, comes out from under ground, when archaeological sources are supplemented by native writings and buildings and pictures which survive to the present. From the mid-eleventh century onwards, in particular, the droplets of sources begin to turn into a steady trickle and then into a flow. Before c.1045 we possess no clearly native narrative, exegetic or administrative documents. By 1125 we have the first sermons, saints' lives, law codes, epistles and pilgrim accounts, as well as a rapidly increasing quantity of brief letters on birch bark and of scratched graffiti on church walls and miscellaneous objects.[2] Before the death of Vladimir Sviatoslavich no component of our main narrative source, the *Primary Chronicle* (*Povest' vremennykh let*) is clearly derived from contemporary Rus' witness; by the early twelfth century, when the chronicle was compiled, its authors could incorporate several decades of contemporary native narratives and interpretations. No building from the age of Vladimir Sviatoslavich or earlier survived above ground into the modern age. Monumental buildings from the mid-eleventh

---

1 On this as the 'Golden Age' see e.g. Boris Rybakov, *Kievan Rus* (Moscow: Progress Publishers, 1984), pp. 153–241. Other general accounts of the period: George Vernadsky, *Kievan Russia*, 7th printing (New Haven and London: Yale University Press, 1972); Simon Franklin and Jonathan Shepard, *The Emergence of Rus 750–1200* (London and New York: Longman, 1996), pp. 183–277.
2 On written sources see Simon Franklin, *Writing, Society and Culture in Early Rus c. 900–1300* (Cambridge: Cambridge University Press, 2002).

to early twelfth centuries can still be seen today – in varying states of complete-ness – the length of Rus', from Novgorod in the north to Kiev and Chernigov in the south. Still more survived until the mid-twentieth century, when they were destroyed either by German invaders or by Stalinist zealots.[3] These early writ-ings and buildings came to acquire – and in some cases were clearly intended to convey – an aura of authority, a kind of definitive status as cultural and political and ideological models, as the foundations of a tradition.

Between 1015 and 1125, then, for subsequent observers Rus' emerged into the light, and immediately contemplated and celebrated its own enlightenment. Such perceptions are real and significant facts of cultural history. However, their documentary accuracy is debatable and our own retelling of the period is necessarily somewhat grubbier than the image.

Dynastic politics

Political legitimacy in Rus' resided in the dynasty. The ruling family managed to create an ideological framework for its own pre-eminence which was main-tained without serious challenge for over half a millennium. To this extent the political structure was simple: the lands of the Rus' were, more or less by definition, the lands claimed or controlled by the descendants of Vladimir Sviatoslavich (or, in more distant genealogical legend, by the descendants of the ninth-century Varangian Riurik). But the simplicity of such a formulation hides its potential complexity in practice. It is one thing to say that legiti-macy resided in the dynasty, quite another to determine how power should be defined and allocated within it. Legitimacy was vested in the family as a whole, not in any individual member of it. Power was distributed and redistributed, claimed and counter-claimed, among members of a continually expanding kinship group, not passed intact and by automatic right from father to son. The political history of the period thus reflects, above all, the interplay of two factors, the dynastic and the regional: on the one hand the issue of precedence or seniority within the ruling family; on the other hand – as a consequence of the distribution of power – the increasingly entrenched and often conflicting regional interests of its local branches.

The changing patterns of internal politics are most graphically shown at moments of strain resulting from disputes over succession. Succession took place both 'vertically' from an older generation to a younger, and 'laterally'

---

3 See e.g. William Craft Brumfield, *A History of Russian Architecture* (Cambridge: Cambridge University Press, 1993), pp. 9–33.

between members of the same generation, from brother to brother or cousin to cousin. Three times between 1015 and 1125 the dynasty had to adjust to 'vertical' succession: in 1015 on the death of Vladimir himself; in 1054 on the death of his son Iaroslav, and in 1093 on the death of his grandson Vsevolod (see Table 4.1). On each occasion the adjustment to 'vertical' succession introduced a fresh set of 'lateral' problems among potential successors in the next generation, and on each occasion the solutions were slightly different. Through looking at the sequence of adjustments to changes of power we can follow the development of a set of conventions and principles which, though never neat or fully consistent in their application, are the closest we get to a political 'system'.[4]

In 1015 Vladimir's sons were scattered around the extremities of the lands, for it had been his policy to consolidate family control over the tribute-gathering areas by allocating each of his sons to a regional base. One was given Turov, to the west, on the route to Poland; another had the land of the Derevlians, the immediate north-western neighbours of the Kievan Polianians; one was installed at Novgorod in the north, another at the remote southern outpost of Tmutorokan', beyond the steppes, overlooking the Straits of Kerch between the Black Sea and the Azov Sea. There were a couple of postings in the north-east, at Rostov and Murom, and one in Polotsk in the north-west. This was Vladimir's framework for ensuring that each of his sons had autonomous means of support and that the family as a whole could establish and maintain the territorial extent of its dominance.

On Vladimir's death this structure collapsed. Despite their remoteness from each other, the regional allocations were clearly not regarded as substitutes for central power (if we regard the middle Dnieper region as the 'centre'). The only exception was Polotsk, where Vladimir's son Iziaslav had already died and had been succeeded by his own son Briacheslav: there is no indication that Briacheslav competed with his uncles, and this is the first recorded example of a regional allocation coming to be treated as the distinct patrimony of a particular branch of the family. Relations between Vladimir's surviving sons, however, were more turbulent. Three were murdered (two of them, Boris and Gleb, went on to become venerated as saints),[5] and three more – Sviatopolk of Turov,

---

4 On the political conventions of the dynasty see Nancy Shields Kollmann, 'Collateral Succession in Kievan Rus'', *HUS* 14 (1990): 377–87; Janet Martin, *Medieval Russia 980–1584* (Cambridge: Cambridge University Press, 1995), pp. 21–35; Franklin and Shepard, *The Emergence of Rus*, pp. 245–77.
5 On the early cult see Gail Lenhoff, *The Martyred Princes Boris and Gleb: A Socio-Cultural Study of the Cult and the Texts* (Columbus, Oh.: Slavica, 1989); Paul Hollingsworth, *The Hagiography of Kievan Rus'* (Cambridge, Mass.: Harvard University Press, 1992), pp. xxvi–lvii.

Table 4.1. *From Vladimir Sviatoslavich to Vladimir Monomakh (princes of Kiev underlined)*

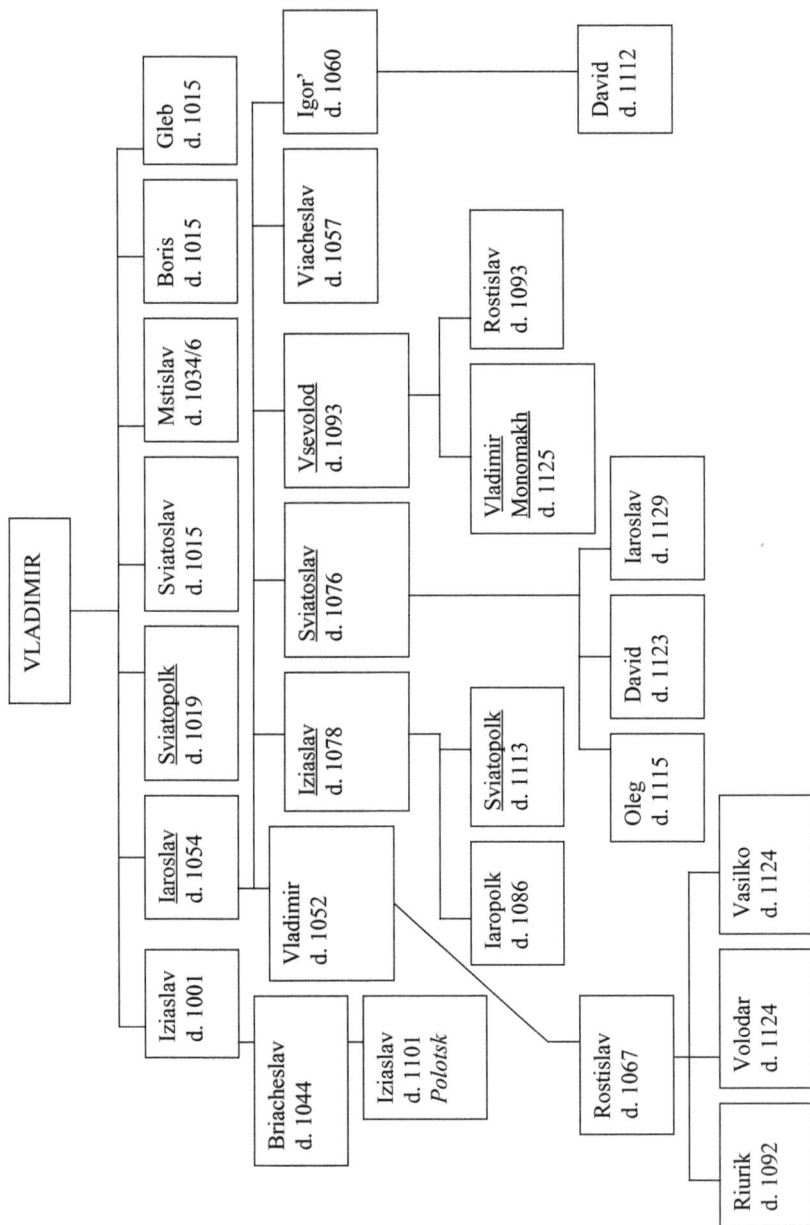

VLADIMIR

- Iziaslav d. 1001
  - Briacheslav d. 1044
    - Iziaslav d. 1101 *Polotsk*
- Iaroslav d. 1054
  - Vladimir d. 1052
    - Rostislav d. 1067
      - Riurik d. 1092
      - Volodar d. 1124
      - Vasilko d. 1124
  - Iziaslav d. 1078
    - Iaropolk d. 1086
    - Sviatopolk d. 1113
  - Sviatoslav d. 1076
    - Oleg d. 1115
    - David d. 1123
    - Iaroslav d. 1129
  - Vsevolod d. 1093
    - Vladimir Monomakh d. 1125
    - Rostislav d. 1093
  - Viacheslav d. 1057
- Sviatopolk d. 1019
- Sviatoslav d. 1015
- Mstislav d. 1034/6
- Boris d. 1015
- Gleb d. 1015
- Igor' d. 1060
  - David d. 1112

Iaroslav of Novgorod, and Mstislav of Tmutorokan' – emerged as the principal combatants. From their widely dispersed power bases each used his own regional resources and contacts to reinforce the campaign for a secure place at the centre. Sviatopolk formed an alliance with the king of Poland, whose multinational force occupied Kiev for a while; Iaroslav augmented his local Novgorodian forces with Scandinavian mercenaries who helped him eventually to defeat and expel Sviatopolk; Mstislav gathered conscripts from his tributaries in the northern Caucasus, with whose aid he was able (in 1024) to negotiate an agreement with Iaroslav: he (Mstislav) would occupy Chernigov and would control the 'left-bank' lands (east of the Dnieper), while Iaroslav would control the 'right bank' lands including Kiev and Novgorod. Only on Mstislav's death (in 1034 or 1036) did Iaroslav revert to his father's status as sole ruler.[6]

Thus the death of Vladimir was followed by multiple fratricide, three years of dynastic war, a further seven years of periodic armed conflict, then a decade of coexistence before the final resolution when just one of Vladimir's numerous sons – Iaroslav – was left alive and at liberty. We can (and scholars do) speculate as to how the succession in 1015 'should have' worked. For such speculations to have any value, we need to be reasonably confident of three things: (i) that we know the seniority of his sons; (ii) that we know Vladimir's own wishes; and (iii) that we know what in principle constituted dynastic propriety at the time. But we know none of these things. Even if we did, and even if we could thereby in theory extrapolate a system to which his sons were meant to adhere, their actions demonstrate that any notional system failed to function. For practical purposes no such system existed.

The next change of generations, on Iaroslav's death in 1054, was more orderly. Like Vladimir, Iaroslav allocated regional possessions to his sons. Unlike Vladimir – according to the *Primary Chronicle* – he specified a hierarchy of seniority both within the dynasty and between the regional allocations, and he laid down some principles of inter-princely relations. The chronicle presents Iaroslav's arrangements in the form of what purports to be his deathbed 'Testament' to his sons, though it is possible that the document itself was composed retrospectively.[7]

6 Franklin and Shepard, *The Emergence of Rus*, pp. 183–207. The precise course of events is contentious: see e.g. I. N. Danilevskii, *Drevniaia Rus' glazami sovremennikov i potomkov (IX–XII vv.)* (Moscow: Aspekt Press, 1998), pp. 336–54; A. V. Nazarenko, *Drevniaia Rus' na mezhdunarodnykh putiakh. Mezhdistsiplinarnye ocherki kul'turnykh, torgovykh, politicheskikh sviazei IX–XII vekov* (Moscow: Iazyki russkoi kul'tury, 2001), pp. 451–503.
7 *Povest' vremennykh let* (hereafter *PVL*), ed. D. S. Likhachev and V. P. Adrianova-Peretts, 2 vols. (Moscow and Leningrad: AN SSSR, 1950), vol. 1, p. 108. See Martin Dimnik, 'The "Testament" of Iaroslav "the Wise": A Re-Examination', *Canadian Slavonic Papers* 29 (1987): 369–86.

As at the death of Vladimir, the offspring of older sons who had pre-deceased their father were not part of the general share-out. Seniority was lateral before it was vertical: that is, it passed down the line of sons before it passed to grandsons. However, whereas in 1015 Polotsk had remained with the family of Vladimir's deceased son, in 1054 Novgorod – the seat of Iaroslav's first son, who had died in 1052 – was not alienated as patrimony but reverted to being in the gift of the prince of Kiev. The oldest of Iaroslav's surviving sons in 1054 were given towns in the middle Dnieper region. Iziaslav and Sviatoslav were to have Kiev and Chernigov (still the two most desirable cities, as in the arrangement between Iaroslav and Mstislav thirty years before), while the third son, Vsevolod, was given the more precarious prize of Pereiaslavl', further south and more exposed to the steppes. As for the conduct of family business, the 'Testament' made two stipulations: first, the eldest son (Iziaslav) was to take the place of the father, was owed the same respect and had similar responsibility for resolving disputes; and second, the territorial allocations were to be inviolate, with no brother entitled to transgress the boundaries of another.

Iaroslav's 'Testament' dealt with an immediate problem of succession, but in the larger dynastic context over time it had to be more aspirational than operational. It only dealt explicitly with a small number of regions. It said nothing about subsequent succession. It was vague about the potential contradiction between its two principal instructions: that the oldest brother had a father's authority, yet that all the brothers' allocated possessions were inviolate (were Chernigov and Pereiaslavl' now the patrimonial possessions of Sviatoslav and Vsevolod respectively, or did Iziaslav have the right to reallocate as a father might?). And of course the 'Testament', like any document, could only be as effective as it was allowed to be by interested parties. Iaroslav's sons do seem to have operated as a reasonably harmonious triumvirate for nearly twenty years (briefly disrupted in 1067–8 when a kinsman from the Polotsk branch of the dynasty, Vseslav Briacheslavich, was installed as prince of Kiev by a faction of the townspeople). Yet in 1073 the two younger brothers, Sviatoslav and Vsevolod, blatantly contravened the provisions of their father's 'Testament' by ousting Iziaslav themselves. Iziaslav returned to Kiev after Sviatoslav's death in 1076, only to be killed in 1078 in battle against a nephew, one of Sviatoslav's sons. Despite the dynastic messiness of Iziaslav's last few years, the result was neat. Kiev passed laterally down the line of brothers and Vsevolod at last found himself in a position similar to that of his father Iaroslav in the mid-1030s: with all his male siblings dead, he was left as 'sole ruler'. The

'Testament' of Iaroslav, blueprint for collective governance, was seemingly dissolved into monarchy. As we shall see, however, in the intervening period the dynasty had developed, and its complexities cannot be reduced to the struggle for Kiev alone.

The next change of generation, on Vsevolod's death in 1093, illustrated and affirmed an important feature of dynastic convention. Vsevolod was succeeded as prince of Kiev by Sviatopolk Iziaslavich. Seniority did not, therefore, pass directly from Vsevolod to his offspring, but reverted to the offspring of his older brother. Or rather, it reverted to the offspring of the oldest of his brothers *who had been prince of Kiev* (the general practice was that one could only succeed to a throne where one's father had already been prince – so those whose fathers died young were at risk of falling off the ladder of succession). Three principles thus emerge: (i) legitimacy in general resides with the dynasty as a whole; (ii) seniority passes laterally down the line of brothers, and then back up to the offspring of the senior brother, except that (iii) a prince of Kiev should be the son of a prince of Kiev (according to the chronicles' formula a prince 'sits on the throne of his father and grandfather').

Although this nuance might be seen as a useful device to limit the number of claimants, the excluded members of the dynasty did not disappear, nor did they cease to be princes, nor did they lose the broader claim to some legitimate share of the family inheritance. Squabbles over Kiev itself are only a small part of the larger pattern of dynastic rule: a pattern which became ever more complex as the family expanded. Regional allocations came to be regarded as patrimonial possessions, within which the senior regional princes could then allocate possessions to their own offspring, approximately reproducing at local level the conventions which emerged in the Kievan succession. Indeed, Kiev and Novgorod remained exceptional in that they always retained, in different ways, a pan-dynastic dimension, never quite being converted into patrimonial principalities. With the dynasty continually expanding, and with every son of a prince remaining a prince, and with no mechanism for limiting the overall numbers, so the regional controversies over succession multiplied. For over forty years from Vsevolod's accession in 1078 there were no serious disputes over the Kievan inheritance, but instead the prince of Kiev and his senior associates on the middle Dnieper had to devote more and more of their time to dealing with conflicts among their junior or dispossessed kinsmen. Regional rivalries among land-hungry princelings were a powerful stimulus for settlement and colonisation and hence gave rise to fresh problems of precedence and demarcation. If in 1015 the princes posted around the periphery had looked inwards to Kiev, by the 1090s there was fierce competition for rights of tribute-gathering or settlement in previously remote areas in the north-east (Rostov, Suzdal') and south-west (Vladimir-in-Volynia, Peremyshl', Terebovl'), which thereby became ever more closely drawn into the political, economic and cultural nexus. The dynastic conventions, messy as they can appear to be (a particularly grisly series of conflicts in the mid-1090s led to an attempt at regulation through an accord at Liubech in 1097),[8] nevertheless helped to drive the process by which the lands of the Rus' gradually expanded outwards from the original north–south axis between the Baltic and the steppes and were consolidated into an increasingly coherent politico-cultural zone.

Returning, however, to Kiev to complete the outline narrative of dynastic politics: Sviatopolk's death in 1113 did not precipitate another change of generations, but it did bring into focus, with respect to Kiev itself, a potential ambiguity in the conventions which had emerged over the second half of the eleventh century. Who was the legitimate successor: Oleg, son of Sviatoslav of Chernigov? or Vladimir Monomakh, son of Vsevolod of Pereiaslavl'? On the one hand: Oleg was a son of the older brother, Vladimir was a son of the younger brother, Oleg's father Sviatoslav had been prince of Kiev before Vladimir's father Vsevolod (1073–6 and 1078–93 respectively), therefore obviously Oleg was senior and had the legitimate claim. On the other hand, Oleg's father Sviatoslav had not become prince of Kiev legitimately according to seniority, nor had he outlasted his older brother as seniority passed down the line of siblings: he had ousted his older brother Iziaslav, whom he had then predeceased, and on both these counts the claims of his offspring were dubious. In 1113 the issue was resolved in favour of Vladimir Vsevolodovich, who (in the chronicle account) recognised the problem but allowed himself to be persuaded by the townspeople of Kiev. However, this ambiguity between the claims of Vladimir and the claims of his cousin Oleg Sviatoslavich was to resurface periodically in disputes over the Kievan succession for at least the next hundred years.

Such, in brief but already sufficiently confusing outline, was the process of improvisation and adaptation through which the dynasty's political culture emerged. Yet whatever the dynasty's own preferences, family agreements in themselves were not enough to ensure their own implementation nor was dynastic seniority in itself a mechanism for the exercise of power. The political culture of a few brothers or cousins or uncles or nephews would have been

---

8 Franklin and Shepard, *The Emergence of Rus*, pp. 265–77; cf. Martin Dimnik, *The Dynasty of Chernigov 1054–1146* (Toronto: Pontifical Institute of Mediaeval Studies, 1994), pp. 191–223.

irrelevant if it were not held in place by structures of coercion and legitimacy involving broader social groups.

Power and governance

The princes of Rus' were warlords, heading a military elite. While prince of Kiev, Vladimir Vsevolodovich Monomakh wrote an 'Instruction' for his sons, a kind of brief *curriculum vitae* presenting as exemplary his own credentials and achievements. What, in Vladimir's presentation, does an exemplary prince do? The answer is simple: he engages in military campaigns, and in their recreational equivalent, the hunt. Vladimir introduces the narrative of his life thus: 'Here I relate to you, my children, the tale of the labours that I have laboured: of my campaigns and of my hunts since I was thirteen years old.' And he concludes the narrative with a summary boast: 'In all [I completed] 83 major campaigns, besides minor campaigns too numerous to recall.'[9] Besides his kin, then, the social group closest to and most vital for the prince was his *druzhina*: his retinue, the protective and coercive basis for his power.

The *druzhina* owed its loyalty to the prince personally. Thus to some extent the *druzhina* could choose whom to support. In 1015 Vladimir Sviatoslavich's son Boris was reputedly on a campaign in the steppes with the *druzhina* of his father. When Vladimir died 'they said to him: "You have your father's *druzhina* and his troops; go to Kiev and sit on your father's throne."' But Boris declined, so the troops dispersed, leaving him with no protection except the singing of psalms, which on this occasion proved ineffectual against the agents of his murderous brother Sviatopolk.[10] Boris was a saint, hence virtuous; but a saint's virtue can be foolhardiness in ordinary men: a wise prince nurtured his *druzhina*, kept it close to him, feasted with it, consulted it and heeded its counsel, rewarded it for its labours on his behalf.[11]

Druzhina was a flexible term and flexible institution.[12] At its core was the 'small' (*malaia*) *druzhina*, the prince's permanent personal bodyguards, but beyond that the *druzhina* merges with the prince's extended household, his *dvor* (the word for a 'court' in all senses) and it formed the nucleus of his

9 *PVL*, vol. I, pp. 158, 162.
10 *PVL*, vol. I, pp. 90–1.
11 See e.g. *PVL*, vol. I, p. 86.
12 See Uwe Halbach, *Der russische Fürstenhof vor dem 16. Jahrhundert: eine vergleichende Untersuchung zur politischen Lexikologie und Verfassungsgeschichte der alten Rus'* (Quellen und Studien zur Geschichte des östlichen Europa, 23; Stuttgart: Steiner Verlag, 1985), pp. 94–113; A. A. Gorskii, *Drevnerusskaia druzhina. K istorii genezisa klassovogo obshchestva i gosudarstva na Rusi* (Moscow: Prometei, 1989).

administration. Perhaps at one stage the *druzhina* had truly corresponded to some egalitarian ideal of military fellowship, with the prince as patron and first among equals, but as the business of being a prince and running a principality in Rus' – especially for one of the senior princes – grew more complex, so the *druzhina* developed its internal hierarchies, its divisions of functions, its structure of offices and responsibilities. It had its own senior members – the boyars – along with the rank-and-file 'youths' (*otroki*) in the junior (*mladshaia*) *druzhina*. Boyar offices spanned military, domestic and urban administration, from general (*voevoda*) to head of household (*kormilets*) to steward or estate manager (*tiun*) to military governor of a city (*tysiatskii*, 'thousander', 'chiliarch'; supported by *sotskie*, 'hundreders', 'centurions'). Lesser functionaries included the domestic manager (*kliuchnik*, literally 'key-man'), enforcement officers such as the *birich*, and – eventually – more specialised servitors such as the 'seal-man' (*pechatnik*) or scribe (*pisets*). In a warrior elite, however, the distinction between military and administrative office is not always clear: thus, for example, the *mechnik* ('swordman') is well attested in Novgorodian inscriptions as having a role in fiscal administration or tribute-gathering.[13]

The political order was not, therefore, just a matter of agreement or dispute within the princely family, the inner circle of his kin. A prince needed his *druzhina*, his inner circle of servitors. And he also needed wider structures of support at least in the towns, an outer circle linked to him more loosely. The pre-Mongol period in general was a time of notable urban economic and demographic growth, and throughout the period the rulers not merely exploited that growth but played a part in stimulating and developing it, whether through early ventures into long-distance trade and diplomacy, or through the cultural initiatives which helped develop local skills and create markets for local craft and manufacture. Around some of the regions, through the establishment and proliferation of patrimonial possessions, princes could often come to be identified intimately with their urban bases, but in Kiev and Novgorod (and perhaps elsewhere) the prince was not integrated into the urban social structure unconditionally. Not that princely rule itself was in question: a city needed a prince as much a prince needed a city; *a* prince; but not necessarily the particular prince. There were significant variations both in the degree of the prince's support from the city, and in the nature and extent of his authority over it.[14]

---

13 See V. L. Ianin, *U istokov novgorodskoi gosudarstvennosti* (Novgorod: Novgorodskii gosu-darstvennyi universitet, 2001).
14 See A. P. Tolochko, *Kniaz' v Drevnei Rusi: vlast', sobstvennost', ideologiia* (Kiev: Naukova Dumka, 1992).

Urban support was embedded in formulae and rituals of political legitimacy. In 1015 Sviatopolk (according to the chronicler antipathetic to him) bribed the Kievans so that they 'received' him, but 'their hearts were not with him', and he asked the men of Vyshgorod whether they would 'receive [him] with [their] heart'.[15] In 1024 Mstislav of Chernigov and Tmutorokan' advanced on Kiev, but the townspeople 'did not receive him'.[16] On 15 September 1068 a faction of the Kievans held a *veche*, a town meeting, on the market square, and the upshot was that a group of them expelled their prince Iziaslav, freed Vseslav Briacheslavich of Polotsk from incarceration, took him to the princely court and 'acclaimed' him there – though a few months later they 'received' Iziaslav again when he returned with an army from Poland.[17] In 1102 Sviatopolk Iziaslavich had an agreement with his cousin Vladimir Vsevolodovich (Monomakh) that his (Sviatopolk's) son should replace Vladimir's son Mstislav as prince in Novgorod. But the Novgorodians would have none of it: 'we do not want either Sviatopolk or his son. Send us [Mstislav] even if he has two heads,' they are reported to have said. And Sviatopolk argued and cajoled but could not persuade them, so the Novgorodians kept Mstislav.[18] In 1113 (according to a chronicler favourable to him) Vladimir Monomakh accepted the Kievan throne not by dynastic necessity but only because the Kievans threatened to riot if he refused; and 'all the Kievans' greeted his entrance into the city.[19] This is all still some way away from the written, contractual form in which Novgorod was to set the terms and conditions for its prince from the latter part of the pre-Mongol period,[20] but to be 'received' or 'acclaimed' by the townspeople, to have the commitment of their 'hearts' (later formalised with an oath on the cross) was important for practical legitimacy.

A prince had a price. In return for protection and prestige, the townspeople surrendered a certain authority. No detailed records of governance survive (most likely none were produced), but we can trace aspects of princely rule through, for example, codes of law. Before the reign of Vladimir Sviatoslavich it is unlikely that any type of written law was formally operational in Rus'. This does not, of course, mean that the country was lawless, merely that

---

15 *PVL*, vol. i, p. 90.
16 *PVL*, vol. i, p. 99.
17 *PVL*, vol. i, pp. 115, 116.
18 *PVL*, vol. i, p. 182.
19 *PVL*, vol. i, p. 196.
20 In the period covered by this chapter it was not unusual for the prince of Kiev to appoint his eldest son to Novgorod while still a child: obviously not as direct ruler but as an emblem of the princely connection to Kiev, while day-to-day authority was vested in an appointed governor (*posadnik*). In the twelfth century the Novgorod *posadnik* became an elected officer, disengaged from Kiev.

dispute resolution and social discipline functioned according to custom. As the chronicle (quoting from a Byzantine source) succinctly puts it: 'ancestral custom is regarded as law for those who have no [written] law'.[21] By the death of Vladimir Monomakh, however, three types of law code had become established, albeit initially on a modest scale: codes issued with the authority of the Church ('canon law'), codes issued under the authority of a prince or princes (*Russkaia pravda*), and joint codes issued by princes with and for the Church. For princely governance the most important of these is *Russkaia pravda*.

Russkaia pravda is the generic name for a series of codes – or one could view it as a cumulative code – whose first version was issued by Iaroslav and which was subsequently adapted and expanded by his successors. *Russkaia pravda* begins with an article prescribing the degrees of kinship within which blood vengeance is permissible ('a brother may avenge [the murder of] his brother, or a son his father, or a father his son, or a brother's son or a sister's son [their uncle]').[22] Subsequently it consists mainly of a list of offences together with the penalty for each, plus a few articles dealing with procedure. The growth of the text of *Russkaia pravda* over this period is evidence for (though not necessarily proof of) the expanding expectations and claims of princely intervention in dispute resolution. Iaroslav's code is very brief, filling barely a page of a modern printed edition. It was chiefly concerned with discipline and disputes within the *druzhina* itself and the urban elite. It includes, for example, penalties for striking someone with a sword or sword-hilt, for cutting off an arm or a finger, for hiding a fugitive slave, for manhandling a Scandinavian, for damaging someone's beard or moustache, for stealing a horse, as well as procedures for recovering a stolen slave who has been sold on several times. The most notable additions to the code under Iaroslav's sons consist of penalties for damage inflicted on the prince's own servitors and property, while articles associated with Vladimir Monomakh are more detailed and also extend the overall scope of the code to deal with, in particular, the regulation of financial dealings including interest rates on loans.[23]

21 *PVL*, vol. 1, p. 15.
22 *RZ*, 9 vols. (Moscow: Iuridicheskaia literatura, 1984–94), vol. 1: *Zakonodatel'stvo Drevnei Rusi*, ed. V. L. Ianin (1984), p. 47; cf. Daniel H. Kaiser (ed. and trans.), *The Laws of Rus' – Tenth to Fifteenth Centuries* (The Laws of Russia. Series 1, Vol. 1; Salt Lake City, Oh.: Charles Schlacks, 1992), p. 15.
23 Iaroslav's *pravda* and that of his sons are combined as the 'short' version in the surviving texts: *RZ*, vol. 1, pp. 7–9; Vladimir Monomakh's additions are incorporated into the 'expanded' version, which also included later accretions: *RZ*, vol. 1, pp. 64–73. Cf. the English translations in Kaiser, *The Laws of Rus'*, pp. 15–34.

The provisions of *Russkaia pravda* are a mixture of custom and innovation. Equivalent types of code can be found in other early medieval north European legal compilations, but the details are specific to Rus'. The introduction and growth of the code seem to reflect princely attempts to advance two processes: the standardisation of practice, and the social extension of princely authority. The very first written code may have been issued for Novgorod while Iaroslav was prince in Kiev, so that the decision to use a written document was a device to promote standard administrative practices in the prince's absence. More revealingly, an article agreed by Iaroslav's sons states that the penalty for killing the prince's stablemaster was to be 80 grivnas 'as Iziaslav established when the people of Dorogobuzh killed his stablemaster'.[24] Here the written code is used to standardise dynastic practice across local jurisdictions. At the same time the nature and number of articles shows changes in the princes' presumptions about their power to intervene. The earliest provisions deal with regulating direct retribution (blood feuds, vendettas) and with specifying sums to be paid in compensation to the victims or their families. The princes never managed fully to prohibit blood-vengeance (although they apparently tried to do so), but gradually compensation was supplemented or replaced by fines: that is to say, the idea that an offender was primarily responsible to the victim made way for the notion that an offender was responsible to the ruler. 'Horizontal', or 'dyadic' judicial practices began to make way for vertical, or 'triadic', relations.[25] Moreover, this was occurring as the princes were broadening the scope of their assumed judicial authority, expanding both the range of people directly affected and the range of behaviours covered by their written rules. Even in its early stages, therefore, the text of *Russkaia pravda* reflects the growing incursion of formal mechanisms of princely authority into the mutual relations and activities of the urban population.

The expansion and harmonisation of rules through written codes was linked to a larger process of political and social integration. The ruling dynasty was only one of the institutions promoting this process through written codes of law. The other relevant institution was the Church. 'We Christians', wrote the chronicler, 'have one law.'[26] Here, however, he is not referring to princely secular law but to the laws of Christianity, the authority of the Church and its teachings: the authority of the Bible in general, and more specifically the authority of the practical codes produced over the centuries under the general

---

24 *RZ*, vol. I, p. 48; cf. Kaiser, *The Laws of Rus'*, p. 17.
25 See, over a longer period, Daniel H. Kaiser, *The Growth of the Law in Medieval Russia* (Princeton: Princeton University Press, 1980).
26 *PVL*, vol. I, p. 16.

heading of canon law. Canon law, combined with Byzantine imperial legislation relating to the Church, was conveyed in reference books known as
nomocanons (*Kormchie knigi* in the Russian tradition). Much of a nomocanon
is concerned with the Church's own internal dogmas and disciplines, but substantial sections are also relevant to the wider community, and one of the
prime responsibilities of churchmen in Rus' was to promote behaviour compatible with canon law, to interpret and apply the rules and guidelines in local
circumstances. In promoting social and cultural integration, the Church was
thus potentially a very significant partner for the princes, for the Church had
pretensions to affect areas of behaviour far beyond the reach of the princes'
writ. The Church took regulation beyond the public sphere and into the home,
into daily life. It prescribed what food could or could not be eaten on which
days through the year, whom and how one could or could not marry, what
to wear or not wear, when to have or not to have sexual intercourse and in
what manner. Clearly these are areas where custom was likely to be powerful and – across the lands of the Rus' – diverse. Some of our most eloquent
sources record the responses of senior churchmen to practical pastoral questions. Thus, for example, Metropolitan Ioann II (c.1077–89) is asked to advise on
a miscellany of issues: whether in the cold northern winters it was permissible
to wear leather undergarments made from the hides of animals which were
considered unclean for eating (answer – yes); or how to deal with those who
married according to local pagan rituals (answer – impose the same penance
that one would impose on fornicators); or whether a ritually unclean mother
should be allowed to breastfeed her sick baby (answer – yes, if the child's life
is otherwise in danger).[27]

The third type of law code brings the secular and the religious institutions
together. Advice, admonition and penances could be meted out by the Church
on its own authority, but the power to impose material sanctions could only
be granted by the prince. A series of 'princely statutes' (*ustavy*) therefore
specified the categories of person and behaviour that came under the Church's
jurisdiction. The two most important statutes are attributed to Vladimir and
Iaroslav respectively, although, like *Russkaia pravda*, these are cumulative
documents preserved in later versions. In principle, however, the basic nature
of each is clear. 'Vladimir's statute' serves as a kind of constitutional statement,
allocating to the Church judicial power over specified categories of people

27 The 'canonical responses' of Ioann II: Slavonic text in *Russkaia istoricheskaia biblioteka*, vol.
vi (St Petersburg: Arkheograficheskaia Kommissiia, 1908), cols. 1–20; Greek version ed.
A. S. Pavlov, 'Otryvki grecheskogo teksta kanonicheskikh otvetov russkogo mitropolita
Ioanna II', *Zapiski Imperatorskoi Akademii nauk* 22 (1873): Appendix 5.

(monks and nuns, the clergy and their families; but also 'displaced' persons such as widows, the lame and the blind) and over specified actions (such as divorce, domestic violence, abduction and rape, sorcery – which may include the use of herbal medicine – and heresy).[28] 'Iaroslav's statute' more closely resembles *Russkaia pravda* in its form: a list of offences and the penalties for each. It is notable for its social differentiation. There was no question of all being equal under the law: the rape or abduction of the daughter of a boyar merited compensation of 5 grivnas in gold and the same sum as a fine to the bishop; but only one grivna of gold was demanded for the rape or abduction of a daughter of 'lesser boyars', and smaller sums further down the social scale. There were fines of 40 grivnas of silver for bigamy, 100 for incest. Sometimes the offender incurred several types of penalty: a man who beat another man's wife had to pay 6 grivnas to the bishop, plus whatever may be due in [secular] law.[29]

Princely power and ecclesiastical authority complemented each other. Moreover, in some ways the Church was better equipped to disseminate and oversee the norms of written law than were the princes, for this was part of its prime mission and in the bishops and the clergy it had a network of trained personnel. Princely administration at this stage was still comparatively rudimentary. The introduction of written law did not, for example, imply the imposition of standard written bureaucratic procedures or the immediate creation of a class of civil administrators.[30] Differentiation of service functions was developing, but eleventh-century Rus' had nothing comparable to the administrative bureaucratic institutions either of contemporary Byzantium or indeed of sixteenth-century Muscovy. Over the period covered by the present chapter, the direction and momentum of change became well established, though the process still had a very long way to go.

Beyond the prince, his retinue and parts of the city, evidence for social or administrative structures becomes very sparse indeed. In other words, we know very little about the vast majority of the population. Lack of knowledge is, of course, no bar to historiographical speculation: just how many of the rural population were or were not 'dependent' or 'free', in which senses? At what stage is it or is it not legitimate to speak of 'feudal' structures and relations? Visions of early Rus' range from a cluster of 'city states' sustained partly by slave labour and partly by the surplus produce of a free peasantry, to

28 *RZ*, vol. I, pp. 139–40; cf. Kaiser, *The Laws of Rus'*, pp. 42–4.
29 See *RZ*, vol. I, pp. 168–70 ('short' version); cf. Kaiser, *The Laws of Rus'*, pp. 45–50 ('expanded' version).
30 See Franklin, *Writing, Society and Culture*, pp. 129–86.

a 'feudal' economy based on the growth of aristocratic manorial estates and a largely dependent peasantry.[31] In addition, the overall picture may have to accommodate wide regional differences. These are, of course, major issues, but the visible pieces of the jigsaw allow too many plausible but conflicting reconstructions to justify full confidence in any of them.

External relations

For most of the history of Rus' there was no such thing as a Rus' foreign policy. In those periods when political power in Rus' was relatively unitary, one can construe the actions of the prince of Kiev, or the agreed joint actions of senior princes, as the policy of Rus'. 'Sole rule' and joint action were more common during the eleventh and early twelfth centuries than at any subsequent period, but still the norm was for the regional princes to pursue their own interests in dealing with their neighbours. Collective diplomacy such as that which had led to the tenth-century trade agreements with Constantinople was increasingly implausible, if not yet wholly impossible.

Our tour of the regions begins in the north. Iaroslav's ties with Scandinavia were established during the decades he spent in Novgorod. He was married to Ingigerd, daughter of the king of Sweden, and in the battles of 1015–19 he may also have formed an alliance with the king of Denmark.[32] Scandinavian sagas speak warmly of the hospitality of Prince Iarisleif of Holmgarthr (= Novgorod) and of the aid he provided to distinguished Vikings on their journeys along the East Way.[33] However, Iaroslav was the last significant Rus' prince to maintain such close traditional ties with Scandinavia. In part the abrupt decline from the mid-eleventh century was due to the strains of the relationship itself. The chronicle hints at antagonism between the mercenaries and the settled Novgorodian population, just as it hints that Vladimir himself had been pleased to offload Scandinavian warriors to Constantinople.[34] In part, however, the

31 For a history of the debates in Russia see M. B. Sverdlov, *Obshchestvennyi stroi Drevnei Rusi v russkoi istoricheskoi nauke XVIII–XX vv.* (St Petersburg: Dmitrii Bulanin, 1996); also Vernadsky, *Kievan Russia*, pp. 143–51.

32 See A. V. Nazarenko, 'O russko-datskom soiuze v pervoi chetverti XI v.', *Drevneishie gosudarstva na territorii SSSR. Materialy i issledovaniia. 1990 god* (Moscow: Nauka, 1991), pp. 167–90.

33 H. R. Ellis Davidson, *The Viking Road to Byzantium* (London: George Allen and Unwin, 1976), pp. 158–73; Henrik Birnbaum, 'Iaroslav's Varangian Connection', *Scandoslavica* 24 (1978): 5–25. For an array of sources see T. N. Dzhakson, *Islandskie korolevskie sagi o vostochnoi Evrope (seredina XI–seredina XIII v.) (teksty, perevod, kommentarii)* (Moscow: Ladomir, 2000).

34 *PVL*, vol. I, pp. 56, 95, 97.

reduced intensity of direct political links with Scandinavia reflects the down-grading, in the second half of the eleventh century, of the autonomy of the Novgorod prince.

For much of the eleventh century the north-eastern settlements such as Rostov and Suzdal' were still remote outposts in the midst of often hostile peoples. A bishop sent in the 1070s was reportedly murdered, the *Primary Chronicle* tells of pagan-led uprisings, and Vladimir Monomakh in his autobi-ography indicates that a march 'through the Viatichi' (the tribe separating the middle Dnieper region from the north-eastern settlements) was particularly hazardous.[35] However, the region had obvious economic potential, with its vast reserves of valuable furs and its strategic position on the trade route between the Baltic and the middle Volga. Towards the end of the century there was already fierce competition among the southern princes of Kiev, Chernigov and Pereiaslavl' for tribute-collecting rights in the north-east. The Liubech agree-ment of 1097 was prompted in part by just such a conflict between Vladimir Monomakh and his cousin Oleg Sviatoslavich of Chernigov. Nevertheless, the relatively low status of Suzdal' is reflected in the fact that Monomakh allocated it to Iurii, the youngest of his many sons. The story of its transformation into a powerful principality under Iurii, later known as Dolgorukii ('Long Arm'), belongs to another chapter.

In the south were the nomadic and semi-nomadic peoples of the steppes, dominated until the 1030s by the Pechenegs, and from the 1060s by the *Polovtsy* (also known as Cumans, also known as Qipchaks).[36] Many of the chronicle narratives, and a fair proportion of subsequent historical writings, imply a state of permanent irreconcilable opposition between the Rus' and the steppe nomads. This is too crude. Certainly there were major clashes, raids and skirmishes in both directions. Yet relations could also be amicable, and on the whole the frontier zones were quite stable. Very rarely did either side have serious territorial designs on the other. There was a limited amount of colonisation by proxy, such as the recruitment and settlement of 'Torks' (Oghuz) in the specially created town of Torchesk as a kind of buffer. Overall, however, it would be hard to show that any Rus' prince spent much more time campaigning against the Pechenegs or the *Polovtsy* than against his own kin within the dynastic lands.

---

35 *PVL*, vol. I, pp. 117–19, 158; Gail Lenhoff, 'Canonization and Princely Power in Northeast Rus': The Cult of Leontij Rostovskij', *Die Welt der Slaven*, NF, 16 (1992), 359–80.

36 See R. M. Mavrodina, *Kievskaia Rus' i kochevniki (pechenegi, torki, polovtsy). Istoriografich-eskii ocherk* (Leningrad: Nauka, 1983); S. A. Pletneva, *Polovtsy* (Moscow: Nauka, 1990); T. S. Noonan, 'Rus', Pechenegs and Polovtsy', *RH* 19 (1992): 300–26.

Relations between the steppe and Chernigov were generally more cordial than those between the steppe and Kiev or Pereiaslavl'. Chernigov had traditional links with the lower Don and the Azov region. When Mstislav of Tmutorokan' and Iaroslav of Novgorod agreed to their division of the lands in 1024, Mstislav settled in Chernigov, and there is no suggestion that he had the worst of the deal. In the decade between 1024 and Mstislav's death, Chernigov looks to have been the dominant power in the middle Dnieper region, and it may be no coincidence that one of Iaroslav's first actions on assuming 'sole rule' was to reassert the pre-eminence of Kiev by undermining Chernigov's relations with the steppe, through mounting what turned out to be the decisive campaign against the Pechenegs. Similarly in 1094 Oleg Sviatoslavich of Chernigov marched from Tmutorokan' with Polovtsian allies to recapture his patrimonial city from his cousin Vladimir Monomakh.[37] In 1096 Oleg refused, under intense pressure from Monomakh and his (Monomakh's) father Vsevolod of Kiev, to join them on a campaign against the *Polovtsy*, and he even sheltered the son of a Polovtsian leader who had been killed on Monomakh's orders.[38] Monomakh did organise a series of highly successful expeditions against the *Polovtsy* in the 1100s and 1110s,[39] yet even he mixed military victory with political alliance, marrying two of his sons (including Iurii Dolgorukii) to Polovtsian brides.[40]

Further south, beyond the steppes, beyond the Black Sea, lay Constantinople. Here we come up against a paradox. In a sense, relations between Kiev and Constantinople ought to have been close and constant. Constantinople was the traditional lure for the Rus' merchants and there is strong documentary evidence of intense (if not always friendly) military, economic, diplomatic and cultural dealings with Constantinople in the tenth century, culminating in the conversion to Christianity which – *inter alia* – should have smoothed the way for ever closer links on all levels. Yet over the course of the eleventh and early twelfth centuries, while ecclesiastical and cultural contacts were of course important, political and diplomatic relations seem to have become more sporadic, and even trade apparently declined after the middle of the century, particularly in manufactured goods, as the Rus' began to acquire some of the skills to switch from import to local production. Finds of Byzantine coins in Rus' become notably rare after *c*.1050.[41] In 1043 Iaroslav sent his eldest

37 *PVL*, vol. i, pp. 101–2, 148.
38 *PVL*, vol. i, p. 149.
39 *PVL*, vol. i, pp. 187, 190–2, 201.
40 *PVL*, vol. i, pp. 187, 202.
41 T. S. Noonan, 'The Monetary History of Kiev in the Pre-Mongol Period', *HUS* 11 (1987): 384–443.

son Vladimir on a military campaign against Constantinople, the last of its kind in the sequence that had started nearly 150 years previously. The cause is not entirely clear (the conflict is supposed to have escalated from the death of a Rus' merchant in an altercation in a Constantinopolitan market). The result was total defeat for the Rus', but the consequences do not seem to have been severe: in the late 1040s Byzantine artists and craftsmen were putting the finishing touches to Iaroslav's main prestige public project, the cathedral of St Sophia, and by the early 1050s Iaroslav's son Vsevolod was married into the family of the reigning Byzantine emperor, Constantine IX Monomachos. The offspring of this union, Vladimir Monomakh, himself impinged on Byzantine authority in 1116–18 by aiding an opponent of Alexios I Komnenos, but this was a minor episode. In 1122 Monomakh's granddaughter married into the ruling Komnenos family.[42]

Perhaps surprisingly, given their Byzantine religious and cultural orientation, political relations between Rus' princes and various parts of Western Europe were more persistent and diverse than political relations with Byzantium. As a crude index one might note the substantially longer list of dynastic marriages, ranging from the elite union of Iaroslav's daughter Anna with Henry I of France, to lower-level unions such as Monomakh's marriage, in the early 1070s, to Gytha, daughter of Harald of England (he who was killed at the Battle of Hastings in 1066). Perhaps, however, the imbalance is not so surprising. In the first place, the comparison is uneven. 'Western Europe' is not a single or homogeneous place, despite its habitual labelling as such. One cannot properly compare the plurality of polities in 'Western Europe' with the unitary polity of Byzantium. Secondly, Byzantium was geographically remote, very rarely did any Rus' prince come face to face with Byzantium by necessity, and no Byzantine military force ever entered or contested Rus' lands. In contrast, more trade routes linked the lands of the Rus' with different parts of Western Europe than with Byzantium, and several Western European peoples and polities shared substantial and periodically contested border zones with the Rus' dynasty. For many of the dynasty political dealings with Byzantium were an option, political dealings with one or more lands of Western Europe were a necessity. Nor did the 1054 schism between Constantinople and Rome (unresolved to the present day) appear to have had much effect on diplomatic

---

42 On these and other reported marriages see Alexander Kazhdan, 'Rus'-Byzantine Princely Marriages in the Eleventh and Twelfth Centuries', *HUS* 12/13 (1988/9 [pub. 1990]): 414–29. Kazhdan stresses that, apart from the marriage of Vladimir Sviatoslavich to the emperor's sister Anna, none of the reported marriages are likely to have been with top-rank Byzantine princes or princesses.

and even personal dealings with 'Latin' countries and peoples. Senior churchmen – notably some of those who came to Rus' from Constantinople – might write stern tracts warning about the errors of the 'Latins' and of the dangers of contact with them,[43] but dynastic marriages continued, and a Rus' monk visiting the Holy Land around 1106–8 could be on perfectly amicable terms with its 'Latin' crusader rulers.[44]

Those princes whose own interests were most directly dependent on relations with one or other of their Western neighbours tended – not surprisingly – to pay the most attention to those neighbours, whether the interest was expressed through friendship or through hostility. Among princes or would-be princes of Kiev this applies particularly to those who were also princes of Turov, on one of the main routes westwards. The first of these was Sviatopolk Vladimirovich, who, as we saw, persuaded Bolesław I of Poland (who happened to be his father-in-law) to put together a force to help him take Kiev in 1018. The second was Iziaslav Iaroslavich, who also persuaded a Polish force, under Bolesław II (who happened to be his wife's nephew) to help him retake Kiev in 1069. After he was ousted again by his younger brother Sviatoslav in 1073, Iziaslav fled westwards again and spent three years trying (unsuccessfully) to solicit material support from Bolesław, the German Emperor Henry IV, and the Pope. By the end of the century, however, Turov had been, so to speak, outflanked, as rival clusters of the proliferating and land-hungry junior princes squabbled for the right to install themselves in the territories still closer to the western border zones, such as Vladimir-in-Volynia, Peremyshl' and Terebovl'. In a particularly vicious and convoluted phase of the conflicts in the late 1090s both Władysław of Poland and Kalman of Hungary were sucked into the dynastic in-fighting which revolved round three descendants of Iaroslav whose fathers had not succeeded to Kiev: Vasilko and Volodar Rostislavichi (grandsons of Iaroslav's eldest son Vladimir, who had died before his father) and David Igorevich (whose father Igor' Iaroslavich had died before his older brothers).[45] This was a prelude to the close involvement of Hungary in the political life of Galich which grew over the first half of the twelfth century.

43 See the works attributed to Leo of Pereiaslavl', Ioann II and Nikofor I: Sophia Senyk, *A History of the Church in Ukraine*, vol. 1: *To the End of the Thirteenth Century* (Orientalia christiana analecta 243; Rome: Pontificio Istituto Orientale, 1993), pp. 316–21; Gerhard Podskalsky, *Christentum und theologische Literatur in der Kiever Rus' (988–1237)* (Munich: C. H. Beck, 1982), pp. 170–84.
44 On the pilgrimage of Daniil in this respect see Senyk, *A History*, pp. 314–15. More broadly on attitudes to 'Latins' see John Fennell, *A History of the Russian Church to 1448* (London and New York: Longman, 1995), pp. 96–104.
45 Franklin and Shepard, *The Emergence of Rus*, pp. 269–70.

Rus' external political relations were thus as unitary or as diffuse as were Rus' domestic politics. During the rare periods of comparatively unitary domestic authority – under Vladimir Sviatoslavich, for example, or under Iaroslav once he became 'sole ruler' after 1036 – it may be possible to identify a comparatively coherent foreign policy. Otherwise the separate princes' dealings with their non-Rus' neighbours were largely – and increasingly – autonomous.

4. Religion, culture, ideology

In the three generations after Vladimir the main implications of the official conversion to Christianity were made manifest. The official baptism was a single, datable event. Christianisation was a long process with profound consequences for social institutions, economic life, structures of authority and power, the urban environment, patterns of employment, manufacturing technology and production, public and private behaviours, diet, visual and written culture, aesthetic and intellectual standards and concepts, ideas and ideology, the understanding of the world.

The Church, including monasteries, provided Christianity's institutional foundations. In the larger administrative structure of Christianity, Rus' was a province of the patriarchate of Constantinople. The Church in Rus' was headed by a metropolitan – properly 'of Rhōsia', or 'of Rus'', but in modern historiography usually labelled 'of Kiev' since that was his residence. Only one metropolitan during this period – Ilarion (c.1051–4) – is known to have been a native of Rus'. The rest were appointees from Byzantium whose first language of religion was Greek.[46] Immediately below the metropolitan were the bishops, in charge of Church organisation in the sub-districts. The spread of bishoprics can serve as one rough indicator of the spread of organised Christianity itself. By the time of Vladimir Monomakh bishoprics were well established in the middle Dnieper region: at Chernigov and Pereiaslavl'; at Belgorod and Iur'ev close to Kiev (possibly to help look after Kiev itself). Moving northwards, there were bishoprics at Turov, Polotsk and Novgorod. Estimates vary as to the date of the foundation of the bishopric of Rostov, in the north-east, but no continuous episcopal presence can be traced there until well into the twelfth century.[47] Over a hundred years after the official conversion,

---

46 See the brief biographies by Andrzej Poppe in Podskalsky, *Christentum*, pp. 282–6.
47 See Andrzej Poppe, 'Werdegang der Diözesanstruktur der Kiever Metropolitankirche in den ersten Jahrhunderten der Christianisierung der Ostslaven', in K. C. Felmy et al. (eds.), *Tausend Jahre Christentum in Russland. Zum Millennium der Taufe der Kiever Rus'* (Göttingen: Vandenhoeck and Ruprecht, 1988), pp. 251–90; J.-P. Arrignon, 'La Création

therefore, organised Christianity was still quite compact: solidly embedded along the north–south, Novgorod–Kiev axis and in a cluster of bishoprics on the middle Dnieper, but not yet institutionally prominent further to the east or west.[48] In other words, organised Christianity followed – with a certain time-lag – the political fortunes of the dynasty.

The first bishops must have come from Byzantium, or from Bulgaria (whence they could bring their experience of Christianity in Slavonic), but by the second half of the eleventh century we know of several who were trained locally, via Rus' monasteries.[49] Monks and bishops had to be celibate, while the parish clergy had to be married, hence bishops were recruited from among monks, not from among the parish clergy (who were also likely to have been educated to a much lower level). The early history of Rus' monasticism is predictably obscure, but again by the late eleventh century some quite substantial foundations were well established in Kiev and the other principal towns.

The Church's most public act was not prayer but building, and the institutions of Christianity transformed the urban landscape. Most churches were small and made of wood. Vladimir's 'Tithe church' of the Mother of God, in his palace compound in Kiev, was the first of the monumental masonry churches,[50] and a more or less continuous tradition of such buildings began from the second quarter of the eleventh century. Mstislav Vladimirovich initiated a building programme in Chernigov but he died when its centrepiece, the church of the Transfiguration of the Saviour, was still only 'as high as a man standing on horseback could stretch with his hands'.[51] From the moment he assumed 'sole rule', Iaroslav Vladimirovich set about turning Kiev into a focus of visible splendour such as no other Rus' city could hope to rival. Taking Constantinople as the model, and importing Byzantine specialists to oversee the job, he commissioned the huge (by the standards of normal East Christian churches) cathedral of St Sophia, as well as churches of St George and St Irene

des diocèses russes au milieu du XII siècle', in *Mille ans de christianisme russe, 988–1988. Actes du colloque international de l'Université Paris-Nanterre 20–23 janvier 1988* (Paris: YMCA, 1989), pp. 27–49.
48 See also the archaeological evidence: A. P. Motsia, 'Nekotorye svedeniia o rasprostranenii khristianstva na Rusi po dannym pogrebal'nogo obriada', in *Obriady i verovaniia drevnego naseleniia Ukrainy. Sbornik nauchnykh trudov* (Kiev: Naukova Dumka, 1990), pp. 114–32; V. V. Sedov, 'Rasprostranenie khristianstva v Drevnei Rusi', *Kratkie soobshcheniia Instituta arkheologii*, 208 (1993): 3–11.
49 See Franklin and Shepard, *The Emergence of Rus*, pp. 311–12.
50 See F. Kämpfer, 'Eine Residenz für Anna Porphyrogenneta', *JGO* 41 (1993): 101–10; *Tserkva Bohoroytsi desiatynna v Kyevi* (Kiev: ArtEk, 1996).
51 *PVL*, vol. i, p. 101.

(patron saints of himself and his wife, but also echoing distinguished imperial foundations in Constantinople). Lesser cathedrals of St Sophia were also built in mid-century in Novgorod and Polotsk. The list of the most prestigious church buildings of the later eleventh century and early twelfth century would include: the church of the Dormition of the Mother of God at the Caves monastery and the church of St Michael at the Vydubichi monastery (both 1070s, both just outside the city), the 'golden-domed' church of St Michael (c.1108) and the church of the Saviour at the princely residence at Berestovo (1115–19). There was a flurry of building at Pereiaslavl' in the 1090s and 1100s, and the main churches of the Novgorodian monasteries of St George and St Anthony date from the 1110s, while the first two decades of the twelfth century also see the start of work on the earliest masonry churches in Suzdal', Smolensk and Peremyshl'.[52] The pattern of church-building, too, mirrors the fortunes of the dynasty.

Churches and large monasteries cost money to build and run. Donations could of course come from all kinds of people, but the main support for the central institutions of the Church was by means of a tithe from specified princely income. Several narrative and documentary sources confirm that payment of a tithe was established practice, though the details vary.[53] By contrast, major donations to monasteries were more likely to be directly in the form of land, including dues from those who lived on the land. Monks could also engage in productive labour, whether on the land or through small-scale crafts and trading. Thus while the metropolitans and bishops were to an appreciable extent dependent on continuing allocations from the surplus wealth of others, a successful monastery enjoyed the benefits of its own endowment and also the opportunity to generate income from its own activities. Nothing substantial is known about support for the lower clergy. One may speculate that they lived mainly off local donations.

Inside the churches and the monasteries were the objects and pictures and sounds and words and smells that created the distinctive atmosphere of East Christian ritual and worship and contemplation. The continuous history of East Slav high culture, of art and literature (terms which are not, however, entirely appropriate to the devotional context), begins in the mid-eleventh century. It would be hard to overemphasise the ambitions of the

---

52 For chronological tables of masonry churches see P. A. Rappoport, *Drevnerusskaia arkhitektura* (St Petersburg: Stroiizdat, 1993), pp. 255–72.

53 See Ia. N. Shchapov, *Gosudarstvo i tserkov' Drevnei Rusi X–XIII vv.* (Moscow: Nauka, 1989), pp. 85–7; B. N. Floria, *Otnosheniia gosudarstva i tserkvi u vostochnykh i zapadnykh slavian* (Moscow: Institut slavianovedeniia i balkanistiki RAN, 1992), pp. 5–20.

mid-eleventh-century patrons and practitioners, who set standards of sophisticated opulence that few could rival for half a millennium: the dazzling mosaics
covering huge surfaces of the upper walls in St Sophia in Kiev (see Plates 3 and
5);[54] the elegant argument and harmonious rhetoric of the *Sermon on Law and
Grace* by Ilarion;[55] the luxurious *Ostromir Gospel* (1056–7), the first surviving
dated Slavonic book, in format the grandest book of the entire pre-Muscovite
age (see Plate 4).[56] These three monuments also happen to exemplify three
distinct types of cultural transmission. The St Sophia mosaics are, in effect,
Byzantine works which happen to have been commissioned in Kiev. Even
their inscriptions are in Greek (see Plate 5). The *Ostromir Gospel* is a copy of a
traditional Greek text in Slavonic translation. Ilarion's sermon uses traditional
Byzantine theological argument to construct a framework of interpretation for
native Rus' history. These are the three principal modes of the Rus' reception
of Byzantine culture: the direct import of objects or personnel; local copying
in Slavonic; and adaptation for local purposes. Throughout the Middle Ages
the specific texture of Rus' Christian culture can be perceived in the nuances
and the interplay of these three modes.

In the mid-eleventh to early twelfth centuries we see the beginnings of such
processes, the establishment of models and precedents which were to become
the foundations of a Rus' tradition. For example, although the mid-eleventh-
century churches of St Sophia were not imitated, the church of the Dormition
at the Caves monastery became the model for many of the most prestigious
churches around the lands of the Rus'.[57] In the eleventh century the Church
formally recognised the first Rus' saints: two of them, – the princes Boris and
Gleb, murdered in 1015 – were, conveniently, members of the ruling dynasty,
which was thereby proved to be especially favoured (see Plate 6); and one
of them – Abbot Feodosii (d. 1074) – was the man who set the communal
rules for the Caves monastery, and his *Life* (as well as one of the accounts
of Boris and Gleb) was written by Nestor, a monk of the Caves.[58] Monks
of the Caves, and possibly Nestor again, were likewise responsible for the
main job of devising and shaping and compiling the *Primary Chronicle*, which
served as the first section of successive East Slav chronicles for centuries, its
narrative thereby becoming accepted as the standard 'foundation myth' of

54 See V. N. Lazarev, *Old Russian Murals and Mosaics* (London: Phaidon, 1966).
55 Simon Franklin, *Sermons and Rhetoric of Kievan Rus'* (Cambridge, Mass.: Harvard University Press, 1991), pp. xvi–xliv, 3–29.
56 *Ostromirovo Evangelie. Faksimil'noe vosproizvedenie* (Leningrad: Aurora, 1988).
57 See Podskalsky, *Christentum*, p. 281.
58 *Biblioteka literatury Drevnei Rusi. Tom I: XI–XII veka* (St Petersburg: Nauka, 1997), pp.
352–432; Hollingsworth, *Hagiography*, pp. lviii–lxviii, 33–95.

the Rus', the tale of their origins and formation.[59] Indeed, if we take into account also a somewhat later Caves compilation known as its *Paterik*, or *Paterikon*, with stories of notable deeds of its monks,[60] then Caves writings constitute a very substantial proportion of all native narrative materials for the period. As a collection of physical and verbal images, therefore, the Kiev-based 'Golden Age' of early Rus' ('Kievan Rus'', as it came to be known in post-medieval writings) was the creation first of the builders and artists and bookmen of Iaroslav Vladimirovich, and then of the monks of the monastery of the Caves. How widely their image of Rus' would have been recognised or accepted as accurate by contemporaries is, of course, open to question, but in retrospect they were extraordinarily successful in shaping the perceptions of their successors.

59 See D. S. Likhachev, *Russkie letopisi i ikh kul'turno-istoricheskoe znachenie* (Moscow and Leningrad: Nauka, 1947).
60 In L. A. Ol'shevskaia and S. N. Travnikov (eds.), *Drevnerusskie pateriki* (Moscow: Nauka, 1999), pp. 7–80; translation (of a slightly different version) in Muriel Heppell, *The 'Paterik' of the Kievan Caves Monastery* (Cambridge, Mass.: Harvard University Press, 1989).

5

The Rus' principalities (1125–1246)

MARTIN DIMNIK

Introduction

The years 1125 to 1246 witnessed the creation of new principalities and eparchies, the flourishing of some and the demise of others. During this period the system of lateral succession governed the political hierarchy of princes within individual dynasties in their promotions to the office of senior prince, and the political hierarchy of senior princes between different dynasties in their rivalries for Kiev, the capital of Rus'.[1]

From the earliest times, it appears, the princes of Rus' followed a system of succession governed by genealogical seniority. It dictated that, after the senior prince of the dynasty died, his eldest surviving brother replaced him. After all the brothers had ruled in rotation, succession went to the eldest surviving nephew. Vladimir Sviatoslavich (d. 1015) had no surviving brothers. Before his death, therefore, he designated his eldest son, Sviatopolk, to rule Kiev. The latter, fearing that his brothers would usurp power from him, waged war against them. In the end, Iaroslav 'the Wise' (Mudryi) was the victor.[2]

Iaroslav, evidently following the example of his father Vladimir, gave hereditary domains to his sons and observed the principle of lateral succession (for a fuller discussion of dynastic politics 1015–1125, see Chapter 4). Hoping to obviate future fratricidal wars, however, he changed the nature of succession to Kiev. He granted his three eldest surviving sons and their descendants, the inner circle so to speak, the right to rule Kiev. Accordingly, his two youngest sons, Igor' and Viacheslav, became debarred or *izgoi*. He

---

1 Chronicles and charters are the main sources of information for the political, ecclesiastical and cultural history of this period. Archaeological, architectural, artistic, sphragistic and numismatic data also give useful information, especially concerning commerce, trades and culture.

2 Martin Dimnik, 'Succession and Inheritance in Rus' before 1054', *Mediaeval Studies* 58 (1996): 87–117.

designated the eldest son, Iziaslav, to replace him in Kiev. After Iziaslav died, Sviatoslav, the next in precedence, would occupy the town. After Sviatoslav, Vsevolod would rule the capital, and after his death succession would pass to the next generation of the inner circle, and so on. Iaroslav also gave the three sons patrimonies adjacent to the Kievan domain: Iziaslav got Turov, Sviatoslav got Chernigov and Vsevolod got Pereiaslavl'.[3] When each occupied Kiev, he would also retain control of his patrimony. This arrangement, Iaroslav believed, would give the prince of Kiev military superiority over the other princes.[4]

Except for one deviation, Iaroslav's revised system worked smoothly during the first generation. Iziaslav succeeded his father but Sviatoslav deposed his brother thus securing for his sons the right to sit on the throne of their father. After Sviatoslav predeceased Iziaslav, the latter returned to Kiev. Following his death, Vsevolod occupied the throne. He was succeeded by his nephew, Iziaslav's eldest son Sviatopolk of Turov. He and Vsevolod's son Vladimir Monomakh of Pereiaslavl', however, violated Iaroslav's design. (See Table 5.1: The House of Iaroslav the Wise.)

After Sviatoslav died in 1076, his eldest surviving son Oleg replaced him as senior prince of the Sviatoslavichi and prince of Chernigov.[5] By 1096, however, Sviatopolk and Monomakh had deprived him of the Chernigov lands. At a congress held at Liubech in 1097, the princes of Rus' penalised the dynasty of Chernigov because Oleg refused to campaign with them against the *Polovtsy*. They apparently demoted him from being sole prince of Chernigov to ruling it jointly with his brother David, and appointed the latter his political superior. The princes evidently also placed David's family ahead of Oleg's in political seniority so that David's sons would rule Chernigov ahead of Oleg's. Even more importantly, Sviatopolk and Monomakh demoted the entire dynasty of Chernigov by placing Monomakh ahead of the Sviatoslavichi on the ladder of succession. Accordingly, after Sviatopolk died, Monomakh and not Oleg would occupy Kiev. In promoting himself, Monomakh violated Iaroslav's so-called 'Testament'. Moreover, by changing the order of political seniority in the inner circle, Monomakh, as it turned out, debarred the Sviatoslavichi.

3 Concerning Iaroslav's family, see N. de Baumgarten, *Généalogies et mariages occidentaux des Rurikides russes du Xe au XIIIe siècle (Orientalia Christiana)* (Rome: Pont. Institutum Orientalium Studiorum, 1927), vol. IX, no. 35, table I.
4 Concerning the controversy over Iaroslav's system of succession, see Martin Dimnik, 'The "Testament" of Iaroslav "The Wise": A Re-examination', *Canadian Slavonic Papers* 29 (1987): 369–86.
5 For Sviatoslav's descendants, see Baumgarten, *Généalogies et mariages*, table IV.

Table 5.1. *The House of Iaroslav the Wise*

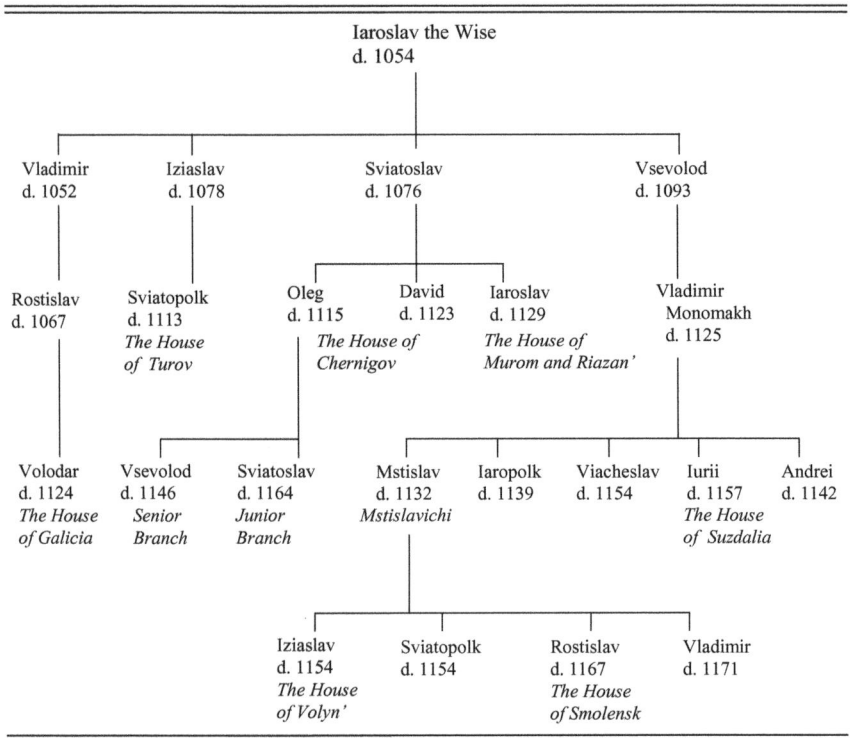

Iaroslav the Wise
d. 1054

| Vladimir d. 1052 | Iziaslav d. 1078 | | Sviatoslav d. 1076 | | | Vsevolod d. 1093 |

| Rostislav d. 1067 | Sviatopolk d. 1113 *The House of Turov* | Oleg d. 1115 *The House of Chernigov* | David d. 1123 | Iaroslav d. 1129 *The House of Murom and Riazan'* | Vladimir Monomakh d. 1125 |

| Volodar d. 1124 *The House of Galicia* | Vsevolod d. 1146 *Senior Branch* | Sviatoslav d. 1164 *Junior Branch* | Mstislav d. 1132 *Mstislavichi* | Iaropolk d. 1139 | Viacheslav d. 1154 | Iurii d. 1157 *The House of Suzdalia* | Andrei d. 1142 |

| Iziaslav d. 1154 *The House of Volyn'* | Sviatopolk d. 1154 | Rostislav d. 1167 *The House of Smolensk* | Vladimir d. 1171 |

Oleg and David would predecease him and their sons would become *izgoi*.

Monomakh's scheme did not stop at demoting the Sviatoslavichi. After Sviatopolk died he formed a pact with Oleg and David to debar Sviatopolk's heirs from ruling Kiev. Thus, two families of the inner circle, the Sviatoslavichi of Chernigov and the Iziaslavichi of Turov, became *izgoi*. Consequently, the three-family system of succession to Kiev created by Iaroslav the Wise failed. Monomakh's descendants remained the only rightful claimants. But he had still other designs for his dynasty. He made a deal with the Kievans to accept the family of his eldest son, Mstislav, as their resident princes.[6] He set the scheme in motion by summoning Mstislav

---

6 For Monomakh's descendants, see Baumgarten, *Généalogies et mariages*, table v.

from Novgorod, giving him Belgorod south-west of Kiev, and naming him co-ruler.[7]

Vladimir Monomakh's successors

Although Mstislav pre-empted the rights of the Iziaslavichi and the Sviatoslavichi by replacing his father in Kiev on 19 May 1125, no prince disputed his action. The Iziaslavichi presented no challenger because they had become politically impotent. The Sviatoslavichi, however, had an eligible candidate in Iaroslav who had succeeded his brothers Oleg and David to Chernigov. According to the Liubech agreement, it seems, he was the rightful claimant. But Iaroslav lacked the leadership qualities for confronting Mstislav. Consequently, he and his sons also became *izgoi*.

Oleg's eldest son, Vsevolod, frustrated with Iaroslav's ineptitude, evicted his uncle from Chernigov in 1127 and declared himself the political head of the dynasty. Mstislav of Kiev, his father-in-law, confirmed his seizure of power. Mstislav and Vsevolod compensated Iaroslav for his loss of Chernigov by giving him Murom and Riazan' as his patrimony. Significantly, in confirming Vsevolod's usurpation, Mstislav violated the lateral order of succession once again.[8] But in doing so, he helped Vsevolod to reclaim for the Ol'govichi their rightful seniority ahead of the Davidovichi. He abrogated the change in political seniority that the princes had dictated at Liubech.

In 1130, in keeping with Monomakh's policy of asserting his family's supremacy, Mstislav subjugated Polotsk by exiling its princes to Byzantium.[9] He was the last ruler of Kiev to impose his control over that dynasty. After his death, the princes of Polotsk would engage in internecine rivalries for some forty years. The chronicles give little information for the Polotsk land for the turn of the thirteenth century, but archaeological evidence suggests that it was a period of intense activity. The princes fought off the encroaching Knights of the Sword (Livonian Order) and the Lithuanians. It was also a period of

---

7 For a detailed examination of the Liubech agreement and for Monomakh's pact with the Kievans, see Martin Dimnik, *The Dynasty of Chernigov 1054–1146* (Toronto: Pontifical Institute of Mediaeval Studies, 1994), pp. 207–23, 271–2, 277, 305–8, 324–5.

8 *PSRL*, vol. II: *Ipat'evskaia letopis'*, 2nd edn (St Petersburg: Tipografiia M.A. Aleksandrova, 1908; photoreproduction, Moscow: Izdatel'stvo vostochnoi literatury, 1962), cols. 290–2; *PSRL*, vol. I: *Lavrent'evskaia letopis'*, 2nd edn (Leningrad: Postoiannaia Istoriko-Arkheograficheskaia Kommissiia AN SSSR, 1926; photoreproduction, Moscow: Izdatel'stvo vostochnoi literatury, 1962), cols. 296–7. For the correct dating in these chronicles, see N. G. Berezhkov, *Khronologiia russkogo letopisaniia* (Moscow: AN SSSR, 1963).

9 *PSRL*, vol. XXV: *Moskovskii letopisnyi svod kontsa XV veka* (Moscow and Leningrad: AN SSSR, 1949), p. 31.

prosperity. In 1229 the prince of Smolensk negotiated a trade agreement with Riga which also benefited Polotsk. Soon after, however, the town came under the sway of the Lithuanians.[10]

Mstislav's reign was extremely successful and none of his descendants would wield as much power. Indeed, some historians call him Mstislav 'the Great'.[11] Before his death he controlled Kiev, Pereiaslavl', Smolensk, Rostov, Suzdal', Novgorod, Polotsk, Turov and Vladimir-in-Volynia. Whereas his father had driven the troublesome *Polovtsy* to the River Don, in 1129 Mstislav drove them beyond the Volga.[12] He died on 15 April 1132.[13]

In keeping with the wishes of his father Monomakh and with the agreement that he and his brother Mstislav had made, Iaropolk, the next in seniority, succeeded Mstislav. But conflicts arose immediately between his brothers, Monomakh's sons (the Monomashichi) and his nephews, Mstislav's sons (the Mstislavichi). Monomakh had intended the Mstislavichi to occupy the patrimonial town of Pereiaslavl' which they could use as a stepping-stone to Kiev after Iaropolk, who had no sons, died. Accordingly, Monomakh had debarred his younger sons: Viacheslav, Iurii, and Andrei. They, however, argued that they had a prior claim to their nephews according to the system of genealogical seniority advocated by Iaroslav the Wise. They won Iaropolk's support and forced the Mstislavichi to seek help from their brother-in-law Vsevolod in Chernigov. The two sides waged war for the remainder of the decade. At the time of Iaropolk's death on 18 February 1139, it appeared that the Monomashichi had won the day. Viacheslav of Turov succeeded him.[14]

Monomakh's younger sons therewith upset his plan to make Kiev the patrimony of the Mstislavichi. Even more importantly, Vsevolod Ol'govich put paid to Monomakh's plan to make his descendants the sole rulers of Kiev. In 1139 he deposed Viacheslav.[15] He refused to submit to Monomakh's injustice in pre-empting the claim of his father Oleg at Liubech. Vsevolod, it is true, could not profess to have the right to sit on the throne of his father because Oleg had never ruled Kiev. Nevertheless, he was the genealogical and political senior prince of his dynasty and usurpation was an acknowledged form of seizing power. With force, therefore, he secured the right for his heirs to rule Kiev.

10 On Polotsk, see L. V. Alekseev, *Polotskaia zemlia (Ocherki istorii severnoi Belorusii) v IX–XIII vv.* (Moscow: Nauka, 1966).
11 John Fennell, *The Crisis of Medieval Russia 1200–1304* (London and New York: Longman, 1983), pp. 10, 119.
12 *PSRL*, vol. xxv, p. 31.
13 *PSRL*, vol. ii, col. 294.
14 Dimnik, *The Dynasty of Chernigov 1054–1146*, pp. 324–48.
15 *PSRL*, vol. ii, cols. 302–3.

Table 5.2. *The House of Galicia*

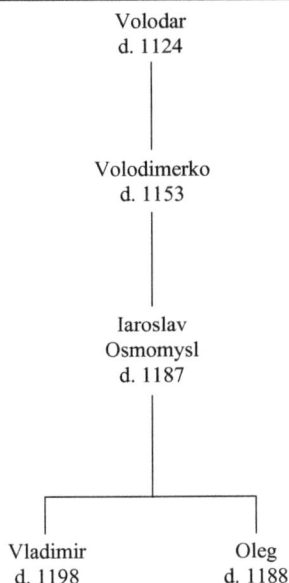

```
                        Volodar
                        d. 1124
                           |
                           |
                       Volodimerko
                        d. 1153
                           |
                           |
                        Iaroslav
                        Osmomysl
                        d. 1187
                  _____|_____
                 |                   |
             Vladimir              Oleg
             d. 1198             d. 1188
```

His authority, like that of Monomakh and Mstislav, was supreme. He appropriated Turov and Vladimir-in-Volynia. He sent his brother Sviatoslav to Novgorod where the latter issued a statute (*ustav*) regulating the relationship between the prince and the Church.[16] After the Novgorodians expelled Sviatoslav, Vsevolod replaced him with Mstislav's son Sviatopolk, one of his brothers-in-law. To another, Iziaslav, he gave Pereiaslavl'. Except for Volodimerko of Galich, who attempted to seize Vladimir-in-Volynia, Vsevolod encountered no serious opposition. (For Volodimerko, see Table 5.2: The House of Galicia.) On one occasion he reconciled his disgruntled brothers and cousins by asking his cousin Sviatosha Davidovich, who had become a monk in the Caves monastery and would later be canonised, to mediate on his behalf. He patronised the Church by building the monastery of St Cyril in Kiev and the church of St George in Kanev.

Before he died on 1 August 1146,[17] Vsevolod also took a page out of Monomakh's book by attempting to make Kiev the patrimony of the Ol'govichi.

---

16 Daniel H. Kaiser, *The Growth of the Law in Medieval Russia* (Princeton: Princeton University Press, 1980), pp. 58–9.
17 *PSRL*, vol. ii, cols. 320–1.

He designated his brother Igor' his successor.[18] Igor', however, failed to assert his rule. The Kievans' preferred candidate, in keeping with their promise to Monomakh, was Mstislav's eldest son Iziaslav of Pereiaslavl'.[19] In supporting the latter, however, the citizens threw the House of Monomakh into turmoil. Iziaslav and his brothers were once again pitted against their uncles.

Iurii Dolgorukii

Iurii their leader was ambitious. To obtain greater independence from the boyars of Rostov, he moved his capital to the smaller Suzdal' after which the region was called Suzdalia. To consolidate his rule he began an energetic town-building programme. There is uncertainty, however, over which towns he founded (e.g. Pereiaslavl'-Zalesskii, Dmitrov and Iur'ev Pol'skii) and over which ones he merely fortified (e.g. Moscow, Galich, Zvenigorod and Kostroma). He initiated the tradition of constructing churches from white Kama limestone and reputedly founded five, including the church of the Transfiguration in Pereiaslavl'-Zalesskii, which he 'filled with books'.[20] In addition to expanding the boundaries of Suzdalia he began asserting his overlordship over the princes of Murom and Riazan'. He campaigned against the Volga-Kama Bulgars to gain control over the trade passing through their lands to the Caspian Sea. To promote his interests in Baltic trade he intervened in Novgorod. In short, Iurii initiated Suzdalia's political ascendancy. He probably received the sobriquet 'Long Arm' (Dolgorukii) after he began laying claim to distant Kiev.[21]

Meanwhile, following the death of one senior prince (Vsevolod) and the eviction of another (Igor') from Kiev, the fortunes of the Ol'govichi plummeted. Their brother, Sviatoslav of Novgorod Severskii, demanded that Iziaslav Mstislavich release Igor', whom he was holding captive. The Davidovichi, who ruled Chernigov, took advantage of their cousins' plight by promising Iziaslav to back his rule in Kiev if, in turn, he helped them to expel Sviatoslav from his domain. In retaliation Sviatoslav, unlike his brother Vsevolod who

---

18 On Vsevolod's reign, see Dimnik, *The Dynasty of Chernigov 1054–1146*, pp. 349–413.
19 *PSRL*, vol. II, col. 327. For a detailed examination of the political rivalries from the death of Vsevolod Ol'govich to the Tatar invasion, see Martin Dimnik, *The Dynasty of Chernigov 1146–1246* (Cambridge: Cambridge University Press, 2003).
20 For church building and culture, see S. Franklin and J. Shepard, *The Emergence of Rus 750–1200* (London and New York: Longman, 1996), pp. 352–63.
21 On Iurii, see A. M. Ianovskii, *Iurii Dolgorukii* (Moscow: Moskovskii rabochii, 1955); V. A. Kuchkin, *Formirovanie gosudarstvennoi territorii severo-vostochnoi Rusi v X–XIV vv.* (Moscow: Nauka, 1984), pp. 3–92; and Iu. A. Limonov, *Vladimiro-Suzdal'skaia Rus': Ocherki sotsial'no-politicheskoi istorii*, ed. B. A. Rybakov (Leningrad: Nauka, 1987), pp. 27–37.

had supported the Mstislavichi, promised to help Iurii win Kiev if the latter helped him to reclaim the lost Ol'govichi lands. Consequently, the two camps went to war.

Iurii challenged his nephew Iziaslav in keeping with the principle of genealogical seniority that governed the practice of succession to Kiev designed by Iaroslav the Wise. He demanded that Monomakh's surviving sons Viacheslav and Iurii occupy Kiev in rotation and that Iziaslav vacate the town. The latter, however, claimed Kiev on the grounds that Monomakh had designated the Mstislavichi his successors. Iziaslav won the day once again, in the main, because he had the support of the Kievans whose backing was vital to any would-be ruler of their town.

In 1147 Iziaslav antagonised many, including his brother Rostislav, by ordering a synod of bishops to install a native of Rus', Klim (Kliment) Smoliatich, metropolitan of Kiev. Some believe that he made the controversial appointment because he was attempting to liberate the Church in Rus' from the domination of the patriarch in Constantinople. Others, however, suggest that he adopted this course of action because there was no patriarch in Constantinople to make the appointment.[22] Meanwhile, the Davidovichi joined their cousin Sviatoslav in a plot to kill Iziaslav and to free the captive Igor'. The Kievans retaliated by murdering Igor'.[23]

Iziaslav struggled to retain control of Kiev by repelling attacks from Iurii and his allies, who included the Ol'govichi, Iurii's son-in-law Iaroslav Volodimerovich 'Eight Wits' (Osmomysl) of Galich, and the ever obliging *Polovtsy*. Iurii's coalition expelled Iziaslav on two occasions. Finally, in 1151 he adopted an unprecedented expedient that mollified Iurii. He invited his uncle Viacheslav, Iurii's elder brother, to be co-ruler.[24] After Iziaslav died on 14 November 1154, his brother Rostislav of Smolensk replaced him as co-ruler with Viacheslav. But the latter died soon after, leaving Rostislav as the sole prince of Kiev.[25]

On 20 March 1155 Iurii deposed him.[26] He consolidated his rule by giving his sons the towns of the Mstislavichi. He sent Andrei to Vyshgorod, Gleb to

---

22 On the controversy over Klim's appointment, see Dimitri Obolensky, 'Byzantium, Kiev and Moscow: A Study in Ecclesiastical Relations', in his *Byzantium and the Slavs* (Crestwood, N.Y.: St Vladimir's Seminary Press, 1994), pp. 142–9; Simon Franklin (trans. and intro.), *Sermons and Rhetoric of Kievan Rus'* (Cambridge, Mass.: Harvard University Press, 1991), pp. xlv–lviii.

23 *PSRL*, vol. II, cols. 347–54.

24 *PSRL*, vol. II, cols. 417–18.

25 *PSRL*, vol. II, cols. 468–9; *Novgorodskaia pervaia letopis' starshego i mladshego izvodov*, ed. A. N. Nasonov (Moscow and Leningrad: AN SSSR, 1950), pp. 215–16.

26 *Novgorodskaia pervaia letopis'*, pp. 29, 216.

Table 5.3. *The House of Suzdalia*

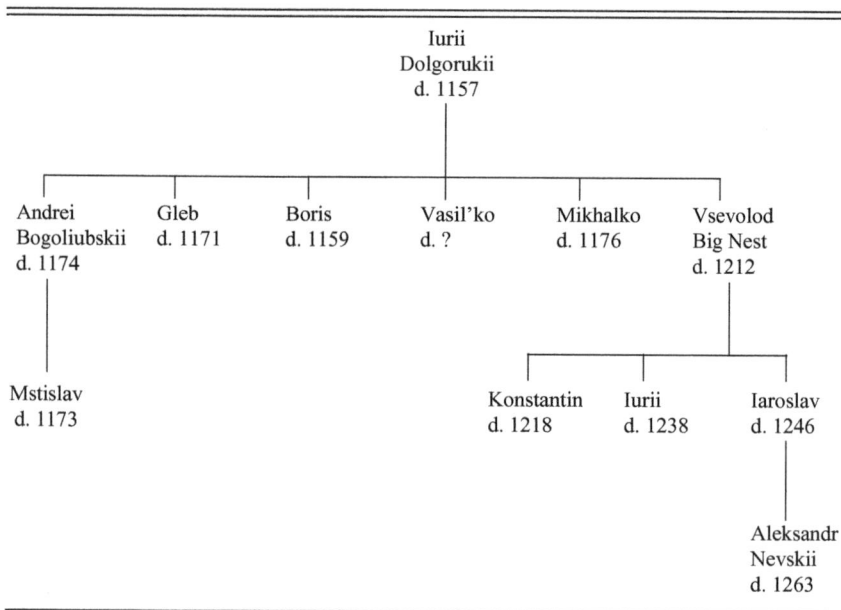

```
                                    Iurii
                                  Dolgorukii
                                   d. 1157


    Andrei          Gleb      Boris      Vasil'ko    Mikhalko    Vsevolod
  Bogoliubskii     d. 1171   d. 1159      d. ?       d. 1176     Big Nest
   d. 1174                                                       d. 1212


   Mstislav                              Konstantin    Iurii     Iaroslav
   d. 1173                                d. 1218     d. 1238    d. 1246


                                                                Aleksandr
                                                                 Nevskii
                                                                 d. 1263
```

Pereiaslavl', Boris to Turov, and Vasil'ko to the River Ros' region. (See Table 5.3: The House of Suzdalia.) He also returned to Sviatoslav the Ol'govichi domains that Iziaslav had appropriated. Moreover, he permitted Sviatoslav to translate Igor''s body to Chernigov where the latter was canonised.[27] Iurii's reign, however, was short-lived because the Kievans despised him. On 15 May 1157 he died after evidently being poisoned at a feast.[28]

After the prince of Kiev died, his allies lost the towns he had allocated to them from the Kievan lands or from debarred families. The towns were seized either by his replacement in Kiev or by the rightful owners. This happened with Turov. Vladimir Monomakh had seized the domain from the sons of Sviatopolk Iziaslavich (d. 1113) and made it the possession of the prince of Kiev. Following the death of Iurii Dolgorukii, however, Sviatopolk's descendant Iurii Iaroslavich recaptured it.[29] After that Turov's politically insignificant princes came increasingly under the influence of Volyn', Galicia and the Lithuanians.

27 *PSRL*, vol. II, col. 408.
28 *PSRL*, vol. II, col. 489.
29 *PSRL*, vol. XXV, p. 63. For Sviatopolk's family, see Baumgarten, *Généalogies et mariages*, table II, 3.

Nevertheless, the town seemingly flourished as a cultural centre. This is testified to by the writings of Kirill (Cyril), Bishop of Turov.[30]

Following Iurii's death the princes of Chernigov briefly reasserted their supremacy. Iziaslav Davidovich seized Kiev.[31] Even though his father David had never ruled the town, he justified his usurpation on the grounds that he was the senior prince of his family and prince of Chernigov. But his rule was short. In 1159 an alliance of princes led by Mstislav Iziaslavich of Volyn' deposed him. Two years later, on 6 April, he was killed while trying to recapture Kiev.[32] After that the Davidovichi died out and the Ol'govichi became the sole dynasty of Chernigov. In 1164, after Sviatoslav Ol'govich died, the Ol'govichi bifurcated into the senior branch descended from Vsevolod Ol'govich, and the junior or cadet branch descended from Sviatoslav Ol'govich.

The Mstislavichi

The system of succession to Kiev that Iaroslav the Wise had envisioned may have been doomed from the start, as some have claimed, but over time it evolved into one forged by political and genealogical vicissitudes. By the middle of the twelfth century, therefore, it once again constituted three families: the senior branch of Ol'govichi in Chernigov, the descendants of Monomakh's eldest son Mstislav in Volyn' and Smolensk, and the family of Monomakh's son Iurii in Suzdalia.[33]

In 1159, after Iziaslav Davidovich fled from Kiev, Mstislav Iziaslavich of Volyn' and his allies invited his uncle Rostislav Mstislavich of Smolensk to rule Kiev.[34] By that time he had secured the political independence of Smolensk from Pereiaslavl'. The town, which lay on the Greek route from Novgorod to Constantinople, enjoyed profitable trade relations. Moreover, despite opposition from Klim Smoliatich to whose appointment as metropolitan Rostislav objected, he established an autonomous eparchy in Smolensk. He issued a charter (*gramota*) stipulating its privileges and those of its bishop. The document is also a valuable source of commercial, geographic and social information.

---

30 On Turov, see P. F. Lysenko, 'Kiev i Turovskaia zemlia', in L. D. Pobol' *et al.* (eds.), *Kiev i zapadnye zemli Rusi v IX–XIII vv.* (Minsk: Nauka i Tekhnika, 1982), pp. 81–108. On Cyril of Turov, see Franklin (trans. and intro.), *Sermons and Rhetoric*, pp. lxxv–xciv.
31 *PSRL*, vol. ii, col. 490.
32 *PSRL*, vol. ii, cols. 517–18.
33 For Iurii's descendants, see Baumgarten, *Généalogies et mariages*, table vi.
34 *PSRL*, vol. ii, col. 504.

Moreover, the 'Life' (*Zhitie*) of Avramii of Smolensk provides valuable data on the social conditions of the time.[35]

Two genealogical considerations were pivotal for Rostislav's successful occupation of Kiev: after the death of his brother Iziaslav he became the eldest surviving Mstislavich; and after the death of his uncle Iurii he became the eldest prince in the entire House of Monomakh. He was therefore the legitimate claimant from both camps. Since all the princes in the House of Monomakh accepted his candidacy, his reign witnessed fewer internecine wars. The *Polovtsy*, however, intensified their attacks. They raided caravans travelling by river and by land from the Black Sea and the Sea of Azov regions. Rostislav organised campaigns against the nomads but failed to curb their forays.

He died on 14 March 1167.[36] After that, the Mstislavichi split into two dynasties: the one in Volyn' descended from Iziaslav who had made that region his family possession, and the one in Smolensk descended from Rostislav.[37] (See Table 5.4: The House of Volyn', and Table 5.5: The House of Smolensk.) Following the latter's death, his nephew Mstislav Iziaslavich of Vladimir-in-Volynia pre-empted the right of his uncle Vladimir Mstislavich of Dorogobuzh to rule Kiev.[38]

At first, Mstislav had the support of the other Mstislavichi because they expected to manipulate him. They discovered that he was no man's lackey, however, after he refused to grant them the towns they demanded. He also antagonised Andrei Bogoliubskii, who had replaced his father Iurii Dolgorukii in Suzdalia. Andrei saw Mstislav's accession as a violation of the traditional order of succession to Kiev. Moreover, Mstislav appointed his son Roman to Novgorod, where Andrei was seeking to assert his influence. Despite Mstislav's unpopularity, he successfully assembled the princes of Rus' against the *Polovtsy*. While in the field, however, he antagonised them further. Without informing them, he allowed his men to plunder the camps of the nomads. After that, we are told, the princes plotted against him.[39]

---

35 On Smolensk, see L. V. Alekseev, *Smolenskaia zemlia v IX–XIII vv. Ocherki istorii Smolenshchiny i Vostochnoi Belorussii* (Moscow: Nauka, 1980). For Rostislav's charter, see Ia. N. Shchapov, *Kniazheskie ustavy i tserkov' v drevnei Rusi XI–XIV vv.* (Moscow: Nauka, 1972), pp. 136–50. For Avramii, see P. Hollingsworth (trans. and intro.), *The Hagiography of Kievan Rus'* (Cambridge, Mass.: Harvard University Press, 1992), pp. lxix–lxxx.
36 *PSRL*, vol. ii, cols. 528–32.
37 For Rostislav's descendants, see Baumgarten, *Généalogies et mariages*, table ix.
38 *PSRL*, vol. ii, col. 535. For Vladimir and Mstislav, see Baumgarten, *Généalogies et mariages*, table v, 30 and 36.
39 *PSRL*, vol. ii, cols. 538–43.

Table 5.4. *The House of Volyn'*

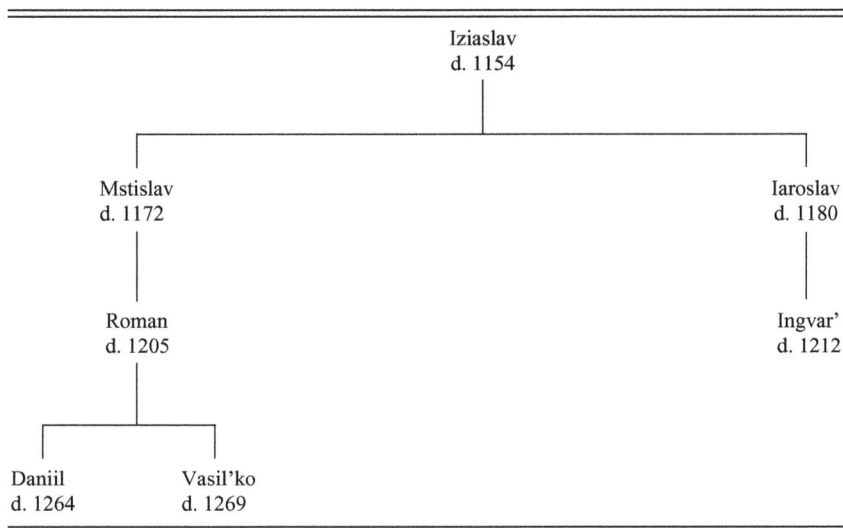

```
                                    Iziaslav
                                    d. 1154
                                       │
        ┌──────────────────────────────────────────────────────┐
     Mstislav                                                 Iaroslav
     d. 1172                                                  d. 1180
        │                                                        │
      Roman                                                   Ingvar'
     d. 1205                                                  d. 1212
        │
    ┌───────┐
  Daniil    Vasil'ko
  d. 1264   d. 1269
```

Table 5.5. *The House of Smolensk*

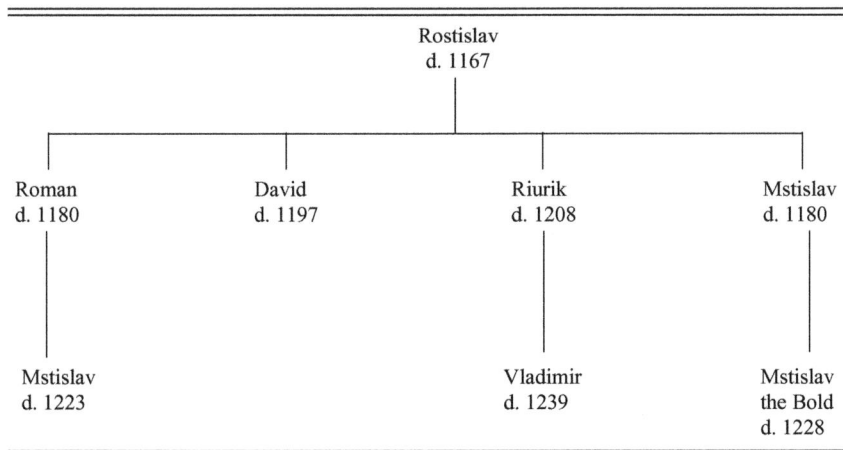

```
                              Rostislav
                              d. 1167
                                 │
   ┌──────────────┬──────────────┬──────────────┐
  Roman          David          Riurik        Mstislav
  d. 1180        d. 1197        d. 1208        d. 1180
   │                              │              │
  Mstislav                      Vladimir       Mstislav
  d. 1223                       d. 1239        the Bold
                                               d. 1228
```

Andrei Bogoliubskii

In 1169 Andrei Bogoliubskii organised a coalition to evict Mstislav from Kiev. Princes from Suzdalia, Smolensk, Volyn' and Chernigov joined the campaign led by Andrei's son Mstislav.[40] Many took part not only because they acknowledged Andrei's prior claim to Kiev, but also because they resented Mstislav for cheating them out of booty. Historians are not agreed on Andrei's objective in attacking Kiev or on the significance of its capture on 8 March. Some claim that his aim was to recover the Kievan throne for the rightful Monomashichi claimants because Kiev was the capital of the land. Others, however, argue that Andrei attempted to subordinate it to Vladimir and that its capture signalled its decline.[41]

Perhaps there is an element of truth in each view. In forcing the usurper Mstislav to flee to Volyn', Andrei, the rightful claimant for the House of Suzdalia, was able to seize control of Kiev. Surprisingly, after his forces captured the town, they sacked it.[42] Their action obviously did not penalise Mstislav in any way. Rather, the attackers vented their spleen against the Kievans. They seemingly ransacked the capital out of envy for its prosperity and out of fury at the arrogance of its citizens. Andrei, of course, had his own reason for condoning the pillaging. He wished to see Kiev wane in magnificence because he was striving to build up his capital of Vladimir as its rival. But his scheme failed. The plundering did not lead to Kiev's decline. It recovered and flourished to suffer even more debilitating sacks in 1203 and in 1240. The evidence that the dynasties which were eligible to rule it continued to covet it as the most cherished plum in Rus' testifies to its continued prosperity.

Meanwhile, Novgorod also remained a bone of contention. Since Suzdalia served as the conduit through which Baltic trade passed from Novgorod to the Caspian Sea, Andrei sought to wrest control of the town from the prince of Kiev and assert his jurisdiction over it. Two years after expelling Mstislav from Kiev, he finally forced the Novgorodians to capitulate by laying an embargo on all grain shipments to their town.[43]

Although historians disagree on Andrei's objectives and achievements, it is safe to assert that he defended the order of succession to Kiev championed

---

40 *PSRL*, vol. II, cols. 543–4.
41 Historians do not agree whether or not Kiev lost its pre-eminence in Rus' after Andrei's alliance sacked it. For the discussions, see P. P. Tolochko, *Drevniaia Rus', Ocherki sotsial'no-politicheskoi istorii* (Kiev: Naukova Dumka, 1987), pp. 138–42; Franklin and Shepard, *The Emergence of Rus*, pp. 323–4; Fennell, *Crisis*, p. 6.
42 *PSRL*, vol. II, cols. 544–5.
43 *Novgorodskaia pervaia letopis'*, pp. 221–2.

by his father. Unlike Iurii, however, he chose to live in Suzdalia. The fate of his father was one deterrent. Moreover, if he occupied Kiev he would remove himself dangerously far from his centre of power in Suzdalia. As Iaroslav the Wise had foreseen, a prince whose patrimony abutted on Kiev had the best chance of ruling it successfully because he could summon auxiliary forces quickly from his patrimony. Nevertheless, realising that ruling Kiev gave its prince a great moral advantage, Andrei could not allow it to fall into a rival's hands. Adhering to the system of genealogical seniority, he gave it to his younger brothers, who also had the right to sit on the throne of their father. First, he sent Gleb from Pereiaslavl', but the Kievans poisoned him, or so Andrei believed. Gleb's alleged murder would have confirmed Andrei's suspicion that the Kievans despised the sons just as vehemently as they had hated Iurii. Next, he appointed Mikhalko. But the latter declined the dubious honour by handing over the town to his brother Vsevolod.[44]

After Mstislav Iziaslavich died in Volyn' in 1170, the Rostislavichi of Smolensk took up the battle for Kiev. They evicted Vsevolod and gave the town to Riurik Rostislavich.[45] Three years later, Andrei formed a coalition with Sviatoslav Vsevolodovich of Chernigov. He was determined to avenge Gleb's death and to punish the Rostislavichi for their insubordination by expelling Riurik. Sviatoslav, for his part, intended to occupy Kiev. Thus, Andrei conceded that Sviatoslav's claim to the capital was as legitimate as his was. He also tacitly admitted his failure to maintain puppets in Kiev. Sviatoslav, the commander-in-chief of the coalition, evicted Riurik and occupied the town. Later, however, Iaroslav Iziaslavich of Lutsk, the younger brother of the deceased Mstislav, brought reinforcements from Volyn', helped Riurik to expel Sviatoslav, and occupied Kiev.[46]

In his patrimony, one of Andrei's main objectives was to raise the political, economic, cultural and ecclesiastical status of Vladimir above that of Kiev. Accordingly, he completed his father's building projects and initiated new ones. He built the Assumption cathedral in Vladimir, its Golden Gates in imitation of those in Kiev, his court at the nearby village of Bogoliubovo (from which he received the sobriquet Bogoliubskii), and the church of the Intercession of Our Lady on the River Nerl. Since he hired artisans from all lands, his churches reflected Romanesque, Byzantine and Trans-Caucasian styles. In striving to create an aura of holiness in Vladimir, he enshrined the relics of Bishop Leontii of Rostov and brought the so-called Vladimir icon of the Mother of God from

44 *PSRL*, vol. ii, cols. 569–70.
45 *PSRL*, vol. ii, cols. 570–1.
46 *PSRL*, vol. ii, cols. 572–8.

Vyshgorod. Hoping to equate the Christian heritage of his capital with that of Kiev, he propagated the pious myth that St Vladimir founded Vladimir. He also attempted, in vain, to create a new metropolitan see.

Andrei adopted autocratic practices in relation to his neighbours. He expanded his domains into the lands of the Volga Bulgars and imposed his will over the princes of Murom and Riazan'. At home he sought to undermine the authority of his subjects in their local assembly (*veche*); he expelled three of his brothers, two nephews and his father's senior boyars; and he spurned the magnates of Rostov and Suzdal' by making the smaller town of Vladimir his capital. After that the region was also referred to as Vladimir-Suzdal'. His overbearing policies evoked great resentment. Finally, on 29 June 1174, while he was waiting for Sviatoslav Vsevolodovich in Chernigov to approve his appointment of Roman Rostislavich of Smolensk to Kiev, his boyars assassinated him.[47]

Sviatoslav Vsevolodovich

After that, Sviatoslav acted as kingmaker in Vladimir-Suzdal'. Earlier, after Andrei had evicted his brothers and nephews from Suzdalia, Sviatoslav had given them sanctuary in Chernigov. Following Andrei's death he helped the refugees to fight for their inheritance. After a bitter rivalry between the uncles and the nephews, Vsevolod, later to be known as 'Big Nest' (Bol'shoe Gnezdo) because of his many offspring, seized Vladimir on the Kliaz'ma.[48] He was indebted for his success, in part, to Sviatoslav's backing. He would rule Vladimir for almost forty years and become the most powerful prince in the land.

After Andrei's death, Roman, the senior prince of the Rostislavichi, replaced Iaroslav Iziaslavich in Kiev.[49] In 1176, however, Sviatoslav found a pretext for attacking Roman with the *Polovtsy*. Not wishing to expose the Christians of Rus' to carnage, Roman ceded control of the town to Sviatoslav.[50] Soon after, the Novgorodians invited the latter to send his son to them.

In the meantime, to strengthen the power of his son-in-law Roman Glebovich of Riazan' against Vsevolod Big Nest, Sviatoslav sent troops

---

47 *PSRL*, vol. II, cols. 580–95. Concerning Andrei's career, see E. S. Hurwitz, *Prince Andrej Bogoljubskij: The Man and the Myth*, Studia historica et philologica 12, sectio slavica 4 (Florence: Licosa Editrice, 1980); and Limonov, *Vladimiro-Suzdal'skaia Rus'*, pp. 38–98.

48 *PSRL*, vol. I, cols. 379–82.

49 *Novgorodskaia pervaia letopis'*, p. 223.

50 *PSRL*, vol. II, cols. 603–5.

Table 5.6. *The House of Chernigov*

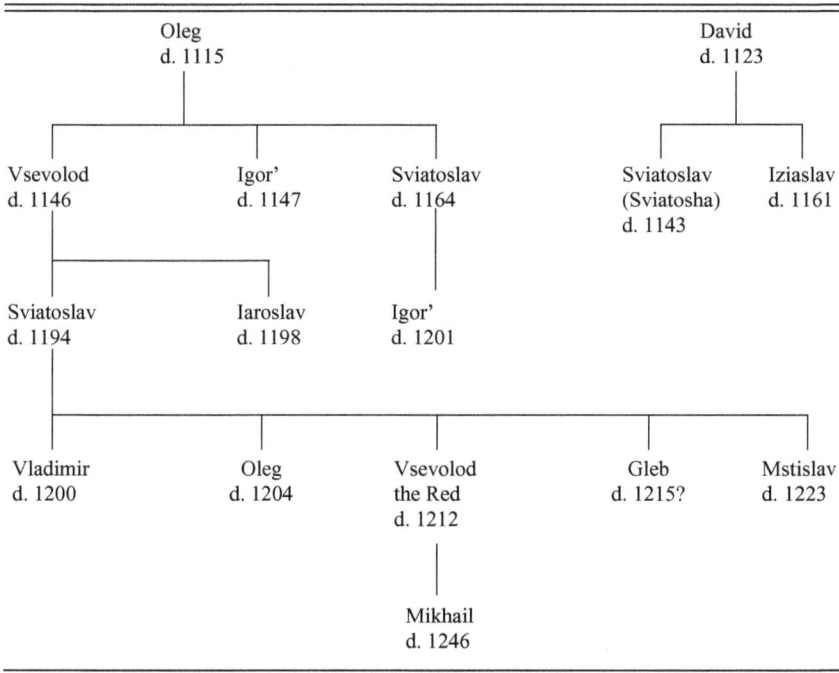

Oleg d. 1115			David d. 1123	
Vsevolod d. 1146	Igor' d. 1147	Sviatoslav d. 1164	Sviatoslav (Sviatosha) d. 1143	Iziaslav d. 1161
Sviatoslav d. 1194	Iaroslav d. 1198	Igor' d. 1201		
Vladimir d. 1200	Oleg d. 1204	Vsevolod the Red d. 1212	Gleb d. 1215?	Mstislav d. 1223
		Mikhail d. 1246		

commanded by his son Gleb to Riazan'.[51] Vsevolod, however, captured the princeling. In his anger, Sviatoslav sought to avenge himself against the House of Monomakh by taking David Rostislavich of Vyshgorod captive while the latter was hunting. After failing to do so, he abandoned Kiev and David's brother Riurik occupied it. Sviatoslav's campaign to free Gleb from Vsevolod was also a fiasco. He therefore joined his son Vladimir in Novgorod and became the town's prince.[52] (See Table 5.6: The House of Chernigov.)

In 1181 he marched south against Riurik and was joined by his brother Iaroslav of Chernigov and his cousin Igor' Sviatoslavich with numerous *Polovtsy*. Riurik prudently vacated Kiev and allowed Sviatoslav to occupy it uncontested. In the meantime, while Igor', Khan Konchak, and their troops

---

51 For Roman Glebovich, see N. de Baumgarten, *Généalogies des branches régnantes des Rurikides du XIIIe au XVIe siècle (Orientalia Christiana)* (Rome: Pont. Institutum Oriental-ium Studiorum, 1934), vol. 35, no. 94, table xiv, 11.

52 *PSRL*, vol. ii, cols. 618–20.

were making merry across the Dnieper from Kiev, Riurik's men routed the revellers. His rival's victory forced Sviatoslav to accept Riurik as his co-ruler.[53]

Duumvirs had administered Kiev in the past. As we have seen, Iziaslav Mstislavich and his uncle Viacheslav Vladimirovich had shared authority over Kiev and all its lands. The partnership between Sviatoslav and Riurik was different. The former was the senior partner and the commander-in-chief, but he ruled only Kiev. Riurik controlled the surrounding Kievan domains and lived in the nearby outpost of Belgorod. His patrimony, however, was Vruchii north-west of Kiev. His control of the towns surrounding Kiev significantly curtailed Sviatoslav's power.

On 1 October 1187, Iaroslav Osmomysl of Galich died.[54] During his reign he had maintained political relations with the Hungarians (his mother was a Hungarian princess), Poles, Bulgarians and Greeks. According to the chronicles, he fortified towns and promoted agriculture and crafts. Commerce prospered, especially in the lower Prut and Danube regions. Galicia also supplied the Kievan lands with much of their salt. Despite his great power, however, Iaroslav never claimed Kiev because he did not belong to a family of the inner circle. Unfortunately for Galicia, on his deathbed he committed a serious political blunder, perhaps at the insistence of boyars who had become more powerful towards the end of his reign. He designated his younger son Oleg, the offspring of his concubine, rather than the elder Vladimir, the offspring of his wife Ol'ga the daughter of Iurii Dolgorukii, his successor.[55] Vladimir challenged Oleg and initiated a general rivalry for Galich.[56] In 1188, taking advantage of the strife, Sviatoslav Vsevolodovich sought to consolidate his control over all the Kievan lands. As he and Riurik rode against Béla III of Hungary who had seized Galich, Sviatoslav proposed to take the town and give it to Riurik in exchange for his Kievan domains and his patrimony of Vruchii. Riurik refused the offer.[57]

The following year Vladimir escaped from Hungary, where the king was holding him captive. After the Galicians reinstated him, he requested Vsevolod Big Nest in Vladimir-Suzdal' to support his rule. In return, he promised to be subservient to his uncle. Vsevolod agreed and demanded that all the princes, notably Roman Mstislavich of Vladimir-in-Volynia, Riurik and

---

53 *PSRL*, vol. ii, cols. 621–4.
54 *PSRL*, vol. ii, cols. 656–7.
55 For Iaroslav's family, see Baumgarten, *Généalogies et mariages*, table iii, 13.
56 For the history of Galicia, see V. T. Pashuto, *Ocherki po istorii Galitsko-Volynskoi Rusi* (Moscow: AN SSSR, 1950).
57 *PSRL*, vol. ii, cols. 662–3.

Sviatoslav pledge not to challenge his nephew's rule. They acquiesced in deference to his military might.[58] Moreover, when making their promises, it appears that all the princes in the House of Monomakh pledged to acknowledge Vsevolod as the senior prince of their dynasty. Sviatoslav, although an Ol'govich, also agreed to obey Vsevolod's directive not to attack Vladimir. In doing so, however, he lost face as the prince of Kiev.[59]

One of Sviatoslav's most important duties as commander-in-chief was to defend Rus' against the *Polovtsy*. In the past, princes like Iurii had used the nomads as their auxiliaries, and they would do so again around the turn of the thirteenth century. For some two decades after the reign of Rostislav Mstislavich, however, relations between the princes and the tribesmen were extremely hostile. The horsemen from the east bank of the Dnieper and those north of the Black Sea raided Pereiaslavl' and the River Ros' region south of Kiev. The tribes living in the Donets basin pillaged, in the main, the Ol'govichi domains in the Zadesen'e and Posem'e regions.[60]

Sviatoslav, Riurik and their allies led many campaigns against the marauders. In 1184 they scored one of their greatest victories at the River Erel' south of the Pereiaslavl' lands, where they took many khans captive.[61] The following year, however, Sviatoslav's cousin Igor' Sviatoslavich of Novgorod Severskii suffered a catastrophic defeat in the Donets river basin (for chronicle illustrations of the battle, see Plate 7).[62] It became the subject of the most famous epic poem of Rus', 'The Lay of Igor''s Campaign' (*Slovo o polku Igoreve*).[63] Despite his valiant efforts, however, Sviatoslav failed to defeat the enemy or to negotiate a lasting peace.

At the peak of his power, Sviatoslav was the dominant political figure in Rus'. In addition to enjoying the loyalty of all the princes, he also maintained diplomatic and commercial relations with the Hungarians, the Poles and the imperial family in Constantinople.[64] Moreover, he was one of the most avid builders of his day. In Kiev he erected a new court, the church of St Vasilii, and restored the damaged St Sophia. In Chernigov, he built a second prince's

58 *PSRL*, vol. II, cols. 666–7.
59 Dimnik, *The Dynasty of Chernigov 1146–1246*, pp. 193–5.
60 S. A. Pletneva, *Polovtsy* (Moscow: Nauka, 1990), p. 146; see also Janet Martin, *Medieval Russia 980–1584* (Cambridge: Cambridge University Press, 1995), pp. 129–32.
61 *PSRL*, vol. II, cols. 630–3.
62 *PSRL*, vol. II, cols. 637–44; see also Martin Dimnik, 'Igor's Defeat at the Kayala: the Chronicle Evidence', *Mediaeval Studies* 63 (2001), 245–82.
63 John Fennell and Dimitri Obolensky (eds.), 'The Lay of Igor's Campaign', in *A Historical Russian Reader: A Selection of Texts from the XIth to the XVth Centuries* (Oxford: Clarendon Press, 1969), pp. 63–72.
64 *PSRL*, vol. II, col. 680.

court and the churches of St Michael and the Annunciation. Vsevolod Big Nest of Vladimir-Suzdal', David Rostislavich of Smolensk and Iaroslav Osmomysl of Galich used the Annunciation as the model for expanding their existing cathedrals and for building new ones.[65] During his reign, it seems, Chernigov grew to its maximum area to match if not to surpass Kiev in size.[66] Sviatoslav died in 1194 during the last week of July and was succeeded, according to their agreement, by Riurik.[67]

Riurik Rostislavich

The following year, Riurik invited David from Smolensk to help him distribute Kievan towns to their relatives. He demonstrated this deference towards his elder brother because, even as prince of Kiev, he was subordinate to David, the senior prince of the Rostislavichi. To his regret, in allocating the towns Riurik neglected Vsevolod Big Nest, whom the Rostislavichi had acknowledged as their senior prince. After Vsevolod threatened Riurik, he gave Vsevolod the towns that he had allotted to his son-in-law Roman Mstislavich of Volyn'. The latter was furious at the turn of events and formed a pact with Iaroslav Vsevolodovich of Chernigov.

Riurik, fearing that Iaroslav would depose him, asked Vsevolod to make Iaroslav pledge not to seize Kiev. What is more, he demanded that the Ol'govichi renounce the claims of their descendants. Iaroslav, proclaiming it to be a preposterous demand, refused to renounce the rights of future Ol'govichi to Kiev. He and Riurik therefore waged war until Vsevolod and David invaded the Chernigov lands. In 1197, Vsevolod, David and Iaroslav reached a settlement. The latter promised not to usurp Kiev from Riurik, but refused to forswear the future claims of his dynasty. While negotiating their agreement, the three senior princes also affirmed the Novgorodians' right to select a prince from whichever dynasty they chose. Moreover, they evidently granted the princes of Riazan' permission to create an autonomous eparchy

65 B. A. Rybakov, 'Drevnosti Chernigova', in N. N. Voronin (ed.), *Materialy i issledovaniia po arkheologii drevnerusskikh gorodov*, vol. 1 (= *Materialy i issledovaniia po arkheologii SSSR*, no. 11, 1949), pp. 90–3.

66 Specialists have estimated that, at its zenith in the late twelfth and early thirteenth centuries, Chernigov covered an area of some 400 to 450 hectares and was arguably the largest town in Rus'. Kiev encompassed some 360–80 hectares; see Volodymyr I. Mezentsev, 'The Territorial and Demographic Development of Medieval Kiev and Other Major Cities of Rus': A Comparative Analysis Based on Recent Archaeological Research', *RR* 48 (1989): 161–9.

67 *PSRL*, vol. 11, col. 680. Concerning Sviatoslav, see Dimnik, *The Dynasty of Chernigov 1146–1246*, pp. 135–212.

independent of Chernigov. Riurik was not present at the deliberations and his demands, in particular that Iaroslav sever his pact with Roman, were largely ignored. Vsevolod's objective was to keep the Rostislavichi dependent on him for military assistance. After Iaroslav Vsevolodovich died in 1198,[68] however, Riurik formed an alliance with his successor Oleg Sviatoslavich.

The following year Roman seized Galich with Polish help. He therewith became one of the most powerful princes in the land. In 1202, he demonstrated his might by inflicting a crushing defeat on the *Polovtsy* and by evicting his father-in-law Riurik from Kiev. He gave it to his cousin Ingvar' Iaroslavich of Lutsk, whose father had ruled the town.[69] Roman himself was not a rightful claimant, even though he was of Mstislav's line, because he belonged to a younger generation than Riurik and Vsevolod Big Nest. The latter, however, learning from the fate of his father Iurii and the example of his brother Andrei, did not occupy Kiev. The Rostislavichi of Smolensk therefore remained the only claimants from the House of Monomakh. Nevertheless, Vsevolod, Roman and their sons would keep a watchful eye on the princes of Kiev and at times try to manipulate their appointments.

In 1203 Riurik, with Oleg of Chernigov and the *Polovtsy*, retaliated by attacking Kiev. Although he would capture it later on several more occasions, his sack of the town is of special significance. The chronicler claims it was the most horrendous devastation that Kiev had experienced since the Christianisation of Rus'.[70] That is, contrary to the views of many historians, it was greater than the havoc inflicted by Andrei Bogoliubskii's coalition. The following year, however, Roman gained the upper hand once again by forcing Riurik to enter a monastery.[71] Then, in 1205, after Roman was killed fighting with the Poles, Riurik reinstated himself in Kiev.[72]

Roman had maintained close ties with the Poles (his mother was a Pole) and Byzantium. After repudiating his first wife Predslava, Riurik's daughter, he married Anna, probably the daughter of Emperor Isaac II Angelus.[73] He also pursued an aggressive policy towards Galich, where he was the first prince to depose the sons of Iaroslav Osmomysl. This gave his own sons, Daniil and Vasil'ko, a claim to Galich because they had the right to sit on the throne of

---

68 *PSRL*, vol. II, cols. 707–8; concerning Iaroslav's career, see Dimnik, *The Dynasty of Chernigov 1146–1246*, pp. 214–32.
69 *PSRL*, vol. I, cols. 417–18.
70 *PSRL*, vol. I, col. 418.
71 *PSRL*, vol. XXV, p. 101.
72 *PSRL*, vol. I, cols. 425–6.
73 Fennell, *Crisis*, p. 24.

their father.[74] Significantly, he captured Galich with the help of boyars many of whom transferred their loyalties to his sons after his death. Unfortunately for the boys, however, they were still minors so that their father's untimely death created a political vacuum in south-western Rus'. They were challenged by princes from Volyn', Smolensk, Chernigov and by the Hungarians.

Vsevolod Big Nest and Vsevolod the Red

When Roman died Vsevolod Big Nest was at the zenith of his power. He avoided meddling in southern affairs and devoted his energies to consolidating his rule over the north-east. He was determined to subjugate the princes of Riazan' who, if allowed to join forces with their relatives in Chernigov, could pose a serious threat to his authority. To secure control of the trade coming from the Caspian Sea, he waged war against the Volga-Kama Bulgars and the Mordva tribes. He destroyed Polovtsian camps along the River Don and strengthened his defences along the middle Volga and the Northern Dvina rivers. Although he seized Novgorodian lands along the upper Volga, he failed to occupy Novgorod itself, where Mstislav Mstislavich 'the Bold' (Udaloi), a Rostislavich, was ensconced. Like Andrei, he pursued a centralising policy in his patrimony by stifling local opposition and by fortifying towns. He also built churches. One of the most striking was that of St Dmitrii in Vladimir, famous for its relief decorations. Finally, the existence of chronicle compilations, like those of his father Iurii and brother Andrei, testifies to flourishing literary activity during his reign.[75]

In 1204, the year before Roman's death, Oleg Sviatoslavich of Chernigov died and was succeeded by his brother Vsevolod 'the Red' (Chermnyi). Unlike most senior princes of Chernigov before him, he tried to seize Galich, but a family from the cadet branch foiled his plan. Igor' Sviatoslavich's sons (the Igorevichi), whose mother was the daughter of Iaroslav Osmomysl, accepted the Galicians' invitation to be their princes. After failing to seize Galich for his own family, but content that his relatives ruled it, Vsevolod expelled Riurik from Kiev. Later, he also evicted Iaroslav, the son of Vsevolod Big Nest, from Pereiaslavl'.[76] For the first time, therefore, an Ol'govich controlled, even if fleetingly, Chernigov, Kiev, Galich and Pereiaslavl'.

---

74 For Roman's family, see Baumgarten, *Généalogies et mariages*, table XI.
75 For Vsevolod, see Fennell, *Crisis*; Limonov, *Vladimiro-Suzdal'skaia Rus'*; D. Wörn, 'Studien zur Herrschaftsideologie des Grossfürsten Vsevolod III "Bol'shoe gnezdo" von Vladimir,' *JGO* 27 (1979): 1–40. For chronicle writing, see Iu. A. Limonov, *Letopisanie Vladimiro-Suzdal'skoi Rusi* (Leningrad: Nauka, 1967).
76 *PSRL*, vol. I, cols. 426–8.

Pereiaslavl' had been the patrimony of Vladimir Monomakh. As noted above, his younger sons and grandsons (Mstislavichi) fought for possession of the town to use it as a stepping-stone to the capital of Rus'. After Iurii Dolgorukii occupied Kiev his descendants gained possession of Pereiaslavl'. During the last quarter of the twelfth century, however, the town and its outposts became favourite targets of Polovtsian raids. Consequently, it declined in importance so that, by the turn of the thirteenth century, it was without a prince for a number of years. Vsevolod expressed greater interest in Pereiaslavl' and sent his son Iaroslav, albeit a minor, to administer it.[77]

Vsevolod the Red's initial success in Kiev was short-lived. Riurik retaliated by driving him out. After that, the town changed hands between them on several occasions. Meanwhile, Vsevolod Big Nest, incensed at Vsevolod the Red for evicting his son Iaroslav from Pereiaslavl', marched against Chernigov. En route, the princes of Riazan' joined him. On learning that they had betrayed him by forming a pact with Vsevolod the Red, Vsevolod attacked Riazan'. He took the princes, their wives and their boyars captive to Vladimir, where many remained until after his death. In 1208 Riurik died and Vsevolod the Red finally occupied Kiev uncontested.[78] Two years later, he formed a pact followed by a marriage bond with Vsevolod Big Nest.[79] Their alliance was the most powerful in the land.

Vsevolod the Red's relatives in Galicia were less fortunate. In 1211 the boyars rebelled against the Igorevichi and hanged three of them.[80] Vsevolod accused the Rostislavichi of complicity in the crime and expelled them from their Kievan domains. He therewith successfully appropriated the lands that his father Sviatoslav had failed to take from Riurik. The evicted princelings, however, turned to Mstislav Romanovich of Smolensk and Mstislav Mstislavich the Bold of Novgorod for help. Meanwhile, on 13 April 1212, Vsevolod Big Nest died depriving Vsevolod the Red of his powerful ally.[81] Taking advantage of

---

77 For Pereiaslavl', see V. G. Liaskoronskii, *Istoriia Pereiaslavskoi zemli s drevneishikh vremen do poloviny XIII stoletiia* (Kiev, 1897); M. P. Kuchera, 'Pereiaslavskoe kniazhestvo', in L. G. Beskrovnyi (ed.), *Drevnerusskie kniazhestva X–XIII vv.* (Moscow: Nauka, 1975), pp. 118–43.

78 Concerning different views on the date of Riurik's death, see Martin Dimnik, 'The Place of Ryurik Rostislavich's Death: Kiev or Chernigov?', *Mediaeval Studies* 44 (1982): 371–93; John Fennell, 'The Last Years of Riurik Rostislavich', in D. C. Waugh (ed.), *Essays in Honor of A. A. Zimin* (Columbus, Oh.: Slavica, 1985), pp. 159–66; O. P. Tolochko, 'Shche raz pro mistse smerti Riuryka Rostyslavycha', in V. P. Kovalenko et al. (eds.), *Sviatyi kniaz' Mykhailo chernihivs'kyi ta ioho doba* (Chernihiv: Siverians'ka Dumka, 1996), pp. 75–6.

79 *PSRL*, vol. i, col. 435.

80 *PSRL*, vol. ii, cols. 723–7. Concerning the controversy over the identities of the three princes, see Dimnik, *The Dynasty of Chernigov 1146–1246*, pp. 272–5.

81 *PSRL*, vol. i, cols. 436–7.

this shift in the balance of power, the Rostislavichi attacked Kiev and drove out Vsevolod. They pursued him to Chernigov where he evidently fell in battle.[82]

Defeat at the River Kalka

The reign of Mstislav Romanovich, who replaced Vsevolod in Kiev, was peaceful, but the north-east was thrown into turmoil. Before his death, Vsevolod Big Nest weakened the power of the senior prince in Vladimir-Suzdal' by dividing up his lands among all his sons. He made matters worse by designating his second son Iurii, rather than the eldest Konstantin, his successor.[83] He therewith antagonised the latter. Meanwhile, Mstislav the Bold ruled Novgorod but Iaroslav of Pereiaslavl'-Zalesskii was determined to evict him. Konstantin joined Mstislav while Iurii backed his brother Iaroslav. The two sides clashed on 21 April 1216 near the River Lipitsa, where Mstislav and Konstantin were victorious.[84] Consequently, Mstislav retained Novgorod and Konstantin replaced Iurii as senior prince.

Two years later, Mstislav the Bold abandoned Novgorod. Soon after, it fell into the hands of Iurii, who became senior prince in 1218 after Konstantin died. Thus, the princes of Vladimir–Suzdal' finally acquired Novgorod, not because they were more powerful than Mstislav the Bold, but because he sought greener pastures in the south-west.[85] Accompanied by his cousin Vladimir Riurikovich of Smolensk and the Ol'govichi, he captured Galich from the Hungarians.[86] After that the Rostislavichi, who controlled Smolensk, Kiev and Galich, were the most powerful dynasty.

In 1223 the Tatars (Mongols) removed the *Polovtsy* as a military power. On receiving this news, Mstislav Romanovich summoned the princes of Rus' to Kiev where they agreed to confront the new enemy on foreign soil. Their forces included contingents from Kiev, Smolensk, Chernigov, Galicia, Volyn' and probably Turov. Vladimir-Suzdal', Riazan', Polotsk and Novgorod sent no men. After the troops set out, Mstislav the Bold quarrelled with his cousin Mstislav of Kiev. Their disagreement was responsible, in part, for the annihilation of their forces on 31 May at the River Kalka.[87]

82 *PSRL*, vol. xxv, p. 109. For Vsevolod the Red's reign, see Dimnik, *The Dynasty of Chernigov 1146–1246*, pp. 249–87.
83 *PSRL*, vol. xxv, p. 108. For Vsevolod's descendants, see Baumgarten, *Généalogies et mariages*, table x.
84 *PSRL*, vol. xxv, pp. 111–14; Fennell, *Crisis*, pp. 48–9.
85 For the controversies in Novgorod, see Fennell, *Crisis*, pp. 51–8; V. L. Ianin, *Novgorodskie posadniki* (Moscow: MGU, 1962).
86 *Novgorodskaia pervaia letopis'*, pp. 59, 260–1.
87 *PSRL*, vol. ii, cols. 740–5. For a discussion of the campaign, see Fennell, *Crisis*, pp. 63–8.

Mstislav the Bold escaped with his life. Mstislav Romanovich of Kiev and Mstislav Sviatoslavich of Chernigov, however, fell in the fray and their deaths necessitated the installation of new senior princes. Vladimir, Riurik's son, occupied Kiev; Mikhail, the son of Vsevolod the Red, occupied Chernigov.[88] The transitions of power worked smoothly according to the system of lateral succession. Given the heavy losses of life that the Ol'govichi had incurred, Mikhail made no attempt to usurp Kiev. Elsewhere, oblivious to or ignoring the threat that the Tatars presented, princes renewed their rivalries: Mstislav the Bold, Daniil Romanovich of Volyn' and the Hungarians fought for Galicia, while in Novgorod the townsmen struggled to win greater privileges from the princes of Vladimir-Suzdal'.

Mikhail Vsevolodovich

In 1224, while Mikhail was visiting his brother-in-law Iurii in the north-east, the latter asked him to act as mediator in Novgorod. Iurii and the townsmen could not agree on the terms of rule because his brother Iaroslav had imposed debilitating taxes on the Novgorodians and appointed his officials over them. As Iurii's agent, Mikhail abrogated many of Iaroslav's stringent measures but in doing so incurred his wrath. Nevertheless, while in Novgorod Mikhail derived benefit for Chernigov by negotiating favourable trade agreements. In the early 1230s, after Iaroslav pillaged his patrimonial domain and because he became involved in southern affairs, Mikhail terminated his involvement in Novgorod.

After that, Iaroslav reasserted his authority over the town through his sons, notably, Aleksandr, later nicknamed Nevskii. Mikhail's withdrawal from the northern emporium also enabled Iurii to restore unity among his brothers and nephews. Just the same, the fragmentation of Vladimir-Suzdal' that Vsevolod Big Nest had initiated by dividing up his lands among his sons, accelerated. Hereditary domains were partitioned even further among new sons.

In the late 1220s, Mikhail's brother-in-law Daniil had initiated an expansionist policy in Volyn' and Galicia. His success in appropriating domains forced Vladimir Riurikovich of Kiev and Mikhail to join forces. In 1228, however, they failed to defeat him at Kamenets and he remained free to pursue his aggression.[89] Meanwhile, the fortunes of the Rostislavichi had waned owing to their manpower losses at the Kalka, to the death of Mstislav the Bold, to succession crises that split the dynasty asunder, to famine in Smolensk and

---

88 For Mikhail's career, see Martin Dimnik, *Mikhail, Prince of Chernigov and Grand Prince of Kiev, 1224–1246* (Toronto: Pontifical Institute of Mediaeval Studies, 1981).
89 *PSRL*, vol. II, cols. 753–4.

to Lithuanian incursions. Despite these setbacks, commerce evidently prospered in Smolensk. In 1229 its prince negotiated a trade agreement with the Germans of Riga and designated a special suburb in Smolensk for quartering their merchants.[90] Nevertheless, two years later, in light of his dynasty's declining fortunes, Vladimir summoned the princes of Rus' to Kiev to solicit new pledges of loyalty.

Soon after, Mikhail besieged Vladimir forcing him to join Daniil, who by then had captured Galich. In 1235, when they invaded Chernigov, Mikhail defeated them with the *Polovtsy*. He evicted Vladimir from Kiev, but later reinstated the Rostislavich as his lieutenant. He therewith imitated Andrei Bogoliubskii who, in 1171, had appointed Roman Rostislavich, the then senior prince of the Rostislavichi, as his puppet in Kiev. After that, Mikhail seized Galich from Daniil. But unlike his father Vsevolod the Red, who had let the Igorevichi rule the town, Mikhail occupied it in person.[91]

His reasons for seeking control of both towns and for occupying Galich in preference to Kiev were, in the main, commercial. Merchants brought luxury goods from Lower Lotharingia, the Rhine region, Westphalia, and Lower Saxony via Galich and Kiev to Chernigov.[92] Ten years later, the Franciscan monk John de Plano Carpini reported that merchants from Bratislava, Constantinople, Genoa, Venice, Pisa, Acre, Austria and the Poles were also visiting Kiev.[93] While Daniil controlled Galich, he could obstruct the flow of merchandise coming through that town to Chernigov. Moreover, after forming his alliance with Vladimir, Daniil probably persuaded him to stem the flow of goods passing through Kiev to Chernigov. Mikhail could ensure that foreign wares reached Chernigov by replacing Daniil in Galich and by making Vladimir his lieutenant in Kiev.

With the support of the local boyars, bishops, the Hungarians, and the Poles, Mikhail retained control of Galich until around 1237. At that time the townsmen invited Daniil to replace Mikhail's son Rostislav while the latter was fighting the Lithuanians.[94] Mikhail had returned to Kiev in the previous year

90 On the Smolensk trade agreement, see R. I. Avanesov (ed.), *Smolenskie gramoty XIII–XIV vekov* (Moscow: AN SSSR, 1963), pp. 18–62.

91 *PSRL*, vol. II, cols. 773–4; *Novgorodskaia pervaia letopis'*, pp. 74, 284–5.

92 V. P. Darkevich and I. I. Edomakha, 'Pamiatnik zapadnoevropeiskoi torevtiki XII veka', *Sovetskaia arkheologiia* 3 (1964): 247–55; V. P. Darkevich, 'K istorii torgovykh sviazei Drevnei Rusi', *Kratkie soobshcheniia o dokladakh i polevykh issledovaniiakh Instituta arkheologii* 138 (1974): 93–103.

93 G. Vernadsky, *The Mongols and Russia* (New Haven: Yale University Press, 1953), pp. 62–4; C. Dawson (ed.), *The Mongol Mission: Narratives and Letters of the Franciscan Missionaries in Mongolia and China in the Thirteenth and Fourteenth Centuries* (New York: Sheed and Ward, 1955), pp. 70–1; Dimnik, *Mikhail*, pp. 76–7.

94 *PSRL*, vol. II, cols. 777–8.

because Iurii and Daniil had joined forces. Fearing that Mikhail had become too powerful, they sought to deprive him of Kiev by evicting Vladimir. The task was made easier following a vicious succession war in Smolensk after which the Rostislavichi became, in effect, the vassals of Vladimir-Suzdal'. Iaroslav, Iurii's brother, left his son Aleksandr in charge of Novgorod and occupied Kiev. After the townsmen refused to support him, however, he returned to Vladimir-Suzdal'.[95] To secure his hold over Kiev, Mikhail occupied it in person.

The Tatars invaded in two phases. First, in December 1237 they overran the lands of Riazan', and in the spring they devastated Vladimir-Suzdal'. Significantly, they spared Novgorod and Smolensk. Second, in 1239 they razed Pereiaslavl' and Chernigov; on 6 December 1240 they captured Kiev and, after that, laid waste to Galicia and Volyn'.[96]

After Baty established Sarai as the capital of the Golden Horde, he commanded every prince to visit him and obtain a patent (*iarlyk*) to rule his domain. In 1243 Iaroslav of Vladimir-Suzdal', who had replaced Iurii as senior prince after the Tatars killed him, was the first to kowtow to Baty. For his reward, the khan named him the senior prince of Rus' and appointed him to Kiev in place of Mikhail.[97] In 1245 Daniil obtained the *iarlyk* for Volyn' and Galicia.[98] The following year Mikhail journeyed to Sarai, but Baty had him put to death because he refused to worship an idol.[99] During the so-called period of the Mongol yoke that followed, the centre of power shifted from Kiev to Muscovy where the descendants of Vsevolod Big Nest, by becoming subservient vassals of the Tatars, attained supremacy.

Conclusion

In conclusion, we have seen that the years 1125 to 1246 gave birth to new principalities (Smolensk, Suzdalia, Murom and Riazan') and new eparchies (Smolensk and Riazan'). They saw the political ascendancy of a number of principalities (Chernigov, Smolensk, Volyn' and Suzdalia) and the decline of others (Turov, Galich, Polotsk, Pereiaslavl', Murom and Riazan') (Map 5.1 shows the Rus'ian principalities around 1246). The princes who shared borders with the Hungarians, the Poles and the Greeks developed political, personal and cultural relations with them. Moreover, dynasties formed commercial ties

---

95 *Novgorodskaia pervaia letopis'*, pp. 74, 285.
96 For the Tatar invasion, see Fennell, *Crisis*, pp. 76–90.
97 *PSRL*, vol. I, col. 470.
98 *PSRL*, vol. II, cols. 805–8; Pashuto, *Ocherki*, pp. 220–34.
99 *Novgorodskaia pervaia letopis'*, pp. 298–303; Dimnik, *Mikhail*, pp. 130–5.

Map 5.1. The Rus' principalities by 1246

with France, Bohemia, Hungary, the Poles, the Germans, the Baltic region, the Near East and Byzantium. They also had dealings, frequently hostile, with the Kama-Bulgars, the Mordva, the *Polovtsy* and the Lithuanians.

These years witnessed the flowering of culture, especially in ambitious building projects. Princes imported artisans from the Greeks, the West and from beyond the Caucasus. The proliferation of churches was accompanied by the growth in the number of native saints, with the concomitant growth in shrines, devotional literature, icons and other religious objects. The period also saw two singular ecclesiastical initiatives. Andrei Bogoliubskii attempted to create a metropolitan see in Vladimir, and a synod of bishops consecrated Klim Smoliatich as the second native metropolitan. Andrei's project failed and Klim's appointment was an isolated instance. Neither had a lasting effect on the organisation of the Church.

During this period Rus' witnessed fierce rivalries as dynasties fought to increase the size of their territories. The principalities of Galicia, Polotsk, Turov, Murom and Riazan' became the main victims of such appropriation. Novgorod was especially desirable for its commercial wealth and because, like Kiev, it had no resident dynasty. But winning Kiev, which enjoyed political and moral supremacy in Rus', was the main object of internecine wars. The princes descended from the powerful dynasties of the inner circle conceived by Iaroslav the Wise were the chief contenders. In their intra-dynastic and inter-dynastic rivalries they acknowledged and, for the most part, faithfully adhered to the system of genealogical seniority that dictated lateral succession.

Disagreements within a dynasty occurred when one prince attempted to debar another from succession or sought to pre-empt his claim (e.g. the Mstislavichi against their uncles). In like manner, two dynasties would go to war when one sought to deprive the other of its right to rule Kiev (e.g. Riurik Rostislavich against Iaroslav of Chernigov). When the senior princes of two dynasties challenged each other's claims, a challenger's success was usually determined by the greater manpower resources of his own dynasty, or by the greater military strength of the alliance that he had forged (e.g. Vsevolod Ol'govich against Viacheslav Vladimirovich; Iurii Dolgorukii against Rostislav Mstislavich; Andrei Bogoliubskii against Mstislav Iziaslavich; Mikhail Vsevolodovich against Vladimir Riurikovich). At times claimants from rival dynasties resolved their disputes by ruling Kiev as duumvirs (e.g. Iziaslav Mstislavich and Viacheslav Vladimirovich; Sviatoslav Vsevolodovich and Riurik Rostislavich). The instances when victorious claimants appointed their puppets to Kiev were failures (e.g. Andrei Bogoliubskii and Mikhail

Vsevolodovich). Finally, on occasion, princes succeeded one another peacefully (e.g. Mstislav Vladimirovich after Vladimir Monomakh; Vsevolod the Red after Riurik Rostislavich; Vladimir Riurikovich after Mstislav Romanovich).

During these years the inner circle created by Iaroslav the Wise evolved into one forged by political realities. Vladimir Monomakh debarred the dynasties of Turov and Chernigov thus making his heirs the only rightful claimants to Kiev. When, however, his younger sons and grandsons (Mstislavichi) both championed their right of succession, they divided the dynasty into two lines of rival contenders. By usurping Kiev from the House of Monomakh, Vsevolod Ol'govich also won the right of succession for his heirs. He therewith raised to three the number of dynasties with legitimate claims. The number increased to four when the Mstislavichi bifurcated into the Volyn' and Smolensk lines. By the beginning of the thirteenth century, however, only two dynasties remained as viable candidates, namely, those of Smolensk (Mstislav Romanovich and Vladimir Riurikovich) and Chernigov (Mikhail Vsevolodovich). The princes of Volyn' had become debarred because they had fallen too low on the genealogical ladder of seniority, and the princes of Suzdalia had found the hostility of the Kievans and the distance that separated them from Kiev to be too great. Finally, in the 1240s, the Tatars terminated the established order of succession to Kiev.

6
North-eastern Russia and the Golden Horde (1246–1359)

JANET MARTIN

On the eve of the Mongol invasion two institutions had given definition to Kievan Rus'. One was the ruling Riurikid dynasty, whose senior prince ruled Kiev. The other was the Orthodox Christian Church headed by the metropolitan, also based at Kiev. Although the component principalities of Kievan Rus' had multiplied and had become the hereditary domains of separate branches of the dynasty, subjecting the state to centrifugal pressures, they all recognised Kiev as the symbolic political and ecclesiastic centre of a common realm and were bound together by dynastic, political, cultural and commercial ties.

The principality that comprised the north-eastern territories of Kievan Rus' was Vladimir, also known as Suzdalia, Rostov-Suzdal', and Vladimir-Suzdal'. Centred around the upper Volga and Oka River basins, its territories were bounded by Novgorod to the north and west, Smolensk to the south-west, and Chernigov and Riazan' to the south. The eastern frontier of Vladimir-Suzdal' stretched to Nizhnii Novgorod on the Volga; beyond lay lands and peoples subject to the Volga Bulgars.

Vladimir-Suzdal' was the realm of the branch of the dynasty descended from Iurii Dolgorukii (1149–57) and his son Vsevolod 'Big Nest' (1176–1212). When the Mongols invaded the Russian lands, Vsevolod's son Iurii, the eldest member of the senior generation of this branch of the dynasty, was recognised, according to principles common to all the principalities of Kievan Rus', as the senior prince of his branch of the dynasty. He was, therefore, the grand prince of Vladimir. Despite his detachment from Kievan politics, the legitimacy of Iurii's rule in Vladimir derived from his place in the dynasty. The sovereignty of the Riurikid dynasty extended to Vladimir and defined it politically as an integral part of Kievan Rus'.

Vsevolod's descendants also ruled in other towns and districts of the principality, which had begun a process of subdivision before the Mongol invasion. Prince Vsevolod had assigned the city and region of Rostov to his son Konstantin; when Konstantin died in 1218, Rostov and its associated towns became the inheritance of his descendants.[1] In 1238, it was ruled by Vasil'ko Konstantinovich (d. 1238).[2] At least half a dozen principalities had been defined in north-eastern Russia, but with the exception of Rostov they had not become the patrimonies of particular branches of the dynasty. They remained attached to the grand principality and were, accordingly, periodically distributed by princes of Vladimir to their relatives.[3]

Affiliation with the Orthodox Church also defined the principality of Vladimir as a component of Kievan Rus'. Until the early thirteenth century the bishop of Rostov was the ecclesiastical leader of the population of the principality of Vladimir. In 1214, while Konstantin, the prince of Rostov, and his younger brother Iurii, appointed prince of Vladimir by their father, were engaged in a dispute over the throne of Vladimir, the eparchy was divided. The bishop of Rostov retained his authority over Rostov, Pereiaslavl', Uglich and Iaroslavl'. But a second bishop, based in the city of Vladimir, assumed ecclesiastical authority over Vladimir, Suzdal' and a series of associated towns.[4] Both bishoprics remained within the larger Russian Orthodox Church, headed by the metropolitan of Kiev.

The Mongol invasion did not immediately destroy the heritage left by Kievan Rus'. The two institutions, the Riurikid dynasty and the Orthodox Church that had given identity and cohesion to Kievan Rus', continued to dominate north-eastern Russia politically and ecclesiastically. But over the next century dynastic, political relations within north-eastern Russia altered under the impact of Golden Horde suzerainty. The lingering bonds connecting north-eastern Russia with Kiev and the south-western principalities loosened in the decades after the Mongol onslaught. North-eastern Russia separated from the south-western principalities of Kievan Rus' while the principality of Vladimir-Suzdal' fragmented into numerous, smaller principalities. During the fourteenth century, furthermore, the Moscow branch of the dynasty,

---

1 *PSRL*, vol. 1: *Lavrent'evskaia letopis', Suzdal'skaia letopis'* (Moscow: Vostochnaia literatura, 1962), cols. 434, 442; John Fennell, *The Crisis of Medieval Russia, 1200–1304* (London and New York: Longman, 1983), pp. 45–6.
2 Fennell, *Crisis*, p. 98; John Fennell, *The Emergence of Moscow 1304–1359* (Berkeley and Los Angeles: University of California Press, 1968), appendix B, table 3.
3 V. A. Kuchkin, *Formirovanie gosudarstvennoi territorii severo-vostochnoi Rusi v X–XV vv.* (Moscow: Nauka, 1984), pp. 101, 110; Fennell, *Crisis*, p. 50.
4 Yaroslav Nikolaevich Shchapov, *State and Church in Early Russia 10th–13th Centuries*, trans. Vic Schneierson (New Rochelle, N.Y., Athens and Moscow: Aristide D. Caratzas, 1993), pp. 50–1; E. Golubinskii, *Istoriia russkoi tserkvi*, vol. 1 (Moscow: Imperatorskoe obshchestvo istorii i drevnostei rossiiskikh, 1901; reprinted The Hague: Mouton, 1969), pp. 336, 338; Fennell, *Crisis*, p. 59 n. 26.

the heirs of Daniil Aleksandrovich, emerged as victors in the competition among the princes for Mongol favour and domestic power. Their political ascendancy violated the dynastic traditions, also inherited from the Kievan era, that had determined dynastic seniority and defined a pattern of lateral succession to the position of prince of Vladimir. In their quest for substitute bases of support and legitimacy the Moscow princes leaned heavily on their Mongol patrons. They also began processes of aggrandising territory, securing dynastic alliances and nurturing ties with the Church that served to secure their hold on the leading political position in north-eastern Russia, the grand prince of Vladimir. These processes also laid the foundations for the state of Muscovy.

Demographic and economic dislocation

The Mongol invasion had a severe impact on the society and economy of north-eastern Russia. During the three-month winter campaign of 1237–8, the city of Vladimir was besieged and burned, and Suzdal' was sacked. Rostov, another of the main cities of the region, as well as Tver', Moscow and a series of other towns, were also listed among those subjected to direct attack.[5] The surrender of towns and defeat of the north-eastern Russian armies did not end the Mongol military assaults. During the quartercentury following the initial invasion, the Mongols conducted fourteen more campaigns against north-eastern Russia. The Golden Horde khans continued to send expeditionary forces, often in the company of Russian princes and at times at the Russian princes' request, into the region. The campaigns tapered off only after the late 1320s.[6]

The military campaigns took a heavy toll on the Russian population. Princes and commoners, urban and rural residents were killed or taken captive. Iurii Vsevolodich of Vladimir and Vasil'ko Konstantinovich of Rostov were among

---

5 *PSRL*, vol. i, cols. 460–7; *PSRL*, vol. iii: *Novgorodskaia pervaia letopis' starshego i mladshego izvodov* (Moscow: Iazyki russkoi kul'tury, 2000), p. 288; *PSRL*, vol. x: *Patriarshaia ili Nikonovskaia letopis'* (St Petersburg: Arkheograficheskaia kommissiia, 1885; reprinted Moscow: Nauka, 1965), pp. 106–9; Fennell, *Crisis*, pp. 79–80; Fennell, *Emergence*, p. 12; Lawrence N. Langer, 'The Medieval Russian Town', in Michael Hamm (ed.), *The City in Russian History* (Lexington: University of Kentucky Press, 1976), p. 15.
6 *PSRL*, vol. x, p. 188; *PSRL*, vol. xv: *Rogozhskii letopisets, Tverskoi sbornik* (St Petersburg, 1863 and Petrograd, 1922; reprinted, Moscow: Iazyki russkoi kul'tury, 2000), cols. 43–4, 416; Langer, 'The Medieval Russian Town', p. 15; Robert O. Crummey, *The Formation of Muscovy 1304–1613* (London and New York: Longman, 1987), pp. 30–1; V. V. Kargalov, 'Posledstviia mongolo-tatarskogo nashestviia XIII v. dlia sel'skikh mestnostei Severo-Vostochnoi Rusi', *VI*, 1965, no. 3: 53, 57; Fennell, *Crisis*, p. 129.

the numerous princes killed during the 1238 campaign.[7] Although population figures are unknown, George Vernadsky estimated that at least 10 per cent of the Russian population died or was taken captive during the invasion of 1237–40.[8] In north-eastern Russia the cumulative result of repeated military incursions was similarly a marked reduction in the size of the population. This effect was compounded by the Mongol khans' demands for human services. Russian princes took part in Mongol military campaigns; commoners were also drafted for military service. Skilled artisans and unskilled labourers were conscripted to participate in the construction of Sarai, the capital city of the Golden Horde built by Khan Baty on a tributary of the lower Volga River. They also contributed to the construction of New Sarai, which was located about seventy-seven miles upstream and replaced Sarai as the Golden Horde capital in the early 1340s. Russian craftsmen were relocated to Sarai also to manufacture goods for its residents and markets. They were sent for similar purposes as far as Karakorum and China.[9]

The Mongol invasion not only depleted the population of north-eastern Russia. It resulted as well in the subordination of the region to Juchi's ulus, known also as the Kipchak Khanate or, more commonly, as the Golden Horde, which formed the north-western sector of the Mongol Empire. The khans of the Golden Horde required the Russian princes to recognise their suzerainty. They also demanded tribute in kind and, by the fourteenth century, in silver from the Russian populace. Mongol administrative agents, known as *baskaki*, were stationed with military contingents in selected north-eastern Russian towns to oversee tax collection and ensure compliance with the khans' decrees.[10] The tribute or *vykhod*, which may have been collected on an annual basis, has been estimated to have reached 5,000 silver roubles per year by 1389, the first year for which calculations are possible; it may have been even larger in earlier decades.[11] That amount has been interpreted as a

---

7 Ibid., pp. 80–1, 98–9.
8 George Vernadsky, *The Mongols and Russia* (*A History of Russia*, vol. III) (New Haven: Yale University Press and London: Oxford University Press, 1953), p. 338.
9 Langer, 'The Medieval Russian Town', p. 23; Thomas T. Allsen, 'Ever Closer Encounters: The Appropriation of Culture and the Apportionment of Peoples in the Mongol Empire', *Journal of Early Modern History* 1 (1997): 2–4; Donald Ostrowski, *Muscovy and the Mongols: Cross-Cultural Influences on the Steppe Frontier, 1304–1589* (Cambridge: Cambridge University Press, 1998), pp. 113–14; Vernadsky, *Mongols*, pp. 88, 123, 201, 213, 227, 338–9. On Sarai, Thomas T. Allsen, 'Saray', in *Encyclopedia of Islam*, 2nd edn., vol. IX (Leiden: E. J. Brill, 1996), 41–2; Vernadsky, *Mongols*, p. 141.
10 Vernadsky, *Mongols*, p. 220; Donald Ostrowski, 'The Mongol Origins of Muscovite Political Institutions', *SR* 49 (1990): 527; Fennell, *Crisis*, pp. 128–9.
11 Michel Roublev, 'The Mongol Tribute According to the Wills and Agreements of the Russian Princes', in Michael Cherniavsky (ed.), *The Structure of Russian History* (New

drain on the economy of northern Russia and a hindrance to its economic development.[12]

Mongol military campaigns, seizures of captives, and demands for labour and tribute were not the only factors that adversely affected the demographic and economic condition of north-eastern Russia. Just over a century after the Mongol invasion, the Black Death or bubonic plague reached the region. Having spread through the lands of the Golden Horde in 1346–7 to Europe, it circled back to northern Russia and reached Pskov and Novgorod in 1352. The following year the epidemic reached north-eastern Russia, where it claimed the lives of the metropolitan, the grand prince, his sons and one of his brothers. After the initial bout, the plague returned repeatedly during the following century. Chronicles reported that as many as a hundred persons died per day at the peak of the epidemic. Scholars estimate that the Russian population declined by 25 per cent as a cumulative result of the waves of plague.[13]

Despite the debilitating effects of conquest and plague, north-eastern Russia experienced a gradual economic recovery. Residents fled from the towns and districts that were favourite targets of Mongol attack. Thus, the capital city of Vladimir lost population and, despite the efforts of its prince Iaroslav Vsevolodich to rebuild it, recovered at a slow pace.[14] But the refugees settled in other towns and districts, such as Rostov and Iaroslavl', that were situated in more remote areas. Five of eight districts that were fashioned into separate principalities between 1238 and 1300 were located beyond the former main population centres of Rostov-Suzdal'. In addition, forty new towns were founded in north-eastern Russia during the fourteenth century. Thus the demographic shift, prompted by the devastation caused by Mongol attacks, also stimulated economic growth. Among the towns and districts that benefited from the

York: Random House, 1970), pp. 56–7; Michel Roublev, 'The Periodicity of the Mongol Tribute as paid by the Russian Princes during the Fourteenth and Fifteenth Centuries', *FOG* 15 (1970): 7.

12 Ostrowski, *Muscovy and the Mongols*, pp. 108–9; Roublev, 'The Periodicity of the Mongol Tribute', 13.

13 *PSRL*, vol. x, pp. 217, 226; *PSRL*, vol. xi: *Patriarshaia ili Nikonovskaia letopis'* (St Petersburg: Arkheograficheskaia kommissiia, 1897; reprinted Moscow: Nauka, 1965), p. 3; Lawrence N. Langer, 'The Black Death in Russia: Its Effects upon Urban Labor', *RH* 2 (1975): 54–7, 62; Gustave Alef, 'The Origins of Muscovite Autocracy. The Age of Ivan III', *FOG* 39 (1986): 22–4; Gustave Alef, 'The Crisis of the Muscovite Aristocracy: A Factor in the Growth of Monarchical Power', *FOG* 15 (1970); reprinted in his *Rulers and Nobles in Fifteenth-Century Muscovy* (London: Variorum Reprints, 1983), 36–8.

14 Fennell, *Crisis*, pp. 119–20; A. N. Nasonov, *Mongoly i Rus' (Istoriia tatarskoi politiki na Rusi)* (Moscow and Leningrad: AN SSSR, 1940; reprinted The Hague and Paris: Mouton, 1969), pp. 38–9.

redistribution of population were Tver' and Moscow, which became dynamic political and economic centres of north-eastern Russia during the fourteenth century.[15]

One visible sign of economic recovery was reflected in production by craftsmen. Despite the transfer of artisans and specialists into Mongol service, carpenters, blacksmiths, potters and other craftsmen continued to manufacture their wares in the thirteenth century; in the fourteenth century they were producing more goods than they had before the invasion.[16] Building construction, particularly of masonry fortifications and churches, was curtailed in the immediate aftermath of the invasion. Only one small church of this type was built in Vladimir in the twenty-five years after the invasion. But half a century later patrons of such construction projects, including princes and, to a lesser degree, metropolitans, were able to muster the finances and skilled labour to undertake them. From the beginning of the fourteenth century new construction was occurring in north-eastern Russia. Appearing first in Tver', building projects were almost immediately also launched in its rival city Moscow. There the church of the Dormition, the cathedral dedicated to the Archangel Michael, and three other stone churches were erected within a decade. By the middle of the century, prosperity was similarly visible in Nizhnii Novgorod.[17]

Economic recovery was attributable, at least in part, to commercial activity. The Golden Horde, known for its brutal military subjugation of the Russians as well as their neighbours in the steppe, was part of the vast Mongol Empire that fostered and depended upon an extensive commercial network that stretched from China in the east to the Mediterranean Sea. Sarai became a key commercial centre in the northern branch of the segment of Great Silk Route that connected Central Asia to the Black Sea. Khan Mangu Temir (1267–81) was particularly active in developing commerce along the route that passed through his domain. To this end he granted the Genoese special trading privileges and encouraged them to found trading colonies at Kafa (Caffa) and

---

15 Janet Martin, *Treasure of the Land of Darkness: The Fur Trade and its Significance for Medieval Russia* (Cambridge: Cambridge University Press, 1986), p. 88; Kuchkin, *Formirovanie gosudarstvennoi territorii*, pp. 121–2; Ostrowski, *Muscovy and the Mongols*, p. 127; Vernadsky, *Mongols*, p. 241; Nasonov, *Mongoly i Rus'*, pp. 36–8.

16 Langer, 'The Medieval Russian Town', pp. 23–4; Vernadsky, *Mongols*, pp. 338–41; Ostrowski, *Muscovy and the Mongols*, p. 112.

17 Langer, 'The Medieval Russian Town', pp. 21, 23; David B. Miller, 'Monumental Building as an Indicator of Economic Trends in Northern Rus' in the Late Kievan and Mongol Periods, 1138–1462', *American Historical Review* 94 (1989): 368–9; N. S. Borisov, 'Moskovskie kniaz'ia i russkie mitropolity XIV veka', *VI*, 1986, no. 8: 38; N. S. Borisov, *Russkaia tserkov' v politicheskoi bor'be XIV–XV vekov* (Moscow: Moskovskii universitet, 1986), pp. 58–61; Fennell, *Crisis*, p. 89; Ostrowski, *Muscovy and the Mongols*, pp. 128–31.

Sudak (Surozh, Soldaia) on the Crimean peninsula in the Black Sea. Using the bishop of Sarai as his envoy, he also opened diplomatic relations with Byzantium.[18]

Northern Russia was drawn into the Mongol commercial network. Goods collected as tribute and gifts for the khan and other Tatar notables were conducted down the Volga River to Sarai. But the Mongols also encouraged Russian commerce, particularly the Baltic trade conducted by the north-western city of Novgorod. Khan Mangu Temir pressured Grand Prince Iaroslav Iaroslavich (1263–71/2), despite his unpopularity in Novgorod, to promote that town's commercial interaction with its German and Swedish trading partners and to guarantee its merchants the right to travel and trade their goods freely throughout Vladimir-Suzdal'.[19] Through the next century a commercial network developed that brought imported European goods through Novgorod into north-eastern Russia, then down the Volga River to Sarai. By the late thirteenth and first half of the fourteenth century Russian merchants were conveying those imports as well as their own products down the Volga River by boat and appearing not only at Sarai, but also Astrakhan' and the Italian colonies of Tana, Kafa and Surozh. At those market centres European silver and textiles as well as Russian luxury furs and other northern goods joined the commercial traffic in silks, spices, grain and slaves that were being conducted in both eastward and westward directions along the Great Silk Road.[20] The steady flow of tribute and commercial traffic through north-eastern Russian market towns from Tver' to Nizhnii Novgorod stimulated their economic recovery and development.

It was within the framework of the economic demands and opportunities created by the Golden Horde that north-eastern Russia recovered. It was similarly under the pressures of Mongol hegemony that north-eastern Russia underwent a political reorganisation during the century following the invasion.

18 Vernadsky, *Mongols*, p. 170; Martin, *Treasure*, p. 31; Ostrowski, *Muscovy and the Mongols*, pp. 110–11, 117; John Meyendorff, *Byzantium and the Rise of Russia. A Study of Byzantino-Russian Relations in the Fourteenth Century* (Cambridge: Cambridge University Press, 1981), p. 46; Nasonov, *Mongoly i Rus'*, p. 46.

19 *PSRL*, vol. III, pp. 88–9, 319; *Gramoty Velikogo Novgoroda i Pskova*, ed. S. N. Valk (Moscow: AN SSSR, 1949), nos. 13, 30, 31, pp. 13, 57, 58–61; Langer, 'The Medieval Russian Town', pp. 16, 17, 20; Vernadsky, *Mongols*, pp. 170–1; V. L. Ianin, *Novgorodskie posadniki* (Moscow: Moskovskii universitet, 1962), p. 156; V. N. Bernadskii, *Novgorod i Novgorodskaia zemlia* (Moscow and Leningrad: AN SSSR, 1961), p. 21; Ostrowski, *Muscovy and the Mongols*, p. 118.

20 Langer, 'The Medieval Russian Town', pp. 20–1; Martin, *Treasure*, pp. 31, 90, 192 n. 132, 218 n. 17.

Table 6.1. *The grand princes of Vladimir 1246–1359*

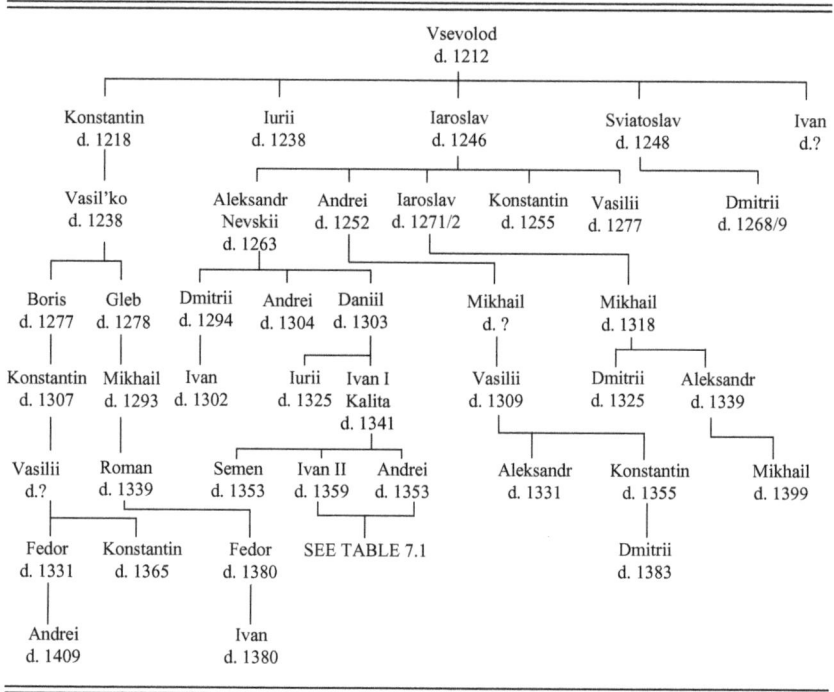

- **Vsevolod** d. 1212
  - **Konstantin** d. 1218
    - **Vasil'ko** d. 1238
      - **Boris** d. 1277
        - **Konstantin** d. 1307
          - **Vasilii** d.?
            - **Fedor** d. 1331
              - **Andrei** d. 1409
      - **Gleb** d. 1278
        - **Mikhail** d. 1293
          - **Roman** d. 1339
            - **Konstantin** d. 1365
  - **Iurii** d. 1238
  - **Iaroslav** d. 1246
    - **Aleksandr Nevskii** d. 1263
      - **Dmitrii** d. 1294
        - **Ivan** d. 1302
          - **Semen** d. 1353
            - **Fedor** d. 1380
              - **Ivan** d. 1380
          - **Ivan II** d. 1359
            - SEE TABLE 7.1
          - **Andrei** d. 1353
    - **Andrei** d. 1252
    - **Iaroslav** d. 1271/2
      - **Andrei** d. 1304
      - **Daniil** d. 1303
        - **Iurii** d. 1325
        - **Ivan I Kalita** d. 1341
    - **Konstantin** d. 1255
      - **Mikhail** d. ?
        - **Vasilii** d. 1309
          - **Aleksandr** d. 1331
    - **Vasilii** d. 1277
      - **Mikhail** d. 1318
        - **Dmitrii** d. 1325
          - **Konstantin** d. 1355
            - **Dmitrii** d. 1383
        - **Aleksandr** d. 1339
          - **Mikhail** d. 1399
    - **Dmitrii** d. 1268/9
  - **Sviatoslav** d. 1248
  - **Ivan** d.?

Dynastic reorganisation and the Golden Horde

By 1246, when Prince Mikhail of Chernigov was killed during his visit to Khan Baty (d. *c*.1255), the princes in north-eastern Russia had already paid homage to their Mongol suzerain and had been confirmed in their offices.[21] Prince Iaroslav Vsevolodich succeeded his brother Iurii Vsevolodich, who had died in 1238, to become the prince of Vladimir. His appointment conformed to the traditional, lateral pattern of dynastic succession. Iaroslav's brother Sviatoslav received Suzdal' along with Nizhnii Novgorod. Another brother, Ivan, became prince of Starodub. Iaroslav's son, Aleksandr Nevskii, was sent to Novgorod. (See Table 6.1.)

It nevertheless took several years for the political situation in north-eastern Russia to stabilise. When Iaroslav appeared for a second time before Baty in 1245, he was sent to the Great Khan at Karokorum. He died on the return

---

21 Nasonov, *Mongoly i Rus'*, p. 26.

journey.[22] He was succeeded by his brother Prince Sviatoslav (1247), who divided his realm among Iaroslav's sons. Konstantin Iaroslavich received Galich and Dmitrov. Iaroslav Iaroslavich received Tver'. The six-year-old Vasilii Iaroslavich became prince of Kostroma.[23] Starodub remained in the possession of Ivan Vsevolodich's descendants. The descendants of Konstantin Vsevolodich, who had died in 1218, continued to rule Rostov, which subsequently fragmented into the principalities of Beloozero, Iaroslavl', Uglich and Ustiug.

This arrangement lasted only until 1249, when Iaroslav's sons Andrei and Aleksandr returned from Karakorum. At that time Andrei replaced his uncle Sviatoslav, who fled from Vladimir.[24] Andrei held his position for only two years. In 1251, when Mongke became the new great khan, the Russian princes were required to attend the khan of the Golden Horde to renew their patents to hold office. Although Aleksandr made the journey, Andrei did not. Aleksandr returned to Vladimir in the company of a Tatar military force and evicted Andrei, who fled first to Novgorod and then to Sweden. Aleksandr Nevskii became the prince of Vladimir in 1252.[25]

Initially, as Baty and his successors established their suzerainty over north-eastern Russia, they respected the dynastic legacy inherited by the Vladimir princes from Kievan Rus'. They confirmed the Vsevolodichi as ruling branch of the dynasty in Vladimir. In their selection of princes of Vladimir they also observed the principles determining dynastic seniority and succession that had evolved during the Kievan Rus' era. But Mongol suzerainty altered the process of succession. Although they tended to uphold Riurikid tradition, the Mongol khans assumed the authority to issue patents to princes for their thrones. They also demanded tribute from their new subjects, and established their own agents, the *baskaki*, at posts in north-eastern Russia to oversee its collection and to maintain order. As the princes of north-eastern Russia adjusted to these conditions over the next century, dynastic politics altered. Succession to the position of grand prince of Vladimir came to depend less on traditional definitions of dynastic seniority and more on the preference of the khan; the khan's favour could, in turn, be earned by the demonstration of a prince's ability to collect and successfully deliver the required tribute.

---

22 *PSRL*, vol. I, col. 471; Vernadsky, *Mongols*, pp. 61, 142–3; Fennell, *Crisis*, pp. 100–1; Christopher Dawson (ed.), *The Mongol Mission* (London and New York: Sheed and Ward, 1955), pp. 58, 65.
23 *PSRL*, vol. I, col. 471.
24 *PSRL*, vol. I, col. 472.
25 *PSRL*, vol. I, col. 473.

Aleksandr Nevskii's reign in Vladimir (1252–63) was marked by co-operation with the Golden Horde. One of the clearest examples of his policy related to Novgorod, located in north-western Russia beyond the borders of the principality of Vladimir. The city of Novgorod controlled a vast northern empire that stretched to the Ural mountains. It was also a commercial centre that conducted trade with Swedes and Germans of the Baltic Sea. Unlike other principalities in Kievan Rus', Novgorod did not have its own hereditary line of princes. But by the early thirteenth century it regularly recognised the authority of the prince of Vladimir. It was in conformity with that practice that Prince Iaroslav Vsevolodich had sent his son Aleksandr Nevskii to govern Novgorod in the aftermath of the invasion.[26]

Novgorod had not been subjected to attack during the Mongol invasion, but in 1257, the Mongols attempted to take a census there for purposes of recruitment and tax collection. The Novgorodians refused to allow the officials to conduct the census. Nevskii, who had accompanied the Tatar officials, inflicted punishment on Novgorod, but was nevertheless summoned along with the princes of Rostov to the horde in 1258. Upon their return Prince Aleksandr, his brother Andrei and the Rostov princes joined the Tatars to enforce the order to take the census in Novgorod.

After these events and under the guidance of Prince Aleksandr Nevskii north-eastern Russia was drawn increasingly into the orbit of Sarai, the capital city of the Golden Horde built on the lower Volga River. Nevskii's successors, his brothers Iaroslav (1263–1271/2) and Vasilii (1272–7), followed his example of close co-operation with the Mongol khans. The princes of Vladimir lost interest in south-western Russia and confined their domestic focus to northern Russia, that is, Vladimir-Suzdal' itself and Novgorod.[27] In exchange Tatars aided them in their capacity as princes of Novgorod in a military campaign against Revel' (1269); they also helped Vasilii expel his nephew Dmitrii from Novgorod in 1273 and establish his own authority there.[28]

During the last quarter of the century the next generation of princes in north-eastern Russia appears to have taken advantage of political conditions within the Golden Horde to serve their own ambitions and challenge the dynastic traditions they had inherited. During the reign of Khan Mangu Temir (1267–81) another leader, Nogai, emerged as a powerful military commander with virtually autonomous authority over the western portion of the horde's territories. Nogai's power persisted through the reign of Tuda Mengu, who

26 *PSRL*, vol. I, col. 475.
27 Nasonov, *Mongoly i Rus'*, pp. 47–8; Fennell, *Crisis*, p. 143.
28 *PSRL*, vol. III, p. 88; Fennell, *Crisis*, pp. 128–9.

succeeded his brother in 1281, and who abdicated in favour of his nephew Tele Buga in 1287. Tele Buga was challenged, however, by the nephew of Mangu Temir, Tokhta, who eventually sought sanctuary and support from Nogai. Together Nogai and Tokhta succeeded in arranging the assassination of Tele Buga and the establishment of Tokhta as the khan at Sarai (1291). The alliance of Tokhta and Nogai did not survive; hostilities resulted in the defeat and death of Nogai in 1299.[29]

Prince Vasilii died (1277) during the reign of Khan Mangu Temir. The throne of Vladimir passed to Dmitrii Aleksandrovich.[30] Dmitrii was the eldest member of the next generation whose father had also served as prince of Vladimir. His succession thus followed dynastic tradition. But Dmitrii did not display the same willingness to co-operate with the khan that his father and uncles had shown. It is not known whether he presented himself before Mangu Temir to obtain a patent for his throne. When the Mongols called upon the north-eastern Russian princes to join a military campaign in the northern Caucasus, Prince Dmitrii, in contrast to his brother Andrei and the princes of Rostov, who obeyed the order, declined to participate. In 1281, when Tuda Mengu became khan, Dmitrii did not go to Sarai to pay homage and renew his patent for his throne. Tuda Mengu responded by appointing Dmitrii's brother Andrei prince of Vladimir and sending a military force of Tatars with Andrei and the Rostov princes against Dmitrii.[31]

The dual authority within the horde, however, enabled Dmitrii to gain support from Nogai, who issued his own patent to Dmitrii and helped him recover his position in Vladimir as well as control over Novgorod. Despite the ongoing hostilities between the brothers, Dmitrii held his post until Tokhta became khan at Sarai in 1291. Once again, Dmitrii declined to go to Sarai. He was joined in this act of defiance by Princes Mikhail Iaroslavich of Tver' and Daniil Aleksandrovich of Moscow. In contrast, Andrei and the Rostov princes presented themselves before Tokhta, reaffirmed their loyalty to the Sarai khan, and registered their complaints against Dmitrii Aleksandrovich. When Tokhta undertook his campaign against Nogai in 1293, he also sent forces to help Andrei overthrow Dmitrii. Learning of the approaching army, Dmitrii fled. Andrei and the Tatars nevertheless staged attacks on a total of fourteen towns, including Vladimir, Suzdal' and Moscow. It was only Dmitrii's death in 1294, however, that resolved the conflict among the Russian princes. Andrei, who then became heir to the throne according to

29 *PSRL*, vol. i, col. 526; *PSRL*, vol. x, pp. 168, 169, 172.
30 *PSRL*, vol. i, col. 525.
31 *PSRL*, vol. i, col. 525; *PSRL*, vol. x, p. 159.

dynastic tradition and who also enjoyed the support of the khan, became prince of Vladimir. Despite the legitimacy of his position, his rivals prevented him from retaking possession of a key town, Pereiaslavl'-Zalesskii, which was held first by Dmitrii's son Ivan and then, after his death in 1302, by Daniil's son Iurii.[32]

Prince Andrei, supported by the Sarai khans, had unsuccessfully attempted to undermine dynastic tradition and usurp the Vladimir throne. The Rostov princes, who according to that tradition had lost their claim to the Vladimir throne, supported Andrei. But Dmitrii retained the support of his younger brother Daniil Aleksandrovich and, despite earlier conflicts with Tver',[33] of his cousin Mikhail Iaroslavich. The unusual political climate within the horde provided an opportunity for him to gain support from Nogai as well and thus defy both the Sarai khan and Andrei.

Although Daniil Aleksandrovich of Moscow supported Dmitrii and the traditional dynastic definition of seniority, his sons successfully challenged that tradition. Gaining support from the khan at Sarai, who had no rival such as Nogai during the first half of the fourteenth century, the Moscow princes ascended and gained control over the Vladimir throne. To achieve this position the Muscovite princes not only challenged the successor to the throne, but forcibly attached territories that had belonged to Vladimir to their own domain.

Andrei died in 1304. Daniil Aleksandrovich had died the year before, in 1303.[34] The dynasty's candidate to assume the Vladimir throne was thus Mikhail Iaroslavich, the senior member of the next generation; his father, Iaroslav, had been prince of Tver' and also prince of Vladimir (1263–71/2). Khan Tokhta approved Mikhail as grand prince of Vladimir. Despite the fact that Mikhail's legitimacy derived from both traditional dynastic and Mongol sources, Iurii Daniilovich of Moscow opposed him. Mikhail was forced to wage two military campaigns (1305 and 1308) against Iurii to secure his position.[35]

The competition between the princes of Tver' and the princes of Moscow continued through the first quarter of the fourteenth century. The princes of Tver' were the rightful heirs to the Vladimir throne according to the dynasty's

32 *PSRL*, vol. i, cols. 484, 526, 527; *PSRL*, vol. x, pp. 161, 165–6, 168–9, 170; Nasonov, *Mongoly i Rus'*, pp. 72–3, 80; Vernadsky, *Mongols*, pp. 193–4; Fennell, *Emergence*, p. 61; L. V. Cherepnin, *Obrazovanie russkogo tsentralizovannogo gosudarstva v XIV–XV vekakh* (Moscow: Sotsial'no-ekonomicheskaia literatura, 1960), pp. 459–60.
33 E.g. *PSRL*, vol. x, pp. 166–7.
34 *PSRL*, vol. i, col. 486.
35 Nasonov, *Mongoly i Rus'*, p. 81; Fennell, *Emergence*, pp. 64–5; Cherepnin, *Obrazovanie*, p. 462.

traditional pattern of succession. According to those norms, the princes of Moscow were illegitimate. Daniil Aleksandrovich had not served as prince of Vladimir; his descendants were therefore ineligible for the grand-princely throne. Khan Tokhta followed his predecessors' example and confirmed the dynasty's selection for grand prince. Initially, his successor Khan Uzbek (1313–41) also followed this precedent. When Mikhail presented himself at the horde, Uzbek renewed his patent.[36] Mikhail remained at the horde for two years. His rival Iurii, taking advantage of his absence, attempted to enhance his own political power in northern Russia. Novgorod, whose commercial wealth made it particularly significant to the rivals, arrested Mikhail's governors and invited Iurii to become its prince. Uzbek nevertheless continued to support Mikhail and sent him back to Russia with Tatar forces to re-establish his authority; Iurii meanwhile was ordered to appear before the khan.[37] But Iurii Daniilovich won Uzbek's favour as well as the hand of the khan's sister in marriage.[38] Returning from the horde to Russia with his wife, an envoy from the khan, and an army, he waged war to remove Mikhail. Mikhail's forces won the battle. Nevertheless, for his defiance and for the death of Iurii's wife, which occurred while she was in Mikhail's custody, Mikhail was executed by Khan Uzbek. Iurii became the grand prince of Vladimir.[39] With the transfer of the patent to the Daniilovich prince the khan's favour replaced the dynasty's traditions.

Iurii held the Vladimir throne for four years (1318–22), but he did so uneasily and only with repeated military assistance from the horde. In 1322, Khan Uzbek restored the throne of Vladimir to the legitimate heir, as determined by the dynasty's norms of succession, Mikhail's son Dmitrii. Iurii prepared to protest and also present a large treasure, which he gathered in Novgorod, to the khan. But Dmitrii's brother Aleksandr robbed Iurii while he was travelling to the horde. When Iurii finally reached the horde in 1325, Dmitrii murdered him. Uzbek, in turn, condemned Dmitrii to death for his crime. But he transferred the patent for Vladimir to the next legitimate candidate according to the dynasty's norms of succession, Dmitrii's brother Aleksandr Mikhailovich.[40]

The dynasty's candidate lost the khan's favour, however, two years later when the population of Tver' staged a revolt against the khan's envoy who had led a force to that city, possibly to gather funds and recruits for a military

---

36 *PSRL*, vol. x, p. 178.
37 *PSRL*, vol. x, pp. 178–9; Fennell, *Emergence*, pp. 75–81.
38 *PSRL*, vol. x, p. 180.
39 *PSRL*, vol. x, pp. 181–6.
40 *PSRL*, vol. x, pp. 188–90.

campaign against the Ilkhans of Persia.[41] When Iurii's brother Ivan Daniilovich then presented himself before Uzbek, the khan sent an army back to north-eastern Russia with him. Joined as well by Prince Aleksandr Vasil'evich of Suzdal', Ivan launched a campaign against Tver'. Aleksandr Mikhailovich fled to Pskov (1327).[42] But when Metropolitan Feognost (Theognostos) excommunicated the entire population of the town for harbouring the fugitive, he moved on to Lithuania (1329). Aleksandr returned to Pskov in 1331 and served as its prince until 1337. He then once again visited the horde and recovered the throne of Tver'. Two years later, however, he was recalled to the horde and executed.[43]

After Aleksandr Mikhailovich lost the throne of Vladimir in 1327, the political, dynastic legacy inherited by north-eastern Russia from Kievan Rus' lost its potency. The norms of seniority and succession, which had been honoured by the Riurikids in north-eastern Russia as in all of Kievan Rus' for centuries and which had combined with the khan's patent to provide legitimacy for the grand prince, were overruled. They were replaced by the khan's favour, which became the exclusive basis for the selection and retention of the highest political position in north-eastern Russia. Although Uzbek may have divided the principality of Vladimir and Novgorod between Ivan Daniilovich and Aleksandr Vasil'evich of Suzdal' in 1328, by 1331 Ivan Daniilovich was the sole grand prince of Vladimir.[44] Uzbek and his successors with rare exceptions bestowed the position on the Daniilovichi, the princes of Moscow. Thus, Ivan Daniilovich, also known as Ivan I Kalita ('Money-bag'), possessed the throne exclusively from 1331 until his death in 1341. Despite recurrent dynastic opposition, which arose not only from the princes of Tver' but also from princes of Beloozero, Iaroslavl' and Suzdal' as well as from Novgorod, he was succeeded by his sons Semen (1341–53) and Ivan II (1353–9).

Territorial reorientation

As the princes of Vladimir developed close ties with Sarai and particularly as the princes of Moscow gained ascendancy in the principality, the bonds

---

41 *PSRL*, vol. x, p. 194; Charles Halperin, *The Tatar Yoke* (Columbus, Oh.: Slavica, 1986), p. 54.
42 *PSRL*, vol. x, p. 195.
43 Fennell, *Emergence*, pp. 118, 158–69. Cf. Halperin, *The Tatar Yoke*, pp. 85, 87.
44 *PSRL*, vol. iii, p. 469; *PSRL*, vol. x, p. 195; Cherepnin, *Obrazovanie*, pp. 497–8; A. E. Presniakov, *The Formation of the Great Russian State. A Study of Russian History in the Thirteenth to Fifteenth Centuries*, trans. A. E. Moorhouse (Chicago: Quadrangle Books, 1970), pp. 123–4; Fennell, *Emergence*, pp. 112–13, 119.

linking north-eastern Russia with the western and south-western portions of Kievan Rus' weakened. As they concentrated their attention more exclusively on northern Russia, the Daniilovichi also began the process of gathering patrimonial principalities within Vladimir and Rostov under their authority.

The bonds linking north-eastern and south-western Russia had noticeably loosened even before the Mongol invasion of Kievan Rus'. In the immediate aftermath of the invasion, however, Kiev continued for a brief period to be recognised as the symbolic political centre of the realm. Iaroslav, possibly as the first Rus' prince to present himself before Baty, may have been given a patent not only for Vladimir-Suzdal', but also for Kiev.[45] When Aleksandr and Andrei returned from Karakorum, Aleksandr had a mandate for the throne of Kiev. But the north-eastern princes no longer recognised the centrality of Kiev. While Andrei, presumably on the authority of the great khan, claimed the throne of Vladimir and evicted their uncle Sviatoslav, Aleksandr went to Novgorod. He never physically went to Kiev to assume his post.[46]

Although the princes of Vladimir refrained from occupying the throne of Kiev and focused their attention on their north-eastern realm, they did retain personal and political ties with the princes in other parts of Kievan Rus'. Their relationships manifested themselves in a variety of ways. Prince Boris Vasil'kovich of Rostov, for example, displayed solidarity with Chernigov by attending his grandfather, Prince Mikhail, in Sarai in 1246.[47] Prince Fedor Rostislavich of Mozhaisk, the brother of Prince Gleb of Smolensk, married into the Rostov clan and c.1260 became the prince of Iaroslavl'.[48]

The most dramatic demonstration of such associations, however, was the alliance forged between Prince Andrei of Vladimir and Prince Danylo (Daniil) of Galicia-Volynia. Prince Danylo had been confirmed in his position after visiting Khan Baty in 1245. He nevertheless sought assistance against the Tatars from his Western neighbours. Aided by his candidate for metropolitan, Kirill (Cyril), he arranged the marriage of his son Leo to the daughter of King Bela IV of Hungary. Danylo himself married the niece of the Lithuanian king (1251).[49] He also established close ties with Andrei of Vladimir. In 1250, Kirill, having been confirmed as metropolitan, travelled to northern Russia. He escorted

---

45 *PSRL*, vol. II: *Ipat'evskaia letopis'* (Moscow: Iazyki russkoi kul'tury, 1998), col. 806; Fennell, *Crisis*, p. 100.
46 *PSRL*, vol. I, col. 472; *PSRL*, vol. III, pp. 80, 304; *PSRL*, vol. x, p. 137; Fennell, *Crisis*, p. 107; Vernadsky, *Mongols*, p. 147; Kuchkin, *Formirovanie gosudarstvennoi territorii*, p. 111.
47 *PSRL*, vol. III, p. 301.
48 *PSRL*, vol. x, pp. 153–4; Gail Lenhoff, *Early Russian Hagiography: The Lives of Prince Fedor the Black* (Wiesbaden: Harrassowitz, 1997), pp. 41–52; Fennell, *Crisis*, pp. 121–2 n. 2, 125, 143.
49 Vernadsky, *Mongols*, p. 156.

Danylo's daughter to Vladimir, where she married Prince Andrei in 1251.[50] Andrei's refusal to pay homage to the khan the following year was perceived as an act of defiance undertaken in alliance with Prince Danylo. The Tatars sent armies against both princes.[51] Defeated at Pereiaslavl'-Zalesskii in 1252, Prince Andrei fled the country. Danylo persisted in his efforts to muster support from the West. He subsequently accepted a crown from Pope Innocent IV and entertained the possibility of uniting the Church in Galicia-Volynia with Rome in return for aid.[52] But when military support did not materialise, he abandoned those ties. By 1256, he was again at war with the Mongols and was forced to flee to Poland and Hungary in 1260.[53] Danylo received no assistance from the Riurikids of north-eastern Russia. By that time Andrei had returned from exile and accepted a submissive role towards his brother and the Mongols. Metropolitan Kirill too had shifted his allegiance to Prince Aleksandr Nevskii and spent long periods away from Kiev in Vladimir.[54]

Although active political co-operation between north-eastern and south-western Russia ended with the defeat of the allies, Andrei and Danylo, other princes of the two regions maintained relationships. Prince Iaroslav Iaroslavich, prince of Tver' and grand prince of Vladimir (1263–71/2), arranged a marriage for his daughter with Iurii of Galicia. Tver' also developed ties with Lithuania, its expanding Western neighbour. Prince Iaroslav's grandson Dmitrii Mikhailovich, who served as grand prince of Vladimir from 1322 to 1325, married Maria, the daughter of Gedimin of Lithuania. The Daniilovichi of Moscow did not maintain such relations. As they eclipsed the Tver' princes, the range of political interest and involvement of the Vladimir princes narrowed from Kievan Rus' as a whole and its western frontiers to their own domain in northern Russia.[55]

From the late thirteenth century Prince Daniil of Moscow and his heirs also began to reverse the trend of territorial fragmentation by attaching the patrimonial principalities of other Vsevolodichi to their own domain. The

50 *PSRL*, vol. I, col. 472; Joseph Fuhrmann, 'Metropolitan Cyril II (1242–1281) and the Politics of Accommodation', *JGO* 24 (1976): 164; Vernadsky, *Mongols*, p. 147.
51 *PSRL*, vol. II, col. 829; Fennell, *Crisis*, pp. 107, 111; Vernadsky, *Mongols*, p. 148.
52 Martin Dimnik, 'Principality of Galicia-Volynia', in *MERSH*, vol. XII (Gulf Breeze, Fla.: Academic International Press, 1979), p. 68; Michael Zdan, 'The Dependence of Halych-Volyn' on the Golden Horde', *SEER* 35 (1957): 515; Nasonov, *Mongoly i Rus'*, pp. 24–6.
53 Fuhrmann, 'Metropolitan Cyril II', 167; Vernadsky, *Mongols*, p. 158.
54 Nasonov, *Mongoly i Rus'*, pp. 40, 47; Fuhrmann, 'Metropolitan Cyril II', 162–7; Fennell, *Crisis*, p. 112; Donald Ostrowski, 'Why Did the Metropolitan Move from Kiev to Vladimir in the Thirteenth Century?', in Boris Gasparov and Olga Raevsky-Hughes (eds.), *Slavic Cultures in the Middle Ages (California Slavic Studies*, vol. 16) (Berkeley, Los Angeles and Oxford: University of California Press, 1993), pp. 83–8.
55 Fennell, *Emergence*, pp. 103–4.

tendency to create patrimonial principalities had begun before the Mongol invasion. Rostov had become the realm of Konstantin Vsevolodich and his descendants. The trend continued after the invasion. The number of sub-divisions within Vladimir-Suzdal' as well as principalities detached from it multiplied. When Prince Iaroslav Vsevolodich succeeded his brother Iurii, he distributed territories to his nephews. During Aleksandr's reign Iur'ev Pol'skii, which had originally been assigned to Prince Sviatoslav Vsevolodich in 1213, was recognised as a hereditary principality. Upon Sviatoslav's death in 1253, it passed to his son Dmitrii.[56] Pereiaslavl'-Zalesskii became the domain of Alek-sandr Nevskii's son Dmitrii, and Moscow was apparently reserved for his son Daniil. Suzdal' was given to Prince Andrei after his return from his exile in 1255.[57]

Between 1238 and 1300, according to V. A. Kuchkin, eight new principalities were carved out of the north-eastern Russian territories to make a total of fourteen.[58] Some of these principalities became inherited domains, possessed by the descendants of the princes who had received them in these distribu-tions. Thus, Tver' became the realm of the dynastic branch descending from Iaroslav Iaroslavich; Moscow similarly became the possession of the heirs of Daniil Aleksandrovich. Other principalities did not become separate, heredi-tary principalities. Kostroma, for example, was considered a distinct principal-ity by the 1250s and ruled by Prince Vasilii Iaroslavich, who also became grand prince of Vladimir in 1272. When he died in 1277, however, Kostroma ceased to be a separate apanage.[59]

The indefinite status of some principalities gave the princes of Moscow an opportunity to obtain permanent possession of them. The process began in the late thirteenth century, before the princes of Moscow made a bid for the throne of Vladimir. The status of the principality of Pereiaslavl'-Zalesskii, as noted above, was a matter of contention. It had been ruled by Prince Dmitrii Aleksandrovich, who had also been Prince of Vladimir. Despite the challenges from his brother Andrei for the Vladimir throne, Dmitrii had retained his authority in Pereiaslavl'-Zalesskii. When he died in 1294, his son Ivan succeeded him there. But Andrei did not recognise it as the patrimonial principality of Dmitrii and his sons and claimed it as a possession of the grand principality. The dispute persisted for a decade. Although Andrei repeatedly appealed to

56 Fennell, *Crisis*, pp. 47, 111.
57 Kuchkin, *Formirovanie gosudarstvennoi territorii*, pp. 110–13.
58 Kuchkin, *Formirovanie gosudarstvennoi territorii*, pp. 110, 121. The eight were Starodub, Suzdal', Tver', Galich-Dmitrov, Kostroma, Moscow, Nizhnii Novgorod-Gorodets and Beloozero. See also Fennell, *Emergence*, p. 21.
59 Kuchkin, *Formirovanie gosudarstvennoi territorii*, p. 119; Fennell, *Emergence*, pp. 21–2.

Khan Tokhta for assistance, Princes Mikhail of Tver' and Daniil of Moscow successfully secured the town for Ivan Dmitr'evich at princely conferences assembled in 1296 and 1300 and militarily defended his position. When Ivan Dmitr'evich died in 1302, Daniil's forces prevented Grand Prince Andrei from taking control of the town. After Daniil also died in 1303, the town accepted his son Iurii as its prince. Pereiaslavl'-Zalesskii remained a possession of the house of Moscow until Iurii's brother, Ivan I Kalita, died in 1341. It was then once again regarded as a component of the grand principality, which by then was ruled by the princes of Moscow.[60]

Daniil and his son Iurii also added Serpukhov, Kolomna and Mozhaisk to their domain. They thereby not only tripled its size, but also gained control over the entire length of the Moskva (Moscow) River and the section of the Oka River extending from Kolomna to Serpukhov.[61] Although Iurii was unable to establish his authority in Kostroma in 1304, the principality became subject to the Moscow princes after they gained the throne of Vladimir, to which Kostroma was attached.[62] By acquiring these principalities, the Moscow princes increased the size of their own domain and gained control over the strategic and economic assets they contained. By taking possession of territories associated with the Vladimir throne, they also symbolically strengthened their claim to that position.

Prince Ivan I Kalita was credited by his grandson Dmitrii Donskoi with purchasing more principalities, specifically Beloozero and Uglich, which were subdivisions of the Rostov principality, and Galich.[63] There is some evidence suggesting that Ivan sent his officials to oversee Rostov as well.[64] Although some scholars doubt that Ivan actually purchased these territories, he did arrange marriages of his daughters to princes of Beloozero, Iaroslavl' and Rostov and thereby established personal seniority, at least, over three major lines within the Rostov branch of the dynasty.[65] Kalita's heirs added territories north-east of Moscow (Iur'ev Pol'skii) and west of the city (the districts of Vereia and Borovsk) to their domain as well.

60 Cherepnin, *Obrazovanie*, pp. 459–60; Vernadsky, *Mongols*, pp. 193–4; Fennell, *Crisis*, pp. 151–2.
61 Fennell, *Emergence*, pp. 50–1; Crummey, *The Formation of Muscovy*, p. 35; Cherepnin, *Obrazovanie*, pp. 459–60; Vernadsky, *Mongols*, p. 193.
62 Fennell, *Crisis*, pp. 127–8; Fennell, *Emergence*, pp. 62, 112.
63 Wladimir Vodoff, 'A propos des "achats" (kupli) d'Ivan Ier de Moscou', *Journal des Savants* (1974): 95–6; A. I. Kopanev, 'O "kupliakh" Ivana Kality', *IZ* 20 (1946): 24–37; Fennell, *Emergence*, pp. 177, 182–4, 191–3; Crummey, *The Formation of Muscovy*, p. 49; Borisov, 'Moskovskie kniaz'ia', 35; Cherepnin, *Obrazovanie*, pp. 510–11.
64 Ibid., p. 509.
65 Vodoff, 'A propos des "achats"', 109, 123; Kopanev, 'O kupliakh', 27; Fennell, *Emergence*, pp. 177, 180–4, 193, 245; Cherepnin, *Obrazovanie*, p. 509.

In addition to their concerns with north-eastern Russia the grand princes of Vladimir consistently sought to maintain their position as prince of Novgorod. One of the first acts undertaken by Prince Iaroslav Vsevolodich upon assuming the position of grand prince of Vladimir in the midst of the crisis caused by the Mongol invasion was to send his son, Aleksandr Nevskii, to Novgorod. Nevskii undertook a vigorous defence of Novgorod and its neighbour Pskov against Lithuania, which had absorbed Polotsk and was encroaching upon Smolensk. Nevskii defeated Lithuania in 1245 and again in 1248.[66]

But Novgorod was not the hereditary domain of the Vsevolodichi or any other branch of the Riurikid dynasty. Although it had been accepting the princes of Vladimir from the early thirteenth century, it had a long history of selecting and ejecting princes. Thus, when it became dissatisfied with Grand Prince Iaroslav Iaroslavich and tried to evict him as its prince in 1270, it invited another prince, Dmitrii Aleksandrovich, to take his place. Dmitrii declined at that time.[67] But after Iaroslav died (1271/2), he did take the Novgorodian throne in defiance of his uncle Vasilii Iaroslavich, who had become grand prince of Vladimir and was obliged to wage war to secure the Novgorodian throne for himself.[68]

By the fourteenth century, however, Novgorod's continuing efforts to control the appointment of its princes and to limit their authority enabled the princes of Moscow to extend their influence over it. In 1304, Novgorod opposed Mikhail Iaroslavich of Tver' when he became grand prince and sent his governors to represent his authority there. Although Mikhail successfully imposed his rule on Novgorod by 1307, the relationship was an uneasy one. In 1312, the year before he presented himself to the new khan Uzbek, Mikhail was once again engaged in hostilities with Novgorod, which he commercially blockaded in order to force its submission.

Novgorod's discontent with Mikhail provided Prince Iurii Daniilovich of Moscow with an opportunity, which he skilfully exploited. As a result Novgorod became involved in the rivalry between the Tver' and Moscow princes that lasted through the first three decades of the fourteenth century. While Mikhail was attending Uzbek, Novgorod invited Iurii to become its prince. Mikhail returned and, supported by a Tatar military force, was engaged in a lengthy process of forcing Novgorod to submit to him when Uzbek appointed Iurii grand prince. Even when Mikhail defeated Iurii's army in 1317, Iurii retreated to Novgorod. During the four years he served as grand prince, Iurii

---

66 *PSRL*, vol. I, cols. 471–2; *PSRL*, vol. III, pp. 79, 304; Fennell, *Crisis*, pp. 100, 102–3.
67 *PSRL*, vol. III, pp. 88, 320.
68 *PSRL*, vol. III, pp. 88–9, 322; *PSRL*, vol. x, p. 151; Fennell, *Crisis*, p. 129.

continued to devote himself to Novgorod and spent a major portion of his time there rather than in north-eastern Russia. His preoccupation with Novgorod gave his new rival, Dmitrii Mikhailovich, grounds to appeal to Uzbek to reverse himself once again and return the grand princely throne to the prince of Tver'. Dmitrii's plea was guaranteed a favourable response when his brother Aleksandr robbed Iurii of the treasure he had collected in Novgorod and was delivering to the khan (1322). Following that episode, Iurii again returned to Novgorod. He spent the years 1323 and 1324 serving its interests. He built a fortress at Orekhov on Lake Ladoga, concluded a treaty between Novgorod and the Swedes and led an expedition against Ustiug, which had blocked Novgorodians' transit to and from their north-eastern possessions. When he finally returned to the horde with a new treasure in 1325, he was killed by Prince Dmitrii.[69]

The critical importance of Novgorod in this political rivalry derived from its commercial wealth, which was the source of silver that the khan demanded in tribute. By the fourteenth century responsibility for collecting and delivering tribute was passing from the *baskaki* to the grand prince of Vladimir.[70] By successfully gathering and delivering the tribute as well as rich gifts for the khan and other influential Tatar notables a prince could gain credibility and the khan's favour. Failing to do so gave the khan reason to transfer the patent for the grand principality and the responsibility for delivering the tribute that accompanied that honour to another prince. Iurii's attention to Novgorodian affairs reflected his determination to control the sector of the economy that could satisfy the khan's demand for tribute. By securing Novgorod's supplies of luxury fur transported from the distant north-east through Ustiug and the trade routes used by the Swedes and Germans who bought those furs with silver, he supported Novgorod's commercial activities and gained access to its wealth.

When Ivan Daniilovich became grand prince of Vladimir, he too became deeply involved with Novgorod, from which he collected not only regular tribute payments but special assessments. Possibly in response to the Golden Horde's demand for increased revenue prompted by its wars against Ilkhans of Persia during the 1330s, Ivan placed greater pressure on Novgorod. In 1332, just after he received the sole patent for the grand principality, he demanded a special payment from Novgorod (*zakamskoe serebro*) and forced it to comply by setting up a blockade that cut off its contacts with north-eastern Russia.

---

69 *PSRL*, vol. III, pp. 94–7, 335–9; Vernadsky, *Mongols*, pp. 96, 100–1.
70 Ibid., pp. 199, 228.

Novgorod for the first time turned to Lithuania for a prince and welcomed Narimunt, the son of Gedimin, to the city. It again recognised Ivan as its prince only in 1334–5. Ivan also applied pressure on Novgorod's northern empire. Whereas Iurii had compelled Ustiug to keep the transit route to the north-east open for Novgorod's benefit, Ivan attacked Ustiug as well as Novgorod to collect tribute. In 1337, he also sent forces against Novgorod's possession, the North Dvina land. In 1339, Ivan once again demanded unusually high contributions from Novgorod, prompting a renewal of their conflict that lasted until after Ivan's death in 1341.[71]

Despite Novgorod's resistance, the first Daniilovichi gained and held dominance over that city and thus had access to its wealth. There is broad scholarly agreement that the Moscow princes' control over Novgorod's supplies of goods, such as luxury fur, as well as the silver that it received for them enabled them to pay the tribute demanded by the Golden Horde khans. The khans responded by awarding the post of grand prince of Vladimir to the Daniilovichi, who had thus demonstrated their reliability.[72]

By the end of the reign of Grand Prince Ivan I Kalita the territorial orientation of the princes of Vladimir had been substantially altered. Their ties with western and south-western Russia were reduced. They concentrated their attention on north-eastern Russia, on Novgorod, and on the Golden Horde. The Daniilovichi, furthermore, had begun to expand their territories and extend their authority over patrimonial principalities in north-eastern Russia. They thus began to stem the tendency to divide the principalities of Vladimir and Rostov into multiple principalities that had prevailed in the thirteenth century. By curtailing the fragmentation and accumulating territories under their own authority, the Daniilovich princes subordinated and weakened their dynastic opponents while also gaining access to a larger pool of economic and human resources. They were better able to collect taxes, to assemble and support more military retainers, and to enforce the Mongol demand for tribute.

In addition to extending their authority over patrimonial principalities in north-eastern Russia, the Daniilovichi sought the position of prince of Novgorod. An important source of wealth, Novgorod was the object of contention between the princes of Tver' and the princes of Moscow. Even before the

---

71 *PSRL*, vol. iii, pp. 99, 344–8, 350; Janet Martin, *Medieval Russia 980–1584* (Cambridge: Cambridge University Press, 1995), pp. 184–5; Martin, *Treasure*, p. 131; Fennell, *Emergence*, pp. 140, 148, 153, 156–7, 242–3; Bernadskii, *Novgorod*, p. 24.
72 Borisov, 'Moskovskie kniaz'ia', 35; Halperin, *The Tatar Yoke*, p. 81; Fennell, *Emergence*, p. 193; Martin, *Medieval Russia*, pp. 182, 185.

Daniilovichi secured the throne of Vladimir they gained favour in Novgorod by defending its commercial interests and securing its trade routes. But while Iurii Daniilovich, who was competing with the princes of Tver', pursued such policies in the service of Novgorod's need to keep its routes open, Ivan Daniilovich did so to control Novgorod and its commercial resources.

Although in their capacity of grand princes of Vladimir and princes of Novgorod the Daniilovichi engaged in military campaigns against the Swedes and the Livonian Order, their focus was not on the western frontier of the Russian lands. While they were engaged in their struggle with the princes of Tver' and winning the support of the Golden Horde khans for the throne of Vladimir, Prince Gedimin of Lithuania (1316–41) was extending his influence over western Russian principalities. Smolensk, Chernigov and Kiev all pledged their allegiance to him and his successor, Ol'gerd (1345–77). After Iurii II of Galicia and Volynia died in 1340, Volynia also fell under Lithuanian control. Gedimin also arranged the marriage of his daughter to Dmitrii Mikhailovich of Tver' (1320) and responded to Pskov's request for a prince (1323). When Novgorod turned to Lithuania for Prince Narimunt in 1332, it was clear that Novgorod too was considering Lithuania as an alternative to Vladimir. Lithuania's expansion was penetrating into north-western Russia and challenging the pre-eminence of the princes of Moscow.[73]

The Church

Although the Golden Horde had confirmed Iurii Dolgorukii's heirs as the ruling dynastic branch in Vladimir, it negated the Kievan Rus' legacy when it appointed the Daniilovichi to be grand princes of Vladimir. The Daniilovichi adopted policies, furthermore, that weakened bonds with the other principalities that had formed Kievan Rus' while they consolidated their authority within the territorial framework of northern Russia. In contrast to the dynasty, the Church, the other institution that had given identity and definition to Kievan Rus', did not narrow its range of interests or its field of operations. Its metropolitans continued to regard the Orthodox population throughout all the lands of Kievan Rus' as their flock and resisted efforts to divide their ecclesiastical realm.

The first metropolitans to head the Russian Church after the Mongol invasion were Kirill (Cyril; 1242–80/1) and Maksim (Maximus; 1282/3–1305). Despite the reported destruction of the city, Kiev remained their base of operation

---

73 Vernadsky, *Mongols*, pp. 202–3, 238; Fennell, *Emergence*, pp. 98–9, 104, 122–3.

until the end of the century. Their activities and concerns, however, covered the entire see. Thus, Kirill, although nominated for his office by Prince Danylo of Galicia, travelled throughout his domain during his tenure in office. He was reported to have been in north-eastern Russia on at least six occasions. He was in Vladimir to welcome Aleksandr Nevskii on his return to the city in 1252 and he officiated at Nevskii's funeral in 1263; Kirill himself died in Pereiaslavl'-Zalesskii. When not travelling, he remained at Kiev; after his death his body was returned there.[74] Maksim similarly served all sectors of his domain.[75] In 1299, Maksim moved the metropolitan's residence to Vladimir.[76]

Like the princes of Vladimir, the metropolitans attempted to accommodate the Golden Horde. In 1261, Metropolitan Kirill arranged for a new bishopric to be established at Sarai. Shortly after Mangu Temir became khan, he issued special privileges to the Church, relieving its personnel from tax obligations and military service. Clergy, in return, prayed for the khan, and thereby acknowledged him as the legitimate suzerain of their people.[77] In the 1340s, Metropolitan Feognost was obliged to deal with alterations in Church privileges made by Khan Janibek.[78]

But unlike the north-eastern Russian princes, who reduced their interaction with western and south-western Russian principalities and reoriented their political focus to northern Russia and the Golden Horde, Maksim and his successors, Petr (1308–25), Feognost (1328–53) and Aleksei (1354–78), became preoccupied with preserving the integrity of their ecclesiastical realm. Attempts to divide the Rus' metropolitanate were initiated soon after Maksim vacated Kiev. The first challenge to the see's unity came from Galicia c.1303, when a metropolitanate was created for the bishoprics in south-western Rus'.[79] It was short-lived. When Prince Iurii L'vovich of Galicia, Danylo's grandson, proposed Petr as his nominee to become the second metropolitan of that see, his candidate was selected instead to succeed Maksim (d. 1305) as the metropolitan

74 *PSRL*, vol. I, col. 473; *PSRL*, vol. x, pp. 139, 143; Jaroslaw Pelenski, 'The Origins of the Muscovite Ecclesiastical Claims to the Kievan Inheritance (Early Fourteenth Century to 1458/1461)', in Gasparov and Raevsky-Hughes (eds.), *Slavic Cultures in the Middle Ages*, p. 103; Ostrowski, 'Why Did the Metropolitan Move?', 83, 87, 92; Fuhrmann, 'Metropolitan Cyril II', 162–4, 166, 171.

75 Fuhrmann, 'Metropolitan Cyril II', 164; Meyendorff, *Byzantium and the Rise of Russia*, p. 79.

76 Ostrowski, 'Why Did the Metropolitan Move?', 93–4.

77 Nasonov, *Mongoly i Rus'*, p. 45; Vernadsky, *Mongols*, pp. 165–6; Crummey, *The Formation of Muscovy*, p. 31; Fuhrmann, 'Metropolitan Cyril II', 168.

78 Meyendorff, *Byzantium and the Rise of Russia*, pp. 160–1; Borisov, *Russkaia tserkov'*, p. 68.

79 Meyendorff, *Byzantium and the Rise of Russia*, p. 92; Borisov, *Russkaia tserkov'*, p. 39; Fennell, *Emergence*, pp. 68, 125; Pelenski, 'Muscovite Ecclesiastical Claims', 105.

of Kiev and all Rus'. The Galician metropolitanate dissolved and with Galicia's candidate at its head the metropolitanate of Kiev and all Rus' was reunited.[80] Petr maintained that unity. But the Galician challenge did not permanently disappear. Towards the end of Petr's life, the Galician metropolitanate was re-established (1325). The new Russian metropolitan Feognost, however, reclaimed the south-western bishoprics when he passed through Galicia on his way to Vladimir (1327). He successfully defeated yet another attempt to form a separate see for the Galician bishoprics by travelling to that region in 1331, just months after the metropolitanate was re-established, and then to Constantinople in 1332. In 1341 a Galician metropolitanate, which lasted until 1347, formed once again, prompting Metropolitan Feognost to continue to devote his energies to abolishing it.[81]

In addition to the recurrent threat that the Galician bishoprics would be detached from the Kievan metropolitanate, a second challenge arose from Lithuania. By the second quarter of the fourteenth century Lithuania was incorporating Orthodox lands that had been parts of Kievan Rus'. During the reigns of Gedimin (1316–41) and Ol'gerd (1345–77) Lithuania extended its authority over Smolensk, Chernigov, and Kiev itself. After Iurii II of Galicia and Volynia died in 1340, Volynia also fell under Lithuanian control. Lithuania, which had provided Novgorod with Prince Narimunt in 1332, was exercising influence not only over Novgorod, but also Pskov and Tver'.[82] In conjunction with the extension of Lithuanian authority over the Orthodox populations of these principalities, a separate metropolitanate was created c.1315–19. When its metropolitan Theophilus (Feofil) died in 1330, no successor was named. Feognost, who was in Constantinople in 1332, may have influenced the decision to leave the post vacant.[83] In 1352, on the eve of Feognost's death, Lithuania urged the renewal of its own metropolitanate. When its appeals met little sympathy in Constantinople, the Patriarch of Trnovo

---

80 Meyendorff, *Byzantium and the Rise of Russia*, pp. 92–4; Dimitri Obolensky, 'Byzantium, Kiev and Moscow: A Study in Ecclesiastical Relations', *Dumbarton Oaks Papers* 11 (Cambridge, Mass.: Harvard University Press, 1957); reprinted in Dimitri Obolensky, *Byzantium and the Slavs: Collected Studies* (London: Variorum Reprints, 1971), 35; Fennell, *Emergence*, pp. 68–9, 125–6; Borisov, *Russkaia tserkov'*, pp. 39, 43–4; Presniakov, *Formation*, p. 242.

81 Meyendorff, *Byzantium and the Rise of Russia*, pp. 94, 154–8, 161–2; Presniakov, *Formation*, p. 242; Fennell, *Emergence*, pp. 125–9; Borisov, *Russkaia tserkov'*, p. 71; Pelenski, 'Muscovite Ecclesiastical Claims', 105; Dimnik, 'Galicia-Volynia', pp. 68–9.

82 Vernadsky, *Mongols*, pp. 202–3, 238; Fennell, *Emergence*, pp. 104, 122–3.

83 Fennell, *Emergence*, pp. 129–30; Meyendorff, *Byzantium and the Rise of Russia*, pp. 95, 152; Pelenski, 'Muscovite Ecclesiastical Claims', 105.

(Bulgaria) consecrated Theodoret as metropolitan for Lithuania.[84] Theodoret claimed jurisdiction over all the Orthodox bishoprics within the lands ruled by Ol'gerd, including Kiev. Although Theodoret was formally deposed and excommunicated by the Patriarch of Constantinople, he continued to function as metropolitan in the Lithuanian see until 1354, when Constantinople confirmed Aleksei as metropolitan of Rus' and also named a new metropolitan, Roman, for Lithuania (1355).[85] Roman included Kiev, which recognised Lithuanian suzerainty, in his ecclesiastical realm as well. Aleksei undertook intensive efforts to recover the Lithuanian bishoprics. They included trips to Constantinople and Kiev, where he was detained for two years. The metropolitanate of Kiev and all Rus', nevertheless, remained divided until Roman died in 1362.[86]

Thus, while the princes of Moscow were challenging Prince Mikhail Iaroslavich and his sons for the Vladimir throne and ingratiating themselves with the khan at Sarai to overrule the dynastic traditions guiding seniority and succession, the metropolitans were reaffirming the Kievan Rus' heritage as a basis for maintaining the unity of their see and were appealing to the patriarchs of Constantinople to support their position.

Although not necessarily motivated by the same goals as the Daniilovichi, some actions undertaken by the metropolitans aided the princes of Moscow in achieving political dominance in north-eastern Russia. In a general way the metropolitans' recognition of the Mongol khan as the suzerain of the Russian lands obliged them to accept the khans' decrees, including their choice of prince for Vladimir. Petr, who became metropolitan of Kiev and all Rus' when the patriarch selected him over the candidature of Prince Mikhail of Tver', is frequently regarded as a partisan of the Moscow princes.[87] Tensions between Petr, on the one hand, and Mikhail of Tver', who had also recently become

84 PSRL, vol. x, p. 226; Meyendorff, *Byzantium and the Rise of Russia*, pp. 164–5; Presniakov, *Formation*, p. 243; Obolensky, 'Byzantium, Kiev and Moscow', 40; Fennell, *Emergence*, pp. 130, 134; Pelenski, 'Muscovite Ecclesiastical Claims', 105.

85 PSRL, vol. xv, col. 63; John Meyendorff, 'Alexis and Roman: A Study in Byzantino-Russian Relations (1352–1354)', *St Vladimir's Theological Quarterly* 11 (1967), 143; Meyendorff, *Byzantium and the Rise of Russia*, pp. 166–170; Presniakov, *Formation*, p. 243; Dimitri Obolensky, 'Byzantium and Russia in the Late Middle Ages', in J. R. Hale, J. R. L. Highfield and B. Smalley (eds.), *Europe in the Late Middle Ages* (London: Faber and Faber, 1965); reprinted in Dimitri Obolensky, *Byzantium and the Slavs: Collected Studies* (London: Variorum Reprints, 1971), p. 256; Fennell, *Emergence*, p. 302; Borisov, *Russkaia tserkov'*, pp. 79–80; G. M. Prokhorov, *Povest' o Mitiae. Rus' i Vizantiia v epokhu kulikovskoi bitvy* (Leningrad: Nauka, 1978), p. 42.

86 Presniakov, *Formation*, pp. 244–5, 253; Meyendorff, *Byzantium and the Rise of Russia*, pp. 170–1; Meyendorff, 'Alexis and Roman', 139, 144; Prokhorov, *Povest' o Mitiae*, p. 26 (1362); Obolensky, 'Byzantium and Russia', 256; Borisov, *Russkaia tserkov'*, p. 80.

87 Ibid., pp. 43–4.

the grand prince of Vladimir, and Andrei, the bishop of Tver', were intense. They reached a peak when Bishop Andrei brought charges of simony against Petr at a Church council, attended by a representative of the patriarch and the bishop of Rostov, in late 1310 or early 1311.[88] Petr's preference for Moscow was evident in his unofficial transfer of the metropolitan's seat to Moscow[89] and, most visibly, in his collaboration with Ivan Daniilovich in the construction of the church of the Dormition (1325), where he was buried.[90] When, soon after his death (December 1325), he was recognised as a saint, Moscow became the centre of his cult.[91] There is no record, however, as N. S. Borisov has pointed out, that Petr gave assistance to the Moscow princes between 1315 and 1325, the height of their conflict with the Tver' princes.[92]

Feognost's activities also contributed to Moscow's success at the expense of Tver'. When Prince Aleksandr fled to Pskov after the Tver' uprising in 1327, the metropolitan excommunicated the Pskov population for giving sanctuary to Aleksandr. His decision to take action against Aleksandr may have been motivated by Tver''s close ties to Lithuania, where his rival Metropolitan Theophilus claimed jurisdiction over the south-western Russian bishoprics.[93] His action nevertheless added the Church's approval to the khan's removal of the Tver' prince from the grand-princely throne. It thus provided another base of legitimacy to the transfer of that position to the Daniilovichi. By 1354, when Moscow formally became the seat of the metropolitanate, the city was rapidly becoming the ecclesiastical centre of north-eastern Russia.

Whereas these acts appeared to support the Moscow princes in their feud with the Tver' princes, others undertaken by the metropolitans were, if not politically neutral, at least not consistently biased in favour of north-eastern Russia or the Daniilovichi. Donald Ostrowski has suggested that Maksim abandoned Kiev to avoid the dangers associated with the conflict between Nogai and Tokhta in the late thirteenth century. The decision to settle in Vladimir was made in the midst of his flight from Kiev, not to heighten the prestige of any particular princely branch in north-eastern Rus'.[94] N. S. Borisov pointed out that Metropolitan Maksim unsuccessfully tried to discourage Prince Iurii

88 Ibid., p. 45; Pelenski, 'Muscovite Ecclesiastical Claims', 103; Fennell, *Emergence*, pp. 71–2; Presniakov, *Formation*, p. 114.
89 Pelenski, 'Muscovite Ecclesiastical Claims', 103–4; Fennell, *Emergence*, p. 192.
90 *PSRL*, vol. x, p. 190; Presniakov, *Formation*, p. 121; Fennell, *Emergence*, pp. 191–2.
91 Pelenski, 'Muscovite Ecclesiastical Claims', 107; Presniakov, *Formation*, pp. 121–2.
92 Borisov, 'Moskovskie kniaz'ia', 33–4.
93 Fennell, *Emergence*, p. 103; Borisov, *Russkaia tserkov'*, p. 67; Borisov, 'Moskovskie kniaz'ia', 36.
94 Donald Ostrowski, 'Why Did the Metropolitan Move?', 92–5. See also Meyendorff, *Byzantium and the Rise of Russia*, p. 46.

of Moscow from challenging the succession of Mikhail of Tver' in 1304.[95] He also argued that Metropolitans Petr, Feognost and Aleksei did not consistently lend their support to the Muscovite princes. Although the Moscow princes may have benefited politically from some of their actions, the metropolitans' motives were rooted in other concerns. Thus, when Feognost, who was just beginning his career in the Russian lands, excommunicated Prince Aleksandr Mikhailovich, he was acting out of obligation to the Mongol khan, not out of loyalty to Aleksandr's Muscovite rival. Similarly, at the end of his career, when he supported Aleksei to be his successor, he did so not because Aleksei, a boyar by origin, would loyally serve the Muscovite prince, but because he valued Aleksei's ties to both north-eastern and south-western Russia. Borisov similarly drew attention to actions undertaken by the metropolitans that did not serve the interests of the Muscovite princes. Feognost's absence at the consecration of churches identified with the transformation of Moscow into an ecclesiastical centre; his dissociation from the canonisation of Petr, who as a metropolitan and a saint was linked to Moscow; and his disapproval of Semen's third marriage, which was designed to improve Moscow's relations with Tver', are all examples of Feognost's political and ideological aloofness from the interests of the Muscovite princes.[96]

Although some actions undertaken by the metropolitans had the political effect of aiding the princes of Moscow in their quest for the throne of Vladimir, the Church and the Daniilovich branch of the dynasty did not share the same political agenda, nor were they consistent allies before 1359. This conclusion contrasts with the view articulated by A. E. Presniakov and adopted by a range of other scholars that emphasises close co-operation between the metropolitans and the Daniilovich princes.[97] Even after the metropolitans relocated the seat of the metropolitanate from Kiev to Vladimir and then to Moscow and even though they took part in Vladimir's domestic and dynastic politics, there were significant differences between dynastic and ecclesiastic outlooks and policies. In contrast to the princes of Vladimir who narrowed the range of their political attention to northern Russia, the metropolitans maintained a broader perspective. They continued to concern themselves with their entire ecclesiastic realm. Also, in contrast to the princes, who depended upon the

---

95 Borisov, *Russkaia tserkov'*, pp. 39–40.
96 Borisov, 'Moskovskie kniaz'ia', 38–40; Borisov, *Russkaia tserkov'*, pp. 6off.; S. B. Veselovskii, *Feodal'noe zemlevladenie v severo-vostochnoi Rusi* (Moscow and Leningrad: AN SSSR, 1947), pp. 333–4.
97 Presniakov, *Formation*, pp. 114–15, 121–2, 239–40; Pelenski, 'Muscovite Ecclesiastical Claims', 103–4; Fennell, *Emergence*, pp. 191–2; Martin, *Medieval Russia*, p. 390.

khans for support and were closely linked with Sarai politically and commercially, the metropolitans engaged in relations not only with Sarai but continued to look to the Patriarch in Constantinople for guidance and support. The metropolitans' primary objective was not rooted in Vladimir, nor did it revolve around the Daniilovichi; it was to maintain the integrity of their see, to prevent its division in conjunction with changing secular political boundaries.

North-eastern Russia in the mid-fourteenth century

By the middle of the fourteenth century the Daniilovichi had secured the position of grand prince of Vladimir. With the support of Khan Uzbek they were able to overcome the princes of Tver' and Ivan I Kalita had ascended the Vladimir throne. After both Ivan I and Uzbek died in 1341, Uzbek's successors, Tinibek (1341–2), Janibek (1342–57) and Berdibek (1357–9), placed Ivan's sons Semen (1341–53) and Ivan II (1353–9) on the throne of Vladimir. In the absence of firm support from the Church and other branches of the dynasty, which could have provided domestic sources of legitimacy for their rule, the princes of Moscow depended on the khans of the Golden Horde to hold their position.

Dynastic reluctance to accept the seniority of the Moscow princes persisted during and after the reign of Ivan I Kalita. Despite Uzbek's preference for the Daniilovichi, other Riurikid princes, clinging to dynastic tradition, withheld their support. Thus, when Aleksandr Mikhailovich appeared before Khan Uzbek in 1339, the princes of Beloozero and Iaroslavl' accompanied him. Aleksandr was executed during this visit.[98] The fate of the Beloozero prince is unknown. But the prince of Iaroslavl', Vasilii Davydovich, joined the princes of Tver' and Suzdal' in 1341 to oppose the appointment of Semen Ivanovich to the grand-princely throne.[99] In 1353, Novgorod nominated the same prince of Suzdal', Konstantin Vasil'evich, to become grand prince of Vladimir. Khan Janibek nevertheless granted the patent for the throne to Semen's brother, Ivan Ivanovich of Moscow.[100]

To neutralise his dynastic opponents Ivan I Kalita had arranged marriages for his daughters with members of their families. He followed the precedent of his brother Iurii who in 1320 had given his daughter in marriage to Konstantin Mikhailovich, the brother of his rivals Dmitrii and Aleksandr Mikhailovich of Tver'.[101] After Aleksandr fled from Tver' in 1327 until at least

98 PSRL, vol. x, pp. 208–11; PSRL, vol. III, pp. 349–50; PSRL, vol. xv, cols. 418–20; Fennell, Emergence, pp. 244–5.
99 Ibid., pp. 181 n. 2, 213, 225.
100 PSRL, vol. III, p. 363.
101 PSRL, vol. xv, cols. 413–14.

1339, Konstantin ruled his principality in harmony with his wife's uncle, Grand Prince Ivan I Kalita.[102] Ivan I, similarly, gave one daughter in marriage to Prince Konstantin Vasil'evich of Rostov (1328). After the demonstration of support for Aleksandr of Tver' by the princes of Iaroslavl' and Beloozero in 1339, Ivan I arranged for two other daughters to marry the sons of the offending princes. By becoming their father-in-law, Ivan I gained personal seniority over members of those dynastic lines that were most resistant to accepting him as the senior member of the dynasty.[103] In 1347, his son Semen attempted to use the same technique to increase his influence in Tver', which after the death of Prince Konstantin Mikhailovich in 1346 was experiencing inter-princely feuds and civil strife. But Metropolitan Feognost refused to sanction the grand prince's third marriage. Semen's marriage to the daughter of the late Prince Aleksandr Mikhailovich thus took place under the shadow of the Church's disapproval.[104]

Semen and Ivan II were also less successful in the pursuit of the policy of territorial aggrandisement that their grandfather Daniil, their uncle Iurii and their father Ivan had fashioned to gain and consolidate their power in Vladimir. The extension of the Muscovite princes' authority over patrimonial principalities and Novgorod had enriched the assets available to them. They had a broader tax base as well as a larger pool from which to attract military retainers and courtiers.[105] Nevertheless, by the reign of Ivan II, expansion was checked. The Daniilovichi appeared to have a firm hold on the position of grand prince of Vladimir. Within their own patrimonial possessions, they kept to a minimum the internal subdivisions that characterised Rostov and in the 1340s also plagued Tver'. But, the authority of the grand prince of Vladimir was sharply delimited in the mid-fourteenth century. Neither his marriage nor his position of grand prince of Vladimir gave Semen authority over Tver'. Suzdal', which with the approval of Khans Uzbek and Janibek merged with Nizhnii Novgorod to form another grand principality in 1341, similarly continued to function independently and challenge the primacy of the Daniilovich princes of Vladimir. Riazan', which had previously displayed deference to its northern neighbour, engaged Moscow in a border dispute by challenging Moscow's control over the stretch of the Oka River between Kolomna and Serpukhov, which Moscow had incorporated early in the fourteenth century. The princes

---

102 *PSRL*, vol. xv, col. 417; Fennell, *Emergence*, p. 226.
103 Kopanev, 'O kupliakh', 27, 30, 34; Fennell, *Emergence*, pp. 177, 181, 245; Cherepnin, *Obrazovanie*, p. 509.
104 *PSRL*, vol. x, pp. 217–18; Borisov, *Russkaia tserkov'*, p. 67; Fennell, *Emergence*, pp. 225–33.
105 Cf. Fennell, *Emergence*, p. 193.

of Rostov and Iaroslavl' were also trying to remove themselves from Semen's authority.[106]

Semen and Ivan II were also losing the loyalty of Novgorod. The dispute that arose in 1339 between Novgorod and Ivan I Kalita was resolved only after Ivan's death by his son Semen, who threatened Novgorod by sending an army to its borders and obliged it to make a special payment to Moscow. Semen himself only arrived in Novgorod to claim its throne in 1346. Whereas Semen and Ivan II demanded high payments from Novgorod, they did not fulfil their obligations to defend Novgorod to the city's satisfaction. Just as Ivan I had failed to defend Novgorod from Swedish attacks in 1337–8, so Semen provided little effective aid a decade later when Lithuania and Sweden attacked Novgorodian territories in 1346 and 1348, respectively. Although he dispatched his brother to fight the Swedes, who had seized the fortress at Orekhov, which Prince Iurii Daniilovich had erected in 1323, Ivan Ivanovich left Novgorod without embarking on the intended campaign. The Novgorodians recovered Orekhov in February 1349 without assistance from Moscow and only after a six-month siege. They similarly launched their counter-offensive against the Swedish post at Vyborg, which led to a cessation of hostilities between Novgorod and Sweden, without support from the grand prince of Vladimir. Indeed, Iurii Daniilovich had been the last prince to actually lead Novgorod's armies.[107] As a result Novgorod not only objected to the succession of Ivan II to the grand princely throne, but delayed its own acceptance of him as its prince, then basically conducted its affairs without reference to him.[108]

* * * * *

By the time Ivan II died in 1359, the two institutions that had defined Kievan Rus', the Riurikid dynasty and the Orthodox Church, continued to shape north-eastern Russia. But under the suzerainty of the Golden Horde the dynasty in particular had changed significantly. The Daniilovichi, the Moscow branch of the dynasty, illegitimate by traditional standards, held the throne of the grand principality of Vladimir. Their political position was dependent upon the good will and the power of the khans of the Golden Horde. The grand princes accordingly curtailed relations with the south-western Russian principalities, which entered the political sphere of Lithuania, and geared their policies to accommodate the Golden Horde. They strove to dominate tribute

106 Borisov, *Russkaia tserkov'*, p. 65; Cherepnin, *Obrazovanie*, pp. 537–8; Presniakov, *Formation*, pp. 194–5, 238; Fennell, *Emergence*, pp. 50, 65–6, 175–6, 220–1; Vernadsky, *Mongols*, p. 226.
107 *PSRL*, vol. III, pp. 358–61; Presniakov, *Formation*, pp. 236–7; Cherepnin, *Obrazovanie*, pp. 543–4; Fennell, *Emergence*, pp. 154–5, 157, 247–8, 261–2, 265–9; Bernadskii, *Novgorod*, pp. 22, 33–4.
108 *PSRL*, vol. III, p. 99; Bernadskii, *Novgorod*, p. 24; Martin, *Medieval Russia*, pp. 184–6.

collection and control trade as well as to increase the size and strength of their own court and military retinue. The authority of the Daniilovichi over north-eastern Russia was nevertheless circumscribed. They lacked control over the grand principalities of Tver' and Suzdal'-Nizhnii Novgorod as well as Riazan', their neighbour to the south. In addition, Lithuania was demonstrating influence over Novgorod and north-eastern principalities that had previously accepted the leadership of the grand prince of Vladimir.

The Church similarly retained its authority. But unlike the princes of Moscow, the metropolitans attempted to sustain the ecclesiastic unity of all sectors of Kievan Rus'. They repeatedly sought to suppress efforts undertaken by Galicia and Lithuania to divide the metropolitanate of Kiev and all Rus'. Rather than cut ties with south-western Russia, the metropolitans continued to travel to those areas as well as to Constantinople and Sarai. They maintained a broad focus that encompassed the entire Orthodox population inherited from Kievan Rus'.

In 1359, Khan Berdibek was overthrown and the Golden Horde entered a twenty-year period of political turbulence. The base of support upon which Daniilovich authority in north-eastern Russia rested was, correspondingly, destabilised. The heir of Ivan II, his young son Dmitrii, could turn neither to other princes, who had not fully accepted the legitimacy of the Daniilovichi, nor to Metropolitan Aleksei, whose preoccupation with the division of his see had drawn him away from Moscow, to compensate for the weakening of support provided by the Golden Horde. With the Golden Horde in disarray and without reliable support from domestic sources, the dynasty and the Church, the future of Dmitrii Ivanovich and the continued pre-eminence of the House of Moscow in both Vladimir and north-eastern Russia were in jeopardy.

7

The emergence of Moscow (1359–1462)

JANET MARTIN

During the century following the Mongol invasion and subjugation of the Russian lands to the Golden Horde the princes of Moscow, the Daniilovichi, gained prominence in north-eastern Russia. By winning the favour of the khans of the Golden Horde they were able to break dynastic traditions of seniority and succession and become the grand princes of Vladimir. But the Daniilovich princes lacked the full support of other branches of the dynasty in north-eastern Russia, whose members recalled traditional norms of legitimacy, and of the Church, whose hierarchs were preoccupied with securing the unity of the metropolitanate of Kiev and all Rus'. They were, therefore, dependent upon the continuing goodwill of the Golden Horde khans to maintain their position. But in 1359, Khan Berdibek (r. 1357–9) was overthrown and the Golden Horde entered a twenty-year period of civil war. The foundation upon which Daniilovich authority rested was destabilised.

The Daniilovich princes did not, however, lose their grip on the throne of Vladimir. Nor, despite the decline of the Golden Horde and sharp clashes with it, did they renounce their allegiance to the khan or lead north-eastern Russia to independence from Tatar hegemony. On the contrary, the northern Russian princes, including the Daniilovichi, continued, albeit with greater reluctance and less frequency, to travel to the horde to receive their patents for office and to pay tribute to the khan.[1] It was not north-eastern Russia, led by the princes of Moscow, that was emerging as the state prepared to replace the disintegrating horde as the dominant polity in Eastern Europe. Lithuania was a stronger, more dynamic state that assumed that role and exercised influence over western and northern Russia. Within their domain, however, the Daniilovichi came to depend less on the khans

---

1 Gustave Alef, 'The Origins of Muscovite Autocracy. The Age of Ivan III', *FOG* 39 (1986): 40; Donald Ostrowski, 'Troop Mobilization by the Muscovite Grand Princes (1313–1533)', in Eric Lohr and Marshall Poe (eds.), *The Military and Society in Russia, 1450–1917* (Leiden, Boston and Köln: Brill, 2002), pp. 25, 34, 38.

and to develop domestic sources of support, rooted in their own court, in their relationships with former dynastic rivals and in the Church. While the Golden Horde gradually fragmented, Dmitrii Ivanovich, who ruled to 1389, and his successors Vasilii I Dmitr'evich (1389–1425) and Vasilii II Vasil'evich (1425–62) nurtured and developed these foundational elements to establish their legitimacy as rulers of a state of Muscovy and to monopolise for their direct descendants the position of prince of its expanding territorial possessions.

The Daniilovichi and the Golden Horde

The political disorder within the horde was preceded and accompanied by mounting social and economic upheavals. One factor contributing to the disturbances was the Black Plague. In 1346–7, it had appeared in the Tatar capital Sarai as well as in Astrakhan' and port cities on the Black Sea coast. In 1364, the plague attacked Sarai a second time, and a decade later the horde was visited yet again.[2]

In addition, the commercial network that economically sustained the Mongol Empire was fraying. The Ottoman Turk capture of Gallipoli and expansion into the Balkans disturbed sea traffic into and out of the Black Sea. In the east the Yuan dynasty in China collapsed (1368). The Ming rulers who displaced the Mongols were less interested in promoting the intercontinental trade that had transported goods along the Silk Road and had been a major commercial base for the entire empire. As a result of disruptions at both ends of the trade route, the commercial activities of the Golden Horde, which controlled the northern branch of its western segment, and the revenues derived from them declined.[3]

The demographic and economic disturbances experienced by the horde contributed to mounting political tensions that erupted after Khan Berdibek was killed. During the next two decades the Sarai throne changed hands dozens of times. Some Tatar clans, furthermore, withdrew their support from

---

2 Lawrence N. Langer, 'The Black Death in Russia. Its Effects upon Urban Labor', *RH* 2 (1975): 55–6; Gustave Alef, 'The Crisis of the Muscovite Aristocracy: A Factor in the Growth of Monarchical Power', *FOG* 15 (1970); reprinted in his *Rulers and Nobles in Fifteenth-Century Muscovy* (London: Variorum Reprints, 1983), p. 36; *PSRL*, vol. x (St. Petersburg: Arkheograficheskaia kommissiia, 1885; reprinted Moscow: Nauka, 1965), p. 217; *PSRL*, vol. xi (St Petersburg: Arkheograficheskaia kommissiia, 1897; reprinted Moscow: Nauka, 1965), p. 21.

3 David Morgan, *The Mongols* (Oxford and New York: Blackwell, 1986), pp. 134–5, 204; George Vernadsky, *The Mongols and Russia (A History of Russia*, vol. iii) (New Haven: Yale University Press and London: Oxford University Press, 1953), pp. 91–2, 205, 246, 268.

the Sarai khan and recognised local leaders instead. In the most extreme cases as many as seven khans simultaneously ruled different sections of the Golden Horde. The situation was complicated as well by the appearance of powerful non-Chingisid clan leaders and notables, who placed their Chingisid protégés on the throne. The most prominent of them was Mamai, who controlled the western portion of the Golden Horde. Into this turmoil contenders from the eastern half of Juchi's ulus, the most important of whom was Tokhtamysh, entered the contest for dominance over the Golden Horde.[4]

The crisis began to subside when Tokhtamysh seized control of Sarai in 1378. In 1381, he defeated Mamai and brought temporary stability to the Golden Horde. A decade later, however, Tokhtamysh was defeated by his former patron, Timur (Tamerlane), a non-Chingisid conqueror who was fashioning his own empire around his capital Samarkand in Central Asia. Tokhtamysh lost control over the eastern portion of Juchi's ulus, but retained his position at Sarai until 1395–6, when Timur launched a campaign during which he attacked not only Sarai, but also Astrakhan' and Azak (Tana) at the mouth of the Don River. Timur thus inflicted a destructive blow on the major towns and commercial centres of the Golden Horde.[5]

While Tokhtamysh fled to Lithuania, Edigei, another non-Chingisid, assumed the dominant role in the Golden Horde. Ruling through Khan Timur Kutlugh, he defeated Tokhtamysh, who was supported by the Lithuanian Prince Vitovt, in 1399. Edigei remained in power until 1411, when his son-in-law drove him from Sarai. Although he, like Tokhtamysh, had attempted to reunite the Golden Horde, its social and economic foundations had been seriously weakened. During the second quarter of the fifteenth century the Golden Horde fragmented into the Crimean khanate, the khanate of Kazan' and the Great Horde.

The political turmoil in the horde affected political conditions in north-eastern Russia. In 1359, the same year Berdibek was removed, Grand Prince Ivan II died; his heir was his nine-year old son, Dmitrii, later known as Dmitrii Donskoi. Following Berdibek's death, the Russian princes travelled to Sarai

4 PSRL, vol. xv: Rogozhskii letopisets; Tverskoi sbornik (Moscow: Iazyki russkoi kul'tury, 2000), cols. 68–9, 70–1; Vernadsky, Mongols, pp. 204, 245–6; L. V. Cherepnin, Obrazovanie russkogo tsentralizovannogo gosudarstva v XIV–XV vekakh (Moscow: Sotsial'no-ekonomicheskaia literatura, 1960), p. 551; A. N. Nasonov, Mongoly i Rus' (Moscow and Leningrad: AN SSSR, 1940; reprinted The Hague and Paris: Mouton, 1969), pp. 117–24; L. N. Gumilev, Drevniaia Rus' i velikaia step' (Moscow: Mysl', 1989), pp. 617–18.
5 PSRL, vol. xi, pp. 127, 157, 158–9; Vernadsky, Mongols, pp. 269, 270, 271–3, 274–7; Janet Martin, Treasure of the Land of Darkness: The Fur Trade and its Significance for Medieval Russia (Cambridge: Cambridge University Press, 1986), p. 33; Robert O. Crummey, The Formation of Muscovy 1304–1613 (London and New York: Longman, 1987), p. 64.

to receive new patents for their offices. But while they were making their journey, Berdibek's successor was also replaced. The new khan, Navruz, issued the patent for the Vladimir throne not to Dmitrii Ivanovich, but to Dmitrii Konstantinovich, the prince of Suzdal' and Nizhnii Novgorod (1360).[6] After Navruz too was overthrown and replaced by Kudyr', the Russian princes returned again for their patents. Civil strife was so intense, however, that not only was Kudyr' killed, but the princes themselves were subjected to physical abuse and robbed of their goods.[7]

In 1362, the Muscovite prince Dmitrii Ivanovich finally received a patent for the grand principality of Vladimir from one of the two khans then claiming authority over the Golden Horde.[8] The figure behind the khan and Dmitrii's patron was Mamai. A key factor that influenced the extension of Mamai's favour to Dmitrii was his ability to deliver tribute payments, which were particularly critical for Mamai as he was attempting to gain and maintain a position of dominance within the Golden Horde. As in earlier periods, commercial activity was the means by which northern Russia acquired silver. Security along the transportation routes was essential for the flow of goods that were traded to merchants of the Hanseatic League and the Order of the Teutonic Knights for silver and other European goods and for delivery of goods and tribute to the horde. But the discord within the horde had disrupted the trade routes leading southward from the Russian lands. As early as 1360, bandits or pirates, known as *ushkuinniki*, were raiding key centres along the Volga River. After an attack on Nizhnii Novgorod, Dmitrii Ivanovich placed pressure on Novgorod, the home base of the bandits, to control them.[9]

Dmitrii held Novgorod responsible not only for disturbances created by the pirates, but also for reduced imports derived from its trade with the Hansa and the Teutonic Order. By 1367, commercial relations were deteriorating. Novgorod became involved in hostilities against the Order, which was encroaching upon the border of Pskov. In 1369, the Hansa imposed duties on Novgorod's silver imports. In 1373, it banned the export of silver to Novgorod for two years. By 1375, when both Novgorodian and German merchants were being detained and their goods were confiscated, commercial relations had

6 *PSRL*, vol. x, p. 231; *PSRL*, vol. xv, cols. 68–9; Cherepnin, *Obrazovanie*, p. 552; Nasonov, *Mongoly i Rus'*, p. 121; N. S. Borisov, *Russkaia tserkov' v politicheskoi bor'be XIV–XV vekov* (Moscow: Moskovskii universitet, 1986), p. 81; Ostrowski, 'Troop Mobilization', p. 28.
7 *PSRL*, vol. xv, col. 71; Cherepnin, *Obrazovanie*, p. 552; Nasonov, *Mongoly i Rus'*, pp. 118–20, 122.
8 *PSRL*, vol. xi, p. 2; *PSRL*, vol. xv, cols. 72, 74.
9 *PSRL*, vol. xv, col. 69; Janet Martin, 'Les uškujniki de Novgorod: Marchands ou Pirates?', *Cahiers du monde russe et soviétique* 16 (1975), 5–18; Cherepnin, *Obrazovanie*, p. 553.

deteriorated significantly. During this period Mamai, anxious to find an agent who could gather and deliver tribute to him, transferred the patent for grand prince of Vladimir from Dmitrii to Prince Mikhail Aleksandrovich of Tver' (1370), then returned it to Dmitrii (1371). When Dmitrii ceased making tribute payments after 1373, Mamai again issued the patent to Mikhail (1375).[10]

Dmitrii, in defiance of Mamai, refused to cede his throne and the city of Vladimir to Mikhail. Mamai, whose horde had been depleted by a bout with the Black Plague, could not enforce his order. Dmitrii militarily defeated Mikhail and kept his position. In the aftermath of this challenge he joined Prince Dmitrii Konstantinovich of Suzdal'-Nizhnii Novgorod to restore order along the Volga River (1377). He did not resume tribute payments, however, and in 1378, his forces clashed with a band subject to Mamai.[11] In 1378, Tokhtamysh was taking control of Sarai. Mamai's position as the unofficial, yet most powerful leader of the Golden Horde was seriously challenged.

Under these circumstances the tribute from northern Russia was important not only as a symbol of his authority, but as revenue he could use to raise forces against his rival. Arranging for support from Lithuania and Riazan', Mamai demanded the tribute from Dmitrii. When it was not forthcoming, he staged a campaign against Dmitrii. But the grand prince of Vladimir raised an army with contingents from Rostov, Iaroslavl', Beloozero, Ustiug, Kolomna, Kostroma, Pereiaslavl' and other principalities across northern Russia. When the two armies engaged at the Battle of Kulikovo (1380), Dmitrii, who there earned the epithet Donskoi, defeated Mamai. The next year the Tatar leader engaged Tokhtamysh, and was again defeated.[12]

Dmitrii Donskoi's relationship with the Golden Horde was complicated. He recognised the authority of the horde and the legitimacy inherent in a patent from the khan. Yet in the context of the internal discord within the horde,

---

10 *PSRL*, vol. XI, pp. 15–16; *PSRL*, vol. XV, col. 110; A. E. Presniakov, *The Formation of the Great Russian State. A Study of Russian History in the Thirteenth to Fifteenth Centuries*, trans. A. E. Moorhouse (Chicago: Quadrangle Books, 1970), pp. 249, 265; A. L. Khoroshkevich, *Torgovlia Velikogo Novgoroda s pribaltikoi i zapadnoi Evropoi v XIV–XV vekakh* (Moscow: AN SSSR, 1963), pp. 109, 280; A. L. Khoroshkevich, 'Iz istorii ganzeiskoi torgovli (Vvoz v Novgorod blagorodnykh metallov v XIV–XV vv.)', in *Srednie veka. Sbornik*, no. 20 (Moscow: AN SSSR, 1961), p. 108; E. A. Rybina, *Torgovlia srednevekovogo Novgoroda. Istoriko-arkheologicheskie ocherki* (Velikii Novgorod: Novgorodskii gosudarstvennyi universitet, 2001), pp. 135–9.

11 *PSRL*, vol. XI, p. 25; Vernadsky, *Mongols*, p. 258; Charles Halperin, *The Tatar Yoke* (Columbus, Oh.: Slavica, 1986), p. 95; Crummey, *Formation of Muscovy*, p. 52.

12 *PSRL*, vol. XI, pp. 52, 54; Halperin, *Tatar Yoke*, pp. 99–101, 104; Vernadsky, *Mongols*, p. 263; Crummey, *Formation of Muscovy*, pp. 53, 57; Donald Ostrowski, *Muscovy and the Mongols. Cross-Cultural Influences on the Steppe Frontier, 1304–1589* (Cambridge: Cambridge University Press, 1998), pp. 155–6; V. A. Kuchkin, 'Dmitrii Donskoi', *VI*, 1995, nos. 5–6: 75–6.

he depended upon Mamai and the khan Mamai placed in power. But Dmitrii also defied Mamai. He did not accept Mamai's decisions to transfer the patent for Vladimir to Mikhail Aleksandrovich of Tver' and, particularly, when the commercial source of silver had diminished, he did not make the required and promised tribute payments to him. Ultimately, he fought against Mamai and defeated him. But when Tokhtamysh seized Sarai and also defeated Mamai, Dmitrii Donskoi, like the other north-eastern Russian princes, immediately acknowledged his suzerainty as khan of the Golden Horde by sending their messengers and costly gifts. They did not, however, attend him personally. Tokhtamysh responded with a military campaign. In contrast to the situation in 1380, Dmitrii was unable to raise an army to oppose Tokhtamysh. Instead, he fled from Moscow, which Tokhtamysh besieged and sacked. Dmitrii, who remained the grand prince of Vladimir, sent his son Vasilii to Tokhtamysh with tribute payments; Vasilii remained as a hostage at Tokhtamysh's court.[13]

Dmitrii's actions and defeat of Mamai did not change the basic relationship between north-eastern Russia and the Golden Horde. Dmitrii and his successors continued to rely on the khan for a patent that legitimised their right to hold the grand-princely throne of Vladimir. They also continued to pay tribute to the khan. Thus, the coins struck by Dmitrii after 1382 were marked by the words 'Grand Prince Dmitrii Ivanovich' on one side, but the other side bore the inscription 'Sultan Tokhtamysh: Long may he live!' On his coins Vasilii I proclaimed himself to be 'grand prince of all Rus''. But until 1399, when Tokhtamysh and his ally Vitovt of Lithuania were defeated by Edigei at the Battle of Vorskla, he repeated the phrase 'Sultan Tokhtamysh: Long may he live' or variations of it on the reverse side. Symbols honouring the Mongols reappeared on Vasilii's coins after 1408.[14]

The nature of the relationship between the Muscovite princes and the Golden Horde was nevertheless changing. Edigei, the non-Chingisid who became the dominant figure in the horde after Timur deposed Tokhtamysh, once again mounted a campaign against north-eastern Russia (1408). He found it necessary to use force to impress north-eastern Russia with his power and convince Vasilii I to show appropriate deference to his suzerain. Vasilii,

---

13 Crummey, *Formation of Muscovy*, pp. 57–8; Halperin, *Tatar Yoke*, pp. 99–100, 116–17; Cherepnin, *Obrazovanie*, p. 649; Ostrowski, *Muscovy and the Mongols*, p. 156; Presniakov, *Formation*, p. 270; Janet Martin, *Medieval Russia 980–1584* (Cambridge: Cambridge University Press, 1995), pp. 214, 384–5.

14 Thomas Noonan, 'Forging a National Identity: Monetary Politics during the Reign of Vasilii I (1389–1425)', in A. M. Kleimola and G. D. Lenhoff (eds.), *Culture and Identity in Muscovy, 1359–1584* (Moscow: ITZ-Garant, 1997), pp. 495, 501–3; *PSRL*, vol. xi, pp. 172–4.

it was alleged, had failed to appear personally before him, had withheld tribute and had given refuge to his rivals and enemies, the fugitive sons of Tokhtamysh.[15]

Even after the Golden Horde began to disintegrate during the second decade of the fifteenth century, the princes of northern Russia recognised the authority of the khan. In 1430, when Prince Iurii Dmitr'evich challenged his nephew Grand Prince Vasilii II Vasil'evich for the throne of Vladimir and Dmitrov, the two princes turned to Ulu-Muhammed. The khan confirmed the appointment of Vasilii II as grand prince. His decision did not, however, have sufficient authority to resolve the dispute. Vasilii II fought a war against his uncle and cousins that lasted almost a quarter of a century before he secured his position.[16] Vasilii II was the last Daniilovich prince to present himself before a Tatar khan to receive a patent for this throne and the first to name his own successor and bequeath his throne to him without prior approval of the khan.[17]

Several years after Ulu-Muhammed issued the Vladimir throne to Vasilii II, he led his horde northward from the region of the Crimean peninsula, where he had been located.[18] The Tatars encountered a Russian army, led by Vasilii's cousins, near Belev on the Russian–Lithuanian border in 1437. The Tatar horde continued to migrate eastward down the Oka River. After clashing several times with Russian forces, they engaged Vasilii II, who was leading a small force, at the Battle of Suzdal' (1445). Vasilii II was wounded and captured. In return for his promise to pay a ransom of 200,000 roubles, according to one account, and make increased tribute payments, Ulu-Muhammed released him. The grand prince returned to Moscow in November 1445.[19] Ulu-Muhammed's horde continued its migration, settling on the mid-Volga River to found the khanate of Kazan' (1445).

Despite the disintegration of the Golden Horde and the weakened condition of Ulu-Muhammed's horde, Grand Prince Vasilii II continued to acknowledge

15 *PSRL*, vol. XI, pp. 205–6; Ostrowski, 'Troop Mobilization', p. 38; A. A. Gorskii, *Moskva i Orda* (Moscow: Nauka, 2000), pp. 127–33; Charles Halperin, 'The Russian Land and the Russian Tsar: The Emergence of Muscovite Ideology, 1380–1408', *FOG* 23 (1976): 55–6; Crummey, *Formation of Muscovy*, p. 65; Vernadsky, *Mongols*, pp. 286–7; Nasonov, *Mongoly i Rus'*, p. 144.
16 A. A. Zimin, *Vitiaz' na rasput'e. Feodal'naia voina v Rossii XV v.* (Moscow: Mysl', 1991), pp. 43, 45–7.
17 Alef, 'Origins', 40.
18 Vernadsky, *Mongols*, p. 293; Gustave Alef, 'The Battle of Suzdal' in 1445. An Episode in the Muscovite War of Succession', *FOG* 25 (1978); reprinted in Gustave Alef, *Rulers and Nobles in Fifteenth-Century Muscovy* (London: Variorum Reprints, 1983), p. 12.
19 *PSRL*, vol. XII (St. Petersburg: Arkheograficheskaia kommissiia, 1901; reprinted Moscow: Nauka, 1965), pp. 63–5; *PSRL*, vol. III: *Novgorodskaia pervaia letopis'* (Moscow: Iazyki russkoi kul'tury, 2000), p. 426; Alef, 'The Battle of Suzdal', 14–15, 17–19; Ostrowski, 'Troop Mobilization', p. 22; Cherepnin, *Obrazovanie*, p. 787.

the suzerainty of the Tatar khan. But in 1447, two of Ulu-Muhammed's sons, Kasim and Iakub, fled from their brother, who had murdered and succeeded Ulu-Muhammed. They presented themselves to Vasilii II and entered his service. For his services Kasim was granted territory on the Oka River that became known as the khanate of Kasimov, a dependency of the state of Muscovy.[20] Kasim and his brother were only the latest in a series of individual Tatar notables who from the 1330s had entered the service of the Daniilovich princes.[21] The appearance of these Tatars in the service of the princes of Moscow represents the beginning of a shift in the balance of perceived and, possibly, real power between the remnants of the Golden Horde and emerging state of Muscovy.

Although they did not renounce the suzerainty of the Tatar khans or permanently cease paying tribute, the Daniilovich princes gradually changed the nature of their relationship with their overlords whose own domain was disintegrating. If measured by the military victories of Tokhtamysh, Edigei and Ulu-Muhammed at the Battle of Suzdal', the balance of power favoured the Mongol khans. But measured by the tendency of the renegade Tatar notables to seek refuge with the prince of Moscow and to enter his service and by the ability of the prince of Moscow, by the end of the reign of Vasilii II, to ignore rituals of paying homage to the khans and display symbols of his own sovereignty, the balance was shifting in favour of the emerging state of Muscovy.

The Daniilovichi and the dynasty

When Grand Prince Ivan II died in 1359, he was not immediately succeeded by his son Dmitrii. Khan Navruz issued the patent for the grand principality of Vladimir to Prince Dmitrii Konstantinovich of Suzdal' and Nizhnii Novgorod (1360). Despite the marriages that had been arranged by Ivan I Kalita to secure their families' loyalty, Prince Konstantin Vasil'evich of Rostov, an uncle of Dmitrii Ivanovich, and Prince Ivan Fedorovich of Beloozero, a cousin of the Moscow prince, supported Dmitrii Konstantinovich, as did Dmitrii Borisovich of Dmitrov.[22]

When Dmitrii Ivanovich did receive a patent for the grand principality, however, forces loyal to him, including those of his brother Ivan (d. 1364) and

20 Janet Martin, 'Muscovite Frontier Policy: The Case of the Khanate of Kasimov', *RH* 19 (1992): 169–70, 174; Vernadsky, *Mongols*, p. 331.
21 Ostrowski, 'Troop Mobilization', pp. 37–9; Ostrowski, *Muscovy and the Mongols*, p. 54.
22 Martin, *Medieval Russia*, pp. 207–8.

his cousin Vladimir Andreevich, drove his rival from Vladimir (1362–3) and prevented him from recovering the town.[23] Dmitrii Ivanovich then arranged for his rival's supporters to be removed from their thrones. In 1363, Dmitrii Ivanovich expelled the princes of Starodub and Galich from their lands. The next year he forced the transfer of Prince Konstantin Vasil'evich from Rostov to Ustiug. Konstantin's nephew, an ally of Dmitrii Ivanovich, replaced him in Rostov.[24] In 1364, the two Dmitriis reconciled. Their alliance was sealed in 1366 with the marriage of Dmitrii Ivanovich to the daughter of Dmitrii Konstantinovich. Dmitrii Konstantinovich did not become a subordinate of the young grand prince of Vladimir, but having ceded the grand principality of Vladimir, he frequently supported Dmitrii Ivanovich and gave him critical military assistance.[25]

By 1367, Dmitrii Ivanovich had cemented his alliance with the prince of Suzdal', demoted the latter's princely supporters, and asserted his authority over them. He had also been accepted as prince of Novgorod. The strength of his political position was paralleled by stone fortifications he began to construct around Moscow.[26] Grand Prince Dmitrii then turned against another potential challenger, Prince Mikhail Aleksandrovich of Tver'. The hostilities began just after an internecine conflict between two branches of the Tver' dynasty was resolved in favour of Mikhail Aleksandrovich. Dmitrii intervened to reverse that outcome and place Mikhail's rival on the Tver' throne. The conflict that began in 1367 lasted until 1375, when Dmitrii emphatically defeated Mikhail. Dmitrii was not able to unseat Mikhail from the Tver' throne. But neither were Mikhail and his powerful ally Ol'gerd of Lithuania able to defeat Dmitrii. Despite a three-day siege of Moscow (1368), they were unable to penetrate the stone walls protecting the city. Dmitrii's campaign into Tver' territory in 1370 prompted Mikhail to appeal to Mamai, who transferred the patent for Vladimir to the Tver' prince that year.[27] Dmitrii, however, won back the

---

23 *PSRL*, vol. x, pp. 233–4; *PSRL*, vol. xi, p. 2; Cherepnin, *Obrazovanie*, p. 554; Nasonov, *Mongoly i Rus'*, pp. 120, 124; Ostrowski, 'Troop Mobilization', p. 28; Vernadsky, *Mongols*, p. 252.

24 *PSRL*, vol. xi, p. 2; Wladimir Vodoff, 'A propos des "achats" (kupli) d'Ivan Ier de Moscou', *Journal des Savants* (1974): 115; Martin, *Treasure*, p. 132; John Fennell, *The Emergence of Moscow 1304–1359* (Berkeley and Los Angeles: University of California Press, 1968), pp. 182–3.

25 *PSRL*, vol. xi, p. 7; Cherepnin, *Obrazovanie*, pp. 554–5; Nasonov, *Mongoly i Rus'*, pp. 120, 124–5; Vodoff, 'Achats', 115; A. I. Kopanev, 'O "kupliakh" Ivana Kality', *IZ* 20 (1946), 25; Ostrowski, 'Troop mobilization', pp. 28–30.

26 Lawrence N. Langer, 'The Medieval Russian Town', in Michael Hamm (ed.), *The City in Russian History* (Lexington: University of Kentucky Press, 1976), p. 26; Ostrowski, *Muscovy and the Mongols*, p. 129; David B. Miller, 'Monumental Building as an Indicator of Economic Trends in Northern Rus' in the Late Kievan and Mongol Periods, 1138–1462', *American Historical Review* 94 (1989): 370, 377, 379.

27 *PSRL*, vol. xi, p. 14; Kuchkin, 'Dmitrii Donskoi', 68; Presniakov, *Formation*, pp. 247–9; Borisov, *Russkaia tserkov'*, pp. 84–5; Crummey, *Formation of Muscovy*, p. 46.

patent from Mamai, retained the support of the north-eastern Russian princes and Novgorod, and defeated Mikhail (1372).[28] Dmitrii and Mikhail reached an accord that lasted only until 1375, when Mikhail once again obtained a patent for the Vladimir throne. But Dmitrii with the military support of his former rival, the prince of Suzdal', as well as numerous other north-eastern Russian princes and Novgorod, inflicted a decisive defeat on Mikhail.[29] In the subsequent peace treaty the two grand princes formally had equal status. But Mikhail acknowledged Dmitrii's seniority, renounced his claim to the throne of Novgorod, and agreed to refrain from conducting independent relations with Lithuania and the Golden Horde.[30]

Despite his youth and the turmoil within the horde that deprived him of the firm support from a powerful Mongol khan, Dmitrii Ivanovich did not lose the position of grand prince of Vladimir. On the contrary, he overcame challenges from the princes of Suzdal' and Tver', the last two rivals for the Vladimir throne. After the 1370s, no other branch of the dynasty disputed the Moscow princes' claim to the throne of Vladimir. By the end of his reign, Dmitrii Ivanovich was virtually able to name his own heir.

Dmitrii's strength rested on his ability to marshal the military support necessary to overcome his rivals. In the absence of assistance from the Mongol khan, whose forces had previously been used to enforce decisions regarding succession, Dmitrii relied even more heavily than his predecessors had on the military units supplied by his relatives and princely allies. The extension of his authority over some north-eastern Russian princes and conclusion of alliances with others thus had practical as well as symbolic significance. With their aid Dmitrii gained the capacity to raise substantial armies and to pursue even further and more successfully than his father Ivan and uncle Semen his grandfather's policy of extending the authority of the prince of Moscow. By 1360, Kostroma was attached to the Muscovite territories, as was Galich.[31] By establishing Andrei Fedorovich as prince of Rostov in 1364, Grand Prince Dmitrii gained not only his loyalty but also Rostov's military services, which in 1360 had been used to support Prince Dmitrii Konstantinovich.[32]

---

28 *PSRL*, vol. XI, pp. 16, 19; Presniakov, *Formation*, pp. 249–50.
29 *PSRL*, vol. XI, p. 22; Presniakov, *Formation*, pp. 250–1.
30 *Dukhovnye i dogovornye gramoty velikikh i udel'nykh kniazei XIV–XVI vv.*, ed. L.V. Cherepnin (Moscow and Leningrad: AN SSSR, 1950), no. 9, pp. 25–8; Presniakov, *Formation*, pp. 251–2; Wladimir Vodoff, 'La Place du grand-prince de Tver' dans les structures politiques russes de la fin du XIVe et du XVe siècle', *FOG* 27 (1980): 33.
31 Ostrowski, 'Troop Mobilization', p. 30; Fennell, *Emergence*, pp. 67, 112.
32 Martin, *Treasure*, pp. 132, 234 n. 80.

As a result, when Dmitrii confronted Mikhail of Tver' in 1375, he was able to assemble an army consisting of forces of 'all the Russian princes', including the princes of Suzdal', Rostov, Iaroslavl', Beloozero and Starodub.[33] Similarly in 1380, when he faced Mamai at the Battle of Kulikovo, Dmitrii's army was composed of forces collected from Beloozero, Iaroslavl', Rostov, Ustiug, Kostroma, Kolomna, Pereiaslavl' and other principalities as well.[34]

The efforts of Dmitrii's son and successor, Vasilii I, to continue his father's policies were tempered by the expansionist drive of his father-in-law, Vitovt of Lithuania. Vasilii did nothing to prevent Vitovt from seizing the western Russian principality of Smolensk in 1395, and he was unable to curb the extension of Lithuanian influence in the northern Russian centres of Tver' and Novgorod.[35] Vasilii, nevertheless, acquired Nizhnii Novgorod, which in 1391, with the agreement of Tokhtamysh, was detached from Suzdal' and attached to Moscow.[36] He also acquired Murom and Gorodets. Although he failed, despite repeated attempts at the turn of the century and during the first quarter of the fifteenth century, to seize Novgorod's northern territory known as the Dvina land, in the process he did replace the prince of Ustiug with his governor.[37] Vasilii thus added Ustiug, Nizhnii Novgorod, Murom and Gorodets to his father's acquisitions of Galich, Beloozero, Starodub and Uglich. In his will Dmitrii had claimed possession of Vladimir, Pereiaslavl', Kostroma and Iur'ev, all of which he left to Vasilii I.[38]

In addition to military strength the extension of Muscovite domination over north-eastern Russian principalities afforded the grand prince access to greater economic resources. The demands for tribute by the Mongol khans and emirs imposed pressure on the grand prince. The tribute that has been estimated to have been 5,000 roubles per year in 1389, rose to 7,000 roubles by 1401 and remained at that level through the reign of Vasilii I.[39] Despite the pressures, which took the form of military campaigns in 1380 and with devastating results in 1382 and 1408, the princes of Moscow were able to use

---

33 *PSRL*, vol. XI, pp. 22–3.
34 *PSRL*, vol. XI, pp. 52, 54; Alef, 'Origins', 18.
35 *PSRL*, vol. III, p. 400; *PSRL*, vol. XI, pp. 162, 204; Presniakov, *Formation*, p. 280; Vernadsky, *Mongols*, pp. 280, 284.
36 Nasonov, *Mongoly i Rus'*, pp. 138–9; Alef, 'Origins', 19, 152; Presniakov, *Formation*, pp. 226–7; Noonan, 'Forging a National Identity', 511.
37 Martin, *Treasure*, pp. 134–5; Cherepnin, *Obrazovanie*, pp. 697–702.
38 *Dukhovnye i dogovornye gramoty*, no. 12, p. 34; *PSRL*, vol. XI, p. 2; V. A. Kuchkin, *Formirovanie gosudarstvennoi territorii severo-vostochnoi Rusi v X–XV vv.* (Moscow: Nauka, 1984), pp. 143–4, 232, 239, 242, 305–6, 308; Vodoff, 'Achats', 107; Presniakov, *Formation*, p. 274.
39 Michel Roublev, 'The Mongol Tribute According to the Wills and Agreements of the Russian Princes', in Michael Cherniavsky (ed.), *The Structure of Russian History. Interpretive Essays* (New York: Random House, 1970), p. 526.

their responsibility to collect taxes and tribute levied by the Mongols to their economic advantage. Although they sent the required amount of tribute, they managed to keep various taxes, such as customs and transport fees, in their own treasuries.[40] The establishment of Muscovite hegemony over the Rostov principalities in 1364 involved the acquisition of the right to collect tribute from Rostov, Ustiug and portions of the north-eastern region known as Perm'. In 1367, according to one chronicle account, the grand prince acquired similar rights over Novgorod's possessions in the extreme north-east. When Stefan of Perm' converted the inhabitants of Vychegda Perm' to Christianity and a new bishopric was carved out of the Novgorod eparchy for them (1383), Moscow consolidated its tenuous command over tribute and trade in luxury fur from their territory.[41]

The Moscow princes used the wealth they acquired in part to embellish their city. Masonry construction, which had reflected the economic recovery of northern Russia earlier in the fourteenth century, continued during the reigns of Dmitrii Ivanovich and his son Vasilii. David Miller has shown that between 1363 and 1387 sixteen such projects were undertaken in north-eastern Russia; the projects accounted for just over one-quarter of all those in northern Russia. During the next quartercentury another twenty-one masonry structures or 29 per cent of all those in northern Russia were built in north-eastern Russia.[42] The projects included the walls that protected Moscow.

New construction was also associated with the monastic movement that had begun in the mid-fourteenth century, partially in response to outbreaks of plague.[43] Walled monasteries were built to the east, south-east and north of Moscow. Although the walls of the Holy Trinity monastery were insufficient to withstand the attacks of Tokhtamysh and Edigei, the ring of monasteries surrounding Moscow provided defensive protection. Fortified monasteries at

---

40 Ostrowski, *Muscovy and the Mongols*, pp. 119–21; *Dukhovnye i dogovornye gramoty*, no. 4, p. 15 and no. 12, p. 33; S. M. Kashtanov, 'Finansovoe ustroistvo moskovskogo kniazhestva v seredine XIV v. po dannym dukhovnykh gramot', in *Issledovaniia po istorii i istoriografii feodalizma. K 100-letiiu so dnia rozhdeniia akademika B. D. Grekova* (Moscow: Nauka, 1982), p. 178.
41 P. Doronin, 'Dokumenty po istorii Komi', *Istoriko-filologicheskii sbornik Komi filiala AN SSSR* 4 (1958), 257–8; Martin, *Treasure*, pp. 132–3; Ostrowski, *Muscovy and the Mongols*, p. 125; Crummey, *Formation*, p. 121; John Meyendorff, *Byzantium and the Rise of Russia. A Study of Byzantino-Russian Relations in the Fourteenth Century* (Cambridge: Cambridge University Press, 1981), pp. 136–7.
42 Miller, 'Monumental Building', 368, 373; Ostrowski, *Muscovy and the Mongols*, p. 130.
43 Pierre Gonneau, 'The Trinity-Sergius Brotherhood in State and Society', in A. M. Kleimola and G. D. Lenhoff (eds.), *Culture and Identity in Muscovy, 1359–1584* (Moscow: ITZ-Garant, 1997), p. 119.

Table 7.1. *Prince Ivan I Kalita and his descendants (names of grand princes are in capitals)*

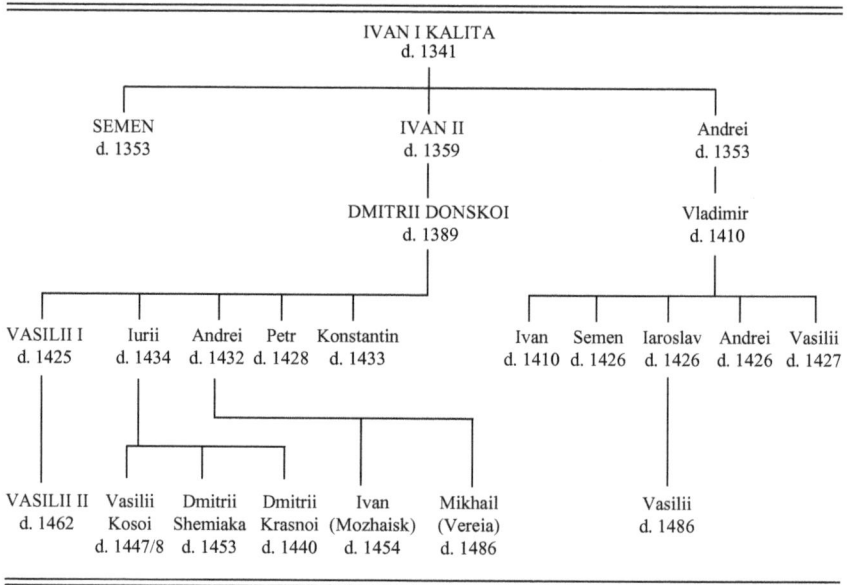

```
                              IVAN I KALITA
                                 d. 1341
        ┌────────────────────────────┼────────────────────────────┐
     SEMEN                         IVAN II                        Andrei
    d. 1353                        d. 1359                        d. 1353
                                      │                             │
                               DMITRII DONSKOI                   Vladimir
                                  d. 1389                        d. 1410
 ┌──────┬──────┬──────┬──────┐        └────────┬──────┬──────┬──────┬──────┐
VASILII I  Iurii  Andrei  Petr  Konstantin   Ivan  Semen  Iaroslav  Andrei  Vasilii
d. 1425  d. 1434 d. 1432 d. 1428  d. 1433   d. 1410 d. 1426 d. 1426 d. 1426 d. 1427
   │        │       │
VASILII II  Vasilii  Dmitrii  Dmitrii   Ivan     Mikhail             Vasilii
d. 1462     Kosoi   Shemiaka  Krasnoi (Mozhaisk) (Vereia)            d. 1486
          d. 1447/8 d. 1453   d. 1440   d. 1454   d. 1486
```

Serpukhov and Kolomna that protected the southern frontier of Muscovy also had defensive functions.[44]

The Muscovite princes' consolidation of power benefited from the small size and cohesiveness of their dynastic branch. Due to the effects of the Black Plague and other demographic factors the Daniilovich family remained small. Although each prince had his own principality, either inherited from his father or dispensed by the grand prince, the family's possessions did not, like those of the Rostov princes, become subdivided into numerous, weak patrimonial principalities. Grand Prince Dmitrii Donskoi shared his realm with only one cousin, Vladimir Andreevich, prince of Serpukhov (see Table 7.1). Relations among the Daniilovich princes also were relatively cordial. Unlike the ruling house of Tver', which divided into two, hostile branches in the mid-fourteenth century, the Daniilovich line not only peacefully shared the family's territorial possessions, but also the revenues derived from them. The courtiers of the

44 Miller, 'Monumental Building', 372; Borisov, *Russkaia tserkov'*, p. 112; Nancy Shields Kollmann, *Kinship and Politics: The Making of the Muscovite Political System, 1345–1547* (Stanford, Calif.: Stanford University Press, 1987), pp. 32–3; Crummey, *Formation of Muscovy*, p. 121.

Daniilovich princes were able to freely transfer their service from one member of the family to another.

This situation prevailed until 1425, when Grand Prince Vasilii Dmitr'evich died. He was survived by four brothers and his son Vasilii. For the first time since the Daniilovichi had become grand princes of Vladimir, a dispute arose within the dynastic branch. The disagreements developed into a civil war that was distinguished by its length and its ferocity. The war took place in three phases and was fought over two related points of contention. The first issue was dynastic seniority and succession.

Tradition established that the senior eligible member of the dynasty should succeed to the position of grand prince when that position became vacant. The senior prince was the eldest member of the senior generation. Succession, confined to those princes whose fathers had been grand princes, thus followed a lateral or co-lateral pattern. The grand-princely station passed from elder brother to younger brother or cousin. When all eligible members of one generation had served as grand prince or died, the position passed to the next generation. The sons of former grand princes then inherited the throne in order of their seniority within their generation. Even when the Mongol khans transferred the grand-princely throne of Vladimir to the Daniilovichi, who were ineligible by these norms because Daniil had never been grand prince, they regularly issued patents according to the lateral, generational pattern of succession.

It was thus according to these norms that Ivan I Kalita came to the throne after his brother Iurii. When Ivan died, his position passed to the next generation and his eldest son Semen became grand prince of Vladimir. Plague claimed the lives of Semen, his sons, and his brother Andrei; his surviving brother, Ivan II, succeeded to the throne. Ivan II was the last member of his generation; when he died, the throne passed to his son Dmitrii. Due to the family's small size and early deaths these successions, while conforming to the lateral pattern, also defined a new vertical pattern of succession from father to son.

Although other members of the dynasty protested against their successions, the Daniilovich princes all accepted their senior members as grand princes. Only when Vasilii I assumed the throne in 1389 was there a weak protest from within the Moscow branch of the dynasty. Prince Vladimir Andreevich of Serpukhov, the cousin of Dmitrii Donskoi, evidently raised an objection to Vasilii's succession. It is not clear that Vladimir Andreevich was seeking the throne of Vladimir for himself. Although he did have seniority as a member of the elder generation, his father Andrei had died from the plague in 1353 and had never served as grand prince. Vladimir was therefore ineligible for succession.[45]

When Vasilii Dmitr'evich died in 1425, his brother Iurii was the legitimate heir according to the lateral pattern of succession. But in his will, dated 1423, Vasilii left the grand principality as well as Moscow and its possessions to his son Vasilii Vasil'evich. He thus asserted a vertical line of succession that bypassed his brothers and denied their seniority. To ensure that his wishes would be honoured, he placed his son, who was ten years old in 1425, under the protection of his brothers Petr and Andrei, two cousins, and Prince Vitovt of Lithuania, who was the boy's maternal grandfather.[46]

The second issue that generated the intra-dynastic war was the prerogatives of the grand prince, his authority over the family's territorial possessions and the relative status of the members of the ruling house. During the fourteenth century relations between the grand prince and his Muscovite relations were co-operative. Grand Prince Semen, for example, shared proceeds from customs fees with his two brothers; as the senior prince, however, he received half of the proceeds, not one-third.[47] Dmitrii Donskoi and his cousin Vladimir Andreevich similarly enjoyed cordial relations. The Serpukhov prince had autonomy within his principality, including the right to collect taxes from its inhabitants. He also had rights to one-third of the revenues collected from Moscow, the seat of the family's shared domain.[48]

The situation changed shortly after Vasilii II became grand prince. Vladimir Andreevich had died in 1410. All of his five sons had died by 1427; four of them were victims of an epidemic of plague in 1426–7. Only one grandson, Vasilii Iaroslavich, survived. When he was to inherit his family's lands, the regents for the grand prince intervened. They confiscated one portion of the Serpukhov patrimonial possessions for Vasilii II and gave another portion to the grand prince's uncle Konstantin Dmitr'evich.[49] In 1428, another of the grand prince's uncles, Petr Dmitr'evich of Dmitrov, died. Once again Vasilii II's government, ignoring the claims of the rest of the family to a share of Petr's principality, seized Dmitrov as a possession of the grand prince.[50]

45 PSRL, vol. XI, p. 121; Presniakov, Formation, pp. 274, 314–15, 320.
46 Dukhovnye i dogovornye gramoty, no. 22, p. 62; Presniakov, Formation, p. 319; Vernadsky, Mongols, p. 294.
47 Dukhovnye i dogovornye gramoty, no. 2, p. 11; Kashtanov, 'Finansovoe ustroistvo', 178.
48 M. N. Tikhomirov, 'Moskovskie tretniki, tysiatskie, i namestniki', Izvestiia AN SSSR, seriia istorii i filosofii 3 (1946): 311–13; Presniakov, Formation, pp. 152–9; Crummey, Formation of Muscovy, pp. 50–1.
49 Zimin, Vitiaz', p. 37.
50 Cherepnin, Obrazovanie, p. 749; Zimin, Vitiaz', pp. 39–40.

The actions of Vasilii's regents secured the loyalty of the young prince's uncle Konstantin. His uncle Andrei, one of the regents, also favoured his nephew. After Andrei died in 1432, his sons, Ivan of Mozhaisk and Mikhail of Vereia, rapidly concluded treaties of friendship with their cousin. Petr died without heirs. But the same actions intensified the opposition of Prince Iurii Dmitr'evich of Zvenigorod and Galich. As the oldest surviving brother of Vasilii I, he regarded himself as the senior member of the dynasty and the rightful heir. He had expressed his discontent in 1425, by refusing to come to Moscow to swear allegiance to his nephew and preparing for war. But he was dissuaded from initiating hostilities by Metropolitan Fotii (Photios), an outbreak of plague and the threat of intervention by Vitovt of Lithuania.[51] Iurii accepted Vasilii as grand prince, but only until the matter was referred to the khan of the Golden Horde.[52]

The issue was not brought before the khan until late summer 1431, after both Vitovt and Fotii had died. In June 1432, Khan Ulu-Muhammed favoured Vasilii with a patent for the grand principality of Vladimir. He determined, however, that Iurii should receive the disputed principality of Dmitrov.[53] When Vasilii refused to cede Dmitrov, Iurii staged a campaign against him. This action, which resulted in the defeat of Vasilii, opened the first stage of the civil war. Iurii replaced Vasilii as grand prince and issued Kolomna to his nephew as an apanage principality. Vasilii, however, retained the loyalty of his courtiers, who moved to Kolomna in support of their prince. Iurii was obliged to withdraw and return the grand principality as well as Dmitrov to Vasilii.[54]

Iurii returned to Galich. But his two elder sons, Vasilii Kosoi (the Cross-Eyed) and Dmitrii Shemiaka, had not supported his decision or his subsequent agreement with Vasilii II. In September 1433, the restored grand prince launched an unsuccessful campaign against them. The renewed hostilities drew Iurii back into the conflict. After suffering another defeat in March 1434, Vasilii II fled to Novgorod, then to Tver' and Nizhnii Novgorod. In the meantime Iurii besieged Moscow and again occupied the capital. This time he received greater support, but he died suddenly in 1434.[55]

51 Vernadsky, *Mongols*, p. 295; Zimin, *Vitiaz'*, pp. 33–7; Crummey, *Formation of Muscovy*, p. 69; Presniakov, *Formation*, p. 323.
52 *Dukhovnye i dogovornye gramoty*, no. 24, pp. 63–7; Zimin, *Vitiaz'*, pp. 39–40; Alef, 'Origins', 34.
53 Zimin, *Vitiaz'*, p. 47; Vernadsky, *Mongols*, pp. 299–300; Presniakov, *Formation*, pp. 325–6.
54 Presniakov, *Formation*, pp. 326–7; Alef, 'Origins', 31; Crummey, *Formation of Muscovy*, p. 70; Zimin, *Vitiaz'*, pp. 57–8, 60; Vernadsky, *Mongols*, p. 300.
55 Zimin, *Vitiaz'*, pp. 62–7; Vernadsky, *Mongols*, p. 300; Alef, 'Origins', 31; Crummey, *Formation of Muscovy*, p. 71; Presniakov, *Formation*, p. 327.

The death of Iurii Dmitr'evich ended the first phase of the civil war. His son, Vasilii Kosoi, launched the second phase (1434–6). His attempt to replace his father ended in failure. Vasilii Kosoi, whose own brothers refused to fight on his behalf, could not gain sufficient support for his claim to the throne. Vasilii Vasil'evich, who had become the legitimate heir by traditional principles of seniority as well as his father's will and the khan's patent, recovered his position as well as Dmitrov and his cousin's principality, Zvenigorod. The two princes reached an accord in 1435. But in the winter of 1435–6, Kosoi attacked Galich, the seat of one of his brothers, Ustiug, and Vologda. He was captured in May 1436, blinded and sent to Kolomna. The defeated Vasilii Kosoi died in 1447/8.[56]

Vasilii II remained at peace with his relatives for the next decade. But in 1445, he was captured by the Tatars of Ulu-Muhammed's migrating horde. This situation provided an opportunity for his cousin, Dmitrii Shemiaka, Kosoi's brother, to renew his family's bid for the grand-princely throne. Dmitrii Shemiaka had not joined his brother Vasilii Kosoi against Vasilii II in 1434–6, and after Kosoi's defeat, he had recognised the seniority of Vasilii II.[57] But the relationship between the cousins was tense. They disagreed about the distribution of lands that had been ruled by another of Iurii's sons, Dmitrii Krasnoi (the Handsome), who died in 1440; about Shemiaka's participation in Vasilii's military campaigns; and about his contributions to the Tatar tribute.[58]

When Vasilii II was taken captive, Dmitrii, the senior member of the dynasty, emerged to fill the vacancy. But Ulu-Muhammed released Vasilii, who promised to pay a large ransom and returned to Moscow with a contingent of Tatars. When he went on a pilgrimage to the Holy Trinity monastery, however, Dmitrii Shemiaka began the third phase of the civil war (1446–53). He seized control of Moscow while forces loyal to him captured Vasilii (1446). Vasilii was blinded and exiled to Uglich. Subsequently, in return for his promise to recognise Dmitrii Shemiaka as grand prince, he received Vologda as an apanage principality.[59]

Shemiaka was not, however, universally accepted as grand prince. The balance of military power had also shifted. The grand prince did not have his own army, but relied, as had his father and grandfather, on a combination of

56 Ibid., pp. 327–8; Alef, 'Origins', 32; Crummey, Formation of Muscovy, p. 71; Vernadsky, Mongols, p. 301; Zimin, Vitiaz', pp. 70, 74–7.
57 Dukhovnye i dogovornye gramoty, no. 35, pp. 89–100; Zimin, Vitiaz', p. 77.
58 Ibid., pp. 72, 95; Alef, 'Origins', 19; Dukhovnye i dogovornye gramoty, no. 38, pp. 107–17.
59 PSRL, vol. XII, pp. 65–9; Presniakov, Formation, pp. 334–5; Zimin, Vitiaz', pp. 105–11; Vernadsky, Mongols, pp. 318–20, 322; Crummey, Formation of Muscovy, pp. 74–5.

forces drawn from military units supplied by family members, independent princes, and the Tatar khans.[60] Although Vasilii II had retained the support of many of his courtiers during the first phase of the war against his uncle Iurii, he did not have the military strength to defeat him. His uncle used the military forces under his own command against Vasilii II. Other princes of north-eastern Russia remained neutral in the Daniilovich family quarrel. And Khan Ulu-Muhammed, who was preoccupied with problems associated with disintegration of the Golden Horde, did not provide military aid to enforce his decision to give the patent for the grand principality to Vasilii.

When Shemiaka seized power, he acted in alliance with Prince Ivan Andree-vich of Mozhaisk. But Prince Vasilii Iaroslavich of Serpukhov disapproved of his action and fled to Lithuania.[61] In addition, Prince Boris Aleksandrovich of Tver', who had previously remained neutral in the conflict among the princes of Moscow, favoured Vasilii in this phase of the dispute and promised his five-year-old daughter in marriage to Vasilii's seven-year-old son.[62] The Tatar tsarevichi Kasim and Iakub joined Vasilii while other supporters gathered in Lithuania and Tver'. Vasilii thus gained support from some of his relatives, independent princes and Tatars. He also won the support of Bishop Iona of Riazan', the most prominent hierarch of the Church.

Vasilii thus had forces strong enough to recapture Moscow. The grand prince triumphantly returned to his capital in February 1447.[63] The combatants concluded a peace agreement in the summer of 1447.[64] Vasilii nevertheless renewed hostilities by capturing Dmitrii's primary seat, the city of Galich, in 1450. Shemiaka fled to Novgorod and pursued the war, mainly in the northern regions of Ustiug, the Dvina land and Vychegda Perm', before returning to Novgorod where he was fatally poisoned in 1453.[65]

In the aftermath of the war Prince Ivan of Mozhaisk fled to Lithuania. Vasilii confiscated his principality as well as Galich, which had belonged to Dmitrii Shemiaka. In 1456, Vasilii also arrested his former ally and supporter, Prince Vasilii of Serpukhov, sent him into exile at Uglich and seized his lands as well.

60 Ostrowski, 'Troop Mobilization', pp. 25–6.
61 PSRL, vol. XII, p. 69; Vernadsky, Mongols, p. 322; Zimin, Vitiaz', p. 111.
62 PSRL, vol. XII, p. 71; Vernadsky, Mongols, pp. 323–4; Presniakov, Formation, pp. 335–6; Vodoff, 'La Place du grand-prince de Tver' ', 50.
63 PSRL, vol. XII, p. 73; Crummey, Formation of Muscovy, p. 75; Vernadsky, Mongols, pp. 323–5; Zimin, Vitiaz', pp. 116, 118–22.
64 Zimin, Vitiaz', p. 125.
65 PSRL, vol. XII, p. 75; Martin, Treasure, pp. 137–8; Vernadsky, Mongols, pp. 325, 328; Zimin, Vitiaz', pp. 139–54; Crummey, Formation of Muscovy, p. 75; Presniakov, Formation, pp. 336–8.

Only Prince Mikhail of Vereia among Vasilii's cousins retained a portion of the Muscovite territories as his own apanage principality.[66]

During and immediately after the war Vasilii II was also able to assert dominance over princes and lands beyond the territories attached to Vladimir and Moscow. In 1449, he concluded a treaty with the prince of Suzdal', in which the latter agreed not to seek or receive patents for their office from the Tatar khan.[67] His position became dependent upon the prince of Moscow, not the khan. When the prince of Riazan' died in 1456, Vasilii II brought his son into his own household and sent his governors to administer that principality. By that time Vasilii had also entered into new agreements with the prince of Tver', who while not acknowledging Vasilii's seniority, nevertheless pledged his co-operation in all ventures against the Tatars as well as their Western neighbours; Boris also recognised Vasilii as the rightful grand prince and as prince of Novgorod.[68]

Vasilii also asserted his authority over Novgorod. In 1431, Novgorod had concluded a treaty with the prince of Lithuania, Svidrigailo, and accepted his nephew as its prince. But even though Svidrigailo was the brother-in-law of Iurii of Galich, Novgorod had been neutral during Iurii's conflict with Vasilii II.[69] When Vasilii II was engaged against Vasilii Kosoi (the Cross-Eyed), he negotiated with Novgorod to enlist its support; he indicated a willingness to settle outstanding disputes over Novgorod's eastern frontier. But after he had defeated Kosoi, he reneged on his agreement. He sent his officers to collect tribute and in 1440–1, after the Lithuanian prince had left the city, he launched a military campaign against Novgorod and forced it to make an additional payment and promise to continue to pay taxes and fees regularly.[70] During the 1440s, however, Novgorod was at war with both of its major Western trading partners, the Hanseatic League and the Teutonic Order. The Hansa blockaded Novgorod and closed its own commercial operations in the city for six years. Novgorod lost commercial revenue. It suffered from high prices and also from a famine. In the midst of these crises Novgorod accepted another prince from

66 Vernadsky, *Mongols*, pp. 327–8; Kollmann, *Kinship and Politics*, p. 157; Zimin, *Vitiaz'*, p. 176; Presniakov, *Formation*, pp. 337–8, 341–2.
67 *Dukhovnye i dogovornye gramoty*, no. 52, pp. 156, 158; Ostrowski, 'Troop Mobilization', p. 34; Zimin, *Vitiaz'*, p. 133.
68 Presniakov, *Formation*, p. 344; Vernadsky, *Mongols*, p. 325.
69 *Gramoty Velikogo Novgoroda i Pskova*, ed. S. N. Valk (Moscow: AN SSSR, 1949; reprinted Düsseldorf: Brücken Verlag and Vaduz: Europe Printing, 1970), no. 63, pp. 105–6; *PSRL*, vol. III, p. 416; Presniakov, *Formation*, pp. 325, 330.
70 *PSRL*, vol. III, pp. 418–21; Presniakov, *Formation*, pp. 330–1; Zimin, *Vitiaz'*, p. 80.

Lithuania (1444).[71] When Vasilii II and Dmitrii Shemiaka took their conflict to the north and disrupted Novgorod's northern trade routes, Novgorod gave support and sanctuary to Shemiaka.

In 1456, as Vasilii II was asserting his authority over other Russian principalities, he also launched a major military campaign against Novgorod and once again defeated it. Novgorod was obliged to accept the Treaty of Iazhelbitsii. According to its terms, it had to cut off its connections with Shemiaka's family as well as with any other enemies of the grand prince. It was to pay taxes and the Tatar tribute to the grand prince; it was to accept the grand prince's judicial officials in the city; and it was to conclude agreements with foreign powers only with the approval of the grand prince. It was obliged, furthermore, to cede key sectors of its northern territorial possessions to the grand prince.[72]

The dynastic war ended in victory for Vasilii II. It resolved in his favour the issues of succession and of the prerogatives of the grand prince. The outcome of the war left Vasilii II with undisputed control over the grand principality and its possessions as well as the territories attached to the principality of Moscow. His relatives, who had shared the familial domain when he took office, had all died or gone into exile or been subordinated. Only one cousin, Mikhail of Vereia, retained an apanage principality. The remainder of the apanage principalities, which had been the territories of Vasilii's Iurevich cousins, of Ivan Andreevich of Mozhaisk, and of Vasilii Iaroslavich of Serpukhov, along with their economic resources and revenues had reverted to the grand prince.

Vasilii's post-war policies towards his relatives and neighbouring princes also provided the grand prince with more secure military power. Although he still relied on them to supply military forces, they had become subordinate to him or had committed themselves by treaty to support him. Vasilii, furthermore, established his Tatar ally, Kasim, on the Oka River. The Tatars of the khanate of Kasimov became available to participate in the military ventures of the Muscovite grand princes. Vasilii II thus ensured that the grand prince would not be as militarily vulnerable as he had been when the wars began. His policies gave him access to larger forces than potential competitors within north-eastern Russia without being dependent on support from independent

---

71 *PSRL*, vol. III, p. 423; *PSRL*, vol. XII, p. 61; Martin, *Treasure*, p. 82; Phillippe Dollinger, *The German Hansa*, trans. D. S. Ault and S. H. Steinberg (Stanford, Calif.: Stanford University Press, 1970), p. 295; Rybina, *Torgovlia srednevekogo Novgoroda*, pp. 158–60; N. A. Kazakova, *Russko-livonskie i russko-ganzeiskie otnosheniia* (Leningrad: Nauka, 1975), pp. 120–6; Cherepnin, *Obrazovanie*, p. 784.
72 *PSRL*, vol. XII, pp. 110–11; V. N. Bernadskii, *Novgorod i Novgorodskaia zemlia* (Moscow and Leningrad: AN SSSR, 1961), pp. 254–9; Cherepnin, *Obrazovanie*, pp. 817–22; Presniakov, *Formation*, p. 343; Zimin, *Vitiaz'*, pp. 173–5; Martin, *Treasure*, p. 138.

princes and the khans of the Great Horde and emerging khanates of Kazan' and Crimea.[73]

Vasilii II emerged from the war as the strongest prince in north-eastern Russia. Shortly after he recovered Moscow, Vasilii asserted his sovereignty by using the title 'sovereign of all Rus" on newly minted coins. In late 1447 or early 1448, he also named his young son, Ivan, his co-ruler; coins then appeared with the inscription 'sovereigns of all Rus".[74] While thereby making it more difficult for co-lateral relatives to challenge his son's succession, Vasilii II also confirmed a vertical pattern of succession for the princes of Moscow. When Ivan III assumed his father's throne in 1462, no other prince within the house of Moscow had the resources or the status to mount a military challenge for the throne, as Iurii Dmitr'evich and his sons had done. The Tatar khans also lost their decisive influence over succession. Vasilii II had appealed to Khan Ulu-Muhammed for a patent to hold the throne of Vladimir. But it was his own military victory over his uncle and cousins that confirmed the replacement of the traditional lateral pattern of succession with a vertical one. Vasilii II was able to leave the grand principality as well as his Muscovite possessions to his son without acquiring prior approval of a Tatar khan. Ivan III, followed by his son and grandson, would expand those core territories to build the state of Muscovy.[75]

The Daniilovichi and the Church

When the Daniilovichi became grand princes of Vladimir during the first half of the fourteenth century, they lacked legitimacy rooted in the dynastic traditions of seniority and succession. They depended upon the authority and favour of the khans of the Golden Horde to hold their position. When the Golden Horde entered a period of internal strife that began with the succession crises of the 1360s, continued with the invasion by Timur, and ultimately resulted in its fragmentation into several khanates during the second quarter of the fifteenth century, the princes of Moscow could no longer rely on the khans' power as a substitute for domestic legitimacy. During the fourteenth

---

73 Ostrowski, 'Troop Mobilization', p. 26.
74 Gustave Alef, 'Muscovy and the Council of Florence', *SR* 20 (1961); reprinted in his *Rulers and Nobles in Fifteenth-Century Muscovy* (London: Variorum Reprints, 1983), 399; Gustave Alef, 'The Political Significance of the Inscriptions of Muscovite Coinage in the Reign of Vasilii II', *Speculum* 34 (1959); reprinted in his *Rulers and Nobles in Fifteenth-Century Muscovy* (London: Variorum Reprints, 1983), 6, 11; Alef, 'Origins', 42; Noonan, 'Forging a National Identity', p. 505; Zimin, *Vitiaz'*, p. 133.
75 Alef, 'Origins', 40; Presniakov, *Formation*, p. 322.

and fifteenth centuries they, therefore, sought to overcome or neutralise their dynastic opponents. They also expanded their own territorial domain and thus increased their economic and military power to become the strongest power in northern Russia. It was the ideological concepts developed by the hierarchs of the Church and the moral authority of the charismatic monastic leaders, however, that conferred a legitimacy on the princes who were shaping a new state of Muscovy.

During the century that followed the Mongol invasion and preceded the reign of Dmitrii Donskoi the outlook of the metropolitans of the Russian Church had diverged from that of the grand princes of Vladimir, particularly the Daniilovich princes. While the princes focused their policies on northern Russia and the Golden Horde, the metropolitans devoted themselves to their entire ecclesiastical realm that included all the lands that had formed Kievan Rus'. The metropolitans, Russians and non-Russians alike,[76] also maintained regular contact with the patriarch at Constantinople. When Ivan II died in 1359, the metropolitan of the Church was Aleksei, who held his office from 1354 to 1378. He began his tenure in office with an outlook that was similar to that of his predecessors. During the next century, however, particularly as the Russian Church assumed an autocephalous status in the mid-fifteenth century, its leaders developed concepts and mythologies that served their ecclesiastical interests, but also imparted a legitimacy to the Daniilovich princes and elevated their status above the other members of the dynasty.

Aleksei had been nominated by Metropolitan Feognost to be his successor. Aleksei's father was Feodor Biakont, who had moved from Chernigov and entered the service of Prince Daniil. His brother was Aleksandr, who became a boyar in the court of Dmitrii Ivanovich. Aleksei, however, had become a monk, but had been selected by Feognost in 1340 to administer the metropolitan's court. In 1352, Feognost named him bishop of Vladimir. He also sent a delegation to Constantinople to nominate Aleksei for the position of metropolitan. By the time the delegates returned to Moscow, Feognost had died (1353). Aleksei personally went to Constantinople where he remained for a year before being confirmed in his office (1354).[77]

76 Dimitri Obolensky, 'Byzantium, Kiev and Moscow: A Study in Ecclesiastical Relations', *Dumbarton Oaks Papers* 11 (Cambridge, Mass.: Harvard University Press, 1957), 33, reprinted in his *Byzantium and the Slavs* (London: Variorum Reprints, 1971) and his *Byzantium and the Slavs* (Crestwood, N.Y.: St Vladimir's Seminary Press, 1994); Dimitri Obolensky, 'Byzantium and Russia in the Late Middle Ages', in J. R. Hale, J. R. L. Highfield and B. Smalley (eds.), *Europe in the Late Middle Ages* (London: Faber and Faber, 1965), p. 254.

77 Obolensky, 'Byzantium, Kiev and Moscow', 37–8; Meyendorff, *Byzantium and the Rise of Russia*, pp. 166–7; Presniakov, *Formation*, pp. 239–40; Crummey, *Formation of Muscovy*,

Later that year, however, another metropolitan, Roman, was named to lead the Orthodox Church in lands under Lithuanian control, including Kiev. The metropolitanate was not reunited until Roman died in 1362. During the first years of his tenure in office Aleksei was thus primarily concerned with ending the division of his see. After his return to Moscow from Constantinople in 1355, he travelled extensively to the horde, back to Constantinople, and in 1358 to Kiev. Prince Ol'gerd of Lithuania held him there for two years.[78]

While Aleksei was in Kiev, Khan Navruz issued the patent for the grand principality of Vladimir to Prince Dmitrii Konstantinovich of Suzdal'.[79] When Aleksei returned, the political competition for the position of grand prince was intensifying. Aleksei used the influence and prestige of his position as well as his close relationship to the Moscow boyars to secure the throne for Dmitrii Ivanovich of Moscow.[80] After Dmitrii Ivanovich successfully ascended his father's throne and Aleksei's rival, Roman, died (1361), the metropolitan devoted more of his attention to guiding the young prince. His unusual attentiveness to the secular affairs of the grand prince provoked complaints from Poland and Lithuania to the patriarch that Aleksei was neglecting their ecclesiastical needs. Tver' too objected that Aleksei displayed unmistakable favour towards Moscow in the conflict between the two principalities that began in 1368. In 1371, the patriarch re-established a metropolitanate for the bishoprics in Galicia, which were subject to the Polish crown. He urged Aleksei to attend to his entire domain, but when complaints persisted, he sent his agent Kiprian (Cyprian) and other envoys to investigate the matter (1373) and then appointed Kiprian to be metropolitan for the lands subject to Lithuania (1375). It was understood, however, that when Aleksei died, Kiprian would succeed him; the metropolitanate of Kiev and all Rus' would be reunified under his leadership.[81]

By the time Aleksei died in 1378, it was Kiprian, the metropolitan in Lithuania, who represented the policy of reunifying the metropolitanate.[82] Aleksei, shifting the policy he had inherited from his predecessors and had pursued

p. 43; S. B. Veselovskii, *Feodal'noe zemlevladenie v severo-vostochnoi Rusi* (Moscow and Leningrad: AN SSSR, 1947), p. 334.

78 Borisov, *Russkaia tserkov'*, pp. 79–80; N. S. Borisov, 'Moskovskie kniaz'ia i russkie mitropolity XIV veka', VI, 1986, no. 8:41; Meyendorff, *Byzantium and the Rise of Russia*, pp. 169–71, 185–6; Presniakov, *Formation*, pp. 243–5, 253–4; Fennell, *Emergence*, p. 302.
79 *PSRL*, vol. x, p. 231.
80 Borisov, *Russkaia tserkov'*, p. 81; Borisov, 'Moskovskie kniaz'ia', 41.
81 Meyendorff, *Byzantium and the Rise of Russia*, pp. 184, 192–201, 287–9; Borisov, *Russkaia tserkov'*, pp. 82, 84–7, 89–90; Obolensky, 'Byzantium and Russia', 256; Presniakov, *Formation*, pp. 253, 257–8, 260; Crummey, *Formation of Muscovy*, pp. 44, 47–9.
82 Presniakov, *Formation*, pp. 297, 299.

in the early years of his tenure in office, led the Church officially centred at Vladimir from 1354 to become closely identified with north-eastern Russia and, more particularly, with the lands subject to the Muscovite prince. Thus, when Kiprian attempted to assume Aleksei's seat, he was ejected from Moscow by Grand Prince Dmitrii Ivanovich. The grand prince nominated his confessor, Michael-Mitiai, to replace Aleksei. When he died on his way to Constantinople, a member of his entourage, Pimen, replaced him.[83]

Although Dmitrii had unceremoniously evicted Kiprian from Moscow when he arrived, he reversed his position after the Battle of Kulikovo. Kiprian assumed the role of metropolitan and remained in Moscow for two years. When Pimen returned from Constantinople, Dmitrii arrested him. Kiprian fled from Moscow, however, when Tokhtamysh approached the city (1382). Although he continued to claim the position, Pimen assumed the functions of metropolitan in north-eastern Russia. Contention between the two persisted until 1389, when a new patriarch in Constantinople confirmed Kiprian as metropolitan and both Pimen and Grand Prince Dmitrii died. Kiprian returned to Moscow in 1390.[84]

Kiprian re-established ecclesiastical unity of all the lands of Rus' in a single metropolitanate. He was supported in his efforts by the new grand prince Vasilii I and the most influential leader of the monastic movement in north-eastern Russia, Sergei of Radonezh. Vitovt of Lithuania, who gave his daughter in marriage to Vasilii I in 1391, the year after Kiprian joined the Lithuanian and Russian Orthodox communities, also regarded Kiprian and his policies with favour.[85] During the remainder of his tenure in office, Kiprian attempted to consolidate the unity of his see ideologically and symbolically. His triumphal entrance into Moscow, during which he was reportedly accompanied by two Greek metropolitans and five bishops representing north-eastern and south-western Russia, dramatically portrayed his commitment to unifying the metropolitanate.[86]

---

83 Meyendorff, *Byzantium and the Rise of Russia*, pp. 209–11, 214–20; Obolensky, 'Byzantium and Russia', p. 257; Borisov, *Russkaia tserkov'*, pp. 79, 100–1, 104–5; A. S. Khoroshev, *Politicheskaia istoriia russkoi kanonizatsii (XI–XVI vv.)* (Moscow: Moskovskii universitet, 1986), pp. 100–2; Presniakov, *Formation*, pp. 294–8; Kuchkin, 'Dmitrii Donskoi', 73–4, 76–7.

84 L. A. Dmitriev, 'Rol' i znachenie mitropolita Kipriana v istorii drevnerusskoi literatury', *TODRL* 19 (1963): 217–19; Crummey, *Formation of Muscovy*, pp. 58–62; Meyendorff, *Byzantium and the Rise of Russia*, pp. 224–41; Borisov, *Russkaia tserkov'*, pp. 108–9.

85 Crummey, *Formation of Muscovy*, p. 62; David B. Miller, 'The Cult of Saint Sergius of Radonezh and Its Political Uses', *SR* 52 (1993), 454; Andrei Pliguzov, 'On the Title "Metropolitan of Kiev and All Rus'"', *HUS* 15 (1991): 351–2.

86 Halperin, 'Russian Land and Russian Tsar', 61.

The same theme was articulated in the *Trinity Chronicle*, compiled at his behest at the end of his life. The chronicle built upon the *Primary Chronicle* from the Kievan Rus' era and the 1305 codex that had been produced in Tver' during the reign of Mikhail Iaroslavich; it added information on events to 1408. Its sources and coverage were consistent with the image of the inclusive, unified Orthodox community promoted by Metropolitan Kiprian. The chronicle, furthermore, set Moscow at the centre of this community. It portrayed early fifteenth-century Moscow, the cultural and ecclesiastical centre of north-eastern Russia, as the historical heir of Kiev, the original seat of the metropolitan of Kiev and all Rus'.[87]

Ecclesiastical unity of all the Orthodox Rus', however, raised the prospect of political unity. Ecclesiastical unity under the metropolitan based in Moscow, who was depicted as the heir of the metropolitans based at Kiev, implied that the grand prince in Moscow was the heir of his Kievan ancestors. This perspective served the interests of the Church hierarchs, who sought to preserve the unity of the metropolitanate under the jurisdiction of the Moscow prelate. It was, perhaps, less acceptable to the Muscovite princes. Political unification of all the northern Russian lands as well as the Orthodox lands under Lithuanian rule was not a realistic option in the early fifteenth century. In addition, although associations with Kievan Rus' endowed the princes of Moscow with status and respect befitting the descendants of the Kievan grand princes, those references also recalled the unsettling fact of the Daniilovich princes' illegitimacy according to the norms of succession that had evolved during the Kievan era.[88]

Representations of the metropolitan at Moscow as the sole legitimate head of the Orthodox community in the Russian lands nevertheless continued to appear and came into sharp focus in the mid-fifteenth century. They were expressed in the context of crises faced by the Church. These accounts, however, not only associated the princes of Moscow with their Kievan ancestors. They imparted to them a moral authority and characterised them as the secular rulers charged with the duty to protect the Orthodox community. They thus provided an ideological foundation for legitimising the grand princes of Moscow.

87 Fennell, *Emergence*, pp. 315–16; Vernadsky, *Mongols*, p. 381; Gonneau, 'The Trinity-Sergius Brotherhood', 138; Ia. S. Lur'e, *Dve istorii Rusi XV veka. Rannie i pozdnie, nezavisimye i ofitsial'nye letopisi ob obrazovanii Moskovskogo gosudarstva* (St Petersburg: Dmitrii Bulanin, 1994), pp. 13, 57–9; Halperin, 'Russian Land and Russian Tsar', 58–9, 63–4; Jaroslaw Pelenski, 'The Origins of the Official Muscovite Claims to the "Kievan Inheritance"', *HUS* 1 (1977): 32–3.
88 Noonan, 'Forging a National Identity', pp. 495, 504.

The population in Muscovite territories faced multiple crises during the second quarter of the fifteenth century. Those who survived the bouts of plague in the early decades of the century (1408–9, 1417, 1419–20) were beset by others, the most severe of which occurred in 1424–7 and 1448, as well as by accompanying famine.[89] War broke out in the 1430s between Vasilii II and his uncle Iurii and then with his cousin Vasilii Kosoi. The Tatars captured Vasilii II (1445); fire destroyed Moscow; and when Vasilii II was released, the war resumed, this time against his cousin Dmitrii Shemiaka.[90] During most of this period the Church was without a metropolitan; leaderless clergy were politically divided; and in the midst of these difficulties the Russian bishops broke with the patriarch in Constantinople.

The crisis within the Church began after Metropolitan Fotii (Photios), Kiprian's successor, died in 1431. His replacement, appointed by the patriarch in Constantinople, died before reaching Moscow. The Russian Church lacked a metropolitan just as the war between Vasilii and his uncle began. Unofficially, Iona, the bishop of Riazan', assumed a leadership role. But the war delayed the formal submission of his nomination to the patriarch. Iona was not able to set out for Constantinople until 1436, after the hostilities between Vasilii II and Vasilii Kosoi were concluded. But by the time he arrived, the patriarch and emperor had named Isidor to head the Russian Church (1437).[91]

Isidor's appointment had political motives. The Ottoman Turks, who had seized most of the territories of the Byzantine Empire during the previous century, were threatening its very existence. The emperor and patriarch desperately sought military aid from Europe, but believed it would not be forthcoming without a resolution of the differences between the Orthodox and the Roman Churches. A council to consider terms for reunifying the two Churches was scheduled. Isidor, who had participated in making arrangements for the council and supported the goal of reconciliation, was chosen to become head of the Russian Church in order to gain its co-operation and to lead its delegation to the council.[92]

---

89 Gonneau, 'The Trinity-Sergius Brotherhood', p. 119; Alef, 'Origins', 24; Langer, 'Black Death', 58, 60–1, 67; Lawrence N. Langer, 'Plague and the Russian Countryside: Monastic Estates in the Late Fourteenth and Fifteenth Centuries', *CASS* 10 (1976): 355.
90 Miller, 'The Cult of Saint Sergius', 689.
91 Alef, 'Muscovy and the Council of Florence', 394; Alef, 'Origins', 43; Michael Cherniavsky, 'The Reception of the Council of Florence in Moscow', *Church History* 24 (1955): 347; Borisov, *Russkaia tserkov'*, p. 142.
92 Alef, 'Muscovy and the Council of Florence', 390, 393–4; Alef, 'Origins', 42–3; Charles Halperin, 'Tverian Political Thought in the Fifteenth Century', *Cahiers du monde russe et soviétique* 18 (1977): 267.

Within six months of his arrival in Moscow, Isidor left, accompanied by a large delegation, to attend the council in Ferrara and Florence, Italy. The Russian Church was once again left without a resident metropolitan. When Isidor did return in 1441, he came, as a consequence of the union achieved by the council in 1439, as a cardinal and a papal legate. Three days later Vasilii II ordered his deposition and arrested him. Although they allowed Isidor to escape six months later and return to Italy, the grand prince and the clergy of Muscovy firmly rejected union with Rome.

For seven more years the Russian Church lacked a metropolitan. In 1448, shortly after he had recovered Moscow, Vasilii II convened the bishops of the Russian eparchies to elect Iona to be metropolitan of the Russian Church. By failing to follow the patriarch into union with Rome and by naming a metropolitan themselves, the bishops with Vasilii's approval were operating autonomously. The fall of Constantinople to the Turks in 1453 appeared to be divine punishment, validating the conviction held by the Russian Church hierarchs that Constantinople's union with Rome had been heretical. It left the Russian Church as the sole bearer of the true Orthodox faith.[93]

Iona's position, which he held by virtue of election by the bishops and appointment of the grand prince but without consecration from the patriarch, was tenuous. He and his supporters thus undertook a variety of measures to bolster his claim to leadership over the entire metropolitanate and to justify the method of his selection. The latter involved depicting the princes of Moscow, particularly Vasilii II, as endowed with divine favour and chosen to rule and defend Muscovy, the bastion of the true Orthodox faith. The techniques employed to solidify the position of the metropolitan also offered an ideological basis for elevating the grand prince just as he was militarily defeating his rivals and politically consolidating his authority over northern Russia. They provided the domestic source of legitimacy that replaced the Tatar patronage on which the Muscovite princes had previously depended.

After his election Iona began to use the title 'metropolitan of Kiev and all Rus'', as Kiprian, Fotii and even Isidor had done. By doing so Iona asserted himself as the rightful heir of these predecessors and the leader of the entire ecclesiastical realm. He used the title until his death in 1461. In 1458, however,

93 Obolensky, 'Byzantium and Russia', 266, 270–1; Cherniavsky, 'Reception of the Council of Florence', 348–9, 351–4; Alef, 'Muscovy and the Council of Florence', 390, 394, 396, 400; Alef, 'Origins', 43–5; Borisov, *Russkaia tserkov'*, pp. 142–3, 156, 158–9; Zimin, *Vitiaz'*, pp. 131–2.

the exiled Uniate patriarch of Constantinople conferred the title on another metropolitan, Gregory (Gregorios Bulgar). Gregory arrived in Lithuania in 1459 and assumed ecclesiastical jurisdiction over the Orthodox eparchies, including Kiev, under the secular rule of the king of Poland and Lithuania. The Russian metropolitanate was once again divided and Iona's goal of keeping it unified and Orthodox was thus frustrated.[94]

Efforts were also made to enhance the spiritual stature of the Russian Church. The sainthood of the monk Sergei of Radonezh (St Sergius) was recognised between 1447 and 1449.[95] In his *vita* of Sergei, the first version of which he produced in the late 1430s, Pakhomii recorded several miracles.[96] In one the Blessed Virgin, long associated with Kiev, appeared to Sergei and assured him that She would protect his monastery.[97] Images portraying this miracle began to be produced at the Trinity monastery in the 1450s.[98] In another Sergei is depicted as blessing Grand Prince Dmitrii Ivanovich and his army on the eve of the Battle of Kulikovo and as thus being instrumental in securing divine assistance for their victory. Scholars doubt that Sergei gave that blessing.[99] But by including it along with the miracle of the Holy Virgin appearing to Sergei, Pakhomii was able to suggest that the divine protection previously extended to Kiev was transmitted through the agency of Sergei to Moscow and its grand prince. This special favour enabled Dmitrii to defeat the infidel, Mamai and his host. This mythical account of Dmitrii's success contrasted sharply with the reality of the failing efforts of the apostate Byzantium to fend off the infidel Turks. The theme was echoed in the *vita*, also written by Pakhomii, of Nikon, a disciple of Sergei. In Nikon's case the infidel was Edigei, who invaded the Russian lands in 1408. Although Edigei's campaign had been devastating, in this account Nikon's prayers resulted in Sergei and also the metropolitans Petr and Aleksei interceding to save the Russian land.[100]

Ecclesiastical supporters of Iona thus made the case that divine protection and saintly intercession were reserved for Muscovy, the centre of the true

---

94 Pliguzov, 'Metropolitan of Kiev and All Rus'', 344, 352; Alef, 'Origins', 45; Obolensky, 'Byzantium and Russia', 272–3.
95 Miller, 'Cult of Saint Sergius', 691.
96 Ibid., 692–3; Crummey, *Formation of Muscovy*, p. 192.
97 Serge A. Zenkovsky (ed.), *Medieval Russia's Epics, Chronicles, and Tales* (New York: E. P. Dutton, 1974), p. 287; Borisov, *Russkaia tserkov'*, pp. 38, 111–12; David B. Miller, 'The Origin of Special Veneration of the Mother of God at the Trinity-Sergius Monastery: The Iconographic Evidence', *RH* 28 (2001): 303.
98 Miller, 'The Origin of Special Veneration', 306–7, 311.
99 E.g. Miller, 'Cult of Saint Sergius', 692; Miller, 'The Origin of Special Veneration', 303.
100 Miller, 'Cult of Saint Sergius', 693.

Orthodox Church. In this context the Muscovite princes were also depicted as divinely selected and endowed with the capacity to defend the Church and the Orthodox community from the infidel. In the *vita* of Dmitrii Donskoi, which may have been composed in the mid-fifteenth century, the prince's ancestry was traced back not just to Ivan I Kalita or even Daniil Aleksandrovich, the founder of the Muscovite line of princes, but to St Vladimir of Kiev.[101]

By the late 1450s and early 1460s, even before chroniclers included Dmitrii's *vita* in their compilations, Vasilii II was also being depicted in chronicle entries and other tracts about the Council of Florence in elevated terms. Vasilii II was compared to St Vladimir. Whereas St Vladimir had introduced Orthodoxy to the Russian lands, Vasilii II had become its defender. He had the insight and the courage to reject the apostate Isidor and preserve Orthodoxy in Russia. He, therefore, also had the spiritual authority to name the metropolitan. The role assigned to the grand prince carried both glory and responsibility. The fall of Byzantium left Muscovy the largest Orthodox realm in the world. Its grand prince assumed the task of protecting the faith previously undertaken by the Byzantine emperor. The grand princes of Moscow, descended from St Vladimir, blessed with divine favour and charged with the responsibility to defend the true Orthodox faith, had acquired the basis for a claim to legitimacy and sovereignty.[102]

* * *

During the period 1359–1462 the princes of Moscow struggled to overcome dynastic opposition and hold the position of grand prince of Vladimir. Surrounded by the Tatar khanates, into which the Golden Horde subdivided, and Lithuania, they faced formidable powers. But by the time Grand Prince Vasilii died in 1462, they had accumulated sufficient territorial, economic and military resources to become the dominant political figures in northern Russia. Their achievements were solidified by the Orthodox Church that, having lost its battle to preserve a unified metropolitanate of Kiev and all Rus', nevertheless

---

101 Gail Lenhoff, 'Unofficial Veneration of the Daniilovichi in Muscovite Rus'', in A. M. Kleimola and G. D. Lenhoff (eds.), *Culture and Identity in Muscovy, 1359–1584* (Moscow: ITZ-Garant, 1997), pp. 405–8; Wladimir Vodoff, 'Quand a pu être le Panégyrique du grand-prince Dmitrii Ivanovich, tsar russe?' *CASS* 13 (1979), 100; Pelenski, 'Origins of the Official Muscovite Claims', 37, 40–2, 44; Jaroslaw Pelenski, 'The Emergence of the Muscovite Claims to the Byzantine-Kievan "Imperial Inheritance"', *HUS* 7 (1983): 521; Halperin, 'Russian Land and Russian Tsar', 76.

102 Cherniavsky, 'Reception of the Council of Florence', 349–50, 352; Joel Raba, 'The Authority of the Muscovite Ruler at the Dawn of the Modern Era', *JGO* 24 (1976): 323; Obolensky, 'Byzantium and Russia', 267–8; Alef, 'Crisis', 24.

supplied the Muscovite princes with the legitimacy that had so long eluded them. Vasilii II, who fought a civil war to break the dynastic traditions of lateral succession and who also ended his ancestors' dependency on the khan for the throne, left his position and possessions to his son, Ivan III, who would transform his inheritance into the state of Muscovy.

8

Medieval Novgorod

V. L. IANIN

It would be difficult to find a medieval Russian city with a more distinctive history than Novgorod.

For the last seventy years medieval Novgorod has been the subject of intensive archaeological investigation. The results of these excavations have provided significant compensation for the regrettable scarcity of conventional sources for the history of early Rus'. This scarcity was caused by environmental factors. Throughout the Middle Ages (and well into modern times, too) Russians lived in wooden houses, and the towns which constituted their cultural centres comprised a collection of wooden structures which regularly fell victim to fires.

It is a distinctive feature of the cultural layer of Novgorod that because of its high humidity and the consequent absence of aeration, all kinds of ancient items have been preserved, including those made from organic materials (wood, bone, leather, cloth and grain) which are usually irreversibly destroyed in normal circumstances. This peculiarity has enabled researchers to establish precise dates for all the objects which have been discovered in the excavations, by means of dendrochronology. It also permitted the great discovery in 1951 of documents written on birch bark, which were preserved in ideal conditions in the cultural strata. By the end of the fieldwork season in 2003, 949 birch-bark documents had been found in Novgorod itself, plus one in nearby Gorodishche, and a further 57 in the surrounding district (38 in Staraia Rusa and 19 in Torzhok). Of these, about 500 were found in strata dating from the eleventh century to the first third of the thirteenth century. This has significantly increased the number of written sources available for the early medieval period, and it has enabled scholars to carry out a fundamental re-examination of many problems which had long been the subject of disputes.

The origins of Novgorod

The vast territory of the Russian north-west has an abundance of forests, lakes and marshes, but a great scarcity of arable land. For a long period (from the Neolithic and Bronze Ages) it was inhabited by tribes of the Finno-Ugrian linguistic group. From the fifth and sixth centuries AD the region was invaded by Slavonic tribes, but this did not lead to any conflict with the indigenous population. While the primary economic activity of the indigenous inhabitants was fishing and hunting, the Slavs tilled the land and cultivated cereals. Thus the two ethnic groups gravitated towards different types of settlement areas and did not interfere with one another.

For a long time historians believed that the Slav immigrants (the Novgorod Slovenes and Krivichi) had come from the middle Dnieper. It was assumed that before the division of Rus' into separate principalities in the twelfth century the eastern Slavs all spoke the same language, and that it was only in the twelfth century that dialects began to form, a development which was accelerated by the Tatar invasion of the thirteenth century. The study of the hundreds of birch-bark documents has, however, shown that the process worked in a completely opposite way. It turned out that the distinctive features of the Novgorod dialect were most evident in texts dating from the eleventh and twelfth centuries, and that subsequently they gradually disappeared as a result of contacts with other East Slav dialects. A search for parallels to the characteristics of the Novgorod dialect led to the conclusion that Slavonic migration to the Russian north-west originated from the territory of modern Poland and northern Germany, and that this was where the ancestors of the medieval Novgorodians came from.[1] This conclusion has been confirmed by archaeological and anthropological evidence.

The most important event in the early history of the north-west region of Rus' was its temporary subjection to the power of the Scandinavians. A later account in the *Novgorod Chronicle* states that the Varangians (i.e. Norsemen) exacted a general tribute (a squirrel-pelt per head) which they collected from the Slavonic tribes of the Slovenes and Krivichi and from the Finno-Ugrian tribe of the Chud', who had not previously been united. Their common misfortune led to an uprising against the Varangians, who were driven out. Once they had obtained their independence, the Slavonic and Finno-Ugrian tribes united and began to build towns, but subsequently they quarrelled among themselves and,

---

1 A. A. Zalizniak, 'Novgorodskie berestianye gramoty s lingvisticheskoi tochki zreniia', in V. L. Ianin and A. A. Zalizniak, *Novgorodskie gramoty na bereste (iz raskopok 1977–1983 gg.)* (Moscow: Nauka, 1986), pp. 89–121.

not wanting to grant pre-eminence to any one of the three tribes (the Slovenes, the Krivichi and the Finno-Ugrians), they decided to invite a Varangian prince from overseas. This plan was put into effect when an invitation was issued in 859 or 862 to the Scandinavian Prince Riurik,[2] who presumably came from Denmark or Friesland. Riurik first settled at Ladoga, but soon moved to a more convenient spot at the source of the River Volkhov,[3] where the main East European trade routes intersected.

The likelihood that this event actually occurred has been confirmed by excavations at Gorodishche (3 kilometres from Novgorod), where the residence of the Novgorod princes was situated until the end of the fifteenth century. The archaeological evidence from Gorodishche proves that the site was indeed founded in the middle of the ninth century. It clearly demonstrates that the inhabitants belonged to the social elite, and that the predominant element was Norman.[4]

When did restrictions on the power of the prince first arise? This is one of the most important problems facing students of the political system of Novgorod. The restrictions were set out as conditions in the invitations issued to princes, and they are found in the oldest of the extant agreements between Novgorod and its prince, which date from the 1260s (the earlier agreements have not survived).[5]

The most important restriction was that the invited prince and his retainers were forbidden to collect state taxes in the Novgorod lands. This right belonged to the Novgorodians themselves, who used the revenues they collected to pay the prince his so-called 'gift', that is, his remuneration for performing his duties. In the course of the Novgorod excavations in strata dating from the end of the tenth century to the first quarter of the twelfth century, wooden seals were frequently found; these were used to safeguard the contents of sacks containing the furs which had been collected as state revenues. These devices have inscriptions on them which indicate that the contents of the sack belonged to the prince or to the tax collectors themselves, who, according to *Russkaia pravda* (the oldest law code of Rus'), were allowed to keep a certain proportion of the collection for themselves. Altogether fifty-one of these items have been found, all of them in the homes of the Novgorodians themselves.

---

2 *Novgorodskaia pervaia letopis' starshego i mladshego izvodov* (Moscow and Leningrad: AN SSSR, 1950), p. 106.

3 *PSRL*, vol. II (St Petersburg: Tipografiia M. A. Aleksandrova, 1908), col. 14.

4 E. N. Nosov, *Novgorodskoe (Riurikovo) Gorodishche* (Leningrad: Nauka, 1990).

5 *Gramoty Velikogo Novgoroda i Pskova* (Moscow and Leningrad: AN SSSR, 1949), nos. 1–3, pp. 9–13.

In several cases these finds were accompanied by birch-bark documents containing detailed information about the revenue collection, addressed to the individuals whose names were inscribed on the seals. Although the earliest of these seals to have survived dates from the end of the tenth century, similar finds in tenth-century strata in Szczecin in Poland, and in Dublin in Ireland, enable us to conclude that the custom of using such devices is of Norman origin; but the limitation of the power of the prince in such an important sphere as tax collection and the preparation of the state budget most probably goes back to the presumed agreement with Riurik.[6]

If this is the case, it explains why Riurik's successors – Oleg, and Riurik's son Igor' – left Novgorod. Breaking his agreement to serve as prince for life, Oleg moved south in order to conquer first Smolensk and then Kiev. His power in Kiev was therefore based not on an agreement, but on the right of a conqueror. Thus the prince was not limited in his actions, and he and his retinue were able to collect revenues (the *poliud'e*) in the lands subject to his authority.

The departure of Oleg and Igor' to the south created a political vacuum in north-western Rus'. As a result of Oleg's breach of the agreement, there was no prince. In his place his representatives, probably headed by a governor appointed by the prince, remained at Gorodishche. But at this period Novgorod itself did not yet exist. Excavations in various parts of the city have not revealed any ninth-century cultural strata. Active settlement of the future territory of Novgorod began, however, at the end of the ninth century and the beginning of the tenth. This process coincided with the abandonment of many settlements in the surrounding district. We must assume that these two processes were interrelated, and that they were caused by the political vacuum created by the absence of a prince, which encouraged the tribal leaders of the Slovenes, Krivichi and Chud' to settle on the future territory of Novgorod, not far from the prince's residence.

The choice of this location, like that of the site of the prince's residence in the middle of the ninth century, was determined by its key position at the crossroads of the main international trade routes. Here, at the point where the River Volkhov flows out of Lake Il'men', the 'road from the Varangians to the Greeks' – the main line of north–south communication – intersected with the Volga–Baltic route – the main line of east–west communication. The active nature of trade movements along these highways is clearly demonstrated by the numerous hoards of Eastern silver coins of the late ninth to the early

---

6 V. L. Ianin, *U istokov novgorodskoi gosudarstvennosti* (Velikii Novgorod: Novgorodskii gosudarstvennyi universitet, 2001).

eleventh centuries and, after the exhaustion of the Asian silver mines – hoards of Western European *denarii* of the eleventh and early twelfth centuries.

Excavations have revealed the nature of the territory of the future Novgorod in the first half of the tenth century. It was not yet a town, but rather three settlements of tribal leaders, separated from one another by uninhabited areas. Around the central farmsteads in these settlements there lay arable lands criss-crossed by dirt-tracks. The names of these settlements, which subsequently provided the basis of Novgorod's administrative-territorial division (its *kontsy,* or 'ends'), indicate their probable original ethnic composition: *Slavenskii* (that is, Slavonic), *Nerevskii* (from the name of a Finno-Ugrian tribe, the 'Noroma' or 'Nereva') and *Liudin* (from the Slavonic word *liudi*, meaning 'people' – most probably this was a Krivichi settlement). The transformation of this loose pre-urban structure into a town took place in the middle of the tenth century.

In 947 the Kievan Princess Ol'ga, while putting the administrative system of her state in order, came to the north-west and carried out campaigns which resulted in the subjugation and unification of the densely inhabited regions along the rivers Msta and Luga. In consequence, the tax system of Novgorod and the amount of the state revenue more than doubled. As a result, the streets began to be paved, and there emerged a system of services and utilities, the construction of homesteads in streets, and other attributes of a town.[7] From this point it is appropriate to use the term, 'Novgorod', since it was then that the social centre of the new formation arose – the kremlin (*Detinets*), which was from the outset called *Novyi gorod* (new town) to distinguish it both from the three original urban-type settlements and from Gorodishche.

The development of boyar power

The newly transformed town exerted a magnetic attraction on the all-Russian princely house. In 970–80 the sons of the Kievan prince Sviatoslav Igorevich, Vladimir and Iaropolk, fought for the right to act as its prince, and sent their governors to Novgorod. In the end Vladimir emerged as the victor, and in his reign (after he had become prince of Kiev) Novgorod followed the example of Kiev in accepting Christianity (around 990) and acquired as its prince Vladimir's son, Iaroslav the Wise. The first churches were constructed in Novgorod at the end of the tenth century – the wooden cathedral of St Sophia and the church

---

7 V. L. Ianin, 'Kniaginia Ol'ga i problema stanovleniia Novgoroda', *Drevnosti Pskova. Arkheologiia. Istoriia. Arkhitektura* (Pskov: Pskovskii gosudarstvennyi ob"edinennyi istoriko-arkhitekturnyi i khudozhestvennyi muzei-zapovednik, 2000), pp. 22–5.

of saints Joachim and Anna, whose dedication is connected with the name of the first bishop of Novgorod, Joachim.

Iaroslav's reign as prince lasted until 1015, when after the death of his father he engaged in a conflict with Sviatopolk the Accursed (Okaiannyi) for control of Kiev. The Novgorodians helped him to achieve victory in this conflict, and Iaroslav rewarded them for their assistance by granting them new privileges. These included the declaration that the Novgorod boyars – the direct descendants of the tribal leaders who had originally invited Riurik to Novgorod – were not subject to the prince's jurisdiction.[8] But even before Vladimir's death, Iaroslav had in 1014 refused to pay the traditional tribute of 2,000 grivnas to Kiev. Only Vladimir's death prevented a military confrontation between father and son.

The privileges which the Novgorod boyars obtained from Iaroslav the Wise laid the basis for the division of Novgorod into two administrative structures. The boyars' homesteads, which were not subject to the jurisdiction of the prince, became the basis of the system of 'ends'. The areas which lay between these 'ends' were settled by inhabitants who were independent of the boyars, including free artisans and merchants. These districts remained within the jurisdiction of the prince. They were divided into 'hundreds' (*sotni*), and were administered by 'thousanders' (*tysiatskie*) and 'hundreders' (*sotskie*), who constituted the machinery of princely governance right up until the end of the twelfth century.

While he was still prince of Kiev, Iaroslav did something that was exceptionally important for Novgorod's cultural development. On a visit to Novgorod in 1030 he 'collected 300 of the elders' and priests' children, in order to teach them book-learning'.[9] Archaeological work has, however, shown that literacy in Novgorod had begun even before this date. In 2000, during excavations in the Liudin 'end' (to the south of the kremlin) in a stratum from the beginning of the eleventh century, there was found a set of three waxed wooden tablets inscribed with several psalms (see Plate 9). Investigations showed that this was designed to teach writing: the teacher wrote something, made the pupils copy what he had written, then rubbed it out and wrote a new text on the smoothed surface. At the present time the 'Novgorod psalter' – so called because the waxed tablets preserve extracts from the psalms – is the oldest dated 'book' in the entire Slavonic world. This was how the very first Novgorod Christians, who had only just been converted (at the end of the

8 V. L. Ianin and M. Kh. Aleshkovskii, 'Proiskhozhdenie Novgoroda: K postanovke problemy', *Istoriia SSSR*, 1971, no. 2: 32–61.
9 *PSRL*, vol. VI, vyp.1 (Moscow: Iazyki russkoi kul'tury, 2000), col. 176.

tenth century), learned to write.[10] Thus when Iaroslav the Wise set up his school in Novgorod, he was following an example which already existed. In the reign of Iaroslav the Wise the prince's position within the power structure of Novgorod was strengthened, and this was reflected in the transfer of his residence from Gorodishche to Novgorod. There it occupied territory on the Trading Side of the town, opposite the kremlin, which to this day is called 'Iaroslav's Court'.

After the wooden cathedral of St Sophia was destroyed by fire, the stone cathedral of St Sophia which survives in Novgorod to the present day was built in 1045–50, on the initiative of Prince Vladimir, the son of Iaroslav the Wise, with the involvement of master-craftsmen from Kiev. This is the oldest stone church on the territory of present-day Russia. At the same time, new fortifications were built in the kremlin, which provided a reliable defence both for the cathedral and for the bishop's palace which was situated alongside it.

In the last quarter of the eleventh century a number of changes took place in Novgorod which testify to the strengthening of the local aristocracy (the boyars) and the weakening of the power of the prince. In 1088–94 the prince of Novgorod was Mstislav, the young son of Vladimir Monomakh. David, the prince sent from Kiev to replace him, was expelled by the Novgorodians, who insisted on the restoration of Mstislav. This was the first clear demonstration of that 'freedom to choose the princes' which was to become the constitutional principle of the Novgorod boyars, who cited the invitation to Riurik as a precedent.

In 1102 the Novgorodians again opposed Kiev's planned replacement of Mstislav by a Kievan client. An analysis of the archaeological evidence relating to imports shows that the city's opposition to Kiev was accompanied by a trade blockade: Kiev cut off the routes by which goods from the south reached Novgorod.

The Novgorodians' concern for Mstislav was accompanied by the introduction during his minority of the most important political institution of boyar rule – the *posadnichestvo* (governorship). If previously the term *posadnik* had been used for the governors sent from Kiev, now the *posadnik* was elected from among the boyars and governed Novgorod jointly with the prince.[11] It was at this time, too, that a second major restriction was placed on the power of the prince – the invited prince was forbidden to own land on a private-property

10 V. L. Ianin and A. A. Zalizniak, 'Novgorodskaia psaltyr' nachala XI veka – drevneishaia kniga Rusi', *Vestnik Rossiiskoi akademii nauk* 71, 3 (2001): 202–9.
11 V. L. Ianin, *Novgorodskie posadniki* (Moscow: Izdatel'stvo Moskovskogo universiteta, 1962), pp. 54–62.

basis anywhere on the territory which was subject to Novgorod. That right was granted only to the Novgorodians themselves.

In addition, the prince and his court returned to Gorodishche, where the prince's residence was restored; it remained there right up until the sixteenth century.

In 1117 Mstislav Vladimirovich, on the instructions of Vladimir Monomakh, departed from Novgorod for Smolensk, leaving his son Vsevolod as prince of Novgorod in his place. In order to make material provision for Vsevolod, Mstislav transferred to Novgorod extensive border territories from his principality of Smolensk, and these became Vsevolod's domain. These lands were transferred on condition that the income derived from them should be placed at the disposal of the prince of Novgorod only if the invited prince was a direct descendant of Mstislav. If a member of another princely line was summoned, the domain's revenues were to be sent to Smolensk.[12]

During Vsevolod's reign the Novgorod boyars introduced yet another restriction of the prince's rights. Originally the prince had performed the functions of the supreme judge of Novgorod. Now a joint judicial court was set up, comprising the prince and the *posadnik*, the head of the boyars. The prince formally retained the main role (he ratified decisions with his seal), but he did not have the right to make a final decision without the *posadnik*'s sanction. In the course of excavations in 1998 the meeting-place of this court was discovered. It had been established in the middle of the 1120s and had functioned for five or six decades, as was shown by more than 100 birch-bark documents which were found there, relating to various types of judicial disputes.[13]

In 1136 a major uprising against the prince led to a complete victory for the boyars, who reorganised the political system and in effect turned the prince into an official of the boyar republic. The prince retained the function of the judge; his decisions, however, acquired force only after they had been definitively confirmed by the *posadnik*. As a result of this uprising Prince Vsevolod was driven out of Novgorod, and Sviatoslav Olegovich was invited from Chernigov to replace him. This turnaround, of course, meant that the issue of the material remuneration of the prince and his retinue had to be resolved again. Sviatoslav was allocated lands in the north, in the region of the Northern Dvina and Pechera rivers. These lands were, however, soon returned to the jurisdiction of the boyars, and the princes were apportioned less prosperous territories.

12 V. L. Ianin, *Novgorod i Litva. Pogranichnye situatsii XIII–XV vekov* (Moscow: Izdatel'stvo Moskovskogo universiteta, 1998).
13 Ianin, *U istokov novgorodskoi gosudarstvennosti*, pp. 6–30.

From the beginning of the twelfth century onwards, problems associated with landholding became the central issues in the economic and political history of Novgorod. The Novgorod lands were deficient in minerals. Iron was found in the region only in the form of marsh ores. All other types of raw material for craft production were obtained by trade: precious and non-ferrous metals were imported from various European countries; amber from the Baltic; valuable types of wood from the Caucasus; and precious and semi-precious ornamental stones from the Urals and from Oriental lands.

In exchange for these imports, Novgorod was able to bring to the international market those resources of the Novgorod lands which were obtained by hunting, fishing and bee-keeping: expensive furs, valuable fish, wax and honey. Their possession of lands which were rich in these valuable export commodities provided the basis of the economic prosperity of the Novgorod boyars. It was precisely in the twelfth century that the system of patrimonial estates (*votchiny*) began to be created in the Novgorod lands.[14]

The layout of every urban boyar homestead included not only living quarters and outhouses, but also the workshops of the craftsmen who were dependents of the householder. The products obtained on the boyar's lands were processed by these craftsmen and taken to the city market, where merchants could sell them in exchange for raw craft materials brought in from abroad. As a result, the main revenue was obtained by the landowners who owned the original products.

In this connection, a major preoccupation of Novgorod's military policy in the twelfth century was the defence of its northern possessions from attacks on them by the Vladimir-Suzdal' principality. Historical chronicles mention numerous military clashes between Novgorod and the Suzdalian claimants to these possessions. The most significant of these was the campaign of the Suzdalians against Novgorod in 1169–70, which resulted in victory for the Novgorodians, whose success was ascribed to a miracle caused by the icon of the 'Mother of God of the Sign', which thereafter became Novgorod's most sacred possession.

The internal politics of the Novgorod boyars was greatly influenced by the rivalry among the territorial groupings which went back to the ancient rivalry among the three original settlements which had formed the basis of Novgorod. Competing with one another for the post of *posadnik*, these groups found allies in the princes of Smolensk, Chernigov and Suzdal', and as a result their internal

---

14 V. L. Ianin, *Novgorodskaia feodal'naia votchina (Istoriko-genealogicheskoe issledovanie)* (Moscow: Nauka, 1981), pp. 200–57.

squabbles were combined with the conflicts among the princes of Rus' for influence in Novgorod. A graphic example of this incessant struggle was the uprising of 1207, in the course of which the boyar grouping of the Liudin end, which was then in power, was expelled from Novgorod; its property, including its landholdings, was distributed among the participants in the uprising; its mansions were burned; and the post of *posadnik* passed into the hands of the rival boyar grouping which had organised the uprising in alliance with the prince of Suzdal'.

A major landmark in the development of the boyar state was the establishment at the end of the twelfth century of the post of republican 'thousander', as a result of which the 'hundreds' system passed out of the jurisdiction of the prince into the jurisdiction of the boyar republic.[15]

In the course of the twelfth century, Novgorod developed its own school of art and architecture. At the beginning of the century the cathedral churches of the monasteries of St Anthony and St George were built and decorated with frescos, and the church of the Annunciation was constructed in princely Gorodishche. These churches served as models for the architects of the entire twelfth century. Among the most significant masterpieces was the church of the Saviour on the Nereditsa, which was built near Gorodishche in 1198 and painted with frescos in 1199. These paintings, which were considered by art historians to be the most significant example of such work in medieval Russia, survived until the twentieth century. Tragically, they were largely destroyed during the Second World War. In the 1960s the church was restored in its original form, but most of its fresco paintings have been preserved only in copies and photographs.[16]

It is worth noting that medieval art in Rus' was usually anonymous. The names of Feofan Grek (Theophanes the Greek), Andrei Rublev and Dionisii, who lived in the fourteenth and fifteenth centuries, are well known, but the names of the artists of the pre-Mongol period were unknown until recent times. Scholars frequently expressed the view that their anonymity would last for ever. In the course of excavations in the 1970s and 1980s, however, archaeologists unearthed the home of an artist of the late twelfth and early thirteenth centuries. His name was discovered from birch-bark letters addressed to him, many of which contained orders for the painting of icons. The artist was called Olisei Grechin; he was also mentioned in the chronicles as a master fresco painter. When his autographs on the birch-bark documents were studied and

15 Ianin, *Novgorodskie posadniki*.
16 *Freski Spasa-Nereditsy* (Leningrad, 1925).

compared with the handwriting of the artist who headed the workshop that
painted the frescos in the church of the Saviour on the Nereditsa, Olisei was
shown to have had the main responsibility for the creation of these murals.[17]

Many birch-bark letters have also been found which were written by Olisei's
father – Petr Mikhalkovich – or received by him. When this group of documents
was studied, it was possible to establish that Petr and his wife Mariia (Marena
in the birch-bark documents) had commissioned the most famous Novgorod
icon of the twelfth century – the icon of the Mother of God of the Sign –
which, as we have already said, played a part in the battle of 1170. It turned out
that this icon was painted for the wedding of Petr Mikhalkovich's daughter
Anastasiia to the Novgorod Prince Mstislav – the son of the famous Prince Iurii
Dolgorukii. This marriage took place in 1155. At the same time Petr and his wife
Mariia commissioned one of the greatest masterpieces of Novgorod applied
art – a silver chalice (communion cup) by the master-craftsman Kosta, which
contains depictions of the Mother of God and saints Peter and Anastasia.[18]

The thirteenth and fourteenth centuries

The thirteenth century was a time of trial for Novgorod. At the very beginning
of the century a permanent military danger arose on the western borders of
the Novgorod lands, from the Teutonic order of knights who had settled on
the Baltic. On the north-western borders no less dangerous a threat was posed
by Swedish aggression. In 1238 in the course of the Tatar–Mongol invasion the
forces of the horde began their incursions into the territory of Novgorod. Baty's
army besieged the Novgorod town of Torzhok for a month, annihilating its
heroic defenders. However, the defence of Torzhok saved Novgorod. Torzhok
was conquered in March; by this time the supplies of fodder for the cavalry
were exhausted, and this frightened the Tatars, as it created a real danger
that they would lose the horses which were their main means of military
transport. The Tatar forces, having come within about a hundred kilometres
of Novgorod, returned to their southern steppes.[19]

After this the Novgorodians managed to concentrate their military forces
for the defence of their western borders, where in 1240 Aleksandr defeated

17 B. A. Kolchin, A. S. Khoroshev and V. L. Ianin, *Usad'ba novgorodskogo khudozhnika XII v.*
   (Moscow: Nauka, 1981).
18 A. A. Gippius, 'K attributsii novgorodskikh kratirov i ikony "Znamenie" ', *Novgorod i Novgorodskaia zemlia. Istoriia i arkheologiia*, vyp. 13 (Novgorod: Novgorodskii gosudarstvennyi
   ob"edinennyi muzei-zapovednik, 1999), pp. 379–94.
19 V. L. Ianin, 'K khronologii i topografii ordynskogo pokhoda na Novgorod v 1238 g.',
   Issledovaniia po istorii i istoriografii feodalizma (Moscow: Nauka, 1982), pp. 146–58.

the Swedes in the Battle on the River Neva for which he received the epithet 'Nevskii'; and in 1242 he vanquished an army of Teutonic knights on the ice of Lake Chud'. This victory was not, however, a decisive one. It was only after a bloody battle at Rakovor (Rakver in Estonia) in 1269 that peace was established on the western borderlands.

At the same time the Tatar–Mongol invasion had had an impact on Novgorod. The traditional system of trade and cultural links with the devastated Russian principalities was destroyed. The building of stone churches was halted until the 1290s. The construction of a stone kremlin in place of the wooden one was begun only in 1302.

Significant changes took place in the relationship between boyar Novgorod and the princes. Previously the principle of 'freedom to choose the princes' had lain at the basis of this relationship; but now the Novgorodians automatically recognised as their prince the man whom the khans of the Golden Horde confirmed as the head of the Rus' princes ('the grand prince'). However, in so far as the main sphere of activity of the grand prince lay outside Novgorod, he came to be represented by governors whom he appointed. Thus the participation of the grand prince in Novgorod affairs was minimal, and this strengthened the boyar republican system.

The behaviour of Grand Prince Aleksandr Nevskii, who required Novgorod to pay tribute to the Mongols even though it had not been conquered by them, and who destroyed some of the boyars' republican prerogatives, provoked the indignation of the Novgorodians, and after Aleksandr's death they set about reorganising the system of government. In an agreement concluded with his brother, Grand Prince Iaroslav Iaroslavich, in the 1260s, the prerogatives which the Novgorodians had previously obtained were confirmed: the prince did not have the right to collect state revenues from the territory of the Novgorod lands (the Novgorodians did that themselves, thereby controlling the state budget); he did not have the right to own any landed estates on the territory of the Novgorod state on a private-property basis; and he also had no right to pronounce judicial decisions without the sanction of the *posadnik*. In the same agreement the prince undertook to refrain from those infringements of the law which had been permitted by his late brother.

After this the functions of the prince in the judicial sphere were restricted even further. If previously all judicial matters had come under his jurisdiction, then at the end of the thirteenth century there was organised a commercial court which came under the jurisdiction of the thousander (a Novgorod boyar), and an episcopal court, which had particular authority over the large group of the population who lived on lands belonging to ecclesiastical institutions.

This situation led to yet another significant reorganisation. From the end of the thirteenth century an immense amount of monastery construction took place in Novgorod. The wealthy boyar families founded monasteries, acted as their patrons and endowed them with considerable wealth, primarily in the form of landholdings. However, in so far as this entire system of landed possessions came within the jurisdiction of the archbishop as head of the Church, the boyars fully realised that any future extension of monastery landholdings might turn the archbishop from a spiritual pastor into the real head of the state, since 'he who controls wealth, holds power'. For that reason a reform was introduced, which resulted in the creation of the office of archimandrite – the head of the entire Novgorod black clergy.

The archimandrite, who acquired as his residence the St George monastery, 4 kilometres outside Novgorod, was in charge of the hegumens (abbots) of the monasteries of the five administrative districts ('ends') of Novgorod. In ecclesiastical and canonical matters the archimandrite was of course subordinate to the archbishop; he was not, however, appointed by the archbishop, but was elected at the boyar *veche* (assembly), like the *posadniki* and other state officials, and he was accountable for his economic activity not to the archbishop, but to the boyar authorities. In other words, the boyar corporation exercised full control over the secular activity of the archimandrite, and it could remove him from office if he turned out to be awkward or incompetent. The boyar groups made full use of this right.[20]

In the last third of the thirteenth century important changes took place in the political system of Novgorod. The boyars, in an attempt to reduce rivalry in the struggle for control of the highest offices of state, created an institution in which the interests of all the territorial groupings were represented. The merchants' organisation acquired its own special administrative system, headed by a thousander who was also elected for a specified period.

In the early 1290s a very important reform of the republican administration was implemented. In essence this amounted to the annual election of the head of state (the *posadnik*); the head of the merchantry and the free artisan population (the thousander); and the head of the black clergy (the archimandrite). It would be difficult to think of a better way of controlling the activity of the highest state leaders. With these new forms of state organisation in place, Novgorod entered the fourteenth century.[21]

20 V. L. Ianin, 'Monastyri srednevekovogo Novgoroda v strukture gosudarstvennykh institutov', *POLYTROPON: k 70-letiiu V. N. Toporova* (Moscow: Indrik, 1998), pp. 911–22.
21 Ianin, *Novgorodskie posadniki*.

In many respects the beginning of the fourteenth century was a watershed in the history of Rus' in general, and of Novgorod in particular. Novgorod's role in the strengthening of the Russian economy must be especially stressed. Having avoided military devastation by the Golden Horde, and having repulsed the aggression of the Swedes and the Teutonic knightly orders on its western borders, Novgorod remained the only region to acquire significant quantities of silver from Western Europe in exchange for the products of its agriculture, hunting, fishing and bee-keeping. The whole of Rus' needed silver, both for its own requirements and for the constant payment of tribute to the Golden Horde. The re-export of silver from Novgorod to Tver', Moscow, Suzdal' and other towns in central Rus' not only strengthened the Novgorodian economy, but it also inspired the aggressive envy of its neighbours, provoking permanent military conflicts with Tver' and then with Moscow.

Incidentally, the constant flow of Western European silver into Novgorod around the beginning of the fourteenth century led to the introduction of a new monetary unit, the rouble, which remains the basis of the Russian coinage to the present day.

A very unusual system for the defence of the state boundaries of the Novgorod lands emerged in the thirteenth and fourteenth centuries. Some of the frontier territories were placed under the dual control of rival factions. For example, the extensive district of Torzhok, situated on the south-western frontiers of Novgorod, was the joint possession of the Novgorodian and the grand-princely authorities. The Novgorodian enclave of Volokolamsk, surrounded on all sides by the lands of the Moscow princes, was in the same position. Tver' made active attempts to detach Torzhok from Novgorod at the beginning of the fourteenth century and in the 1370s, but they were resisted by the Novgorodians.

The system of dual subordination of its frontier territories provided Novgorod with a highly effective means of dealing with Lithuania, which posed a real military threat from the second half of the thirteenth century onwards. In the period from the mid-thirteenth to the first third of the fourteenth century the northern districts of the Smolensk principality which bordered on Novgorod fell into the hands of Lithuania as a result of Lithuanian aggression against Smolensk and Novgorod. After successful military action by Novgorod in 1326 a general peace was concluded amongst Novgorod, the Teutonic order, Smolensk, Polotsk and the grand duchy of Lithuania. The main achievement of this peace treaty was the creation of a long-lasting set of principles which governed border relationships between Lithuania and Novgorod. Lithuania accepted its obligation to observe strictly the sovereignty of Novgorod over the entire territory of its possessions, and in exchange it received the revenues of those Novgorod frontier lands which in 1117, according to the wishes of Mstislav, had been transferred to Novgorod from the Smolensk principality, as the domain of those Novgorod princes who were descendants of Mstislav. Having conquered the Smolensk territories, Lithuania thereby inherited the rights bestowed by the ancient relationships between Smolensk and Novgorod.[22]

In the years immediately following this action, the system of military and political co-operation between Novgorod and Lithuania was extended. The princes of the Lithuanian royal house received 'as feeding (*kormlenie*)' (as a source of revenue) some small Novgorodian towns on the border with Sweden and accepted the obligation to protect the Novgorodian territory there against possible Swedish expansion. Sometimes this system experienced periods of conflict, but in general it operated successfully right up until the loss of Novgorod's independence at the end of the fifteenth century.

Conflict with Moscow

Relations with Moscow turned out to be more difficult. Before the decisive victory of Rus' over the Golden Horde in 1380 at the Battle of Kulikovo, there was a struggle for the grand-princely title between representatives of various Russian centres – in particular, between Tver' and Moscow. The victory of 1380 definitively secured that title for the Moscow princes. But at the same time this outcome meant that Novgorod in effect lost its traditional right to choose its prince, and this exacerbated its relations with Moscow and led to attempts to look to Moscow's opponents as an alternative.

In 1384 the Novgorodians declared that they were no longer under the jurisdiction of the Moscow metropolitan. Two years later the Moscow Prince Dmitrii launched a military campaign against Novgorod in revenge for an attack by the Novgorodians on his possessions. In 1397 Dmitrii's son Vasilii I broke the peace with the Novgorodians, forced the Dvina boyars to recognise his authority over the Dvina lands and also seized Volokolamsk, Torzhok, Vologda and Bezhetsk. The status quo was partially restored only in 1398. In 1419 the Novgorodians declared that their prince was the brother of the Moscow prince, Konstantin Dmitrievich, who had quarrelled with Vasilii I; this conflict was, however, quickly patched up.

22 Ianin, *Novgorod i Litva*.

The complexity of its relations with Moscow was an important reason for the extension of Novgorod's fortifications. In the 1380s a circle of external defensive structures was built – the *Okol'nyi gorod* (the 'outer town'), about 9 kilometres in length, and consisting of an earthen rampart topped with a wooden wall and with stone towers over the entrances.

The growing rivalry with Moscow at this time, in the reign of Dmitrii Donskoi, led Novgorod to adopt the proud name of 'Great' Novgorod, as a kind of equivalent to the title of Grand (literally 'great') Prince.

The loss of their traditional choice of a prince was one of the reasons for the consolidation of the Novgorod boyars. A second and equally serious reason for this process of consolidation was the growth of anti-boyar sentiments among the non-privileged mass of the population of Novgorod. The institution of boyar power was reorganised as early as the middle of the fourteenth century. Before the reform of 1354 each of the five Novgorod 'ends' elected its representative for life, and the *posadnik* was elected annually from among these representatives (and only from their number). Now all five representatives became *posadniki*, and in addition a chief ('*stepennyi*') *posadnik* was elected at the city *veche*.[23]

The new system led to the consolidation of the boyars. Previously they had obtained high state office as a result of conflicts with other boyar families which assumed the form of a competition among the 'ends' of Novgorod. At the same time the boyars largely lost the opportunity to engage in social demagogy. Previously a candidate who was standing for election as *posadnik* could try to persuade the ordinary people that their problems stemmed from the fact that it was his rival who was running the state, and canvass on his own behalf; but now the boyars as a whole accepted collective responsibility for their political actions.

This became even more obvious in the next stage of the reform, at the end of the 1410s. Around 1417 the norms of representation were trebled: the sources testify to the simultaneous existence of eighteen *posadniki* from this date, and re-elections of the head of state began to be held not once but twice a year. However, even this innovation did not remove the social tensions. In 1418 there was a mighty anti-boyar uprising led by a certain Stepanka. The insurgents flocked to plunder the monasteries, saying, 'Here are the boyars' granaries, let us pillage our foes!' The terrified boyars managed to calm the crowd down with the help of the archbishop, but it seems that in the course of this uprising the conflicts among the boyars' territorial groupings

---

23 Ianin, *Novgorodskie posadniki*.

remained, and were criticised by the archbishop, as the spiritual leader of Novgorod.

The great anti-boyar uprising of 1418 encouraged the Novgorod boyars to carry out a new consolidation, in which the number of *posadniki* who were active at the same time was increased to twenty-four, and in 1463 to thirty-six (at that time they also began to elect seven thousanders). Virtually every boyar family in Novgorod had a share in power. The representatives of all of these families not only had the opportunity to be elected to the office of *posadnik* or thousander, but in practice they more or less owned these offices. It is revealing that the chronicle, when describing the events of the third quarter of the fifteenth century, frequently does not unambiguously name the *posadniki*. As a result of the reforms of the fifteenth century, which increased the number of *posadniki* practically to the number of boyar families, the title of *posadnik* was devalued, and the designation of boyar acquired additional weight. It seems that in this period the terms 'boyar' and *'posadnik'* were used interchangeably in everyday usage.

At the same time, the collegial institution of 1417, comprising eighteen *posadniki*, five thousanders, the archimandrite and five hegumens (each of whom supervised the priors of the monasteries in their 'ends' and were subordinate to the archimandrite) acquired a certain resemblance to the senate of the Venetian republic. This similarity was recognised in Novgorod, as the following illustration demonstrates. From 1420, when the Novgorodians began to mint their own silver coinage, and right up until the end of Novgorodian independence, the coins retained the same design, the main element of which was the depiction of a kneeling horseman receiving the symbols of power from the hands of the patroness of Novgorod, St Sophia. This image was undoubtedly modelled on the traditional subject of Venetian coins, which depicted a kneeling Doge receiving the symbols of power from the patron of Venice, St Mark.

At the same time, the emergence of this oligarchic political institution fundamentally altered the relationship between the boyars and the other strata of the Novgorod population. Previously the territorial boyar groupings had fought among themselves for power, but now the consolidated boyar institution as a whole was counter-posed to the non-privileged strata of the Novgorod population. This new disposition of forces is reflected in the chronicle entries of the mid-fifteenth century which speak of the 'unjust boyars' and state that 'we have no justice or fair court proceedings'; and also in the emergence of a whole group of literary works which criticise the self-interest and corruption of the boyars and especially of the *posadniki* ('The tale of the *posadnik*

Dobrynia', 'The tale of the *posadnik* Shchil'). These attitudes were to have fateful consequences in the future, when the power of the Novgorod boyars at the time of its liquidation by Ivan III could not find defenders in the mass of the ordinary population of the city.

Meanwhile the confrontation between Novgorod and Moscow intensified from decade to decade. The famous conflict between Prince Vasilii II Temnyi (the 'Dark') of Moscow and Prince Dmitrii Shemiaka of Galich had an impact on Novgorod. Dmitrii Shemiaka, after he had been defeated by Vasilii, whom he had blinded, found refuge in Novgorod, where Vasilii Temnyi's vengeance caught up with him: Dmitrii was poisoned on the orders of the Moscow prince who soon afterwards – in 1456 – launched a military campaign against Novgorod. The Novgorodians were instructed not to provide any support for Dmitrii Shemiaka's son Ivan and his ally, the Mozhaisk prince Ivan Andreevich. It is significant that it was in 1463, when the Novgorodians defied this prohibition – thereby proclaiming a definitive rift with Moscow – that the final stage in the expansion of boyar representation in the supreme institution of power took place. Such a decisive step could not be taken without a new demonstration of the unity of the boyar groups.

At this time the end of Novgorod's independence was approaching. Ivan III's anti-Novgorod policy was motivated by his claim that Novgorod aimed to transfer to the jurisdiction of Lithuania and renounce the Orthodox faith. Fearing Muscovite expansionism, Novgorod was indeed seeking an alliance with Lithuania and put forward the idea of inviting the Lithuanian Grand Prince Casimir as its prince. However, the drafts of a possible agreement contained special provisions for religious independence and the inviolability of sacred Orthodox objects of veneration. Nevertheless it was under the slogan of the defence of Orthodoxy that Ivan III in 1471 launched a campaign against Novgorod, which suffered a severe defeat in the battle on the River Shelon'. The initiators of the alliance with Lithuania were executed, but the institutions of boyar power were not altered.

In 1475 the Muscovite prince undertook what was this time described as a 'peaceful campaign' against Novgorod. He was met by delegations of Novgorodians all along his route, and thereafter he displayed a certain degree of objectivity in the judicial decisions which he made in response to complaints from the inhabitants of Novgorod.

The end of Novgorod's independence came in 1477, when Ivan III sent numerous troops against Novgorod. It is ironic that, as is evident from several documents, the Muscovite grand prince did not have the explicit intention of subjugating Novgorod. A folder which accompanied him on the campaign has been preserved; it contains documents which justified Moscow's rights only to the possession of territories along the Northern Dvina. The aim of his military expedition was to detach the Dvina lands from Novgorod.[24] However, as has already been noted above, boyar power found no defenders, and Novgorod fell into the hands of the Muscovite prince, who established complete control over the Novgorodians in January 1478. The *veche* was prohibited, *posadnichestvo* was abolished as a symbol of autonomy, and the *veche* bell was taken to Moscow. However, the Moscow prince swore that he would not interfere with the landed property of the Novgorodians. This promise was broken some ten years later, when thousands of Novgorodian landowners were resettled on Muscovite lands and Muscovite service-tenure landholders were brought in to replace them.

Novgorod in the fifteenth century

What was Novgorod like when Moscow liquidated its independence? An answer to this question requires us to examine a number of important aspects of its culture.

Only fifty years ago the conventional view in the scholarly literature was that the population of medieval Rus' was completely illiterate. It was assumed that the only literate people were the clergy and the princes, and that not even all of them could read and write.

Now more than a thousand birch-bark texts dating from the eleventh to fifteenth centuries have been found in the towns of early Rus', 949 of them in Novgorod. Calculations based on the characteristics of the cultural layer of Novgorod enable us to state that the site still contains at least 20,000 similar documents, written by people of the most varied social positions – boyars and peasants, artisans and merchants. They include a considerable number of texts written by women, which for the Middle Ages is the most revealing indicator of the high cultural level of a society. It is clear that the figure cited above reflects only a tiny proportion of all that was written on birch-bark in medieval Novgorod: the majority of such letters must have been burned either in the frequent street fires or in domestic stoves. It has been noted that the majority of texts written by authors of low social status date from the fourteenth and fifteenth centuries.

The rarity of birch-bark texts in other towns, and their abundance in Novgorod, results not only from the fact that extensive excavations have been

24 V. L. Ianin, 'Bor'ba Novgoroda i Moskvy za Dvinskie zemli v 50–kh - 70-kh gg. XV v.', *IZ* 108 (1982): 189–214.

conducted in Novgorod from 1932 onwards. There were other reasons for the high level of literacy in Novgorod, including the peculiarities of its political system. As we have already noted, the annual re-elections to the highest offices of state created the opportunity for every boyar to be elected to these coveted posts. The economic base of the Novgorod boyars was very large-scale landownership. In the central and southern Rus' principalities, with their monarchical political systems, the boyars displayed centrifugal tendencies, aspiring to live far away from the prince on their own estates, where they themselves could behave like monarchs towards their vassals. But the Novgorod boyar was centripetal. To leave Novgorod and live on one's own estate, dozens or hundreds of kilometres away from Novgorod, meant turning into a hermit, cut off from the hotbed of political passions, and renouncing any claims to power. The fifteenth-century cadastres show that the Novgorod boyars lived in Novgorod itself, far from their landed possessions and from their peasants. But these possessions required the boyar's constant attention. He had to issue instructions to his stewards, to receive reports from them about the progress of agricultural work and the prospects for the harvest, and of course about the income from his estate. The birch-bark letters of the fourteenth and fifteenth centuries are largely concerned with these issues. But such correspondence required literacy not only from the master, but also from the servant. And amongst the letters from this period we find a considerable number which were written by peasants, containing various complaints, including some about the activities of their master's estate stewards.

There is another important factor which helped to create the high cultural level of the citizens of Novgorod. Unlike Venice, where the senate met in an enclosed building which guaranteed the confidentiality of its sessions, the Novgorod *veche*, at which the top leaders of the boyar republic were elected, at first once and then twice a year, discussed their problems in the open air near the cathedral of St Nicholas, in the vicinity of the city market. The members of the *veche*, who had the right to vote on important decisions, were representatives of the city's elite, the owners of large city homesteads, and primarily boyars. Incidentally, a fourteenth-century German source refers to the Novgorod *veche* as '300 gold belts', which corresponds to the approximate number of owners of large urban homesteads. But the public had open access to the *veche* assembly: the Novgorod plebs who congregated in the *veche* square had an opportunity to influence the conduct of the assembly with cries of approval or dissent, thereby creating for themselves the illusion of participation in the political life of the city and the state. It may have been illusory, but this sense of involvement was undoubtedly an important component of the mentality of the medieval Novgorodian.

Novgorod's busy international contacts were another significant influence. A. S. Pushkin famously wrote of Peter the Great, that he 'cut a window through to Europe' by annexing the Baltic coast of the Gulf of Finland. The contemporary writer Boris Kiselev, rephrasing Pushkin, expressed the important idea that, 'Where Peter cut a window through to Europe, in medieval Novgorod the door was wide open'.

Certainly from the time of its foundation Novgorod was very closely linked with the Baltic region. Even before the creation of the Hanseatic League Novgorod conducted active trade with the countries of northern and western Europe. At the beginning of the twelfth century on the Trading Side of the city there was built the Gothic Court, where merchants from the island of Gotland stayed. At the end of the twelfth century the German merchants, who were soon to become the leading figures in Baltic trade, built themselves a similar merchant court. After the formation of the Hanseatic League both of these foreign courts, the Gothic and the German, came under the jurisdiction of the Hanseatic merchants and formed a single Hanseatic office. In Hanseatic sources they are referred to as the Court of St Peter, after the Catholic church which stood in the German Court. In addition to Novgorod there were Hanseatic offices in three other European cities: London, Bruges and Bergen.[25]

Novgorod's contacts with Western Europe were not limited to trade. The entrance to the main Novgorod cathedral of St Sophia was adorned with wonderful bronze doors, which remain to the present day. These doors were made in Magdeburg in the twelfth century and came to Novgorod in the fourteenth century, when a Russian craftsman added some new reliefs to them and provided Russian translations of their Latin inscriptions. The chronicle states that the Novgorod archbishop's palace was built in 1433 by German craftsmen who worked alongside Novgorod craftsmen. We have already noted that Novgorod coins adopted the motif of Venetian coins, adapted to the local patron saint.

The high level of Novgorod's cultural attainment in the fourteenth and fifteenth centuries is indicated by the number of churches listed in an inventory which was compiled at the end of the fifteenth century, immediately after the annexation of Novgorod by Moscow. Altogether there were eighty-three

---

25 E. A. Rybina, *Inozemnye dvory v Novgorode XII–XVII vv.* (Moscow: Izdatel'stvo Moskovskogo universiteta, 1986).

operational churches in the city, almost all of which were built of stone. They included such masterpieces of the Novgorod style as the fourteenth-century churches of St Theodore Stratelates on the Brook and the Transfiguration of the Saviour on Il'in Street, both of which were decorated with frescos. The artist responsible for the Transfiguration church was the great Feofan Grek (Theophanes the Greek). In 1407 the church of Saints Peter and Paul – the high-point of medieval Novgorodian architecture – was built at Kozhevniki.

Novgorod was surrounded by a tight circle of outlying monasteries, including the fourteenth-century churches at Volotovo and Kovalevo and the church of the Nativity in the Cemetery, whose interiors retain outstanding sets of frescos of the same period. This circle of surrounding monasteries began to be built in the eleventh century. It included such outstanding twelfth-century masterpieces of art and architecture as the cathedrals of the St George and St Anthony monasteries, and of the monasteries of the Annunciation and the Saviour on the Nereditsa.

An interesting episode in the history of Novgorodian architecture was the period of activity of Archbishop Evfimii II (1428–54). A strong opponent of Moscow, he became the main ideologue of anti-Muscovite sentiments. Harking back to the twelfth century, when Novgorod had witnessed its greatest successes in its struggle against princely power and in strengthening its boyar institutions, Evfimii revived the architectural style of that period, which was markedly different from that of the fourteenth and early fifteenth centuries. By that date the style of the single-apsed church with a slanted (*lopastnyi*) roof had become standard, but Evfimii II encouraged the restoration of twelfth-century churches 'on the old basis', with their characteristic three apses and roofs with arched gables. When the Muscovites established themselves in Novgorod they took these revivalist churches to be examples of the latest fashion and they based the future development of architecture in Novgorod on these models.

Epilogue

The annexation of Novgorod by Moscow in 1478 interrupted building activity in the city for a long time. Construction was abandoned in the last years of Novgorod's independence, during the turbulent times of the final conflict with Moscow. The last church before the annexation was built in 1463, and the next one only in 1508. The main efforts of the Muscovites when they took over in Novgorod were directed towards fortifying the city as the most important border fortress in north-west Rus'. At the end of the fifteenth century the walls and towers of the kremlin were rebuilt. Then it was the turn of the

Okol'nyi gorod – the outer fortifications of Novgorod – to be rebuilt. Moscow was preparing for a protracted war for the acquisition of an extensive outlet to the Baltic Sea.

In 1570 a new tragedy occurred in Novgorod, when Ivan the Terrible inflicted bloody reprisals on the city, suspecting its inhabitants of treason.[26] The Livonian war (1558–83) inflicted another harsh blow on Novgorod. The cadastres compiled in the 1580s reveal a picture of devastation of the once flourishing city. At the very end of the century, however, Novgorod was getting back on to its feet. An Italian architect whose name remains unknown to us was invited to the town and drew up the plans for an additional line of fortification which was built around the stone-built kremlin. The so-called 'Earthen Town' was one of the first structures in Europe to have bastions. However with the onset of the seventeenth century and the 'Time of Troubles' Novgorod came under Swedish control for seven whole years (1611–17). These years completed its destruction,[27] which was compounded by the transfer of the main centre of Russian trade with Western Europe to Archangel.

The Soviet–German war of 1941–5 virtually wiped Novgorod from the face of the earth, turning dozens of its historic buildings into ruins. But yet again, because of its cultural significance both for Russia and for Europe as whole, Novgorod was raised from its ruins, like the mythical phoenix which is born again from the ashes. For its very name – *Novyi gorod*, the new town – seems to symbolise the youth and immortality of this great city.

Translated by Maureen Perrie

26 R. G. Skrynnikov, *Tragediia Novgoroda* (Moscow: Izdatel'stvo imeni Sabashnikovykh, 1994).
27 *Opis' Novgoroda 1617 goda*, vyp. 1–2 (Moscow: AN SSSR, 1984).

PART II

*

THE EXPANSION, CONSOLIDATION AND CRISIS OF MUSCOVY (1462–1613)

9

The growth of Muscovy (1462–1533)

DONALD OSTROWSKI

During the period between 1462 and 1533, Muscovy underwent substantial growth in land and population, virtually tripling in size (see Map 9.1). The Muscovite state gained a significant amount of land and population to the southwest in treaties with Lithuania, and annexed the principalities and republics of Iaroslavl' (1471), Perm' (1472), Rostov (1473), Tver' (1485), Viatka (1489), Pskov (1510), Smolensk (1514) and Riazan' (1521). But by far its greatest acquisition was through the annexation of Novgorod in 1478. At the same time, the ruling order – that is, the grand prince, princes, boyars and other landlords – consolidated its hold on the populace and countryside. One should not focus on the enormous expansion as the result of some kind of Muscovite 'manifest destiny' (the so-called 'gathering of the Russian lands'), because the expansion itself occurred as the result of a significant refashioning and implementation of internal policies by the grand princes and ruling elite. These policies transformed Muscovy from a loosely organised confederation, roughly equivalent in structure to any of the neighbouring steppe khanates, into a monarch-in-council form of government with a quasi-bureaucratic administrative structure equal to that of any European dynastic state. These policies included more effective and uniform administrative institutions and methods, the creation of a ready and mobile military force, and the building of a spectacular citadel in the capital to impress all and sundry with the ruling power. Non-Russian princes and nobles were incorporated in large numbers. Added to these developments was an implacable aggrandisement of power on the part of those who ran the state. In short, they made the Muscovite dynastic state. These changes were begun under Vasilii II, brought to fruition under Ivan III and developed further under Vasilii III.

Throughout this process, the grand princes worked with the consensus support of the ruling class. Although individual boyars could be punished for crimes against the ruler, the boyars as a whole contributed to the propagation of Muscovite power. Parallel with the state, the Church also instituted

Map 9.1. The expansion of Muscovy, 1462–1533

standardised policies and practices. In addition, churchmen developed an anti-Tatar ideology that soon came to permeate all their writings about the steppe and has heavily influenced historians' interpretation of this period. Eventually, the increase and spread of civil administration began to interfere with the Church's practices, and the Church's search for heretics affected some state personages, but on the whole the state and Church worked together, although not always completely harmoniously.

In what follows, I will describe the situation and conditions in Muscovy at the time of the ascension to the throne of Ivan III in 1462; how that situation and those conditions were affected by the reigns of Ivan III and Vasilii III; and sum up the differences that occurred in Muscovy by 1533.

Muscovy in 1462

In the middle of the fifteenth century, Muscovy was one of a number of independent Rus' principalities and republics that had the potential for expansion and for incorporating other Rus' principalities and republics. Riazan', to the south-east on the other side of the Oka River from Muscovy, had maintained its viability and sovereignty despite being located in the northern reaches of the western steppe and often caught in battles between the Qipchaq (Kipchak) khans and Muscovite grand princes. The grand prince of Tver', just to the west of Muscovy, was nominally a vassal of the Muscovite grand prince, but he could still manoeuvre relatively independently in diplomatic relations. An alliance of Tver' with Lithuania against Muscovy was an ongoing possibility and if successful could have advanced the Tver' grand prince to first place among the Rus' princes. Novgorod further to the west of Tver' was a prosperous merchant republic that held nominal possession of vast lands to the north and north-east all the way to the White Sea and coast of the Arctic Ocean. In addition, four other principalities and republics had managed to remain independent of neighbouring larger entities. Iaroslavl' and Rostov were virtually surrounded by Muscovite holdings, and their incorporation into Muscovy seemed to be only a matter of time. The republic of Pskov, situated between Novgorod and Lithuania, tended to remain closely allied with Novgorod but could and did on occasion use its proximity with Lithuania for political leverage. Finally, the republic of Viatka, located to the north-east of the Muscovite domain and north of Kazan', also played off its two more powerful neighbours to maintain its independence.

In domestic terms, the grand prince of Muscovy ruled with sharply circumscribed powers. He had no standing army and was dependent on his relatives and vassal princes to raise military forces. Since he had insufficient economic resources to maintain a large-scale standing force, he was subject to more or less constant armed threats, both external and internal, to his crown. The grand prince, thus, had a tenuous hold on power. Vasilii II barely survived capture by the Kazan' Tatars in 1445, as well as a civil war with his uncle and nephews that disrupted the Muscovite realm for almost twenty years.

By 1462, when Vasilii II died, he had defeated his rivals in the civil war, consolidated the support of the ruling class, and reached agreement with the

Table 9.1. *Vasilii II and his immediate descendants*

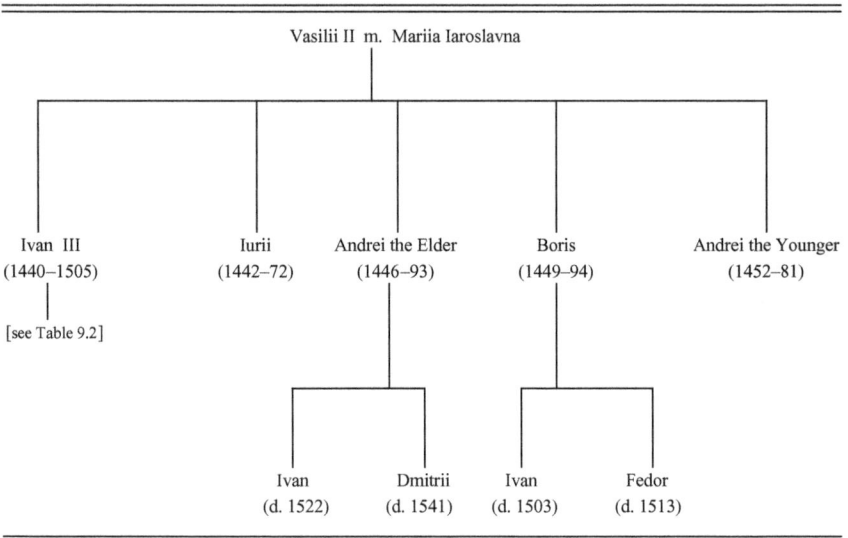

		Vasilii II m. Mariia Iaroslavna		
Ivan III (1440–1505)	Iurii (1442–72)	Andrei the Elder (1446–93)	Boris (1449–94)	Andrei the Younger (1452–81)
[see Table 9.2]				
		Ivan (d. 1522) — Dmitrii (d. 1541)	Ivan (d. 1503) — Fedor (d. 1513)	

Rus' Church leaders. His son Ivan III inherited a domain that was relatively prosperous being able to extract tolls along the Moskva River and along those sections of the Oka and Volga rivers that it controlled, as well as tax peasant farmers who cultivated and harvested grain and forest products, such as honey, flax, wax and timber.

Among the indigenous continuities that laid the basis for further developments were the social structure of Muscovy and the Church of Rus'. The social structure itself and categories within the Muscovite domains remained fairly consistent while the composition within certain categories changed significantly.

Vasilii II made it clear in his will that his eldest son Ivan III should succeed him as grand prince. Nonetheless, he distributed his lands among his five sons (see Table 9.1: Vasilii II and his immediate descendants). Although Ivan received the bulk of Vasilii's lands (fourteen towns versus twelve towns divided among the other four sons), the younger sons, Iurii, Andrei the Elder, Boris and Andrei the Younger received substantial holdings. In effect, Ivan was *primus inter pares* among his brothers, and Ivan still had to call on his brothers to help him raise troops.

During this period, the Muscovite grand princes successfully ended the independence of other Rus' princes. In part they did so by forbidding them independent contact with the Tatar khans so as to prevent them from receiving the *iarlyk* (patent) for their principality. And any *iarlyk* they had received had to be turned over to the grand prince. Thus, the Muscovite grand prince became the sole source of authority for these princes' legitimacy as rulers in their own domains.

Not having the means to gather large-scale forces themselves, the grand princes relied on the support of others to mobilise armies, at least until the end of the fifteenth century. During the fourteenth century, the grand princes relied mainly on the Tatar khans to supply large numbers of forces for major campaigns. The grand princes supplemented those troops with forces supplied by members of their own family (brothers, uncles and cousins) as well as by independent Rus' princes. On those occasions when the Tatar khan did not supply troops, the grand princes relied on the support given by independent Rus' princes. Early in the fifteenth century, the Tatar khans and independent Rus' princes stopped supplying forces to the Muscovite grand prince altogether,[1] so he had to rely more on members of his own family as well as on semi-independent 'service' princes (including Lithuanian, Rus'ian and Tatar), who contributed their own retinues and warriors.

Muscovy's internal governmental operation relied on reaching decisions through institutional consultation and consensus-building among the elite and, through that elite, with the ruling class. The Muscovite grand prince and the boyars made the most important laws of the realm in consultation with each other, and these laws were promulgated only with the consent of the boyars. The boyar duma was thus a political institution that had a prominent governmental role as a council of state. It had the same three functions as the divan of *qarachi beys*, the steppe khanate council of clan chieftains, and was most likely modelled on it. The approval of the boyars was required for all important governmental endeavours and the signatures of its members were mandatory on all matters of state-wide internal policy. Treaties and agreements had to be witnessed by boyars, and could also include brothers and sons of the ruler, close advisers, other prominent clan members, as well as religious leaders. Representatives of the boyars had to be present at any meetings the grand prince had with foreign ambassadors

---

1 The second *Sofiia Chronicle* contains a warning from Iona, the archbishop of Novgorod, to the Novgorodians not to kill Vasilii II upon his visit there in 1460 because 'his eldest son, Prince Ivan . . . will ask for an army from the khan and march against you': *PSRL*, vol. VI.2 (Moscow: Iazyki russkoi kul'tury, 2001), col. 131. Although the khans had stopped sending forces to aid the Muscovite grand prince after 1406, the notion that the grand prince could theoretically call on such troops apparently still existed fifty-four years later.

and envoys.[2] The ruler was thereby prevented from making agreements with foreign powers without the knowledge and approval of the boyar duma.

Since the grand prince had no standing army to speak of, his armies had to be gathered anew for each campaign, and demobilised after that campaign was over. The Muscovites of this period seem to have fought using steppe tactics and weapons, which depended on mounted archers with composite bows. Gravures in Sigismund von Herberstein's mid-sixteenth-century published version of his *Notes on Muscovy* show Muscovite mounted archers with the steppe recurved composite bow, which delivered an arrow more powerfully and at a greater distance than either the crossbow or the English longbow, and was superior to any firearm before the nineteenth century in terms of range, accuracy and rate of fire (see Plate 11). The military register books (*razriadnye knigi*) tell us the kind of regimental formations in which the Muscovite army fought. These formation arrangements were similar to those of Mongol and Tatar armies. But by the second half of the fifteenth century, Muscovy was already beginning to take part in the gunpowder revolution of the West. The chronicles describe the Muscovites using arquebuses against the Tatars in 1480. The men shooting these weapons were the forerunners of the *strel'tsy* (musketeers) of the sixteenth and seventeenth centuries.

During the fifteenth century, commercial activity placed Moscow in the middle of a large merchant trade network that reached from the Black Sea well into the forests of the north. Three main trade routes cut across the steppe to the Black Sea. The most easterly one ran down the Don River to Tana. The middle route was mainly an overland route to Perekop and the Crimea. The westerly route ran from Moscow through Kaluga, Bryn, Briansk, then east of Kiev to Novgorod Severskii and Putivl'.[3] Our main sources of information about those trade routes come from the end of the fifteenth century when Muscovy began taking over protection of Rus' merchants plying those routes. Forest products for trade, as well as customs duties (*tamga, kostki*) and tolls (*myt*) on commerce passing through the territory Moscow controlled were the basis of fifteenth- and sixteenth-century Muscovite prosperity.

---

2 See Donald Ostrowski, 'Muscovite Adaptation of Steppe Political Institutions', *Kritika* 1 (2000): 288–9.

3 V. E. Syroechkovskii, 'Puti i usloviia snoshenii Moskvy s Krymom na rubezhe XVI veka', *Izvestiia AN SSSR. Otdelenie obshchestvennykh nauk*, no. 3 (1932): 200–2 and map. See also Janet Martin, 'Muscovite Relations with the Khanate of Kazan' and the Crimea (1460s to 1521)', *CASS* 17 (1983): 442.

As in most other countries of the time, over 85 per cent of the population of Muscovy was engaged in agricultural pursuits. Much of the peasantry were not free farmers but lived on the estates of magnates or the monasteries. Peasants' relationship with the landlords could be complex and acrimonious, resulting in court cases. Peasants, accustomed to being mobile from engaging in slash-and-burn agricultural methods, began to be restricted in their movements through state regulations.

About 10 per cent of the Muscovite population consisted of slaves. Different categories of slaves existed in Muscovy and some, considered elite slaves, served in governmental, provincial and estates administration.[4] Elite slaves occupied such positions as treasurer (*kaznachei*), administrative assistant (*tiun*), rural administrator (*posel'skii*), estate steward (*kliuchnik*), state secretaries and estate supervisors (*d'iaki*) and various other positions from translator (*tolmach*) to archer (*strelok, luchnik*).[5] During the time of Ivan III and Vasilii III there were few or no restrictions on who could own slaves. Such restrictions began to come later in the sixteenth century. People could also move in and out of slave status. When Ivan III introduced *pomest'e* (see below), he converted a number of elite military slaves into military servitors.[6]

Muscovy was a vital trade centre for the forested area north of the western steppe region. As a result, the Muscovite ruling class, military, administration and culture were subject to outside influences. Until the fifteenth century, the major influence flow across the Eurasian land mass was from east to west. Inventions and administrative practices and innovations came from China and spread westward. In the fifteenth century, the direction of influence flow began to reverse, and we see the first signs of a west-to-east flow. Muscovy, located on the cusp between East and West started to experience Western influences at this time.

Finally, the ideal of the relationship between grand prince and metropolitan was inherited from Byzantium as a reflection of the relationship between the basileus and patriarch, which was to be one of harmony between state and Church. According to Byzantine political theory the head of the state and the head of the Church were two arms of the same body politic. Their spheres of influence, although differing, also overlapped to an extent. While the ruler of the state took as his sphere of influence civil administration and

---

4 Richard Hellie, *Slavery in Russia 1450–1725* (Chicago: University of Chicago Press, 1982), p. 15.
5 *Ibid.*, p. 462, table 14.1.
6 *Ibid.*, p. 395.

direction of military forces, the head of the Church could and did act as an adviser in that sphere. Likewise, the sphere of the head of the Church was internal Church matters, such as dogma and ritual. Yet, the head of the state could advise on those matters. In the overlapping sphere, which concerned the external Church administration, the two were to act together. As in Byzantium, this ideal of symphony of powers was striven after but not always attained.

Ivan III and Vasilii III

We have little historical evidence concerning the personal characteristics of Ivan III. Perhaps the only contemporary evidence is Ambrogio Contarini's description of Ivan when he was thirty-seven years old: 'he is tall, thin, and handsome.'[7] If we extrapolate from the evidence of Ivan's policies and actions, we get an image of Ivan III as an individual intent on expanding his power yet at times faltering, at other times unsure how to attain his goal, trying one policy for a while only to abandon it for another. He endures the Novgorod–Moscow heretics much to the chagrin of the Church leaders, then turns against the heretics and aids the Church in bringing them to trial and punishment in 1504. He had his grandson Dmitrii crowned co-ruler in 1498 and executed six conspirators while arresting a number of others who were allegedly plotting to set up a centre of rebellion under his son Vasilii in the northern provinces of Beloozero and Vologda.[8] Ivan changed his mind four years later when he placed Vasilii on the throne as his co-ruler, and he put Dmitrii and Dmitrii's mother Elena under house arrest. According to the ambassador from the Holy Roman Empire Sigismund von Herberstein, who visited Muscovy in 1517 and 1526, Ivan III again changed his mind on his deathbed and wanted Dmitrii to succeed him.[9] In his actions toward the Qipchaq khan in 1480, he received the opprobrium of Archbishop Vassian Rylo for his indecisiveness and lack of courage.[10] And Stephen, the Palatine of Moldavia, is reported by Herberstein

---

7 Ambrogio Contarini, 'Viaggio in Persia', in *Barbaro i Kontarini o Rossii. K istorii italo-russkikh sviazei v XV v.*, ed. E. Ch. Skrzhinskaia (Leningrad: Nauka, 1971), p. 205.

8 The information about the execution of the conspirators can be found in *PSRL*, vol. VI. 2, col. 352; *PSRL*, vol. VIII (Moscow: Iazyki russkoi kul'tury, 2001), p. 234; *PSRL*, vol. XII (Moscow: Nauka, 1965), p. 246; *Ioasafovskaia letopis'*, ed. A. A. Zimin (Moscow: AN SSSR, 1957), p. 134. In addition, according to one copy of the *Nikon Chronicle*, certain 'women [*babi*] were coming to her [Sofiia] with herbs' (presumably poisonous) and they were 'drowned by night in the Moskva River': *PSRL*, vol.XII, p. 263.

9 Sigismund von Herberstein, *Notes upon Russia*, 2 vols., trans. R. H. Major (New York: Burt Franklin, 1851–2), vol. I, p. 21.

10 *Pamiatniki literatury drevnei Rusi. Konets XV – pervaia polovina XVI veka* (Moscow: Khudozhestvennaia literatura, 1984), pp. 522–37.

Table 9.2. *Ivan III and his immediate descendants*

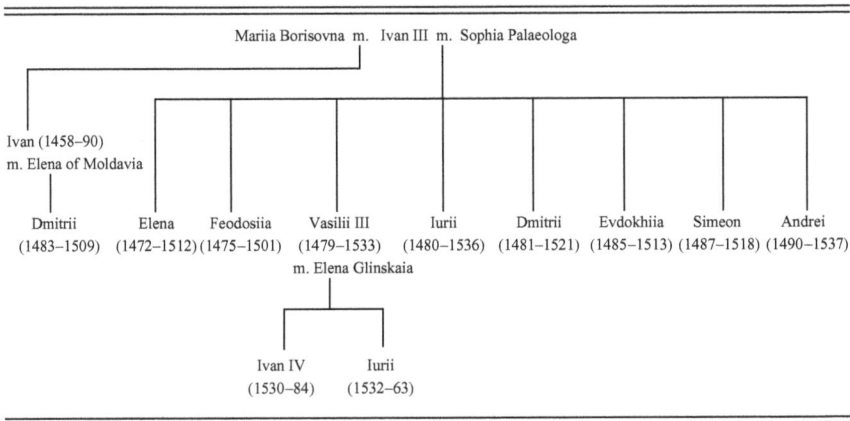

Mariia Borisovna m. Ivan III m. Sophia Palaeologa

Ivan (1458–90) m. Elena of Moldavia

Dmitrii	Elena	Feodosiia	Vasilii III	Iurii	Dmitrii	Evdokhiia	Simeon	Andrei
(1483–1509)	(1472–1512)	(1475–1501)	(1479–1533)	(1480–1536)	(1481–1521)	(1485–1513)	(1487–1518)	(1490–1537)

Vasilii III m. Elena Glinskaia

Ivan IV	Iurii
(1530–84)	(1532–63)

to have often said about Ivan: 'That he increased his dominion while sitting at home and sleeping, while he himself could scarcely defend his own boundaries by fighting every day'.[11] Nonetheless, the reign of Ivan III and the actions he did take had a decisive impact on the creation of the Muscovite state.

At the age of six years, Ivan was betrothed to Mariia, the daughter of Boris Aleksandrovich, the grand prince of Tver', as part of a treaty Vasilii II arranged in 1446 in order to regain the grand-princely throne from his cousin Dmitrii Shemiaka. The marriage took place six years later in 1452 and Mariia Borisovna gave birth to a male heir, Ivan, in 1458. She died in 1467. Mariia does not seem to have played any direct role in the politics of the time in contrast to her mother-in-law Mariia Iaroslavna and her successor as wife, Sofiia Palaeologa, whom Ivan III married in 1472. Sofiia gave birth to eight children (see Table 9.2: Ivan III and his immediate descendents): Elena (who married Alexander, the grand duke of Lithuania); Feodosiia (who married Prince V. D. Kholmskii); Vasilii III; Iurii of Dmitrov; Dmitrii of Uglich; Evdokhiia (who married the Tsarevich Peter Ibraimov); Simeon of Kaluga; and Andrei of Staritsa. Meanwhile, Ivan, the son of Ivan III and Maria Borisovna, married Elena of Moldavia, who gave birth to a son Dmitrii. The question whether his grandson Dmitrii by the son of his first wife or his son Vasilii by his second wife should succeed him vexed Ivan during his last years. In addition, in 1503, Ivan III suffered a debilitating stroke and appears to have been severely incapacitated until his death two years later on 27 October 1505.

11 Herberstein, *Notes*, vol. I, p. 24.

Vasilii III, like his father, strove to expand his own personal power along with that of the state, and, also like his father, depended on advisers within the ruling elite rather than on his own brothers. Within two months of succeeding to the throne in October 1505, he had Kudai Kul, a Kazanian tsarevich who had been in protective custody under Ivan III since 1487, convert to Christianity as Peter Ibraimov. Within another month Kudai Kul/Peter married Vasilii's sister Evdokhiia. From then until his death in 1523, Kudai Kul/Peter was Vasilii's closest associate,[12] and possibly was to be his successor.[13] Only after Kudai Kul/Peter's death did Vasilii III begin proceedings to divorce his wife Solomoniia because she had not produced an heir. On 28 November 1525, she went to the Pokrov monastery in Suzdal' and was veiled as a nun. Within two months, Vasilii married Elena Glinskaia, who produced two sons – Ivan in 1530 and Iurii in 1532. Vasilii III died on 21 September 1533, from a boil on his left thigh that had become infected.

Domestic policies

The domestic policies of both Ivan III and Vasilii III focused on reducing the power of their brothers and on maintaining good relations with the boyars and the Church. The relationship between Ivan III and Vasilii III, on one side, and their respective brothers, on the other, was often a tense and suspicious one. Both grand princes, however, required their brothers' help in mobilising troops. Each grand prince had four brothers and each brother could be expected to muster about 10,000 men for a campaign.

On 12 September 1472, Ivan's eldest brother, Iurii, died childless without having completed his will. The draft form of the will revealed only lists of goods, monetary wealth and villages that were to be distributed among his mother, brothers, separate individuals and monasteries. Nothing in the will mentioned what should happen to his lands in Dmitrov, Khotun', Medyn', Mozhaisk and Serpukhov. Ivan decided to absorb Iurii's holdings into his own instead of (as was traditionally done) dividing them with the other remaining brothers.

---

12 See my 'The Extraordinary Career of Tsarevich Kudai Kul/Peter in the Context of Relations between Muscovy and Kazan' ', in Janusz Duzinkiewicz, Myroslav Popovych, Vladyslav Verstiuk and Natalia Yakovenko (eds.), *States, Societies, Cultures: East and West. Essays in Honor of Jaroslaw Pelenski* (New York: Ross Publishing, 2004), pp. 697–719.

13 On this point, see A. A. Zimin, 'Ivan Groznyi i Simeon Bekbulatovich v 1575 g.', *Uchenye zapiski Kazanskogo gosudarstvennogo pedagogicheskogo universiteta* 80: *Iz istorii Tatari* 4 (1970): 146–7; A. A. Zimin, *Rossiia na poroge novogo vremeni (Ocherki politicheskoi istorii Rossii pervoi treti XVI v.)* (Moscow: Mysl', 1972), p. 99; A. A. Zimin, *V kanun groznykh potriasenii. Predposylki pervoi Krest'ianskoi voiny v Rossii* (Moscow: Mysl', 1986), p. 25.

This action upset the brothers who received nothing, for they, according to the chronicles, then complained and were given additional lands by Ivan and his mother, Mariia. The next year, 1473, Ivan concluded treaties with Boris (February) and Andrei the Elder (September) in which they acknowledged Ivan and his son Ivan as 'elder brothers'. The treaty prohibited Boris and Andrei the Elder from carrying on diplomatic or military relations with any other ruler without the knowledge of Ivan III. They, in turn, were to be kept informed of Ivan's dealings with foreign princes. In addition, they obligated themselves to protect each other and their estates. No record of such a treaty with Andrei the Younger is preserved.

In the summer of 1480, Andrei the Elder and Boris withdrew their forces and headed for Lithuania. This potential defection came at a critical moment because Khan Ahmed of the Great Horde was advancing with his army on Muscovy. After much negotiation, Andrei and Boris returned to help in the defence of Moscow. In 1481, when Andrei the Younger died, he left everything to Ivan, who may have required Andrei to draw up his will this way so he would not have to repeat the disagreement with Boris and Andrei the Elder that had occurred eight years earlier when their brother Iurii died. Significantly, one of the witnesses of Andrei's will was the grand-princely boyar Prince Ivan Patrikeev.

Ivan arrested Andrei the Elder for not supplying him with troops to aid the Crimean Tatars against an attack from the Great Horde in 1491. Andrei died in prison in 1493, and Ivan took over his estates. Boris died in 1494 and divided his estates between his two sons: Fedor and Ivan. When Ivan Borisovich died in 1503, his lands reverted to Ivan III, and when Fedor Borisovich died in 1515, his lands reverted to Vasilii III.

Mutual dislike and distrust seem to have been characteristic of the relationship between Vasilii and his brothers. In 1511, his brother Simeon was caught trying to go over to Lithuania. Vasilii's concern that his brothers would succeed him after Tsarevich Peter Ibraimov died may have led him to divorce the barren Solomoniia and marry Elena.[14] Vasilii managed to complete the task started by his father of isolating the brothers of the grand prince from power and eliminating his dependency on them for troop mobilisation.

From the mid-fifteenth century on, the grand princes placed their armies predominantly under the command of service princes. On the occasion of Ivan's visit to Novgorod in 1495, in his entourage of 170 individuals listed in

14 *PSRL*, vol. v.1 (Moscow: Iazyki russkoi kul'tury, 2000), p. 103.

the *razriadnaia kniga,* 60 (35.3 per cent) had princely titles. It is likely that their prominence in the sources reflects their military importance as well. At the time of the accession of Ivan III, the only prince to hold a semi-independent apanage within the Muscovite realm was Prince Mikhail Andreevich of Vereia, who had shown great loyalty to Ivan's father. Nevertheless, Ivan pressured him to give up part of his apanage granted him by Vasilii II. After the disagreement over who held proper jurisdiction of the Kirillo-Belozerskii monastery in 1478, Ivan required Mikhail to cede to him the district of Belozersk, which was part of Mikhail's apanage. When Mikhail died in 1486, Ivan took the rest.

In 1473, one of the stipulations in Ivan III's agreements with his brothers Boris and Andrei the Elder was that Danyar Kasimovich and other Tatar service princes were to be considered 'equal in status' (*s odnogo*) with Ivan – that is, above the grand prince's brothers. Earlier in the century, in 1406, Vasilii I had established that the grand prince's brothers were to have a higher ranking than Rus' princes coming under Muscovite grand-princely domination or into Muscovite service.[15] Vasilii III maintained this ranking of brothers above service princes, and tsarevichi above brothers, as he preferred to have his brother-in-law, the tsarevich Peter Ibraimov, to be his closest adviser, to accompany him on campaigns, and to defend Moscow when it was attacked by the Crimean khan in 1521.

Ivan III and Vasilii III completed the process of incorporating the service princes as integral parts of their armies along with their own boyars. In 1462, we have the attestation of nine boyars, four of whom were princes, and in 1533, we have the attestation of twelve boyars, six of whom were princes (and three *okol'nichie,* one of whom was a prince). These numbers indicate that the service princes were already being merged with the boyars under Vasilii II. His son and grandson merely continued and reinforced the practice. Both Ivan III and Vasilii III treated their boyars well, let them manage their estates unhindered and regularly consulted with them on the formulation of state policies. For example, the three law codes from 1497 to 1589 include the boyars along with the grand prince/tsar as compiling or issuing the code. The Law Code (*Sudebnik*) of 1497 begins: 'In the year 7006, in the month of September, the Grand Prince of all Rus' Ivan Vasil'evich, with his sons and boyars, compiled a code of law . . . '[16] Numerous decrees contain the formula

15 *PSRL,* vol. xv.2 (Moscow: Iazyki russkoi kul'tury, 2000), cols. 476–7.
16 *Sudebniki XV–XVI vekov,* ed. B. D. Grekov (Moscow and Leningrad: AN SSSR, 1952), p. 19. The *Sudebnik* of 1550 begins similarly: 'In the year 7058, in the month of June, Tsar and Grand Prince of All Rus' Ivan Vasil'evich, with his kinsmen and boyars, issued this Code of Law': *Sudebniki XV–XVI vekov,* p. 141. The *Sudebnik* of 1589 (long redaction) includes

'the Grand Prince decreed with the boyars . . .' or similar formulas indicating that the boyars and the grand prince on certain important matters decreed together.[17] These formulas demonstrate that the boyars were fulfilling more than a mere advisory role and that their approval was required for the issuing of these acts.

The acts that the boyars participated in decreeing were the most significant acts of the government – namely, law codes, foreign treaties, and precedent-setting measures. Other, less important decrees, such as *kormlenie* ('feeding'), *votchina*, and *pomest'e* grants, judicial immunities, local agreements, etc., were clearly the prerogative of the ruler alone. As we might expect, there was always an in-between area – one of ambiguity – and this ambiguity could on occasion be the source of friction between the ruler and his boyars when one thought the other was transgressing the proper bounds.

In 1489, Ivan III told Nicholaus Poppel, the ambassador of the Holy Roman Emperor, that he could not meet him without the boyars present.[18] This declaration followed the steppe principle that the ruler could meet with foreign envoys only in the presence of representatives of the council of state. The minutes of the Ambassadorial Chancellery (*Posol'skii prikaz*) as well as accounts of foreign ambassadors to Muscovy attest that this practice was rarely violated. Vasilii was also accused by the court official I. N. Bersen-Beklemishev of ignoring the old boyars and of making policy 'alone with three [others] in his bedchamber'.[19] But this criticism was from someone who was not a boyar and was an isolated one. Vasilii and the boyars seem to have been much in accord throughout his reign.

Through the introduction of *pomest'e*, the grand princes were able to maintain a group of cavalry (estimated at around 17,500 by the time of the reign of Ivan IV)[20] who were ready at a moment's notice (at least in principle) to

---

top Church prelates along with 'all the princes and boyars' as deciding and issuing the code together with the tsar: *Sudebniki XV–XVI vekov*, p. 366.

17 See e.g. *Sbornik Imperatorskogo Russkogo istoricheskogo obshchestva*, vol. 35 (1882), p. 503, no. 85; p. 630, no. 93; *PRP*, 8 vols. (Moscow: Gosiurizdat, 1952–63), vyp. IV: *Pamiatniki prava perioda ukrepleniia russkogo tsentralizovannogo gosudarstva XV–XVII vv.*, ed. L. V. Cherepnin (1956), pp. 486, 487, 495, 514, 515, 516, 517–518, 524, 526, 529; *PRP*, vyp.v: *Pamiatniki prava perioda soslovno-predstavitel'noi monarkhii. Pervaia polovina XVII v.*, ed. L. V. Cherepnin (1959), p. 237; *Tysiachnaia kniga 1550 g. i Dvorovaia tetrad' piatidesiatykh godov XVI veka*, ed. A. A. Zimin (Moscow and Leningrad: AN SSSR, 1950), p. 53.

18 *Pamiatniki diplomaticheskikh snoshenii drevnei Rossi s derzhavami inostrannymi*, 10 vols. (St Petersburg: Tipografiia II Otdeleniia Sobstvennoi E. I. V. Kantselarii, 1851–71), vol. 1 (1851), col. 1.

19 *AAE*, 4 vols. (St Petersburg: Tipografiia II Otdeleniia Sobstvennoi E. I. V. Kantselarii, 1836), vol. 1, p. 142.

20 Richard Hellie, *Enserfment and Military Change in Muscovy* (Chicago: University of Chicago Press, 1971), p. 267.

muster for combat and who were beholden to the Muscovite grand prince for
providing them with a means of financial support. In addition, other servitors
were maintained as vicegerents (*namestniki* and *volosteli*) through *kormlenie*
grants, which were of limited tenure, and through outright stipends given by
the grand prince.[21]

Contemporary evidence tells us of a thriving commercial life in Muscovy
during this period. Pastoral nomads brought tens of thousands of horses to
Moscow each year. In 1474, the chronicles state that 3,200 merchants and 600
envoys arrived in Moscow from Sarai with 40,000 horses for sale.[22] The 'Chronicle Notes of Mark Levkeinskii' mentions the Nogais' coming to Moscow with
80,000 horses in 1530; with 30,000 horses in 1531; and with 50,000 horses in 1534.[23]
Also under 1534, the Voskresenie and Nikon chronicles report another trade
contingent from the Nogai Tatars of 4,700 merchants, 70 *murzy* (gentry), 70
envoys, and 8,000 horses.[24] Although such economic information in the chronicles is rare and not subject to verification, we can find some confirmation of
the numbers of horses the Tatars sold annually in Moscow in the account of
Giles Fletcher from the late sixteenth century: 'there are brought yeerely to
the *Mosko* to be exchanged for other commodities 30. or 40. thousand *Tartar*
horse, which they call *Cones [koni]*'.[25] Rus' merchants were also active in other
cities. On 24 June 1505, for example, the khan of Kazan', Muhammed Emin,
precipitated a war with Muscovy when he arrested Muscovite merchants in
Kazan', executing some of them and sending others into slavery.[26]

Perhaps the only contemporary estimate of the size of the Muscovite economy comes from George Trakhaniot (Percamota), a Greek in the employ of
the Muscovite grand prince. On a diplomatic mission in 1486 to the court of
the duke of Milan, he reported that the income of the Muscovite state 'exceeds
each year over a million gold ducats, this ducat being of the value and weight
of those of Turkey and Venice'.[27] Trakhaniot goes on to report that

21 Herberstein, *Notes*, vol. I, p. 30.
22 *Ioasafovskaia letopis'*, p. 88; *PSRL*, vol. VIII, p. 180; *PSRL*, vol. XII, p. 156; *PSRL*, vol. XVIII
   (St Petersburg: Tipografiia M. A. Aleksandrova, 1913), p. 249; *PSRL*, vol. XXVI (Moscow
   and Leningrad: AN SSSR, 1959), p. 254; *PSRL*, vol. XXVIII (Moscow and Leningrad: AN
   SSSR, 1959), p. 308; and 'Letopisnye zapisi Marka Levkeinskogo', in A. A. Zimin, 'Kratkie
   letopisi XV–XVI vv.', *Istoricheskii arkhiv* 5 (1950): 10.
23 'Letopisnye zapisi Marka Levkeinskogo', 12–13.
24 *PSRL*, vol. VIII, p. 287; *PSRL*, vol. XIII (Moscow: Nauka, 1965), p. 80. Cf. *PSRL*, vol. XX (St
   Petersburg: Tipografiia M. A. Aleksandrova, 1910), p. 425.
25 Giles Fletcher, *Of the Russe Common Wealth, or Maner of Governement by the Russe Emperour,
   (Commonly Called the Emperour of Moskovia) with the Manners, and Fashions of the People of
   That Country* (London: T. D. for Thomas Charde, 1591), fo. 70v.
26 *PSRL*, vol. VI.2, col. 373; *PSRL*, vol. VIII, pp. 244–5; *PSRL*, vol. XII, p. 259.
27 George Trakhaniot, 'Notes and Information about the Affairs and the Ruler of Russia',
   in Robert M. Croskey and E. C. Ronquist, 'George Trakhaniot's Description of Russia

[c]ertain provinces . . . give in tribute each year great quantities of sables, ermines, and squirrel skins. Certain others bring cloth and other necessaries for the use and maintenance of the court. Even the meats, honey, beer, fodder, and hay used by the Lord and others of the court are brought by communities and provinces according to certain quantities imposed by ordinance . . .[28]

Trakhaniot's descriptions corroborate the earlier statement of Contarini about Moscow's significance as a fur-trading centre:

Many merchants from Germany and Poland gather in the city throughout the winter. They buy furs exclusively – sables, foxes, ermines, squirrels, and sometimes wolves. And although these furs are procured at places many days' journey from the city of Moscow, mostly in the areas toward the northeast, and even maybe the northwest, all are brought to this place and the merchants buy the furs here.[29]

The large amounts of wealth reported by our sources derived mainly from commercial activity along the major rivers of the area – the Volga, Oka and Moskva and their tributaries.

In Church affairs, this period saw the dominance of councils, beginning with councils in 1447 and, especially, 1448, where the Rus' bishops chose their own metropolitan. A number of the councils (1488, 1490, 1504, 1525 and 1531) were concerned with questions of heresy and the investigation of alleged heretics. Councils in 1455, 1459, 1478, 1492, 1500, 1503 and 1509 discussed other ecclesiastical issues. The Council of 1503, for example, made decisions on matters of ecclesiastical discipline and procedure, including forbidding the payment of fees for the placement of priests and deacons, establishing the minimum age for clerics, prohibiting a priest from celebrating Mass while drunk or the day after being drunk, stipulating that widowered priests must enter a monastery and forbidding monks and nuns from living in the same monastery. The prohibition against taking fees for clerical placement appears to have been in response to the claims of the heretics that fees were uncanonical.

The issue of secularisation of Church and monastic lands has been traditionally associated with the 1503 Church Council, but that association is based on faulty and unreliable polemical sources of the mid-sixteenth century. There

in 1486', *RH* 17 (1990): 61. Trakhaniot most likely is referring to the equivalent amount of wealth in terms that his listeners could understand and should not be taken to mean that gold coins circulated in Muscovy.

28 Trakhaniot, 'Notes and information', 61. According to Croskey, the ermine in the portrait *Lady with an Ermine* by Leonardo da Vinci may have been among the gifts of furs and live sables that Trakhaniot brought to Milan: Croskey and Ronquist, 'George Trakhaniot's Description of Russia', 58–9.

29 Contarini, 'Viaggio in Persia', p. 205.

is no contemporary or reliable evidence that discusses such an occurrence at the council. And there is no clear or reliable evidence that Ivan III planned in any way to extend his extensive confiscation of Church and monastic lands in Novgorod to the rest of Muscovy.[30]

During this time, Nil Sorskii (d. 1508) and Iosif Volotskii (d. 1515) were the most prominent representatives of two of the three forms of monasticism in the Eastern Church. They represented the *skete* life and communal monastic life, respectively (the third form was the solitary monk). Rather than being in conflict, their two forms of monasticism complemented each other, and Nil and Iosif seem to have held each other in mutual respect. It was only subsequent antagonism among monastic factions as well as between Nil's disciple Vassian Patrikeev and Iosif's disciple Metropolitan Daniil that led to the notion some kind of opposition existed between Iosif and Nil.

Iosif Volotskii is often credited with instigating the council decision of 1504 against the heretics. His lengthy polemical work the *Prosvetitel'* ('Enlightener') presented his understanding of their faults. He also may have been instrumental in bringing about the removal from office of Metropolitan Zosima in 1494.[31] Besides his attacks on heretics, Iosif is important for his articulation of parts of a political theory that concerned the role of wise advisers: (1) non-critical and silent obedience when the ruler is acting according to God's laws; (2) vocal criticism but obedience if the legitimate ruler was transgressing God's laws; (3) vocal criticism and passive disobedience if the legitimate ruler was commanding the adviser to transgress God's laws; and (4) vocal and active opposition when the ruler was not legitimate. In Discourse 16 of his *Prosvetitel'*, Iosif recommends non-critical and silent obedience whereas in Discourse 7 he recommends disobedience to the 'tormentor' (*muchitel'*) who is a tyrant transgressing God's laws.[32] One should not focus on one or the other Discourse as Iosif's 'true' view exclusive of the other, but understand them as part of a consistent political theory that had its origins in Byzantine political thought.[33]

30 See my 'A "Fontological" Investigation of the Muscovite Church Council of 1503', unpublished Ph.D. dissertation, Pennsylvania State University, 1977 (Ann Arbor: UMI, 1977, AAT 7723262); and my '500 let spustia. Tserkovnyi Sobor 1503 g.', *Palaeoslavica* 11 (2003): 214–39.
31 He accused Zosima of being sympathetic to the heretics and of engaging in sodomy. The only contemporary evidence for Zosima's dismissal comes from the second *Sofiia Chronicle*, which refers simply to his being an alcoholic and thereby neglecting the Church: *PSRL*, vol. VI. 2, col. 341.
32 Iosif Volotskii, *Prosvetitel'*, *ili oblichenie eresi zhidovstvuiushchikh*, 3rd edn, ed. A. Volkov (Kazan': Tipografiia Imperatorskogo universiteta, 1896), pp. 547, 287.
33 See my *Muscovy and the Mongols: Cross-Cultural Influences on the Steppe Frontier* (Cambridge: Cambridge University Press, 1998), pp. 203–7.

Both Ivan III and Vasilii III were actively involved with the Church as befitted their positions as head of state. They presided with their respective metropolitans over Church councils. They also recognised the Church's spiritual role. According to the *Typography Chronicle*, Metropolitan Simon imposed a penance on Ivan III, which he seems to have accepted, for bringing about the death of his brother Andrei the Elder in 1493. In 1502, if we can accept Iosif Volotskii's account, Ivan confessed that he had not been hard enough on the heretics and those who sympathised with them, including his daughter-in-law Elena and his grandson Dmitrii. But he could also act in his role as keeper of the external Church. In a jurisdictional dispute concerning the Kirillo-Belozerskii monastery in 1478, he decided in favour of his own confessor, Archbishop Vassian of Rostov, against the hegumen of the monastery as well as the apanage Prince Michael of Vereia and Metropolitan Gerontii. In 1479, he undertook a three-year investigation of the proper direction for processing around a church, when he thought Gerontii was leading a procession the wrong way (Ivan later apologised). And in 1490, he showed up at the end of a Church council proceedings to have Metropolitan Zosima investigate what the canon laws were concerning heretics.[34]

Vasilii III also abided by the Church's prerogatives and actively punished heretics. As befitted his role, Vasilii sent a letter to the patriarch of Constantinople in 1516 requesting him to send someone to assist in the translation of Greek books into Russian, which resulted in the coming of Maksim Grek to Muscovy. But Vasilii III refused, according to his own prerogative, to appoint an archbishop to Novgorod after Serapion was asked to step down in 1509. Finally, seventeen years later he appointed Makarii, the archimandrite of the Luzhetsk monastery near Mozhaisk, to that post. Vasilii divorced his wife in 1525, but this had provoked opposition both within and outside the Church. Makarii's support for Vasilii during the divorce could have contributed to his being promoted to the position of archbishop.

The Law Code of 1497 has the distinction of being the first Muscovy-wide law code. Apparently intended as a guide for judges in deciding cases and assessing fees, it made uniform the laws throughout all newly acquired territories and the old holdings of the grand prince. Through its provisions we glimpse a well-developed system of judicial administration. Most cases were decided at the local level in an ecclesiastical court or in a common court (*obshchii sud*), but three kinds of higher courts are mentioned: (1) court of the vicegerent

---

34 N. A. Kazakova and Ia. S. Lur'e, *Antifeodal'nye ereticheskie dvizheniia na Rusi XIV–nachala XVI veka* (Moscow and Leningrad: AN SSSR, 1955), p. 385.

(i.e. *namestniki* and *volosteli* and their deputies); (2) courts in which a boyar or *okol'nichii* presided (it was then the responsibility of the clerk [*d'iak*] to report the results to the grand-princely court for its approval); and (3) the court of the grand prince and his sons. Among the sixty-eight articles in the Law Code are: stipulations of punishment for various crimes such as murder, robbery and arson; and rules for litigation concerning lands and loans, for relations between employers and employees and for relations between landholders and peasants. Fifteen of the articles deal with damages and payments to individuals, and thirty-six of them stipulate payments and fees to the court. Article 30 is particularly relevant for our discussion for it provides the 'riding-distance fees' to be paid to bailiffs (*nedel'shchiki*) to fifty-three places within the Muscovite domain, virtually all the towns the grand princes of Moscow had acquired in the previous 180 years.

Article 57 of the Law Code of 1497 regulated the peasants' movements in accord with the needs of an agricultural community. They could move once a year, in November after the harvest. If peasants lived in a house built by the owner of the estate, they had to pay up to half a rouble for a house in the forest and up to one rouble for a house in the steppe. This article was meant to protect the landholder from precipitous comings and goings of the peasants on his lands and thus ensure him sufficient labour at least for the year. In the late sixteenth and early seventeenth centuries, these restrictive regulations were expanded to tie the peasants to the soil as serfs.

The Law Code of 1497 may appear somewhat primitive and unsystematic to us today, but it was an extremely important initiative in transforming Muscovy from a loose confederation of separate territories into a relatively well-organised state.

At the beginning of the reign of Ivan III, landholding in Muscovy generally fell into one of four categories: (1) court lands, administered by a high government official and subordinate officials, usually slaves; (2) black lands, which were administered by second-level officials, the *namestniki* and the *volosteli*; (3) *votchiny*, which could be bought, sold, mortgaged, or given away; and (4) ecclesiastical lands, which the Church had the right to administer.[35] To these categories of landholding was added *pomest'e* in 1482 when the first known grant for *pomest'e* landholding was issued. *Pomest'e* (or military fief) was usually given as a reward for some courageous deed or compensation for faithful service. In the *pomest'e* grants, there is no suggestion of any kind of free contractual arrangement in which the servitor offered his services in return for

---

35 R. E. F. Smith, *Peasant Farming in Muscovy* (Cambridge: Cambridge University Press, 1977), pp. 100–2.

the *pomest'e*. Instead, the grand prince could choose to which of his servitors he would grant a *pomest'e* estate or to withhold such a grant as he pleased. Similarly the grand prince could grant *pomest'ia* to those from whom he had taken their *votchiny*, such as the Novgorodian landholders.

Pomest'e was similar to *votchina* in most respects. It, like *votchina*, could be and was inherited, and this was so from its inception.[36] The condition for inheritance was that someone in the family, a son or brother, could continue to provide service to the grand prince. Otherwise, the *pomest'e* reverted to the grand-princely land fund to be granted to someone else. The rates of turnover from one family to another were similar for both *pomest'e* and *votchina*. The holder considered the land to be his indefinitely; it was not temporary or provisional as long as a suitable heir could provide military service. *Pomest'e* land could be exchanged for other *pomest'e* land, just as *votchina* land could be exchanged for other *votchina* land. The historian V. B. Kobrin has, however, pointed out three differences between *pomest'e* and *votchina*. A *pomeshchik* could not, as a *votchinnik* could do, sell his estate; nor could he mortgage it (say, to obtain cash) or give it away (say, to a monastery).[37] These three prohibitions associated with *pomest'e* indicate its origins in the need for Ivan III to provide a livelihood for his military servitors. Its similarity to *iqta* landholding among the Muslims has led to the suggestion that Ivan III borrowed the principles and concepts of *iqta* for his system of military land grants. Such a borrowing would have been facilitated by advice from the Chingisid princes and other Tatars then coming into the Muscovite military system.[38]

Although the establishment of *pomest'e* created a ready-made military force that owed allegiance directly to the grand prince, both Ivan III and Vasilii III still found themselves having to rely on service princes and family members to mobilise troops. They could, however, now call on an ever-greater number of warrior-servitors without any intermediaries. As a result, grand-princely family members and service princes began to lose their semi-independent

36 Iu. G. Alekseev and A. I. Kopanev, 'Razvitie pomestnoi sistemy v XVI v.', in *Dvorianstvo i krepostnoi stroi Rossii XVI–XVIII vv. Sbornik statei, posviashchennyi pamiati Alekseia Andree-vicha Novosel'skogo*, ed. N. I. Pavlenko et al. (Moscow: Nauka, 1975), p. 59; A. Ia. Degtiarev, 'O mobilizatsii pomestnykh zemel' v XVI v.', in *Iz istorii feodal'noi Rossii. Stat'i i ocherki k 70-letiiu so dnia rozhdeniia prof. V. V. Mavrodina*, ed. A. Ia. Degtiarev et al. (Leningrad: Izdatel'stvo Leningradskogo universiteta, 1978), pp. 85–9; V. B. Kobrin, 'Stanovlenie pomestnoi sistemy', *IZ* 105 (1980), 151–2; V. B. Kobrin, *Vlast' i sobstvennost' v srednevekovoi Rossii (XV–XVI vv.)* (Moscow: Mysl', 1985), pp. 92–3; and my 'Early *pomest'e* Grants as a Historical Source', *Oxford Slavonic Papers* 33 (2000): 36–63.
37 Kobrin, 'Stanovlenie', 180; and Kobrin, *Vlast' i sobstvennost'*, p. 134.
38 See my 'The Military Land Grant along the Muslim-Christian Frontier', *RH* 19 (1992): 327–59; and 'Errata', *RH* 21 (1994): 249–50.

military and political status. The *pomest'e* system in effect gave the grand prince, if not a standing army, at least a military force available to be called up quickly for whatever purpose he together with the boyar duma deemed necessary.

Foreign influences

Both Ivan III and Vasilii III sought out and adapted foreign institutions and technical skills to their policy needs. A few of these influences are mentioned below.

Most of the steppe influences on Muscovy had already occurred by 1462.[39] Both Ivan III and Vasilii III actively maintained the *iam*, a network of way stations for travel, inherited from the Mongols. Herberstein describes this system: 'The prince has post stations in all parts of the dominions, with a regular number of horses at the different places, so that when the royal courier is sent anywhere, he may immediately have a horse without delay . . . On one occasion, a servant of mine rode on such post horses from Novgorod to Moscow, a distance of six hundred versts [642.1 km] . . . in seventy-two hours.'[40] During the reign of Ivan III the introduction of *pomest'e*, as mentioned, was based on Islamic *iqta* introduced via refugee Tatars from the Qipchaq khanate. Certain Tatar record-keeping practices, such as the use of scrolls, were introduced into Muscovite chanceries at this time.

A major influence from the West was the influx of Lithuanian nobility into Muscovite service in the fifteenth and sixteenth centuries. The Patrikeevs, for example, were a prominent princely family in Lithuania whose members dominated the boyar duma during most of the reign of Ivan III.[41] One estimate of the number of families of the ruling class in the seventeenth century with Polish-Lithuanian and 'Western European' names places it at 49.4 per cent (452 of 915 families).[42] The transformation of Muscovy into something more than just a government of personal rule and allegiances but also a government of laws and institutions correlates with the influx of Lithuanian nobility into Muscovite service and was accomplished with their active support.

39 For a list of steppe influences on Muscovy, see table 2 in Ostrowski, 'Muscovite Adaptation', 295.
40 Herberstein, *Notes*, vol. 1, pp. 108–9.
41 It has been suggested that the dynastic crisis of the late 1490s, in which a number of the Patrikeevs were arrested and disgraced, was the result of an attempt on the part of other boyars to reduce their power: Nancy Shields Kollmann, 'Consensus Politics: The Dynastic Crisis of the 1490s Reconsidered', *RR* 45 (1986): 235–67.
42 The estimate is N. P. Zagoskin's as reported in M. F. Vladimirskii-Budanov, *Obzor istorii russkogo prava*, 3rd edn. (Kiev: N. Ia. Ogloblin, 1900), p. 135, n. 1.

Initial contacts between Italy and Muscovy occurred at the Council of Florence in 1438–9. Rus' merchants had contact with Italian merchants in Kaffa and Tana until the Italians were expelled by the Ottoman Turks in 1475. The marriage of Ivan III to Zoe (Sofiia) Palaeologa in 1472 brought many Italicised Greeks in her entourage to Moscow who took government positions.[43] What these Italicised Greeks may have brought was an understanding of an organised state structure that had not existed in Muscovy previously and did not exist among Muscovy's immediate neighbours.

A major visible act of state-building – the makeover of the Muscovite Kremlin – involved the contracting of Italian architects and engineers. The Italian architect Aristotle Fioravanti was brought in by Ivan III to design and oversee the construction of the Dormition cathedral from 1475 to 1479. Italian architects Marco Ruffo and Pietro Antonio Solario designed and oversaw the construction of the Hall of Facets (*Granovitaia palata*) from 1487 to 1491. In 1505, the cathedral of the Archangel Michael, designed by Alevisio Lamberti da Montagnana of Venice, was completed. The present crenellated walls and towers of the Moscow Kremlin also owe their design to Italians such as Solario and Antonio Friazin.[44] The magnificent set of court and church buildings that resulted is still an imposing sight today. At the time it was more than enough to proclaim the message of state power the Muscovite rulers and elite wished to convey, especially to foreign ambassadors, who were also subjected to majestic court rituals.

Foreign policies

Both Ivan III and Vasilii III had far-ranging foreign policies. Their predominant concern was with the steppe and Moldavia[45] but also extended far westward. Ivan III, for example, reached an agreement with King Jan of Denmark against Sweden, and he negotiated with the Holy Roman Emperor in regard to a treaty directed against Poland-Lithuania. Vasilii III continued negotiations with the Holy Roman Emperor engaged in diplomatic contact with France.

As early as 1314, Novgorod had asked Iurii Daniilovich, grand prince of Moscow, to serve as prince. The idea was to protect Novgorod from the

---

43 See e.g. Robert Croskey, 'Byzantine Greeks in Late Fifteenth- and Early Sixteenth[-] Century Russia', in *The Byzantine Legacy in Eastern Europe*, ed. Lowell Clucas (Boulder, Colo: East European Monographs, 1988), pp. 35–56.

44 For further information about Italian architectural influence in the Moscow Kremlin, see William Craft Brumfield, *A History of Russian Architecture* (Cambridge: Cambridge University Press, 1993), pp. 95–106; and William Craft Brumfield, *Gold in Azure: One Thousand Years of Russian Architecture* (Boston: David R. Godine, 1983), pp. 139–57.

45 Knud Rasmussen, 'On the Information Level of the Muscovite Posol'skij prikaz in the Sixteenth Century', *FOG* 24 (1978): 91, 94.

inroads and exorbitant demands of Mikhail Iaroslavich, grand prince of Tver' and Vladimir. But in 1317, the Novgorodians concluded a separate treaty with Mikhail. Nonetheless, in the mid-fifteenth century, Vasilii II and then his son Ivan III used the invitation to their ancestor Iurii and other fourteenth-century agreements that Novgorod reached with the Moscow grand princes against Tver', to claim that Novgorod was part of their patrimony. In 1456, by the Treaty of Iazhelbitsii, Novgorod agreed to submit its foreign policy to the approval of Muscovy. Subsequently, Vasilii II was the first grand prince of Moscow to claim Novgorod as his patrimony in his will (1462). Novgorod tried to break free of the constraints of this treaty by declaring Mikhail Olelkovich of Lithuania its prince in 1470. Ivan III advanced on Novgorod in 1472 and re-established the terms of Iazhelbitsii. In 1475, in a 'peaceful' visit to the city, Ivan arrested and deported to Muscovite lands a number of Novgorodian boyars. He took over Novgorod completely in 1478 when he became suspicious of further intrigue. He prohibited meetings of the *veche* (town assembly) and confiscated the bell that convoked such meetings. By 1500, he had confiscated close to 1 million hectares (2.5 million acres) of Novgorodian boyar and Church lands, removed a number of landholders and merchants, and ended Novgorod's association with the Hansa.

After the conquest of Novgorod and the taking of Torzhok in 1478, Muscovite territory completely surrounded the principality of Tver'. The Tver' prince, Mikhail Borisovich, the brother of Ivan III's first wife, acknowledged a subordinate relationship with the Muscovite grand prince in 1483.[46] When Mikhail sought a political alliance with Casimir IV of Poland and Lithuania in 1484, Ivan moved to pre-empt it. Tver' was formally annexed a short time later, in 1485.

Between 1462 and 1533, the western steppe area of the Eurasian heartland witnessed a balance of power among five political entities of medium economic and military might: the Crimean khanate, the Great Horde (replaced in 1502 by the khanate of Astrakhan'), the Kazan' khanate, the khanate of Tiumen' (soon to be replaced by the khanate of Sibir') and Muscovy. These five political entities occupied a frontier zone between three relatively distant major powers (or core areas): the Ottoman Empire, Poland-Lithuania and Safavid Persia. None of these three major powers was strong enough or close enough to exert hegemony over the western steppe or its accompanying savannah and forest border area.

---

46 *Dukhovnye i dogovornye gramoty velikikh i udel'nykh kniazei XIV–XVI vv.*, ed. L.V. Cherepnin (Moscow and Leningrad: AN SSSR, 1950), pp. 295–301.

Muscovy's first direct diplomatic contact with the Ottoman Empire came in 1496 although indirect relations had been conducted through the Crimean khan for twenty years before that. The Ottoman and Muscovite governments had good relations with each other despite the desire of many to get Muscovy involved in a war against the Ottoman Empire in order to free the Orthodox Christians there. Trade relations developed such that Turkish merchants purchased furs, iron tools, flax, walrus tusks and mercury from Muscovy while Russian merchants purchased brocades, taffeta and silk from Turkey.

Nonetheless, during the latter half of the fifteenth century, Muscovy was in a vulnerable position where it could be threatened by a possible coalition of Poland-Lithuania with one or the other of Muscovy's competitors – in particular, the Great Horde or the Crimean khanate. Kazan', however, found itself even more vulnerably placed in an intermediate frontier zone between Muscovy, the Tiumen' khanate, the Great Horde, and the Crimean khanate as well as the Nogai horde. This intermediate position, which made it vulnerable to military attack from one or a combination of the surrounding intermediate powers, also gave the Kazan' khanate its vitality as a commercial power.

From 1475, the Crimean khan was the nominal vassal of the Ottoman sultan, but operated independently in the western steppe. The Great Horde was no longer the major power it had been – that is, as the pre-break-up Qipchaq khanate. Yet, the khan of the Great Horde was, until 1502, still the nominal suzerain of Muscovy. And in the Astrakhan' khanate, a successor to the Great Horde, the khan continued to receive tribute from the Muscovite grand prince, as did the khans of the other successor khanates. As long as the Kazan' khanate remained favourable to Muscovy or at least neutral but independent, the Muscovite grand prince could feel relatively secure concerning eastern approaches to Muscovy, because Kazan' was not strong enough to defeat Muscovy alone. When Kazan' fell under the direct influence of one of the other neighbouring khanates, it could then be used as an advance base and provide additional forces for an attack on Moscow, as was done in 1521 by the Crimean khan Muhammed Girey.

Throughout this period the Muscovite grand princes continued to pay tribute to the khans as their nominal vassal. Among other evidence that this was so are the wills of the grand princes. The will of Ivan III (1504), for example, specifies that tribute be sent to the khanates of Astrakhan', Crimea and Kazan', as well as to the 'tsareviches' town' (Kasimov).[47]

---

47 *Dukhovnye i dogovornye gramoty*, p. 362.

In great part, we must attribute the dramatic reversal of western steppe power relations subsequently in the sixteenth century to the successful military strategies of the Muscovite leaders – in particular, in terms of mobilisation of troops and other military resources. During the period from the middle of the fourteenth century to the fifteenth century, the Muscovite grand princes were adept at getting Lithuanian princes and nobility and their attendant service people to come over into grand-princely service,[48] although by the sixteenth century some princes in the service of the Muscovite ruler would flee to the Lithuanian grand duke.[49] The Muscovite grand princes were also equally adept if not more so, especially during the period from the middle of the fifteenth century to the sixteenth century, in getting *tsarevichi* and other Tatar nobility and their attendant service people to enter grand-princely service.[50] Ivan III, for example, set up a puppet khanate in Kasimov where Tatar refugees could escape without violating their allegiance to Islam or Chingisid rule.

When Casimir IV died in 1490, Poland and Lithuania were once again under separate rulers. Ivan III took advantage of the resultant weakened position of Lithuania to follow an aggressive military policy against towns across the Lithuanian border. In 1494, Lithuania ceded Viaz'ma to Muscovy. The marriage in 1495 between Grand Duke Alexander and Elena, the daughter of Ivan, sealed the bargain. An outbreak of hostilities between Muscovy and Lithuania from 1500 to 1503 spread to involve the Livonian knights and the Great Horde (both on the side of Lithuania), and the Crimean khanate (on the side of Muscovy). Muscovy made further territorial gains, including the Chernigov-Seversk area, and the Great Horde was routed by Mengli Girey. During the reign of Vasilii III, Lithuania and Moscow were at war on two occasions: 1507–8 and 1512–22. It was during the latter war that Muscovy annexed Smolensk in 1514.

---

48 See Oswald P. Backus, *Motives of West Russian Nobles in Deserting Lithuania for Moscow, 1377–1514* (Lawrence: University of Kansas Press, 1957), p. 98, where he provides thirteen reasons given in the sources for Lithuanian nobles going over to Muscovy between 1481 and 1500. The most prominent Lithuanians to join Muscovite service were the Gediminovich princes Fedor Ivanovich Bel'skii, Mikhail L'vovich Glinskii and Dmitrii Fedorovich Vorotynskii.
49 Oswald P. Backus, 'Treason as a Concept and Defections from Moscow to Lithuania in the Sixteenth Century', *FOG* 15 (1970): 119–44.
50 See my 'Troop Mobilization by the Muscovite Grand Princes (1313–1533)', in Eric Lohr and Marshall Poe (eds.), *The Military and Society in Russia, 1450–1917* (Leiden: Brill, 2002), pp. 37–9; see also Craig Gayen Kennedy, 'The Juchids of Muscovy: A Study of Personal Ties between Émigré Tatar Dynasts and the Muscovite Grand Princes in the Fifteenth and Sixteenth Centuries', unpublished Ph.D. dissertation, Harvard University, 1994 (Ann Arbor: UMI, 1994, AAT 9520971).

The term 'Great Horde' is the name we find in the sources after the middle of the fifteenth century until 1502 for the remnants of the Qipchaq khanate that remained after the splitting off of the Kazan' khanate and the Crimean khanate. By 1480, Ivan III had already been acting autonomously for many years without any need to gain approval for his policies from the khan of the Great Horde. In that year in the late summer and early autumn, Khan Ahmed of the Great Horde advanced with a large force to the south-west of Muscovy. He was apparently hoping for military help from Casimir, the king of Poland and grand duke of Lithuania. That help never arrived. Ivan, for his part, was without the support of two of his brothers, Andrei the Elder and Boris, or their accompanying armies. Ivan convened a war council made up of the boyar duma, the top Church prelates (including Metropolitan Gerontii and Archbishop Vassian Rylo), and Ivan's mother, Mariia, to discuss how to conduct the campaign. Prince Ivan Patrikeev was left in charge of the defences of Moscow.

The army of the Great Horde and the army of Muscovy faced each other across the River Ugra for some two weeks with arrows being shot and some arquebuses being fired. On 11 November Ahmed retreated and peace was restored. The contemporary chronicles present an unflattering account of the two armies being afraid to fight. Archbishop Vassian Rylo wrote a sharply worded letter to Ivan accusing him of vacillation and lack of will. Yet, the encounter on the Ugra was similar to other such encounters between Tatar and Muscovite forces, when neither side could gain a military advantage. The churchmen, who were not military leaders, however, saw things differently at the time. Nevertheless, a subsequent Church account of the 'stand on the Ugra', a work of the 1550s, described it as one of the most significant events in world history.[51] And the author of the *Kazanskaia istoriia* ('History of Kazan'') added numerous fictional details that made the 'overthrow of the Tatar yoke' in 1480 an irresistible invention for historians to adopt. All this was part of the creation by Rus' churchmen of an 'ideological package' of anti-Tatar writings, which placed a hostile spin on chronicle and other Church historical accounts of Muscovy's relations with the steppe peoples.[52] Rather than represent any kind of 'overthrow of Tatar yoke' the event on the Ugra changed relations between Muscovy and the Great Horde little if at all. It did, however, mark

51 D. P. Golokhvastov and Archimandrite Leonid, 'Blagoveshchenskii ierei Sil'vestr i ego poslaniia', ChOIDR 1874, kn. 1, pp. 71–2. This work, in the form of a letter addressed to Ivan IV, is generally attributed either to Metropolitan Makarii or to the priest Sil'vestr.

52 For more on this 'ideological package', see my *Muscovy and the Mongols*, pp. 135–98.

the last time the Great Horde attacked Muscovy, although not the last time it attacked Muscovy's ally, the Crimean khanate.

During the reign of Ivan III, Muscovy and the Crimean khanate had friendly relations. The Crimean khan Mengli Girey considered himself a 'brother' of the grand prince, and Mengli Girey's wife, Nur Sultan, considered herself his 'sister'. Ivan III was thus able to preclude any alliance of the grand duke of Lithuania with the Crimean khan. Under Vasilii III, in contrast, relations with the Crimean khanate deteriorated. Muhammed Girey, the son of Mengli Girey, followed an aggressive foreign policy towards Muscovy, which resulted in Kazan' 's forming a long-term alliance with the Crimean khanate, and ultimately in the devastating attack on Moscow in 1521. One effect of the attack was that Muscovy had to pay an additional yearly tribute to the Crimean khan. In this respect, Vasilii III's steppe policy was not as successful as that of his father.

Muscovy in 1533

The Church's attempts to seek out and have the state authorities punish heretics can be seen as part of a larger movement on the part of both secular and ecclesiastical authorities to standardise practices and beliefs within the Muscovite realm. A significant part of this larger movement was the creation by the Church of an anti-Tatar ideology, which served to put a different framework on relations of Muscovy with the steppe khanates than the one the secular leaders had operated within. The huge incorporation of new territories required the extension of administrative procedures and laws to these areas. The transfer of Novgorodian landholders to areas closer to Moscow and their replacement with middle servitors who were given *pomest'e* for their support was part of this process. At first, Ivan III was reluctant to pursue heretics with as much zeal as Archbishop Gennadii wanted. Towards the end of his life, however, Ivan agreed to the heretics' being executed. Under his successor, Vasilii III, the expansion of the state administrative apparatus began to impinge on the freedom the Church had experienced until then in terms of land acquisitions. It was under Vasilii that the first stipulations concerning the need for churches and monasteries to register their land acquisitions with state agents began to appear. The grand prince and his agents had been able to confiscate particular ecclesiastical lands under the grand prince's role as keeper of the external Church. But the inculcation into law of the right of the state agents to do so led to a strong reaction on the part of Church leaders, which was to be played out later, in the second half of the sixteenth century.

In 1533, Muscovy was on the verge of becoming the dominant power in the western steppe region. This circumstance resulted from the success of the grand prince and the ruling elite in incorporating new resource areas, in creating an enlarged and greatly modified (in terms of composition) ruling class, in the ability of Muscovy to adapt and borrow what it needed from neighbouring cultures, in the creation of a readily mobilisable military force and in the reshaping of the Muscovite principality into a dynastic state.

10

Ivan IV (1533–1584)

SERGEI BOGATYREV

One of the longest reigns in Russian history, the rule of Ivan IV was a period of ambitious political, military and cultural projects. The ruling family sought to utilise all the material and human resources of the realm to strengthen its political power and to integrate territories with diverse cultural and economic traditions into a single state. These aims did not always complement each other. As a result of integration the Muscovite state became increasingly complex, both socially and politically. This, in turn, put the dynasty under pressure from various forces operating in the centre, in the provinces and on the international arena. As the leader of the dynasty, Ivan responded decisively to the challenges of integration, though his reaction was often erratic and inconsistent.

Safeguarding the royal family

Ivan Vasil'evich, the future Ivan IV 'the Terrible' (Groznyi), was born into the family of Grand Prince Vasilii III of Moscow, the head of the ruling branch of the Riurikid dynasty, on 25 August 1530. Ivan's mother was Elena Glinskaia, the niece of Prince Mikhail L'vovich Glinskii, who came to serve Vasilii III from Lithuania in 1508. Ivan IV nominally became grand prince at the age of three after the death of his father in December 1533. Soon Elena noticeably increased her political activities and freed herself from the tutelage of her relatives and the regents appointed by Vasilii III. Courtiers began to refer to Elena as sovereign (*gosudarynia*) alongside the nominal ruler, Ivan.[1]

Our knowledge of the early years of Ivan's life comes largely from later sources, which were politically biased. Some observations on the formative period of his life, however, can be made from a reconstruction of the physical and cultural environment in which the boy grew up. Under Elena Glinskaia, court rituals took place either in the state rooms set aside for

---

1 A. L. Iurganov, 'Politicheskaia bor'ba v 30-e gg. XVI veka', *Istoriia SSSR*, 1988, no. 2: 106–12.

official ceremonies or in her private apartments, where she lived with Ivan.[2] Built by a Milanese architect, these apartments had a distinctly Renaissance appearance.[3] The spatial arrangement of the Kremlin palace, however, was based not on inter-connecting rooms (enfilades), as it was in Western Renaissance palaces, but on a typical Muscovite combination of confined clusters of three rooms.[4] Another local peculiarity was that the architectural ensemble of the Kremlin palace included several churches. The immediate proximity of the court churches, as well as the cultural traditions of the family, undoubtedly contributed to the formation of Ivan's Orthodox identity. At the same time, Ivan spent his formative years in a rather cosmopolitan atmosphere. His physical environment was a mixture of Muscovite and Western architecture. He also became familiar with Eastern customs and perhaps even learned some elementary Tatar during receptions of Tatar dignitaries.[5]

The ruling circles were highly concerned that the heads of collateral branches of the dynasty, Vasilii III's brothers Prince Iurii Ivanovich of Dmitrov and Prince Andrei Ivanovich of Staritsa, would claim power during Ivan's minority. In December 1533, Prince Iurii was taken into custody, where he died three years later.[6] Between 1534 and 1536 Elena Glinskaia also exerted pressure on Prince Andrei Ivanovich by imposing new terms to define their mutual relationship.[7] These conditions reflected profound changes in the relations between the grand-princely family and the collateral line of the dynasty. Unlike previous agreements between members of the dynasty, the grand princess did not recognise traditional responsibilities such as respecting Andrei as a close relative and guaranteeing his land possessions. Elena also forbade Andrei to receive grand-princely servitors, though previous agreements allowed servitors to choose masters at their will.

---

2 See *PSRL*, vol. xiii (Moscow: Iazyki russkoi kul'tury, 2000), p. 104, left column.
3 The present design of the palace is a result of seventeenth-century renovations. See S. S. Pod"iapol'skii, G. S. Evdokimov, E. I. Ruzaeva, A. V. Iaganov and D. E. Iakovlev, 'Novye dannye o Kremlevskom dvortse rubezha XV–XVI vv.', in A. L. Batalov et al. (eds.), *Drevnerusskoe iskusstvo. Russkoe iskusstvo pozdnego srednevekov'ia, XVI vek* (St Petersburg: Dmitrii Bulanin, 2003), pp. 51–98.
4 Ivan later reproduced a similar spatial arrangement in his residence in Kolomna in 1577. See I. E. Zabelin, *Domashnii byt russkikh tsarei i tsarits v XVI i XVII stoletiiakh*, vol. iii: *Materialy* (Moscow: Iazyki russkoi kul'tury, 2003), p. 458 (first pagination).
5 See *PSRL*, vol. xiii, p. 104, left column.
6 On various interpretations of Prince Iurii Vasil'evich's position towards the grand-princely family in the tendentious official chronicles, see *PSRL*, vol. xiii, pp. 77–8, 90. On Iurii, see also M. M. Krom, 'Sud'ba regentskogo soveta pri maloletnem Ivane IV. Novye dannye o vnutripoliticheskoi bor'be kontsa 1533–1534 goda', *Otechestvennaia istoriia*, 1996, no. 5: 40–2.
7 *SGGD*, vol. i (Moscow: Tipografiia N. S. Vsevolozhskogo, 1813), pp. 451–2.

The new terms thus facilitated a redistribution of power within the dynasty in favour of the ruling family. It is very likely that it was precisely this dictated agreement that made Andrei rise in rebellion against Elena Glinskaia in 1537.[8] Despite having military forces at his disposal, Andrei eventually preferred to negotiate with the Moscow authorities rather than to fight. Elena Glinskaia used this situation to her own advantage by inviting Andrei to the capital and imprisoning him, his wife Efrosin'ia and his son Vladimir. Andrei died in custody in December 1537, but the members of his family would remain a source of concern for Ivan IV for decades to come.

Elena's death at the age of around thirty on 3 April 1538 gave rise to much speculation about her poisoning. The archaeologist T. D. Panova, who carried out an autopsy of the remains of members of the dynasty buried in the Kremlin, also believes that many of them, including Elena, were poisoned.[9] Panova's conclusion is based on the findings of large amounts of arsenic and mercury in the bodies. However, we know very little about the background chemistry of Muscovites in regard to their nutrition, medicines and cosmetics. This is why relative estimations seem to be more revealing than absolute ones. The content of such a typical poisonous substance as arsenic in Elena's remains was substantially lower than in those who were definitely poisoned (the Staritsa family, see below). On the whole, accusations of poisoning were typical of political struggle in the sixteenth century and are hardly trustworthy.[10]

As long as Elena Glinskaia was alive, the ruling line of the dynasty had enough political power to impose its will on those whom it considered dangerous pretenders to the throne. Her death was followed by the so-called 'boyar rule' (1537–47). Despite the minority of the ruler, the administration and courts continued to function in the realm. At the same time, the 'boyar rule' saw an escalation of conflict between court groupings headed by the princely clans of the Shuiskiis, Bel'skiis, Kubenskiis and Glinskiis, and the boyar Vorontsov clan. The reason for the political crisis was the absence of capable leadership in the ruling family and the political ineffectiveness of the Church hierarchs who could not mediate between the conflicting parties at court.[11]

---

8 On Andrei's rebellion, see I. I. Smirnov, *Ocherki politicheskoi istorii Russkogo gosudarstva 30–50kh godov XVI veka* (Moscow and Leningrad: AN SSSR, 1958), pp. 56–74; A. L. Iurganov, 'Staritskii miatezh', *VI*, 1985, no. 2: 100–10.

9 There is no scholarly publication of the results of the autopsy to date. The main results of the autopsy can be found in a popular article: Denis Babichenko, 'Kremlevskie tainy: 33-i element', *Itogi*, no. 37 (327), 17 September 2002: 36–9.

10 See Andrei Pavlov and Maureen Perrie, *Ivan the Terrible* (Harlow: Longman, 2003), p. 29.

11 M. M. Krom believes that the main reason for the crisis was the minority of the ruler. See his 'Politicheskii krizis 30–40kh godov XVI veka. Postanovka problemy', *Otechestvennaia istoriia*, 1998, no. 5: 13, 15.

There were, however, certain cultural mechanisms which would secure the position of an under-age monarch in Muscovy. The ruling circles propagated an image of Ivan as a capable monarch and a brave warrior. The practice dated back to Vasilii III, who saw Ivan not only as a child, but also as a representative of the dynasty, even though of small physical proportions. Vasilii ordered a helmet for the under-age Ivan, to symbolise the concept of the infant eventually becoming a mighty sovereign. The helmet, which reproduced the design of adult ones in miniature, featured inscriptions propagating the autocratic power of Vasilii III and glorifying Ivan as his successor (see Plate 12a).[12] The same cultural model of the authority of the crown assuming a life apart from the human form of the ruler was employed in the official chronicles and government documents. According to these sources, the orphaned under-age monarch was responsible for all governmental decisions in the late 1530s and 1540s. Nancy Shields Kollmann thinks that the discrepancy between the image of the ruler in the official propaganda and the powerlessness of the child Ivan reflects the weak position of every monarch, whatever his or her age, in Muscovite politics.[13] However, the official documents did acknowledge the fact that the grand prince was still a defenceless minor, who could not take part in military actions and needed the guidance of adults.[14] Part of dynastic policy, such calculated propaganda contributed to the succession of power within the ruling family.

The first signs of political stabilisation became visible in the early 1540s. In 1540–1, Efrosin'ia and Vladimir of Staritsa were released from captivity and Vladimir was restored to his father's landed possessions. The dynasty finally received an effective protector in 1542, when Makarii became the new metropolitan.[15] The generally accepted view is that Makarii was a client of the Shuiskii princes, who belonged to the Suzdal' line of the dynasty and had

12 See N. S. Vladimirskaia (ed.), *Orel i lev. Rossiia i Shvetsiia v XVII veke. Katalog vystavki. Gosudarstvennyi istoricheskii muzei, 4.04–1.07.2001* (Moscow: Gosudarstvennyi istoricheskii muzei, 2001), pp. 56–7, no. 3.
13 See Nancy Shields Kollmann, 'The Grand Prince in Muscovite Politics: The Problem of Genre in Sources on Ivan's Minority', *RH* 14 (1987): 293–313.
14 *PSRL*, vol. VIII (St Petersburg: Tipografiia Eduarda Pratsa, 1859; reprinted Moscow: Iazyki russkoi kul'tury, 2001), pp. 297–301; *Pskovskie letopisi*, ed. A. N. Nasonov, vol. I (Moscow and Leningrad: AN SSSR, 1941; reprinted Düsseldorf and The Hague: Brücken-Verlag GMBH, Europe Printing, 1967), p. 110; *Sbornik Imperatorskogo Russkogo istoricheskogo obshchestva*, vol. LIX (St Petersburg: Tipografiia F. Eleonskogo i K., 1887), pp. 33, 34, 37, 43–4, 66–7, 95. I am grateful to Charles J. Halperin for these references.
15 On Makarii, see Arkhimandrit Makarii (Veretennikov), *Zhizn' i trudy sviatitelia Makariia, mitropolita Moskovskogo i vseia Rusi* (Moscow: Izdatel'skii sovet Russkoi pravoslavnoi tserkvi, 2002).

matrimonial ties with the ruling family.[16] At the same time, Makarii had already accumulated substantial political and moral weight prior to his enthronement when he was archbishop of Novgorod, the second-ranking figure in the Church hierarchy. Makarii's tenure in Novgorod (1526–42) coincided with A. M. Shuiskii's vicegerency in Pskov (1539/40–winter 1540/1). In Pskov, A. M. Shuiskii was very hostile to the locals and caused many Pskovian abbots to flee to Novgorod.[17] He planned to give Makarii a solemn reception in Pskov, but the Pskovian chronicles do not mention such a visit by the hierarch.[18] Makarii apparently cancelled his trip to Pskov because of the misdeeds of the vicegerent. Makarii, who demonstrated a keen interest in Church affairs in Pskov, would hardly have accepted such harsh treatment of the local clergy.[19] This is why it is unlikely that the Shuiskiis promoted Makarii. When he became metropolitan, Makarii resolutely interfered in court feuds acting against the Shuiskiis.[20] In 1543, A. M. Shuiskii was thrown to the court kennelmen. Various sources attribute the order to kill Shuiskii to the grand prince or unnamed boyars. Whoever was behind this cruel murder, Makarii did not use his considerable moral power to stop the humiliating death of Shuiskii. The metropolitan apparently had no interest in saving the life of the boyar.

According to the official chronicle, after the murder of Shuiskii, 'the boyars began to fear the sovereign'.[21] It seems that the sphere of Ivan's ritual and social activities did indeed become wider then. Beginning in 1543, the chamber for official receptions in the Kremlin was referred to in the official sources as *stolovaia*, which alluded to the throne (*stol*) or, more widely, to the hereditary power of the grand prince.[22] The new appellation implies that Ivan began on a regular basis to utilise these premises, which were specially designated for the ritual activities of the ruler. In 1543 the ruling circles also began propagating abroad the idea that Ivan was ready for marriage. The Kremlin sent requests for a bride to several foreign royal houses and waited for responses.[23]

16 See e.g. A. A. Zimin, *Reformy Ivana Groznogo* (Moscow: Izdatel'stvo sotsial'no-ekonomicheskoi literatury, 1960), p. 264. Krom notes that the Shuiskiis did not enjoy a monopoly on power in 1542–3: see his 'Politicheskii krizis', 14.

17 See *Pskovskie letopisi*, vol. 1, p. 110; T. I. Pashkova, *Mestnoe upravlenie v Russkom gosudarstve v pervoi polovine XVI v. Namestniki i volosteli* (Moscow: Drevlekhranilishche, 2000), p. 154.

18 Makarii (Veretennikov), *Zhizn'*, pp. 67, 346–7. Veretennikov seems to believe that Makarii visited Pskov under A. M. Shuiskii, but does not explain the silence of the Pskovian chronicles about such a visit.

19 On Makarii's approach to Pskov, see Makarii (Veretennikov), *Zhizn'*, pp. 64–5.

20 *PSRL*, vol. xiii, p. 145.

21 *PSRL*, vol. xiii, p. 145.

22 S.S. Pod"iapol'skii, 'Moskovskii Kremlevskii dvorets XVI v. po dannym pis'mennykh istochnikov', in Batalov et al. (eds.), *Drevnerusskoe iskusstvo*, p. 113.

23 *Sbornik Imperatorskogo Russkogo istoricheskogo obshchestva*, vol. lix, p. 228.

Ivan IV's official chronicle also mentions his initial intention to take a wife from abroad. The chronicle's explanation that the ruler abandoned this idea for fear that his and a foreign woman's temperaments would be too different strikes the reader as an attempt to hide the failure of such matrimonial plans.[24] Foreign monarchs were apparently reluctant to conclude a union by marriage with the Muscovite dynasty, whose prestige among its Western and Eastern neighbours had declined during Ivan's minority.[25] Later, Ivan repeatedly tried to find a foreign bride, but succeeded only in marrying the Caucasian Princess Mariia (Kuchenei) in 1561.[26]

To restore the prestige of the dynasty at home and abroad, Ivan embarked on an ambitious and politically controversial plan to be crowned as tsar of all Rus'. Church texts described Old Testament kings as 'tsars' and Christ as the Heavenly Tsar. Muscovite political vocabulary reserved the title of tsar for the rulers of superior status, the Byzantine emperor and Tatar khan. In the Muscovite view, the moral authority of the Orthodox emperor and the political might of the Muslim khan derived from the will of God. Given the strong religious connotation of the title of tsar, it is almost certain that the main driving force behind the coronation was Metropolitan Makarii. Familiar with descriptions of Byzantine imperial coronations, the metropolitan acted as the mastermind of Ivan's coronation, which took place in the Dormition cathedral in the Kremlin on 16 January 1547.[27]

During the coronation, the ruling circles claimed continuity between Ivan's rule and the rule of the Byzantine emperors and the Kievan princes. Even before the times of Ivan IV, Muscovite ideological texts anachronistically applied the title of tsar to Vladimir I of Kiev and Dmitrii Donskoi of Moscow to proclaim a direct and uninterrupted dynastic continuity from Kiev to Moscow. The public declaration of the growing political ambitions of the Muscovite ruler at the 1547 coronation caused an adverse reaction from his western neighbour, Sigismund II of Poland and Lithuania, whose possessions included Kiev and other lands of Kievan Rus'. As a result, the coronation was followed by a long

---

24 *PSRL*, vol. XIII, p. 450.
25 See Krom, 'Politicheskii krizis', 13; A. L. Khoroshkevich, *Rossiia v sisteme mezhdunarodnykh otnoshenii serediny XVI veka* (Moscow: Drevlekhranilishche, 2003), p. 65; Pavlov and Perrie, *Ivan*, p. 41.
26 See Hugh F. Graham, 'Paul Juusten's Mission to Muscovy', *RH* 13 (1986): 44, 89; Jerome Horsey, 'Travels', in Lloyd E. Berry and Robert O. Crummey (eds.), *Rude and Barbarous Kingdom. Russia in the Accounts of Sixteenth-Century English Voyagers* (Madison: University of Wisconsin Press, 1968), pp. 279–80; Khoroshkevich, *Rossiia*, p. 275.
27 See David B. Miller, 'Creating Legitimacy: Ritual, Ideology, and Power in Sixteenth-Century Russia', *RH* 21 (1994): 298–302; Pavlov and Perrie, *Ivan*, pp. 34–6.

diplomatic struggle between Muscovy and Poland-Lithuania over Ivan IV's new title.[28]

The fact that the ritual of the coronation included a considerable Byzantine element, as well as Ivan's aggressive foreign policy after 1547, has generated much debate about whether Ivan's power was of an imperial character. It would be inaccurate to describe Ivan's coronation as imperial in a strict historical sense. In Byzantium, the head of the Church anointed the aspiring emperor, marking thereby his symbolical rebirth into a Christ-like status. Since the act of anointing transformed the ruler into a sacred figure, the emperor was proclaimed holy. The most accurate accounts of Ivan's coronation, however, do not mention anointing.[29] Leaving anointing out of the ritual was probably in the interests of Makarii, who sought to secure his own spiritual authority during the coronation. In his speech at the ceremony, Makarii stressed that the tsar had his own judge in Heaven and that the ruler could enter the heavenly tsardom only by properly fulfilling his tasks of protecting the Christian faith and the Orthodox Church. Such moral prescriptions that urged the ruler to protect the Church and to listen to wise advisers were essential elements of Muscovite political culture.[30]

Ivan's coronation was followed in February 1547 by his marriage to Anastasiia Romanovna, a member of the established boyar clan of the Zakhar'in-Iur'evs. Following in Edward L. Keenan's footsteps, Kollmann sees Ivan's marriage in the context of the 'marriage politics' of senior boyar clans, which were purportedly responsible for running the Muscovite polity and manipulated the ruler in their own interests.[31] However, Ivan's marriage was preceded by a wide search for a royal bride. As mentioned above, a foreign woman was possible and, apparently, even more desirable than a Muscovite one. Among the local candidates were not only daughters of boyars and other members

---

28 See Jaroslaw Pelenski, 'The Origins of the Official Muscovite Claims to the "Kievan Inheritance"', *HUS* 1 (1977): 29–52; A. L. Khoroshkevich, 'Tsarskii titul Ivana IV i boiarskii "miatezh" 1553 goda', *Otechestvennaia istoriia*, 1994, no. 3: 23–42.

29 For earlier versions of the description of the coronation, see *PSRL*, vols. XIII, pp. 150–1; XXIX (Moscow: Nauka, 1965), pp. 49–50. On the missing elements of the ritual, see A. P. Bogdanov, 'Chiny venchaniia rossiiskikh tsarei', in B. A. Rybakov et al. (eds.), *Kul'tura srednevekovoi Moskvy XIV–XVII vv.* (Moscow: Nauka, 1995), p. 217; B. A. Uspenskii, *Tsar' i patriarkh: Kharisma vlasti v Rossii. Vizantiiskaia model' i ee russkoe pereosmyslenie* (Moscow: Iazyki russkoi kul'tury, 1998), pp. 109–13 (includes a review of the historiography).

30 Daniel Rowland, 'Did Muscovite Literary Ideology Place Limits on the Power of the Tsar, 1540s–1660s?', *RR* 49 (1990): 125–55; Sergei Bogatyrev, *The Sovereign and his Counsellors: Ritualised Consultations in Muscovite Political Culture, 1350s–1570s* (Helsinki: Finnish Academy of Science and Letters, 2000), pp. 38–98.

31 Nancy Shields Kollmann, *Kinship and Politics. The Making of the Muscovite Political System, 1345–1547* (Stanford, Calif.: Stanford University Press, 1987), pp. 121–45, 174.

of the court, but also those of provincial rank-and-file cavalrymen and church servitors. The sources suggest that the age, appearance and health of a bride were as important as her pedigree.[32] Ivan's numerous later wives were from a Muscovite elite clan (Mariia Nagaia), from relatively obscure gentry families (Marfa Sobakina, Anna Koltovskaia, Anna Vasil'chikova) and from a foreign dynasty (Mariia Kuchenei). The wide ethnic and social background of the royal wives shows that the choice was not only a matter of the 'marriage politics' of a handful of boyar clans. Royal marriages were essential for sustaining the relations between the dynasty and the wide circles of servitors and for maintaining the international relations of the day.

Ivan's coronation and his marriage were major contributions to the strengthening of his position as the head of the dynasty in the Muscovite polity. Though the coronation did not turn Ivan into a sacred ruler, it signified a major transformation of Muscovite political institutions. The coronation changed the status of the ruling family and affected its domestic, international and cultural policy. Ivan's old title of grand prince made him *primus inter pares* among other members of the dynasty. By assuming the title of tsar, Ivan acquired the status of a ruler chosen by God and received supreme authority over other princes and members of the court.

The elevated position of the dynastic head allowed the ruling circles to launch an ideological programme of consolidation of the elite around the figure of the monarch. The main thesis of the official propaganda contrasted the anarchy of the boyar rule during the minority of Ivan with the harmony prevailing under Tsar Ivan. The Church actively contributed to the 'policy of reconciliation', though the role of particular clerics in this process is a matter of controversy. The received wisdom is that the priest Sil'vestr was an influential adviser to the tsar in both spiritual and political matters in the 1550s. Carolyn Johnston Pouncy, however, has argued that Sil'vestr was a well-educated and well-connected person, but was not such an influential adviser as some later sources describe him.[33] Unlike Sil'vestr, Metropolitan Makarii surely had an entrée to the closest entourage of the tsar. He was responsible for the formulation of the idea of militant Orthodoxy at the end of the 1540s and early 1550s and participated in administrative and diplomatic affairs. Metropolitan Makarii was probably a key architect of the new ideology, as is apparent from the documents of the so-called Council of a Hundred Chapters (*Stoglav*). This convocation of top-level ecclesiastics and some elite courtiers was held in

---

32 See V. D. Nazarov, 'Svadebnye dela XVI veka', VI, 1976, no. 10: 118–20.
33 Carolyn Johnston Pouncy, ' "The blessed Sil'vestr" and the Politics of Invention in Muscovy, 1545–1700', *HUS* 19 (1995): 548–72.

1551 to enact measures to improve ecclesiastical life and the morals of the clergy and Church members. In line with Makarii's views expressed during the coronation, the *Stoglav* defended the interests of the clergy, capitalising on the idea of a union between the tsar and the Church.

The proceedings of the *Stoglav* also included a speech by the tsar which presented the court feuds of Ivan's minority in a favourable light to the dynasty. In his speech, Ivan recalled his childhood as a period of revolt and blamed the boyars for seizing power and eliminating his uncles.[34] Since the extant text of Ivan's speech has been edited, it is not easy to determine who personally was behind this attempt to absolve Elena Glinskaia of any responsibility for the deaths of Iurii of Dmitrov and in particular of Andrei of Staritsa. Nevertheless, the speech can be seen as Ivan's contribution to the reinterpretation of recent dynastic history. The utilisation of personal information about Ivan's early years and about his closest relatives for ideological purposes at least required his sanction. Furthermore, it is very likely that Ivan participated in the compilation of the speech, since its original text was written, according to the surviving documents of the council, in Ivan's own hand or was signed by him.[35] There was a tradition of literacy in the royal family, and so the evidence of Ivan's involvement in the preparation of the speech is highly plausible.[36]

Makarii's model of harmony between the ruling family and the Church, however, was not always as effective as at the *Stoglav*. In 1553, a dynastic crisis broke out when Ivan was seriously ill and ordered his boyars to swear an oath of allegiance to his infant son Dmitrii. The crisis, which was highly reminiscent of the last days of Vasilii III, caused quarrels between various groups of courtiers, some of whom considered Vladimir of Staritsa, son of the late Andrei, a better candidate. It was up to the metropolitan to act as a mediator in the conflict, but Makarii for some reason refrained from any interference.[37] Makarii's involvement in government activities began decreasing from the mid-1550s, apparently due to his ambiguous position during the 1553 crisis and active intercession with the tsar on behalf of some of Ivan's courtiers.[38]

34 E. B. Emchenko, *Stoglav. Issledovanie i tekst* (Moscow: Indrik, 2000), p. 246.
35 Emchenko, *Stoglav*, p. 242.
36 On the literacy of Vasilii III and Andrei of Staritsa, see V. V. Kalugin, *Andrei Kurbskii i Ivan Groznyi. Teoreticheskie vzgliady i literaturnaia tekhnika drevnerusskogo pisatelia* (Moscow: Iazyki russkoi kul'tury, 1998), pp. 138–9.
37 See I. Gralia (Hieronim Grala), *Ivan Mikhailov Viskovatyi: Kar'era gosudarstvennogo deiatelia v Rossii XVI v.* (Moscow: Radiks, 1994), pp. 136–8. Dmitrii died in an accident shortly after the crisis.
38 See Smirnov, *Ocherki*, pp. 194–202; S. O. Shmidt, 'Mitropolit Makarii i pravitel'stvennaia deiatel'nost' ego vremeni', in S. O. Shmidt, *Rossiia Ivana Groznogo* (Moscow: Nauka, 1999), pp. 239–45; Makarii (Veretennikov), *Zhizn'*, pp. 143–54.

A further step in the changing relationship between the monarch and the head of the Russian Church was the obtaining of a sanction for Ivan's title of tsar from the patriarch of Constantinople in the second half of the 1550s. As part of this project, Ivan's ideological advisers prepared new instructions on the ritual of coronation for the tsar's heir, Ivan Ivanovich. Unlike the 1547 coronation masterminded by Makarii, the new version of the ritual included the anointing of the ruler, that is, likening him to Christ. Capitalising on this idea, Ivan soon began treating his subjects, including many Church hierarchs, with unprecedented violence (see below). After Makarii's death in 1563, the tsar resolutely deposed and sometimes even executed those metropolitans who did not accept his erratic domestic policy.

The strengthening of the position of the ruler was reflected in the official heraldry and the design of Ivan's coins.[39] In 1560–3, the Church ideologists produced the *Imperial Book of Degrees (Stepennaia kniga)*, a work that glorified the Muscovite dynasty.[40] Starting from the mid-1560s, Ivan also began promoting the concept of the divine nature of his power and his hereditary right to the title of tsar in his letters addressed to the fugitive boyar Prince Andrei Mikhailovich Kurbskii and the rulers of Poland, Sweden and England.[41] In his letters to Kurbskii, Ivan elaborated on the ideas of the *Stoglav* concerning the danger of boyar rule to the state. He again blamed the boyars for their aspirations to seek power during his minority and made similar accusations against his entourage of the 1550s.

Keenan argues that Ivan was illiterate and never wrote the works attributed to him, but most historians now disagree.[42] Keenan's assumption is based primarily on his controversial study of the correspondence between Ivan and Kurbskii. At the same time, there are other letters of Ivan. Many of them, full of irony, parody and mockery of opponents, have survived in sixteenth-century copies in the archives of the Foreign (Ambassadorial) Chancellery. Keenan fails to offer an alternative attribution for or any cultural explanation

---

39 Uspenskii, *Tsar'*, pp. 20, 109–13; Khoroshkevich, *Rossiia*, pp. 66, 186–8, 288–9, 348; A.S. Mel'nikova, *Russkie monety ot Ivana Groznogo do Petra Velikogo. Istoriia russkoi denezhnoi sistemy s 1533 po 1682 god* (Moscow: Finansy i statistika, 1989), p. 41.
40 David B. Miller, 'The Velikie Minei Chetii and the Stepennaia Kniga of Metropolitan Makarii and the Origins of Russian National Consciousness', *FOG* 26 (1979), 263–382.
41 D. S. Likhachev and Ia. S. Lur'e (eds.), *Poslaniia Ivana Groznogo* (Moscow and Leningrad: AN SSSR, 1951); J. L. I. Fennell (ed. and trans.), *The Correspondence between Prince Kurbsky and Tsar Ivan IV of Russia* (Cambridge: Cambridge University Press, 1955).
42 See Edward L. Keenan, *The Kurbskii–Groznyi Apocrypha. The Seventeenth-Century Genesis of the 'Correspondence' Attributed to Prince A. M. Kurbskii and Tsar Ivan IV*, with an appendix by Daniel C. Waugh (Cambridge, Mass.: Harvard University Press, 1971). See also Charles J. Halperin's review article, 'Edward Keenan and the Kurbskii–Groznyi Correspondence in Hindsight', and Keenan's response, both in *JGO* 46 (1998): 376–415.

of the appearance of these documents. Judging by the excessive formality of Muscovite diplomatic practice, it would be unrealistic to assume that anyone except the tsar could have had enough authority to write such unusual letters to foreign rulers. Though we can hardly trust the romantic stories about Ivan IV's Renaissance library, it is obvious that he was familiar with literary culture. Ivan's treasury included a typical Muscovite selection of Church books, some chronicles, and a Western book of herbal remedies. Contemporary sources show that Ivan frequently borrowed books from clerics and courtiers, read them and also donated books to churches and monasteries.[43]

The 1550s policy of reconciliation had little application to the collateral branches of the dynasty. Ivan elevated his family at the expense of the Dmitrov and Staritsa lines of the dynasty. The tsar's chancellery promoted the ancient roots of the dynasty by preparing a special list (*sinodik*) of its members, starting with the medieval princes of Kiev and ending with Ivan's deceased children, to be commemorated by the patriarch of Constantinople.[44] Neither Iurii of Dmitrov nor Andrei of Staritsa was mentioned in the tsar's *sinodik*, though Ivan did make donations to the monasteries in memory of Iurii.[45] Ivan's attitude to Vladimir of Staritsa was also very circumspect. In the 1550s and 1560s, the tsar regularly involved Vladimir in military campaigns and provided him with experienced foreign architects.[46] At the same time, after the 1553 crisis, the tsar demanded from Vladimir unconditional support for the ruling family, ordered him to reside in Moscow and limited the size of his court.[47] During the 1560s, Ivan increased pressure on the Staritsa family. Many historians have seen Vladimir and Efrosin'ia of Staritsa as leaders of conservative political forces opposing the centralising policy of the tsar, but this interpretation relies

43 For a list of books from the tsar's private treasury, see 'Opis' domashnemu imushch-estvu tsaria Ivana Vasil'evicha, po spiskam i knigam 90 i 91 godov', in *Vremennik Impera-torskogo Moskovskogo obshchestva istorii i drevnostei rossiiskikh* 7 (Moscow: Universitetskaia tipografiia, 1850), smes': 6–7. The list is incomplete as it is part of an inventory of items that were missing from the treasury after the death of Ivan IV. See G. V. Zhari-nov, 'O proiskhozhdenii tak nazyvaemoi "Opisi domashnemu imushchestvu tsaria Ivana Vasil'evicha . . ." ', *Arkhiv russkoi istorii* 2 (Moscow: Roskomarkhiv, 1992): 179–85. On books donated and borrowed by Ivan, see N. N. Zarubin, *Biblioteka Ivana Groznogo. Rekonstruk-tsiia i bibliograficheskoe opisanie*, ed. A. A. Amosov (Leningrad: Nauka, Leningradskoe otdelenie, 1982), p. 22.

44 S. M. Kashtanov, 'The Czar's Sinodik of the 1550s', *Istoricheskaia Genealogiia/Historical Genealogy* 2 (Ekaterinburg and Paris: Yarmarka Press, 1993): 44–67. The patriarch blessed Ivan's assumption of the title of tsar with some reservations in 1560.

45 S. M. Kashtanov, *Finansy srednevekovoi Rusi* (Moscow: Nauka, 1988), p. 141.

46 See *Razriadnaia kniga 1475–1598 gg.*, ed. V. I. Buganov (Moscow: Nauka, 1966), pp. 127–230; G. S. Evdokimov, E. I. Ruzaeva and D. E. Iakovlev, 'Arkhitekturnaia keramika v dekore Moskovskogo velikokniazheskogo dvortsa v seredine XVI v.', in Batalov et al. (eds.), *Drevnerusskoe iskusstvo*, p. 126.

47 *SGGD*, vol. 1, pp. 460–8.

too heavily on Ivan's official propaganda. Vladimir did not need to have any political views to arouse Ivan IV's suspicion since distrust of their own kin was typical of pre-modern monarchs. Ivan's relationship with the Staritsa family was a result of his dynastic policy and his own concept of personal power. Equipped with the idea of the divine nature of his authority, Ivan took to extremes the traditional repressive policy of the ruling family towards collateral branches of the dynasty.

Metropolitan Makarii's death in 1563 apparently freed Ivan's hands. Beginning in 1564, the tsar several times forced Vladimir of Staritsa to exchange his hereditary possessions, which eventually led to the destruction of the Staritsa apanage (udel). Ivan IV also compelled Vladimir's mother, Efrosin'ia, who was an influential figure at the Staritsa court, to become a nun and peopled Vladimir's court with the tsar's loyalists. In 1569, the tsar accused Vladimir and his family of high treason and poisoned them.[48]

After the death of his infant son Dmitrii in 1553, Ivan IV paved the way to the throne for his next son, Ivan Ivanovich. The tsar promoted his son in line with the traditions of the royal family, adapting them for the new political and cultural circumstances. Following the lead of Vasilii III, the tsar ordered a helmet for his three-year-old son in 1557, to emphasise the continuity of power within the family (see Plate 12b). At the same time, the inscriptions on the helmet of Ivan Ivanovich included new rhetoric which stressed the piety of the tsar and his son, and Ivan IV's love of God, and exalted Moscow as the capital of the tsardom.[49] Together with the heraldic images of double-headed eagles reproduced on the helmet, this rhetoric revealed the new political status of the dynasty and its close association with divine forces. In the early 1560s, the tsar presented his under-age son as a ruler capable of issuing state documents and created a small court for him.[50] The heir, however, never became tsar. Ivan IV accidentally killed his son during a brawl on 9 November 1581. Numerous speculations about what caused this accident are unverifiable, but it is clear that the tsar did not intend to kill Ivan Ivanovich.

Deeply shocked by the tragedy, Ivan IV died of natural causes on 18 March 1584. His death gave rise to typical rumours about his assassination, but, judging

48 For new archaeological material on the burial of members of the Staritsa family, see T. D. Panova, 'Opyt izucheniia nekropolia Moskovskogo Kremlia', in V. F. Kozlov et al. (eds.), Moskovskii nekropol'. Istoriia, arkheologiia, iskusstvo, okhrana (Moscow: Nauchno-issledovatel'skii institut kul'tury, 1991), pp. 101–4; T. D. Panova, Nekropoli Moskovskogo Kremlia (Moscow: Muzei-zapovednik 'Moskovskii Kreml'', 2003), p. 31, no. 94.
49 I. A. Komarov et al. (eds.), Armoury Chamber of the Russian Tsars (St Petersburg: Atlant, 2002), pp. 44, 300.
50 A. V. Antonov, 'Serpukhovskie dokumenty iz dela Patrikeevykh', Russkii diplomatarii 7 (Moscow: Drevlekhranilishche, 2001): 304–5.

by the archaeological evidence, there is little basis for such gossip. The remains of a poisoned infant from the Staritsa family buried in the Kremlin have very high arsenic content in comparison with the bodies of other members of the dynasty. At the same time, the poisoning did not affect the mercury level of the victim. A high level of arsenic in comparison with other bodies can thus be seen as circumstantial evidence of poisoning. As the content of arsenic in Ivan IV's remains is one of the lowest among those examined by archaeologists in the Kremlin, the probability that he was poisoned should be minimised.[51] The autopsy on Ivan IV also revealed spinal disease and large amounts of mercury in his body. However, it would be risky to attribute Ivan's unpredictable political actions and erratic family life to mercury poisoning, since there is no direct connection between the chemistry of a person's body and his or her behaviour. As the autopsy shows, the chemical composition of Ivan Ivanovich's remains is highly similar to that of the tsar, including the same high level of mercury. Ivan Ivanovich, however, never demonstrated such extravagant behaviour as his father did.

Ivan IV's next son, Fedor, inherited the throne. When his elder brother was alive, Fedor occupied a rather modest position in the family. Foreign and later Muscovite sources suggest that Fedor was retarded, though L.E. Morozova questions the reliability of this evidence.[52] Whatever his mental health, Fedor was capable of participating in military campaigns and court ceremonies. Fedor became the last member of the Riurikid dynasty on the throne.

Building the realm

At the beginning of Ivan's reign, the population of his realm, which received in English the established but somewhat inaccurate name of Muscovy, was predominantly Russian-speaking and Orthodox. Non-Russian ethnic groups resided in the periphery of the realm and were numerically rather small. Language and religion were important consolidating factors, which, however, did not remove substantial regional differences across the country. In the northern part of the country, remote territories along the White Sea coast sported self-sufficient communities of peasants and fishermen, which enjoyed much autonomy in local affairs throughout Ivan's reign. In the north-west, the towns of Novgorod and Pskov boasted developed urban communities. The local elites of the Trans-Volga, Riazan' and Trans-Oka regions often retained

---

51 See M. M. Gerasimov, 'Dokumental'nyi portret Ivana Groznogo', in *Kratkie soobshcheniia Instituta arkheologii AN SSSR* 100 (1965): 139; Babichenko, 'Kremlevskie tainy', 38.
52 See L. E. Morozova, 'Fedor Ivanovich', *VI*, 1997, no. 2: 49–71.

their hereditary lands and local affiliations, provided they remained loyal to Moscow.

During Ivan's minority, the ruling circles took a series of measures with the aim of integrating the vast realm. The central authorities carried out a large programme of land surveying in the late 1530s and 1540s. During the surveys, the authorities extended common tax burdens and other obligations to various segments of the local population. The surveys also shaped the local landscape by defining and describing all of its significant elements.[53] The government-sponsored surveys, therefore, not only registered local peculiarities, but also contributed to the formation of local identities. In the first half of the sixteenth century, the authorities replaced various quit-rents in kind with payments in money. To keep up with the growing role of money in the economy of Muscovy, Elena Glinskaia successfully implemented a currency reform by unifying monetary units across the realm in the second half of the 1530s. The new monetary system effectively incorporated the local currencies of Novgorod and Pskov and facilitated the integration of these economically important regions into the realm.[54]

The central authorities experimented with various methods of involving different regional groups in maintaining law and order in the provinces. Though these attempts were not limited to the provincial cavalrymen, it was precisely this group that became the chief agent of the government in local affairs. Cavalrymen had sufficient military skills and organisational experience as military servitors and estate owners. Beginning in the 1550s, the provincial cavalrymen started dominating the local district (*guba*) administration, which was responsible for law and order in the provinces, control over the local population's mobility, the distribution of service lands, the gathering of taxes, the mustering of local military forces and the certifying of slavery contracts. Since the authority of the *guba* elders covered various groups of the local population, the *guba* administration was an important factor in consolidating local communities. The *guba* administration was also open to cavalrymen of non-Muscovite origin and thereby facilitated their integration. The state thus actively participated in the formation of local identities and made use of them for its own political needs.

The townsmen and peasant communities also received limited autonomy in local affairs during the reforms of the 1550s. These changes in provincial

---

53 Those lands and meadows that were not covered by surveys often remained nameless. See Kashtanov, *Finansy*, p. 28. Such objects with no names could not have a significant meaning for the local perception of an area.

54 Mel'nikova, *Russkie monety*, pp. 14–28.

administration led to some redistribution of authority in favour of urban and rural communities at the expense of the local representatives of the central authorities (vicegerents or *namestniki*). Contrary to widespread opinion, the vicegerent administration, however, was not abolished in the middle of the sixteenth century.[55] In the 1550s, the ruling circles attempted to standardise judicial and administrative practices across the country by introducing a new law code (1550) and delegating routine administrative and financial tasks to the increasingly structured chancelleries (*prikazy*).[56]

The position of elite military servitors became more stable thanks to the standardisation of the terms of their service, improved registry, and the regulation of service relations among them during campaigns. As a result of the reforms of the 1550s, the sovereign's court, a hierarchical institution made up of the ruler's elite servitors, acquired a complicated rank structure.[57] Service relations between courtiers were subject to rules of precedence (*mestnichestvo*), a complex system that defined the status of a courtier on the basis of the prominence and service appointments of his ancestors and relatives. There are different opinions about who benefited from *mestnichestvo*. Kollmann sees it more as a means of consolidating the elite in the traditional patrimonial political system than as a means for the affirmation of the tsar's power. According to S. O. Shmidt, the system of precedence functioned on the basis of a mixture of the traditional principles of family honour and the principles of service relations that were formulated by the royal power. The monarchy could thus use *mestnichestvo* for controlling the elite. In line with this view, Ann M. Kleimola notes that *mestnichestvo*, which took its final shape during the minority of Ivan, caused a fragmentation of the elite and prevented the formation of a cohesive hereditary aristocracy which could have checked the autocratic power of the ruler. Shmidt's and Kleimola's points of view may explain why the elite

---

55 On the local administration, see N. E. Nosov, *Ocherki po istorii mestnogo upravleniia Russkogo gosudarstva pervoi poloviny XVI veka* (Moscow and Leningrad: AN SSSR, 1957); N. E. Nosov, *Stanovlenie soslovno-predstavitel'nykh uchrezhdenii v Rossii. Izyskaniia o zemskoi reforme Ivana Groznogo* (Leningrad: Nauka, Leningradskoe otdelenie, 1969); Carol B. Stevens, 'Banditry and Provincial Order in Sixteenth-Century Russia', in Ann M. Kleimola and Gail D. Lenhoff (eds.), *Culture and Identity in Muscovy, 1359–1584* (UCLA Slavic Studies, n.s., vol. 3; Moscow: ITZ-Garant, 1997), pp. 578–9; Sergei Bogatyrev, 'Localism and Integration in Muscovy', in Sergei Bogatyrev (ed.), *Russia Takes Shape. Patterns of Integration from the Middle Ages to the Present* (Helsinki: Finnish Academy of Science and Letters, 2004), pp. 59–127. For a revision of the history of the vicegerent administration, see Brian L. Davies, 'The Town Governors in the Reign of Ivan IV', *RH* 14 (1987): 77–143; Pashkova, *Mestnoe upravlenie*.
56 See Horace W. Dewey, 'The 1550 Sudebnik as an Instrument of Reform', *JGO* 10 (1962): 161–80; Peter B. Brown, 'Muscovite Government Bureaus', *RH* 10 (1983): 269–330.
57 On the sovereign's court, see Bogatyrev, *Sovereign*, pp. 16–26; Pavlov and Perrie, *Ivan*, pp. 23, 70.

servitors failed to effectively oppose the tsar's transgressions and his personal interference with the system of precedence.[58]

It is hard to determine who personally was responsible for the reforms. Historians sometimes call the ruling circles of the 1550s 'the chosen council', but this vague term is apparently irrelevant to governmental institutions.[59] B. N. Floria has suggested that the reforms were the results of a collective effort by the ruling elite, whose members were finally united after the long period of conflict during the boyar rule.[60] It is true that Ivan granted top court ranks to a wide circle of elite servitors, which especially benefited the tsarina's relatives, the Zakhar'in-Iur'evs. At the same time, there was no complete harmony among the elite. Their matrimonial ties with the ruler did not save the Zakhar'ins from falling out of favour after the 1553 dynastic crisis. The wide admission to the upper strata of the court apparently facilitated a certain social mobility at court. This situation was favourable for such functionaries as the courtier Aleksei Fedorovich Adashev and the secretary Ivan Mikhailovich Viskovatyi. They did not belong to the highest strata of the elite, but actively contributed to the running of the polity. Adashev had enough authority to revise the official genealogical records in favour of his clan. He was also involved in writing the official chronicle. Though his role in the 1550s government may be exaggerated in later sources, it is obvious that Adashev was a very important figure of the day.[61]

Limited and inconsistent as they were, the reforms allowed Ivan to reach a certain degree of consolidation of his realm and to pursue an aggressive policy towards his neighbours. With the taking of the Tatar states of Kazan' (1552) and Astrakhan' (1556), Ivan acquired vast territories populated with a multi-ethnic, predominantly Muslim population with distinctive cultural and economic traditions. The conquest was thus a major step in turning Ivan's

58 Nancy Shields Kollmann, *By Honor Bound. State and Society in Early Modern Russia* (Ithaca, N.Y., London: Cornell University Press, 1999), pp. 166–7; S. O. Shmidt, *U istokov rossiiskogo absoliutizma. Issledovanie sotsial'no-politicheskoi istorii vremeni Ivana Groznogo* (Moscow: Progress, 1996), pp. 330–80; Ann M. Kleimola, 'Status, Place, and Politics: The Rise of mestnichestvo during the boiarskoe pravlenie', *FOG* 27 (1980): 195–214. On Ivan's intrusion in *mestnichestvo*, see A. A. Zimin, *Oprichnina* (Moscow: Territoriia, 2001), p. 221; Pavlov and Perrie, *Ivan*, pp. 187–8.

59 A. N. Grobovsky, *The 'Chosen Council' of Ivan IV. A Reinterpretation* (New York: Gaus, 1969); A. I. Filiushkin, *Istoriia odnoi mistifikatsii. Ivan Groznyi i 'Izbrannaia Rada'* (Moscow: Voronezhskii gosudarstvennyi universitet, 1998).

60 Boris Floria, *Ivan Groznyi*, 2nd edn (Moscow: Molodaia gvardiia, 2002), p. 50.

61 On A. F. Adashev, see D. M. Bulanin, 'Adashev Aleksei Fedorovich', in *Slovar' knizhnikov i knizhnosti Drevnei Rusi*, vyp. 2: *Vtoraia polovina XIV–XVI v.* (Leningrad: Nauka, Leningradskoe otdelenie, 1988), pt. 1, pp. 8–10; Filiushkin, *Istoriia*. On I. M. Viskovatyi, see Gralia, *Ivan*.

realm into a multi-ethnic empire. By annexing the khanates, the tsar established control of the Volga waterway and gained access to the Caspian Sea and
the markets of Iran. The official propaganda presented the conquest of the
Tatar states as a triumph of militant Orthodoxy over the infidels. Conquering
the Kazan' and Astrakhan' khanates, which the Muscovite political tradition
saw as tsardoms, also contributed to the legitimisation of Ivan's assumption of
the title of tsar. The ruling circles used a variety of methods of integration in the
annexed territories, including the use of violence against the rebellious, Christianisation, which, however, was not very deep or systematic, incorporation
of the loyal local elite into the tsar's court and giving the annexed territories
special status in the administrative system.[62]

The victory over Kazan' triggered the expansion of Muscovy into Siberia.
After the taking of Kazan', the Siberian khan acknowledged the suzerainty
of Ivan IV and became his tributary. The ruling circles employed the
entrepreneurial merchant family of Stroganovs for the colonisation of Siberia.
The annexation of Astrakhan' enabled Muscovy to increase its presence in the
North Caucasus. Ivan's marriage to Mariia Kuchenei of Kabarda, mentioned
above, was part of this policy.[63]

The conquering of the lands of Kazan' and Astrakhan' escalated the tension
between Muscovy and the powerful Muslim states of Crimea and Turkey. The
Crimean khan saw Kazan' as a hereditary possession of his dynasty. The Turkish
sultan, in his turn, was particularly concerned about Muscovy's penetration
of the North Caucasus. Despite somewhat different political perspectives,
these powerful states concluded a union against Muscovy and jointly attacked
Astrakhan' in 1569. Thanks to the protective measures of the Russian side,
its diplomatic manoeuvring and the logistical miscalculations of the Turkish
commanders, the campaign failed.[64] Despite the failure, the Crimean khan
continued his aggressive policy towards Muscovy. He devastated Moscow in
1571, but Ivan's commanders inflicted a defeat on him at the Battle of Molodi
in 1572. This victory halted the revanchist plans of the Crimean khan.

Ivan IV failed to avoid simultaneous involvement in military conflicts on
several fronts. Without settling the conflict in the south, he launched a war
against his western neighbour, Livonia, in 1558. Historians traditionally interpret the Livonian war (1558–83) in geopolitical terms, asserting that Ivan was

62 Andreas Kappeler, *The Russian Empire: A Multiethnic History* (Harlow: Longman, 2001), pp.
24–32; M. B. Pliukhanova, *Siuzhety i simvoly Moskovskogo tsarstva* (St Petersburg: Akropol',
1995), pp. 177–90, 199–202.
63 See Janet Martin, *Medieval Russia, 980–1584* (Cambridge: Cambridge University Press,
1995), pp. 354–5; Kappeler, *The Russian Empire*, pp. 33–6.
64 See Martin, *Medieval Russia*, pp. 355–7; Khoroshkevich, *Rossiia*, pp. 508–14.

looking for a passage to the Baltic Sea to expand overseas trade. Revisionists explain the war's origins in terms of Ivan's short-term interest in getting tribute to replenish his treasury. They note that the geopolitical interpretations of the Livonian war are somewhat anachronistic and marked by economic determinism. The widely accepted view that the tsar began the war to gain access to the Baltic Sea derives from the Livonian and Polish sources. At the same time, there are no Muscovite sources corroborating the idea that the Muscovite authorities aspired to develop their own commercial and transport infrastructure in the Baltic region.[65]

The Muscovite ruling circles showed no intention of escalating the military operation in Livonia after a series of victories in the late 1550s. The situation, however, dramatically changed in the early 1560s when the Polish-Lithuanian state, Sweden and Denmark partitioned Livonia and became directly involved in the ongoing struggle. The main opponents of Muscovy, Poland and Lithuania, considerably strengthened their political and military resources when they united into a single monarchy by concluding the Union of Lublin in 1569. From 1579, Stefan Batory of Poland and Lithuania, an energetic politician and gifted commander, repulsed Muscovite forces and invaded the Novgorod and Pskov regions. In the last stage of the war, the Swedes captured a number of Muscovite strongholds along the coast of the Gulf of Finland. The Livonian war only resulted in human and material losses for Muscovy.

In his deliberate search for allies, Ivan actively supported commercial relations between Muscovy and England by granting generous privileges to English merchants. The English were interested in furs and a number of Muscovite commodities required for shipbuilding (timber, rope fibres, tallow, tar). Muscovites, in turn, benefited from English supplies of armaments, non-precious metals, clothes and luxury items. The tsar's attempts to conclude a political union with Elizabeth I of England were, however, in vain.

Muscovy's growing involvement in international affairs and the greater complexity of its social and administrative structures put increasing strain on the limited political resources of the monarchy. By the mid-1560s, Ivan's fears of court feuds and his failures in Western policy were added to his constant trepidation about his family.[66] In his search for security, Ivan left Moscow with his family and took up residence at Aleksandrovskaia Sloboda, north-east of

---

65 See Maureen Perrie, *The Cult of Ivan the Terrible in Stalin's Russia* (Houndmills: Palgrave, 2001), pp. 89–92; Aleksandr Filiushkin, 'Diskursy Livonskoi voiny', *Ab Imperio* 4 (2001): 43–80.

66 On the role of foreign policy in the establishment of the *oprichnina*, see Khoroshkevich, *Rossiia*, p. 416.

Moscow, in December 1564. Aleksandrovskaia Sloboda, which was founded by Vasilii III, was the largest grand-princely residence in the countryside. It was designed as an isolated fortified stronghold and as a place of pilgrimage. The site included a cathedral, one of the biggest in the country, and a palace with late Gothic architectural features. Despite the Western borrowings, the overall design of the residence was archaic even for the times of Vasilii III.[67] Ivan IV thus chose for his refuge a very conservative spatial environment. Having settled at Aleksandrovskaia Sloboda, he accused his old court of treason and the clerics of covering up for the traitors. The tsar demanded the right to punish his enemies. He divided the territory of his realm, his court and the administration into two: the *oprichnina* (from 'oprich'', 'separate') under the tsar's personal control; and the *zemshchina* (from 'zemlia', 'land'), officially under the rule of those boyars who stayed in Moscow.

The ideology of the *oprichnina* was never fully articulated. Ivan surely capitalised on the political ideas of the 1550s about anarchy prevailing during the boyar rule.[68] It is also very probable that the concept of the divine nature of Ivan's power, which received its final shape in the early 1560s, also played a major part in the formation of the *oprichnina*. The official chronicle stresses that God guided Ivan on his way out of Moscow.[69] Priscilla Hunt interprets the semiotic behaviour of Ivan during the *oprichnina* as an extreme manifestation of the official ideology of sacred kingship. According to Hunt, the cult of Holy Wisdom, which embodied the severity and meekness of Christ, was particularly relevant to Ivan's policy in the 1560s.[70] Ivan indeed paid special attention to his campaigns against places that sported cathedrals dedicated to the cult, in particular against Polotsk in 1562 and Novgorod in 1570. The official propaganda and court rituals presented these campaigns as acts of restoring Orthodoxy in the towns and protecting their holy churches from heretics and traitors.[71]

---

67 V. V. Kavel'makher, 'Gosudarev dvor v Aleksandrovskoi slobode. Opyt rekonstruktsii', in Iakob Ul'feldt, *Puteshestvie v Rossiiu*, ed. Dzh. Lind and A. L. Khoroshkevich (Moscow: Iazyki slavianskoi kul'tury, 2002), pp. 457–87.

68 Accusations against boyars who disobeyed Ivan during his minority are prominent in the official account of the establishment of the *oprichnina*: see *PSRL*, vol. XIII, p. 392.

69 *PSRL*, vol. XIII, p. 392.

70 See Priscilla Hunt, 'Ivan IV's Personal Mythology of Kingship', *SR* 52 (1993): 769–809. Hunt believes that the concept of the tsar's power derives directly from Makarii's views, but the process of the formation of this concept could have been multi-phased.

71 On the Polotsk campaign, see Sergei Bogatyrev, 'Battle for Divine Wisdom. The Rhetoric of Ivan IV's Campaign against Polotsk', in Eric Lohr and Marshall Poe (eds.), *The Military and Society in Russia, 1450–1917* (Leiden: Brill, 2002), pp. 325–63. On the Novgorod punitive campaign, see Floria, *Ivan*, p. 239.

The idea that Ivan acted as an exclusive judge, treating his subjects with awe and mercy, like God, may explain why the *oprichnina* policy was a peculiar combination of bloody terror and acts of public reconciliation. During the *oprichnina*, numerous executions, which, according to the incomplete official records, took the lives of more than 3,000 people, were often followed by amnesties. The mass exile of around 180 princes and cavalrymen to Kazan' and the confiscation of their lands (1565) were counterbalanced when they were pardoned and their property was partially restored. In 1566, in the middle of the *oprichnina* terror, the tsar convened a large gathering, the so-called 'Assembly of the Land' (*zemskii sobor*), of his elite servitors, provincial cavalrymen, the clergy and the merchants to discuss whether he should continue the Livonian war. Many scholars see this meeting as an 'estate-representative' institution, on the lines of a Western Parliament, which provided representation for various social groups. Others note that the participants did not represent their local communities or estates (*sosloviia*) because there were no elections to the assembly.[72] Judging by the surviving document of the meeting, its members indeed saw themselves primarily as servitors of the tsar rather than delegates of constituencies. They interacted with the monarchy in a rather traditional manner by expressing support for the policy of the ruler and swearing an oath of allegiance to him, like many courtiers had done before.[73]

The *oprichnina* has received various interpretations in the literature. Some historians have seen it as a conscious struggle among certain social groups, others suggest that it was an irrational outcome of Ivan's mental illness. Hunt and A. L. Iurganov offer cultural explanations of the *oprichnina* which do not exclude the possibility that Ivan's personality deeply affected his policy. Since the *oprichnina* involved a peculiar symbolism that alluded to the tsar and his *oprichniki* as punitive instruments of divine wrath, Iurganov explains the *oprichnina* in terms of possible eschatological expectations and imitations of biblical descriptions of the Heavenly Kingdom.[74] This interpretation is in accord with the complex symbolism of a military banner ordered by Ivan shortly before the *oprichnina*, in 1559/60. The images of Christ, the Archangel Michael and St John the Apostle, and quotations from the Book of Revelation that are reproduced in the banner allude to the tsar waging the final battle with cosmic evil (see

72 For the historiography of the 1566 *zemskii sobor*, see Pavlov and Perrie, *Ivan*, pp. 131–2.
73 *SGGD*, vol. 1, pp. 545–56. On the practice of swearing an oath of allegiance in Muscovite political culture, see H. W. Dewey and A. M. Kleimola, 'Promise and Perfidy in Old Russian Cross-Kissing', *Canadian Slavic Studies* 3 (1968): 334.
74 A. L. Iurganov, 'Oprichnina i strashnyi sud', *Otechestvennaia istoriia*, 1997, no. 3: 52–75; A. L. Iurganov, *Kategorii russkoi srednevekovoi kul'tury* (Moscow: MIROS, 1998), pp. 382–98.

Plate 13).[75] Judging by a contemporary provincial chronicle which parallels the rule of Ivan with an apocalyptic kingdom, such eschatological imagery may have found a response among Ivan's cultured subjects.[76]

The *oprichnina* affected various local communities in different ways. The authorities deported non-*oprichnina* servitors from the *oprichnina* lands and granted their estates to the *oprichniki*, but the extent of these forced resettlements remains unclear. Despite such relocations, the *oprichnina* did not deprive provincial cavalrymen of room for manoeuvre. It might take the authorities a year and a half to begin relocating cavalrymen from a region included in the *oprichnina*. During this period many local cavalrymen managed to obtain tax exemptions from the central authorities and to secure possession of desirable lands in their new places of residence. Furthermore, some of them did not go to specified destinations, but to places chosen because of ties of kinship (*dlia rodstva*). In these cases, the authorities accepted their wishes.[77] The *zemshchina* territories bore the heavy financial burden of funding the organisation and actions of the *oprichnina*; some *zemshchina* communities were pillaged and devastated. In early 1570, the tsar and his *oprichniki* sacked Novgorod, where they slaughtered between 3,000 and 15,000 people. At the same time, the lower-ranking inhabitants of Moscow escaped Ivan's disgrace and forced resettlements. For taxpayers in the remote north, the establishment of the *oprichnina* mostly meant a change of payee.

The tsar abolished the *oprichnina* in 1572 after its troops proved to be ineffective during a devastating Tatar raid on Moscow. Nevertheless, he returned to the practice of dividing his court during the 'rule' of Simeon Bekbulatovich in the mid-1570s. This episode shows how the growing complexity of the ethnic composition of the tsar's court affected Ivan's dynastic policy. The increasing involvement of Muscovy in Eastern diplomacy resulted in the growing presence of Tatar servitors in Muscovy. Starting from the times of Vasilii III, Tatar dignitaries descending from Chingis Khan (Chingisids) occupied very prominent positions at the court of the grand prince of Moscow. In accordance with the traditional Muscovite practice, these elite Tatar servitors received the title of tsar. Thanks to their mobility and military skill, Tatar forces led by the

75 Lukian Iakovlev, *Drevnosti Rossiiskogo gosudarstva. Dopolnenie k III otdeleniiu. Russkie starinnye znamena* (Moscow: Sinodal'naia tipografiia, 1865), pp. 8–10; D. Strukov and I. Popov, *Risunki k izdaniiu 'Russkie starinnye znamena' Lukiana Iakovleva* (Moscow: Khromolitografiia V. Bakhman, 1865).

76 The Stroev copy of the third *Pskov Chronicle*, dating to the 1560s: *Pskovskie letopisi*, ed. A. N. Nasonov, vol. ii (Moscow: AN SSSR, 1955; reprinted Moscow: Iazyki russkoi kul'tury, 2000), p. 231.

77 See V. N. Kozliakov, 'Novyi dokument ob oprichnykh pereseleniiakh', in *Arkhiv russkoi istorii* 7 (Moscow: Drevlekhranilishche, 2002): 197–211.

Chingisids became important elements of the tsar's army operating on the western front.[78]

By the mid-1570s, only one of such Tatar tsars, the baptised Tatar Khan Simeon Bekbulatovich, was alive. He actively participated in the tsar's campaigns and became Ivan IV's nephew by marriage. In 1575, Ivan unexpectedly installed Simeon on the Muscovite throne in his stead. For a year, Simeon was a nominal ruler as grand prince of Moscow. Scholars usually see this bizarre act as Ivan's attempt at abdication, a cultural experiment or a political parody. According to the Soviet historian A. A. Zimin, Ivan IV was planning to pass on the throne to Simeon.[79] The historian justly focuses on the close relations between the Muscovite dynasty and the descendants of Chingis Khan, but he seems to underestimate such an essential element of dynastic policy as Simeon's title. In the second half of the 1560s, Ivan IV himself bestowed on Simeon the title of tsar.[80] Given his pedigree and title, Simeon could indeed become a pretender for the Muscovite throne, something which apparently caused Ivan's suspicion in the intense political situation of the mid-1570s. At the same time, Ivan could not resort to violence in his dealings with Simeon because of his title of tsar. The use of violence against the bearer of the title would compromise the idea of the divine origin of the tsar's power. This is why Ivan consistently lowered Simeon's status in the dynastic hierarchy. First he made Simeon grand prince of Moscow and shortly after that, grand prince of Tver'.[81] The episode with Simeon thus seems to be an elaborate means of precluding a possible Chingisid succession to the throne.

At the end of Ivan's reign, Muscovy's human and economic resources were exhausted. The Livonian war, the *oprichnina*, famines and epidemics led to human losses and the country's economic decline. The economic crisis was especially grave in the Novgorod region, which was devastated during the war and the *oprichnina*. The population of the region fell by more than 80 per cent in the early 1580s when compared to the mid-sixteenth century. The

---

78 See Janet Martin, 'Tatars in the Muscovite Army during the Livonian War', in Lohr and Poe (eds.), *The Military and Society*, pp. 365–87.

79 A. A. Zimin, *V kanun groznykh potriasenii. Predposylki pervoi krest'ianskoi voiny v Rossii* (Moscow: Mysl', 1986), p. 27. For a review of the historiography, see Pavlov and Perrie, *Ivan*, pp. 172–3.

80 A. A. Zimin (ed.), *Gosudarstvennyi arkhiv Rossii XVI stoletiia. Opyt rekonstruktsii*, vol. III (Moscow: Institut istorii SSSR, 1978), p. 451.

81 A later piece of evidence suggesting that Simeon was crowned as tsar in 1575 is not reliable, because from 1575 till Ivan's death in 1584 contemporary working documents refer to Simeon as grand prince. Only after Ivan IV's death was the title of tsar restored to Simeon. See *PSRL*, vol. xxxiv (Moscow: Nauka, 1978), p. 192; *Razriadnaia kniga 1475–1598 gg.*, p. 363.

economic hardship caused many peasants to flee to the periphery of the realm. By the end of Ivan's reign, peasants had abandoned 70–98 per cent of arable land throughout the country. The authorities sought to stop this practice by limiting the mobility of the peasants at the end of Ivan's reign. Irregular at first, such measures later resulted in the establishment of serfdom in Russia.

* * *

Was Ivan IV's reign important in a long-term perspective? The traditional view is that Ivan created a centralised state which assumed control over its subjects through the political regime of autocracy. Historians also often juxtapose the first half of Ivan's reign, which was a period of reforms, to the second one, when he unleashed a campaign of terror. Recent studies with their accent on continuities, localities, minorities and informal relations within the elite argue that Ivan's regime remained medieval and personal. Ivan and his advisers did indeed use some traditional forms of dynastic and court policies. It is also clear now that the social and political structure of the Muscovite polity under Ivan IV never was as homogenous as the notion of a 'centralised state' implies.

Nevertheless, Ivan changed Muscovy. The period from the end of the 1540s to the early 1560s was formative for Ivan's reign. The royal family received a new status during a multi-phase transformation of the concept of its power, which began with Ivan's coronation as tsar and culminated in turning him into a sacred figure. The 1550s policy of reconciliation also contributed to the strengthening of the dynasty. Capitalising on the commonly agreed reinterpretation of the period of boyar rule, the monarchy articulated its central role in Muscovite politics. The elite became carefully arranged in a rank order; the functionaries received clearly defined procedures and forms of documents. Thanks to these reforms, the sovereign's court, the chancellery system and the local administration turned into complex organisations which facilitated the functioning of the military-fiscal state.[82]

Ivan valued the political and organisational instruments that he received in the 1550s. It is true that his policy later became extravagant and unpredictable, probably as a result of mental illness. Ivan's transgressions, however, were not signs of full debility, because they had their own logic which was based on the ideas formulated in the 1550s: the divine sanction for the tsar's power, and precluding the boyars from restoring their rule, which could lead to anarchy.

---

82 On the fiscal-military state, see Jan Glete, *War and the State in Early Modern Europe. Spain, the Dutch Republic and Sweden as Fiscal-Military States, 1500–1660* (London and New York: Routledge, 2002), *passim*; Chester S. L. Dunning, *Russia's First Civil War: The Time of Troubles and the Founding of the Romanov Dynasty* (University Park, Pa.: Pennsylvania State University Press, 2001), p. 19.

Despite the notorious experiments with his court, Ivan never relinquished his title of tsar and was obsessed with bequeathing it to his heir. It is obvious that Ivan exaggerated, if not imagined, various threats to his power and to his family. This is why much of Ivan's characteristic activity was in fact defensive. However erratic his dynastic policy was, Ivan eventually succeeded in its implementation, since he secured the succession of power for one of his sons despite all the tragic events in the family. The assumption and active propaganda of the title of tsar, transgressions and sudden changes in policy during the *oprichnina* contributed to the image of the Muscovite prince as a ruler accountable only to God. Though succeeding Muscovite rulers never went to the extremes reached by Ivan, they benefited from the idea of the divine nature of the power of the Russian monarch which crystallised during Ivan's reign.

How far was Ivan personally in charge of policy during his long reign? The relationship between the ruler and his counsellors was complex and varied according to circumstances. Ivan the boy surely depended on his mentors. At the same time, all evidence of the influence of one or another courtier on the adult ruler should be treated with caution, because passages about good and evil advisers are commonplaces in the literary and documentary sources. At the height of the terror, Ivan could subject every courtier to suspicion and punishment.[83] Ivan's reign thus revealed the vulnerability of the social and legal mechanisms for personal protection when confronted by authorities exceeding the political system's normal level of violence.

Ivan was also generally successful in integrating various territories into a single state. Despite the failure in the Livonian war, his regime had enough political, military, economic and cultural resources to annex large territories. Ivan's state also sustained its presence in the provinces and accommodated localism. The centre established in the provinces a local government system which was based on a combination of centrally appointed and locally elected officials. Despite later modifications, this form of local administration proved to be functional and durable. Ivan left to his successors a devastated but coherent state that retained its territorial integrity even in spite of the stormy events of the Time of Troubles. As a result of Ivan's rule, Muscovy became a self-sufficient polity at an immensely high price.

83 See the revealing records of an investigation held by Ivan in S. K. Bogoiavlenskii (ed.), 'Dopros tsarem Ioannom Groznym russkikh plennikov, vyshedshikh iz Kryma', in *ChOIDR* 2 (Moscow: Sinodal'naia tipografiia, 1912), Smes': 26–33.

II

Fedor Ivanovich and Boris Godunov
(1584–1605)

A. P. PAVLOV

At the end of Ivan the Terrible's reign Russia experienced an acute political, social and economic crisis. The protracted Livonian war and natural disasters had brought the economic life of the country to a complete collapse. The Novgorod tax cadastres depict a catastrophic decline in the population by the beginning of the 1580s (by almost 80 per cent) and the neglect of arable land (the proportion of untilled land was more than 90 per cent).[1] The crisis affected not only the north-west but the entire territory of Russia.[2] The economic decline had a deleterious effect on the military capability of the army – many noblemen were unable to provide service from their devastated estates. After Groznyi's death the Polish King Stefan Batory nurtured plans to invade Russia. He counted on finding support in some circles of Russian society. When M. I. Golovin defected to Lithuania he assured the king that he would not encounter any serious resistance in Russia. The country faced a real threat of foreign invasion and internal unrest.

The situation was compounded by a profound crisis in the ruling elites. A power struggle began immediately after the death of Tsar Ivan. On the very night of his death (the night of 18/19 March 1584) conflicts occurred in the duma, as a result of which Tsarevich Dmitrii's kinsmen, the Nagois, were arrested and banished from court.[3] Shortly afterwards Tsarevich Dmitrii was dispatched to his apanage at Uglich. Groznyi's elder son Fedor was elevated to the throne. A sickly and weak-willed individual, he was not capable of ruling independently and, according to contemporaries, he found the performance even of formal court ceremonies to be a burden. The fate of the throne and the state lay in the hands of competing boyar groupings. The viability of Groznyi's protracted efforts to establish 'autocratism' was to be put to the test. In the

1 *Agrarnaia istoriia Severo-Zapada Rossii XVI veka: Novgorodskie piatiny* (Leningrad: Nauka, 1974), pp. 291–2.
2 E. I. Kolycheva, *Agrarnyi stroi Rossii XVI veka* (Moscow: Nauka, 1987), pp. 178–95.
3 *PSRL*, vol. xiv (Moscow: Nauka, 1965), p. 35.

opinion of S. F. Platonov, the struggle among the elites at the beginning of Tsar Fedor's reign amounted only to simple conflicts for influence at court.[4] But this point of view does not take into account all the complexity and gravity of the situation. At such a time the future political development of the country was in question. At the beginning of Tsar Fedor's reign there were two diametrically opposed positions in the political struggle. At one extreme there stood the upper tier of the hereditary princely aristocracy. The logic of the political struggle created an alliance between the former *oprichnina* ('court') magnates, the Shuiskii princes, and some former *zemshchina* men – the Princes Mstislavskii, Vorotynskii, Kurakin and Golitsyn. These boyars could lay claim to the role of the tsar's leading counsellors on the basis of their exclusively eminent lineage rather than of court favouritism. It seems that the political aim of this group was to limit the tsar's power in favour of the premier princely aristocracy. It is not surprising that these 'princelings' should have displayed open sympathy for the system in the Polish-Lithuanian Commonwealth (*Rzeczpospolita*), where the king was elected and his power depended on the will of the great magnates.[5]

The social and political antithesis of this princely grouping were the low-born *oprichnina* ('court') nobles who were concerned with preserving the rights and privileges they had enjoyed in Groznyi's lifetime. At the beginning of April 1584 the most energetic of these men – B. Ia. Bel'skii – attempted to seize power and to force the tsar to continue the *oprichnina* policy. Bel'skii's venture was unsuccessful, and the former favourite was forced into 'honourable exile' as governor of Nizhnii Novgorod. With Bel'skii's removal the position of the former 'court' nobles was seriously undermined.

Neither the 'princely' nor the '*oprichnina*' faction managed to gain the upper hand in the political struggle. A third political force, headed by the Godunovs and the Romanovs, moved to the fore and emerged victorious. By the summer of 1584 these two clans had effected a rapprochement. They concluded a 'testamentary alliance of friendship' in which the ageing boyar Nikita Romanovich Iur'ev, Tsar Fedor's uncle on his mother's side, entrusted the guardianship of his young sons – the Nikitich Romanov brothers – to the tsar's brother-in-law, Boris Godunov. This agreement was an advantageous one for Godunov. In all probability it was largely as a result of the support of N. R. Iur'ev that Boris obtained the high boyaral rank of equerry by the time of the new tsar's

4 S. F. Platonov, *Ocherki po istorii Smuty v Moskovskom gosudarstve XVI–XVII vv.*, 5th edn (Moscow: Pamiatniki istoricheskoi mysli, 1995), pp. 125–7.
5 B. N. Floria, *Russko-pol'skie otnosheniia i politicheskoe razvitie Vostochnoi Evropy* (Moscow: Nauka, 1978), pp. 133–40.

coronation (31 May 1584). From then onwards the Godunovs' ascent was meteoric. By the summer of 1584 there were already five members of the clan in
the duma. In Vienna in November 1584 Luka Novosil'tsev, the Russian ambassador to the Holy Roman Empire, referred to Boris Godunov as 'the ruler of
the land, a great and gracious lord'.[6] Thus in the summer of 1584 Godunov
emerged from the shadows and was officially recognised as the ruler of the
state and de facto regent for Tsar Fedor. For the next twenty years, until his
death, he was the central political figure in Muscovy.

The regency of Boris Godunov

Boris grasped the reins of government at an extremely difficult time. Ivan
Groznyi had left a burdensome legacy for his successors, and it was necessary
to lead the country out of a profound political and economic crisis.

One of the most immediate tasks was to overcome the division in the ruling
elite and restore the weakened authority of central government. Godunov was
unable to resolve this problem fully as long as the Shuiskiis and their supporters
stood in his way. Once he had established himself in power, he conducted a decisive struggle against them. The first to suffer were the Shuiskiis' supporters –
the Golovins, the Princes Kurakin, Golitsyn and Vorotynskii and the most
senior duma boyar, Prince I. F. Mstislavskii. Then, at the end of 1586, came
the turn of the Shuiskiis themselves. In May 1586 the Shuiskiis, with the backing of the head of the Russian Church, Metropolitan Dionisii, and of the
Moscow townspeople, organised a petition in the name of the estates of the
realm. It was addressed to Tsar Fedor, and begged him to divorce his childless
wife, Irina Godunova. But the tsar rejected this proposition. Godunov was
not at that time prepared to persecute the Shuiskiis directly. He waited for a
more favourable opportunity and collected compromising information against
them. The removal of the Shuiskiis occurred soon after the return (on 1 October 1586) of a Russian embassy from Poland, when Boris might have received
confirmation of his suspicions that the Shuiskiis were in contact with Polish
lords.[7] In the autumn of 1586 the Shuiskiis were banished from the capital, and
in the following year they suffered severe persecution. The most prominent
and active of them – Ivan Petrovich and Andrei Ivanovich – were killed in prison
by their jailers, probably not without Godunov's knowledge.[8] Metropolitan
Dionisii and Bishop Varlaam of Krutitsa were removed from their posts. The

6 Platonov, *Ocherki po istorii Smuty*, p. 134.
7 Floria, *Russko-pol'skie otnosheniia i politicheskoe razvitie Vostochnoi Evropy*, p. 140.
8 R. G. Skrynnikov, *Rossiia nakanune 'Smutnogo vremeni'* (Moscow: Mysl', 1981), pp. 58–9.

'trading peasants' who had supported the Shuiskiis were disgraced and then executed.

The end of the 1580s was a major watershed in the political struggle which ended in the complete victory of Boris Godunov. Its main result was the defeat of the elite of the high-born 'princelings' and the removal of the low-born *oprichnina* guard from power.

Like Ivan the Terrible, Boris Godunov directed all his efforts towards strengthening the autocratic power of the tsar, subordinating all the various estates of the realm, and the princely-boyar elite in particular. But Godunov pursued this aim by different means. Contrary to widespread opinion, although he himself was a former *oprichnik* and the son-in-law of the notorious *oprichnina* leader Maliuta Skuratov, Boris was not opposed in principle to the princely elite as a whole. An examination of the composition of the boyar duma leads to a conclusion which is unexpected from the traditional point of view – throughout the entire period of Boris Godunov's rule, both as regent for Tsar Fedor and in his own reign, the highest-ranking princely-boyar elite clearly predominated in the duma.

The essence of Godunov's policy in relation to the boyars becomes clearer if we study the reform of the sovereign's court which was carried out under his rule in the second half of the 1580s. As a wise and hard-headed politician, he realised that neither the continuation of the *oprichnina* policy nor the establishment of a regime of 'boyar rule' could resolve Russia's political crisis. The regent looked back at the constructive reforms of the court in the middle of the sixteenth century, and especially at the ideas behind the Thousander Reform of 1550, which was intended to consolidate the upper strata of the service class around the throne. Boris Godunov followed this model when he reorganised and reviewed the personnel of the sovereign's court. There is a great similarity between the decrees of 1550 and 1587 concerning the allocation of service estates close to the capital to members of the sovereign's court.[9] In the course of the reform of the court in the second half of the 1580s its membership was thoroughly reviewed. The government's aim was to bring the hierarchical structure of the court into line with the social origins of its members, and to remove low-born individuals. The surviving list of members of the sovereign's court from 1588/9 indicates that representatives of the most eminent princely-boyar families clearly predominated in the highest court ranks – the boyar

9 *Tysiachnaia kniga 1550 g. i Dvorovaia tetrad' 50-kh godov XVI v.*, ed. A. A. Zimin (Moscow and Leningrad: AN SSSR, 1950), pp. 53–4; *Zakonodatel'nye akty Russkogo gosudarstva vtoroi poloviny XVI–pervoi poloviny XVII veka: Teksty* (Leningrad: Nauka, 1986), p. 63.

duma and the Moscow nobility.[10] The court retained its aristocratic composition throughout the years of Godunov's rule, both as regent and as tsar. At the same time, at the end of the sixteenth century and at the beginning of the seventeenth century there was a marked numerical increase in the provincial nobility and a growth in its political activity. The provincial nobility was, however, largely excluded from participation in governance. The highest posts in the state apparatus were concentrated in the hands of the predominantly aristocratic elites of the sovereign's court, and also of the secretarial heads of the chancellery bureaucracy. At the end of the sixteenth century the role of the boyars in the governance of the central and local administrative apparatus increased; the boyars and the Moscow nobles played a more noticeable part than before in the work of the chancelleries, and the power of the provincial governors was strengthened. In the years of Godunov's regency we can clearly observe the consolidation of the 'boyar' elite, both at court and in the chancellery secretariat, into a special privileged ruling group of servitors.

This consolidation did not, however, lead to any weakening of the power of the autocrat. By the end of the sixteenth century the princely-boyar elite had lost most of their hereditary lands and their previous links with the provincial nobility, and they did not constitute any kind of stratum of great magnates who were all-powerful in the localities. The Russian aristocracy was totally dependent on state service, and it was riven by precedence disputes; it was incapable of acting as a united force in defence of its corporate interests.[11] Many of even the most eminent princes sought the friendship of the powerful regent Boris Godunov, who largely controlled service appointments and land allocations, and they provided him with their support. Godunov did not need to resort to disgrace and execution on a large scale in order to retain the obedience of the elite. But he managed to avoid resorting to the methods of the *oprichnina* mainly because he was able to take advantage of the results of the *oprichnina* itself and the achievements of the centralising policies of previous Muscovite rulers.

One of the most important events of Godunov's regency was the establishment of the Russian patriarchate in 1589. This helped to strengthen the authority of the Russian sovereign and of the Russian Church both within the country and beyond its borders. The introduction of the patriarchate led to a further rapprochement of Church and state. It is revealing that the main

---

10 *Boiarskie spiski poslednei chetverti XVI–nachala XVII v. i rospis' russkogo voiska 1604 g.*, comp. S. P. Mordovina and A. L. Stanislavskii, pt. 1 (Moscow: TsGADA, 1979), pp. 104–76.

11 A. P. Pavlov, *Gosudarev dvor i politicheskaia bor'ba pri Borise Godunove (1584–1605 gg.)* (St Petersburg: Nauka, 1992), pp. 202–3.

role in the negotiations with Patriarch Jeremiah of Constantinople, when he came to Russia to discuss the establishment of the patriarchate, was played by representatives of the secular power – the regent, Boris Godunov, and the conciliar ambassadorial secretary, A. Ia. Shchelkalov.[12] At the same time, at the end of the sixteenth century the clergy came to play an increasingly active role in defending the interests of the state. For example, the leaders of the Church hierarchy played a prominent role in the election of Godunov as tsar and the legitimisation of his autocratic power, and in the denunciation of the First False Dmitrii as an impostor. Boris Godunov's supporter Metropolitan Iov became patriarch, and other Church leaders were promoted. They largely owed the strengthening of their position to the regent.

By implementing this policy of consolidating the upper tiers of the service class and of the clergy under the aegis of the autocracy, Boris Godunov managed to resolve the country's internal political crisis, to restore the authority of the Russian monarchy and to establish himself firmly in power.

With the aim of strengthening state power, Godunov's government carried out a restructuring of central and local institutions of government. At the end of the sixteenth century and the beginning of the seventeenth, further measures were introduced to improve and extend the chancellery system of administration, and the number of secretaries was expanded.[13] The control of the centre over the districts was again perceptibly increased. An important indicator of this was the development and consolidation of the power of the provincial governors (*voevody*). A new feature in this period was the appearance of governors not only in the peripheral border towns, but also in the northern and central regions of the country.[14] At the same time, we find a decline in the role of the *guba* and *zemskii* ('land') institutions of local self-government by the social estates.

In the realm of foreign policy, Boris Godunov's government aimed to overcome the onerous consequences of the Livonian war and to restore the international prestige of the Muscovite state. After the death of Ivan the Terrible, Russian diplomats conducted tense negotiations with the Poles, as a result of which they managed to prevent a potentially damaging military confrontation with Poland and to conclude a prolonged fifteen-year truce, which was extended for a further twenty years in 1601. Taking advantage of a favourable

12 A. Ia. Shpakov, *Gosudarstvo i tserkov' v ikh vzaimnykh otnosheniiakh v Moskovskom gosudarstve* (Odessa: Tipografiia Aktsionernogo Iuzhno-russkogo obshchestva pechatnogo dela, 1912), pp. 245–341; R. G. Skrynnikov, *Gosudarstvo i tserkov' na Rusi XIV–XVI vv.* (Novosibirsk: Nauka, 1991), pp. 351–61.

13 A. P. Pavlov, 'Prikazy i prikaznaia biurokratiia (1584–1605 gg.)', *IZ* 116 (1988): 187–227.

14 Pavlov, *Gosudarev dvor*, pp. 239–49.

international situation and of internal difficulties in Sweden, in the winter of 1589/90 Russia began military action against the Swedes, with the aim of regaining her former towns on the Baltic coast. In 1595 in the village of Tiavzino a peace treaty was signed with the Swedes, in which Sweden returned to Russia Ivangorod, Iam, Kopor'e, Oreshek and Korela. This was a major victory for Russia, although it should not be overstated – the problem of an outlet to the Baltic Sea was not fundamentally resolved, and the sea-route known as the 'Narva sailing' remained in Swedish hands.[15] Russia's trade with the countries of Western Europe was conducted, as before, mainly through the north of the country. As a result of Godunov's efforts, relations with England were revived. The Russian government extended its patronage to the English merchants and gave them tariff privileges, but it refused to grant them monopoly rights to trade through the White Sea and opened its ports to the merchants of other countries.

If in the west Moscow had managed to stabilise the situation, then in the east and south its policy was more active and aggressive. One of Russia's main foreign-policy successes under Boris Godunov was the final consolidation of its control over Siberia. After the death of Ermak Siberia had again come under the power of the local khans. At the beginning of 1586 government forces headed by the commander V. B. Sukin were sent beyond the Urals. The Russian generals did not engage solely in military actions and organised the construction of a whole network of fortified towns in Siberia. In 1588 the Siberian khan Seid-Akhmat was taken prisoner, and ten years later the Russian generals routed the horde of Khan Kuchum. At the end of the sixteenth century the vast and wealthy territory of Siberia became an integral part of the Russian state (see Map 11.1).

Russia's position on the Volga was considerably strengthened. In the 1580s and 1590s a number of new towns were built – Ufa, Samara, Tsaritsyn, Saratov and others. The consolidation of Russian influence on the Volga led the khans of the Great Nogai Horde to recognise the power of the Muscovite sovereigns. An entire system of fortified towns (Voronezh, Livny, Elets, Kursk, Belgorod, Kromy, Oskol, Valuiki and Tsarev Borisov) was also built on the 'Crimean frontier'. The borders of the state were extended much further south. The international situation was favourable for Russia's southward expansion. The Crimean Horde had been drawn into numerous wars on the side of Turkey against Persia, the Habsburgs and the *Rzeczpospolita*, and it did not have

15 B. N. Floria, *Russko-pol'skie otnosheniia i baltiiskii vopros v kontse XVI–nachale XVII v.* (Moscow: Nauka, 1973), pp. 61–2.

Map 11.1. Russia in 1598

sufficient forces to undertake any major campaign against Rus'. Only on one occasion in the combined period of Godunov's regency and reign did the Crimeans manage to penetrate far into the Russian interior. In the summer of 1591 Khan Kazy-Girey came as far as Moscow with a large army. But having encountered a substantial Russian force blocking his advance, he decided not to risk the main body of his troops in battle, and was obliged to retreat.

The period of Boris Godunov's regency marked an important stage in the development of cultural contacts with the countries of Western Europe. Godunov was keen to recruit foreign specialists into Russian service. Seventeenth-century Russian writers even accused him of excessive fondness for foreigners. Boris himself had not had the opportunity to receive a systematic 'book-learning' education in his youth, but he gave his son Fedor a good education. Endowed with a lively and practical mind, Boris Godunov was no stranger to European enlightenment and he cherished plans to introduce European-style schools into Russia. In order to train up an educated elite, he sent groups of young people – the sons of noblemen and officials – to be educated abroad.

Overcoming the economic collapse and the acute social crisis was a task of primary importance and complexity. The central problem of internal policy at the end of the sixteenth and the beginning of the seventeenth centuries was to satisfy the economic interests of the noble servicemen (at that time the cavalry, comprising the service-tenure nobility, constituted the fighting core of the Russian army). In the first year of the reign of Tsar Fedor Ivanovich (on 20 July 1584) the government got the Church council to approve a resolution which confirmed a previous decision of 1580 forbidding land bequests to monasteries, and introduced an important new point abolishing the tax privileges (*tarkhany*) of large-scale ecclesiastical and secular landowners.[16] Encountering opposition from the Church authorities, however, Boris Godunov's government chose not to go for the complete abolition of the *tarkhany* and restricted itself to the adoption of Ivan Groznyi's practice of the 1580s of collecting extraordinary taxes from 'tax-exempt' lands. The act of 1584 legalised this practice. The council's resolution forbidding land bequests to monasteries was also put into practice in an inconsistent way. In the sources we find numerous cases of the violation of this law.[17] The measures of the 1580s and 1590s did not halt the growth of monastery landownership and did not fundamentally eliminate the tax privileges of the large landowners. They did not really guarantee either the uniformity of taxation or the creation of a supplementary fund of land for allocation as service estates. Moreover, the government continued to make extensive land grants to monasteries and to prominent boyars. Not wanting to quarrel with the influential clergy, Godunov's government tried to minimise its concessions to the nobility at the expense of the monasteries.

16 *Zakonodatel'nye akty*, p.62
17 S. B. Veselovskii, *Feodal'noe zemlevladenie v severo-vostochnoi Rusi* (Moscow and Leningrad: AN SSSR, 1947), p. 107.

The most important measure designed to satisfy the interests of the nobility was the issuing and implementation of laws about the enserfment of the
peasants. Boris Godunov's government at first continued the practice of the
so-called 'forbidden years', which had been introduced in Ivan Groznyi's reign
at the beginning of the 1580s ('forbidden years' were years in which peasants
were deprived of their traditional right to leave their landlords on St George's
Day). In the 1580s and 1590s a district land census was undertaken. However,
the land census of the end of the sixteenth century did not have such a comprehensive character as is usually assumed. The absence of complete up-to-date
surveys of many regions delayed the process of peasant enserfment. The practice of 'forbidden years' was not in itself sufficiently effective to retain the
peasant population in place. It contained a number of contradictions. On the
one hand, the landowner had the right to search for his peasants throughout
the entire period of operation of the 'forbidden years', and the duration of
the search period was not stipulated; on the other, the regime of 'forbidden
years' was regarded as a temporary measure – 'until the sovereign's decree'.
In addition, the 'forbidden years' were not introduced simultaneously across
the whole territory of the country, and this introduced further confusion
into judicial transactions. After 1592 the term, 'forbidden years', disappears
from the sources. V. I. Koretskii expressed the opinion that in 1592/3 a single all-Russian law forbidding peasant movement was introduced.[18] But other
scholars have expressed serious doubts as to whether such a major law of enserfment existed.[19] Great interest has been aroused by documents discovered by
Koretskii which contain information about the introduction at the beginning
of the 1590s of a five-year limit on the presentation of petitions about abducted
peasants. By establishing a definite five-year limit for the return of peasants the
government was trying to introduce some kind of order into the extremely
confused relationships among landowners in the issue of peasant ownership.
The new practice annulled the old system of 'forbidden years' and negated
the significance of the district land-survey, which remained incomplete in the
1580s and early 1590s, although it had arisen out of the recognition of the fact of
the prohibition of peasant transfers. The policies of the early 1590s described
above were developed further in a decree of 24 November 1597, which is the
earliest surviving law on peasant enserfment. According to this decree, in the

18 V. I. Koretskii, *Zakreposhchenie krest'ian i klassovaia bor'ba v Rossii vo vtoroi polovine XVI v.*
(Moscow: Nauka, 1970), pp. 123ff.
19 V. M. Paneiakh, 'Zakreposhchenie krest'ian v XVI v.: novye materialy, kontseptsii, perspektivy izucheniia (po povodu knigi V. I. Koretskogo)', *Istoriia SSSR*, 1972, no. 1: 157–65;
R. G. Skrynnikov, 'Zapovednye i urochnye gody tsaria Fedora', *Istoriia SSSR*, 1973, no. 1:
99–129.

course of a five-year period fugitive and abducted peasants were subject to search and return to their former owners, but after the expiry of these five 'fixed' years they were bound to their new owners. The introduction of the norm of a five-year search period for peasants was advantageous primarily for the large-scale and privileged landowners, who had greater opportunities to lure peasants and to conceal them on their estates.

Alongside these measures relating to the enserfment of the peasants, legislation was enacted at the end of the sixteenth century concerning slaves. The most important law on slavery was the code (*Ulozhenie*) of 1 February 1597 which required the compulsory registration of the names of slaves in special bondage books. According to the code of 1597 debt-slaves (*kabal'nye liudi*) were deprived of the right to obtain their freedom by paying off their debt, and were obliged to remain in a situation of dependency until the death of their master. The law prescribed that deeds of servitude (*sluzhilye kabaly*) should be taken from 'free people' who served their master for more than six months, thereby turning them into bond-slaves. Thus slave-owners acquired the possibility of enslaving a significant number of 'voluntary servants', and thereby compensating significantly for the labour shortage.

Boris Godunov's government was thus greatly concerned to satisfy the economic needs of the nobility. But at the same time, in trying to secure the support of the influential boyars and clergy, Godunov clearly did not intend to cause serious damage to their interests in order to please the rank-and-file nobility, and this explains the notorious inconsistency of his 'pro-noble' policy.

In the towns Godunov's government conducted a policy of so-called 'trading-quarter construction', which satisfied the economic interests of the townspeople, since the 'tax-paying (*tiaglye*) traders' (those townspeople who paid state taxes) included artisans and tradesmen who belonged to monasteries and to servicemen. But at the same time, 'trading-quarter construction' was implemented by coercive methods and it led to a greater binding of the townsmen to the trading quarters.[20]

The government's economic policy, together with the securing of peace on its borders, soon bore fruit, and in the 1590s the economy revived significantly. At the end of the 1580s and the beginning of the 1590s the tax burden was also reduced to some extent.[21] Contemporaries are unanimous that the reign of Fedor Ivanovich was a period of stability and prosperity. Boris Godunov deserves much of the credit for this. 'Boris is incomparable', the Russian envoys

---

20 P. P. Smirnov, *Posadskie liudi i ikh klassovaia bor'ba do serediny XVII veka*, 2 vols. (Moscow and Leningrad: AN SSSR, 1947–8), vol. 1 (1947), pp. 160–90.
21 Kolycheva, *Agrarnyi stroi*, p. 168.

to Persia said, referring not only to the regent's remarkable intelligence, but also to his unique role in government. At the end of the 1580s Godunov acquired the right to deal independently with foreign powers. He buttressed his exceptional position with a number of high-sounding titles. In addition to the rank of equerry which he had obtained in 1584 he also called himself 'vicegerent and warden' of the khanates of Kazan' and Astrakhan' and 'court [privy] governor', and he adopted the title of 'servant'. Russian envoys to foreign courts explained this last title as follows: 'That title is higher than all the boyars and is granted by the sovereign for special services.'[22]

Slowly but surely, Godunov rose to the summit of power, which he reached by carefully calculated moves. He did not resort to disgrace and bloodshed on any significant scale. In the entire period of his rule, both as regent and as tsar, not a single boyar was executed in public. But Boris was by no means a meek and kindly person. He was both cunning and ruthless in his dealings with his most dangerous opponents. His reprisals against his enemies were clandestine and pre-emptive. The chancellor P. I. Golovin was secretly murdered en route to exile, evidently not without Godunov's knowledge.[23] Boris also disposed covertly of the Princes Ivan Petrovich and Andrei Ivanovich Shuiskii. He played a skilful political game, planning his moves well in advance and eliminating not only immediate but also potential rivals. For example, with the help of a trusted associate – the Englishman Jerome Horsey – Godunov persuaded the widow of the Livonian 'king' Magnus, Mariia Vladimirovna (the daughter of Vladimir Staritskii and Evdokiia Nagaia), to come back to Russia. But when she returned, Mariia and her young daughter ended up in a convent.

In May 1591 Tsarevich Dmitrii, the youngest son of Ivan the Terrible, died in mysterious circumstances at Uglich. The inhabitants of Uglich, incited by the tsarevich's kinsmen, the Nagois, staged a disturbance and killed the secretary Mikhail Bitiagovskii (who was the representative of the Moscow administration in Uglich), together with his son and some other men whom they held responsible for the tsarevich's death. Soon afterwards a commission of inquiry, headed by Prince V. I. Shuiskii, came to the town from Moscow. It reached the conclusion that the tsarevich had stabbed himself with his knife in the course of an epileptic fit. But the version that Dmitrii had been killed on the orders of Boris Godunov enjoyed wide currency among the people. In the reign of

---

22 G. N. Anpilogov, *Novye dokumenty o Rossii kontsa XVI–nachala XVII veka* (Moscow: Izdatel'stvo Moskovskogo universiteta, 1967), pp. 77–8.
23 Dzherom Gorsei, *Zapiski o Rossii: XVI–nachalo XVII v.* (Moscow: MGU, 1990), p. 101; cf. Lloyd E. Berry and Robert O. Crummey (eds.), *Rude and Barbarous Kingdom: Russia in the Accounts of Sixteenth-Century English Voyagers* (Madison, Milwaukee and London: University of Wisconsin Press, 1968), p. 322.

Tsar Vasilii Shuiskii this version received the official sanction of the Church when Dmitrii of Uglich was canonised as a saint. For a long time the view that Boris Godunov was responsible for the tsarevich's death was unchallenged in the historical literature. The situation changed after the publication of studies by S. F. Platonov and V. K. Klein.[24] Platonov traced the literary history of the legend about Tsarevich Dmitrii's 'murder' and noted that contemporaries who wrote about it during the Time of Troubles refer in very circumspect terms to Boris's role in the killing of Dmitrii, and that dramatic details of the murder appear only in later seventeenth-century accounts. Klein carried out extensive and fruitful work examining and reconstructing the report of the Uglich investigation of 1591. He demonstrated that what has come down to us is the original version, in the form in which it was presented by Vasilii Shuiskii's commission of inquiry to a session of the Sacred Council on 2 June 1591 (only the first part of the report is missing). The version contained in the investigation report has received the support of I. A. Golubtsov, I. I. Polosin, R. G. Skrynnikov and other historians.[25] But doubts concerning the validity of the way the investigation report was compiled have still not been dispelled. A. A. Zimin made a number of serious criticisms of this source.[26] The investigation report is undoubtedly tendentious. But its critics have not managed to advance arguments which would decisively refute the conclusions of the commission of inquiry. The sources are such that the indictment against Boris remains unproven; but neither does the case for the defence give him a complete alibi.

Would the death of the tsarevich have been in Godunov's interests? It is difficult to give an unambiguous answer to this question. On the one hand, the existence of a centre of opposition at Uglich, with Tsarevich Dmitrii as its figurehead, could not have failed to arouse the regent's anxiety. But, on the other hand, Boris could have achieved 'supreme power' without killing the tsarevich. Dmitrii had been born from an uncanonical seventh marriage, which enabled Godunov to question his right to the throne. At the same time Boris took pains to enhance the status of his sister, Tsaritsa Irina, as a possible heir to the throne. In a situation where Boris Godunov was the de facto sole ruler of the state, Tsar Fedor's 'lawful wife in the eyes of God' could quite justifiably challenge the right to the throne of Tsar Ivan's son, born 'of an

24 S. F. Platonov, *Boris Godunov* (Petrograd: Ogni, 1921), pp. 96–7; V. K. Klein, *Uglichskoe sledstvennoe delo o smerti tsarevicha Dimitriia* (Moscow: Imperatorskii Arkheologicheskii institut imeni Imperatora Nikolaia II, 1913).
25 I. A. Golubtsov, ' "Izmena" Nagikh ', *Uchenye zapiski instituta istorii RANION*, 4 (1929): 70 etc.; Skrynnikov, *Rossiia nakanune 'Smutnogo vremeni'*, pp. 74–85.
26 A. A. Zimin, *V kanun groznykh potriasenii* (Moscow: Mysl', 1986), pp. 153–82.

Table 11.1. *The end of the Riurikid dynasty*

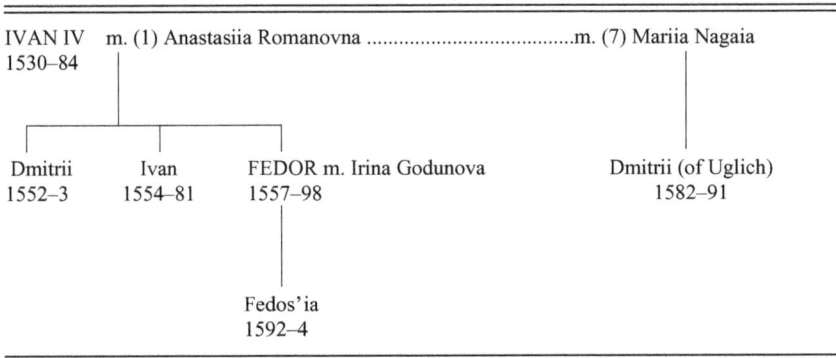

IVAN IV 1530–84	m. (1) Anastasiia Romanovna	....m. (7) Mariia Nagaia

Dmitrii 1552–3	Ivan 1554–81	FEDOR m. Irina Godunova 1557–98	Dmitrii (of Uglich) 1582–91

Fedos'ia
1592–4

unlawful seventh wife'. It is quite possible that Godunov was hatching some kind of plan to dispose of the tsarevich and his kin.[27] But if he had intended to murder Dmitrii, May 1591 was not the most appropriate time to make the attempt. In April and May there was worrying news that the Crimean khan was preparing to invade, and things were not entirely calm in the capital in the spring of 1591. In general we do not have sufficiently strong arguments either to reject or to confirm the findings of the report of the Uglich investigation, and the question of the circumstances of Tsarevich Dmitrii's death remains an open one.

In May 1592 the court ceremoniously celebrated the birth of a daughter – Tsarevna Fedos'ia – to Tsar Fedor and Tsaritsa Irina. But the tsarevna died on 25 January 1594, before her second birthday (see Table 11.1). Her death clearly revealed that the ruling dynasty was facing a crisis, and it made the question of the succession urgent. The Godunovs blatantly promoted their claims to the throne. From the middle of the 1590s Boris began to involve his son Fedor in affairs of state. But Boris Godunov was not the only candidate for the throne. His former allies, the Romanovs, stood in his way. Their advantage lay in the fact that Tsar Fedor himself had Romanov blood (from Tsar Ivan's marriage to Anastasiia Romanovna). As Fedor's brother-in-law, Boris Godunov could not boast a blood relationship with the tsar. Gradually the Romanovs advanced themselves at court and acquired influential positions in the duma. Around them there gathered a close-knit circle of their kinsmen and supporters. From

27 Dzhil's Fletcher, *O gosudarstve Russkom* (St Petersburg: A. S. Suvorin, 1906), p. 21; cf. Berry and Crummey, *Rude and Barbarous Kingdom*, p. 128.

then onwards there was strife and rivalry between the Godunovs and the Romanovs. This was not a conflict over different directions in policy, but a struggle for power and for the throne between two mighty boyar clans. Like the Godunovs, the Romanovs exercised an exceptional degree of influence at court, but the latter's role was primarily that of honoured courtiers, and it could not be compared with the Godunovs' role in governance. Boris Godunov possessed real power. He was able to count on the support of a significant number of members of the boyar duma and the sovereign's court, the secretarial apparatus, the influential clergy and the merchant elite, and this is what guaranteed his success in the contest for the throne.

On 7 January 1598 Tsar Fedor died. After the expiry of the forty-day period of mourning, an Assembly of the Land was convened in Moscow, and on 21 February it elected Boris Godunov as tsar. The traditional view among historians was that the assembly was stacked with Godunov's supporters and that his election was a 'farce' played out to a pre-written script.[28] V. O. Kliuchevskii, however, studied the signatures on the main document produced by the assembly – the confirmatory charter – and concluded that the elective assembly of 1598 was entirely conventional in its composition. If there had been some kind of campaigning in favour of Boris, Kliuchevskii commented, it had not altered the composition of the Assembly of the Land.[29] In the more recent historiography there are various views about the authenticity and completeness of the signatures on the surviving copies of the confirmatory charter, and about the actual membership of the assembly.[30] We have no reason to doubt, however, that an electoral Assembly of the Land did in fact convene in February 1598 and legitimately elect Boris Godunov as tsar.[31] What was considered illegitimate by contemporaries of the Time of Troubles was not the 'juridical' but the 'moral' aspect of Boris Godunov's election – a 'saint-killer' (the person responsible for the death of Tsarevich Dmitrii) could not be a 'true' tsar. As far as the assembly of 1598 itself is concerned, the writers of the Time of Troubles did

28 See e.g. V. N. Latkin, *Zemskie sobory drevnei Rusi* (St Petersburg: Izdatel'stvo L. F. Panteleeva, 1885), pp. 94–5.
29 V. O. Kliuchevskii, 'Sostav predstavitel'stva na zemskikh soborakh drevnei Rusi', in his *Sochineniia*, 8 vols. (Moscow: Izdatel'stvo sotsial'no-ekonomicheskoi literatury, 1956–9), vol. VIII (1959), pp. 59–61.
30 S. P. Mordovina, 'Kharakter dvorianskogo predstavitel'stva na zemskom sobore 1598 g.', *VI*, 1971, no. 2: 55–63; L.V. Cherepnin, *Zemskie sobory Russkogo gosudarstva v XVI–XVII vv.* (Moscow: Nauka, 1978), p. 146; R. G. Skrynnikov, 'Zemskii sobor 1598 goda i izbranie Borisa Godunova na tron', *Istoriia SSSR*, 1977, no. 3: 141–57; Zimin, *V kanun groznykh potriasenii*, pp. 212–33.
31 A. P. Pavlov, 'Sobornaia utverzhdennaia gramota ob izbranii Borisa Godunova na prestol', *Vspomogatel'nye istoricheskie distsipliny* 10 (1978): 206–25.

not doubt its 'correctness' and they even contrasted the legitimate election of Godunov by 'all the towns' to the 'sudden' accession of Vasilii Shuiskii without any consultation of the 'land'.

Tsar Boris

On 1 September Boris was solemnly crowned as tsar. His coronation was accompanied by a number of lavish ceremonies and formalities. The new tsar made all kinds of efforts to acquire popularity among his ordinary subjects, and solemnly promised to care even for the poorest beggars. On his accession to the throne he granted numerous privileges and favours to various groups of the population. There is even evidence that Tsar Boris intended to regulate the obligations of the seigniorial peasants.[32] But although he courted the estates of the realm, Boris had no desire to become dependent on them. His aim of becoming the 'great and gracious lord' of his people was an expression of the credo of an autocratic monarch rather than a ruler dependent on his 'electorate'. While granting various favours to his subjects, Boris at the same time demanded their loyalty, and encouraged them to denounce 'villains' and 'traitors'.[33]

But the power of the Russian autocrats in the sixteenth and seventeenth centuries was not absolute. As he consolidated his position on the throne, Boris was obliged to conduct a cautious and flexible policy in relation to the boyar elite. If the new-made tsar had acted too decisively and rashly, all the results of his previous policy of consolidating the magnates around the throne would have been negated and he would have encountered serious opposition. As an experienced politician, Boris Godunov understood the danger of a radical break with tradition in his relations with the ruling boyar group, and of exerting direct pressure on the aristocracy. To mark the occasion of his coronation in September 1598 Boris Godunov made generous allocations of duma ranks to the top tier of the aristocracy. Towards the end of Godunov's reign the size of the boyar duma was reduced, and the relative weight of the princely aristocracy within it was increased. Of the twenty duma boyars in 1605, twelve belonged to the premier princely clans or were eminent foreigners.[34] It is generally thought that Boris unduly promoted his relatives and supporters and ruled the state with their help. But the actual picture was more complex. In the first year of

---

32 *Donesenie o poezdke v Moskvu M. Shilia 1598 g.* (Moscow, 1875), p.17.
33 *Russkaia Istoricheskaia Biblioteka*, vol. II (St Petersburg: Arkheograficheskaia Kommissiia, 1875), cols. 63–6.
34 Pavlov, *Gosudarev dvor*, p. 66.

Boris's reign four new members of the Godunov clan entered the duma, but they were all awarded not the highest duma rank of boyar, but the rank of *okol'nichii*. In Boris's reign only two new Godunovs became boyars (via the rank of *okol'nichii*), but at the same time two older Godunov boyars left the stage. None of the Godunovs who was newly promoted into the duma possessed any great qualities of statesmanship. As in the years of his regency, Boris when he was tsar tried to find support in various boyar groupings, including the premier princely aristocracy. And in this he succeeded. The tsar made clever use of precedence conflicts among the princely-boyar aristocracy in order to further his own interests. S. F. Platonov's view that Tsar Boris was politically isolated in the boyar milieu cannot be accepted as correct. The circle of boyars who came to court and enjoyed the tsar's favour was fairly wide, but – and in this respect Platonov is right – they did not comprise a single cohesive party, and there were few among them who possessed any political talent.[35] This gave rise to the internal weakness in the Godunovs' government which manifested itself after Boris's death.

Weakened by the repressions of the 1580s and lacking support from the boyars, the Church and the townspeople, the Shuiskiis and other eminent 'princelings' were unable to act openly against Godunov. The main threat to Godunov was posed by the boyar clan of the Romanovs, who had not reconciled themselves to their defeat in the electoral struggle. In November 1600 the Romanovs were subjected to harsh forms of disgrace. The eldest of the brothers – Fedor Nikitich Romanov – was tonsured as a monk and exiled under the name of Filaret to the northerly Antoniev-Siiskii monastery. His brothers and followers were dispersed to various towns and places of imprisonment, and many of them died in exile. R. G. Skrynnikov has persuasively suggested that the persecution of the Romanovs was linked with Boris's illness.[36] Concerned about the fate of his heir, he decided to strike a blow against them, taking advantage of a denunciation which a slave of the Romanovs made against his masters. The Romanovs' case was the most important political trial in Boris's reign, but it directly affected only a few boyars and noblemen. At the beginning of the 1600s Godunov's old opponent B. Ia. Bel'skii was also subjected to repression and disgrace, as was the secretary V. Ia. Shchelkalov.

There is a widespread view in the historical literature that the idea of setting up a pretender was developed by the boyar opposition with the aim of overthrowing the Godunovs. But we do not have any sources which provide direct

35 Platonov, *Ocherki po istorii Smuty*, pp. 161, 175.
36 R. G. Skrynnikov, *Boris Godunov*, 3rd edn (Moscow, 1983), pp. 137–8.

and reliable evidence of this. S. F. Platonov's speculation that the Romanovs were party to the pretender intrigue is somewhat dubious.[37] The fact that the pretender (Grigorii Otrep'ev) lived in the court of the Romanovs and their followers the Cherkasskiis does not in itself provide a basis for such a view. If we accept this proposition, it is difficult to explain why the custody regime imposed on the disgraced Romanovs should have been relaxed at the end of Godunov's reign, or why many of their supporters were allowed to return from exile. We know that in 1604–5 Tsar Boris appointed the boyars and eminent princes F. I. Mstislavskii, V. I. and D. I. Shuiskii and V. V. Golitsyn to head his regiments against the False Dmitrii, and these commanders inflicted a crushing defeat on the pretender at Dobrynichi. The army openly defected from the Godunovs only after Boris's death. And even then by no means all the boyars and commanders betrayed them, and some of the commanders (the princes M. P. Katyrev-Rostovskii, A. A. Teliatevskii and others) returned to Moscow with the loyal regiments. The decisive role in the transfer of the troops to the side of the False Dmitrii was played by the servicemen of the southern towns. Russian and foreign sources unanimously testify that the initiative for surrendering the towns of the Seversk 'frontier district' came not from their governors but from the lower classes of the population. In contrast to the opinion of V. O. Kliuchevskii and S. F. Platonov, who considered that the Time of Troubles began 'from above' (in the boyar milieu), the unrest on the eve of the Troubles occurred not at the top of the social ladder but at the lower levels of the social pyramid.

In spite of the recovery in the economy, the consequences of the economic and social crisis had not been entirely overcome by the end of the sixteenth century: most of the arable land and farmsteads in the majority of districts remained unworked, and the rural population had not returned to its pre-crisis level.[38] Before it had recovered from the post-*oprichnina* crisis, Russia's economic system suffered a new blow at the beginning of the seventeenth century – a terrible famine which lasted for three years and which affected the entire territory of the country. The famine of 1601–3 cost hundreds of thousands of human lives. Godunov's government enacted energetic measures to alleviate the consequences of this natural disaster. It took steps to combat speculation in grain: royal decrees prescribed fixed prices for grain and the punishment of speculators; large sums of money were distributed in the capital and in other towns to help the starving; and public works were organised. But these measures failed to bring about a significant improvement in the situation.

37 Platonov, *Ocherki po istorii Smuty*, p. 160.
38 Kolycheva, *Agrarnyi stroi*, p. 201; *Agrarnaia istoriia*, p. 296.

Against the background of famine and economic crisis, social conflicts were exacerbated, and a widespread flight of peasants and slaves took place. In order to alleviate the build-up of social tensions, in the autumn of 1601 the government issued a decree which solemnly announced that the peasants' traditional right of departure on St George's Day was being restored.[39] But this arrangement was re-established only on the lands of the provincial nobility and the lowest-ranking courtiers. Peasants on court and state lands did not gain the right to move, nor did peasants who belonged to large-scale ecclesiastical and secular landowners. As before, Boris Godunov did not want to infringe the interests of the influential ruling elite. By making concessions to the enserfed peasantry and to the large-scale landowners, the government damaged the interests of the mass of the gentry. In order to prevent the complete ruination of the petty servicemen, the decree permitted nobles to transfer no more than one or two peasants 'among themselves'. The terms of the 1601 decree were reaffirmed in a new decree of 24 November 1602. The practical implementation of the decrees of 1601 and 1602 not only failed to reduce the social discord, but significantly increased it. The peasants interpreted the laws in their own interests, as granting them complete freedom from serfdom, while the noble landowners defied the provisions of the legislation by obstructing peasant movement in every way. The law was not reissued in 1603, and at the end of his reign Boris Godunov returned to his old policy of enserfment.[40] This increased the discontent of the peasantry. At the same time, the popularity of Godunov's government among the nobility was significantly undermined.

In a situation characterised by famine and economic crisis, disturbances began among the lower social classes. In the autumn of 1603 a large-scale bloody battle took place on the outskirts of Moscow between government forces and a substantial detachment of insurgents led by a certain Khlopko. The government repeatedly sent troops of noble servicemen to suppress disturbances in various towns. In Soviet historiography all of these events were considered to be symptoms of class struggle on the part of the peasantry, and to mark the beginning of a Peasant War.[41] This interpretation was convincingly challenged by R. G. Skrynnikov, who demonstrated that the popular

39 *Zakonodatel'nye akty*, p. 70.
40 V. I. Koretskii, *Formirovanie krepostnogo prava i pervaia krest'ianskaia voina v Rossii* (Moscow: Nauka, 1975), p. 365.
41 I. I. Smirnov, *Vosstanie Bolotnikova* (Moscow: Gosudarstvennoe Izdatel'stvo politicheskoi literatury, 1951), pp. 77–83; Koretskii, *Formirovanie krepostnogo prava*, pp. 192–235.

unrest of 1601–3 had been on a smaller scale than previously thought, and that the disturbances themselves did not amount to much more than ordinary banditry.[42]

The situation on the southern frontiers was particularly tense. At the beginning of the seventeenth century great hordes of fugitive peasants and slaves had fled southwards from the central and northern regions of the country and had joined the ranks of the 'free' cossacks. Their numbers were swelled not only by agricultural workers, but also by the boyars' military slaves and even by impoverished nobles. The cossack hosts were fairly numerous; battle-hardened in conflicts with the Tatars and Turks, they represented a military force to be reckoned with. What is more, the cossacks were unhappy about the construction of the new towns on the southern frontier, which drove a wedge into their lands. The sharp increase in grain prices during the famine had encouraged the cossacks to make more frequent raids into Crimean and Turkish territory, which threatened to bring about international complications for Russia. The cossacks also attacked Russian settlements and merchant caravans. All of these developments forced Boris Godunov's government to introduce a number of repressive measures against them, and, in particular, to prohibit the sale of gunpowder and food supplies to the Don.[43] But Godunov's repressions were not able to pacify the 'free cossackry' and merely accelerated the outbreak of its dissatisfaction.

In an attempt to safeguard the food supply of its newly annexed southern lands, the government introduced a widespread initiative to compel the local population to perform labour services (*barshchina*) on state lands (the so-called *gosudareva desiatinnaia pashnia*, or sovereign's tithe ploughlands). But because the peasant population in this region was small, the tilling of the land was mainly carried out by the servicemen 'by contract' (*pribornye*) and by the petty gentry, who had to combine the burden of military service with heavy agricultural labour. All of this could not fail to provoke protest from the servicemen of the southern towns. The small-scale southern landholders were greatly enraged by the expansion of large-scale boyar landownership on to the fertile lands of the south. The proximity of these big landowners, who were influential at court, harmed the economy of the petty servicemen, and this provoked their hatred towards the 'boyar' government in Moscow.

42 R. G. Skrynnikov, *Rossiia v nachale XVII v. 'Smuta'* (Moscow: Mysl', 1988), pp. 58–73.
43 A. L. Stanislavskii, *Grazhdanskaia voina v Rossii XVII v. Kazachestvo na perelome istorii* (Moscow: Mysl', 1990), pp. 17–20.

At the end of Boris Godunov's reign the southern frontier was a powder keg, ready to explode from any spark. The spark was provided by the incursion into Russian territory of a pretender claiming to be Tsarevich Dmitrii, who had supposedly escaped from the assassins sent by Godunov to kill him. Godunov's government claimed that he was Grigorii Otrep'ev, a fugitive unfrocked monk and former nobleman from Galich, and this remains the most convincing explanation of the identity of the man who posed as Ivan the Terrible's son, Dmitrii.[44]

At the time when it crossed the Russian frontier in the autumn of 1604, the False Dmitrii's army consisted only of 2,000 Polish noblemen and a few thousand Zaporozhian and Don cossacks. However, as it advanced further towards the Russian heartland, it recruited impressive new forces. The pretender's success was guaranteed primarily by the extensive support he received from the free cossacks and from the population of the southern frontiers who rebelled against Godunov. The townspeople of the south voluntarily recognised the 'true' Tsar Dmitrii and handed their governors over to him.

On 13 April 1605, at the height of the war against the pretender, Tsar Boris Godunov died suddenly. His son, Tsarevich Fedor, was named as his successor. But in the inexperienced hands of Boris's young heir the wheel of government began to spin out of control. In the final days of his reign Boris Godunov placed great hopes on his talented and ambitious general P. F. Basmanov. But when drawing up the new service register after Boris's death, the influential courtier and boyar Semen Nikitich Godunov appointed his own son-in-law Prince A. A. Teliatevskii 'above' Basmanov, which provoked an angry protest from the latter and led him to betray the Godunovs. But it was not boyar treason, but the stance adopted by the numerous detachments of servicemen from the southern towns (Riazan', Tula, etc.) that had the decisive influence on the course of events. After the defection of the army at Kromy to the pretender in May 1605, the fate of the Godunov dynasty was sealed. On 1 June 1605 supporters of the False Dmitrii instigated an uprising in Moscow which led to the overthrow of the Godunovs. A few days later, on 10 June, the young Tsar Fedor Borisovich and Boris's widow, Tsaritsa Mariia Grigor'evna, were killed by a group of men, headed by Prince V. V. Golitsyn, who had been specially sent by the False Dmitrii; Boris's daughter, Tsarevna Kseniia, was confined in a convent. Thus the dynasty that Boris Godunov had founded

44 R. G. Skrynnikov, *Samozvantsy v Rossii v nachale XVII veka: Grigorii Otrep'ev* (Novosibirsk: Nauka, 1987).

came to a tragic end. The devastating and bloody Time of Troubles had begun.

* * *

The tempestuous events of the Time of Troubles have to a considerable extent diverted the attention of historians from the significance of Boris Godunov's reformist activity. It is important to bear in mind that thanks to Godunov's efforts Russia enjoyed a twenty-year period of peace at the end of the sixteenth century and the beginning of the seventeenth. In place of exhausting wars and the bacchanalia of the *oprichnina* there was a period of political stability and a partial economic boom. The country's international prestige was strengthened. The period also witnessed such significant events for the future of the country as the establishment of the patriarchate and the definitive annexation of Siberia. Boris Godunov's policy for consolidating the ruling elite of the service class around the throne had far-reaching consequences. It was under Boris Godunov that the future direction of Russia's political development was largely determined, and the specific features of the state structure were established, in which strong autocratic power coexisted and co-operated with the boyar service aristocracy. Yielding to the demands of the broad mass of the service class, Godunov continued the policy of enserfment of the peasantry. But his policy possessed little consistency. The dissatisfaction of the numerous lower classes and also of the petty servicemen, whose interests had had to be sacrificed by Boris Godunov's government, led in the end to civil war and a Time of Troubles in Russia.

Translated by Maureen Perrie

12

The peasantry

RICHARD HELLIE

Peasant farming and material culture

One way to focus sharply on this topic is to compare the situation of the Russian peasant with that of the American farmer. The American farmer was a completely free man who lived in his own house with his family on an isolated farmstead/homestead that belonged to him. The stove in his log cabin vented outside through a chimney and he owned everything in his cabin. Because land was free, he could farm as much land as his physical capacity permitted. His land was comparatively rich and harvests were relatively abundant. He was able to accumulate and store wealth in many forms: grain, cattle, material possessions and cash. Typically he had no landlord and was solely responsible for his own taxes. In contrast, by the end of this period the Russian peasant was for most practical purposes enserfed (see Chapters 16 and 23) and he lived in a village and farmed land that was not his own. Although he may have believed that the land was his, in fact the state believed that the land belonged to it and could be confiscated for a monastery, other Church institution or a private landholder/owner who was in full-time state military or civil service employ.[1] His hut was roughly the same size as the American's log cabin, and it was built in roughly the same way: notched logs stacked on top of one another and chinked with moss and/or clay. The Russian peasant's land, although abundant, was of poor quality and the crop yields were extraordinarily low. As will be described further below, the interior of the Russian peasant's hut was considerably different from that of his American counterpart. Russian livestock, work implements, and crops were significantly different from the

---

[1] A. D. Gorskii, *Bor'ba krest'ian za zemliu na Rusi v XV–nachale XVI veka* (Moscow: MGU, 1974); L. I. Ivina, *Krupnaia votchina Severo-Vostochnoi Rusi kontsa XIV–pervoi poloviny XVI v.* (Leningrad: Nauka, 1979), p. 105. Suits between peasants and others over land are the main sources of information for these claims. See also Iu. G. Alekseev, *Agrarnaia i sotsial'naia istoriia Severo-Vostochnoi Rusi XV–XVII vv. Pereiaslavskii uezd* (Moscow and Leningrad: Nauka, 1966), p. 167 *et passim*.

American. For climatological and socio-political reasons, the Russian peasant found it difficult to accumulate wealth, and the collective system of taxation made it dangerous for one peasant to appear more prosperous than another. Lastly, the dress of the Russian peasant was different from that of the American farmer.

During the time period covered by this chapter the area inhabited by the Russian peasant expanded enormously, as detailed in Chapters 9, 10 and 11. In brief, in 1462 the Russian peasant inhabited the area between Pskov in the west and Nizhnii Novgorod in the east, the Oka River in the south and the Volga River in the north. By 1613 Russian habitation had moved well across the Volga and the Urals into Siberia in the east, down the Volga to Astrakhan' in the south and also some distance south of the Oka, and finally north of the Volga all the way to the White Sea. Most of this area provided crucial constraints on peasant agriculture and material life that could not be overcome. The frost-free period began around the middle of May and ended towards the end of September, which provided a short frost-free growing season of 120 days or so.[2] Snow covered the ground nearly half the year.[3] Not only was the growing season short, but the soil throughout most of the area was thin (7.5 cm thick), acidic podzol with very little (1 to 4 per cent) humus.[4]

These factors dictated that rye was by far the predominant cereal crop, whose yields were extraordinarily low: the Russians were lucky to harvest three seeds for each one sown. The yields for oats were even lower. In the West those were pre-Carolingian yields, which had risen to 6 : 1 by the end of the fifteenth century. The low Russian yields were to a major extent the result of downward selection: instead of saving and sowing the biggest seeds, the Russians used those to pay rent and taxes, and planted either the smallest seeds or the middle-sized ones, and ate the others. As wheat was rarely grown in this period, winter rye was the most important grain crop because it escaped the limitations of the short growing season.[5] (It was planted in the autumn, germinated before snowfall, and was harvested in the summer.) Oats were grown for human consumption, but primarily for the horses. Nearly as much land was devoted to cultivating oats as rye.[6] Barley and wheat were also occasionally grown. The

2 I. A. Gol'tsberg (ed.), *Agroklimaticheskii atlas mira* (Moscow and Leningrad: Gidrome-teoizdat, 1972), pp. 41, 48, 55.
3 Ibid., p. 105.
4 V. K. Mesiats (ed.), *Sel'sko-khoziaistvennyi entsiklopedicheskii slovar'* (Moscow: Sovetskaia entsiklopediia, 1989), p. 403; A. I. Tulupnikov (ed.), *Atlas sel'skogo khoziaistva SSSR* (Moscow: GUGK, 1960), p. 8.
5 V. D. Kobylianskii (ed.), *Rozh'* (Leningrad: Agropromizdat, 1989), p. 259 *et passim*.
6 A. L. Shapiro et al., *Agrarnaia istoriia severo-zapada Rossii. Vtoraia polovina XV–nachalo XVI v.* (Leningrad: Nauka, 1971), pp. 39, 44, 249.

major industrial crop was flax, sown in some western areas, and occasionally hemp and hops.

The Russians typically kept gardens, in which they raised cabbage (their major source of Vitamin C), cucumbers, carrots, beets, radishes, turnips, peas, garlic and onions. The harsh climate was not favourable for raising fruit trees, but some Russians grew apples (as many as ten varieties). Much rarer were cherries, plums and raspberries. Mushrooms, berries and nuts were brought in from forests.[7]

As mentioned, Russian peasants lived in villages, not on isolated home-steads. The villages ranged in size from a few households to several dozen.[8] Water for drinking, washing and cooking was either carried from a river or brook or drawn from a village well. Each hut was enclosed in a yard (*dvor*) by a wooden fence.[9] There was no general system of 'village planning' applicable everywhere. In some places the common ancestor's yard was in the centre of the village with those of his descendants surrounding it, in other places yards were next to each other facing a common 'street' in a land with neither streets nor roads that a modern person would recognise.[10] The peasant's garden might be in his yard, or outside of it.[11] The purpose of the fence was to keep the peasant's livestock from straying at night. In the daytime, the village's livestock were put out to pasture in a common meadow where one or more of the peasants tended the flock. A typical peasant had one horse for draught purposes, a cow or two for milk, cheese and meat, a calf (the horses and cattle were very small), occasionally sheep or goats, maybe pigs and some chickens

7 N. A. Gorskaia et al. (eds.), *Krest'ianstvo v periody rannego i razvitogo feodalizma (Istoriia krest'ianstva SSSR s drevneishikh vremen do velikoi oktiabr'skoi sotsialisticheskoi revoliutsii*, vol. II) (Moscow: Nauka 1990), pp. 160, 214, 230, 240; A. D. Gorskii, *Ocherki ekonomicheskogo polozheniia krest'ian Severo-Vostochnoi Rusi XIV–XV vv.* (Moscow: MGU, 1960), pp. 61–4.
8 A. Ia. Degtiarev observed that around 1500 in the Novgorod region 90 per cent of the villages contained only one to five households: *Russkaia derevnia v XV–XVII vekakh* (Leningrad: LGU, 1980), pp. 23, 37. S. B. Veselovskii calculated that Volga–Oka settlements were villages of only one to three households apiece: *Selo i derevnia v Severo- Vostochnoi Rusi XIV–XVI vv.* (Moscow and Leningrad: OGIZ, 1936), p. 26. These low numbers have been attributed to the Mongol conquest: the way to avoid being raided was to live in villages so small that they were not worth raiding. In general, these figures rose by 1550. In 1588, Nizhnii Novgorod villages contained almost nine households apiece (Degtiarev, *Russkaia derevnia*, p. 116). Low figures in the two-to-five households per village range can also be found in E. I. Kolycheva, *Agrarnyi stroi Rossii XVI veka* (Moscow: Nauka, 1987), p. 105. See also N. N. Voronin, *K istorii sel'skogo poseleniia feodal'noi Rusi. Pogost, svoboda, selo, derevnia* (Leningrad: OGIZ, 1935).
9 A. A. Shennikov, *Dvor krest'ian Neudachki Petrova i Shestachki Andreeva. Kak byli ustroeny usad'by russkikh krest'ian v XVI veke* (St Petersburg: Russkoe geograficheskoe obshchestvo, 1993).
10 Gorskaia, *Krest'ianstvo v periody*, p. 158.
11 Gorskii, *Ocherki*, pp. 60–2.

which could be expected to lay less than one egg a week.[12] All of this provided a poor, monotonous diet occasionally enlivened by alcohol. Mead (near-beer) was a popular drink and at the end of the sixteenth century many peasants had from two to five hundred beehives, whence came the mead.[13] The origins of vodka are unclear. It was first mentioned in 1174, and probably came into its own as a popular commodity in the relatively prosperous second half of the fifteenth century.[14] Meat was rarely served in peasant households, but fish was much more common.[15]

Also in the yard was a privy, an outbuilding or barn for the livestock in cool weather, a grain drier, a threshing floor and a shed for storing agricultural implements, hay and grain reserves (including seed for the next growing season). The famous Russian bathhouse typically was not in a peasant yard (for fear of fire, for one reason), but close to a source of water, such as a pond, lake or river.

When it became bitterly cold, much (maybe all) of the livestock and food stores such as cabbage moved inside. The major structure inside every peasant hut was the stove, a structure built in one of the corners that occupied much of the room in the hut. It was built of rock and mortar and had three chambers for maximum extraction of heat. Had the Russian stove had a chimney, 80 per cent of the heat would have gone out of the chimney, so there was only a smoke hole in the back of the stove which vented the smoke into the room. The heating season was about six months of the year,[16] so that for six months of the year the peasants breathed a toxic mixture of carbon monoxide and over two hundred wood-smoke particles that clogged their throats and lungs. The product was the infamous Russian smoky hut, one of the major features of Russian civilisation from the time the Slavs moved east into Ukraine in the sixth century, and then into the Volga–Oka mesopotamia in the eleventh–thirteenth centuries, down until the 1930s. The smoke was so dense that it left

12 A. L. Shapiro et al., *Agrarnaia istoriia severo-zapada Rossii XVI veka. Sever. Pskov. Obshchie itogi razvitiia severo-zapada* (Leningrad: Nauka, 1978), p. 25. I must thank the authors for sending me a copy of this book. See also their *Agrarnaia istoriia* (1971), pp. 33, 35, 168. Gorskaia makes the salient point that, although peasants raised chickens, chicken meat, eggs and geese were typically reserved as rent payments for landlords (Gorskaia, *Krest'ianstvo v periody*, p. 160). For poignant examples, see Kolycheva, where peasants' eggs and cheese are a major part of the rent obligation (*Agrarnyi stroi* , pp. 85, 88).
13 G. M. Karagodin, *Kniga o vodke i vinodelii* (Cheliabinsk: Ural LTD, 2000), p. 31; Gorskii, *Ocherki*, pp. 75–81.
14 Ibid., p. 45. Gorskaia opted for the sixteenth century (Gorskaia, *Krest'ianstvo v periody*, p. 160).
15 Ibid., p. 160; Gorskii, *Ocherki*, pp. 82–6.
16 Richard Hellie, *The Economy and Material Culture of Russia* (Chicago: University of Chicago Press, 1999), p. 117 (Fig. 4. Monthly sales of firewood).

a line around the wall about shoulder-high, where the bottom of the smoke cloud hung. The air was so toxic that it disinfected the hut to the extent that not even cockroaches could survive. The Russians had a saying: 'If you want to be warm, you have to suffer the smoke.'[17]

Besides the stove, there were benches around the walls of the hut on which the peasants sat during the day and slept at night, on mattresses stuffed with hay or straw. Early tables were made of clay and immovable; movable tables made of wood date from the seventeenth century.[18] Some huts had primitive stools, but usually there were no chairs or other furniture except a trunk (made of wood, leather, and/or woven bark, reeds and other materials) in which the peasants kept their extra and out-of-season clothing. There was a shelf protruding from one of the walls on which cooking utensils were kept. Clay pots were used for storage or mixing. There were typically three or four small windows (to prevent the heat from escaping) covered sometimes with mica (in huts of the more well-to-do), more often with parchment made of bull's bladder. (The huts of the poor had no windows at all.) The windows did not open, and during the coldest weather were covered over with mats to conserve heat. Also to conserve heat, the front door was low and narrow. Internal lighting, such as there was (and the peasant hut was always dark inside), was provided by splinters set alight or a burning wick in oil. Smoky, tallow candles were used first in the seventeenth century, and more expensive wax candles were used where there were many bees.[19] Most huts had dirt floors, probably to facilitate cleaning up the excrement slurry during the coldest months when all the livestock as well as the peasant family lived full time in the hut.[20] Feeding the livestock over the winter was a real chore. Supplies often ran out during the late winter or early spring, and the cries of the starving animals could be heard throughout the village. Some animals were so weak by spring that they could not stand and had to be carried out to pasture.

Thanks to the prominence of rye in the Russian diet, the nutritional state of the 'average Russian' was almost certainly better than one might have imagined. That does not mean, however, that Russian nutrition was ideal. One

17 Richard Hellie, 'The Russian Smoky Hut and its Possible Health Consequences', *RH* 28 (2001): 171–84.
18 D. A. Baranov et al., *Russkaia izba. Illiustrirovannaia entsiklopediia. Vnutrennee prostranstvo izby. Mebel' i ubranstvo izby. Domashniaia i khoziaistvennaia utvar'* (St Petersburg: Iskusstvo, 1999), pp. 114–15.
19 Ibid., pp. 306–7.
20 Ibid. This volume is concerned primarily with the period 1700–1825, but much of it is relevant to the earlier period because traditional life changed very slowly. As this book notes, many huts did not have wooden floors even in the 1920s–1930s (p. 55).

problem was an inadequate quantity of meat, caused primarily by the inability of Russians to winter sufficient numbers of livestock. Although the elite (clergy and laymen) had access to adequate quantities of fish, it is not clear that the 'average Russian' did. The quantity and variety of fruits and vegetables available to the 'average Russian' was also inadequate. Thus Russians well may have been deficient in Vitamin A, niacin, cobalamin, Vitamin D, calcium and selenium. These deficiencies almost certainly made the Russians' bodies function at less than optimum levels, made them susceptible to disease and diminished their energy levels. These factors, combined with the impact of the smoky hut, contributed mightily in making the Russian the short-lived, lethargic, marginally productive, minimally creative (original) person he was.

Peasant clothing was simple, nearly all of it home-made out of homespun wool or flax/linen, sometimes hemp. On his head the peasant wore a cap (*kolpak*) or felt hat (*shapka*). The woman wore a kerchief. The man's coat was a caftan (*kaftan*), a woman's coat or long jacket was called a *telogreia*, a man's tunic was called an *odnoriadka* and his heavy-duty winter coat a sheepskin *shuba*. A man's basic garment was a shirt (*rubakha, rubashka*) and trousers (*porty, shtany*); a woman's a dress (*rubakha, sarafan* or *letnik*). Both sexes wore stockings (*chulki*), linden bast shoes (*lapti*) in summer, ordinary leather shoes in less clement weather (*bashmaki* (men's) or *koty* (women's)), and felt boots (*valenki*) in snowy weather. Gloves (*perchatki*) and mittens (*rukavitsy*) completed the peasant outfit. Unmarried girls/women wore one braid, married women two. Women also wore earrings, beads and necklaces. Wealthy peasants, relatively few and far between, wore furs and expensive jewellery and their houses contained metal utensils and other items purchased in the market, even books.[21] Exhibiting wealth was risky, for the collective system of taxation provided an incentive for poorer peasants to shift their burden to the more prosperous.

The peasant's agricultural inventory was his personal property and its nature was determined by agricultural conditions and his crops. Because the podzolic soil was so thin, there was no need for a plough that would turn over a deep furrow. The famous two-pronged scratch plough (the *sokha*) was adequate to stir up the soil for planting. It was smoothed out by a harrow, a lattice of four or five boards crossing each other at right angles out of which protruded a peg at each intersection to break up the clods of dirt. Both the scratch plough and the harrow were light implements which could easily be pulled by one

21 A. I. Kopanev, *Krest'ianstvo Russkogo Severa v XVI v.* (Leningrad: Nauka, 1978), pp. 211–13.

horse, unless it was so mal-nourished that it could barely walk. The horse was also employed to pull a sleigh in the winter, and a four-wheeled cart in the summer. The peasant also possessed a scythe and sickle for harvesting grain and cutting hay. It is likely that they were almost the only metal items in the peasant's possession, along with a flail, a chain at the end of a stick used to beat the grains out of the stalk. Instead of stacking the harvested grain in shocks to dry, the peasant probably put it into a drier, where moving air removed the moisture while keeping post-harvest rain, hail and snow off the cut grain. An axe completed the peasant's inventory; this he used for cutting down trees in the forest, fashioning logs for his house, cutting firewood for the stove and preparing other wooden objects. Peasants living near navigable bodies of water typically owned a variety of vessels: canoes, barges, flat-bottomed boats and so on. Water mills are known to have appeared at least as early as the thirteenth century.[22]

The nature of peasant farming changed significantly more than once during the period covered by the timespan of this chapter. At the end of the civil war between Grand Prince Vasilii II and first his uncles and then his cousins in 1453, population density throughout Muscovy was very low, which led to the initiation of the enserfment process. For our purposes right here, however, this meant that free land was everywhere, a fact observed by foreign travellers. This allowed slash-burn/assartage agriculture to be practised everywhere. While it involved quite a bit more strenuous labour than other forms of agriculture, it was also more productive. A peasant moved into a plot of forest and cut it down. He could use the felled trees for housing and fuel. The main point was, however, that he set fire to what remained after the logs had been removed. The resulting ashes produced a comparatively rich topsoil into which the peasant could broadcast his seeds and harvest a fairly high yield. The high soil productivity lasted about three years, and then the peasant moved on to another newly burned-over plot. It took about forty years for the soil to recover its fertility in this extensive slash/burn agriculture, but while there was free, forested land available, it was the most profitable form of farming available to the Russian peasant.

With the rise of Moscow and the consolidation of the Muscovite state in the decades after 1453, internal wars ceased and the population began to expand. The years 1480–1570 are generally termed in the literature as a period of economic upsurge.[23] Extensive agriculture of the slash-burn type became

22 Gorskaia, *Krest'ianstvo v periody*, p. 214.
23 A. L. Shapiro, *Russkoe krest'ianstvo pered zakreposhcheniem (XIV–XVI vv.)* (Leningrad: LGU, 1987), p. 3.

less possible. That this was happening was readily observable by 1500.[24] By 1550 the movement from slash-burn agriculture[25] to the more intensive three-field system had progressed to the point that it was expressed in the Law Code (*Sudebnik*) (see Chapter 16).[26] In the traditional three-field system, one field was planted in the spring and harvested in the autumn; a second field was planted in the autumn and harvested the following summer; and the third field was fallow. What is here called 'the second field' produced the highest yields because there was no frantic rush to plant in the spring or to harvest in the autumn because of the short growing season, but rather leisurely sowing could be done in the summer/autumn and rather leisurely harvesting in the mid-summer. In the winter field the sown seeds typically sprouted before snowfall; in the absence of snow cover, the sprouts might freeze and die, but this happened infrequently enough so that it was not a major risk factor. Article 88 of the *Sudebnik* of 1550 permitted peasants who had moved on St George's Day (26 November), after the winter crop had been sown, to return in the following summer to harvest that crop.[27] Historians assume that the use of the three-field system was fairly widespread by 1550. Along with this went a system of strip-farming in which fields were divided into long, narrow strips. The strips were allotted to the peasants in a fashion which spread the risks of farming (insect infestations, blights, hail storms) equally among the peasants of a given locale.[28]

This, however, was not fated to last. Paranoid Tsar Ivan the Terrible launched his psychotic *oprichnina* in 1565 in which he split the Muscovite tsardom into two parts: the *oprichnina*, which he ran himself, and the *zemshchina* (the rest of the state), run by the seven boyars who typically were in charge of the state when the sovereign was absent. Ivan's henchmen, the notorious *oprichniki*, among their many barbarous acts 'collected as much rent from their peasants in one year as usually was collected in ten years'.[29] By 1572 this put the peasants

24 G. E. Kochin, *Sel'skoe khoziaistvo na Rusi v period obrazovaniia Russkogo tsentralizovannogo gosudarstva, konets XIII–nachalo XVI v.* (Moscow and Leningrad: Nauka, 1965), pp. 129–75, 431–4; Gorskii, *Ocherki*, pp. 32–7, 55.

25 V. P. Petrov, *Podsechnoe zemledelie* (Kiev: Naukova Dumka, 1968).

26 Gorskaia, *Krest'ianstvo v periody*, pp. 230–2.

27 Richard Hellie (ed. and trans.), *Muscovite Society* (Chicago: University of Chicago Syllabus Division, 1967, 1970), pp. 105–6.

28 Donald N. McCloskey, 'Scattering in Open Fields', *Journal of European Economic History* 9 (1980): 209–14, among many other essays on the same theme.

29 Richard Hellie, 'What Happened? How Did he Get away with it? Ivan Groznyi's Paranoia and the Problem of Institutional Restraints', *RH* 14 (1987): 199–224; Gorskaia, *Krest'ianstvo v periody*, pp. 263–5; Kolycheva gives examples from the 1570s where 80 to 100 per cent of the land was fallow, in the years 1584–86 in Moscow province 86.6 per cent (*Agrarnyi stroi*, pp. 182–3, 191).

to flight, much as had done Vasilii II's civil war, as the agriculturalists moved north of the Volga,[30] east of Kazan' into the Urals and Siberia, south along the Volga and to some extent into the lands south of the Oka. The result was that ensuing censuses found up to 85 per cent of the heartland of Muscovy, especially around Moscow and Novgorod, abandoned and the right of peasants to move on St George's Day was gradually abolished.[31] Also often abandoned was the three-field system of agriculture, which was not to become widely used again until the second half of the eighteenth century.[32]

Slavery and the beginnings of enserfment

The vast majority of the population in the years 1462–1613 were peasants who were becoming serfs, perhaps 85 per cent. Of the rest, perhaps 5 to 15 per cent were slaves.[33] Relatively insignificant numbers of townsmen, clergy and government servicemen comprised the rest of the population. This balance reflected the very low productivity of agriculture, which required nearly every-one to farm. Even townsmen, most clergymen and even many servicemen raised much of their own food.

As discussed in Chapter 16, slavery was one of the oldest social institutions in Russia and one of the major concerns of law. As a proportion of all law, the quantity dedicated solely to slavery can only be described as staggering. Slavery in fact was so important in Russia that a special central governmental office was created around 1550 to deal solely with slavery matters. Russia

---

30 Relatively precise numbers for the beginning and middle of the sixteenth century, the 1580s, and 1620s can be found in Shapiro et al., *Agrarnaia istoriia* (1978), pp. 9, 136.

31 Richard Hellie, *Enserfment and Military Change in Muscovy* (Chicago: University of Chicago Press, 1971), pp. 96–7 *et passim*; Degtiarev, *Russkaia derevnia*, pp. 77, 88.

32 Gorskaia notes that in the 1570s and 1580s much of the land lay fallow, but contends that this was only because of a shortage of labour and did not represent an abandonment of the three-field system per se (Gorskaia, *Krest'ianstvo v periody*, p. 235).

33 Richard Hellie, *Slavery in Russia 1450–1725* (Chicago: University of Chicago Press, 1982). Alekseev presents evidence that at least on one occasion slaves comprised from 17 to 30 per cent of the population (*Agrarnaia istoriia*, p. 122), but that was exceptional. The major problem with counting slaves in this period is that the only reliable numbers are of the slaves who engaged in agriculture, and they comprised about 2 per cent of rural households. While occasionally the sole 'farmer' a cavalryman had was a slave, the vast majority of slaves were not engaged in production, but were household slaves who were not counted in the 'census records' (land cadastres) of the time. As discussed more in Chapter 23, productive (= farming) slaves presented a real problem to the government. The general rule was that slaves owned nothing, could produce nothing, and therefore could not be taxed. That farming slaves produced nothing was blatantly false, of course, so the government gradually began to tax them. A 1678 census revealed that many serfs had nominally / legally been converted into slaves, so in 1679 the government solved the problem by converting all farming slaves into taxpaying serfs.

was the sole country in history to have one governmental department in the capital devoted solely to the issue of slavery. Major changes in the institution occurred during the period covered by this chapter. As has been discussed, society was in chaos after the reign of Ivan IV, and Boris Godunov, acting in the name of the mentally challenged Tsar Fedor Ivanovich, tried to stabilise the situation by history-making measures enacted in the 1590s involving both slaves and peasants. The one involving slaves radically changed the nature of the institution. By this time the major slavery institution was limited service contract slavery (*kabal'noe kholopstvo*). A Russian – typically a low-energy, low-initiative down-and-outer – approached another Russian and asked him to buy him. The transaction was phrased in terms of a loan: the 'borrower' took a sum (perhaps 1, 2 or 3 roubles) from the 'lender' and agreed to work for him for a year in lieu of paying interest on the loan.[34] In ancient Parthia, this was known as *antichresis*. If the borrower failed to repay the loan in a year, he became the full slave of the lender. Almost no such 'loans' were ever repaid, and both parties realised from the start that the transaction was in reality a self-sale into perpetual slavery. Over the course of the sixteenth century limited service contract slavery replaced full slavery as the major relief institution for those desiring to sell themselves into slavery. The difference was that *kabal'noe kholopstvo* offered hope for a year of manumission, whereas full slavery from the outset was for life and hereditary. The trouble for the government was that slavery usually took an individual off the tax rolls, which the government did not like. Therefore on 25 April 1597, the typically activist government, by fiat, changed the nature of *kabal'noe kholopstvo*. The sale / loan was no longer for a year, but for the life of the creditor. Upon the death of the creditor, the slave was freed – presumably to go back onto the tax rolls. What the government did not understand was that the dependency created by slavery made it impossible for the freedman to exist on his own, with the result that he soon sold himself back into slavery, often to the heirs of the deceased. The government was unable to 'solve' this problem until Peter the Great by fiat in 1724 converted all household slaves into household serfs (all males, from newborns to decrepit geriatrics, were called 'souls') who all had to pay taxes.

The farming peasantry were also in chaos as a result of Ivan's psychotic reign. Serfdom dates back to the 1450s, with the introduction of St George's Day (26 November) for indebted monastery peasants, who could only move on that date.[35] The *Sudebnik* of 1497 extended St George's Day to all peasants.

---

34 Hellie, *Muscovite Society*, pp. 240–2.
35 Ibid., ch. 7; Hellie, *Enserfment*, chs. 4–6; V. V. Mavrodin (ed.), *Materialy po istorii krest'ian v Rossii XI–XVII vv. Sbornik dokumentov* (Leningrad: LGU, 1958), pp. 39–110; A. E. Vorms

Then in the 1580s the government began to repeal the right of peasants to move on St George's Day who lived on the lands of selected landholders. In 1592 this prohibition was extended 'until further notice' to all peasants. The purpose was to stabilise the labour force of the provincial middle service-class cavalry, who could not render military service in the absence of peasant rent-payers. Thus with a flourish of the pen Boris Godunov's hypertrophic government changed the legal status of more than nine-tenths of the Russian population. Enserfment, especially as it descended into a slave-like condition, unquestionably would have been impossible without the fact that the Russians were accustomed to enslaving their own people.

Boris did not end his 1590s social legislative spree with the above. He added another provision to the enserfment decree, a statute of limitations on the recovery of fugitive serfs. There was no statute of limitations on the recovery of fugitive slaves, but Boris decided that hunters of fugitive serfs should be given five years to locate their chattels and file a suit for their recovery. Five years seems like a long time, but Russia is a big country, and was getting bigger all the time as mentioned above. Once a Russian serf had fled into any of the areas outside the Volga–Oka mesopotamia, finding him became almost impossible. Various elements of the Russian government wanted all of those areas inhabited by scarce Russians, and in fact encouraged migration into those areas. The struggle for scarce labour resources had yet another element: serfs could and did flee not only to the new territories, but also to lands of larger lay and monastic landlords. Such magnates (in the 1630s called 'contumacious people' – *sil'nye liudi*, literally, 'strong people') had estates in many places, and could move fugitives from one estate to another so that a pursuer could never find them. The five-year statute of limitations was a licence to the magnates and regional recruiters to recruit the peasant labour force of the Moscow heartland middle service-class cavalry. The sequel to this is discussed in Chapter 23.

In 1607 Tsar Vasilii IV Shuiskii promulgated an important edict on fugitive serfs and slaves.[36] The first important thing was that he linked the two categories of population. Secondly, he extended the statute of limitations to fifteen years for the hunting down and filing suits for fugitive serfs. The linking of serfs with slaves by Shuiskii was an important landmark in the abasement of the Russian peasantry. The St George's Day measures 'only' bound the peasants to the land so that they would be there as rent-paying fixtures for the next

et al. (eds.), *Pamiatniki istorii krest'ian XIV–XIX vv.* (Moscow: N. N. Klochkov, 1910), pp. 14–50. The literature on enserfment is vast. See the bibliography for additional titles.
36 Hellie, *Muscovite Society*, pp. 137–41.

tenants of the land, rather like immovable structures left by one holder of the land for the next one. This was 'legalised' by the state in two forms of state charters. One, issued to the landholder, called a *vvoznaia gramota*, informed him that the peasants of such-and-such a parcel were to pay him traditional rent. In the first half of the sixteenth century, it is likely that the landholder did not even collect the rent himself, but a third party did. The second charter, called an 'obedience charter' (*poslushnaia gramota*), was issued to the peasants, and informed them that so-and-so was now the holder of the land and that they should pay him the traditional rent. But Ivan IV during his mad *oprichnina* introduced a dramatic change into the 'obedience charter': instead of ordering the peasants to pay traditional rent, they were ordered to 'obey their landholder in everything'. This gave the landholders complete control over their peasants. This was responsible for much of the peasant chaos that led to the repeal of the right to move on St George's Day. But for the long run, the personal abasement of the peasant was equally important. The 1607 Shuiskii decree enhanced this abasement, which was adumbrated by the simultaneity of the 1592 and 1597 decrees changing the status of the slaves and the peasants.

The period 1462–1613 witnessed intervention by the 'Agapetus state' (see Chapter 16) in the lives of its subjects unparalleled in previous history. Much of the institution of slavery was radically changed, while the freedom of the peasantry was radically abased. At the end of his reign Peter the Great abolished slavery by converting slaves into serfs. Peter's heirs by the end of the eighteenth century converted the serfs into near-slaves, the property of their lords (owners). The 'Agapetus state' was so powerful because it claimed and exercised control over – almost without opposition – two of the three basic factors of the economy, all the land and labour.[37] This had little impact on peasant methods of farming or material culture, but it laid down the course for Russian history until 1991.

37 Richard Hellie, 'Thoughts on the Absence of Elite Resistance in Muscovy', *Kritika* 1 (2001): 5–20. The third factor, capital, was almost irrelevant in this period.

13

Towns and commerce

DENIS J. B. SHAW

'It remaineth that a larger discourse be made of Moscow, the principal city of that country. – Our men say that in bigness it is as great as the city of London with the suburbs thereof. There are many and great buildings in it, but for beauty and fairness nothing comparable to ours. There are many towns and villages also, but built out of order and with no handsomeness: their streets and ways are not paved with stone as ours are, the walls of their houses are of wood, the roofs for the most part are covered with shingle boards.'[1]

Richard Chancellor's somewhat disdainful description of the city of Moscow, which he first visited in 1553, fairly reflected European reactions to that and other Russian towns in the period before Peter the Great. Russian towns were different from, and much inferior to, the towns of Europe. This is a tradition which has endured down to our own day. Both pre-1917 Russian and modern Western scholars have contrasted the commercial dynamism and political liberties enjoyed by European towns in the medieval and early modern periods with the limited and restricted commercial development and politically repressed character of Russian towns at that time.[2] Few if any Russian towns developed the 'urban community' described for the medieval European city by Max Weber.[3] Such an emphasis, needless to say, ultimately stems from a

---

1 Richard Chancellor, 'The First Voyage to Russia', in Lloyd E. Berry and Robert O. Crummey (eds.), *Rude and Barbarous Kingdom: Russia in the Accounts of Sixteenth-Century English Voyagers* (Madison: University of Wisconsin Press, 1968), p. 23.
2 I. I. Ditiatin, *Ustroistvo i upravlenie gorodov Rossii* (St Petersburg: Tipografiia Merkul'eva, 1875); P. Miliukov, *Ocherki po istorii russkoi kul'tury. Chast' pervaia: naselenie, ekonomicheskii, gosudarstvennyi i soslovnyi stroi* (St Petersburg: Mir Bozhii, 1896); Samuel H. Baron, 'The Town in "Feudal" Russia', *SR* 28 (1969): 116–22; Samuel H. Baron, 'The Weber Thesis and the Failure of Capitalist Development in "Early Modern" Russia', *JGO* 18 (1970): 320–36; V. Murvar, 'Max Weber's Urban Typology and Russia', *Sociological Quarterly* 8 (1967): 481–94; Richard Pipes, *Russia under the Old Regime* (Harmondsworth: Penguin Books, 1977), pp. 191–211.
3 Max Weber, *The City*, trans. and ed. Don Martindale and Gertrud Neuwirth (New York: The Free Press, 1958); Jan de Vries, *European Urbanization, 1500–1800* (London: Methuen,

much broader issue: to what extent has Russia ever been, or could it hope to become, European?

Whilst specialists on Russia thus focused on the extent to which Russian towns exhibited fully urban characteristics, students of comparative urbanism increasingly challenged some of the assumptions lying behind such debates. Thus the meaning of concepts like Weber's 'urban community' or the distinctive 'urban civilisation' which supposedly characterised medieval and early modern European cities has been questioned with particular reference to their empirical applicability and the degree of generalisation involved.[4] Marxists have argued that, far from being islands of freedom in a sea of serfdom as many earlier scholars had asserted, towns were in fact important bolsters of the feudal nexus.[5] Furthermore, the assumption that European cities (and European modernity more generally) should be regarded as the standard against which cities (and modernities) elsewhere should be measured has been widely challenged.[6] Some scholars urge that what should be compared is not cities as separate units but the evolution of urban networks and hierarchies acting as integrators of entire societies and thus as measures of social development.[7]

This chapter will refrain from entering the debate about the 'essential' nature of urbanism and approach Russian towns less as individuals than as interconnected nodes within a network having complex interlinkages with society, economy and government.[8] The emphasis, in other words, will be less on towns as commercial foci and more on their multifunctional character. But their significance as commercial centres will also be highlighted before the chapter opens out into a broader discussion of commerce in this period.

1984), pp. 3–13; Don Martindale, 'Prefatory Remarks: The Theory of the City', in Weber, *The City*, pp. 9–62; Murvar, 'Max Weber's Urban Typology'.

4 Paul Wheatley, 'The Concept of Urbanism', in P. Ucko, R. Tringham and G. W. Dimbleby (eds.), *Man, Settlement and Urbanism* (London: Duckworth, 1972), pp. 601–37; Christopher R. Friedrichs, *The Early Modern City* (London: Longman, 1995), pp. 3–15.

5 J. Merrington, 'Town and Country in the Transition to Capitalism', in R. Hilton (ed.), *The Transition from Feudalism to Capitalism* (London: NLB, 1976), pp. 170–95; R. H. Hilton, 'Towns in English Feudal Society', in *Class Conflict and the Crisis of Feudalism: Collected Essays of R.H. Hilton* (London: Hambledon Press, 1984), pp. 175–86.

6 V. Liebermann, 'Transcending East–West Dichotomies: State and Culture Formation in Six Ostensibly Different Areas', in V. Lieberman (ed.), *Beyond Binary Histories: Reimagining Eurasia to c. 1830* (Ann Arbor: University of Michigan Press, 1999), pp. 19–102; G. Rozman, *Urban Networks in Russia, 1750–1800 and Pre-Modern Periodization* (Princeton: Princeton University Press, 1976).

7 Ibid.; de Vries, *European Urbanization*, pp. 3–13; G. William Skinner, 'Regional Urbanization in Nineteenth-Century China', in G. William Skinner (ed.), *The City in Late Imperial China* (Stanford, Calif.: Stanford University Press, 1977), pp. 211–49.

8 de Vries, *European Urbanization*, p. 9.

The urban network

The number and relative importance of Russian towns in this period is a matter of uncertainty, a reflection of the patchy and ambiguous nature of the sources. The Russian term for 'town' (*gorod*) meant little more than a fortified settlement. In the sixteenth century the official sources generally used the word to refer to a place having some administrative and military significance. There is no definitive list of towns in the sources, and scholars of Russian urbanism have been forced to scour such records as cadastres (*pistsovye knigi*), military rolls and accounts, decrees, chancellery documents, charters and patents to try to construct a definitive list.[9] It is on the basis of such sources that scholars such as Nevolin, Chechulin, Smirnov and more recently French and others have calculated the number of towns.[10] French argues that there were at least 130 towns in the Russian network at the beginning of the sixteenth century, and implies that Chechulin's total of 218 towns existing at some point in the century (not counting Siberian towns) may be slightly too low for the century's end. However, the absence of agreement on how many of these constituted 'real' towns (for example, how many had genuine commercial functions) leaves plenty of scope for dispute.

The unification of the Russian state led to the decline or disappearance of many fortress towns located along the boundaries between the different principalities. But these losses were more than compensated by the addition of new towns to the network as suggested by the totals given above. Some of the gains came from the acquisition of already existing towns in newly conquered territories along the western border and down the Volga (Kazan', 1552; Astrakhan', 1556). In the west, in addition to towns in the Russian principalities annexed by Muscovy (Novgorod, 1478; Tver', 1485; Pskov, 1510), significant territories were taken from Lithuania and Livonia including the towns of Viaz'ma (1494), Toropets, Chernigov and others (1503), Smolensk (1514) and Narva (1558–81). In 1492 Ivan III built the fortress of Ivangorod on the opposite bank of the River Narva to try to overawe the latter city and entice away its trade. Other forts were built further south along the border. In the north few new towns appeared in this period, but important foundations included Pustozersk, at

9 See e.g. A. A. Zimin, 'Sostav russkikh gorodov XVI v.', *IZ* 52 (1955): 336–47.
10 K. A. Nevolin, 'Obshchii spisok russkikh gorodov', in his *Polnoe sobranie sochinenii*, vol. vi (St Petersburg, 1859), pp. 27–96; N. D. Chechulin, *Goroda Moskovskogo gosudarstva v XVI veke* (St Petersburg: Tipografiia I. N. Skorokhodova, 1889), pp. 14–23; P. P. Smirnov, *Goroda Moskovskogo gosudarstva v pervoi polovine XVII veke*, vol. i, pt. 2 (Kiev: A. I. Grossman, 1919); R. A. French, 'The Early and Medieval Russian Town', in J. H. Bater and R. A. French (eds.), *Studies in Russian Historical Geography* (London: Academic Press, 1983), pp. 263–4.

the mouth of the Pechora (1499) and Archangel at that of the Northern Dvina (1583–4).

By far the most significant town founding in the period occurred as a consequence of the Russian occupation of the Volga valley. Upstream from Kazan' several new towns (Vasil'sursk, Sviiazhsk, probably Cheboksary) had been founded before the former's capture in 1552. The occupation of the valley down to Astrakhan' was secured by the establishment of fortress towns at Samara (1586), Tsaritsyn (1588) and Saratov (1590). Meanwhile further west, and following the devastating Tatar raid on Moscow in 1571, the government decided to try to overawe the principal Tatar tracks or invasion routes from the open steppe grasslands by building new military towns at Livny, Voronezh (both 1585), Elets (1592), Kursk, Belgorod (both 1596) and several other places.[11] East of the Volga, new territories were also now open to Russian occupation as a result of the fall of Kazan'. In 1586, in the same year that they built Samara, the Russians established Ufa, and also Tiumen' in western Siberia, followed by Tobol'sk a year later. Verkhotur'e was founded in the Urals in 1598, and Turiisk two years after. Several towns were constructed along the Ob, culminating in the founding of Tomsk nearby in 1604.[12]

The sixteenth century was thus a dynamic period for the founding of new towns, and especially the latter half. The same cannot be said of the commercial life of towns for which the second half of the century was to prove particularly difficult. Unfortunately the available statistics make tracing the expansion and contraction of towns over this period especially problematic and there are severe uncertainties about urban population levels and the character of the urban hierarchy. There can, however, be no doubt that the pinnacle of the urban hierarchy was Moscow. In the absence of cadastres and census books for the city, population estimates rely upon crude guesses by travellers like Herberstein, who related the tale that a recent official count had recorded 41,500 houses in the city.[13] This has been interpreted as referring more correctly to the number of adult males in the city. For the end of the century a total population of 80,000–100,000 has been suggested.[14] If this is accurate, it means that Moscow was one of the largest cities in Europe at the time (only nine

---

11 D. J. B. Shaw, 'Southern Frontiers of Muscovy, 1550–1700', in J. H. Bater and R. A. French (eds.), *Studies in Russian Historical Geography* (London: Academic Press, 1983), pp. 117–42.

12 V. I. Kochedatov, *Pervye russkie goroda Sibiri* (Moscow: Stroiizdat, 1978), pp. 20–1.

13 Sigismund von Herberstein, *Description of Moscow and Muscovy, 1557*, ed. B. Picard, (London: J. M. Dent, 1969), p. 20.

14 M. N. Tikhomirov, *Rossiia v XVI veke* (Moscow: AN SSSR, 1962), p. 66; *Istoriia Moskvy*, vol. 1, *Period feodalizma, XII – XVII vv.* (Moscow: AN SSSR, 1952), p. 179; *Ocherki istorii SSSR, period feodalizma, konets XVv. – nachalo XVIIv.* (Moscow: AN SSSR, 1955), p. 266. Herberstein's visits were made in 1517–18 and 1526–7.

West European cities had populations in excess of 80,000 in 1600: London, Paris, Milan, Venice, Naples, Rome, Palermo, Seville and Lisbon).[15] Moscow was, of course, the seat of the tsar and government with all the activities which these implied. It was also a major commercial and trading centre, a pivot of military and religious activity and much besides. In other words, it was the geographical focus of the realm.

By comparison with Moscow, other Russian cities paled in size and importance, though the evidence on population sizes is extremely patchy. Novgorod, for example, was no longer the leading commercial centre it had been before its annexation by Moscow in 1478 but nevertheless retained a significant role at least down to its sacking by Ivan IV's *oprichniki* in 1570. According to Chechulin's calculations, Novgorod had over 5,000 households in the late 1540s which, he believed, indicated a population of over 20,000.[16] Kazan' on the newly annexed south-eastern frontier had considerable commercial and military significance when it was described in a cadastre in the late 1560s. From this source Chechulin estimated a population of up to 15,000.[17] Other sizeable towns included Smolensk, Nizhnii Novgorod, Pskov, Kaluga, Kolomna, Vologda, Kostroma and Kholmogory. All appear to have contained at least 500 households at various points in the sixteenth century.[18] Iaroslavl', which was to become a major centre in the seventeenth century, may also have been in their number but the sources are uncertain.[19] Apart from the capital, therefore, Russia's larger towns included the centres of formerly and recently independent states or principalities (Kazan', Novgorod and Pskov), provincial centres (Nizhnii Novgorod, Kaluga, Kolomna, Vologda and Kostroma), and peripheral or border towns whose populations reflected the size of their commerce and/or of their garrisons (Novgorod, Smolensk, Kazan', Pskov and possibly Nizhnii Novgorod). Compared to Western Europe, Russian towns were relatively small at this time, with the important exception of Moscow. Russia lacked sizeable regional centres compared to Western Europe (though it was not unlike England and Scotland in this respect).[20] However, Gilbert Rozman argues that the settlement hierarchy reflected a society which was moving beyond a process of purely administrative integration to a stage where

15 de Vries, *European Urbanization*, pp. 270–8.
16 Chechulin, *Goroda*, p. 52.
17 Ibid., p. 206.
18 Tikhomirov, *Rossiia v XVI veke*; Henry L. Eaton, 'Decline and Recovery of the Russian Cities from 1500 to 1700', *CASS* 11 (1977): 220–52.
19 Tikhomirov, *Rossiia v XVI veke*, pp. 217–18. Astrakhan' was probably a significant centre also, but the sources are imprecise.
20 de Vries, *European Urbanization*, pp. 269–87.

commercial integration was becoming more significant. In his view, Russia had thus reached a stage of development at which countries like England and France had arrived 100–150 years previously.[21]

While cadastres, census books and similar materials can give us an idea of a town's relative size at a particular point, very rarely are they frequent or comparable enough to allow growth or decline to be accurately gauged in this period. Other kinds of evidence can, however, give some notion of general trends. The issue of to what extent Russian towns flourished or declined has been debated, with Soviet historians inclined to take an optimistic view as towns participated in the move towards the 'all-Russian market' postulated by Lenin for the seventeenth century. Clearly, in and of itself, the proliferation in the number of towns described above does seem to point towards some degree of urban dynamism. At the same time, from at least the middle of the sixteenth century, many towns appear to have suffered, especially in central and north-western Russia. Various kinds of evidence seem to point to the view that Russia shared in the economic upswing which apparently affected much of Europe from the latter part of the fifteenth century. But from the middle of the next century conditions in Russia, unlike Europe, seem to have deteriorated. The most frequently cited reason for this situation is the policies of Ivan IV.[22] Ivan's plunging of the country into the long and disastrous Livonian war (1558–83) and his reign of terror known as the *oprichnina* (1565–72) both brought destruction on a large scale with few areas escaping completely. The sacking of Novgorod and Pskov (1570), the Crimean Tatar attack on Moscow (1571), the devastation of large areas of the countryside, and the large-scale migrations of peasants are some of the more memorable episodes in this grim period. Then, following Ivan's death (1584) and a brief period of recovery, the 1590s witnessed further war culminating in the disasters of Boris Godunov's reign (1598–1605) including famine in 1601–3, and the period of anarchy and warfare known as the Time of Troubles (1604–13).

Giles Fletcher, who visited Russia in 1588–9, was a witness of some of the depredations which resulted from the troubles of Ivan IV's reign. In Moscow, for example, he noted that 'there lieth waste a great breadth of ground which before was well set and planted with buildings –', the after-effects of the Tatar raid of 1571. Having mentioned a handful of other places, he asserts that 'the other towns have nothing that is greatly memorable save many ruins within their walls, which showeth the decrease of the Russe people under this government'. In the same vein he notes the desertion of many villages and towns, for

21 Rozman, *Urban Networks in Russia*, pp. 33–42, 56–66.
22 Richard Hellie, 'Foundations of Russian Capitalism', *SR* 26 (1967), 148–54.

example between Vologda and Iaroslavl', where 'there are in sight fifty *derevni* or villages at the least, some half a mile, some a mile long, that stand vacant and desolate without any inhabitant'. According to Fletcher, his informants, some better travelled than he, assured him that 'the like is in all other places of the realm'.[23]

Whether or not Fletcher exaggerated, other evidence confirms his general picture of economic and social depression in the latter part of the sixteenth century. Thus Eaton has estimated that the average number of urban taxpaying households per town declined from 231 to 151, or by 35 per cent, between about 1550 and the 1580s; in 25 towns for which household data are available for both periods he calculates an overall decline of 61 per cent.[24] Kolomna, which is believed to have had a population of up to 3,000 in the 1570s, had only 12 urban taxpaying households whilst 54 dwellings were recorded as empty and there were 249 vacant lots. Serpukhov in 1552 had 623 taxpaying households and 143 vacant lots; Murom in 1566 recorded 587 and 151 respectively, and by 1574 only 111 taxpaying households, 157 empty dwellings, and 520 vacant lots.[25] Economic depression is believed to have struck the north-west especially hard, since this was the region where much of the warfare and disorder occurred. But there can also be little doubt that matters varied regionally and that the losses incurred in the centre and the north-west were to some degree balanced by gains on the new peripheries. Voronezh, for example, was founded in 1585 and by the time of its first cadastre in 1615 it had a population of over 800 households including those of 76 urban taxpayers and 87 monastic dependents, most of the latter engaged in trade and crafts. The town had 63 trading stalls (*lavki*) and half stalls, 23 of which were run by state servitors.[26] Clearly many of the inhabitants of the town had migrated from further north, perhaps in part fleeing from economic difficulties being experienced elsewhere in the country.

Urban society and administration

In much the same way that de Vries regards early modern European cities as points of co-ordination for a whole range of social activities,[27] Russian towns

23 Giles Fletcher, 'Of the Russe Commonwealth', in Lloyd E. Berry and Robert O. Crummey (eds.), *Rude and Barbarous Kingdom: Russia in the Accounts of Sixteenth-Century English Voyagers* (Madison: University of Wisconsin Press, 1968), pp. 125, 170.
24 Eaton, 'Decline and Recovery', p. 229.
25 Chechulin, *Goroda*, pp. 156–9, 173; *Ocherki istorii SSSR*, p. 263.
26 L. B. Veinberg and A. A. Poltoratskaia, *Materialy dlia istorii Voronezhskoi i sosednikh gubernii*, vol. II (Voronezh, 1891), pp. 1–26.
27 de Vries, *European Urbanization*, p. 12.

(other than the most insignificant) were multifunctional nodes performing a series of vital tasks in the developing and expanding state. Thus they were administrative centres, points of control over the surrounding territory. They were military and defensive nodes, directed against both internal and external foes. They were commercial foci at various scales. Most of them had handicraft and manufacturing activities. All had a religious role. And not a few had intensive gardening and even agrarian functions. Towns were not only vital to the needs of the state but they also had a significant part to play in wealth creation. They were thus places in which many social actors were keenly interested.

The multifunctional character of the town was reflected in its physical morphology.[28] The typical sixteenth-century Russian town had a fortified core, usually called the kremlin (*kreml'*) or *gorod*, which contained the major administrative and military offices and sometimes the residences of the elite or even of a portion of the population. Outside this was the commercial suburb or *posad*, often again walled and sometimes subdivided by walls into various sections. Beyond the *posad*, and either adjacent to it or at times separated from it by open space, there might be other suburbs (fortified or not, and sometimes referred to by the term *slobody*). Occasionally the whole settlement or a major part of it might be contained within a single wall which was sometimes described as the *ostrog*.[29] The typical town therefore had a cellular structure. The morphology of the town will be further explored in Chapter 25.

Urban social structure was usually complex. Towns with any degree of commercial life generally had a population of 'taxpaying' or *posad* people. This part of the population earned its basic livelihood from handicrafts, trade and similar activities and, for the privilege of being allowed to pursue these activities in towns, they were subject to a tax burden (*tiaglo*) imposed by the state. As well as paying taxes, the *tiaglo* might include the obligation of performing various services, such as acting as customs officials, guards, watchmen and the like, which obligations could be exceedingly troublesome. The *tiaglo* was generally imposed on the taxpaying community as a group (sometimes structured into several groups) who were then obliged, by means of an assembly (*skhod*) or other mechanism to elect officials to administer the burden. The *posad* community, however, was by no means a group of equals. Rather members were differentiated according to their wealth. At one extreme, in Moscow,

28 French, 'The Early and Medieval Russian Town', pp. 268–74; L. M. Tverskoi, *Russkoe gradostroitel'stvo do kontsa XVII veka* (Moscow and Leningrad: AN SSSR, 1953).
29 As at Voronezh in 1615; see Veinberg and Poltoratskaia, *Materialy*, pp. 1–26.

were the *gosti*, the richest and most significant merchants in the realm who were engaged in state service at the highest level. Also wealthy and performing important tasks for the government were members of the Moscow 'hundreds' – by the late sixteenth century, the *gostinaia sotnia* (merchants' hundred) and the *sukonnaia sotnia* (cloth hundred). Most members of the *posad* were divided into three ranks (*stati*) according to their wealth, but the details seem to have varied from town to town. Also resident in the *posad* in many cases were cottars (*bobyli*), labourers and others who seem to have earned a living through lowly trading activities, acting as yard keepers, through casual labour and by other means. These people do not appear to have been full members of the *posad* community but paid a quit-rent (*obrok*) to the state. *Posad* people were most common in towns of the north-west, north and centre although, as we have seen, many in the centre had fled south by the latter part of the sixteenth century. There, however, they often joined the service ranks, a social transition made much easier by the fluid life of the frontier.

Members of the *posad*, and the land that they occupied, were designated 'black', meaning that such persons were liable to the *tiaglo*. But not all traders and craftspeople in the sixteenth-century town were designated 'black'. Others were 'white', meaning that they lived in suburbs owned by members of the higher nobility, middle-ranking servicemen, the Church, monasteries and others. Such people were relieved of the *tiaglo* on the grounds that they owed their obligations not to the state but to their lords. Many towns had such 'white' suburbs (often called *slobody*), which were in many ways the remnants of past political subdivisions in Russia when princes, monasteries, high churchmen and others customarily derived income from their urban possessions. From the time of Ivan III the tsars had been trying to eradicate them on the grounds that they denied important revenues to the state, while the 'black' people generally resented them because of their tax privileges and the unfair competition which they consequently promoted. Also a problem for the tsars were the private towns, often situated on monastic or patrimonial estates. Smirnov calculated that there were about fifteen fortified private towns in the sixteenth century, reduced to about ten in the first half of the seventeenth.[30]

An important element in the populations of many towns (and also designated 'white') were the military men, for the most part members of the lower-ranking service contingents, including musketeers (*strel'tsy*), cossacks and others. Unlike middle-ranking servitors (*deti boiarskie* and others), the

---

30 Smirnov, *Goroda*, p. 110.

lower ranks either had no land and were paid in cash or kind, or they held land in communal fields with others in the same group. Few had serfs or other dependents. Moscow had a large element of service people in its population. They were less common in the north and parts of the north-west, but very common in the southern frontier towns where they often constituted the biggest element of the urban population. Here, in addition to their military duties, servicemen engaged in agriculture with their families, and many engaged in trades and crafts as well. They settled in their own suburbs close by the fortified towns where they were administered by their own regimental structures and communal organisations.

Towns also had other groups in their populations. Members of the clergy, monks, monastic and church servitors were an important element, in addition to the already-mentioned monastic dependents living in 'white places'. Moscow naturally contained all social ranks, from the tsar downwards. The social elite tended to live in the capital where they maintained their homes but also held estates elsewhere. Their life in the city was eased by the ministrations of dependents – serfs, slaves and others. Some other towns, Kazan' for example, also had members of the middle-ranking service class living in town where they had services to perform. It was more common, however, for such groups to live on their country estates, but they were generally required to maintain dwellings ('siege dwellings') in town, officially for occupation during times of disturbance or conflict. The dwellings were usually cared for in the absence of the owner by a housekeeper (*dvornik*), often a slave or other dependent who frequently engaged in commercial activity. Other groups included non-Russians (European soldiers, ambassadors, merchants and some others in Moscow; European merchants in some other places, notably Archangel and Vologda; Tatar and other minority representatives and groups in Moscow, Kazan', Astrakhan' and other towns), and non-official elements (runaways, beggars, criminal groups).

There is no sense in which the disparate members of the urban population constituted an 'urban citizenry' or could provide any unified political voice or identity for the town. Each group was administered separately, with different interests, and the only unity was provided by the town governor who represented the tsar and whose remit extended over the nearby region as well as the town. In this sense, then, the town barely represented a separate entity from its surrounding milieu, was disunited within itself and fell very much under the aegis of the state. Liberal scholars of the past thus lamented the lack of commercial opportunity, entrepreneurial spirit and civic freedom which, they believed, flowed from the imposition upon towns of the centralised, Muscovite model of control rather than a more 'democratic' model like the one they postulated for early Novgorod.[31]

From the point of view of a hard-pressed and financially constrained Muscovite state, however, strict control had many advantages. The problem was that the state was barely in a position to enforce it. The sixteenth century was a time of transition between the fragmented polity which had characterised the post-Mongol period and the more centralised system inaugurated by Peter the Great. As towns had been absorbed by the expanding Muscovite state their princes or other rulers had been replaced by the tsar's representatives (*namestniki*), often members of the Muscovite elite. The latter were maintained by a system of 'feedings' (*kormlenie*) or payments and provisions derived from local sources. Similar payments were made to subordinate officials. As centralisation proceeded, these payments were regulated more strictly, and certain of the functions of the *namestnik* were transferred to other centrally appointed officials. But some *namestniki* proved disturbingly independent, incompetent and corrupt, influenced by oscillations in the power of elite families at court. From the 1530s, therefore, various reforms were inaugurated. The first, the *guba* reform (1538–9), removed the duty of suppressing lawlessness and disorder from the hands of the *namestniki* into those of elected local officials. A new law code (1550) regulated provincial administration. The 1550s witnessed the inauguration of new local officials to oversee tax collection and civil administration and then, in 1555–6, the abolition of *kormlenie* and with it provincial administration by the *namestniki*.[32] What eventually replaced the latter was a system of administration by military governors (*voevody*) based on the towns and responsible for civil and military affairs within their towns and the surrounding districts (*uezdy*). Military governors were usually members of the service class rather than of the central elite. The new system was pioneered on the southern frontier before the end of the sixteenth century. However, strict and systematic central control of the towns and their subsidiary districts was vitiated, among other things, by the chaotic structure of central government departments (*prikazy*) which supervised different facets of urban life, and towns in different locations, in a seemingly random

31 J. Michael Hittle, *The Service City: State and Townsmen in Russia, 1600–1800* (Cambridge, Mass.: Harvard University Press, 1979), pp. 5–9.

32 Janet Martin, *Medieval Russia, 980–1584* (Cambridge: Cambridge University Press, 1995), pp. 284–6, 344–7; Brian L. Davies, 'The Town Governors in the Reign of Ivan IV', *RH* 14 (1987): 77–144.

fashion. This was a problem which was to persist until the reforms of Peter the Great.[33]

Urban and regional commerce

The great majority of Russians during this period were peasants, involved in a largely subsistence economy and resorting to the market only where it became necessary to earn money to pay taxes and duties or to purchase essential goods. Many town dwellers also supported themselves to greater or lesser degree by engaging in agriculture and various kinds of primary production. Wealthy landowners, including those engaged in political, administrative, military and other tasks in Moscow and lesser towns, could often rely on their serfs and other dependents to supply their needs from their country estates. Other urban dwellers, however, including many administrative and military personnel, clergy, merchants, traders and craftsmen, were more or less dependent on the market. The rise and growth of towns, and particularly the stimulus provided by the burgeoning state and its growing needs in raw materials and manufactured goods, were important impulses to market and commercial activity. Especially significant in this regard was the role of Moscow, as commercial as well as political and administrative centre of the country and, as has been seen, dominant over all other towns in the realm. The major communications routes (rivers and roads) radiated from the capital to all the populated parts of the territory, and also beyond via ports and frontier posts. A number of scholars have thus seen the basis for an 'all-Russian market' with Moscow as its nodal point being established in this period.[34] The significance of the international market place in Russia's development, whilst impossible to establish with any certainty because of scanty evidence, should probably not be exaggerated. Whilst Russian state-building was clearly partly a response to the dangers and challenges posed by potential or actual enemies beyond the frontiers, the country was unable to benefit fully from the expanding commercial network based on Western Europe and the North Atlantic which

33 Tikhomirov, *Rossiya v XVI veke*, p. 30; for details of central administration of towns and districts in the seventeenth century, see A. S. Lappo-Danilevskii, *Organizatsiia priamogo oblozheniia v Moskovskom gosudarstve so vremen smuty do epokhi preobrazovanii* (St Petersburg: Tipografiia I. N. Skorokhodova, 1890), pp. 542–50.

34 *Ocherki istorii SSSR*, pp. 249–61; Artur Attman, 'The Russian Market in World Trade, 1500–1800', *Scandinavian Economic History Review* 29 (1981): 177–80; Kristoff Glamann, 'The Changing Patterns of Trade', in *Cambridge Economic History of Europe*, vol. v (Cambridge: Cambridge University Press, 1977), pp. 217, 228.

was becoming apparent about this time.[35] Not only was Russia geographically peripheral to many of the new developments, but access was hindered by poor communications and its limited coastline.[36]

By clustering around the towns commerce and manufacture were able to benefit from the military protection, access to important officials and geographical nodality available in urban centres. At the same time the state itself encouraged such patterns since it eased the problems of regulation and tax collection. Moreover, particularly from the time of Ivan III (1462–1505) the tsars pursued a regular policy of relocating wealthy merchants and craftspeople from peripheral towns to Moscow and other places. Such crude actions seem to have been motivated more by political than by economic considerations and they may well have been to the detriment of commerce. But they do indicate the importance accorded by the tsars to commerce in general and to merchants and craftspeople in particular. The financial significance of the towns to the state was, of course, one of the reasons why the latter attempted to eradicate the privately owned suburbs and towns from the fifteenth century onwards.

Crafts and manufactures were a key feature of the *posad* of many towns, as well as of many of the 'white' suburbs. Moscow in particular was characterised by numerous suburbs owned by the court, the state and private owners (including the Church) whose inhabitants lived not (or not only) by selling their products on the marketplace but by fulfilling the orders of their respective masters. Thus Moscow had its armaments manufacturers (most notably, the cannon foundry, established by Ivan III) and other metalworkers, some of whom were engaged in fine metalwork for the court, those engaged in textile and clothes production, the preparation of food, workers in wood and stone, those engaged in specialist crafts like icon-painting, printing and jewellery manufacture, and many others, often directly serving the needs of court, government or private landowner. But the key point is that the presence of manufacture did not necessarily imply market relations. Moscow's court (or palace and treasury) suburbs originally developed to supply the needs of the court and the government and worked in response to specific orders. Their inhabitants fulfilled the latter on the basis of their obligations as residents of the

35 I. Wallerstein, *The Modern World-System*, vol. ii: *Mercantilism and the Consolidation of the European World-Economy, 1600–1750* (New York: Academic Press, 1980).
36 But for a positive assessment of the situation before the 1560s, see D. P. Makovskii, *Razvitie tovarno-denezhnykh otnoshenii v sel'skom khoziaistve russkogo gosudarstva v XVI veke* (Smolensk: Smolenskii gosudarstvennyi pedagogicheskii institut, 1963); N. E. Nosov, 'Russkii gorod i russkoe kupechestvo v XVI stoletii (k postanovke voprosa)', in *Issledovaniia po sotsial'no-politicheskoi istorii Rossii* (Leningrad: Nauka, 1971), pp. 152–77.

court suburbs. By the late sixteenth century, however, many of these people seem to have been working for the market also (which might include the state as purchaser) like other residents of the 'black' and 'white' suburbs.

Crafts and manufactures generally took place in the urban suburbs in the homes of the various artisans. The sources rarely permit an insight into the location of different kinds of manufacturing and craft activities in different towns, but in Moscow's case it seems that a few of the suburbs were specialised in this sense, including some of the court suburbs.[37] A prominent feature of many towns was the trading square (*torg*), usually located at a central and accessible point. In Moscow's case this was to the east of the Kremlin by the Moscow River on the site of the present-day Red Square, sometimes supplemented in winter by trading on the actual ice of the river itself. Much of what is now the open space of the square was occupied in the sixteenth century by a series of specialised trading rows (*riady*) consisting of individual shops (*lavki*), stalls and sometimes cellars and stores owned or rented by merchants, craftsmen, Church and monastic dependents and others. Shops were predominantly of wood, occasionally of stone. Sixteenth- or early seventeenth-century Moscow rows seem to have included a Surozhskii row (trading mainly in foreign goods), shoe row, ironmongery row, cloth row, glove row, women's row, kaftan row, iron row, silver row, tinkers' row and numerous others. Towards the end of the century one or more trading courts (*palaty*) are recorded which incorporated shops and rows, including a merchants' bazaar (*gostinnyi dvor*) where visiting or foreign merchants could trade. The streets of the Kitai gorod, Moscow's oldest *posad* to the east of the trading square, had many trading establishments, including the houses of foreign merchants, whilst some trading bazaars and markets were located in other parts of the city. The latter included markets for horses, cattle, timber and construction materials.[38]

The detailed geographical patterns of trade and commerce across Russia in the sixteenth century cannot be established because of the lack of adequate source materials. The exact nature of the links between Moscow and the rest of the country, for example, is only known in part, thanks to the researches into often difficult source material by a handful of scholars.[39] The character of

---

37 V. Snegirev, *Moskovskie slobody* (Moscow: Moskovskii rabochii, 1947), pp. 56ff., 78; French, 'The Early and Medieval Russian Town', p. 270.

38 *Istoriia Moskvy*, vol. I, pp. 156–61.

39 See e.g. M.V. Fekhner, *Torgovlia russkogo gosudarstva so stranami Vostoka v XVI veke* (Moscow: Izdatel'stvo Gosudarstvennogo Istoricheskogo muzeia, 1952); N. Kostomarov, *Ocherki torgovli Moskovskogo gosudarstva v XVI i XVII stoletiiakh* (St Petersburg: N. Tiblen, 1862); S. V. Bakhrushin, *Nauchnye trudy*, 4 vols. (Moscow: AN SSSR, 1952–9); G. S. Rabinovich, *Gorod soli: Staraia Russa v kontse XVI–seredine XVIII vekov* (Leningrad: Izdatel'stvo

commerce and trade in Russia's regions and their towns is also known only in part. Very little is known about trade and commerce taking place below the level of the official towns, even though there is plenty of evidence to suggest the rise of trading centres and villages in various parts of the country from at least the fifteenth century. In the north-west, for example, the Novgorod cadastres record the existence of numerous small trading points or *riady* from this time whilst in the north similar places, often dealing in furs, were sometimes described as *pogosti*. The term *posad* could also be used to describe such centres, as in the case of Tikhvin Posad in the north-west.[40] Their inhabitants were often traders and craftspeople rather than agriculturalists. Many settlements of this type were monastic centres. Serbina collected evidence for a hundred or more small trading and commercial centres for various sixteenth-century dates in thirty-four districts (*uezdy*) of the Russian state. For the ninety-three centres for which it was possible to ascertain ownership, 82 per cent were monastic, a quarter of these belonging to one monastery, the Trinity-Sergius (Troitse-Sergiev), north-east of Moscow.[41] What became of all these centres during the vicissitudes of the later sixteenth century is unknown, although it is apparent that several of those located in the north-west and near the western frontier disappeared, perhaps in consequence of the Livonian war.[42]

Towns often acted as commercial foci for their surrounding regions and many manufactures were oriented to the meeting of local and everyday needs. These included the provision of food, clothing, footwear, fuel, building materials, horses and so on to urban and rural inhabitants. In this sense urban economies bore the unspecialised character which was typical of early modern towns throughout Europe. Where they also engaged in more specialised activities, this reflected their locations relative to such features as localised resources, important trading routes, coasts, borders and the like. One example was the fur trade which had once been the basis of the wealth of the city of Novgorod. By the second half of the fifteenth century Novgorod's leading role

Leningradskogo universiteta, 1973); K. N. Serbina, *Ocherki iz sotsial'no-ekonomicheskoi istorii russkogo goroda: Tikhvinskii posad v XVI–XVII vv.* (Moscow and Leningrad: AN SSSR, 1951); Paul Bushkovitch, *The Merchants of Moscow, 1580–1650* (Cambridge: Cambridge University Press, 1980).
40 French, 'The Early and Medieval Russian Town', pp. 265–6; R. A. French, 'The Urban Network of Later Medieval Russia', in *Geographical Studies on the Soviet Union: Essays in Honor of Chauncy D. Harris* (Chicago: University of Chicago, Department of Geography, Research Paper no. 211, 1984), p. 45; Serbina, *Ocherki*; V. N. Vernadskii, *Novgorod i Novgorodskaia zemlia v XV veke* (Moscow and Leningrad: AN SSSR, 1961), p. 112.
41 K. N. Serbina, 'Iz istorii vozniknoveniia gorodov v Rossii XVI v.', in *Goroda feodal'noi Rossii* (Moscow: Nauka, 1966), pp. 135–8.
42 French, 'The Urban Network', p. 46.

had been eclipsed by competition from Moscow and new organising centres for the trade had become significant, such as Velikii Ustiug, Vologda,[43] and Tobol'sk in western Siberia.[44] Likewise the salt trade played an important part in the life of many northern centres as well as others towards the Urals and further south along the Volga.[45] Iron ore, fish or important agricultural products like flax and hemp helped define the characters of other centres. For towns in central Russia the looming presence of Moscow and the many demands of its marketplace were significant and helped mould the economies of towns across a wide area.

Long-distance and international trade

Referring to Europe's regional economies in the sixteenth and seventeenth centuries, Kristof Glamann has written that 'it is isolation, not interaction, that leaps to the eye'.[46] Everywhere the costs and risks of long-distance trade militated against its easy development. Travel by land was particularly problematic. Only where the sea penetrated deeply into the European land mass, as it did most notably in the cases of the Mediterranean and the Baltic and their associated gulfs and bays, or where the land was crossed by great and easily navigable rivers, as was the case on the East European plain, was communication somewhat easier. In the Baltic the rise of the Hanseatic League of north German cities had fostered commercial relations with the Russian principalities of Novgorod and Pskov in particular. Hanseatic dealings with the Russians were facilitated by their factories in such centres as Novgorod, Riga, Vitebsk, Polotsk and Dorpat.[47] But Russia's commercial relations were not only with the West. It also had extensive dealings with the East, whose importance for Russia had been enhanced by the latter's dependence on the Golden Horde for two and a half centuries. Communications in this direction were eased by the possibility of using navigable rivers like the Don, the Dnieper and, especially

---

43 J. Martin, *Treasure of the Land of Darkness: The Fur Trade and its Significance for Medieval Russia* (Cambridge: Cambridge University Press, 1986), pp. 92–109.

44 O. N. Vilkov, 'Tobol'sk – tsentr tamozhennoi sluzhby Sibiri XVII v.', in *Goroda Sibiri: ekonomika, upravlenie i kul'tura gorodov Sibiri v dosovetskii period* (Novosibirsk: Nauka, Sibirskoe otdelenie, 1974), pp. 131–69.

45 E. I. Zaozerskaia, *U istokov krupnogo proizvodstva v russkoi promyshlennosti XVI–XVII vv.: k voprosu o genezise kapitalizma v Rossii* (Moscow: Nauka, 1970); N. V. Ustiugov, *Solevarennaia promyshlennost' Soli Kamskoi v XVII veke* (Moscow: AN SSSR, 1957); R. E. F. Smith and David Christian, *Bread and Salt: A Social and Economic History of Food and Drink in Russia* (Cambridge: Cambridge University Press, 1984), pp. 27–73.

46 Glamann, 'The Changing Patterns', p. 186.

47 Walther Kirchner, *Commercial Relations Between Russia and Europe, 1400–1800: Collected Essays* (Bloomington: Indiana University Press, 1966), p. 92.

later, the Volga. In the opinion of Fekhner, Russia's commercial links with the East were more significant than its Western ones in the sixteenth century.[48]

Russia's trade with the West, and its policies with respect to that trade, were moulded by two major factors in this period. One was the opportunities for trade and development presented by the more dynamic European economies, particularly from the fifteenth century. The other, and not unrelated to the first, was the growing political instability along Russia's western borders and the eastern Baltic as various powers began to compete for both territory and commercial advantage. Traditionally the German Hanse with its principal centre at Lübeck had dominated the Baltic trade in such goods as grain, salt and salt fish, woollen cloth, furs, timber and forest products. Baltic products like furs, hides, honey, flax, hemp and wax were in constant demand in Central and Western Europe. From the early fifteenth century, however, the Hanse monopoly was increasingly challenged as the cities of the eastern Baltic attempted to bypass the dominance of Lübeck and its associates. A complicating factor was Moscow's annexation of Novgorod (1478) followed by Tver' (1485) and Pskov (1510). This appeared to threaten the balance of power in the region, especially when Ivan III's founding of Ivangorod opposite Narva in 1492 signalled Muscovy's commercial ambitions in the Baltic in no uncertain manner. Two years later, however, Ivan closed down the Hanse's major factory at Novgorod which proved a severe blow to those ambitions, hardly compensated for by Ivangorod and the opening up of Russian trade to other foreign merchants. Nevertheless the Muscovite state found itself in increasing need of Western goods as well as of Western technical expertise whilst Russian goods continued to find a market there. The situation therefore encouraged further contacts. In addition to the Baltic, Russia had links to the West via the traditional overland route through Lithuania and Poland though commerce was frequently interrupted by difficult political relations and border changes.[49] Smolensk, taken by the Russians in 1514, was an important trading centre in this direction.

The beginning of the Livonian war in 1558 proved an important milestone in Russia's commercial relationships with the West. The capture of Narva by Russian forces in that year meant that Russia now had a secure port on the Baltic which proved attractive to merchant vessels from many parts of northern and western Europe. In Kirchner's view, within ten years Narva had developed into one of the Baltic's wealthiest ports as well as one of its most significant

---

48 Fekhner, *Torgovlia*, pp. 5–6.
49 Bushkovitch, *The Merchants of Moscow*, pp. 87–91.

political focal points.[50] Kirchner argues that, had the Russians retained Narva for longer than they did, it might have proved a most potent instrument in the country's Westernisation and that its loss to the Swedes in 1581 was a serious setback which was only rectified by Peter the Great. But this argument appears to give too much weight to the importance of a single port – compared to the disasters of the Livonian war, the *oprichnina* and the other calamities which befell Russia in the late sixteenth century Narva's loss appears a relatively minor affair. Nevertheless the loss did mean that Russia now lacked its own Baltic port, becoming dependent on Sweden for its Baltic trade links via Revel' and Narva. This fact severely restricted the country's Baltic connections down to Peter the Great's time.

It is in this context that the arrival of an English merchant fleet under Richard Chancellor at the mouth of the Northern Dvina on the White Sea in 1553 assumes significance. The English had participated to some degree in the Baltic trade but their northern venture had been directed more at discovering a north-east passage to Asia than at finding a new route to Russia. Nevertheless within two years an English Muscovy Company had been established to exploit this new commercial opportunity. The English were soon joined by the Dutch, the French and others. At first the trade involved a rather difficult transhipment and transit of goods to Kholmogory, situated some way up the river at a point which could not be reached by larger vessels. In 1583–4, however, the government, possibly responding to the loss of Narva, decided to build the new port of Archangel close to the river's mouth and accessible to the large sea-going ships used by the English and Dutch to negotiate the difficult passage around the North Cape. Within a few years, it seems, Archangel had become Russia's most important port.[51] According to Bushkovitch, the importance of Archangel lies not so much in the kinds of goods traded there but in the fact that Russia now had direct contact with West European states, bypassing the Swedish middleman. Statistics for the early years of trade at Archangel are almost completely missing, but some for the English Muscovy Company in the mid-1580s seem to show that agricultural products (flax and hempen cordage, tallow) were more important exports than the traditional forest products by this stage.[52] This may reflect some of the ways in which the Russian economy had changed during the course of the sixteenth century. Archangel, though remote, was destined to play an important role in Russian commerce down to

50 Kirchner, *Commercial Relations*, pp. 70–1.
51 Bushkovitch, *The Merchants of Moscow*, p. 69.
52 T. S. Willan, *The Early History of the Russia Company, 1553–1603* (Manchester: Manchester University Press, 1956), pp. 182–3; Bushkovitch, *The Merchants of Moscow*, pp. 65–7.

the eighteenth century. Its communications links with central Russia via the Northern Dvina and Sukhona routes and then via Vologda and Iaroslavl' to Moscow, and its link to Siberia via Velikii Ustiug, Viatka and Perm', brought the benefits of long-distance trade to a significant number of northern centres.

The meagre sources recording Russian trade with countries to the south allow only the most general picture to be presented.[53] Down to 1530 or so the Ottoman Empire seems to have been the main trading partner and Russian merchants regularly travelled to Kaffa in Crimea either via the Don or another route. Later, routes through Poland and Moldavia to the Ottomans seem to have been favoured. But trade with the Ottomans appears to have declined from 1580 or so whilst that with Persia via the Volga and Astrakhan' flourished. Persian silks and other textiles were in demand by the Russians whilst Russian leather and furs travelled towards Persia. Many of the Volga towns and also Moscow itself benefited from this trade.

Conclusion

Sixteenth-century Russia and its towns underwent many vicissitudes. From apparent buoyancy in the late fifteenth and early sixteenth centuries the towns, and commercial life in general, seem to have entered a more problematic phase after about 1560. Yet Russia continued to expand territorially and this expansion was accompanied by the spread of urbanism and commercial activity into new regions. Unfortunately the nature of the source material is such as to make the detailed study of such apparently contradictory processes extremely difficult. What can be said is that the growing network of towns was of central importance for the whole process of Russian state-building. Whilst the towns may not have compared with those of Western Europe in their commercial dynamism and civic development, their overall significance for Russia's quest to build a strong and expansive empire is clear.

53 V. E. Syroechkovskii, *Gosti-surozhane (Izvestiia gosudarstvennoi Akademii Istorii Material'noi Kul'tury*, 127) (Moscow and Leningrad: OGIZ, 1935); Fekhner, *Torgovlia*; Bushkovitch, *The Merchants of Moscow*, pp. 92–101.

14

The non-Christian peoples on the Muscovite frontiers

MICHAEL KHODARKOVSKY

When Ivan III was crowned as grand prince of Moscow in 1462, he became the ruler of a small but ambitious principality. First among equals, the grand prince of Moscow was one among several Russian Orthodox princes who ruled over the East Slavic lands. By the time of his death in 1505, Ivan III was the ruler of a sovereign Muscovite state which now subsumed most of the other Russian Orthodox principalities, and was an heir to the Byzantine emperors. The long reign of Ivan III marked two important phases in Muscovite history: political unification of the Russian Orthodox Christian lands under a single sovereign, and territorial expansion into the neighbouring lands populated by non-Christians.

The conquest in the north and north-east

The rise of Moscow had always been closely connected with its expansion in the north and north-east. There, the dense woods and numerous lakes and rivers of the north offered abundant supplies of precious furs and the primitive hunters of the region could be easily compelled to pay such tribute. From the late fourteenth century, Moscow was attempting to establish its control around the Dvina River in the north and in the Perm' region in the north-east. Moscow fought several wars with Novgorod over control of the northern region and its inhabitants who had already been paying tribute to Novgorod. Throughout the fifteenth century, Novgorod was forced to cede more and more of its northern colonies to Moscow until Novgorod's final defeat by Moscow in 1478 brought the region under Moscow's sway.[1]

---

1 Janet Martin, 'Russian Expansion in the Far North', in *Russian Colonial Expansion to 1917*, ed. Michael Rywkin (London: Mansell Publishing, 1988), pp. 35–40; Andreas Kappeler, *The Russian Empire: A Multiethnic History*, trans. Alfred Clayton (Harlow: Longman, 2001), pp. 6–18; M. K. Liubavskii, *Istoricheskaia geografiia Rossii v sviazi s kolonizatsiei* (Moscow: I. I. Liubimov, 1909; reprinted St Petersburg: Lan', 2001), pp. 155–62.

The newly risen Orthodox Muscovy stood alone against Roman Catholic Sweden in the north-west and Lithuania in the west, the Islamic Golden Horde and its successor khanates of the Crimea and Astrakhan' in the south and Kazan' in the east. Except for the western borderlands which were overwhelmingly populated by the Christian communities, Moscow was surrounded by a vast non-Christian world. It is here, on its non-Christian frontiers, that Moscow enjoyed its major military successes, acquired new confidence, crystallised its own identity, and built its first empire.

Before the ultimate collapse of the Golden Horde in the early sixteenth century allowed for Moscow's expansion south and east, the natural direction of Muscovite expansion was the north-east. Moscow's increasing appetite for furs, salt and metals led to Muscovite penetration of the distant lands populated by various animist peoples.

In contrast to Novgorod, which was solely interested in exacting tribute from the native population of the north, the Muscovites undertook a full-scale colonisation of the region. The traditional landscape of the northern region, previously dominated by primordial wilderness and the hunting and fishing societies of the aboriginal population, was undergoing a thorough transformation. New villages, forts, towns and monasteries emerged with the arrival of Russian peasants, soldiers, townsmen, traders and bureaucrats who were to settle and colonise the lands, and clergy seeking to convert the pagan population. North of the Urals, the construction of Pustozersk allowed Moscow to set foot in the arctic tundra populated by the Nenets (Samoed), while the Muscovite towns of Ust'-Vym, Cherdyn' and Solikamsk had firmly put the Great Perm' region populated by Komi (Zyrians) under Moscow's control. Previously sporadic missionary activity of the Russian Orthodox Church received a new impetus with the foundation in 1462 of the first large monastery in the Urals, the Ioanna-Bogoslovskii monastery in Cherdyn'.[2]

In the 1550s, the title of the recently crowned tsar of all Russia, Ivan IV, began to include the territories east of the Urals, 'Obdor, Konda and all Siberian lands'. More often than not, such claims over new lands and peoples were premature, and Moscow's limited influence in the region continued to rely on exchange treaties with the natives. The Muscovites would have to wait until the 1590s, when the construction of the forts and towns of Berezov, Obdorsk and Verkhotur'e did indeed give Moscow greater control over lands east of the Urals mostly populated by the Khanty (Ostiaks) and Mansi (Voguls).[3]

---

2 *Istoriia Urala s drevneishikh vremen do 1861 g.* (Moscow: Nauka, 1989), p. 146.
3 James Forsyth, *A History of the Peoples of Siberia* (Cambridge: Cambridge University Press, 1992), p. 10.

By the middle of the sixteenth century the Muscovite expansion in the north-east was encroaching on the various peoples in the Volga–Kama Mesopotamia. These were the northern boundaries of the magnificent Muslim khanate of Kazan'. At the same time Moscow's expansion brought it directly to the gates of the city of Kazan', which remained the main barrier preventing Moscow's expansion east into Siberia and south towards the Caucasus.

The conquest of Kazan' and Astrakhan'

The conquest and annexation of the Kazan' khanate was one of the critical watersheds in Russian history. It set the stage for Moscow's relentless territorial aggrandisement throughout the following centuries. The upstart Muscovite state was rapidly turning into an empire, whose ruler claimed to be a Universal Emperor destined to rule over the diverse multitudes of pagan and Muslim peoples.

The long-term strategic and economic importance of the conquest of Kazan' was obvious: to control the riches of the mid-Volga area, to gain access to the wealth of Siberia and to dominate the commercial routes to Central Asia and China as well as Iran and the Caucasus. In other words, Kazan' was Moscow's window on the East.

But even greater was its immediate symbolic significance. Kazan' was one of the successor states of the Golden Horde and its rulers were the Chingisids, the direct descendants of Chingis khan. Given the centuries of humiliation and the grand princes' subservience to the khans of the Golden Horde, Moscow undoubtedly saw the conquest of Kazan' as an ultimate testimony to its newly won sovereignty, the superiority of its arms and, most importantly, a Divine Indication that Moscow had become the centre of Christendom.

Of course, Ivan IV was not the only one claiming to be a Universal Christian ruler, and his Habsburg contemporaries, the Holy Roman Emperor, Charles V, and his son Philip II, king of Spain, had laid similar claims prior to Ivan IV. Is it possible that Ivan IV was, in fact, inspired by the Spanish feats which followed in short succession: the Reconquista of the Iberian peninsula from the Muslims, the swift conquest of America and its animist population and finally Charles V's conquest of Tunis in 1535, celebrated as a crusading triumph against the World of Islam?

Immediately after Kazan''s conquest, Moscow showed a zeal similar to its Spanish counterpart: the mosques were destroyed and the Muslim population faced slaughter, expulsion, forced resettlement and conversion to Orthodox

Christianity.[4] Those who were converted at the initial stage of conquest become known as the old converts (*starokreshchennye*). Yet Moscow's rule over the conquered Muslim domains proved to be very different from that of Spain. Shortly after the annexation of Kazan', Moscow changed its policy to a mixture of carrots and sticks, choosing to rely more on accommodation and co-optation than on concerted violence. The Muscovite rulers never resorted to the sort of violent campaign which characterised the Spanish Reconquista: wholesale conversion to Christianity and massive expulsion.

Belatedly and unconvincingly Moscow also tried to make Kazan' into its own Reconquista, claiming that Kazan' had always been a patrimony of the Russian princes. Such a claim could justify the conquest to Muscovite and Western audiences, but it certainly found little appeal among the population of the Kazan' khanate and Muslims outside it. Unlike Spain, which was a part of a larger Roman Catholic Europe, Moscow was surrounded by powerful Islamic states and numerous non-Christian peoples whom it simply could not afford to antagonise, even less to dispense with. To legitimise its conquest among the population of the former Golden Horde, Moscow had to take the mantle of the khans and to claim to be an heir to their glory. It would not be the last time that Moscow's political theology of a crusading state destined to rule and convert the pagans and the Muslims was moderated by the reality mandating a more accommodating approach. For a long time to come, Moscow's pragmatic political concerns continued to coexist uneasily with its theological visions.

Annexation of the Kazan' khanate added numerous non-Christians to the Muscovite realm. These were the Mordva, Chuvash, Mari (Cheremis) and Udmurts (Votiaks) who comprised prosperous agricultural communities along the banks of the Volga, Viatka and Kama rivers and remained predominantly pagan. But most significantly, for the first time Moscow acquired large numbers of Muslims who were to become the subjects of the Christian tsar. These were Tatars mostly residing in and around Kazan' and Bashkirs in the territory east of the Volga.

The conquest and annexation of Kazan' in 1552 was the culmination of a long process: Moscow's incremental but determined territorial aggrandisement, driven above all by its growing economic and military might on the one hand and the increasing rivalry and debilitation among the successor khanates of the Golden Horde on the other. Moscow's expansion was also based on a complex

4 *Prodolzhenie drevnei rossiiskoi vivliofiki*, 11 vols. (St Petersburg: Imperatorskaia Akademiia Nauk, 1786–1801; reprinted in Slavic printings and reprintings, 251, ed. C. H. van Schooneveld, The Hague and Paris: Mouton, 1970), vol. IX (1793), pp. 60–5.

set of its ever-changing relationships with the various constituent parts of the former Golden Horde.

Thus, it was no secret that Moscow's measured military successes between 1480 and 1509 were due to its alliance with the Crimea. Of course, what was de facto an alliance was seen in the world of steppe politics as a relationship of two unequals. The Crimean khans claimed to be the heirs to the heritage of the Golden Horde and referred to themselves as the Great Khans of the Great Horde (Ulug Ordugunun Ulug Khan), while continuing to regard the grand princes as the rulers of a subservient tributary state. Such indeed was the status of the Russian princes since the mid-thirteenth century, when they had been pressed into submission by the khans of the Golden Horde. The Muscovite grand princes tacitly agreed with such assumptions and never challenged them openly as long as the Crimea and Moscow had common enemies: Poland-Lithuania and the Great Horde.

In the middle of the fifteenth century several branches of the Chingisids seceded from the Golden Horde. They used traditional commercial hubs to establish new political centres on the fringes of the Golden Horde: thus emerged the khanates of the Crimea, Kazan', Astrakhan' and Siberia. What was left of the Golden Horde was the Great Horde, a nomadic confederation deprived of its vital economic centres, whose khans could claim to be the heirs of the Golden Horde with greater legitimacy than any other members of the Chingis dynasty and were therefore the main rivals of the Crimean khans. In 1502, having suffered the last devastating blow by the Crimeans, the Great Horde ceased to exist, its people and herds captured and brought to the Crimea. With their common antagonist gone, the interests of Moscow and Crimea began to diverge. In their effort to establish Crimean authority over the parts of the former Golden Horde, the Crimean khans sought to control Kazan', Kasimov and Astrakhan' and continued to demand tribute and military assistance from Muscovy.

In the meantime, Moscow had its own agenda. With its hard-won sovereignty, Moscow was in no mood to have the Crimea replace Sarai, the former residence of the khans of the Golden Horde. It slashed the payments of customary tribute, procrastinated in helping the Crimeans against Astrakhan' and, most importantly, zealously guarded its influence over Kazan' where, however intermittently and indirectly, Moscow had exercised control since 1487. When in 1519 Moscow installed in Kazan' Shah Ali, a member of the rival branch of the Chingisid dynasty and a nephew of Ahmed, the deceased khan of the Great Horde, the Crimean khan Muhammed Girey had had enough. In 1521, Muhammed Girey approached his arch-rival, the khan of Astrakhan', and offered peace and alliance against Moscow. At the same time, pro-Crimean forces in Kazan' organised a coup and successfully installed on the throne Sahip Girey, the son of the deceased Crimean khan, Mengli Girey. The deferred hostility which had characterised the relationship between Moscow and the Crimea since 1509 now turned into an open war. The military campaign launched against Muscovy from both the Crimea and Kazan' was one of the most devastating in the history of the Muscovite state.[5]

With the final dissipation of the Golden Horde, the steppe lost any semblance of central authority, which led to further turmoil and the emergence of new actors and new alliances. From the mid-1520s Moscow's military success was, in no small degree, based on its alliance with the Nogais, a powerful nomadic confederation of Turko-Mongol tribes. Throughout the sixteenth century, the Nogais found themselves under increasing pressure from other nomadic peoples, the Kazakhs and Kalmyks, and were forced to move further west, approaching the Muscovite zone of influence. De facto crucial players in the turbulent politics of the steppe, the Nogais had no claims to the throne of the Great Khan of the Horde because their rulers were not descendants of Chingis khan. The Nogais played a critical role in annihilating the Great Horde and assisting Moscow in the conquests of Kazan' and Astrakhan'.[6]

Moscow's annexation of Kazan' represented more than a military victory; it was also an ultimate challenge to the Crimean pretensions to rule and control the territories of the former Golden Horde in the name of the horde's khans. Vocabulary of images spoke louder than words. To celebrate his victory over Kazan', Ivan IV ordered the construction of the most unusual cathedral. Erected in the Red Square near the Kremlin, St Basil's cathedral, with its eclectic architecture, stood as the ultimate symbol of Moscow's place in its self-construed theological and political universe. Moscow was to be the New Jerusalem and the New Sarai, both at the same time.

The deluge of foreign embassies and envoys in the wake of Moscow's military victory was a further confirmation of Moscow's rise to international prominence. The author of the *Kazan' Chronicle* did not doubt the biblical importance of Moscow's victory over Kazan', when he included the Babylonians among many foreign envoys arriving to honour the Muscovite tsar.[7]

5 M. Khudiakov, *Ocherki po istorii Kazanskogo khanstva* (Kazan': Gosudarstvennoe izdatel'stvo, 1923; reprinted Kazan': Fond TIAK, 1990), pp. 49–80; Michael Khodarkovsky, *Russia's Steppe Frontier: The Making of a Colonial Empire, 1500–1800* (Bloomington: Indiana University Press, 2002), pp. 91–100.

6 Ibid., pp. 81, 100–7.

7 L. A. Iuzefovich, '*Kak v posol'skikh obychaiakh vedetsia . . .*' (Moscow: Mezhdunarodnye otnosheniia, 1988), p. 5.

The first ones to recognise the new status of the tsar as a successor to the khans of the Golden Horde were those most interested in seeking Moscow's economic and military assistance. After the conquest of Kazan', recognising the sovereignty and supremacy of the Muscovite ruler, the Nogais began to refer to Ivan IV as the 'White Tsar' more frequently, while one Nogai mirza, Belek-Bulat, decided to surpass others in his flattery and called Ivan IV 'the son of Chingis'.

The Nogais of Ismail and Belek-Bulat mirzas, whose pastures were located along the banks of the Volga, remained Moscow's crucial allies. The fact that Moscow's ambitions did not end with the annexation of Kazan' was made clear in Ivan's letters to Ismail mirza in early 1553. Ivan asked Ismail to let him know of an opportune moment to begin their campaign against Astrakhan' and to advise him how best to conquer the Crimea.[8]

In the spring of 1554, following Ismail's advice, Ivan sent an army of 30,000 men down the Volga to rendezvous with Ismail's Nogais and to install on the Astrakhan' throne a Muscovite and Nogai protégé, Dervish Ali from the Astrakhan' dynasty. Unlike the conquest of Kazan', the conquest of Astrakhan' took place without much struggle or drama. The Astrakhan' khan, Yamgurchi, fled to Azov with no attempt to resist the Muscovite siege of the city, and Moscow declared Dervish to be the new khan of Astrakhan'. Ismail was given thirty Muscovite musketeers and expected to guard the land approaches to Astrakhan', while Ivan was to secure the water routes.

Ismail's delivery of Astrakhan' into Muscovite hands set off anew the dormant hostilities between the Nogai chiefs. As in the past, the internal wars among the Nogais were waged along the factional lines of a pro-Russian versus an anti-Russian coalition. In early 1555 the members of the victorious pro-Russian coalition assumed the leadership positions among the Nogais and Ismail became their *beg* (a supreme chief). When in the following year the recalcitrant Nogai nobles rebelled against Ismail *beg* and Dervish khan chose to forge close ties with the Crimea, Ivan IV dispatched his army against Astrakhan' once again. Dervish khan fled and Astrakhan' fell without any resistance. This time, however, as in his experience with Kazan', Ivan decided to rely on the puppet Chingisids no longer. Astrakhan' was now annexed and was henceforward ruled by the appointed Muscovite *voevodas* (military governors).[9]

8 *Prodolzhenie drevnei rossiiskoi vivliofiki*, vol. IX, pp. 64–6, 80, 81.
9 Ibid., pp. 122–6, 152–6, 163–8; V. V. Trepavlov, *Istoriia Nogaiskoi Ordy* (Moscow: Vostochnaia literatura, 2001), pp. 263–4, 297–9.

A foothold in the North Caucasus

The Muscovite annexation of Astrakhan' transformed Moscow overnight into a significant player in the Caucasus region. Throughout the early 1550s, the envoys of various Kabardinian princes from the Piatigorsk region in the North Caucasus arrived in Astrakhan' and Moscow. They came to explore the possibility of a military alliance against their adversaries: the Crimeans in the west and the Kumyks in the east. The Crimean khan continued to demand a levy of Kabardinian boys and girls, who were in high demand at the Ottoman court. Any refusal to supply the youths invited punitive raids from the Crimea. On the other side, to the east, the Kabardinian villages suffered from the debilitating raids of the Kumyks. Ruled by the *shamkhal* (a title of a Kumyk ruler) from his residence in Tarki in northern Daghestan and closely allied with the Crimeans and Ottomans, the Kumyks were one of the most significant military and economic powers in the North Caucasus. The slave trade in captured Kabardinians, Georgians, and other peoples of the Caucasus was a vital source of revenue for the Kumyks, who sold their human booty to the merchants from Persia and Central Asia at the thriving slave markets in the Kumyk town of Enderi (Andreevskaia in Russian). Enderi together with Kaffa, the Ottoman port in the Crimea where the human cargo from the Slavic lands had been sold and shipped to distant lands, were the two most important slave-trading centres in the region.

One group of the Kabardinian nobles led by their grand prince Temriuk Idarov was particularly enthusiastic about the newly founded alliance with Moscow. In exchange for serving Moscow's interests, Temriuk expected Moscow's help in protecting his people from the Kumyk raids and in suppressing the rival Kabardinian princes. Perceived in terms of traditional political culture, Temriuk was to be Ivan IV's *kunak,* that is, a valued guest, friend or ally. From Moscow's point of view, however, Temriuk's relationship with the tsar could only be that of a subject with his ruler. The notion that the Kabardinians became Muscovite subjects as early as the 1550s was construed by the Muscovite chroniclers of the latter day and uncritically accepted into the historiographical tradition. More than two centuries later, after the Ottoman Porte was compelled to concede that the Kabardinians were now in Russia's sphere of influence, the Kabardinian nobles refused to swear allegiance to Russia insisting that they had always been Russia's *kunaks*, but not subjects.[10]

---

10 *Akty, sobrannye Kavkazskoi Arkheograficheskoi kommissiei*, 12 vols. (Tiflis, 1866–83), vol. 1 (1866), p. 91.

Whatever the differences in the interpretation of their relationship, both the Kabardinians and Muscovites were keenly interested in establishing close ties between them. Probably few expected at the time that these ties would become so close. In 1561, shortly after the death of his first wife, Ivan IV married the daughter of Temriuk Idarov. She was brought to Moscow, baptised, named Mariia and remained Ivan IV's wife until her death in 1569.[11] The marriage was the most eloquent testimony to Moscow's ambitions in the Caucasus and its first attempt to establish a foothold there through the loyal Kabardinian princes.

The royal marriage with the Kabardinian princess may have been prompted by more than geopolitical goals. The Muscovite officials believed that Kabardinians were Orthodox Christians before they became Muslims, and because the influence of Islam on the Kabardinians was barely discernible, Moscow hoped to have them converted or reconverted without much difficulty. In 1560, when dispatching Muscovite troops to assist the Kabardinians against the Kumyks, Ivan also included several priests, who were instructed to baptise the Kabardinians. But if any major conversion of the Kabardinians was indeed envisioned, it did not happen. Achieving Moscow's missionary goals as well as military objectives proved to be a more formidable task than Moscow expected.[12]

Moscow's increasing activity in the North Caucasus had finally attracted the attention of the Ottoman sultan, Süleyman the Magnificent. Despite initial concern over Moscow's conquests of Kazan' and Astrakhan', the issue of containing Muscovite ambitions did not become a priority while the Porte was engaged in a protracted struggle with the Habsburgs in the West and Safavid Persia in the East. By the early 1560s, however, it became apparent that Moscow's rapid expansion southward along the Volga and Don rivers was threatening Ottoman strategic interests in the area and could no longer be ignored. The Don cossacks' raids disrupted land communications with the Ottoman fort of Azov (Azak), and the Russian military governors in Astrakhan' did not allow safe passage of Muslim pilgrims from the Central Asian khanates to Mecca.

In 1567, the sultan and khan discovered that the Muscovites were constructing Fort Tersk on the Terek River in the eastern corner of the North Caucasus. Moscow's expansion further south now suddenly endangered the Porte's vital

11 *Kabardino-russkie otnosheniia v XVI–XVIII v. Dokumenty i materialy*, 2 vols. (Moscow: AN SSSR, 1957), vol. 1, p. 9.
12 Ibid., p. 8: Michael Khodarkovsky, 'Of Christianity, Enlightenment, and Colonialism: Russia in the North Caucasus, 1500–1800', *Journal of Modern History* 71 (1999): 412–13.

communications with its newly acquired possessions on the western shore of the Caspian Sea and threatened the Crimea's control of parts of the North Caucasus and its Kabardinian subjects. The Porte revived the plan to send an expeditionary force in order to construct a canal connecting the Don and the Volga rivers. Ottoman success in building such a canal would have allowed Istanbul to conquer Astrakhan', to dominate the entire North Caucasus region and to control the trade routes connecting Bukhara, Khiva, Urgench and Tashkent with the Ottoman markets.

In 1567 news reached Moscow that the new Ottoman sultan, Selim II, was preparing an armada of 7,000 ships to sail to Azov under his personal command, and then he and the Crimean khan would set out against Astrakhan'. The Crimean khan, Devlet Girey, expressed his concern over Moscow's expansion to the Muscovite envoy in the Crimea: 'Before Ivan used to send tribute (shuby, literally fur coats) to Kazan', and then he seized Kazan' and Astrakhan', and now he founded Tersk.' With the support of an Ottoman army behind him, the Crimean khan wrote to Ivan raising the price of peace with Moscow. Devlet Girey demanded that Ivan return Kazan' and Astrakhan' to the Crimea ('because from the old days Astrakhan' and Kazan' were part of the Muslim world and the iurt [apanage] of the khans of our dynasty'), send valuable and numerous presents and give up building a fort on the Terek River. Otherwise, the khan warned, there would be no peace.[13]

In the spring of 1569 a large Ottoman–Crimean force set out on the campaign. Digging a canal between the Don and the Volga at their nearest point proved to be too difficult an undertaking, and the work was soon abandoned. The Ottoman–Crimean expeditionary force approached Astrakhan' in September 1569. Instead of continuing the campaign so late in the season, the decision was made not to storm the city but to build a fort nearby and winter there in anticipation of reinforcements in the following year. In the end, rumours of a large Russian army sailing down the Volga and a Persian army dispatched to assist Astrakhan' forced the Ottoman retreat.

Although a military fiasco, the Astrakhan' campaign of 1569 convinced Moscow that the Porte's concerns had to be taken more seriously. Ivan IV's assurances that he meant no harm to Muslims and the Islamic faith, and that he had conquered the Volga khanates merely to ensure their loyalty, did not

13 *Rossiiskii gosudarstvennyi arkhiv drevnikh aktov*, Moscow, Krymskie dela, f. 123, kn. 13, ll. 57, 66ob., 67, 71ob., 82, 83; E. I. Kusheva, 'Politika russkogo gosudarstva na Severnom Kavkaze v 1552–1572 gg.', *IZ* 34 (1950): 279–80; A. A. Novosel'skii, *Bor'ba Moskovskogo gosudarstva s tatarami v pervoi polovine 17 veka* (Moscow and Leningrad: AN SSSR, 1948), pp. 23–7; P. A. Sadikov, 'Pokhod tatar i turok na Astrakhan' v 1569 g.', *IZ* 22 (1947): 143–50.

satisfy Selim II. The sultan insisted that the regions of Astrakhan' and Kabarda in the Caucasus were traditional Ottoman domains with Muslim residents. He demanded that the pilgrims and merchants from Bukhara and elsewhere be allowed to proceed through Astrakhan' en route to Mecca. In 1571, eager to prevent another campaign against Astrakhan', which Moscow could ill afford to defend at the time, Ivan IV informed the sultan that Fort Tersk was being demolished and the Astrakhan' route reopened.[14] Propelled almost instantly into the forefront of a struggle with Islam, Moscow was not yet prepared for such a confrontation. For the time being, the government refrained from missionary or any other activity that could provoke the Ottomans.

The conquest of Siberia

While Moscow's ambitions in the Caucasus collided with the interests of its powerful regional contenders, the Islamic states of the Crimea, the Ottomans and the Persians, no such major power stood in Moscow's way in Siberia. Here no other state insisted on its sovereignty over the indigenous peoples or claimed religious affinity with the predominantly animist population. It was not until the Russians reached the distant frontiers on the Amur River in the second half of the seventeenth century that they were confronted with the competing interests of another powerful state, Ming China.

This absence of a rival sovereign state extending its claims to the Siberian lands and the commercial nature of the Siberian frontier may explain why the conquest and colonisation of Siberia were put into private hands, the powerful family of the Novgorod merchants and entrepreneurs, the Stroganovs. After all, the royal charters to the Stroganovs to colonise Siberia in the sixteenth century and a charter to the Russian-American Company to exploit Alaska in the nineteenth century are the only two known instances, short-lived as they were, when the colonisation of the new frontiers was entrusted to large commercial companies similar to the better-known cases in the history of the Western European expansion.

The Stroganovs' success in colonising the Kama River region, which Ivan IV had entrusted to them in a charter of 1558, encouraged Ivan IV to issue a series of similar charters granting the Stroganovs a twenty-year exemption from customs and taxes and the right to construct the forts and recruit its own military in order to colonise the region east of the Urals.

14 *Kabardino-russkie otnosheniia v XVI–XVIII vv.*, vol. i, no. 10, p. 20; no. 13, p. 26; no. 16, pp. 27–9; *Puteshestviia russkikh poslov XVI–XVII vv. Stateinye spiski* (Moscow and Leningrad: AN SSSR, 1954), p. 76.

Moscow's plans for further expansion were impeded by the forces of Kuchum Khan, the ruler of the rising Siberian khanate. A former part of the Golden Horde, the Siberian khanate mostly comprised the territory between the Tobol' and Irtysh rivers. When in 1563 Kuchum seized the throne of the khan, he only rightfully restored the rule of the Chingisid dynasty over the Siberian khanate, which was wrested away from Kuchum's grandfather Ibak (Abak) in 1495 by the local nobles of the Toibugid clan. In the following decades, relying on the military force of the Nogais and Bashkirs, Kuchum imposed tribute on the local Khanty and Mansi peoples and created a powerful khanate, which he ruled from his winter residence in Sibir' located at the confluence of the Tobol' and Irtysh rivers.[15]

It was not long before the reach of the Stroganovs' entrepreneurial activity encroached on the borders of the khanate. The disputes over tribute-paying Khanty and Mansi led to clashes and raids against the Muscovite forts and settlements. Kuchum and his khanate represented a direct challenge to Moscow's claims of sovereignty over the newly vanquished peoples and to a Muscovite monopoly on the fur trade. Moreover, the privileges granted to the Stroganovs over the Kama region had expired, and the Stroganovs had strong incentives to expand and defend their enterprises east of the Urals. With these goals in mind, Grigorii Stroganov undertook to finance and organise a military expedition deep into Kuchum's khanate.

In the autumn of 1581, a Volga cossack named Ermak set out at the head of a 500-strong band of mercenaries to confront Kuchum Khan. Like the Spanish kings, who had hardly expected that the small bands of conquistadors under Hernando Cortez and Francisco Pizarro sent in the early sixteenth century to explore the Americas would in fact conquer the entire continent, neither the Stroganovs nor Ivan IV could have anticipated that Ermak's expedition would lay the foundation for a conquest of Siberia.

Sailing down the rivers, Ermak's mercenaries plundered the natives' villages and met no resistance until they reached the estuary of the Tobol' River. Here, in the autumn of 1582 the first major battle between the cossacks of Ermak and Kuchum Khan was fought. Kuchum's army was devastated by the cossack firepower and the subsequent battles proved again that the arrows of Kuchum's armed men were no match for the cossacks' muskets and cannon.

Kuchum fled and the cossacks triumphantly entered the khan's capital, the town of Sibir'. The joy of easy victory did not last for too long, however, and

15 Trepavlov, *Istoriia Nogaiskoi Ordy*, pp. 118–19; *Istoriia Sibiri*, 5 vols. (Leningrad: Nauka, 1968), vol. I, pp. 363–72; vol. II, pp. 26–35; Forsyth, *A History of the Peoples of Siberia*, pp. 19–27.

what the Tatar arrows failed to accomplish, the diseases and inhospitable environment did. In time, some of the local chiefs, who initially sided with Ermak, abandoned him after they began to realise that Ermak came simply to replace their former Tatar overlords. In the summer of 1585, isolated and lacking supplies and ammunition, Ermak and his followers were ambushed and killed.[16]

Moscow was caught unaware of the Stroganovs' expedition of 1581 and its initial reaction was that of outrage. Ivan IV chastised the Stroganovs for hiring a band of the unruly Volga cossacks without Moscow's consent. Equating their action with treason, Ivan IV accused the Stroganovs of needlessly provoking Kuchum Khan and causing the natives to raid the Muscovite forts and towns. He instructed the Stroganovs to have Ermak and his cossacks return to the Perm' region, and to make sure that it was done promptly, he dispatched a detachment of Muscovite troops with orders to bring Ermak's cossacks back to Perm'.[17] Ivan IV's reluctance to support the Stroganovs' adventure in Siberia eventually doomed Ermak and his companions.

Ivan IV's death in 1584 brought about a complete reversal of the government attitude towards the Siberian campaign. Without further delay, Moscow declared an annexation of Siberia and promptly dispatched the troops to secure Ermak's success. In 1586 the Muscovite troops laid the foundation of Fort Tiumen' and a year later of Tobol'sk. Both forts were built near the traditional and now ravaged residences of the Siberian khans: Tiumen' on the Tura River near Chimga Tura and Tobol'sk near the last residence of the khan, Sibir'.

In the following three decades, while the rival factions of the Chingisids and Toibugids continued to be at war with each other, the Muscovites consolidated their power in the region and expanded rapidly into central Siberia, reaching the western banks of the Enisei River. A sprawling network of the abundant Siberian rivers provided a perfect transportation. The mushrooming Muscovite towns and forts were witnesses to both the direction and the rapidity of the Muscovite advance. After the founding of Tobol'sk in 1587, the Muscovites sailed south-east erecting towns up the Irtysh River (Tara, 1594), up the Ob River (Surgut, 1594, Narym, 1596, Tomsk, 1604), and on the Enisei River (Eniseisk, 1619). Built on the edge where the Siberian forests receded into an open steppe, these forts became Russia's outposts in dealing with the various Turko-Mongol nomads of the steppe. In the north, the forts of Mangazeia, built on the Taz River in 1601, and of New Mangazeia on the Enisei in 1607, laid the ground for Muscovite dominance over the local Nenets.

16 *Istoriia Urala s drevneishikh vremen do 1861 g.*, pp. 153–9.
17 Aleksandr Andreev (comp.), *Stroganovy. Entsiklopedicheskoe izdanie* (Moscow: Belyi volk–Kraft, 2000), pp. 245–6.

In some sense, Siberia was conquered in spite of the Muscovite government, which preferred a slow and cautious pace of expansion. But when Kuchum's armies proved to be ineffective, Moscow quickly moved to build on the cossacks' bold actions. The colonisation of Siberia was no longer left in the hands of the Stroganovs but became a government enterprise similar to Muscovy's other frontiers. Another part of the former Golden Horde had been conquered and annexed by the Muscovite state. By the end of the sixteenth century, with the exception of the Crimea, the Muscovite rulers could claim control over the entire territory of the former Golden Horde.

The structure of the indigenous societies

Throughout its relentless expansion in the sixteenth century Moscow came across a variety of peoples, who spoke different languages, worshipped different gods and abided by different laws and customs. Yet along the entire expanse of the Muscovite frontiers in the north, east and south, the indigenous peoples had one undeniable feature in common: they were not organised into sovereign states but were instead traditional, kinship-based societies with non-existent or weak central authority. The degree of their social and political organisation varied from the perpetually fragmented kinship groups under the local chiefs of the reindeer-herding Nentsy of the arctic north, to the socially more complex agricultural societies of the Mordva, Chuvash, Mari and Udmurts of the Volga and Kama rivers, to the hunting and fishing societies of the Khanty and Mansi of western Siberia, and finally to the more socially stratified and centralised societies of the pastoral nomads of the Bashkirs or Nogais in the southern regions of the steppe.

The authority of the local chiefs was limited to their own *iurt* (an apanage; a territory controlled by a group of kin) or some other tribal unit. At times of war, one chief could become the supreme leader, but he was rarely able to sustain his authority after the military campaigns were over. One such Mansi chief of Pelym rose to power when he united local forces against the Muscovite forts and settlements after Ermak's departure in 1581 exposed the Muscovite rear. More centralised were the Nogais, whose society was a more cohesive confederation of tribes and clans with the established social and administrative hierarchy led by the supreme chief (*beg*).

The most complex and developed societies, socially and politically, were the Muslim khanates of Kazan', Astrakhan' and Siberia. The Turkic peoples, commonly known as Tatars, were the dominant element in these khanates ruled by the khans of a Chingisid lineage. Deprived of political power after the Muscovite conquests, the Turkic peoples and the Kazan' Tatars, in particular, remained an important part of the Islamic civilisation and the most sophisticated society among Muscovy's new and numerous subjects.

The terms of encounter

By the late sixteenth century the boundaries of the former Golden Horde in the east and south had largely become Muscovite boundaries and the ruling Turko-Mongol elites had been replaced by the Muscovite administrators. From the beginning, Moscow relied on the existing concepts and structures to rule over the vanquished population. The three basic concepts on which the relationship with the indigenous population was based were all of Turkic provenance: *shert'*, *amanat* and *iasak*. The first one implied an oath of allegiance and vassalage to the tsar, the second intended to secure such an oath by delivering the native hostages into the Muscovite hands and the third emphasised economic subservience to Moscow through the payment of fur or some other sort of tribute. Such at least was Moscow's view, which was not always shared by the natives.

In 1483 a military band of Muscovites crossed the Iron Gates or the Rocky Belt, as the Ural Mountains were referred to at various times. It was not the first time that various adventurers, mostly from the city of Novgorod, had crossed the Urals in order to explore the riches of the unknown lands and to establish trade with the local peoples. However, when they did so again in 1483, they arrived as representatives of Ivan III, the ruler of the rapidly expanding and self-consciously Orthodox Muscovite state. The Muscovite officials described one such encounter and the ceremony involved in striking a peace treaty between the chiefs of the Khanty and Mansi peoples and the Muscovites:

> And their custom of making peace is as follows: they put a bear skin under a thick trunk of a cut pine tree, then they put two sabres with their sharp ends upwards and bread and fish on the bear skin. And we put a cross atop the pine tree and they put a wooden idol and tied it up below the cross; and they began to walk below their idol in the direction of the sun. And one of them standing nearby said: 'that who will break this peace, let him be punished by God of his faith'. And they walked about a tree three times, and we bowed to the cross, and they bowed to the sun. After all of this they drank water from the cup containing a golden nugget and they kept saying: 'you, gold, seek the one who betrays'.[18]

18 S. V. Bakhrushin, 'Ostiatskie i vogul'skie kniazhestva v XVI–XVII vv.', in his *Nauchnye trudy*, 4 vols. (Moscow: AN SSSR, 1952–9), vol. III, pt. 2 (1955), p. 152.

The same event was registered in the Russian chronicle, but described quite differently: 'and the local princes swore not to bear any ill-will, not to exhibit any violence, and to be loyal to the Grand Prince of Muscovy'.[19] Obviously, things did not look the same from the banks of the Siberian rivers and from Moscow. What the local chiefs considered a peace treaty struck with the newly arrived strangers, Moscow regarded as the chiefs' oath of allegiance to the grand prince, their submission to Moscow. The opening salvo of Russia's conquest of Siberia was made and continued to be based on mutual misconceptions. While Moscow attempted to perpetuate an image of the natives as the subjects of the tsar, the natives saw in Russians another military and trading partner.

It is likely that to some of the indigenous peoples, who were former subjects to the khans of the Golden Horde and later its splinter khanates, the terms of engagement were less ambiguous. Some simply continued the established practices, switching their allegiances and tribute from the old Turko-Mongol overlords to the new one in Moscow. This was typical of the peoples of the middle Volga region, or most of the Khanty and Mansi in western Siberia. Yet for many others Moscow's demands of unconditional vassalage, hostages and tribute were both incomprehensible and offensive.

Moscow's policy of demanding an immediate submission to the tsar was typical for both the southern and eastern frontiers. In 1589, for example, following his orders from Moscow, the commander of the recently rebuilt Fort Tersk in the North Caucasus instructed the Kumyk *shamkhal* to dispatch the envoys and to petition to become the tsar's subject or otherwise face military retribution.[20] In the same year, in response to the Muscovite demands for pledging loyalty and submitting hostages, the Kabardinian chief, Alkas, replied: 'I have reached an old age, and hitherto people believed my word in everything, and I have never given hostages or taken an oath to anyone.'[21] A few years later, on the Siberian frontier, the Muscovites received a more dramatic reply from the Kalmyk chief Kho-Urlük. Upon the first encounter with Kho-Urlük in 1606, the envoys from the Siberian town of Tara presented him with an ultimatum to swear allegiance to the Muscovite suzerain and surrender hostages, or else to vacate the land. Insulted by such demands, Kho-Urlük ordered the Muscovite envoys put to death.[22]

19 Ibid.; *PSRL*, vol. xxvi: *Vologodsko-Permskaia letopis'* (Moscow: AN SSSR, 1959), p. 277.
20 *Snosheniia Rossii s Kavkazom. Materialy izvlechennye iz Moskovskogo Ministerstva Inostran-nykh del, 1578–1613*, comp. S. L. Belokurov (Moscow: Universitetskaia Tipografiia, 1889), no. 10, p. 79; no. 12, p. 112.
21 Ibid., no. 11, pp. 142–3.
22 Ibid., no. 4, pp. 28–9.

In the end, however, the Kabardinian, Kalmyk and numerous other chiefs chose to comply with the Muscovite demands, which were accompanied by the irresistible offers of presents, annuities and military aid. In return for their oath of allegiance and hostages, the local chiefs were rewarded with cash, woollens, furs and various luxury items, 'so that other peoples would follow the example and come into submission. . .' Thus, Alkas consulted with his nobles (*uzden*) and agreed to Muscovite conditions, provided that Moscow paid him an annuity, let his people hunt and fish along the rivers freely, ferried them across the rivers and helped them against adversaries.[23]

Yet Moscow's objective of turning the natives into loyal, tribute-paying subjects remained unrealised for a long time. The natives continued to construe their relationship with Moscow in their own terms, which were pointedly different from Moscow's. The *shert'*, which Moscow conceived of as an oath of allegiance, was seen by the local chiefs as a peace treaty with mutual obligations. Providing hostages was one of the concessions offered by the local chiefs to Moscow's adamant demands for such human surety. Moscow's assurances to treat the hostages as honourable guests and reward them upon return helped the chiefs to convince their kin that this was the only way to secure a peace treaty and receive benefits from Moscow. In the North Caucasus, for example, such 'hostages' appeared to be more military liaisons than hostages. For several years they resided in Fort Tersk with their retinues and joined Muscovite military campaigns in return for generous rewards and payments.[24]

Even *iasak*, which is usually considered to be a tribute or tax paid by the natives to Moscow and an unquestionable sign of their submission, was in reality a fur trade, an unequal exchange between the equal parties. One contemporary observer commented that the native chiefs were collecting furs from their own people and bringing them to the Muscovite officials voluntarily. And many a Muscovite official bemoaned the fact that without the expected payments in kind, or presents in Muscovite vocabulary, the natives refused to offer their furs.[25]

Finally, annual payments and intermittent presents which in Moscow's eyes were annuities and favours granted by the tsar to the local chiefs in exchange for their allegiance, had been regarded by the natives as a rightful form of tribute or payments due to them as a condition of a peace treaty. When such payments did not arrive on time or were brought in insufficient amounts, the

23 Ibid., no. 10, p. 77; no. 11, pp. 142–3.
24 Ibid., no. 11, pp. 142–3; no. 19, p. 305.
25 *Istoriia Sibiri*, vol. 1, p. 369; S. V. Bakhrushin, 'Iasak v Sibiri v XVII v.', in his *Nauchnye trudy*, 4 vols. (Moscow: AN SSSR, 1952–9), vol. III, pt. 2 (1955), pp. 71–5.

Nogai, Kabardinian, Kalmyk and other chiefs felt free to launch raids against Muscovy to demand the restoration of the status quo.

In the seventeenth century, Moscow and its restless neighbours along the frontiers would continue to struggle in defining and redefining the terms of their relationship. Time, however, was on Moscow's side. We shall revisit these issues at greater length in Chapter 22. Suffice it to recapitulate here that from the time of the initial encounter Moscow and the natives perceived each other in different terms and construed different realities which continued to coexist along the Muscovite frontiers.

Methods of conquest

Contested vocabularies and terms of engagement notwithstanding, one undeniable reality remained: Moscow's expansion in the sixteenth century was made possible by its overwhelming military, economic and political superiority vis-à-vis the disparate peoples along Muscovy's northern, eastern and southern frontiers. Everywhere the conquests were facilitated by an almost perpetual state of warfare between and among the tribal societies and the rival chiefs. Some chiefs sought Moscow's assistance against the contenders for power and before long found themselves completely dependent on Moscow. Other chiefs were won over by various forms of early modern economic aid: payments, presents, trade privileges, exemptions from customs, and bribes. Often the local chiefs requested that the Muscovites build a nearby fort for their protection. Thus, the construction of Fort Sviiazhsk near Kazan' could not have taken place without the co-operation of some of the Chuvash and Mari chiefs, Fort Tersk in the North Caucasus without the Kabardinian chief, Temriuk Idarov and his descendants, Forts Tomsk and Eniseisk in central Siberia without the Mansi chief, Alachev, and Fort Mangazeia in northern Siberia without the chief of the Nenets tribe of the Mongkansi.[26]

While some native chiefs and princes chose to serve Moscow's interests so they could aggrandise their power among their own people, numerous others preferred to leave their kin and settle in the Muscovite lands. Indeed, it was Moscow's long-standing policy to employ and actively recruit the services of the native elites. At first, content to join the Moscow grand princes on occasional military campaigns in return for rewards, various indigenous princes were soon ready to settle in Muscovy and perform military service in exchange

26 *Kabardino-russkie otnosheniia v XVI–XVIII vv.*, vol. 1, no. 10, p. 20; *Narody Sibiri*, ed. M. G. Levina and L. P. Potapova (Moscow: AN SSSR, 1956), pp. 573–4; Forsyth, *A History of the Peoples of Siberia*, p. 36.

for a stable income: grants of land, supplies of grain, cash and generous gifts. The increasing number of such renegade native princes in Moscow's service was directly proportional to the increasing turmoil in their own societies.

One of the best-known, if somewhat exceptional, cases was the arrival in Moscow of Kasim, the son of the khan of the Golden Horde, Ulu-Muhammed. In 1452, Grand Prince Vasilii II granted Kasim a frontier town in the Meshchera lands (Meshcherskii gorodok). Later known as Kasimov, it became the residence for numerous members of the Chingisid dynasty for over two centuries. At first an autonomous Muslim enclave on the Muscovite frontier ruled by the legitimate khans, it soon became a puppet khanate within Muscovy and a convenient springboard to install the loyal Chingisids in Kazan' and Astrakhan'.[27]

After the initial conquest of Kazan', Moscow chose to resort to the same policy of forced resettlement and exchange of populations which it traditionally applied in the Muscovite lands proper. Thus, the Tatars were expelled and some resettled as far as Novgorod and Russian Orthodox townsmen and peasants were brought in to settle in the Kazan' area. However, the incendiary nature of such policies became apparent shortly thereafter. The government realised that expanding into lands with non-Russian and non-Christian populations required a more gradual approach.[28]

Likewise, the initial zeal in asserting the victory of the Christian arms over the Muslim khanate by burning the mosques of Kazan' and converting the Muslims by force had quickly abated. Facing local revolts and the threat of the Ottoman–Crimean intervention, Moscow had to postpone any immediate plan for transforming the Muslim lands into Christian ones. The religious conversion of the non-Christians did not cease, but any large-scale evangelisation had to wait for better times. Moscow was compelled to resort to a more gradual and pragmatic approach which prevailed until the early eighteenth century. (For a more detailed discussion of the issue of the religious conversion in the seventeenth century, see Chapter 22 below.)

While the threat of conversion to Christianity by force was avoided for the time being, the fears and rumours that such conversion was imminent

27 V. V. Vel'iaminov-Zernov, *Issledovanie o Kasimovskikh tsariakh i tsarevichakh*, 4 vols. (St Petersburg: Imperatorskaia Akademiia Nauk, 1863–87), vol. 1 (1863), pp. 13–28. Edward Keenan observes correctly that Kasimov must have been given to Kasim upon agreement between Vasilii II and Ulu-Muhammed ('Muscovy and Kazan, 1445–1552: A Study in Steppe Politics', unpublished Ph.D. thesis, Harvard University, 1965, p. 397). The role of Kasimov in the Muscovite–Crimean relations under Ivan III is discussed by Janet Martin, 'Muscovite Frontier Policy: The Case of the Khanate of Kasimov', *RH* 19 (1992): 169–79.

28 M. K. Liubavskii, *Obzor istorii russkoi kolonizatsii*, reprint edn (Moscow: Izdatel'stvo Moskovskogo Universiteta, 1996), pp. 246–7; Janet Martin, 'The Novokshcheny of Novgorod: Assimilation in the Sixteenth Century', *Central Asian Survey* 9 (1990): 13–38.

drove many non-Christians to flee their lands. Some were expelled, others chose to flee to avoid the new landlords, administrators and tax collectors. The Muscovite conquests, particularly in the most densely populated mid-Volga region, resulted in a massive migration of the native population further east and south-east. By the early eighteenth century, some of the migrant Mari, Chuvash, Udmurts and others in the Bashkir lands formed a special social category of registered peasants, known as *tepter* (from *defter* – a registry book, in Turkic languages). By the middle of the nineteenth century, there were about 300,000 of them: they were all Muslim and were now listed as Bashkirs.

The newly conquered territories were ruled haphazardly. The official policies were a typical combination of carrots to those nobles and chiefs who proved to be loyal and sticks to the recalcitrant ones. Of course, the ultimate 'carrots' were reserved for those who chose to convert to Orthodox Christianity: the nobles could retain their lands, status and privileges and the commoners were promised temporary exemptions from taxes and one-time payments in cash or in kind.

Moscow's policies towards its new non-Christian subjects and Muscovite practices often happened to be far apart. The reality of governing the remote frontier regions populated by different peoples who spoke different tongues and abided by different laws proved to be far more ambiguous than the government's decrees allowed. The Muscovite government in the frontier regions was rife with corruption with the frontier administrators often subverting the very laws they were supposed to enforce. Thus, despite the government order banning the construction of new mosques in the Kazan' region, many new mosques were erected and the Church officials squarely laid the blame on the shoulders of the local governors. In Siberia, to secure the supplies of furs, the government tried to limit the conversion of the natives, who would otherwise be resettled among the Muscovites and stop delivering *iasak*. But the conversion of the natives to Christianity was one of the surest ways for the corrupt local officials to enrich themselves: the converts were often enslaved by the government officials, sold into slavery to others, or exploited in a number of different ways. In the seventeenth century, the instructions to each new governor sent to administer Siberian towns strictly forbade the government officials to enslave or sell the new converts.[29] It may not be much of an exaggeration

---

29 *AI*, 5 vols. (St. Petersburg: various publishers, 1841–2), vol. I (Tipografiia Ekspeditsii zagotovleniia Gosudarstvennykh bumag, 1841), no. 209, p. 449; vol. III (Tipografiia II Otdeleniia Sobstvennoi E. I. V. Kantseliarii, 1841), no. 1542, pp. 244–5.

to suggest that Moscow expended no less an effort in fighting the corruption of its own officials than it did in subduing the natives.

* * *

By the end of the sixteenth century Muscovy was dramatically transformed from the backwater principality ruled by the grand prince to one of the largest empires, whose rulers could no longer be dismissed as over-ambitious upstarts by other major powers. At the time, unable to challenge its neighbours in the west, Moscow pursued relentless expansion in all other directions. Building on the previous colonisation of the northern regions undertaken by Novgorod, Moscow's expansion in the north and north-east came across little notable resistance. The native population was quickly overwhelmed by a combination of state, peasant and monastery colonisation of their lands.

In the east and particularly in the south, the challenges were more formidable. In the east, Moscow's expansion was largely driven by commercial concerns with the primary goal to secure the supplies of furs at all costs: trade, tribute or whatever combination of the above. In the south, Moscow's objectives were military and geopolitical: to secure its frontiers from constant predations and to turn their restless nomadic and semi-nomadic neighbours into reliable auxiliaries. With the exception of the brief interlude by the Stroganovs, the matters of colonisation in the east and south were entirely in the hands of the state.

The expansion of Muscovy was occurring at the same time as other European empires were expanding overseas. The New Worlds of both the Europeans and Muscovites included the territories occupied by large numbers of animists. What set the Muscovite empire apart from its European counterparts, however, was that it expanded into the contiguous territories populated by Muslims in addition to the animists. Only one other European power, Spain, found itself in the same situation in the fifteenth century when it expanded into the lands occupied by the Muslims. Spain's 'final solution' of purging itself of any non-Christian elements, Muslims and Jews, was quite different from Moscow's. Unable and unwilling to apply the Spanish solution, the Christian rulers of Russia would continue to rule over a heterogeneous empire with a large number of Muslim subjects. In this sense, Russia was much more like an Ottoman empire, where Muslim sultans ruled over their many Christian subjects.

15

The Orthodox Church

DAVID B. MILLER

In 1448 Grand Prince Vasilii II of Moscow and a council of bishops of the see of Kiev and all Rus' within his control elevated Bishop Iona of Riazan' to the office of metropolitan. They did so to forestall the appointment of a metropolitan unsympathetic to Moscow and, worse, sympathetic to the union with Rome concluded at Florence in 1438. Vasilii and the bishops expected that an Orthodox patriarch of Constantinople would consecrate Iona, but in 1453 Constantinople fell to the Turks. By the time Iona died in 1461, Vasilii and his bishops agreed that his elevation without the patriarch's approval was canonical. Moscow's rulers and their prelates chose Feodosii (1461–4) and Filipp (1464–73) to succeed Iona with the title 'metropolitan of all Rus''. But the Rus' they administered was commensurate with the authority of the Muscovite state. Moscow's metropolitans continued to claim jurisdiction over the Lithuanian and Novgorod eparchies, but they were to administer only those coming under Muscovite rule. Yet Muscovites interpreted Iona's elevation in a manner that accorded the see an exceptional destiny. In one of many letters demanding that they accept him, Iona told the Orthodox bishops of Lithuania that, when Constantinople accepted union with Rome, it forfeited divine protection and fell to the Turks. Another letter said that Iona was 'by God's will installed in this great office . . . by all the archbishops and bishops of the present Orthodox great Russian autocracy of the sovereign and my son the Grand Prince Vasilii Vasil'evich'.[1]

The structure of the Church was as rudimentary when its Council of One Hundred Chapters (*Stoglav*) met in 1551 as it had been in Iona's time. Nine bishops and archbishops were in attendance. A tenth eparchy was created in 1552 for Kazan'. By 1589 Pskov became the eleventh. The vastness of the metropolitanate and its eparchies, and eparchial traditions of autonomy, made

---

1 *Russkaia Istoricheskaia Biblioteka*, 39 vols. (St Petersburg: Arkheograficheskaia kommissiia, 1872–1927), vol. VI (1908), cols. 622–3, 627–32.

supervision of the parish clergy impossible. The Church's solution resembled that of Moscow's rulers. It appointed plenipotentiaries called 'tenth men' (*desiatel'niki*) to administer the ten districts of each eparchy. The 'tenth men' collected tithes from parishes and adjudicated cases falling under Church law. Their courts had jurisdiction over the clergy and, in cases of heresy, witchcraft, sexual infractions and family law, also over the laity. On Church lands they shared jurisdiction with civil courts in matters pertaining to Church properties and crimes threatening public order. Like the ruler's governors, they had arbitrary powers and, given the inability of the Church to pay them, lived from a share of the tithe and from fees for court judgements. Most were laymen and their titles – boyars, junior boyars (*deti boiarskie*), clerks – mimicked those of the ruler's officialdom. Parishioners or estate owners recruited priests who went to bishops for ordination. Most priests married locally and lived in rural settlements. They supported themselves by farming lands provided by the community, from fees for administering sacraments and from modest state subsidies. Priests viewed 'tenth men' as rapacious and resented being managed by laymen.[2] Needless to say, they were ill equipped to instruct the clergy, let alone their parishioners, in what it meant to be Christian.

In 1914 E. V. Anichkov, equating an understanding of confessional theology with religious belief, wrote that only from the fifteenth century did the peasantry become Christian. Anichkov might have included elites in his indictment, because most evidence of religious culture concerns princes, landowners, prelates and monks.[3] It was a culture in which the literacy of the clerical elite, judging by the manuscript legacy extant in Rus', was within a narrow range of liturgical books, collections of sermons and homilies, chronicles and lives of saints. Until about 1500 little was translated locally and, excepting hagiography, original works were few. Prelates, originally from monastic brotherhoods, might obtain grounding in canon law and theology, and the aristocracy and urban well-to-do may have had a functional literacy in the language of clerks; but the populace, Archbishop Gennadii Gonzov of Novgorod complained to Metropolitan Simon about 1500, was so ignorant that 'there is no one to select to be a priest'.[4] Although they were not to ordain priests or deacons lacking

2 E. B. Emchenko, *Stoglav: Issledovanie i tekst* (Moscow: Indrik, 2000), p. 255; Evgenii Golubinskii, *Istoriia russkoi tserkvi*, 2 vols. (Moscow: Universitetskaia Tipografiia, 1900–22), vol. II, pt. 2, pp. 7–61; Paul Bushkovitch, *Religion and Society in Russia* (New York: Oxford University Press, 1992), pp. 22–3.
3 E. V. Anichkov, *Iazychestvo i Drevniaia Rus'* (St Petersburg: M. M. Stasiulevich, 1914), p. 306.
4 *AI*, vol. I (St. Petersburg: Arkheograficheskaia kommissiia, 1841), p. 147; Francis J. Thomson, 'The Corpus of Slavonic Translations Available in Muscovy', in Boris Gasparov and

a proper education, prelates had little choice but to do so. Yet it would be a mistake to view popular religiosity as other than rich, diverse and, by the sixteenth century, distinctive.

Popular religiosity

Russian Orthodoxy added many feasts to the liturgical cycle inherited from Constantinople. But without regular or centralised procedures of canonisation, no calendar was the same. The *Stoglav* warned of lay persons who were false prophets of miracles or revelations, but central authorities, when confronted with popular cults promoted by local clerics, usually capitulated.[5] Thus, in 1458 the clergy in Ustiug reported healings at the grave of the holy fool Prokopii (d. 1303). In 1471 a church went up at his gravesite; by 1500 there was a biography reporting miracles and powers of prophecy. Finally, in 1547 a council designated Prokopii a local saint (8 July). Nor could authorities ignore the Muscovite cult of the holy fool Vasilii the Blessed (d. 1552?). His ostensibly foolish behaviour and insults – even to the ruler – followed from an ability to see truths invisible to others. When his grave became known for healings, Tsar Fedor I had Vasilii reburied in a chapel adjoining the church of the Intercession on Red Square in 1588. So great was his following that the church to which his chapel was attached to this day is known by his name (St Basil's).[6] But most saints entering the calendar in the sixteenth century – sixteen of at least twenty-one – were monastic founders whose successors exhumed their relics and promoted their miracles. For example, Hegumen Gelasii initiated the cult of Savva Visherskii who had founded a monastery near Novgorod in the 1450s. It became famous because Archbishop Iona had hagiographer Pakhomii the Serb write Savva's biography. The Church recognised Savva a 'national' saint by 1550. Of fourteen 'earlier' saints about whom hagiographers wrote biographies, eight were monks and one a nun.

Muscovite expansion shaped the accretion of new feasts. After its conquest by Moscow, Novgorod prelates refused to observe feast days of Muscovite

Olga Raevsky-Hughes (eds.), *Slavic Cultures in the Middle Ages* (*Christianity and the Eastern Slavs*, vol. 1) (Berkeley: University of California Press, 1993), pp. 179–86; Emchenko, *Stoglav*, pp. 285–6; Jack E. Kollmann, Jr., 'The Stoglav Council and Parish Priests', *RH* 7 (1980): 66–7, 74–6.

5 Richard D. Bosley, 'The Changing Profile of the Liturgical Calendar in Muscovy's Formative Years', in A. M. Kleimola and G. D. Lenhoff (eds.), *Culture and Identity in Muscovy, 1359–1584* (Moscow: ITZ-Garant, 1997), pp. 26–38; Emchenko, *Stoglav*, pp. 311–12.

6 *Slovar' knizhnikov i knizhnosti Drevnei Rusi*, vol. 11, ed. D. S. Likhachev (St Petersburg: Nauka, 1988–9), pt. 1, pp. 322–4; Natalie Challis and Horace W. Dewey, 'Basil the Blessed, Holy Fool of Moscow', *RH* 14 (1987): 47–59.

saints. Thus, hegumens of its major monasteries refused to participate when Gennadii, the archbishop appointed by Moscow, organised a procession on 8 December 1499 during which he conducted services to Moscow's metropolitan saints Peter and Aleksei. Gennadii thereupon compromised; in a procession a week later the hegumens joined him in a procession that included services to the Muscovites, but also to St Varlaam Khutynskii of Novgorod.[7] Metropolitan Makarii vigorously promoted the nationalisation of the calendar. In 1547 a council recognised as 'all-Russian' saints eighteen persons whose feasts had been celebrated locally. Makarii gained recognition for at least fifteen more 'all-Russian' saints, probably at a council in 1549. Reflecting on the canonisations in his 'Life of Savva Krypetskii of Pskov' (1555), hagiographer Vasilii wrote that the Russian land, like Constantinople, the second Rome, radiated with feasts of many saints. 'There', he said, 'Mohammedan falsehoods of the godless Turks had destroyed Orthodoxy, while here the teachings of our holy fathers ever more illuminate the Russian land.'[8] The councils failed to establish procedures for canonisation and no calendar of 'all-Russian' saints resembled another. But universal calendars reflecting these canonisations henceforth were celebrated throughout Russia.

To celebrants the original meaning of numerous feasts became intertwined or confused with traditional rites coinciding with the summer and winter solstices or with periods in the agricultural cycle. On the eve of the Epiphany, for the Orthodox a celebration of Christ's baptism, revellers proceeded to the river to immerse themselves symbolically in the river Jordan in a rite of purification.[9] Passion Week, with its promise of renewal, and Trinity Saturday (the eve of Pentecost), contained echoes of reverence for the Slavic pagan sun god Iarilo, who in the spring was reborn to assure bountiful crops. On these occasions celebrants commemorated ancestors with offerings and enquired of the dead about prospects for their salvation. Peasants drove livestock to pasture on St Gregory's day and prayed to Elijah against drought. Russians also prayed to icons of saints and inscribed them on amulets integrating folkways – in which signs, portents and intercessions were phenomena capable of upsetting, or setting right again, the moral order – with faith that Christian saints possessed powers to heal, to benefit the salvation of souls or to keep

7 *Novgorodskie letopisi* (St Petersburg: Akademiia Nauk, 1879), pp. 59–64.
8 V. O. Kliuchevskii, *Drevnerusskie zhitiia sviatykh kak istoricheskii istochnik* (Moscow: Tipografiia Gracheva, 1871), pp. 227–8; G. Z. Kuntsevich, 'Podlinnyi spisok o novykh chudotvortsakh, *Izvestiia Otdela russkogo iazyka i slovesnosti Akademii nauk* 15 (1910), bk. 1, pp. 255–7; Bushkovitch, *Religion*, pp. 75–89.
9 Emchenko, *Stoglav*, pp. 313–15, 399–402; Bushkovitch, 'The Epiphany Ceremony of the Russian Court in the Sixteenth and Seventeenth Centuries', *RR* 49 (1990): 12–14.

families and communities in equilibrium. Mary, as Mother of God, was an intercessor for or against just about anything. Women turned to St Paraskeva-Piatnitsa, venerated originally as a martyr, to secure a marriage or a birth and to guide them in domestic matters. Women prayed to Saints Gurios, Samonas and Abibos to suppress hostile thoughts towards their husbands, to St Conon to cure children of smallpox.[10]

Muscovite liturgical practices changed constantly. In Pskov in the early fifteenth century the priest Iov, citing Photios, the Greek metropolitan of Rus', contended that the triple-hallelujah was prevalent throughout Orthodoxy while the monk Evfrosin insisted one should chant the hallelujah twice. But by 1510 Evfrosin was recognised locally as a saint and in 1551 the *Stoglav* ruled as canonical the double-hallelujah and the related custom of crossing oneself with two fingers instead of three. Complaints entered at the *Stoglav* Council reveal other examples of how folkways permeated liturgical practices: the 'desecration' of the altar with offerings of food used for banqueting, cauls thought to be favourable omens for the newborn, soap for washing the sanctuary and salt placed on the altar before sunrise on Holy Thursday, then used to cure ailments in persons and cattle. In dispensing holy water to parishioners for protections and cures, the line between priest and sorcerer blurred. To shorten services, clergy chanted different parts of the liturgy simultaneously (*mnogo-glasie*) making it incomprehensible. Believers acquiesced, revering the 'magic' of the service. Priests also transformed the spoken liturgy into a 'continuous song' and began to walk in deasil, or with the sun, in rites and processions in a manner informed by tradition. When Metropolitan Gerontii, citing Greek practice, questioned the canonicity of proceeding in deasil in consecrating the Dormition cathedral in 1479, Grand Prince Ivan III rebuked him.[11] By 1600 the liturgical cycle had become 'national'. Wedding rituals, like those described in the manual written in the 1550s 'On the Management of the Household' (*Domostroi*), were unions of clans carried out according to ancient custom. Their rites, such as the bride donning a matron's headwear (*kika*) symbolising her transformation from maiden into married woman, were anything but Christian. A priest sanctioned the ceremony, but a best man (*druzhka*) and a

10 V. G. Vlasov, 'The Christianization of the Russian Peasants', in Marjorie Mandelstam Balzer (ed.), *Russian Traditional Culture* (Armonk, N.Y.: M. E. Sharpe, 1992), p. 17; N. M. Nikol'skii, *Istoriia russkoi tserkvi*, 4th edn. (Moscow: Izdatel'stvo politicheskoi literatury, 1988), pp. 43–4, 47, 50–1; Eve Levin, 'Supplicatory Prayers as a Source for Popular Religious Culture in Muscovite Russia', in S. H. Baron and N. S. Kollmann (eds.), *Religion and Culture in Early Modern Russia and Ukraine* (DeKalb: Northern Illinois University Press, 1997), p. 101.
11 Emchenko, *Stoglav*, pp. 290–3, 304, 309–10, 313–15, 319; Vlasov, 'Christianization', pp. 24–6; Nikol'skii, *Istoriia*, p. 43; *Slovar'*, vol. II, pt. 1, pp. 262–4.

matchmaker (*svakha*) presided. Church weddings became common only in the fourteenth century, and were followed by folk rituals for bedding, announcing a coupling and the purification of the couple. Still, by the sixteenth the binding of unions with a sacrament performed by an authority above and outside the clans had become customary. Rituals for commoners in the *Domostroi* and accounts of imperial weddings were similar.[12]

In the building boom of the sixteenth century a 'national' style of church architecture emerged. One of its elements was the construction of masonry churches with sharply vertical 'tent' roofs and rows of arched gables inspired by wooden tower churches built by village craftsmen. The first (1529–32) was the church of Ascension in Kolomenskoe built by Grand Prince Vasilii III. Another element of the new style was the appearance of icon screens separating the nave from the chancel with rows of intercessory figures turned towards a central icon *Christ in His Powers* over the holy doors to the sanctuary. Some trace its inspiration to late Byzantine spirituality; others to the Russian manner of decorating wooden churches. The oldest extant high iconostasis, painted in the 1420s, is in the Trinity church of the Trinity-Sergius monastery. New technologies of masonry construction and design also appeared. When Metropolitan Filipp's new cathedral church of the Dormition in the Kremlin collapsed before it was completed in 1474, Ivan III brought in Pskov builders and an engineer from Bologna, Aristotle Fioravanti. Fioravanti's five-domed church, completed in 1479, resembled Russian cross-in-square churches, while using Italian engineering techniques and exhibiting tastes and skills of Pskov builders in working limestone, brick and decorative tile (see Plate 15). Pskov builders also introduced the belfry to Muscovite church complexes, the first being that in the single tall drum on the church of the Holy Spirit (1476) at the Trinity-Sergius monastery. In 1505 Ivan commissioned the Venetian Alevisio the Younger to build the cathedral of the Archangel Michael as a family burial church. In its pilasters, cornices and scalloped gables, it resembled Venetian churches. New cathedrals such as that in the Novodevichii convent in Moscow (1524–5) or the Dormition cathedral in Rostov (*c.*1600), replicated these innovations. In churches of St John the Baptist in Diakovo (*c.*1547), Saints Boris and Gleb in Staritsa (1558–61) and the Intercession (St Basil's, 1555–61) on Red Square, builders produced a complex variant to this style. The Intercession church consisted of eight chapels surrounding a central altar with a tent roof. Exaggerated helmet cupolas, replacing traditional shallow domes, capped the heightened

---

12 Daniel H. Kaiser, 'Symbol and Ritual in the Marriages of Ivan IV', *RH* 14 (1987): 247–62; Carolyn J. Pouncy (ed.), *The Domostroi* (Ithaca, N.Y.: Cornell University Press, 1994), pp. 204–39.

drums over each altar. Ideological schemes and Western models inspired its layout, and a Pskov builder oversaw its construction. By 1600 churches with multiple altars, tent roofs and helmet cupolas went up everywhere.[13] They blended forms, materials and techniques developed in many places, elements of popular religiosity and Renaissance innovations in engineering and design.

The huge quantity, variety and opulence of reliquaries, icons and other religious objects that laity donated to monasteries belie the view that its religiosity was a formality. Chronicle entries, such as that recording the appearance of an image of the Mother of God in 1383 over the River Tikhvinka in the Obonezhskaia territory of Novgorod, tell the same story. Its purported miracles attracted pilgrims. A century later bookmen entered new miracle tales into the Novgorod chronicle and Archbishop Serapion (1504–9) built a brick church to house the icon. In Moscow the cult entered the liturgical calendar and in 1524 Metropolitan Daniil wrote it into his 'history of Russia' known as the *Nikon Chronicle*. Complaints about the ubiquity of uncanonical or blasphemous icons reflected the Church's ambivalence about such 'appearances'. Even the court was complicit. Ivan Viskovatyi, Ivan IV's Keeper of the Seal, complained about icons with unprecedented imagery with which painters from Pskov and Novgorod redecorated Ivan IV's family church of the Annunciation after the fire of 1547.[14]

Reports of fires provide evidence that towns were filled with churches in which ordinary people shared liturgical experiences. The frequency of religious processions was another form of popular religiosity. They might be provincial celebrations like that in Ustiug in 1557 when its inhabitants proceeded with a cross to honour the raising of the church of St. Nicholas Velikoretskii. Or they could be great affairs like Metropolitan Filipp's processions on 30 April and 23 May, 1472, to inaugurate construction of the Dormition cathedral and to translate there the relics of metropolitans Photios, Kipriian and Iona.[15] No later than 1548 Metropolitan Makarii fashioned a court procession to celebrate Palm Sunday. Based upon a ritual he had observed in Novgorod, it re-enacted Jesus's

13 William Craft Brumfield, *A History of Russian Architecture* (Cambridge: Cambridge University Press, 1993), pp. 89–140, 501–15; cf. A. M. Lidov (ed.), *Ikonostas* (Moscow: Progress-Traditsiia, 2000); and George Majeska, 'Ikonostas', unpublished paper presented May 2003 at Dumbarton Oaks, Washington, DC.
14 *Slovar'*, vol. II, pt. 2, pp. 365–7; Emchenko, *Stoglav*, p. 376; David B. Miller, 'The Viskovatyi Affair of 1553–54', *RH* 8 (1981): 293–332.
15 K. N. Serbina (ed.), *Ustiuzhskii letopisnyi svod* (Moscow and Leningrad: AN SSSR, 1950), p. 109; *Ioasafovskaia letopis'*, ed. A. A. Zimin (Moscow: AN SSSR, 1957), pp. 76–7.

entry into Jerusalem by having the tsar, afoot, lead the metropolitan, mounted on a horse and followed by nobles and clerics, to the Intercession church on Red Square. For the Epiphany Feast of 1558, Ivan IV led the hierarchy and the court onto the Moscow River to a hole in the ice where Makarii blessed the water with a cross. After that he splashed Ivan's son and the nobility, commoners filed by to fill pots, children and the ill were immersed, some Tatars baptised and Ivan's horse brought to drink. The baptism on the symbolic River Jordan, the animals and the healings were elements of popular feasts.[16] Although many rural settlements lacked churches, peasants also primarily and most deeply expressed their religiosity in communal celebrations. When they could not, they resented it. In a petition to the archbishop of Novgorod in 1582 peasants and *deti boiarskie* in a remote parish requested they be allowed to attend a neighbouring church. The petitioners said their priest could not communicate with them because his church was far away and required a boat to get there; as a result their ill died without confessing, there were no prayers when mothers gave birth and the young were not baptised.[17]

Popular religiosity is incomprehensible apart from monasteries. No one knows how many existed at one time, but E. I. Kolycheva estimates that 486 monasteries were founded between 1448 and 1600. Typically, they began as hermitages or *sketes*. As they grew, metropolitans encouraged them to organise with rules of communal living. Monasteries were subordinate to a bishop or were patrimonial (*ktitorskie*) houses like the Kirillo-Belozerskii monastery, initially supported by Princes Andrei (d. 1432) of Mozhaisk and his son Mikhail (d. 1486) of Vereia.[18] Great houses maintained donation books recording gifts, copybooks with records of land grants and feast books that recorded names of benefactors. The names of provincial landowners predominate, but benefactors came from every category of free people. Donors made grants in return for prayers for their souls and those of family members and ancestors. Although the Orthodox never formulated a doctrine of purgatory, death rituals provided for memorial prayers for forty days. About 1400 believers began to think this inadequate to assure the salvation of kin, whether they had died recently or

16 Bushkovitch, 'Epiphany', pp. 1–14; Michael S. Flier, 'Breaking the Code: The Image of the Tsar in the Muscovite Palm Sunday Ritual', in Michael S. Flier and Daniel Rowland (eds.), *Medieval Russian Culture*, vol. II (Berkeley: University of California Press, 1994), pp. 214–32.
17 P. S. Stefanovich, *Prikhod i prikhodskoe dukhovenstvo v Rossii v XVI–XVII vekakh* (Moscow: Indrik, 2002), pp. 250–1.
18 E. I. Kolycheva, 'Pravoslavnye monastyri vtoroi poloviny XV–XVI veka', in N. V. Sinitsyna (ed.), *Monashestvo i monastyri v Rossii, XI–XX veka* (Moscow: Nauka, 2002), pp. 82–9.

long before. Their solution was to request commemorations at monasteries containing relics of intercessors and which could perform prayer rituals presumably in perpetuity. In exchange they gave monasteries gifts.[19] By 1500 the culture of commemoration became institutionalised in *sinodiki*, recording the names of those for whom donations were made. Iosif Volotskii founded a monastery in 1479 with a system in which a small sum bought a place in an 'eternal' (*vechnyi*) *sinodik*, a list read independently of the liturgical cycle. Fifty roubles purchased entry in a 'daily' (*posiavdnevnyi*) *sinodik*, a shorter list read at places in the liturgy for commemorations. Anniversary feasts cost 100 roubles. Other houses maintained analogous systems. The rich arranged commemorations at several houses. Requests for tonsure and burial near a miracle worker began in the late fifteenth century.[20]

Moscow's rulers made pilgrimages to monasteries to pray, underwrite feasts and give presents. Ivan IV often went on extended pilgrimages. Thus, on 21 May 1545 he visited the Trinity-Sergius monastery, houses in Pereiaslavl', Rostov and Iaroslavl', the Kirill and Ferapont monasteries near Beloozero, and the Dmitrii-Prilutskii monastery and three other houses near Vologda. Spouses of Muscovite rulers created a gendered cult of St Sergius. In 1499 Sophia Palaeologa, Ivan III's second wife, donated an icon cloth to the Trinity-Sergius monastery giving credence to a story that Sergius's intercession allowed her to give Ivan an heir, Vasilii III. Sixteenth-century ideologues wrote that the miracle resulted from a pilgrimage. Tsaritsa Anastasiia went on foot to Trinity in 1547 to pray for an heir, as did Tsaritsa Irina in 1585.[21] Elites, who scheduled memorial feasts and made tonsure and burial at monasteries part of their death rituals, sought by public displays to reinforce family and social identities. But it is useless to distinguish between popular and noble religiosity. Peasant visits are attested in miracle tales and in charters that show monasteries dispensed beer to ordinary folk at feasts by which they celebrated transition rites and commemorated ancestors. Laity constantly visited cenobite houses;

19 Daniel H. Kaiser, 'Death and Dying in Early Modern Russia', in Nancy Shields Kollmann (ed.), *Major Problems in Early Modern Russian History* (New York: Garland, 1992), pp. 217–57; Ludwig Steindorff, 'Klöster als Zentren der Tötensorge in Altrussland', *FOG* 50 (1995): 337–53.
20 Ludwig Steindorff, 'Sravnenie istochnikov ob organizatsii pominaniia usopshikh v Iosifo-Volokolamskom i Troitse-Sergievom monastyriakh v XVI veke', *Arkheograficheskii Ezhegodnik za 1996 g.* (Moscow: Nauka, 1998), pp. 65–78.
21 Nancy S. Kollmann, 'Pilgrimage, Procession and Symbolic Space in Sixteenth-Century Russian Politics', in Michael S. Flier and Daniel Rowland (eds.), *Medieval Russian Culture*, vol. II (Berkeley: University of California Press, 1994), pp. 163–81; Isolde Thyrêt, *Between God and Tsar: Religious Symbolism and the Royal Women of Muscovite Russia* (DeKalb: Northern Illinois University Press, 2001), pp. 21–39ff.

their faith blended folkways and Christian practice in a harmonious culture of commemoration.[22]

As much for economic and political reasons as out of piety, princes granted monasteries immunities from taxes and tariffs on their commerce, salt works, agriculture and fisheries. Ivan III halted the practice and even confiscated monastic lands in Novgorod. Thenceforth he and his successors controlled the appointment of hegumens to big houses and periodically inventoried monastic charters, causing some to be revoked. Paradoxically, Vasilii III gave monasteries generous gifts and Ivan IV lavish ones. During the prosperous 1530s–1550s and in the aftermath of the *oprichnina*, there were no restraints on the accumulation of property and the wealth of the great houses skyrocketed. By 1600 the Simonovskii monastery near Moscow owned over fifty villages in nineteen *uezdy* and the Trinity-Sergius monastery owned an estimated 118,000 hectares in forty *uezdy* and commercial and industrial holdings in over fifteen towns. Monasteries held at least 20 per cent of all arable land.[23]

All this wealth and the presence of monks from aristocratic families could not but undermine rules of communal property, equality of status and a simple life. Iosif Volotskii accorded the Simonovskii and Kirillo-Belozerskii monasteries a reputation for austerity, one he initially emulated at his monastery. Monks wore simple attire, ate and prayed as one and had no personal property. Unable to maintain this order, Iosif, or during the illness that killed him in 1515 co-hegumen Daniil, wrote a new rule. It provided for three classes of monks with graded privileges for food, dress and personal effects, and a more relaxed regime. At most monasteries monks from landowning families constituted a large component and most of the officers. Those who made donations in return for tonsure enjoyed incomes from donated property until they died; those without property were artisans, low-level managers or did menial tasks.[24] The career and writings of Nil Sorskii (d. 1508) explain why Iosif singled out the Kirillo-Belozerskii monastery for austerity. Nil was tonsured there and before 1489 travelled to centres of Orthodox spirituality on

22 Emchenko, *Stoglav*, pp. 330–5, 339–43; Vlasov, 'Christianization', pp. 20–1; Eve Levin, '*Dvoeverie* and Popular Religion', in Stephen K. Batalden (ed.), *Seeking God: The Recovery of Religious Identity in Orthodox Russia, Ukraine, and Georgia* (DeKalb: Northern Illinois University Press, 1993), pp. 45–6.
23 Kolycheva, 'Monastyri', pp. 99–109.
24 A. A. Zimin and Ia. S. Lur'e (eds.), *Poslaniia Iosifa Volotskogo* (Moscow and Leningrad: AN SSSR, 1959), pp. 296–319; K. I. Nevostruev (ed.), 'Zhitie prepodobnogo Iosifa Volokolamskogo, sostavlennoe Savvoiu, episkopom krutitskim', *Chteniia Obshchestva Liubitelei drevnei pis'mennosti* 2 (1865): 15–18, 24–31, 49–53, 61–5; and K. I. Nevostruev (ed.), 'Zhitie prepodobnogo Iosifa Volokolamskogo, sostavlennoe neizvestnym', ibid., 88–108; Kolycheva, 'Monastyri', pp. 89–95.

Mount Athos. This set Nil on a new spiritual path. He founded a semi-hermitic *skete* on the Sora River modelled on that of early holy men and on what Kirill's hermitage once was like; its monks supported themselves, prepared their own food and ate it in solitude; they had no property other than icons and books to guide their devotions. Nil wrote that silence and a simple life provided the only environment in which a monk might bring God into his heart. The means, citing Simeon the New Theologian and Gregory of Sinai, was to recite the prayer, 'Lord Jesus Christ Son of God, have mercy on me, a sinner'. In Byzantium it was a prayer of Hesychast mystics.[25] About 14 per cent of all monasteries were convents. Subsidiaries of male houses were small and possessed little property. Others were patrimonial houses like the Kremlin convent of the Ascension which Grand Prince Dmitrii I's widow Evdokiia (the nun Efrosiniia) founded in 1407. Vasilii III assured it a permanent existence in 1518/19 by building a masonry church to house Evdokiia's relics and by making it the burial church for grand princesses. The Novodevichii monastery, which Vasilii founded near Moscow in 1525, housed nuns from well-born families and a miracle-working icon, assuring it rich donations. By 1602–3 it had 141 nuns. Wealthy convents had social hierarchies reflecting that outside their walls. For a donation elite families entered female relatives on their rolls, or donors to male houses specified that on their death they or their widows be given cells. This elite controlled property, came and went on family business, had servants and ruled, subject to their patrons. Nuns, whose entry was not connected with a grant, were common sisters who did necessary labour and lived communally with less rations.[26]

Heresy

While Iosif and Nil refined their ideals, others were criticising traditional beliefs, rituals and institutions. In 1467 Metropolitan Filipp wrote to Archbishop Iona of Novgorod about popular animosity in Iona's eparchy towards the Church and its wealth. Archbishop Gennadii told Metropolitan Zosima that a Jew in the entourage of Mikhail Olel'kovich, who came from Kiev to be Novgorod's prince in 1471, had caused the unrest. He warned prelates that it had infected priests, deacons, officials and simple people. In 1487 Gennadii charged four men with heresy and sent them to Moscow for judgement. Ivan III and

25 M. S. Borovkova-Maikova, 'Nil Sorskogo predanie i ustav', *Pamiatniki drevnei pis'mennosti i iskusstva*, no. 179 (St Petersburg, 1912), esp. pp. 21–2, 88–9.
26 E. B. Emchenko, 'Zhenskie monastyri v Rossii', in N. V. Sinitsyna (ed.), *Monashestvo i monastyri v Rossii, XI–XX veka* (Moscow: Nauka, 2002), pp. 90, 245–84.

Metropolitan Gerontii exonerated one, found the others guilty of execrating icons and had them whipped. Gennadii thought this lenient and complained to Zosima that Gerontii (d. 1489) had allowed heretical priests Gavrilko and Denis to serve in Moscow, the latter at the Kremlin church of Michael the Archangel, and that Ivan's diplomat Fedor Kuritsyn protected them. Mobilising other bishops, Gennadii drove Aleksei from his church and compelled Zosima to convene another council. It met 17 October 1490, convicting some of desecrating icons and of the 'judaising' denial of Christ's divinity, and the monk Zakarii as a *strigol'nik*, referring to a Pskov heresy that denied the authority of simoniacal prelates. The council excommunicated and anathematised the heretics and sent them to Novgorod for punishment.[27] As long as Ivan favoured the governing faction that included Kuritsyn, freethinkers were immune from punishment in Moscow.

Gennadii and Iosif Volotskii were alarmed. By Gennadii's account, heretical preachers had reached credulous Christians throughout the eparchy. Moreover, Ivan appointed Kuritsyn's confederate Kassian archimandrite of Novgorod's Iur'ev (St George) monastery. The Moscow heretics were few in number, but influential. Grand Princess Elena was reputed to be one. It must have galled Gennadii and Iosif too that the heretics were literate clerics and laymen whose views were not supposed to count in religious affairs. It is certain they preached that it was idolatry to worship man-made symbols of the faith, that venerating relics was superstition and monasticism unnecessary. Gennadii also likened their beliefs to those of heretics who had denied the Trinity, saying they prayed like Jews. In their arguments, he complained, they cited passages from the Old Testament and texts called 'The Logic' (*Logika*) and 'The Six Wings' (*Shestokril*) unknown to him. 'The Logic' was informed by a rationalist approach to theology; the latter, an astronomical work, became important as the year 7000 approached, by our reckoning 1491/2. In eschatological lore, because the Lord created the world in seven days, it would be followed by 7,000 years of faith, after which Christians might expect chaos, Christ's second coming and a day of judgement. Its approach caused unease; when it passed without a stir, free thinkers ridiculed religious authority. Kuritsyn's version of a pseudo-letter of St Paul to the Laodicians, one of few surviving heretical writings, expressed a humanist Christianity.[28] Other heretics may have shared Kuritsyn's conviction that Christian piety derived from an individual conscience that privileged

27 *Russkaia Istoricheskaia Biblioteka*, vol. VI, cols. 715–20; N. A. Kazakova and Ia. S. Lur'e, *Antifeodal'nye ereticheskie dvizheniia na Rusi XIV – nachala XVI veka* (Moscow and Leningrad: AN SSSR, 1955), pp. 309–115, 373–86, 468–73.
28 Kazakova and Lur'e, *Dvizheniia*, pp. 265–9, 309–13, 315–73, 391–414.

human rationality. But most of the accused were clerics, so it is wrong to think of the heresy as a secular critique of Orthodoxy.

To confound the heretics Gennadii recruited bookmen, including two Greeks, the Dominican Veniamin, and two Lübeckers, printer Bartholomäus Ghotan and doctor Niklaus Bülow. Their great achievement was assembling the first complete Slavonic Bible in Muscovy in 1499. It was the source of later editions and the first printed Bible of Ivan Fedorov in West Bank Ukraine in 1580/1. Bülow translated Latin calendars and astronomy texts to compute a new paschal canon reaffirming Christ's second coming, and a translation of a medieval Latin refutation of Judaism.[29] Iosif Volotskii was the scourge of Moscow freethinkers. In the 'Book about the New Heresy' or 'Enlightener' (*Prosvetitel'*), which he wrote between 1502 and 1504 from reconstituted sermons, Iosif accused Ivan of abetting the heresy and said Zosima treated heretics lightly because he was a heretic. It was exceptional in equating the heresy with Judaism, an evil external to Orthodoxy. Gennadii said that Kuritsyn became a heretic after an embassy to Hungary in 1482–6.[30] Iosif's charge that the heretics proselytised Judaism under the guise of reforming Orthodoxy long has caused controversy because of its implication of unsavoury Jewish influences in Russia and counter-charges of Russian anti-Semitism. Ia. S. Lur'e has argued against Jewish influences, but Moishe Taube makes the case that the *Shestokril* and the *Logika* were translated from medieval Hebrew texts, identifies Gennadii's Kievan Jew as Zacharia ben Aharon and argues that Kuritsyn relied on a translation from Hebrew of the *Secretum secretorum* in the first section of the Laodicean Letter. No one disputes that the heretics solicited translations out of very Christian concerns.[31]

Having removed the court faction that included Kuritsyn, jailed his co-ruler Dmitrii and Dmitrii's mother Elena, and recognised Vasilii as sole heir in April 1502, Ivan III summoned Iosif to discuss what to do about heresy. According to Iosif, Ivan asked forgiveness for shielding heretics. In December 1504, Vasilii, Ivan and Metropolitan Simon convened a council that condemned Ivan-Volk Kuritsyn (sources last mentioned brother Fedor in 1500) and two others as

29 Ibid., pp. 137–46.
30 Ibid., pp. 320–73, 377, 391–414, 427–38, 466–77; Iosif Volotskii, *Prosvetitel' ili oblichenie eresi zhidovstvuiushchikh*, 4th edn (Kazan': Kazan'skii universitet, 1903), pp. 27–304.
31 Kazakova and Lur'e, *Dvizheniia*, pp. 74–91, 109–93; Ia. S. Lure', 'Istochniki po istorii "novoiavivsheisia novgorodskoi eresi" ("Zhidovstvuiushchikh")', *Jews and Slavs* 3 (1995): 199–223; M. Taube, 'The Kievan Jew Zacharia and the Astronomical Works of the Judaizers', *Jews and Slavs* 3 (1995): 168–98; M. Taube, 'The "Poem of the Soul" in the *Laodicean Epistle* and the Literature of the Judaizers', *HUS* 19 (1995): 671–85; M. Taube, 'Posleslovie k "Logicheskim terminam" Maimonida i eres' zhidovstvuiushchikh', in *In Memoriam: Sbornik Pamiati Ia. S. Lur'e* (St Petersburg: Atheneum-Feniks, 1997), pp. 239–46.

heretics and burnt them at the stake. In Novgorod heretics were burnt or imprisoned. Nil Sorskii's hostility to the heresy is documented. But Nil's disciple Vassian Patrikeev wrote that monks of the northern hermitages believed that, while the irreconcilable should be imprisoned, the Church should forgive the repentant. One disciple said Nil shared this view.[32] Nil probably concurred with Iosif about trying heretics, but parted company with him over the punishments.

Iosifites and non-possessors

In 1499 Ivan raided Novgorod's eparchial treasury. Blaming Ivan's heretical advisers, Archbishop Gennadii prepared a *sinodik* anathematising all who seized Church property and commissioned Veniamin's 'Short Sermon' (*Slovo kratka*) which used the legend that Roman Emperor Constantine I had issued a charter to the Pope that made Church lands sacrosanct.[33] Then, in August–September 1503 Ivan apparently convened a Church council and placed before it the question of Church lands. Ivan hardly contemplated anything as drastic as his Novgorod confiscations. The hierarchy was a necessary ally and his servicemen, by reason of grants to monasteries for memorial prayers, had a stake in the existing order. Replying to Ivan's purported agenda, Metropolitan Simon cited Constantine's charter and claimed that Ivan's 'ancestors' Grand Princes Vladimir (d. 1015) and Iaroslav (d. 1054) of Kiev had upheld it. The anonymous 'Other Sermon' (*Slovo inoe*), written then or soon after ostensibly to defend the Trinity-Sergius monastery's jurisdiction over the village of Ilemna, provides a gloss on the 'reply', saying Ivan sought to make the Church dependent on the state treasury and granaries. Towards this end, it said, Ivan summoned Nil Sorskii who testified that 'it is not becoming to monks to own villages'. Most likely the anonymous 'Quarrel with Iosif Volotskii' had it right, saying Ivan ordered Nil and Iosif to be present and that they took opposing sides.[34] The

32 Kazakova and Lur'e, *Dvizheniia*, pp. 217–22, 436–8; Iu. V. Ankhimiuk, 'Slovo na "Spisanie Iosifa" – pamiatnik rannego nestiazhatel'stva', *Zapiski Otdela rukopisei Russkoi gosudarstvennoi biblioteki* 49 (1990): 115–46; N. A. Kazakova, *Vassian Patrikeev i ego sochineniia* (Moscow and Leningrad: AN, 1960), pp. 253–77; A. I. Pliguzov, *Polemika v russkoi tserkvi pervoi treti XVI stoletiia* (Moscow: Indrik, 2002), pp. 57–80.
33 *Pskovskie letopisi*, vol. II, ed. A. N. Nasonov (Moscow: AN SSSR, 1955), p. 252; ' "Slovo kratka" v zashchitu monastyrskikh imushchestv', *ChOIDR* (1902), no. 2: pp. 31–2.
34 Zimin and Lur'e (eds.), *Poslaniia Iosifa*, pp. 322–6, 367; Kazakova, *Vassian*, p. 279; Nevostruev (ed.), 'Zhitie, sostavlennoe neizvestnym', pp. 112–20; Iu. K. Begunov, ' "Slovo inoe" – novonaidennoe proizvedenie russkoi publitsistiki XVI v. o bor'be Ivan III s zemlevladeniem tserkvi', *TODRL* 20 (1964): 351–2; *PSRL*, vol. VI (St Petersburg: Tipografiia Eduarda Pratsa, 1853), p. 49.

lack of an official record, the late provenance of sources mentioning a council and their tendentiousness, has troubled historians.[35] Yet, the council certainly took place. In the absence of a record, one must conclude that the Church's opposition caused Ivan to draw back. Given the stakes, it is understandable why contemporaries treated the abortive council with silence, and why Iosif's disciples and Nil's, with their own agendas, provided biased accounts of it.

For fifty years these factions contested what constituted Orthodox tradition. Monks from Iosif's monastery and other large houses defended monastic property rights and autonomy, shared Iosif's hatred of heresy and extended its definition to include their rivals. Most defenders of Nil's heritage were from northern hermitages. Known as Non-possessors (*nestiazhateli*) for their dedication to vows of poverty, they were willing to forgive heretics who repented. Their leader was Vassian, whom Ivan III tonsured and sent to the Kirillo-Belozerskii monastery when he disgraced his father Ivan Patrikeev in 1499. Vassian became Nil's disciple and returned to Moscow in 1509–10 when Vasilii III's officials re-examined monastic immunities. For contemporaries he interpreted the meaning of the councils of 1503 and 1504. A monk, he argued, should empty himself of material burdens to cultivate piety, Nil's inner way. Neither Greek saintly monks, Saints Antonii and Feodosii of the Kiev Pecherskii (Caves) monastery, nor Saints Varlaam Khutynskii, Sergius Radonezhskii and Kirill Belozerskii, he said, acquired property. Vassian's compilation of canon law (*kormchaia kniga*) was also hostile to landed monasticism.[36]

In 1518 Vassian found an ally in Maximos 'the Greek' (Maksim Grek), whom Vasilii recruited as a translator. Maximos was born Michael Tivolis into a noble family in Epirus. About 1492 Michael joined Greek émigrés in Italy. He knew John Lascaris and Marsilio Ficino, studied with Pico della Mirandola, helped Aldus Manutius print Greek classics, saw Savonarola in power and became a Dominican monk. Returning to Orthodoxy, Michael became the monk Maximos at the Vatopedi monastery on Mount Athos in 1505–6. Vasilii III refused to allow Maximos to return to Mount Athos. Subsequently, with a learning previously unknown in Russia, Maximos carried on a wide correspondence, wrote treatises on translation, onomastics and grammar, sermons about astrology, prophecy and apocryphal works, monographs on governance and polemics against other faiths. Iosifites viewed his learning with a suspicion reinforced by reports that he found Russian services provincial and liturgical

35 Pliguzov, *Polemika*, pp. 21–56, 330–86; R. G. Skrynnikov, *Krest i korona. Tserkov' i gosudarstvo na Rusi IX–XVII vv.* (St Petersburg: Iskusstvo, 2000), pp. 172–84.
36 Kazakova, *Vassian*, pp. 36–64, 232–3, 256–7, 272–4, 276–9; Pliguzov, *Polemika*, pp. 57–178, 253–7.

books full of errors, and because of his association with Vassian. Also, Max-imos's descriptions for Vasilii and Vassian of monasteries on Mount Athos and of the Franciscan and Dominican orders, favourably reported that they supported themselves and owned no villages.[37]

In 1525 the Iosifite Metropolitan Daniil convened a court that on the slender-est evidence convicted Maximos of heresy and treasonous relations with the Turks. He was excommunicated and put in irons in the Iosifo-Volokolamskii monastery. Daniil brought Maximos to trial again in 1531 on charges designed to entrap Vassian. His jailers said Maximos and Vassian had denigrated Muscovite liturgical innovations and that he doubted the sanctity of Pafnutii of Borovsk and other monks who owned villages. The council also detected 'Jewish' pas-sages in Maximos's translation of Simeon Metaphrast's 'Life of the Mother of God'. Maximos's copyist, the monk Isak Sobaka, said he gave Vassian the translation; others attributed the errors to Vassian. The council excommuni-cated Vassian and confined him at the Iosifo-Volokolamskii monastery, where he died. It sent Maximos to the Otroch' monastery in Tver'. Although the Iosifites equated Non-possessors with 'judaisers', they could not isolate them. Bishop Akakii of Tver' removed Maximos's irons and allowed him books and to write. Ioasaf Skripitsyn, hegumen of the Trinity-Sergius monastery, replaced Daniil as metropolitan in 1539, lifted Isak's excommunication and made him hegumen of the Simonovskii monastery, then of the Kremlin Chudovskii (Miracles) monastery. But in 1542 a court faction replaced Ioasaf with Makarii. From a Moscow clerical family related to Iosif Volotskii, like Iosif, tonsured at the Pafnut'ev monastery, and Daniil's archbishop of Novgorod, Makarii abhorred heterodoxy. In 1549 he informed Vasilii III of Isak's complicity in Maximos's and Vassian's heresy and convicted him again.[38]

Reform

Maximos, judged by diplomat Ivan Beklemishev, his intimate and co-defendant in 1525, a 'wise man, able to assist us and enlighten us when we inquire how a sovereign should order the land, how people should be treated, and how a

37 Dimitri Obolensky, 'Italy, Mount Athos, and Muscovy: The Three Worlds of Maximos the Greek (c. 1470–1556)', *Proceedings of the British Academy* 67 (1981): 143–9; Maksim, *Sochineniia*, 3 vols., 2nd edn (Kazan': Kazan'skii universitet, 1894–7), vol. II, pp. 89–118, vol. III, pp. 182–3, 203; V. F. Rzhiga, 'Neizdannye sochineniia Maksima "Greka"', *Byzantinoslavica* 6 (1935–6): 96, 100.
38 N. N. Pokrovskii, *Sudnye spiski Maksima Greka i Isaka Sobaki* (Moscow: Glavnoe arkhivnoe upravleniia, 1971), pp. 90–125, 130–9; Kazakova, *Vassian*, pp. 285–318; Pliguzov, *Polemika*, pp. 207–52.

metropolitan should live', was the progenitor of a new literature exploring how to live a Christian life.[39] Addressing the interest in astrology generated by court doctor Niklaus Bülow, Maximos warned that man-made science offered the seductive delusion that external forces determined one's fate. It was dangerous because it relieved the believer of the God-given gift of free will. In a Sermon on Penitence he counselled that 'neither withdrawal from the world, donning a monk's habit . . . are so pleasing to God as a pure faith, an honest life and good works'.[40] Clerics, so diverse in their beliefs as the Non-possessor monk Artemii and Metropolitan Daniil, also addressed this theme. Artemii, like religious radicals in Poland-Lithuania, told correspondents Scripture was a better guide than miracles to living virtuously, stressing that the onus was on the seeker to let Scripture shape his or her existence. Daniil's sermons were more conventional; yet, he was the first Muscovite hierarch to write in this vein. His sermons, like Artemii's, privileged moral instruction along with ritual and devotional practices.[41] The *Domostroi* usually is cited to demonstrate that servicemen, state functionaries and townspeople valued moral instruction. Sil'vestr, a priest and icon painter in the Kremlin church of the Annunciation, dedicated a copy of this anonymous work to his son Anfim, telling him that a Christian household would shine in the esteem of others. Orthodoxy supplied the rituals structuring a system of deference defining the sexes, parents and children, master and slave. In chapters on child-rearing the father's role was protector of children and mentor in behaviour and trades to sons, his wife so educating daughters. They quoted Scripture to counsel against spoiling with kindness.[42] In Novgorod Makarii took reform in a different direction, the production by 1538 of an encyclopedia organised as a menology, that is, with texts celebrating saints on their feast days. Organised in twelve books, one for each month, it was called a 'great menology' (*velikie minei chetii*) because it contained full biographies of saints, and because it appended other writings to the calendar. As metropolitan Makarii sponsored an expanded edition with biographies of those he had canonised and materials from his archive. Thus, to selections for July and August were appended the final edition of Iosif's 'Enlightener', a partial translation from Greek of Ricoldus of Florence's hostile account (*c*.1300) of Muslim beliefs, the Sermon compiled from Holy Writings

39 *AAE*, vol. 1 (St. Petersburg: Tipografiia II Otdeleniia Sobstvennoi E. I. V. Kantseliarii, 1836), p. 141.
40 Maksim, *Sochineniia*, vol. 1, pp. 387, 400–1; vol. 11, p. 149.
41 *Russkaia Istoricheskaia Biblioteka*, vol. 1V, cols. 1407–12; V. I. Zhmakin, 'Mitropolit Daniil i ego sochineniia', *ChOIDR* (1881), no. 2, app., pp. 1–39, 44–55, 62–76.
42 Pouncy (ed.), *Domostroi*, pp. 177, 93, 145, 176–90.

(*c.*1462), excoriating those who had accepted union with Rome and praising Grand Prince Vasilii II for saving Muscovy, the earliest epistle by Filofei of Pskov (in 1524 to Misiur' Munekhin) describing Moscow as the third Rome, and letters of Russian prelates. Claiming he had preserved every sacred writing, Makarii retained a copy and presented the other to Ivan IV in 1552 as a reference book of authoritative texts.[43]

Ivan IV, however, working with a new favourite, Artemii, had in mind more radical reforms. Artemii was from Pskov, a city touched by reformation currents in Poland-Lithuania. Ivan summoned him from a northern hermitage and compelled the Trinity-Sergius monastery to accept him as hegumen. Simultaneously, he convened the *Stoglav* Council in January 1551. In his opening address Ivan said monasticism, founded to save souls, had become worldly; people became monks and nuns to live comfortably and to carouse with laity to the disregard of their calling. Ivan reminded the council that the acceptance of gifts and villages had brought monasteries to such a state. This caused Makarii and the Iosifite majority to answer that, since Constantine, Byzantine emperors, Church fathers and councils, Russian princes and Tatar khans had respected Church property. In the end no one was satisfied. The Iosifites conceded many points: the council recognised the government's right to inventory monastic lands; it promised to obey the provision in the Law Code of 1550 ending the issuance of immunity charters; it agreed to limitations of its right to acquire estates and to reductions in state subsidies for monasteries; and it recognised the tsar's decree of 15 September 1550 which re-established state taxation and jurisdiction in Church suburbs of Russian towns and banned the creation of new ones.[44] But the monasteries retained their considerable autonomy and the right to acquire property.

The council also committed itself to improving the behaviour of parish clergy and laity. To deal with human failing, it admonished people to attend church and open their hearts to God by confession. Decrying the ignorance or disregard of marriage laws, it repeated relevant canons. The clergy was to hold services and requiems regularly and put the fear of God into parishioners. So the laity would have no excuse to evade observances, it forbade the clergy to charge unreasonable fees for sacraments; parishioners who ignored admonitions to behave and disrupted or failed to attend services might be excommunicated. So the clergy understood its obligations, the council ordered seminaries be

43 V. A. Kuchkin, 'O formirovanii Velikikh Minei Chetii mitropolita Makariia', in A. A. Sidorov (ed.), *Problemy rukopisnoi i pechatnoi knigi* (Moscow: Nauka, 1976), pp. 86–101.
44 Emchenko, *Stoglav*, pp. 256–9, 328–35, 343–56, 358–72, 376–80, 407–9.

established in towns and reminded clerics of their mentoring duties. Unworthy clerics might be dismissed. The reforms were of little consequence, primarily because the Church failed to found seminaries or upgrade its administration. Ivan told the council that 'tenth men' were venal and that their levies impoverished parishioners, leaving the churches empty. Its answer was to replace them with senior priests (*popovskie starosty*) chosen from among and by local clergy. With their parishes, they were responsible for paying tithes.[45] Whether it produced more revenue is unclear; as a means to enhance the moral and theological acuity of the clergy and its ability to minister to parishioners, it was a step backward. Senior priests, autonomous of eparchial supervision, were hardly better educated than their juniors.

Artemii's tenure as a reformer ended with flight to the northern hermitages in July 1551. Retribution followed when Makarii in 1553–4 convened councils to hear charges tying him to heresies of serviceman Matvei Bashkin, runaway servant and monk Feodosii Kosoi and the official Ivan Viskovatyi. Viskovatyi was convicted of lesser charges, the others found guilty of heresy and excommunicated. In 1555 and 1556–7 courts convicted their disciples. Bashkin was sent to the Iosifo-Volokolamskii monastery, the others to the Solovetskii monastery whence they fled to Lithuania. Feodosii became an anti-trinitarian preacher; Artemii remained an Orthodox monk.[46] Official sources said the accused, apart from Viskovatyi, believed Jesus was less than God, and denied the efficacy of religious rites, symbols and the worship of saints and relics. It is difficult to know what Feodosii Kosoi espoused in the early 1550s, because refutations of his theology appeared after his flight and addressed his preaching in Lithuania where, according to one critic, he told crowds the Church was a union of all believers; before God, Tatars and Germans, and Christians were equal. The court heard testimony that Bashkin had enquired why believers owned slaves while professing to love others as they would have others love them. Although not unaware of reformation currents, Artemii's theology was in the Non-possessor tradition. He denied doubting the efficacy of requiems and symbols of faith, urging Ivan to expropriate monastic lands, that he 'wrote like a Jew' or refused to curse the Novgorod heretics, saying only that salvation depended primarily on living righteously, and that the heretics' punishment had been unjust. This criticism of Iosif's *Enlightener* caused an uproar when

45 Emchenko, *Stoglav*, pp. 239, 244–5, 255, 281–7, 297–302, 390, 394–7, 399–405; Jack Kollmann, 'The Stoglav', 66–91.
46 *AAE*, vol. I, pp. 240–56; M. V. Dmitriev, *Dissidents russes*, 2 vols. (vols. XIX, XX of André Séguenny, ed., *Biblioteka Dissidentium*, Baden-Baden: V. Koerner, 1998–9), vol. I, pp. 73–5; vol. II, pp. 15–18, 22, 37, 61–3.

Bishop Kassian of Riazan', the only non-Iosifite on the court, agreed. Ivan and Makarii endorsed the book and removed Kassian from office.[47]

There was no mass movement for religious reform. Most believers were attached to rituals and institutions the heretics criticised. Moreover, sources circulated only in handwritten copies. The lack of a print culture, and a concomitant information revolution such as that sweeping Western Europe, guaranteed that Maximos's translations, sermons and polemics, the Church's pedagogical mission or the teachings of its critics would reach but a small number of people. The only press was that founded by Ivan IV and Makarii in 1553 and run by Kremlin deacons Ivan Fedorov and Petr Mstislavich. It printed six anonymous scriptural texts, and Fedorov's 'The Acts and Letters of the Apostles' (1564) and 'Book of Hours' (1565). Fedorov left in 1568 for Lithuania, one report saying that a mob, incited by clergy, burnt his press. However, that press produced thirteen more works either of Scripture, liturgical books or menologies between 1568 and 1606.[48]

Church and state

Soon after 1504 Iosif Volotskii exalted Moscow's ruler, utilising the double-edged maxims of the deacon Agapetus to Byzantine Emperor Justinian I. A familiar text within Orthodoxy, it taught that a ruler deserved the obedience of his subjects if he upheld Orthodox notions of virtue and justice. Iosif was the first to celebrate Moscow's emergence in a way that explored its implications for the relationship between Church and state. In 1519 Maximos referred Vasilii III to Justinian I's view that the spiritual power of the Church and the political power of the state must be in harmony.[49] Makarii reiterated this principle in crowning Ivan IV tsar in 1547. Modelled on Byzantine rites, the rite proclaimed the ruler's office divine, meaning that it involved sacerdotal obligations and the duty to uphold the faith. In 1561 the patriarch of Constantinople recognised Ivan's title and Fedor's imperial coronation in 1584 ended with a procession through Moscow. Like the Palm Sunday and Epiphany processions, its imperial imagery was steeped in Christian humility. To restore harmony between ranks of ruler and head of Church, Boris Godunov, acting for Tsar Fedor, in 1586

47 *AAE*, vol. I, pp. 249, 251–3; A. N. Popov (ed.), 'Poslanie mnogoslovnoe, sochinenie inoka Zinoviia', *ChOIDR* (1880), bk. 2, pp. 143–4; *Russkaia Istoricheskaia Biblioteka*, vol. IV, cols. 1439–40.
48 A. S. Zernova, *Knigi kirillovskoi pechati, izdannye v Moskve v XVI–XVII vekakh* (Moscow: Gosudarstvennaia biblioteka SSSR, 1958), pp. 11–25.
49 Iosif, *Prosvetitel'* (4th edn), p. 547; Zimin and Lur'e (eds.), *Poslaniia Iosifa*, pp. 183–5, 229–32; Maksim, *Sochineniia*, vol. II, pp. 297–8.

importuned Patriarch Joachim of Antioch, then visiting Moscow for alms, to arrange a synod to elevate Metropolitan Iov of Moscow to the rank of patriarch. Nothing happened, so when Patriarch Jeremiah II of Constantinople came to Moscow for alms in 1589, Boris detained him until he consecrated Iov as patriarch and proclaimed the Russian *tsarstvo* the third Rome. In May 1590 a synod, including all the Eastern patriarchs, confirmed Iov's ordination.[50] The reality of Iov's dignity was more tenuous. In 1448 Grand Prince Vasilii II had initiated Iona's installation as metropolitan. His successors also decided who became metropolitan or patriarch, oversaw his choice of prelates and often intervened to elevate or depose them. They proceeded more cautiously in ecclesiastical matters. In 1479 Metropolitan Gerontii retired to the Simonovskii monastery and refused to hold services, to protest against Ivan III's interference in the consecration of the Dormition cathedral. Ivan had to come to him before he would return. But when Gerontii repeated the tactic in 1483, it failed to evoke the same response. Subsequently, rulers intervened more boldly in internal affairs of the Church, Ivan IV especially so, but such acts still resembled Byzantine notions of a harmony of spiritual and secular power. Ivan IV shattered this image when in 1569 he had Metropolitan Filipp killed. It was then remarkable that in 1590 a monk of the Solovetskii monastery wrote a life of Filipp proclaiming him a saint, and used Agapetus's words to condemn Ivan for martyring him.[51]

Time of Troubles

The Church found the Time of Troubles perplexing. Patriarch Iov, who had helped Godunov become tsar, was deposed by the first pretender. Reflecting on this in 1606, the monk Terentii of the Kremlin Annunciation church described a dream in which the Lord lamented that there was no true tsar, patriarch, clergy or people in His 'new Israel'.[52] When Prince Vasilii Shuiskii overturned the pretender at the end of 1606, he selected Germogen (Hermogen) as patriarch. Germogen was to lead resistance to the Polish occupation of Moscow and crown Michael Romanov tsar in 1613. The careers of his rival, Metropolitan Filaret of Rostov, and of Avraamii Palitsyn, the monk-narrator of

50 *SGGD*, vol. II (St Petersburg: Tipografiia Vsevolozhskogo, 1819), pp. 94–103; Skrynnikov, *Krest i korona*, pp. 316–26.
51 Paul Bushkovitch, 'The Life of Saint Filipp: Tsar and Metropolitan in the Late Sixteenth Century', in Flier and Rowland (eds.), *Medieval Russian Culture*, vol. II, pp. 29–46.
52 A. I. Pliguzov and I. A. Tikhoniuk (eds.), *Smuta v Moskovskom gosudarstve* (Moscow: Sovremennik, 1989), p. 64.

the ordeal of the Trinity-Sergius monastery during the *smuta* (Time of Troubles), however, better typified the conflicted loyalties of prelates. Filaret had been Fedor Nikitich, the doyen of the Romanov family, thus related by marriage to Ivan IV. In 1600 Tsar Boris tonsured him to end his political life. The first pretender freed Filaret, making him metropolitan of Rostov; the second pretender installed him as patriarch, a rival to Germogen. When his candidacy collapsed, Filaret negotiated with King Sigismund of Poland to make Sigismund's son Władysław tsar. Filaret was in a Polish jail when Russian forces liberated Moscow and crowned his son Michael. Palitsyn, a failed serviceman, became a monk no earlier than 1597 and in 1608 was cellarer of the Trinity-Sergius monastery. Early in Michael's reign, he wrote a tale of the *smuta*. Its core was a description of a siege of the monastery, September 1608–January 1610, by the second pretender and the Poles. Authentic details, visions and miracles, and an anti-Polish patriotism informed its narrative. Yet, during the siege Palitsyn was in Moscow, intriguing to replace Shuiskii with Władysław. For a time he favoured Sigismund's candidacy. The Polish occupation, however, consolidated for ordinary folk a faith-based national consciousness. Konrad Bussow, a German eyewitness, wrote that on 29 January 1611 commoners, resentful of Polish mockery of their services and dishonour to their saints, besieged them in the Kremlin. That spring, after the Poles forbade the Palm Sunday ritual, an angry crowd staged *its* version of the feast. What once was an elite affair had become a popular celebration in which an ersatz tsar, symbolically the humble Christ, led the Church, symbolised by Patriarch Germogen, to the Jerusalem chapel of the Intercession church, a symbolic renewal of the promise of salvation.[53]

53 Konrad Bussov, *Moskovskaia khronika, 1584–1613* (Moscow and Leningrad: AN SSSR, 1961), pp. 317, 320–1.

16

The law

RICHARD HELLIE

There were significant changes in the law in this period. First, it completed the evolution from a dyadic process to a triadic process. Second, it made significant progress in the shift from a law based primarily on oral evidence to one based on written evidence. Third, it featured four major law codes, *Sudebniki*, which were major advances over what Russia had known previously.

The medieval legal compilation, the *Russkaia pravda*, which was initiated in 1016 and was completed in the 1170s, remained the 'fundamental law' of Russia through to 1549. What follows is a summary of the provisions of the *Pravda*.[1] This will be used for comparison to illustrate the evolution of middle Muscovite law, as the era of the *Sudebniki* is sometimes called.

Russkaia pravda

The *Pravda* began as a court handbook to facilitate the protection of the people of Novgorod against mercenary Viking oppression. Accretions added around 1072 by Iaroslav's sons, probably based on estate codes, were motivated by an attempt to protect representatives of the princely administration and their property with sanctions of various fines for homicide or theft or destruction of princely property. The so-called 'Statute of Vladimir Monomakh' (1113–25) dealt particularly with debt. Accretions added during the reign of Vsevolod around 1176 included a 'slavery statute' (in which it was observed that a slave was not an animal, but had human characteristics – '*a to est' ne skot*'), plus articles on court procedure, penal law and inheritance.

---

1 The literature on the *Russkaia pravda* is enormous. The fundamental edition remains the three volumes edited by B. D. Grekov et al., *Pravda russkaia* (Moscow and Leningrad: AN SSSR, 1940–63). The best translation into English is by Daniel H. Kaiser in his *The Laws of Rus' – Tenth to Fifteenth Centuries* (Salt Lake City, Ut.: Charles Schlacks, 1992), pp. 14–40. My favourite article is L. V. Cherepnin's 'Obshchestvenno-politicheskie otnosheniia v drevnei Rusi i Russkaia pravda', in A. P. Novosel'tsev et al., *Drevnerusskoe gosudarstvo i ego mezhdunarodnoe znachenie* (Moscow: Nauka, 1965), pp. 128–278.

The *Pravda* was quite thorough on the matter of evidence. Witnesses could be either an eyewitness (*vidok*) or character/rumour witness (*poslukh*). Direct evidence, such as the testimony of a kidnapped or stolen slave or black and blue marks left by an assault, was considered definitive. The confrontment/confrontation also produced good evidence. Various forms of divine revelation were also considered possible evidence, such as the oath and ordeal by iron and water. The *Pravda* was compiled for an oral society in which written evidence was so sparse that it was not worth mentioning.

Inheritance norms were also relatively elaborate. Wills (typically oral) were recognised. Guardianship was permitted. When there were no heirs, property escheated to the prince. Wives could not inherit, and children of female slaves could not inherit. A homestead was passed to the youngest son (presumably as a reward for having looked after the parents) and could not be divided.

Crimes were those against property, plus arson, murder and assault. The ordinary remedies were fines, but in addition banishment and exile were possible, as were confiscation of property, corporal punishment and execution.

The functions of law in the half-millennium *Pravda* era were the following: to limit the circle of relatives who could get vengeance; to expropriate from the relatives of the deceased for the prince the obligation to punish a killer; to protect citizens from the prince's retinue; to protect society against offenders; to protect the lower classes from the upper classes; to preserve order; and to establish harmony in a multi-ethnic society. The law also took on the obligation of protecting Christianity, preserving social hierarchy and male superiority while protecting helpless women, and enforcing collective responsibility. Law was also a centralising device, extending capital norms throughout the rest of Rus'. The law tried to support institutions of private property and protect commerce and business. One of the main functions of law was to provide financial support for officialdom and, in a minor way, maintain the army. Finally, like all law everywhere, the *Russkaia pravda* served as a device for resolving conflicts, regulating compensation for damages, and creating a more humane society – replacing the law of the jungle. Below this will be contrasted with the functions of middle Muscovite law.

The sources of the *Russkaia pravda* have been debated for centuries, with no resolution. Some have looked to Byzantium as the source of inspiration of the *Pravda*, but in fact not a single article in the Russian code can be traced to a Byzantine document. Scandinavian law might be another source.[2] The

---

2 The late Professor Oswald Prentiss Backus told me shortly before his death that he had discovered on an island in the Baltic a volume which might have been a Scandinavian prototype for the *Russkaia pravda*, but I have heard no more of this since his demise.

logical solution to this problem seems to be to assign authorship of the *Pravda* to the East Slavs themselves. When problems arose, they knew how to solve them. They could not read Greek, Latin or Swedish, so had nowhere to look for precedents and solution but within themselves.

Another hold-over from Kievan Russian law into this period was Church law. Two documents allegedly from the beginning of the eleventh century must be mentioned. The first was Vladimir's *Church Statute*.[3] An elegantly simple document, it proclaimed a few universals that lasted down into the early modern period. One was that 'Church people' were not subject to state legal jurisdiction. 'Church people' included not only the obvious folk such as metropolitans, bishops, monastery elders, monks and priests, but also society's helpless, such as widows, beggars, wanderers, freedmen and the like. The second document was Iaroslav's *Church Statute*, which gave the Church jurisdiction over family law and numerous aspects of communal relations, what sometimes has been determined a usurpation of communal law.[4] The latter was quite complex, and not destined to last very long. It was soon replaced by the *Rudder* or *Pilot's Book* (the *Kormchaia kniga*), translations into Church Slavonic of the Byzantine *Nomocanon*, the Church law.[5] The *Rudder* began to be used in the last quarter of the thirteenth century and assumed the areas of jurisdiction that earlier had been claimed by Iaroslav's *Church Statute*. In addition to the *Nomocanon*, the *Kormchaia kniga* contained Byzantine civil law, such as the *Ekloga* and the *Procheiros nomos*.

Perhaps the major evolution between the *Russkaia pravda* and middle Muscovite law was that the legal process changed from a dyadic one to a triadic one.[6] The dyadic legal process is a feature of societies that are largely consensual with minimal government. In such societies 'the state' offers judicial conflict resolution services for a fee. However, 'the state' has no or minimal interest in the judicial process other than the fee it generates for its official. 'The state' does not originate or prosecute cases, has no or few enforcement mechanisms, and has no jails. In such legal processes the aggrieved in both 'civil' and 'criminal' cases (the distinction did not exist) initiates the case as plaintiff, and the defendant is obliged to respond. The entire process is accusatorial, with

3 Kaiser, *Laws of Rus'*, pp. 42–4.
4 Ibid., pp. 45–50.
5 Denver Cummings (trans.), *The Rudder (Pedalion) of the Metaphorical Ship of the One Holy Catholic and Apostolic Church of the Orthodox Christians* (Chicago: Orthodox Christian Education Society, 1957).
6 Daniel H. Kaiser, *The Growth of the Law in Medieval Russia* (Princeton: Princeton University Press, 1980). For much greater detail on the dyadic-triadic evolution, see his unpublished Ph.D. dissertation, 'The Transformation of Legal Relations in Old Rus' (Thirteenth to Fifteenth Centuries)', University of Chicago, 1977.

the 'plaintiff' bearing the entire burden of carrying the case forward. If the defendant fails to respond, he / she loses the case by default and must pay the fine decreed by the official acting as judge. Failure to pay the fine in such a society resulted in enslavement or banishment. The twenty-first-century model of dyadic law is international law and the World Court, where potential litigants appear only if they want to.

The triadic legal process is much different. The state has an interest in the case, and has officials to move the case along. The state itself is likely to initiate 'criminal cases', and, as the process becomes inquisitional, the official / judge sometimes assumes the role of prosecutor. In a 'civil case', the plaintiff must press his case, but the judge is not obliged to be a neutral arbiter. The state is present to enforce verdicts. The jail, which appeared in Russia around 1550, becomes an important instrument of the process. Besides imprisonment, other sanctions supplement fines, such as corporal and capital punishment and mutilation.

The evolution from the dyadic to the triadic legal process was a gradual one. The consensual society gradually disappeared as *Gemeinschaft* yielded to *Gesellschaft*. This process had already made considerable headway in Novgorod, a city of at least 20,000 people before it was annexed by Moscow in 1478; in Pskov, a city of perhaps 15,000 people before it was annexed by Moscow in 1510; and in Moscow itself, which purportedly had 40,000 houses in the first half of the sixteenth century. The 'great break' in the move to the triadic legal process occurred in the 1520s, when law and order broke down throughout much of Muscovy, and what remained of the consensual society went with it. Numerous petitions were submitted to the capital demanding that action be taken against crime. In response, Moscow sent agents to the provinces to stop the crime wave. This brought the state directly into the criminal process in a way inconceivable earlier. From this time on the triadic process reigned supreme.

This was preceded by another series of events which had a major impact on the course of the law. At the end of the fifteenth century and in the first decade of the sixteenth century, three independent strands came together whose second-order consequence had a lasting impact on Russia.[7] The first issue was the dynastic controversy over who should succeed Ivan III, which was resolved at the end of the fifteenth century in favour of the son of his second marriage, Vasilii III. The second issue was that of the so-called Judaisers, a group of dissident clergymen who adhered to many of the tenets of the

---

7 Aleksandr Ianov, *Rossiia: U istokov tragedii 1462–1584* (Moscow: Progress, 2001), pp. 122–53.

Old Testament but also represented advanced knowledge in Muscovy. Their adherents worked their way into the entourage of Ivan III, but were finally purged at Church councils at the outset of the sixteenth century. The third issue involved the role of the Russian Orthodox Church in the world. Since the middle of the fourteenth century the Church, and especially monasteries, had been accumulating lands, and by 1500 owned close to a third of all the populated land of Muscovy. This brought the Church in a major way into 'the world', which offended purists who believed that the role of the Church should be the salvation of souls, not the accumulation of property. The camps were divided into non-possessors / non-acquirers and possessors / acquirers. The former were also called 'the trans-Volga [north of the Volga] elders' and were led by Nil Maikov Sorskii. Their major antagonist was the elder of the Voloko-lamsk monastery, Iosif (Ivan Sanin). The trans-Volga elders were defeated at the same councils which liquidated the Judaisers. Iosif was the victor in all three contests: the dynastic succession, Judaiser controversy and the issue of Church lands. Out of gratitude to Ivan III and Vasilii III, over the course of several tortured years he reformulated teachings of the Byzantine deacon Agapetus (fl. 527–48) into the doctrine 'in his body the sovereign is a man, but in his authority he is like God'.[8] This Russian version of the divine rights of kings underpinned Russian law and the monarchy down to its fall in 1917, and was then taken up in another format by the Soviets. For our purposes here, the Iosifite slogan, which was widely debated at the time and known to many people, served to legitimise Moscow's formalisation of the triadic legal system.

Before commencing the discussion of the Muscovite *Sudebniki*, a few words must be said about two other previous Russian law codes, the *Pskov Judicial Charter* (120 articles compiled between 1397 and 1467) and the *Novgorod Judicial Charter* (42 articles compiled sometime shortly after Moscow's 1478 annexation of the republic).[9] They represent the best of north-west Russian law of the

---

8 Ihor Ševčenko, 'A Neglected Byzantine Source of Muscovite Political Ideology', *Harvard Slavic Studies* 2 (1954): 141–79.

9 Richard Hellie, 'Russian Law From Oleg to Peter the Great', the Foreword in Kaiser's *Laws of Rus'*, pp. xxiii–xxiv. Kaiser's translations of the two codes can be found on pp. 66–105. Other relatively recent editions can be found in *PRP*, 8 vols. (Moscow: Gosiurizdat, 1952–63), vyp. II: *Pamiatniki prava feodal'no-razdroblennoi Rusi XII–XV vv.*, comp. A. A. Zimin (1953), pp. 210–44 and 282–381 and *RZ*, 9 vols. (Moscow: Iuridicheskaia literatura, 1984–94), vol. I: *Zakonodatel'stvo Drevnei Rusi*, ed. V. L. Ianin (1984), pp. 299–389. The *Pskov Judicial Charter* (*Pskovskaia sudnaia gramota*) will henceforth be cited as *PSG*, and the *Novgorod Judicial Charter* (*Novgorodskaia sudnaia gramota*) as *NSG*. The Muscovite *Sudebniki* can be found in *Sudebniki XV–XVI vekov*, ed. B. D. Grekov (Moscow and Leningrad, AN SSSR, 1952) and in other collections such as *PRP* and *RZ*. They are cited henceforth as: *1497 Sudebnik*; *1550 Sudebnik*, etc.

time, which was considerably more advanced than the contemporary law of Muscovy.

The *Pskov Judicial Charter*

The *Pskov Judicial Charter* had its origins in the *Russkaia pravda*, in laws by rulers Aleksandr (r. 1327–30, 1332–7) and Konstantin (r. 1407–14), in decrees of the popular assembly (*veche*) and town ruling council (*gospoda*), and in Pskov customary or common law. It was one of the most important sources of the Muscovite *Sudebnik* of 1497. In Pskov the transition from dyadic to triadic law was under way, but by no means complete. The transition was evident in the office of the 'police officer, bailiff, guard' (*pristav*, from the verb *pristaviti* – to bring, to deliver, to issue an order, to appoint), who had the obligation to investigate criminal offences. The plaintiff was expected to be with him during an investigation, when he was his assistant in prosecuting his case.[10] He represented society, the community and the political authorities who appointed him (the prince and the mayor) when he witnessed agreements, investigated criminal offences, arrested a thief or debtor to enforce appearance in court and when he served as executioner.[11]

If it is accurate to generalise that the *Russkaia pravda* concentrated on procedural and criminal law, then by contrast one may state in summary that the Pskov statute was concerned primarily with civil norms: contract, property, inheritance and the legal status of the peasant.

Because landownership was almost irrelevant in Kievan Rus', the *Pravda* hardly distinguished immoveable from moveable property. Apparently urban property conflict resolution was not deemed sufficiently significant to codify. The situation was obviously different in Pskov, where the distinction between immoveable property and moveable property was sanguine.

By the fifteenth century the hereditary estate (*votchina*) was well established in Pskov. The law distinguished various forms of hereditary estate on the basis of who owned it (princely, monastic, boyaral, clan) and on the basis of how it had come into being (purchase or grant from the ruler). Pskov law theoretically permitted the sale of any property, moveable or immoveable. Land, however, was rarely a commodity in late medieval and early modern Russia because members of the seller's clan had the right to inherit the estate and could buy it back almost without any restrictions. This greatly inhibited the mobilisation

---

10 *PSG*, arts. 67, 98.
11 *PSG*, arts. 34, 98.

of land because the market was suffocated by the redemption restrictions. In Pskov a land sale contract had to specify the last date on which a seller or his heirs could redeem a hereditary estate.[12] This was a modest concession to the market, but fundamentally the interest of the clan triumphed. Even the seller himself could redeem immoveable property unless he foreswore the right to do so in his sale document. The clan also could sue for the return of land willed to outsiders without its consent. Individualism was almost unheard of anywhere in Russia until after the mid-seventeenth century, but property law was just another factor hindering the development of individualism, in this case in the interest of the clan as a collective.

From a legal economic history perspective, an interesting provision allowed the possessor and tiller of land to gain ownership of the property after four or five years. Even if an owner had written documents on such land, he lost it if he did not use it for half a decade.[13] This did not apply to forests, where written documents were supreme. The goal here was to keep agricultural land in production. If an owner failed to do so, he could lose it to someone who would. This provision was frequently resorted to in suits.

The law of Pskov strove to protect the interests of owners. A sale made while drunk was void should either seller or buyer challenge it when sober.[14] A seller had to guarantee that the item being sold was not stolen.[15] Almost astonishingly advanced was the declared right of a buyer to void the transaction if the item was defective.[16] The *Russkaia pravda* stated that a finder owned whatever he had found, but Pskov legislation provided for the loser to sue the finder, who had to prove that he had not stolen the item in contention.[17] This evolution made sense, because in Kiev documentation was nearly absent and unreliable oral testimony would have had to have been resorted to, whereas Pskov had a much more sophisticated legal climate with the result that the costs of protecting the rights of the owner were bearable.

The Pskov law of contract was the most sophisticated in this period. The *Pravda* did not know written contracts, all were oral in the presence of witnesses. Pskov, however, prohibited oral contracts for over a rouble.[18] Pskov knew four kinds of contracts: (1) Oral. (2) A written document called a *zapis'*, a copy of which was preserved in the Trinity cathedral archive. Such a document

---

12 *PSG*, art. 13.
13 *PSG*, art. 9.
14 *PSG*, art. 114.
15 *PSG*, arts. 46, 47, 56.
16 *PSG*, art. 118, here a diseased cow.
17 *PSG*, arts. 46, 47.
18 *PSG*, arts. 30, 33.

could not be disputed in court. (3) Another written document, the *riadnitsa*, which was a record of monies paid, loans repaid, filed in the Trinity archive. This also could not be contested. (4) Something called a *doska*, etymologically probably something written on a tablet or board, but by the fifteenth century a private document not filed in the Trinity archive and something which could be contested at trial.[19] None of this entered mainstream Muscovite law.

Pskov provided a generally favourable legal climate for commerce, not surprising in the most 'Western' of the cities of Rus'. Storage, pawns and loans were all protected.[20] Interest on loans (*imanie*) was legal and no maximum was prescribed. Disputes were to be litigated before the ruling council (*gospoda*) of Pskov, which is assigned judicial responsibilities in many of the other articles of the statute.[21]

Labour law was introduced in Pskov. A worker (*naimit* – 'hireling') explicitly had the right to claim his wages. He was a free man who entered an oral contract with his employer whom he could sue. He also could leave whenever he wanted and get paid for the work done. The worker had to announce publicly his claims against the employer.[22]

Russian inheritance law became more sophisticated in the journey from Kiev to Pskov. In the earlier period wills were oral, and they still could be in Pskov. However, while still vital or on his deathbed in the presence of witnesses, a man could give away any moveable or immoveable property to whomever he wanted and that was a legal transaction.[23] However, written testaments came to be preferred, and they could be secured by depositing a copy in the Trinity cathedral archive. When a wife who owned land died, her widower husband could keep her property until his death or remarriage, at which time it reverted to her family. The same applied for a widow. Relatives could claim the clothes of a deceased wife if the widower remarried or of a deceased husband and the widower or widow was obliged to hand them over. Neither was required to take an oath that there were no more clothes. A widow could claim her moveable property from her father-in-law or brother-in-law and they were obliged to hand it over.[24]

---

19 *PSG*, arts. 30, 31, 32, 36, 38.
20 *PSG*, arts. 16, 17, 29–32.
21 *PSG*, arts. 73, 74.
22 *PSG*, arts. 39, 40. Moscow was less favourable to the worker, who lost all his wages if he failed to fulfil the contract by leaving early: *1497 Sudebnik*, art. 54, *1550 Sudebnik*, art. 83, *1589 Sudebnik Short*, art. 16, *1589 Sudebnik Expanded*, art. 148.
23 *PSG*, art. 100.
24 *PSG*, arts. 88–91.

'Criminal law' was definitely a minor – although necessary – interest in the *Pskov Judicial Charter*. Treason, punishable by death, was unknown in the *Pravda*. The death penalty was also prescribed for a third theft, horse-stealing, theft of property in the Pskov fortress churches (which, incidentally, were used by merchants for storage of their wares), arson and for flight abroad. For violating court decorum, the culprit could be placed in the stocks (*dyba*) and also fined.[25] Fines were also prescribed for a first and second theft.

The goal of criminal law punishments was primarily fourfold: (1) deterrence, the enunciation of threats to discourage other potential criminals; (2) incapacitation, to protect society by removing dangerous individuals, by capital punishment (note that jails did not exist and that banishment was not employed); (3) by raising the penalties, to discourage recidivism; (4) composition, to compensate those damaged.

Pskov used law to define and regulate society. Particularly important for the long run of Russian history was the condition of the tenant farmer (*izornik*). He might have taken a loan (*pokruta*) of grain, tools or cash from his lord, who also gave him land for a garden plot. If the farmer fled without repaying the loan (a form of theft), the master could seize his property. When he died, his obligations passed to his heirs, who got the rest of his estate after the loan was paid back. If he paid back the loan, he could move on St Phillip's Fast Day, 14 November, the ancestor of the Muscovite St George's Day (26 November), which was the major instrument initiating the enserfment of the peasantry in Russia. The *izornik* had the right to sue in court. In the absence of documents, the lord could make a public declaration of his claims against the *izornik*, take an oath to prove his claims and provide witnesses to prove that the farmer was a tenant on his property. Then a judgement would be entered against the *izornik*.[26]

The rules of evidence in Pskov were much more 'modern' than in Kiev. As repeatedly shown above, written evidence was definitely preferred in Pskov, a development that was not to occur in Muscovy until after 1550. Also important in Pskov was the written legal decision (*pravaia gramota*),[27] a summary of the case with the verdict which was given to the winning litigant.[28] The winner could use this document to advance his claims in case of further disputes. Oral

25 *PSG*, art. 58.
26 *PSG*, arts. 42, 44, 51, 63, 74–6, 84–7.
27 The oldest known *pravaia gramota* dates from 1284, in Smolensk.
28 *PSG*, art. 61. See also *1497 Sudebnik*, art. 27.

marketplace declarations (*zaklikan'ia*) about lost items or slaves were still in use, as were *zaklikan'ia* when a hireling was trying to exact his wages from an employer[29] or a lord was attempting to exact a loan from a peasant.[30] Other important forms of evidence were witnesses and the oath. Property boundary disputes could be resolved by taking an oath on the cross.[31]

Article 37 of the *Pskov Judicial Charter* laid down the provisions for trials by combat to resolve judicial disputes. Trial by combat by the thirteenth century had driven out the *Pravda*'s ordeal by iron and water.[32] Assistants were permitted at a trial by combat. Should the loser be killed in the combat, the winner could take his armour or whatever else he wore to the field, but nothing more. If the loser survived, he had to pay various fees to the officials present, nothing to the prince, and the winning litigant's claims.[33] By the end of the fifteenth century, trial by combat was being abandoned almost everywhere except in Muscovy in favour of written evidence (see below). In 1410 the Russian Orthodox Church had expressed opposition to trial by combat, supposedly an expression of divine judgement that was obviously a farce when the winner often proved to be the litigant who could hire the strongest brute to fight his case.

Article 71 makes it appear as though a legal profession was developing by forbidding an 'attorney' (*posobnik*) from conducting more than one trial a day. The term *posobnik* means 'aide', but one may assume that semi-professional lawyers were emerging because otherwise the issue of someone taking more than one case per day would not arise. The *posobnik* in the case of representation for women, monks, minors, the aged and the deaf in most cases was just an aide, presumably a relative, not one of the attorneys who could only handle one case a day. Further evidence that professional lawyers were beginning to appear can be found in the stipulations that no mayor (*posadnik*) or other official (*vlastel'*)

29 *PSG*, art. 39. In Muscovy, a worker who quit before his contract was completed lost all of his wages (*1497 Sudebnik*, art. 54). Half a century later, however, a provision was added that an employer who did not pay his employee his due had to pay double that sum (*1550 Sudebnik*, art. 83; *1589 Sudebnik*, art. 148 increased the penalty to triple).
30 *PSG*, art. 44.
31 *PSG*, art. 78. This replaced the traditional East Slavic practice of walking the boundaries with a piece of turf on the litigant's head. See Elena Pavlova, 'Private Land Ownership in Northeastern Russia during the Late Appanage Period (Last Quarter of the Fourteenth through the Middle of the Fifteenth Century)', unpublished Ph.D. dissertation, University of Chicago, 1998.
32 A good discussion of trial by combat (*pole*) can be found in Grekov, *Sudebniki*, pp. 47–50. *Pole* appeared only at the end of the fourteenth century, in a Novgorodian Church statute book (*kormchaia kniga*).
33 See also *PSG*, arts. 10, 13, 17, 18, 21, 36, 37, 101, 117, 119.

was permitted to litigate for anyone else. Both were permitted to litigate for themselves, and the mayor could argue a case for a church of which he was an elder.[34] This development was aborted, and sixteenth-century Russian sources only mention slaves who hung around the court offering advice to litigants – one presumes for a fee.[35] Only in 1864 did the Russian autocracy permit a bar to develop.

Pskov developed a sophisticated system of specialised courts. The court of the prince, mayors and hundreders handled the 'big cases': homicide, robbery, theft, assault and battery, fugitive debtors (another form of theft) and landownership disputes. The court of the mayor and judges elected by the popular assembly dealt with contracts. Courts of fraternal societies processed fights, disputes and other conflicts that occurred during feasts.

The legal process in Pskov was primarily a dyadic one. Moreover, there was no distinction between the criminal and civil process. The trial was accusatory, both parties were present, it was not an inquisition with the judge taking a major role. In the horizontal process, citizens brought all cases. The primary goal of procedure was the speedy resolution of conflicts (and, incidentally, the rapid payment of fees). 'Justice' was probably secondary. In petty cases, there was no summons with force at its disposal to bring the accused to trial. After five days, a defendant who did not appear just lost the case.[36]

Besides regulating conflict, a major function of the *Pskov Judicial Statute* was to provide income for officialdom. Law as a cash source was crucial in the development of triadic relations as the law took on a life of its own independent of the regulation of conflict. The apparatus of judges, bailiffs and scribes were all paid. A crucial function of law became the regulation of the income of this horde. Along with this went the issue of bribery. Article 4 forbade the taking of secret, that is, illegal, bribes. To the modern mind, this seems like an oxymoron, but in the East Slavic late-medieval era this was just a form of regulating income-gathering, one of the major functions of the justice system.

Other functions of law in Pskov were to support and protect the Church; to maintain sex distinctions (sex discrimination was noticeably less than in later Muscovite law); and to support the family: a son who would not feed his parents was disinherited automatically.[37]

---

34 *PSG*, arts. 68–9.
35 Richard Hellie, *Slavery in Russia 1450–1725* (Chicago: University of Chicago Press, 1982), pp. 477–8. A poignant quotation from a 1582 report to Ivan IV on slaves in the courtroom is quoted in the above text.
36 *PSG*, arts. 25, 26, 39.
37 *PSG*, art. 53.

The law

The *Novgorod Judicial Charter*

The *Novgorod Judicial Charter* is extant in only one copy, and is incomplete. It is generally assumed that it had some relation to the law of the Republic of Novgorod, but the extant copy was clearly written under Moscow's dictation after the Republic's annexation in 1478. Sorting out what were Novgorodian norms prior to 1478 from what was mandated by the Moscow occupation forces seems to be impossible – with one exception: a number of articles dictate that the Muscovites and the Novgorodians were to function together. The Novgorodian mayor was to try cases together with the governor sent from Moscow, and the Moscow grand prince had the right to hear appeals of any verdict rendered in Novgorod.[38] Moscow's governor could also hear cases independently.[39]

Many of the Novgorodian provisions were the same as or variations on what existed in Kiev and Pskov. The judicial process was to be orderly, with no intimidation or use of force.[40] Only two friends could accompany a litigant to trial. If there were more than two, the two allowed had to pay a fine.[41] Anyone who assaulted a bailiff delivering a summons automatically lost the case.[42] Trials had to be expeditious, no longer than a month.[43] Land disputes had to be resolved in two months. In what must have been a Muscovite addition, local officials (a mayor or military commander) were to be fined the ruinous sum of 50 roubles for any delay. The plaintiff had the right to use bailiffs to compel the judge to complete the case on time.[44] In another sign that the Novgorodian legislators were aware of the harm resulting from 'the law's delay' (Shakespeare's phrase), any litigant who failed to show up on time when a case had been postponed automatically lost the case. Similarly, if a litigant had a representative/attorney to represent him and the representative died, the litigant had to choose another one, appear himself or lose the case.[45] These provisions allowed only one postponement of a case.

The central issue of fees for judicial services was spelled out, including the delivery of summonses. The loser had to pay the court fees promptly.[46] A losing defendant had a month to pay the plaintiff, or the latter could seize his

38 *NSG*, arts. 2–3.
39 *NSG*, art. 25.
40 *NSG*, arts. 6, 7.
41 *NSG*, art. 42.
42 *NSG*, art. 40.
43 *NSG*, art. 9.
44 *NSG*, arts. 28–9.
45 *NSG*, arts. 31, 32.
46 *NSG*, arts. 8, 23, 33, 34.

371

person, presumably to enslave him. If the loser hid, then all Novgorod was to punish him.[47] This is a wonderful statement of the essence of the dyadic process: either the loser does what the court decrees, or the entire community will punish him.

A new principle was introduced in land disputes. First, the plaintiff had to sue on the issue of forcible seizure of the property, and then about the issue of actual ownership.[48] This resembled English common law, which prescribed that suits had to be prosecuted one at a time and that they could not be mixed. One might note here also that Novgorod did not adopt the Pskov four- or five-year land possession rule. This was probably for several reasons: Novgorod had far more land than did Pskov, so someone who wanted to farm could easily find land no one else was using. Moreover, Pskovian land was of higher quality and thus more valuable than was the case in the Republic of Novgorod, which overall was more concerned about urban issues than was Pskov.

Another new procedural rule was that a plaintiff had to take an oath on the cross (kiss the cross) before a suit would be heard. Failure to do so by either the plaintiff or the defendant resulted in automatic loss of the case.[49] Oath-taking was not decisive in such cases, but Novgorod had more faith in such evidence than did earlier legislators, which reflects the fact that Christianisation made considerable progress in Russia among the 'masses' between 1350 and 1480. Presumably this was also an 'efficiency' measure: if a superstitious litigant would not even kiss the cross before the case began, it saved the trouble of hearing the case itself. Representation, by an 'attorney' or a relative, was allowed, but the litigant had to kiss the cross first. A son could kiss the cross for his widowed mother, but if he refused, she had to do it at home. In suits over boat ownership, the 'attorney' and witnesses had to kiss the cross.[50] Officials also were required to swear that they would be honest in court.[51] Honesty was mentioned in the context of the Moscow agent's (*tiun*) court, where it was mentioned that each litigant had to be attended by a Novgorodian bailiff (*pristav*) and again the matter of the oath was mentioned, this time for the judges.[52] One may assume that the bailiffs were to assist the litigants in matters such as bringing witnesses to court.

In an ambiguous article, the *Novgorod Judicial Charter* enumerates what today would be termed 'felonies': theft, robbery, battery, arson and homicide,

47 *NSG*, art. 34.
48 *NSG*, arts. 10, 11, 13.
49 *NSG*, arts. 14–15.
50 *NSG*, arts. 16–19.
51 *NSG*, art. 27.
52 *NSG*, art. 25.

as well as the people who might commit them. The ambiguity lies in whether the accused in these felonies was a slave, or all kinds of other Novgorodians. The issue of slavery – presumably whether or not someone was a slave – was added to the list. Slavery was an extraordinarily prominent institution in Novgorod, and it is surprising that more of the charter is not devoted to that issue.[53] (Perhaps it was in parts that don't survive.) Cases could be initiated by citizens (part of the dyadic process) by swearing an oath and signing the accusation. Once a complaint had been made, officials were to bring the accused to court. Force (*sila*) could not be used to bring in the accused, one assumes because the defendant was still only accused but not yet found guilty. Officials who employed unnecessary force were themselves guilty of a crime.[54] A similar uncertainty is present in article 37, where the issue seems to be felonies committed by slaves, claims against them leading to enslavement by the victim-plaintiffs and relationship to the previous slave-owner. As in most slave systems, the former slave-owner is liable for the conduct of his slave and must compensate the victim for any wrongs committed by his slave. Slave systems varied in the degree to which they recognised the humanity of slaves (as Pskov said, the slave is not an animal), his responsibility for his actions, his ability to be a witness in court and so on, but all systems held the owner ultimately responsible for the actions of his chattel. Novgorodian law did not allow such an accused to sell himself to a fourth person, who had to assume liability for his chattel's wrongs. Similar ambiguity is inherent in article 38, which seems to say that a slave accused of a crime must kiss the cross or else settle the case without the aid of his owner. One assumes that a slave who opted to defend himself risked becoming the slave of the plaintiff. As many slaves had chosen their owners to whom they sold themselves, the law seems to say that, if the slave wanted to stay with his former master, he had to help him out by mounting a credible defence, or else risk being transferred to an owner he did not know or choose. For a slave who was innocent of the charges,

---

53 Hellie, *Slavery in Russia*. See also A. I. Iakovlev (ed.), *Novgorodskie zapisnye kabal'nye knigi 100–104 i 111 godov (1591–1596 i 1602–1603 gg.)* (Moscow and Leningrad: AN SSSR, 1939), which includes the registration of a number of sixteenth-century documents. Another indicator of the importance of slavery in pre-1478 Novgorod is the fact that the famous archaeological excavations took place at the intersections of Slave and High streets. The so-called birch-bark charters were found there because the slave market was one of the most active places in Novgorod and a reader-writer set up business at that busy intersection to serve the needs of the largely illiterate population of the city. Once the professional reader had read the birch-bark message to his illiterate customer, the latter threw it into the muck, which preserved the letter for more than half a millennium.

54 *NSG*, art. 36.

this presented a dilemma – either defend yourself properly, or fall into alien hands.

Immunities

The immunity was an important institution in late-medieval and early modern Russia. The immunity charter was issued by a ruling prince to a private individual or Church body (typically, an important magnate or monastery) granting the immunity holder exemption either from taxation or from the jurisdiction of the issuer's court, or both. There is a major issue in the historiography over whether this signified the weakness of the state authority (the issuer could not do everything himself, so contracted it out to others) or was a sign of state authority strength (as a privilege, the state allowed the immunity holder to reap the financial windfall resulting from the cancellation of selected taxes or from holding trials from which otherwise the state officials would gain income).[55] Vast numbers of immunity charters have been published and their exemptions serve as the primary source for the types of taxation that existed – if the grantee of the immunity was freed from paying such and such a tax, the assumption is that everyone else had to pay it. Here we are more interested, however, in judicial immunities, which again illustrated the types of crimes the issuer of the immunity was interested in. When immunities first appeared, there were no limitations on the exemption from the officials of the princely court and only the landlord holding the immunity could conduct trials in that jurisdiction. But those rights began to be limited from the end of the fourteenth century with the rise of Moscow. Murder and red-handed robbery cases were reserved for the prince's officials. By 1425 so-called 'joint courts', presided over by an official of the grand prince and someone representing the immunity holder, had to issue verdicts and punish thieves and robbers. After the Muscovite civil war, in the 1450s, judicial rights were further limited and murder became universally exempted from immunity jurisdiction, and robbery and red-handed theft were also occasionally exempted.

As a rule, Ivan III limited judicial immunities further as he desired that his own officials should be able to collect the fees from all legal cases. His immunities granted to monasteries at the end of the 1480s and beginning of the 1490s typically reserved for the prince only murder trials, but in such documents issued to lay lords the area of exclusion was larger: murder, robbery

55 S. M. Kashtanov, *Sotsial'no-politicheskaia istoriia Rossii kontsa XV–pervoi poloviny XVI veka* (Moscow: Nauka, 1967), pp. 4–5.

and red-handed theft.[56] In the period of Ivan IV's minority, 'the period of boyar rule', the issuance of immunities was renewed to the point that 238 such documents are still extant.[57] Most of them were tax and customs immunities, but many were judicial as well. A really generous judicial immunity would allow a monastery to hold trials involving all offences, a more limited one would reserve the major felonies for the officials of the grand prince. In 1551 all immunities were reviewed and those not renewed lapsed.[58] Immunities were revived during the *oprichnina* (1565–72), but Ivan's death in 1584 marked the end of an era for immunities.[59] Although both article 43 of the 1550 *Sudebnik* and article 92 of the 1589 *Sudebnik* forbade the granting of immunity charters and demanded their recall, limited immunities continued to be granted into the seventeenth century, but essentially they died out with the strengthening of the Muscovite chancellery (*prikaz*) system.

The Muscovite *Sudebniki*

Nothing is known about the origins of the *Sudebnik* of 1497. The succession crisis had just passed. Civil disorders were a frequent reason for the compilation of law in Russia, but almost certainly not that time. A number of rulers liked to see themselves as latter-day Constantines or Justinians, but there is no evidence that the declining Ivan III could be included in those numbers. All we know is that the document is extant and that it initiated certain threads which were to be central in Middle Muscovite law, such as serfdom and the claim that officials could not make law: when the law did not give a precise solution to a precise problem, the case had to be sent to Moscow for resolution. We must also recall that there is only one copy extant of the 1497 *Sudebnik*, whereas many pre-1550 copies of the *Russkaia pravda* are still available. The number of surviving texts is assumed to correspond to the use of the relative law codes. The compiler (someone in the circle of Fedor Vasil'evich Kuritsyn) of the code borrowed eleven of its articles from the *Pskov Judicial Charter*, two from the *Russkaia pravda*, and a dozen of them from grand-princely orders to provincial governors working on three-year rotations in the 'feeding' system (*kormlenie*).

---

56 Ibid., pp. 14–15.
57 S. M. Kashtanov, 'Feodal'nyi immunitet v gody boiarskogo pravleniia (1538–1548 gg.)', *IZ* 66 (1960): 240.
58 S. M. Kashtanov, 'K voprosu ob otmene tarkhanov v 1575/76 g.', *IZ* 77 (1965): 210–11.
59 For a superb history and analysis of judicial immunities, see Marc David Zlotnik, 'Immunity Charters and the Centralization of the Muscovite State', unpublished Ph.D. dissertation, University of Chicago, 1976, pp. 113–64.

The 1550 *Sudebnik* (two-thirds of which originated in the 1497 code) does not have anyone's signature on it, but the assumption is that it was one of the fruits of attempts to restore order after the chaos of Ivan IV's minority, which included uprisings in Moscow. Around 1550 Ivan's inner kitchen cabinet (known in the literature as 'the chosen council') instituted a number of reforms, both military and judicial. The 100-article *Sudebnik* was one of the reforms. Another seventy-three supplemental articles were added between 1550 and 1607. These 173 articles were the basis of Russian law until the *Ulozhenie* (Law Code) of 1649, supplemented by the chancelleries' scroll records of their own practices. About fifty copies of the 1550 code are extant.

In 1589 people in the Russian north (the White Sea littoral region, also known as the Dvina Land) decided that they needed a *Sudebnik* to meet their needs. They produced a short version (fifty-six articles, which were conceived of as an addition to the 1550 code) and an expanded version (231 articles). They might have been ignored were it not for the fact that surviving evidence indicates that the 1589 *Sudebnik* was used for conflict resolutions whose paper trail ended in Moscow. About 64 per cent of the expanded version came from the 1550 predecessor, a handful of others from various statutes of 1556, and 27 per cent were compiled to meet the needs of the north. They are largely grouped at the end of the code.

The last *Sudebnik* was presumably compiled in 1606 by the invading Polish forces accompanying False Dmitrii I to the Moscow throne. This 'Composite *Sudebnik*', as it is known, was probably never used anywhere by anyone – although the fact that it now exists in five copies implies that people were sufficiently interested in it to copy it. The 1606 document made an effort to group the articles into logical categories that comprised twenty-five chapters. The West Russian *Lithuanian Statute of 1588* contained twenty-five chapters, and it is possible that some West Russians had a hand in drafting the 1606 code. Incidentally, the great *Ulozhenie* of 1649 also had twenty-five chapters. The Composite *Sudebnik* incorporated the 1550 code and its supplements mentioned above, decrees of 1562 and 1572 on princely estates, and laws of 1597, 1602, and 1606 on slaves and peasants. Anachronistically, it ignores the two major 1592 pieces of social legislation: (1) the 'temporary' repeal of the right of peasants to leave their lords on St George's Day (26 November) and (2) the placing of a five-year-statute of limitations on the right to sue for the recovery of fugitive peasants. Peasants were not free in the *Rzeczpospolita*, and so this was not a 'comparative oversight'. Perhaps the invading Poles hoped to woo the Russian peasants to their side by pitting them against their masters and the officialdom of Boris Godunov. This is something we will never know.

The *Sudebniki* were primarily court handbooks. Thus it is not surprising that fees which could be charged for judicial services were among their major concern, as well as who those officials were who were entitled to collect the fees.[60] Procedures were prescribed,[61] and almost incidentally the delicts which were subject to the prince's jurisdiction.[62]

The years 1497–1606 witnessed as much change in Russian local administration as any other period one can think of. In the fifteenth century the prince's agent in any locale was his governor (*voevoda, namestnik*) to govern a precise area on rotation for periods of one to three years. The governor was expected to take in sufficient revenue (called 'feeding' – *kormlenie*) to allow him to support himself for another period in Moscow, where he probably served in the cavalry.[63] *Voevoda*-justice was a dyadic process supreme. The governor went to his assignment and took his slaves with him. Depending on his personal energy level, each governor apportioned the duties between himself and his slaves. There are transcripts extant in which all the people in a trial were slaves: the judge, the plaintiff and the accused. To simplify, by 1556 the Moscow-sent governor was phased out, in favour of locally elected officials who were to manage criminal and civil cases. This was not total decentralisation because Moscow demanded that the elected officials report to the capital immediately upon election and then required them to submit records of their practice either annually or biannually. This was how the Poles found the situation when they arrived in 1606. The 1589 *Sudebnik* still mentioned the *voevoda* for reasons that no one comprehends.

Also for reasons no one comprehends, the *Sudebniki* prohibited bribe-taking. Earlier that form of revenue raising was just regulated.[64]

The hordes of officials had their fees spelled out for almost anything imaginable – for holding of trials, for writing and sealing documents, for travelling on foot and on horseback to perform their missions (such as delivering

60 *1497 Sudebnik*, art. 51. See also below, n. 66.
61 *1497 Sudebnik*, arts. 26, 36–8, 45, 51; *1550 Sudebnik*, arts. 15, 20, 22, 23, 28-30, 48, 49, 62, 68, 74, 75; *1589 Sudebnik*, arts. 20–2, 31, 32, 34, 35, 75, 78, 97–9, 116, 122, 133, 134.
62 *1497 Sudebnik*, arts. [theft] 34, 36, 39; [assault] 48, 53; [robbery] 48; [insult] 53; *1550 Sudebnik*, arts. [arson] 12, 61, 62; [assault] 11, 16, 25, 31; [brigandage] 53, 59, 60, 62, 89; [church theft] 55, 61; [destroying land boundary markers] 87; [espionage, treason] 61; [false accusation, slander] 59, 72; [forgery] 59; [insult, injuring someone's honour] 25, 26, 31, 62, 70; [kidnapping] 55; [murder] 12, 59, 60, 62, 71, 72; [notorious criminal] 52, 53, 59–61, 71; [official malfeasance] 3–5, 18, 21, 28, 32, 53, 54; [robbery] 16, 25; [swindling] 58; [theft] 52–55, 57, 60, 62, 71. The 1589 list is the same.
63 *1497 Sudebnik*, art. 41; *1550 Sudebnik*, arts. 22, 24, 48, 60, 62–4, 66–8, 70–2, 75, 96; *1589 Sudebnik*, arts. 34, 36, 37, 97, 114, 116–18, 125–9, 133, 134, 198.
64 *1497 Sudebnik*, arts. 1, 33, 34, 38, 67; *1550 Sudebnik*, arts. 1, 32, 53, 62, 68, 99; *1589 Sudebnik*, arts. 1, 80, 96, 104, 122, 202.

summonses or bringing someone in for trial); for registering loans and slaves. The *Sudebniki* also prescribed the percentage of suits to be turned over to the court as well as a host of other fees, all of which were to assure that those carrying out Middle Muscovite law would not go hungry.[65]

As mentioned earlier, Russian law especially worried about 'the law's delay'. Expeditious resolution of conflicts and payment of the required fees was almost always uppermost in the oral society of 1497,[66] which was becoming increasingly literate after 1550.[67] Delaying the process, which by 1550 had become triadic, was something the state (at least in theory) would not tolerate.[68]

The most elemental point of the *Sudebniki* was that judges in no way could make law, by interpretation, by analogy, by 'flexibility' or any other means. The judge had to resolve the case in front of him on the basis of what was presented at trial. Any other case had to be sent to Moscow for resolution.[69] The degree of centralisation called for in 1550 is extraordinary: many cases had to be sent to Moscow for final resolution.[70] The 'Agapetus state' (in which the sovereign believed he was God's vicegerent on earth and most of his subjects concurred in that belief) could not tolerate norms being established anywhere other than in Moscow. In the eighteenth century, this led to a clogging of the Russian courts, which was only undone by Alexander II's famous Judicial Reform of 1864.

There were different levels of courts in early modern Russia – local, peasant, provincial, capital, the ruler's court – but there was no system of appeal.[71] The verdict a litigant got was the verdict the litigant was stuck with. The law's assumption (and also its demand) was that the judge was a disinterested person who weighed the testimony and, following the rules, rendered a verdict which any reasonable person in the same circumstances would issue. A litigant could sue a judge for malfeasance, but that was another matter – which did not reopen the case. Official malfeasance was a major concern in 1550, and much of the

---

65 *1497 Sudebnik*, arts. 3–8, 15–18, 21–6, 28–30, 36, 38–40, 44, 48, 50, 53, 64, 65, 68; *1550 Sudebnik*, arts. 8–12, 15, 16, 18, 28, 30–1, 33–42, 44–6, 49–51, 55, 59, 62, 65, 74, 75, 77; *1589 Sudebnik*, arts. 10–17, 21, 27, 29, 77–9, 81–91, 94–6, 99, 102, 116, 133, 134, 139. On summonses, see *1497 Sudebnik*, art. 26; *1550 Sudebnik*, arts. 21, 41; *1589 Sudebnik*, arts. 168, 171.

66 *1497 Sudebnik*, arts. 27, 32.

67 *1550 Sudebnik*, arts. 62, 69 mention that some officials are literate, others are not. See also *1589 Sudebnik*, arts. 116, 123.

68 *1550 Sudebnik*, arts. 41, 42, 49, 69, 72, 75; *1589 Sudebnik*, arts. 98, 99, 124, 129, 134.

69 *1550 Sudebnik*, arts. 7, 98; *1589 Sudebnik*, arts. 8, 201.

70 *Inter alia*, see *1550 Sudebnik*, arts. 39, 54, 63, 66, 67, 69, 71, 72, 76, 77, 100; *1589 Sudebnik*, arts. 117, 119, 120, 121, 126, 128, 129, 136–40, 204.

71 *1497 Sudebnik*, arts. 19, 21; *1550 Sudebnik*, arts. 28, 37, 38, 60, 97; *1589 Sudebnik*, arts. 75, 86, 200.

code's severe punishments (high fines, public flogging, jailing) were reserved for officials who abused their positions.[72] A litigant also could appeal to the sovereign (grand prince until 1547, tsar after that), and the ruler, employing what we might call his 'Agapetus powers', could reverse the case. That was not spelled out in the law at all, and if such a reversal occurred, it was an expression of his arbitrariness, not because anyone believed he had divine knowledge of the case. Whether this happened, and, if so, how often, is unknown. The law itself in 1550 became frequently an expression of arbitrariness. Instead of laying down a sanction for an offence, it just said that the culprit would be punished as the tsar decreed, a legal expression of the Agapetus state.[73]

The evolution of the rules of evidence is one of the most interesting developments in the *Sudebniki*. As just mentioned, the society was making a radical transition in this period from one based primarily on oral tradition[74] to one in which written documents could (it is too early to say 'should') play a major role (already seen in the *Pskov Judicial Charter*). The major force propelling this forward was the introduction of the chancelleries (*prikazy*) in 1550, which themselves kept records and demanded that their agents in the provinces keep them informed with a constant flow of information. By the 1570s–1580s all officials of the Provincial Felony Administration were required to be literate. Those men were elected by their peers from among the ranks of the middle service class, the provincial cavalrymen.

Another form of evidence was divine revelation, such as the casting of lots,[75] the oath,[76] and the judicial duel (*pole*), the subject of a surprising number of articles.[77] Trial by combat seems to have been almost the premier form of evidence/proof in 1497 and 1550. At some time at the end of the sixteenth century it went out of use. No one knows why, but a good suggestion has been that the introduction of firearms (especially pistols) cast aspersion on notions that whoever was the better shot was the person designated by God as the righteous one. Another factor putting the duel out of business may have been

72 *1550 Sudebnik*, arts. 3–5, 18, 21, 32, 38, 53, 54, 71; *1589 Sudebnik*, arts. 3–5, 29, 80, 104–6, 126. In some sense, the worst official sanction was disgrace (*opala*), whereby an official became a nobody (*1550 Sudebnik*, art. 7; *1589 Sudebnik*, art. 8).

73 *1550 Sudebnik*, arts. 3, 25, 26, 44, 53, 67, 69, 75; *1589 Sudebnik*, arts. 39, 43, 105, 123.

74 *1497 Sudebnik*, art. 34; *1550 Sudebnik*, arts. 53, 69, 95, 99. Art. 99 demanded that oral witnesses could report only what they had actually seen (also *1589 Sudebnik*, art. 203).

75 *1550 Sudebnik*, art. 27.

76 *1497 Sudebnik*, arts. 46–8, 52, 58; *1550 Sudebnik*, arts. 16, 19, 25, 27, 93; *1589 Sudebnik*, arts. 27, 30, 40, 74.

77 *1497 Sudebnik*, arts. 4–7, 38, 48–9, 52, 68; *1550 Sudebnik*, arts. 9–17, 19, 62, 89; *1589 Sudebnik*, arts. 12–22, 27, 28, 30, 180.

the introduction of the concept of dishonour in the 1550 *Sudebnik*,[78] which expanded to the point in 1649 that everyone from the lowest slave or peasant to the highest boyar in Muscovy had a dishonour value either stated in the law or based on his governmental compensation entitlement level. Thus instead of having to fight a physical duel, a person who felt he had been dishonoured could go to court and the court would determine whether or not this was so. The oath suffered a decline in prestige as presumably the populace began to have increasing doubts that the Russian Orthodox Church was the sole source of truth. Material evidence (the stolen goods, for example) was used, as were varying forms of human evidence. One was witnesses (presumably primarily eyewitnesses; character, rumour or hearsay witnesses were no longer distinguished),[79] another was the judicial confrontation (the plaintiff had to confront the defendant face to face and repeat his charges). The last form of evidence was the investigation (a special subset of which was the 'general investigation' (*poval'nyi obysk*) in which an entire community was interrogated about 'Who owned the cow with the crooked horn?'; the litigant who got the most 'votes' won the case).[80]

Primitive societies had troubles deciding what to do with people between the time an accusation was initiated and a court verdict was rendered. Such societies did not have jails to detain the accused, which many would say is punishing the accused before he is found guilty in any case. An alternative to jail was to let a contract to someone to keep chained to the wall a detainee, who then had to pay a 'chaining fee' (*pozheleznoe*) for the detention as well as somehow pay for his keep (or perhaps have relatives bring him food).[81] The *Sudebnik* of 1497 provided an alternative: an accused could post bail or satisdation (*poruka*) in lieu of being chained to a wall.[82]

By 1613 'crimes' and especially punishments differed markedly from what had been the practices in the 1170s. Most of this can be viewed as part of the evolution from the dyadic to the triadic legal process. In the *Pravda*, 'crimes' were torts in which the wronged was supposed to receive composition and compensation. The more modern notion of 'society' as the real victim was

---

78 A forerunner can be seen in *1497 Sudebnik*, art. 53. See especially *1550 Sudebnik*, art. 26, which lists a dishonour sum for most residents of Muscovy, including peasants and slaves. See also arts. 25, 31, 62, and 70. *1589 Sudebnik*, arts. 39, 41–73. These last articles amount essentially to a *bezchest'e* (dishonour) statute, anticipating chapter 10 of the 1649 *Ulozhenie*.

79 *1497 Sudebnik*, arts. 46, 47, 52; *1550 Sudebnik*, arts. 15–18; *1589 Sudebnik*, arts. 20–2, 27–9.

80 On the investigation (*obysk*), see *1497 Sudebnik*, arts. 14, 34; *1550 Sudebnik*, arts. 52, 56, 57, 72; *1589 Sudebnik*, art. 205 et al.

81 *1550 Sudebnik*, arts. 3, 70; *1589 Sudebnik*, arts. 3, 125.

82 *1497 Sudebnik*, arts. 14, 31, 35; *1550 Sudebnik*, arts. 12, 47, 49, 54, 55, 58, 70, 72; *1589 Sudebnik*, arts. 10, 17, 81, 96, 98, 99, 106, 107, 125, 128, 129.

totally absent. The notion that society was the victim of crime became prevalent in the *Sudebniki*. Then the question arises: how is the criminal to pay his debt to society? Sitting in prison is one answer, but Muscovy did not have prisons until 1550,[83] and they were not used very much for penal incarceration until decades later. Exile and banishment are other useful social sanctions, but are very expensive in labour-short societies such as was Muscovy. The same holds for capital punishment:[84] who can benefit from a dead man (unless he is so heinous that society can tolerate him under no circumstance)? Corporal punishment proved to be the answer.[85] There were any number of forces pushing Muscovy in the direction of corporal punishment savagery (which peaked in the 'Felony Statute' of 1663, combining chapters 21 and 22 of the *Ulozhenie* of 1649), including more 'Western' law such as the West Russian *Lithuanian Statutes* of 1529, 1566 and 1588, but the major impetus was certainly the domestic requirement of 'getting tough' on crime. The Byzantine legal heritage may have played a role in the increasing savagery of Muscovite law, but it is fairly evident that the Mongol hegemony (1237–1480) did not.

Prior to 1497, capital punishment was reserved for few offences. But the 1550 *Sudebnik* lengthened the list to include some homicides, arson, horse theft, theft from a church, theft of a slave, treason, brigandage, rebellion, recidivism for lesser felonies.[86] The issue of intent did not enter into Muscovite sanctions until the *Ulozhenie* of 1649. A thief with a criminal reputation and apprehended with stolen goods was put to death if accused by five or six men. Plaintiffs' claims were exacted from his property. The 'burden of proof' for execution in 1550 was expanded to a general inquest of the population. If the inquest recorded that he was a good person, he was to be tried by normal procedures. Regardless, he was to be tortured.[87] If he confessed, he was to be executed. If he failed to confess, he was to be jailed for life. In 1589 torture was made more precise: 100 blows with the knout (which certainly would have killed an ordinary person). In 1589, if the inquest reported the accused to be a good person, he was to be acquitted immediately.[88]

---

83 *1550 Sudebnik*, arts. 7–11, 13, 33, 34, 46, 53, 55, 58; *1589 Sudebnik*, arts. 8, 11, 16, 18, 105, 107.
84 *1550 Sudebnik*, arts. 56, 57, 59–61; *1589 Sudebnik*, arts. 108, 109, 113–15. See also the earlier discussion of various delicts.
85 *1550 Sudebnik*, arts. 5, 6, 8, 9, 28, 32–4, 42, 47, 53, 54, 58, 99; *1589 Sudebnik*, arts. 5, 6, 11, 12, 80, 81, 104–6, 110.
86 *1497 Sudebnik*, arts. 8, 39. See also n. 62 above. Most interesting is the stress that deserving felons had to be executed and could not be turned over to their victims as slaves to compensate the victims for their losses, even if the felons' property was insufficient to compensate the victims.
87 See *1497 Sudebnik*, art. 34 [torture]; *1550 Sudebnik*, arts. 52, 56, 57, 72. 74.
88 *1589 Sudebnik*, art. 103.

Other punishments ranged from flogging with the knout (for a first theft, plus a fine), incarceration, to the old-fashioned fine.[89] A most visible element in the criminal sphere was the increasing introduction of the government. Ordinary subjects could still file complaints, but anything 'interesting' was soon taken over and prosecuted by the state.

The 'Agapetus state' came to believe that it had enhanced responsibilities not only in the political and criminal spheres, but increasingly in all other spheres of life as well. The three factors in any economy are land, labour and capital. By 1613 the government laid claims to nearly complete control over the first two, and probably would have over capital as well had there been much to control. (See Chapter 23.) Control over land prior to 1480 was primarily a political exercise, not an economic one. Land was so sparsely populated that control over any particular parcel (except in the few urban areas) was hardly something to be contested. Control over large areas was important because the state and its agents could travel around and find people to tax, occasionally to levy military recruits from, and to be present to offer conflict resolution services to on demand. Monasteries were really the sole exception. They could collect rents only from peasants living on *their* parcels of lands and estates. This was why it was the monasteries which introduced St George's Day to control the mobility of their peasant debtors during the chaotic labour situation after the civil war of 1425–53.

But by the 1497 *Sudebnik* much had changed. On the issue of land, the government of Ivan III discovered after the annexation of Novgorod and the deportation of its landowners that land could be mobilised to enhance its military might. Thus the first 'service-class revolution' was initiated by replacing the Novgorodian landowners with Muscovite cavalrymen, who were assigned service landholdings on which lived about thirty peasant households to pay them rent to enable them to render military service. Each landholding (*pomest'e*) was tenureable only while service was being rendered; after service ceased, the *pomeshchik* had to surrender his assigned lands to another serviceman. The system was mentioned in the 1497 *Sudebnik*.[90] As Moscow grew in size, many of the annexed lands were put into the *pomest'e* system. In 1556, as part of the campaign to raise troops to annexe the lower Volga (south of Kazan', annexed in 1552), the government got the idea that it could demand service from all land

---

89 1497 *Sudebnik*, arts. 10, 62; 1550 *Sudebnik*, arts. 5, 6, 28, 55, 58, 87, 99; 1589 *Sudebnik*, arts. 4–6, 11, 12, 13, 16, 80, 81, 102, 103, 105–7, 112, 113, 170, 172, 203, 212, 213. The considerable expansion of savage flogging between 1550 and 1589 is evident just in this list.
90 1497 *Sudebnik*, arts. 29, 63; 1550 *Sudebnik*, art. 84. There were no service landholdings in the Dvina Land, so it is not surprising that the 1589 *Sudebnik* did not mention the subject.

(previously service from the other major form of landholding, landownership – the *votchina* – had been in some respects optional). The 1556 edict prescribed that one outfitted cavalryman had to be provided from each 100 *cheti* (1 *chet'* = 1.39 US acres or half a hectare) of populated land.[91] This forced estate owners into the market to hire military slaves to meet their recruiting quotas and the military muster records are full of lists of these slave cavalrymen. By the 1580s perhaps 80 per cent of the military land fund was *pomest'e* land and it appeared as though the *votchina* might die out. This did not happen because every *pomeshchik*'s aspiration was to become a *votchinnik* who could pass his estate to his heirs, which became often practice in the second half of the seventeenth century and *de jure* reality in the eighteenth century. Prior to 1450 East Slavic princes regarded all land in their domains as their personal patrimonial property which they were free to dispose of as they pleased. After 1556, most usable land de facto was land which could be mobilised by the state for military purposes.[92]

Mobilising the land, the hypertrophic state set about controlling all labour. This began with St George's Day limitations for monastery debtors in the 1450s. That demonstrated what could be done, and in the 1497 *Sudebnik* it was applied to all peasants.[93] As discussed in considerably greater detail in Chapter 12, in 1592 all peasants were forbidden to move at all. As also discussed in Chapter 12, having decided that it had the power to control the legal status of the peasantry, the state decided that it could alter the status of the slaves. Slaves were the subject of a remarkable number of articles in 1497, far more than any other sector of society.[94] Except for emancipations, such dramatic state interventions in the institution of slavery are rare in human history. Full slavery was melded into limited service contract slavery, and then in the 1590s the nature of the 'limitation' changed from an *antichresis* (see Chapter 12) of one

91 Richard Hellie, *Enserfment and Military Change in Muscovy* (Chicago: University of Chicago Press, 1971), pp. 37–8.

92 Even today, fences are not as common in Eastern Europe as they are in America. One may assume that the appearance of fences reflects a desire to save labour on herding livestock and to protect crops from grazing livestock, as well as an increasing value of land. See *1497 Sudebnik*, art. 61; *1550 Sudebnik*, arts. 86, 87; *1589 Sudebnik*, arts. 168, 171.

93 *1497 Sudebnik*, art. 55. This was elaborated on in *1550 Sudebnik*, art. 88, which reflected the introduction of the three-field system of agriculture.

94 *1497 Sudebnik*, arts. 17, 18, 23, 40–3, 55, 56, 66. The centrality of slavery in Muscovy is further reflected in *1550 Sudebnik*, arts. 26, 35, 40, 54, 59–63, 65–7, 71, 77–81. Article 76 is a miniature slavery statute, and article 90 reflects the increasing use of slaves in military operations; a slave who was captured by enemy forces was freed if he returned to Muscovy. The fact that there were so many articles on slavery in *1589 Sudebnik* (arts. 88, 113, 115, 117, 119–21, 136–46, 182) is a manifestation of how omni-present the institution was in Muscovy.

year that defaulted to hereditary full slavery upon inability after a year to repay a loan to slavery for the life of the owner, followed by compulsory emancipation upon his death. In 1550 the government decreed that able-bodied townsmen had to live in the juridical towns, not on monastery urban property.[95] In the 1590s the government decided that it had the right to control the mobility of townsmen (paralleling the control over peasant mobility),[96] which culminated in the 1649 *Ulozhenie*'s prohibition against townsmen's leaving their place of urban residence. This is a perfect example of how the 'Agapetus monarchy' developed the maximalist state which found few areas of Russian life where it could not intervene.[97] Comparatively, what is interesting is the use of law in this evolution. In America, for example, law is often seen as a very conservative institution that is the codification of a reality that sometimes has already passed. In early modern Russia, on the other hand, law became the statement of social programmes that the state was hoping to enact; and it usually could enforce most of what it had enacted. In this respect Muscovy was the perfect ancestor of the Soviet Union, a radical political organisation with a programme of social change it was constantly attempting to enact. The result was the first service-class revolution.

A few more words need to be said about landed property. The conditional service landholdings (*pomest'ia*) have been mentioned. Hereditary estates (*votchiny*) were of various kinds: princely, boyaral, monastery, clan, granted and purchased. Each had its own rules for sale and the possibility of redemption. Monastery estates in practice were inalienable, but most *votchiny* could be given away, willed by testament, sold, exchanged and mortgaged. In reality, landed property was rarely mobilised in the economy because service landholdings were state property reserved for military service and private hereditary estates could be redeemed for up to forty years after sale at the price the seller had received for it.[98] Thus it made no sense for any private person to buy land, and as a result it is impossible to find agricultural land prices in Muscovy.[99]

By the end of the fifteenth century the land in Muscovy was beginning to fill up, and contests over landownership became more frequent. In the interests

95 *1550 Sudebnik*, art. 91; *1589 Sudebnik*, arts. 184, 188, 189. This had no 1497 precedent.
96 Richard Hellie (ed. and trans.), *Muscovite Society* (Chicago: University of Chicago Syllabus Division, 1967 and 1970), pp. 33–47.
97 Richard Hellie, 'The Expanding Role of the State in Russia', in Jarmo T. Kotilaine and Marshall T. Poe (eds.), *Modernizing Muscovy: Reform and Social Change in Seventeenth-Century Russia* (London: Routledge, 2003), pp. 29–56.
98 *1550 Sudebnik*, art. 85. This had no 1497 antecedent. See also *1589 Sudebnik*, arts. 164, 165.
99 Richard Hellie, *The Economy and Material Culture of Russia 1600–1725* (Chicago: University of Chicago Press, 1999), pp. 391–3, 411.

of efficiency seen throughout this chapter, the 1497 *Sudebnik* imposed statutes of limitations on the filing of suits over landownership between monasteries, members of the service class, and peasants (three years) and between the sovereign, monasteries and servicemen (six years).[100] Here one can see the ancestor of the five-year statute of limitations on the filing of suits for the recovery of fugitive serfs of 1592. There were no statutes of limitations on the filing of suits for moveable property, including slaves.

The rules of inheritance were spelled out in the *Sudebniki*. An oral or written will had precedence. In its absence, a son inherited. Next was a daughter, then other members of the clan. Failing that, property escheated to the prince.[101]

As observed by D. P. Makovskii some decades ago, prior to Ivan's *oprichnina* (1565–72) Muscovy was developing into a commercial society.[102] This is evident in the law, where numerous articles deal with loans.[103] Of particular interest is the provision permitting borrowing with the payment of interest.[104] New legislation on branding horses may or may not reflect an increasing commoditisation of horses.[105]

By 1613 Russian law had changed considerably from the law of the late Middle Ages, but elements of continuity must also be stressed. First and foremost was the fact that law remained a major revenue-raising device for officialdom. Law remained a device for cleaning up social messes, be they felonies or civil disputes. The major distinction between the earlier era and the pre-Romanov decades was that the distinction between felonies – in which the state took an increasing interest – and civil disputes, about which the state ordinarily could not care less, was heightened by changes in the essence of society that required a change in the legal process from a dyadic one to a triadic one as well as changes in the nature of the state power, from a relatively benign and weak organism with few pretensions, to an increasingly assertive autocracy that recognised few limitations on its authority. This was facilitated by increasing literacy both in the capital and in the provinces among the handfuls of people who mattered and who were essential for keeping the records required for keeping track of slave ownership, land allocation and possession, military service and compensation, foreign relations and accusations of domestic treason,

---

100 *1497 Sudebnik*, art. 63; *1550 Sudebnik*, arts. 24, 84; *1589 Sudebnik*, arts. 37, 149, 150, 156.
101 *1497 Sudebnik*, art. 60; *1550 Sudebnik*, art. 92; *1589 Sudebnik*, art. 190.
102 D. P. Makovskii, *Razvitie tovarno-denezhnykh otnoshenii v sel'skom khoziaistve Russkogo gosudarstva v XVI veka* (Smolensk: Smolenskii pedagogicheskii institut, 1963).
103 *1497 Sudebnik*, arts. 53, 55. Note the *1550 Sudebnik* expansion: arts. 11, 15, 16, 31, 36, 82, 90. See also *1589 Sudebnik*, arts. 15, 84, 146, 147, 181, 182.
104 *1550 Sudebnik*, art. 36; *1589 Sudebnik*, art. 84. This had no precedent.
105 *1550 Sudebnik*, arts. 94–6; *1589 Sudebnik*, arts. 195–8.

post roads, and what happened at trial. Law still had the function of determining inheritance and preserving male superiority and regime dominance, but almost to an astonishing extent it became the government's mouthpiece for directing social change towards a rigidly stratified, almost-caste society. Law became a major instrument in preserving what the legislators wanted to keep from the past while simultaneously serving as a major instrument in assisting change in desired directions.

17

Political ideas and rituals

MICHAEL S. FLIER

Shortly after the dedication of Moscow's cathedral church in 1479, Grand Prince Ivan III accused Metropolitan Gerontii of contravening ritual tradition by leading the cross procession around the church counterclockwise (*protiv solntsa*) instead of clockwise (*po solon'*) during the dedication service. Perhaps Ivan was motivated by superstition, given the collapse of the previous reconstruction. Or perhaps he was influenced by the Catholic-orientated entourage around his second wife, Sophia Palaeologa, a former ward of the Pope. Whatever the cause, he forbade the consecration of any church in Moscow for three years while he investigated previous practice. Finding no conclusive protocols, he was obliged to recant in 1482 to prevent the metropolitan's resignation.[1] This rare personal episode involving ritual and political control reveals a connection that merits further enquiry.

Ritual, with its attendant symbols and actions, powerfully expresses the ways in which members of a society, especially its elites, see themselves and wish themselves to be seen. The present chapter seeks to describe and analyse the function of ritual in representing political ideas in Muscovy before the seventeenth century. Political ritual refers to that set of conventionalised events ruled by protocol and consisting of separate acts performed *in public* whose purpose is to confirm or restore links to a commonly held political concept or belief for the ritual's participants and observers. The interlocking spheres of politics and religion in medieval society presuppose the presentation of political ideology within a spiritual framework. Religious symbolism approximates the harmony of political structure with the providence of God.

As with any rite, the successful performance of a ritual is understood to be transformative. A grand prince is made tsar; water is made holy to benefit those in need of grace; a subject is confirmed in his loyalty and politically

---

1 *PSRL*, vol. VI, pt. 2 (Moscow: Iazyki russkoi kul'tury, 2001), pp. 286–7, 313–14; *PSRL*, vol. XX, pt. 1 (St Petersburg: Tipografiia M. A. Aleksandrova, 1910), pp. 335, 348.

inferior position; a society is rededicated to the possibility of resurrection after death. Such are the psychological and spiritual transformations rituals bring about.

The political life of Muscovite society was replete with rituals. Perhaps the most daunting was kissing the cross (*krestnoe tselovanie*) in a church to solemnify an oath or declaration as true. Princes forged alliances, confirmed treaties and attested wills by kissing the cross. Litigants in court disputes without clear evidence faced the terrifying prospect of standing before the cross, kissing it the fateful third time, and swearing the truth of their testimony. Frequently they opted for other forms of resolution.[2]

The ritual of petition produced different relationships. In describing ritual practice at the Muscovite court in the early sixteenth century, Sigismund von Herberstein, the ambassador of the Holy Roman Emperor, wrote:

> whenever anyone makes a petition, or offers thanks, it is the custom to bow the head; if he wishes to do so in a very marked manner, he bends himself so low as to touch the ground with his hand; but if he desires to offer his thanks to the grand-duke for any great favour, or to beg anything of him, he then bows himself so low as to touch the ground with his forehead.[3]

This ritual, combined with references to petitioners as slaves (*kholopy*) and the ruler as master (*gosudar'*), convinced many foreigners, including Herberstein, that Muscovy was a despotic state. *Bit' chelom* 'to beat one's forehead' was, after all, the Muscovite term for paying obeisance and the source for *chelobitie* (*chelobit'e*) 'petition', literally beating of the forehead.

Cross kissing was a Kievan and Muscovite ritual that confirmed a relationship of obeisance before God, rendering all persons, high and low, equal before their creator. The beating of the head, by contrast, was a ritual that confirmed an asymmetrical relationship, rendering petitioner and petitioned unequal in status and affirming the political and social hierarchy of Muscovite life.

Muscovy and the ideology of rulership

The correlation of ritual and political ideas begins with the historical transformation of Muscovy and the development of a myth to account for it. By

---

2 Giles Fletcher, 'Of the Russe Commonwealth', in Lloyd E. Berry and Robert O. Crummey (eds.), *Rude and Barbarous Kingdom: Russia in the Accounts of Sixteenth-Century English Voyagers* (Madison: University of Wisconsin Press, 1968), pp. 174–5; Nancy Shields Kollmann, *By Honor Bound: State and Society in Early Modern Russia* (Ithaca, N. Y.: Cornell University Press, 1999), pp. 119–20.

3 Sigismund von Herberstein, *Notes upon Russia*, 2 vols., trans. R. H. Major (New York: Burt Franklin, 1851–2), vol. ii, pp. 124–5.

the mid-fifteenth century, Moscow was adjusting to an altered position in the world of Eastern Orthodoxy. Rejecting the Union of Florence and Ferrara, the Muscovites refused to consult the Greeks when selecting their new metropolitan in 1448 and in effect formed an autocephalous Orthodox Church. Thereafter, the Muscovite Church promulgated an anti-Tatar, anti-Muslim campaign in the chronicles in counterpoint to the pure Christian tradition represented by Moscow.[4] Moscow was increasingly portrayed as inheriting the legacy of Kievan Rus' and with it, the myth of the Rus'ian Land, which was ultimately incorporated into the myth of the Muscovite ruler.[5] Constantinople's capture by the Turks in 1453 and the seemingly providential expansion of the Muscovite principality thereafter opened new vistas for Ivan III when he ascended to the throne in 1462. By 1480, Archbishop Vassian Rylo was urging him to become the great Christian tsar and liberator of the Rus'ian Land, the 'New Israel', in its struggle against the Golden Horde, the 'godless sons of Hagar'.[6]

The ideology that crystallised in Muscovy during the reigns of Ivan III (1462–1505), his son, Vasilii III (1505–33) and grandson, Ivan IV (1533–84) presented the Byzantine notion of the emperor-dominated realm as the Kingdom of Christ on Earth. If allusion to Agapetus gave the ruler absolute political authority over the state ('though an emperor in body be like all other men, yet in power he is like God'), the *Epanagōgē* of Patriarch Photius and other Byzantine political literature known in Muscovy at the time broadly demarcated spheres of authority apportioned among temporal and spiritual leaders.[7] Church polemicists such as Iosif Volotskii in *The Enlightener* praised the power and authority of the grand prince, but insisted on the mobilisation of wise advisers – temporal and spiritual – against authority that transgressed the laws of God.[8]

Muscovite rulership and the Kievan legacy were expressed most clearly in the invented tradition of *The Tale of the Princes of Vladimir* (c.1510). The

---

4 Donald Ostrowski, *Muscovy and the Mongols: Cross-Cultural Influences on the Steppe Frontier, 1304–1589* (Cambridge: Cambridge University Press, 1998), pp. 164–70.
5 Charles J. Halperin, 'The Russian Land and the Russian Tsar: The Emergence of Muscovite Ideology, 1380–1408', *FOG* 23 (1976): 79–82; Jaroslaw Pelenski, 'The Origins of the Official Muscovite Claims to the "Kievan Inheritance"', *HUS* 1 (1977): 40–2, 51–2 and 'The Emergence of the Muscovite Claims to the Byzantine-Kievan "Imperial Inheritance"', *HUS* 7 (1983): 20–1.
6 *PSRL*, vol. VIII (Moscow: Iazyki russkoi kul'tury, 2001), pp. 212–13.
7 Deno John Geanakoplos, *Byzantine East & Latin West: Two Worlds of Christendom in Middle Ages and Renaissance, Studies in Ecclesiastical and Cultural History* (New York: Harper Torchbooks, 1966), pp. 63–5; Ostrowski, *Muscovy and the Mongols*, pp. 207–8.
8 David M. Goldfrank, *The Monastic Rule of Iosif Volotsky*, rev. edn, Cistercian Studies Series, no. 36 (Kalamazoo, Mich., and Cambridge, Mass.: Cistercian Publications, 2000), p. 42; Daniel Rowland, 'Did Muscovite Literary Ideology Place Limits on the Power of the Tsar (1540s–1660s)?', *RR* 49 (1990): 126–31; Ostrowski, *Muscovy and the Mongols*, pp. 199–218.

Roman genealogy that traced the Riurikid dynasty back to Prus, a kinsman of Augustus Caesar, may have been included to assure Europeans that the use of the term 'tsar' for the Muscovite ruler was legitimate. The Monomakh legend provided a Byzantine pedigree for Muscovite Orthodox rulership in the form of concrete royal symbols of authority sent by Byzantine emperor Constantine Monomachos to Vladimir Monomakh to be used at the latter's installation as Kievan grand prince.[9]

In theory the Muscovite ruler had unlimited power and authority in rendering God's will, but in practice he governed with the support and close involvement of a secular and ecclesiastical elite.[10] It was this ruling elite that faced the imminent Apocalypse at the approach of 1492, the portentous year 7000 in the Byzantine reckoning. In this context, the city of Moscow itself was reconceptualised in Orthodox Christian terms as the New Jerusalem and Muscovy came to be understood as the embodiment of the Chosen People, whose ruler chosen by God was prepared to lead them to salvation.[11]

Ritual and setting

In three centuries Moscow had evolved from a mere outpost to a city with a walled fortress and pretensions to greatness. By the 1470s, the earlier structures built to mark the rise of a city – limestone walls, stone churches, royal palace and halls – were dilapidated.[12] Ivan III, better than any of his immediate predecessors, understood how setting and ritual might serve to integrate the notions of the emerging Muscovite state and a ruling elite. In an impressive environment, solemn rituals could elevate the person of the ruler and help confirm his position at the apex of society. There was no place more suitable for rituals of high purpose than the Kremlin, the fortress of Moscow.

Cathedral Square was one of the semiotically most charged spaces within the Kremlin (see Figure 17.1). It was bounded on the north by the cathedral

---

9 Ostrowski, *Muscovy and the Mongols*, pp. 171–6.
10 Edward L. Keenan, 'Muscovite Political Folkways', *RR* 45 (1986): 128–36; Nancy Shields Kollmann, *Kinship and Politics: The Making of the Muscovite Political System, 1345–1547* (Stanford, Calif.: Stanford University Press, 1987), pp. 146–87; Kollmann, *By Honor Bound*, pp. 169–202; Ostrowski, *Muscovy and the Mongols*, pp. 85–107, 135–43, 199–218.
11 Ostrowski, *Muscovy and the Mongols*, p. 218; Michael S. Flier, 'Till the End of Time: The Apocalypse in Russian Historical Experience before 1500', in Valerie A. Kivelson and Robert H. Greene (eds.), *Orthodox Russia: Belief and Practice under the Tsars* (University Park, Pa.: Pennsylvania State University Press, 2003), pp. 152–8.
12 I. E. Grabar' (ed.), *Istoriia russkogo iskusstva*, 13 vols. (Moscow: AN SSSR, 1953–64), vol. III (1955), pp. 282–333; T. F. Savarenskaia (ed.), *Arkhitekturnye ansambli Moskvy XV–nachala XX vekov: Printsipy khudozhestvennogo edinstva* (Moscow: Stroiizdat, 1997), pp. 17–53.

Figure 17.1. Cathedral Square, Moscow Kremlin

KEY: 1. Cathedral of the Dormition
      2. Cathedral of Archangel Michael
      3. Cathedral of Annunciation
      4. Faceted Hall
      5. Golden Hall
      6. Beautiful (Red) Porch
      7. Palace
      8. Bell Tower 'Ivan the Great'
      9. Tainik Tower

of the Dormition (primary cathedral church), on the east by the bell tower 'Ivan the Great', on the south by the cathedral of the Archangel Michael (royal necropolis), and on the west by the cathedral of the Annunciation (palace church), the Golden Hall (throne room), the adjacent Beautiful (Red) Porch and Staircase, and the Faceted Hall (reception hall).

The cathedral of the Dormition (1475–9) was designed by Bolognese architect Aristotele Fioravanti after the Muscovite effort to rebuild resulted in a disastrous collapse in 1474.[13] Fioravanti reshaped the older Vladimir Dormition plan in a Renaissance compositional key, maintaining modified medieval Vladimir-Suzdal' features on the exterior. He created a dramatic southern portal facing Cathedral Square, harmonised the dimensions of the bays, flattened the apses, and produced a characteristically north-eastern limestone façade that prompted contemporaries to describe the building as though carved 'from a single stone'.[14] He opened up the internal space to the highest vaults, eliminating the gallery that would traditionally have ensconced the royal family. The place of the grand prince was relocated to the ground floor near the southern portal, which became an effective alternative point of egress for the ruler during processions.

The Metropolitan's Pew, mentioned in many of the Dormition's rituals, was apparently installed between 1479 and the mid-1480s in a space adjacent to the south-east pillar of the nave facing the iconostasis.[15] More than seven decades passed before the self-standing Tsar's Pew was installed on 1 September 1551, four years after Ivan IV was officially crowned as the first tsar. Better known as the Monomakh Throne, the Pew boasted twelve carved wooden panels based on excerpts from the Monomakh legend taken from *The Tale of the Princes of Vladimir*. Apart from military forays against the Byzantines, the panels depicted Monomakh in consultation with a boyar council, the arrival of the royal Byzantine regalia in Kiev, and their use in the crowning of Vladimir Monomakh as grand prince, all messages immediately relevant to Muscovite ideology. The theme of Jerusalem was represented in the inscription around the cornice, which reproduced God's injunction about dynastic continuity and wise rulership to King David and King Solomon. Furthermore, the composition of the Pew bore a clear affinity to the Dormition's Small Zion, a silver

---

13 See historical survey with source references in V. P. Vygolov, *Arkhitektura Moskovskoi Rusi serediny XV veka* (Moscow: Nauka, 1988), pp. 177–210.

14 *PSRL*, vol. xxv (Moscow and Leningrad: AN SSSR, 1949), p. 324.

15 T. V. Tolstaia, *Uspenskii sobor Moskovskogo Kremlia* (Moscow: Nauka, 1979), p. 30; G. N. Bocharov, 'Tsarskoe Mesto Ivana Groznogo v Moskovskom Uspenskom sobore', in *Pamiatniki russkoi arkhitektury i monumental'nogo iskusstva: Goroda, ansambli, zodchie*, ed. V. P. Vygolov (Moscow: Nauka, 1985), p. 46.

liturgical vessel representing Jerusalem's Holy Sepulchre and carried in solemn processions.[16]

The cathedral of Archangel Michael (1505–8) was designed by another Italian architect, Alevisio the Younger. He retained the asymmetrical bays from the earlier medieval plan, but added striking Renaissance ornament, including limestone articulation against a red-brick façade and distinctive, large scallop-shell gables signifying rebirth. This was fitting symbolism for a site devoted to the memory of the royal dynasty, whose sarcophagi occupied the southern and later northern part of the nave and a side chapel near the sanctuary.

The cathedral of the Annunciation (1484–9) had been rebuilt by native Psko-vian architects, who skilfully combined the basic Suzdalian articulated cube with its blind arcade frieze and ogival gables together with brickwork and design redolent of Pskov and Novgorod, a stylistic marriage signalling Mus-covite success in 'the gathering of the Rus'ian lands'.

The Faceted Hall (1487–91) was designed by Italians Marco Ruffo and Pietro Antonio Solario in the style of a northern Italian Renaissance palazzo, but with an obvious allusion to its namesake in Novgorod. Named after the carved facets on the eastern façade facing the Square, it was notable for its internal design with a huge central pier supporting groined vaults. The pier served as a staging area for official receptions and banquets hosted by the grand prince. The Faceted Hall is often mentioned in foreign accounts as the site of numerous rituals of status and conciliation as regards foreign audiences, seating protocol, the tasting and distribution of food and the proposing of toasts.[17]

The Golden Hall was planned by Ivan III but completed by his son, Vasilii III, in 1508. Reached off a great landing, the Beautiful (Red) Porch overlooking Cathedral Square, the Golden Hall consisted of a vestibule, where dignitaries gathered, and the throne room. The name was apparently inspired by the *Chrysotriklinos*, the Golden Hall throne room of the Byzantine emperor in Constantinople. Severely damaged in the Moscow fire of 1547, the Golden Hall was completely rebuilt by order of the newly crowned tsar, Ivan IV, and decorated with elaborate and controversial murals that referred to allegories and historical events important to Muscovite ideology.[18]

16 I. A. Sterligova, 'Ierusalimy kak liturgicheskie sosudy v Drevnei Rusi', in *Ierusalim v russkoi kul'ture*, ed. Andrei Batalov and Aleksei Lidov (Moscow: Nauka, 1994), p. 50; Michael S. Flier, 'The Throne of Monomakh: Ivan the Terrible and the Architectonics of Destiny', in James Cracraft and Daniel Rowland (eds.), *Architectures of Russian Identity 1500 to the Present* (Ithaca, N.Y.: Cornell University Press, 2003), pp. 30–2.

17 Herberstein, *Notes*, vol. ii, pp. 127–32; Richard Chancellor, 'The First Voyage to Russia', in Berry and Crummey (eds.), *Rude and Barbarous Kingdom*, pp. 25–7.

18 O. I. Podobedova, *Moskovskaia shkola zhivopisi pri Ivane IV: Raboty v Moskovskom Kremle 40-kh–70-kh godov XVI v.* (Moscow: Nauka, 1972), pp. 59–68; David B. Miller, 'The

The major architectural innovation beyond the Kremlin itself was the church of the Intercession on the Moat, later known as St Basil's cathedral. Built in Beautiful (Red) Square in celebration of Ivan IV's victory over the Kazan' khanate in 1552, the church underwent a slow progression in 1555 from individual shrines to a composite set of correlated chapels, which, taken together, resemble Jerusalem in microcosm.[19] Completed in 1561 on a site adjacent to the central marketplace and the world of the non-elite, the Intercession stood as an antipode to the core structures of Cathedral Square behind the Kremlin walls.

In 1598/9, just to the north of the Intercession, a raised round dais was built in stone, possibly replacing an earlier wooden structure.[20] Called Golgotha (*Lobnoe mesto* 'place of the skull'), it was a site for major royal proclamations, including declarations of war, announcements of royal births and deaths and the naming of heirs apparent, perhaps replacing the original city tribune. It was also used as a station for major cross processions led by the chief prelate and the tsar, rituals featuring the palladium of Moscow, the icon of the Vladimir Mother of God, in honour of her benevolent protection. Golgotha, by its very name and placement near the Intercession 'Jerusalem', made manifest Moscow's self-perception as the New Jerusalem.

The political rituals that realised most directly the myth of the Muscovite ruler and his realm were either *contingent*, prompted by circumstance, or *cyclical*, governed by the ecclesiastical calendar. They were *direct*, requiring the presence of the ruler, or *indirect*, referring to his office. In addition to the actual protocols of ceremony, the locus of performance, whether inside or outside Moscow and its golden centre, provided significant points of reference that guided and enriched the message intended. Nowhere is this better demonstrated than in the etiquette involving foreign diplomats, from whom we have quite extensive responses.[21]

Viskovatyi Affair of 1553–54: Official Art, the Emergence of Autocracy, and the Disintegration of Medieval Russian Culture', *RH* 8 (1981): 298, 308, 314–20; Michael S. Flier, 'K semioticheskomu analizu Zolotoi palaty Moskovskogo Kremlia', in *Drevnerusskoe iskusstvo. Russkoe iskusstvo pozdnego srednevekov'ia: XVI vek* (St Petersburg: Dmitrii Bulanin, 2003), pp. 180–6; Daniel Rowland, 'Two Cultures, One Throneroom: Secular Courtiers and Orthodox Culture in the Golden Hall of the Moscow Kremlin', in Kivelson and Greene (eds.), *Orthodox Russia: Belief and Practice under the Tsars*, pp. 40–53.

19 Michael S. Flier, 'Filling in the Blanks: The Church of the Intercession and the Architectonics of Medieval Muscovite Ritual', *HUS* 19 (1995): 120–37; Savarenskaia (ed.), *Arkhitekturnye ansambli Moskvy*, pp. 54–99.

20 *PSRL*, vol. xxxiv (Moscow: AN SSSR, 1978), p. 202; B. A. Uspenskii, *Tsar' i patriarkh: Kharizma vlasti v Rossii (Vizantiiskaia model' i ee russkoe pereosmyslenie)* (Moscow: Iazyki russkoi kul'tury, 1998), p. 455 (n. 52).

21 Marshall Poe, 'A People Born to Slavery': *Russia in Early Modern Ethnography, 1476–1748* (Ithaca, N.Y.: Cornell University Press, 2000), pp. 39–81.

Contingent rituals

Foreign diplomatic rituals

In a report that resonates with others from sixteenth- and seventeenth-century writers, Herberstein commented on the indirect but nonetheless elaborate ritual etiquette that faced foreign embassies upon approaching Muscovite territory.[22] Each part of the protocol – initial contact, local interview, delay for instructions from Moscow, escort, entrance into Moscow, sequestering and audience with the Muscovite ruler – confirmed relative status. Ritual gestures such as dismounting from horses or sledges, or the baring of heads in anticipation of verbal exchange, were carried out in a specific order, designed to place the prestige of the Muscovite representative, and indirectly that of the grand prince, above that of the foreign visitor and his master.

Royal escorts rode ahead of and behind the embassy along the entire route, allowing no one to fall behind or join the entourage. Symbolically the royal reach extended to the very borders of the realm, enveloping the foreign element and drawing it towards the centre. At each station new representatives were dispatched from the centre to receive the members of the embassy and greet them in the name of the ruler until at last, after several days or even weeks of waiting outside the city, they were escorted into Moscow past crowds of people intentionally brought there. Entering the Kremlin on foot, they encountered huge numbers of soldiers and separate ranks of courtiers – enough people, so Herberstein reasoned, to impress foreigners with the sheer quantity of subjects and the consequent power of the grand prince. The closer the envoys came to the site of the grand prince, the more frequent were the successions of ever more highly placed ranks of nobility, each rank moving into position directly behind the embassy as the next higher one waited to greet them.

Once ushered into the throne room itself, the envoys descended several steps to the floor. From this position they were obliged to look up at the sumptuously attired ruler on a raised throne. Additionally they confronted his numerous courtiers, clad in golden cloth down to their ankles, the boyars resplendent in their high fur hats, and all seated on benches above the steps against the other three walls in an orderly array.[23] The English merchant Richard Chancellor reported that 'this so honorable an assembly, so great a majesty of the emperor and of the place, might very well have amazed our men and have dashed them out of countenance. . .'[24] The papal legate to

22 Herberstein, *Notes*, vol. II, pp. 112–42.
23 Chancellor, 'First Voyage', p. 24.
24 Ibid., p. 25.

Ivan IV, Antonio Possevino, judged that in the splendour of his court and those who populate it, the tsar 'rivals the Pope and surpasses other kings'.[25] The English commercial agent Jerome Horsey noted with admiration Ivan IV's four royal guards (*ryndy*) flanking the throne, dressed in shiny silver cloth and bearing ceremonial pole-axes.[26] The carefully arranged hierarchy of courtiers dominated by the tsar was all-encompassing and meant to impress visitors with the size, authority and immeasurable wealth of the Muscovite court. All petitioners were required to repeat the ruler's lengthy series of titles, a list based on rank and geographic spread. Omission of any title on the list was not tolerated.[27] The most important ceremonial act during the audience was the diplomat's kissing of the tsar's right hand, if it was offered.[28] Ritual enquiries about health were then followed by the formal presentation of gifts by the diplomat.

Royal progresses

As a complement to the ritualised travel of diplomats towards the centre, the royal progress from centre to periphery allowed the ruler himself to promulgate Muscovite ideology by travelling to cities, towns and monasteries in elaborate processions, with icons and other ecclesiastical accoutrements.[29] Such a ritual stamping out of territory and creation of royal space tied the land to the ruler through contiguity. Participating in impressive ceremonies of entrance (*adventus*) and departure (*profectio*), the ruler was able to take possession of the site physically and spiritually by means of an awe-inspiring display of the sort demonstrated by Ivan IV when he captured and entered Kazan' in 1552 and then returned to Moscow in a triumphant procession.[30]

Bride shows

The authority of the ruler was represented directly or indirectly in rituals intended to preserve harmony and balance among the court elite. Marriage

---

25 Antonio Possevino, *The Moscovia of Antonio Possevino, S.J.*, ed. and trans. Hugh F. Graham, UCIS Series in Russian and East European Studies, no. 1 (Pittsburgh: University Center for International Studies, University of Pittsburgh, 1977), p. 47.
26 Sir Jerome Horsey, 'Travels', in Berry and Crummey (eds.), *Rude and Barbarous Kingdom*, p. 303.
27 Fletcher, 'Russe Commonwealth', pp. 131–2; cf. Herberstein, *Notes*, vol. II, pp. 34–8.
28 L.A. Iuzefovich, 'Kak v posol'skikh obychaiakh vedetsia' (Moscow: Mezhdunarodnye otnosheniia, 1988), pp. 115–16.
29 Nancy Shields Kollmann, 'Pilgrimage, Procession, and Symbolic Space in Sixteenth-Century Russian Politics', in Michael S. Flier and Daniel Rowland (eds.), *Medieval Russian Culture*, 2 vols. (Berkeley: University of California Press, 1994), vol. II, pp. 163–6.
30 *PSRL*, vol. XIII (Moscow: Iazyki russkoi kul'tury, 2000), pp. 220–8.

arrangements, for instance, helped maintain a tenuous power network among specific clans at court. The intricate organisation of bride shows, performed ritually before the ruler, guaranteed him and his family firm control over the selection process and the relationships to be strengthened, weakened or ended.[31]

Surrender-by-the-head ritual

The indirect ritual of surrender by the head (*vydacha golovoiu*) was intended to confirm the hierarchy among elites established by the rules of precedence (*mestnichestvo*) and is described in Kotoshikhin's seventeenth-century account of the Muscovite court.[32] Violators of precedence were sent in disgrace on foot instead of on horseback from the Kremlin, a metonym of the tsar's power, to the house of the offended party, where the tsar's representatives announced the ruler's decision to the winner as he stood on an upstairs porch. The semiotic oppositions of low and high were complemented by the loser's permission to insult the winner for emotional release without retaliation. The ritual reinforced the image of the ruler as charismatic and autocratic, and that of the noble elite as accommodating and supportive advisers committed to preserving the order and stability that made government by consensus possible.[33]

Coronation ritual

Although we have no record of the investiture ceremony of the grand princes of Kievan Rus' or of their counterparts in Muscovite Rus' before the late fifteenth century, some form of installation ceremony surely existed. The direct formula that appears in chronicle accounts simply notes that such-and-such a prince assumed authority (*siede* lit. 'sat') in a given capital or that a more highly placed ruler installed him on the throne (*posadi* lit. 'seated').

The earliest evidence of an actual coronation ceremony in Muscovy dates from 4 February 1498, when a ritual based on the Byzantine ceremony for co-emperors was used to lend legitimacy to Ivan III's naming a controversial heir apparent – grandson Dmitrii rather than second son Vasilii – to the Muscovite throne. By 1502, Vasilii had regained favour and was named grand prince and thus entitled to succeed his father. Interestingly, the performance of the coronation ceremony had not guaranteed the succession to Dmitrii, thus

---

31 Russell E. Martin, 'Dynastic Marriage in Muscovy, 1500–1729', unpublished Ph.D. dissertation, Harvard University, 1996, pp. 30–110.
32 Grigorij Kotošixin, *O Rossii v carstvovanie Alekseja Mixajloviča: Text and Commentary*, ed. A. E. Pennington (Oxford: Clarendon Press, 1980), fos. 63–64v, 67, 149, 150.
33 Nancy Shields Kollmann, 'Ritual and Social Drama at the Muscovite Court', *SR* 45 (1986): 497–500.

revealing its culturally compromised status as a political device. This point was driven home when Vasilii himself assumed the role of heir apparent in 1502 and ascended to the throne of his late father in 1505, in both instances without the ritual of coronation.

The accession of Ivan IV in 1533, however, proved a turning point in the conception of the Muscovite ruler. Surviving several court intrigues, Ivan found an ally in Makarii, archbishop of Novgorod, and from 1542, metropolitan of Moscow. Through a number of cultural initiatives, the revision of the Great Reading Menology and the writing of the Book of Degrees among the most significant, Makarii sought to elevate the position and authority of the tsar as a messianic figure, in effect, to sacralise him and accord him special charisma.[34] In 1547, Makarii was prepared to declare Ivan not simply grand prince, but tsar and autocrat, a God-chosen sovereign. Accordingly, he devised an appropriate coronation ceremony based on the Byzantine model used for Dmitrii, a ritual appropriate for transforming the sixteen-year-old prince into a tsar.

Ivan was officially crowned on 16 January 1547 in the Dormition cathedral in a ritual that had many implications for the historical and eschatological significance of the Muscovite ruler. The date was significant because it fell on the first Sunday after the final observance of Epiphany, which celebrates God's satisfaction with Christ's baptism by John ('the Forerunner') in the River Jordan. Ritually 'anointed', Christ begins his ministry in the Holy Land with this event, an appropriate analogue to Ivan's official beginning as tsar of Muscovy, the New Israel.[35]

The coronation ceremony in the Dormition cathedral combined high solemnity with the symbolism of legend and Scripture to create an effect with universal impact. Ordered ranks of the clergy flanked chairs set up for Makarii and Ivan on a specially built dais in the centre of the cathedral. Gold brocades covered the space between the dais and the Royal Doors of the iconostasis, where a stand was placed to hold the royal regalia, which the grand prince's confessor had brought high on a golden plate 'with fear and trembling', accompanied by a highly placed entourage that stood guard. As bells began to ring across Moscow some thirty minutes later, Ivan left his quarters in a solemn procession, preceded by his confessor sprinkling holy water along the path and followed by his brother and members of the nobility.

---

34 David B. Miller, 'The Velikie minei chetii and the Stepennaia kniga of Metropolitan Makarii and the Origins of Russian National Consciousness', *FOG* 26 (1979): 264–7, 312–13, 362–8; V. M. Zhivov and B. A. Uspenskii, 'Tsar' i Bog: Semioticheskie aspekty sakralizatsii monarkha v Rossii', in *Iazyki kul'tury i problemy perevodimosti* (Moscow: Nauka, 1978), pp. 56–7, 84; Possevino, *Moscovia*, p. 47.

35 Daniel Rowland, 'Moscow – the Third Rome or the New Israel?', *RR* 55 (1996): 602–3.

The regalia were tangible links to the Monomakh legend, overt signs of the ruler's Kievan and Byzantine pedigrees. Significantly, their number changed over the course of the sixteenth century, apparently to embellish the ceremony with more visible symbols of power and authority. In Dmitrii's coronation, only the *barmy*, an elaborately embroidered and bejewelled neck-piece, and a cap (*shapka*) were mentioned, the same combination found in grand-princely testaments from the time of Ivan I Kalita (*c.* 1339).[36] In the ceremony for Ivan IV, a cross made from the True Cross was included. This inventory matches three of the five items in Monomakh's regalia specifically enumerated in *The Tale of the Princes of Vladimir* and correlated texts.[37] Of the remaining two, a gold chain was added to the Extended version of Ivan's ceremony, but the carnelian box much enjoyed by Caesar Augustus was never incorporated into the ceremony. Perhaps its exclusion was an explicit sign that as relevant as Roman genealogy might be for foreign recognition of the title 'tsar', only 'Byzantine' artefacts were deemed suitable for the spiritual confirmation of the Muscovite ruler.[38]

Ordered ranks of the clergy and the nobility lined Ivan's way to the dais. All were commanded to stand silent and not dare transgress the ruler's path. The bells stopped on his arrival. After introductory prayers, Metropolitan Makarii lifted the cross from the golden plate, placed it on Ivan's neck, and addressed the God of Revelation. He associated the anointing of David by Samuel as king over Israel with the anointing of Grand Prince Ivan Vasil'evich as tsar of all Rus'. He wished the grand prince a long life, his reign now legitimised by the Byzantine regalia. Makarii invested Ivan with the *barmy*, and the cap of Monomakh, and after a blessing of the tsar, admonished him on the duties of an Orthodox Christian ruler, the text based largely on Pseudo-Basil's Instruction to his son Leo.[39] The liturgy ended with communion before the iconostasis.

Ivan left the Dormition through the south portal and stood at the exit while a shower of gold and silver coins was poured over his head three times. He then processed over a path strewn with velvet and damask cloth to the Archangel Michael cathedral to hear a litany and pray before the graves of his royal predecessors. Leaving that cathedral through the western door, he

---

36 *Dukhovnye i dogovornye gramoty velikikh i udel'nykh kniazei XIV–XVI vv.*, ed. L. V. Cherepnin (Moscow and Leningrad: AN SSSR, 1950), p. 8.

37 R. P. Dmitrieva, *Skazanie o kniaz'iakh vladimirskikh* (Moscow and Leningrad: AN SSSR, 1955), pp. 164, 177, 190.

38 In general, the importance of the notion Moscow – Third Rome is grossly exaggerated in the historiography of sixteenth-century Muscovy; see Ostrowski, *Muscovy and the Mongols*, pp. 219–43.

39 Ihor Ševčenko, 'A Neglected Byzantine Source of Muscovite Political Ideology', in his *Byzantium and the Slavs in Letters and Culture* (Cambridge, Mass.: Harvard Ukrainian Research Institute, 1991), p. 72.

was again showered three times with gold and silver coins. He processed over a cloth-strewn path to the Annunciation cathedral, where he heard a litany. Descending the stairs onto the square again, he walked to the central staircase leading up to the Golden Hall and was showered once again with gold and silver coins three times before leaving for his own quarters in the palace.[40] He hosted a magnificent banquet for the high clergy and nobility in the Faceted Hall. Meanwhile those remaining behind in the Dormition were permitted to break up the specially built dais and take away material keepsakes sanctified by the ritual itself.[41]

An additional ceremony, the anointing of the new tsar, was apparently introduced only in 1584 for the coronation of Fedor Ivanovich, as represented in the Extended version of the ritual. Performed before communion, it was not equivalent to the Byzantine anointing of the forehead with sacred myrrh, but rather identical with the sacrament of chrismation, as performed at baptisms, with anointing of the head, the eyes, the ears, the chest and both sides of the hands (see Plate 17).[42] This additional act not only likened the Muscovite tsars to the Byzantine emperors and the Old Testament kings they were emulating, but to Christ himself at his baptism, a further sacralisation of the Muscovite ruler.[43]

The act of showering the tsar with coins provided a visible connection between locale and function. He acted as Christ's representative on earth at the Dormition, heir of a noble dynasty at the Archangel Michael and ruler of the realm at the Annunciation, with the symbolic values of fecundity and longevity signified by the showering of coins at each station. Ironically, the inclusion of this ritual act is based on error contained in a pilgrim's description of the 1392 Byzantine coronation ceremony, apparently used as a source in composing the Muscovite ritual. Either Ignatii of Smolensk misinterpreted the Byzantine custom of showering coins on the milling crowd out of imperial largesse, or a later scribe misread his copy of Ignatii's text, mistaking a particle for an object pronoun, thereby showering *him* (the emperor) with the coins.[44]

The coronation, the most important of the contingent rituals for conveying the sacred foundation of the office of tsar, occurred only once for each reign.

40 *PSRL*, vol. XIII, pp. 150–1, 451–3.
41 E. V. Barsov, *Drevne-russkie pamiatniki sviashchennogo venchaniia tsarei na tsarstvo* (Moscow: Universitetskaia tipografiia, 1883), pp. 66, 90; *PSRL*, vol. XIII, p. 150.
42 Barsov, *Drevne-russkie pamiatniki*, pp. 61–4; Uspenskii, *Tsar' i Patriarkh*, pp. 14–29, 111–12.
43 Uspenskii, *Tsar' i Patriarkh*, p. 20.
44 George P. Majeska, 'The Moscow Coronation of 1498 Reconsidered', *JGO* 26 (1978): 356–7, and his *Russian Travelers to Constantinople in the Fourteenth and Fifteenth Centuries*, Dumbarton Oaks Studies, no. 19 (Washington, DC: Dumbarton Oaks Research Library and Collection, 1984), pp. 112–13, 435–6; Ostrowski, *Muscovy and the Mongols*, p. 186 (n. 104).

It was the royal rituals performed at regular intervals that helped promulgate for the secular and spiritual elite the myth of the Muscovite ruler, especially through reference to artefacts and sites associated with his transformation.

Cyclical rituals

The Church calendar dominated life throughout Muscovy. Apart from the numerous Church services that the tsar and the nobility regularly attended, there were five rituals of especial importance. These demarcated major junctures in the annual cycle and expressed the fundamental values of the Muscovite myth in highly marked settings. Two were non-narrative – the New Year's ritual and the Last Judgement ritual; three contained dramatised narrative – the Fiery Furnace ritual, the Epiphany ritual and the Palm Sunday ritual. All five entailed the presence of the heads of Church and state in Moscow and underscored various perspectives on the relationship between the God-ordained ruler, the Church and the ruler's spiritual and secular advisers. Each of the five rituals highlighted particular portions of the semiotically sacred space demarcated by the Kremlin and its immediate environs, and each was marked by a special tolling of bells that resonated across the Kremlin.[45]

New Year's ritual

The celebration of the Valediction of the Year (*Letoprovozhdenie*) took place on the morning of 1 September.[46] The metropolitan preceded two deacons, each carrying a Gospel lectionary, and the remaining clergy in a cross procession from the Dormition to the space between the Annunciation and the Archangel Michael cathedrals, where two chairs had been placed for the metropolitan and the tsar. In an apparent sign of humility, the tsar without the royal regalia proceeded from the porch of the Annunciation to the centre space. The ceremony represented a farewell to the old year and a greeting to the new, a transition symbolised by antiphonal choirs and two Gospel lectionaries. The books were placed on separate lecterns, flanking an icon of St Simeon the Stylite, whose feast is celebrated on 1 September.

45 The discussion of these rituals in Moscow is based on information from foreigners, Russian chronicles, published archival documents, and seventeenth-century ceremonial books from Moscow's Dormition cathedral, which reflect directly or indirectly practices from the preceding century (Aleksandr Golubtsov, 'Chinovniki Moskovskogo Uspenskogo sobora', *ChOIDR*, 1907, bk. IV, pt. I).

46 Golubtsov, 'Chinovniki', 1–4, 147–50, 214, 279; Konstantin Nikol'skii, *O sluzhbakh Russkoi tserkvi byvshikh v prezhnikh pechatnykh bogosluzhebnykh knigakh* (St Petersburg: Tipografiia Tovarishchestva 'Obshchestvennaia pol'za', 1885), pp. 98–158.

The prescribed psalms concerned the redemption and destiny of the Chosen People (Ps. 73 [74] and 2) and the covenant between the Chosen People and God (Ps. 64 [65]), the last including the proclamation 'Thou crownest the year with thy goodness'. The reading from Isaiah 61: 1–9 includes his declaration 'The spirit of the Lord God is upon me, because the Lord has anointed me to bring good tidings to the afflicted . . . to proclaim the year of the Lord's favour.' Prayers and thanksgiving for kings (1 Tim. 2: 1–7) were followed by a Gospel reading, in which Christ refers to Isaiah's declaration (Luke 4: 16–22). The passages were read twice, line for line, first by the metropolitan from one lectionary, then by the archdeacon from the other. The ritual doubling appears to emphasise the union of beginning and ending, the year to come, as the year of the Lord's favour. Immersing the cross in holy water, the metropolitan initiated the new year by signing to the four corners of the earth, and, after wishing the tsar many long years, he sprinkled him with holy water, and then the nobility by rank, and finally all others gathered. The tsar returned to the Annunciation to celebrate the Eucharist.

The transition to a new age, the blessings conferred on the ruler and the Chosen People, the anointing of Christ as emblematic of the year of the Lord's favour were all positive signs that expressed the relationship between ruler and ruled under the benevolent protection of God. It is noteworthy that two of the three major inscriptions surrounding the enormous image of Christ Emmanuel as Final Judge on the ceiling of the Golden Hall throne room were taken from the New Year service.[47] This connection between ritual and throne room reinforced the perception of the reign of Ivan IV as a new age in Muscovite Rus'.

The Last Judgement ritual

Meatfare Sunday, the day before Shrovetide (*Maslenitsa*), is devoted to the most fateful event awaiting all Christians, the Last Judgement.[48] In a ceremony reminiscent of the New Year ritual, the heads of Church and state walked in cross processions from their respective churches, the Annunciation and Dormition, to the north-eastern part of Cathedral Square behind the Dormition apses, where chairs for each were set up alongside lecterns that held two Gospel lectionaries flanking an icon of the Last Judgement. Following hymns devoted to the Last Judgement, the archdeacon read Old Testament

---

47 Frank Kämpfer, ' "Rußland an der Schwelle zur Neuzeit": Kunst, Ideologie und historisches Bewußtsein unter Ivan Groznyj', *JGO* 23 (1975): 509.
48 Golubtsov, 'Chinovniki', 82–5, 242; Nikol'skii, *O sluzhbakh*, pp. 214–36.

excerpts, warning of the impending days of destruction and despair but holding out salvation for God's Chosen People (Joel 2: 1–27 and 3: 1–5, Isa. 13: 6) and describing the terrifying vision of the Ancient of Days and the Last Judgement (Dan. 7: 1–14). For the Gospel readings, the metropolitan faced east, the direction of the resurrection, and read about the fates of the righteous and the sinful at the Last Judgement (Matt. 25: 31–46). The archdeacon standing opposite him read the same passage facing west, the direction associated with the Last Judgement.[49] The doubled reading, analogous to that performed in the New Year ritual, underscored the transformative juncture of the Apocalypse.

The tsar was singled out as the primary representative whose good health and blessings would redound to the Chosen People as a whole, and especially to the nobility, who followed him in receiving a sprinkling of holy water before dismissal. The ritual was performed beneath the east-facing outside murals of the Dormition with the central image of the New Testament Trinity, iconography closely associated with the Last Judgement.[50] Through annual ritual, the destiny of Moscow and its ruler were confirmed before the beginning of the Great Fast leading up to Easter.

Fiery Furnace ritual

December 17 is a feast day that celebrates the three Hebrew youths Hananiah, Mishael and Azariah (Shadrach, Meshach and Abednego). Refusing to bow to the golden idol of King Nebuchadnezzar, they were cast into a fiery furnace on orders of the ruler, spurred on by his evil advisers, the Chaldeans. Visited by an angel, the youths remained unharmed, but the Chaldean jailers who had cast them in were themselves destroyed by the flames. Astonished at the youths' deliverance, Nebuchadnezzar ordered their release and praised God, recognising his superiority (Daniel 3).

The Fiery Furnace ritual was performed in the presence of the tsar on the first or second Sunday before Christmas during matins and included the seventh and eighth canticles, which refer to the three youths. A raised dais (*peshch'* 'furnace') was placed in front of the Royal Gates of the Dormition iconostasis. In the sanctuary, a deacon used a long cloth to bind the necks of the three boys performing the roles of the three youths and led them

49 In Eastern Orthodox church decoration, the Last Judgement depicted on the western wall is typically the final image encountered by the faithful as they leave the nave.
50 V. G. Briusova, 'Kompozitsiia "Novozavetnoi Troitsy" v stenopisi Uspenskogo sobora', in E. S. Smirnova (ed.), *Uspenskii sobor Moskovskogo Kremlia* (Moscow: Nauka, 1985), pp. 88–97.

through the north doors and into the custody of the waiting Chaldeans. After they were taken into the centre of the furnace, 'The Song of the Three Holy Children' (Dan. 3) was sung. When the archdeacon uttered the words 'the angel of the Lord came down into the oven', the image of an angel painted on parchment was lowered from above into the furnace to the accompaniment of loud noise simulating thunder. After bowing to the angel, the three youths traced the inner circumference of the furnace three times, singing the 'Prayer of Azariah'. The Chaldeans bowed to the spared youths and led them out of the furnace. The youths approached the metropolitan and wished him and the royal family many long years of life. Then, in order, the officiating clergy and then the boyars sang 'many long years' to the tsar.

The narrative itself served as an allegory of the relationship between the ruler, his advisers, and God's chosen. The transformation of the ruler from evil to good is carried out in the face of the destruction of the Chaldean advisers by fire and the salvation of the youths. In its allusion to the evil potential of bad advisers on the ruler, the Fiery Furnace ritual can be grouped with other Muscovite cultural artefacts that underscore the ruler's duty before God and his people, for example, the Golden Hall vestibule murals and the Monomakh Throne.

Epiphany ritual

The Christmas season ended with a major ritual celebrating the baptism of Christ in the River Jordan. The Blessing of the Waters was the climax of a solemn ceremony on the morning of 6 January that began with a cross procession as much as a mile in length, involving the heads of Church and state, moving from the Moscow Dormition, through the then passable Tainik tower out of the Kremlin, and onto the ice of the Moscow River.[51] A hole some 18 feet square had been made in the ice to reveal the river beneath, ceremonially renamed the 'Jordan' (*Iordan'*). The clergy arranged themselves around the hole with a platform set up on one side to hold the metropolitan's throne. The tsar stood bare-headed on the ice. After the 'Jordan' was hallowed, the metropolitan took up some water in his hands and cast it first on the tsar, then in similar fashion on the other nobles in order. Once the tsar and his entourage had departed, the crowds of onlookers rushed to partake of the newly sanctified water. The English merchant Anthony Jenkinson describes their joyful plunge in 1558: 'but y preasse that there was about the water when

51 Golubtsov, 'Chinovniki', 35–7, 176, 218, 294–5; Nikol'skii, *O sluzhbakh*, pp. 287–96; Fletcher, 'Russe Commonwealth', p. 233.

the Emperour was gone, was wonderful to behold, for there came about 5000. pots to be filled of that water: for that Muscovite which hath no part of that water, thinks himselfe unhappy.'[52]

The Epiphany ritual impressed all foreigners who witnessed it.[53] Like the New Year ritual, it marked a major transformation, a purification and regeneration. But with the procession extending beyond the walls of the Kremlin, the ritual invited all Muscovites, regardless of station, to participate. The regenerative blessing of the holy water cast first upon the tsar and then his elites accrued symbolically to the people of Muscovy as well, inviting their clamour to immerse themselves, their loved ones, and even their valued animals in the newly sanctified water.[54]

Jenkinson misread the symbolism of the ritual when he concluded that the tsar's baring of his head and standing while the metropolitan and the clergy sat must signal a lesser dignity on the part of the ruler.[55] He was unaware that liturgically, the clergy were required to sit during the Old Testament readings and stand for the New Testament lections. Furthermore he failed to realise that the ritual gave overt expression to one of the chief characteristics contained in the image of the tsar as representative of Christ on earth, namely, his humility, a virtue lauded by contemporary writers.[56] The iconography of the baptism itself shows Christ standing in the River Jordan with John's right hand blessing his bare head. Just as Christ humbled himself in that ritual, so too did the tsar humble himself in the course of universal spiritual renewal.

Palm Sunday ritual

The Palm Sunday ritual was the most impressive of all the royal rituals in Moscow (see Plate 18).[57] We have no Muscovite account of it prior to the seventeenth century, but members of the Russia Company described it in their ethnographic reports. In 1558, one of Anthony Jenkinson's entourage wrote:

52 Richard Hakluyt, *The Principall Navigations Voiages and Discoveries of the English Nation*, 2 vols., ed. David Beers Quinn and Raleigh Ashlin Skelton (Cambridge: Cambridge University Press, 1965), vol. I, p. 341; Fletcher, 'Russe Commonwealth', pp. 233–4.

53 Poe (*People*, p. 48, n. 41) provides a complete list of foreign references for the Epiphany and Palm Sunday rituals.

54 Fletcher, 'Russe Commonwealth', pp. 233–4.

55 Hakluyt, *Principall Navigations*, vol. I, pp. 343–4. Cf. Paul A. Bushkovitch, 'The Epiphany Ceremony of the Russian Court in the Sixteenth and Seventeenth Centuries', *RR* 49 (1990): 1–4.

56 Rowland, 'Limits', 135.

57 Golubtsov, 'Chinovniki', 103–8, 250–3; Nikol'skii, *O sluzhbakh*, pp. 45–97; Michael S. Flier, 'Breaking the Code: The Image of the Tsar in the Muscovite Palm Sunday Ritual', in Flier and Rowland (eds.), *Medieval Russian Culture*, vol. II, pp. 213–18, 227–32.

– First, they have a tree of a good bignesse which is made fast upon two sleds, as though it were growing there, and it is hanged with apples, raisins, figs and dates and with many fruits abundantly. In the midst of ye same tree stand 5 boyes in white vestures, which sing in the tree before the procession.

The float was followed in turn by a long cross procession of acolytes, numerous richly attired prelates, and half of the Muscovite nobility. The central focus of the procession was a re-enactment of Christ's triumphant entry into Jerusalem on Palm Sunday.

– First, there is a horse covered with white linnen cloth down to ye ground, his eares being made long with the same cloth like to an asses ears. Upon this horse the Metropolitane sitteth sidelong like a woman: in his lappe lieth a faire booke [the Gospels], with a crucifix of Goldsmiths worke upon the cover, which he holdest fast with his left hand, and in his right hand he hath a crosse of gold, with which crosse he ceaseth not to blesse the people as he rideth.

Some thirty sons of priests spread large pieces of cloth in the path of the approaching Christ, picking them up as soon as the horse passed over them and running ahead to spread them out again.

– One of the Emperores noble men leadeth the horse by the head, but the Emperour himselfe going on foote leadeth the horse by the ende of the reine of his bridle with one of his hands, and in the other of his hands he had a branch of a Palme tree: after this followed the rest of the Emperours Noble men and Gentlemen, with a great number of other people.[58]

Beginning at the Dormition, the procession apparently moved to a chapel dedicated to the Entry into Jerusalem within the Kremlin (Annunciation cathedral?),[59] before returning to the Dormition for dismissal, whereupon the ceremonial tree was broken apart and distributed to the assembled throng. The tsar was given 200 roubles by the metropolitan, which some foreigners interpreted as payment for service rendered.[60] The lower position of the tsar vis-à-vis the metropolitan was taken by many foreign observers as yet another sign of the ruler's lesser status, without considering the tsar's identification with Christ through humility, as seen in the Epiphany ritual.[61]

58 Hakluyt, *Principall Navigations*, vol. 1, pp. 341–2.
59 Ibid., p. 342.
60 Fletcher, 'Russe Commonwealth', p. 234.
61 Hakluyt, *Principall Navigations*, vol. 1, pp. 343–4. Cf. Robert O. Crummey, 'Court Spectacles in Seventeenth-Century Russia: Illusion and Reality', in Daniel C. Waugh (ed.), *Essays in Honor of A.A. Zimin* (Columbus, Oh.: Slavica Publishers, 1985), p. 134.

Sometime after completion of the church of the Intercession on the Moat in 1561, the procession extended out of the Kremlin onto Beautiful (Red) Square and in view of the people. The tsar and metropolitan participated in a short ceremony in the Intercession's Chapel of the Entry into Jerusalem before returning to the Dormition. This re-enactment of Christ's *adventus* near the microcosm of Jerusalem outside the walls of the Kremlin encouraged those in attendance, participants and observers, to see the city re-entered as Moscow transformed, the New Jerusalem. The emotional and spiritual power of the ceremony was amply demonstrated in 1611, when the Polish forces occupying Moscow cancelled the Palm Sunday ritual: they were obliged to reinstate it to avoid a riot.[62]

Typological characteristics

These five rituals presented distinct aspects of the political ideas that made up the myth of the Muscovite ruler. All required the presence of the ruler, but one, the Fiery Furnace ritual, was performed as a liturgical drama and afforded him a passive, observer's role. It was also the only one of the five performed completely inside the Dormition and the only one that alluded to a distinction between good and evil emperors, and good and evil advisers, elements of a typology realised in contemporary literature.[63] Two of the rituals were limited to the outside spaces within the Kremlin (New Year and Last Judgement rituals in Cathedral Square) and featured the contemplation of crossing temporal boundaries, from the year ending to the 'year of the Lord's favour', and from history to eternity, respectively. Both alluded to Kremlin iconography, in the Golden Hall and outside the Dormition cathedral, respectively.

The two most significant and solemn of the royal rituals were much more complex in nature, revealing not only protocols of performance but semiotic representation on the iconographic, historical and eschatological levels. The Epiphany ritual and the revised Palm Sunday ritual utilised space inside and outside the Kremlin, emblematic of their more extensive, universal significance. Both used performance to re-enact events in the life of Christ, thereby introducing immediate association with the Holy Land: the Moscow River with the River Jordan, and the city of Moscow with the New Jerusalem. Both were influenced by the iconography of the Baptism and the Entry into Jerusalem. And both recalled pivotal historical events: the baptism of Vladimir, which

62 Konrad Bussov, *Moskovskaia khronika, 1584–1613*, ed. I. I. Smirnov, trans. S. A. Akuliants (Leningrad: AN SSSR, 1961), pp. 185, 320–1.
63 Ostrowski, *Muscovy and the Mongols*, pp. 203–10.

launched the Christian history of the Rus', and Ivan IV's defeat of Kazan', which resulted in his triumphant entry into Moscow. As though at communion, observers of both rituals could partake of material objects made holy in the presence of the prelate and ruler: the water of the Moscow River and the constructed tree.

The contingent rituals were concerned primarily with matters of the present; the cyclical rituals with issues of fate and deliverance. This is especially true for the rituals thematically tied to Jerusalem. With the microcosmic Jerusalem as a site of pilgrimage, the River Jordan as an annual source of regeneration, and Golgotha as pulpit, the leaders of Church and state declared their intention by century's end to supplement the political ideas of Muscovy with a clearer vision of its messianic destiny following the Last Judgement and the Apocalypse. It was this conception of Muscovite ideology that survived the demise of the Riurikid dynasty and was carefully nurtured by its Romanov successors as the seventeenth century unfolded.

18

The Time of Troubles (1603–1613)

MAUREEN PERRIE

Historians have used the term, 'The Time of Troubles' (*smutnoe vremia*, *smuta*), to refer to various series of events in the late sixteenth and early seventeenth centuries. The classic study by S. F. Platonov, first published in 1899, dated the start of the Troubles to the death of Ivan the Terrible in 1584, when a power struggle among the boyars began. It ended, according to Platonov, with the election of Michael Romanov to the throne in 1613.[1] In the Soviet period, the term, 'Time of Troubles', was abandoned in favour of the concept of a 'peasant war', derived from Friedrich Engels's study of the events in Germany in 1525.[2] I. I. Smirnov's account of the Bolotnikov revolt of 1606–7 identified that episode alone as the 'first peasant war' in Russia, but after Stalin's death some Soviet historians argued that the entire sequence of events from 1603 (the Khlopko uprising) to 1614 (the defeat of Zarutskii's movement) constituted a 'peasant war'.[3] Towards the end of the Soviet era, Russian historians rejected the notion of a 'peasant war' and either reverted to the use of the older term, 'Time of Troubles', or introduced the idea of a 'civil war'.[4] Western historians were never persuaded by the 'peasant war' concept for this period, preferring to retain the term, 'Time of Troubles'.[5] Chester Dunning's adoption of 'civil war' terminology, like that of the Russian historians R. G. Skrynnikov and

---

1 S. F. Platonov, *Ocherki po istorii smuty v Moskovskom gosudarstve XVI–XVII vv.*, [4th edn] (Moscow: Gosudarstvennoe sotsial'no–ekonomicheskoe izdatel'stvo, 1937); 5th edn (Moscow: Pamiatniki istoricheskoi mysli, 1995).

2 I. I. Smirnov, *Vosstanie Bolotnikova, 1606–1607*, 2nd edn (Leningrad: Gosudarstvennoe izdatel'stvo politicheskoi literatury, 1951), pp. 493–4.

3 For example, A. A. Zimin, 'Nekotorye voprosy istorii krest'ianskoi voiny v Rossii v nachale XVII veka', *VI* 1958, no.3: pp. 97–113.

4 R. G. Skrynnikov, *Rossiia v nachale XVII v. 'Smuta'* (Moscow: Mysl', 1988); R. G. Skrynnikov, *Smuta v Rossii v nachale XVII v. Ivan Bolotnikov* (Leningrad: Nauka, 1988); A. L. Stanislavskii, *Grazhdanskaia voina v Rossii XVII v. Kazachestvo na perelome istorii* (Moscow: Mysl', 1990).

5 Maureen Perrie, *Pretenders and Popular Monarchism in Early Modern Russia. The False Tsars of the Time of Troubles* (Cambridge: Cambridge University Press, 1995); Chester S. L. Dunning, *Russia's First Civil War. The Time of Troubles and the Founding of the Romanov Dynasty* (University Park, Pa.: Pennsylvania State University Press, 2001).

A. L. Stanislavskii, involves a conscious rejection of 'class struggle' approaches to the period, and stresses vertical rather than horizontal divisions in Russian society. The 'civil war' approach also plays down the significance of foreign intervention – which was heavily stressed both in Stalin-era Soviet historiography and in some pre-revolutionary accounts – and finds the origins of the Troubles primarily in internal Russian problems.

This chapter presents the 'Time of Troubles' as beginning with the First False Dmitrii's invasion of Russia in the autumn of 1604. In the aftermath of the famine of 1601–3, the pretender's challenge to Boris Godunov's legitimacy as tsar interacted with the social grievances of the population of the southern frontier to produce a highly explosive mixture.

The First False Dmitrii

In the summer of 1603 a young man appeared on the estate of Prince Adam Vishnevetskii at Brahin in Lithuania. He claimed to be Tsarevich Dmitrii, Ivan the Terrible's youngest son, who had died under mysterious circumstances at Uglich in 1591. The youth explained that he had escaped from assassins sent by Boris Godunov to kill him, and was now seeking help to gain his rightful throne. Vishnevetskii apparently found his story credible, and reported it first to the Polish chancellor, Jan Zamoyski, and then to King Sigismund himself. The pretender obtained the patronage of Adam Vishnevetskii's cousin, Prince Constantine Vishnevetskii, and of Prince Constantine's father-in-law, Jerzy Mniszech, the Palatine of Sandomierz, whose family seat was at Sambor, in Poland. Mniszech offered Dmitrii military aid in return for the promise of territorial gains at the expense of Russia. Their agreement was cemented by the pretender's betrothal to Mniszech's daughter, Marina, and by his secret adoption of Roman Catholicism. In March 1604 the self-styled Dmitrii had an audience with the king in Cracow, where they discussed the prospect of Russia's conversion to Catholicism. The king, however, faced strong opposition in the Sejm to a military adventure in support of the pretender, which would have infringed the peace treaty that had been concluded between Poland and Russia in 1601. Sigismund was able to offer only unofficial encouragement to the undertaking. Dmitrii returned with Mniszech to Sambor, and spent the summer gathering military support. At the end of August they began their march on Muscovy to topple the 'usurper' Boris Godunov from the throne.

Who was this pretender who has become known as the 'First False Dmitrii'? Boris Godunov's government identified him as Grigorii Otrep'ev, a renegade monk of noble origin. This view has predominated in subsequent scholarship, although there have been some dissenting voices: Chester Dunning not only rejects the view that the pretender was Otrep'ev, but has even revived the idea that he may indeed have been Dmitrii of Uglich.[6] Although Dmitrii's real identity is impossible to prove definitively, the argument that he was Otrep'ev continues to be the most persuasive in the eyes of most modern historians.[7] It is also true, however, that the pretender performed his role with such self-confidence that he himself may well have believed that he really was Tsarevich Dmitrii.

Various conspiracy theories name certain boyar clans as the pretender's patrons, who aimed to use him as a lever to unseat Godunov. The families most frequently mentioned in this connection are the Romanovs, the Cherkasskiis, the Shuiskiis and the Nagois. But, as A. P. Pavlov has noted, there is little convincing evidence of boyar involvement in a plot to set up a pretender.[8] It is more likely that Otrep'ev acted on his own initiative, perhaps motivated by a desire for revenge against Godunov for the tsar's persecution of his patrons, the Romanovs, in 1600.[9]

In the autumn of 1604 the pretender crossed the Russian frontier near Kiev with a small army of Polish troops and cossacks. The first Russian border fortress, Moravsk (Monastyrevskii Ostrog) surrendered without a struggle, and it was followed by other towns in the Seversk (south-west) region: Chernigov, Putivl', Ryl'sk and Kursk. Dmitrii also gained the support of the peasants of the prosperous Komaritskaia district. The fortress of Novgorod Severskii, however, was well defended by Godunov's general P. F. Basmanov, and at the beginning of January 1605 the pretender's Polish mercenaries mutinied, angered by his failure to pay them. But by this time Dmitrii had been joined by several thousand Don and Zaporozhian cossacks. He pressed on towards the Russian heartland, occupying Sevsk without opposition, but on 21 January he encountered an army commanded by Prince F. I. Mstislavskii, and suffered a severe defeat at Dobrynichi. In spite of this military setback, the rising in Dmitrii's favour continued to spread through the towns of the southern steppe, where his support came primarily from the petty military servitors who were dissatisfied with Godunov's policies towards them. The governors of these frontier fortresses who remained loyal to Godunov were overthrown by the townspeople and the garrison troops as traitors to the 'true tsar' Dmitrii. Apart

---

6 Dunning, *Russia's First Civil War*, pp. 131–2.
7 Skrynnikov, *Rossiia v nachale XVII v.*, pp. 79–103: Perrie, *Pretenders*, pp. 44–50.
8 A. P. Pavlov, *Gosudarev dvor i politicheskaia bor'ba pri Borise Godunove (1584–1605 gg.)* (St Petersburg: Nauka, 1992), pp. 78–9.
9 Perrie, *Pretenders*, pp. 55–8.

from the Komaritskaia district, the region contained few peasants, and the 'peasant war' formula of Soviet historiography has little relevance to this stage of the pretender's campaign. Although he obtained support primarily from the lower classes, including the minor servicemen, Dmitrii based his appeal on his claim to be the 'true tsar', and did not make a specific bid for the backing of the poor. His only proclamation to survive from this period, dated November 1604, is addressed to all social groups in the conventional descending hierarchical order.[10] The function of pretence, as Dmitrii's success clearly demonstrated, was to unite all those with grievances against the reigning tsar under the banner of a candidate for the throne who could claim an alternative – and superior – basis for his political legitimacy.

Boris Godunov died suddenly in Moscow on 13 April 1605, when the pretender was encamped at Putivl', where he had retreated after his defeat at Dobrynichi in January. At the time of his death, Boris's army was besieging the small fortress of Kromy, to the north-east of Putivl', which was held for the pretender by the Don cossack ataman Korela. The boyars in Moscow swore allegiance to Boris's young son, Fedor, but uncertainty about the stability of support for Fedor Borisovich undermined the morale of the government troops at Kromy. On 7 May the army mutinied, and many of its commanders, including Peter Basmanov, went over to Dmitrii. A deputation led by Prince Ivan Golitsyn was sent to Putivl' from Kromy to report that the troops had defected to 'Tsar Dmitrii', and the pretender marched unopposed towards Moscow.

From Krapivna, near Tula, Dmitrii sent two envoys to Moscow with a proclamation calling on the inhabitants of the capital to recognise him as their tsar. They were escorted into the centre of the city by insurgents from the outskirts. On the morning of 1 June, Dmitrii's proclamation was read out to the people of Moscow who had assembled on Red Square. Many of the boyars, most of whom had by now abandoned the cause of Fedor Godunov, were present to hear the pretender's fulsome promises of rewards for the transfer of their loyalty.[11] The proclamation triggered a popular uprising in the capital which was directed primarily against the Godunovs and their supporters. The administration of the city in Dmitrii's name was taken over by Bogdan Bel'skii, who had been disgraced in 1600 and had returned to Moscow only as a result of a political amnesty declared on Boris's death. Before the pretender entered the capital his agents murdered Fedor Borisovich and his mother; and Patriarch Iov,

10 *AAE*, vol. ii (St Petersburg: Tipografiia II Otdeleniia Sobstvennoi E. I. V. Kantseliarii, 1836), no. 26, p. 76.
11 *AAE*, vol. ii, no. 34, pp. 89–91.

who had been attacked during the popular uprising for his continued loyalty to the Godunovs, was stripped of his office.

On 20 June 1605 the pretender made a triumphal entry into Moscow, where he was greeted as the 'true sun' shining on Russia.[12] According to some contemporary sources, many of those who continued to oppose him, and to express scepticism about his identity, were secretly arrested, imprisoned and put to death; but only two public executions took place. The brothers Shuiskii were brought to trial, accused of plotting to kill the new tsar. All three were found guilty. Prince Vasilii Shuiskii was sentenced to death, but he was reprieved at the last moment and sent into exile with his brothers. Soon after this, the pretender's credibility received an important boost when the former Tsaritsa Mariia Nagaia (now the nun Marfa), the mother of Dmitrii of Uglich, publicly recognised him as her son. On 21 July, three days after Marfa's arrival in the capital, Dmitrii was crowned in the Dormition cathedral in the Kremlin.

Historians have offered conflicting assessments of Dmitrii's achievements as tsar. The problem of reaching a balanced evaluation is complicated not only by the brevity of his reign, but also by the lack of official sources, since many documents were destroyed after his overthrow in May 1606. Some scholars have presented him as an enlightened reformer, who brought a refreshing element of Westernising modernisation into the traditional world of Muscovite politics, before being swept from power by a backlash of conservative boyar opposition to his innovations; others have seen him as an opportunist who was unable to cope with the complexities of power, and paid the price for his failures. A recent Russian study suggests that Dmitrii relied on a boyar duma whose aristocratic composition was not too dissimilar from that of Boris Godunov, and that his domestic policy was fairly traditional. In the end he was overthrown as a result of the machinations of the most powerful faction in the duma, which no longer found him to be a useful figurehead.[13] Chester Dunning, too, stresses continuity in policy between Tsar Dmitrii and his immediate predecessors; and he argues that the pretender's opponents were only a small and unrepresentative group of boyars.[14]

There has been particular controversy among historians about Dmitrii's social legislation which affected the position of slaves and peasants. A law of 7 January 1606 forbade the joint assignment of a bondsman to more than one owner, thereby ensuring that slaves would be freed on the deaths of their

12 Conrad Bussow, *The Disturbed State of the Russian Realm*, ed. and trans. G. Edward Orchard (Montreal: McGill–Queen's University Press, 1994), p. 50.
13 V. I. Ul'ianovskii, *Rossiiskie samozvantsy: Lzhedmitrii I* (Kiev: Libid', 1993), pp. 41–124.
14 Dunning, *Russia's First Civil War*, pp. 201–25.

master. A decree of 1 February 1606 stated that those peasants who had fled
during the famine years of 1601–2 because their masters were unable to feed
them were not to be returned to their old lords, but were to remain as slaves or
serfs of their new masters.[15] There is a general scholarly consensus that these
two pieces of legislation represented minor concessions to the slaves and
peasants respectively.[16] There is no convincing evidence, however, to support
V. I. Koretskii's assertion that Dmitrii was planning to issue a new law code
which would have restored the peasants' right of departure on St George's
Day from the autumn of 1606.[17] In general, Dmitrii preserved the institutions
of slavery and serfdom, and was more concerned to protect the interests
of the slave- and serf-owning nobles than those of their bondsmen. He also
rewarded the petty servicemen of the southern and south-western towns who
had provided the main base of his support in the course of his march on
Moscow. They were granted lands and money; their obligation to till the land
for the state was abolished; and they were exempted from the payment of
taxes for ten years. The gentry of other regions, however, did not benefit
significantly, in terms of land and money payments, from Dmitrii's rule.[18]

In some other spheres, Dmitrii's policies were more innovative. He planned
to promote science and education, and introduced new types of military
training for his troops. He sought to raise Russia's international prestige by
adopting the title 'tsesar'' (emperor). In his foreign policy he at first gave
some indications that he was willing to support Poland in its war against
Sweden, but he subsequently abandoned this scheme in favour of an ambitious plan to launch a crusade against the Crimean Tatars and the Turks, a
project which was encouraged by the Pope and King Sigismund. Before the
campaign could be launched, however, the pretender was overthrown and
killed.

After Dmitrii's coronation, the initial doubts about his identity seemed to
have been appeased, and by the end of 1605 he was sufficiently confident of his
position to pardon the Shuiskiis and permit them to return to the capital. There
they soon resumed their plotting against him: some sources refer to a number
of abortive assassination attempts in early 1606. In March, a conspiracy against
Dmitrii was uncovered in the ranks of his own bodyguard of musketeers; the
pretender himself incited the strel'tsy to tear the 'traitors' to pieces. After this

15 Zakonodatel'nye akty Russkogo gosudarstva vtoroi poloviny XVI – pervoi poloviny XVII veka.
Teksty (Leningrad: Nauka, 1986), nos. 54–5, pp. 73–4.
16 Ul'ianovskii, Rossiiskie samozvantsy, pp. 170–230; Perrie, Pretenders, pp. 87–9.
17 V. I. Koretskii, Formirovanie krepostnogo prava i pervaia krest'ianskaia voina v Rossii (Moscow:
Nauka, 1975), pp. 243–9.
18 Ul'ianovskii, Rossiiskie samozvantsy, pp. 125–230.

episode, organised opposition appeared to subside; but the Shuiskiis and their allies were only biding their time.

Aspects of the new tsar's behaviour created favourable soil for his opponents. In spite of promises that he had made when he was a penniless fugitive in Poland, Dmitrii made no attempt in his short reign to convert Russia to Catholicism. He did, however, have Polish favourites, including his secretaries Jan and Stanisław Buczynski; he was tolerant of non-Orthodox believers; and he disregarded many traditional court practices, adopting Western-style dress, and furbishing his new palace in the Kremlin in the latest Polish style. The main pretext for the conspirators' action against the 'heretical' tsar, however, was provided by his marriage to Marina Mniszech. The new tsar's choice of a foreign bride, who was unwilling to convert to Orthodoxy, antagonised many Russians; and the arrogant behaviour of Marina's Polish escort when they arrived in Moscow on 2 May 1606 played into the hands of the pretender's enemies. Early on the morning of 17 May, a week after Dmitrii's wedding, the conspirators raised the cry that the Poles were attacking the tsar. The Muscovites rushed to the Kremlin, and fell upon the hated foreigners. Meanwhile, the tsar was murdered by the assassins as he tried to escape from his apartment.

Two days after the pretender's death, Prince Vasilii Shuiskii was declared tsar. A senior member of the Suzdal' princely clan, Shuiskii had some claim to the throne on the basis of his Riurikid lineage; but the legitimacy of his 'election' as tsar was very dubious from the outset. Opposition to Shuiskii soon mobilised under the slogan of restoring Tsar Dmitrii – who, it was claimed, had not in fact perished in the uprising of 17 May – to the throne. The rumours about Dmitrii's escape from death were spread by his Russian supporters, and were of course welcomed by Marina Mniszech, who had been arrested along with her father and the Polish envoys to Moscow after her husband's death.

The Bolotnikov revolt

The main centre of opposition to Shuiskii was the town of Putivl', which had been an important base of support for the pretender in the course of his march towards Moscow in 1605. Immediately after his arrival in Putivl', Prince Grigorii Shakhovskoi, the new governor appointed by Shuiskii, defected to 'Tsar Dmitrii'; and many other towns in the Seversk region also refused to acknowledge Shuiskii as tsar. The belief that Dmitrii had escaped death – which served to legitimise the townspeople's rejection of Shuiskii – was not based only on rumours from Moscow. It was also strengthened by the actions of Michael Molchanov, one of Tsar Dmitrii's closest confidants, who had fled from the capital on the day of the pretender's murder. Molchanov rode to Putivl', where he promoted the idea that Dmitrii was still alive; from Putivl' he went to Sambor, in Poland – the home of the Mniszech family – where he began to play the role of the late tsar. He did not, however, appear in public as Dmitrii, probably because he bore no physical resemblance to the first pretender, who had been a familiar figure at Sambor.

At some time in the summer of 1606 a certain Ivan Isaevich Bolotnikov arrived in Putivl', claiming that he had met Tsar Dmitrii at Sambor and had been appointed by him as commander of his army. Bolotnikov was a former military bondsman and cossack who had been captured by the Turks and served as a galley-slave before escaping and returning to Russia through Poland. Shakhovskoi accepted his claims, and put him in charge of one of the two armies which marched from Putivl' towards Moscow by separate routes in the autumn of 1606. The leaders of the second army were of higher social status than Bolotnikov: it was commanded by the petty nobleman Istoma Pashkov, and it was later joined by the servicemen of Riazan' under Prokopii Liapunov. At the beginning of November the two armies joined forces at Kolomenskoe, on the outskirts of Moscow, and began to besiege the capital.

The siege lasted for about a month. The anti-Shuiskii forces sent various messages to the inhabitants of the city. Pashkov, who was the first to reach Moscow, appealed to the inhabitants to surrender, and to hand over the Shuiskiis as traitors to Tsar Dmitrii. Some sources suggest that later, after Bolotnikov's arrival, the besiegers called on the lower classes in the capital to rise up against the rich. Patriarch Germogen claimed that the rebels distributed leaflets inciting bond-slaves to kill their masters, and promising them their wives and lands; encouraged the city's 'rogues' to kill the merchants and seize their property; and promised high court ranks to those who joined them.[19] Some scholars doubt, however, whether Germogen's pro-Shuiskii propaganda accurately reflected the rebels' appeals;[20] even if it did, the insurgents' programme – with its promises of landed estates and noble ranks – hardly amounted to the call for an 'anti-feudal' social revolution which the older historiography detected in it. In spite of the fears which were aroused among the upper classes, no popular uprising materialised in the capital – perhaps because Shuiskii managed to persuade the Muscovites that the rebels held them collectively responsible for the events of 17 May, and planned to massacre them all. The insurgents' position was also weakened by their inability to produce

19 *AAE*, vol. II, no. 57, p. 129.
20 Skrynnikov, *Smuta v Rossii*, pp. 134–5; Dunning, *Russia's First Civil War*, pp. 304–5.

Tsar Dmitrii in person. Finally, divisions within the besiegers' camp led to the defection of Liapunov and Pashkov to Shuiskii's side: it is unclear whether these divisions reflected purely personal rivalries among the commanders, or whether social tensions also played a part. On 2 December, Tsar Vasilii's troops launched an attack on the besieging forces. Pashkov and his men deserted to Shuiskii in the course of the battle, and Bolotnikov retreated to Kaluga with the remains of the rebel army, still in fairly good order. In spite of this military defeat, the revolt continued across an extensive swathe of territory from the south-west frontier to the Volga basin.

Another pretender had appeared on the Volga even before the death of the First False Dmitrii. In the spring of 1606 a young cossack called Il'ia Korovin was chosen by a band of Terek cossacks to play the part of 'Tsarevich Peter', a non-existent son of Tsar Fedor Ivanovich. Although any real son of Tsar Fedor's would have had a better claim to the throne than Dmitrii of Uglich, the cossacks do not seem to have wanted to replace Dmitrii with Peter; they always acted in Dmitrii's name. They evidently felt that they had not been adequately rewarded for their services to Dmitrii, but they blamed the boyars for this, rather than the tsar.[21] Peter's pretence was clearly modelled on that of Dmitrii; its function, however, was not to overthrow the tsar, but rather to enhance the cossacks' bid to persuade him to grant them a suitable reward. Peter and his supporters rampaged upriver, looting merchant ships as they went; but when they heard of Dmitrii's overthrow and murder, they retreated back down the Volga, before crossing over to the rivers Don and Donets. Around November 1606 they moved to Putivl' at the invitation of Prince Grigorii Shakhovskoi, who was still holding the town for Bolotnikov. Here Peter launched a reign of terror against 'traitors to Tsar Dmitrii': he ordered the execution of many noblemen who had been captured by the insurgents during their march on Moscow and were imprisoned at Putivl'. In February 1607 Peter moved his troops from Putivl' to Tula in order to offer support to Bolotnikov, who was besieged by Shuiskii's army in nearby Kaluga. In May, Bolotnikov managed to break out of Kaluga and join Peter's forces in Tula.

After Tsarevich Peter's departure from the Volga, the region continued to support Tsar Dmitrii. The rebellion which developed on the lower Volga from the summer of 1606 was largely independent of the revolt in the Seversk lands. The first major town to reject Shuiskii was Astrakhan', the great commercial port at the mouth of the Volga, on the Caspian Sea. On 17 June 1606 its

---

21 *Vosstanie I. Bolotnikova. Dokumenty i materialy*, comp. A. I. Kopanev and A. G. Man'kov (Moscow: Izdatel'stvo sotsial'no-ekonomicheskoi literatury, 1959), p. 225.

inhabitants staged an uprising against Shuiskii, and the city governor, Prince I. D. Khvorostinin, transferred his loyalty to Dmitrii. Pro-Shuiskii troops under the command of F. I. Sheremetev took up camp on the island of Balchik, a few miles upstream from Astrakhan', where they remained for more than a year. A number of new pretenders, apparently modelling themselves on Tsarevich Peter, appeared in Astrakhan' at around this time: Tsarevich Ivan Augustus, who claimed to be a son of Ivan the Terrible; Osinovik, a son of Tsarevich Ivan Ivanovich; and Lavr (or Lavrentii), another supposed son of Tsar Fedor Ivanovich.[22] None of these pretenders had a real historical prototype. Ivan Augustus's relationship with Prince Khvorostinin, the governor of Astrakhan', appears to have been similar to that of Tsarevich Peter with Prince Shakhovskoi at Putivl'; like Peter, Ivan Augustus acted in the name of Tsar Dmitrii, and his sphere of influence extended up the Volga at least as far as Tsaritsyn.[23]

Bolotnikov's forces had been united with those of Tsarevich Peter at Tula in May 1607; on 30 June, Tsar Vasilii arrived outside the gates of the town at the head of a large army, and laid siege to it. By the autumn of 1607 the defenders of the town found themselves in a desperate situation. Shuiskii had built a dam on the River Upa downstream from Tula, which caused the town to flood. All communications were cut off, and the inhabitants suffered terrible hardship and hunger. Eventually Tsarevich Peter and Bolotnikov opened negotiations with Shuiskii, and on 10 October Tula surrendered. Tsarevich Peter was tortured and interrogated before being executed in Moscow in January 1608. In February 1611 Bolotnikov was exiled to Kargopol', where he was imprisoned for a time, and then blinded and drowned. Prince Shakhovskoi was banished to a monastery, but soon escaped and subsequently joined the supporters of the Second False Dmitrii.

The Second False Dmitrii

The failure of Tsar Dmitrii to put in an appearance had greatly demoralised Bolotnikov's forces, but a second False Dmitrii had in fact surfaced in Russia well before the fall of Tula. This new pretender revealed himself in the town of Starodub, in the Seversk region, in June 1607.

By the autumn of 1606 Michael Molchanov had abandoned his attempt to adopt the identity of Tsar Dmitrii and had left Sambor.[24] The rebel camp,

22 *PSRL*, vol. XIV (Moscow: Nauka, 1965), p. 89, para.195.
23 Perrie, *Pretenders*, pp. 131–4, 144–9.
24 I. O. Tiumentsev, *Smuta v Rossii v nachale XVII stoletiia: dvizhenie Lzhedmitriia II* (Volgograd: Volgogradskii Gosudarstvennyi Universitet, 1999), p. 72.

however, was still in urgent need of a new Dmitrii. There is some evidence that at the end of December 1606 Tsarevich Peter travelled from Putivl' to Lithuania, supposedly in search of his 'uncle' Dmitrii, and that this journey may have been linked to the first stages of the setting up of a new pretender-tsar: the earliest traces of the Second False Dmitrii can be found in the winter of 1606–7 in the Belorussian lands of Poland-Lithuania which were visited by Tsarevich Peter at about the same time.[25]

There is still no agreement about the identity of the Second False Dmitrii. Many older historians depicted him as a puppet of the Polish government; but some recent scholars have argued that his sponsors were Russians involved in the Bolotnikov revolt. They give greatest credence to sources which suggest that he was a poor schoolteacher from Lithuanian Belorussia who was coerced into playing the role of Dmitrii by some minor Polish noblemen who were in contact with Tsarevich Peter and other Russian insurgents based in Putivl'.[26] There is evidence to indicate, however, that the Second False Dmitrii may have initiated the intrigue himself (there were by now several precedents for him to follow), or at least participated in it willingly.[27] Certainly the new pretender acquired Russian supporters as soon as he crossed the border from Lithuania, and they helped to stage the revelation of his 'true' royal identity at Starodub. There he was also 'recognised' by Ivan Martynovich Zarutskii, a cossack leader from the Ukraine, who had been sent by Bolotnikov to search for Tsar Dmitrii. Zarutskii was subsequently to become one of the most important commanders in the pretender's service.

At Starodub Dmitrii and his accomplices began to recruit troops to go to the assistance of Bolotnikov and Tsarevich Peter in besieged Tula. Most of the towns in the Seversk region soon acknowledged the new Tsar Dmitrii and provided him with servicemen, but much of his small army comprised mercenaries from Poland-Lithuania. In September 1607 Dmitrii left Starodub, but he had advanced no further than Belev when he learned that Tula had fallen on 10 October. The pretender retreated to Karachev, and then to Orel, where he set up camp. During the winter of 1607–8 he recruited new forces. Some of these were the remnants of Bolotnikov's army from Tula; cossack reinforcements came from the Don, Volga, Terek and Dnieper; and new bands of mercenaries from Poland-Lithuania also joined him.[28]

25 Skrynnikov, *Smuta v Rossii*, pp. 191–3; Tiumentsev, *Smuta v Rossii*, pp. 72–9; Dunning, *Russia's First Civil War*, pp. 372–3.
26 Skrynnikov, *Smuta v Rossii*, pp. 190–202; Tiumentsev, *Smuta v Rossii*, pp. 74–9; Dunning, *Russia's First Civil War*, pp. 368–72.
27 Perrie, *Pretenders*, p. 165.
28 Tiumentsev, *Smuta v Rossii*, pp. 112–16.

While encamped at Orel, Dmitrii made a bid for the support of the slaves of
Shuiskii's supporters, promising them their masters' lands, wives and daughters if they transferred their allegiance to him. There has been considerable
scholarly controversy about the pretender's policy towards peasants and slaves
at this time. It seems most probable that, like Bolotnikov, the Second False
Dmitrii was hoping to attract military bondsmen into his service by offering
them a share of the property confiscated from their 'traitor' lords. Certainly
the pretender did not pursue an 'anti-feudal' policy: he granted lands and peasants to the Russian servicemen and foreign mercenaries who supported him.
Shuiskii responded with measures of his own in February and March 1608.
These have also been the subject of conflicting interpretations, but they seem
to have been designed to attract both servicemen and slaves to his side.[29]

In March 1608 the Polish commander Prince Roman Różyński arrived in
Orel with a large detachment of cavalry, and ousted the hetman Mikołaj
Miechowicki as commander-in-chief of Dmitrii's army. Perhaps as a result
of Różyński's influence, the pretender began to tone down the more socially
divisive elements of his propaganda. From the spring of 1608 onwards, he tried
to bid for the support of noble servicemen rather than that of military slaves.
In a proclamation to Smolensk in April 1608, Dmitrii condemned the reign of
terror which Tsarevich Peter had introduced at Putivl' and Tula, and dissoci-
ated himself from the various cossack 'tsareviches' who had appeared on the
Volga and on the steppe.[30] He had already executed one of these – 'Tsarevich
Fedor Fedorovich' – at the end of 1607; he later hanged the Astrakhan' pretenders Ivan Augustus and Lavrentii at Tushino, probably in the summer of
1608. What happened to the other seven pretenders who were named in his
proclamation is unknown.

At the end of April 1608 Dmitrii marched from Orel towards Bolkhov,
where Tsar Vasilii's army, commanded by his brother, Prince Dmitrii Shuiskii,
was encamped. Różyński inflicted a major defeat on Shuiskii, and occupied
Bolkhov, before advancing on the capital via Kozel'sk, Kaluga, Borisov and
Mozhaisk. The pretender's troops set up camp in the village of Tushino, just
outside Moscow. On 25 June they defeated Shuiskii again at Khodynka, but
were unable to take the capital. Dmitrii entrenched himself at Tushino, where
he was to remain until the end of the following year.

Although the Polish troops who had joined the pretender's camp had done
so without the official sanction of King Sigismund, Tsar Vasilii hoped to

<hr/>

29 Perrie, *Pretenders*, pp. 171–3; Tiumentsev, *Smuta v Rossii*, pp. 116–26; Dunning, *Russia's First Civil War*, pp. 391–2.
30 *Vosstanie I. Bolotnikova*, pp. 229–31.

persuade the king to put pressure on his fellow countrymen to leave Russia. In a treaty signed in July 1608 Shuiskii agreed to release the Mniszechs and other Poles imprisoned in Russia; in return, Sigismund promised that all Polish troops at Tushino would be withdrawn. In practice, after their release the Mniszechs ended up at Tushino, where Marina was 'reunited' with her 'husband'; and not only did the Polish soldiers fail to leave Tushino, but others soon joined them. The most notable of the new arrivals was Jan-Piotr Sapieha, a nephew of the Lithuanian chancellor Leo Sapieha.

The initial successes of the pretender's troops undermined support for Tsar Vasilii in Moscow, and from the autumn of 1608 many boyars and noblemen transferred their allegiance to Tushino. Subsequently some of these men switched sides more than once (they were described by a contemporary as 'migratory birds'),[31] but Dmitrii managed to acquire a boyar duma and sovereign's court which included some eminent Muscovite aristocrats, including the Princes D. T. and Iu. N. Trubetskoi, and the boyar M. G. Saltykov. In October 1608 Metropolitan Filaret of Rostov (the former Fedor Nikitich Romanov) was brought to Tushino as a prisoner, and was appointed patriarch. Various kinsmen of the Romanovs – Prince A. Iu. Sitskii, Prince R. F. Troekurov and I. I. Godunov – became Tushino boyars.[32]

At the end of September 1608 Sapieha and his men left Tushino to lay siege to the great Trinity-Sergius monastery, north-east of the capital. The siege was to last until January 1610, and the heroic resistance of the defenders constituted one of the most celebrated episodes of the Time of Troubles. The rest of Dmitrii's army remained at Tushino. Their blockade of Moscow was not complete, since Riazan', to the south-east, remained loyal to Shuiskii, and supplies were able to enter the capital by the Riazan' road, which led through Kolomna.

In the autumn of 1608 Dmitrii's commanders concentrated on securing the allegiance of the towns which lay to the north and east of Moscow. Most of these towns recognised the pretender as a result of the use or threat of force by raiding parties from Tushino or from Sapieha's camp outside the Trinity monastery. Recent detailed research indicates that, contrary to the claims of some older historians, there is little evidence that popular uprisings in favour of Dmitrii took place in these towns. Pskov is a possible exception, but there the social conflicts pre-dated the formation of the Tushino camp and were in

31 A. Palitsyn, *Skazanie Avraamiia Palitsyna* (Moscow: AN SSSR, 1955), p. 117.
32 Tiumentsev, *Smuta v Rossii*, pp. 298–305, 543–5.

any case less polarised than the chronicle picture of 'little people' versus 'big people' suggests.[33]

By the end of 1608, the only major cities to remain loyal to Shuiskii were Novgorod in the north-west and Smolensk in the west. On the Volga, Nizhnii Novgorod and Kazan' were still held by Shuiskii's commanders, but overall Tsar Vasilii's position seemed fairly hopeless. At the beginning of 1609 the Kolomna road was briefly blocked, impeding the supply of food to the capital from the Riazan' region. As food prices increased in Moscow, so did discontent with Shuiskii. In February some of his courtiers made an attempt to overthrow him, but the plot was thwarted, mainly as a result of Patriarch Germogen's stout defence of the tsar. The boyar I. F. Kriuk-Kolychev organised another conspiracy on Palm Sunday, but this was discovered and the ringleader was executed.

In many parts of northern Russia, support for the pretender turned out to be short-lived. In the north-west, Pskov continued to acknowledge 'Tsar Dmitrii', but the towns of the north-east began to revolt against him from the beginning of 1609 onwards. Kostroma rebelled against the Tushinites as early as December 1608, but there, and in Galich, the popular revolt was soon suppressed by Polish troops. The situation in many places was confused, with some towns changing sides more than once. The uprisings against the Tushinites were fuelled by the rapacity of the Poles and the cossacks, who imposed heavy taxes and other exactions on the townspeople, and sometimes resorted to blatant looting. Government propaganda also played a part. Shuiskii denounced Dmitrii as an impostor, and claimed that the Catholic Poles presented a threat to Orthodoxy; these assertions helped to gain him support. In most districts the anti-Tushino movement had a broad social base, comprising servicemen as well as townspeople and peasants.[34]

At the beginning of 1609 Shuiskii acquired additional forces from abroad. In August 1608 Tsar Vasilii had sent his nephew, Prince Michael Skopin-Shuiskii, to Novgorod to negotiate with Karl IX for Swedish military assistance against the Poles. In February 1609 the Swedish commander Jacob Pontus de la Gardie arrived in Novgorod and concluded an agreement with Skopin-Shuiskii. In early May a combined Russian and Swedish army defeated troops that had been sent from Tushino against Novgorod. On 10 May Skopin-Shuiskii left Novgorod to march on Moscow and lift the siege of the capital. News of his advance encouraged those northern towns which still recognised Dmitrii to

33 *Pskovskie letopisi*, ed. A. N. Nasonov, vol. II (Moscow: AN SSSR, 1955), p. 268; cf. Tiumentsev, *Smuta v Rossii*, pp. 198–202, 219–55.
34 Tiumentsev, *Smuta v Rossii*, p. 419.

transfer their allegiance to Tsar Vasilii; but Pskov held out, in spite of an attempt by Prince Michael's forces to capture the town on 18 May. In July 1609 Skopin occupied Tver', and then moved east to link up with the troops sent by the north-eastern towns. At Aleksandrovskaia Sloboda they awaited the arrival of the boyar Fedor Sheremetev, who had been liberating the Volga towns to the south-east. Sheremetev had left his camp outside Astrakhan' in the autumn of 1607, and had gradually moved up the Volga. He reached Nizhnii Novgorod in the spring of 1609, and joined Skopin-Shuiskii at Aleksandrovskaia Sloboda towards the end of that year.

In the summer of 1609 King Sigismund, angered by Swedish support for Shuiskii, decided to intervene directly in the Russian civil war in order to obtain the Muscovite throne either for himself or for his son Władysław. In September he laid siege to Smolensk. The Poles who were encamped at Tushino did not welcome Sigismund's action, and sent envoys to Smolensk to try to dissuade the king from his undertaking. But Sigismund in his turn made a bid for the support of the Tushinites. A delegation from Smolensk arrived at Tushino in December 1609 to conduct negotiations with Różyński. The pretender was excluded from these talks. Fearing treachery, and aware that Skopin-Shuiskii's army was now close to Moscow, Dmitrii fled to Kaluga.

The pretender's flight demoralised and divided the Tushino encampment. Some of the Russians defected to Shuiskii in Moscow; some returned to their homes; while others followed Dmitrii to Kaluga. In January 1610 Jan-Piotr Sapieha abandoned the siege of the Trinity monastery and retreated to Dmitrov, where Marina Mniszech joined him from Tushino. Marina subsequently moved to Kaluga to be reunited with Dmitrii, while Sapieha retreated further west after Dmitrov fell to Skopin-Shuiskii's forces. At the end of January 1610 a group of Russian boyars at Tushino sent a delegation to Smolensk, headed by M. G. Saltykov, who agreed terms with King Sigismund on 4 February for the offer of the Russian throne to Prince Władysław. Finally, on 6 March Różyński burned the Tushino camp to the ground and withdrew its remaining occupants to Volokolamsk.

Soon after the abandonment of Tushino, Skopin-Shuiskii entered Moscow in triumph. On 23 April, however, he died suddenly in the capital: according to rumour, he was poisoned either by Tsar Vasilii or by Prince Dmitrii Shuiskii, who were thought to be jealous of their nephew's success and fearful that he might become a rival candidate for the throne. Vasilii Shuiskii's enemies, led by Prokopii Liapunov, the governor of Riazan', exploited these rumours in order to mobilise further opposition to the tsar. The military situation also began to deteriorate for Shuiskii after Prince Michael's death. Tsar Vasilii appointed his brother Dmitrii as commander-in-chief of his army and sent him, with the Swedish general de la Gardie, against King Sigismund's camp at Smolensk. The Polish commander Stanisław Żółkiewski advanced to meet them, defeated them at Klushino, and occupied Mozhaisk. At the same time, the Second False Dmitrii, who had successfully recruited a new army of cossacks and Poles, including Sapieha's mercenaries, left Kaluga and marched on the capital.[35] On 16 July 1610 he set up camp at Kolomenskoe, just outside Moscow. Some of the pretender's supporters approached Shuiskii's opponents in the capital and suggested that both sides overthrow their tsars and elect a new sovereign. On 17 July Shuiskii was deposed and tonsured as a monk, but Dmitrii's men failed to keep their side of the bargain.

The situation in Moscow after Shuiskii's removal was critical. Attempts to organise the election of a new tsar proved abortive, and power passed into the hands of a council of seven boyars who acted as a provisional government. Żółkiewski advanced to the outskirts of the capital, and began to negotiate terms with the boyars for the offer of the Russian throne to Władysław, in return for Polish military assistance against Tsar Dmitrii. An agreement was reached on 17 August, and Moscow and most of the towns which had recognised Shuiskii swore an oath of allegiance to Władysław. Żółkiewski managed to persuade Sapieha's troops to defect from Dmitrii's camp, and the pretender fled back to Kaluga. Żółkiewski moved quickly to consolidate his position. He ensured that the Russian delegation which was sent to Smolensk to offer the throne to Władysław included both Prince Vasilii Golitsyn, who had been one of the leading Russian candidates for election to the throne, and Filaret Romanov, whose young son Michael was another favoured contender. Then, on the pretext that the people of Moscow might revolt in favour of the pretender, Żółkiewski moved his troops into the capital, in direct contravention of his agreement of 17 August with the boyars. Soon afterwards Żółkiewski left for Smolensk, escorting the deposed tsar, Vasilii Shuiskii, and his brothers into captivity, and leaving the Polish commander Alexander Gosiewski in charge of the capital. At Smolensk, however, it became clear that King Sigismund had no intention of sending Władysław to Moscow, but planned to become tsar of Russia himself. When this proposition was rejected by the Russian envoys, they were imprisoned, and the king resumed his siege of Smolensk.

By the autumn of 1610 most Russians realised that their prospective new tsar was not the potential convert to Orthodoxy, Prince Władysław, but the ardently Catholic King Sigismund; the Poles, moreover, had occupied Moscow and

35 Ibid., pp. 493–5.

were continuing hostilities elsewhere. In these circumstances, the popularity of the Second False Dmitrii again began to grow. At Kaluga, the pretender's supporters were at first primarily cossacks – including Don cossacks under the command of the ataman I. M. Zarutskii – and Tatars. By December, Dmitrii had recruited some mercenaries, and a number of new towns, such as Viatka and Kazan', had recognised him as tsar.[36] Feuding, accompanied by the torture and execution of suspected 'traitors', had however become endemic in the Kaluga camp. On 11 December the pretender was murdered by the Tatar prince Peter Urusov, in a revenge attack for Dmitrii's killing of the khan of Kasimov, another Tatar leader who had entered Dmitrii's service. A few days later, Marina Mniszech gave birth to a son, Ivan Dmitrievich, who became a 'hereditary pretender' (K. V. Chistov has described him as 'an involuntary pretender (*samozvanets*) by birth').[37]

The national liberation campaign

Even before the murder of the Second False Dmitrii, other elements in Russian society had begun to mobilise opposition to the Polish occupation of Moscow. The death of the pretender, who had been a controversial and divisive figure, provided an additional impetus to their efforts. In Moscow itself Patriarch Germogen refused to swear loyalty to King Sigismund, and was placed under virtual house arrest by the boyar government. None the less, Germogen was able to have his appeals for resistance smuggled out of the capital. The patriarch's letters found the soil particularly well prepared in Riazan', where Shuiskii's old enemy Prokopii Liapunov was governor. Nizhnii Novgorod was also responsive to the call. Liapunov began to recruit an army of servicemen from various towns, and he also bid for the support of the forces that had previously recognised Tsar Dmitrii. Prince Dmitrii Trubetskoi, the most senior of the Second False Dmitrii's boyars, brought troops from Kaluga; and Zarutskii, who had fled from Kaluga with Marina and her son after the pretender's murder, led his Don cossacks from Tula.

As the liberation army approached Moscow, the people of the capital staged an unsuccessful uprising against the Poles on 19 March 1611. The occupiers withdrew into the Kremlin, burning the outlying parts of the city as they retreated and making much of the population homeless. The national militia set up camp outside the capital and took an oath to elect a tsar. But the

36 Ibid., pp. 508–14.
37 K. V. Chistov, *Russkie narodnye sotsial'no–utopicheskie legendy XVII–XIX vv.* (Moscow: Nauka, 1967), p. 66.

forces besieging Moscow were very heterogeneous in their composition, and were plagued by disputes and disagreements. They could not even agree on the choice of a single leader, creating instead a triumvirate of Liapunov, Trubetskoi and Zarutskii. On 30 June an agreement was signed by the triumvirs and by representatives of the troops, which was designed to resolve conflicts over the remuneration of servicemen and cossacks.[38] New disputes soon broke out, however, over their preferred candidate for the throne. Liapunov favoured one of the sons of Karl IX, in the hope that this would guarantee military assistance from Sweden against the Poles. Zarutskii, by contrast, promoted the cause of Marina Mniszech's infant son, 'Tsarevich' Ivan Dmitrievich. The two leaders' support for rival candidates for the throne contributed to a conflict which resulted in Liapunov's murder by the cossacks on 22 July 1611. After Liapunov's death, many of the noble servicemen deserted the besiegers' camp. Zarutskii and Trubetskoi continued to blockade the capital with their predominantly cossack forces, but their attempts to capture the city in the autumn were unsuccessful. By the end of the year many cossacks too had drifted away from Moscow.[39]

In the course of 1611 the foreign intervention forces made considerable advances. Smolensk finally fell to King Sigismund on 3 June, but a subsequent offensive by the Lithuanian hetman Jan Karol Chodkiewicz failed to dislodge Zarutskii and Trubetskoi from their camp outside Moscow. In July 1611 the Swedish commander de la Gardie occupied Novgorod, but instead of coming to the assistance of the liberation forces besieging the capital, the Swedes pursued their own interests, and annexed many Russian towns in the Novgorod region.

A Third False Dmitrii was active in the north-west in 1611–12. The real identity of this pretender is unknown: the official chronicler describes him as Sidorka or Matiushka, a deacon from Moscow.[40] He first appeared in Novgorod at the beginning of 1611, before moving to Ivangorod, where he made an unsuccessful attempt to gain support from the Swedes. He was soon recognised by the neighbouring towns of Iam, Kopor'e and Gdov. Pskov at first resisted him, but after Novgorod had surrendered to de la Gardie the Pskovans invited the new Tsar Dmitrii to their town, in the hope that he would defend them against the Swedes. The pretender arrived in Pskov on 4 December 1611, and established his headquarters there. By this time, however, the name of Tsar Dmitrii had lost its broad social appeal, and only a handful of towns recognised his new incarnation. The cossacks remained susceptible

38 Stanislavskii, *Grazhdanskaia voina*, pp. 36–9; Dunning, *Russia's First Civil War*, pp. 425–6.
39 Stanislavskii, *Grazhdanskaia voina*, pp. 40–2; Dunning, *Russia's First Civil War*, pp. 429–30.
40 PSRL, vol. XIV, p. 115, para. 279.

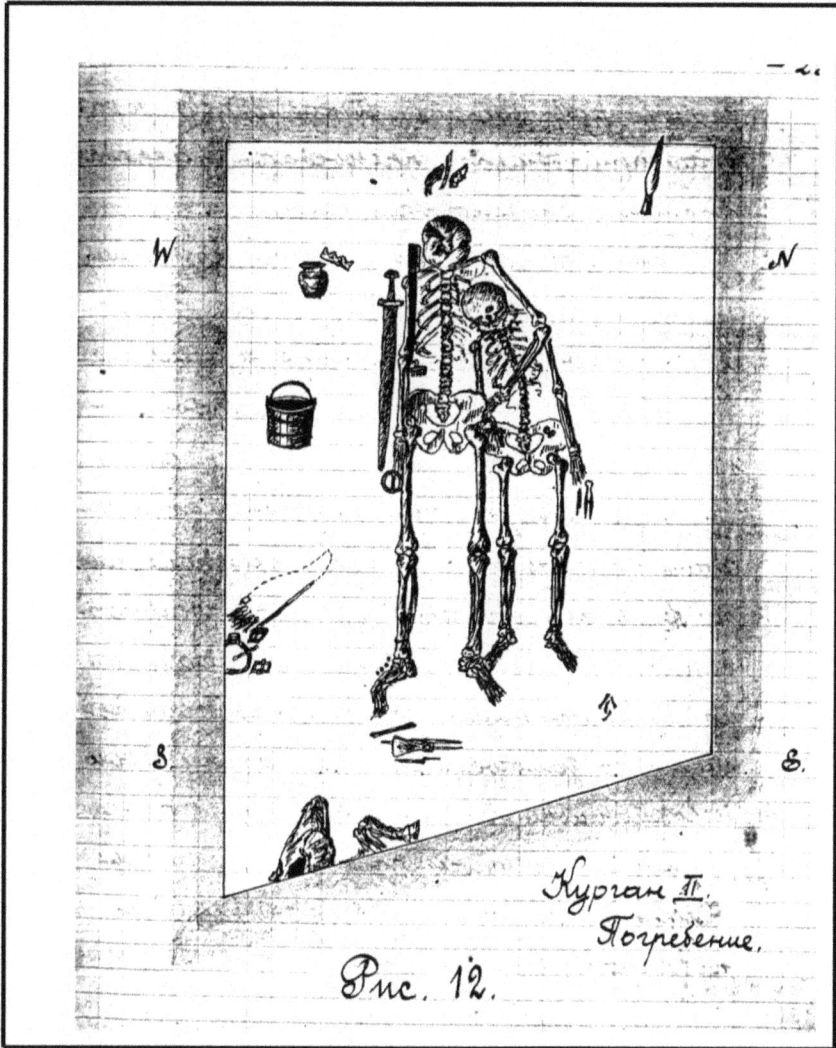

Plate 1. Warrior and woman. This couple was buried in a chamber grave in the burial ground at Shestovitsa, near Chernigov, around the mid-tenth century. The woman was almost certainly a slave – perhaps a favourite – put to death at the time of the warrior's funeral. A horse was also slaughtered and placed in the grave. The warrior's sword is of 'H-type' (Petersen's classification) and was probably manufactured in Western Europe, perhaps the Rhineland. The rich inventory includes a battle knife; quiverful of arrows; weights for balances; and a kind of tool kit. See p. 58.

2a (i)   2a (ii)

2b (i)   2b (ii)

Plate 2. Coins of Vladimir I. Like contemporary leaders in Scandinavia and Poland, Vladimir issued coins soon after adopting Christianity. All his gold coins, and Type I of his silver coins (*srebreniki*) copy the design of the gold *nomismata* of his brothers-in-law, Emperors Basil II and Constantine VIII (976–1025). Vladimir's gold coins, few in number and struck over a fairly short period, are generally competently executed. See p. 69.

Plate 2a. *Srebrenik* of Vladimir, Type I

Plate 2a (i). Christ the Lord of All (Pantokrator), crudely rendered, but features such as the cross-nimbus behind Christ's head and His Gospel Book are still recognisable. The legend is in mirror-writing and reads from right to left.

Plate 2a (ii). Vladimir's crown and its pendants are schematic, his body stunted, but – like the Byzantine emperors in the original design – he holds a cross with a long staff. Over his left shoulder is a trident-like authority symbol, most probably adapted from Khazar usage.

Plate 2b. *Srebrenik* of Vladimir, Type II. Vladimir's *srebreniki*, which were issued in sizeable quantities, underwent substantial debasement in silver content and degradation from the Byzantine-derived design. Type II is of slightly later date than Type I, *c.*1000–1015.

Plate 2b (i). Vladimir's face and crown have merged into a cross encircled by a nimbus.

Plate 2b (ii). Vladimir's authority symbol – probably a familiar sight to the Rus' moneyer – has replaced the Pantokrator and is rendered clearly and competently.

Plate 3. Monumental mosaic of the Theotokos (Mother of God) in the apse of the church of St Sophia in Kiev; mid-eleventh century. See p. 96.

Plate 4. St Luke the Evangelist. Manuscript miniature; 1057; from the *Ostromir Gospel*, the oldest surviving dated Slavonic book. See p. 96.

Plate 5. Mosaic of St Mark writing his Gospel, in the church of St Sophia in Kiev; mid-eleventh century. All the inscriptions (the evangelist's name, and the text of his Gospel on the lectern) are in Greek. See p. 96.

Plate 6. Icon of Saints Boris and Gleb; early fourteenth century. Boris and Gleb were sons
of Prince Vladimir Sviatoslavich (the Kievan prince who made Christianity the official
religion of Rus'). Murdered in 1015 by their brother, Boris and Gleb were among the very
earliest natives of Rus' to be venerated as saints. See p. 96.

7a

7b

Plate 7. The defeat of Prince Igor' Sviatoslavich by the *Polovtsy* at the Battle of the Kaiala River in 1185. See p. 115. Miniatures from the fifteenth-century *Radzivil Chronicle*.
Plate 7a. Sviatoslav Ol'govich pursuing the fleeing *Polovtsy*.
Plate 7b. Vsevolod Sviatoslavich fighting on foot (left scene) and Igor''s capture (right scene).

Plate 8. The reconstructed church of St Paraskeva Piatnitsa, Chernigov (early thirteenth century).

Plate 9. The 'Novgorod psalter', one of a set of three waxed wooden writing tablets with texts from the psalms, discovered by archaeologists in July 2000. Novgorod, early eleventh century. See p. 193.

Plate 10. Grand Prince Vasilii III. From the first (Latin) edition of Baron Sigismund von Herberstein's account of Russia, published in Basel in 1556.

11a

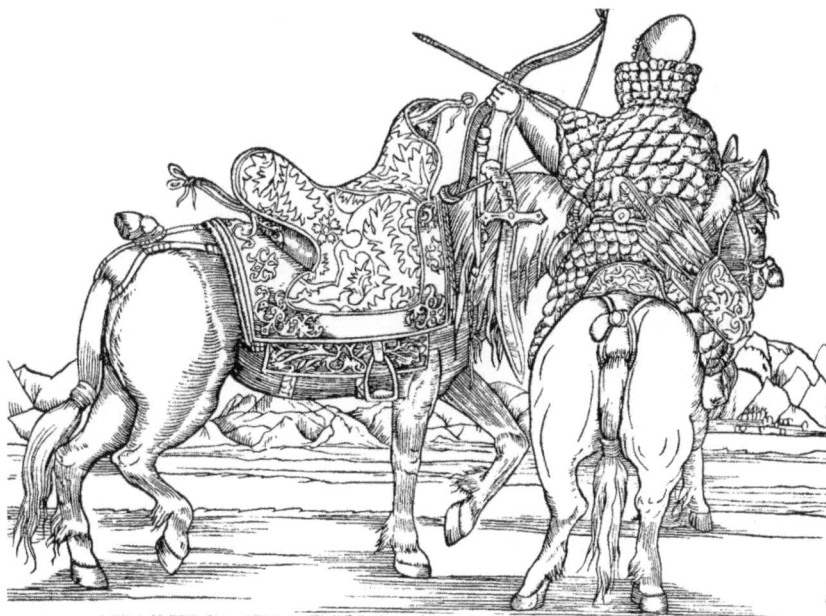

11b

Plate 11a. and 11b. Russian cavalrymen. From the 1556 edition of Herberstein. See p. 218.

12a   12b

Plate 12. Royal helmets in the sixteenth century.
Plate 12a. Helmet of Ivan IV (*c.*1533). Inscribed: 'Helmet of Prince Ivan Vasil'evich, son of
Grand Prince Vasilii Ivanovich, Sovereign of All Russia and Autocrat'. See p. 243.
Plate 12b. Helmet of Ivan Ivanovich, son of Ivan IV, decorated with images of
double-headed eagles and lions (1557). Inscribed: 'This helmet was made on the order of
the faithful and Christ-loving Tsar, Great Sovereign Ivan Vasil'evich of All Russia,
Autocrat, for his faithful son, Tsarevich Ivan Ivanovich in the fourth year after his birth, in
the glorious ruling city of Moscow on the 8th day of July, in the year 7065'. See p. 251.

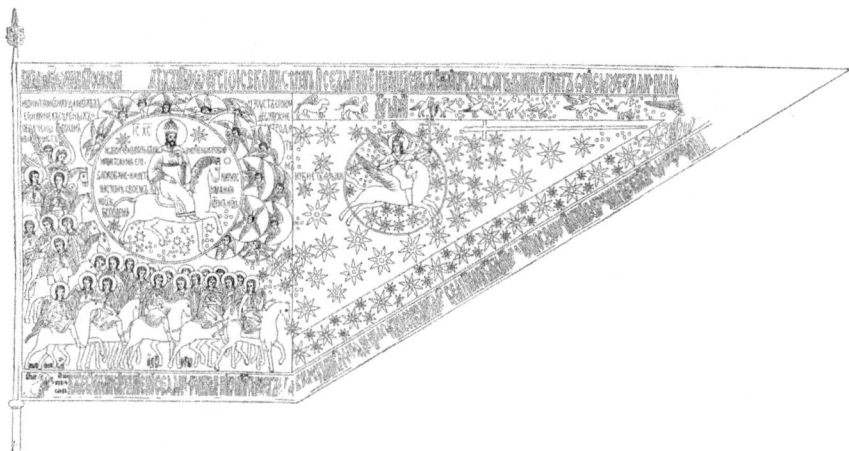

Plate 13. The Great Banner of Ivan IV, with apocalyptic images and quotations from Revelation (1559/60). The central mounted figure is Jesus Christ; the winged horseman on the right is the Archangel Michael. See pp. 259–60.

Plate 14. A Russian merchant. From a sixteenth-century German engraving in the collection of P. Ia. Dashkov, reproduced in the 1908 Russian translation of Herberstein.

Plate 15. Cathedral of the Dormition (1475–9), north and east façades. Moscow Kremlin. Photograph by William Brumfield. See p. 343.

Plate 16. A ceremony in front of St Basil's cathedral in Moscow (built 1555–61), as witnessed by the Holstein envoys on 1 October 1634. On the left, the patriarch extends a cross to the tsar. From the second (1656) edition of Adam Olearius's account of the embassy.

Plate 17. Anointing of Tsar Michael during the coronation ritual in the cathedral of the Dormition, 1613. The regalia seen on gold plates are the Cap of Monomakh, the sceptre and the orb. From a 1672 account. See p. 400.

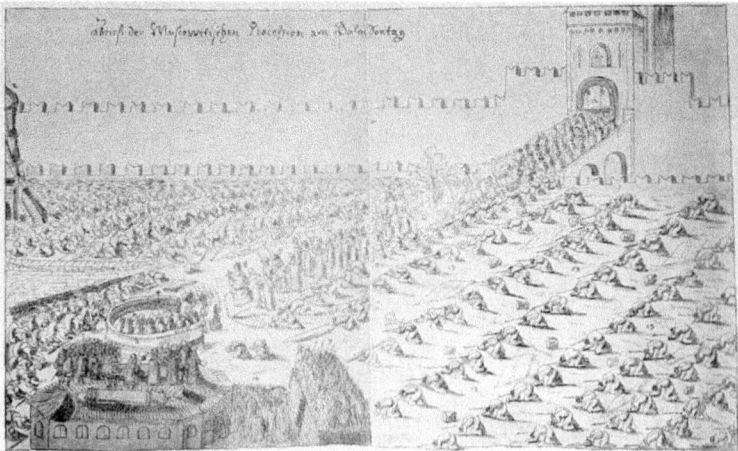

Plate 18. Palm Sunday ritual in Moscow, 1662. The procession returns to the Kremlin from Golgotha (foreground). The church of the Intercession (St Basil's) is at the left. Engraving from Baron von Meyerberg's account of the embassy of the Holy Roman Emperor to Moscow in 1661–2. See p. 405.

Plate 19. Tsar Michael Romanov at the age of forty-two (i.e. in 1638). Portrait from the first (1647) edition of Adam Olearius's account of Russia.

Plate 20. Engraved portrait of Tsar Alexis. Vienna (1660s–1670s).

Plate 21. Various types of corporal punishment, depicted against the background of the Moscow Kremlin. From the 1656 edition of Olearius. See p. 571.

Plate 22. Russian dress in the seventeenth century. A variety of types of costumes, reflecting differences in gender and social status. From the second (1656) edition of Olearius's account of Russia.

LADOGA

23a

23b

Plate 23. Popular entertainments. The Church disapproved of such entertainments, and *skomorokhi* were banned in 1648. See p. 626.

Plate 23a. *Skomorokhi* (folk minstrels) singing and dancing to amuse the envoys from Holstein at Ladoga in 1634. From Adam Olearius's account of the embassy, first published in 1647.

Plate 23b. In the foreground, a showman wrapped in a blanket operates a puppet theatre above his head. From the second (1656) edition of Olearius's account.

Plate 24. Church of the Holy Trinity at Nikitniki, Moscow (1631–53). Detail of the façade.
See p. 644.

Plate 25. 'Moscow Baroque' church of the Intercession at Fili (1690s). See p. 645.

Plate 26. The wooden palace at Kolomenskoe (1660s–1670s). Anonymous eighteenth-century engraving. See p. 646.

Plate 27. *Lubok* (wood block print): *The Mice Bury the Cat*. Late seventeenth century. See p. 649.

Plate 28. Engraved portrait of Tsarevna Sophia Alekseevna, Amsterdam, 1680s. Anonymous nineteenth-century copy. See p. 652.

to pretenders, however, and the Pskovan tsar soon established links with their encampments outside Moscow. In March 1612 they swore allegiance to the Third False Dmitrii.[41]

After the death of Liapunov some of the towns which had previously supported the liberation army expressed their distrust of its two remaining commanders, Trubetskoi and Zarutskii. They were particularly concerned that Zarutskii and his cossacks might plan to place Marina Mniszech's son on the throne. Patriarch Germogen sent a proclamation to Nizhnii Novgorod calling on the townspeople to reject the infant 'Tsarevich' Ivan Dmitrievich.[42] The receipt of the patriarch's letter in Nizhnii, in August 1611, served as the impulse for the organisation of a new liberation army. The collection of resources to fund its recruitment was undertaken by Koz'ma Minin, a local butcher and elected representative of the townspeople; the command of the troops was entrusted to Prince Dmitrii Pozharskii, one of Liapunov's generals, who had been wounded outside Moscow in March 1611 and was convalescing near Nizhnii Novgorod. Over the winter of 1611–12 Minin and Pozharskii mobilised their forces. The nucleus of the 'second national militia', as it is sometimes called, was provided by the garrison of Nizhnii Novgorod and neighbouring Volga towns, together with some refugee servicemen from the Smolensk region. At the beginning of March 1612 Minin and Pozharskii left Nizhnii and headed towards Moscow. At Iaroslavl' they learned that the cossack encampments outside the capital had taken an oath to the Third False Dmitrii. Pozharskii immediately sent proclamations to various towns, condemning Zarutskii and Trubetskoi for recognising the Pskov pretender and calling on all true Christians to renounce the new Tsar Dmitrii as well as Marina and her son.

The cossack encampments soon deserted the cause of the Third False Dmitrii, who had in any case made himself very unpopular in Pskov, by ruling through terror and intimidation. In May the townspeople overthrew him and sent him under escort to Moscow, where he was held prisoner by the cossacks. Trubetskoi and Zarutskii wrote to Pozharskii at Iaroslavl' to assure him that they had repudiated Dmitrii, and had also abandoned the claim of Marina's son to the throne. They were prepared to join forces with Pozharskii in liberating Moscow from the Poles and electing a new tsar by common agreement.[43] Pozharskii, however, reacted coldly to these conciliatory approaches. He had established his headquarters at Iaroslavl', where he headed a provisional government and continued to recruit servicemen into

---

41 Perrie, *Pretenders*, pp. 211–16.
42 *AAE*, vol. II, no. 194.ii, pp. 333–4.
43 Perrie, *Pretenders*, pp. 216–18.

his army. In discussions about a future tsar, Pozharskii seemed to favour the Swedish prince Karl Filip (whose brother, Gustav Adolf, had succeeded their father Karl IX as king). Pozharskii's assurances to the Swedes about Karl Filip's prospects of obtaining the Russian throne helped to neutralise the military threat from Sweden, which was still occupying Novgorod and other parts of the north-west.

After securing his rear as a result of the agreement with the Swedes, Pozharskii finally left Iaroslavl' on 27 July 1612. On the following day Zarutskii fled from the encampment outside Moscow, apparently fearing that he would be deposed from his command by the leaders of the new national militia. Zarutskii was accompanied by about half of his army, probably around 2,500 men. At Kolomna he collected Marina and her son, and they then rode with their cossacks to the Riazan' district, where Zarutskii rallied support for Tsarevich Ivan's claim to the throne. Pozharskii's army arrived outside Moscow in mid-August, just in time to play a major part in the rout of Chodkiewicz's Polish forces, which had advanced on the capital from the west. Zarutskii's flight removed a major obstacle to the creation of a single army of liberation, and at the end of September Pozharskii and Trubetskoi agreed to form a united command. A month later, the occupiers of the Kremlin surrendered, and Moscow was liberated at last. But the danger from the Poles was not yet over. After the defeat of Chodkiewicz, King Sigismund himself marched on Russia in the hope of obtaining the crown for his son Władysław. The Polish army advanced rapidly and a detachment commanded by Adam Żółkiewski reached the outskirts of Moscow by mid-November. But military failures and the onset of winter forced the Poles to retreat.

At the end of 1612 the liberators of Moscow, headed by Minin, Pozharskii and Trubetskoi, summoned an Assembly of the Land to elect a new tsar. The delegates gathered in the capital at the beginning of January 1613. One of their first resolutions was to reject any foreign candidates for the throne, a decision which was directed not only against the Polish and Swedish princes, but also against Marina and her son. This left three main Russian contenders: Prince Ivan Golitsyn, Prince Dmitrii Trubetskoi and Michael Romanov, Filaret's sixteen-year-old son. Of these, the cossacks favoured the latter two, because of their connection with Tushino. The young Romanov also enjoyed broad support from other sections of the population, and he was the eventual choice of the electoral assembly in February 1613. The Romanovs' association by marriage with the old dynasty undoubtedly helped Michael's election (his father was the nephew of Anastasiia Romanovna, the first wife of Ivan IV); and the fact that the ambitious and energetic Filaret was in Polish captivity made his teenage son more acceptable to the boyars.

One of the first actions of Tsar Michael's government was to send troops in pursuit of Zarutskii. After a battle with government forces at Voronezh in June 1613 the cossack ataman headed for Astrakhan', where he was welcomed with great enthusiasm. Zarutskii spread the rumour that Tsar Dmitrii was still alive, and he and Marina acted as the guardians of the young 'tsarevich' Ivan Dmitrievich. In the winter of 1613–14 Zarutskii initiated a reign of terror in Astrakhan', killing the governor, Prince I. D. Khvorostinin, and many of the 'good' (wealthy) citizens, perhaps because they opposed his plans to seek assistance from the Persian Shah and the Turkish Sultan. At Easter 1614 there was a popular uprising against Zarutskii's rule, and soon afterwards he fled the city with Marina and her son, accompanied by a small band of cossacks. A few days later, government troops commanded by Prince I. N. Odoevskii entered Astrakhan', and the city transferred its allegiance to Tsar Michael. Zarutskii and his followers were captured on the River Iaik; they were returned to Astrakhan' and then sent to Moscow. Zarutskii was impaled; the three-year-old Tsarevich Ivan was hanged; and Marina died in captivity soon afterwards.[44]

The execution of Zarutskii and Ivan Dmitrievich eliminated the last serious challenge to Tsar Michael's legitimacy within Russia. Unrest continued for some time, however, and in 1614–15 the government was preoccupied with mopping-up operations against various roving cossack bands whom they perceived as a major threat to social and political stability.[45] Foreign intervention continued for several more years. Peace was concluded with Sweden only in 1617, when Novgorod was returned to Russia as a result of the Treaty of Stolbovo. Hostilities with Poland lasted even longer. Chodkiewicz invaded Russia again in 1617 in a further attempt to place Prince Władysław on the throne. The Poles were obliged to retreat, but in the Treaty of Deulino, signed in December 1618, Russia ceded Smolensk and other western borderlands to King Sigismund. In accordance with the terms of the treaty, Filaret Romanov was released from captivity, and he returned to Russia in 1619 to become patriarch and de facto ruler of the country. Some have seen this event as the real end of the Time of Troubles.[46] But the Poles still refused to drop Władysław's claim to the title of tsar. In 1632, on the death of King Sigismund, the Russians

44 Ibid., pp. 218–28.
45 Stanislavskii, *Grazhdanskaia voina*, pp. 93–152.
46 Dunning, *Russia's First Civil War*, p. 459.

went on to the offensive against Poland, in an attempt to reconquer Smolensk. They failed to achieve this goal, but in the 'perpetual' Peace of Polianovka, of 1634, Władysław – who had been elected King of Poland in succession to his father – formally renounced his claim to the Russian throne, thereby tying up that remaining loose end from the Time of Troubles.

Conclusion

According to S. F. Platonov's classic account of the Time of Troubles, the social groups at both the top and bottom of Russian society lost out at the expense of the middle strata. The old princely-boyar aristocracy was totally discredited, first by Vasilii Shuiskii's attempt to establish an oligarchic regime and then by the boyars' collaboration with the Poles. At the other end of the spectrum, the cossacks and the fugitive peasants and slaves who swelled their ranks also suffered a defeat with the suppression of Zarutskii's movement. The 'middle classes' – the ordinary servicemen and the more prosperous townsmen, who liberated Moscow from the Poles and elected Michael Romanov as their tsar at the Assembly of the Land – emerged victorious.[47] Recent scholarship has, however, questioned several of Platonov's conclusions, contesting in particular his claim that the position of the old aristocracy was significantly weakened as a result of the Troubles.[48]

Perhaps the most remarkable consequence of the Time of Troubles was the fact that the autocratic monarchical system survived more or less unchanged from the late sixteenth century, with no significant new restrictions on the power of the tsar. It is highly revealing that the conflicts of the early seventeenth century were fought out under the banners of competing claimants for the throne, rather than of competing types of monarchy. Of course the various candidates represented different styles and systems of rule; but they all based their claims to the throne on their legitimacy as the 'true' tsar rather than on any programme of social or political reform. The basis of legitimacy was contested (hereditary versus elective), but not the autocratic nature of monarchical rule itself. The dynastic crisis of 1598, occurring as it did in a system based on hereditary succession, gave rise to the First False Dmitrii; and his triumphs in their turn inspired new pretenders. The proliferation of cossack 'tsareviches', however, and the killing and looting committed by

47 Platonov, *Ocherki* [4th edn], pp. 429–33.
48 A. P. Pavlov, 'Gosudarev dvor v istorii Rossii XVII veka', *FOG* 56 (2000): 227–42; Dunning, *Russia's First Civil War*, pp. 461–80.

their followers, served to discredit pretence in the eyes of most ordinary Russians. After the Time of Troubles, no further Russian *samozvanets* was able to obtain the type of broad social support which had accrued to the first two False Dmitriis: later pretenders who achieved any significant backing did so almost exclusively from the lower classes, and from cossacks and peasants in particular.

PART III

RUSSIA UNDER THE FIRST ROMANOVS (1613–1689)

19

The central government and its institutions

MARSHALL POE

For the Muscovite state, the seventeenth century was one of evolution and growth, rather than radical change.[1] The century experienced no political revolutions of the magnitude seen during the reigns of Ivan III and Ivan IV. Russia, having recovered from the confusion of the Time of Troubles, remained a strong autocracy held firmly in the hands of a small, martial ruling class. This is not to say that there was general stasis. Things still fell apart, though only for brief moments. And one can detect a single important political trend – the remarkable inflation of honours begun under Tsar Aleksei (Alexis) Mikhailovich and radically amplified by his weak successors. Nonetheless, the general picture was one of continuity, punctuated by momentary fits of confusion and gradual change.

The case is much the same in the realm of institutions.[2] Seventeenth-century Muscovy was administered by the same fundamental types of organisation that it had been before the great upheaval of the beginning of the century. The most important institutions remained the royal family, its court and courtiers (*gosudarev dvor*) and the administrative chancelleries (*prikazy*). Similarly, the boyar council and the Assembly of the Land – both inventions of an earlier age – continued to operate in the seventeenth century much as they had before. All of these institutions grew, but not so much as to fundamentally alter their essential character.

---

1 The best general history of seventeenth-century Russia remains V. O. Kliuchevskii, *A Course in Russian History: The Seventeenth Century* (Chicago: Quadrangle Books, 1968). For a survey of primary and secondary sources, see S. A. Kristensen [Christensen], *Istoriia rossii XVII v. Obzor issledovanii i istochnikov* (Moscow: Progress, 1989). On high politics, see Robert O. Crummey, *Aristocrats and Servitors: The Boyar Elite in Russia, 1613–1689* (Princeton: Princeton University Press, 1983), and Paul Bushkovitch, *Peter the Great: The Struggle for Power, 1671–1725* (Cambridge and New York: Cambridge University Press, 2001).

2 For an overview of governmental institutions, see N. P. Eroshkin, *Ocherki istorii gosudarstvennykh uchrezhdenii dorevoliutsionnoi Rossii* (Moscow: Gosudarstvennoe Uchebno-Pedagogicheskoe izdatel'stvo Ministerstva prosveshcheniia RSFSR, 1960).

Finally, we might note that the state existed for the same purpose as it had in the sixteenth century and earlier – to serve the interests of the Muscovite ruling class.[3] Though one occasionally finds biblical tropes in Muscovite ornamental texts about monarchs 'tending their flocks' and such, the truth is that the elite did not hide the fact that they were a self-interested ruling class and that the state was the instrument of their domination. They showed open contempt for peasants, merchants and often clergymen, and almost never missed an opportunity to fleece them – a point made and bemoaned by the well-travelled, well-educated and well-informed political philosopher (and proto-Slavophile!) Iurii Krizhanich in the 1660s.[4] Any attempt at protest that was not couched in the most subservient terms was met with a rush of horrific violence (violence that only the state could muster, since it was the only organised interest in early modern Russia). As visiting foreigners often noted, there was no talk of the 'commonwealth', the 'common good', or common anything (that would come with Peter and from Europe). Muscovites high and low believed the tsar owned everything – land and those occupying it – by heavenly proclamation.[5] That he distributed his largesse unequally (and predominantly to the elite) bothered not a soul. No one could conceive of any other order, no one objected to it (at least for very long . . .) and no one even thought it wrong. It was the way of things, and that was that.

The tsar in his court

Muscovites had an entire catalogue of sayings to the effect that the tsar was like God (and, one might add, the God of Moses rather than Jesus),[6] so it is only appropriate that we begin our survey of seventeenth-century institutions with the ruler and his court.

Let us begin with the royal person, for he was an institution in his own right. In contrast to some monarchies, the Russians do not seem to have recognised or even known about the 'king's two bodies' doctrine.[7] The clergy said and

3 For an extended discussion of the Russian ruling class and its interests, see Marshall T. Poe, *The Russian Moment in World History* (Princeton: Princeton University Press, 2003).
4 Iurii Krizhanich, *Politika*, ed. A. Gol'dberg (Moscow: Nauka, 1965), pp. 583–4.
5 P. V. Lukin, *Narodnye predstavleniia o gosudarstvennoi vlasti v Rossii XVII veka* (Moscow: Nauka, 2000), *passim*.
6 On these dicta, see Marshall T. Poe, 'A People Born to Slavery': *Russia in Early Modern European Ethnography, 1476–1748* (Ithaca, N.Y., and London: Cornell University Press, 2000), appendix 1.
7 On the European concept, see E. H. Kantorowicz, *The King's Two Bodies* (Princeton: Princeton University Press, 1957). For an explicit contrast, see Michael Cherniavsky, 'Saintly Princes and Princely Saints', in his *Tsar and People: A Historical Study of Russian National and Social Myths* (New Haven: Yale University Press, 1961), pp. 28–30.

commoners believed that the tsar was selected by the Lord, not *to hold the office* of tsar, but *to be* tsar. This is why one finds so much talk of the 'true tsar' and 'pretenders', particularly during the Time of Troubles when it was hard to tell the difference, but also after the ascension of the Romanovs.[8] Just how one could know the 'true tsar' was anybody's guess, but that there was a 'true' – that is, divinely appointed – tsar was never seriously questioned. There was, then, no office of 'tsar'; there was just the 'true tsar', a person and family ordained by the hand of the All Mighty.

We know, of course, that Michael Romanov was elected or, rather, his family won out in a rough and tumble competition dominated by occupying cossacks in 1613. But it was not considered polite (or even safe)[9] to mention this after the fact. That is because Michael was the 'true tsar'. His family and their propagandists spent a lot of effort to drive this point home. They went so far as to argue that they were not only the very descendents and rightful heirs to the Riurikids (via one of Ivan IV's marriages), but that they were in some mystical sense Riurikids themselves. This effort to cloak themselves in other-worldly divinity appealed to the Muscovite mind, but it doubtless had little effect on the men who actually engineered the Romanov 'succession'. They knew, as politicians always know, what had actually happened. Nonetheless, it made no sense for them to do anything but play along. The tsar, after all, was one of them and would – if he were wisely selected – protect their interests. Michael and his successors did just this, and they became 'true tsars' as a result.

Though one reads occasionally in Muscovite didactic texts that the tsar should do this or that (take council, be merciful, be wise),[10] he really had only two hard and fast duties: to produce a suitable heir and to rule the country in consultation with his boyars. There were, naturally, rules about how he would perform these two tasks, the former governed by Christian doctrine and the latter by custom. Since the rights and obligations of Orthodox marriage are

---

8 On pretenderism, see Chester Dunning, *Russia's First Civil War: The Time of Troubles and the Founding of the Romanov Dynasty* (University Park, Pa.: Pennsylvania State University Press, 2001) and Maureen Perrie, *Pretenders and Popular Monarchism in Early Modern Russia: The False Tsars of the Time of Troubles* (Cambridge and New York: Cambridge University Press, 1995).

9 On the Romanovs' campaign to stamp out pretenderism, see Mark C. Lapman, 'Political Denunciations in Muscovy, 1600 to 1649: The Sovereign's Word and Deed', unpublished Ph.D. dissertation, Harvard, University, 1982; N. I. Novombergskii, *Slovo i delo gosudarevy: Protsessy do izdaniia Ulozheniia Alekseia Mikhailovicha 1649 g.* (Moscow: A. I. Snegireva, 1911), and G. G. Tel'berg, *Ocherki politicheskogo suda i politicheskikh prestuplenii* (Moscow: Tipografiia Imperatorskogo Moskovskogo Universiteta, 1912).

10 See Daniel Rowland, 'The Problem of Advice in Muscovite Tales about the Time of Troubles', *RH* 6 (1979): 259–83, and his 'Did Muscovite Literary Ideology Place Limits on the Power of the Tsar (1540s–1660s)?', *RR* 49 (1990): 125–56.

Duma ranks
Boiare
↑
Okol'nichie
↑
Dumnye dvoriane
↑
Ceremonial ranks
↑
Dumnye d'iaki

Sub-duma court ranks
Stol'niki
↑
Dvoriane moskovskie
↑
Striapchie
↑
Zhil'tsy

Administrative ranks
D'iaki
↑
Pod'iachie

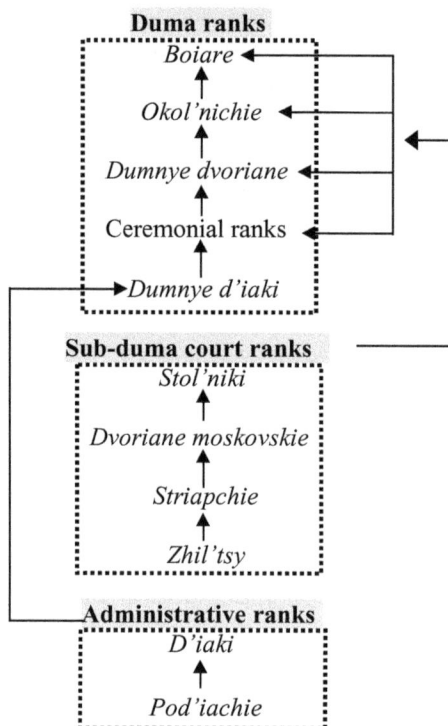

Figure 19.1. The sovereign's court in the seventeenth century

sufficiently well known (one wife, or at least one at a time), as is the process by which an heir is begotten, let us discuss the rules of Muscovite politics as they were practised in their principal arena, the sovereign's court (*gosudarev dvor*).[11]

The sovereign's court was the locus of political power in Muscovy. It was not a place (though the royal family did have quarters in the Kremlin called a 'court' or *dvor*), but rather a hierarchy of ranks. Figure 19.1 outlines them.

As one would expect, higher ranks were more honourable than lower ranks, and generally less populous. To some degree, different rank-holders did different things: the men in the duma ranks (*boiare i dumnye liudi*) advised the tsar in the royal council (duma), an ill-defined customary body whose power

---

11 For a bibliography of works on the *gosudarev dvor*, see O. Kosheleva and M. A. Strucheva, *Gosudarev dvor v Rossii: konets XV–nachalo XVIII vv.: katalog knizhnoi vystavki* (Moscow: Gosudarstvennaia publichnaia istoricheskaia biblioteka Rossii, 1997).

waxed and waned depending on the age of the tsar, the authority of those around him and the number of counsellors present. Those below the duma ranks (the sub-duma court ranks in Figure 19.1) generally worked as footmen of various sorts at court – serving at table, guarding the palace, performing in ceremonies, escorting emissaries and so on. Despite their modern 'servile' connotations, these lines of employ were considered very honourable duty by high-born Muscovites (and certainly better than serving in the provinces). Finally, the administrators served in the chancelleries (*prikazy*). Because they performed servile work (writing), they were drawn from a less honourable class (*sluzhilye liudi po priboru*, or 'service people by contract') rather than from the ranks of hereditary servitors (*sluzhilye liudi po otechestvu*, or 'service people by birth').[12]

As Figure 19.1 suggests, servitors sometimes moved through the ranks. The rules for entry into and promotion through the upper ranks were as follows.[13] The men in the three duma ranks above *dumnyi d'iak* (*boiarin, okol'nichii, dumnyi dvorianin*) were generally recruited from hereditary servitors in the sub-duma court ranks. Elected hereditary servitors could be appointed to any of these three ranks (that is, not *dumnyi d'iak*). Once they had assumed a rank, they could progress upward, for example, from *dumnyi dvorianin* to *okol'nichii* or from *okol'nichii* to *boiarin*. Ranks could not be skipped after entry – one could not go directly from *dumnyi dvorianin* to *boiarin*. *Dumnye d'iaki* were generally recruited from the ranks of *d'iaki* who were themselves recruited from clerks (*pod'iachie*), all of whom were men of lower birth.[14] Like their hereditary counterparts in the duma cohort, they could progress through ranks after appointment, again, without skipping.

To simplify a bit, the game of Muscovite politics had as its goal either advancement to the high ranks (for individuals and their families) or control of the composition of these ranks (for the royal family, or blocs of allied families). It bears mentioning that seventeenth-century politics had very little to do with policies and everything to do with persons. There may have been debate on this or that issue, but, as we have noted, everyone in the sovereign's court was (to continue our metaphor) on the same team and pursued the same

12 On this distinction, see N. P. Pavlov-Sil'vanskii, *Gosudarevy sluzhilye liudi. Liudi kabal'nye i dokladnye*, 2nd edn (St Petersburg: Tipografiia M. M. Stasiulevicha, 1909), pp. 128–208.
13 This system is described in Crummey, *Aristocrats and Servitors*, pp. 23–4, as well as in Marshall T. Poe, *The Russian Elite in the Seventeenth Century*, 2 vols. (Helsinki: Academia Scientiarum Fennica, 2003), vol. ii, passim.
14 On the administrative class, see N. F. Demidova, *Sluzhilaia biurokratiia v Rossii XVII v. i ee rol' v formirovanii absoliutizma* (Moskva: Nauka, 1987).

goal – the maintenance and, if possible, the expansion of the elite's interests.[15] Certainly there was conflict over issues. But it is telling that the Muscovites never developed a formal institution that might represent differing political agendas among notables. None was needed. The prime political question, it appears, was always *who* would pursue this common agenda, and only rarely *whether* it should be pursued.

There were, in essence, three players in this contest.[16] First, there was the tsar himself. In theory, he made all appointments to and promotions through the ranks. Yet in fact he did not rule alone, but rather with the aid of close relatives, advisers and mentors.[17] The existence of a small retinue of advisers around the tsar was recognised by the Muscovites themselves: Grigorii Kotoshikhin, the treasonous scribe who penned the only indigenous description of the Muscovite political system, explicitly calls them the 'close people' (*blizhnie liudi*).[18] These confidants would and could bend the tsar's ear when it came to appointments and promotions. The second major class of players at the Muscovite court were old elite servitors, that is, men of very high, heritable status whose families traditionally held positions in the duma ranks. These were Muscovy's aristocrats: for centuries, they had commanded Muscovy's armies, administered Muscovy's central offices, and governed Muscovy's far-flung territories.[19] Their right to high offices was guarded by *mestnichestvo*,

15 On consensus among the elite, see: Edward L. Keenan, 'Muscovite Political Folkways', *RR* 45 (1986), 115–81; Nancy Shields Kollmann, *Kinship and Politics: The Making of the Muscovite Political System, 1345–1547* (Stanford, Calif.: Stanford University Press, 1987), pp. 2, 7–8, 18, 44, 149–52, 184. The degree of consensus is the subject of some debate. See the exchange between Valerie Kivelson and Marshall Poe in *Kritika* 3 (2002): 473–99.
16 This is not to say that these were the only political actors in Muscovy. Certainly there were others (the Church, elite women etc.). These three, however, are the most significant for our limited purposes. On the Church in politics, see: Georg Bernhard Michels, *At War with the Church: Religious Dissent in Seventeenth-Century Russia* (Stanford, Calif.: Stanford University Press, 1999). On elite women in politics, see: Isolde Thyrêt, *Between God and Tsar: Religious Symbolism and the Royal Women of Muscovite Russia* (DeKalb, Ill.: Northern Illinois University Press, 2001).
17 There are a number of well-known examples: Michael and his father, Patriarch Filaret; the young Alexis and Boris Ivanovich Morozov; Sophia and Prince Vasilii Vasil'evich Golitsyn; Peter and his assembly of friends.
18 Grigorij Kotošixin [G. K. Kotoshikhin], *O Rossii v carstvovanie Alekseja Mixajloviča. Text and commentary*, ed. A. E. Pennington (Oxford and New York: Clarendon Press, 1980), fos. 34–36v. On Kotoshikhin's understanding of governmental institutions, see Benjamin P. Uroff, 'Grigorii Karpovich Kotoshikhin, "On Russia in the Reign of Alexis Mikhailovich": An Annotated Translation', unpublished Ph.D. Dissertation, University of Illinois, 1970, and Fritz T. Epstein, 'Die Hof- und Zentralverwaltung im Moskauer Staat und die Bedeutung von G.K. Kotosichins zeitgenoessischem Werk "Über Russland unter der Herrschaft des Zaren Aleksej Michajlovic" für die russische Verwaltungsgeschichte', *Hamburger Historische Studien* 7 (1978): 1–228.
19 On them, see Crummey, *Aristocrats and Servitors*, passim.

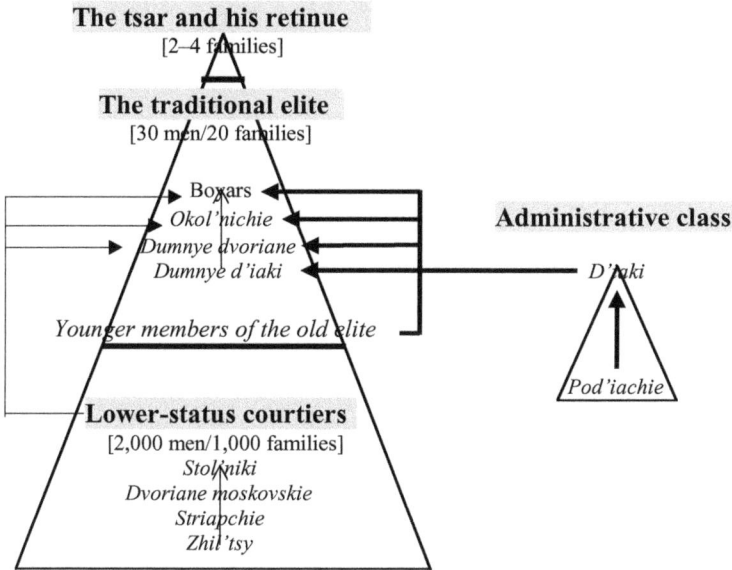

Figure 19.2. The sovereign's court (c.1620)

early Russia's mechanism for protecting the order of precedence.[20] Finally, we have men and families serving in the lower orders of the sovereign's court – the thousands of *stol'niki*, *dvoriane moskovskie*, and *striapchie* who occupied minor offices in Moscow and the provinces. They could never reasonably hope to win appointments to the duma. Figure 19.2 describes the three interest groups within the system of ranks.

The contest over the duma ranks was not a fair one. The tsar held the most power – he, as we have said, made all the appointments. The old elite had considerable though less power – by Muscovite tradition, elite families had a special claim on the upper ranks, often passing them on through several generations. And the mass of courtiers had the least power – only very occasionally would the tsar reach down into the lower rungs of the court to elevate a common *stol'nik*, but the possibility was always open.

Each of these parties deployed different strategies to gain victory. The tsar's course was one of balance: he attempted to distribute just enough of the ranks to elite servitors so as to guarantee their allegiance, while at the same time reserving a portion for the purposes of patronage, reward of merit, or some

20 The literature on *mestnichestvo* is large. For a recent treatment, see Nancy Shields Kollmann, *By Honor Bound: State and Society in Early Modern Russia* (Ithaca, N.Y., and London: Cornell University Press, 1999), pp. 131–68.

other end. Members of the old elite pursued a strategy of maintenance: they fought to preserve their hold on the duma ranks by keeping new servitors out of existing positions and preventing the tsar from creating new posts. The common courtiers' strategy was offensive: they used a variety of mechanisms to win favour with the tsar or elite (service, marriage alliances, etc.) in order to gain a place among the duma men.

Who won? A brief overview of seventeenth-century high politics

As Michael Romanov ascended the throne in 1613, he and the coalition of forces that supported him faced serious difficulties. There were several claimants to the crown (some arguably more legitimate than Mikhail Fedorovich), the country was occupied by Swedes, Poles and numerous rebel bands, and the economy was in shambles after many years of bloody civil war. No one was really sure who the 'true tsar' was. The Romanov party did the only thing it could to maintain power: issue a 'national' call to eject the foreigners, declare a de facto amnesty to those in other camps and begin the slow and painful process of reducing its opponents – alien and domestic – one at a time. First, the rebels were defeated (Zarutskii, Mniszech), then the otherwise distracted Swedes were pacified (the Treaty of Stolbovo, 1617) and finally the Poles were ejected (the Truce of Deulino, 1618). These measures shored up the Romanovs' hold on power. The return of Michael's father, soon-to-be Patriarch Filaret, from Polish captivity in 1619 solidified it. For the first and last time in Russian history, father and son – the head of the Church and head of the state – ruled together.

Aside from this single (albeit dramatic) innovation, the diarchy pursued a moderate course aimed at cultivating political support and recouping the considerable losses incurred during and after the Troubles. Even after the situation had stabilised, there was no general purge of elements who had fought for the 'wrong' side in the previous decades (though the Romanovs did turn hard on their former allies the cossacks). Rather, the sins of the Time of Troubles were forgotten for all but a few. The old boyars returned to their high places, irrespective of what port they had sought in the storm of the Troubles. The administrative class took its station as well, again without suffering for its prior allegiances. And the central and provincial military servitors were prepared for the imminent reckoning with Poland, which finally came in 1634.

Indeed, after the Romanov political settlement, Russian high politics were marked by a general peace for over thirty years. Certainly there were intrigues, schemes and plots (many of which are unknown to us, hidden by the habit of not writing anything of importance down), but these were the quotidian affairs of every court in every country. The political quiet was shattered, finally, in 1648. Three years earlier, the young Aleksei Mikhailovich succeeded his much venerated father (see Table 19.1). Alexis's former tutor, Boris Ivanovich Morozov, became regent and packed the court and council with his cronies. Though a capable man, he was surrounded by the corrupt Miloslavskii clique (Alexis's first wife was a Miloslavskii; Morozov married her sister, thereby becoming the tsar's brother-in-law). Calls of government corruption grew louder until Moscow and several other cities exploded in riots aimed at bringing Morozov and the Miloslavskiis down. The mob lynched officials, burnt houses and looted shops. At one point, the tsar himself was threatened by the angry crowd. By all reports, this episode had a powerful effect on the youthful, pious ruler.[21] Bowing to pressure, Morozov and the tsar's father-in-law were exiled (only to return shortly), corrupt officials (or at least those the crowd said were corrupt) were brutally executed and the tsar resolved to reform the state in such a way as to make sure such things never happened again.

Alexis turned to the able Prince N. I. Odoevskii for help. He headed a commission designed to solve all the unattended problems faced by Muscovy at one bold, legislative stroke. Perhaps recalling his father's fondness for public input (it had saved them in 1613), Alexis called a massive assembly of 'all kinds of people' in Moscow for this purpose. In hindsight, it was a risky move for an immature leader still reeling from his first taste of popular protest. But the commission did its monumental work, the public acclaimed it, and Muscovy had a roadmap to permanent order – the *Sobornoe Ulozhenie* of 1649, one of the largest law codes of the early modern period. Like all successful compromises, there was something in it for everyone (or at least everyone who mattered): the powerful had their places next to the tsar affirmed; the gentry received the right to pursue runaway serfs and slaves as long as necessary to return them; and the common urban folks were promised that the corruption would be punished to the fullest extent of the law (which was, we should note, quite far).[22] Again, peace reigned at court and in the country. Save two periods of

---

21 Philip Longworth, *Alexis, Tsar of all the Russias* (London: Secker and Warburg, 1984), pp. 38–45.

22 On the *Ulozhenie*, see A. G. Man'kov, *Ulozhenie 1649 goda–kodeks feodal'nogo prava Rossii* (Leningrad: Nauka, 1980); L. I. Ivina (ed.), *Sobornoe ulozhenie 1649 goda: tekst, kommentarii* (Leningrad: Nauka, Leningradskoe otdelenie, 1987), and Richard Hellie (trans. and ed.), *The Muscovite Law Code (Ulozhenie) of 1649* (Irvine, Calif.: Charles Schlacks, 1988). For an excellent treatment of the general context, see Richard Hellie, *Enserfment and Military Change in Muscovy* (Chicago: University of Chicago Press, 1971).

Table 19.1. *The early Romanovs*

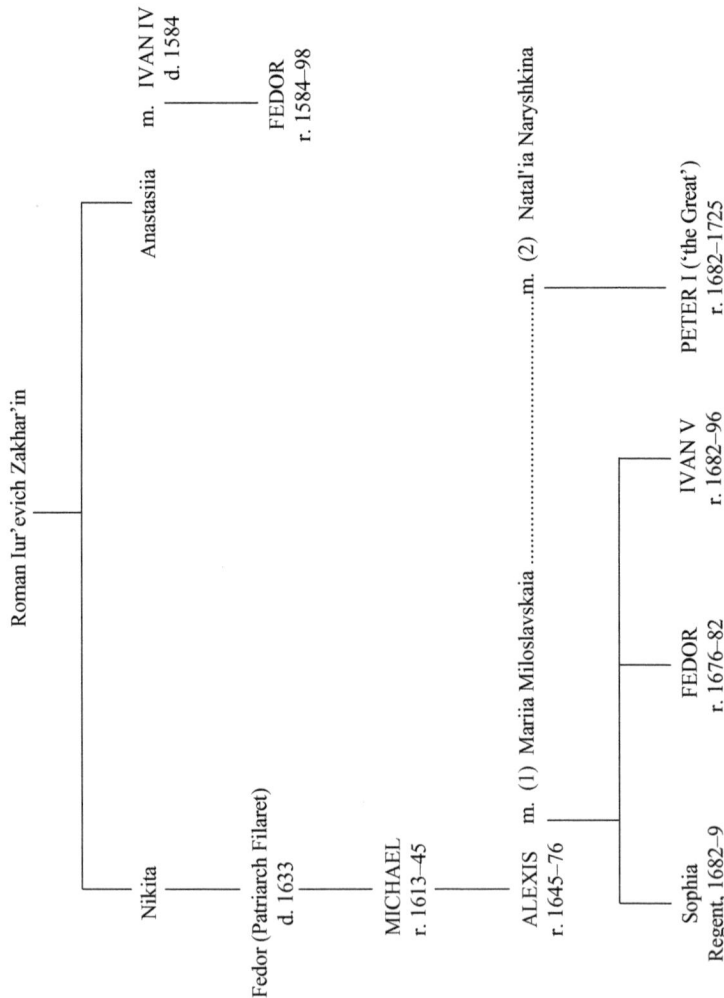

Roman Iur'evich Zakhar'in

Nikita

Anastasiia   m.   IVAN IV
d. 1584

Fedor (Patriarch Filaret)
d. 1633

FEDOR
r. 1584–98

MICHAEL
r. 1613–45

ALEXIS   m. (1) Mariia Miloslavskaia .... m. (2) Natal'ia Naryshkina
r. 1645–76

Sophia
Regent, 1682–9

FEDOR
r. 1676–82

IVAN V
r. 1682–96

PETER I ('the Great')
r. 1682–1725

urban unrest brought on by debasement of the silver with copper (1656 and 1662), all was quiet. Or so it appeared. Under the calm surface, however, an important struggle was occurring at the very heart of Muscovite high politics.

The greatest cause of Alexis's reign (and his greatest triumph) was the Thirteen Years War, his effort to recoup the losses suffered at the hands of the hated Poles. Personally marching off to battle in 1654, he took a direct interest in making sure his crusade was brought off successfully. In the course of his campaigning, Alexis must (and here we are speculating) have judged for himself the merits (and demerits) of his soldiers, for he came back to the capital devoted to the idea of reforming, if not overturning, the existing political order.[23] In the context of a rapidly evolving administrative and military situation, the traditional boyar elite had become distinctly less useful. Even men of low status did not respect them, as Kotoshikhin's unflattering portrait demonstrates.[24] Talented men – regardless of birth – who were willing to serve and serve well were needed. Given the rules of appointment to the boyar ranks, such 'new men' had no chance to attain the highest honours. Merit was not being rewarded, at least not in the way Alexis believed it should be. Obviously, the rules had to be changed so as to allow the entry of the 'new men'.[25]

The tsar did not bring the 'new men' into the duma all at once. He could not do so without risking a costly and dangerous political battle with the old elites. Rather, he pursued a conservative approach, appointing a few 'new men' at time. But even here his options were limited by the hold of the old elites over the upper ranks. Alexis knew that they would probably grumble if he promoted men of lower status to the highest ranks in the duma orders, for these were the traditional preserve of the old elite. Neither could Alexis make the more honourable of the 'new men' conciliar secretaries (*dumnye d'iaki*), for that rank was deemed too low for the hereditary servitors in the sovereign's court. Therefore Alexis opted for a strategy that would at once appease the hereditary *boiarstvo* and permit him to promote the 'new men': he transformed

23 Longworth, *Alexis, Tsar of all the Russias*, pp. 136–7. Muscovy was under significant military pressure in the seventeenth century, and Alexis initiated a number of important military reforms. See Hellie, *Enserfment and Military Change in Muscovy*, pp. 181–201.
24 Kotoshikhin writes: 'in many cases boyar rank is conferred not for intelligence but for exalted lineage, and many of them are unlettered and uneducated' (Kotošixin, *O Rossii*, fo. 35v).
25 The following paragraphs are adapted from Marshall T. Poe, 'Tsar Aleksei Mikhailovich and the Demise of the Romanov Political Settlement', *RR* 62 (2004): 537–64; Marshall T. Poe, 'Absolutism and the New Men of Seventeenth-Century Russia', in J. Kotilaine and M. Poe (eds.), *Modernizing Muscovy: Reform and Social Change in Seventeenth-Century Russia* (London: RoutledgeCurzon, 2004), pp. 97–115; and Marshall T. Poe, *The Russian Elite in the Seventeenth Century*, vol. II, *passim*.

the rank of conciliar courtier (*dumnyi dvorianin*). The chronology of events is telling. In 1650, Alexis took the unprecedented step of appointing a fifth man to *dumnyi dvorianin*. Prior to that act, the largest number of *dumnye dvoriane* had been four (in 1634 and 1635), and ordinarily there had only been one. By the first year of the war, there were eight of them. During the war, he promoted sixteen more. Among them we find many of Alexis's 'new men'.[26] During the war the tsar began to promote his *dumnye dvoriane* into the ranks of *okol'nichie*.[27] One of them, A. L. Ordin-Nashchokin, was made boyar in 1667 and served as effective prime minister until 1671. In that year another 'new man', A. S. Matveev, took his place, though he was not promoted to boyar until 1674.[28]

Under Alexis, then, two prominent 'new men' came to rule Russia. Others exercised less visible but no less important roles as leaders in the chancellery system. In all, Alexis appointed forty-eight low-status 'new men' to the duma ranks. As we can see in Figure 19.3, the tsar entrusted them with a great number of Muscovy's highest administrative offices.[29]

Particularly notable is the fact that Alexis placed his 'new men' in the most important *prikazy*: the Military Service Chancellery (*Razriad*), arguably the most powerful *prikaz* in seventeenth-century Muscovy; the Service Land Chancellery (*Pomestnyi prikaz*), which administered estates given to the gentry throughout Russia; and the Ambassadorial Chancellery (*Posol'skii prikaz*), which controlled Muscovy's foreign affairs.[30]

Alexis began the process of supplementing hereditary rank-holders with competent 'new men'.[31] It is difficult to overestimate the impact of these appointments on the Muscovite political system. Alexis's alteration of duma appointment policy destroyed the equilibrium between the tsar and the elite families that ended the Time of Troubles. By the end of the Thirteen Years War, the tsar clearly had the upper hand in political matters. Alexis had successfully transformed the duma ranks from a royal council controlled by hereditary clans into a fount of royal patronage to be distributed as the tsar desired. The

26 I. P. Matiushkin, A. O. Pronchishcheev, I. F. Eropkin, P. K. Elizarov, I. I. Baklanovskii, V. M. Eropkin, A. L. Ordin-Nashchokin, I. A. Pronchishchev, Z. F. Leont'ev, I. I. Chaadaev, G. B. Nashchokin, D. M. Bashmakov, Ia. T. Khitrovo, G. S. Karaulov, L. T. Golosov.
27 Z. V. Kondyrev in 1655, F. K. Elizarov in 1665; A. L. Ordin-Nashchokin in 1665; A. S. Matveev in 1672; I. B. Khitrovo in 1674.
28 On the rule of Ordin-Nashchokin and Matveev, and its impact on court politics, see Bushkovitch, *Peter the Great*, pp. 49–79.
29 Data in this table was drawn from S. K. Bogoiavlenskii, *Prikaznye sud'i XVII veka* (Moscow and Leningrad: AN SSSR, 1946). The abbreviations DD, DDv, Ok and B refer to the positions of *dumnyi d'iak*, *dumnyi dvorianin*, *okol'nichii* and boyar respectively.
30 On the *prikaz* system, and the importance of these chancelleries in particular, see Peter B. Brown, 'Muscovite Government Bureaus', *RH* 10 (1983): 269–330.
31 Crummey, *Aristocrats and Servitors*, p. 28.

Name	Ranks			Chancelleries led
	DD > DDv > Ok > B			
Elizarov, F. K.	1646	1650	1655	Service Land [1643/4–63/4]
Anichkov, I. M.		1646		Tsar's Workshop [1635/6–46/7]
Chistoi, N. I.	1647			Grand Treasury [1630/1–46/7]; Ore [1641/2]; Ambassadorial [1646/7–47/8]
Narbekov, B. F.		1648		Grand Revenue [1648/9–51/2]
Zaborovskii, S. I.	1649	1664		Military Service [1648/9–63/4]; Monastery [1667/8–75/6]; New Tax District [1676/7]
Lopukhin, L. D.	1651	1667		Kazan' Palace [1646/7–71/2]; Ambassadorial [1652/3–64/5]; Novgorod Tax District [1652/3–64/5]; Seal [1653/4–63/4]; Provisions [1674/5]
Kondyrev, Z. V.		1651	1655	Equerry [1646/7–53/4]
Ianov, V. F.		1652		Patriarch's Court [1641/2–46/7, 1648/9–52/3]
Matiushkin, I. P.		1653		Great Treasury [1634/5–61/2]; Ore [1641/2]
Ivanov, A. I.	1653			Treasury [1639/40–44/5]; Ambassadorial [1645/6–66/7]; Novgorod Tax District [1645/6–63/4]; Seal [1653/4–68/9]; Monastery [1654/5]; Seal Matters [1667/8]
Pronchishchev, A. O.		1654		Investigative [1654/5–56/7]
Eropkin, I. F.		1655		NONE
Elizarov, P. K.		1655		Moscow (*Zemskii*) [1655/6–71/2]; Kostroma Tax District [1656/7–70/1]; Financial Investigation [1662/3–64/5]
Baklanovskii, I. I.		1655		Moscow Judicial [1630/1–31/2]; Grand Revenue [1632/3–37/8]; Artillery [1658/9–62/3, 1672/3–77/8]; Grand Treasury [1663/4–68/9]
O.-Nashchokin, A. L.	1658	1665	1667	Ambassadorial [1666/7–70/1]; Vladimir Tax District [1666/7–70/1]; Galich Tax District [1666/7–70/1]; Little Russian [1666/7–68/9]; Ransom [1667/8]
Anichkov, G. M.		1659		Grand Palace [1657/8–64/5]; Palace Judicial [1664/5]; New Tax District [1664/5–68/9]

Figure 19.3. Alexis's new men in the chancelleries

Name	Ranks			Chancelleries led
	DD > DDv > Ok > B			
Pronchishchev, I. A.	1661			Grand Treasury [1661/2–62/3]; Monastery [1664/5]; Grand Revenue [1667/8–69/70]; Ransom [1667/8–69/70]; Criminal [1673/4–74/5]
Leont'ev, Z. F.	1662			NONE
Chaadaev, I. I.	1662			Moscow (*Zemskii*) [1672/3–73/4]; Foreign Mercenaries [1676/7–77/8]; Dragoon [1676/7–86/7]; Siberian [1680/1–82/3]
Nashchokin, G. B.	1664			Vladimir Judicial [1648/9]; Slave [1658/9–61/2]; Postal [1662/3–66/7]
Khitrovo, I. T.	1664			NONE
Bashmakov, D. M.	1664			Tsar's Workshop [1654/5]; Grand Palace [1655/6]; Privy Affairs [1655/6–63/4]; Lithuanian [1657/8]; Ustiug Tax District [1657/8–58/9]; Financial Investigation [1662/3]; Military Service [1663/4–69/70, 1675/6]; Ambassadorial [1669/70–70/1]; Vladimir [1669/70–70/1]; Galich [1669/70–70/1]; Little Russian [1669/70–70/1]; Petitions [1674/5]; Seal [1675/6–99/1700]; Treasury [1677/8–79/80, 1681/2]; Investigative [1676/7, 1679/80]; Financial Collection [1680/1]
Karaulov, G. S.	1665			Service Land [1659/60–69/70]; Grand Palace [1669/70]; Postal [1669/70–71/2]; Kazan' [1671/2–75/6]; Moscow (*Zemskii*) [1679/80]; Criminal [1682/3]; Investigative [1689/90]
Durov, A. S.	1665			Postal [1630/1–31/2]; Equerry [1633/4]; Grand Revenue [1637/8–39/40]; Musketeers [1642/3–44/5, 1661/2–69/70]; Ustiug Tax District [1653/4, 1669/70–70/1]; New Tax District [1660/1–61/2]
Khitrovo, I. B.	1666	1674		Grand Palace [1664/5–69/70]; Palace Judicial [1664/5–69/70]
O.-Nashchokin, B. I.	1667			NONE

Figure 19.3 *(cont.)*

Name	Ranks	Chancelleries led
	DD > DDv > Ok > B	
Golosov, L. T.	1667	Patriarch's Court [1652/3–58/9, 1660/1–62/3]; Ambassadorial [1662/3–69/70, 1680/1]; Novgorod [1662/3–69/70, 1680/1]; Ransom [1667/8]; Tsarina's Workshop [1659/60–60/1]; Vladimir [1667/8–69/70, 1680/1]; Galich [1667/8–69/70, 1680/1]; Little Russian [1667/8–69/70, 1680/1]; Pharmaceutical [1669/70–71/2]; Smolensk [1680/1]; Ustiug [1680/1]
Dokhturov, G. S.	1667	Postal [1649/50–51/2]; Grand Palace [1651/2–53/4]; Musketeers [1653/4–61/2]; Grand Treasury [1661/2–63/4]; New Tax District [1664/5, 1666/7, 1669/70–75/6]; Ambassadorial [1666/7–69/70]; Vladimir Tax District [1667/8–69/70]; Galich Tax District [1667/8–69/70]; Novgorod Tax District [1667/8–69/70]; Little Russian [1667/8–69/70]; Seal [1668/9–75/6]; Service Land [1669/70–75/6]; Military Service [1673/4–75/6]; Ransom [1677/8]
Tolstoi, A. V.	1668	NONE
Rtishchev, G. I.	1669	Tsar's Workshop [1649/50–68/9]
Ivanov, L. I.	1669	New Tax District [1662/3–63/4]; Grand Palace [1663/4–69/70, 1680/1]; Armoury [1663/4–69/70]; Musketeers [1669/70–75/6, 1677/8]; Ustiug Tax District [1672/3–75/6, 1679/80]; Lithuanian [1674/5]; Investigative [1675/6]; Ambassadorial [1675/6–81/2]
Titov, S. S.	1670	Musketeers [1655/6–56/7]; Vladimir Tax District [1655/6–56/7]; Galich Tax District [1655/6–56/7]; Criminal [1656/7]; Military Service [1657/8–58/9, 1669/70–73/4]; Financial Collection [1662/3–63/4]; Grand Palace [1663/4–69/70]; Vladimir Judicial [1663/4]
Solovtsov, I. P.	1670	Provisions [1669/70–70/1]
Sokovnin, F. P.	1670	Tsarina's Workshop [1666/7–69/70, 1676/7–81/2, 1681/2]; Petitions [1675/6]
Nesterov, A. I.	1670	Gun Barrel [1653/4, 1655/6, 1657/8, 1660/1, 1665/6]; Armoury [1659/60–67/8]; Gold Works [1667/8]

Figure 19.3 *(cont.)*

Name	DD	DDv	Ok	B	Chancelleries led
		DD > *DDv* > *Ok* > *B*			
Matveev, A. S.		1670	1672	1674	Little Russian [1668/9–75/6]; Ambassadorial [1669/70–75/6]; Vladimir Tax District [1669/70–75/6]; Galich Tax District [1669/70–75/6]; Novgorod Tax District [1669/70, 1671/2–75/6]; Ransom [1670/1–71/2]; Pharmaceutical [1671/2–75/6]
Leont'ev, F. I.		1670			Artillery [1672/3–76/7]
Khitrovo, I. S.		1670	1676		Provisions [1667/8–69/70]; Ustiug Tax District [1670/1–71/2]; Monastery [1675/6–77/8]; Judicial Review [1689/90]
Poltev, S. F.		1671			Dragoons [1670/1–75/6]; Foreign Mercenaries [1670/1–75/6]
Naryshkin, K. P.		1671	1672	1672	Ustiug Tax District [1676/7]; Grand Treasury [1676/7–77/8]; Grand Revenue [1676/7–77/8]
Khitrovo, A. S.		1671	1676		Grand Palace [1669/70–78/9]; Court Judicial [1669/70–75/6, 1677/8–78/9]
Bogdanov, G. K.	1671				Military Service [1656/7–60/1]; New Tax District [1660/1–65/6]; Ransom [1666/7, 1668/9, 1670/1–71/2]; Ambassadorial [1670/1–75/6]; Little Russian [1668/9–75/6]; Vladimir [1670/1–75/6]; Galich [1670/1–75/6]; Grand Treasury [1675/6–76/7]; Grand Revenue [1675/6–76/7]
Polianskii, D. L.	1672				Privy Affairs [1671/2–75/6]; Provisions [1675/6–77/8]; Grand Revenue [1675/6]; Investigative [1675/6, 1677/8]; Musketeers [1675/6–77/8, 1681/2]; Ustiug Tax District [1675/6–77/8]; Judicial [1680/1]; Moscow (*Zemskii*) [1686/7–89/90]; Treasury [1689/90]
Naryshkin, F. P.		1672			NONE
Mikhailov, F.	1672				Artillery [1655/6]; Foreign Mercenary [1656/7–57/8]; Grand Treasury [1659/60–63/4]; Grand Revenue [1662/3]; Privy Affairs [1663/4–71/2]; Grand Palace [1671/2–76/7]
Matiushkin, A. I.		1672			Equerry [1653/4–63/4]; Gun Barrel [1653/4]
Lopukhin, A. N.		1672			Tsarina's Workshop [1669/70–76/7]
Panin, V. N.		1673			NONE

Figure 19.3 (*cont.*)

tsar no longer ruled exclusively with the duma men, but instead via special conciliar and executive bodies. Kotoshikhin described two of them. The first was a kind of privy council chosen from the 'closest boyars and *okol'nichie*' (*boiare i okol'nichie blizhnie*). Here Alexis discussed affairs 'in private', outside the large council.[32] Second, Kotoshikhin detailed the workings of the Privy Chancellery (*Prikaz tainykh del*), where the 'boyars and duma men do not enter . . . and have no jurisdiction'.[33] 'And that chancellery', he wrote, 'was established in the present reign, so that the tsar's will and all his affairs would be carried out as he desires, without the boyars and duma men having any knowledge of these matters.'[34] Kotoshikhin's understanding of Alexis's relation to hereditary duma men is clear: while he honoured them, he did his real business with the 'closest people'. He was, it is true, hardly the first Russian ruler to surround himself with an inner circle of powerful advisers.[35] He was, however, the first to do so since the political settlement that ended the Time of Troubles. For one of the few times in Muscovite history, the tsar had succeeded in liberating himself from the elite of which he was a part. Muscovy became an autocracy – or at least less of an oligarchy – as it had been under Ivan III and Ivan IV.

But only for a moment, for Alexis's new order proved untenable. He was strong enough and clever enough to use his novel tool of patronage sparingly. His successors were neither. As a result of their political insecurity, Fedor, Sophia and young Peter – together with those who urged them on – were forced to 'go to the well' of duma patronage often in order to win support among the *boiarstvo*. They made hordes of appointments from the ever-expanding court in a desperate effort to curry favour. The result can be seen in Figure 19.4.

The duma ranks ballooned, and thereby lost their meaning even as royal patronage. Alexis's weak successors had, in essence, devalued the currency bequeathed to them by their father. What Alexis had carefully designed as a mechanism to bring new talent into the political class resulted, under his children, in the destruction of that class. Confusion reigned among the elite; *mestnichestvo* – a nuisance from the point of view of the crown and meaningless from the point of view of the old elite – died an unmourned death.[36] As early

---

32 Kotošixin, *O Rossii*, fo. 36.
33 Ibid., fo. 123v.
34 Ibid., fo.124.
35 On the existence of such 'inner circles' in previous eras, see A. I. Filiushkin, *Istoriia odnoi mistifikatsii: Ivan Groznyi i 'Izbrannaia Rada'* (Moscow: VGU, 1998), and Sergei Bogatyrev, *The Sovereign and His Counsellors. Ritualised Consultations in Muscovite Political Culture, 1350s–1570s* (Helsinki: Finnish Academy of Science and Letters 2000).
36 Marshall T. Poe, 'The Imaginary World of Semen Koltovskii: Genealogical Anxiety and Falsification in Seventeenth-Century Russia', *Cahiers du monde russe* 39 (1998): 375–88.

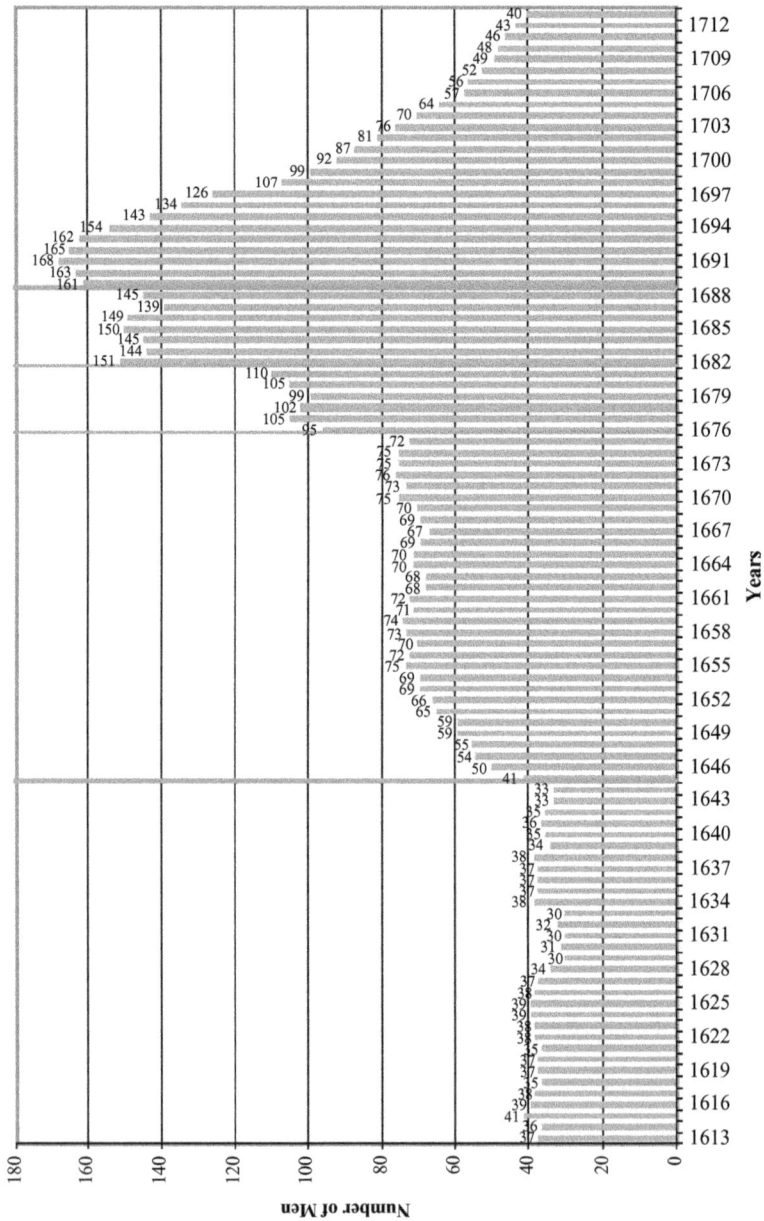

Figure 19.4. The size of the duma ranks, 1613–1713

Number of Men (x-axis): 180, 160, 140, 120, 100, 80, 60, 40, 20, 0

Years (y-axis): 1613, 1616, 1619, 1622, 1625, 1628, 1631, 1634, 1637, 1640, 1643, 1646, 1649, 1652, 1655, 1658, 1661, 1664, 1667, 1670, 1673, 1676, 1679, 1682, 1685, 1688, 1691, 1694, 1697, 1700, 1703, 1706, 1709, 1712

as 1681, even the wise old men of the traditional elite – led in this instance by Vasilii Golitsyn – were actively searching for a new order to replace what had obviously been broken.[37] They failed, and it would be up to Peter, who personally witnessed the corruption of his father's legacy, to forge a new and profoundly monarchical political system.

The chancelleries

While the boyar and court elite led Muscovy, chancellery personnel – the *prikaznye liudi* – administered it. They were, as we have seen, distinctly second-class citizens at court, 'employees at will' serving at the pleasure of the tsar – or not. But the state was growing rapidly in the seventeenth century, and with it the administrative burden of far-flung, complex operations. Since the *prikaz* personnel needed organisational skill and a deep knowledge of affairs, the elite generally kept them employed and reasonably satisfied – the state could not run without them. If a chancellery man performed well and had the proper connections, he could advance, first, through the administrative ranks (*pod'iachii* to *d'iak*) and, then, to the duma (though very rarely and almost always to *dumnyi d'iak*, no further). This *cursus honorum* was steep: only a small proportion of all clerks (*pod'iachie*) were made *d'iaki* (secretaries) and few *d'iaki* were made *dumnye d'iaki*.[38] As we have noted, late in the century some of the *prikaz* people occupied important positions in the government, and one served as de facto prime minister. This remarkable shift upward was a reflection of the growing importance of administrative work for the state.

The world of the *prikaz* people was different from that of any other Muscovite in a number of ways. First, the chancellery employees were literate, a fact that differentiated them from even most members of the elite (Koto-shikhin called the latter 'unlettered and uneducated').[39] As the century drew to a close, a few of them would even develop a taste for something we might

37 A. I. Markevich, *Istoriia mestnichestva v Moskovskom gosudarstve v XV–XVII vekakh* (Odessa: Tipografiia Odesskogo Vestnika, 1888), pp. 572ff.; V. K. Nikol'skii, 'Boiarskaia popytka 1681 g.', *Istoricheskie izvestiia izdavaemye Istoricheskim obshchestvom pri Moskovskom universitete* 2 (1917): 57–87; G. Ostrogorsky, 'Das Projekt einer Rangtabelle aus der Zeit des Tsaren Fedor Alekseevich', *Jahrbücher für Kultur und Geschichte der Slaven* 9 (1933): 86–138; M. Ia. Volkov, 'Ob otmene mestnichestva v Rossii', *Istoriia SSSR*, 1977, no. 2: 53–67; P. V. Sedov, 'O boiarskoi popytke uchrezhdeniia namestnichestva v Rossii v 1681–82 gg.', *Vestnik LGU* 9 (1985): 25–9; Kollmann, *By Honor Bound*, pp. 226–31; and Bushkovitch, *Peter the Great*, pp. 118–19.
38 S. K. Bogoiavlenskii, 'Prikaznye d'iaki XVII veka', *IZ* 1 (1937): 220–39; Demidova, *Sluzhilaia biurokratiia*, pp. 23–4.
39 Kotošixin, *O Rossii*, fo. 35v.

sensibly call 'literature' (almost all of it imported), a first for Muscovy.[40] Second, the *prikaz* people worked in offices run in quasi-rational fashion. The chancelleries had many of the trademarks of the classic Weberian bureaucracy: written rules, regular procedures, functional differentiation, reward to merit.[41] This is not, of course, to say that *prikaz* employees were insulated from the winds of nepotism, favouritism and even caprice. Far from it: most *prikaz* people were the sons of *prikaz* officials, all had patrons and not a few were summarily dismissed without cause. Nevertheless, the rudiments of the modern administrative office were all present in the *prikazy*. Finally, chancellery workers lived in Moscow cheek-by-jowl with the elite: the *prikazy* were located in the Kremlin and Kitai gorod and their employees lived in the environs. This proximity gave them access to power that was unimaginable for the typical Russian.

As the interests of the state expanded, so too did the ranks of the *prikazy*.[42] The number of *prikaz* people grew significantly in the seventeenth century, from a few hundred in 1613 to several thousand in 1689. The vast majority of them were lowly clerks (*pod'iachie*). These men did most of the work in the offices, and their numbers expanded mightily during the century: in 1626 there were around 500 of them in the Moscow offices; by 1698 there were nearly 3,000.[43] As in all Muscovite institutions, we find hierarchy among the clerks – junior (*mladshii*), middle (*srednii*) and senior (*starshii*). If a man were particularly lucky, he might be appointed to *d'iak*. *D'iaki* ordinarily commanded the chancelleries, serving together with an extra-administrative servitor (usually a man holding duma rank). They could be tapped for other services as

40 This development is discussed in S. I. Nikolaev, 'Poeziia i diplomatiia (iz literaturnoi deiatel'nosti Posol'skogo prikaza v 1670–kh gg.)', *TODRL* 42 (1989): 143–73, and Edward L. Keenan, *The Kurbskii–Groznyi Apocrypha: The Seventeenth-Century Genesis of the 'Correspondence' Attributed to Prince A. M. Kurbskii and Tsar Ivan IV* (Cambridge, Mass.: Harvard University Press, 1971), pp. 84–9.

41 This is emphasised in Peter B. Brown, 'Early Modern Russian Bureaucracy: The Evolution of the Chancellery System from Ivan III to Peter the Great, 1478–1717', unpublished Ph.D. dissertation, University of Chicago, 1978; Peter B. Brown, 'Muscovite Government Bureaus', *RH* 10 (1983): 269–330; and B. Plavsic, 'Seventeenth-Century Chanceries and their Staffs', in D. K. Rowney and W. M. Pintner (eds.), *Russian Officialdom: The Bureaucratization of Russian Society from the 17th to the 20th Century* (Chapel Hill: University of North Carolina Press, 1980), pp. 19–45.

42 On the chancellery personnel and their growth in the seventeenth century, see Demidova, *Sluzhilaia biurokratiia*; N. F. Demidova, 'Gosudarstvennyi apparat Rossii v XVII veke', *IZ* 108 (1982): 109–54; N. F. Demidova, 'Biurokratizatsiia gosudarstvennogo apparata absoliutizma v XVII–XVIII vv.', in N. M. Druzhinin (ed.), *Absoliutizm v Rossii (XVII–XVIII vv.). Sbornik statei k semidesiatiletiiu so dnia rozhdeniia i sorokapiatiletiiu nauchnoi i pedagogicheskoi deiatel'nosti B. B. Kafengauza* (Moscow: Nauka, 1964), pp. 206–42; and N. F. Demidova, 'Prikaznye liudi XVII v. (Sotsial'nyi sostav i istochniki formirovaniia)', *IZ* 90 (1972): 332–54.

43 Demidova, *Sluzhilaia biurokratiia*, p. 23.

well, as Kotoshikhin tells us: 'they [*d'iaki*] serve as associates of the boyars and *okol'nichie* and duma men and closest men in the chancelleries in Moscow and in the provinces, and of ambassadors in embassies; and they . . . administer affairs of every kind, and hold trials, and are sent on various missions.'[44] Like the *pod'iachie*, the numbers of *d'iaki* grew in the seventeenth century: in 1626 there were around fifty serving in the chancelleries; by 1698, there were roughly twice that many.[45] Of the roughly 800 men who served as *d'iaki* in the century, only forty-seven ever achieved the exalted status of *dumnyi d'iak*. These men were super-secretaries: they attended the royal council (though they were required to stand during the proceedings), advised the tsar, and administered the most sensitive affairs.[46] Of them, thirteen achieved the rank of *dumnyi dvorianin*; four, *okol'nichii*; and one, boyar.[47] Naturally, all of these men were advanced late in the century, after Aleksei Mikhailovich had 'opened the ranks to merit'.

The number of chancelleries themselves grew in the seventeenth century as well. In the ten years following the accession of Michael, the number rose from around 35 to around 50; thereafter, the number varied between 45 and 59.[48] These figures are, however, misleading on a number of counts. First, most chancelleries were quite short-lived, reflecting the fact that they were often created on an ad hoc basis to fulfil a specific mission (for example, the collection of a tax, or the investigation of a particular affair). Only the largest chancelleries administering the most central functions – the Military Service, Service Land, the Ambassadorial and so on – operated continuously throughout the century.

Though the chancelleries were not officially arranged in any 'organisational chart', we can gauge their administrative scope by placing them in functional categories (see Figure 19.5: Numbers and type of chancelleries per decade, 1610s–1690s).[49] What is most apparent in Figure 19.5 is the concentration on military and foreign affairs – the *prikazy* were primarily instruments of war-making. Most of them were either directly engaged in provisioning the army (the military chancelleries, and we should include the Service Land Chancellery here as well) or funding the army (the financial chancelleries). Though

44 Kotošixin, *O Rossii*, fo. 37v.
45 Demidova, *Sluzhilaia biurokratiia*, p. 23.
46 Kotošixin, *O Rossii*, fos. 33ff.
47 See Poe, *The Russian Elite in the Seventeenth Century*, vol. II, p. 35.
48 On all that follows concerning the *prikazy*, see Brown, 'Early Modern Russian Bureaucracy' and his 'Muscovite Government Bureaus'.
49 Peter B. Brown, 'Bureaucratic Administration in Seventeenth-Century Russia', in J. Kotilaine and M. Poe (eds.), *Modernizing Muscovy: Reform and Social Change in Seventeenth-Century Russia* (London: RoutledgeCurzon, 2004), p. 66. Sub-headings such as 'Manpower mobilisation' indicate areas of competence, and the numbers do not add up to the sub-totals above them.

	1610s	1620s	1630s	1640s	1650s	1660s	1670s	1680s	1690s
CHANCELLERIES OF THE REALM	**44**	**50**	**48**	**47**	**50**	**54**	**51**	**40**	**46**
MILITARY AFFAIRS	12	9	17	15	15	17	15	11	15
• Manpower mobilisation	3	4	5	7	7	4	4	4	5
• Weapons production	3	3	3	4	4	4	3	3	5
• Fortification	1	1	2	2	1	1	1	1	1
• Finance and supply	4	1	5	2	3	5	6	3	3
• Prisoner of war redemption	0	0	2	0	0	2	1	0	0
• Military administration	2	1	1	1	1	2	1	1	2
FINANCE	12	12	10	11	11	12	12	9	11
• Taxation	11	11	11	11	11	11	11	9	10
• Treasuries	2	3	3	3	3	3	3	2	2
• Minting	1	1	0	0	1	2	1	0	0
• Mining	0	0	0	1	0	0	0	0	1
SERVICE LAND	1	1	1	1	1	1	1	1	1
FELONY PROSECUTION	1	1	1	1	1	1	1	2	1
FOREIGN AND COLONIAL AFFAIRS	2	2	3	5	7	9	6	5	5
• Diplomacy	1	1	1	2	1	2	1	1	1
• Southern and western territories	0	0	0	0	2	3	2	2	2
• Colonial administration	1	1	2	2	2	3	3	2	2
• Judicial instance for foreigners	1	1	1	2	3	2	1	1	1
POSTAL SERVICE	1	1	1	1	1	1	1	1	1
URBAN AFFAIRS	2	2	2	3	3	2	2	1	1
• Townsmen	1	1	1	2	1	0	0	0	0
• Moscow	1	1	1	1	1	1	1	1	1
• Health statistics	0	0	0	0	1	0	0	0	0
• Social welfare	0	0	0	0	0	1	1	0	0
LITIGATION	7	10	6	5	5	7	7	7	8
• Petitioning	2	2	2	1	1	1	1	1	0
• Upper and middle service classes	11	13	9	9	9	11	11	11	11
DOCUMENTS AND PRINTED MATTER	2	2	2	2	2	2	3	2	2
ECCLESIASTICAL AFFAIRS	3	2	0	1	2	1	1	0	0
MISCELLANEOUS	1	8	5	2	2	1	2	1	1

Figure 19.5. Numbers and type of chancelleries per decade, 1610s–1690s

PALACE CHANCELLERIES	10	14	14	13	12	7	8	9	8
COURT AND ITS LANDS	3	3	3	2	1	1	1	3	2
CARE OF THE TSAR	5	5	5	5	3	2	3	2	2
PRECIOUS METALS AND OBJECTS	2	5	5	5	6	3	3	3	3
MEMORIAL SERVICES AND HISTORY	0	1	1	1	2	1	1	1	1
PRIVY CHANCELLERIES OF THE TSAR	0	0	0	0	1	1	1	3	3
ALEKSEI MIKHAILOVICH	0	0	0	0	1	1	1	0	0
PETER THE GREAT	0	0	0	0	0	0	0	3	3
PATRIARCHAL CHANCELLERIES	3	4	3	3	3	4	5	4	4
TOTAL	57	68	65	63	66	66	65	56	61

Figure 19.5 (*cont.*)

the foreign affairs chancelleries were fewer in number, one of them – the massive Ambassadorial Chancellery – was a locus of state power which controlled far-flung territories. Chancelleries in these categories were the largest, best funded, most powerful and most honourable of all the administrative organs in the central government.

Like the workaday lower-court nobility, the chancellery personnel grew more powerful during the course of the century for the simple reason that the tsar found their services increasingly indispensable. Modern states cannot operate without relatively efficient – or at minimum, effective – bureaucracies. They collect the taxes, recruit personnel, and organise complex affairs generally. Throughout early modern Europe, states were travelling a road that made them more and more dependent on the offices of well-trained, skilled administrators. So it was in Muscovy. By the close of the century, the status of both administrators and administrative work had risen appreciably. More and more of them were elevated to the royal council, and increasingly hereditary military servitors of very high status (the old boyars and 'new men') opted to serve the tsar in the *prikazy*.[50] The once entirely martial ruling class gained a hybrid character, working with near equal frequency in the court, army and

50 Robert O. Crummey, 'The Origins of the Noble Official: The Boyar Elite, 1613–1689', in D. K. Rowney and W. M. Pintner (eds.), *Russian Officialdom: The Bureaucratization of*

offices. It was a common story, one that has parallels in Prussia, France and all other successful early modern states.[51]

Other central institutions: the 'boyar council' and 'Assembly of the Land'

The tsar, the court and the *prikazy* were the central stable elements of Muscovite governance throughout the seventeenth century. This being said, there were two other institutions, quite different in character, that we find in this era: the so-called 'boyar council' (*boiarskaia duma*) and 'Assembly of the Land' (*zemskii sobor*). Both have been the subject of considerable controversy. Early historians, with their eyes to the West, saw in them formal counselling and even representative bodies, the Russian analogues to peer councils and parliaments. Later historians called these views into question, noting that both terms were invented by eighteenth-century Russian historians and that there is very little in law or custom that defined the competence or operation of these bodies. With this in mind, let us look at what is known about these institutions today.

The phrase *boiarskaia duma*, though a later coinage, has come to stand for the regular high councils held at the courts of Kievan, apanage and particularly Muscovite princes from the ninth to the early eighteenth century.[52] It appears in no medieval or early modern Russian source. The terms 'council' (*duma*), 'privy council' (*blizhniaia duma*) and 'tsar's senate' (*tsarskii sinklit*) appear in Muscovite sources and refer to a royal council of some sort. In early Muscovy, dependent service families, not princes or independent lords, staffed the council. Consistent with this fact, the council seems to have evolved into an

Russian Society from the Seventeenth to the Twentieth Century (Chapel Hill: University of North Carolina Press, 1980), pp. 46–75. Also see Bickford O'Brien, 'Muscovite Prikaz Administration of the Seventeenth Century: The Quality of Leadership', *FOG* 24 (1978): 223–35.

51 On the All-European context, see Marshall T. Poe, 'The Military Revolution, Administrative Development, and Cultural Change in Early Modern Russia', *Journal of Early Modern History* 2 (1998): 247–73, and his 'The Consequences of the Military Revolution in Muscovy in Comparative Perspective', *Comparative Studies in Society and History* 38 (1996): 603–18.

52 The literature on the boyar elite (what we have called the duma ranks of the sovereign's court) is immense, while studies of the duma per se are few (largely due to a lack of sources). The standard treatments, all somewhat dated, are: V. O. Kliuchevskii, *Boiarskaia duma drevnei Rusi. Opyt istorii pravitel'stvennogo uchrezhdeniia v sviazi s istoriei obshchestva*, 3rd edn (Moscow: Sinodal'naia tipografiia, 1902); S. F. Platonov, 'Boiarskaia duma – predshestvennitsa senata', in his *Stat'i po russkoi istorii* (1883–1912), 2nd edn (St Petersburg: M. A. Aleksandrov, 1912), pp. 447–94; V. I. Sergeevich, *Drevnosti russkogo prava*, vol. II: *Veche i kniaz'. Sovetniki kniazia*, 3rd edn (St Petersburg, 1908). The best modern treatment is Bogatyrev, *The Sovereign and his Counsellors*.

instrument of the prince's private administration (his 'patrimony' (*votchina*)). Officers of the domain ('chiliarchs' (*tysiatskie*)), 'major-domos' (*dvoretskie*), 'seal-bearers' (*pechatniki*), 'treasurers' (*kaznacheia*)) are identified among his counsellors. Classes appear among the boyars in the council early on: the 'privy boyars' (*vvedennye boiare*) and 'departmental boyars' (*putnye boiare*), for example, are distinguished from all others. These men were probably agents of the prince's private administration, but this is not certain. The competence of the council appears to have been extensive but is indistinguishable from that of the prince. No formal definition of powers is found in any source. Similarly, nothing is known of the internal operation of the council in the early period.

The princely council underwent considerable development in connection with the rise of Muscovy in the fifteenth and sixteenth centuries. To the old Muscovite service families were added immigrants from defeated apanages, the Lithuanian Commonwealth, and the Tatar khanates. These new arrivals were at first given minor positions in the grand-princely administration and later, after they had been tested, were given high court rank and served as councillors. Records of this era permit the identification of most of those holding these ranks, something impossible in the Kievan and Apanage periods.[53] The evidence suggests that the number of men holding 'conciliar ranks' (*dumnye chiny*) was small, hovering around fifteen members in the years of Ivan III and Vasilii III, though it increased in size to about fifty under Ivan IV. In this period the competence of the duma – or at least of certain members of the council – is suggested in legislation and legal documents for the first time. The Law Code (*Sudebnik*) of 1497 directs that the 'boyars and *okol'nichie* are to administer justice' (*suditi sud boiaram i okol'nichim*), and it is known from surviving cases that they did so.[54] In like measure, the duma seems to have had some legislative authority, as can be seen in the often-repeated Muscovite formula 'the sovereign orders and the boyars affirm' (*gosudar' ukazal i boiare prigovorili*). Despite these hints, the exact boundaries of the duma's independent competence, if any, remained unregulated.

53 On the membership of the duma (or at least the identity of those holding duma ranks) in the fifteenth and sixteenth centuries, see: S. B. Veselovskii, *Issledovaniia po istorii klassa sluzhilykh zemlevladel'tsev* (Moscow: Nauka, 1969); A. A. Zimin, *Formirovanie boiarskoi aristokratii v Rossii vo vtoroi polovine XV–pervoi treti XVI v.* (Moscow: Nauka, 1988); Kollmann, *Kinship and Politics*; A. P. Pavlov, *Gosudarev dvor i politicheskaia bor'ba pri Borise Godunove* (Moscow: Nauka, 1992); M. E. Bychkova, *Sostav klassa feodalov Rossii v XVI v.* (Moscow: Nauka, 1986).

54 *Sudebniki XV–XVI vekov*, ed. B. D. Grekov (Moscow: AN SSSR, 1952), p. 19. Also see Ann M. Kleimola, *Justice in Medieval Russia: Muscovite Judgment Charters (pravye gramoty) of the Fifteenth and Sixteenth Centuries* (Philadelphia : American Philosophical Society, vol. 65, 1975).

Towards the end of the sixteenth century foreigners provided some sketchy evidence of the operation of the council.[55] They report seeing the council arrayed during ambassadorial audiences. However, it is evident that on such occasions the members played highly scripted roles that probably did not reflect the proceeding of 'private' council meetings. According to the English ambassador Giles Fletcher, central and provincial administrators, as well as private suitors, appeared before the duma on Mondays, Wednesdays and Fridays at seven in the morning.[56] The foreigners generally dismissed the duma as an ineffectual body, but this is not entirely accurate.[57] The council was very active during the Time of Troubles and succeeded in imposing an oath on Tsar Vasilii Shuiskii in 1606. According to Kotoshikhin, a similar oath was taken by Michael Romanov in 1613, but this is uncorroborated.[58]

In the seventeenth century, the competence of the council, as well as its exact composition and mode of operation, remained undefined – there was no constitution or even coherent (and inscribed) custom detailing who was (or should be) on it, or what it was to do (other than deliberate with the tsar). Kotoshikhin thoroughly describes general congresses of council members in which affairs were discussed and legislation was considered, affirmed and sent to the chancelleries for promulgation.[59] He tells us that 'although [Tsar Mikhail Fedorovich] used the title "autocrat", [he] could do nothing without the boyars' council'.[60] His son, in contrast, did quite a bit without their council. He favoured smaller groups of familiars (the *blizhnie liudi*) over the mass of courtiers who were coming to occupy the duma ranks.[61] By the second half of the century, the number of men who held these ranks was in all probability too large for all of them to serve as councillors, and there is no evidence that they did so. The duma ranks, as we have said, had turned into a source of patronage for weak monarchs and thus the councillors – at least most of them – were deprived of their council.

The history of the *zemskii sobor* is just as controversial and murky.[62] The phrase itself was coined by the radical Slavophile Konstantin Aksakov around

55 Poe, 'A People Born to Slavery', pp. 66–7, 103–4.
56 Giles Fletcher, *Of the Russe Commonwealth*, ed. John V. A. Fine and Richard Pipes (Cambridge, Mass.: Harvard University Press, 1966), pp. 34–6.
57 Poe, 'A People Born to Slavery', pp. 63–6, 101–3, 203.
58 Kotošixin, *O Rossii*, fos. 184–185v.
59 Ibid., fos. 35v–36.
60 Ibid., fos. 185v–186.
61 Ibid., fos. 36–36v.
62 On the historiography of the *zemskii sobor*, see L. V. Cherepnin, *Zemskie sobory russkogo gosudarstva v XVI–XVII vv.* (Moscow: Nauka, 1978), pp. 5–47, and Peter B. Brown, 'The *Zemskii Sobor* in Recent Soviet Historiography', *RH* 10 (1983): 77–90.

1850.[63] It is found in no Muscovite source. Nineteenth-century Russian historians of a liberal bent tried their best to make out of the thin evidence a 'proto-parliamentary' body that – but for the unbridled power of self-seeking tsars and boyars – might have led Russia to enlightened liberal democracy. More sober historians, focusing on the evidence rather than projecting their fantasies on bygone eras, contradicted this rosy interpretation. The battle continues.

What can be said with confidence is this.[64] Some sort of popular assembly was first called by Ivan IV and, thereafter, occasionally by his successors. The regime of Michael Romanov – weak and attempting to establish its legitimacy – seemed particularly fond of them (he was 'elected' by one), though his father was not. Though the assemblies (usually called *sobory*) could be assigned very specific tasks – for example, ratification of the *Ulozhenie* of 1649 (called '*Sobornoe*' because it was affirmed by a *sobor*) – they were generally organised by the government to take stock of opinion on affairs domestic and international.

The composition of the assemblies was never set, though they appear to have had two salient characteristics – they were elite (almost entirely composed of high-born military servitors) and they were ad hoc (the government often simply gathered servitors and clerics already in Moscow). Some were large – several hundred delegates; others were small – several dozen delegates. The assemblies were not regularly conferred according to any schedule. Rather, they seem to have been called in moments of doubt or crisis. Delegates almost always supported the government; there was no forceful 'debate' as far as we know. Their exact competence – like the royal council – was never defined in law or custom, though they were consulted on a wide range of affairs. As we can see in Figure 19.6, some acclaimed tsars, others declared war, while others still adopted legislation.[65]

Delegates were called as a matter of service obligation (and sometimes viewed said service as onerous), not as a matter of 'right'. Neither in years

---

63 K. S. Aksakov, *Polnoe sobranie sochinenii K. S. Aksakova*, 3 vols. (Moscow: P. Bakhmetev, 1861–80), vol. I, p. 11.

64 The following is drawn from: Ellerd Hulbert, 'Sixteenth-Century Russian Assemblies of the Land: Their Composition, Organization, and Competence', unpublished Ph.D. dissertation, University of Chicago, 1970; Hans-Joachim Torke, *Die staatsbedingte Gesellschaft im moskauer Reich: Zar und Zemlja in der altrussischen Herrschaftsverfassung 1613–1689* (Leiden: E. J. Brill, 1974); Cherepnin, *Zemskie sobory*; Ira L. Campbell, 'The Composition, Character and Competence of the Assembly of the Land in Seventeenth-Century Russia', unpublished Ph.D. dissertation, University of Illinois, 1984, and Donald Ostrowski, 'The Assembly of the Land as a Representative Institution', in J. Kotilaine and M. Poe (eds.), *Modernizing Muscovy: Reform and Social Change in Seventeenth-Century Russia* (London: RoutledgeCurzon, 2004), pp. 117–42.

65 Ostrowski, 'The Assembly of the Land', pp. 135–6.

Year	Primary activity
1613	Chose Michael as tsar
1614	Advised on stopping movements of Zarutskii and the cossacks
1616	Discussed conditions of peace with Sweden and a monetary levy
1617	Advised on a monetary levy
1619	Advised on raising of Filaret to the patriarchal throne
1621	Advised on war with Poland
1622	Advised on war with Poland
1632	Advised on the collection of money for the Polish campaign
1634	Advised on the collection of money and on the Polish campaign
1637	Advised on an invasion of the Crimean Khan Sefat Girey and the collection of money
1639	Advised on response to Crimean treatment of two Muscovite envoys
1642	Recommended support of Don cossacks in relation to the taking of Azov
1645	Chose Alexis as tsar
1648	Advised the composition of a new law code
1648–9	Approved the new law code
1650	Advised on the movement of people into Pskov
1651	Advised on Russo-Polish relations and Bohdan Khmel'nyts'kyi
1653	Advised on war with Poland and support of Zaporozhian cossacks
1681–2	Advised on military, financial and land reforms
1682	Chose Peter as tsar (27 April); chose Peter and Ivan as co-tsars (May)
1683–4	Advised on peace with Poland

Figure 19.6. Seventeenth-century 'Assemblies of the Land' and their activities

without assemblies, nor in the year they were extinguished finally, was there any protest or even mention of them in Muscovite sources. Foreigners, who were often careful observers of Russian politics, very rarely note them and when they do attribute little importance to them.[66]

Concluding remarks

In the end, the seventeenth-century Muscovite state proved to be quite robust. Even after it was almost totally taken apart in the maelstrom of the Time of Troubles, the triptych tsar–court–*prikazy* re-emerged rapidly and in full form. The ruling class wasted no time or effort on costly government experimentation in 1613. It simply picked itself up and got down to business. And its business was rule, plain and simple. For the tsar, his court and the men of offices, the

66 Poe, *A People Born to Slavery*, pp. 66–7.

entire point of the state was to rule over others and live off them. Never was this point seriously questioned. One must admire the single-minded purpose this sort of concentration bespeaks. While other early modern states (whatever their form) might pursue any number of goals – fostering science, patronising the arts, educating the public, spreading the Good Word – the Muscovite elite focused nearly all its energy in ruling others or conquering others so that they might rule them. Domination was their *raison d'être*.

As the century closed, this focus was, for good or ill, lost. Peter and his cohort were enamoured of a different vision of the state and its goals, one that was as new to Russia as it was profoundly alien to the Muscovite spirit. Aleksei Mikhailovich could no more have said he was the 'first servant of the state' than he could have sworn off the Orthodox faith. He could not serve the state because he owned the state. It was his instrument to do with as his master – God in Heaven – commanded. Neither could his servitors have said they were serving anything like the 'common good'. Such a thing was impossible, for they were honourable men and truly honourable men served only God and his representative, the tsar. As for the rest – all those who were neither tsars nor servants of tsars – they just did not matter.

20

Local government and administration

BRIAN DAVIES

There were two important developments affecting local government in the period 1613–89. The first was the spread of the town governor system of local administration. In the sixteenth century annually appointed town commandants (*godovye voevody*) with some civil as well as military authority had been found in some districts on the southern and western frontier. But by the 1620s most districts were under commandants turned town governors (*gorodovye voevody*), with staffs of clerks and constables, and exercising authority over the *guba* and *zemskii* elders, fortifications stewards, siege captains and other local officials. Responsibility for most aspects of defence, taxation, policing, civil and criminal justice, the remuneration of servicemen and the regulation of *pomest'e* landholding at the district level was now concentrated in the town governors' offices. The second development was the increasing reliance of town governor administration on codified law, written instructions and regular reporting and account-keeping. This enhanced central chancellery control over local administration and partly compensated for the avocational nature of town governor service.

The spread of town governor administration

The universalisation of *gorodovyi voevoda* administration had been a response to the breakdown of the political order in the Time of Troubles. On the one hand, the spread of town governor administration across the southern frontier in the late sixteenth century had helped to fuel the Troubles: mass discontent with the heavy burdens of defence duty and agricultural corvée on the 'Sovereign's tithe ploughlands' had led to the overthrow of several southern frontier town governors and placed much of the south in the hands of the First False Dmitrii and successor insurgents. On the other hand, after the disintegration of Tsar Vasilii Shuiskii's regime in 1608 the tasks of defeating the rebels and foreign invaders and re-establishing strong central authority fell by default to other town governors, notably P. P. Liapunov of Riazan' and D. M. Pozharskii of Zaraisk, who had the military experience and political connections to lead the governors and lesser officials of the towns of the north-east into forming an army of national liberation and a provisional government. In coalition with certain boyars and cossack leaders Pozharskii's army drove the Poles from Moscow (1612) and restored the Russian monarchy under the new Tsar Mikhail Fedorovich (1613). It was natural that the new Romanov monarchy should see its continued survival in the utmost centralisation and militarisation of provincial government – the logical agents of which were the town governors, appointed by and accountable to the central chancelleries, selected from the court nobility, and given broad authority over district military, fiscal, judicial and police affairs. Upon Tsar Michael's accession his government was supposedly deluged with collective petitions from the provinces, 'from many towns, from the *dvoriane* and *deti boiarskie* and various servicemen and inhabitants', begging that town governors be placed in charge of their districts, for 'without town governors their towns would not exist'.[1] Whether these petitions really represented local will or its ventriloquism by the central government cannot be determined, but three days later the central government authorised the general restoration and expansion of town governor rule, to all districts in need of town governors. Whereas town governor administration had been confined mostly to the western and southern frontiers before the Troubles, it came to prevail throughout the centre and north as well by the 1620s. By 1633 there were 190 governors' offices, and 299 by 1682.[2]

After 1613 most of the local administrative organs common before the Troubles were liquidated or were absorbed into town governor administration. The title of vicegerent (*namestnik*) was still used at court as a ceremonial honorific, but vicegerents no longer governed in the provinces. The fortifications and siege stewards declined in number and became subordinate officials (*prikaznye liudi*) of the town governors' offices. Customs and tavern administration remained in the hands of elected community representatives or tax-farmers, but they came under the supervision of the town governors, who supervised their operations and gave them quarterly or annual accountings. District-level and canton-level elected *zemskii* offices for tax collection and justice continued to exist in the north, but most of them were subordinated to the town governors, so that *zemskii* officials no longer dealt with the chancelleries

---

1 P. Ivanov, *Opisanie gosudarstvennogo razriadnogo arkhiva* (Moscow: Tipografiia S. Silivanskogo, 1842), pp. 156, 209.
2 N. F. Demidova, *Sluzhilaia biurokratiia v Rossii XVII v. i ee rol' v formirovanii absoliutizma* (Moscow: Nauka, 1987), p. 31.

directly but only through their local governor; the more important kinds of court cases traditionally heard in the district-level *zemskii* court were now held in the governor's court, which also became a court of second instance over those matters still heard in *zemskii* courts; and the tax-collection activities of *zemskii* officials were subject to especially tight control from the governor's office, for the governor had the authority to beat *zemskii* officials under righter (*pravezh*), that is, in the stocks, for any tax arrears or irregularities and the tendency was towards requiring *zemskii* collections to be turned in to the governor's office.

For some time the *guba* constabulary offices for policing and investigating felonies were permitted greater autonomy, for Moscow saw some advantage in keeping the defence of the community against banditry and violent crime in the hands of elected community representatives – especially as those elected as chief constables were supposed to be the communities' 'best men', ideally prosperous *dvoriane* or *deti boiarskie*, reporting their investigations directly to the Robbery Chancellery (*Razboinyi prikaz*) at Moscow for pronouncement of verdict. Besides reducing the need to send down special inquisitors from Moscow, this would have the advantage of shifting blame for policing failures from state officials to community representatives. Moscow's preference for the continued independence of the *guba* system was indicated in the 1649 *Ulozhenie* and 1669 New Decree Statutes as well as in a 1627 decree that announced that *guba* chief constables should be elected in all towns. But this came up against fiscal and manpower concerns: maintaining *guba* offices cost the community additional taxes, and in wartime prosperous *dvoriane* and *deti boiarskie* were needed in the army, not at home performing constabulary duties which could be assumed by the town governors or, in worst cases, by inquisitors from the Robbery Chancellery. The *guba* system was therefore not expanded; the town governors increasingly sought to subordinate the *guba* officials de facto; and in 1679 all *guba* offices were closed.[3]

Enhanced control through improved record-keeping

Town governor administration operated under closer central chancellery control than had vicegerent administration in the previous century because the town governors' offices were held to higher expectations of written reporting

3 V. N. Glaz'ev, *Vlast' i obshchestvo na iuge Rossii XVII v.: Protivodeistvie ugolovnoi prestupnosti* (Voronezh: Voronezhskii gosudarstvennyi universitet, 2001), p. 141.

and compliance with written instructions. The town governors were guided in their general or long-term responsibilities by written working orders (*nakazy*), and in more particular and non-routine matters by decree rescripts from the chancelleries; they were expected to submit frequent reports, even if all they had to relate was their progress in implementing relatively routine directives; and they had to maintain an increasingly wide range of rolls, inventories, land allotment and surveying books, court hearing inquest transcripts and account books for various indirect and direct revenues. Inventories of the archives of governors' offices generally show a significant increase in the rate of record production, especially from mid-century. This reflected the increasing demands upon the governors' offices by the central chancelleries, but also the demands upon them from the community in terms of litigation and petitioning of needs and grievances.[4]

Because the primary purpose of the governor's office was to gather and systematise information to facilitate executive decision-making in the central chancelleries and duma, the clerical staffing of the governor's offices was a crucial concern. It was the governor's clerks (*pod'iachie*) who produced, routed and stored all this information and kept order in the town archive and treasury. The clerks also performed important tasks in the field – supervising corvée, conducting *obysk* polling at inquests, conveying cash to and from Moscow, or surveying property boundaries. In some districts the governor's clerical staff was too small, too inexperienced or too poorly remunerated to maintain the flow of information required by the chancelleries. The smaller governors' offices might have only one or two clerks in permanent service and so be forced to turn over some tasks to public notaries or even press passing travellers into temporary clerical service. In the 1640s the clericate of the provincial governors' offices officially numbered no more than 775, slightly fewer than the number of clerks staffing the central chancelleries.[5] However, the total clerical manpower at work in provincial administration may have been significantly larger because this total does not include the clerks serving in the customs, liquor excise, *guba* and *zemskii* offices. Furthermore, the small clerical staffs of the smaller governorships could be compensated for by making these governorships satellites of the larger offices found in the bigger towns of the region or the capitals of regional military administrations (*razriady*). The

4 On record-keeping in the governors' offices, see: N. N. Ogloblin, 'Provintsial'nye arkhivy v XVII veke', *Vestnik arkheologii i istorii izdavaemyi Arkheologicheskim institutom* 6 (1886): 74–206; D. Ia. Samokvasov, *Russkie arkhivy i tsarskii kontrol' prikaznoi sluzhby v XVII veke* (Moscow, 1902); N. N. Ogloblin, 'Obozrenie stolbtsov i knig Sibirskogo prikaza', 4 parts, *ChOIDR* 2 (1895): i–viii and 1–422; 1 (1898): 1–162; 3 (1900): i–iv and 1–394; 1 (1902): 1–288.
5 Demidova, *Sluzhilaia biurokratiia*, p. 37.

larger governors' offices came to have nearly as many clerks as some Moscow chancelleries and to imitate chancellery internal organisation by distributing them among bureaux (*stoly*, 'desks') for specialised functions under the general direction of an experienced senior executive clerk. In the 1640s the Pskov governor's office had twenty-one clerks and by 1699 it would have fifty-four clerks, some of whom had thirty or forty years' experience.[6]

The demand for clerical manpower in the provinces after the end of the Troubles had made it necessary for Moscow to give its town governors a free hand in appointing clerks and to accept as eligible men of all kinds of backgrounds: church clerks, the sons of priests, servicemen, merchants' sons, the sons of taxpaying townsmen and state peasants and déclassé itinerants. After about 1640 this was no longer affordable, for taxpayers or servicemen enrolled as clerks thereby left the tax and military service rolls. The central chancelleries therefore began tightening their control over the appointment of clerks (eventually all appointments would be controlled by the Military Chancellery). The chancelleries moved towards standardising clerical pay rates, and they gradually reduced the range of social estates and ranks eligible for clerical appointment. Cossacks and musketeers were forbidden to take service as clerks; by the 1660s–1670s it was the rule that *deti boiarskie* could be appointed as clerks only if they had retired from military service, lacked the *pomest'e* lands to render military service or had not yet received formal initiation into military service. By the end of the century not even this was permitted: now no candidate could be appointed whose father had been registered in military service or on the tax rolls; only those whose fathers had been clerks were allowed to continue clerking in the governors' offices.

Thus the clericate became a closed hereditary corporation. Although this probably had the effect of slowing the growth rate of the provincial clericate, it had the advantage of improving clerical training and *esprit de corps* and making clerical service a life profession. Local clerical 'dynasties' emerged, with clerks accumulating decades of experience in the local governor's office and passing their training on to their sons, some of whom eventually worked their way up into the clericate of the central chancelleries. There was increased likelihood that clerical dynasties would tend to conduct themselves as local elites and exploit their neighbours, but clerical dynasties at least were motivated to attend closely to apprentice training out of self-interest.[7]

6 V. A. Arakcheev, *Pskovskii krai v XV–XVII vekakh: Obshchestvo i gosudarstvo* (St Petersburg: Russko-Baltiiskii informatsionnyi tsentr BLITs, 2003), p. 310.
7 As there were no universities or academies to train clerks, all clerical training had to be obtained through apprenticeship within the chancellery or governor's office.

Local government in reconstruction and reform

The spread and systematisation of town governor administration was crucial to Patriarch Filaret's reconstruction programme (1619–33): the town governors helped reassemble and update chancellery cadastral knowledge, review the monasteries' fiscal immunities, return fugitive townsmen to the tax rolls, introduce new extraordinary taxes for military exigencies, suppress banditry and rebuild the *pomest'e*-based cavalry army by expediting response to petitions for entitlement award and land allotment.

In the period 1633–48 policy was made by the succession of cliques led by I. B. Cherkasskii, F. I. Sheremetev and B. I. Morozov. They gave priority to accelerating colonisation of the southern frontier and eliminating the tax-exempt social categories and enclaves in the towns. Town governor administration played an essential role in both projects.

The years 1648–54 saw town governor authority used to implement several important reforms strengthening the southern frontier defence system: the completion of most of the Belgorod Line; levies into the newly revived foreign formation infantry and cavalry regiments; the subjection of southern servicemen to the grain taxes (quarter grain, siege grain etc.) previously paid only by peasants and townsmen; and the laying of foundations for the vast Belgorod regional military administration (*Belgorodskii razriad*), which subordinated several town governors' offices in the south to the senior commander's office at Belgorod, not only for mobilisations and joint military operations but also for review of judicial, fiscal and land allotment matters. An equally significant reform in this period affected civil and criminal justice in governors' courts across the realm: the *Ulozhenie* law code (1649) greatly expanded and standardised instructions for investigations and hearings in the local courts and streamlined and further centralised judicial administration by giving the duma functions of an appellate court and by further concentrating the supervision of criminal justice matters in the Robbery Chancellery. The *Ulozhenie* also ended the time limit for the recovery of fugitive peasants, thereby completing the process of peasant enserfment, and provided instructions for the governors' offices to enforce enserfment by conducting mass dragnets of fugitive peasants and townsmen as well as holding hearings for fugitive remands. The fact that the *zemskii sobor* was no longer convened after 1653 may testify to the centre's confidence in town governor administration by this point: apparently the flow of information from governors' reports and accounts and community petitions was now considered regular and reliable enough to support decision-making in the duma and chancelleries without any need to supplement it by periodically assembling representatives of the estates to solicit their views.

During the Thirteen Years War expenditure on army pay (particularly upon the more expensive foreign formation regiments, which accounted for some 75–80 per cent) increased enormously, exceeding a million roubles annually by 1663, about four times what army service allowances had totalled in 1632.[8] The sharp rise in tax rates and infantry levy quotas in the war years was all the harder to bear because grain taxes and infantry conscription no longer fell only upon men of draft (*tiaglye liudi*) traditionally defined, and because ruinous inflation had resulted from the government's decision to debase coinage. The governors' offices came under great pressure to keep cash, grain and manpower resources flowing while at the same time policing against desertion, taxpayer flight and riot. To tighten central control over their accounting and policing two new chancelleries with broad investigatory powers were created: a Privy Chancellery (founded in 1654) and an Auditing Chancellery (founded in 1656). A second great regional military administration was also established at Sevsk to further co-ordinate resource mobilisation and military operations on the southern frontier.

The Andrusovo Armistice (1667) did not lead to any significant relief from high grain taxation and infantry conscription rates. It remained necessary to garrison eastern Ukraine, to keep Moscow's puppet hetmans Mnogogreshnyi and Samoilovich in power and hold Hetman Doroshenko at bay; it was also necessary to defend against the Crimean Tatars by reinforcing the Belgorod Line and sending troops down the Don to assist (and control) the Don cossacks; and in 1674 a Muscovite army had to take the field in western Ukraine to defeat Doroshenko, who was now actively supported by Ottoman forces. The defeat of Doroshenko led immediately to the first Russo-Turkish war (1676–81), which depopulated much of eastern Ukraine and deterred the Ottomans from invading western Ukraine but also revealed the need to reform Muscovite military and fiscal practices. More regional military administrations were therefore formed (the Riazan', Tambov, Kazan', Smolensk and Vladimir *razriady*). A new Iziuma Line was built to extend the southern frontier defence a further 160 kilometres southward and shield military colonisation in Sloboda Ukraine. In 1678–80 six new foreign formation cavalry and ten new foreign formation infantry regiments were created, while the number of southern servicemen in the traditional formation cavalry was reduced by limiting eligibility to

---

8 J. L. H. Keep, *Soldiers of the Tsar: Army and Society in Russia, 1462–1874* (Oxford: Clarendon Press, 1985), p. 91.

prosperous men holding at least twenty-four peasant households and therefore presumably able to maintain themselves in service from their *pomest'ia* alone, without cash allowances. To meet the higher costs for new foreign formation troop pay, a major reform of state finances was undertaken. It started with a new general cadastral survey (1677–9), the first since 1646; led to the decision (1679) to shift to the assessment of direct taxes by household, thereby abandoning the old method of assessing by *sokha* (i.e. by area and productive capacity of cultivated land); saw the amalgamation of a number of minor direct taxes into a single 'musketeers' money' tax for the army; and culminated in the founding of the Grand Treasury and the production of the first rudimentary state budget (1680). The simplification of direct taxation enhanced central chancellery control and permitted a further division of labour over fiscal matters at the local level, with the town governors' offices made responsible largely for recording and actual collection of taxes left to elected community representatives.

Efforts at bureaucratic rationalisation

Over the course of the seventeenth century *voevoda* administration came to display more of the characteristics of rational bureaucratic organisation. It was already significantly differentiated: official duties were distinguished from the pursuit of personal interests, it being an already long-established principle that the governor's office (the *s"ezzhaia izba*, assembly house) was separate from his residence (*voevodskii dvor*) and that he was forbidden to hold documents or the town seal at the latter; and there was some formal division of labour, at least within the larger offices – horizontally, in the form of discrete clerkships or even bureaux with specialised functions, and vertically, with supervising signatory clerks, document clerks and secretaries reporting in turn to the governor. By mid-century it had even become the tendency to rename the governor's office a *prikaznaia izba* in recognition that its organisation was increasingly resembling that of a small chancellery. Office work was subject to various integrating mechanisms promoting standardised practice: there was a comprehensive and fairly consistent repertory of routines for handling incoming business, recording expenditures and services performed and reporting up important information and unresolved business; and although there was as yet no uniform written General Regulation covering all aspects of office work, that sphere of activity where written regulations were most necessary – the administration of justice – had finally received a comprehensive code of procedures with the promulgation of the *Ulozhenie*. Surety bonding, oaths of conduct, annual and end-of-term audits and investigations went some way towards tightening constraints over the conduct of governors and their staffs. To enhance co-ordination and compensate for the limited effectiveness of central control mechanisms, most executive decision-making was removed from the governors' offices and located above them in the chancelleries, with ultimate executive policy-making removed to an even higher level, above the central chancellery bureaucracy, in the duma counselling circle.

But in one important respect *voevoda* administration resisted full bureau-cratic rationalisation. Although clerical staffs were expanding and office work undergoing further regulation in the governors' offices, neither process was sufficiently advanced to fully compensate for the fact that the organising link between the central and provincial clericates – the *gorodovye voevody* – were not themselves career administrative specialists. Those appointed as town governors were court notables serving only avocationally, without any special training for the task, as an occasional respite from their field army and court duties. There was no Muscovite *noblesse de robe*, trained in the law and seeking promotion to nobility through the path of judicial and administrative service, from which to draw in filling town governorships.

This by itself presented an obstacle to further centralisation of command-and-control, as avocational administration by notables is generally thought to have been slower, less precise, and less unified than fully bureaucratised administration, being 'less bound to schemata and more formless . . . and also because it is less dependent upon superiors'.[9] Notables were more inclined to ignore bureaucratic rules and abuse their authority because they were not permanently subordinated to bureaucratic superiors, had not internalised a bureaucratic ethos of impersonalised objectivised service to the organisation and its larger mission, and meanwhile claimed social status above that of pro-fessional bureaucrats. And in Muscovy the problem was further exacerbated by the fact that town governor duty carried less honour and less remuneration than other forms of state service and so was less likely to be sought by notables pursuing promotion and influence at court.

There were various reasons to seek appointment as a town governor. It offered a rest from the rigours and risks of campaign duty, which is why measures had to be taken in wartime to tighten the Military Chancellery's control over appointments lest the provincial governors' offices become havens for shirkers. Those appointed to certain distant towns were immune from

9 Max Weber, *Economy and Society*, ed. Guenther Roth and Claus Wittich, 2 vols. (Berkeley: University of California Press, 1978), vol. II, p. 974.

lawsuit for the duration of their terms. Governorships 'in array' (*v razriade* – as when one was appointed to govern a larger town with some authority over the governors of nearby lesser satellite towns) offered the opportunity to demonstrate higher *mestnichestvo* precedence over certain other nobles. Many seeking governorships were probably drawn by the opportunity to collect 'feeding' income in kind and cash (*kormlenie*, see below) to supplement their regular annual bounties from the sovereign's treasury.

Petitioners for appointment therefore usually cited as grounds their need for relief: they had been on campaign duty for many years with no real respite, held inadequate service lands, had fallen into debt and so sought governorships 'for their poverty'.[10] There were at any time many metropolitan nobles feeling themselves in need of relief, so there were usually multiple candidates available to take over vacant governorships. The chancelleries therefore had some choice as to whom to appoint – indeed, probably greater choice than in appointments to army commands, which were by nature 'in array' and therefore more subject to *mestnichestvo* precedence considerations.

But these motives for seeking appointment all treated town governor duty as merely avocational, a temporary surcease from the proper vocations of a metropolitan nobleman, duty in the field army and in the court. The Muscovite state service system had traditionally valorised field army and court duty over administrative duty in the provinces, so that rank promotions and raises to service bounties were much more often awarded for the former than for the latter. When town governors did see raises or royal gifts in honorarium, it was less likely to be as a reward for governor duty than part of a general distribution of largesse across the entire upper service class in commemoration of a special event such as a great military victory or the birth of a tsarevich. Nor was town governor duty as good a path to rank promotion or political influence as army and court duty, which were more visibly meritorious – performed in proximity to the sovereign and one's fellow nobles – and did not require long absence from the circles of gossip, counsel and patronage at court that were so important to career advancement. Strictly speaking, town governor duty was not even routinely formally remunerated; it did not ordinarily carry its own salary precisely because it was considered a respite from vocational service. A notable appointed to a town governorship was usually expected to live off the annual *zhalovanie* bounty he already received in accordance with his rank

---

10 For petitions seeking the governor's post at Pereiaslavl'-Riazan' see A. A. Kabanov, 'Akty o naznachenii i smene voevod v Pereiaslavle Riazanskom', 2 pts., *Trudy Riazanskoi uchenoi arkhivnoi kommissii* 25, 2 (1912), 1–28, and 26, 1 (1914), 15–35.

and entitlement rating.[11] Whatever feeding arrangement he could negotiate with those he governed was his own concern, unless the chancelleries received complaint that he was extorting too much of it.

Therefore, although governorships were reserved for servitors of Moscow rank, that is, members of the metropolitan nobility, and the governorships of especially important towns like Novgorod and Astrakhan' might go to the elite of duma rank, the vast majority of governorships were given out to the middle and lower Moscow ranks; and while examination of service career patterns shows many metropolitan nobles taking turns at town governor duty, it presents few instances of them specialising in it. Those serving as town governors did so only avocationally, and most of them only on infrequent occasions, with little or no prior experience. There was little opportunity for them to familiarise themselves fully with bureaucratic routines and norms, and little reason for them to internalise a professional bureaucratic ethos.

Fortunately there were mechanisms partly compensating for the avocational character of town governor service.

While the discipline of career bureaucratic service was largely alien to the Muscovite metropolitan nobility, the discipline of general state service was not. Since the mid-fifteenth century the metropolitan nobility had been liable for compulsory life service to the sovereign – if not so much for provincial administrative service, certainly for court service and especially service in the field army. The Muscovite notable therefore differed from the Western European notable in accepting to a far greater degree the notion that rank and entitlements derived from service to the sovereign (even if town governor duty was not the preferred service track for winning them); more importantly, even while he was resting from campaign duty by feeding in the provinces as a town governor he remained under a military discipline which provided penalties for malfeasance.

In districts where the governor's office had direct responsibility for tax collection as well as tax recording the governor could be held accountable to the central chancelleries for any arrears or deficits caused by unfair or negligent collection measures as well as by embezzlement. Even for minor deficits he could be fined, deprived of rank, subjected to corporal punishment, imprisoned or exiled. When such irregularities had been caught at Moscow during

11 In some instances notables appointed to hard postings – governorships in underdeveloped regions far off in Siberia – did receive special maintenance subsidies out of the treasury, usually in grain or spirits, but these were only in supplement to their regular service bounties.

examination of records submitted from the governor's office, the task of exacting the missing sum and imposing a fine or other penalty was entrusted to chancellery clerks and constables sent down for the purpose. In general, though, irregularities were not so easily discovered this way because until late in the century most chancelleries were not insistent that governors regularly send in full copies of their income and expenditure books (the Military Chancellery, for example, began requiring this only from 1685); they only required regular submission of short summaries (*smety*) comparing the current year's balance with that of the previous year and brief projections (*pomety*) of revenue and expenditure for the coming year. This may be why, when chancellery officials were sent down to exact arrears and deficits, it was sometimes to several districts in succession, arrears and deficits having been found to have accumulated undetected for some time across a broad region. In 1646, for example, the Ustiug Territorial Chancellery authorised that 35,000 roubles of missing revenues be exacted from the governors of several districts in its jurisdiction.[12]

The chancelleries recognised that central control could not rely entirely on quarterly or annual account submissions and therefore they continued to place greater reliance on subjecting outgoing governors to end-of-term audits by their replacements. The outgoing governor was required to give his replacement full assistance in conducting a general inventory and audit. This could take many days to complete, as it involved inspections of fortifications and troops, counting and weighing cash and grain stores, examining *s"ezzhaia izba* logbooks and archive inventories, reviewing income and expenditure accounts and conducting interrogations into expenditures that appeared to lack authorisation from Moscow. In some cases the centre expected this audit to assess the profitability of the outgoing governor's administration compared to previous governors' terms, in which case a profit report (*pribyl'naia kniga*) as well as audit report had to be prepared. The outgoing governor was not allowed to depart until the chancelleries had received these audit results and ruled on whether he had to pay any fines, make restitution of missing funds, or pay any damages to local inhabitants. Fines of a hundred roubles or more were common enough; restitution of missing funds sometimes was ordered at double rate, to the total value of thousands of roubles.

The end-of-term audit was also recognised as an opportunity for the inhabitants to file complaint against the outgoing governor and ask his replacement to

12 P. P. Smirnov, *Posadskie liudi i ikh klassovaia bor'ba do serediny XVII veka*, 2 vols. (Moscow and Leningrad: AN SSSR, 1947–8), vol. II, pp. 37–8.

begin an investigation. In the Siberian towns the opportunity to file complaint was an especially important supplement to other central control measures and was accompanied by a special ritual: each new governor was under instruction to invite community representatives to a *bienvenue* feast, ply them with food and drink – expressly identified as largesse provided by the tsar himself, not by his governor – and then read them the 'sovereign's declaration of vouchsafe' (*gosudarevo zhalovannoe slovo*), an address promising them the new governor would protect them against extortion and oppression and investigate whatever complaints they chose to bring against the outgoing governor.

The chancelleries sometimes sent down from Moscow special inquisitors (*syshchiki*) to investigate specific complaints of corruption or abuse of authority made in collective petitions from the community or in denunciations by associate governors, clerks or other subordinate officials. The inquisitors made audits, took witness testimony, polled the community by *poval'nyi obysk*, reported up, and then implemented whatever penalty Moscow decreed. A good number of inquest records have been preserved, especially from Siberia, and some are quite long and painstaking and produced verdicts giving victims of governor corruption meaningful relief. But when victims failed to get redress they charged the inquisitor with failing to take particular crucial testimonies or misrecording or forging testimonies. In other instances inquests dragged on for years without result.

The struggles against governor malfeasance therefore had to employ preventive measures as well. The tendency over the course of the century was towards standardising the length of town governor terms – to two years in most towns under the authority of the Military Chancellery, with extensions of one or two years for merit or upon the petition of local inhabitants unwilling to risk possibly greater exploitation under a new governor. Besides providing more appointment opportunities to nobles seeking respite from army and court duty, appointing for shorter terms gave governors less time to build local clientage machines and drive their districts to revolt with their extortion and oppression. Governor terms in the larger and more strategic towns, in territorial *razriad* capitals and in distant Siberian towns were usually longer, to provide greater continuity in frontier defence and diplomatic operations and to reduce opportunities for governors homebound from Siberian posts to smuggle contraband furs in their baggage.

To check abuse of power it was also frequent practice to appoint to the larger towns and *razriad* capitals a senior governor and one to three associate town governors (*tovarishchi*) or secretaries on instruction to operate collegially, 'acting together as one, without dissension'.[13] Actual procedures for collegial decision-making were not spelled out (and so may not always have been observed in practice), but it was usually stipulated that the senior governor could put his seal on official acts only in the presence of his associates, that court cases had to be heard by senior governors and their associates together and resolved by unanimous verdict and that a senior governor or one or more of his associates had the right to challenge other kinds of decisions reached unilaterally without consultation.

An especially important means of minimising opportunities for governor malfeasance was sharpening the division of labour between central and local government. Maximum separation of policy-making from policy implementation was sought, with the former centralised in the chancelleries and duma at Moscow and the latter left to the town governors. Governors were forbidden to set entitlement rates on their own initiative, without express authorisation from Moscow. Even many routine expenditures could not be made without prior chancellery authorisation. The 1670s saw efforts to remove the governors' offices further from the business of collecting taxes and entrusting collection to elected elders and deputies. In most capital criminal cases sentence of death could be made only by the Robbery Chancellery, and the governors of middling and smaller towns were usually restricted from hearing civil cases over a certain rouble value. Some of these restrictions were routinised in governors' working orders, while others were imposed in particular circumstances, by special decree. The centre reserved for itself practically any decision which, if left entirely up to the governor's discretion, might become a *tiagost'*, that is, a ruinous burden on the community. The exceptions were matters requiring immediate local response, such as military emergencies. Working orders tried to specify such circumstances in advance and instruct governors that in responding to these exigencies they could consider themselves free to act 'according to the matter at hand, and as God so enlightens them', provided they make immediate report to Moscow afterwards.

The practice of concentrating executive decision-making in the central government did not much reduce the range of tasks the governor was responsible for implementing – he still investigated and heard court cases and carried out sentences on them, even if the sentence was pronounced at Moscow – so it could be said the governor was still expected to be omni-competent even

---

13 *Polnoe sobranie zakonov Rossiiskoi imperii. Sobranie pervoe*, 45 vols. (St Petersburg: Tipografiia II Otdeleniia S.I.V. Kantseliarii, 1830–43), vol. III, no. 1670; *AI*, vol. III (St Petersburg: Tipografiia II Otdeleniia Sobstvennoi E. I. V. Kantseliarii, 1841), nos. 134, 154.

if forbidden opportunities tempting him to assert omnipotence. Centralising decision-making at Moscow of course had the disadvantage of encouraging prevarication among the town governors, who instead of acting in timely fashion would write repeatedly to Moscow asking for further clarification as to what they were supposed to do. But the sacrifice of speed to central control was exactly the kind of cost an autocracy was willing to pay, preferable to accepting increased abuse of authority, the higher price that would have attached to entrusting greater discretion to the governors.

Given that executive decision-making was increasingly concentrated at Moscow, ever greater emphasis had to be placed on the reportorial function of the *s"ezzhaia izba* clericate. The governors and their clerks had to make more frequent and detailed reports to Moscow and submit extracts from or copies of their account books. More attention was given to documenting other matters in which the chancelleries had shown less interest in the first half of the century: keeping accurate trial records and *obysk* polling records, updating prisoner lists, inventorying confiscated property, compiling logs of interrogations of travellers and new settlers, issuing travel passes (now detailed enough to serve almost as passports) and submitting more informative protocols on the elections of customs deputies and jail guards. Ideally, the increased flow of information from such record-keeping would support the centralisation of decision-making at Moscow, making it more realistic and proactive; any contradictions or omissions discovered in audits and record checks would expose instances of governor malfeasance; and by making information-gathering and reporting the primary function of the *s"ezzhaia izba* some further devolution of district-level administrative authority from the governors to their clerks could be expected, thereby partly compensating for the governors' comparative inexperience.

The results of this push for greater documentation from the governors' offices were mixed. There was clearly a great increase in the volume of *s"ezzhaia izba* record production after mid-century, especially in the larger towns; some of it was in response to the chancelleries' increased demands for documentation, but some of it was also in response to expanded grievance and need petitioning from the local population. There are some signs already by the 1660s that the flow of information to Moscow had so expanded as to exceed the processing capabilities of certain chancelleries. This was dealt with by restructuring higher administration, in three ways: by forming new territorial *razriady* so that financial accounting and supervision of judicial matters could be undertaken at the regional level, by *razriad* commanders standing between the town governors and the central chancelleries; by further subordinating other military-function chancelleries to the great Military Chancellery, so as to streamline and improve co-ordination of military administration; and by creating a Privy Chancellery and Auditing Chancellery to gather intelligence on commanders and town governors, conduct audits of the governors' offices and other chancelleries and investigate malfeasance and red tape.

On the other hand many *s"ezzhaia izba* and *guba, zemskii,* customs and excise offices were not up to the chancelleries' demands for fuller, more reliable and timelier reporting and accounting. They fell months or years behind in submitting annual accounts, failed to record important information like vacant entitlements or property boundaries, or miscounted when tallying servicemen or cash and grain reserves. Governors blamed these failures on clerks who were 'drunkards and brawlers . . . stupid and unable to write'.[14] The clerks in turn could complain of the unreliable information provided by the lower *prikaznye liudi* and elected officials, who were often outright illiterate (at Kazan' in 1627 the fortifications steward, one of the two musketeer captains, the customs chief, one of the two tavern chiefs, one of the two *zemskii* elders and eighteen of the nineteen customs and tavern deputies were illiterate).[15] We also find instances of governors accused by their own clerks and other subordinates of seriously neglecting their responsibilities.

A large part of chancellery communications to the provinces therefore comprised warnings and rebukes about delays or errors in submitting annual accounts. The chancelleries obviously could not afford to rely entirely upon official reporting and accounting to catch error, and certainly not to expose abuse of authority and corruption in local administration. B. N. Chicherin and other liberal historians attributed the persistence of error and malfeasance to the underdevelopment of bureaucratic rationality in central administration, to the centre's inability to articulate a General Regulation and enforce it through regular control mechanisms.[16] Actually, the central chancelleries had developed and were continuing to develop a wide range of measures to enhance central control and combat malfeasance. The system's real weakness was at the local level, and derived from cadre inadequacy rather than insufficient attention to central control measures: the centre still did not receive enough reliable and timely information because most districts

---

14 S. V. Bakhrushin, 'Ocherki po istorii krasnoiarskogo uezda v XVII v.', in his *Nauchnye trudy*, 4 vols. (Moscow: AN SSSR, 1952–9), vol. IV (1959), pp. 167–9.

15 S. I. Porfir'ev, *Neskol'ko dannykh o prikaznom upravlenii v Kazani v 1627 g.* (Kazan', 1911), p. 4.

16 B. N. Chicherin, *Oblastnye uchrezhdeniia Rossii v XVII veke* (Moscow: Tipografiia Aleksandra Semena, 1856), pp. 577–9.

had too few experienced clerks, and too often inattentive as well as inexperienced governors; and for lack of revenue the centre was unable adequately to remunerate either governors or clerks, thereby giving them greater reason to embezzle and especially to prey upon the community through bribe-taking, extortion and excessive feeding.

The political economy of corruption

The practice of permitting officials in the provinces to take part of their remuneration in the form of feedings in cash and kind collected from the communities they governed had not actually been abolished everywhere in the reform of 1555–6. Only certain cantons and districts, mostly in northern Muscovy, appear to have availed themselves of that reform by purchasing their removal from vicegerent jurisdiction and the right to elect their own *zemskii* officials in exchange for quit-rent payments, equivalent to the old feeding norms, paid into the central chancelleries. The military exigencies of the Livonian war and Troubles discouraged the further expansion of *zemskii* self-government: it was more important to free up the middle service class for campaign duty and to militarise local government in the frontier districts by expanding the powers of their fortifications stewards or placing them under annually appointed commandants or town governors. In fact the practice of feeding enjoyed a revival from the 1570s. Vicegerents and feeding obligations were now officially restored in certain towns and districts which had gone on feeding quit-rent just a few years before. Shares of feeding quit-rent revenues from particular regions were officially awarded to certain powerful boyars (the Shuiskiis, Boris Godunov). In most instances, however, the revival of feeding was not officially decreed but privately arranged between officials and the communities they governed, the feeding rates set by custom and negotiation. The centre now exercised less direct control over feedings than before, since feeding arrangements were no longer defined by charter or revenue list as those before 1556 had been. A 1620 decree attempted to criminalise feeding but quickly proved unenforceable, above all because of the treasury's continued need to keep down costs for salary remuneration; so the central government thereafter had to content itself with threatening penalties upon officials convicted of illegal exactions, without any clear identification in the law of what constituted these.[17] Determining what was an acceptable feeding rate and what was an illegal feeding

---

17 *Zakonodatel'nye akty Russkogo gosudarstva vtoroi poloviny XVI – pervoi poloviny XVII veka. Teksty* (Leningrad: Nauka, 1986), no. 68.

exaction was left up to the community; the central government did not intervene unless it received complaints of extortionate feeding demands so heavy
as to leave the community with too little to meet its tax obligations to Moscow.

Because feeding transactions were no longer regulated by charter or revenue
list one can only guess as to the spread and scale of feeding of town governors
and their staffs in the seventeenth century. Anecdotal evidence from investigation records and the expenditure books kept by *zemskii* officials in the north
suggest the practice was common there and the amounts involved often considerable. If Moscow's toleration of feeding was only tacit, it was not much
concealed. It was not unknown for a servitor to petition for appointment as
town governor on grounds he needed feeding income ('I beg leave to go out
and feed') and to request posting to a particular district on the basis of its
feeding yield. Upon completing his term as town governor of Kostroma, one
Moscow *dvorianin* complained his appointment had yielded him far less than
the 500–600 roubles' feeding previous governors had received; Moscow agreed
to find him another appointment after its investigation confirmed that the 400
roubles of feeding he had received at Kostroma had been with community
consent: 'He took what they brought him, and plundered no one.'[18]

Many other town governors and *prikaznye liudi* did plunder the communities
in their charge, using their power to quash petitions and order jailings and
beatings of community representatives in order to extort wildly excessive
feedings. This appears to have happened on such a scale as to suggest the town
governors treated feeding as a strategy of semi-feudal rent-taking – further
evidence that feudal techniques of governance had not been fully supplanted
by state bureaucratic techniques.

But there may have been a second reason for the persistence of feeding: the
possibility that communities were unwilling to demand its outright abolition
or at least a return to its charter regulation because feeding could be turned to
some community advantage under the right circumstances. Feeding deliveries
were made in the name of the entire community (as what Marcel Mauss called
'total prestations') and were conducted with some ceremony as gestures of
obsequy towards the person of the receiving official. Feeding payments not
fixed by charter but 'negotiated' between community representatives and the
receiving official, arranged at sufficiently generous rates and delivered on time
in a confident and ungrudging spirit, could therefore be represented as community gifts and used to partly disarm the official (countering his demand that

18 V. N. Tatishchev, *Istoriia rossiiskaia*, vol. VII (Moscow and Leningrad: Nauka, 1968),
   p. 296.

he be dealt with solely as an outsider present in impersonal superior official capacity, responsible only to the central government), to take his measure (gauging the limits of his greed and his readiness to bargain), to familiarise him (drawing him into a kind of honorary kinship with the community) and finally to obligate him (first in a general sense, and later, at the right moment, to specific favours reciprocating the community's hospitality). The favour sought might be permission for a delegation of petitioners to travel to Moscow, or the governor's favourable report upon the community's petition of need, but occasionally it could go as far as requesting that fines or corporal punishment be mitigated or the collection of tax arrears be postponed. In the latter instances there was the danger that feeding was suborning officials, undermining chancellery control over them. But because the centre had decided to tolerate feeding remuneration freely offered, the only means it had of counteracting this effect was to engage in its own kind of ritual gifting to the community past the suborned official. Thus the ritual of the sovereign's vouchsafe had the purpose of using gift prestation to re-establish direct personalised reciprocity of trust between sovereign and subjects and to reassert the autocracy's claim that all bounty issued from the sovereign, not from his officials, who merely distributed it on his command.

The same expenditure concerns that left the central government unwilling to suppress feeding complicated its struggle against bribery; and because tolerance of feeding permitted open collective gift prestation to officials, it was harder to ban outright other more private and particular forms of gifting that could be used to camouflage bribery. Black corruption – obvious embracery and extortion – could be prosecuted, but a large sphere of activity taking the forms of grey and white corruption (purchasing influence and services through tips, gratuities, honorances and feeding prestations) escaped regulation.

The government's commitment to struggle against bribe-taking and bribe-giving in its courts had already been proclaimed in the 1497 *Sudebnik*, although it took longer for the law to specify penalties and extend them to judges of the highest rank. The 1550 *Sudebnik* had got around to specifying punishments for litigants caught bribing judges or witnesses and for bailiffs, clerks, and secretaries falsifying bonds and court transcripts for bribes; and the 1649 *Ulozhenie* finally prescribed punishment for witnesses who perjured themselves for bribes (knouting) and for judges who convicted the innocent or exculpated the guilty for bribes (judges of duma rank were to be deprived of rank, while those below duma rank were to be knouted). By that point it could be said that Muscovite law clearly forbade bribes of embracery (*posuly*). The bribe of embracery aimed at establishing a relationship between giver and recipient which was prejudicial to state interests and to the interests of the community; it purchased influence or judgements which were denied to others and adversely affected others; and it enabled the bribe-taking official to abuse for his own gain the authority delegated to him by the sovereign, thereby defaming the reputation for impartiality of the sovereign's justice. By these tests, nearly any gift offered or accepted in the courts could potentially result in embracery if complaint of it had been made. Hence the law was most explicit in condemning bribery in judicial settings.

The law also made it a crime for officials to extort illegal payments (*vziatki* or *nalogi i nasil'stvo*). There were frequent complaints, especially in Siberia, of governors unjustly imprisoning and tormenting innocent men in order to extort ransoms, and the cash value of some of these ransoms was considerable – 20 or 30 roubles or more. If subjects were willing to press a charge that they had been victims of such extortion it was possible to convict a governor and get him deprived of rank or knouted and forced to make restitution to the victims and pay a fine to the treasury.

But there were also various common gift transactions which had the effect of bribes, purchasing some form of official influence yet falling short of obvious discriminatory embracery and deriving from no obvious extortion. The law continued to recognise petitioners' rights to offer officials earnest money and gratuities (*pochesti, pominki*) to expedite processing of their requests or express their thanks for a service performed. Earnest money and gratuities were in fact such widely accepted income for officials that clerks working in particular chancelleries which traditionally handled a heavy load of court cases or petitioners' requests were usually given lower salary entitlements on the assumption they were better positioned to supplement their pay with gifts. Naturally these clerks came to expect particular gifts for particular services rendered, that is, came to set their own schedules of fees, and such fee-charging in turn received legitimation by analogy with the *kormlenie* feeding tradition; it even came to be known as 'feeding from services' (*kormlenie ot del*).[19] Only in one context did the *Ulozhenie* equate the acceptance of gratuities with the crime of bribe-taking: when a commander discharged troops from service in exchange for gratuities.

This meant it was easy enough, even in a judicial setting, to disguise a bribe as an innocent gratuity provided both giver and recipient connived to support the illusion; and even if such a transaction left an injured party, he might find

---

19 Demidova, *Sluzhilaia biurokratiia*, pp. 141–2.

it difficult to demonstrate the bribe had purchased a judgement that would not have otherwise been forthcoming.

Muscovite law was not unique in struggling to maintain some distinction between innocent gift and corrupting bribe; this problem persisted elsewhere in early modern Europe, especially wherever officials depended at least in part upon fees and gratuities for remuneration. On the one hand, Moscow could not afford to ignore the problem of corruption, as it undermined central control and bureaucratic discipline and discredited the sovereign's claim to offer his subjects protection and redress; therefore there was some chance that community complaints against particularly egregious official corruption could bring about special investigations. On the other hand, Moscow recognised the remuneration of its officials depended partly upon feeding prestations, earnest money and gratuities, so it could not afford a policy of aggressive 'zero tolerance' prosecuting any kind of gifting on the grounds that it had the potential to encourage embracery or extortion; therefore Moscow continued to receive collective petitions complaining that its central chancelleries and governors' offices in general remained too easily bribable by 'strong people', and foreign observers (Olearius, Mayerberg, Perry) continued to consider the selling of verdicts common practice in Muscovite courts.

The community's attitude towards bribery in the governor's office may have been ambivalent. Much of the time, when bribery worked against their own interests, they would have had cause to decry it; but, as with feeding, there would also have been opportunities to exploit it. Whether bribery damaged or served community interests depended on the structure of the local market for bribe-subornable government services. If the governor and his staff set cheap enough rates for their own subornment and bribes could be tendered at low risk, the bribe economy underwent some democratisation and those of modest means and status could purchase some of the favours connected elites enjoyed as a matter of course. Where the risk of bribe-giving was greater and bribe prices were higher, only the wealthier strong men of the community were likely to be able to purchase services – which they might use to prey upon their weaker neighbours. Under some circumstances the community could counter the bribes tendered by local strong men by increasing the value of the community's own collective prestations of *kormlenie*; otherwise the community's only resort was to petition the central chancelleries for an investigation.

Travel to Moscow to present a petition in person was generally restricted to those given travel passes by the governor; some chancelleries held audiences for petitioners only at Christmas time; and after 1649 it was illegal to bypass the chancelleries by trying to petition the tsar directly. But the centre could not afford to deny its subjects altogether the right to petition against local strong men or malfeasant officials. The tsar owed his subjects some defence against official malfeasance. This was not seen as limiting his autocratic power, but rather as strengthening it, for by eliminating malfeasance by officials who defied his will he reinforced and re-legitimated his power as autocrat and ultimate source of all justice and bounty. This was another indication of the transitional character of the Muscovite state in this period: when techniques of bureaucratic centralisation failed it, it freely reverted to traditional centralisation techniques invoking the personal patriarchal authority of the tsar. Therefore the sovereign's vouchsafe invited subjects to voice complaints against their outgoing governor; governors caught quashing petitions against themselves could be prosecuted for crimes against the tsar; and petitioners charging their governor or his staff with abuses betraying the sovereign's interest (*gosudarevo delo*) could circumvent their governor and come to Moscow without his pass to petition the chancelleries in person.

21

Muscovy at war and peace

BRIAN DAVIES

At the end of the sixteenth century Muscovite territory covered about 5.4 million square kilometres and carried a population of about seven million inhabitants. During the Troubles its territory and population probably contracted significantly, for much of the north-west and west fell under Swedish or Polish occupation and Moscow's control over much of the south was contested by rebel cossack bands and the Tatars. But by 1678 Muscovite territory had tripled and its population had recovered and expanded to about 10.5 million souls.[1]

Much of this territorial expansion had occurred east of the Urals, on land that was sparsely populated and unable to mount much resistance. The real demonstration of revived Muscovite imperial power had been made on the southern steppe frontier and in the south-west and west. Through protracted war, military colonisation and more adroit diplomacy the government of the early Romanov tsars had recovered the lost provinces of Smolensk and Seversk, placed Kiev and eastern Ukraine under protectorate and moved the realm's southern frontier from the forest-steppe zone into the depths of the steppe. In the process two traditional enemies of Muscovite imperial power, the Polish-Lithuanian Commonwealth and the Crimean khanate, found their own military and diplomatic power considerably reduced. Two more powerful challengers, Sweden and the Ottoman Empire, had also been fought, but for relatively brief periods and with mixed results (failure to wrest control of the Livonian coast, but success at deterring Ottoman attack on left-bank Ukraine). Recognition that Muscovy was becoming a great power in northern and eastern Europe was apparent in Swedish and Ottoman efforts in the 1620s–1630s to enlist her in coalition against the Commonwealth and German Empire and in Polish and Austrian efforts in the 1680s to bring her into the Holy League.

---

1 Ia. E. Vodarskii, *Naselenie Rossii za 400 let* (Moscow: Prosveshchenie, 1973), pp. 27–8: Richard Hellie, *Slavery in Russia, 1450–1725* (Chicago: University of Chicago Press, 1982), pp. 1–2.

Muscovy's recovery from the humiliating foreign occupations of the Troubles and her emergence as a great power owed a great deal to her ability to learn the art of patience: her greatest gains were won through readiness to wait until the opportune geopolitical moment to exploit her rivals' weaknesses and readiness to devote long-term attention to working out ways to overcome friction in the mobilisation and use of military power.

Recovery and revanche, 1613–34

The first task facing the government of Tsar Michael was to assure its survival. The Swedes still occupied Novgorod and King Gustav II Adolf was bent on occupying north-west Muscovy from Narva down to Pskov, holding Karelia, conquering the White Sea coast as far as Archangel, and placing his brother Karl Filip on the Moscow throne. Cossack insurgencies remained a threat: although Zarutskii's cossack army was destroyed on the lower Volga in 1614, a new cossack army under Balovnia had just appeared in Pomor'e. The Polish-Lithuanian Commonwealth still presented a mortal danger; Sigismund III held to his plan of driving on Moscow to place his son Władysław on the throne, and a Polish army under Chodkiewicz and Władysław stood ready for this purpose at Smolensk. Lisowski's force of cossacks and Polish and foreign mercenary freebooters engaged Muscovite armies at Orel and Kaluga.

Fortunately Gustav Adolf's long siege of Pskov had failed by early 1616 and with the encouragement of Dutch and English diplomats he began to shift his attention to a project for war against the Commonwealth that would assist the Protestant cause of weakening Habsburg power in Central Europe. Peace talks mediated by John Merrick finally produced a Russo-Swedish peace treaty at Stolbovo in February 1617. By its terms Gustav Adolf abandoned Novgorod and restored it and Staraia Rusa, Porkhov and Sumersk canton to the tsar; in return the tsar ceded him Korela, Kopor'e, Oreshek, Iam and Ivangorod, thereby surrendering direct trade access to the Baltic. Sweden now controlled the Baltic coast from Livonia to Finland.[2]

In the early autumn of 1618 the Poles made their assault upon Moscow. The army of Chodkiewicz and Władysław advanced upon Moscow from Mozhaisk while a second army of Ukrainian cossacks under Sahaidachnyi moved up from the south. They were beaten back from the gates of Moscow in September, but fears that they would attack again brought Tsar Michael's government

---

2 G. A. Sanin et al. (eds.), *Istoriia vneshnei politiki Rossii: Konets XV–XVII vek* (Moscow: Mezhdunarodnye otnosheniia, 1999), pp. 218–19.

to sue for truce. In December 1618 a fourteen-year armistice was signed at Deulino. This treaty's terms were even harsher for Muscovy: the western Rus' territories of Smolensk, Chernigov and most of Seversk – holding about thirty towns in all – were ceded to the Commonwealth, bringing its frontier as far east as Viaz'ma, Rzhev and Kaluga (Russia's western borders in 1618 are shown in Map 21.1). Władysław also maintained his claim to the Muscovite throne.[3]

The Stolbovo and Deulino treaties at least bought Muscovy time for reconstruction and rearmament. Muscovy's reconstruction occurred in two stages. In the first stage (1613–18) the boyar duma worked with the Assembly of the Land to restore basic order by re-establishing chancellery control over the town governors, appointing town governors to districts which had not had them before, suppressing banditry in the provinces, co-opting cossack bands, pressuring communities to resubmit to taxation and militia levies and imposing extraordinary taxes to raise revenue for further reconstruction. The second phase (1619–30) proceeded under the leadership of the young tsar's powerful father Patriarch Filaret (F. N. Romanov), newly returned from nine years' captivity in Poland; it devoted further effort to these tasks while also attempting to repair and improve resource mobilisation for war. Filaret's administration gave priority to repopulating state lands and *posad* communes with taxpayers, updating cadastres and restoring accounting for arrears and future regular taxes, issuing commercial privileges to European merchants and restoring chancellery control over the distribution of service lands and service salaries. In both stages there were also unsuccessful attempts to secure large loans from England, the Netherlands, Denmark and Persia in exchange for free transit trade rights.

Filaret was strongly committed to a revanchist campaign to recover the western Rus' territories that had been lost to the Commonwealth during the Troubles. Regaining control of Smolensk was especially important to him, for its massive fortress commanded the main road from the frontier to Moscow. The first few years of his government produced no opportunity to undertake this, however; reconstruction had to take priority, there was some opposition to a war of revanche in the Ambassadors' Chancellery, and Filaret was as yet unable to get assurance that Sweden and the Ottoman Empire would join Muscovy in coalition against the Commonwealth. After their defeat at Chocim (1621) the Ottomans had negotiated a peace with the Poles and were making some effort to restrain the Crimean khan from raiding Commonwealth

---

3 Ibid., p. 220.

FINLAND

Lake
Onega

Baltic
Sea

Gulf of
Finland

Korela

Lake
Ladoga

Beloozero

LIVONIA

Ivangorod

Lake
Chud'

Novgorod

Pskov

Tver'

Polotsk

Rzhev

Moscow

Smolensk

Viaz'ma

POLAND-
LITHUANIA

Kaluga

Novgorod
Severskii

Chernigov

Kiev

Territory ceded to
Sweden, 1617

Territory ceded to
Poland–Lithuania, 1618

0   100   200   300   400 km

Map 21.1. Russia's western borders, 1618

territory; Gustav Adolf was interested in alliance with Muscovy, but on terms of commercial concessions too high for Moscow to pay.

But by the end of the decade opportunity had finally presented itself. Gustav Adolf's war against the Poles had ended in an armistice, the Dutch and French having pressed him to sign a peace at Altmark (1629) so he would carry his war into northern Germany instead. But to be free to concentrate his forces in Germany Gustav Adolf now needed a guarantee that the Poles would not break their armistice and drive his garrisons out of Livonia and Ducal Prussia. A Muscovite invasion of eastern Lithuania to reconquer Smolensk could provide the diversion needed to prevent this.

In 1630 Monier, Gustav's ambassador to Moscow, negotiated a commercial agreement of great potential benefit to the Swedish campaign in Germany: Sweden would be given the right to purchase duty-free 50,000 quarters of Muscovite rye annually, for resale at Amsterdam; given that war had disrupted the traditional pattern of the Baltic grain trade, this would yield Sweden a considerable windfall; and in return Sweden would export arms to Muscovy for its invasion of the Commonwealth. The Monier Agreement paved the way for an active Swedish–Muscovite alliance. By 1632 this alliance had expanded into a tentative broader coalition with the Ottomans and Crimean Tatars. Filaret's campaign to recover Smolensk thereby became part of a more ambitious coalition war conducted simultaneously on the German, Hungarian and southern and eastern Commonwealth fronts.[4]

In 1630 the Muscovite government began issuing large cash bounties to hire mercenary officers in Sweden, the Netherlands and Scotland to train a new foreign formation force (*inozemskii stroi*) in the new tactics used so effectively by the armies of the United Provinces and Sweden. Six regiments of infantry (*soldaty*), a regiment of heavy cavalry pistoleers (*reitary*), and a regiment of dragoons (*draguny*) were formed from Muscovite peasant militiamen, cossacks, novitiate middle service class cavalrymen and free volunteers from various social categories. These regiments would comprise about half the force operating in the Smolensk theatre in 1632–4. Unlike the traditional formation troops the new regiments were outfitted and salaried at treasury expense – at very considerable expense, in fact, the cost of maintaining just 6,610 *soldaty* in 1633 exceeding 129,000 roubles.[5] Such a heavy investment in units of European type

4 B. F. Porshnev, *Muscovy and Sweden in the Thirty Years War, 1630–1635*, ed. Paul Dukes and trans. Brian Pearce (Cambridge: Cambridge University Press, 1995), pp. 28–35.

5 A. V. Chernov, *Vooruzhennye sily Russkogo gosudarstva* (Moscow: Ministerstvo oborony SSSR, 1954), pp. 114–15, 157–8; Richard Hellie, *Enserfment and Military Change in Muscovy* (Chicago: University of Chicago Press, 1971), pp. 168–72.

was necessary, though, because the recent Polish–Swedish war had given the Commonwealth reason to begin expanding and modernising its own foreign formation (*cudzoziemski autorament*).

The death of Sigismund III in April 1632 was followed by an interregnum which Filaret thought would last at least several months and provide a window of opportunity for war to recover Smolensk. Filaret therefore launched an invasion in August 1632, sending M. B. Shein into Lithuania with 29,000 men. By October Shein had managed to capture over twenty towns and place Smolensk, his main objective, under siege. But then the Russian offensive stalled. Muddy roads delayed the arrival of Shein's heavy artillery. Władysław IV finally took the throne in February 1633 and immediately began assembling an army of 23,000 men to relieve Smolensk. Because Shein's troops had neglected their lines of circumvallation Władysław's army was able to surround them and place the besiegers under siege in August 1633. In January 1634 Shein sued for armistice in order to evacuate what was left of his army. As Moscow had not authorised this, and because a scapegoat was needed for the collapse of the campaign, the boyar duma charged Shein with treason and had him beheaded.[6]

Continuing the war against the Commonwealth was unthinkable now. The war's chief architect, Patriarch Filaret, had died in October 1633; Gustav Adolf had fallen at Lutzen in November 1632 and Swedish forces in Pomerania were now left more vulnerable to a Polish attack; help from the Ottomans could no longer be expected, for internal revolts and war with Persia had prevented the sultan from carrying out the invasion of Poland scheduled for spring 1634. Above all Muscovy again faced a major threat from the Crimean khanate – not so much from Khan Janibek Girey as from certain Crimean Tatar beys and mirzas hungry for plunder opportunities after several years of harvest failure, heavy inflation, and civil war in Crimea. In the spring and summer of 1632 some 20,000 Tatars ravaged southern Muscovy. In 1633 they came in even greater strength – over 30,000 strong – and this time circumvented the fortifications of the Abatis Line and crossed the Oka into central Muscovy, taking thousands of captives in Serpukhov, Kolomna, Kashira and Riazan' districts. This invasion may have contributed to Shein's defeat at Smolensk by provoking mass desertion by those of his troops whose home districts had come under Tatar attack.

The Ambassadors' Chancellery and boyar duma had already decided to seek armistice in November 1633. But Shein's capitulation at Smolensk made

---

6 For accounts of the Smolensk war see E. D. Stashevskii, *Smolenskaia voina 1632–1634. Organizatsiia i sostoianie moskovskoi armii* (Kiev, 1919), and William C. Fuller, Jr., *Strategy and Power in Russia, 1600–1914* (New York: Free Press, 1992), pp. 7–14.

it impossible for them to demand that the Poles should evacuate Smolensk and Dorogobuzh as the price of peace. The armistice signed at Polianovka on 4 June 1634 therefore left the Smolensk, Chernigov and Seversk lands in Polish hands. Filaret's project of recovering the western Rus' territories had failed. For Muscovy there was some partial compensation in Władysław IV's agreement to abandon his claims to the Moscow throne, but it was no longer realistic for Władysław to pursue these claims through war.

The Crimean khanate and the Don cossack host

The peace established by the Polianovka Treaty was undisturbed for two decades. Resumption of war between the Commonwealth and Muscovy was deterred by both sides' recognition that their simultaneously reformed military establishments had put them at rough parity; and after 1634 Władysław IV was preoccupied with Sweden, cossack unrest in Ukraine, pay arrears in his army and his magnates' fears of royal military absolutism.

After the Polianovka Treaty Muscovy could no longer expect active support from Sweden. The cheap Russian grain exports Gustav Adolf had counted on to help subsidise Swedish operations had been cut back; Władysław IV was freer to concentrate his forces against Swedish garrisons on the Baltic coast; and meanwhile most of Sweden's allies against the German Empire were suing for peace with Ferdinand II. Oxenstierna therefore had begun withdrawing Swedish forces from Germany in anticipation of a Polish or Danish attack somewhere on the Baltic front. Queen Christina's other regents were even more alarmed and made several important concessions, including Swedish evacuation of Prussia, in order to obtain a truce with the Commonwealth (the Treaty of Stuhmsdorf, 1635).

This shift in the balance of power in the Baltic made it necessary for Moscow to disentangle itself from northern European affairs and maintain cautious neutrality vis-à-vis both Sweden and the Commonwealth. For the most part it kept to this course, departing from it only briefly, in 1643, when Denmark and the Commonwealth tried to tempt Muscovy into coalition against Sweden by holding out the possibility of a marriage between Tsar Michael's daughter Irina and the Danish crown prince Waldemar. Entering such a coalition would have been unwise, for Swedish military power had revived by that point, strengthened by alliance with France and generous French subsidies. The tsar and his councillors fortunately realised this just in time, when a Swedish army under Torstensson invaded and overwhelmed Denmark on the eve of Waldemar's arrival in Moscow. The tsar immediately abandoned the marriage project and even placed Waldemar under house arrest to reassure the Swedes he would no longer listen to Danish blandishments.

As there were no opportunities for territorial expansion or influence on the Baltic and western Rus' fronts, Muscovite diplomatic and military activity in 1635–54 focused almost entirely on defending the southern frontier against the threat from the Crimean khanate.

It was logical and necessary to give the Crimean problem priority because the khanate was now more dangerous than ever, its behaviour more unpredictable and more resistant to traditional means of containment. The Crimean Tatar invasions of southern and central Muscovy in 1632–3 showed that the khan was losing control of his beys and Nogai confederates, that they were willing to defy him and launch attacks on Muscovite border towns with nearly as many troops as the khan could mobilise on his own authority. Furthermore, less could now be expected from Moscow's traditional diplomatic approach to deterring Crimean aggression – appealing to the Ottoman sultan to rein in the khan – for the Crimean nobility was increasingly anti-Ottoman and even separatist in spirit and the khans under greater pressure to play to this spirit in order to keep themselves in power.[7]

Meanwhile Muscovy had lost much of its leverage over its own vassal polities on the Kipchak steppe. It could not count on the fealty of the Great Nogai beys as a counterweight to the khanate, for the Great Nogai Horde was in disintegration and many of its elements driven west across the Volga by the invading Kalmyks and forced into alliance with the Crimean Tatars and Lesser Nogais. The Don cossack host remained implacably hostile to the khanate and the Porte, but also ready to defy Moscow whenever their interests diverged; it had baulked when called upon to support an expedition out of Astrakhan' to punish the Lesser Nogais in 1633, and it repeatedly ignored Moscow's urgings to cease making naval raids on Crimean and Ottoman territory. Don cossack raiding activity thereby risked provoking retaliation not only by the Crimean Tatars but by the Turks. But there was little Moscow could do to prevent it; reducing the semi-annual cash and stores subsidy (Don shipment, *Donskoi otpusk*) sent down the Don just had the effect of giving the host more reason to turn to raiding to make up its lost revenue. In fact throughout this period the independent political-military course taken by the host would be nearly as much a problem for Moscow as the hostility of the Crimean khanate.

---

7 Mykhailo Hrushevsky, *History of Ukraine-Rus'*. Vol. VIII: *The Cossack Age, 1626–1650* (Edmonton: Canadian Institute of Ukrainian Studies, 2002), pp. 179–80; A. A. Novosel'skii, *Bor'ba Moskovskogo gosudarstva s tatarami v pervoi polovine XVII veka* (Moscow: AN SSSR, 1948), pp. 245–8.

As diplomacy could accomplish little, security on the southern frontier came to depend all the more on military measures: resuming military colonisation in the forest-steppe and steppe, on a vastly expanded scale and using new, more cost-effective manpower categories; strengthening and expanding defence lines; experimenting with new military formations and tactics, and reorganising command-and-control; and giving greater attention to small-scale offensive operations, sending small forces down the Don to put more pressure on the Crimean Tatars while tightening Moscow's control over the Don cossack host.

During the Smolensk war the total strength of the Borderland and Riazan' arrays had been reduced to about 5,000 men. It was now substantially increased, to 12,000 men by 1635 and 17,000 men by 1636. This made it easier for the corps of the Borderland and Riazan' arrays to reinforce each other and for the Great Corps (*Bol'shoi polk*) finally to begin providing a forward defence, to march south from Tula to the relief of the towns south of the Abatis Line. The Military Chancellery also undertook a general inspection of the Abatis Line, and in 1638–9 it put 20,000 men to work rebuilding some 600 kilometres of the line. The forces manning the repaired Abatis Line now included foreign formation infantry and dragoons – some from regiments that had served in the Smolensk campaign, others newly enlisted – and although their deployment was only seasonal, this at least set the precedent for using foreign formation units on the southern frontier against the Tatar enemy.[8]

Military colonisation beyond the Abatis Line was resumed in order to establish an outer perimeter far to the south of the Oka. Several new garrison towns were built in 1635–7 (Chernavsk, Kozlov, Verkhnii Lomov, Nizhnii Lomov, Tambov, Userdsk, Iablonov, Efremov), mostly in the south-east, to secure the territory threatened from the Nogai Road. An earthen steppe wall built from Kozlov to the Chelnova River proved especially effective in blocking Tatar raids up the Nogai Road. By early 1637 this had convinced the tsar and duma to authorise 111,000 roubles to build similar new garrison towns and steppe wall segments to the south-west, to stop Tatar movement up the Muravskii, Iziumskii and Kal'miusskii trails. These new towns and steppe wall segments were built in such proximity that it was an easy matter to link them with the older steppe town of Belgorod to form a single defence line network, the central length of the future Belgorod Line.[9]

8 A. I. Iakovlev, *Zasechnaia cherta Moskovskogo gosudarstva v XVII veke* (Moscow: Tipografiia G. Lissnera i D. Sobko, 1916), pp. 45–6, 57, 62–3.
9 V. P. Zagorovskii, *Belgorodskaia cherta* (Voronezh: Voronezhskii gosudarstvennyi universitet, 1969), pp. 93–4.

The Military Chancellery wanted to settle these new garrison towns as rapidly and cheaply as possible, so it took up new methods and formats of military colonisation. It mobilised thousands of volunteers by relaxing standards of social eligibility for enlistment in military service, even to the point of permitting the enlistment of ruined former servicemen who had been forced by poverty or calamity to take up residence under lords as peasant tenants; and it altered standards and procedures in court hearings for the remand of fugitive peasants, to make it harder for lords to recover peasant tenants who had fled south to enrol illegally in the new garrison towns. Revolt in Commonwealth Ukraine was driving thousands of Ukrainian refugees into southern Muscovy; many of them were settled in special new service colonies in the south-west, on the steppes below Belgorod and Valuiki, in what would come to be called Sloboda Ukraine, while others were distributed among the new garrison towns of the Belgorod Line, even as far east as Kozlov. Their cossack experience and their skills at milling, distilling and mouldboard plough farming would contribute significantly to the success of the Muscovite drive to colonise the southern steppe. And in a decision very consequential for the subsequent social history of southern Muscovy, the Military Chancellery chose not to reproduce in the new southern frontier districts the kind of middle service class – *deti boiarskie* with service lands of over 200 quarters per field and peasant tenants – traditionally encountered in central and northern Muscovy. Instead it reconfigured the middle service class, adapting it to southern frontier economic and service conditions, by enrolling *deti boiarskie* who were also *odnodvortsy* and *siabry* – yeomen with much smaller service land entitlement rates and land allotments, lacking peasant tenant labour and holding their service lands as repartitionable allotments within collective block grants administered by their village communes.

These measures strengthening southern frontier defences helped Muscovy weather the crisis that broke out in spring 1637 when the Don cossacks murdered the Ottoman diplomat Foma Cantacuzene and besieged and captured the Ottoman fortress of Azov. Azov had been left suddenly vulnerable to a Don cossack attack because Khan Inaet Girey's forces were mostly off in Bucak fighting Khantimur and Sultan Murad IV was preoccupied with wars in Persia and Hungary. The Don host could justify seizing Azov because its garrison had provided support for Tatar raids upon Don cossack settlements on the lower Don, and Ataman Ivan Katorzhnyi may also have calculated that possessing Azov would allow him to bargain for more generous treatment from the tsar and larger Don shipment subsidies. But Moscow had no reason to authorise the seizure of Azov. While Azov's Ottoman garrison was too small to pose a threat to the towns of southern Muscovy, its presence had been enough to serve as a tripwire providing the sultan with cause, if he chose to make use of it, to retaliate directly against Don cossack or Muscovite aggression. If the sultan should get the impression that Moscow was in any way complicit in the attack on Azov it would damage Muscovite trade at Azov and Kaffa and might even drag Muscovy into war with the Porte.

As long as the Don cossacks occupied Azov (1637–42) Moscow therefore followed the policy of strengthening its southern frontier defence while simultaneously using diplomacy to absolve the tsar of any blame for the crisis. Tsar Michael sent some grain and munitions to the host but refused their request to send troops and place Azov under his protection. An Assembly of the Land convened in 1642 was all for going to war, but Tsar Michael ignored it and resumed paying tribute to the new Crimean khan even while Muscovite envoys sent to Crimea were being abused. Missions were sent to Sultan Murad IV and, after his death in 1640, to Sultan Ibrahim, to give reassurance that the murder of Cantacuzene and seizure of Azov had been the work of brigands acting 'for reasons unknown . . . without our instruction'.[10] In June–September 1641 a large Ottoman army commanded by the pasha of Silistria besieged the cossacks in Azov; although it failed to retake Azov, it clearly demonstrated how important recovery of Azov was to Sultan Ibrahim, so when Ibrahim issued a new ultimatum to Moscow in March 1642 Tsar Michael complied and ordered the Don cossacks to evacuate Azov. Ottoman forces reoccupied Azov in September 1642 and reinforced its garrison.

War with the Ottoman Empire had been avoided. The new Turkish garrison at Azov carried out some retaliatory raids on Don cossack settlements but left the southern Muscovite border towns alone. There had been Crimean Tatar raids into southern Muscovy in 1637 and 1641–3, but they had been undertaken by beys and princes acting on their own, driven by famine and livestock epidemics in Crimea (Inaet Girey's successors Begadyr Girey, r. 1637–41, and Mehmed Girey, r. 1641–4, were no more able to curb the Crimean nobility).

Muscovite–Ottoman relations had suffered serious damage, however. The Don cossacks had rebuilt their forts and settlements near Azov and were again attacking Turkish troops; Sultan Ibrahim demanded the tsar remove the host from the lower Don, a request beyond the tsar's power to fulfil. The new Crimean khan Islam Girey III (r. 1644–54) decided the best way to tame the Crimean nobility was to realign with the Ottoman sultan and put himself

10 S. I. Riabov, *Voisko Donskoe i rossiiskoe samoderzhavie* (Volgograd: Peremena, 1993), p. 24.

at the head of major invasions against the Commonwealth and Muscovy. Therefore 20,000 Tatars invaded the Commonwealth and another 20,000 swept across southern Muscovy in the summer of 1644, carrying off about 10,000 prisoners. Another 6,000 Muscovite captives were taken the following year. Sultan Ibrahim gave his approval for these operations.[11] By unleashing Islam Girey III and threatening direct Ottoman military retaliation Ibrahim was able to stop the Polish–Muscovite rapprochement. In 1646 Władysław IV renewed peace with the Porte and resumed tribute gifts to the khan.

Moscow therefore had to increase investment in its southern frontier defence system. The Tatar incursions of 1644–5 had taken advantage of particular weaknesses in that system: the absence of unified command in the corps of the southern field army, and the over-centralisation of command initiative in the Military Chancellery; the inability of the field army (still stationed along the Abatis Line) to offer a forward defence for the districts to its south; large gaps in the Belgorod Line, especially between Voronezh and Kozlov and between the Tikhaia Sosna and Oskol' rivers; and Moscow's inability to stop Don cossack raids further provoking the Tatars and Turks.

The new government of Tsar Aleksei Mikhailovich addressed each of these weaknesses in 1646–54. Several more garrison towns were built and linked up with the Belgorod Line. Most of the gaps in the line were filled by 1654; by 1658 the line extended all along the southern edge of the forest steppe zone, from Akhtyrka on the Vorskla River to Chelnavsk about 800 kilometres to the east, and a second defence line some 500 kilometres long extended from Chelnavsk to the Volga. Twenty-five garrison towns stood on or just behind the Belgorod Line; thousands of *odnodvortsy deti boiarskie*, service cossacks and musketeers had been settled on ploughlands in these new garrison districts.

In 1646 the corps previously deployed far to the north in the Borderland and Riazan' arrays were restationed along the new perimeter formed by the Belgorod Line. The Great Corps, Vanguard and Rear Guard now stood at Livny, Kursk and Elets each spring and shifted in June to Belgorod, Karpov and Iablonov. Garrison contingents and small field units south of the Abatis Line no longer had to march north to rendezvous with the corps but could move south to join them on the Belgorod Line.

This in turn led to new command-and-control practices along the Belgorod Line. Because southern garrison forces could now play a larger role in reinforcing corps operations, it became necessary for the corps commander at Belgorod to take up broader year-round operational and logistics authority

11 Hrushevsky, *History of Ukraine-Rus'*, vol. VIII, pp. 264–8.

over all the troops residing in the Belgorod Array territory, those in the garrisons as well as the Belgorod corps. The town governors of the southern garrison towns were thereby subordinated in military affairs, and gradually in broader administrative affairs, to the commander at Belgorod, to whom the Military Chancellery could now devolve resource logistic and monitoring functions that had previously been centralised at Moscow. By 1653 one can speak of a large Belgorod Line regional military administration (*Belgorodskii razriad*) operating out of the corps commander's headquarters at Belgorod or Kursk. During the Thirteen Years War this new principle of regional military administration would take on even greater importance: similar territorial *razriady* would be formed on the north-western front at Novgorod and Smolensk and the westernmost districts of the Belgorod *razriad* spun off into a separate Sevsk *razriad*.

After the Smolensk war most but not all of the expensive foreign formation regiments had been disbanded. A few thousand foreign formation *soldaty* and dragoons had manned the Abatis Line in 1638, 1639 and 1642, but it had not been considered cost-effective to deploy them every year. But in 1646 the government decided to make foreign formation units an important permanent element in the southern frontier defence system. A number of officers were hired abroad, especially in the Netherlands; a *kriegsbuch* on the exercise of musket and pike was translated into Russian, to help in training Muscovite infantry; a new census was conducted to levy troops by household rather than from inhabited *chetvert'*; and Tsar Alexis endorsed the Military Chancellery's recommendation that the southern garrisons cease relying on irregularly levied peasant militia to help defend the Belgorod Line and instead place entire peasant communities in standing service as 'settled' dragoons and infantry, drilled in their villages year-round under foreign officers. In Komaritskaia canton in 1646 5,125 state peasants were taken into three dragoon regiments; the next year several private *votchina* villages along the Voronezh River west of Kozlov were likewise put in dragoon service.[12]

In 1648 a new cossack revolt in Ukraine, led by Bohdan Khmel'nyts'kyi and in alliance with the Crimean Tatars, dealt devastating defeats to Polish armies at Zhevty Vody and Korsun'. The massacre of another Polish army at Batih in May 1652 placed Khmel'nyts'kyi in control of most of Ukraine as far west as Kamienets in Podol'ia and made the prospect of Muscovite alliance with rebel Ukraine more attractive and war with the Commonwealth

---

12 Brian Davies, 'Village Into Garrison: The Militarized Peasant Communities of Southern Muscovy', *RR* 51 (1992): 481–501.

in Ukraine and Belarus' more likely. The Military Chancellery therefore began organising foreign formation units for the southern field army, not just for local defence. Four regiments (8,000 men) of *soldaty* were formed at Iablonov, in the Belgorod *razriad*, filled largely from conscripts levied from the non-taxpaying populations of eighteen southern districts. The next year some *soldat* regiments were also formed near Smolensk on the north-western front.[13]

Moscow also took steps to tighten its control over the Don cossack host. Larger Don shipment subsidies were dispatched in 1644, 1646 and 1647, but there were also attempts in 1646 and 1648 to 'reinforce' the host with new Muscovite manpower in such a way as to bind it to Moscow-directed operations. Larger expeditions, resupplied by river flotillas built on the Voronezh and upper Don, were sent down in 1659–62; although they still held back from assaulting Azov, they did join the Don cossacks in land and sea raids to harass Ottoman forces building new fortresses on the Mertvyi Donets and Kalancha rivers. From 1662 to 1671 Muscovite forces on the lower Don refrained from operations against the Turks and devoted their attention to distributing the Don shipments and keeping the host under surveillance.

All of these Don expeditions suffered heavy losses to hunger and desertion, and they did not accomplish much against the Tatars and Turks. But they did give the Muscovite army valuable experience in land–sea operations and did begin to restrict the Don cossack host's freedom of initiative. By the late 1660s the host was in transformation. Muscovite military colonisation of the Belgorod Line had set off a cascade migration of thousands of deserters and fugitive peasants southward into the Don host. The resources provided by the Don agricultural economy and Don shipments were not enough to support them. Meanwhile Moscow's diplomacy to get the sultan and the khan to stop attacks in Ukraine on behalf of Hetman Doroshenko (see below) meant that Moscow could no longer sanction Don cossack raids on the khanate or on Ottoman coastal towns. Denied plunder opportunities on the Black Sea, part of the host rebelled and followed Stepan Razin on a campaign of piracy on the Caspian and then on a revolt against Ataman Kornilo Iakovlev and Muscovite garrisons on the lower Volga. Razin's defeat in 1671 left the host further servilised to Moscow.[14]

---

13 Hellie, *Enserfment*, p. 193.
14 On the Don expeditions, see V. P. Zagorovskii, 'Sudostroenie na Donu i ispol'zovanie Rossieiu parusnogo-grebnogo flota v bor'be protiv Krymskogo khanstva i Turtsii', Kandidatskaia dissertatsiia, Voronezhskii Gosudarstvennyi Universitet, 1961. On the Razin Rebellion, see E. V. Chistiakova and V. M. Solov'ev, *Stepan Razin i ego soratniki* (Moscow: Mysl', 1988), and Michael Khodarkovsky, 'The Stepan Razin Uprising: Was it a "Peasant War"?', *JGO* 42 (1994): 1–19.

The Thirteen Years War, 1654–67

As early as 1649 Bohdan Khmel'nyts'kyi had tried to convince Moscow to assist his revolt against the Commonwealth and put Ukraine under the tsar's protection. At that time Moscow had not been interested; taking responsibility for Ukraine as a client or vassal polity had been a major objective of Muscovite grand strategy, and joining the Ukrainians in war upon the Commonwealth also meant going to war against the Crimean Tatars, who had left their alliance with Khmel'nyts'kyi. By late 1652, however, the tsar's government was ready to ally with Khmel'nyts'kyi. Khmel'nyts'kyi's great victory at Batih meant that Muscovite intervention in Ukraine was likely to meet a greatly reduced Polish military threat, and there was still hope that Ukrainian and Muscovite diplomacy could convince the Crimean khan to rejoin the alliance against the Poles. But the primary reason Tsar Alexis accepted Khmel'nyts'kyi's alliance proposal in June 1653 and formalised it in the Pereiaslav (Pereiaslavl') Treaty in January 1654 had much less to do with Ukraine than with Muscovite designs upon Lithuanian Belarus'. The Commonwealth's war against Khmel'nyts'kyi's cossacks had left very few troops defending Lithuania and the west Rus' territories – Smolensk, Seversk, Chernigov – wrested from Muscovy during the Troubles. Reconquering these territories promised to be considerably easier than in 1632–4, particularly now that Khmel'nyts'kyi promised to send thousands of cossack troops north to assist such a campaign. Furthermore, Moscow felt that the window of opportunity to accomplish this was closing, for Lithuanian Grand Hetman Janusz Radziwiłł, aware of Lithuania's vulnerability to Muscovite invasion, was trying to get the hospodar of Moldavia to mediate a peace treaty between the Commonwealth and Khmel'nyts'kyi's hetmanate.

There was therefore an impulsive element in Moscow's decision to intervene in Ukraine. Muscovite military preparations for the war were thorough: the invasion of Lithuania was soundly planned, and it was decided that foreign formation units would comprise a larger part of the field armies on the Lithuanian and Ukrainian fronts, towards which end 40,000 muskets were bought from the Dutch and Swedes and more enlistees and conscripts were taken into the *soldat* regiments of the Belgorod *razriad*.[15] But the full strategic consequences of placing Ukraine under Muscovite protection were not yet apparent. Bohdan Khmel'nyts'kyi had created a de facto independent hetmanate across most of Ukraine in six years of war; it was Khmel'nyts'kyi's military leadership and diplomatic cunning which held this hetmanate together;

---

15 A. N. Mal'tsev, *Rossiia i Belorussiia v seredine XVII veka* (Moscow: MGU, 1974), p. 23.

and it was Khmel'nyts'kyi's vision of an autonomous Ukraine in loose confederation and military alliance with Muscovy that his colonels understood to be the objective of the Pereiaslav Treaty. But once Khmel'nyts'kyi passed from the scene the hetmanate would be riven by conflicts between the cossack elite and rank-and-file, between cossacks and townsmen and peasants and between the cossack colonels and the Muscovite commanders garrisoning the larger Ukrainian towns. The task of protecting Ukraine would inevitably give Moscow reason to increase the number of its garrisons, make greater demands upon Ukrainian revenue sources to provision them and thereby encroach upon Ukrainian liberties. Furthermore, because Khmel'nyts'kyi had been pursuing an imaginative but complicated diplomacy since 1648 before turning to Moscow for protection, the Crimean Tatars, Moldavians, Wallachians, Transylvanians, Ottomans and Swedes had come to have stakes in what happened to Ukraine. Muscovite protectorate over Ukraine therefore had serious repercussions for Muscovy's relations with these nations, and Ukrainian cossacks growing disillusioned with Muscovite protectorate would have alternative alliance models (Ottoman–Tatar protectorate, reincorporation in the Polish-Lithuanian Commonwealth, and later, Swedish protectorate) to which to turn.

On 15 May 1654 Muscovite armies invaded Lithuanian Belarus' and entered eastern Ukraine. The primary objective in this opening campaign was clearly the recapture of Smolensk and the west Rus' territories annexed to the grand duchy of Lithuania. Three large army groups entered Lithuanian territory: a main army of 40,000 men under the command of the tsar himself, moving from Viaz'ma towards Smolensk; a second army of 15,000 under V. P. Sheremetev, advancing from Velikie Luki against Polotsk and Vitebsk; and another army of 15,000 under A. N. Trubetskoi, moving from Briansk towards Minsk. A smaller force under L. Saltykov also advanced from Pskov, and Khmel'nyts'kyi sent some 20,000 Ukrainian cossacks under Colonel Zolotarenko to invade Belarus' from the south. Muscovite troop deployments in Ukraine were considerably smaller: 4,000 troops under A. V. Buturlin were sent to reinforce Zolotarenko, and 2,500 troops went to garrison Kiev. Another 7,000 Muscovite troops held the Belgorod Line against Tatar attack.[16]

The invasion of Belarus' and Lithuania was strikingly successful. The Muscovites had overwhelming numerical superiority (Lithuanian Grand Hetman Janusz Radziwiłł, charged with the task of throwing them back, had no more than 6,000–7,000 effectives); their operation had been planned long in advance;

16 Ibid., pp. 26–37.

and the tsar's presence with the army provided better command-and-control than if supreme command had remained back at Moscow. In June the Muscovites took Belaia, Dorogobuzh and Roslavl'; by late August they had captured Mstislavl', Orsha, Mogilev and the capital at Vilnius; Smolensk fell to them in September, and Vitebsk in November.

In the summer of 1655 Sweden's King Karl X Gustav (r. 1654–60) began his own invasion of the Commonwealth in order to exploit the Muscovites' successes in Lithuania while pre-empting their advance towards his own intended sphere of influence in the region. As most Polish and Lithuanian troops were already engaged against the Muscovites the invading Swedes were able to make remarkable progress in just a few months – and their sudden gains threatened to usurp everything the Muscovites had won to that point. On 13 June Swedish troops landed in Riga and seized Dunaburg, then under siege by the Muscovites; on 17 August, a week after Muscovite troops had taken Vilnius, Lithuanian Grand Hetman Janusz Radziwiłł signed the Treaty of Niejdany, recognising Karl Gustav as grand duke over all of Lithuania; and on 8 September the Swedes entered Warsaw, forcing Jan Kazimierz to flee into exile in Silesia.

Karl Gustav had no desire to see the Muscovites seize Riga or any other part of the Baltic coast, but he had been prepared to accept Muscovite control over the southern Lithuanian hinterland if this kept his peace with Muscovy while he finished off the Poles.[17] But Moscow was not interested in such a compromise, for it had revised its original war aims: A. L. Ordin-Nashchokin, the rising star of Muscovite diplomacy, now considered it paramount that Muscovy secure its dominion over occupied Lithuania and win access to the Baltic, and he therefore urged the tsar to negotiate a peace with Jan Kazimierz and an alliance with him against the Swedes. This was against the advice of Khmel'nyts'kyi, who was seeking to form a Swedish–Ukrainian alliance which would finish off the Commonwealth and guarantee the liberation of right-bank Ukraine. In fact Ordin-Nashchokin so felt the need for haste that Muscovy declared war upon Sweden in May 1656 while peace talks with the Poles at Vilnius were still in their preliminary stage. A treaty with the Commonwealth was finally signed in November, but it was only for an armistice, not a permanent peace and true alliance, for the Muscovite envoys at Vilnius had not been satisfied with Jan Kazimierz's offer to cede Smolensk and Seversk and had held out for even larger concessions: the cession of Lithuania, or the 'election' of Tsar Alexis as Poland's king upon the death of Jan Kazimierz.

17 L. V. Zaborovskii, *Rossiia, Rech' Pospolitaia, i Shvetsiia v seredine XVII v.* (Moscow: Nauka, 1981), pp. 118, 121.

Muscovy's war with Sweden mostly took the form of operations against small Swedish garrisons in Karelia, Izhorsk and Livonia. In the summer and autumn of 1656 Muscovite forces were able to capture Dunaburg, Koknes and Iur'ev (Dorpat), but they failed to take Riga even after three months' siege because they had no fleet to blockade its reinforcement by sea. The Swedes launched a counter-offensive the next year, defeating the Muscovites at Walk but failing to capture Gdov.

In December 1658 the breakdown of peace talks with the Commonwealth and Vyhovs'kyi's betrayal in Ukraine forced Tsar Alexis to sign a three-year armistice with the Swedes. Sweden was ready for truce; the Polish and Lithuanian hetmans had joined in *confederatio* against the Swedes and had brought back Jan Kazimierz, who had regained the military initiative; and Karl X Gustav's operations against Prussia and Denmark had provoked the Danes, Prussians, Austrians and Dutch to join the Commonwealth in coalition against him. His sudden death in February 1660 gave his successor, Karl XI, the opportunity to sue for peace while terms were still favourable. The Treaty of Oliva (May 1660) recognised Hohenzollern sovereignty over Prussia in exchange for recognition of Swedish control over Livonia and Jan Kazimierz's abandonment of his claim to the Swedish throne. The Treaty of Kardis (June 1661) established a permanent peace between Sweden and Muscovy and compelled Tsar Alexis to return to Swedish control the Baltic towns and territories he had captured since 1656.

The 1656–8 armistice between Muscovy and the Commonwealth had not bound Bohdan Khmel'nyts'kyi from continuing his operations against the Poles, or the Crimean Tatars from continuing their raids into Ukraine and southern Muscovy. Khmel'nyts'kyi's attempts to bring Moldavia and Wallachia into alliance with him and George II Rakoczi, along with Zaporozhian and Don cossack raids on Azov, had the effect of provoking a rapprochement between the Poles and the Turks and Tatars. The sultan and khan launched a punitive invasion of Moldavia and Wallachia and offered Jan Kazimierz detachments to strike against the Ukrainians and the Don cossacks.

Bohdan Khmel'nyts'kyi died in July 1657. His secretary Ivan Vyhovs'kyi was proclaimed the new hetman. From the start three problems confronted Vyhovs'kyi: it was now clear that any chance for resumed alliance with the khanate required reconciliation with the Poles as well; his own authority was being challenged by Pushkar, the colonel of the Poltava regiment, and by Barabash, the Zaporozhian ataman, who enjoyed the protection of the Muscovite general Romodanovskii; and there was growing dissatisfaction in Ukraine with the Muscovite protectorate. Moscow diplomats had been ready at the Vilnius talks (from which Ukrainian envoys had been excluded) to trade Ukraine for Polish recognition of Tsar Alexis's future right to the Polish throne; and in preparation for resumed hostilities with the Commonwealth Moscow was establishing more garrisons in Ukraine and requisitioning army provisions and transport at ruinous rates.[18]

When Muscovy's war with the Commonwealth resumed in Lithuania in September 1658 it was therefore without a secured Ukrainian rear. On 6 September Vyhovs'kyi signed a treaty with the Poles at Hadiach, by terms of which Jan Kazimierz agreed to reincorporate Ukraine in the Commonwealth as a grand duchy of Ruthenia, recognise Vyhovs'kyi as grand duke subject to the king alone, and dismantle the Uniate Church (although the Sejm ratified but never honoured this treaty, Hadiach henceforth served as an alternative model of Ukrainian autonomy for those cossacks unable to trust in Muscovite protectorate).

Military alliance with Vyhovs'kyi's cossacks allowed Jan Kazimierz to redouble his efforts against the Muscovites on the Lithuanian front. The war here took an increasingly brutal turn involving long sieges and ambushes provoking the Muscovites to cruel reprisals against the local population – thereby intensifying resistance to Muscovite occupation. Fighting Vyhovs'kyi and his Tatar and Polish allies in Ukraine also required much larger Muscovite forces than the Ukrainian theatre had previously seen. G. G. Romodanovskii's corps had some success against them at Lokhvitsa, but S. I. Pozharskii's corps was ambushed and crushed at Konotop in July 1659. Muscovite forces then began to withdraw from Ukraine to regroup at Sevsk. Fortunately for Moscow, its protectorate over Ukraine – at least over its left bank – was saved at this moment by a cossack revolt against Vyhovs'kyi. Muscovite armies exploited this revolt and re-entered Ukraine. In September 1659 Vyhovs'kyi was deposed and Muscovite troops awarded the hetmanate to Bohdan Khmel'nyts'kyi's son Iurii.

Iurii Khmel'nyts'kyi was inexperienced and easily led, and Moscow was determined to do the leading; the chance that the new hetman might also turn renegade had to be prevented. Moscow therefore took his accession as the opportunity to redefine its protectorate responsibilities so as to limit the hetman's authority. The kind of Ukrainian autonomy Moscow had intended to recognise in the 1654 Pereiaslav Treaty can still be debated; but it is very clear that the revised Pereiaslav Articles promulgated in 1659 aimed at greatly

---

18 N. I. Kostomarov, 'Getmanstvo Vygovskogo', in his *Kazaki* (Moscow: Charli, 1995), pp. 49–50, 59, 74, 101.

reducing Ukraine's autonomy. Chernigov, Starodub and Novgorod Severskii were declared part of Muscovy, not of Ukraine, and were put under full Muscovite administration; the hetman could no longer receive foreign envoys or undertake his own campaigns without the tsar's permission; and a successor hetman could not be chosen without 'report' to Moscow.[19]

Not surprisingly the 1659 Pereiaslav Articles had the opposite effect to what Moscow intended: they heightened cossack discontent with the Muscovite protectorate and increased the pressure on Iurii Khmel'nyts'kyi to follow the example of Vyhovs'kyi and turn renegade. In the autumn of 1660 a large Muscovite army under V. B. Sheremetev drove into Volynia with the objective of crushing the Polish-Lithuanian field army and capturing L'viv. Iurii Khmel'nyts'kyi's army was supposed to reinforce Sheremetev at Chudnov, but Iurii instead signed a peace treaty with the Poles and pledged to restore Ukraine to the Commonwealth. Sheremetev's army of 40,000 men, surrounded by Polish and Crimean forces, was forced to surrender.

Operations in Ukraine in 1660–2 generally took the form of raids and counter-raids across the Dnieper. Polish and Tatar attacks on the left bank did the greatest damage; Khmel'nyts'kyi's cossacks were less effective because their ranks were increasingly divided by doubts over the ultimate intentions of their Polish and Tatar allies. Khmel'nyts'kyi's army suffered a serious defeat in July 1662 when the Crimean Tatars failed to come to his rescue from Romodanovskii. In January 1663 a cossack assembly at Chyhyryn deposed Iurii Khmel'nyts'kyi and elected Pavel Teteria hetman. Teteria, a supporter of the Hadiach Articles and alliance with the Poles, was rejected by the Zaporozhian host and the cossacks of the left bank, who in June 1663 proclaimed Ivan Briukhovets'kyi, a client of Moscow, as their hetman.

November 1663 to January 1664 saw the last great campaign of the war. Three large corps under King Jan Kazimierz, Stefan Czarniecki and Hetman Teteria crossed the Dnieper, sacked a number of small towns on the left bank, and pushed as far east as Hlukhiv and Novgorod Severskii before being thrown back by Romodanovskii's and Briukhovets'kyi's forces.

Both sides were now too exhausted to continue major operations. There were no major battles in Belarus' or Lithuania in 1665, and, except for some raids near Korsun' and Bila Tsirkva, no Muscovite attempt to push deep into right-bank Ukraine.

In 1666 Petro Doroshenko, Teteria's successor as hetman on the right bank, provided further reason for the Commonwealth and Muscovy to begin

---

19 N. I. Kostomarov, 'Getmanstvo Iuriia Khmel'nitskogo', in his *Kazaki*, pp. 176–80.

peace talks: he suddenly broke with the Poles and allied with the Crimean khan in a campaign to liberate and unite both banks of Ukraine. In January 1667 the Commonwealth and Muscovy signed a thirteen-year armistice at Andrusovo. With the signing of the Andrusovo Armistice the Poles finally conceded Smolensk, Seversk and Chernigov to Muscovy (a concession they had been ready to make in 1656 at Vilnius) and confirmed Muscovite sovereignty over left-bank Ukraine. They also left Muscovy in temporary control of Kiev, having agreed to postpone final resolution of the Kiev question to expedite signing of the armistice and free their forces for campaign against Doroshenko.

The strain the war had placed on Muscovite finances and manpower mobilisation had been considerable but not as permanently damaging as the strain upon the Commonwealth's resources. The Tsar's government was not under the same political restraints as the Polish crown; its ability to mobilise troops and provisions did not depend upon the vote of a Sejm fearful of feeding a royal military absolutism. The decision to increase the relative weight in the army of the foreign formation troops (7 per cent of the Muscovite military establishment in 1651, 79 per cent in 1663) had been sound. With the exception of the better-trained elite guards regiments based in Moscow the *soldat* infantry were still of limited tactical effectiveness on the battlefield. More importantly, though, the *soldat* regiments were conscripted from politically subaltern commoners, so it was easier to rebuild them than damaged units of traditional middle service class cavalry. Over the course of the war about 100,000 men were conscripted into the *soldat* regiments; the original rate of one conscript from every twenty-five households (1658) was soon increased to one from every twenty (1660) and in many districts on the Belgorod Line this rate was ignored and men taken from nearly every household. Furthermore, although the government was still unable to collect cash taxes on a scale sufficient to pay its growing foreign formations (and the inflation of the early 1660s made this all the harder), it was free to compensate by switching to payment in grain and imposing new grain taxes, even on social categories previously considered exempt.[20] For these reasons it did not take long after Andrusovo for Muscovite military resource mobilisation to recover and demonstrate its ability to meet the even greater demands of the continuing war in Ukraine.

---

20 Hellie, *Enserfment*, pp. 175, 194–6, 200–10, 269; Carol Belkin Stevens, *Soldiers on the Steppe: Army Reform and Social Change in Early Modern Russia* (De Kalb: Northern Illinois University Press, 1995), pp. 33, 56.

Conflict with the Ottomans and Crimean Tatars, 1667–89

After the Andrusovo Armistice the Muscovite government pursued a very cautious policy towards Sweden. It did press for right of free trade at Riga and Revel' in 1673 and significantly reinforced its border near Narva in 1677, but throughout the Scanian war (1674–9) it rebuffed Denmark's efforts to drag it into conflict with Sweden, even though this might have provided Moscow an opportunity to regain Livonian territory. Sweden eventually prevailed in the Scanian war, but at the cost of some temporary weakening of its military power, so the Swedish threat to Muscovy through the 1680s was considerably reduced.[21]

Muscovite attention in this period was instead focused largely upon the situation in Ukraine, where it faced four major threats to its control of the left bank: the emergence of a rival right-bank hetmanate bent on rolling back the Muscovites and reunifying Ukraine; the Commonwealth's resistance to Ordin-Nashchokin's project of a permanent peace and alliance and, worse, the possibility the Commonwealth might break the Andrusovo Armistice and resume war with Muscovy; the continuing problems of Crimean Tatar raiding; and the growing danger of Ottoman invasion.

By 1663 the military and political stalemate had already resulted in the de facto division of Ukraine along the Dnieper. This division was formalised at the peace talks at Andrusovo in 1667, from which Ukrainian cossack representatives had been excluded. Cossacks on both banks of the Dnieper were therefore deeply dissatisfied with the outcome of the Andrusovo talks. By 1666 many cossacks on the left bank had come to resent the tsar's protectorate: there were now over 11,000 Muscovite troops garrisoning Kiev and the left-bank towns, Muscovite *voevoda* administration was spreading, mill and tavern revenues now went to the tsar's treasury and Hetman Briukhovets'kyi was unsuitably obsequious towards Moscow. Meanwhile cossack colonels on the right bank had abandoned any hope of relying on Polish assistance to reunify Ukraine under their own hetman, Petro Doroshenko, and had instead chosen to pursue alliance with Crimean khan Aadil Girey and Ottoman sultan Mehmed IV.

Hetman Doroshenko's acceptance of Ottoman political and military support threatened the Polish–Muscovite armistice as well as Muscovite control over the left bank. This gave Doroshenko the freedom to campaign against either Muscovy or the Commonwealth while holding out to each the possibility

---

21 Robert I. Frost, *The Northern Wars, 1558–1721* (London, New York: Longman, 2000), pp. 216–17.

that the right concessions might give him reason to break with the Turks and reconcile.

Ordin-Nashchokin, by this time in declining health, had limited options in dealing with the Doroshenko problem. The missions he sent to Istanbul and Edirne to get the sultan to accept Andrusovo were rebuffed, and his efforts to negotiate with the sultan through Crimean Tatar mediation were blocked by the Zaporozhian host, which went so far as to assassinate the Crimean and Muscovite envoys. This left him no real alternative but to concentrate on diplomacy with Warsaw, communicating his willingness to negotiate some kind of shared Polish–Muscovite suzerainty over the right bank in order to transform the Andrusovo Armistice into a permanent peace and a mutual defence pact against the Ottomans. He also sent missions to Vienna, to enlist at the least the emperor's mediation and optimally his agreement to join in coalition against the sultan.

But besides risking giving Doroshenko, the khan, and the sultan provocation to declare war, these negotiations caused alarm among the left-bank cossacks, who feared Ordin-Nashchokin might give back Kiev or even part of the left bank to the Poles in order to achieve his alliance project. Many of those left-bank cossacks losing faith in Muscovy's readiness to stand firm for a unified Ukraine freed from Polish rule began defecting to Doroshenko, who appeared at the time a more resolute defender of these principles even with his troubling ties to the Turks and Tatars. Support for Doroshenko on the left bank reached such proportions that eventually even Briukhovet'skyi recognised the extent of his delegitimation, turned renegade, and began expelling the Muscovite garrisons. Briukhovets'kyi apparently expected that Doroshenko and the sultan would reward him by confirming him as vassal hetman over the left bank and Zaporozhia. But Briukhovets'kyi was deceived: Doroshenko crossed the Dnieper and overthrew him, replacing him with commissioned hetman Demian Mnogogreshnyi.

Ordin-Nashchokin retired in 1671. Within a year the new director of the Ambassadors' Chancellery, Artamon Matveev, confronted a simpler if starker and more dangerous situation in Ukraine. Muscovite control over the left bank had been partly restored: Mnogogreshnyi had shifted his allegiance to Moscow and had ratified the Hlukhiv Articles (February 1669). The Hlukhiv Articles had the effect of quelling anti-Muscovite feeling while putting the left-bank hetman on a tighter leash: they conceded some greater autonomy to the hetman's administration (revenues to maintain the Muscovite garrisons and *voevody* were once again to be collected into the hetman's treasury, not into the tsar's) yet reaffirmed the tsar's right to maintain garrisons for the time being in other towns besides Kiev and to control the Hetmanate's foreign relations.[22] When Mnogogreshnyi began chafing under these restraints Moscow easily deposed him (June 1672) and replaced him with the more compliant Ivan Samoilovich.

Furthermore, support for Doroshenko was now ebbing on the right bank as well as on the left. He was perceived as having gone too far in servilising himself to the sultan, his Korsun' Articles (April 1669) having pledged his full alliance with the Porte and khanate and even his formal vassalage to the sultan. The terms of these Korsun' Articles were meant to commit Ottoman and Crimean Tatar forces to joint operations with Doroshenko's regiments without compromising the autonomy of Ukraine, but the sultan and the khan did not send quick and unequivocal assurance they accepted these terms. The right-bank colonels therefore began falling away from Doroshenko, leaving him all the more dependent upon his Ottoman and Tatar auxiliaries and all the more isolated from the Ukrainian population.

The most important development of all, however, was the escalation of Ottoman military support for Doroshenko into a full-blown Ottoman invasion of the Polish-Lithuanian Commonwealth in the summer of 1672. On 17 October King Michał signed a peace treaty at Buczacz ceding all of Podol'ia to the sultan and recognising the independence of right-bank Ukraine under Hetman Doroshenko.

Podol'ia thereby came under an Ottoman occupation that would last until 1699. And Doroshenko was emboldened to step up agitation on the left bank to unite all Ukraine under his leadership. Muscovite commitment to a protectorate over a left-bank hetmanate now carried much greater risk of provoking war with the Ottoman Empire, the most imposing military power in Eastern Europe.

Yet Artamon Matveev accepted this risk and reaffirmed Moscow's commitment to Samoilovich's left-bank hetmanate. Ironically, Doroshenko's own intransigence had made this possible. Doroshenko was still talking to Muscovite envoys and presenting himself as amenable to reconciliation with Moscow, but he had raised the price for this reconciliation: not only the cession of Kiev, the left bank and Zaporozhia, but also now Moscow's pledge it would assist him militarily to protect Ukraine from the Turks.[23] Thus Muscovy now

22 V. Gorobets, 'Ukrainsko-rossiiskie otnosheniia v politiko-pravovoi status getman-shchiny', in A. I. Miller et al. (eds.), *Rossiia-Ukraina: istoriia vzaimootnoshenii* (Moscow: Iazyki mirovoi kul'tury, 1997), p. 9; N. I. Kostomarov, *Ruina. Mazepa. Mazepintsy* (Moscow: Charli, 1995), pp. 158–65.
23 Ibid., p. 267.

ran the risk of war with the sultan regardless of whether it accepted or rejected Doroshenko's sovereignty over all Ukraine. War against the Ottomans was a frightening prospect, but Muscovy was at least better prepared for it now. The Muscovite army had had time to recover from the revenue and manpower shortfalls that had produced stalemate in the Thirteen Years War (by 1669 the total strength of the Belgorod and Sevsk army groups had expanded to over 112,000);[24] G. G. Romodanovskii had emerged as a competent commander capable of carrying the war over to the right bank; Moscow knew it could count on the loyalty of the Zaporozhian host; great numbers of refugees were crossing the Dnieper to resettle on the left bank; and Samoilovich was as intent on conquering the right bank as Doroshenko was on subjugating the left. The Turks were at the time too preoccupied in Podol'ia to offer Doroshenko much help in holding the eastern reaches of the right bank. Furthermore, Matveev could still hope for alliance with the Commonwealth: the Sejm had refused to ratify the shameful Buczacz Treaty and a number of Polish commanders had joined Crown Hetman Sobieski in a *confederatio* to resume military operations against the Turks. The wretched King Michał died on 10 November 1673; that same day Sobieski dealt the main Ottoman army a crushing blow at Chocim and forced it to withdraw across the Danube.

In early 1674 Moscow therefore abandoned negotiations with Doroshenko. Romodanovskii and Samoilovich invaded the right bank, captured Cherkassk and a number of other towns, and put Doroshenko's capital of Chyhyryn under siege. An assembly (*rada*) at Pereiaslav proclaimed Samoilovich het-man of all Ukraine – prematurely, it turned out, for Chyhyryn was well fortified and able to withstand long siege and a large Ottoman army under Kaplan Pasha finally began marching to Doroshenko's relief in the summer. Romodanovskii and Samoilovich were forced to lift the siege and withdraw across the Dnieper. The real damage to Doroshenko's cause was done by his own ally, Kaplan Pasha, whose massacres of civilians at Lodyzhin and Uman' drove thousands of refugees eastward across the Dnieper, and by Hetman Sobieski, recently elected king of Poland, who re-entered right-bank Ukraine and captured a number of important towns as soon as Kaplan Pasha's army had withdrawn.

By December 1676 Doroshenko's forces numbered no more than 2,000 and Doroshenko was compelled to surrender. But Samoilovich was unable to exploit this to establish his control over the right bank, for the Ottomans still claimed sovereignty over Ukraine, now as a principality of Lesser Sarmatia

---

24 Hellie, *Enserfment*, p. 271.

under their new puppet, Iurii Khmel'nyts'kyi, and they appeared to be ready to campaign on Iurii's behalf to seize not only Chyhyryn but Kiev and thereby eliminate any Muscovite military presence on the eastern side of the Dnieper. Sufficient provocations for an Ottoman attack had already been given – Zaporozhian cossack raids on the Crimean coast and small-scale operations by Don cossacks and Muscovite forces against the Ottoman fortresses on the lower Don. And the Poles could no longer be counted on to divert the Ottomans on the right bank: now that he was king, Sobieski found it harder to raise armies of the size he had commanded while in *confederatio* revolt, so in October 1676 he had signed an armistice with the Turks at Zorawno and ceded the right bank to them. The Turks seem to have led him to expect that Smolensk would be restored to the Commonwealth once Samoilovich and the Muscovites were defeated. Moscow was unable to present Sobieski with a compelling counter-offer, especially as Tsar Alexis had just died and Matveev's influence over foreign policy was fading.

In June 1677 an Ottoman army of 45,000 under Ibraim Pasha crossed the Danube and marched towards Chyhyryn, the symbolic capital of the Hetmanate. Muscovy now risked being dragged into full-scale war with the Ottoman Empire. But Romodanovskii and Samoilovich were able to convince Moscow to reinforce the Muscovite–Ukrainian garrison at Chyhyryn and to let them lead a large relief expedition of over 50,000 men. Samoilovich was especially adamant about holding Chyhyryn, without which he could not maintain the loyalty of the Zaporozhian host much less extend his sovereignty over the towns and villages of the right bank. Moscow was probably more convinced by Romodanovskii's argument – that the capture of Chyhyryn would give the Turks and Tatars a staging area for attacks upon Kiev and the towns of the left bank – and by the realisation that failure to endorse Samoilovich's projects could weaken Samoilovich's support for Muscovite occupation over the left bank.

In late August Romodanovskii and Samoilovich succeeded in routing the Ottoman and Crimean forces besieging Chyhyryn. Their victory appears to have been one of the more striking Muscovite military successes to date: total Muscovite and Ukrainian casualties were reported at just 3,000 dead and 5,000 wounded, while the Turks and Tatars allegedly lost about 20,000 men.[25] The sultan subsequently expressed his displeasure by imprisoning both Ibraim Pasha and Khan Selim.

25 A. N. Popov, 'Turetskaia voina v tsarstvovanie Fedora Alekseevicha', *Russkii vestnik* 6 (March 1857): 167–70; V. N. Zaruba, *Ukrainskoe kazatskoe voisko v bor'be s turetskoi-tatarskoi agressiei* (Kharkov: Osnova, 1993), pp. 46–50.

In June 1678 the Ottomans made a second bid to seize Chyhyryn. This time the invading Ottoman army numbered 70,000 (not counting Crimean Tatar auxiliaries), had a much larger artillery train and was commanded by Kara Mustafa Pasha, the grand vizier. Romodanovskii and Samoilovich again marched to the relief of Chyhyryn, with the same forces and nearly the same plan of operations as the year before. The crucial difference this time was that they halted their armies on the far side of the Tias'min River, nearly four kilometres from Chyhyryn, on 4 August, ostensibly to await reinforcements, and meanwhile made no serious effort to harass the Ottoman camp. This gave the Turks time to continue their bombardment of Chyhyryn and move their trenches up to its walls. On 11 August Romodanovskii ordered Chyhyryn evacuated and burned to prevent it from falling into enemy hands. He and Samoilovich then withdrew across the Dnieper.

Given Romodanovskii's insistence the year before on the strategic necessity of holding Chyhyryn, this had the appearance of a major defeat, and it led many Ukrainians to blame Romodanovskii for incompetence or even treason. Actually Moscow had issued Romodanovskii secret orders to do everything to avoid battle with the Turks, to seek peace talks with them and to be prepared to sacrifice Chyhyryn rather than his army so as not to leave Kiev and the left bank under-defended. Chyhyryn was of greater importance to Samoilovich than to Moscow, which placed higher priority on defending Kiev and the left bank.[26]

The Russo-Turkish war of 1676–81 is usually seen as a stalemate or even as a Russian defeat because Chyhyryn had to be destroyed and the right bank was thereby lost to the Turks and Iurii Khmel'nyts'kyi. In fact the right bank did not fall to them. The higher Ottoman priority at the time was consolidating control over Podol'ia, to hold the Moldavian and Wallachian hospodars in line and block Sobieski from invading Moldavia. A massive Muscovite force build-up on the left bank, in Sloboda Ukraine, and along the Belgorod Line provided sufficient deterrent against an Ottoman attack across the Dnieper or a Crimean Tatar invasion from the south: in 1679 70,000 Muscovite troops and 30,000 of Samoilovich's cossacks defended Kiev and the left bank, while 50,000 Muscovite troops held the Belgorod Line; roughly equal numbers were fielded in 1680.[27] The Ottomans therefore made no effort to rebuild Chyhyryn as a base for operations against Kiev and the left bank, and most of the Ottoman and

26 Brian Davies, 'The Second Chigirin Campaign (1678): Late Muscovite Military Power in Transition', in Eric Lohr and Marshall Poe (eds.), *The Military and Society in Russia, 1450–1917* (Leiden: E. J. Brill, 2002), pp. 101–2, 104–5.
27 Ibid., pp. 115–19.

Crimean troops supporting Khmel'nyts'kyi were soon withdrawn. By January 1681 the pasha of Azov was signalling the Sultan's interest in armistice talks.

Chyhyryn proved far less decisive in shaping the destiny of the right bank than the spring 1679 raids on right bank towns and villages undertaken by Samoilovich's son Semen and Muscovite troops out of the Kiev garrison and the regiment of Grigorii Kosagov. This operation came to be called the Great Expulsion. Several of the larger right-bank towns were burned and about 20,000 of their inhabitants were driven across the Dnieper into the left-bank hetmanate. This depopulated most of the right bank as far as the Bug River, turning it into a no man's land buffering the Dnieper frontier of the left-bank hetmanate. Iurii Khmel'nyts'kyi was left only with the western part of Bratslav palatinate as a resource base. The Turks deposed him in 1681 and tried to set Moldavian hospodar Gheorghe Duca over Podol'ia and the right bank, but this was frustrated by a cossack revolt supported by the Poles. Sulimenko, the next pro-Ottoman hetman on the right bank, was overthrown in 1685.

The 20,000 refugees pushed across the Dnieper could not all be resettled on the territories of Samoilovich's cossack regiments, where competition for ploughland was already intense, so two-thirds of them were transferred to Sloboda Ukraine, to perform cossack service from virgin steppe land along the Northern Donets and Oskol' rivers. This strengthened the Sloboda Ukraine cossack regiments serving in the Muscovite army and encouraged further Muscovite and Ukrainian colonisation of the region, to safeguard which the Military Chancellery began erecting a new defence line, the Iziuma Line, running 530 kilometres in all, linking up twenty garrison towns, enclosing an area of 30,000 square kilometres, and thereby extending the Muscovite frontier another 160 kilometres southward. With the construction of the towns of Maiatsk and Tor Muscovy now had garrisons within 150 kilometres of the Black Sea coast.[28]

The build-up in Sloboda Ukraine and link-up of the Iziuma Line with the Belgorod Line provided much greater protection against Crimean Tatar raids. Khan Murad Girey was compelled to negotiate at Bakhchisarai a twenty-year armistice with Muscovy (1681), formally recognising Kiev and the left bank as Muscovite possessions and a 10-kilometre-wide strip of the right bank along the Dnieper as a neutral zone closed to territorial aggrandisement by any power. The khan subsequently induced Sultan Mehmed IV to ratify these same terms.

It could therefore be argued that Muscovy won its first great war with the Ottoman Empire. It had secured its position on the left bank, eliminated for

28 On the construction and colonisation of the Iziuma Line, see V. P. Zagorovskii, *Iziumskaia cherta* (Voronezh: Voronezhskii gosudarstvennyi universitet, 1980).

some time the danger of a rival right-bank hetmanate, and further reduced the Crimean Tatar threat. A further indication that the war had strengthened Muscovy's military and political standing was the new foreign policy pursued by the Commonwealth after the collapse of the Gninski mission to Istanbul in 1678. The Sejm finally ratified a fifteen-year extension of the Andrusovo Armistice (on terms less advantageous to the Commonwealth than previously demanded) and King Jan Sobieski abandoned attempts to ally with the Porte and returned to his project of driving the Turks from Podol'ia and Moldavia. He therefore began negotiations to induce Tsar Fedor to join him, Emperor Leopold I and Venetian Doge Alvise Contarini in coalition to drive the Turks from Europe.

By 1684 Moscow was ready to join this Holy League. Sobieski's surprising victory over the army of Grand Vizier Kara Mustafa at the gates of Vienna (12 September 1683) undoubtedly helped to convince the Muscovite government, but there were other reasons. The most important consideration was the Commonwealth's clear eagerness for Muscovite alliance, which showed Golitsyn the time had come to demand that the Poles renounce all claim to Kiev, the left bank, the Zaporozhian Sech' and the regions of Smolensk, Chernigov and Seversk. Golitsyn demanded the Commonwealth sign a treaty of permanent peace on these terms, and to the Sejm's dismay King Jan Sobieski's envoys signed it (26 April 1686).[29] Hetman Samoilovich was also angered by this, for the treaty had the effect of recognising Polish claims over the right bank and frustrating his campaign to unite all Ukraine under his own mace.

The Treaty of Eternal Peace can be said to mark the point at which Muscovy achieved lasting geopolitical preponderance over the Polish-Lithuanian Commonwealth (Map 21.2 shows territory ceded by Poland-Lithuania after 1667). Sobieski had hoped to compensate the Commonwealth for these lost territories by driving the Turks out of Podol'ia and Moldavia, but neither of these objectives was accomplished in his lifetime and the lives and revenue he squandered on them ultimately provoked a backlash by the magnates, who further reduced the military power available to the crown. Nor was he able to re-establish control over the right bank; efforts by Polish magnates to recolonise the region drove the majority of right-bank cossacks into a new revolt led by Colonel Semen Palii.

Ratification of the Eternal Peace now obligated Muscovy to make good its pledge to the Holy League and wage war upon the Crimean khanate. Golitsyn

---

29 Andrzej Sulima Kaminski, *Republic vs. Autocracy. Poland-Lithuania and Russia, 1686–1697* (Cambridge, Mass.: Harvard Ukrainian Research Institute, 1993), p. 12.

FINLAND

Gulf of
Finland

Lake
Ladoga

LIVONIA

● Narva

● Novgorod

●Pskov

Polotsk ●

● Moscow

● Smolensk

POLAND-
LITHUANIA

● Starodub

Chernigov●

●Novgorod
Severskii

Kiev● ●Pereiaslav

● Belgorod

Chyhyryn ●

Don

Dnieper

OTTOMAN
EMPIRE

ZAPOROZHIA

CRIMEAN KHANATE

● Cherkassk

Azov

Perekop ●

Sea of
Azov

Kaffa

Black Sea

Territory ceded by
Poland–Lithuania
from 1667

0   400 km

Map 21.2. Russia's western borders, 1689

undertook two expeditions against Perekop (1687, 1689) to pin the Tatars down in Crimea while the Poles invaded Moldavia, the Austrians engaged the Turks in Transylvania and the Venetians campaigned in Dalmatia. On both of these expeditions Golitsyn led an enormous army of over 110,000 Muscovite troops and 30,000–50,000 Ukrainian troops across hundreds of kilometres of empty and arid steppe; both expeditions failed to besiege Perekop and withdrew with heavy casualties, mostly from drought and lack of fodder; and Golitsyn contributed to his own downfall and the downfall of regent Sophia by trying to pass off both campaigns as successes, to the disgust of his officers and the court. In fairness to Golitsyn, a successful expedition across the steppe to capture Perekop was probably beyond the capabilities of any other power of the age and may not even have been Golitsyn's real objective. The Crimean expeditions did divert the Crimean Tatars from reinforcing Ottoman operations on other fronts and did show the Holy League the tremendous powers of resource mobilisation Muscovy now possessed (if also of its ability to waste resources); they did establish two important garrisons and supply depots (Novobogorodit-skoe and Novosergeevsk) for future expeditions against the khanate and the Ottoman fortresses on the Dnieper; and they had the effect of tightening Moscow's control over the Zaporozhian host and the left bank, by planting Muscovite garrisons just across the Dnieper from the host and by creating the opportunity to scapegoat and depose Samoilovich and replace him with Ivan Mazepa.

Besides profiting politically from the discrediting of Golitsyn's Crimean expeditions, Tsar Peter and his circle initially saw no advantage to campaigning on behalf of the Holy League; they were convinced the Poles and Austrians were already bogged down in Moldavia and Hungary and inclining to a separate peace with the Ottomans, so it would be better for Muscovy to seek its own reconciliation with the Porte and khanate lest it be left struggling on alone. For the time being, then, the new government would distance itself from Warsaw and Vienna and soften its demands upon the sultan and khan in hope of negotiating an armistice. It was not until 1694 that Peter would renew commitment to the Holy League by preparing a major expedition against Azov.

Muscovy's emergence as a great power

In Tsar Alexis's reign Muscovite foreign policy had played for very high stakes but had run high losses in the process. Tsar Alexis had entered the Ukrainian quagmire in 1654 in order to obtain Bogdan Khmel'nyts'kyi's aid in Belarus' and Lithuania; he had prolonged the war with the Commonwealth by setting unrealistic terms for peace, including his election to the Polish throne; and he had left the conflict with the Commonwealth unresolved in order to suddenly open an unsuccessful war upon the Swedes for control of the Baltic coast.

Muscovite foreign policy after 1676 was generally more cautious but sure-footed. The 1677 Chyhyryn campaign (which ended very fortunately) or Golitsyn's Crimean expeditions (which wasted lives but did not leave the southern frontier more vulnerable) cannot be compared with Tsar Alexis's gambles. Yet several major strategic objectives were achieved by 1689. Muscovy had won Polish and Ottoman recognition of the Tsar's sovereignty over left-bank Ukraine and had begun to exercise greater control over the Zaporozhian and Don cossack hosts. It no longer faced any significant threat from a right-bank hetmanate (the right bank's pro-Polish hetmans could seldom mobilise more than 5,000 men, its pro-Ottoman hetmans no more than a few hundred). The Polish-Lithuanian Commonwealth was no longer Muscovy's mortal enemy; it had finally signed a treaty of permanent peace and abandoned its claims to the long-contested territories of Smolensk and Chernigov in return for Muscovite entry into the Holy League. The Crimean khanate remained a threat to the towns of Sloboda Ukraine and the Belgorod Line, but no longer to the Muscovite heartland; more of the steppe had come under Muscovite military colonisation, advancing the front to just a few hundred kilometres of the khanate and encouraging Muscovite and cossack forces to go on the offensive with a series of operations on the lower Don and Dnieper. Muscovy still did not have mastery over the Livonian coast of the Baltic but had been able to enjoy a long respite from conflict with Sweden.

These successes were owed in part to blunders by Muscovy's rivals. A contributing factor was the greater experience and enlarged scope of Muscovite diplomacy. Now that Muscovy had demonstrated its military usefulness to the Ottoman Empire's enemies it became practical to send frequent missions to most of the European powers. Muscovy finally had its first permanent mission, at Warsaw, which served as a clearing house for reports from its envoys in other European capitals as well as a source of improved intelligence on foreign efforts to manipulate Polish political factions. The Little Russian Chancellery (*Malorossiiskii prikaz*) had also taken on great importance for managing political relations with the hetmans, colonels and towns of the left bank. Its work made it possible to reduce the ability of the later hetmans (Samoilovich, Mazepa) to pursue their own foreign policies while maintaining their loyalty for longer than had been possible before; by further servilising the hetmans it was possible in turn to force the colonels and *starshina* to accept Muscovite garrisons as an essentially permanent fact.

Muscovite military power, near exhaustion by the end of the Thirteen Years War, had revived very quickly and grown to impressive new proportions. The number of effectives for field army service reached 164,600 men in 1680 (55 per cent of these were in the foreign formation infantry and cavalry).[30] Thousands more performed garrison duty on the Belgorod Line and the new Iziuma Line. The two Chyhyryn operations, the great defensive deployment of 1679, and Golitsyn's Perekop expeditions demonstrated Muscovite ability to mobilise and maintain campaign armies of extraordinary size.[31] The campaigns of the 1670s–1680s also show more authority for command-and-control being moved out of the Military Chancellery at Moscow and closer to the front. The Chyhyryn campaigns also show the foreign formation infantry finally fulfilling its tactical potential, especially in their 26 August 1677 night descent across the Sula River and their 3 August 1678 assault on Strel'nikov Hill.[32]

During or immediately after the Russo-Turkish war there were a number of important reforms further addressing the needs of the army. In 1678 the Military Chancellery issued revised standards for assignment to the traditional and foreign formation cavalry units in the Belgorod corps, limiting eligibility for service in these units to those holding a certain minimum number of peasant households, that is to men prosperous enough to maintain themselves in cavalry service from their *pomest'ia* alone. This made it possible to eliminate the need to pay cash allowances to cavalrymen and reassign less prosperous servicemen from cavalry units to the infantry regiments. Over the next two years the infantry regiments were further expanded through a drive to enrol thousands of vagrants, pardoned shirkers, impoverished *deti boiarskie* and cossacks and musketeers. By 1681 these measures had succeeded in increasing the relative weight of foreign formation troops in the field army and establishing a ratio of infantry to cavalry of nearly 2:1. The *strel'tsy* were not abolished but their units were restructured along the lines of the foreign formation infantry, reformed into companies under captains and regiments under colonels, so that they could be put to drilling in foreign formation infantry evolutions. The centuries of traditional cavalry were likewise reorganised as companies.[33]

To raise more revenue for paying the expanded foreign formation infantry a major reform of state finances was undertaken in 1677–81. A new general

30 Chernov, *Vooruzhennye sily*, pp. 187–9.
31 Stevens, *Soldiers on the Steppe*, pp. 113–16, 120.
32 Davies, 'The Second Chigirin Campaign', pp. 108–11.
33 Stevens, *Soldiers on the Steppe*, pp. 77–84.

cadastral survey was undertaken; a number of minor direct taxes were amalgamated into one army maintenance cash tax (*streletskie den'gi*, 'musketeers' money'); this cash tax, along with the army grain tax, was now assessed by household (no longer by *sokha*, i.e. by area and productive capacity of cultivated land); and authority over direct taxation was further centralised in the Grand Treasury to reduce collection costs and facilitate budgeting.

Command-and-control was strengthened in two ways. The *razriad* principle of territorial army group command and administration was extended across the rest of European Russia by creating five new territorial army groups, for a total of nine, and assigning to them all troops in field army service, either in traditional or foreign formation units. This had the effect of simplifying muster procedures (each army group had two or more permanent designated muster points), devolving more authority for logistics to the territorial level, and reinforcing the tendency to use army groups as large corps in operations. The abolition of *mestnichestvo* in 1682 was in part motivated by the need to improve command-and-control; the tasks of modernising force structure (reorganising traditional cavalry and *strel'tsy* units into companies and regiments) and mounting more complex operations (by territorial corps, and by multiple corps together) made it necessary to eliminate precedence suits and discourage quarrels over precedence honour that might undermine such efforts.

These reforms constituted a foundation for Peter I's programme of military modernisation just as the expansion of diplomatic activity paved the way for Peter's efforts to make Russia a leading player in the concert of European nations.

22

Non-Russian subjects

MICHAEL KHODARKOVSKY

From 1598 to 1613 Muscovy experienced the most severe crises known as the Time of Troubles. Despite the ravages of civil war and foreign interventions which marked the Time of Troubles, some in the Muscovite government continued to attend dutifully to their daily routines and obligations. The local *voevodas* on the frontiers proceeded to govern their forts and towns and construct new ones. The Foreign Office in Moscow continued to receive and dispatch envoys to the peoples on the distant frontiers and churn out reports about them. The pace of Russian colonisation might have been slowed down but it did not stop. The ascension to the Russian throne of the Romanov dynasty in 1613 put an end to the Time of Troubles. Russia emerged from the Time of Troubles with a rediscovered sense of national identity and a newly found confidence in its incessant territorial expansion.

Throughout the seventeenth century the Russian government expended great resources and energy on consolidating its hold over annexed territories and moving into new ones. By the end of the century, Moscow could boast of enduring success in expanding further east, where the Russians reached the shores of the Pacific Ocean, and south and south-east, where the newly built forts and towns pushed the imperial boundaries further into the steppe. The seventeenth century also marked the beginning of Russia's expansion in the west, where Moscow's acquisition of territories in Ukraine added a new dimension to the Russian imperial foundation. No longer did Moscow expand into lands populated by non-Christians: Muslims, animists, and Buddhists. In its western borderlands, Russia had come to acquire a large population of Orthodox Christians who were non-Russian. The ever-growing number of Russia's subjects now included non-Christians in the east and non-Russians in the west.

The steppe

Russia's steppe frontier remained ambiguous and ill defined. To the extent that this frontier was defined, it represented a boundary between Russia and those who were deemed hostile to it. A peace treaty (*shert'*) prepared in 1604 by the government officials for the ruler of the Greater Nogai Horde, *beg* Ishterek, gave a clear indication of where Moscow believed its southern frontier to lie. Ishterek was expected to have no contacts with the Ottoman sultan, the Crimean khan, the Persian shah, the Bukharan khan, Tashkent, Urgench, the Kazakh Horde, the Kumyk shamkhal or the Circassians. In other words, Moscow roughly delineated its southern boundaries stretching from the Crimea to the North Caucasus to Central Asia.[1]

By the early seventeenth century, Russia's policies in the steppe, which were meant to encourage the Nogais' dependence on Russia and to weaken them by promoting the factional struggle among their leaders, proved to have the desired effect. Once a powerful confederation of Turkic nomads, the Nogais' significance had been greatly reduced by the debilitating internal struggle. In the early seventeenth century, the Nogais of the Greater Horde were no longer capable of mounting any serious challenge to the Russian state in the south and instead grew desperately dependent on Russia's economic and military aid.

But the stability and relative safety on Russia's southern frontier was always short-lived, subject to the rapidly changing situation in the steppe. Continuing the centuries-old pattern, the steppes of Inner Asia disgorged another powerful nomadic confederation which came to replace the Nogais in the Caspian steppe. The intruders shared with their new neighbours neither the overlapping structures of related Turkic clans nor their Islamic religion. The newly arrived steppe nomads were a Mongol people and avowed Tibetan Buddhists guided by the Dalai Lama. Their neighbours called them Kalmyks.

Even early exploratory forays by the Kalmyks used to send the Nogais fleeing in panic from their formidable foe. Moscow's attempts to arrest the movement of the Kalmyks further west and to control the situation in the steppe proved to be futile. In the first decade of the seventeenth century, most of the Kalmyks roamed along the Irtysh, Ishim and Tobol' rivers of south-western Siberia. In the second decade they had crossed the Iaik River, and by the early 1630s they reached the vicinity of Astrakhan', routed the Nogais and the Russian musketeers dispatched to help them, and occupied the pastures

---

1 'Akty vremeni Lzhedmitriia 1-go (1603–1606), Nogaiskie dela', ed. N. V. Rozhdestvenskii, *ChOIDR* (Moscow, 1845–1918), vol. 264, pt.1 (1918): 105–9, 136, 139–42.

along the Volga. Russia's inability to protect the Nogais from the Kalmyk raids led some of the Nogais to join the Kalmyks, while the majority chose to flee further west towards Azov, seeking the protection of the Ottoman Porte.

The arrival of the Kalmyks in the 1630s had a dramatic impact on the entire southern region. The decades of Moscow's careful strategies of weakening, dividing and impoverishing the Nogais and its significant expenditures to implement such policies, seemed to have been wasted. The Nogais, whom Moscow considered long pacified, had now joined the Crimean Tatars and the Lesser Nogai Horde near Azov. Together they launched devastating raids into Russia's southern borderlands. Only in the three years of 1632, 1633 and 1637 the Nogais and Crimeans captured and brought to the Crimea more than 10,000 Russian prisoners. The newly colonised southern region with its towns and peasants urgently needed protection.

The danger of the Nogais and Crimeans breaking through the southern defences and approaching Moscow was no exaggeration. The intentions of the Kalmyks, who came to replace the Nogais in the Caspian steppe, remained unknown. It is unlikely that Russia's previous historical experiences in the steppe left Moscow sanguine about the prospect of peace with the Kalmyks. Faced with the new and dangerous situation along the southern frontier, Moscow hastened to conclude a peace treaty with Poland in 1634 and to turn its attention to the south. Indeed, this time Moscow decided to embark on a new strategy and to invest unprecedented resources in order to secure the lands already settled and populated by the Russians and to end the threat of nomadic invasion once and for all.

In a change from previous policies Moscow decided to play the 'cossack card'. The cossacks were the ultimate 'melting pot' in early modern Russia. Among several cossack hosts which Moscow claimed to control, the Don cossacks were the most powerful. In the seventeenth century, they included a motley crowd of Russians, new converts, Zaporozhian cossacks, Poles, Lithuanians, peasants and various fugitives from justice.[2] Mirroring the lifestyle and the military organisation of the steppe societies, the cossacks were a perfect antidote to the nomadic peoples of the steppe. And like many non-Russian peoples, the cossacks proved to be some of Russia's most mutinous subjects.

In a shift from the previous policy of restraining the Don cossacks to avoid provoking the Ottoman Porte, Moscow was now prepared to further arm the cossacks and encourage their raids. Such raids, however, were to be carefully

---

2 Grigorii Kotoshikhin, *O Rossii v tsarstvovanie Alekseia Mikhailovicha* (St Petersburg: Tipografiia Glavnogo upravleniia udelov, 1906), p. 135.

calibrated, and the cossacks were instructed to limit their attacks to the Nogais and Crimeans alone, and not to raid Ottoman possessions, Azov and Kaffa in particular.[3]

To be sure, controlling the cossacks was no easy matter, as the interests of the government and the cossacks did not always coincide. After all, it was not the impoverished Nogais that the cossacks were after. Their eyes were set on the wealthy Ottoman and Crimean towns and villages along the Black Sea coast. The only obstacles between the cossacks and the promise of rich booty and numerous captives were the fortifications of Azov, the Ottoman fortress in the estuary of the Don, which prevented the cossacks from sailing down the river to the sea.

When in 1636, enticed by the Crimean khan and under continuous pressure from the Kalmyks and cossacks, the Nogais abandoned the area around Azov and crossed the Don on the way to the Crimea, the Don cossacks quickly moved to lay siege to Azov. In June 1637, Azov was in the hands of the triumphant cossacks. In the next five years, taken aback by this unexpected and undesired development, Moscow was presented with an unpalatable dilemma: to support the cossacks and thus enter war with the Ottoman Empire, or to avoid war by having the cossacks abandon the fortress. After much hesitation and deliberation, the government chose avoidance over confrontation.

But the cossacks' degree of independence from Moscow and a history of their unruliness and participation in popular revolts made the government suspicious of their true intentions, and, as the Azov affair proved, not unreasonably so. Use of the cossacks along the frontier had to be supplemented by a more reliable strategy. In 1635, the government undertook a new and bold initiative; it began the construction of the fortification lines in the south. The duration of the construction, the expenditures on these extensive fortification networks, and the utilisation of human and natural resources for this purpose made the project the single most ambitious and important strategic undertaking in seventeenth-century Russia. It was to become Moscow's own Great Wall to fend off the 'infidels' from the southern steppe.

Constructing a fortification line in the southern region was not an entirely novel idea. Such fortification lines were already known in tenth-century Kievan Rus', and more recently, in the middle of the sixteenth century, they had been constructed just south of the Oka River. By the 1630s numerous forts and towns emerged far south of Moscow. Still, these proliferating vanguard military outposts had to be supplied from the central regions of Russia because agriculture

---

3 A. A. Novosel'skii, *Bor'ba Moskovskogo gosudarstva s tatarami v pervoi polovine XVII veka* (Moscow and Leningrad: AN SSSR, 1948), pp. 237–8, 296.

remained a dangerous undertaking on the frontier. It was paramount to provide further security, if a peasant colonisation of the region were to take place. The fortification lines were to serve exactly that purpose, becoming, in time, both the primary means of Moscow's defence against predations and an effective tool of Russia's territorial expansion.

In the decade from 1635 to 1646, Moscow moved its frontier defences much further south, connecting, in one uninterrupted defence line, the natural obstacles, such as rivers and swamps, with man-made fortifications: several rows of moats, felled trees and palisades studded with advance warning towers and forts armed with cannon and other firearms. The first such fortification line (*zaseka* or *zasechnaia cherta*), stretching for more than 800 kilometres from the Akhtyrka River in the west to Tambov in the east, became known as the Belgorod Line. It took the government another decade to extend the fortification line further east, from Tambov to Simbirsk on the Volga. By the mid-seventeenth century, both the colonists arriving in the southern regions of Russia and the residents of Kazan' province found themselves in relative safety behind the Belgorod and Simbirsk fortification lines.[4]

The Kalmyks were seen as the dangerous outsiders whose raids disrupted the status quo in the region and thus, in addition to Russia, threatened the interests of other regional powers from the Crimea to the North Caucasus, to the Central Asian khanates. At first invincible, the Kalmyks suffered a major debacle in the steppe and mountains of the North Caucasus in 1644. A large Kalmyk contingent was decimated by the combined forces of the Nogais and Kabardinians with the help of Crimean Tatar and Russian detachments which provided the crucial fire power. Driven by mutual interests, the Russians and Crimeans succeeded in pushing the Kalmyks back east of the Iaik River.

A few years later the Kalmyks were back in force. Led by their new chief *tay-ishi*, Daichin, the Kalmyks ravaged the Kazan' and Ufa provinces, routed the Crimean troops, and demanded the return of the remains of Daichin's father

---

4 On the evolution of the fortification lines see A. I. Iakovlev, *Zasechnaia cherta Moskovskogo gosudarstva v XVII veke* (Moscow: Tipografiia I. Lisnera, 1916); V. P. Zagorovskii, *Belgorodskaia cherta* (Voronezh: Voronezhskii Gosudarstvennyi Universitet, 1969); A. V. Nikitin, 'Oboronitel'nye sooruzheniia zasechnoi cherty XVI–XVII vv.', in *Materialy i issledovaniia po arkheologii SSSR*, vol. 44 (1955): 116–213; Novosel'skii, *Bor'ba*, pp. 293–6. For works in English which discuss the situation and fortifications in the south see Brian Davies, 'The Role of the Town Governors in the Defense and Military Colonization of Muscovy's Southern Frontier: The Case of Kozlov, 1635–38', 2 vols., unpublished Ph.D. dissertation, University of Chicago, 1983; Richard Hellie, *Enserfment and Military Change in Muscovy* (Chicago: University of Chicago Press, 1971), pp. 174–80; Carol Belkin Stevens, *Soldiers on the Steppe: Army Reform and Social Change in Early Modern Russia* (DeKalb: Northern Illinois University Press, 1995), pp. 19–36.

and brothers killed in 1644. When a Russian envoy approached Daichin with demands to confirm the Kalmyks' allegiance and submit hostages, Daichin called him a liar for making such grotesque claims. A realisation that the Kalmyks' arrival in the Caspian steppe was irreversible prompted the Russian authorities to drop some of their customary demands and to adopt a more conciliatory tone. To enlist the Kalmyks as a counterforce to the Crimeans, Moscow returned the remains of Daichin's father and brothers, offered Kalmyks payments and rewards for their military campaigns, and trade privileges in the frontier towns. In 1654, after Moscow annexed parts of Ukraine, the rival alliances took shape: Poland and Crimea were facing Russia and its new ally, the Kalmyks.

Similar to Moscow's relationship with other nomadic peoples, Russia's alliance with the Kalmyks remained precarious. While the written treaties (*shert'*) prepared in Moscow and written in Russian were inevitably phrased as the Kalmyks' oath of allegiance, they were, in fact, peace treaties with mutual obligations by both parties to maintain peace, trade and military co-operation. Insisting that the Kalmyks were the subjects of the tsar, Moscow objected to the Kalmyks' independent relations with the Crimea, Ottomans or other powers potentially hostile to Moscow, suspecting, and correctly so, that the Kalmyks' allegiances could be easily bought and sold. The Kalmyks, however, believed that Moscow often failed to live up to its commitments when the Russian officials did not deliver payments, demanded custom duties and bribes, did not protect Kalmyks from the raids of Russia's purported subjects, cossacks and Bashkirs, and above all, converted to Christianity fugitive or captured Kalmyks.

Throughout the seventeenth century, the Kalmyks' relationship with Russia continued to alternate between that of a military alliance against the Crimea and openly hostile acts against Russia. By the end of the century, a more pragmatic attitude prevailed in Moscow. In July 1697, a Kalmyk khan, Ayuki, and the high-ranking Russian envoy, the boyar Prince B. A. Golitsyn, signed a treaty which was strikingly different from the previous ones. This time it was the Russian side which undertook commitments to assist the Kalmyks, to put a stop to the Bashkir and cossack raids, not to dictate the boundaries of Kalmyks' pastures, and neither give refuge, nor convert the runaway Kalmyks.[5]

With the Russian conquest of the Ottoman fort of Azov in 1696, the Kalmyks realised that, for the time being, their fortunes lay with Russia.

---

5 Michael Khodarkovsky, *Where Two Worlds Met: The Russian State and the Kalmyk Nomads, 1600–1771* (Ithaca, N.Y.: Cornell University Press, 1992), pp. 105–33.

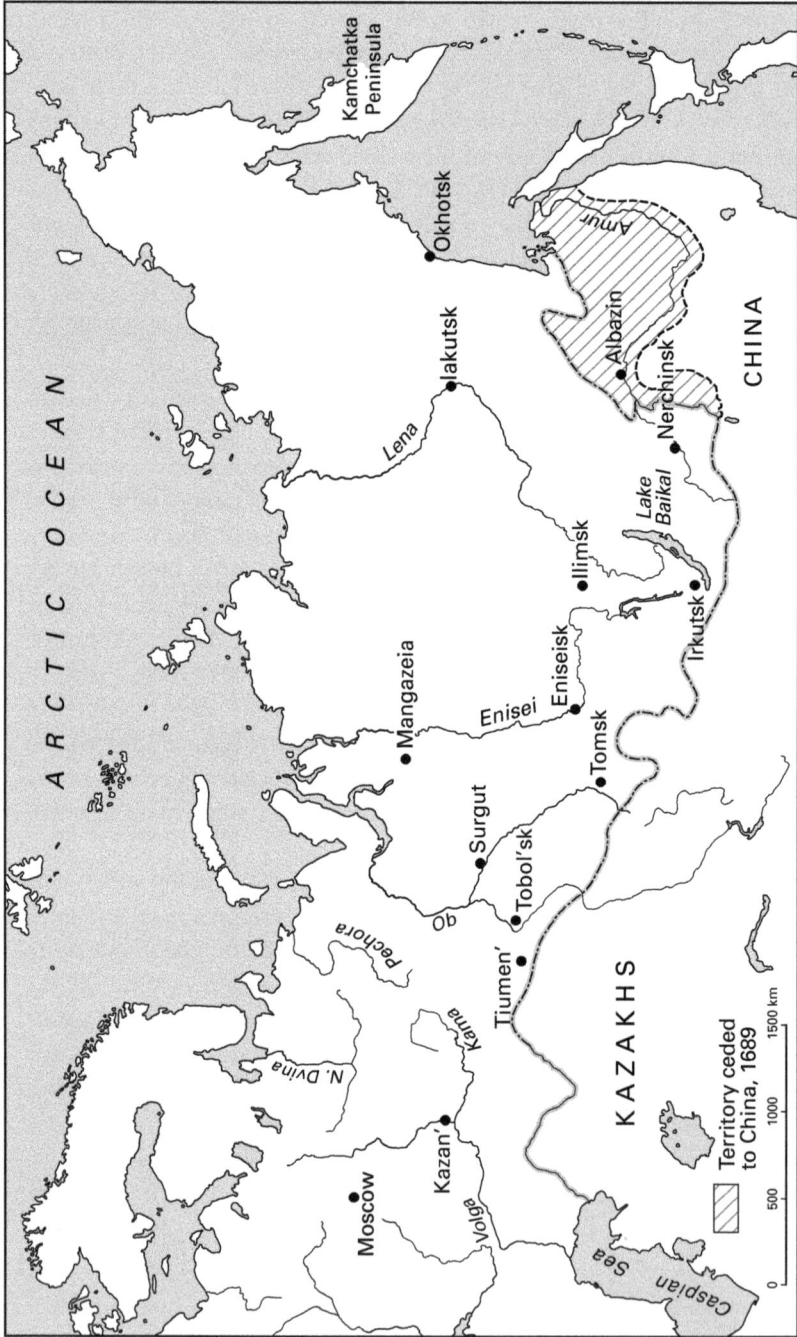

Map 22.1. Russian expansion in Siberia to 1689

At the same time, Moscow also concluded that it would gain more by mollifying the Kalmyks than confronting them. In addressing the Kalmyk grievances and putting down in writing its own obligations, the government was ready to admit that assuring the co-operation of the Kalmyks and achieving a modicum of peace along the frontier required more than emphasising the Kalmyks' submissive status and their obligations. Rather, it required a clearly articulated recognition that such a relationship was a two-way street with mutual obligations and commitments. Such an understanding of their relationship would last for the next two decades, when the newly confident Russian authorities would once again impose a new set of restrictions on the Kalmyks and insist on their explicit submission to the Russian emperor.

Siberia

By the beginning of the seventeenth century, Moscow was well established in western Siberia and reached the banks of the Enisei River. Russia's further expansion in Siberia skirted a careful line between the northern boundaries of the steppe and the southern boundaries of the Siberian forest, thus avoiding the inhospitable terrain of the permafrost wilderness in the north and the open arid steppe in the south. Russia had to wait for another hundred years before undertaking an incremental expansion into the steppe lands (presently northern Kazakhstan), dominated by two powerful nomadic confederations, the Kazakhs and the Oirats.

In the meantime, the Russians moved south-east reaching the Ili River where in 1630 they founded Fort Ilimsk. From here, Russia's first colonists took two different paths. One route of colonisation took the Russians down the Lena River into central Siberia, the other moved south down the Ilim river towards Lake Baikal and the Amur River. In the first instance, the Russians met little resistance and advanced speedily to the shores of the Pacific Ocean. In two years, the Russian colonists sailed down the Lena River across the lands populated by the Evenk (Tungus) and Sakha (Iakut) to found Fort Iakutsk in 1632. In 1647, the Russians reached the Pacific coast and founded Fort Okhotsk in 1649. In the second half of the century, Russian forts and settlements emerged in the lands populated by the Even (Lamut), Yukagir, Chukchi and Koriak of north-eastern Siberia. By the end of the century several Russian forts dotted the landscape of the Kamchatka peninsula (see Map 22.1).

Russia's expansion along this northern route was no different from other parts of Siberia where the native population could offer sporadic but ultimately ineffective resistance, the local elites could be easily co-opted, divided and manipulated and the furs would be collected either in form of a tribute or trade. The native peoples were to become 'the *iasak*-paying subjects eternally' and the only choice they had was to 'enter the sublime protection of the Grand Sovereign, the Tsar' voluntarily or to be reduced into submission by Russian arms.[6]

The second route of Russia's expansion into Siberia took the Russians into the lands of the Buriats and Evenk around Lake Baikal and the Daurs of the Amur River. Then Russia's advance had quickly come to a halt. Here, the Russians encountered another sovereign state and empire, whose ruler too claimed suzerainty over numerous native residents of the area. The Russians approached the imperial boundaries of Ch'ing China.

It was not uncommon for both sides to claim suzerainty and the right to collect *iasak* from the same native people and for the natives to pay tribute to both Russians and Chinese. Russia's encroachment into the Chinese sphere of influence and the numerous arguments and disputes over the loyalty and tributary payments of the native peoples were annoying enough for the Manchu rulers of China. But when the rebellious Russian cossacks arrived to found Fort Albazin on the Amur River in 1665 and Russian settlers, attracted by the stories of the Amur region's fabulous riches, began to arrive in larger numbers, Beijing realised that negotiations alone would not resolve the contentious issues. Chinese armies marched towards the Russian forts of Albazin and Nerchinsk, eventually forcing the Russians to raze most of their forts and settlements and to abandon any further expansion in the region. The Treaty of Nerchinsk signed in 1689 established a boundary between the Russian and Chinese empires along the Argun and Shilka rivers and the Stanovoi mountain range, effectively denying Russia any access to the Amur region. The Russians had to wait for over 150 years before annexing the Amur region and turning it into the far-eastern corner of the Russian Empire.[7]

---

6 *AI*, 5 vols. (St Petersburg: various publishers, 1841–2), vol. IV (Tipografiia II Otdeleniia Sobstvennoi E. I. V. Kantseliarii, 1842), no. 219, pp. 473–4.
7 George Lantzeff and Richard Pierce, *Eastward to Empire: Exploration and Conquest on the Russian Open Frontier, to 1750* (Montreal: McGill–Queen's University Press, 1973), pp. 127–83; James Forsyth, *A History of the Peoples of Siberia* (Cambridge: Cambridge University Press, 1992), pp. 48–109; Mark Bassin, *Imperial Visions, Nationalist Imagination and Geographical Expansion in the Russian Far East, 1840–1865* (Cambridge: Cambridge University Press, 1999), pp. 19–24.

The North Caucasus

Throughout the seventeenth century Russia could boast of no visible territorial expansion in the North Caucasus. Russia's advance here had been stalled for the same reasons as its march eastward into south-eastern Siberia was halted in the 1650s. In the Caucasus, Moscow approached the sphere of influence of two sovereign states, the Ottoman and Persian empires. At the time when Russia's unquestionable military and economic superiority enabled it to expand with relative ease into the lands inhabited by various tribal societies, Moscow had to take a long pause before it was able to confront the similarly organised and dynamic empires of the Chinese, Persians and Ottomans.

Since its first penetration of the Caucasus in the 1560s Moscow struggled to maintain a foothold there. Forced to raze Fort Tersk several times, Moscow had decided to build a fort at a new location further north in the estuary of the Terek River. In 1588, Moscow dispatched a contingent of musketeers and cossacks to defend the newly built fort at the site of the old Turkic town of Tiumen'. Initially named Fort Tiumen', it was quickly renamed Fort Tersk. The survival of Tersk remained precarious for a few more years under the renewed Ottoman demands to raze the fort and the rumours of the impending Crimean campaign. But the Ottomans were busy prosecuting their successful war against Safavid Persia and their priorities were to maintain the newly won possessions along the Caspian coast: Derbent, Shemakha and Baku. The issue seemed to have been raised by the Ottomans for the last time in 1593. When Moscow assured the Ottomans of its peaceful intentions and promised not to interfere with the Ottoman interests in the region, the Porte stopped demanding the demolition of Tersk.[8]

If anything, Russia's presence in the North Caucasus in the seventeenth century was a testimony to its tenacity and determination. Moscow's attempts to move south of Tersk proved to be unsuccessful. Several large-scale military campaigns into Daghestan were a failure. Twice Moscow built and rebuilt Fort Sunzhenskii on the Sunzha River where it flows into the Terek River, and twice Moscow was forced to abandon it. The small cossack settlements which emerged in the foothills of the Caucasus along the Terek River (the Greben' Mountains) had to be razed in the 1650s. Only Tersk stayed and remained Russia's principal base in the North Caucasus throughout the seventeenth century.

8 *Kabardino-russkie otnosheniia v XVI–XVIII vv. Dokumenty i materialy*, 2 vols. (Moscow: AN SSSR, 1957), vol. I, nos. 21 (pp. 34–5), 41 (pp. 67–8), 43 (p. 69).

The absence of a visible territorial expansion notwithstanding, Russia succeeded in establishing itself as a major power in the north-eastern corner of the Caucasus. Throughout the seventeenth century, Moscow cultivated ties with the numerous chiefs and nobles among the local peoples: the Kumyks, Nogais, Chechens and particularly the Kabardinians. Occasionally, the Russian troops marched from Tersk to assist a loyal native chief against his rivals. But most of the time, Moscow extended its influence through a system of payments, rewards and other benefits to those who represented Russian interests in the region.

Throughout the seventeenth century, a growing number of native nobles chose to seek refuge in Tersk from their rivals and foes. They often arrived with their retinue and were given land, grain and cash in exchange for their military service. Native commoners too fled to Tersk in ever-increasing numbers fleeing justice, or heavy taxation or simply lured by promises of better life. Many of the commoners became converts to Christianity. By the 1620s, four large quarters populated solely by the indigenous people grew outside the walls of Tersk: Circassian (Kabardinian), *Okochane* (members of the Ingush clan of Ako who came to Tersk in the 1590s), New convert and Tatar. The Kabardinian quarter was the largest with about 175 households by the end of the century. All in all, the population of these four quarters was almost three times larger than the Russian population of Tersk.[9]

Perhaps the most celebrated example of the natives' co-operation with Russia was the Kabardinian dynasty of the Cherkasskiis, whose members for several generations faithfully served Russian interests in the region. With the construction of Fort Tersk in 1588, several Kabardinian chiefs offered their service to Moscow and arrived at Tersk to reside there with their retinues. Among these chiefs, one, Sunchalei Ianglychev, earned the complete trust of the Russian government. He travelled to Moscow several times, was granted an annuity, and in 1615 was appointed a ruling prince over the non-Christian population of Tersk. His son Mutsal and grandson Kaspulat continued to serve Russia faithfully.

In the last half of the seventeenth century, Kaspulat Mutsalovich Cherkasskii proved to be Russia's indispensable liaison in the entire southern region. He ensured that important chiefs in Daghestan and various Kabardinian nobles were at peace with Russia. His sister's marriage to a Kalmyk chief *tayishi* accounted for his special relations with the Kalmyks. On numerous occasions,

9 Ibid., p. 402, n. 165; *Istoriia narodov Severnogo Kavkaza s drevneishikh vremen do kontsa XVIII v.*, ed. B. B. Piotrovskii (Moscow: Nauka, 1988), pp. 330–1.

his motley contingent of the Kabardinians, Kumyks, Nogais and others in Russian service joined the Kalmyks in their campaigns against the Crimea and in Ukraine against the Ottomans. Handsomely rewarded for his service, Kaspulat Cherkasskii was put in charge of all the non-Christians of Tersk, had fortified houses near Astrakhan' and Tersk and was granted for life the right to collect customs duties in Tersk.[10]

By the end of the century Tersk grew into an important frontier town. The Russian government was making sure that Tersk was adequately protected. In 1650 alone, 1,379 musketeers and cossacks were transferred to Tersk from other frontier towns and settled there with their families.[11] Tersk remained Russia's principal frontier garrison in the Caucasus until the second quarter of the eighteenth century when the advancing Russian forts and cossack settlements turned this once strategic frontier town into a provincial backwater.

The Baltics and Ukraine

Like its double-headed eagle, the symbol of the Russian monarchy, Russia faced simultaneously two very different worlds: one in the east with its animist, Muslim and Buddhist populations and the other in the west with a predominantly Christian population. Unlike its rapid advance in the east, Russia's numerous attempts to expand in the west were frustrated by the superior militaries of its neighbours: the Polish-Lithuanian Commonwealth and Sweden. Two wars in the Baltic region (1558–83, 1656–61) brought Moscow in control of some parts of Livonia and Estonia, only to be given up shortly thereafter. Only in the early eighteenth century was Russia able to establish itself in the Baltic region. The significance attributed to the Baltics was inescapable when Peter the Great imposed his vision on the region and founded a new imperial capital on the Baltic shores.

In the second half of the seventeenth century, Moscow's newly claimed subjects in the west came from eastern Ukraine. They were also Orthodox and, in Moscow's view, shared the same historical traditions of Kievan Rus'. Yet for centuries, the residents of Ukraine had remained cut off from Moscow and instead subjected to influences from Poland and Lithuania. Linguistically and culturally, they clearly possessed an identity different from their Orthodox co-religionists in Moscow. Given their common confessional identity, Moscow

---

10 *Kabardino-russkie otnosheniia v XVI–XVIII vv.*, vol. i, nos. 28 (pp. 50–1), 52 (pp. 84–5), 208 (pp. 325–6), 232 (pp. 360–1), 236 (pp. 364–5); Khodarkovsky, *Where Two Worlds Met*, pp. 95, 113–18.
11 *AI*, vol. iv, no. 141, p. 285.

considered the Ukrainians to be Russian, but with a small nod to their difference it referred to them as 'little Russians'.

Russia's acquisition of eastern Ukraine was very similar to its annexation of Siberia in the sense that Russia's involvement and expansion here was equally hesitant and cautious. The annexation of Ukraine might also have had to await the early 1700s, when the modernised Russian military proved superior to its western neighbours, had not the opportunity presented itself in 1654. For decades the Dnieper cossacks who resided in the well-fortified territory called the Zaporozhian Sech' enjoyed their freedom and privileges like their counterparts on the Don, Volga and Iaik rivers. But when the Polish government attempted to increase its control over the Zaporozhian cossacks, they revolted. The largest such uprising took place in 1648–9 under the leadership of Bohdan Khmel'nyts'kyi, who was able to unite the cossacks and the Ukrainian peasants under the anti-Polish, anti-Jewish and anti-Catholic banner.

First and foremost the cossacks were opportunists. Their sense of shared Orthodox Christian identity with the Russians mattered less than their independence and privileges. It was only after failing to form an alliance with the Ottomans and the Crimean Tatars that the cossacks approached Moscow. Realising that the support of the Zaporozhian host would mean a war with Poland-Lithuania, Moscow rebuffed Khmel'nyts'kyi and his cossacks. Yet a few years later in a momentous decision, the tsar, the Church and the boyars felt that they could no longer pass the opportunity to liberate their co-religionists from Catholic oppression and finally to acquire the lands of ancient Kievan Rus'.

In January of 1654, in the town of Pereiaslav the Zaporozhian hetman Khmel'nyts'kyi and other cossack leaders affixed their signatures to a document which the cossacks regarded as the terms of their military alliance with Russia and which Moscow considered an affirmation of the cossacks' new status as the subjects of the tsar. Such divergent understanding of their relationship inevitably led to a speedy fall-out. Two years later, in 1656, the cossacks entered an alliance with Sweden, and in 1658 chose to revert to the protection of the Polish king. But Moscow was no longer shy about its ambitions in Ukraine. The fate of Ukraine was decided in a war between Russia and Poland and the truce which the two concluded at Andrusovo in 1667. Ukraine would become divided: the left bank of the Dnieper River would come under Russian control and the right bank would remain in Polish hands.

Several other cossack revolts in the seventeenth century failed to change the status quo and to unify the cossacks again. For some time, the cossack hetmanate on the left bank of the Dnieper retained most of its privileges and sufficient autonomy. Typical incongruities of Russia's policies which were in evidence elsewhere were also present in Russia's relationship with the cossack hetmanate. While considering the occupants of the left bank to be Russian subjects, Moscow dealt with the hetmanate via the Little Russian Chancellery which was part of Russia's Foreign Office.

In many ways Moscow's relationship with the cossacks fell into a pattern of Russia's relations with the peoples elsewhere on its expanding frontiers. Like various non-Christian peoples along the Russian frontier, the cossacks too interpreted their treaty with Moscow as a military alliance with mutual obligations. They too initially were allowed autonomy which then was slowly eroded as Moscow engaged in co-opting the elites, manipulating the local rivalries and resettling those who chose to serve Russia and enrolling them in the Russian military (thus, the eastern part of the hetmanate became known as the Sloboda Ukraine and was settled with the Ukrainian cossacks who were organised into the regular regiments under the military command of the Russian governor in Belgorod). It seems that the nature of Russian autocracy allowed no exceptions, and the Russian imperial policies applied to both the non-Christians and Christians alike.

The fate of the hetmanate was likewise similar to many of its steppe neighbours. The Ukrainian hetmanate too was slowly stripped of its autonomy. By the 1720s the hetmanate was increasingly drawn into the Russian administrative and social structures, a process which was completed by the end of the eighteenth century.

The mid-Volga region

While rapidly expanding into the new areas, Russia also continued to consolidate its control in the regions conquered in the previous century. By far the most diverse and important was the middle Volga region. Here, in addition to the conquered peoples – Tatar, Bashkir, Mari, Mordva, Chuvash and Udmurt – others arrived to settle and colonise the region. By the end of the seventeenth century, not only did many towns have a sizeable Slavic population, but the countryside too was transformed by the arrival of Russian landlords and peasants and exiled Polish prisoners of war. If in the frontier regions Moscow's objectives did not go beyond the initial demands of political loyalty, in the mid-Volga region the previously vanquished population was already thoroughly integrated into the Russian administrative system. Some non-Christians were enlisted into the Russian military and occupied a special position known as the service Tatars. Other non-Christians were levied specific *iasak* or other payments and performed sundry state services.

The natives had several choices: to succumb to the Russian dominance, resist it or to flee further away; and they exercised all of these options. The majority of the non-Christians stayed on their ancestral lands, but their acceptance of Russian domination was hardly peaceful. Throughout the centuries the non-Christians of the Volga region together with the cossacks of Russia's southern borderlands were the main source of resistance to Moscow and its policies. The mid-Volga region was systematically rocked by both small-scale popular disturbances and large-scale uprisings. Among numerous peoples of the regions, the Bashkirs unquestionably took the prize and suffered the consequences of being the most rebellious subjects of the tsar.[12]

The Russian conquest and colonisation policies of the mid-Volga region also triggered a large-scale migration of the non-Christians. Some reported fleeing to avoid onerous taxation, others were fearful of forceful conversion to Christianity, whether real or rumoured. Thousands of those who fled and settled on the Bashkir lands eventually formed two social categories of registered peasants (*tepter*) and unregistered migrant peasants, who later became state peasants (*bobyl'*). In 1631–2, there were 8,355 *tepter* and *bobyl'* households residing on the Bashkir lands.[13]

While some among the native elites with the status of *tarkhan* had their traditional privilege of tax exemption confirmed and others were bestowed with it anew, a great number of the native population found itself labouring under the increased burden of taxation, corvée, state services and various legal restrictions. The impoverishment of the native peoples was evident in the flight of the population, numerous rebellions and a ceaseless paper trail of formal complaints to the governing Russian authorities. One desperate measure to which the natives resorted at the hard economic times was selling their children and kin into slavery to their wealthy co-religionists or the Russians.[14]

Russian policies of incremental integration of the conquered native population in the Russian Empire and their consequences were best described by the fugitive Bashkirs. In 1755, in the wake of yet another Bashkir uprising, a group of more than 1,500 Bashkir households came to seek refuge among the Kazakhs and warned them about the dangers of submitting to Russia. The

12 *Materialy po istorii Bashkirskoi ASSR*, vol. I: *Bashkirskie vosstaniia v XVII i pervoi polovine XVIII vekov* (Moscow and Leningrad: AN SSSR, 1936), pp. 26–40, 150–212.
13 *Ocherki po istorii Bashkirskoi ASSR*, vol. I, pt.I (Ufa: Bashkirskoe izdatel'stvo, 1956), p. 97.
14 Ibid., pp. 132–4; *Materialy po istorii Bashkirskoi ASSR*, vol. III: *Ekonomicheskie i sotsialnye otnosheniia v Bashkirii v pervoi polovine XVIII veka* (Moscow and Leningrad: AN SSSR, 1949), pp. 9–25.

fugitive Bashkirs explained that they had become Russian subjects of their own volition, had agreed to pay *iasak* and had provided numerous services and labour. In the beginning they too, like the Kazakhs, had been granted privileges, but then the government had begun to demand from them more than from their ancestors. Every year they were getting worse off, and now they were brought into such misery that they could not even feed themselves. Their petitions did not reach the empress, and their petitions to the governor remained unheeded. The governor forbade them to petition the empress, and seized, tortured and killed many of their people; they were no longer free in their own lands and waters. How could they live without the land? Military regiments came and ruined them; they cut their trees with the beehives, built forts and forced Bashkirs to fell trees, dig soil, cut stones, provide transportation, join the military patrols and buy salt at a higher price. Finally, the desperate Bashkirs resolved to flee, even though the Russian authorities tried to prevent them from fleeing by ordering executions of one remaining Bashkir resident for each fugitive. The Bashkirs warned that the same fate would soon befall the Kazakhs.[15]

Methods of conquest and colonisation

Russia's methods of conquest and colonisation appear to have formed a clear pattern. The newly encountered peoples were expected to submit an oath of allegiance seeking the tsar's protection and favour and pledging their eternal loyalty. These oaths of allegiance were prepared in Moscow and were often available only in Russian. After the native rulers, either coerced or beguiled by Russian promises, had agreed to affix their signatures to the *shert'*, Moscow held them responsible and insisted that they became Russia's subjects. A disingenuity on the part of both Moscow and the native chiefs was obvious. The chiefs were mostly interested in economic largesse and political advantages, but never considered such documents binding. Moscow too understood very well the precarious nature of its relationship with the various peoples on its frontiers. It might have claimed them as subjects, but it treated them as foreigners and considered all related matters through Russia's Foreign Office. In a further sign of Moscow's conscious and deliberate obfuscation, the royal titles which claimed suzerainty over various peoples in the frontier regions were mentioned only in correspondence with the Western Christian rulers

---

15 *Kazakhsko-russkie otnosheniia v XVI–XVIII vekakh. Sbornik dokumentov i materialov* (Alma-Ata: AN Kazakhskoi SSR, 1961), no. 210, p. 539.

and were carefully omitted in letters to the Ottoman sultans and Persian shahs.[16]

In the initial stages, Moscow relied heavily on the local elites, winning them over through a system of payments and rewards and retaining their privileges. In time, however, the growing military and economic dependence of these elites on Russia and increasing proximity of the Russian settlements, towns, monasteries and forts allowed Moscow to move into a more intrusive stage of bringing the native population under a tighter Russian rule. In other words, Moscow proceeded cautiously from indirect rule in the borderlands to direct rule once the borderlands were more firmly integrated.

Of course, such an evolution of Russia's rule over the non-Russian peoples was not a straight line, and Moscow had to overcome numerous pitfalls along the way. One of the typical dilemmas confronted by the Russian authorities along the frontiers was whether to unite a native people by supporting a single authority of a strong local ruler or to divide them by encouraging the rivalry among their elites. Both approaches were deployed at different times: the former when Moscow was in a weak position and chose to rely on the non-Russians' military aid, the latter when such aid was no longer needed and Moscow's goals then were to weaken and subdue its new non-Russian subjects.

Other issues seemed to have worked at cross-purposes. It was well understood in Moscow that winning over the native elites was critical to Russia's interests and Moscow pursued the policies of co-optation. At the same time, other Russian policies served to undermine the collaboration of the native elites. One of the major issues which emerged throughout the seventeenth century was the flight of native slaves and commoners to seek freedom and a better life in Russia. While the arrival of the native elites to seek military service and protection in Russia was an old and established practice, the exodus of commoners was a new and disturbing phenomenon in the view of the non-Russian elites.

The native nobles bitterly complained that they were losing their people to their great detriment and demanded the fugitives' return or a monetary compensation. Such complaints were most of the time dismissed by the authorities in neighbouring Russian towns under the pretext that the fugitives had been converted to Christianity and therefore could not be returned. Even in Siberia, where the increased number of fugitives meant diminished quantities of fur *iasak*, the Russian authorities accepted such fugitives and converted them to

---

16 Kotoshikhin, *O Rossii v tsarstvovanie Alekseia Mikhailovicha*, pp. 39, 40, 87.

Christianity as long as their conversion was 'voluntary'. The drain of the natives into Russia remained an issue of great importance throughout the centuries and continued to undermine Russia's relations with various native chiefs along the frontiers.[17]

Even when, compelled by political circumstances, Moscow instructed its governors to return such fugitives unconverted, few of them found their way back home. The unaware native fugitives, who could be profitably exploited or sold, represented an attractive source of profit to the corrupt local Russian authorities. Half a century later, in 1755, responding to the undeniable reality of massive exodus, purchase and conversion of the natives, the government gave a green light to those who wished to purchase and convert the natives in the frontier regions of Astrakhan', Orenburg and Siberia. In a remarkable violation of the exclusive privilege of the Russian nobility to purchase and own serfs, the government permitted priests, merchants, cossacks and others to buy, convert and teach non-Christians, who were to remain their serfs until the owners' death. The Senate sanctioned the purchase of Kalmyks, Kumyks, Chechens, Kazakhs, Karakalpaks, Turkmens, Tomuts, Tatars, Bashkirs, Baraba Tatars and other Muslims and idol-worshippers. Thus, the non-Christians would be acquired without force, 'so that they could be converted to Christianity'. Such transactions were to take place only with written permission from the native chiefs or parents of those offered for sale, and with the reasonable assurances that those to be sold had not been kidnapped.[18] Of course, given the desperate situation of many natives and the corruption of both the Russian officials and the native chiefs, these conditions were unlikely to prevent any illegal sales. What was in the seventeenth century still a cautious government policy by the mid-eighteenth century had developed into a direct encouragement of a wide-ranging enserfment and Christianisation of the non-Christians in the frontier regions.

Whether through deliberate policies or the circumstances of its overwhelming dominance, Russia's impact on the indigenous societies was destabilising and destructive. In time, the native elites found themselves drawn into the orbit of Russia's influence, becoming dependent on Moscow in political, military and economic matters. The attraction of the Russian market and access to a

---

17 *AI*, vol. I (Tipografiia Ekspeditsii zagotovleniia Gosudarstvennykh bumag, 1841), no. 209, p. 449; vol. III (Tipografiia II Otdeleniia Sobstvennoi E. I. V. Kantseliarii, 1841), no. 1542, pp. 236, 244–5; no. 1594, pp. 355–6; Michael Khodarkovsky, *Russia's Steppe Frontier: The Making of a Colonial Empire, 1500–1800* (Bloomington: Indiana University Press, 2002), pp. 201–10.
18 *Arkhiv vneshnei politiki Rossiiskoi imperii* (Moscow), f. 119, op. 5, *Kalmytskie dela*, 1755 g., d. 17, ll. 17–20.

variety of goods, cash and loans compelled the native elites to increase the tax burden on their own population in order to obtain various items of prestige and luxury. This in turn led to the problem of 'the labour drain', that is, the fleeing of the native commoners to Russia to escape their plight at home. The commoners in the indigenous societies had found themselves overburdened by the increasing demands of both their own elites and the Russian government.

What followed was the interminable civil wars between the elites vying for power and closer ties to Moscow on the one hand, and popular uprisings against the Russian government and those native elites who collaborated with Moscow on the other. The ultimate result was continuous and irreversible political and economic debilitation of the native societies, their increased dependence on Russia and their eventual incorporation into the imperial structures.

For many non-Russian peoples, the seventeenth century marked the beginning of their integration into the Russian Empire. At the time, the Russian government was still struggling to close a large gap between the rate of Moscow's expansion and its ability to control and govern the new territories and peoples. The under-governed nature of Russia's new territories and frontiers meant that the government preferred to rely on indirect control and mostly a set of non-coercive policies and incentives. It was in the eighteenth century, after the Petrine revolution, that the new Westernised generations of Russian bureaucrats and officers brought with them to the Russian frontiers the conviction of Russian and Christian superiority and their determination to achieve both the submission of the natives in no uncertain terms and a change in their way of life. In relative terms, the events of the seventeenth century were less traumatic and destructive for the native societies than the following century would prove to be.

23

The economy, trade and serfdom

RICHARD HELLIE

Commerce and the merchantry

The Russian economy in the period 1613–89 was quite sophisticated. The leaders of the hypertrophic Muscovite state were basically monetarists à la Milton Friedman who understood well that the quantity and quality of the money in circulation determined the price level. The currency was based on silver, primarily reminted thalers imported from other countries in Europe because Muscovy in that period mined no precious metals, which did not exist on its territory. By manipulating the quantity and quality of silver in the currency, the government could make the price level rise, fall or remain constant.

Throughout these decades of the 'short Russian seventeenth century', the price level of commodities varied wildly for brief periods, but always returned sooner or later to the median for the period.[1] Events such as famines and wars also had an impact on the price level, but they were not nearly as dramatic as the monetary impacts. Thus prices tended to rise for the Smolensk war (1632–4) and the Thirteen Years War (1654–67), but the major inflationary swing in prices in 1662–3 was caused not by the war, but by the government's devaluing the currency. This commenced at the end of the 1650s, when the government decided to try to pay for the war by replacing the silver currency with copper coinage.[2] Probably because faith in the government was strong, the 'bogus currency' was accepted at 'face value' for four years. A crisis occurred only when the government began to refuse to accept the copper coinage for tax payments and when word began to circulate that government leaders were minting copper coins for their own profit. Then bedlam broke loose, prices

1 This is evident for the most common commodity, rye, but holds for nearly everything else as well. See Richard Hellie, *The Economy and Material Culture of Russia 1600–1725* (Chicago: University of Chicago Press, 1999), p. 14 (see Fig. 2.1) *et passim*.
2 Richard Hellie, 'Russia, 1200–1815', in Richard Bonney (ed.), *The Rise of the Fiscal State in Europe, c.1200–1815* (Oxford: Oxford University Press, 1999), p. 494 *et passim*.

skyrocketed and the populace of Moscow rebelled in the famous Copper Uprising. Almost immediately the government increased the silver content of the currency by 2 per cent, all protest subsided and prices fell back to the median. Aside from war years, prices generally were stable for long periods of time. Of course crop failures caused temporary, localised price spikes. The general rule of the data on this period is that whenever an agricultural commodity price veers far from the median (i.e. looks 'wrong'), the source will typically say that the high price was the result of a crop failure.

All commerce in Russia was based on cash or barter. Russia had no banks until the middle of the eighteenth century,[3] and the merchants were not Rothschild-types who could proffer loans to the government or to each other. The Russian merchantry had a reputation for dishonesty, and the level of trust was certainly very low. Monasteries had reserves, which sometimes the government would 'borrow': there is no evidence that such 'loans' were ever repaid. The nexus between the mercantile monasteries, integrated vertical conglomerates which engaged in production and trade and the merchant class is not fully understood.

The government understood that its capacity to control prices generally was extraordinarily limited. One might expect that a government with pretensions akin to those of the Muscovite 'Agapetus state'[4] would have been in and out of the market all the time, but this was not the case. In its purchases, the government both in Moscow and at the local level generally was a 'price taker', that is, it paid market prices if it wanted to buy something. Only very rarely did the government impose price controls on ordinary traded goods, such as sturgeon in 1623 on the lower Volga.[5] The major exception was the price of slaves: the government set the price of limited service contract slaves at 2 roubles apiece during the Time of Troubles and raised it to 3 roubles apiece in the mid-1620s.[6] Earlier the price for slaves had been set by the market;[7] the intervention by the government changed the composition of slaves. Forcing a buyer to pay the same price for a young child as for a prime-age worker motivated buyers to bypass the over-priced slaves who thus could not get the

---

3 Arcadius Kahan, *The Plow, the Hammer, and the Knout. An Economic History of Eighteenth-Century Russia*, ed. Richard Hellie (Chicago: University of Chicago Press, 1985), pp. 311–18.

4 See 'Agapetos', in *The Oxford Dictionary of Byzantium*, ed. A. P. Kazhdan, 3 vols. (New York: Oxford University Press, 1991), vol. I, p. 34.

5 Hellie, *Economy*, pp. 80–1.

6 Richard Hellie, *Slavery in Russia 1450–1725* (Chicago: University of Chicago Press, 1982), p. 63.

7 There was one exception: as noted in Chapter 16 above, the *Sudebnik* of 1550 had placed a price cap of 15 roubles on military slaves.

welfare which the institution of slavery provided. Whether the government had anticipated this consequence of its action is unknown. The government was able to intervene in the pricing of slaves because all purchases of slaves had to be registered with the government. Without registration of the slave in the Slavery Chancellery (see Chapter 12 above), the buyer had no legal claim to his chattel, who then would have been able to flee with impunity. The government was not similarly involved with any other sale transactions in Muscovy. One might imagine that the government, which by the time of this chapter had complete control over the economic factors of land and labour, would have been similarly involved with registration of the sale of immovable property, but the fact is that sales of agricultural land were almost non-existent.[8] As shown in Chapter 16 above, government control over most of the agricultural land fund plus the right of clan redemption combined to stifle free sales transactions in land.

The vast quantity of price data permit the calculation of costs for almost anything when quantitative data are available. Thus the cost of the great Smolensk fortress, built between 1596 and 1600, perhaps the largest construction project in the sixteenth-century world, can be calculated at about 1.5 million roubles.[9] One can further calculate that the government saved vast quantities of money by abandoning that stationary form of defence in favour of the system of the fortified lines south of the Oka in the seventeenth century, and that, moreover, around mid-century, the army cost about one-eighth of Muscovy's GDP.[10]

Muscovite legislation did much of what it could to facilitate commerce. Interest on loans in common law was limited to 20 per cent in the sixteenth century.[11] In 1649, however, it was forbidden.[12] Although Russia was in the Roman law tradition in many respects because much of its law came from Byzantium, Russia for some reason never developed the Roman law of

---

8 So far, no one has produced any Muscovite land transaction between non-relatives with both the units of lands and the prices paid – presumably the definition of a market. This is most evident in the work of Valerie Kivelson: see her *Autocracy in the Provinces: The Muscovite Gentry and Political Culture in the Seventeenth Century* (Stanford, Calif.: Stanford University Press, 1996). This makes comparison between the prices of farm land in Muscovy and elsewhere impossible. See also Hellie, *Economy*, pp. 392, 631.

9 Richard Hellie, 'The Costs of Muscovite Military Defense and Expansion', in Eric Lohr and Marshall Poe (eds.), *The Military and Society in Russia 1450–1917* (Leiden: Brill, 2002), p. 49.

10 Ibid., p. 66.

11 E. I. Kolycheva, *Agrarnyi stroi Rossii XVI veka* (Moscow: Nauka, 1987), p. 117.

12 Richard Hellie (trans. and ed.), *The Muscovite Law Code (Ulozhenie) of 1649* (Irvine, Calif.: Charles Schlacks, 1988), ch. 20, art. 39. (Cited henceforth as Hellie, *Ulozhenie*.)

contract.[13] Other areas of law of interest to merchants, such as the storage of goods, however, were well developed and it would be fair to say that the legal climate for trade was generally favourable. Throughout most of this period access to courts was inexpensive, trials were expeditious and judges seem to have been relatively (if not totally) honest. Muscovite law helped to lower commercial transaction costs.

Muscovy had a well-developed group of merchants of all types, ranging from petty merchants who traded in local market stalls to long-distance merchants such as the Stroganovs who traded in salt, furs, precious objects and imported goods. The long-distance merchants used slaves to expand their family firms as was done in other countries, especially in Africa. The merchants were greatly facilitated by a number of institutional factors which considerably ante-dated this period. Most crucial was the practice stressed during Ivan IV's minority that Russia had 'one faith, one unit of currency and one measure'. This was strengthened in 1653 by a proclamation of standard units as well as a rationalisation of internal customs fees. Although internal customs collections were not abolished until 1753, they seem to have been relatively few and seem not to have inhibited commerce significantly. Given these factors, it is not surprising that Russia had something approximating a single market in the seventeenth century: costs of any similar item were similar throughout Russia, with differences being accounted for by the cost of transportation. Merchants had sufficient information to learn of differences in the costs of similar items throughout the country, and took advantage of arbitrage opportunities wherever they might arise by shipping goods from low-cost areas to higher-cost areas whenever it would have been profitable. By 1689 merchants, who created dynasties often lasting three generations, could trade unhindered throughout much of the Eurasian land mass, from the White Sea in the north to the Caspian Sea in the south, from Smolensk in the west to the Pacific Ocean in the east. This trade provided opportunities for significant accumulation of capital – which was spent on large houses, the Church, luxury goods and household slaves, who produced little or nothing and consumed much.

The elite merchants were organised by the government into three groups: the *gosti*, the *gostinaia sotnia* and the *sukonnaia sotnia*.[14] The assignments were based on capital. Rather than being an honour, such assignments were something to be avoided and even dreaded, for the government regarded them as

13 Richard Hellie, 'Russian Law from Oleg to Peter the Great', in Daniel H. Kaiser (trans. and ed.), *The Laws of Rus' – Tenth to Fifteenth Century* (Salt Lake City, Ut.: Charles Schlacks, 1992), pp. xi–xl.
14 Hellie, *Ulozhenie*, preamble, ch. 13, art. 1; ch. 19, art. 34.

members of the service class who could be pressed into government service as needed. This service took them away from their businesses and had the potential to bankrupt them. The first, the *gosti*, were based in Moscow and were the leading merchants of the realm. There were only a handful of them and they were assigned to run the major customs houses, such as at Archangel, in Astrakhan', and elsewhere. The second group, the *gostinaia sotnia* (sometimes translated as 'the merchants' hundred') were also Moscow-based and ran lesser customs houses. If collections did not match anticipation, they could be charged the difference. The third group, the *sukonnaia sotnia* ('the cloth hundred') were the elite of the provincial merchants and were assigned lesser government tasks. All of these merchants from time to time were assigned to trade the tsar's goods, particularly sables.

Chapter 19 of the Law Code (*Sobornoe Ulozhenie*) of 1649 made the merchantry into a privileged estate or caste. Except for monasteries and the tsar himself, town merchants faced little competition. Peasants, landowners and landholders, clergymen and most military servitors were forbidden to engage in trade, manufacturing and the ownership of urban property. Townsmen, those juridically on the urban tax rolls, had an exclusive monopoly on trade, manufacturing and the ownership of urban property. A small exception was made for members of the upper and middle service-class capital and provincial cavalry: they could own one house in town and keep one slave there. Such properties could not be used as bases for enterprises which would compete with the townsmen.[15] Armed musketeers were allowed to engage in petty trade and urban employment to supplement their inadequate wages. Church establishments had to surrender their urban properties and keep outside a wide greenbelt around towns, where the townsmen could keep gardens and pasture livestock. In exchange for these monopolies, the townsmen, who were largely either craftsmen or merchants, had to provide the government with the cash it needed. This arrangement, the product of disturbances in many Russian towns in June 1648, produced a settlement that kept the townsmen from rioting for over a century while providing the government with its needed revenues.[16]

Although the Russian merchants did comparatively well domestically, they could not compete in the international sphere. The larger merchants expressed this in an elaborate petition to the government in 1649 in which they requested the expulsion of Western merchants from the interior of Russia and their

15 Ibid., ch. 19.
16 Richard Hellie, 'The Stratification of Muscovite Society: The Townsmen', *RH* 5 (1978): 119–75.

confinement to the ports and frontier cities. The petition rehearsed foreign trade in Muscovy for the previous century and its dominance by the English and Dutch. They noted that the English gave local Russian merchants loans, which the Russians themselves could not do, and employed them as their factors. The foreigners kept the Russians confined to their White Sea ports.[17] The fact is that the English were just better merchants. This was proved in the Mediterranean in the last quarter of the sixteenth century when in two decades the English seized all long-distance trade from all competitors.[18] It was also proved in the period 1740–1810, when the French dominated Russian culture but were a poor third in the trade sector. The French complained about English loans to Russian factors, just as the elite Russians had complained a century earlier. In all of these cases, the Mediterranean, the pre-1649 era and the post-1740 era, the key to English success was communications.[19] This was high on the list of the things the Russians said that they just were unable to compete with.

Without any assistance from the government, by 1613 the Russians were able to borrow the names and styles of much of their clothing from the Turkic peoples who had been their southern neighbours for the previous millennium.[20] But when it came to major technology transfer after 1613 from the West, nothing happened without governmental intervention. Moscow hired not only medical doctors, linguists, translators, astronomers and painters, but also architects, silk weavers, ship builders, food specialists, paper makers, vintners, iron makers and ore prospectors from the West. Metal specialists were requested from abroad in 1621, and the Dutch in the 1620s and 1630s enjoyed monopoly hegemony in the iron industry. In 1623 Dutch entrepreneurs established a rope works, complementing that set up by the English at the end of the sixteenth century. The Dutch got a pitch monopoly in the 1620s and a potash monopoly in the 1630s. Dutch and Holstein shipwrights built a fleet on the Caspian in the 1630s. In 1634, the Dutch got a monopoly on the manufacture of velvet. In the same year, the first glass factory was established. Westerners also organised a temporary postal system and taught the Russians how to dig deeper wells. The first paper mill was built in 1655, and foreigners established

17 Richard Hellie (ed. and trans.), *Muscovite Society* (Chicago: University of Chicago Press, 1967, 1970), pp. 63–91.
18 Maria Fusaro, 'Commercial Networks of Cooperation in the Venetian Mediterranean: The English and the Greeks, a Case Study', unpublished paper, October 2001.
19 Richard Hellie, 'Le Commerce russe dans la deuxième moitié du XVIIIe siècle (1740–1810)', in *L'Influence française en Russie au XVIII siècle*, ed. Jean-Pierre Poussou et al. (Paris: Presses de l'Université de Paris-Sorbonne, 2004), pp. 73–82.
20 Hellie, *Economy*, ch. 18.

a rag paper factory six years later. In 1667 foreigners set up woollen mills and a decade later an Italian set up a silk factory. In the late 1660s, at the invitation of the government, foreign prospectors discovered copper ores in the north, north of the Volga, and began to mine and process them for the state. These people were in addition to the mercenaries who modernised the Russian army for the Smolensk war (1632–4) by introducing the new formation regiments. About half of the Russian army at Smolensk consisted of these mercenaries and their men. They proved to be a tremendous drain on the treasury, so the majority were sent home after the war. Recruitment was initiated again in 1647 in preparation for the Thirteen Years War (1654–67), but this time was largely limited to officers.[21] In 1654 the government, primarily at the urging of the Orthodox Church, closed one of the last openings in the caste society created by the *Ulozhenie* of 1649 (see below) when it forced the foreigners, almost all of whom were very highly compensated, to live in the Northern European Settlement (*nemetskaia sloboda*: the Foreign – literally German – Quarter). This later served as the incubator for Peter the Great's Western orientation.

In the mid-seventeenth century mercantilism (a slight variation on the French Colbertism) came to Russia. The first mercantilist was Fedor Rtishchev, but its major spokesman was A. L. Ordin-Nashchokin. A native of Pskov, Ordin-Nashchokin wrote the Pskov merchant charter of 1665 and the New Trade Regulations of 1667. He advocated Western-style efficiency and gaining an outlet in the Baltic to the West. *Inter alia*, he was a mild protectionist who advocated keeping as much specie as possible in Russia, which may have been partially responsible for the general decline in the price level between 1663 and 1689.[22]

The process of enserfment, 1613–49

The Muscovite economy did not provide well for most Russians. As mentioned, there are no useful minerals between the Volga and the Oka and all had to be imported. The thin podzol topsoil is acidic and provides very low yields, in this period three seeds harvested for each one sown. The growing season was too short and the precipitation typically considerably more than would have been ideal. Lesser yields led to famine and starvation, which occurred roughly once in every seven years in Russia.

Most people lived in smoky huts, log cabins with a large brick or stone and mortar stove which vented their lethal smoke into the room rather than

---

21 Hellie, *Enserfment*, chs. 10 and 11.
22 See most of the figures in Hellie, *Economy*.

outside via a chimney, to save heat. One may surmise that most people had very little energy, both because they were gassed six months of the year by their own air-polluting stoves and because of inadequate nutrition. Most people lived at a subsistence level with a life expectancy of less than thirty years. Per capita income was probably less than $600 (£350). The median wage for the entire population was 4 kopecks per day, and for the 'working class' it was 3 kopecks per day. A smoky hut's median price was 3.25 roubles, or about 100 days' pay.[23] Frequent fires meant that housing was replaced often. As discussed in Chapter 12 above, there was little inside most of the huts: the three-chambered stove (which could be large enough for two people to sleep on the top), benches around two-plus walls of the room to sit and sleep on, occasionally a table, perhaps a trunk for extra clothing and little more.

The vast majority of the population in the years 1613–89 were serfs, perhaps 85 per cent. Of the rest, perhaps 5 to 15 per cent were slaves. Then the clergy, townsmen and military forces comprised around another 2 per cent each. These were of the roughly five million inhabitants in 1613, perhaps nine or ten million in 1689.[24]

For reasons that are still not clear, the Time of Troubles had little impact on the process of enserfing the peasantry. Shuiskii's 1607 decree seems to have gone into limbo, and the legal situation reverted to the decrees of 1592: the peasants were bound to the land with the repeal of the right to move on St George's Day until further notice and the five-year statute of limitations on the filing of suits for the recovery of fugitive serfs. What may be called 'the Soviet' explanation for this was that the government was so terrified by first the Khlopko uprising (1601–3) and then the Bolotnikov uprising (1606–7) that it lacked the spirit to repress the peasants any further. I would be inclined towards another interpretation: the 1592 provisions satisfied those who were running the government, so they were not about to make any changes unless forced to do so.[25]

Other elements, however, were restive with the status quo. In the social stratification sweepstakes, the townsmen held a special place. Their problem was the Russian system of collective taxation. The census takers came around

23 Hellie, *Economy*, ch. 20; pp. 388, 404–5.
24 Ia. E. Vodarskii reckons the 1678 population at ten million, of whom 92 per cent were peasants (V. A. Aleksandrov et al., *Krest'ianstvo perioda pozdnego feodalizma (seredina XVIIv. – 1861 g.) (Istoriia krest'ianstva Rossii s drevneishikh vremen do 1917 g.,* vol. III) (Moscow: Nauka, 1993), p.18). This seems to minimise excessively the slave population, which was not counted in the censuses because slaves paid no taxes. See my *Slavery* volume for my calculations of the numbers of slaves.
25 Hellie, *Enserfment*, chs. 6 and 7.

and would find *x* number of people living in an urban area. Assuming that *x* number of people lived in the area, the tax collectors assessed the area *y* roubles until the next census. Problems arose when some townsmen moved away or fled. The tax collectors still insisted that the area pay *y* roubles, even though there were fewer taxpayers than there had been when the census was taken. As a result, the remaining townsmen began to ask the government to forbid any further people from moving away and that those who had moved away be returned to share in the tax burden. An early example of this was in 1590/1, when the people of Toropets (on the western frontier) asked that their fellow townsmen be forbidden to move. The government complied by extending the forbidden years concept from the peasantry to the townsmen of Toropets.[26]

The Time of Troubles was brutal to the Russian towns. Townsmen were sent scurrying in all directions, much as Ivan IV's savage reign had sent the peasants scattering. By 1613 many towns were completely depopulated.[27] 'Recovery economics' is an important branch of economics, and it is probably correct to infer that Russia had recovered from the Time of Troubles by 1629. The year 1613 became the reference point for urban residence. After then, when townsmen asked that their peers who had departed be returned, the reference point always was back to 1613. By the late 1630s, townsmen were being returned who had fled a quarter-century earlier. This example played a major role in the campaign to have peasants returned who had fled more than five years previously. Also exemplary for the institution of serfdom was the fact that the government in the late 1630s became directly involved in the search for and return of fugitive townsmen.[28] For fugitive serfs and slaves, on the other hand, the government took no role until after the *Ulozhenie* of 1649.

Monasteries also suffered from the dislocations caused by the Time of Troubles. This recalls the time in the 1450s, when monasteries initiated the limitation of indebted peasants to the period around St George's Day, the very first steps on the road to serfdom. Shortly after 1613 elite monasteries were the first to be heard from on the issue of fugitive serfs. They complained that five years were inadequate for the recovery of their fugitive serfs, and the government extended the time to ten and more years, depending on when the peasants had fled.[29]

26 Hellie, *Muscovite Society*, pp. 33–47.
27 P. P. Smirnov, *Posadskie liudi i ikh klassovaia bor'ba do serediny XVII veka*, 2 vols. (Moscow and Leningrad: AN SSSR, 1947–8).
28 Ibid.; Hellie, 'Stratification'.
29 Hellie, *Muscovite Society*, pp. 144–56, A. E. Vorms et al. (eds.), *Pamiatniki istorii krest'ian XIV–XIX vv.* (Moscow: N. N. Klochkov, 1910), pp. 50–2.

Other than these developments, the social stratification front was relatively quiet between the end of the Time of Troubles and the end of the Smolensk war. Recovery took most of the social energy there was, and Patriarch Filaret, father of Tsar Michael, ran a tight ship while he was at the helm of the Russian state between 1619 and 1633. After his death, self-serving and corruption became the order of the day in the Russian government between 1633 and 1648. The ruling elite were occupied with allotting lands to themselves and looting the treasury. Witnessing that orgy of corruption, the members of the middle service class decided that it was time to get theirs. So, in 1637 they initiated perhaps the most famous petition campaign in Russian history for the completion of the enserfment of the peasantry.[30] They enumerated the troubles the five-year statute of limitations on the recovery of fugitive serfs caused them. They noted that 'contumacious (literally, strong) people' (sil'nye liudi) used the statute of limitations to conceal fugitives; once the statute of limitations had expired, the 'contumacious people' would send the fugitives back whence they had come to recruit other fugitives. The only solution, said the petitioners, was to repeal the statute of limitations. The government responded by extending the statute of limitations from five to nine years.[31]

The provincial cavalrymen found this concession to be of little help, so in 1641 again petitioned for a repeal of the statute of limitations. The government responded by extending the statute of limitations from nine to fifteen years.[32] Here one must stop to examine the context of these petitions. After the conclusion of the Smolensk war, which ended in a 'draw' because the Poles surrendered their claim to the Russian throne but refused to return the great fortress of Smolensk to the Russians, the government turned its attention from the western front to the southern front. The Crimean Tatars were still a major threat to Muscovy; their annual slave raids had carried off tens of thousands of Russians into the slave markets of the Crimea, and their raids diverted the Russians during the Smolensk war from concentrating their full attention on Smolensk. So the Muscovites began to wall off the southern frontier by constructing what became known as the Belgorod fortified line in the years 1636–54. This moved the formal frontier of Muscovy hundreds of miles south of the Oka and added tens of thousands of hectares of some of the best agricultural land in the world to Muscovite control. Those directing

30 N. A. Gorskaia et al., *Krest'ianstvo v periody rannego i razvitogo feodalizma (Istoriia krest'ianstva SSSR s drevneishikh vremen do velikoi oktiabr'skoi sotsialisticheskoi revoliutsii,* vol. II) (Moscow: Nauka, 1990), pp. 379–80.
31 Hellie, *Muscovite Society,* pp. 167–76.
32 Ibid., pp. 178–91.

the Belgorod Line operation wanted the region between the line and the Oka settled for strategic purposes. The new settlers could be recruited for military purposes for service on the fortified line if necessary, and as farmers added significantly to the GNP of Muscovy while providing ready food to the frontier forces. Peasants were delighted to oblige by migrating to the frontier because their incomes rose farming the rich *chernozem* vis-à-vis what they could get from the poor podzol soils north of the Oka; besides that, south of the Oka, they had no landlords to worry about or pay rent to. Government officials behind the Belgorod Line were reluctant to return fugitives to their places of origins north of the Oka.

Thus in the years after 1636 the middle service-class cavalry landholders north of the Oka came to know that every time they would report for their annual military service, their peasants would use their absence to move to a frontier region where they could not possibly locate them, both because of the distances involved and because of the hostility of the frontier officials should by some stroke of luck they manage to find their fugitives. Slaves registered in the Moscow Slavery Chancellery were accurately enough described so that in a judicial contest for the return of a fugitive slave, the central records could be brought to the courtroom and a reasonable decision made whether the person being contested was the slave described in the government document. But in the case of peasant serfs, no such records existed.[33] In a hostile frontier courtroom, a serf-hunter could claim that the contested person x was his fugitive serf Ivan son of Pavel, x could respond that he was Nikolai son of Aleksei, that this was a case of mistaken identity – and the judge almost certainly would throw out the plaintiff's claim for x. The provincial cavalrymen, who only had 5.6 peasant households apiece, were hardly wealthy to begin with. When their labour force began to vanish, they became desperate.

Fifteen years proved to be of no more use to the middle service class than had nine or five. So, in 1645 they submitted a third petition asking for the repeal of the statute of limitations. This time, the government, in transition from Tsar Michael to Tsar Alexis, caved in and promised to repeal the statute

33 A decree of 30 March 1688 tried to compensate for this inadequacy by requiring the registration of purchased and ceded/exchanged hereditary estate and service landholding serfs in the Service Landholding Chancellery (SLC) while loans and similar documents were to be registered in the Slavery Chancellery (SC). This measure could not be effective because the SLC was already overburdened with trying to keep track of the ownership and possession of much of the land in Russia, and could not possibly cope with keeping records on all the serfs as well. The SC's task was much more manageable. See *RZ*, 9 vols. (Moscow: Iuridicheskaia literatura, 1984–94), vol. IV: *Zakonodatel'stvo perioda stanovleniia absoliutizma*, ed. A. G. Man'kov (1986), pp. 102–3.

of limitations – once a new census had been taken.[34] The census was taken, in 1646–7, but the government was taken over (in the name of Alexis) by his tutor, Boris Ivanovich Morozov. Morozov was one of the most able men ever to head a Russian government, but also one of the most greedy and corrupt. Contemporaries reported that he had a 'thirst for gold as others thirst for water'. Morozov tried to rationalise and simplify the taxation system, which consisted of countless imposts on almost everything that moved or was stationary. Morozov got the idea of annulling many of them and consolidating them into a tax on salt. What Morozov forgot was that the demand for salt is elastic. With a dramatic rise in the price of salt because of the new tax, the consumption fell dramatically, and the reform collapsed. The rage against Morozov, however, did not collapse, but was only strengthened by many of his other activities. Of a rather minor if ancient Muscovite family, but not a noble, he began life with modest peasant holdings and ended it as the largest serf-holder in Muscovy. He enriched himself both with lands and peasants and with state property. He surrounded himself with a loyal cadre of equally rapacious individuals. Not only did he 'forget' the 1645 promise to repeal the statute of limitations, all the while he was luring away other landholders' peasants and dispatching them to distant properties he appropriated for himself on the Volga. He issued orders to his estate stewards to conceal fugitives even as his days in active government service were expiring in 1648.[35]

Morozov was so corrupt that the townsmen of Moscow could no longer endure it. They composed a petition to Alexis and tried to present it to him on 1 June 1648, as he rode through Moscow. That monumental document was translated into Swedish by a visitor at the time in Moscow and survives both in the original Middle Russian and in Swedish.[36] When the petitioners tried to present the document to Alexis, his accompanying musketeer guards tore it up and threw it into their faces. This touched off two days of rioting in Moscow in which a considerable portion of the city was burned, and two of Morozov's collaborators were torn to bits by the mob and their remains cast on some of the many dung heaps gracing the city's streets.[37] Morozov was saved from a similar fate only by the personal intervention of the tsar, who promised that Boris Ivanovich would never again serve in the Muscovite government.

34 Ibid., pp. 191–6.
35 Hellie, *Enserfment*, pp. 133–8, 188–9.
36 Hellie, *Muscovite Society*, pp. 198–205.
37 Richard Hellie, 'Patterns of Instability in Russian and Soviet History', *Chicago Review of International Affairs* 1 (1989): 3–34.

In their petition the people of Moscow complained about the Morozov gang corruption and asked for the compilation of a new law code, with references to the Byzantine lawgivers Constantine and Justinian. The government, which was frightened out of its wits as the rioting spread to a dozen other towns, made several responses. First, Morozov and his cohort were permanently purged from the government and replaced with another group. Second, a commission of five men, headed by N. I. Odoevskii, was appointed to compile the laws. And third, calls were issued for the election of delegates to an Assembly of the Land (*zemskii sobor*), a proto-parliamentary body which originated in 1566 and was called at times when major national issues needed to be resolved, such as war and peace, dynastic succession and major legal issues. A full Assembly of the Land consisted of two chambers. The upper chamber contained members of the upper service class and the clergy. The lower chamber had elected delegates from the towns and the provincial middle service class. It is known that at least some of the 1648 delegate elections were vigorously contested.[38]

The Ulozhenie of 1649

The Odoevskii legislative commission was one of the most efficient in all Russian history. Its members sent requests to the major chancelleries requesting that they send them their statute books, scrolls on which laws were entered as they were made. About ten of the forty chancelleries participated in that process. The commission extracted the most relevant provisions from the statute books and grouped them into what became the twenty-five chapters of the Law Code of 1649 (*Sobornoe Ulozhenie*), the most important written monument in all of Russian history before the nineteenth century – with perhaps the exception of the chronicles. On 1 October 1648, the delegates to the Assembly of the Land assembled with the petitions and demands of their constituents. About 7 per cent of the 968 articles of the *Ulozhenie* resulted from the petitions brought to the Assembly of the Land, including one for the repeal of the statute of limitations for filing suits for the recovery of fugitive serfs. The Odoevskii Commission read its draft to the delegates of each chamber, who voted each article either up or down. The provisions demanded by the delegates were integrated in with the Odoevskii Commission's draft extracted from the chancellery records. The whole project was completed in January 1649, and on 29 January the delegates who were willing signed the

---

38 Hellie, *Enserfment*, pp. 134–45, *et passim*; Richard Hellie, 'Zemskii sobor', in *MERSH*, vol. xlv (Gulf Breeze, Fla.: Academic International Press, 1987), pp. 226–34.

scroll copy of the *Ulozhenie*. This point must be stressed, for it is known that a number of the upper chamber clerics refused to sign the document to protest against the beating the Church had taken in the document on issues ranging from a semi-secularisation of the Church (a lay governmental chancellery, the Monastery Chancellery, was appointed to manage much of the Church; this was an ancestor of Peter the Great's Holy Synod) to issues on Church property discussed at the beginning of this chapter. The scroll copy, which is still extant, was taken to the state typography, and then 1,200 copies were published. This was the second civil (non-religious) book published in Muscovy. The 1,200 copies sold out rapidly, and a second printing of another 1,200 copies was ordered immediately, which sold out in a couple of years.[39] The entire *Ulozhenie* is a printed manifestation of the dictum of the Nobel Prize-winning economist James Buchanan that governments will acquire more power whenever the opportunity arises. The *Ulozhenie* gave the government power over nearly all of society, thus consolidating its almost total control over two of the major economic factors (land and labour).[40] The third factor, capital, was

---

39 Richard Hellie, 'Muscovite Law and Society: the *Ulozhenie* of 1649 as a Reflection of the Political and Social Development of Russia since the *Sudebnik* of 1589', unpublished Ph.D. dissertation, University of Chicago, 1965; Richard Hellie, 'The *Ulozhenie* of 1649', *MERSH*, vol. XL (Gulf Breeze, Fla.: Academic International Press, 1985), pp. 192–8; Richard Hellie, 'Early Modern Russian Law: The *Ulozhenie* of 1649', and '*Ulozhenie* Commentary: Preamble and Chapters 1–2', *RH* 15 (1988): 155–224; Richard Hellie, 'Commentary on Chapters 3 through 6', *RH* 17 (1990): 65–78; Richard Hellie, 'Commentary on Chapters 7–9', *RH* 17 (1990): 179–226; Richard Hellie, 'Commentary on Chapter 11 (The Judicial Process for Peasants)', *RH* 17 (1990): 305–39; Richard Hellie, 'The Church and the Law in Late Muscovy: Chapters 12 and 13 of the *Ulozhenie* of 1649', *CASS* 25 (1991): 179–99.

40 Perhaps a chapter such as this should discuss in detail the evolution of the exploitation of the peasants / serfs in this period, but space limitations and other considerations prevent such a presentation. Soviet scholars did much work on this issue, but never systematised their findings. The problems are immense. One is the passage of time, and the facts that rents were always changing. Another is the fact that there were numerous forms of rent, ranging from labour rent (*barshchina*) in which a serf farmed his lord's land to money or in kind rent (*obrok*) to any possible combination of these forms of rent. Geographical variations were important. Perhaps most important was the variety of landowners and landholders ranging from the state itself to the tsar, from the Church (consisting of the patriarch, monasteries, individual institutions) to magnate landowners down to provincial cavalry landholders. With the passage of time, pure 'rent' gets mixed up with taxes. The general assumption is that rent and taxes took about a third of a peasant's harvest and his time (if properly priced), the peasant could consume about a third of what he produced, and he had to save about a third of his harvest for seed for the following year. See e.g. A. N. Sakharov, *Russkaia derevnia XVII v. Po materialam Patriarshego khoziaistva* (Moscow: Nauka, 1966), pp. 66–7; N. A. Gorskaia, *Monastyrskie krest'iane Tsentral'noi Rossii v XVII veke. O sushchnosti i formakh feodal'no-krepostnicheskikh otnoshenii* (Moscow: Nauka, 1977), pp. 239–339; Iu. A. Tikhonov, *Pomeshchich'i krest'iane v Rossii. Feodal'naia renta v XVII – nachale XVIII v.* (Moscow: Nauka, 1974), pp. 117–305. Tikhonov's table 59 shows the vast variations in rents on service landholdings in this period (p. 297). See also L. V. Milov, *Velikorusskii pakhar' i osobennosti rossiiskogo istoricheskogo protsessa* (Moscow:

still largely in private hands, although the discussion above about technology transfers indicates that the government, which also was the largest merchant, had considerable control over this factor as well.

The *Ulozhenie* became known everywhere almost immediately and was referred to by those with legal interests for decades thereafter. The major changes in the law were announced by public criers. For the purposes of this chapter, the major items of interest were contained in the *Ulozhenie*'s chapter 11 (serfdom, 34 articles), chapter 19 (townsmen, 40 articles), and chapter 20 (slaves, 119 articles). The Assembly of the Land added little to chapter 20, which was a codification of the practices of the Slavery Chancellery. On the other hand, much of chapters 11 and 19 came from petitions by the delegates to the Assembly of the Land. The principles of these three chapters interacted with one another in the production of the system which was to last in Russia – even beyond the abolition of personal serfdom in 1861 – until the reforms of 1906 onwards.

The first principle of serfdom was that the peasant could not move without his lord's permission. The same was true for the townsmen (for whom the town was the 'lord'). According to articles 1 and 2 of chapter 11, this was true for all peasants, regardless of whether they lived on lay or Church seigniorial land, or on land that had no lord, 'taxable land', that still belonged to the peasants or to the state. Later on, in the eighteenth century, the provisions for seigniorial and state peasants diverged, but this was not the case in 1649. Second, there was the issue of the return of fugitives. Here the measures for serfs resembled more those for slaves than for townsmen. For the return of slaves, there had never been a statute of limitations for the filing of suits for the recovery of fugitives. Now, the same applied to serfs. As mentioned earlier, however, the evidentiary bases for the status of slavery and serfdom differed dramatically. Slaves were registered in the Moscow Slavery Chancellery; otherwise they were not slaves. There was no formal registration for serfs, so the issue arose of what evidence would apply in the case of disputes involving serfs. The *Ulozhenie* preferred written evidence, and mentioned the land cadastres compiled in 1626, the recently compiled 1646–7 census, or records transmitting possession of lands to servicemen. In practice, such written evidence overrode the clause in the *Ulozhenie* which declared that a peasant was supposed to live where his/her grandfather had lived. On the other hand, there were no provisions for the return of townsmen who had fled prior to the *Ulozhenie*; for them,

Rosspen, 1998), pp. 483–5; Z. A. Ogrizko, *Iz istorii krest'ianstva na Severe feodal'noi Rossii XVII v. (Osobye formy krepostnoi zavisimosti)* (Moscow: Sovetskaia Rossiia, 1968), pp. 26–57; Aleksandrov et al., *Krest'ianstvo*, p. 154.

the binding process began on 29 January 1649, and continued indefinitely into the future. No definitive explanation for the difference has ever been offered, but one may surmise that the Odoevskii commission believed that townsmen were involved in a trade whose disruption would be economically deleterious, whereas peasants moved their agricultural site regularly because of soil exhaustion and thus transportation back to a legal lord's estate would be little more disruptive than moving to a new site on the same estate in slash/burn (assartage) agriculture, or rotating around in the three-field system. Of course the explanation may have been more political than economic, that the delegates from the middle service-class cavalry at the Assembly of the Land were more persuasive/intimidating than were the urban delegates.

A major issue that concerned all three population categories was that of marriage. If one or two fugitives wed while one or both were in flight from their lawful owners or places of residence, what should happen to the couple? The Russian Orthodox Church was adamant that marriage was inviolable. In response to this simple dogma, a simple solution for fugitives was found: receiving fugitive slaves, serfs and townsmen was illegal, so whoever received the fugitive was penalised by losing the couple. However, the family was not inviolable, so that if they had children, the law-breaking harbourer of the fugitive could keep the offspring born while in his 'care' even though he (or it: a town) lost the parents. If the fugitives married while on 'neutral ground', such as on the frontier where there were no lords, then the lords cast lots to determine possession. The winner got the couple and had to pay the loser 10 roubles. If a female fugitive serf married a frontier serviceman, he could keep her for 50 roubles. This was an impossible sum, presumably meant to deter servicemen from marrying fugitive women and the women from fleeing to the frontiers.

One final issue, the abasement of the person of the serf which began in the reign of Ivan IV (see Chapter 12 above) remains to be discussed. The *Ulozhenie* surprisingly has little to say about that, even though the chapter on slaves is the second longest in the law code and thus the Odoevskii commission cannot be suspected of having been squeamish on this topic. One may surmise that the legislators wanted to concentrate on the principle at hand, the perpetual binding of the peasants to the land, not its possible derivative which could easily enough turn into its opposite, the binding of the peasant to the person of a lord. The culmination of this fate of the serfs waited until the early eighteenth century, to last until 1861. But the forebodings of what was to come are evident in the *Ulozhenie*. Ominous is article 3 of chapter 15 which permits a hereditary landowner (*votchinnik*) to issue a manumission charter freeing his serf, but denies that privilege to a service landholder (*pomeshchik*). This, of course, equates one category of serfs with slaves, both of whom can become freedmen (nearly the sole category of free people in Muscovy). This also served as a vehicle for an owner of a hereditary estate to transfer his peasants to another holding. Article 7 of chapter 16 permits outright someone who acquired waste lands to move peasants from his other lands to populate those waste lands. Nothing is said about the consent of the serfs in this process, which probably enhanced economic efficiency at the expense of the personal freedom of the serfs.

Another ominous sign of the abasement of the peasant is in article 141 of chapter 10. It had long been assumed that a slave was an extension of his owner, and that putting pressure on a slave would force his owner to comply with the law. This article extends that provision to the serf: if a defendant hid from a bailiff, the bailiff could detain either his slave or his serf to force him to appear. Chapter 10, article 161 establishes the procedures for conducting a general investigation (*poval'nyi obysk*). Members of the middle service class (*dvoriane* and *deti boiarskie*) were to be interrogated separately, and their testimony was to be recorded separately from that of their slaves and serfs. Notice here that again the serfs are linked with slaves, and both are less full witnesses than their masters. (Further on, however, article 163 decrees that serfs who lied in such investigations were to be fined a rouble, but nothing was said about slaves who lied at all; their owners were fined 30 roubles for their own perjury. Article 261 contains further evidence that slave status had not yet been fully extended to serfs. A member of the middle service class who did not pay his debts could be placed in a righter (*pravezh*), a form of stocks, where force would be used to compel the debtor to pay. His slave could be put in the righter instead of the debtor, but this did not extend to serfs.) On the other hand, debts could be collected both from the slaves and the serfs of a landholder or estate owner (art. 262). In 1642 peasants had been denied the right to make contracts which, upon default, would have led to their formal enslavement.

At the request of the provincial cavalry delegates to the Assembly of the Land, a practice borrowed from the history of the townsmen was soon adopted: the mass dragnet. The difficulty of finding fugitive serfs in the condition of constant labour shortage and the willingness of other lords to take them in was a constant theme of Russian history.[41] The same was true, of course, for townsmen, except that townsmen were likely to flee from one town to another;

---

41 Richard Hellie, 'Migration in Early Modern Russia, 1480s–1780s', in David Eltis (ed.), *Coerced and Free Migration. Global Perspectives* (Stanford, Calif.: Stanford University Press, 2002), pp. 292–323.

the number of urban settlements was limited, and it was comparatively easy for a dragnet to go through urban areas and identify those who did not legally belong there. The magnitude of the difficulty of such endeavours in the vast Russian countryside and the new frontier areas can only be imagined. It was modestly facilitated by the Russian practice of living in villages, however, rather than on isolated farmsteads. Be that as it may, after the *Ulozhenie*, the government formed dragnet teams which scoured the countryside for fugitive peasants.[42] No doubt the legal practice of the mass inquisition (*poval'nyi obysk*) gave the Russian government practice in running dragnets; the mass inquisition could be called for by litigants, and a team of investigators would go out to the area to survey the region to ask up to several hundred people such a question as, 'Who owned the spotted cow with the crooked horn?' Whichever litigant got the majority won the case. When hunting for fugitive serfs (slaves were thrown in, too), the interrogators asked everyone to prove that he/she lived where he/she was at the moment. If no proof could be offered, the assumption was that the object of the inquisition must belong somewhere else. Torture could be used to find out where that somewhere else was. Then the fugitives were loaded on carts and returned where they belonged. Records survive revealing that some investigators returned more than a thousand runaways.

Creating a legal caste of peasant serfs, the *Ulozhenie* forbade them to leave their caste. Earlier, a down-and-out peasant could sell him/herself into slavery, but this was now forbidden. The government was always short of military personnel, and occasionally peasants joined the middle service-class cavalry or the lower service-class musketeers, artillerymen or cossacks. That was also categorically forbidden. Becoming a townsman had also been an option. It is doubtful that the townsmen reproduced themselves, and they always welcomed additions to their numbers who would share the tax burden. Moreover, there were no guilds to keep interlopers out. But rural to urban migration was also forbidden. Nevertheless, it persisted, in spite of the law. After the *Ulozhenie*, the townsmen on several occasions asked that amnesties be granted to fugitive peasants currently living in their midst. The government, anxious to collect the cash taxes paid by townsmen, agreed in 1684, 1685 and 1688 not to return fugitive serfs who had been registered in a town in the 1678 census. In 1693,

---

42 This practice continued for years thereafter, for without continuing enforcement the legal stratification of society would have been a farce. The distinguished Leningrad/St Petersburg historian A. G. Man'kov claimed that the fifty-two article decree of 2 March 1683 to the state's fugitive serf and slave hunters was the most important legislative document of the second half of the seventeenth century (*RZ*, vol. iv, p. 79).

this date was moved up to 1684.[43] Regrettably, I know of no way to calculate the economic cost to the Russian economy up until 1689 of the prohibition against rural–urban migration, but there must have been some – just as there unquestionably must have been economic costs from the stratification of the entire society. The fact was that the Muscovite state exhibited its maximalist tendencies in the social sphere, regardless of the economic costs.

In spite of the *Ulozhenie*, peasants continued to flee, both to other landlords and to the frontiers. About the latter little could be done, and it is not clear that the government was opposed to the settling of the frontier areas in any case.[44] But the government learned that there was something it could do to inhibit lords from receiving fugitives. The first step was a fine, which had no impact. Then the government decided to confiscate an additional peasant besides the fugitive being returned. This had no impact. So the government raised the number to two. This also had no impact. But when the number was raised to four, would-be recipients of others' fugitive serfs drove them out en masse.[45] Historians have been able to learn of only a handful of enforcements of this sanction. For the savage Peter the Great, this was still insufficient, so he decreed the death penalty for the receiver of another's serf. Whether this sanction was ever effected is unknown.

The post-*Ulozhenie* era was replete with legislation on serfs, as we have seen. The last measure which must be mentioned came about as a result of the census of 1678, which uncovered the fact that vast numbers of serfs, now differing little from slaves, had left the tax rolls by selling themselves into slavery. The following year the government solved this problem on 2 September 1679 by unilaterally converting all slaves engaged in agriculture into serfs, that is, putting them on the tax rolls.[46] This left household slavery as the sole exit for the exploited peasantry, a fact uncovered in the census of 1719. Peter liquidated that problem on 5 February 1722, and again on 19 January 1723, by making all household slaves subject to the soul tax (a head tax on all males), thus extinguishing the institution of slavery in favour of serfdom.[47]

---

43 Ibid., pp. 146–7; *PRP*, 8 vols. (Moscow: Gosiurizdat, 1952–63), vyp. VII: *Pamiatniki prava perioda sozdaniia absoliutnoi monarkhii. Vtoraia polovina XVII v.*, ed. L. V. Cherepnin (1963), pp. 298–301. See also the decree of 5 March 1677, permitting peasants of the Saviour monastery who had settled in the town of Iaroslavl' after the *Ulozhenie* to remain there (*PRP*, vyp. VII, p. 297). In 1699 a similar decree was issued for Kazan' (ibid., p. 302).

44 Hellie, *Enserfment*, p. 250.

45 Ibid., pp. 252–3. Additionally, fines of 20 roubles per year per fugitive were to be collected, and offending estate stewards were to be beaten with the knout: Vorms, *Pamiatniki*, pp. 84–6.

46 Hellie, *Slavery*, pp. 686, 697.

47 Ibid., p. 698.

The census of 1678 changed the method of assessment of taxation. Previously, peasants had been taxed on the basis of the quantity and quality of the land they tilled. As one might expect, this led to a diminution of agricultural tillage. So the government decided to tax on the basis of households. The mean household size had been four. The new provision changed the nature of the peasant/serf household. Like all economic creatures, the Russians soon figured out a way to 'beat' the tax collector: to crowd as many people into a house as possible. The smoky hut had limited capacity, but fundamentally solitaries disappeared and the three-generational family was created. The same thing had happened earlier in the Balkans, when the Ottomans had introduced household taxation a few centuries earlier. Mean household size increased to ten, as surviving grandparents, their male children and spouses and their children all crowded into one hut. Nineteenth-century Slavophiles believed that the extended family was a primordial Slavic peasant institution, but in fact it had been created, really unknowingly, by the powerful Muscovite state. Peter figured out what had happened, and shifted to the system of soul taxation. Crowding so many people into one hut was undoubtedly deleterious for both health and social relations, but it saved money (first, on heat, like the stove ventilating into the room), so that the extended family persisted to 1861, and in many cases to the end of the tsarist regime. This was done under pressure from landlords desiring to maximise rents and peasant communes desiring each household to have maximum disposable income to pay its share of the collectively assessed taxes. Recall that the soul tax was imposed on all males. Only working males actually could pay the tax burden, whereas a widow with five small boys paid nothing, even though five 'souls' were entered in the tax records. Thus the tax burden of a community was collectively assessed and paid by the able-bodied males, who were interested in every household's taxpaying ability to support the demands of the hypertrophic state.

24

Law and society

NANCY SHIELDS KOLLMANN

Addressing the interconnections of 'law and society' in seventeenth-century Muscovy is challenging, because of the complexity of the judicial system. Russia was far from the uniformity in law, adjudication and procedure that the contemporary European *Polizeistaat* was striving for (and even there the goal was achieved more in the breach than the norm).[1] In its multiplicity of venues and legal norms and in the flexibility of the enforcement of those norms, Russian justice was decidedly medieval.

This is not to say that the state was passive in the legal arena. Codification and centralisation of judicial power were, indeed, key goals of seventeenth-century rulers. But their ambition exceeded reality. Moscow's rulers were hindered by the challenge of administering an empire that was immense, ethnically diverse and riddled with pockets of immunity. This chapter will explore that complexity by surveying the multiple venues of legal proceedings in Muscovy, then by examining judicial practice and finally by surveying changes in the positive law.

Judicial venues

In principle a centralised bureaucratic structure of chancelleries in Moscow and regional governors in the provinces provided the judicial system in the seventeenth century. Chancelleries sent governors, called *voevody*, to appointed regions. They exercised administrative, fiscal and judicial authority; they often oversaw subordinate officials and courts in smaller towns. On paper the system was hierarchical and empire wide. In practice, however, many groups and regions fell out of range of the governor's authority because of explicit or

---

1 Bruce Lenman and Geoffrey Parker, 'The State, the Community and the Criminal Law in Early Modern Europe', in V. A. C. Gatrell, Bruce Lenman and Geoffrey Parker (eds.), *Crime and the Law. The Social History of Crime in Western Europe since 1500* (London: Europa Publications, 1980), pp. 11–48.

implicit charters of judicial immunity, religious, ethnic or colonial status, or personal dependency.

The Russian Orthodox Church was a key beneficiary of judicial immunity. Collectively the largest landholder in Muscovy in the seventeenth century, the Church had enjoyed fiscal and judicial privileges since the time of Christianisation in 988.[2] The most undisputed immunity enjoyed by the Church was the right to adjudicate cases involving spiritual issues over all Orthodox Christians. In the seventeenth century spiritual issues were defined widely, ranging from blasphemy, heresy and witchcraft to family law, inheritance and divorce. These cases were tried in bishops' courts, with the patriarch as appeal.

More problematic was secular jurisdiction over the Church's dependants. In the seventeenth century the state claimed a role here, providing in the Chancellery of the Great Palace a higher instance for trials of Church dependants and clergy (except for the patriarch's people) in secular cases. In practice, however, Church people litigated in a dizzying array of venues.

Since at least the fifteenth century Muscovite grand princes regularly granted charters of judicial, fiscal and/or administrative immunity, or privileges of appeal directly to the tsar, to monasteries, private individuals, collectives of artisans and the like, reserving to the tsar only criminal law. The patriarch adjudicated over laymen and clergy in the parishes and monasteries on his lands under an immunity received in 1625 and affirmed throughout the century. Metropolitans, archbishops and bishops or the patriarch also granted immunities to monasteries or communities from their own courts, allowing monastic hierarchs to judge their dependants or allowing appeal to the tsar, not the bishop. Immunities could be limited to a certain type of crime or value of suit; the options were myriad and almost every imaginable combination can be encountered. Although the state proclaimed a policy of curtailing immunities in the mid-sixteenth century, they continued to be awarded through the seventeenth. The result was that almost each ecclesiastical community had a different relationship with Church and state courts, often preferring high-level secular courts to Church courts.

In the seventeenth century the state tried to gain jurisdiction over Church people. The Conciliar Law Code of 1649 (hereafter *Ulozhenie*) affirmed the patriarch's judicial autonomy (chapter 12), but created a Monastery Chancellery

---

2 Hieromonach Nikolai Iarushevich, *Tserkovnyi sud v Rossii do izdaniia sobornogo ulozheniia Alekseia Mikhailovicha (1649 g.)* . . . *Istoriko-kanonicheskoe issledovanie* (Petrograd: Sinodal'naia tipografiia, 1917); F. Dmitriev, *Istoriia sudebnykh instantsii i grazhdanskogo appelliatsionnogo sudoproizvodstva ot sudebnika do uchrezhdeniia o guberniiakh* (Moscow: Universitetskaia tipografiia, 1859), pp. 93–100, 324–33.

(chapter 13) for clergy and laymen in all but spiritual suits.[3] This prompted the 1667 Church Council to claim judicial authority over clergy in all affairs, even in criminal cases, where it established the primacy of Church investigators in a shared Church–state criminal trial. The Monastery Chancellery lost its juridical authority and was abolished in 1677, only to be reinstated in 1701 by Peter the Great.

As landlords, Church institutions exercised legal jurisdiction over their lay staff and peasants in petty crime. In principle, criminal cases involving Church dependants were to be judged by the tsar's courts. Even here, however, some immunity charters allowed criminal jurisdiction, and many monasteries routinely usurped this authority and judged and punished criminal suits in-house.[4] In monasteries the hegumen often delegated the task of adjudication to the treasurer or cellarer, who presided over court with a council of monastic brothers; very large monasteries also maintained a network of local judicial officials. Bishops similarly divided their lands into 'tenths' and appointed an official (*desiatinnik*) in each area. These local judges were so harsh that bishops often awarded immunities from them to monasteries or parish churches.[5] The patriarch maintained a hierarchy of central and local judicial offices in his dominions as well. Church courts used Byzantine canon law for spiritual issues and a combination of Church and secular law for secular jurisdiction.[6]

All in all, never in the seventeenth century did one single principle govern the issue of jurisdiction for people associated with the Church. All depended upon one's social status, institutional affiliation and its immunity rights, physical location and type of crime.

A second large incidence of immunity from the tsar's judicial authority related to dependant status, that is, serfdom and slavery. The vast majority of the Muscovite population were peasants and in the seventeenth century a growing portion of them were transferred (by purchase, by tsar's grant) to private landholders. Perhaps 10 per cent of the population were slaves.[7] The right to own peasants and slaves was limited to the Church, the traditional cavalry army (Moscow ranks and provincial gentry) and Moscow merchants

---

3 Richard Hellie (trans. and ed.), *The Muscovite Law Code (Ulozhenie) of 1649*, pt. 1: *Text and Translation* (Irvine, Calif.: Charles Schlacks, 1988).
4 A. P. Dobroklonskii, 'Solotchinskii monastyr', ego slugi i krest'iane v XVII veke', *ChOIDR*, 1888, no. 144, kn. 1, ch. 5.
5 For discussion of bishops' authority, see Georg B. Michels, 'Ruling without Mercy: Seventeenth-Century Russian Bishops and their Officials', *Kritika* 4 (2003): 515–42.
6 George G. Weickhardt, 'Pre-Petrine Law and Western Law: The Influence of Roman and Canon Law', *HUS* 19 (1995): 756–83.
7 Richard Hellie, *Slavery in Russia, 1450–1725* (Chicago and London: University of Chicago Press, 1982), pp. 679–89.

(*gosti*), who also had exclusive rights to ownership of hereditary (*votchina*) and service tenure (*pomest'e*) land. Landlords traditionally enjoyed jurisdiction over dependant peasants and slaves in petty disputes and the culmination of enserfment in the 1649 *Ulozhenie* simply intensified their coercive control. Landlords relied on village communal institutions for basic law and order, overseen by their bailiffs; in the largest estates a bailiff would hold court in a formal venue.[8]

Large areas of the Russian Empire, however, did not know serfdom. Serfdom was limited to the most fertile agrarian lands – the centre, the north-west and the expanding southern borderlands. In the north and Siberia the challenges of distance, low yields and labour scarcity made it impossible to keep peasants fixed to land and landlord. In areas without serfdom, peasants enjoyed local self-governance, subordinate to the governor's administration. Similarly enjoying more judicial autonomy than serfs were groups who stood midway between peasants and the privileged military elite, the so-called 'contract servitors'. These included military or quasi-military units such as engineers, artillery, cossacks, musketeers, postal riders. In addition to their military functions, they farmed (land was often granted communally to the group, rather than to individuals) and/or produced and sold goods. They could not own populated land or dependent labour. As we shall see below, jurisdiction over them was complex.

In addition to Church and landlord jurisdiction, much of the population of seventeenth-century Russia was exempt from the central administration in all but criminal cases because of ethnic, religious and colonial status. Muscovy's colonial policy was laissez-faire in the seventeenth century, tolerating diversity in law, judicial institutions and elites.

The acquisition of the key trade depot of Kazan' in 1552 served as a springboard for Russian expansion into the middle Volga and steppe.[9] Expansion into the steppe was in full swing by the seventeenth century, with fortified lines and frontier outposts staffed by Russians and elites of the Tatar, Mari, Mordva and other native peoples. Such border troops were granted *pomest'e* as cavalrymen or were enlisted into contract servitor ranks. In the 1650s and 1660s the state also transferred to the southern frontier servitors from recently conquered Smolensk and Polotsk, often also transferring peasants from the

8 See the extensive correspondence of boyar B. I. Morozov with his bailiffs in A. I. Iakovlev (ed.), *Akty khoziaistva boiarina B. I. Morozova*, 2 vols. (Moscow and Leningrad: AN SSSR, 1940–5).
9 Although dated, this Stalinist-era collective work has good coverage of middle Volga and Siberia: *Ocherki istorii SSSR. Period feodalizma. XVII vek* (Moscow: AN SSSR, 1955), pp. 787–869.

centre to populate their lands. All these military servitors and non-enserfed peasants were subject to the governor's authority. But indigenous communities were permitted to use their own administrative and judicial institutions and Islamic or customary law. Natives were subject to the governor only in criminal cases.

Siberia presented an equally complex task of governance when Russia subdued the west Siberian khanate in the late sixteenth century. By the mid-seventeenth, Russians had settled in thin lines along the southern steppe frontier and had established trade depots along the Ob, Enisei and other rivers to their mouths in the Arctic. The Russian population in Siberia was small, estimated by the end of the century at 25,000, including around 11,000 military servitors, about 2,500 urban dwellers (*posadskie*) and the rest peasants.

Peasants fled to Siberia from the Russian north, the heartland, the middle Volga area and southern frontier. They farmed their own land and a portion of the tsar's grain fields (which provided military grain supplies). Enserfment did not develop to any great extent, although the Church did own some peasants (by the end of the century about 1,500 peasant households belonged to Siberian monasteries). Russian peasants in Siberia governed themselves in local communes (on the model of the north discussed below) and were subject to the local governor in criminal affairs. Because of the sparseness of settlement and distance from Moscow, governors in Siberia were given longer terms (two to three years) and broader authority than governors in the centre. They were renowned for corruption, ruling like satraps far from Moscow's controlling hand.[10]

Siberian governors also oversaw a far-flung, sparsely settled population of ethnic groups, who were taxed primarily in precious furs. In economy these peoples ranged from settled forest exploitation and hunting to pastoral nomadism of horses and cattle in the steppe to reindeer pastoralism in the Arctic to hunting ocean mammals. Their communities were tiny, their languages numbered in the hundreds, most Paleo-Asiatic, unrelated one to the other. Siberian governors prosecuted natives for major crimes and made Russian courts available to Siberian natives as they wished, often making concessions to native customs, even in criminal cases. For petty crimes, governors allowed native communities to govern themselves with native elites, laws and councils.

The situation was equally complex in Russia's relations with the Bashkirs south of the Urals in the seventeenth century. The area was diverse in economy

10 V. A. Aleksandrov and N. N. Pokrovskii, *Vlast' i obshchestvo. Sibir' v XVII v.* (Novosibirsk: Nauka, 1991), and George V. Lantzeff, *Siberia in the Seventeenth Century* (Berkeley: University of California Press, 1943).

and ethnic groups. The more northern area was primarily agricultural, while Bashkirs settled to the south in the steppe practised pastoral nomadism. The judicial landscape was highly complex. Newly arrived Russians, Tatar peasants and military men, Chuvash, Udmurts, forcibly transferred Polotsk noblemen, all settled in the northern agricultural area, each with different social and political statuses. Some, like the Russian cavalrymen and Polotsk noblemen, received *pomest'e* with serfs. Service Tatars were equated with contract servitors and farmed land that they rented from native Bashkirs. Russian peasants fell into serfdom to military men or the Church, or settled state lands. Bashkir peasants, meanwhile, maintained their traditional customs, institutions and elites.

When Moscow acquired significant lands in left-bank Ukraine and Belarus' in the Khmel'nyts'kyi uprising and the subsequent Russo-Polish wars (ended by peace treaties of 1667, 1687), it faced an administrative challenge far different from that posed by the sparsely settled farming, forest and steppe communities east of Moscow. The Ukrainian and Belarusian lands, previously part of the parliamentary noble democracy of the Commonwealth of Poland and Lithuania, were densely and diversely populated. The cossack state, or hetmanate, governed most of the left bank from 1648 into the last third of the eighteenth century. Muscovy placed governors in key centres such as Kiev, Chernigov and Pereiaslav and administered Ukraine through the Little Russian Chancellery, or *Malorossiiskii prikaz* (to 1722). But through treaties renegotiated with each new hetman Moscow allowed the cossack administration to remain essentially unchanged. The hetmanate was divided into approximately sixteen regimental units, run by cossack colonels, who served as head appellate judges for the regional courts in their area. In adjudication they used diverse law codes – decrees of hetmans and tsars, Lithuanian Statutes of 1566 and 1588 and customary law. The result was so complex that the cossack administration commissioned a codification of laws in 1728. The new code – submitted to the Russian Senate in 1743 but not approved – was nevertheless used in the Ukrainian lands in the second half of the eighteenth century.[11]

Pockets of judicial practice outside the hetmanate still existed in Ukraine. Landlords operated their own manorial courts with authority over civil and minor criminal affairs; so also did the Church, which was the largest single proprietor of land. The Ukrainian Orthodox Church (led by the Metropolitan of Kiev) maintained ecclesiastical courts for clerics, using Church law, and also

---

11 A. I. Pashuk, *Sud i sudnichestvo na Livoberezhnii Ukraini v XVII–XVIII st.* (L'viv, 1967), chs. 2–3.

for general issues of marriage, divorce and morality. Uniate Church institutions were almost unknown in this part of the Commonwealth.

Outside the hetmanate Muscovy ruled more directly through governors in Sloboda Ukraine and Zaporozhia. In the sixteenth and seventeenth centuries municipal self-government through German law was granted to major towns in Ukraine and Belarus'. About twelve towns in the hetmanate enjoyed such privileges, while smaller towns were privately governed by landlords or ruled by cossack administration. Magdeburg law was maintained for at least a century after Muscovy took over, finally falling into disuse in favour of the hetmanate's law codes by the end of the eighteenth century. After Moscow acquired the Smolensk and upper Oka areas in Belarus', it revoked municipal privileges and transferred the areas to governor control. But tsars affirmed the landholdings and privileges granted to Smolensk noblemen by Polish kings; special rights for the Smolensk nobility were revoked only in 1761.

So, large areas and groups stood beyond the tsar's courts. The judicial arena that *was* covered by the tsar's centralised system reflected his claims to power. A principal area was criminal law – murder, robbery, theft with material evidence, treason, heresy, arson. The tsar also claimed authority over immoveable property, dispensing land in service or hereditary tenure. Accordingly, great attention in seventeenth-century law codes was devoted to the issues of ownership and inheritance of land. By the same token, to support the landed cavalry and to produce steady revenues for state expansion, the state concerned itself extensively with social legislation. Not only did it enforce enserfment but it also regulated slavery and limited the mobility of the urban populace. These key areas – criminal, property and social law – were adjudicated by the tsar's governors.

As judge the governor in the seventeenth century tried civil cases.[12] Governors with large jurisdictions who were accompanied by a state secretary (*d'iak*) appointed by Moscow could judge cases beyond 20 roubles in value and also land and slave disputes. Governors of smaller towns, without a state secretary, were limited to cases up to 20 roubles in value, after which their corresponding chancellery took over (*Ulozhenie* chapter 13: article 3).[13] In theory criminal cases were done by locally elected criminal officers – the *guba* elders and swornmen. But by the mid-seventeenth century the *guba* system

12 Two classic surveys of local government and the *guba* administration are: Boris Chicherin, *Oblastnye uchrezhdeniia Rossii v XVII veke* (Moscow: Tipografiia Aleksandra Semena, 1856); and Hans-Joachim Torke, *Die staatsbedingte Gesellschaft im moskauer Reich. Zar und Zemlja in der altrussischen Herschaftsverfassung, 1613–1689* (Leiden: E. J. Brill, 1974).
13 Hereafter references to chapters and articles in the *Ulozhenie* will be provided in the text, and abbreviated, e.g. '13:3'.

was falling under the authority of governors. *Guba* officers might develop a case and turn it over to the governor to judge, or resolve it jointly with him. Whole areas of the realm did not have *guba* institutions, and often did not want them. V. N. Glaz'ev shows that in the seventeenth century communities often refused to support both a governor and a *guba* apparatus, since it was too expensive.[14]

The legal system embraced by the system of governors was uniform across the state in law and procedure, but not in judicial venue. Leaving aside the many areas of immunity discussed above, legal jurisdiction was complex even within the tsar's system. F. Dmitriev argued that the *Ulozhenie* of 1649 had simplified legal jurisdiction from sixteenth-century complexity to three principles – jurisdiction by residence, by social status or by type of crime.[15] His simplification is deceptive: the resulting system still provided multiple court systems and judicial personnel, resulting in frequent transfer of venue and quarrels between centre and periphery over jurisdiction.

Residence was the principal determinant of judicial venue. Different chancelleries administered discrete regions of the country, and sent out governors to their delegated parts of the realm. The Military Service Chancellery (*Razriad*) administered the southern frontier; the Kazan' Palace and Siberia Chancellery oversaw those areas. A handful of territorial chancelleries called *chetverti* (Novgorod, Ustiug, Kostroma and Galich) oversaw the north-west and northern areas to the Urals. The chancellery that oversaw the governor provided the higher instance for local cases. A significant exception was the city of Moscow, which did not have a governor. There the Moscow Administrative Chancellery enforced law and order for the taxpaying populace of the town.

A governor's administration varied according to the region he governed. Siberia, the middle Volga and the southern frontier were sparsely populated, had a high percentage of servitors of a contract service type, and relatively few taxpaying peasants to pay the costs of elected administration such as the *guba* system. The governor therefore ruled rather autonomously. But in the north – the lands stretching from the Novgorodian hinterland, to the Dvina watershed, eastward to the Urals and north to the White and Arctic Seas – peasant communities balanced meagre farming with forest exploitation, fishing, hunting, modest artisan work and trade and they organised themselves into self-governing communes at the regional (*volost'*) and village levels here. Those belonging to the large monasteries so dominant in the north

---

14 V. N. Glaz'ev, *Vlast' i obshchestvo na iuge Rossii v XVII veke: Protivodeistvie ugolovnoi prestupnosti* (Voronezh: Voronezhskii gosudarstvennyi universitet, 2001).

15 Dmitriev, *Istoriia sudebnykh instantsii*, p. 348.

(Solovetskii, Kirillo-Belozerskii monasteries) were dependant on them, but the majority of the population was not enserfed, subject only to the tsars. For petty crimes, such as minor theft, brawls, land disputes, disagreements between neighbours, drunkenness, these communities handled their own affairs, with limited oversight by the governor. In criminal affairs they were overseen by governors and sometimes by *guba* institutions, although these were weakly developed in the north.[16]

Following Dmitriev's second principle – social status – many corporate groups were subordinate in fiscal, administrative and judicial matters to one of the chancelleries in Moscow, bypassing the jurisdiction of the local governor. The Foreign Affairs Chancellery had jurisdiction over most foreigners visiting Moscow as well as the Don cossacks, while the Foreign Military Chancellery had jurisdiction over European soldiers in Russian service. The Postal Chancellery had jurisdiction over post riders, the Stonework for stone and brick-workers on the southern frontier, the Armoury for factory workers, the Musketeer for musketeers and cossacks serving in towns, the Engineers' Chancellery for artillerymen. Privileged Moscow merchants were granted jurisdiction by the Chancellery of the Great Treasury, while the Moscow and Vladimir Judicial Chancelleries judged the higher ranks of landed servitors in civil issues. The Chancellery of the Great Palace was court of appeal for the tsar's (*dvortsovye*) properties, for non-enserfed communes, and in principle for Church people. When a plaintiff presented a case, he followed the rule that the venue was determined by the defendant's jurisdiction.

Finally, Dmitriev's third principle – type of crime – also determined jurisdiction. As we have seen, the Church claimed jurisdiction over spiritual issues. The Felony Chancellery had authority over the criminal law through the *guba* system. The Slavery Chancellery handled disputes about slave ownership, while the Service Land Chancellery handled probably the greatest volume of litigation in the seventeenth century, over land.

All in all, the Muscovite state was riddled with pockets of judicial autonomies within the overarching law asserted by the centre. These pockets included ethnic, religious and political communities in non-Russian colonial areas; courts of private landlords and the Church; ecclesiastical courts for religious and moral issues. The law interacted with 'society' in myriad venues and laws depending upon one's social status, religion, ethnicity and crime.

16 A classic study of government in the north: M. M. Bogoslovskii, *Zemskoe samoupravlenie na russkom severe v XVII veke*, in *ChOIDR* 1910, no. 232, kn. 1, pp. i–viii, 321 pp. and 105 pp. of addenda; and 1912, no. 214, 2, pp. i–iv, 311 pp.

The practice of the law

The 1649 *Ulozhenie* declared itself authoritative over 'all people of the Muscovite state, from highest to lowest rank' (10: 1). In practice we see the full social range active in litigations. Even slaves could initiate suits, testify and offer evidence. Landlords also represented their dependants in court. Women could participate in court cases, although they were often represented by male kinsmen and spouses when such were available. Widows could litigate on their own behalf. Some limitations were introduced in this century: minors could not take an oath or sue (10: 185; 14: 5); the mentally incompetent could not litigate; peasants could not sue their landlords, nor spouses their partners, nor children their parents; freed slaves could not sue their former masters (10: 174, 176–7).[17]

A striking aspect of Muscovite judicial practice in the seventeenth century was the lack of a specialised class of lawyers serving as judges or advocates. Muscovy had no professional legal schools. Most judges did not specialise in judging – provincial governors were jacks of all trades and relied upon the expertise of local under-secretaries or state secretaries assigned from Moscow chancelleries. The situation was somewhat different in the chancelleries, particularly by the second half of the century, when judges began to serve consistently in one chancellery, building up expertise.

Moscow's bureaucratic stratum – state secretaries (*d'iaki*) and under-secretaries (*pod'iachie*) – constituted a repository of practical judicial knowledge.[18] These men wrote the documentation for stages of a suit, selected relevant excerpts from law codes to advise the judge and hired themselves out to write petitions for litigants. We also find parish priests writing petitions and signing documents in place of illiterate litigants. But in the seventeenth century these literate judicial experts did not develop into a notarial class or a stratum of lawyers and legal advocates.

Corruption and bribery were constants in this judicial system, so much so that we do well to reorient our thinking on the topic. Local governors lived off fees collected in judicial and bureaucratic activities and from payments in cash and kind from their communities. They stood in a gift-exchange relationship with their community: they expected gifts from their subjects and the subjects

17 Good surveys include A. G. Man'kov, *Zakonodatel'stvo i pravo Rossii vtoroi poloviny XVII v.* (St Petersburg: Nauka, 1998); V. S. Nersesiants (ed.), *Razvitie russkogo prava v XV–pervoi polovine XVII v.* (Moscow: Nauka, 1986), and E. A. Skripilev (ed.), *Razvitie russkogo prava vtoroi poloviny XVII–XVIII vv.* (Moscow: Nauka, 1992).
18 N. F. Demidova, *Sluzhilaia biurokratiia v Rossii XVII v. i ee rol' v formirovanii absoliutizma* (Moscow: Nauka, 1987).

in turn expected attention and concern. Muscovites recognised several types of gifts to judges and officials, only one of which – excessive fees for services not rendered – was considered illegal. The others – gifts at holidays, gifts to the official's family – were just considered the cost of doing business.[19]

For reasons of lack of specialisation, or the press of other duties, or conflicts over venue, or corruption or a host of other causes, the law was not a highly professional arena in seventeenth-century Russia. Delay was endemic, as well as complaints against judges for favouritism and enmity. Moscow chancelleries were responsive to replacing a judge when a litigant complained, and law codes are replete with exhortations, incentives and punishments to ensure speedy and honest justice. The late seventeenth century saw several efforts to reform governors' authority to make it less predatory on the taxpaying and merchant populations, and in a few celebrated cases governors were punished for excessive graft and corruption.[20]

Muscovite law in the seventeenth century knew two types of procedure – accusatory (sud) and inquisitorial (sysk), the latter being used primarily but not exclusively in criminal cases. In an accusatory trial, litigants presented witnesses and evidence, while in the inquisitorial the judge directed the search for evidence. Accusatory suits, discussed in Ulozhenie chapter 10, were used primarily for material loss – land disputes, damage to crops and farm equipment, contracts and debts. A typical litigation began, even in criminal cases, with a complaint that listed the circumstances and value of the loss. The plaintiff couched his petition in formulaic language suggesting his personal dependency on the tsar. Each social class used a self-deprecating diminutive to describe itself – servitors styled themselves the 'slaves' of the tsar, clergy, the tsar's 'pilgrims', peasants and urban taxpayers, the tsar's 'orphans'. Litigants used the diminutive version of first names: Ivan presented himself as 'Ivashko', Vasilii as 'Vaska'. The conceit was that the tsar was personally bestowing his justice and mercy on the litigant, through his representative, the judge.

In an accusatory trial, the judge summoned the litigants, itself a complex process due to the expanse of the realm and demands of military service. Laws of the seventeenth century established detailed rules about time limits for appearing for trial, default for late appearance and norms for delay of trial.

19 Brian L. Davies, 'The Politics of Give and Take: Kormlenie as Service Remuneration and Generalized Exchange, 1488–1726', in Ann M. Kleimola and Gail Lenhoff (eds.), Culture and Identity in Muscovy, 1359–1584, UCLA Slavic Studies, n.s. 3 (Moscow: ITZ-Garant, 1997), pp. 39–67, and P. V. Sedov, 'Podnosheniia v moskovskikh prikazakh XVII veka', Otechestvennaia istoriia, 1996, no. 1: 139–50. See also Chapter 20 in the present volume.
20 Christoph Shmidt, Sozialkontrolle in Moskau : Justiz, Kriminalität und Leibeigenschaft, 1649–1785 (Stuttgart: F. Steiner Verlag, 1996), pp. 76–92.

Once assembled, both sides of the story were heard and the litigants presented evidence. Written documentation was preferred; each side could also present witnesses and reject any of the other's proposed witnesses.[21] The law mandated that if they agreed on a small number of witnesses, they were to abide by that testimony. In the absence of documents and definitive witnesses, judges put litigants into a face-to-face confrontation (*ochnaia stavka*), or as a last resort asked the litigants to submit to an oath, which usually resulted in one side settling with the other before taking the oath.[22]

Many cases were not carried to conclusion, judging by extant records. Some of this might be loss of records over time. But a great proportion of cases were settled out of court, demonstrating the persistence of traditional concepts of distributive justice. Community sentiment valued social harmony and stability over strife and vindication. Even criminal cases were settled, contravening the law. Murder cases, for example, might be settled so that an aggrieved widow would be provided with upkeep for herself and her children. Other cases would be abandoned before conclusion because of expense, or preoccupations of military service, or waning of interest.

In an inquisitorial suit, the judge took the active role. When a complaint of major crime came to him, he swung into action, ordering the arrest of the accused, the investigation of the crime scene, corpse or injured party, and the defendant and other important parties to be put on surety bond (*poruka*; whereby a group of friends, neighbours and/or kinsmen guaranteed that they will show up for trial). Depending upon the alleged crime, the defendant was held in jail or released on surety.

The judge collected evidence through a few means of questioning. Witnesses could be questioned individually or the judge could order a survey of the community. Traditionally reputation and standing in the community had been a factor in assessing guilt and punishment in Muscovite litigation. By the mid-seventeenth century, however, the community inquest was declining in significance in favour of more 'rational', that is, eyewitness, evidence. The inquest was finally abolished in 1688 because of abuses.

The judge's most powerful weapon in questioning the accused and others implicated by him was torture, regarded as an ordeal of God. Such questioning proceeded in stages: simple questioning, questioning in the presence of executioner and instruments of torture and under torture. The goal was to

21 George G. Weickhardt, 'Due Process and Equal Justice in the Muscovite Codes', *RR* 51 (1992): 463–80.
22 For more detail on trial procedures, see my *By Honor Bound: State and Society in Early Modern Russia* (Ithaca, N.Y.: Cornell University Press, 1999), ch. 3.

elicit confession and information about intent and accomplices. The methods of torture were not ornate, usually flogging, but for very serious accusations burning with fire was done.

A judge resolved a case after the entire transcript of the proceedings had been copied afresh and read to him. This lengthy document included copies of the initial and subsequent petitions presented by litigants in the course of the trial, all the judge's orders to subordinates, all their reports, copies of surety documents, excerpts of relevant laws and transcripts of torture sessions and community investigations. In most criminal trials the governors or *guba* authorities sent the case to Moscow for decision, although the 1669 Criminal Articles allowed investigators (*syshchiki*) for very serious crimes to resolve cases and carry out punishments, including execution, on the spot.

In criminal cases, judges rarely invoked the full terror of the law. They often sentenced felons to punishments less severe than prescribed by law, taking into account the circumstances of the crime, intent and community standing. In 1650, for example, a woman who admitted conspiring to murder her husband was spared execution because the community vouched for her character and maligned that of the deceased.[23] Extending the fiction that the litigant was appealing to and being judged by the tsar, after sentencing judges often proffered 'mercy' in his name, reducing punishments. Exceptions to this flexible sentencing pattern concerned the most serious crimes – political treason, heresy and witchcraft and the like – for which punishments were very severe.

In cases where material damage was at stake, losing defendants paid court fees, the value of the suit and sometimes a fine for losses incurred in the trial process (*volokita*). In cases of physical or symbolic harm (dishonour), sanctions ranged from fines to short periods of incarceration, exile to hard labour and a range of corporal punishment from beating to flogging to execution (various types of corporal punishment in this period are illustrated in Plate 21). Punishment was not administered equally across social classes. Although the military servitors did not enjoy explicit protections from corporal punishment, de facto they were rarely subject to it, either because of a provision of 'mercy' or because the law avoided it.

When cases were appealed, it usually took the form of judges applying to a higher instance – for example, from the governor to his chancellery to the boyar council and the tsar – to resolve a disputed or difficult case. Corporal

23 Nancy S. Kollmann, 'The Extremes of Patriarchy: Spousal Abuse and Murder in Early Modern Russia', *RH* 25 (1998): 133–40.

punishment, even execution, was administered promptly. The collection of fees and fines could drag on for years, either because of poverty or vindictiveness. Many case transcripts end with repeated appeals to the court to force a losing litigant to settle his obligations.

Muscovite judicial practice was in many ways more medieval than early modern in its distributive justice: it widely used settlement out of court, countenanced reputation and community standards as evidence or mitigating factors; it bestowed mercy to lessen sentences and considered torture a credible form of evidence collection. Nevertheless, as the century developed, similarities with contemporary European practice emerged, such as a rationalisation of forms of evidence, standardisation of norms and procedure, a heightening of punishments and a more extensive claim of tsarist power.

Codifications of the law

The seventeenth century was remarkable for the generation and codification of secular law. Going into the seventeenth century, judges had available to them several codes of law. The Russian Law (*Russkaia pravda*), dating to Kievan times, was edited in an abbreviated version around 1630, but where and how its norms, that emphasised debt, slaveholding and punishments, were current is unclear. The Law Code (*sudebnik*) of 1550 of 100 articles, which extended the 1497 Law Code and was later extended by over seventy-three supplementary articles, clearly remained in force. It was primarily an advisory to judges, setting fees for services in an attempt to limit judicial corruption, decreeing punishments for some crimes and setting out procedural rules and standards of evidence. The 1550 *sudebnik* was followed by a longer (231 articles) edition of 1589 for the north and a compiled *sudebnik* of 1606–7 that added later decrees on landholding, debts and enserfment and developed the inquisitorial procedure. It was notable for being divided into thematic chapters, a first step towards more rational codification.[24] In addition, the Lithuanian Statute of 1588 was translated and disseminated in Moscow chancelleries, and Byzantine secular law became influential by the 1620s.[25]

In the seventeenth century the law proliferated. Moscow chancelleries kept books of laws and precedents that guided their work; these were occasionally

24 Three *sudebniki*: PRP, 8 vols. (Moscow: Gosudarstvennoe izdatel'stvo iuridicheskoi literatury, 1952–63), vyp. IV: *Pamiatniki prava perioda ukrepleniia russkogo tsentralizovannogo gosudarstva XV–XVII vv.*, ed. L. V. Cherepnin (1956), pp. 229–350, 409–570.
25 I. I. Lappo (ed.), *Litovskii statut v moskovskom perevode-redaktsii* (Iur'ev: Tipografiia K. Mattisena, 1916).

compiled and then added to; at mid-century they became the basis for relevant portions of the 1649 *Ulozhenie*. Such *ustavnye knigi* from the first half of the seventeenth century are known from the Felony, Slavery, Great Palace, Moscow Administrative, Service Land and Postal chancelleries.[26]

Local governors made do with handwritten copies of the *sudebniki* and of decrees they received from the centre. The 1649 *Ulozhenie* was the first law code to be issued in print (about 2,500 copies by 1651) and it was distributed to local governors. Another body of law relevant in the seventeenth century comprised charters granting immunities and privileges to various corporate entities, as we have seen.

The 1649 *Ulozhenie* codified the preceding half-century of law and added some innovations, based on legal sources enumerated above. It was massive – in twenty-five thematic chapters, it included 967 articles. The second half of the century saw feverish legislation, presaging Peter the Great's legislative blitz of the early eighteenth century. By one count, 1,583 new decrees were issued in the second half of the seventeenth century, reflecting the state's desire to regulate society and mobilise resources through the law. Many new decrees concerned public order, reflecting European concepts of *Polizeistaat*.

New compendia appeared in various fields: in 1653 and 1667, tariff and trade regulations; in 1669, a new criminal code; in 1676, 1680 and 1681, codifications on service tenure and hereditary land.[27] General codifications to replace the *Ulozhenie* were ordered in 1681 and 1695, to no avail. In 1700 Peter the Great created a commission to codify the laws but it too was fruitless. The *Ulozhenie* remained the standard in most areas of the law until late in the eighteenth century.

The most significant changes in positive law were made in the realm of social legislation.[28] Laws defined social groups and limited access into privileged ranks and egress from dependent ranks. The *Ulozhenie*'s list of compensation for insult to honour is telling: longer (almost eighty articles) than those of the 1550 and 1589 *sudebniki*, it included ecclesiastical and lay social ranks from the patriarch and boyars to peasants and slaves (10: 26–99). Its guiding principle – that all people have honour, but higher ranks deserve greater compensation – reflects the law code's resolute emphasis on social hierarchy.

---

26 *PRP*, vyp. iv, pp. 353–405 and *PRP*, vyp. v: *Pamiatniki prava perioda soslovno-predstavitel'noi monarkhii. Pervaia polovina XVII v.*, ed. L. V. Cherepnin (1959), pp. 185–532.

27 1669 criminal law and land decrees: *PRP*, vyp. vii: *Pamiatniki prava perioda sozdaniia absoliutnoi monarkhii. Vtoraia polovina XVII v.*, ed. L. V. Cherepnin (1963), pp. 57–100, 396–434.

28 Richard Hellie, 'Muscovite Law and Society: The Ulozhenie of 1649 as a Reflection of the Political and Social Development of Russia since the *Sudebnik* of 1589', unpublished Ph.D. dissertation, University of Chicago, 1965.

The military service class cemented its position with the *Ulozhenie* by the full enserfment of the peasantry, a particularly direct benefit to the provincial gentry, strapped for land and labour. Wealthy landholders (including the Church) were inconvenienced by the *Ulozhenie*'s new prohibitions on their taking in runaway peasants or purchasing lands in the provinces, but were by no means severely hampered in their social and economic ascendancy.

The *Ulozhenie* devoted significant attention to the needs and duties of the privileged military elite, Moscow-based and provincial. Chapter 7 of the *Ulozhenie* concerned itself with their conduct during service, including strict punishment for desertion from service and from battle. Laws prohibiting gentry to sell themselves into slavery were repeated, as was the requirement of mandatory service (it was gradually reduced in the last quarter of the century, only to be reinstated by Peter I). Landed servitors enjoyed economic and legal privileges: preferential access to the grain market in time of shortage, lower tax rates on many commercial transactions, a higher rate of ransom if captured in war.

Major attention was given to landholding in the *Ulozhenie* (chapters 16 and 17) and legislation of 1676, 1680 and 1681. Norms, generally more theoretical than enforceable, were established for land grants to servitors. Over the course of the century service tenure and hereditary types of land converged in law and practice; there was an active market in the sale, mortgaging and devolution of service-tenure land and purchased hereditary estates. Norms of inheritance recognised this, and widened women's access to landholding despite legal attempts to limit it. By law widows and minor children and unmarried daughters were granted portions of their deceased husband's or father's *pomest'e* for upkeep but had very limited access to hereditary lands. As Valerie Kivelson has shown, however, families disregarded the law to ensure that widows, sons and daughters were taken care of. Practising partible inheritance, they awarded almost as much land of all types to women for upkeep or dowry as to male kin.[29]

Other groups – the Church, merchants – benefited from legal change in the seventeenth century. Since the mid-sixteenth century the state had been legislating against donating *votchina* land to the Church; these laws were repeated in the *Ulozhenie*, but ignored. Church landholding boomed in the seventeenth century. Church institutions continued to enjoy immunities from the local courts, despite the brief tenure of the Monastery Chancellery. Laws of the seventeenth century extended the privileges of Moscow merchants (*gosti*) and

---

29 Valerie A. Kivelson, 'The Effects of Partible Inheritance: Gentry Families and the State in Muscovy', *RR* 53 (1994): 197–212.

the other two merchant corporations (*gostinnaia* and *sukonnaia sotni*). Of the three groups, only *gosti* could trade abroad. Otherwise, all enjoyed the right to own hereditary land, to be immune from governors' courts, to distil and keep spirits and to enjoy various tax breaks and privileges. The tax privileges of the musketeers and cossacks were affirmed in the *Ulozhenie* as well (chapters 23–4).

The townsmen, like the provincial gentry, received significant attention in the *Ulozhenie* (chapter 19), resulting from their persistent petitioning to the state in the first half of the century. It provided that townsmen who had fled to join other social groups – musketeers, cossacks, merchant corporations – should be returned to their taxpaying town commune. Laws forbade townsmen to put themselves in dependent status. Most importantly, the *Ulozhenie* abolished the tax-exempt neighbourhoods of Church and wealthy landlords that had caused unfair competition to urban taxpayers, awarding taxpaying townsmen monopolies on urban trade, manufacturing and landholding. But, on the other hand, townsmen were in effect enserfed by the *Ulozhenie* – they were registered in their town commune and the statute of limitations to track down runaway townsmen was abolished. They had become a hereditary social class, but, like the peasants, an immobile one.

In the area of trade the seventeenth century saw significant codification, in response to Russian merchants' petitions against foreign competition and as manifestation of the state's developing mercantilism. The *Ulozhenie* of 1649 devoted little attention to foreign trade, but it addressed some domestic trade and taxation issues. It regulated tolls, ferry fees and bridge fees, assuring exemption from them to servitors and foreigners and prohibiting fraudulent tolls (chapter 9); it established a sliding scale of rates to ransom Russian captives in war according to social status (chapter 8); it regulated illicit taverns, production of spirits and sale and use of tobacco (chapter 25).

Soon after the *Ulozhenie*, trade regulations of 1653 addressed issues of foreign trade. They instituted a single trade tariff for the transit of commercial goods for domestic merchants, and a higher, uniform rate for foreign merchants. These norms were included in the much broader 1667 New Commercial Regulations. Authored in part by the progressive reformer A. L. Ordin-Nashchokin, the articles also removed trade and the customs service from the jurisdiction of local governors, and further restricted foreigners to trading at the border towns in a limited range of goods and only at certain times of the year. Its protectionist norms remained in force until 1755.[30]

---

30 1667 Trade Regulations: *PRP*, vyp. VII, pp. 303–28.

Peasants and slaves suffered most from seventeenth-century social legislation. The *Ulozhenie* culminated the process of enserfment that began in earnest in the late sixteenth century. By the seventeenth century, laws forbade peasants to move from their landlords; the *Ulozhenie* capped the process by ending the statute of limitations on the recapture of runaways (chapter 11). Thereafter the state committed significant resources into sending investigators (*syshchiki*) to chase down fugitive serfs and townsmen. In the second half of the seventeenth century peasants could sue and be a witness in courts; they paid taxes, could be tried for crimes and could hold local elected offices. But gradually, in a process that reached its apex in the eighteenth century, peasants fell into more servile dependency on their lords. Serf owners could judge and corporally punish their peasants for all but criminal offences, they could force their serfs and slaves to pay their debts and, although serfs were legally supposed to be tied to their lands, de facto landlords moved them at will.

Even more dependent on their lords were slaves. Of the many categories of slavery cited in Muscovite sources, in the seventeenth century the most common was limited contract slavery (*kabal'noe kholopstvo*). In the seventeenth century this was hereditary slavery for the life of the owner. The state's interest in slavery in the seventeenth century was to reap fees from the registration of slaves and to limit the phenomenon, since slavery deprived the state of labour power and tax revenues. The *Ulozhenie* devoted its second-longest chapter to slavery (chapter 20). After 1649 the state captured more of the productive power of slaves by including rural slaves in taxation when the household basis was introduced in the late 1670s and by merging household slaves with serfs in 1722.

Social legislation in the seventeenth century mobilised productive resources by binding people to a limited number of social ranks. Practice, however, often contradicted this trend. Slavery persisted, despite attempts to keep individuals from selling themselves into it. Peasants fled from serfdom to the frontier and to Siberia; contract servitors on the frontier transgressed the monopolies on landholding, serf ownership or trade guaranteed to other groups. Fanatic in the heartland at tracking down runaway serfs and townsmen and fixing people to social categories because of its great needs for labour and income, in the colonies the state tolerated social and legal diversity. Seventeenth-century legislation did not pursue a single goal of social control or *Polizeistaat* uniformity, but profited from an expedient diversity.

Nevertheless the state's ambition to aggrandise its stature through the law is striking in seventeenth-century legislation. The first several chapters of the 1649 *Ulozhenie* constitute an innovation. Borrowed from the 1588 Lithuanian Statute and motivated most likely by the social unrest of the 1640s, they introduce the concept of *lèse majesté*, focusing on assaults to the state's dignity, embodied in the Church hierarchs and cathedrals, the tsar and his palaces, and in seals and official documents representing his authority (chapters 1–6).

Criminal law became harsher in comparison with sixteenth-century codes, under the influence of foreign, probably Byzantine, law codes (*Ulozhenie* chapters 21 and 22; 1669 New Articles). Harsher corporal punishments were introduced – burying alive, nose-splitting, branding and other forms of mutilation. Torture was prescribed more widely, the death penalty was applied to over sixty crimes (almost twice that number in codes of Peter the Great's time). Public floggings and executions were prescribed to deter others but the death penalty was not used as widely as in some West European countries of the time and was not carried out with such 'spectacle of suffering'.[31] Executions were usually performed by hanging within a day of sentencing. The Church schism in the second half of the century elicited an escalation in corporal punishment. Secular courts judged schismatics as traitors as well as heretics and inflicted extreme punishments. Similarly punishments for witchcraft and sorcery, as well as for recidivist crime, were harsher than those for less charged criminal acts.

For lesser crimes, the death penalty was often commuted to exile to capture the labour power of criminals. Long-term imprisonment was rarely used as punishment, but towns kept jails for the detention of criminals awaiting trial and people could stay in prison many years paying off fines from court cases (21: 92).

In the seventeenth century various principles affecting responsibility for crime were introduced into Russian law that were developed more thoroughly in the eighteenth century. Notions of intent, negligence and malice first appeared; the law found defence of self and property to be exonerating, and punished unintentional assault and homicide more leniently than intentional. Drunkenness was considered a mitigating circumstance (21: 69, 71, 88). In the realm of civil law, unlike criminal, much regularisation but little substantive change occurred. Chapters in the *Ulozhenie* (14, 15, 18) concerned oathtaking, settled cases and fees for documents. The *Ulozhenie*'s longest chapter (10) addressed judicial corruption, courtroom procedure and civil suits. By the end of the century Moscow's legal heritage was rich and complex, but scattered in a panoply of thematic compendia and individual decrees and precedents.

---

31 Pieter Spierenburg, *The Spectacle of Suffering. Executions and the Evolution of Repression: From a Preindustrial Metropolis to the European Experience* (Cambridge and London: Cambridge University Press, 1984).

Society interacted with law in a multitude of ways in seventeenth-century Muscovy. Traditional distributive justice shaped adjudication; the multiplicity of norms and venues undermined judicial consistency. But the trend was nevertheless towards a greater rationalisation. Codification was proceeding, standardised norms of record-keeping were being established; standards of evidence favoured rational proof. Scholars have deemed these trends 'absolutist'. So also might one term the concept of 'the common good' that appears in the law by the end of the century. The concept that the state uses law to serve the public good came to court circles from Ukraine by the 1680s and inspired many of the projects of military and bureaucratic reform of that decade. Despite its complexity, seventeenth-century law provided Peter the Great with a firm foundation when he launched his bold effort to standardise law and administration on the 'well-ordered police state' model in the next century.

25

Urban developments

DENIS J. B. SHAW

The seventeenth century was a difficult period for Russia, as it appears to have been for much of Europe. Yet this is a very broad generalisation, difficult to substantiate from the limited evidence and paying scant heed to geographical and chronological differences. After 1613 Russia was able to enjoy the benefits of a stable dynasty, a situation in marked contrast to the anarchic times which went before. And it was a realm still undergoing vigorous expansion and colonisation. Such discordant processes were naturally reflected in the life of Russia's towns. Fortunately the sources which permit the study of urban developments are richer and fuller for this period than they are for the sixteenth century and they have been better explored by historians. But they are all too often sporadic and uneven, and their meaning sometimes obscure. This chapter will consider a number of facets of urbanism in the period. It will also address two issues, namely the symbolic and religious role of towns and their physical morphology, which do not figure in Chapter 13 on the sixteenth century but which can be profitably studied for both periods taken together.

The urban network

As was the case in the sixteenth century, the legal status of towns in the seventeenth remained uncertain and the places referred to as 'towns' (*goroda*) in the sources were often fortresses with little or no commercial function, or sometimes they did have a trading function but lacked a *posad* population.[1] Some 'towns' even had no subsidiary district (*uezd*), such as the three *gorodki* (literally, 'little towns') of Kostensk, Orlov and Belokolodsk built on the Belgorod Line near Voronezh in the middle of the century or, it appears, the nearby private

---

1 That is, a tax-bearing population attached to a legal commercial suburb. Conversely, other towns had a legal *posad* but lacked commercial activity.

town of Romanov which belonged to the tsar's kinsman, boyar N. I. Romanov.[2] Equally other places, like the monastic settlement of Tikhvin Posad towards the north-west, had commercial functions but were not referred to as towns. Adopting a catholic definition of the term, French has argued that there were around 220 towns in Russia at the beginning of a century which witnessed the appearance of about a hundred new ones during its course.[3] Vodarskii, however, argued for a stricter, Marxist definition of a town as a place having both a legal commercial suburb (*posad*) and a commercial function. On this basis he recognised 160 towns in 1652, rising to 173 in 1678 and 189 by 1722.[4]

The appearance of many new towns in Russia during the course of the seventeenth century is largely explained by the process of frontier expansion and colonisation of new territories. In the west many towns were acquired as the state expanded its frontiers in that direction. To the east numerous new towns were built as the Russian state took control of more and more of Siberia. The first Russian town on the Pacific, Okhotsk, was founded in 1649. Many Siberian towns remained quite small, however. Thus Vodarskii names nineteen principal administrative centres in Siberia for 1699, only thirteen of which were towns by his definition. According to his figures, at the end of the century Siberia had a total of only 2,535 *posad* households.[5] More significant in terms of town founding was Russia's southern frontier west of the Urals. Here a concerted effort was made from the 1630s to 1650s to set up a series of fortified towns along and behind the new Belgorod and Simbirsk military lines.[6] Subsequently, in the second half of the century, many new towns appeared in the forest-steppe and steppe south and east of these lines.

A number of studies have been made of the broad population data for towns, using the rather richer sources which are available for this period.[7]

2 V. P. Zagorovskii, *Belgorodskaia cherta* (Voronezh: Izdatel'stvo Voronezhskogo universiteta, 1969), pp. 211, 227–9.
3 R. A. French, 'The Early and Medieval Russian Town', in J. H. Bater and R. A. French (eds.), *Studies in Russian Historical Geography* (London: Academic Press, 1983), pp. 249–77; R. A. French, 'The Urban Network of Later Medieval Russia', in *Geographical Studies on the Soviet Union: Essays in Honor of Chauncy D. Harris* (Chicago: University of Chicago, Department of Geography, Research Paper no. 211, 1984), pp. 29–51.
4 Ia. E. Vodarskii, *Naselenie Rossii v kontse XVII v–nachale XVIII v.* (Moscow: Nauka, 1977), p. 133.
5 Ibid., p. 127; Ia. E. Vodarskii, 'Chislennost' i razmeshchenie posadskogo naseleniia v Rossii vo vtoroi polovine XVII v.', in *Goroda feodal'noi Rossii* (Moscow: Nauka, 1966), p. 290.
6 D. J. B. Shaw, 'Southern Frontiers of Muscovy, 1550–1700', in Bater and French, *Studies*, pp. 117–42.
7 P. P. Smirnov, *Goroda Moskovskogo gosudarstva v pervoi polovine XVII veke*, vol. 1, pt. 2 (Kiev: A. I. Grossman, 1919); Vodarskii, 'Chislennost' '; Henry L. Eaton, 'Decline and Recovery of the Russian Cities from 1500 to 1700', *CASS* 11 (1977): 220–52.

The latter include cadastral surveys, census books and associated enumerations which provide statistics on numbers of *posad* households, most notably in censuses of 1646–7 and 1678–9. Additionally there are enumerations dating from 1649–52 which record the households of traders and handicrafts people, many in 'white places',[8] which were added to the *posady* of towns as a result of the 1649 Legislative Commission (see below). Also important are enumerations of military servitors and 'able-bodied' personnel undertaken for towns in various years, usually under the auspices of the Military Chancellery (*Razriadnyi prikaz*). Most notable among these is a military census for 1678.[9] Vodarskii has provided urban household data for 212 towns (plus Siberian towns taken together) for 1630–50, 1670–80 and 1722 based on Smirnov's data for 1646–7 and 1649–52 and on his own analyses for the later dates.[10] Figure 25.1 reproduces his data for towns having 500 or more *posad* households in the seventeenth century. His data for 1722 are omitted. For comparison the table also lists numbers of *posad* households recorded for the latter part of the sixteenth century where available, based on the study by Eaton.[11]

The data are too uncertain and too scanty to allow solid conclusions to be drawn about urban growth trends, though perhaps the apparent sharp fall in the size of the *posad* in some commercial centres (Kaluga, Nizhnii Novgorod, Novgorod, Suzdal') between the late sixteenth century and the 1640s is worthy of note. Moscow was clearly dominant, as in the previous century, although once again the sources are sparse.[12] In addition to Moscow, the largest towns, with over 1,000 *posad* households (Vologda, Kazan', Kaluga, Kostroma, Nizhnii Novgorod, Iaroslavl') were all old towns which dated from before the sixteenth century and, apart from Kazan', all having a long history of connection with Muscovy. They were all situated on major river and trading routes. The fall of Novgorod from this group over the previous century no doubt reflects the troubles of the latter half of the sixteenth century and the early seventeenth, together with the problems of accessing the Baltic (see Chapter 13). The disappearance of Smolensk is also significant, connected to its loss to Poland down to the middle years of the century. The wars with

---

8 'White places' were parts of towns which were free of the normal tax and service obligations.
9 *DopAI*, vol. IX (St Petersburg: Tipografiia II Otdeleniia Sobstvennoi E. I. V. Kantseliarii, 1875), no. 106, pp. 219–314.
10 Vodarskii, 'Chislennost' ', pp. 282–90; Smirnov, *Goroda*, pp. 32ff.
11 Eaton, 'Decline and Recovery', pp. 235–46.
12 Ibid., pp. 250–1.

Town	I	2	3	4	5	6	7	8
Archangel and Kholmogory		645	1,018	263	715	835	4	138
Arzamas		430	2	135	559	560	—	98
Balakhna		637	—	112	661	642	9	140
Galich		729	(41)	46	788	481	19	46
Iaroslavl'	259[a]	2,871	174	564	3,042	2,310	57	468
Kaluga	723	588	339	105	694	1,015	—	45
Kargopol' and Turchasov	476	538	20	6	—	666	—	—
Kazan'	598	1,191	1,600	200	—	310	—	—
Khlynov	247	624	1	26	661	616	20	142
Kolomna	34	615	8	261	740	352	—	79
Kostroma		1,726	54	414	2,086	1,069	—	106
Kursk		270	396	20	—	538	104	11
Moscow		1,221[b]	(20,000)[b]	8,000[b]	3,615	7,043[c]	—	—
Nizhnii Novgorod	2421[a]	1,107	500	666	1,874	1,270	—	600
Novgorod	4157	640	1,050	145	770	862	153	344
Olonets	376	—	—	155	155	637	—	—
Pereslavl'-Zalesskii		525	(80)	104	624	408	—	110
Pskov		940	(1,306)	51	997	912	372	1,043
Rostov	16[a]	416	(15)	167	552	491	—	217
Simbirsk		—	—	—	19	504	—	114
Sol' Kamskaia		549	9	146	686	831	25	20
Suzdal'	414	360	(14)	495	435	519	7	596
Torzhok	89[a]	486	8	58	508	659	—	—
Tver'		345	53	250	497	524	—	110
Uglich		447	—	226	603	548	—	49
Ustiug Velikii		744	53	36	—	920	—	119
Vladimir		483	58	405	703	400	—	290
Vologda	591	1,234	175	363	1,674	1,196	13	284
Zaraisk		446	(127)	65	587	254	—	1

Key: 1. *Posad* households, *c.*1550–1590s; 2. *Posad* households, 1646; 3. Servitor households, 1650 (figures in parentheses – 1632); 4. Other households, 1646; 5. *Posad* households, 1652; 6. *Posad* households, 1678; 7. Servitor households, 1670s (partial data); 8. Other households, 1678 (partial data).

a. Data for 1610s

b. Data for 1638

c. Data for 1700

Sources: Henry L. Eaton, 'Decline and recovery of the Russian cities from 1500 to 1700', *Canadian-American Slavic Studies* 11 no. 2 (1977): 220–52; Ia. E. Vodarskii, 'Chislennost' i razmeshchenie posadskogo naseleniia v Rossii vo vtoroi polovine XVIIv.', in *Goroda feodal'noi Rossii* (Moscow, 1966), pp. 271–97.

Figure 25.1. Urban household totals in the sixteenth and seventeenth centuries (towns with 500 or more households in the *posad* in the seventeenth century)

Poland badly affected Russo-Polish trade, which did not in fact recover until after about 1750.[13]

Eaton has ascribed the apparent fall in the size of the *posad* in some of the biggest towns (Vologda, Kazan', Kostroma, Nizhnii Novgorod and Iaroslavl') between 1652 and 1678 to general lack of economic buoyancy in the latter half of the century compared to the apparent recovery in the first half. He thus questions those Soviet scholars who took a more optimistic view, regarding the century as the time when the 'all-Russian market' appeared, following Lenin's dictum. It may be that Vodarskii exaggerated the overall growth in the total number of *posad* dwellers in Russia between the two dates, although numbers do seem to have grown absolutely. The sluggish growth or even stagnation of some of the older towns in central Muscovy was probably offset by greater economic vigour on some of the frontiers.[14]

The official *posad* dwellers were, of course, by no means the only residents of Russian towns in the seventeenth century. According to Vodarskii, they constituted only 34 per cent of the total urban population in 1646, 44 per cent in 1652 (after the addition of the 'white places'), and 41 per cent in 1678. Of greater numerical significance were the state servitors or military personnel who formed 53 per cent in 1652 and 45 per cent by 1678.[15] Figure 25.1, which shows only the towns with 500 *posad* households or more, omits some of those with really big urban garrisons. Belgorod, for example, recorded only 44 *posad* households in 1646 but 459 servitor households in 1650. Kursk recorded 270 and 396 respectively, Sevsk none and 6,017, Voronezh 85 and 1,135, and Astrakhan' none and 3,350.[16] Servitors often engaged in trade and craft activity, especially before 1649, though many were paid and others lived by agrarian pursuits, particularly in the south. In the 1640s the bigger urban garrisons were clearly located in Moscow, along the vulnerable western and southern frontiers, and at three strategic points on the Volga (Nizhnii Novgorod, Kazan' and Astrakhan') (see Map 25.1).

In addition to the *posad* dwellers and military personnel, towns had other elements in their populations, not all of whom were recorded in the various censuses. Depending on the size and location of the town, these would include state officials and higher or middle-ranking servitors, their dependents, clergy and their dependents, cottars (*bobyli*), peasants, beggars and other unofficial

13 Paul Bushkovitch, *The Merchants of Moscow, 1580–1650* (Cambridge: Cambridge University Press, 1980), pp. 87–91.
14 J. Pallot and D. J. B. Shaw, *Landscape and Settlement in Romanov Russia, 1613–1917* (Oxford: Clarendon Press, 1990), pp. 241–64, esp. 242–4, and also 308–9.
15 Vodarskii, 'Chislennost' ', p. 279.
16 Ibid., pp. 282–90.

Map 25.1. Towns in mid-seventeenth-century European Russia

584

groups, and sometimes foreigners and non-Russian peoples. To measure the level of urbanisation in Russia by considering only the proportion of the total population who were *posad* dwellers (a legal rather than an occupational or social category) is therefore quite misleading.[17]

Russian towns of this period have often been described as static with little commercial vivacity and, at best, sluggish in growth. There is some truth in this picture for, as we have noted already, the seventeenth century was a difficult period. Sluggishness in a demographic sense, however, was a normal characteristic of early modern (pre-industrial) towns all over Europe.[18] Furthermore such assessments often overlook a most important feature of Russian towns in this period – their significance not as individual places but in the broader urban network which was developing across the Russian state. In other words towns had a pivotal role in the building of the state, acting as co-ordinating points for all kinds of activities which helped bind the state together. It is in this sense that de Vries talks of 'structural urbanisation'.[19] It is this issue which forms the focus of the rest of this chapter.

Urban society and administration

The establishment of the Romanov dynasty in 1613 was quickly followed by moves to pacify and control the extensive territories of the state. Towns played a significant role in this process. Towns had long been regarded as administrative centres for their surrounding districts or *uezdy*. This function was now strengthened as the office of *voevoda*, or military governor, which was an appointment of the central government, was now extended from the frontier regions to central and northern towns. The *voevoda* was now the tsar's representative in the locality, charged with upholding the state's interests and overseeing both military and civil matters within his area of jurisdiction. In these tasks he was aided by a small bureaucracy of officials centred in the governor's office (*prikaznaia izba*). Nowhere perhaps was the *voevoda's* function more apparent than on the vulnerable southern frontier where the entire defensive and civilian life of each town and its district was meant to be

---

17 See Vodarskii, *Naselenie*, pp. 129–34. On the basis of Vodarskii's data, the 'urban' population in 1678 (*posad* dwellers plus other urban residents – nobility, administration, clergy, housekeepers and others) can be estimated at around 4 per cent of the total. However, this does not appear to include the servitors, or the elements (peasants and others) who resided in towns illegally. The data excludes Ukraine.

18 J. de Vries, *European Urbanization, 1500–1800* (London: Methuen, 1984), pp. 254–8.

19 Ibid., p. 12.

organised by the *voevoda* with the strictest eye on security.[20] It was also on the frontier that the closer co-ordination of the town's functions as nodes in the state's military and administrative structures at local level was pioneered. Here the founding and development of each town, and its subsequent life and defensive role, was the immediate concern of the Military Chancellery in Moscow. By the middle of the century that chancellery was attempting to improve defensive co-ordination between the towns by designating military districts (*razriady*) under the jurisdiction of one central town. The first permanent one was established in the 1640s and 1650s centred on Belgorod. This was followed by other frontier districts (Sevsk, Smolensk, Novgorod, Kazan', Tambov) and, in the last quarter of the century, by some in the country's interior (Moscow, Vladimir, Riazan'). This move was clearly a harbinger of Peter the Great's provincial reform in the early eighteenth century and was motivated by some of the same goals – to improve control and co-ordination over localities.[21]

The office of *voevoda*, characterised by a continual tendency to interfere in local affairs and not a little corruption, rarely sat well with the felt interests of urban communities or with the functions of locally elected officials like the police elders (*gubnye starosty*) and land elders (*zemskie starosty*) who were invested with the responsibility of carrying out certain key functions on behalf of the state. As has been remarked so often, the latter's elected status did not imply any real measure of urban autonomy. But numerous tensions arose out of the primitive character of the system of administration as well as from the conflicting nature of the state's goals – for example, between the need to raise as much revenue as possible from the towns, on the one hand, and the desire to foster urban trade and commerce on the other. Most towns, except the smaller frontier forts, were multifunctional, but the different functions were not always easily reconcilable.

The fragmented character of urban society which characterised sixteenth-century towns continued to be a feature of the seventeenth. However, as explained in Chapter 23, the situation was somewhat simplified by the *Ulozhenie* of 1649 which abolished the 'white' (tax privileged) status of many ecclesiastical and private suburbs and added them to the *posad*. According to Vodarskii's calculations, the total number of male *posad* dwellers in Russian towns rose from about 83,000 in 1646 to some 108,000 in 1652, a rise very largely accounted for by the effects of the *Ulozhenie*. The great majority of the households confiscated

---

20 Pallot and Shaw, *Landscape*, pp. 23–4.
21 Ibid., p. 246.

by the state in 1649 were in fact Church and monastic ones.[22] There had long been resentment on the part of the 'black' *posad* dwellers over commercial competition from their more privileged neighbours in the 'white' suburbs, and the 1649 reform was stimulated by a series of urban riots over this and other issues the previous year. However, another effect of the reform was to strengthen the attachment of the *posad* dweller to the *posad* where he lived. Henceforth the *posad* dweller was to stay put and share the burden of taxation and service laid upon the *posad* community as a whole by the government. He was not to move elsewhere, even if superior commercial opportunities seemed to warrant it. Similarly, those *posad* traders who were discovered to be living in non-urban centres (often engaged in trade there) were to be returned to their own *posad*, whilst no *posad* dweller was to 'commend' himself (sell himself into slavery, usually by reason of debt) to a wealthy landowner or to the Church.[23] In this way not only was the *posad* consolidated as a source of revenue for the state but its role as a co-ordinator of the commercial life of the country was strengthened.

Urban commerce

We have seen that the 1649 *Ulozhenie* abolished the 'white places', added their inhabitants to the ranks of the 'black' *posad* dwellers and tied the latter to the *posad* by forbidding migration. It also had a number of other implications. Thus article 6 of chapter 19 (the chapter dealing with the townspeople) orders any agricultural peasants from hereditary or service estates who have shops, warehouses or salt boilers in Moscow or other towns to sell them to members of the *posad* community and return to their estates. 'Henceforth no one other than the sovereign's taxpayers shall keep shops, warehouses and salt boilers.'[24] Thus the *posad* community was guaranteed a virtual monopoly over urban trade. This monopoly was constrained by two exceptions. Firstly, article 11 permitted the minor servitors of provincial towns, namely musketeers, cossacks and dragoons who were engaged in commercial enterprises and kept shops to continue with those activities provided they paid customs duties and the annual shop tax. Since, however, they were not members of the *posad* community but engaged in the tsar's service, they were freed from other urban taxes and

---

22 P. P. Smirnov, *Posadskie liudi i ikh klassovaia bor'ba do serediny XVII v.*, 2 vols. (Moscow and Leningrad: AN SSSR, 1947–8), vol. ii, pp. 701–18.

23 R. Hellie (ed. and trans.), *The Muscovite Law Code (Ulozhenie) of 1649*, pt. 1: *Text and Translation* (Irvine, Calif.: Charles Schlacks, 1988), ch. 19, art. 9, 13, pp. 154–5 (hereafter Hellie, *Ulozhenie*).

24 Ibid., p. 153.

the compulsory service obligations of the townsmen.[25] Commercial activity was probably essential to the livelihoods of such poorly paid groups. By contrast, other minor servitors (gunners, artillerymen, gatekeepers, state carpenters and smiths) who were engaged in commerce and trade were obliged to pay the same taxes and render the same services as the townsmen (perhaps because their military duties were such that they had more opportunity to engage in commercial activities).[26] The indulgence granted to the musketeers and other minor servitors was particularly important to the southern frontier towns where the 'black' *posad* dwellers were at first a minority and much trade was in the hands of servitors.[27] The other exception to the *posad* dwellers' monopoly over trade was made in article 17 of chapter 19 which permitted peasants coming to town with goods for sale to trade those goods in the marketplace from their carts or from boats but forbade them to buy or rent shops.[28] Peasants were similarly prevented from holding taxable houses in town.

Moscow remained the centre of Russian commercial life in this period. Some scholars assert that the city's population rose to 200,000 people during the course of the century, but this seems high.[29] The sources are incomplete and ambiguous and the population seems to have fluctuated considerably in any case.[30] A spectacular instance of the latter came in 1654 when the city was devastated by plague, killing up to 80 per cent of the population in the opinion of some.[31] Nevertheless it is clear that the city, with its mixed population and enormous range of occupations and activities, was a focus for trade and production of all kinds. Moreover, Moscow merchants played a major role in linking the various parts of the country's commercial network together, as with the northern trade via Archangel, the Volga trade, that towards the Urals and Siberia, and to a lesser extent that with the north-west and the Baltic.[32] Moscow's role was clearly a reflection of its status as the country's capital and the fact that it was the home of the country's wealthiest merchants.

25 Ibid., p. 155.
26 Ibid.
27 E. V. Chistiakova, 'Remeslo i torgovlia na Voronezhskom posade v seredine XVII v.', *Izvestiia Voronezhskogo Gosudarstvennogo universiteta* 25 (1954): 46–63; V. A. Aleksandrov, 'Streletskoe naselenie iuzhnykh gorodov Rossii v XVIIv.', in *Novoe o proshlom nashei strany* (Moscow: Nauka, 1967), pp. 235–50.
28 Hellie, *Ulozhenie*, p. 157. See also art. 15, p. 156; art. 9, p. 155.
29 *Istoriia Moskvy*, vol. 1: *Period feodalizma, XII–XVIIvv.* (Moscow: AN SSSR, 1952), p. 446; see P. V. Sytin, *Istoriia planirovki i zastroiki Moskvy. Materialy i issledovaniia*, vol. 1: 1147–1762 (Moscow: Trudy Muzeia Istorii i Rekonstruktsii Moskvy, vyp. 1, 1950), p. 121.
30 Eaton, 'Decline and Recovery', pp. 250–1.
31 *Istoriia Moskvy*, p. 453; Eaton, 'Decline and Recovery', p. 250.
32 Bushkovitch, *The Merchants of Moscow*, pp. 69, 83–4, 101, 125–6, 168–9.

Outside the Kremlin seventeenth-century Moscow was subdivided into a series of 'hundreds' (*sotni*) and suburban settlements (*slobody*) which were the habitations of different social groups. Their exact number appears to have varied through time, and the sources disagree. According to Snegirev, however, they included suburbs belonging to the court and treasury, those of the military servitors, monastic and Church settlements, foreign suburbs and the 'black' suburbs.[33] Basic to the commercial life of the city were the 'black' hundreds and suburbs, the core of the *posad* community. Whatever may have been the original difference in meaning between *sotnia* and *sloboda*, by the seventeenth century the two words were synonymous, designating a settlement populated by people of one status or origin (or sometimes occupation). In principle a *sloboda* also had one communal organisation, but this was not always the case in Moscow.[34] In 1649, as a result of the *Ulozhenie*, nineteen private ('white') suburbs with 1410 households were transferred to the 'black' hundreds and suburbs, thus enhancing the significance of the latter to the commercial life of the city as a whole.[35] According to one source, eleven years earlier in 1638 the 'black' and 'white' commercial suburbs together with those belonging to the court and treasury accounted for 48.7 per cent of the city's population.[36] This population formed the core of the city's commercial life.

An important feature of Moscow's economy in the seventeenth century was the extensive 'in house' production for the benefit of the court, government, army and other central agencies. Much of this took place in the court and treasury suburbs located mainly to the west of the Kremlin. The residents of these suburbs had a status which was rather similar to that of minor state servitors, being obliged to supply the court or government agencies with necessary goods and services in return for payments made in money or in kind. Whenever possible, they might supplement their income by producing for the market or in response to private orders. Many court craftsmen, for example, worked for the Armoury, making firearms or other kinds of light weaponry, or engaged in other skilled pursuits like joinery, cabinet-making, icon-painting, map-making and ornamental arts. The Great Palace chancellery was responsible for provisioning the court, whilst those working for the Treasury Court prepared costume and cloth, and also furs for diplomatic exchanges. Treasury craftsmen worked for the various government chancelleries as smiths, carpenters, carriage makers, furriers, coinage makers, builders, brick makers,

---

33 V. Snegirev, *Moskovskie slobody* (Moscow: Moskovskii rabochii, 1947), p. 18.
34 Ibid., pp. 19–20.
35 *Istoriia Moskvy*, pp. 373, 462–3.
36 Ibid., p. 450.

stonemasons, furriers, costumiers, jewellers, workers in precious metals and gems, cloth makers and so on. To the extent that such craftspeople also produced for the marketplace their relatively privileged situation caused resentment among the 'black' *posad* dwellers.

Craftspeople among the latter group, working mainly for the market, engaged in a wide variety of pursuits. Thus Moscow had many metalworkers. An inventory of 1641 lists sixty-nine smithies in the Earth Town[37] beyond the Tver' Gate, thirty-five in different parts of the White Town,[38] twenty-nine south of the river in Zamoskvorech'e and various others.[39] Other metalworkers worked in copper, tin, gold and silver, all metals which were lacking in seventeenth-century Muscovy. Carpentry in various forms employed many in the city. For large projects like court or government buildings teams of carpenters were sometimes brought to Moscow from other towns and regions. Workers with hemp and flax and their derivatives were limited in number, perhaps because of the significance of such crafts as rural pursuits, but Moscow did provide a market for some specialists. Workers in leather were many – perhaps 200 in 1638 – whilst there were about 100 furriers.[40] Other significant crafts in the *posad* included wool-working, working in tallow and wax (there were thirty-five candle makers and ten soap makers in 1638), producing food (about 600 producers and traders of various kinds in 1638, including those working for the court) and cloth (about 250 producers and traders in 1638).

Large-scale activity in the seventeenth-century city was essentially restricted to that under the aegis of the government. It included the cannon foundry, which dated from the fifteenth century but which expanded from the 1620s, the already-mentioned Armoury with its offshoots the Gold and Silver Chambers (*palaty*), state powder mills, state brickworks, the mints, two paper mills, and others. Such manufactories worked predominantly to state orders rather than to the market.

Something was said in Chapter 13 about the hierarchy of merchants and *posad* traders which characterised sixteenth-century Russian towns. This hierarchy continued to be significant in the seventeenth century and nowhere more so than in Moscow where the richest merchants of the realm lived. At one extreme, wealthy merchants (*gosti* and members of the *gost'* hundreds) traded over wide regions and also with foreigners, and sometimes controlled or had interests in local trade as well. At the other were minor traders, selling

---

37 For the location of the Earth Town, see below.
38 For the location of the White Town, see below.
39 *Istoriia Moskvy*, p. 373.
40 Ibid., pp. 386–8.

their wares in local shops (bought or rented), from mere temporary stalls and carts in the marketplace, or working in shops belonging to others. The organisation of trade lagged behind that of a growing number of European states. Merchants lacked capital, there were no banks or modern credit facilities, and Russian merchants sometimes found it difficult to compete with foreigners. Not until the New Trade Statute of 1667 did they enjoy a measure of protection from foreign competition, particularly in local and retail trade.

The essential geographical patterns of trade in seventeenth-century Moscow did not greatly differ from those of the sixteenth century, for the city continued to be a great consumer of food and other necessities as well as of the many raw materials needed by its manufactories. As before, the Kitai gorod with its large trading square adjacent to the Kremlin continued to be the focus of activity. Retail trade was still conducted through shops organised into specialised trading rows (and also through warehouses, cellars and other outlets). The names of about 120 trading rows are known from the seventeenth century. Wholesale trade and trade by foreign merchants was also conducted through the two merchants' bazaars (*gostinnye dvory*), completed in 1641 and 1667. Olearius and other travellers noted the liveliness and diversity of trade in the city – of the ancestor of Red Square, for example, he asserts that 'all day long it is full of tradespeople, both men and women, and slaves and idlers'.[41] But his account also makes it clear that there was a lively trade in other parts of the city, notably in the White Town ('Tsargorod'). In the latter, he asserts 'are located the bread and flour stalls, the butchers' blocks, the cattle market, and taverns selling beer, mead and vodka'.[42]

The seventeenth-century geography of trade and commerce outside Moscow can only be reconstructed in part thanks to the patchy nature of the evidence. Something has been said already about the location of the towns with the largest *posad* communities along the major trading routes. Space will allow a brief discussion of towns on only one of these routes.

The route northwards from Moscow to Archangel was the most important seventeenth-century route for trade with Western Europe. After 1600 this trade was dominated by the Dutch. Although the English had first arrived at the mouth of the Northern Dvina in the 1550s, the town itself was constructed only in 1583–4 close to the nearby monastery. At first the foreign trade had mainly taken place at Kholmogory, the goods being transferred upriver to that town by shallow draft vessels from the anchorages in the mouth of the river.

---

41 Adam Olearius, *The Travels of Olearius in Seventeenth-Century Russia*, ed. and trans. Samuel H. Baron (Stanford, Calif.: Stanford University Press, 1967), p. 114.

42 Ibid., p. 114.

Gradually, however, Archangel assumed the character of a proper port. In the 1620s it contained 115 *posad* households,[43] and the 1622–4 cadastre describes government offices, warehouses and trading establishments.[44] A proportion of the trade was in the hands of local servitors. It has been estimated that foreign trade at Archangel increased by two to three times on average between the beginning and the middle of the century.[45] The liveliest time for commerce was the annual fair between June and September when the foreign ships arrived and merchants and traders came from many parts of Russia, especially Moscow, various northern towns and the important northern monasteries. Between 1668 and 1684 a large new stone merchants' bazaar was constructed to government order to cope with the trade. A community of foreign merchants resided permanently in the town. But the overall population remained small, no doubt reflecting the restricted period for trading. In fact Archangel's seventy shops in the 1620s (not counting the trading spaces in the merchants' bazaar) and limited number of trades contrasted poorly with nearby Kholmogory which had 316 shops and a much wider variety of craft activities. The latter was the true centre of the region for local commerce.[46]

From Archangel the main trading route ran up the Northern Dvina and then up the Sukhona to the transhipment point at Vologda. Before reaching Vologda, however, traders would arrive at Ustiug Velikii, where the main route to Siberia began. Ustiug Velikii had played an important role in the fur trade, connecting Siberia with Archangel, and was also noted for a range of manufacture and commerce including metalworking, carpentry and woodworking, leather, fur-dressing, clothing, food and others.[47] Nearby Tot'ma, also on the Sukhona, was a centre for salt production.[48] Vologda itself was the principal commercial point on the route to Moscow because merchants would wait here for the winter freeze before proceeding overland to the capital by sledge. In the 1620s it had a population of perhaps 5,000 and contained the houses of eleven foreign traders and five Moscow *gosti*. It had a wide variety of crafts, over 300 shops, a large merchants' bazaar and other commercial facilities.[49]

43 Eaton, 'Decline and Recovery', p. 235.
44 Iu. A. Barashkov, *Arkhangel'sk: arkhitekturnaia biografiia* (Arkhangel'sk: Severo-Zapadnoe knizhnoe izdatel'stvo, 1984), p. 18.
45 Bushkovitch, *The Merchants of Moscow*, pp. 51, 56.
46 O. V. Ovsiannikov, 'Kholmogorskii i Arkhangel'skii posady po pistsovym i perepisnym knigam XVII v.', in *Materialy po istorii Evropeiskogo Severa SSSR*, vol. 1 (Vologda, 1970), pp. 197–211.
47 A. Ts. Merzon and Iu.A. Tikhonov, *Rynok Ustiuga Velikogo v period skladyvaniia vserossi-iskogo rynka (XVII vek)* (Moscow: AN SSSR, 1960).
48 R. E. F. Smith and David Christian, *Bread and Salt: A Social and Economic History of Food and Drink in Russia* (Cambridge: Cambridge University Press, 1984), pp. 46–8.
49 A. E. Mertsalov, *Ocherki goroda Vologdy po pistsovoi knige 1627 goda* (Vologda, 1885).

The final important point on the road to Moscow was Iaroslavl' on the Volga, a major centre for leather and other kinds of manufacturing and a centre of trade interlinking the Volga and routes to Siberia with those to the north-west, as well as Moscow and the centre with Archangel and the north.

As noted in Chapter 13, not all commerce took place in towns. Monastic centres like Tikhvin Posad were also significant, as were numerous villages. Not until the eighteenth century, however, do the statistics on trade at this level permit anything like a comprehensive picture of the geography of trade to be drawn.[50]

The symbolic and religious role of towns

Religion was central to the life of Russian towns in the seventeenth century. Something of its significance for the individual town emerges in the 1627 cadastre for Vologda, as discussed by Mertsalov.[51] In that year, the town of about 5,000–6,000 inhabitants had sixty churches, including the cathedral, and three monasteries. In addition to more than eighty inhabited houses of priests and other church officials, there were the houses and homes of monastic personnel, their dependents and the servants and dependents of the archbishop. Monasteries outside Vologda, including some of Russia's most important, maintained establishments in the town. All this infrastructure underpinned the elaborate life of religious observance and regulation which characterised all Russian towns in this period. Thus the lives of urban dwellers were punctuated by the round of religious holidays, festivals, fasts and days of abstinence which marked the Orthodox year. For the devout both public religious worship and private devotion were regular and demanding. Processions and pilgrimages were normal parts of urban life. The town itself, furthermore, was an assemblage of sacred spaces. Whether in the individual house, which might devote a sacred corner to a holy icon, or in church confronted by the cosmic symbolism of its architecture and its elaborate arrays of mosaics, icons and other decorations, to say nothing of the verbal, musical and dramatic enactments of its rituals, the town dweller was constantly reminded of religious truth, and his or her behaviour was affected accordingly. Chapter 1 of the *Ulozhenie*, for example, specifies the severest penalties for blasphemy or for any

---

50 See e.g. B. N. Mironov, *Vnutrennii rynok Rossii vo vtoroi polovine XVIII – pervoi polovine XIX v.* (Leningrad: Nauka, 1981).
51 Mertsalov, *Ocherki*, pp. 12ff.

kind of unruly behaviour in church.[52] Chapter 10 enforces the observance of Sundays and the principal religious holidays, and restricts trade during religious processions.[53] And chapter 19 forbids foreign churches from locating in central Moscow – they were to be located beyond the Earth Town 'in places distant from God's churches'.[54] In a similar spirit of spatial exclusiveness and religious purity, legislation forced Europeans to sell their property in Moscow and move to a new suburb north-east of the city (1652), and also forbade unconverted foreigners to wear Russian dress, enter Orthodox churches or employ Orthodox servants.[55] Whilst foreigners might be tolerated, the Russian town was meant to radiate values which were at one and the same time Russian and Orthodox. Those towns which served as episcopal centres, moreover, were charged with the task of upholding those values in their surrounding regions.

Numerous social thinkers, among them Elman Service and Paul Wheatley,[56] have argued for the close relationship between political power and sacred authority in traditional complex societies, and Wheatley in particular has noted how cities in such societies were frequently structured to reflect prevailing notions of cosmic order. The claim by the Russian tsars to divine sanction for their rule has been noted by many writers, and in particular the quest by the sixteenth-century tsars to have Moscow recognised as the 'Third Rome', successor to Rome itself and to Constantinople as the centre of world Christendom.[57] The location of the palace of the patriarch, or head of the Russian Orthodox Church, in the seventeenth-century Moscow Kremlin next to the palace of the tsar himself may be taken to symbolise the 'symphony' between Church and state which supposedly reigned under Orthodoxy. The life of the seventeenth-century tsars and of their court was saturated with religious symbolism, observances and practices, as noted by many foreign visitors who were generally hard put to understand the significance of what they saw. The tsars, for example, partook of numerous religious pilgrimages and on particular feast days, notably on Palm Sunday and at Epiphany, the

---

52 Hellie, *Ulozhenie*, ch. 1, pp. 3–4.
53 Ibid., ch. 10, art. 25–6, pp. 28–9.
54 Ibid., ch. 19, art. 40, p. 161.
55 Olearius, *Travels*, pp. 29, 51, 73, 129, 263, 281 etc.; S. H. Baron, 'The Origins of Seventeenth-Century Moscow's Nemeckaja sloboda', *California Slavic Studies* 5 (1970): 1–17.
56 E. Service, *Origins of the State and Civilization: the Process of Cultural Evolution* (New York: Norton, 1975), p. 51; Paul Wheatley, *The Pivot of the Four Quarters: A Preliminary Enquiry into the Origins and Character of the Ancient Chinese City* (Edinburgh: Edinburgh University Press, 1971).
57 G. Hosking, *Russia: People and Empire* (London: HarperCollins, 1997), pp. 4–8; D. B. Rowland, 'Moscow – the Third Rome or the New Israel?', *RR* 55 (1996): 591–614.

city itself formed the setting for the acting out of the elaborate ceremonials which were performed.[58] How far such ceremonials derived some of their meaning from a symbolism which was enshrined within the actual fabric of the city – in the orientation of certain of its streets, for example, or in the religious imagery associated with certain buildings (for example, the imagery of the 'new Jerusalem' associated by some writers with St Basil's Cathedral in Red Square or with Boris Godunov's plans to reconstruct the Kremlin) – is a matter which deserves further research.[59] What seems quite clear is that Russian towns were, to use Wheatley's phrase, 'generators of sacred space' and as such helped underpin the prevailing political and religious order. That being so, it is hardly surprising that the founding of a new town, as of Archangel in 1583–4, or Tsarev Borisov in 1599, was an act invariably inaugurated in religious ceremonial.[60]

But that, of course, cannot be the full story, for what has been said above in a sense reflects the outlook of the state and of its rulers, rather than that of ordinary people. It is by no means certain, for example, that Christianity had in fact entirely managed to eradicate the remnants of paganism, even by the seventeenth century.[61] Moreover, the seventeenth century was itself a time of change and that fact was bound to be reflected in the heterogeneous life of towns, especially the biggest ones. The mixing of foreigners with Russians in Moscow and other towns meant the mixing of Orthodoxy with new ideas and perhaps with 'heresy', no matter how much the latter might be resisted by religious conservatives. The period was one of growing controversy. The deposition of the Patriarch Nikon, and the schism in the Orthodox Church, split society asunder. But such events were mere harbingers of the much greater challenges to traditional religious authority and to the religious unity of Russia which would follow from the time of Peter the Great. The religious symbolism of the town, in other words, no longer reflected the beliefs of all Russians. It seems likely that it had never done so.

---

58 Ivan Zabelin, *Domashnii byt russkikh tsarei*, vol. 1 (Moscow: Iazyki russkoi kul'tury, 2000), pp. 393–453.
59 Robin Milner-Gulland, *The Russians* (Oxford: Blackwell, 1997), pp. 212–20; A. L. Batalov and T. N. Viatchanina, 'Ob ideinom znachenii i interpretatsii Ierusalimskogo obraza v russkoi arkhitekture XVI–XVII vv.', *Arkhitekturnoe nasledstvo* 36 (1988): 22–42.
60 G. V. Alferova, *Russkii gorod XVI–XVII vekov* (Moscow: Stroiizdat, 1989), pp. 56–61; D. I. Bagalei, *Materialy dlia istorii kolonizatsii i byta stepnoi okrainy Moskovskogo gosudarstva v XVI–XVII vekakh*, vol. I (Khar'kov, 1886), p. 9; Barashkov, *Arkhangel'sk*, p. 17.
61 G. P. Fedotov, *The Russian Religious Mind*, vol. 1 (Cambridge, Mass.: Harvard University Press, 1966), pp. 344–62; Milner-Gulland, *The Russians*, pp. 96–103; W. F. Ryan, *The Bathhouse at Midnight: An Historical Survey of Magic and Divination in Russia* (Stroud: Sutton Publishing, 1999), p. 14.

The physical form of towns

The great majority of Russian towns in the sixteenth and seventeenth centuries were fortified. Not until the end of the latter century did fortification begin to lose its significance.[62] This fact tells us much about the nature of life in Russia at the time – a realm which was open to the threat of invasion from many directions and within which the tsar's writ was constantly frustrated. Nowhere was such frustration liable to be felt more keenly than towards the frontiers. Towards the end of the sixteenth century, for example, a series of northern centres, including Archangel, Kargopol', Kholmogory and Sol'vychegodsk, began to be fortified.[63] They were felt to be vulnerable from the west and also, in the case of those close to the White Sea, from the northern coast. The two centuries also witnessed considerable efforts to fortify towns close to the western frontier.[64] And the energy which was expended upon the defence of the southern frontier and on the building of fortified towns as an integral component of that defence was particularly intense. It was in these regions in particular where the military role of towns became dominant as every effort was made to make all aspects of life subservient to it.[65]

The tendency to fortify particular parts of the town as it expanded – first, perhaps, the *gorod*, then the nearby *posad*, then perhaps individual *slobody,* or newer parts of the *posad* as the latter expanded beyond the old walls – gave rise to the characteristic 'cellular' structure of towns which has been alluded to by many writers.[66] Moscow provides a characteristic example. From 1485 the Kremlin began to be fortified in brick thanks to the efforts of Italian architects. These walls replaced earlier ones. Some years later in 1535 what is now the Kitai gorod (then known as the 'Great *Posad*') was also walled in stone. What is now known as the Boulevard Ring was guarded by an earthen rampart. This was rebuilt in brick in 1586–93, the space within it gradually becoming known as the 'White Town'. After the 1591 raid by the Crimean Tatars, a fourth fortification line in earth with a wooden wall was built along what is now the Garden Ring.[67] The area within this final rampart became known as the 'Earth Town'. Thus arose the ring and radial pattern which is still a feature of Moscow's plan today. In other towns, however, the cells were less concentric or regular. And

62 Alferova, *Russkii gorod*, p. 180.
63 O. V. Ovsiannikov, 'Oboronitel'nye sooruzheniia severorusskikh gorodov XVI–XVII vekov', in *Letopis' Severa*, vi (Moscow, 1972), pp. 211–23.
64 See e.g. G. V. Alferova and V. A. Kharlamov, *Kiev vo vtoroi polovine XVII veke* (Kiev: Naukova Dumka, 1982).
65 Pallot and Shaw, *Landscape*, pp. 23–4.
66 French, 'The Early and Medieval', pp. 268–74.
67 Sytin, *Istoriia planirovki*, pp. 42, 52, 58–9.

in many cases, especially in the south, the fortifications were wooden rather than of stone.

From a distance Russian towns typically made a great impression on foreigners. Thus, encountering Plesko (Pskov) in 1661, the Scottish mercenary Patrick Gordon noted that it 'had a glorious show, being environed with a stone wall, with many towers. Here are many churches and monasteries, some whereof have three, some five steeples or towers, whereon are round globes of six, eight or ten fathoms circumference, which – make a great and pleasant show.' On closer acquaintance, however, Gordon was much less impressed. 'Having lodged in the town', he noted that it 'stunk with nastiness, and was no wise answerable to the glorious show it hath afar off, and our expectations –'.[68] To foreigners Russia's towns seemed dirty, unplanned, badly maintained and primitive. Only the churches called forth praise, but even they were vitiated by superstition and their strange architecture. Other buildings were predominantly wooden and seemed quite unimpressive when compared to those common in the West.

The towns, of course, suffered from severe disadvantages. Most of the building, as noted already, was in wood, which had the great advantage of being cheap and readily available but the supreme disadvantage of being vulnerable to fire. In fact so frequent and so devastating did urban fires tend to be that rebuilding had to be done as quickly as possible and at minimum expense, paying little attention to aesthetics or to style. No wonder the results failed to inspire admiration. But the towns were not in fact quite as disordered as they often appeared to foreign observers, particularly in the case of Moscow. From the time of Ivan III, for example, measures were taken to provide fire patrols and also to uphold law and order through forms of policing and controls over traffic, especially at night. From the sixteenth century the tsars gave encouragement to building in stone. Some attention was paid to drainage and to the planking of unpaved and often barely passable streets. From the early seventeenth century concerted efforts were made to widen and straighten certain important streets, especially in the city centre, and to prevent infringements of the building line. This was partly as a fire protection measure.[69] Wells were constructed to give easy access to water in cases of fire. The security and well-being of the capital, where the tsar himself resided, was naturally of crucial importance to the government. Much less seems to have been done in other towns.

68 *Passages from the Diary of Patrick Gordon of Auchleuchries in the Years 1635–1699* (London: Frank Cass, 1968), pp. 43–4.
69 Sytin, *Istoriia planirovki*, pp. 84–90, 162ff.

Moscow and other towns remained quite 'medieval' in appearance down to the end of the century. The typical house or 'court' (*dvor*), for example, consisted of a wooden structure, perhaps accompanied by outbuildings, and the whole surrounded by a high wooden fence. A gate gave access to the street. But Moscow had begun to change its appearance to some degree by the mid-century when new stone and brick homes and mansions of some of the wealthier were noted by the visiting Paul of Aleppo.[70] According to some scholars, the stone and brick houses and mansions which began to appear in the latter part of the century reflected evidence of an interest in new architectural forms and a departure from those based on traditional wooden construction.[71] By European standards Russian towns spread over enormous areas, necessitating the construction of very lengthy walls in order to encompass them. Towns typically included considerable areas of open space between their built-up areas, used for growing food and pasturing livestock. They also tended to sprawl beyond their walls into the countryside beyond and many activities, especially some of those involving fire, were confined to those regions.

There has been considerable debate among scholars over the extent to which Russian towns were subject to planning. L. M. Tverskoi, for example, argued for a degree of regularity in street patterns and suggested that towns were generally planned even when their street patterns seemed irregular.[72] Regularity is particularly noticeable in the layout of some of the southern military towns. Other scholars have spoken of the 'spontaneous' development of towns.[73] A somewhat original argument has been advanced by G. V. Alferova.[74] According to her, towns were planned, but the planning took a different form from the regular, geometrically based system of much Western planning from medieval times onwards which ultimately derived from the Greek conceptions of Hippodamus. Alferova believed that Russian ideas on planning took their origin from Byzantine laws and practices which were translated and appeared in Russian legal anthologies and similar texts from an early period. The latter were used in princely law courts, but it is unclear how far the laws applying to urban affairs were applied, at least before the seventeenth century (there is a faint echo of Byzantine urban conceptions in

70 *Istoriia Moskvy*, p. 509; Olearius, *Travels*, p. 154.
71 A. V. Ikonnikov, *Tysiachia let russkoi arkhitektury* (Moscow: Iskusstvo, 1990), pp. 182–95.
72 L. N. Tverskoi, *Russkoe gradostroitel'stvo do kontsa XVII veka: planirovka i zastroika russkikh gorodov* (Moscow and Leningrad: AN SSSR, 1953).
73 V. A. Shkvarikov, *Ocherk istorii planirovki i zastroiki russkikh gorodov* (Moscow: Gosudarstvennoe Izdatel'stvo Literatury po Stroitel'stvu i Arkhitekture, 1954).
74 Alferova, *Russkii gorod*.

the *Ulozhenie*).[75] The argument is that the Byzantine tradition paid less heed to regularity of form than to such matters as heights of and distances between buildings (views, ventilation, effects of shadow), the width of streets, property boundaries, hygiene, vegetation, drainage and water supply. There was, according to Alferova, overall concern with the profile of the townscape. After about the fourteenth century, she avers, towns were founded and developed according to a well-regulated procedure which included proper documentation and adherence to ritual practice. The problem is that there appears to be only limited documentary evidence to support some of these assertions. What may or may not have appeared in legal texts may tell us little or nothing about actual practice. Moreover, some of Alferova's claims almost amount to a belief in a sophisticated form of landscape architecture long before such a thing was possible. Clearly this is an area which demands more research. It may be that Alferova's study points the way to a deeper understanding of the symbolism enshrined in townscape than has been usual to date. But whether what she writes about is 'planning' is quite a different matter.

Conclusion

Whereas a traditional approach to the study of Russian towns has emphasised their sluggish development and particularly their backwardness relative to European towns of the period, this chapter has emphasised another angle, following the thought of Jan de Vries.[76] This is to view towns as elements in a network and to consider their role as co-ordinators of a growing series of activities across the state. By the seventeenth century most Russian towns were multifunctional and acted as important nodes (albeit varying in their individual importance) for the organisation of commercial, administrative, military, cultural and sacred space. This process of growing nodal significance is termed by de Vries 'structural urbanisation'.[77] To view the towns only in terms of their commercial role, in other words, is to miss one of the most important things about them. And it is to overlook the vital role they played in the building of the Russian state.

75 Hellie, *Ulozhenie*, ch. 10, arts. 278, 279.
76 de Vries, *European Urbanization*.
77 Ibid., p. 12.

26

Popular revolts

MAUREEN PERRIE

The election of Michael Romanov as tsar in 1613 is conventionally seen as marking the end of the Time of Troubles, but social unrest continued for some time. The cossack leader Ivan Zarutskii based himself in Astrakhan' in 1613–14 with his mistress Marina Mniszech, the widow of the First and Second False Dmitriis, and promoted the claim to the throne of her infant son, 'Tsarevich' Ivan Dmitrievich. Zarutskii and the little pretender were executed in the summer of 1614 and, although the cossacks continued to create problems for the government in 1614–15, subsequent protests against the new regime were only sporadic. The conclusion of peace with Sweden in 1617 and with Poland in 1618 brought an end to foreign intervention, and the next decade and a half was a period of relative stability for Russia, both internally and externally.

In 1632 Tsar Michael's government took advantage of the interregnum in Poland-Lithuania which followed the death of King Sigismund III. An army led by the boyar M. B. Shein was dispatched to the western frontier in a bid to regain Smolensk, which had been ceded to the Poles in the Treaty of Deulino of 1618. Thereafter Russia was to be involved almost continuously in warfare (see Chapter 21); the economic and social strains created by these wars contributed in large part to the series of popular revolts which caused the period to be described as 'the rebellious century'. The principal urban uprisings occurred in Moscow and other towns in 1648–50, and in the capital in 1662 and 1682; the most extensive revolt was the great cossack–peasant uprising led by Sten'ka Razin, in 1670–1. The first part of this chapter will provide a chronological overview of the revolts; the second will examine the social composition of their participants; and the third will consider the aims and demands they embodied, within the common framework of 'rebellions in the name of the tsar'.

The sequence of revolts

The first symptoms of unrest occurred against the background of the unsuccessful Smolensk war of 1632–4. The government called for volunteers to supplement the regular army, and many peasants and bondsmen rallied to the appeal, calling themselves 'free cossacks' and acting semi-independently as partisans in the vicinity of the front, sometimes in association with bands of Don cossacks. Their actions were often directed against the property of local Russian landowners rather than against the Poles, and their ranks were swollen by deserters from Shein's army. Soviet historians called this movement the 'Balashovshchina' after one of its early leaders, Ivan Balash, an enserfed monastery peasant from Dorogobuzh *uezd* who died in captivity in 1633. The rural unrest soon subsided, and its remnants were suppressed by government troops after the conclusion of the Peace of Polianovka with Poland in June 1634. The episode had echoes in the capital. When the irregular 'cossack' leaders Anisim Chertoprud and Ivan Teslev came to Moscow for negotiations with the government, many discontented slaves and other members of the lower orders took advantage of the opportunity to escape from the city by volunteering to join their bands.[1] The Russians' failure to capture Smolensk provoked allegations that the army commanders had turned traitor; according to the Holstein envoy Adam Olearius, the government was obliged to execute Shein under pressure from the Moscow mob, who threatened a popular uprising.[2] Two years later, a fire in the central Kitai-gorod district of the capital in March 1636 was followed by extensive looting of merchants' property; but this seems to have been primarily a case of criminal opportunism rather than a significant episode of social or political conflict.[3]

The events of 1648–50 were much more serious. The uprising which began in Moscow in June 1648 is often known as the 'salt riot'. In fact the unpopular tax on salt, introduced in 1646, had been abolished at the end of 1647, but other direct taxes were tripled to compensate for the loss of revenue, and resentment of the tax burden was an important underlying cause of the subsequent unrest. On 1 June the young Tsar Alexis was returning from a pilgrimage when he

---

1 B. F. Porshnev, 'Sotsial'no-politicheskaia obstanovka v Rossii vo vremia Smolenskoi voiny', *Istoriia SSSR*, 1957, no.5: pp. 112–40; B. F. Porshnev, 'Razvitie "Balashovskogo" dvizheniia v fevrale-marte 1634 g.', in *Problemy obshchestvenno-politicheskoi istorii Rossii i slavianskikh stran. Sbornik statei k 70-letiiu akademika M. N. Tikhomirova* (Moscow: Izdatel'stvo vostochnoi literatury, 1963), pp. 225–35.

2 Adam Olearius, *The Travels of Olearius in Seventeenth-Century Russia*, ed. and trans. Samuel H. Baron (Stanford, Calif.: Stanford University Press, 1967), p. 153.

3 E. V. Chistiakova, *Gorodskie vosstaniia v Rossii v pervoi polovine XVII veka (30-40-e gody)* (Voronezh: Izdatel'stvo Voronezhskogo universiteta, 1975), pp. 59–61.

was met on the outskirts of the capital by a crowd who attempted to present him with a petition. The citizens were complaining about abuses committed by L. S. Pleshcheev, the head of the *Zemskii prikaz*, the chancellery which had primary responsibility for the administration of Moscow. The fact that the tsar – in defiance of the traditionally paternalistic relationship between ruler and subject in Muscovy – not only refused to accept the petition, but also ordered the arrest of some of the petitioners, angered the crowd. The next day Alexis again found himself surrounded by indignant Muscovites, who heckled and jostled the boyars and officials who were sent out to negotiate with them. On 2 and 3 June the crowds, now joined by many of the *strel'tsy* (musketeers) stationed in the capital, began to attack the homes and property of the most unpopular members of the ruling elite. These included not only Pleshcheev, but also the tsar's brother-in-law B. I. Morozov, and P. T. Trakhaniotov, the head of the *Pushkarskii prikaz* (Artillery Chancellery). Nazarii Chistyi, who was held responsible for the hated salt tax, was lynched by the mob – he was cut to pieces and his body was dumped on a dung heap. On 3 June Alexis sent a new delegation of boyars, including his kinsman N. I. Romanov, to speak to the people. The boyars agreed to hand Pleshcheev over, and he was butchered by the crowd. On 5 June, in response to the insurgents' demands, Trakhaniotov was executed. Fires broke out in various parts of Moscow – leading to predictably contradictory accusations of arson – and much of the city was burned to the ground. The disturbances continued, and a week later Morozov was exiled to the Kirillo-Belozerskii monastery, after the intervention of some nobles and merchants who persuaded the government to convene an Assembly of the Land. A broadly representative assembly met in September, and in January 1649 it approved the new Law Code known as the *Ulozhenie*, which finally enserfed the peasantry and abolished the tax-immune 'white quarters' in the towns. By a judicious combination of concessions and repressions, the government gradually restored its authority; Morozov was allowed to return from his northerly place of exile in October 1648, and by the beginning of the following year he had regained the reins of power.[4]

4 *Gorodskie vosstaniia v Moskovskom gosudarstve XVII v. Sbornik dokumentov*, ed. K. V. Bazile-vich (Moscow: Gosudarstvennoe sotsial'no-ekonomicheskoe izdatel'stvo, 1936), pp. 35–92; P. P. Smirnov, *Posadskie liudi i ikh klassovaia bor'ba do serediny XVII veka*, 2 vols. (Moscow and Leningrad: AN SSSR, 1947–8), vol. ii, pp. 158–248; S. V. Bakhrushin, 'Moskovskoe vosstanie 1648 g.', in his *Nauchnye trudy*, 4 vols. (Moscow: AN SSSR, 1952–9), vol. ii (1954), pp. 46–91; Chistiakova, *Gorodskie vosstaniia*, pp. 62–106; Valerie A. Kivelson, 'The Devil Stole his Mind: The Tsar and the 1648 Moscow Uprising', *American Historical Review* 98 (1993): 733–56.

Uprisings also occurred in various provincial towns in 1648–9: in Kozlov, Kursk, Voronezh, Novosil' and others in the south; in Sol'vychegodsk and Ustiug Velikii in the north; and in several parts of Siberia.[5] The Siberian town of Tomsk remained in the hands of insurgents for a particularly long period: a revolt against the governor, Prince O. I. Shcherbatyi, which had begun in April 1648 (even before the uprising in Moscow) continued until August 1649.[6]

In some cases the revolts in provincial towns were triggered by news of the events in Moscow. In Kozlov the local servicemen had been complaining to the Moscow authorities about abuses by the town governor and other officials since 1647. On 11 June 1648, when a group of petitioners returned from Moscow with news of the uprising in the capital, attacks were launched on the 'best people' (the wealthy and privileged), and the governor and many of the gentry fled from the town.[7] In Kursk the conflict arose over the government's right to search for runaway *strel'tsy* and cossacks who had found refuge in the town as monastery peasants. The musketeer captain Konstantin Teglev was murdered on 5 July when he tried to enforce the search, and an indignant crowd threatened the lives and property of other representatives of the local authorities. The townspeople cited the killing of 'traitors' in Moscow as a precedent for the lynching of Teglev: 'Better men than he are being killed in Moscow,' affirmed the monastery peasant Kuz'ma Vedenitsyn, who had just returned from the capital.[8] In Voronezh, Novosil', Sol'vychegodsk and Ustiug Velikii, too, there is evidence that the disturbances were stimulated by the arrival of news that boyars and officials were being attacked in Moscow. Reports that the insurgents in the capital had not been punished, and that concessions had been made to their demands, produced a strong impression in the provinces, and led to 'copycat' actions in some towns.[9] In parts of the south-west, urban disturbances may have been influenced not only by news of the events in Moscow, but also by the cossack rising led by Bohdan Khmel'nyts'kyi, which broke out in 1648 in the neighbouring Ukrainian and Belarusian territories of the Polish-Lithuanian Commonwealth.[10]

The risings of 1650 in Pskov and Novgorod, in the north-west of Russia, had a specific context of their own. In 1649 a Russian embassy to Stockholm

5 Chistiakova, *Gorodskie vosstaniia*, pp. 107–234.
6 N. N. Pokrovskii, *Tomsk. 1648–1649 gg. Voevodskaia vlast' i zemskie miry* (Novosibirsk: Nauka, 1989).
7 *Gorodskie vosstaniia*, pp. 93–108; Brian L. Davies, *State Power and Community in Early Modern Russia: the Case of Kozlov, 1635–1649* (Houndmills: Palgrave Macmillan, 2004), pp. 225–42.
8 *Gorodskie vosstaniia*, p. 113.
9 Ibid., pp. 29–30.
10 Chistiakova, *Gorodskie vosstaniia*, pp. 156–64.

agreed to pay compensation to the Swedes for fugitives who had settled in Muscovy from territory ceded to Sweden in the Peace of Stolbovo of 1617. Part of the payment was to be made in the form of rye, and the Pskov merchant Fedor Emel'ianov was entrusted by the Moscow government with the task of buying up this grain. As a result of Emel'ianov's transactions the price of rye soared, creating severe hardship and subsequent discontent in both Pskov and Novgorod. The unrest in Pskov came to a head when the Swedish agent Login Nummens arrived in the town on 28 February to collect the grain; the appearance in Novgorod on 15 March of the Danish envoy Evert Krabbe, who was suspected of being a Swedish agent, triggered a similar reaction. In both towns the homes of rich merchants were raided and the city governors were placed under house arrest. The Moscow authorities dispatched the military commander Prince I. N. Khovanskii against the rebellious cities. Novgorod surrendered on 13 April, but Pskov remained defiant and withstood a siege from Khovanskii's troops until a settlement was negotiated in August.[11]

The next major uprising in the capital, the 'copper riot' of 1662, occurred against the background of the protracted war with Poland (which had been under way since 1654), exacerbated by a conflict with Sweden in 1656–8. In its search for revenue to fund its military operations, the government resorted not only to increased taxation, but also to a currency reform which substituted copper coinage for silver. Counterfeit coins also came into circulation, adding to price inflation. Measures taken by the government against the forgers, many of whom occupied prominent positions in the chancelleries, did little to appease the citizens; rather, they simply fuelled suspicion of treason in high places. On 25 July the musketeer Kuz'ma Nagaev summoned the citizens to assemble on Red Square. A large contingent marched to the village of Kolomenskoe, on the outskirts of Moscow, where the tsar and his court were in residence. Alexis managed to persuade the protestors that their allegations would be fully investigated, and they returned to Moscow. In the capital, meanwhile, attacks had already begun on the homes of the wealthy merchants Vasilii Shorin and Semen Zadorin. The tsar sent Prince I. A. Khovanskii to calm the situation in the city centre, but his mission was unsuccessful and another crowd of insurgent Muscovites headed for Kolomenskoe. Alexis again tried to appease them with promises,

11 M. N. Tikhomirov, *Klassovaia bor'ba v Rossii XVII v.* (Moscow: Nauka, 1969), pp. 23–169, 234–396; *'Miatezhnoe vremia'. Sledstvennoe delo o Novgorodskom vosstanii 1650 goda*, comp. G. M. Kovalenko, T. A. Lapteva, T. B. Solov'eva (St Petersburg and Kishinev: Nestor-Historia, 2001).

but when words failed he used loyal troops to disperse and bloodily repress the rebels.[12]

The 'copper riot' lasted for only a single day, and was confined to Moscow; but the next major upheaval – the Razin revolt – was much more protracted and extensive.[13] After the legal enserfment of the peasantry in 1649 the government took active measures to prevent peasants from fleeing to the southern and eastern frontier regions, where they had traditionally found refuge with the cossack bands who frequented the basins of the rivers Don, Volga, Terek and Iaik. Pressure was exerted on the Don cossacks, in particular, to return peasant fugitives to the centre. The government cut its supplies of food, money and weaponry to the Don host. This policy resulted in considerable hardship for the poorer cossacks, and symptoms of their distress soon appeared. In 1666 a detachment of several hundred Don cossacks, led by Vasilii Us, rode northwards; from their encampment near Tula they sent a delegation to Moscow with a request that they be taken into state service. While they awaited the tsar's response, their ranks were swollen by runaway peasants and bondsmen from the Tula and Voronezh regions, and even from Moscow itself. In order to obtain provisions, they raided and looted landowners' estates. The government mustered regular troops against them, and the cossacks retreated to the Don, accompanied by significant numbers of their new recruits from the central districts. Many of them, including Vasilii Us himself, were to participate in the Razin revolt which broke out soon afterwards.

In 1667, on the conclusion of the prolonged war with Poland, the situation on the Don deteriorated further, as cossacks returned from fighting in the Ukraine, and there was a further influx of refugees. It was in this context that the ataman (chieftain) Stepan Timofeevich (Sten'ka) Razin organised a piratical expedition in which several hundred cossacks crossed to the Volga above Tsaritsyn and sailed downstream to the Caspian Sea, where their raids went north to Iaitsk at the mouth of the Iaik River, and then south into Persian waters. In the late summer of 1669 Razin left the Caspian and returned to the Don by the Volga route, having been allowed to pass through Astrakhan' and Tsaritsyn unmolested by the tsarist authorities. He wintered on an island

12 V. I. Buganov, *Moskovskoe vosstanie 1662 g.* (Moscow: Nauka, 1964); *Vosstanie 1662 g. v Moskve. Sbornik dokumentov*, comp. V. I. Buganov (Moscow: Nauka, 1964).

13 *Krest'ianskaia voina pod predvoditel'stvom Stepana Razina. Sbornik dokumentov*, 4 vols. (in 5) (Moscow: AN SSSR, 1954–76); I. V. Stepanov, *Krest'ianskaia voina v Rossii v 1670–1671 gg. Vosstanie Stepana Razina*, 2 vols. (Leningrad: Izdatel'stvo Leningradskogo universiteta, 1966–72); Michael Khodarkovsky, 'The Stepan Razin Uprising: Was it a "Peasant War"?', *JGO* 42 (1994): 1–19.

in the Don near Kagal'nik, where he attracted a host of impoverished and discontented followers.

In the spring of 1670 Razin decided on a much bolder enterprise than his primarily piratical expedition of 1667–9: an attack on the Russian heartland to eradicate the 'traitor-boyars' in Moscow. In May Razin and his cossacks crossed again from the Don to the Volga, and captured Tsaritsyn. But instead of heading up the Volga towards Moscow, they decided to consolidate their rear, and moved downriver to take Astrakhan'. The cossacks' capture of the fortress was facilitated by a popular uprising in the city. There ensued a massacre of the privileged elites of Astrakhan': the governor, Prince I. S. Prozorovskii, was thrown to his death from the top of a tower, and his two young sons were tortured. In July Razin again headed upstream, the mid-Volga towns of Saratov and Samara surrendering to him without resistance. As the cossacks moved up the Volga, they distributed 'seditious letters' in the surrounding villages, provoking a widespread peasant revolt. Estates were looted, manor houses burned and landowners murdered. Some of the non-Russian peoples of the Volga were also drawn into the rising, especially the Mordva, the Mari and the Chuvash. The rebels' triumphant advance was eventually arrested at Simbirsk. The town's garrison held out against the rebel siege for more than a month, before being relieved by fresh troops from Kazan', who defeated Razin at the beginning of October. At about the same time Sten'ka's brother Frol, who was sailing up the Don in a parallel enterprise, was halted south of Voronezh by government troops. By the winter of 1670–1, although the rebellion continued to spread in some regions, its back had been broken, and the government was on the offensive. Punitive expeditions were sent down the Volga and the Don, brutally repressing the revolt. Razin himself was captured on the Don by service cossacks in April 1671 and executed in Moscow in June.

A major uprising, often known as the 'Khovanshchina' (and depicted in Musorgskii's opera of that name) occurred in the capital in 1682.[14] Although the eponymous Khovanskii princes played an important part in the events, the main role in the revolt belonged to the *strel'tsy*, nearly 15,000 of whom were stationed in Moscow at the beginning of the year. The musketeers had complained about harsh treatment by their officers in the winter of 1681–2, but they failed to obtain satisfactory redress from the authorities. The situation was

14 V. I. Buganov, *Moskovskie vosstaniia kontsa XVII veka* (Moscow: Nauka, 1969), pp. 87–318; *Vosstanie v Moskve 1682 goda. Sbornik dokumentov*, comp. N. G. Savich (Moscow: Nauka, 1976); Lindsey Hughes, *Sophia, Regent of Russia, 1657–1704* (New Haven: Yale University Press, 1990), pp. 52–88.

exacerbated by a dynastic crisis. On 27 April Tsar Fedor died childless, creating a problem for the succession to the throne. The choice lay between Ivan, Fedor's only surviving full brother (from their father's first marriage to Mariia Miloslavskaia), and Peter, the only son of Tsar Alexis's second wife, Natal'ia Naryshkina. Ivan was sixteen, but physically and mentally handicapped; Peter was intelligent and healthy, but not yet ten years old. On the day of Fedor's death, a hastily convened Assembly of the Land chose the younger brother as tsar; custom therefore dictated that his mother should be regent. This resolution of the succession issue was controversial, however, and the grievances of the *strel'tsy* against their commanders were soon extended to the Naryshkins and their supporters, who had – it was claimed – usurped the throne from Ivan, the rightful heir, in order to establish boyar rule during Peter's minority.

On 30 April, in response to a petition from the rank-and-file *strel'tsy*, Tsaritsa Natal'ia ordered that some of their most corrupt officers should be flogged. This did not satisfy the *strel'tsy*, and on 15–17 May they rioted, bursting into the Kremlin and brutally murdering members of the Naryshkin clan and their allies. A compromise solution to the dynastic crisis was provided by the novel arrangement that Ivan and Peter should rule jointly, but with Ivan as the 'first' tsar and his full sister Sophia as de facto regent. The *strel'tsy* continued to influence events throughout the summer. They insisted on being renamed 'court infantry', and on 6 June they erected a large column on Red Square on which they listed the victims of the uprising of 15–17 May and justified their 'execution' as traitors. Prince I. A. Khovanskii, who had become head of the Musketeer Chancellery (*Streletskii prikaz*) after the uprising, tried to use the situation to promote his own interests. In July he organised a debate between a deputation of Old Believers (who enjoyed considerable support among the *strel'tsy*) and representatives of the official Church, in the presence of Tsarevna Sophia and her sisters. Sophia, however, soon gained the upper hand. Khovanskii and his son Andrei were accused of treason and executed in September. In October the regent was able to muster regular troops to protect her, the *strel'tsy* submitted to her authority and she established control over the capital.

Unrest continued for some time on the Don and in other parts of the south. This had begun before the Moscow events, when the Peace of Bakhchisarai of 1681 with Turkey and the Crimea blocked the cossacks' access to the Black Sea. In the spring of 1682 some Don cossacks planned to follow Razin's example and attack the Russian heartland; news of the unrest in the capital subsequently encouraged them to go to the aid of the *strel'tsy* against the boyars.

The initiative was nipped in the bud by government troops, but sporadic disturbances occurred in a number of south-western districts in 1682–3.[15]

The social composition of the rebels

What was the nature of these revolts, and how much did they have in common? Soviet historians drew a distinction between the Razin revolt, on the one hand, which was characterised as a 'peasant war' (more specifically, as the 'second peasant war', following that of Bolotnikov in 1606–7), and the urban revolts, such as those of 1648–50, on the other. In practice this distinction is somewhat artificial. The term 'peasant war' is just as problematic in its application to the Razin revolt as it is to the Bolotnikov episode.[16] Not only was the main leadership provided by cossacks, but the rebellion also involved uprisings in the lower Volga towns, from Astrakhan' to Tsaritsyn, whose participants were similar to those of the urban revolts in 1648–50, 1662 and 1682. But if the 'peasant war' of 1669–71 included urban participants, some of the urban risings of 1648–50 spilled over into the surrounding countryside and involved peasants in neighbouring villages.

Let us look first at the uprisings in the capital. The initial impulse for the revolt in Moscow in 1648 was provided by the ordinary townspeople (artisans and tradesmen) whose petition was rejected by the tsar; the strel'tsy also became involved at an early stage. The gentry took advantage of the unrest to present their own petitions, and they ended up as the main beneficiaries when the government made a major concession to them (the convening of the Assembly of the Land which approved the Ulozhenie of 1649) in order to split the opposition. The social composition of the revolt was therefore fairly heterogeneous, including representatives of relatively privileged groups, such as the gentry and merchants. The main participants in the 1662 'copper riot' were artisans and tradesmen, and petty military servitors; the strel'tsy played only a minor role. The 1682 uprising, by contrast, was largely dominated by the strel'tsy. For both the 1648 and 1682 revolts, there is some evidence that these were not purely spontaneous outbursts of protest by the lower classes, but that various individuals from the ruling elites incited or influenced the course of events. In 1648 the popular protests about Morozov benefited his enemies, N. I. Romanov and Prince Ia. K. Cherkasskii; in 1682 Tsarevich Ivan's kinsmen, the Miloslavskiis, were thought to have encouraged the protests of the

15 Buganov, *Moskovskie vosstaniia*, pp. 318–47.
16 Khodarkovsky, 'The Stepan Razin Uprising'.

strel'tsy against Peter's election as tsar, while the subsequent conflict between Tsarevna Sophia and Prince I. A. Khovanskii affected the outcome of the affair.[17]

The role of the bond-slaves in the Moscow revolts was a somewhat ambiguous one. In terms of their social position, the bondsmen themselves ranged from impoverished domestic servants to the relatively privileged military slaves. The latter were likely to support their masters against the insurgents, while the house-slaves, even if they sympathised with the poorer sections of the townspeople, were often too dependent on their lords to risk participating in any challenges to their authority. Nevertheless, there is some evidence of the involvement of slaves in the revolts. One source indicates that runaway slaves participated in the looting which followed the fires in Moscow in early June 1648, and another claims that on 27 June the boyars' slaves in the capital demanded their freedom, as a result of which six of them were executed and seventy-two were imprisoned.[18] In 1662 there were relatively few slaves among the insurgents, while some actively participated in the suppression of the revolt.[19] In 1682 the 'boyars' people' (slaves) presented a petition to the two tsars on 26 May, asking for freedom, but they received little support from the *strel'tsy*, whose grievances had been largely assuaged by the election of Ivan as 'first tsar'.[20]

The composition of the participants in the urban revolts in the provinces in 1648–50 reflected the varied social structures of the towns affected. The frontier towns in the south and in Siberia were primarily fortresses, and here the main role in the uprisings was played by the petty servicemen 'by contract', such as the *strel'tsy* and urban cossacks. Many of these servicemen were engaged in crafts and trades, and even in peasant-style agriculture, in order to supplement the inadequate monetary payments they received from the state. Their interests and grievances were therefore very similar to those of the taxpaying townspeople in other regions. The northern towns of Ustiug and Sol'vychegodsk, where unrest occurred in 1648, were important manufacturing and trading centres. Here the main participants in the disturbances were the poorer townspeople, such as artisans and traders, and their actions were directed primarily against local officials responsible for tax collection, and against those merchants who were regarded as the closest allies of the

---

17 Robert O. Crummey, *Aristocrats and Servitors. The Boyar Elite in Russia, 1613–1689* (Princeton: Princeton University Press, 1983), pp. 82–97.
18 Chistiakova, *Gorodskie vosstaniia*, pp. 88–90.
19 Buganov, *Moskovskoe vosstanie 1662 g.*, pp. 41–2.
20 Buganov, *Moskovskie vosstaniia*, pp. 198–9.

town authorities. Pskov and Novgorod were the two largest commercial cities of the north-west. In both cases in 1650 the townspeople as a whole, together with the musketeers from the garrison, rose up against the city governors and rich merchants who were implicated in the sale of grain to Sweden. In Pskov, where the uprising continued for six months, sharp divisions developed between the richer merchants and hereditary servicemen, on the one hand, and the poorer townspeople and *strel'tsy*, on the other, concerning the terms on which they would surrender to the besieging government forces. During the siege of Pskov the peasants in some neighbouring villages joined raiding parties of insurgent townspeople in attacking Khovanskii's troops and looting landlords' estates.[21]

The Razin revolt was the most heterogeneous of all the later seventeenth-century uprisings. Its main leadership was provided by cossacks. For Soviet historians, this was not inconsistent with their designation of the rebellion as a 'peasant war', since many cossacks were of peasant origin. But, as other scholars have recognised, cossacks had a very different identity from peasants. The Don cossacks who spearheaded the Razin revolt were independent mercenary cavalrymen who voluntarily offered their services to the tsar in return for the supplies they received from his government. Razin himself belonged to the more prosperous section of the cossacks, but most of his followers came from the poorer strata. Many of these destitute cossacks had only recently come to the Don, and settled in its upper reaches. In the summer of 1670, as Razin conquered the lower Volga, his cossacks were joined by *strel'tsy*, soldiers and other petty servicemen from the garrisons of the occupied towns, together with some sailors from the ports, and townspeople who had taken part in the urban uprisings which were triggered by the rebels' approach. Non-Russians from the mid-Volga – Chuvash, Mordva, Mari and Tatars – gave the rebellion a distinctively multi-ethnic character. Russian peasants played a part only in the latter stages of the insurrection, as the rebels moved into the mid-Volga region with its gentry estates farmed by serf labour. One of the few recorded examples of female involvement in these seventeenth-century revolts is the case of Alena, a nun of peasant origin from the town of Arzamas, who commanded a detachment of 7,000 men before being captured and burned alive on the orders of the tsar's general, Prince Iu. A. Dolgorukii.[22]

21 Tikhomirov, *Klassovaia bor'ba*, pp. 93–8.
22 *Zapiski inostrantsev o vosstanii Stepana Razina*, ed. A. G. Man'kov (Leningrad: Nauka, 1968), pp. 99, 124.

Soviet historians sometimes defined 'peasant wars' as 'civil wars of the feudal period',[23] but in comparison to the Time of Troubles (and even to the Bolotnikov episode within it) the geographical scope of the Razin revolt was relatively limited, focusing on the river basins of the Volga and Don. Thus it is more appropriate to describe it as a 'frontier rebellion' rather than a 'civil war': in that respect – and in its social composition – it is more similar to the Pugachev revolt of 1773–5 than to the Time of Troubles. Like Pugachev's, Razin's uprising had professional military leadership, provided by the cossacks, and the insurgents formed large armies which engaged in open conflict with government troops. To that extent it constituted a more significant threat to political stability than the urban insurrections; and it was met with a much harsher and less conciliatory response from the authorities.

Finally, it is worth noting that religious issues played a part in some revolts. The non-Russian peoples of the mid-Volga who supported Razin were mostly Muslims, and their grievances against the Russian government's policy of forcibly converting them to Christianity had fuelled the constant series of rebellions which they had staged since Muscovy's annexation of the Volga khanates in the mid-sixteenth century. Razin made a bid for their support, and one of his appeals to the Kazan' Tatars invoked the Prophet Mohammed.[24] After the schism in the Orthodox Church, Old Belief became an issue in some of the uprisings. There is evidence that Razin had contacts in the Old-Believer stronghold of Solovki, the island monastery in the White Sea which held out against a siege by government forces for eight years, from 1668 to 1676. But Razin's religious appeal was somewhat inconsistent: not only did he invoke the Prophet, but he also presented himself as a champion of Nikon, who had been deposed as patriarch in 1666 and imprisoned in the Ferapontov monastery. The rebels claimed that Nikon accompanied them on their voyage up the Volga. The cossacks believed that Nikon, whom they described as their 'father', had been removed from office by the boyars. They cursed his successor Ioasaf, and planned to restore Nikon to the patriarchate.[25] In 1682 Khovanskii appealed to Old-Believer sympathies among the *strel'tsy* when he organised the debate with the schismatics; and Old Belief among the Don cossacks was an influence on their unrest in 1682–3.

23 See e.g. V. Nazarov, 'The Peasant Wars in Russia and their Place in the History of the Class Struggle in Europe', in *The Comparative Historical Method in Soviet Mediaeval Studies* (Problems of the Contemporary World, no. 79) (Moscow: USSR Academy of Sciences, 1979), pp. 115–16.
24 Khodarkovsky, 'The Stepan Razin Uprising', pp. 13, 15–16.
25 *Krest'ianskaia voina*, vol. ii.i, no. 22, p. 31; no. 29, p. 44.

'Rebellions in the name of the tsar'

All of these revolts, to a greater or lesser extent, assumed the form of 'rebellions in the name of the tsar': that is, they were directed primarily against the 'traitor-boyars' rather than against the reigning tsar. In this respect they differed significantly from most of the rebellions during the Time of Troubles, which were aimed against rulers, such as Boris Godunov or Vasilii Shuiskii, who were identified as usurpers; the insurgents sought to replace them with pretenders whom they claimed to be the 'true' tsar, treacherously removed from the throne or from the succession (the first two False Dmitriis).

In the revolts which took place under the first Romanovs, the rebels commonly described their main targets as 'traitor-boyars'. These were not exclusively 'boyars' in the narrow sense of the tsar's highest-ranking counsellors; rather, they belonged to a category sometimes identified as 'the strong men'. In addition to boyars and *okol'nichie*, this group included high chancellery officials, rich merchants and provincial governors. In Moscow in 1648 the chief 'traitors' whose deaths the crowds demanded were the boyar Boris Morozov, the *okol'nichie* Petr Trakhaniotov, the conciliar secretary (*dumnyi d'iak*) Nazarii Chistyi and the judge Leontii Pleshcheev.[26] In 1662 the eight 'traitors' listed in the insurgents' proclamation were the boyars I. D. and I. M. Miloslavskii, the *okol'nichie* F. M. Rtishchev and B. M. Khitrovo, the secretary D. M. Bashmakov and the merchants V. G. and B. V. Shorin and S. Zadorin.[27] Sten'ka Razin called on his cossacks 'to go to Rus' against the sovereign's enemies and traitors and to eradicate the traitor boyars and counsellors from the Muscovite state, and the governors and officials in the towns'.[28] The seventeen victims of the revolt of 15–17 May 1682 included five boyars (the Princes Iu. A. and M. Iu. Dolgorukii, Prince G. G. Romodanovskii, A. S. Matveev and I. K. Naryshkin); and the conciliar secretaries L. I. Ivanov and A. S. Kirillov.[29]

Not all boyars were regarded as traitors, however. On 3 June 1648 the Moscow crowd cried out that N. I. Romanov should rule them alongside the tsar, in place of B. I. Morozov; and in Pskov, in 1650, Romanov was identified as a boyar who 'cared about the land'.[30] Prince I. A. Khovanskii was described as a 'good' person by the Moscow insurgents of 1662; and in 1682 the *strel'tsy* referred to

26 *Gorodskie vosstaniia*, pp. 54, 56–7, 61, 75.
27 Buganov, *Moskovskoe vosstanie 1662 g.*, pp. 44–7.
28 *Krest'ianskaia voina*, vol. I, no. 171, p. 235.
29 Buganov, *Moskovskie vosstaniia*, p. 151.
30 Chistiakova, *Gorodskie vosstaniia*, pp. 69–70; Tikhomirov, *Klassovaia bor'ba*, p. 70.

him as their 'father'.[31] In his address to the cossack circle at Panshin Gorodok in May 1670, Razin described some boyars as 'good', because they provided the cossacks with food and drink when they visited Moscow.[32]

The insurgents therefore distinguished between 'good' and 'bad' members of the ruling elite, so that the revolts were not simply indiscriminate attacks on all 'feudal' lords, as some of the cruder Soviet Marxist class-struggle interpretations implied, but were directed only against those who were most detested by the ordinary people. In some cases the rebels invited the crowd to pass judgement on their proposed victims. Razin asked the people of Astrakhan' to decide who should be put to death; and in Moscow in 1682 the strel'tsy called for the crowd's approval before killing their enemies.[33]

The cruelty of the insurgents' punishment and killing of their victims is a common theme in contemporary accounts of these revolts. The 'traitors' were sometimes literally torn apart in an explosion of mob violence; after death their bodies were frequently defiled and abused. The looting of the victims' property may be seen as a crude form of redistribution of wealth; its burning and destruction was a more symbolic form of popular rejection of privilege. For all the understandable indignation expressed in elite sources about the violence involved in the rebels' reprisals against their victims, the forms assumed by popular retribution often resembled those of official punishments, especially the torturing and execution of 'traitor-boyars' during Ivan the Terrible's oprichnina.[34] And it should be borne in mind that the tsarist government's repression of the revolts – especially the Razin uprising – involved much greater and more extensive cruelty than that practised by the rebels themselves.

In order to legitimise their attacks on their chosen victims, the rebels regularly accused them of treason. They commonly alleged that the 'traitor-boyars' exploited and oppressed the peasants and townsfolk. The complaints of the insurgents in Moscow in 1648, for example, focused on abuses and maladministration by the power holders.[35] Exploitation of the ordinary people was frequently associated with harm to the interests of the state, as the Russian historian N. N. Pokrovskii has noted in his detailed

---

31 Grigorij Kotošixin, *O Rossii v carstvovanie Alekseja Mixajloviča. Text and commentary*, ed. A. E. Pennington (Oxford: Clarendon Press, 1980), p. 115; Buganov, *Moskovskie vosstaniia*, p. 251.

32 *Krest'ianskaia voina*, vol. 1, no. 171, pp. 235–6.

33 Stepanov, *Krest'ianskaia voina*, vol. ii.i, p. 89; Buganov, *Moskovskie vosstaniia*, pp. 113, 152–3.

34 S. K. Rosovetskii, 'Ustnaia proza XVI–XVII vv. ob Ivane Groznom – pravitele', *Russkii fol'klor* 20 (1981): 90–92.

35 *Gorodskie vosstaniia*, pp. 35, 46–7.

study of the uprising of 1648–9 in Tomsk, where the petitioners accused the town governor, Prince O. I. Shcherbatyi, of reducing the tsar's revenue through his impoverishment of the peasants and indigenous peoples of the district.[36]

Other types of treason were also alleged – although often these allegations had little or no foundation. Claims of plots against the life of the tsar and other members of the royal family were very common. In 1648–50 rumours spread to provincial towns that the boyars had tried to kill Tsar Alexis. Razin blamed the boyars for the recent deaths of Tsaritsa Mariia Il'inichna and the tsareviches Aleksei and Simeon Alekseevich. In 1682 the rebel Muscovites accused the 'traitors' of having murdered Tsar Fedor and Tsarevich Ivan, in order to clear the way for Peter's succession to the throne.[37]

Finally, the insurgents' adversaries were regularly accused of 'external' treason, that is, of secret dealings with Russia's foreign enemies. In Pskov and Novgorod in 1650 the dispatch of grain and money to Sweden led to suspicions that the city governors and local merchants were Swedish agents, and that the conspiracy also involved some of the boyars in Moscow, including B. I. Morozov. In 1662 the boyars were accused of corresponding with the Polish king and planning to surrender Muscovy to the Poles; and rumours circulated that officials in the Musketeer Chancellery had substituted sand for gunpowder in supplies of ammunition sent to the army at the front. In 1682 the boyar Prince G. G. Romodanovskii was said to have sympathised with the Turkish sultan and the Crimean khan in the recent Chyhyryn campaign.[38] In their choice of allegations against their enemies, as well as in the forms of cruel punishment they inflicted upon them, the seventeenth-century insurgents may have modelled themselves on state terror directed against 'traitors': in the period of the *oprichnina*, Tsar Ivan IV had made accusations of both 'internal' and 'external' treason against the boyars, and their 'internal' treason was said to have involved oppression of the people as well as harm to the prosperity of the state.[39] More broadly, protestors often made use of the same type of rhetoric against corruption as was employed in official statements by the Moscow government.

---

36 Pokrovskii, *Tomsk*, pp. 97–8, 107–8. See also Davies, *State Power and Community*, pp. 215–16.
37 Bakhrushin, 'Moskovskoe vosstanie 1648g.', p. 79; Tikhomirov, *Klassovaia bor'ba*, p. 379; *Krest'ianskaia voina*, vol. 1, no. 171, p. 235; Buganov, *Moskovskie vosstaniia*, p. 156.
38 Tikhomirov, *Klassovaia bor'ba*, pp. 254, 362; Buganov, *Moskovskoe vosstanie 1662 g.*, pp. 44–6; Buganov, *Moskovskie vosstaniia*, pp. 154–5.
39 M. Perri, 'V chem sostoiala "izmena" zhertv narodnykh vosstanii XVII veka?', in *Rossiia XV–XVIII stoletii. Sbornik nauchnykh statei*, ed. I. O. Tiumentsev (Volgograd and St Petersburg: Volgogradskii gosudarstvennyi universitet, 2001), p. 217.

In most popular revolts, the 'evil' traitor-boyars were contrasted with the 'good' tsar. In 1648–50, however, there is some evidence that the rebels criticised the ruler himself. In Moscow, Alexis was described as 'young and foolish', and even as a 'traitor'; similar 'unseemly words' were recorded in Pskov and Novgorod. Rumours had circulated in Tsar Michael's reign that Alexis and his younger brother, Tsarevich Ivan, were changelings, non-royal boys substituted for baby daughters born to Tsaritsa Evdokiia. But the tsar's critics in 1648–50 do not appear to have questioned his legitimacy as ruler, or to have rejected the monarchy as an institution: rather, Alexis was depicted as a tool of the traitor-boyars, and pressure was exerted on him to replace them with 'wise advisers'.[40] Young and inexperienced tsars were evidently seen as particularly susceptible to the influence of 'wicked counsellors': in 1682 the *strel'tsy* expressed fears that the nine-year-old Peter's election as tsar would mean that unjust and corrupt boyars would be the real rulers.[41]

Doubts about the legitimacy of the new dynasty had been expressed in the reign of Tsar Michael, when the authorities reported numerous cases of 'sovereign's word and deed' (*slovo i delo gosudarevy, lèse-majesté*) allegations criticising the Romanovs. Rumours even spread that 'Tsar Dmitrii' was still alive. In spite of these concerns, royal impostors (*samozvantsy*), who had played such a prominent part in the Time of Troubles, were much less evident in Russia in subsequent decades. Pretenders claiming to be Tsarevich Ivan Dmitrievich, Marina Mniszech's son by the Second False Dmitrii, were reported in Poland and the Crimea in the 1640s; and false Shuiskiis (including the notorious Timoshka Ankudinov, who claimed various royal identities) appeared in Poland and Moldavia – but none of these had any connection with the popular revolts within Muscovy itself.[42] Some cases were recorded of Russians calling themselves tsars or tsareviches; but, according to a recent study, this 'popular pretence' was more of a cultural than a political phenomenon: a reflection of the notion that to be a tsar meant the possession of exceptional superiority over ordinary people.[43] The apparently non-political nature of many of these claims to royal status did not, however, mean that the tsarist government considered them

40 Maureen Perrie, 'Indecent, Unseemly and Inappropriate Words: Popular Criticisms of the Tsar, 1648–50', *FOG* 58 (2001): 143–9.
41 Sil'vestr Medvedev, *Sozertsanie kratkoe let 7190–92* (Kiev: Tipografiia Imperatorskogo Universiteta Sv. Vladimira, 1895), p. 44.
42 Maureen Perrie, *Pretenders and Popular Monarchism in Early Modern Russia: The False Tsars of the Time of Troubles* (Cambridge: Cambridge University Press, 1995), pp. 229–36.
43 P. V. Lukin, *Narodnye predstavleniia o gosudarstvennoi vlasti v Rossii XVII veka* (Moscow: Nauka, 2000), pp. 103–69.

to be innocuous: on the contrary, they were rigorously prosecuted as political crimes.

The first evidence of pretence associated with popular revolt is found in the Razin uprising. Although the revolt had begun in May 1670 as a classic 'rebellion in the name of the tsar' against the 'traitor-boyars', by the late summer, as the cossacks moved up the Volga, Razin was spreading rumours that they were accompanied by Tsarevich Aleksei Alekseevich (who had died in 1670) as well as by the deposed patriarch Nikon. It is not clear whether there was an actual pretender-tsarevich in Razin's flotilla, or whether the cossacks were simply using his name in order to justify their actions. Certainly there is no evidence that the rebels planned to overthrow Tsar Alexis and replace him with his 'son' – rather, it seems that they were claiming that the tsarevich would lead them to Moscow to attack the 'traitor-boyars' who had supposedly plotted to kill him. In 1673 a false Tsarevich Simeon Alekseevich appeared in Zaporozh'e (the real Simeon had died in 1669 at the age of four): he too seemed to be hostile to the boyars rather than to his 'father', Tsar Alexis. These pretender-tsareviches were not counterposed to the reigning tsar, but served to provide legitimacy for popular revolts against the 'traitor-boyars'.[44]

Other forms of 'popular monarchism' in this period involved rumours about official documents. The disturbances in Voronezh and Ustiug Velikii in 1648 were triggered by (unfounded) reports that official letters had been received calling on the townspeople to follow the example of the Muscovites and attack rich merchants: the alleged existence of such documents served to legitimise attacks on the local elites. In other cases, for example in Tomsk in 1649 and in Novgorod and Pskov in 1650, when real documents condemning the revolts arrived from Moscow, the rebels maintained that they had been falsified by the boyars or officials: these claims rationalised the insurgents' refusal to obey orders instructing them to surrender to the authorities. Such rumours reflected the popular belief that true justice would be sanctioned by the tsar, and that letters in his name must embody such justice.[45]

* * *

44 C. S. Ingerflom, 'Entre le mythe et la parole: l'action. Naissance de la conception politique du pouvoir en Russie', *Annales: histoire, sciences sociales* 51 (1996): 733–57; Maureen Perrie, 'Pretenders in the Name of the Tsar: Cossack "Tsareviches" in Seventeenth-Century Russia', *FOG* 56 (2000): 249–53.

45 Maureen Perrie, 'Popular Monarchism in Mid-17th-Century Russia: the Politics of the "Sovereign's *gramoty*"', in Gyula Szvák (ed.), *Muscovy: Peculiarities of its Development* (Budapest: Magyar Ruszisztikai Intézet, 2003), pp. 135–42.

The evidence which we have considered in this chapter suggests that these seventeenth-century revolts were directed primarily against individuals rather than against institutions, and that their participants were mainly concerned with the redress of specific grievances rather than with the advocacy of any coherent programme of reform, let alone revolution. Only in the case of the Razin revolt do we find an indication of broader aims. In his speech to the cossacks at Panshin Gorodok, Razin called on them all 'to drive the traitors out of the Muscovite state and to give the common people freedom'.[46] According to a contemporary English account of his Volga campaign: 'Every where he promised Liberty, and a redemption from the Yoak (so he call'd it) of the Bojars or Nobles; which he said were the oppressors of the Countrey . . . '.[47] The aim of 'liberty' and freedom from oppression is rather vague; but some indication of what it meant in practice is provided by accounts of the rebels' sojourn in Astrakhan', indicating that they destroyed the documents which registered slaves, thereby granting the bondsmen their freedom. Similar actions are recorded in the Moscow risings of 1648 and 1682.[48] In some towns which were under the insurgents' control, cossack-style 'circles' replaced the existing authorities.[49] But it would be rash to conclude on the basis of this kind of evidence that the rebels aimed to abolish slavery and serfdom as institutions, or to introduce some type of grass-roots democracy.

In so far as there was a common factor in the very diverse popular revolts which occurred under the first Romanovs, it may be identified as protest against the expansion of the state, against its infringement of the traditional rights and freedoms of townspeople, peasants and cossacks, and against the increased burden of taxation which it imposed upon them. These protests took place in the name of good tsars with wise advisers, who would protect their people against traitor-boyars and corrupt officials (an idealised version of the paternalistic monarchy of the sixteenth century); but they did little to prevent the further growth of the bureaucratic state under Peter the Great and his successors.

46 *Krest'ianskaia voina*, vol. I, no. 171, p. 235.
47 *Zapiski inostrantsev*, p. 97.
48 Stepanov, *Krest'ianskaia voina*, vol. II.i, p. 102; Chistiakova, *Gorodskie vosstaniia*, pp. 72–3; Buganov, *Moskovskie vosstaniia*, pp. 158–61.
49 Chistiakova, *Gorodskie vosstaniia*, p. 242.

27

The Orthodox Church and the schism

ROBERT O. CRUMMEY

The seventeenth century was a time of bitter conflict and wrenching change in the Orthodox Church of Russia and its relationship with the tsars' government and society. In this respect, the Church reflected the fissures in Muscovite society and culture of which it was an integral part. After the successful building of a 'national' Church in the fifteenth and sixteenth centuries, described in an earlier chapter, its leaders faced grave challenges. Critics from within demanded liturgical purity and moral reform and representatives of other branches of Eastern Orthodoxy challenged the legitimacy of Russian national tradition. At critical moments – especially in the pivotal years, 1649–67 – the clashing interests of the tsars' government and Church's leaders disrupted the 'symphony' that, in Orthodox tradition, ideally characterises the relations of Church and state. And laymen and women increasingly rebelled against the Church's claims and its economic power and social privilege. By the first decades of the eighteenth century, the results of these conflicts included a radical redefinition of the relationship between Church and state and a schism among the faithful.

The legacy of the past

Several of the most important themes in the history of the Russian Church after 1613 can be traced to pivotal events at the end of the sixteenth century and beginning of the seventeenth. First, in 1589, while visiting the Russian capital in search of financial support, Patriarch Jeremiah of Constantinople agreed, under extreme pressure, to the creation of the Patriarchate of Moscow and, in 1590 and 1593, the other Orthodox patriarchs accepted the *fait accompli*. This act both culminated and symbolised the changing relationship between the Greek and Russian branches of Orthodoxy. Even after 1589, the Greeks who came to Moscow for alms remained convinced that the Greek 'mother Church' was still the ultimate arbiter of Eastern Orthodox belief and practice.

For their part, the leaders of the Muscovite government and Church were acutely aware of the fact that, after the fall of Byzantium in 1453, the tsardom was the only major Orthodox state left on earth and thus primary guardian of true Christianity.

Second, in the late sixteenth century, the Orthodox Church in the Polish-Lithuanian Commonwealth faced many threats. The Roman Catholic hierarchy and missionary orders, in alliance with the government of Sigismund III, worked energetically to convert Orthodox believers as did various Protestant groups. The Orthodox response took two forms. Lay leaders established centres of Orthodox scholarship and publishing and founded schools. The Ostrih Bible of 1581, the first published translation of the Old and New Testaments into Church Slavonic, is the best-known result of these early initiatives. In 1596, however, all but two members of the Orthodox hierarchy of the Commonwealth accepted the Union of Brest under which they recognised the supremacy of the Pope in return for the right to retain the Orthodox liturgy in Slavonic.

From the outset, many Orthodox believers, particularly the leaders of the laity, rejected the union. A network of confraternities spread to all the main urban centres in the Orthodox regions of the Commonwealth and everywhere founded schools modelled on the best pedagogical practices of Roman Catholic Europe. By 1633, moreover, the revitalised Orthodox hierarchy had won legal recognition from the crown. In short, the Orthodox Church in Ukraine successfully rebuilt itself as an institution and developed networks of schools and scholars fit to defend Eastern Orthodoxy against its enemies, especially post-Tridentine Roman Catholicism. For the rest of the century, the Orthodox Church in Muscovite Russia had the opportunity to draw upon these experiences and cultural resources.

Third and last, the experience of the Time of Troubles (1598–1613) shaped the later history of the Muscovite Church in two important ways. First, Russia's sufferings undermined the conviction that, as the last Orthodox realm on earth, Muscovy enjoyed God's special blessing. Again and again, contemporaries asked why God had allowed His people to suffer such devastation. Second, the Troubles emphasised the potential role of the Russian patriarch as leader in revitalising the community. However accurately, tradition holds that Patriarch Hermogen (Germogen) (1606–12) sent out pastoral appeals urging Russians to hold fast to the native tradition of Orthodoxy, reject all compromise with foreigners and their ways, and give their lives to restore the tsardom. Hermogen's three most powerful seventeenth-century successors – Filaret (1619–34), Nikon (1652–8 or 1666) and Ioakim (1674–90) – all followed his lead, attempting to use their office to impose their convictions and agendas on the Church.

Patriarch Filaret

The election in 1613 of Michael Romanov, teenage scion of a powerful boyar clan related by marriage to the old Riurikid dynasty, traditionally marks the end of the Time of Troubles. The new tsar's father, Filaret, would have been a far stronger candidate for the throne but for the fact that in 1600 he had been tonsured against his will on Boris Godunov's orders – vows that were irrevocable by Eastern Orthodox tradition even though made under duress. Thereafter, although by origin a lay politician and courtier, he could hold only ecclesiastical office. Filaret's career as a prince of the Church was both meteoric and confusing: the First False Dmitrii appointed him Metropolitan of Rostov, and both Vasilii Shuiskii and the Second Pretender recognised him as patriarch, at least temporarily.

In 1619, on his return to Moscow, Filaret ascended the vacant patriarchal throne and, in practice, also acted as effective head of his son's government. Historians have usually characterised him as a forceful, but unimaginative conservative and, after years of imprisonment in Poland, a staunch defender of Muscovite Orthodoxy against Roman Catholic influence.

Filaret strove to strengthen the Church in three ways. First, beginning with his consecration by Patriarch Theophanes of Jerusalem, he systematically built up the power and prestige of the Moscow Patriarchate. He adopted the title *Velikii Gosudar'* (Great Sovereign), normally applied only to tsars, and, on many occasions, used it in decrees issued jointly with his son. In light of Filaret's position as head of the ruling family, this practice made sense, but set a dangerous precedent. He also took practical steps to make the patriarch the most powerful and richest man in Muscovy other than the tsar himself. Through royal grants, he built up an impressive portfolio of estates in all parts of Russia from which he collected revenue and in which he had judicial authority over all but the most serious crimes. To administer these territories and collect revenue from the clergy, Filaret created separate patriarchal chancelleries for administration, finances and judicial affairs, parallel to the offices of the state bureaucracy, and a corps of servitors – laymen as well as clergy – to manage them and also to serve as his retinue. In short, as patriarch, he virtually made himself ruler of a separate principality within the realm, a precedent that the more ambitious of his successors eagerly followed.

Second, he adopted practical and symbolic measures to preserve the purity of Muscovite Orthodoxy. Rebuking his immediate predecessor, Metropolitan Iona of Krutitsy, *locum tenens* in his absence, he insisted, for example, that only Orthodox baptism by triple immersion was valid and therefore that all foreigners – even Eastern Orthodox believers from the Polish Commonwealth – had to be baptised again in order to be received into the Russian Church. In 1620, a Church Council in Moscow adopted his policy. The driving force behind this exceptionally rigorous stance was probably fear of the corrupting influence of the Uniate movement in the Commonwealth: the anti-Union Orthodox in Ukraine took the same position.

Although Filaret saw Roman Catholicism as Orthodoxy's most dangerous foe, he also tried to shelter his flock from the pernicious influence of freethinkers and Protestants. As is well known, he had two intellectuals from prominent aristocratic families, S. I. Shakhovskoi and I. A. Khvorostinin, imprisoned temporarily in monasteries for disrespect to Orthodoxy or immoral conduct. As for Protestants, many of whom had come to Moscow as mercenary soldiers, he ordered them in 1633 to live exclusively in their own settlement – a foreign, non-Orthodox enclave within the city, later nicknamed 'The German Quarter' (*nemetskaia sloboda*). Military exigencies, however, ruled out any additional limitations on their freedom to work and worship in Moscow.[1]

Third, the 'Gutenberg revolution' belatedly took root in Muscovite Russia at the beginning of the seventeenth century. Printing presented the Church with both an opportunity and a challenge. Well aware of the dangers of open public discussion in print, tsars and patriarchs maintained a virtual monopoly over this revolutionary technology: the official Printing Office (*Pechatnyi dvor*) published the overwhelming majority of books that appeared in Russia during the seventeenth century. Printing made it possible to provide parishes and monasteries with reliable copies of the service books that the Orthodox liturgy requires. Even so, there were perils, for publishing uniform editions of liturgical books requires the editors to establish authoritative texts. Given centuries of evolving liturgical practice within the Orthodox Commonwealth, leading to different practices in different communities, and the inevitable variations in

---

1 Metropolitan Makarii, *Istoriia russkoi tserkvi*, 12 vols. (Düsseldorf: Brücken-Verlag, 1968–9), vol. XI, pp. 3–8, 23–33; A. V. Kartashev, *Ocherki po istorii russkoi tserkvi*, 2 vols. (Moscow: Nauka, 1991), vol. II, pp. 96–9; Pierre Pascal, *Avvakum et les débuts du raskol*, 2nd edn (Paris, The Hague: Mouton, 1969), pp. 25–7; Serge A. Zenkovsky, *Russkoe staroobriadchestvo; dukhovnye dvizheniia semnadtsatogo veka* (Forum Slavicum, Bd. 21) (Munich: W. Fink, 1970), pp. 70–4; Paul Bushkovitch, *Religion and Society in Russia: The Sixteenth and Seventeenth Centuries* (New York: Oxford University Press, 1992), pp. 52–3.

hand-copied manuscripts, how were editors to decide which variant was truly Orthodox?

As soon as he returned to Moscow, Filaret faced a crisis over this issue. In his absence, Tsar Michael had turned to the leaders of the Holy Trinity monastery, the only important centre of learning in a devastated cultural landscape, and commissioned Abbot Dionysii to prepare new editions of fundamental liturgical texts beginning with the *Sluzhebnik* (Missal). He and his collaborators, Arsenii Glukhoi and Ivan Nasedka, compared recent Muscovite editions with a selection of earlier Slavonic and Greek texts and found a number of passages that, in their eyes, were illogical or tinged with heresy. Their work elicited a violent reaction. In 1618, led by Metropolitan Iona, an ecclesiastical council attacked their editions, particularly for small changes in the ceremony of blessing the waters at Epiphany, condemned Dionysii and the others as heretics and defrocked them.

Filaret immediately made clear that the Printing House would continue to publish new editions of the liturgical books prepared by the best native scholars. Accordingly, at the urging of Patriarch Theophanes, he pardoned the disgraced editors and sent them back to work. At the same time, he remained vigilant for signs of heresy, particularly Latin influence. He refused to publish the catechism of the Ruthenian monk, Lavrentii Zyzanii; condemned the *Evangelie uchitel'noe* (Gospels with commentary) of another Ruthenian, Kyryl Tranquillon Stavrovetsky; and attempted to prohibit the importation of all books from the Polish Commonwealth. The patriarch's caution meant that the *Pechatnyi dvor* published a very modest number of books in his lifetime. But, by setting the programme in motion and assembling the scholars, he laid the groundwork for the flowering of ecclesiastical publishing under his unimposing successors, Ioasaf I (1634–40) and Iosif (1642–52).[2]

The Church in the seventeenth century

At this point, let us pause for a very brief survey of the institutional structure and economic position of the Russian Orthodox Church in the seventeenth century. This is no easy task: historians have given remarkably little systematic attention to these subjects. We can therefore present only general impressions, supported by fragmentary or anecdotal information. One thing is clear, however. Like the secular administration, the seventeenth-century

2 Pascal, *Avvakum*, pp. 8–14, 21–4; Zenkovsky, *Russkoe staroobriadchestvo*, pp. 91–6; Kartashev, *Ocherki*, vol. ii, pp. 85–94.

Church appeared to be an imposing institutional structure, but, in practice, the patriarch and the metropolitans, archbishops and bishops who served under him had very little effective control over monastic communities or the parish clergy and their flocks to say nothing of the many self-appointed priests, monks and nuns who reported to no human authority. The crises that shook the seventeenth-century Church arose, in considerable measure, from the attempts of the hierarchy to exercise more effective control over the body of Christ.[3]

The enormous size of Russian eparchies (dioceses) – compared, for example, with those of the Greek Church – is one obvious reason why the hierarchy had so little impact on the day-to-day life of its flock. The leaders of the Church had long recognised the problem, but, over the course of the seventeenth century, Church Councils consistently resisted proposals to create new dioceses by subdividing existing jurisdictions, presumably because bishops feared the loss of revenue and power that reform would inevitably entail. In 1619, for example, the Russian hierarchy consisted of Patriarch Filaret, four metropolitans, six archbishops and one bishop.[4] Obvious pastoral needs, created by the territorial expansion of the Russian state and the challenge of religious dissent, however, led to the creation of some new jurisdictions, Tobol'sk in Siberia (1620), Viatka (1656), Belgorod (1667), Nizhnii Novgorod (1672) and four in 1682 – Ustiug Velikii, Kholmogory, Voronezh and Tambov. By 1700, the size of the hierarchy had risen to twenty-four – the patriarch, fourteen metropolitans, seven archbishops and two bishops.

By and large, seventeenth-century parish priests, like their predecessors, lived far from their bishops both geographically and socially. Anecdotal evidence indicates that the parish priesthood was usually an ascribed occupation, handed down from father to son with the approval of the local community. At best, its members' education consisted of the customary instruction in reading and writing, using familiar religious texts, and hands-on training in the liturgy. The parish clergy were intimately interconnected with local society. As a married man – unlike his celibate bishop – a priest had to provide for his family through farming and collecting the customary fees for his services. He was vulnerable to pressure from officials of the crown, at the mercy of the nobles who owned land nearby, and could easily become the enemy of

---

3 A central theme in Georg B. Michels, *At War with the Church. Religious Dissent in Seventeenth-Century Russia* (Stanford, Calif.: Stanford University Press, 1999).

4 P. M. Stroev, *Spiski ierarkhov i nastoiatelei monastyrei rossiiskoi tserkvi* (St Petersburg: Tipografiia V. S. Balasheva, 1877).

his parishioners if he attempted to challenge the syncretism of Christian and traditional folk beliefs and practices that shaped their lives.

In the second half of the century, however, these conditions began to change. Patriarchs and bishops began to insist that all candidates for priestly office be literate and receive formal ordination charters from them. Moreover, having installed new priests, the hierarchy attempted to make sure that they followed the official policies of the Church.[5] The success of these initiatives naturally varied widely from place to place depending on the energy of the bishop and the responsiveness or resistance of the parish priests involved. In addition, as Daniel Kaiser's studies show, diocesan courts conscientiously investigated alleged breaches of canon law on marriage, the family and sexual mores and, in most cases, strictly upheld the Church's traditional teachings.[6]

In the seventeenth century, monasteries remained a vital force in Russian Orthodoxy: at the same time, the emergence of competing centres of authority, especially the patriarchate, probably reduced their relative power within the Church as compared with earlier centuries. Monasteries such as the Holy Trinity, the Kirillo-Belozerskii and the Solovetskii were still very wealthy and influential, each one a complex hierarchical organisation of monks and lay dependents that functioned largely independently of outside control. Foundations like these stood out as exceptional, however: the vast majority of the 494 men's and women's communities which owned populated land in 1653 were very small.[7] All, large and small, depended heavily on the patronage of laymen and women of all stations, from the imperial family to peasants and townspeople.

In the seventeenth century, monastic estates continued to grow in spite of repeated legal prohibitions on new acquisitions of land. The pace of acquisition through bequests, however, slowed to a trickle after mid-century.[8] In addition, all members of the hierarchy, above all the patriarch, likewise controlled extensive tracts and the revenues they produced.[9] A summary of the landholdings of the hierarchy, the monasteries and the lay elite in 1678 provides a rough

5 Michels, War, pp. 31–2, 163–70, 187.
6 Most recently, Daniel H. Kaiser, ' "Whose Wife Will She Be at the Resurrection?" Marriage and Remarriage in Early Modern Russia', SR 62 (2003): 302–23.
7 Ia. E. Vodarskii, 'Tserkovnye organizatsii i ikh krepostnye krest'iane vo vtoroi polovine XVII – nachale XVIII v.', in Istoricheskaia geografiia Rossii. XII – nachalo XX v. (Moscow: Nauka, 1975), p. 76.
8 S. V. Nikolaeva, 'Vklady i vkladchiki v Troitse-Sergiev Monastyr' v XVI–XVII vekakh. (Po vkladnym knigam XVII veka)', in Tserkov' v istorii Rossii, 3 vols. (Moscow: Institut rossiiskoi istorii Rossiiskoi akademii nauk, 1997–9), vol. II (1998), pp. 81–107.
9 Vodarskii, 'Tserkovnye organizatsii'; Iu. V. Got'e, Zamoskovnyi krai v XVII veke (Moscow: Gosudarstvennoe sotsial'no-ekonomicheskoe izdatel'stvo, 1937), pp. 230–53.

indication of the relative wealth of the leaders of the Church. At that time, the patriarch owned lands with 7,128 peasant households, the six metropolitans a total of 7,167 – of which the Metropolitan of Rostov owned 3,909 – and six archbishops a total of 4,494. Monasteries and churches owned lands with almost 100,000 peasant households, led by the Holy Trinity with close to 17,000. To be sure, the overwhelming majority of monasteries on the list had fewer than 200 households. By comparison, the members of the boyar council, the tsar's most prominent officials and courtiers, controlled a total of 46,771 households. The richest layman on the list, I. M. Vorotynskii, owned 4,609. Thus the data from 1678, however flawed they may be, show the great wealth, in laymen's terms, of the hierarchy and the largest monasteries. No wonder the provincial gentry and townspeople considered them 'strong people' against whose power and privileges they complained so bitterly in the 1630s and 1640s!

Liturgy and public ceremony also brought the leaders of the Church and the secular elite together. In the most dramatic example, tsar and patriarch acted out the 'symphony' of Church and state in the public rituals of Epiphany and Palm Sunday, commemorating Christ's baptism and entry into Jerusalem. These ceremonies, created by sixteenth-century Muscovite churchmen from the repertoire of ecumenical Christian symbolism, underwent some alterations in detail and emphasis during the seventeenth century. Their central message did not change. Moscow, capital of the only powerful Eastern Orthodox monarchy, was the centre of the Christian world and its ruler, consecrated and supported by the Church, justified his authority by defending the true faith. The ceremonies' symbolic complexity, however, left the issue of the relative importance of tsar and patriarch in the economy of salvation open to differing interpretations.[10]

These great festivals formed only a small part of the ritual tapestry that shaped the life of the hierarchy and the imperial court. As Orthodox Christians, the tsars and their families and attendants took part in all the main services of the liturgical calendar, celebrating the most solemn feasts such as Easter in the cathedrals of the Moscow Kremlin with full magnificence. And the imperial

---

10 Robert O. Crummey, 'Court Spectacles in Seventeenth Century Russia: Illusion and Reality', in Daniel Clarke Waugh (ed.), *Essays in Honor of A. A. Zimin* (Columbus, Oh.: Slavica, 1985), pp. 130–58; Michael S. Flier, 'Breaking the Code: The Image of the Tsar in the Muscovite Palm Sunday Ritual', in Michael S. Flier and Daniel Rowland (eds.), *Medieval Russian Culture*, vol. II (California Slavic Studies, 19) (Berkeley: University of California Press, 1994), pp. 213–42; Michael S. Flier, 'Court Ceremony in an Age of Reform. Patriarch Nikon and the Palm Sunday Ritual', in Samuel H. Baron and Nancy Shields Kollmann (eds.), *Religion and Culture in Early Modern Russia and Ukraine* (DeKalb, Ill.: Northern Illinois University Press, 1997), pp. 74–95; Paul Bushkovitch, 'The Epiphany Ceremony of the Russian Court in the Sixteenth and Seventeenth Centuries', *RR* 49 (1990): 1–18.

family continued the tradition of regular pilgrimages to the Holy Trinity and other monasteries to venerate their saintly founders.[11]

Pressure for reform

After the relatively uneventful tenure of Patriarch Filaret, the Muscovite Church began to feel pressure for change from within and from without. Like their counterparts in Roman Catholic and Protestant Europe, would-be reformers among the clergy strove for consistency and good order in the celebration of the liturgy and attempted to raise the moral tone of parish life. Many of their complaints were not new. In 1636, for example, Ivan Neronov and other parish priests in Nizhnii Novgorod sent a petition to Patriarch Ioasaf, asking for his support in restoring order and dignity to services of worship. The petitioners recited a litany of long-standing abuses – *mnogoglasie* (the practice of chanting up to 'five or six' different parts of the service simultaneously) and other liturgical short-cuts. They also complained at length about rowdy behaviour during services.[12] In a series of pastoral instructions, Patriarch Ioasaf strongly supported their demands for pious behaviour during the liturgy. Ten years later, his successor, Iosif, issued a general decree that all priests, deacons and 'all Orthodox Christians fast . . . and refrain from drunkenness, injustice and all kinds of sin'. Worshippers 'should stand in God's church with fear and trembling . . . silently . . .' and pray 'over their sins with tears, humble sighs and contrite hearts . . .'

The Nizhnii Novgorod petitioners also attacked the laity's boisterous celebration of non- or pre-Christian festivals such as Rusalii and Koliada at the most solemn times of the liturgical year. Folk minstrels (*skomorokhi*) drew their particular ire (for depictions of *skomorokhi* and other popular entertainers, see Plate 23). On this issue too, the hierarchy agreed but could see no way to uproot these ancient practices.[13]

Attacking *mnogoglasie* was more controversial. Liturgical short-cuts had crept into Russian Orthodoxy for good reason. Over the centuries, monastic services had become the norm in parishes, putting severe demands on the

---

11 I. Zabelin, *Domashnii byt russkikh tsarei v XVI i XVII st.* (Moscow: Tipografiia A. I. Mamontova, 1895), pp. 376–435; Nancy Shields Kollmann, 'Pilgrimage, Procession, and Symbolic Space in Sixteenth-Century Russian Politics', in Flier and Rowland (eds.), *Medieval Russian Culture*, vol. II, pp. 163–81.

12 N. V. Rozhdestvenskii, 'K istorii bor'by s tserkovnymi bezporiadkami, otgoloskami iazychestva i porokami v russkom bytu XVII v.', *ChOIDR* 201 (1902, kn. 2), pp. 19–23.

13 *AAE*, 4 vols. (St. Petersburg: Tipografiia II Otdeleniia Sobstvennoi E. I. V. Kantseliarii, 1836), vol. IV, pp. 481–2 (no. 321).

patience and stamina of even the most devout laypeople.[14] When the first attempts to set some limits to these traditional practices encountered vigorous opposition, Iosif retreated and, in 1649, to the reformers' chagrin, an ecclesiastical council chose to maintain the status quo.[15]

Paradoxically, the reformers' desire for an orderly and consistent liturgy opened the Muscovite Church to books and scholars from Ukraine – precisely what Filaret had feared. From the late 1630s to the early 1650s, the *Pechatnyi dvor* published new editions of the most important service books, a number of saints' lives and classics of Eastern Christian spirituality such as writings of St John Chrysostom, St Efrem the Syrian and St John Climacus, works in which the editors avoided offending Muscovite sensibilities. In the 1640s, however, the *Pechatnyi dvor* also published a number of works from Ukraine including Petr Mohyla's catechism, the *Nomokanon* of Zakhariia Kopystenskii and the pioneering Slavonic grammar of Meletii Smotritskii. Moreover, since the Printing Office desperately needed more editors who knew Greek and Latin, three scholars from Ukraine joined its staff in 1649. Finally, from Ukraine came a book that stimulated apocalyptic reflection among the cultural elite of Moscow, Hegumen Nafanail's compilation of apocalyptic writings, the *Book of Faith*, an Orthodox interpretation of the Union of Brest as a prelude to the End Time. The Muscovite miscellany, the *Kirillova kniga*, and the writings of St Efrem also contributed to the climate of apocalyptic speculation.[16]

In 1645, Aleksei (Alexis) Mikhailovich became tsar. His decisive role in the stormy events of the following decades demonstrates the extent to which, long before Peter I, the attitudes and choices of the secular ruler ultimately determined the fate of the Russian Orthodox Church. Strong supporters of reform, the young ruler and his confessor, Stefan Vonifat'ev, gathered like-minded men, traditionally known as the Zealots of Piety, including parish priests such as Neronov and his protégé Avvakum, and in time the future patriarch Nikon. Everyone in this diverse group agreed that parish life must be revitalised through effective preaching, the full and orderly celebration of the liturgy, and strict enforcement of the Church's moral teachings.

Before long, Alexis and his allies in the Church made several of the reformers' demands official policy. The tsar, already known for his personal antipathy towards folk entertainment, issued a series of decrees, beginning in December

14 Pascal, *Avvakum*, pp. 58–9.
15 'Deianiia Moskovskogo tserkovnogo sobora 1649 goda', ed. S. A. Belokurov, *ChOIDR* 171 (1894, kn. 4): 1–52.
16 A. S. Zernova, *Knigi kirillovskoi pechati izdannye v Moskve v XVI–XVII vekakh* (Moscow: Gosudarstvennaia Ordena Lenina biblioteka SSSR imeni V. I. Lenina, 1958), pp. 46–77; Pascal, *Avvakum*, pp. 65–71, 128–32; Zenkovsky, *Russkoe staroobriadchestvo*, pp. 91–101.

1648, ordering local governors to ban *skomorokhi* and suppress the folk customs associated with them in every village and hamlet in their jurisdictions.[17]
Issuing decrees, however, was much easier than changing deep-rooted patterns of behaviour: scattered evidence suggests that the *skomorokhi* continued
to practise their ancient trade in the remote countryside into the eighteenth
century and many of the agrarian rites and folk festivals survived long enough
for modern ethnographers to record them.[18]

The reformers also won their battle for *edinoglasie* (celebrating the liturgy
with no overlapping or short-cuts). Reversing the decision of 1649, another
ecclesiastical council, in February 1651, made the practice obligatory in parish
churches as well as in monasteries.[19]

Not surprisingly, the implementation of the Zealots' programme aroused
violent opposition among the laity. Avvakum's hagiographic autobiography,
written roughly twenty years after the events, describes his clashes with a
prominent aristocrat, other local notables, and ordinary parishioners while
parish priest of Lopatitsy. Twice, in 1648 and 1652, in fear for his life, he fled
his parish for the safety of Moscow. The second time, he received a major
promotion to become dean of the cathedral in Iurevets on the Volga, but could
serve only eight weeks until '. . . the priests, peasants and their women . . .' beat
him and drove him out of town. As he recalled them, Avvakum's methods of
enforcing liturgical and moral order and rebuking sinners were hardly subtle.[20]
Moreover, his clashes with his parishioners took place at a time of extreme
unrest in many urban centres of Russia. Nevertheless, his problems with his
parishioners ultimately arose from his commitment to radical change. Other
reformist priests suffered through similar tribulations. As foot soldiers in a
campaign of reform from above, they took the brunt of parishioners' anger at
the demand that they abruptly change their traditional way of life.

Legal and economic issues also threatened the reformers' campaign. The
Law Code of 1649 significantly changed the legal relationship of Church and

17 N. Kharuzin, 'K voprosu o bor'be moskovskogo pravitel'stva s narodnymi iazycheskimi
obriadami i sueveriiami v polovine XVII v.', *Etnograficheskoe Obozrenie*, 1879, no. 1, 143–51;
AI, vol. IV (St Petersburg: Tipografiia II Otdeleniia Sobstvennoi E. I. V. Kantseliarii, 1842),
pp. 124–6.
18 Russell Zguta, *Russian Minstrels: A History of the Skomorokhi* (Philadelphia: University
of Pennsylvania Press, 1978), pp. 63–5; M. M. Gromyko, *Mir russkoi derevni* (Moscow:
Molodaia Gvardiia, 1991), pp. 325–9, 345–60.
19 Pascal, *Avvakum*, pp. 156–8.
20 Archpriest Avvakum, *Zhitie Protopopa Avvakuma im samim napisannoe i drugie ego sochineniia*, ed. N. K. Gudzii (Moscow: Goslitizdat, 1960), pp. 61–4; Archpriest Avvakum,
The Life Written by Himself: With the Study of V. V. Vinogradov, trans. and ed. Kenneth N.
Brostrom (Michigan Slavic translations, no. 4) (Ann Arbor: University of Michigan Press,
1979), pp. 45–50.

state. It created a Monastery Chancellery (*Monastyrskii prikaz*) and gave it authority to try criminal and civil cases involving clergymen and inhabitants of Church lands except the patriarchal domain.[21] Moreover, under pressure from urban taxpayers, the government confiscated the tax-exempt urban settlements in which the Church's dependents conducted trade. Although neither the judgement of churchmen by the secular government nor the confiscation of ecclesiastical property was unprecedented – the Great Court Chancellery had previously handled legal cases involving the clergy – the sweeping provisions of the Code made clear that neither the Church's judicial privileges nor its lands were sacrosanct.

Patriarch Nikon

When Nikon became patriarch in 1652, many of the latent tensions within the Russian Church erupted into open conflict. Nikon aroused enormous controversy in his own day and still fascinates and perplexes us. Born into a peasant family in the Nizhnii Novgorod area, he served briefly as a parish priest before taking monastic vows in the Anzerskii Skit on an island in the White Sea. In this small idiorrhythmic community, he followed a severely ascetic rule of life. He also displayed great energy and administrative talent, qualities that ultimately brought him to the position of abbot of the Kozheozerskii monastery on the coast of the mainland. In this capacity, he travelled to Moscow in 1646 and was introduced to Tsar Alexis.

From that moment, Nikon became a favourite of the tsar and an ally of the Church reformers at his court. Although his long-term relationship with Alexis was very complex, his meteoric rise to the patriarchal throne unquestionably required the unconditional support of the tsar and his advisers. Alexis immediately appointed him archimandrite of the Novospasskii monastery in Moscow, a favourite foundation of the Romanov family. In 1649, he was consecrated Metropolitan of Novgorod, the second most powerful position in the hierarchy. In both of these capacities, he carried out the programme of the reformers with characteristic determination. In 1650, he also displayed great physical courage and political astuteness in quelling an uprising in Novgorod with minimal bloodshed.

---

21 *Sobornoe ulozhenie 1649 goda: tekst, kommentarii*, ed. L.I. Ivina, G.V. Abramovich et al. (Leningrad: Nauka, Leningradskoe otdelenie, 1987), pp. 69–70, 242–6; M. I. Gorchakov, *Monastyrskii prikaz, 1649–1725 g. Opyt istoriko-iuridicheskogo issledovaniia* (St. Petersburg: A. Transhel', 1868), pp. 40–90.

During his tenure in Novgorod, Nikon made it clear that, in his opinion, the ecclesiastical hierarchy was the natural leader in the campaign to revitalise Russian Orthodoxy. He did everything he could to increase his own effective power and ceremonial dignity as metropolitan and to emphasise that the ultimate responsibility for the spiritual well-being of Russia lay with the Church's leaders, not the secular ruler. For example, in 1652, as part of a campaign to canonise martyred leaders of the Russian Church, he brought the relics of Metropolitan Filipp, already recognised as a saint, from the Solovetskii monastery to Moscow. While in Solovki, he publicly read Tsar Alexis's statement of contrition for the sin of his predecessor, Ivan IV, in ordering Filipp's murder. At the same time, it is difficult to be sure how accurately Nikon's fullest statements of his theories on the relations of Church and state reflect his views during his active ministry since he wrote them years later while in self-imposed exile. For example, in his *Refutation*, he repeatedly attacked the *Ulozhenie* of 1649 for usurping the Church's legal autonomy and property rights.[22] In 1649, however, he had signed the new law code – under duress, he later insisted – and his scruples had not prevented him from accepting the patriarchal dignity in the hope, he subsequently claimed, of reversing the policies to which he expressed such strong aversion.

Once enthroned as patriarch with the enthusiastic support of the tsar and the rest of the reformers, Nikon immediately took steps to assert his authority. According to his later testimony, at his consecration he made the tsar, the boyars and the bishops swear to obey him as their pastor. In his capacity as patriarch, Nikon evidently saw himself as the personification of the Church. He strove to transform its organisational structure into an effective hierarchical administration with the patriarch at the top: he reacted with particular ruthlessness to any sign of opposition from other members of the hierarchy. Like Filaret, he added extensive lands to the patriarch's own domain and, in addition to building or repairing other churches, maintained three important monasteries – the Iverskii, the Kretnyi and the Voskresenskii (also known as the New Jerusalem) – as his own foundations. A man of imposing appearance, he impressed visiting clergymen with his magnificent vestments, his long sermons and his dramatic manner of celebrating the liturgy. Moreover, beginning in 1653, with the tsar's consent, he began to use the epithet, *Velikii gosudar'* (Great

---

22 William Palmer, *The Patriarch and the Tsar*, 6 vols. (London: Trübner and Co., 1871–6), vol. 1 (1871), pp. 292–548; Patriarch Nikon, *Patriarch Nikon on Church and State – Nikon's 'Refutation' (Vozrazhenie ili razorenie smirennogo Nikona, Bozhieiu milostiiu Patriarkha, protivo voprosov boiarina Simeona Streshneva)*, ed. Valerie A. Tumins and George Vernadsky (Berlin, New York, Amsterdam: Mouton, 1982), pp. 351–601.

Sovereign), previously used by only one patriarch – Filaret, father of a tsar and effective head of state.

He also continued the reformers' campaign to purify Russian Orthodoxy. Within weeks of his consecration, to protect the faithful from temptation, decrees prohibited the sale of vodka on holy days and required all non-Orthodox foreigners in Moscow to move to a new 'German Quarter' on the Iauza River further from the centre of the city.[23]

The long-standing campaign to publish accurate liturgical books and distribute them throughout Russia, however, quickly took a fateful turn. The tsar, the new patriarch and some of their collaborators decided that the best way to revitalise Russian Orthodoxy was to forge closer ties with ecumenical Eastern Orthodoxy, especially the Greek mother Church. In 1649, the latest of a long line of Greek visitors, Patriarch Paisios of Jerusalem and a scholar of dubious background, known as Arsenius the Greek, appeared in Moscow and tried to convince the tsar and Nikon that, in so far as they differed, Greek liturgical practices were faithful to the Orthodox tradition and Russian customs were erroneous local innovations. To test this claim, a Russian monk, Arsenii Sukhanov, made two journeys in 1649–50 and 1651–3 to investigate the condition of the Greek Church. His findings included a report that monks on Mount Athos had burned Russian liturgical books as heretical and his experiences led him to conduct a bitter debate with visiting Greeks in Moscow in 1650 on the orthodoxy of Russian practices.[24] Following the advice of the Greeks took the tsar and Nikon down a dangerous path, for, as their contemporaries were well aware, it was the Greeks' apostasy at the Council of Florence that had thrust Orthodox Russia into the centre of world history. Moreover, in the mid-seventeenth century, the main centres of Greek Orthodox learning and publishing were in the Roman Catholic world, especially Venice.

Against this background, on 11 February 1653, the Printing Office published a new edition of the Psalter which omitted the customary article instructing worshippers on the correct way to cross themselves. Then, within days, Nikon filled the gap with an instruction (*pamiat'*) to the faithful to use the so-called three-finger sign of the cross, holding their thumb, index and middle fingers together. Muscovite tradition, embodied in the protocols of the *Stoglav* Council of 1551, held to the two-finger sign with only the index and middle fingers extended. Then, in early 1654, a council of the Russian Church approved the principle of revising Russian liturgical books 'according to ancient parchment

23 Zenkovsky, *Russkoe staroobriadchestvo*, pp. 193–5.
24 Kartashev, *Ocherki*, vol. II, pp. 126–31.

and Greek texts (*po starym kharateinym i grecheskim knigam*)'. New editions followed one another in rapid succession – missals (*Sluzhebniki*) in 1654 and 1655 and, in 1654, the *Skrizhal*, a treatise on the nature of liturgy along with Nikon's justification of his reforms.

In addition to the sign of the cross, the most controversial changes in the details of the liturgy included the four-pointed instead of eight-pointed cross on the sacred wafer and on church buildings; the triple rather than double Alleluia after the Psalms and the Cherubic hymn; the number of prostrations and bows in Lent; a new transliteration of 'Jesus' into Slavonic ('*Iisus*' instead of '*Isus*'); and small, but significant alterations in the wording of the Nicene Creed.

As Nikon's contemporary opponents and the best modern scholars have argued, the new editions of the service books were based, not on ancient manuscripts, but on very recent Greek editions and mandated the substitution of contemporary Greek practices for traditional Russian usages.[25] The standardisation of Russian and Greek liturgies arose from the desire, shared by Tsar Alexis's government and Nikon, to build a more united Orthodox commonwealth with Russia at its head. The Orthodox hierarchy in Ukraine had made similar changes decades earlier without significant opposition. Recently, scholars have also argued that Nikon's liturgical reforms arose from a new understanding of the nature and function of liturgy as a commemoration of Christ's life, death and resurrection in which words, gestures and ritual objects may legitimately have several different levels of meaning simultaneously.[26]

Whatever their deeper meaning, the new service books altered some of the most frequently repeated words, gestures and visible symbols in the liturgy. Even more jarring was the autocratic manner in which Nikon introduced the new editions: against the advice of the Patriarch of Constantinople and his royal protector, he insisted that only the reformed usage was acceptable. In 1656, he repeatedly branded the two-finger sign of the cross and other traditional Russian practices as heretical.[27]

25 On the reforms, N. F. Kapterev, *Patriarkh Nikon i Tsar' Aleksei Mikhailovich*, 2 vols. (Sergiev Posad: Tipografiia Sviato-Troitskoi Sergievoi Lavry, 1909–12); Paul Meyendorff, *Russia, Ritual, and Reform: the Liturgical Reforms of Nikon in the 17th Century* (Crestwood, N.Y.: St Vladimir's Press, 1991).

26 Karl Christian Felmy, *Die Deutung der Göttlichen Liturgie in der russischen Theologie: Wege und Wandlungen russischer Liturgie-Auslegung* (Arbeiten zur Kirchengeschichte, 54) (Berlin, New York: de Gruyter, 1984), pp. 80–111; Boris A. Uspensky, 'The Schism and Cultural Conflict in the Seventeenth Century', in Stephen K. Batalden (ed.), *Seeking God: The Recovery of Religious Identity in Orthodox Russia, Ukraine, and Georgia* (DeKalb: Northern Illinois University Press, 1993), pp. 106–43.

27 Kapterev, *Patriarkh Nikon*, vol. I, pp. 192–8; Meyendorff, *Russia*, pp. 61–2.

Resistance to Nikon's reforms

The reforms and the patriarch's intransigence in enforcing them split the reform coalition. In a series of increasingly agitated letters written in late 1653 and early 1654 to the tsar and Vonifat'ev, Ivan Neronov severely criticised Nikon's abandonment of Russia's heritage and the arrogance with which he was treating his former friends. The three-finger sign of the cross and the altered number of deep bows (*poklony*) in services were specific examples of these destructive policies. In one letter to Vonifat'ev, he told of hearing a voice from an icon urging him to resist Nikon's reforms, a story later retold in his friend Avvakum's autobiography.[28] For their outspoken protests, the authorities excommunicated Neronov and imprisoned him in a remote northern monastery and exiled Avvakum to Siberia. According to tradition, the one bishop who in 1654 openly questioned the reforms, Pavel of Kolomna, lost his see and his life for his stand.[29]

As these examples indicate, resistance to the liturgical reforms began with individuals and small, scattered groups. Beginning with Spiridon Potemkin in 1658, a few prominent clergymen, members of the ecclesiastical elite, wrote detailed critiques of Nikon's reforms. They received valuable support from Bishop Aleksandr of Viatka who, although he did not write any polemics of his own, encouraged those who did and collected a library of texts to support the anti-reform position. Despite some differences in details, the works of Potemkin, Nikita Dobrynin 'Pustosviat', the priest Lazar' and others all attacked the internal inconsistencies in the new service books and raised fundamental questions about the legitimacy of Russian Orthodoxy. For if traditional Russian usages were heretical, were all previous generations of Russian Christians – saints and sinners alike – damned as heretics? Although these manuscripts had very limited circulation, they served as a valuable resource for later generations of polemicists against the reformed Church.

Nikon's critics faced formidable polemical opponents armed with the two weapons they lacked – the resources of the Printing Office and the support of the hierarchy and government. In addition to the *Skrizhal*, Simeon Polotskii, resident court poet and tutor to the tsar's children, published *Zhezl pravleniia* in 1668. Afanasii of Kholmogory's *Uvet dukhovnyi* of 1682 was to be the next in a long succession of attacks on critics of the reformed Church.[30]

---

28 *Materialy dlia istorii raskola za pervoe vremia ego sushchestvovaniia*, ed. N. Subbotin, 9 vols. (Moscow: Redaktsiia 'Bratskoe slovo', 1874–90), vol. I, pp. 51–78, 99–100; Avvakum, *Zhitie*, p. 65.
29 *Materialy*, vol. I, pp. 100–2.
30 Michels, *War*, pp. 112–15.

Small numbers of uneducated laypeople also expressed opposition to the reforms. In 1657, the ecclesiastical and governmental authorities imprisoned the Rostov weaver, Sila Bogdanov, and two companions for publicly condemning the new service books.[31]

More radical still were the small groups that made up the Kapiton movement. Beginning in the 1620s or 1630s, Kapiton and his followers rejected the Orthodox Church and its clergy as corrupt and practised extreme forms of asceticism, such as rigorous fasting in all seasons and, if official accusations can be believed, some even starved themselves to death. In 1665 and 1666, the authorities investigated several informal monastic communities that followed his fundamental teachings. And although not their central concern, these later followers of Kapiton included the new liturgical books in their list of grievances against the Church.

In the short run, isolated objections to the new liturgical texts did nothing to shake Nikon's overwhelming power over the Church and influence at court. The only threat to his position lay in his dependence on his royal patron, Tsar Alexis. Historians have advanced many hypotheses, none completely convincing, to explain the deterioration of their relationship. Many of the tsar's courtiers, much of the hierarchy – and perhaps Alexis himself – had probably become weary of the patriarch's imperious manner and jealous of his influence and wealth. Be that as it may, Alexis and Nikon abruptly parted ways in 1658. After the tsar refused to settle several seemingly trifling conflicts to Nikon's satisfaction, on 10 June, the patriarch withdrew from Moscow to the New Jerusalem monastery and left the day-to-day business of the Church in the hands of the usual second-in-command, the Metropolitan of Krutitsy. At the same time, Nikon still thought of himself as the patriarch. For example, in 1659, he attempted to anathematise Metropolitan Pitirim of Krutitsy for replacing him in the role of Christ in the annual Palm Sunday procession.

Nikon's self-imposed exile without abdicating from the patriarchal office created an extremely awkward situation. As messages and emissaries shuttled back and forth between Moscow and New Jerusalem, it became clear that there was no hope of reconciliation, for, in addition to intense personal animosity, Nikon and Alexis's government had radically different ideas about the relations of Church and state in a Christian monarchy. In his lengthy *Refutation* of 1664 Nikon insisted in the strongest possible terms on the superiority of the

31 *Dokumenty Razriadnogo, Posol'skogo, Novgorodskogo i Tainogo Prikazov o raskol'nikakh v gorodakh Rossii, 1654–1684 gg.*, ed. V. S. Rumiantseva (Moscow: AN SSSR, Institut istorii SSSR, 1990), pp. 29–58; Michels, *War*, pp. 33–8.

spiritual power to the secular arm.[32] Therefore, in matters of principle such as, for example, the complete judicial independence of the Church from lay justice, the Church and its primate should prevail. Was Nikon, as he claimed, simply restating fundamental Orthodox principles? Many of his arguments and examples do indeed come from classic Orthodox texts. Nevertheless, the vehemence with which he made his case stretched the elastic notion of 'symphony' beyond the breaking point. And, as many scholars have noted, Nikon borrowed some of his most telling images – for example, likening the Church to the sun and secular government to the moon – from Papal polemics of the high Middle Ages.[33] Finally, Nikon's attitudes ran counter to the tendency of governments and ecclesiastical leaders all across sixteenth- and seventeenth-century Europe to collaborate in making the Church a force for maintaining political cohesion and social order.

In this situation, Alexis had no choice but to replace Nikon. But with what procedures and on what grounds could a patriarch be deposed? It is a measure of the tsar's desperation that his most valuable agent in arranging Nikon's deposition was Paisios Ligarides, a former apostate to Roman Catholicism who styled himself Metropolitan of Gaza, an office from which he had been deposed. After a local ecclesiastical council in 1666 was unable to reach a compromise whereby Nikon would abdicate the patriarchate, but maintain his episcopal dignity and administrative control of his favourite monasteries, the government chose a more radical solution, an 'ecumenical' council of Eastern Orthodoxy with the participation of the other patriarchs, only two of whom actually appeared. Its decisions were a foregone conclusion. On 12 December 1666, the council deposed Nikon for dereliction of duty, insulting the tsar and mistreating the clergy, reduced him to the rank of an ordinary monk, and imprisoned him in the remote Ferapontov monastery.

Old Belief and the official Church after 1666

The government and its ecclesiastical allies dealt with the critics of the reformed liturgy in a similar fashion. Taking a reconciliatory position, the local council of 1666 had proclaimed that the new rites were correct, but avoided condemning

---

32 Palmer, *Patriarch and Tsar*, vol. 1; Nikon, *Refutation*.
33 Contrast M. V. Zyzykin, *Patriarkh Nikon. Ego gosudarstvennye i kanonicheskie idei*, 3 vols. (Warsaw: Sinodal'naia Tipografiia, 1931–8) with Kapterev, *Patriarkh Nikon*.

traditional Russian practices. Several of the leaders of the opposition, particularly Ivan Neronov and Aleksandr of Viatka, reconciled themselves with the new dispensation in order not to divide the body of Christ. Others resisted to the bitter end.

The ecumenical council of 1666–7 settled the issue simply and radically. It declared that only the reformed liturgy was true Orthodox usage and condemned traditional Russian practices and the *Stoglav* which sanctioned them as heretical. Simultaneously, its representatives exerted intense pressure on the recalcitrant critics of the new liturgy to recant. One, Nikita Dobrynin, yielded – temporarily as it turned out. Five others – Avvakum, Lazar', Epifanii, Nikifor and deacon Fedor – held out. All were defrocked, two had their tongues cut out for insulting the tsar, and all were sent to prison in Pustozersk on the Arctic coast.

The councils of 1666–7 had far-reaching implications for the future of the Russian Church. They made clear that Tsar Alexis and his advisers – the secular government and its ecclesiastical allies – had decisive power over the Church. Thereafter any religious dissenters understood correctly that the state was also their enemy. Moreover, for better or worse, in exercising its leadership of ecumenical Orthodoxy, Alexis's government chose to make scholars from Ukraine and the Greek world and their local disciples the intellectual leaders of the Russian Church.

The decisions of 1666–7 appeared to have restored peace and uniformity to the Russian Church. Reality soon proved to be far more complicated. Even in disgrace and prison, Nikon retained the allegiance of many of the faithful who revered him as the true patriarch and turned to him for spiritual counsel. He remained intransigent in his belief that the state – the agent of the Antichrist – had trampled on the rights of the Church. Nevertheless, in 1681, Alexis's son, Fedor, gave him permission to return to his beloved New Jerusalem although he died before reaching it.

The enforcement of the reformed liturgy seemed to proceed successfully. As Michels has shown, the Printing Office quickly sold each printing of the new service books and, by 1700, the new liturgical texts had spread to even the most remote parts of the realm.[34] Once again, however, matters were not so simple.

The determined defenders of traditional Russian practices – the Old Believers – understood full well that, after 1667, there could be no compromise with

---

34 Michels, *War*, pp. 28–30, 143–4.

the official Church or the state. Avvakum and his fellow prisoners smuggled virulent attacks on the new order to small groups of supporters in Moscow and elsewhere. Their execution at the stake in 1681 only added the authority of martyrdom to their teachings. Ironically, they agreed with Nikon, their old enemy, that the reign of the Antichrist, precursor of the End Time, had begun. During the 1670s, persecution and intimidation – or widespread indifference to the liturgical reforms, as Michels argues – limited the number of open adherents of the Old Belief.

Yet the decisions of 1666–7 had brought not peace but the sword. Outbursts of violent resistance to the state and the Church became a regular feature of the Russian landscape in the last decades of the seventeenth century. Local grievances fuelled each uprising: opposition to the reformed Church and its new liturgy also played a prominent part in the rebels' demands. In the most dramatic instance, the Solovetskii monastery, long a law unto itself, rebelled against the imposition of the new liturgy and held out against besieging government troops from 1668 until 1676. Even though its surviving defenders were massacred, its example strengthened the determination of other opponents of the new order in state and Church. For example, Old Belief was a significant element in the resistance of the Don cossacks to Moscow's administrative control.

The bloody uprising in Moscow in 1682, in which Old Believers led by Nikita Dobrynin joined forces with the mutinous garrison, made the explosive mixture of political and religious opposition unmistakably clear. When Sophia emerged from the crisis as regent for her two brothers, her government issued the decree of December 1684 which mandated death at the stake for all unrepentant Old Believers and severe penalties for anyone who sheltered them. Her government sent troops to enforce the law even in the most remote areas of the country.[35]

The government's intransigence elicited equally militant responses. Scattered groups of religious radicals had already demonstrated the ultimate form of protest against the powers of this world – suicide by fire. Following their lead, in the 1680s and 1690s, groups of militants seized isolated monasteries and villages – notoriously the Paleostrovskii monastery in 1687 and 1689 and Pudozh in 1693 – and, when government forces attacked them, burned themselves alive rather than surrender. These episodes of mass suicide which combined social banditry and religious fanaticism profoundly shocked the government,

35 *Polnoe sobranie zakonov Rossiiskoi Imperii*, Sobranie pervoe, 45 vols. (St Petersburg: Tipografiia II Otdeleniia S.I.V. Kantseliarii, 1830–43), vol. II, pp. 647–50 (no. 1102).

the Church and more moderate Old Believers, one of whom, Evfrosin, in 1691 wrote a denunciation of the practice as a violation of the traditional Christian prohibition of suicide.[36]

The second response of the opponents of the reformed Church was less spectacular but ultimately more successful. Many fled to remote corners of the realm or beyond the borders of the empire, founded unofficial communities, and began to adapt Orthodox liturgical observances to their new circumstances. Some fugitive groups soon fell victim to governmental persecution; others, such as the Vyg community, managed to survive and became the principal centres of the Old Belief in the first decades of the eighteenth century.

The official Church after 1667

In the last years of the century, Patriarch Ioakim (1674–90) set the agendas for the official Church. By background a member of the service nobility, he proved to be a strong-willed leader who, like Nikon, saw the patriarch as the personification of the Church. At the same time, he understood the necessity of collaboration with the governments that followed one another in rapid succession during his tenure and recognised the practical limitations of his position. For example, when Tsar Fedor insisted on pardoning Nikon, he acquiesced in spite of grave personal misgivings. In the crises of 1682 and 1689, he supported the claims of Peter I to the throne.

Within the ecclesiastical administration, he strove for a disciplined, clearly organised hierarchy free from the routine interference of the state. Following the recommendation of the councils of 1666–7 and the decision of a local council in 1675, Ioakim abolished the *Monastyrskii prikaz* in 1677 and replaced it with a system under which members of the clergy conducted trials of churchmen and supervised the administration of Church lands. The elaborate plan of Tsar Fedor's government to address the enormous size of Russian dioceses achieved very limited success, however, thanks to the resistance of the episcopate, led by Ioakim, who feared a system in which bishops would report to archbishops and not directly to the patriarch. In the end, the Church created eleven new dioceses by dividing the territory of existing jurisdictions and, in 1682, succeeded in filling only four.

---

36 Robert O. Crummey, *The Old Believers & the World of Antichrist. The Vyg Community and the Russian State, 1694–1855* (Madison: University of Wisconsin Press, 1970), pp. 39–57; Georg B. Michels, 'The Violent Old Belief: An Examination of Religious Dissent on the Karelian Frontier', *RH* 19 (1992): 203–29.

Ioakim's greatest achievement, however, may well be the agreement, concluded with the support of Hetman Samoilovych in 1686, that the new Metropolitan of Kiev, Gedeon, would recognise the ultimate jurisdiction of the Patriarch of Moscow, not of Constantinople as previously. Since then, the fates of the Orthodox Churches in Ukraine and Russia have been inextricably linked, with profound consequences for both.[37]

Ioakim's understanding of the Church required that the hierarchy, under the patriarch's leadership, control devotional life and ecclesiastical culture. In dealing with popular religion, as part of his crusade against the Old Believers and other dissidents, Ioakim and his supporters sponsored miracle cults that gave divine sanction to the three-finger sign of the cross, but suppressed unofficial and unverifiable saints' cults, notably the veneration of Anna of Kashin. He also believed that, since an embattled Church required educated priests, it was vital to found a theological academy in Moscow. The first two attempts, however, collapsed because of the theological and political controversies between the so-called Latinophile and Grecophile parties within the ecclesiastical elite – both of which, in reality, adapted international Latin scholarship to Orthodox uses.

In 1700 when Ioakim's successor, Adrian, died, Peter I chose to leave the patriarchal throne vacant, a harbinger of radical changes to come. Looking back over a century of dramatic events, many of the Church's fundamental characteristics had changed little. In spite of attempts to strengthen the office of patriarch and the role of Church Councils, the tsars' government repeatedly took the initiative in establishing ecclesiastical policy and intervened to settle disputes among the faithful. At their best, the clergy provided the population with spiritual guidance and social and cultural leadership. Yet attempts to create an orderly hierarchical system of administration and to respond to the cultural changes in other branches of Eastern Orthodoxy had only limited success. As a wealthy landowner, moreover, the Church attracted popular discontent and was an inviting target for a cash-starved state. And, most dangerously, the Russian Orthodox community had fallen into schism. In competition with the state-supported official Church, the Old Believers had begun to build their own organisations, select their own cadre of leaders and create their own religious culture. Thus, for all its apparent strength, the Russian Orthodox Church soon had to bend before the onslaught of a wilful reforming autocrat.

37 K. V. Kharlampovich, *Malorossiiskoe vliianie na velikorusskuiu tserkovnuiu zhizn'*, vol. 1 (Kazan': Izdanie knizhnogo magazina M. A. Golubeva, 1914), pp. 214–32.

Cultural and intellectual life

LINDSEY HUGHES

Culture 'in transition'

Modern historians have categorised Russia's seventeenth century as a 'transitional period' (*perekhodnyi vek*), when tradition vied with innovation, indigenous culture with imported trends. The conceptual framework of binary oppositions has proved particularly fruitful.[1] High culture in particular underwent changes that have been explained with reference to Westernisation, modernisation and secularisation. Some scholars have argued that developments in art, architecture and literature constituted a Muscovite version of the Baroque,[2] others, adopting Dmitrii Likhachev's formula, that they represented something 'close to the significance of the Renaissance in the cultural history of Western Europe'.[3] Such phenomena as the illusionistic use of light, shade and perspective in icons, portrait-painting from life, elements of a modified classical order system in architecture and new genres and subjects in literature are treated as curtain-raisers to the eighteenth century, when Russia would begin to fulfil its destiny by catching up with Western Europe with the assistance of Peter the Great.

If we accept the view that Russia had to 'catch up' with the West, with preconceptions about what Russia *ought* to have been, we may well conclude that, culturally speaking, here was a 'blank sheet' waiting to be filled. By the

---

1 See Iu. M. Lotman and B. A. Uspenskii, 'Binary Models in the Dynamics of Russian Culture to the End of the Eighteenth Century', in A. D. and A. S. Nakhimovsky (eds.), *The Semiotics of Russian Cultural History* (Ithaca, N.Y.: Cornell University Press, 1985), pp. 30–66.

2 See A. I. Nekrasov (ed.), *Barokko v Rossii* (Moscow: GAKhN, 1926) and summaries of debates in James Cracraft, *The Petrine Revolution in Russian Architecture* (Chicago: University of Chicago Press, 1988) and in his *The Petrine Revolution in Russian Imagery* (Chicago: University of Chicago Press, 1997). Also Natalia Kostotchkina, 'The Baroque in 17th-Century Russian Art: Icon-Painting, Painting, Decorative and Applied Art', unpublished M.Phil. thesis, SSEES, University of London, 1994.

3 D. S. Likhachev, 'Barokko i ego russkii variant XVII veka', *Russkaia literatura*, 1969, no. 2: 18–45, and his *Razvitie russkoi literatury X–XVII vekov* (Leningrad: Nauka, 1973), p. 214.

start of the seventeenth century the Renaissance had made little impact on Muscovy. In the figurative arts there was no free-standing portraiture, still life, landscapes or urban scenes, history painting or domestic genre. There were icons, wood prints and illuminated manuscripts, but no painting in oil on canvas. Sculpture deep chiselled in stone or cast in metal (bell-making excepted) was unknown. Printing (introduced in 1564) was in its infancy. Muscovy had no theatres or universities. It had produced no poets, dramatists, philosophers, scholars or even theologians. It lacked both theoretical concepts of 'the arts' and political theory. Historians who prioritise written records will search in vain for a scholarly rationale of autocracy, for example. If we go on to play the 'great names' game, Muscovy will not figure in the world pantheon. The special emphases and prohibitions of Orthodoxy, a dependent nobility, weak urbanisation and economic backwardness created a climate that distinguished Russian elite culture sharply from that of Protestant and Catholic Europe.

To understand Muscovite high culture (peasant culture and its regional variations are beyond the scope of our survey) we must initially abandon the search for the genres, activities and practitioners defined by Western experience. Political ideology, for example, was expressed first and foremost not in erudite tracts but in images and rituals. The combined efforts of artists and craftsmen created and embellished 'sacred landscapes' in a complex interaction of architecture, iconography, fabrics and vestments, choreography (of processions), and sacred chant. This culture was conservative, but it was not impervious to the contemporary events described elsewhere in this volume. Indeed, in the seventeenth century 'a transformation of cultural consciousness' was to occur.[4]

Culture after the Time of Troubles

The resolution of the Time of Troubles was, on the face of it, backward-looking. Official rhetoric emphasised the restoration of God's favour and of old values through a universally acclaimed new ruling dynasty with strong links with the old. The violation of the sacred Kremlin by Poles (bearers of demonic culture) was interpreted as punishment for sins. The visible evidence of repentance were rituals that mirrored the harmonious realm with the restored tsar at its divinely ordered centre, enhanced by new churches, icons and religious artefacts.

4 Viktor Zhivov, 'Religious Reform and the Emergence of the Individual in Seventeenth-Century Russian Literature', in Samuel H. Baron and Nancy Shields Kollmann (eds.), *Religion and Culture in Early Modern Russia and Ukraine* (DeKalb: Northern Illinois University Press, 1997), pp. 184–98.

Muscovite ceremonial customs were revived, for ritual continuity was more necessary than ever as a buttress of royal authority. Michael was crowned in 1613 according to the Byzantine-influenced rite of 1547. Courtly pomp was particularly impressive during the reign of Tsar Alexis (1645–76). Among the annual highlights was the Palm Sunday parade to St Basil's cathedral, when the tsar on foot and the patriarch seated on a colt enacted the 'symphony' of tsardom and priesthood, and the feast of Epiphany on 6 January, when the patriarch blessed the waters of the Moskva River at a sacred spot designated 'the Jordan'.[5] On such occasions the skills of craftsmen were displayed in all their brilliance in icons, crosses, vessels and vestments, banners, ceremonial saddles, harnesses and weapons. Family events were also treated with great solemnity. For example, the name-days of Alexis's numerous relatives were celebrated by processions and liturgies for the feasts of patron saints.[6]

The meticulous records of the tsars' progresses (*vykhody*) do not dwell on secular diversions. Since women were excluded from most public occasions, the masques and balls of Western court life were out of the question.[7] We should not draw a rigid line between sacred and profane activities, however. After name-day liturgies special pastries were distributed to courtiers and churchmen. Weddings and royal births were marked by lavish banquets with singing and games. Alexis maintained country palaces for summer recreations, for example at Kolomenskoe (see below) and Izmailovo, which boasted gardens with hothouses and a menagerie. He was particularly devoted to hunting and devised a ceremonial book of rules for the 'glorious sport' of falconry.[8]

Michael instituted a programme of building in the historic centre. In the 1630s Russian masters constructed the Kremlin's Terem palace. Not only its numerous chapels but also the royal living quarters were decorated with religious frescos that drew parallels between Moscow's rulers and their biblical predecessors. There was no clear boundary between sacred and secular space.

5 See Robert O. Crummey, 'Court Spectacles in Seventeenth-Century Russia: Illusion and Reality', in D. C. Waugh (ed.), *Essays in Honor of A. A. Zimin* (Columbus, Oh.: Slavica, 1985), pp. 130–46; Paul Bushkovitch, 'The Epiphany Ceremony of the Russian Court in the Sixteenth and Seventeenth Centuries', *RR* 49 (1990): 1–18.
6 See Philip Longworth, *Alexis Tsar of All the Russias* (London: Secker and Warburg, 1984); Lindsey Hughes, 'The Petrine Year: Anniversaries and Festivals in the Reign of Peter the Great (1682–1725)', in Karin Friedrich (ed.), *Festive Culture in Germany and Europe from the 16th to the 20th Century* (Lewiston, N.Y.: Mellen Press, 2000), pp. 148–68.
7 See Isolde Thyrêt, *Between God and Tsar. Religious Symbolism and the Royal Women of Muscovite Russia* (DeKalb: Northern Illinois University Press, 2001).
8 Longworth, *Alexis*, pp. 118–20.

In the same period the cathedral of the Icon of Our Lady of Kazan' on Red Square was built to commemorate the national resistance of 1612.[9] Processions for the feasts of this and other wonder-working icons were staged several times a year throughout the century. In 1625 Muscovites celebrated the acquisition of a fragment of Christ's garment. The feast of the Deposition of the Robe of Our Lord (10 July) was one of several added to the liturgical calendar that formed the basis of cultural life at court.[10] In 1642–3 teams of artists from all over Russia repainted the murals in the Kremlin Dormition cathedral, following the outlines of older images. Frescos depicting the princes and tsars of Rus' in the Archangel cathedral were similarly renovated, beginning in 1652.[11] But we have no authentic likeness of Tsar Michael, although there are records of his image (*obraz*, suggesting a Byzantine-style effigy) being made in the Kremlin workshops for presentation abroad.[12]

The Romanov succession was backward-looking but it also drove innovation. National recovery and independence required armies, alliances, trade and foreign expertise. The primary need was for military specialists, but others came too. In the 1620s the Scottish engineer Christopher Galloway added ornate upper portions with Gothic and Renaissance features to the Kremlin's Saviour tower and installed a clock. The Swede Johann Kristler designed a never-completed bridge over the Moskva River.[13] The first Western painter to arrive, in 1643, was Hans Deters (Deterson) from the Netherlands. Among the elite a taste grew for foreign 'novelties' and cunning technical devices (*khitrosti*). At the same time, Patriarch Filaret banned books published in Lithuania to combat the 'Latin' influences that had proliferated during the Time of Troubles. Tension between opening access to new ideas and protecting Orthodoxy from heresy was a defining characteristic of the seventeenth century.

9 William C. Brumfield, *A History of Russian Architecture* (Cambridge: Cambridge University Press, 1993), pp. 141–5.
10 See Hughes, 'Petrine Year' and her 'The Courts of Moscow and St Petersburg. c. 1547–1725', in John Adamson (ed.), *The Princely Courts of Europe 1500–1750* (London: Weidenfeld and Nicolson, 1999), pp. 294–313.
11 I. L. Buseva-Davydova, *Khramy Moskovskogo Kremlia: sviatyni i drevnosti* (Moscow: Nauka, 1997), pp. 42–3, 103–4.
12 B. N. Floria, 'Nekotorye dannye o nachale svetskogo portreta v Rossii', *Arkhiv russkoi istorii* 1 (1992): 137–9; Frank Kämpfer, *Das russische Herrscherbild von den Anfängen bis zu Peter dem Grossen. Studien zur Entwicklung politischer Ikonographie im byzantinischen Kulturkreis* (Recklinghausen: A. Bongers, 1978), pp. 211–12.
13 Jeremy Howard, *The Scottish Kremlin Builder: Christopher Galloway* (Edinburgh: Manifesto, 1997); Lindsey Hughes, 'The West Comes to Russian Architecture', in Paul Dukes (ed.), *Russia and Europe* (London: Collins and Brown, 1991), pp. 24–47.

Architecture and sculpture

The first masonry churches to be built after the Troubles continued sixteenth-century trends, displaying tiers of *kokoshnik* gables beneath the elongated drums of their cupolas or capped with tent (*shater*) roofs. (In the 1650s Patriarch Nikon banned 'tent' churches as uncanonical.) A sort of compendium of seventeenth-century ecclesiastical architecture is provided by the five-domed church of the Holy Trinity in Nikitniki (1631–53), built for a wealthy merchant not far from Red Square (see Plate 24).[14] The architect's imaginative flair was expended on picturesque annexes (a bell-tower and porch surmounted by tents) and on the exterior decoration. *Kokoshnik* gables and ornamental brickwork jostle with modified elements of the Western-order system, such as recessed half-columns and classically profiled window surrounds, pediments and cornices. The interior, constructed without internal piers, was covered in frescos. Similar churches were built all over Russia in towns, villages and monasteries, visible evidence of economic recovery. In the commercial city of Iaroslavl' on the Volga merchants built dozens of churches, richly decorated outside with a veritable 'encrustation' of carved brickwork and polychrome ceramics, inside with brilliantly coloured frescos.[15] Impressive architectural projects were carried out in Rostov Velikii and in the new monasteries founded by Patriarch Nikon.

Soviet scholars associated such architecture with 'secularisation' (*obmirshchenie*). By reducing domes to mere decorative appendages, they argued, and articulating façades with carved window frames, builders made their churches look like palaces and hence undermined their sacredness. But clearly neither builders nor congregations thought in such terms. Their distinctive silhouettes and lavish decorativeness made these churches highly visible landmarks in praise of God.

The culmination of the 'ornamental' style came with the 'Moscow Baroque' (a late nineteenth-century term) that flourished in and around the capital from the late 1670s and in the provinces into the 1700s.[16] Builders demonstrated a refined sense of symmetry and regularity in their ordering of both structural and decorative elements, replacing Russian ornament almost entirely with motifs derived from the classical orders: half-columns with pediments and

14 Brumfield, *History*, pp. 147–9.
15 Ibid., pp. 158–64.
16 See Cracraft, *Architecture*, pp. 85–109; Lindsey Hughes, 'Western European Graphic Material as a Source for Moscow Baroque Architecture', *SEER* 55 (1977): 433–43; and her 'Moscow Baroque – a Controversial Style', *Transactions of the Association of Russian-American Scholars in USA* 15 (1982): 69–93.

bases, window surrounds and portals with broken pediments, volutes, fluted and twisted columns and shell gables. A particularly impressive concentration of such buildings was commissioned from unknown Russian craftsmen in the 1680s by Tsarevna Sophia for the Moscow Novodevichii convent. Civic buildings were constructed on similar principles, for example Prince Vasilii Golitsyn's Moscow mansion (1680s) and the Pharmacy on Red Square (1690s).

Structural innovation appeared in the so-called 'octagon on cube' churches in Moscow Baroque style. One of the finest examples, the church of the Intercession at Fili, built in 1690–3 by unknown architects for Peter I's uncle Lev Naryshkin, has a tower of receding octagons flanked by four annexes, each capped with a cupola and decorated with intricately carved limestone details (see Plate 25). Inside an ornate gilded iconostasis holds round and octagonal, as well as 'standard' rectangular icons, all painted in a distinctly 'Italianate' style far removed from traditional Russo-Byzantine painting.[17] This and other tower churches such as the Trinity at Troitse-Lykovo and the Saviour at Ubory (by Iakov Bukhvostov, the leading exponent of the style) may owe something to prototypes in Russian wooden architecture, as well as to 'Ruthenian' influence. Craftsmen from Belorussia and Ukraine introduced Polish Baroque and Renaissance architectural elements through the medium of wood-carving and decorative ceramics. The theory of the cultural interaction of the 'fraternal' nations fitted comfortably into the Soviet ideological framework, but Russia's 'elder brother' status limited the extent to which such borrowing could be acknowledged, as did its mainly religious character.[18] The topic requires fuller investigation.

Western architectural ideas emanated from the Armoury (see below) and Foreign Office workshops, where craftsmen had access to prints, maps and illustrated books.[19] Tsar Alexis owned a book of 'the stone buildings of all German states' and works by Vignola, Palladio and other theoreticians of the Renaissance and Baroque eras. Russian builders (*zodchie*)[20] were unacquainted with the theoretical underpinnings of the five orders of architecture and none, as far as we know, had first-hand experience of Western buildings, although

17 See N. Gordeeva and L. Tarasenko, *Tserkov' Pokrova v Filiakh* (Moscow: 'Izobrazitel'noe iskusstvo', 1980); Brumfield, *History*, pp. 184–93.

18 See Lindsey Hughes, 'Byelorussian Craftsmen in Seventeenth-Century Russia and their Influence on Muscovite Architecture', *Journal of Byelorussian Studies* 3 (1976): 327–41. On wider issues, Max Okenfuss, *The Rise and Fall of Latin Humanism in Early-Modern Russia: Pagan Authors, Ukrainians, and the Resiliency of Muscovy* (Leiden and New York: Brill, 1995), and editors' introduction to Baron and Kollmann (eds.), *Religion and Culture*, pp. 3–16.

19 S. P. Luppov, *Kniga v Rossii XVII veka* (Leningrad: Nauka, 1970); Hughes, 'Western European Graphic Material'.

20 The borrowed words *arkhitektor* and *arkhitektura* first appear in the late 1690s–early 1700s.

some had been to Ukraine. But a few potential patrons picked up ideas abroad, not least Alexis himself, whose encounters with city architecture and magnates' estates while on military campaigns in Lithuania and the Baltic in the 1650s inspired him, according to his English doctor Samuel Collins, to remodel his residences.[21] Some Russians may even have ventured into Moscow's Foreign Quarter (*nemetskaia sloboda*) and gazed at its Protestant churches, shops and taverns, although restrictions on access limited the Quarter's impact.[22]

The hybrid nature of seventeenth-century Russian architecture is demonstrated by Tsar Alexis's wooden palace at Kolomenskoe (1660s–1670s) (see Plate 26). Simon Petrov, the director of works, was not an architect, but a master carpenter. He and his men employed traditional timber construction, but also added broken pediments and twisting columns. Ceilings were painted with signs of the Zodiac and the Seasons and Ruthenian craftsmen made such 'curiosities' as automata in the shape of lions. The tsar's wooden palace was an idiosyncratic example of the carpenters' skills that dominated both urban and rural landscapes in seventeenth-century Russia. Because so few timber buildings survive intact from the period and because there were no Russian Canalettos to record them, we can only reconstruct the urban scene from stylised images in miniatures and icons and foreigners' sketches.[23]

Woodwork, especially iconostases, survives mostly from interiors. Away from Moscow craftsmen made not just carvings but also three-dimensional religious images, rather like high-relief icons. Popular subjects were St Nicholas of Mozhaisk and St Paraskeva.[24] The first known examples of free-standing stone sculpture in Russia are the statues of saints outside the tower church of the Sign at Dubrovitsy (1690–1704). The church's design also departed radically from traditional Orthodox conventions by dispensing with cupolas in favour of an open-work crown. Inside there were Latin inscriptions.[25] The Westernised tastes of its owner, Peter I's tutor Prince Boris Golitsyn, who knew Latin and had access to Italian craftsmen, place the church at Dubrovitsy at the very limits of 'transitional' culture. There would be strong resistance to 'graven images' well into the eighteenth century.

21 Samuel Collins, *The Present State of Russia* (London, 1671), pp. 64–5.
22 See Lindsey Hughes, 'Attitudes towards Foreigners in Early Modern Russia', in Cathryn Brennan and Murray Frame (eds.), *Russia and the Wider World in Historical Perspective: Essays for Paul Dukes* (Basingstoke: Macmillan, 2000), pp. 1–23.
23 Cracraft, *Architecture*, pp. 40–2.
24 See T. M. Kol'tsova (ed.), *Reznye ikonostasy i dereviannaia skul'ptura Russkogo Severa. Katalog vystavki* (Archangel and Moscow: MKRF, 1995).
25 Brumfield, *History*, pp. 189–90; T. A. Gatova, 'Iz istorii dekorativnoi skul'ptury Moskvy nachala XVIII v.', in T. V. Alekseeva (ed.), *Russkoe iskusstvo XVIII veka* (Moscow: 'Iskusstvo', 1968), pp. 40–1.

The Armoury: icons, portraits, applied art

The Kremlin Armoury Chamber (*Oruzheinaia palata*), established at the beginning of the sixteenth century, comprised a complex of studios making, storing and repairing high-quality items for the tsars' ceremonial and everyday use. Under the directorship of the boyar Bogdan Khitrovo from 1654 to 1680 it emerged as a virtual 'academy of arts'.[26]

The royal churches and residences swallowed up icons by the dozen and the Armoury's studios employed some of the best icon painters (*ikonopistsy*) in the land. The most famous was Simon Ushakov (1629–86), who is regarded as the very embodiment of 'transition', a pioneer of new effects in icon-painting, but never a fully-fledged easel painter.[27] In particular, he was known for his ability to apply chiaroscuro effects, especially to faces in such traditional compositions as *Christ Not Made by Hands*. Ushakov was acquainted with Western art. The classical arch in the background of his icon *The Old Testament Trinity* (1671), for example, was copied from a print of a painting by the Italian Paolo Veronese. In his epistle to Ushakov, written some time between 1656 and 1666, fellow icon painter Iosif Vladimirov asked: 'How can people possibly claim that only Russians are allowed to paint icons and only Russian icon-painting may be revered, while that of other lands should neither be kept nor honoured?' In the reply attributed to him, Ushakov wrote of the usefulness of image-making for commemorating the past and recording the present, comparing the painter's skill with the properties of a mirror.[28] But he remained firmly within an Orthodox context.

His icon *The Planting of the Tree of the Muscovite Realm* (1668) demonstrates several aspects of his art. It includes images of Tsar Alexis, his first wife Mariia and two of their sons, the only surviving 'portrait' of the tsar known for sure to have been produced during his lifetime and signed by the artist. (The signing of icons, hitherto anonymous, is itself evidence of the growth of artistic autonomy.) The icon also contains accurate representations of the walls of the Kremlin and the *Spasskii* (Saviour) tower. But far from being a vehicle for

---

26 See Lindsey Hughes, 'The Moscow Armoury and Innovations in 17th-Century Muscovite Art', *CASS* 13 (1979): 204–23; Cracraft, *Imagery*, pp. 107–15.

27 For a popular Soviet view, see N. G. Bekeneva, *Simon Ushakov 1626–1686* (Leningrad: Khudozhnik RSFSR, 1984). Also V. G. Briusova, *Russkaia zhivopis' XVII veka* (Moscow: Iskusstvo, 1984); Lindsey Hughes, 'The Age of Transition: Seventeenth-Century Russian Icon-Painting', in Sarah Smyth and Stanford Kingston (eds.), *Icons 88* (Dublin: Veritas Publications, 1988), pp. 63–74.

28 'Poslanie nekoego izografa Iosifa k tsareva izografu i mudreishemu zhivopistsu Simonu Ushakovu' and 'Slovo k liuboshchatel'nomu ikonnogo pisaniia' (*c*.1667), as cited in Cracraft, *Imagery*, pp. 82–8.

'realism' that 'undermines the religious-symbolic basis of early Russian art',[29] the iconography conventionally ignores the laws of time, space and perspective, bringing together heaven and earth and architecture and holy men of different epochs, presided over by an image of the twelfth-century Vladimir Mother of God.[30] Notional likenesses of rulers and their families in poses of supplication or prayer, as here, were in the Byzantine tradition. Another example is the icon *Honouring the Life-Giving Cross* (1677–8), by another Armoury painter, Ivan Saltanov, in which Constantine the Great and St Helena venerate the cross together with Alexis, Mariia and Patriarch Nikon.[31]

Clearly neither Ushakov nor Saltanov had any intention of depicting the 'struggle between the secular and the religious' detected by some modern historians.[32] More recently Russian scholars have shifted the emphasis from the novelty of Ushakov's work to its traditional elements – Byzantine, Kievan and Muscovite – categorising it as 'late medieval'.[33] The painter Fedor Zubov (d. 1689) copied some of his icons directly from foreign religious paintings, for example, his *Crucifixion* of 1685, in which blood, usually omitted from the Orthodox iconography of this subject, drips from Christ's hands and sides. But he also worked in a strictly Orthodox idiom. Icons such as *Nativity of the Mother of God* (1688) are remarkable for their stylised ornamentation, intricate details of architecture and landscapes and the application of highlights to fabrics.[34] Other leading painters of the era, such as Karp Zolotarev, Ivan Bezmin and Kirill Ulanov, remained true to Orthodox iconography, while adopting certain 'Italianate' stylistic features.[35] But subjects such as landscapes and still life that in Western art had long been treated independently in a secular context, in Russia remained within the framework of icons and frescos.

29 E. S. Ovchinnikova, *Portret v russkom iskusstve XVII veka* (Moscow: Iskusstvo, 1955), p. 13. Also I. E. Danilova and N. E. Mneva, 'Zhivopis' XVII veka', in I. E. Grabar' (ed.), *Istoriia russkogo iskusstva*, 12 vols. (Moscow: AN SSSR, 1953–61), vol. IV (1959), p. 380.
30 Lindsey Hughes, 'Simon Ushakov's Icon "The Tree of the Muscovite State" Revisited', *FOG* 58 (2001): 223–34; Thyrêt, *Between God and Tsar*, pp. 70–8; Kämpfer, *Herrscherbild*, pp. 227–30.
31 Ibid., plate 138, and pp. 233–4.
32 Ovchinnikova, *Portret*, p. 22. See Cracraft, *Imagery*, p. 19, on the exaggeration of 'the degree to which such painting was "secular" in either subject or style'.
33 E. S. Smirnova, 'Simon Ushakov—"Historicism" and "Byzantinism": On the Interpretation of Russian Painting from the Second Half of the Seventeenth Century', in Baron and Kollmann (eds.), *Religion and Culture*, pp. 170–83.
34 See V. G. Briusova, *Fedor Zubov* (Moscow: 'Izobrazitel'noe iskusstvo', 1985), pp. 150–4.
35 A. A. Pavlenko, 'Karp Zolotarev i Moskovskie zhivopistsy poslednei treti XVII v.', in *Pamiatniki kul'tury. Novye otkrytiia.1982* (Leningrad: Nauka, 1984), pp. 301–16; A.A. Pavlenko, 'Evoliutsiia russkoi ikonopisi i zhivopisnoe masterstvo kak iavlenie perekhodnogo perioda', in *Russkaia kul'tura v perekhodnyi period ot Srednevekov'ia k novomu vremeni* (Moscow: Institut rossiiskoi istorii RAN, 1992), pp. 103–8; Kostotchkina, 'Baroque', pp. 100–31.

Soviet scholars attempted to identify distinct 'schools' of icon-painting beyond Moscow, for example, in the Kostroma workshops of Gurii Nikitin,[36] but their studies were compromised by the ideologically motivated quest for 'progressive' features in 'democratic' art away from the oppressiveness of the tsar's court. Fine-quality icons were produced in Iaroslavl', Ustiug, Vologda and other regional centres. Small icons rich in miniaturised detail are often attributed to the Stroganov school. The intricately decorative effects, lavish application of gold and glowing colours that are hallmarks of seventeenth-century icons had analogies in applied art. Coloured enamelling on gilded silver (a speciality of Sol'vychegodsk), decorative leather work and fabrics sown with gold and silver thread and seed pearls displayed a mixture of traditional floral and Western motifs.[37]

The most 'democratic' form of religious art were the single-sheet wood block prints (*lubki*) of icon subjects, often with decorative borders of flowers and geometric patterns, that circulated widely among all classes of the population. A whole collection of such prints makes up Vasilii Koren's illustrated Bible and Apocalypse (1692–6), fusing folk and Baroque motifs. Some served liturgical purposes, for example, printed *antiminsy* for use at the altar, others featured non-devotional topics, for example *The Feast of the Pious and Impious* and *The Mice Bury the Cat* (see Plate 27).[38] The most sophisticated prints came from Ukraine, where artists produced illustrations from wood and metal blocks for religious books and also allegorical *conclusiones*, engraved programmes for debates in the Kiev Academy.[39] In the 1680s these spread to Moscow. One of the most ambitious official graphic projects was Karion Istomin's illustrated Alphabet (*Bukvar'*), which was first made in manuscript for the royal children, then printed in 1694. Many of the illustrations for each letter of the Cyrillic alphabet were copied from Western sources.

In the Armoury and other studios Russian artists worked alongside foreign painters, including the Pole Stanisław Loputskii and the Germans (or Dutch?) Daniel Wuchters (in Russia 1663–7) and 'master of perspective' Peter Engels (1670–80s).[40] Western artists introduced oil painting on canvas and new biblical and historical subjects, including scenes from classical history, for the

36 V. G. Briusova, *Gurii Nikitin* (Moscow: 'Izobrazitel'noe iskusstvo', 1982).
37 Anne Odom, *Russian Enamels* (Baltimore: Walters Art Gallery, 1996); Kostotchkina, 'Baroque', pp. 191–266.
38 See E. A. Mishina, *Russkaia graviura na dereve XVII–XVIII vv.* (St Petersburg: Dmitrii Bulanin, 2000 [?]).
39 M. A. Alekseeva, 'Zhanr konkliuzii v russkom iskusstve kontsa XVII – nachala XVIII v.', in T. V. Alekseeva (ed.), *Russkoe iskusstvo barokko* (Moscow: Nauka, 1977), pp. 7–29.
40 Cracraft, *Imagery*, pp. 115–19.

interiors of secular buildings. Unfortunately, too little of their work survives to pass judgement on their skills or to define precisely their influence. Russian artists' receptiveness to the outside world and ability to work in a fully-fledged Western style were limited by Orthodox artistic conventions, lack of travel opportunities, inadequate technical knowledge and ignorance of classical history and mythology. As far as we know, there were no master works for them to copy. Where the use of foreign models is well documented, for example, simplified imitations of plates from Piscator's illustrated Bible, they worked mainly in a religious context.[41]

In 1683 a separate Armoury workshop for non-religious art (*zhivopisnaia palata*) was established under Ushakov's directorship.[42] Armoury employment rolls for 1687–8 record twenty-seven *ikonopistsy* and forty *zhivopistsy*, the latter making maps and charts, prints, banners, theatrical scenery (for Tsar Alexis's short-lived theatre: see below) and decorating such items as furniture, Easter eggs, chess sets and children's toys. Icon painters diversified their skills. In a petition of 1681, for example, Vasilii Poznanskii announced that he was adept at both *ikonopis'* and *zhivopis'* and could do historical subjects, 'perspective' studies and portraits.[43]

The introduction of the secular portrait (*parsuna* or *persona*, the term borrowed from Latin via Polish) was a significant innovation.[44] The earliest known examples, posthumous images of Prince Mikhail Skopin-Shuiskii and Tsar Fedor Ivanovich (1630s?), were icon-like studies in tempera on wood.[45] Freestanding likenesses of Russians painted in oils on canvas depicting persons detached from an iconic composition or a dynastic cycle are extremely rare before the 1680s. Although there is documentary evidence of *parsuny* being painted in the 1650s–1660s, extant examples are elusive. Not one of Ushakov's portraits survives, for example. The first written reference to a Russian artist doing a portrait *from life* is Fedor Iur'ev's non-extant study of Tsar Alexis of 1671.[46] The largest surviving collection of portraits are the Russian and foreign rulers in the *Book of Titled Heads* (*Tituliarnik*), a sort of dynastic reference work produced for the Foreign Office by Armoury artists in 1672–3. The images are highly stylised, identifying individuals by inscriptions and appropriate regalia.

---

41 For example, the *Theatrum Biblicum*, first published Amsterdam, 1643. See Hughes, 'Moscow Armoury', p. 212; Cracraft, *Imagery*, pp. 94–6.
42 Hughes, 'Moscow Armoury', pp. 208–9.
43 Ovchinnikova, *Portret*, p. 29.
44 See Lindsey Hughes, 'Images of the Elite: A Reconsideration of the Portrait in Seventeenth-Century Russia', *FOG* 56 (2000): 167–85.
45 See Kämpfer, *Herrscherbild*, pp. 174–6; illustrations in Ovchinnikova, *Portret*, p. 59.
46 Ibid., p. 27.

Little distinguishes Tsar Alexis from twelfth-century Prince Vladimir Mono-makh.[47]

A key period in the evolution of the *parsuna* portrait was the short reign of Tsar Fedor Alekseevich (1676–82), which saw the further spread of Polish cultural influences. In 1677 Fedor ordered portraits for the tombs of Tsars Michael and Alexis from Fedor Zubov and in 1682 two half-length portraits of his father from Ivan Saltanov. Rare 'naive' equestrian studies of Michael and Alexis, painted in tempera on canvas but with gold icon-like backgrounds, also date from Fedor's reign.[48] In 1678 Ivan Bezmin went to the palace to paint the tsar (*pisal gosudarskuiu personu*).[49]

The best-known surviving oil painting of Tsar Alexis may date from this time. This stiff and stylised Byzantine image of the tsar in his regalia suggests some development towards three-dimensionality in the background and in the moulding of the face. Both it and a posthumous portrait on a wooden panel of Fedor himself, made for placing by his tomb, are reminiscent of similarly static and decorative panel portraits of Tudor kings and queens painted in England more than a century earlier, with attention devoted to sumptuous fabrics, gems and regalia.[50]

From the 1680s boyars, too, appear in easel portraits modelled on the stiffly formal 'Sarmatian' portraits of nobles in Poland-Lithuania and Ukraine.[51] An image engraved from a painting of Prince Vasilii Vasil'evich Golitsyn (*c.* 1687), attributed to the Ukrainian Leontii Tarasevich, with its coat of arms and heraldic verses, is wholly in this Polish-Ukrainian manner.[52] Golitsyn, one of the few Russians to know Latin, also owned 'German' prints, maps, musical instruments, foreign books, clocks, furniture and mirrors. He amassed a portrait gallery, as did another boyar, Artamon Matveev. Matveev, who had a Scottish wife, also staged home theatricals and hired a foreign tutor to teach his son Latin and Greek.[53]

47 See V. Kostsova, 'Tituliarnik sobraniia Gosudarstvennogo Ermitazha', *Trudy Gosu-darstvennogo Ermitazha* 3 (1959): 16–40; Cracraft, *Imagery*, pp. 68–70; Kostotchkina, 'Baroque', pp. 82–4.

48 Ovchinnikova, *Portret*, pp. 27–8; Danilova and Mneva, 'Zhivopis'', p. 457.

49 A. E. Viktorov, *Opisanie zapisnykh knig i bumag starinnykh dvortsovykh prikazov, 1584–1725 g.*, 2 vols. (Moscow: Arkhipov, 1883), vol. II, p. 446.

50 Hughes, 'Images', 177; Kämpfer, *Herrscherbild*, pp. 214, 242; Briusova, *Russkaia zhivopis'*, plate 36.

51 See L. I. Tananaeva, 'Portretnye formy v Pol'she i v Rossii v XVII v. Nekotorye sviazi i paralleli', *Sovetskoe iskusstvoznanie '81* (1982), pp. 85–125; Cracraft, *Imagery*, pp. 190–1; Hughes, 'Images', 172–3.

52 Lindsey Hughes, *Sophia Regent of Russia 1657–1704* (New Haven: Yale University Press, 1990), pp. 144–5.

53 On Golitsyn: Lindsey Hughes, *Russia and the West, the Life of a Seventeenth-Century West-ernizer, Prince V. V. Golitsyn (1643–1714)* (Newtonville, Mass.: ORP, 1984); A. Smith, 'The

Both these men were exceptional. Even allowing for high rates of destruction of noble property over the centuries, the meagre evidence of portraits from
the seventeenth century undermines attempts to demonstrate their 'wide distribution . . . not only in the capital but also in the provinces'.[54] James Cracraft
describes Muscovite *parsuny* as 'exceedingly provincial and even regressive by
contemporary Western European standards'.[55] We should add, however, that
'Western European standards' were by no means uniformly professional and
that 'naive' portraits painted by semi-trained or untaught provincial artists
remained the norm outside court circles all over Europe. The point is that in
Russia portraits were still a novelty whereas in much of Western Europe they
were commonplace.

The gap between Russia and the West was at its widest in respect of female
portraits. Recent studies argue that Muscovite royal women were empowered
by religious symbolism and rhetoric; for example, the murals in their reception
chamber in the Kremlin featured images of strong female rulers from the Bible
and Byzantium.[56] But likenesses of living women remained a rarity as long as
elite women were kept in semi-seclusion. The first known free-standing female
portraits in Muscovy depict the exceptional figure of Tsarevna Sophia, regent
1682–9. A version engraved in Amsterdam was even surrounded by seven
allegorical Virtues and verses in Latin (see Plate 28). All Sophia's portraits
emphasised traditional attributes of rulership, as symbolised by regalia in the
setting of a double eagle.[57] Celebrations of female beauty and sexuality were
out of the question in Russia and remained so for some time. While late
seventeenth-century England enjoyed the 'age of the pin-up', with prints of
royal mistresses and assorted actresses (sometimes nude) widely available
for sale, most Muscovite women remained faceless.[58] The few known oil

Brilliant Career of Prince Golitsyn', *HUS* 19 (1995): 639–54; Richard Hellie, *The Economy
and Material Culture of Russia 1600–1725* (Chicago: University of Chicago Press, 1999),
pp. 571–627. Robert O. Crummey writes: 'Only one boyar . . . Golitsyn, could claim to
be a whole-hearted devotee of the new cultural standards': *Aristocrats and Servitors: The
Boyar Elite in Russia, 1613–1689* (Princeton: Princeton University Press, 1983), p. 161. On
Matveev, Paul Bushkovitch, *Peter the Great. The Struggle for Power, 1671–1725* (Cambridge:
Cambridge University Press, 2001), pp. 43–79.
54 Ovchinnikova, *Portret*, p. 101.
55 Cracraft, *Imagery*, p. 192.
56 See Thyrêt, *Between God and Tsar*; Lindsey Hughes, 'Women and the Arts at the Russian
Court from the 16th to the 18th Century', in J. Pomeroy and R. Gray (eds.), *An Imperial
Collection. Women Artists from the State Hermitage* (Washington, DC: National Museum of
Women in the Arts, 2003), pp. 19–49.
57 See Hughes, *Sophia*, pp. 139–44, and her 'Sophia, "Autocrat of All the Russias": Titles,
Ritual and Eulogy in the Regency of Sophia Alekseevna (1682–89)', *Canadian Slavonic
Papers* 28 (1986): 266–86.
58 David Piper, *The English Face* (London: National Gallery, 1978), pp. 103–4.

paintings of seventeenth-century women, for example, Tsar Fedor's widow Martha, in modest Muscovite robe and headdress, and Peter I's mother Natalia Naryshkina, her hair hidden by a severe black scarf like a nun's veil, date from the 1690s.[59]

Theatre and music

In October 1672 Alexis sat down at Preobrazhenskoe outside Moscow to watch a company of German amateur actors directed by a Lutheran pastor perform the 'Play of Ahasuerus and Esther', the first such spectacle to be staged at court. The tsar was aware of fellow monarchs' enthusiasm for theatre and a decade earlier had instructed the agent John Hebdon to bring players to Moscow. He was persuaded to revive this unfulfilled plan by Artamon Matveev, a pioneer of amateur dramatics, who staged a production of the ballet *Orpheo* at Shrovetide 1672.[60] The repertoire of Alexis's theatre was largely religious and moralising, with biblical stories providing the plots; but contemporary references and slapstick humour were built in. All plays, regardless of content, had spectacular lighting effects, 'perspective' scenery and colourful costumes. *The Comedy of Bacchus* even featured drunkards, maidens and performing bears.[61] Staged within the confines of royal palaces before restricted audiences, these performances were extensions of courtly spectacle. The theatre was in operation only until the tsar's death, after which it was closed under pressure from the patriarch. There is no basis for the legend that Tsarevna Sophia wrote and performed plays.[62] The first public theatre in Russia opened in Moscow in 1701, but was not a great success.

The tsar's theatre accelerated the importation of Western instruments and musical scores, previously virtually unknown. It also featured traditional vocal music, which in the course of the century assimilated a number of 'novelties' via Ukraine, including linear (five-line) notation and the increased use

59 Cracraft, *Imagery*, pp. 206–8; Hughes, 'Women' and her 'Images of Greatness: Portraits of Peter I', in *Peter the Great and the West: New Perspectives*, ed. L. Hughes (Basingstoke: Palgrave, 2000), pp. 250–70.
60 Simon Karlinsky, *Russian Drama from its Beginnings to the Age of Pushkin* (Berkeley: University of California Press, 1985). Documents on this topic were published in S. K. Bogoiavlenskii, *Moskovskii teatr pri tsariakh Aleksee i Petre* (Moscow: Russkaia starina, 1914).
61 For texts see O. A. Derzhavina et al. (eds.), *Ranniaia russkaia dramaturgiia XVII – pervaia polovina XVIII v.*, 5 vols. (Moscow: Nauka, 1972–6). Also L. A. Sofronova, *Poetika slavianskogo teatra XVII – XVIII vv.* (Moscow: Nauka, 1981).
62 Hughes, *Sophia*, pp. 173–5.

of polyphonic (part-singing) compositions. The two most prestigious church choirs belonged to the tsar and the patriarch. They and smaller ensembles maintained by monasteries and private individuals performed not only liturgical music, but also 'interludes' (*kontserty*) in church and spiritual chants (*dukhovnye kanty*), which could be sung at home. One of the most prolific composers in the medium of sacred music was the singer Vasilii Titov, who set Simeon Polotskii's rhymed Psalter to music.[63] Another composer, Nikolai Diletskii, a Ukrainian who studied in Vilna, produced *Ideia grammatiki musiki-iskoi*, the first treatise on music to be translated into Russian. Many vocal scores from the period await analysis and publication.

Instrumental music was restricted by the Church, which permitted only vocal music during the liturgy. A campaign spearheaded early in Alexis's reign by the Zealots of Piety prompted an edict of 1645: 'Take great care that nowhere should there be shameful spectacles and games, and no wandering minstrels with tambourines and flutes either in the town or the villages.' Tambourines, flutes and horns were to be smashed 'without exception'. A foreign witness reported that about five cartloads of instruments were confiscated and burnt.[64] The Zealots' targets were pagan entertainers, but 'seemly' musical entertainments were permissible at court functions and diplomatic receptions. In 1664, for example, musicians from the suite of the English ambassador Charles Howard gave some private performances. Tsar Alexis employed a Polish organist, Simeon Gutkovskii. Organs, pipes and drums were played at the tsar's wedding to Natalia Naryshkina in 1671.[65] Even so, Alexis was at first hesitant about permitting instrumental music in his new theatre 'as being new and in some ways pagan, but when the players pleaded with him that without music it was impossible to put together a chorus, just as it was impossible for dancers to dance without legs, then he, a little unwillingly, left everything to the discretion of the actors themselves'. Foreign musicians supplied the accompaniment, some specially hired from abroad.[66] The entry of the Dutch embassy of Konraad van Klenk into Moscow in 1676 was greeted by 'the continual and unceasing sounds of trumpets and percussion', as well as pipes and

---

63 See Olga Dolskaya, 'Choral Music in the Petrine Era', in A. G. Cross (ed.), *Russia in the Reign of Peter the Great: Old and New Perspectives* (Cambridge: Study Group on 18th-century Russia, 1998), pp. 173–4; and her 'Vasilii Titov and the "Moscow Baroque"', *Journal of the Royal Musical Association* 118 (1993): 203–22.

64 Adam Olearius, *The Travels of Olearius in Seventeenth-Century Russia*, ed. and trans. S. Baron (Stanford, Calif.: Stanford University Press, 1967), pp. 262–3.

65 See C. R. Jensen, 'Music for the Tsar: a Preliminary Study of the Music of the Muscovite Court Theatre', *Musical Quarterly* 79 (1995): 371–2.

66 Jacob Reutenfels, quoted ibid., 373.

flutes.[67] Such music was to become a regular feature of Peter I's parades and entertainments.

Literary and intellectual life: publishing and printing

Anthologies and surveys generally include the seventeenth century and the first decades of the eighteenth as the last chapter of Early Russian literature. There was indeed much continuity from the sixteenth century. Russian traditional literature – lives of saints, miracle stories of the Virgin Mary, folk tales – was enjoyed by most classes. Increasingly, however, these were supplemented by new 'high' genres – poetry, drama, sermons – for selected readers. The separation of elite from popular literature continued, as the concept of *belles lettres* emerged.[68] Little of this was reflected in print, however. In the whole of the seventeenth century the Moscow Press (*Pechatnyi dvor*), for most of the period the only one in Russia, published fewer than ten books that were not wholly religious in content. These included the 1649 Law Code, Meletii Smotritskii's *Grammar* and a manual for training infantry regiments. The Press's best-sellers were alphabet primers for teaching basic literacy, closely followed by the Psalter. Its total output between 1601 and 1700 amounted to only 483 editions, of which more than 80 per cent were for liturgical use.[69] In other words, the medium of print was virtually reserved for sacred texts, mostly heavy tomes for use in church, while profane or secular works were confined to manuscripts or oral transmission.

Historians who measure Russia with a Western yardstick generally link low achievements in 'book culture' with lack of learning. The idea runs like a refrain through accounts written by Western travellers, many of whom had some form of higher education. The absence of Russian names among the luminaries of the so-called 'scientific revolution' is hardly surprising when we consider that not only did Muscovy have no universities or academies, but also apparently lacked even elementary schools. Some Orthodox churchmen magnified the negative impression by equating foreign learning with 'guile' and 'deception'. At the same time, we should not exaggerate the gap. Even Isaac Newton, a devout Christian, studied topics such as astrology and alchemy that today would be regarded as 'unscientific'. For the mass of people all

---

67 Ibid., 375, 377, 382.
68 See E. K. Romodanovskaia, *Russkaia literatura na poroge novogo vremeni* (Novosibirsk: Nauka, 1994), esp. pp. 3–11.
69 Luppov, *Kniga*, p. 29.

over Europe the world was explained by divine providence, not the laws of physics. Everywhere book learning, an urban phenomenon, was for the few. Even noblemen often had a minimal grasp of classical languages and Latin humanism.[70]

Books printed in Cyrillic in foreign centres of Orthodox learning reached Russia, as well as secular books in foreign languages. Translations on secular topics such as medicine and mathematics were commissioned in government departments and works in manuscript on diverse subjects circulated among literate people, while a flourishing oral tradition brought a variety of texts even to the remote countryside. After the Time of Troubles many historical narratives appeared that retold real-life events and showed an interest in personalities, for example Avraamii Palitsyn's *Skazanie* of the Troubles and Katyrev-Rostovskii's *Book of Chronicles*. Such works circulated alongside fictional tales of adventure and mystery. Particularly popular were translations via the Polish from the *Great Mirror* (*Magnum speculum exemplorum*) and *Deeds of the Romans*. Nobles and townspeople read chivalric romances, picaresque tales and parodic works like *Liturgy to the Ale House* and *Shemiaka's Judgement*. A new genre was the 'literature of roguery' in which characters constantly transform themselves and adopt new identities.[71] Tales in this category include *Savva Grudtsyn* and *Frol Skobeev*, the latter remarkable for its lack of a moral message. Soviet historians exaggerated the significance of such tales, treating them as 'democratic satires' that criticised the status quo. A more nuanced reading is now possible, revealing a mixture of hagiographic framing, foreign borrowings and local embellishments. Redating has pushed these stories to the very end of the century and to the 'margins' of the literary scene.[72]

Traditional forms could accommodate new content, for example the 'Life' of the pious laywoman Iuliania Lazarevskaia written by her son, who stressed her humility and charity rather than her asceticism or devotion to the liturgy.[73] The autobiographical 'Life' of Archpriest Avvakum, composed in the 1670s,

---

70 See arguments in Paul Bushkovitch, 'Cultural Change among the Russian Boyars 1650–1680. New Sources and Old Problems', *FOG* 56 (2000): 89–111. On astrology and other pseudo-sciences in Muscovy, W. F. Ryan, *The Bathhouse at Midnight. An Historical Survey of Magic and Divination in Russia* (University Park, Pa.: Pennsylvania State University Press, 1999); W. F. Ryan, 'Aristotle and Pseudo-Aristotle in Kievan and Muscovite Russia', in J. Kraye et al. (eds.), *Pseudo-Aristotle in the Middle Ages* (London: Warburg Institute, 1986), pp. 97–109.

71 Marcia A. Morris, *The Literature of Roguery in Seventeenth- and Eighteenth-Century Russia* (Evanston, Ill.: Northwestern University Press, 2000).

72 Zhivov, 'Religious Reform', pp. 188–9.

73 See discussion in Paul Bushkovitch, *Religion and Society in Russia. The Sixteenth and Seventeenth Centuries* (Oxford: Oxford University Press, 1992), pp. 140–7.

contained earthy scenes of family life written in a robust vernacular alongside rhetorical passages underlining the theme of personal struggle.[74]

The emergence of literature as an activity with distinct aesthetic and formal requirements carried out by named authors is reflected in the work of the so-called 'chancellery' or Printing Office poets of the first half of the century, who specialised in didactic verse, epistles and appeals in syllabic metre derived from Ruthenian models.[75] The first translated treatise on rhetoric in Russian dates from 1623. The assimilation of new literary forms and a genre system was accelerated by the Church's programme for correcting service books. A major pioneer of sermons, for example, was the Ukrainian scholar and corrector Epifanii Slavinetskii.

The career of Simeon Polotskii (Samuil Gavrilovich Petrovskii-Sinianovich, 1629–80) exemplifies new trends in Latin / Slavonic literary culture.[76] This Kiev-educated monk came to Moscow in 1664 to serve as tutor to Tsar Alexis's children. He left a massive legacy of sacred and secular writings in manuscript, while his published works make him one of the rare authors active in Muscovy whose name appeared in print during his lifetime or very shortly after his death.[77] Most of his publications were produced in the Palace Typography (*Verkhniaia tipografiia*), which in the 1670s to early 1680s operated alongside the Moscow Press. His *Psalter in Verse* (1680) was a best-seller. Writings preserved in manuscript include *Vertograd mnogotsvetnyi*, a massive anthology of 2,763 didactic poems written in syllabic verse, the content borrowed from Latin originals by Jesuit writers, and the *Rifmologion* of occasional verses for royal events. Polotskii makes frequent reference to classical authors and tales from antiquity. The title page to his *History of Barlaam and Josaphat* (1681), designed by Ushakov, has been hailed as 'the first example of the use of Classical symbolism by a Russian artist'.[78] In general, poetry was still regarded as a higher form of spiritual activity. Even secular poems concentrated on moral improvement, especially the curbing of pride and avarice.

---

74 See N. S. Demkova (ed.), *Sochineniia protopopa Avvakuma i publitsisticheskaia literatura rannego staroobriadchestva* (St. Petersburg: Izdatel'stvo S.-Peterburgskogo universiteta, 1998).

75 See A. M. Panchenko (ed.), *Russkaia sillabicheskaia poeziia XVII–XVIII vv.* (Leningrad: Sovetskii pisatel', 1970); A. M. Panchenko, *Russkaia stikhotvornaia kul'tura XVII veka* (Leningrad: Nauka, 1973); Bushkovitch, *Religion*, pp. 140–5; D. I. Luburkin, *Russkaia novolatinskaia poeziia: materialy k istorii XVII – pervaia polovina XVIII veka* (Moscow: RGGU, 2000).

76 Simeon Polotskii, *Simeon Polockij. Vertograd mnogocvetnyj*, ed. Anthony Hippisley and Lydia I. Sazonova, 3 vols. (Cologne: Böhlau, 1996–2000); L. I. Sazonova, *Poeziia russkogo barokko* (Moscow: Nauka, 1991).

77 Bushkovitch, *Religion*, pp. 150–1.

78 Cracraft, *Imagery*, pp. 127, 155.

Along with acceptance of poetry came some sponsorship of education. Some boyars learned Latin and Polish from foreign tutors.[79] The young Tsar Alexis's early lessons were from primers and biblical texts, but later he read cosmographies, astronomy and mechanics, ancient history and travel accounts. A few schools sprang up, attached to monasteries (Miracles (Chudovskii), St Andrew's and Zaikonospasskii), to the Moscow Printing House and government departments, although information about them is fragmentary.[80] Tsar Alexis's son Alexis, instructed by Polotskii, in 1667 was able to deliver a speech in Latin and Polish to a delegation from Poland. In 1682 another son, Tsar Fedor, approved a charter of privileges for an academy in Moscow to teach grammar, poetics, rhetoric, dialectics, rational, natural and legal philosophy and the 'free sciences'. The prototype was the Mohyla academy in Kiev, founded in the 1630s on the Jesuit model. Fedor's plan was implemented under Sophia in 1685–7 when the Slavonic-Greek-Latin academy opened its doors. All its classes were conducted in Latin. The teachers were churchmen. The curriculum included Aristotelian cosmology in the context of Jesuit natural philosophy in an attempt to harmonise secular learning with faith.[81]

Conclusion: secularisation revisited

Our knowledge of seventeenth-century Russian culture is far from complete. Attributions and dating are often imprecise, especially in the case of icons. Surviving monuments may be too few to allow generalisations – wooden buildings, for example – or there may be no examples left at all, as in the case of 'history' paintings executed on the walls of royal palaces. New literary texts in manuscript continue to be discovered and scholars constantly revise the dating of the known ones. Provincial culture in particular requires further study.[82] We may conclude that, by and large, 'high' Russo-Byzantine Orthodox models and 'low' folk culture met most of the needs of the sort of society that Muscovy was in the seventeenth century and reflected the sort of view of the world that most Muscovites still held. Hence, tsars in their portraits, including the young Peter the Great, looked more like Byzantine emperors than French or English kings; Orthodox church design remained distinct from

79 Bushkovitch, 'Cultural Change', 104–5.
80 A. Sakharov, et al. (eds.), *Ocherki po istorii russkoi kul'tury XVII veka*, 2 vols. (Moscow: MGU, 1979), vol. II, pp. 149–52.
81 See N. Chrissides, 'Creating the New Educational Elite. Learning and Faith in Moscow's Slavo-Greco-Latin Academy, 1685–1694', unpublished PhD thesis, Yale University, 2000.
82 See Valerie Kivelson, *Autocracy in the Provinces. The Muscovite Gentry and Political Culture in the Seventeenth Century* (Stanford, Calif.: Stanford University Press, 1996).

Catholic or Protestant; you could buy an icon or an edition of the Psalter in most towns, but not an oil painting or a book of poetry. At the same time, there is compelling evidence of growing receptiveness to selected aspects of Western culture, for example, in the desire of the boyar elite to acquire portraits with coats of arms. Patterns of borrowing and receptiveness suggest a timid but growing attachment to 'the West' as a desirable source of new ideas, filtered through 'fraternal' cultures (notably Ukraine), contradicted by discourses of the dangers of alien customs and limited by economic and social realities. Hence seventeenth-century Muscovites failed to assimilate many things that were commonplace for members of the European elites, including statues, classical mansions and pictures of their wives and daughters. Boyars still had to adhere to the royal calendar and independent, participatory cultural life outside the tsar's household was extremely restricted. Unlike many of his Western contemporaries, the average Russian boyar did not compose or play music, read or write poetry or philosophy, speak foreign languages, travel abroad or take an interest in architecture (as opposed to building), horticulture or science. There were exceptions, such as Matveev and Golitsyn, but by and large in their accomplishments and culture Muscovite nobles were closer to the rest of the population than to their European counterparts. A consistently 'Westernising' programme for the arts was patently absent during the reigns of the seventeenth-century tsars. Foreign 'novelties' belonged to 'closed' society; they were not intended for and still less imposed upon a wider public as later were Peter I's dress reforms, for example. Religion dominated high culture.

Soviet historians, obliged to demonstrate an atheistic world-view, dealt with the awkward fact of the prolonged control of established religion over seventeenth-century Russian culture by emphasising the 'discovery of the value of the human personality' (*lichnost'*) behind religious façades. They minimised or denied the religiosity of religious art, underlining instead its humane (*gumanitarnye*), popular (*narodnye*) and 'life-enhancing' (*zhizneradostnye*) qualities.[83] Icons and frescos were scrutinised for evidence of realism, naturalistic landscapes, peasant physiognomies and everyday (*bytovye*) details. Soviet architectural historians detected 'progress' in an increase in the number of domestic and civic buildings constructed of stone and brick rather than wood. Cult architecture could be the bearer of advanced features, too. Churches, for example, were said to have 'drawn closer' to civic buildings in their design. Soviet scholars, particularly during the Stalin period, played down foreign borrowing

---

83 See, for example, Grabar', *Istoriia*, vol. 1 (1953), p. 504.

and exaggerated the indigenous roots of new ideas, especially 'democratic' ones.[84]

The evidence presented above shows that traditional religious culture remained strong and that Western, secular trends operated within limits. Tsar Alexis conducted experiments in horticulture with the help of foreign experts, but he also had holy water sprinkled to form signs of the cross on fields. He employed foreign medics, but carried around a tooth of St Sabbas to cure toothache. Simeon Polotskii wrote his works explicitly 'for the spiritual benefit of Orthodox Christians' (polzy radi dushevnyia pravoslavnykh khristian). Literature and art were firmly rooted in the acceptance of well-defined hierarchies and in a world of opposites in which a constant struggle is waged between good and evil and where ultimately people must renounce worldly things.

There was fierce opposition to what were perceived as 'Latin and Lutheran' innovations in religious art. In 1674, for example, Patriarch Ioakim banned the sale of paper prints 'made by German heretics, Lutherans and Calvinists, according to their own damned persuasion, crudely and wrongly'. He and his predecessors denounced icons that 'depict everything after the manner of earthly things'.[85] Their Old Believer opponents agreed with them in this respect. The most frequently quoted pronouncement on the subject is Archpriest Avvakum's complaint that some icon painters made Christ 'look like a German, big-bellied and fat, except that no sword is painted on his hip'.[86] Henceforth Old Believers strove to preserve ancient artistic traditions. Warnings were aimed at both non-canonical compositions and non-traditional, three-dimensional depictions that added improper 'worldliness' to images which, according to Orthodox tradition, should intimate the divine world beyond the icon, not imitate the flesh and blood of the here and now. The Church had no quarrel with secular painting as such. Indeed, Patriarch Nikon had his portrait painted several times.[87] In general, seventeenth-century debates demonstrate a new awareness of the shifting boundaries between the sacred and profane and an attempt to establish what was permissible for the

84 For discussions of the problems of Soviet scholarship, see Cracraft, Architecture, pp. 9–18, and Cracraft, Imagery, pp. 95–106; also Lindsey Hughes, 'Restoring Religion to Russian Art', in G. Hosking and R. Service (eds.), Reinterpreting Russia (London: Arnold, 1999), pp. 40–53.
85 D. A. Rovinskii, Russkie gravery i ikh proizvedenie s 1564 do osnovaniia Akademii Khudozhestv (Moscow: Izdatel'stvo grafa Uvarova, 1870), pp. 135–6.
86 See N. E. Andreyev, 'Nikon and Avvakum on Icon-Painting', in his Studies in Muscovy (London: Variorum, 1970), essay XIII, p. 43.
87 Ovchinnikova, Portret, p. 98. Discussion in Cracraft, Imagery, pp. 117–18.

devout Orthodox. There was an increased concern with individual morality as opposed to asceticism.[88]

In 1690 Patriarch Ioakim was still appealing to Tsars Ivan and Peter to 'resist new Latin and alien customs and not to introduce the wearing of foreign dress'.[89] The culture of the 1690s, still inadequately studied, bears witness to the proliferation of Western influences. Among the royal family's orders from the Armoury we find images of patron saints not on wooden panels but in oils on canvas,[90] battle paintings 'after the German model' and pictures on canvas depicting 'troops travelling by sea' copied from German engravings.[91] Armoury artists found themselves making regimental banners and decorating the new ships that Tsar Peter built at Voronezh. The victory parade held in Moscow in 1696 to celebrate the capture of Azov from the Turks took place against a backdrop of classical architectural devices, allegorical paintings and wooden sculptures set on triumphal gates inscribed with the words of Julius Caesar: 'I came. I saw. I conquered.'[92]

Peter's Great Embassy to Western Europe (1697–8) consolidated his view of what constituted 'civilised' art and architecture. In January 1698 he became the subject of the first portrait of a Russian ruler wholly in the Western manner, painted in London by Sir Godfrey Kneller.[93] By 1701 only two icon painters remained on the Armoury payroll and by 1711 nearly all Armoury personnel were transferred to the new capital of St Petersburg.[94] Yet we are still far from the 'liberal' atmosphere that Western thinkers such as David Hume regarded as essential for the flourishing of the arts.[95] There was still no sign of an independent public sphere. The arts in Russia remained firmly harnessed to higher authority, even though power shifted from the Church to the state.

From the early eighteenth century most things 'pre-Petrine' were regarded as a blank. Russia must achieve cultural salvation by imitating and assimilating

---

88 Zhivov, 'Religious Reform', p. 193.
89 Full text in N. Ustrialov, *Istoriia tsarstvovaniia Petra Velikogo*, 6 vols. (St Petersburg: Tipografiia II Otdeleniia S. I. V. Kantseliarii, 1858–63), vol. II (1859), appendix 9, pp. 467–77. Also Hughes, 'Attitudes towards Foreigners'.
90 G. V. Esipov (ed.), *Sbornik vypisok iz arkhivnykh bumag o Petre Velikom*, 2 vols. (Moscow: Universitetskaia tipografiia, 1872), vol. I, p. 127. Lindsey Hughes, *Russia in the Age of Peter the Great* (New Haven: Yale University Press, 1998), pp. 12–20.
91 Esipov (ed.), *Sbornik*, vol. I, pp. 143–4, 161–2.
92 See Richard Wortman, *Scenarios of Power. Myth and Ceremony in Russian Monarchy*, 2 vols. (Princeton: Princeton University Press, 1995–2000), vol. I, pp. 42–4.
93 Cracraft, *Imagery*, pp. 133–4; Hughes, 'Images of Greatness', pp. 253–4.
94 Esipov (ed.), *Sbornik*, vol. I, p. 154.
95 Gianluigi Goggi, 'The Philosophes and the Debate over Russian Civilization', in Maria Di Salvo and Lindsey Hughes (eds.), *A Window on Russia* (Rome: La Fenice Edizioni, 1996), pp. 299–305.

Western culture. The idea that Russian art began with Peter held sway for the next century and a half, roughly coinciding with the period that classicism dominated the arts in Russia and most of Europe. Only from the mid-nineteenth century did Russia's seventeenth century begin to be rehabilitated and recreated in the Russian imagination. Its buildings were widely imitated in the Neo- or Pseudo-Russian style. Artists, illustrators and designers – Ivan Bilibin, Apolinarii Vasnetsov, Andrei Riabushkin, Viacheslav Shvarz – tried to capture the century's spirit. Fabergé and Ovchinnikov recreated the shapes and colours of seventeenth-century *objets de vertu* for elite clients.[96] A romanticised seventeenth-century style became the fashion preference at the court of Nicholas II, who liked to see himself as a latter-day Tsar Alexis. This imagined seventeenth century is a fairy-tale world of turrets and cupolas, exotic fabrics, elaborate carvings and jewel-like surfaces that awakes nostalgia for a pre-Western, pre-classical world. In this vision, far from being the period that prepared the ground for Westernisation, the seventeenth century remains the last bastion of true Russian culture.

96 See E. I. Kirichenko, *The Russian Style* (London: L. King, 1991), ch. 3.

Bibliography

This Bibliography includes all of the works cited in the footnotes, with the exception of those of a general, comparative or theoretical nature which do not relate primarily to the history of Russia in the period. It also includes a number of relevant works, recommended by the contributors, which are not cited in their footnotes.

The Bibliography has been subdivided as follows:

I. PRIMARY SOURCES
II. SECONDARY SOURCES
   1. Political history
      (a) *c.*900–1462
      (b) 1462–1613
      (c) 1613–89
   2. Economic and social history
   3. The Orthodox Church
   4. Cultural and intellectual history

The subdivisions of the secondary material are necessarily somewhat arbitrary. Political history (II.1) includes general works, and works relating to military and diplomatic history, popular uprisings, and Russians' relations with non-Russians within their borders, as well as the development of central and local government institutions. Where individual items cover periods longer than the chronological subdivisions chosen (II.1.a–c), they are normally listed only under the earliest of these. Economic and social history (II.2) includes archaeology, law, demography, ethnography, gender and historical geography. The section on the Orthodox Church (II.3) excludes religious art and architecture, which is covered in II.4 (Cultural and intellectual history).

I. PRIMARY SOURCES

AAE, 4 vols. (St Petersburg: Tipografiia II Otdeleniia Sobstvennoi E. I. V. Kantseliarii, 1836).

Adalbert, *Continuatio Reginonis*, ed. A. Bauer and R. Rau, in *Quellen zur Geschichte der sächsischen Kaiserzeit* (reprinted Darmstadt: Wissenschaftliche Buchgesellschaft, 2002), pp. 185–231.

Adelung, Friedrich, *Augustin Freiherr von Meyerberg und seine Reise nach Russland, nebst einer von ihm auf dieser Reise veranstalteten Sammlung von Ansichten, Gebräuchen, Bildnissen u.s.w.* (St Petersburg: Karl Kray, 1827).

Adrianova-Peretts, V. P. (ed.), *Slovo o polku Igoreve* (Moscow: AN SSSR, 1950).

AI, 5 vols. (St Petersburg: various publishers, 1841–2).

Akty, sobrannye Kavkazskoi Arkheograficheskoi kommissiei, 12 vols. (Tiflis, 1866–83, vol. I., Tiflis, 1866).

'Akty vremeni Lzhedmitriia 1-go (1603–1606), Nogaiskie dela', ed. N. V. Rozhdestvenskii, *ChOIDR*, vol. 264, pt. 1 (1918).

Andreev, Aleksandr, comp., *Stroganovy. Entsiklopedicheskoe izdanie* (Moscow: Belyi volk – Kraft, 2000).

Ankhimiuk, Iu. V., 'Slovo na "Spisanie Iosifa" – pamiatnik rannego nestiazhatel'stva', *Zapiski Otdela Rukopisei Russkoi gosudarstvennoi biblioteki* 49 (1990): 115–46.

Annales Bertiniani, ed. F. Grat, J. Vielliard and S. Clémencet (Société de l'histoire de France 470) (Paris: C. Klincksieck, 1964).

Anpilogov, G. N., *Novye dokumenty o Rossii kontsa XVI–nachala XVII veka* (Moscow: Izdatel'stvo Moskovskogo Universiteta, 1967).

Antonov, A. V., 'Serpukhovskie dokumenty iz dela Patrikeevykh', *Russkii diplomatarii* 7 (Moscow: Drevlekhranilishche, 2001): 299–309.

Avanesov, R. I. (ed.), *Smolenskie gramoty XIII–XIV vekov* (Moscow: AN SSSR, 1963).

Avvakum, Archpriest, *Zhitie protopopa Avvakuma, im samim napisannoe, i drugie ego sochineniia*, ed. N. K. Gudzii (Moscow: Goslitizdat, 1960).

    Archpriest Avvakum, the Life Written by Himself: With the Study of V. V. Vinogradov, trans. and ed. Kenneth N. Brostrom (Michigan Slavic translations; no. 4) (Ann Arbor: Michigan Slavic Publications, University of Michigan Press, 1979).

Bagalei, D. I., *Materialy dlia istorii kolonizatsii i byta stepnoi okrainy Moskovskogo gosudarstva v XVI–XVII vekakh*, vol. 1 (Khar'kov, 1886).

Barsov, E. V., *Drevne-russkie pamiatniki sviashchennogo venchaniia tsarei na tsarstvo* (Moscow: Universitetskaia tipografiia, 1883).

Begunov, Iu. K., ' "Slovo inoe" – novonaidennoe proizvedenie russkoi publitsistike XVI v. o bor'be Ivan III s zemlevladeniem tserkvi', *TODRL* 20 (1964): 351–2.

Belokurov, S. A., 'Razriadnye zapisi za Smutnoe vremia (7113–7121 gg.)', *ChOIDR* 221 (1907), kn. 2, otd. 2: 1–80.

Berry, Lloyd E., and Crummey, Robert O. (eds.), *Rude and Barbarous Kingdom: Russia in the Accounts of Sixteenth-Century English Voyagers* (Madison: University of Wisconsin Press, 1968).

Biblioteka literatury Drevnei Rusi. Tom I: XI–XII veka (St Petersburg: Nauka, 1997).

Bogoiavlenskii, S. K. (ed.), 'Dopros tsarem Ioannom Groznym russkikh plennikov, vyshedshikh iz Kryma', *ChOIDR* 2 (Moscow: Sinodal'naia tipografiia, 1912), *Smes'*: 26–33.

Boiarskie spiski poslednei chetverti XVI – nachala XVII v. i rospis' russkogo voiska 1604 g., comp. S. P. Mordovina and A. L. Stanislavskii, 2 parts (Moscow: TsGADA, 1979).

Bond, E. A. (ed.), *Russia at the Close of the Sixteenth Century* (London: Hakluyt Society, 1896).

Borovkova-Maikova, M. S., 'Nila sorskogo predanie i ustav', *Pamiatniki Drevnei pis'mennosti i iskusstva*, no. 179 (1912).

Bronevskii, S. M., *Istoricheskie vypiski o snosheniiakh Rossii s Persiei, Gruziei i voobshche s gorskimi narodami, v Kavkaze obitaiushchimi, so vremen Ivana Vasil'evicha donyne*, ed. I. K. Pavlova (St Petersburg: Peterburgskoe Vostokovedenie, 1996).

Bussov, Konrad, *Moskovskaia khronika 1584–1613 gg.*, ed. I. I. Smirnov (Moscow and Leningrad: AN SSSR, 1961).

Bussow, Conrad, *The Disturbed State of the Russian Realm*, ed. and trans. G. Edward Orchard (Montreal: McGill-Queen's University Press, 1994).

Chancellor, Richard, 'The First Voyage to Russia', in Lloyd E. Berry and Robert O. Crummey (eds.), *Rude and Barbarous Kingdom: Russia in the Accounts of Sixteenth-Century English Voyagers* (Madison: University of Wisconsin Press, 1968), pp. 9–41.

The Chronicle of Novgorod, 1016–1471, trans. Robert Mitchell and Nevill Forbes (Camden Society Third Series, no. 25) (London: Royal Historical Society, 1914).

Collins, Samuel, *The Present State of Russia* (London, 1671).

Constantine VII, *De administrando imperio*, ed. and trans. G. Moravcsik and R. J. H. Jenkins (Corpus fontium historiae byzantinae 1) (Washington: Dumbarton Oaks, 2nd edn., 1967).

De cerimoniis aulae byzantinae, ed. J. J. Reiske, vol. 1 (Corpus scriptorum historiae byzantinae) (Bonn: E. Weber, 1829).

Contarini, Ambrogio, 'Viaggio in Persia', in *Barbaro i Kontarini o Rossii. K istorii italo-russkikh sviazei v XV v.*, ed. E. Ch. Skrzhinskaia (Leningrad: Nauka, 1971), pp. 188–210.

Cross, Samuel Hazard, and Sherbowitz-Wetzor, Olgerd P. (trans.), *The Russian Primary Chronicle. Laurentian Text*, 3rd printing (Cambridge, Mass.: Mediaeval Academy of America, 1973).

Cummings, Denver (trans.), *The Rudder (Pedalion) of the Metaphorical Ship of the One Holy Catholic and Apostolic Church of the Orthodox Christians* (Chicago: Orthodox Christian Education Society, 1957).

Dawson, Christopher (ed.), *The Mongol Mission* (New York: Sheed and Ward, 1955).

'Deianiia Moskovskogo tserkovnogo sobora 1649 goda', ed. S. A. Belokurov, *ChOIDR* 171 (1894, kn. 4): 1–52.

Demkova, N. S. (ed.), *Sochineniia protopopa Avvakuma i publitsisticheskaia literatura rannego staroobriadchestva* (St Petersburg: Izdatel'stvo S.-Peterburgskogo universiteta, 1998).

De-Pule, M., *Materialy po istorii Voronezhskoi i sosednikh gubernii. Orlovskie akty XVII–XVIII stoletii* (Voronezh, 1861).

Derzhavina, O. A., et al. (eds.), *Ranniaia russkaia dramaturgiia XVII – pervaia polovina XVIII v.*, 5 vols. (Moscow: Nauka, 1972–6).

Dewey, Horace W. (ed.), *Muscovite Judicial Texts 1488–1556 (Michigan Slavic Materials, no. 7)* (Ann Arbor: University of Michigan, Department of Slavic Languages and Literatures, 1966).

Dmitrieva, R. P., *Skazanie o kniaz'iakh vladimirskikh* (Moscow and Leningrad: AN SSSR, 1955).

Dnevnik Mariny Mnishek, trans. V. N. Kozliakov (St Petersburg: Dmitrii Bulanin, 1995).

Dokumenty Razriadnogo, Posol'skogo, Novgorodskogo i Tainogo Prikazov o raskol'nikakh v gorodakh Rossii, 1654–1684 gg., ed. V. S. Rumiantseva (Moscow: AN SSSR, Institut istorii SSSR, 1990).

Donesenie o poezdke v Moskvu M. Shilia 1598 g. (Moscow, 1875).

DopAI, 12 vols. (St Petersburg: various publishers, 1846–75).

Doronin, P., 'Dokumenty po istorii Komi', *Istoriko-filologicheskii sbornik Komi filiala AN SSSR* 4 (1958): 241–71.

Dukhovnye i dogovornye gramoty velikikh i udel'nykh kniazei XIV–XVI vv., ed. L. V. Cherepnin (Moscow and Leningrad: AN SSSR, 1950).

Dzhakson, T. N., *Islandskie korolevskie sagi o vostochnoi Evrope (seredina XI–seredina XIII v.) (teksty, perevod, kommentarii)* (Moscow: Ladomir, 2000).

Emchenko, E. B., *Stoglav. Issledovanie i tekst* (Moscow: Indrik, 2000).

Esipov, G. V. (ed.), *Sbornik vypisok iz arkhivnykh bumag o Petre Velikom*, 2 vols. (Moscow: Universitetskaia tipografiia, 1872).

Fennell, J. L. I. (ed. and trans.), *The Correspondence between Prince A.M. Kurbsky and Tsar Ivan IV of Russia, 1564–1579* (Cambridge: Cambridge University Press, 1955).

(ed. and trans.), *Prince A.M. Kurbsky's History of Ivan IV* (Cambridge: Cambridge University Press, 1965).

and Obolensky, Dimitri (eds.), 'The Lay of Igor's Campaign', in *A Historical Russian Reader: A Selection of Texts from the XIth to the XVth Centuries* (Oxford: Clarendon Press, 1969), pp. 63–72.

Fletcher, Giles, *Of the Russe Common Wealth, or Maner of Governement by the Russe Emperour, (Commonly Called the Emperour of Moskovia) with the Manners, and Fashions of the People of That Country* (London: T. D. for Thomas Charde, 1591).

[Fletcher, Dzhil's], *O gosudarstve Russkom* (St Petersburg: A. S. Suvorin, 1906).

Of the Russe Commonwealth, ed. John V. A. Fine and Richard Pipes (Cambridge, Mass.: Harvard University Press, 1966).

'Of the Russe Commonwealth', in Lloyd E. Berry and Robert O. Crummey (eds.), *Rude and Barbarous Kingdom: Russia in the Accounts of Sixteenth-Century English Voyagers* (Madison: University of Wisconsin Press, 1968), pp. 85–246.

Franklin, Simon (trans. and intro.), *Sermons and Rhetoric of Kievan Rus'* (Cambridge, Mass.: Harvard University Press, 1991).

Glazyrina, G. V., *Saga ob Ingvare puteshestvennike. Tekst. Perevod. Kommentarii* (Moscow: Vostochnaia literatura, 2002).

Golb, N. and Pritsak, O., *Khazarian Hebrew Documents of the Tenth Century* (Ithaca, N.Y.: Cornell University Press, 1982).

Goldfrank, David M., *The Monastic Rule of Iosif Volotsky*, rev. edn, Cistercian Studies Series, no. 36 (Kalamazoo, Mich., and Cambridge, Mass.: Cistercian Publications, 2000).

Golokhvastov, D. P., and Archimandrite Leonid, 'Blagoveshchenskii ierei Sil'vestr i ego poslaniia', *ChOIDR* (1874), kn. 1: 71–2.

Golubtsov, Aleksandr, 'Chinovnik Novgorodskogo Sofiiskogo sobora', *ChOIDR* (1899), kn. 2: otd. 2: i–xx, 1–272.

'Chinovniki Moskovskogo Uspenskogo sobora', *ChOIDR* (1907), kn. 4, otd. 1: 1–312.

Gordon, Patrick, *Passages from the Diary of Patrick Gordon of Auchleuchries in the Years 1635–1699* (London: Frank Cass, 1968).

Gorodskie vosstaniia v Moskovskom gosudarstve XVII v. Sbornik dokumentov, ed. K.V. Bazilevich (Moscow: Gosudarstvennoe sotsial'no-ekonomicheskoe izdatel'stvo, 1936; reprinted Moscow: Gosudarstvennaia Publichnaia Istoricheskaia Biblioteka Rossii, 2003).

Gorsei, Dzherom [Jerome Horsey], *Zapiski o Rossii: XVI–nachalo XVII v.*, ed. and trans. A.A. Sevast'ianova (Moscow: MGU, 1990).

Graham, Hugh F., 'Paul Juusten's Mission to Muscovy', *RH* 13 (1986): 41–92.

Gramoty Velikogo Novgoroda i Pskova, ed. S. N. Valk (Moscow: AN SSSR, 1949; reprinted Düsseldorf: Brücken Verlag and Vaduz: Europe Printing, 1970).

Grekov, B. D., et al. (eds.), *Pravda russkaia*, 3 vols. (Moscow and Leningrad: AN SSSR, 1940–63).

Hakluyt, Richard, *The Principall Navigations Voiages and Discoveries of the English Nation*, 2 vols., facs. edn, ed. David Beers Quinn and Raleigh Ashlin Skelton (Cambridge: Cambridge University Press, 1965).

Hellie, Richard (ed. and trans.), *Muscovite Society* (Chicago: University of Chicago, 1967, 1970).

(ed. and trans.), *The Muscovite Law Code (Ulozhenie) of 1649*. Part 1: *Text and Translation* (Irvine, Calif.: Charles Schlacks, 1988).

Heppell, Muriel (trans.), *The 'Paterik' of the Kievan Caves Monastery* (Cambridge, Mass.: Harvard University Press, 1989).

Herberstein, Sigismund von, *Notes upon Russia*, 2 vols., trans. R. H. Major (New York: Burt Franklin, 1851–2).

Description of Moscow and Muscovy, 1557, ed. B. Picard (London: J. M. Dent, 1969).

Hollingsworth, Paul (trans. and intro.), *The Hagiography of Kievan Rus'* (Cambridge, Mass.: Harvard University Press, 1992).

Horsey, Jerome, 'Travels', in Lloyd E. Berry and Robert O. Crummey (eds.), *Rude and Barbarous Kingdom. Russia in the Accounts of Sixteenth-Century English Voyagers* (Madison: University of Wisconsin Press, 1968), pp. 262–369.

Iakovlev, A. I. (ed.), *Novgorodskie zapisnye kabal'nye knigi 100–104 i 111 godov (1591–1596 i 1602–1603 gg.)* (Moscow and Leningrad: AN SSSR, 1939).

(ed.), *Akty khoziaistva boiarina B. I. Morozova*, 2 vols. (Moscow and Leningrad: AN SSSR, 1940–5).

Iakovlev, Lukian, *Drevnosti Rossiiskogo gosudarstva. Dopolnenie k III otdeleniiu. Russkie starinnye znamena* (Moscow: Sinodal'naia tipografiia, 1865).

Iakubov, K. I. (ed.), *Rossiia i Shvetsiia v pervoi polovine XVII veka* (Moscow: Universitetskaia tipografiia, 1897).

Ianin, V. L., *Aktovye pechati Drevnei Rusi X–XV vv.*, vol. 1: *Pechati X–nachala XIII v.* (Moscow: Nauka, 1970).

and Gaidukov, P. G., *Aktovye pechati Drevnei Rusi X–XV vv.*, vol. III: *Pechati, zaregistrirovannye v 1970–1996 gg.* (Moscow: Intrada, 1998).

Ibn Fadlan, *Risāla*, ed. T. Lewicki, *Źródła arabskie do dziejów słówiańszczyzny*, vol. III (Wrocław, Warsaw, Cracow, Gdansk, Łodz: Polska Akademia Nauk, 1985).

Ibn Rusta, *Kitāb al-A'lak an-nafisa*, ed. T. Lewicki, *Źródła arabskie do dziejów słówiańszczyzny*, vol. II.2 (Wrocław, Warsaw, Cracow, Gdansk: Polska Akademia Nauk, 1977).

Ilarion, 'Slovo o zakone i blagodati', in D. S. Likhachev et al. (eds.), *Biblioteka literatury drevnei Rusi*, vol. 1 (St Petersburg: Nauka, 1997), pp. 26–60.

Inostrannye izvestiia o vosstanii Stepana Razina, ed. A. G. Man'kov (Leningrad: Nauka, 1975).

Ioasafovskaia letopis', ed. A. A. Zimin (Moscow: AN SSSR, 1957).

Ivina, L. I., et al. (eds.), *Sobornoe ulozhenie 1649 goda: tekst, kommentarii* (Leningrad: Nauka, Leningradskoe otdelenie, 1987).

'Iz l'vovskogo arkhiva kn. Sapegi', *Russkii arkhiv*, 1896, vol. 1, bk. 4.

Kabanov, A. A., 'Akty o naznachenii i smene voevod v Pereiaslavle Riazanskom', 2 pts., *Trudy Riazanskoi uchenoi arkhivnoi kommissii* 25, 2 (1912): 1–28; and 26, 1 (1914): 15–35.

Kabardino-russkie otnosheniia v XVI–XVIII vv. Dokumenty i materialy, 2 vols. (Moscow: AN SSSR, 1957).

Kaiser, Daniel H. (ed. and trans.), *The Laws of Rus' – Tenth to Fifteenth Centuries (The Laws of Russia*, series I, vol. 1) (Salt Lake City, Ut.: Charles Schlacks, 1992).

Kashtanov, S. M., 'The Czar's Sinodik of the 1550s', *Istoricheskaia Genealogiia/Historical Genealogy* 2 (Ekaterinburg and Paris: Yarmarka Press, 1993), pp. 44–67.

Kazakhsko-russkie otnosheniia v XVI–XVIII vekakh. Sbornik dokumentov i materialov (Alma-Ata: AN Kazakhskoi SSR, 1961).

Kazakova, N. A., *Vassian Patrikeev i ego sochineniia* (Moscow and Leningrad: AN SSSR, 1960). and Lur'e, Ia. S., *Antifeodal'nye ereticheskie dvizheniia na Rusi XIV – nachala XVI veka* (Moscow and Leningrad: AN SSSR, 1955).

Kharuzin, N., 'K voprosu o bor'be moskovskogo pravitel'stva s narodnymi iazycheskimi obriadami i sueveriiami v polovine XVII v.', *Etnograficheskoe Obozrenie*, 1879, no. 1: 143–51.

Klein, V. K., *Uglichskoe sledstvennoe delo o smerti tsarevicha Dimitriia* (Moscow: Imperatorskii Arkheologicheskii institut imeni Imperatora Nikolaia II, 1913).

Kokovtsov, P. K., *Evreisko-khazarskaia perepiska v X veke* (Leningrad: AN SSSR, 1932).

Komarov, I. A., et al. (eds.), *Armoury Chamber of the Russian Tsars* (St Petersburg: Atlant, 2002).

Kotoshikhin, Grigorii, *O Rossii v tsarstvovanie Alekseia Mikhailovicha* (St Petersburg: Tipografiia Glavnogo upravleniia udelov, 1906).

'On Russia in the Reign of Alexis Mikhailovich: An Annotated Translation', trans. Benjamin Phillip Uroff, unpublished Ph.D. diss., Columbia University, 1970.

Kotošixin, Grigorij, *O Rossii v carstvovanie Alekseja Mixajloviča. Text and commentary*, ed. A. E. Pennington (Oxford: Clarendon Press, 1980).

O Rossii v tsarstvovanie Alekseia Mikhailovicha, ed. G.A. Leont'eva (Moscow: ROSSPEN, 2000).

Kozhanchikov, D. E. (ed.), *Stoglav* (St Petersburg: Tipografiia Imperatorskoi Akademii Nauk, 1863).

Kozliakov, V. N., 'Novyi dokument ob oprichnykh pereseleniiakh', in *Arkhiv russkoi istorii* 7 (Moscow: Drevlekhranilishche, 2002): 197–211.

Krest'ianskaia voina pod predvoditel'stvom Stepana Razina. Sbornik dokumentov, 4 vols. (in 5) (Moscow: AN SSSR, 1954–76).

Krest'ianstvo i natsionaly v revoliutsionnom dvizhenii. Razinshchina, ed. S. G. Tomsinskii (Moscow and Leningrad: Gosudarstvennoe sotsial'no-ekonomicheskoe izdatel'stvo, 1931).

Krizhanich, Iurii, *Politika*, ed. A. Gol'dberg (Moscow: Nauka, 1965).

Russian Statecraft. The Politika of Iurii Krizhanich. An Analysis and Translation of Iurii Krizhanich's Politika, by John M. Letiche and Basil Dmytryshin (Oxford and New York: Basil Blackwell, 1985).

Kuntsevich, G. Z. 'Podlinnyi spisok o novykh chudotvortsakh', *Izvestiia Otdela russkogo iazyka i slovesnosti Akademii nauk* 15 (1910), bk. 1, pp. 252–7.

Lappo, I. I. (ed.), *Litovskii statut v moskovskom perevode-redaktsii* (Iur'ev: Tipografiia K. Mattisena, 1916).

Lavochnye knigi Novgoroda-Velikogo 1583g., ed. S. V. Bakhrushin (Moscow: RANION, 1930).

'Letopisnye zapisi Marka Levkeinskogo', in A. A. Zimin, 'Kratkie letopisi XV–XVI vv.', *Istoricheskii arkhiv* 5 (1950): 9–14.

Likhachev, D. S., and Lur'e, Ia.S. (eds.), *Poslaniia Ivana Groznogo* (Moscow and Leningrad: AN SSSR, 1951).

Louis II, *Epistola ad Basilium I.*, Monumenta Germaniae Historica, Epistolae Karolini Aevi, V (Berlin: Weidmann, 1928), pp. 389–94.

Loviagin, A. M. (ed.), *Albom Meierberga. Bytovye kartiny Rossii XVII veka* (St Petersburg: A. S. Suvorin, 1903).

Majeska, George P., *Russian Travelers to Constantinople in the Fourteenth and Fifteenth Centuries*, Dumbarton Oaks Studies, no. 19 (Washington, D C: Dumbarton Oaks Research Library and Collection, 1984).

Maksim Grek, *Sochineniia prepodobnogo Maksima Greka*, 2nd edn, 3 vols. (Kazan': Kazanskii universitet, 1894–7).

Man'kov, A. G. (ed.), *Materialy po istorii krest'ian v russkom gosudarstve XVI veka. Sbornik dokumentov* (Leningrad: LGU, 1955).

Margeret, Jacques, *The Russian Empire and Grand Duchy of Muscovy: A 17th-Century French Account*, ed. and trans. Chester S. L. Dunning (Pittsburgh: University of Pittsburgh Press, 1983).

Massa, Isaak [Isaac], *Kratkoe izvestie o Moskovii nachala XVII v.* (Moscow: Gosudarstvennoe Sotsial'no-ekonomicheskoe izdatel'stvo, 1937).

A Short History of the Beginnings and Origins of These Present Wars in Moscow under the Reigns of Various Sovereigns down to the Year 1610, ed. and trans. G. Edward Orchard (Toronto: University of Toronto Press, 1983).

Materialy dlia istorii raskola za pervoe vremia ego sushchestvovaniia, ed. N. Subbotin, 9 vols. (Moscow, Redaktsiia 'Bratskoe Slovo', 1874–90).

Materialy po istorii Bashkirskoi ASSR, vol. i: *Bashkirskie vosstaniia v XVII i pervoi polovine XVIII vekov* (Moscow and Leningrad: AN SSSR, 1936).

Materialy po istorii Bashkirskoi ASSR, vol. iii: *Ekonomicheskie i sotsial'nye otnosheniia v Bashkirii v pervoi polovine XVIII veka* (Moscow and Leningrad: AN SSSR, 1949).

Mavrodin, V. V. (ed.), *Materialy po istorii krest'ian v Rossii XI–XVII vv. (Sbornik dokumentov)* (Leningrad: LGU, 1958).

Medvedev, Sil'vestr, *Sozertsanie kratkoe let 7190–92* (Kiev: Tipografiia Imperatorskogo Universiteta Sv. Vladimira, 1895).

'Miatezhnoe vremia'. *Sledstvennoe delo o Novgorodskom vosstanii 1650 goda*, comp. G. M. Kovalenko, T. A. Lapteva, T. B. Solov'eva (St Petersburg and Kishinev: Nestor-Historia, 2001).

Minorsky, V., *Sharaf al-Zamān Tāhir Marvazī on China, the Turks and India* (James G. Forlong Fund 22) (London: Royal Asiatic Society, 1942).

Narodnoe dvizhenie v Rossii v epokhu Smuty nachala XVII veka, 1601–1608. Sbornik dokumentov, ed. N. M. Rogozhin et al. (Moscow: Nauka, 2003).

Nazarov, V. D., 'Svadebnye dela XVI veka', *VI*, 1976, no. 10: 110–23.

Nevostruev, K. I. (ed.), 'Zhitie prepodobnogo Iosifa Volokolamskogo, sostavlennoe Savvoiu, episkopom krutitskim', 'Zhitie prepodobnogo Iosifa Volokolamskogo, sostavlennoe neizvestnym', 'Nadgrobnoe slovo prepodobnomu Iosifu Volokolamskomu uchenika i srodnika ego Dosifeia Toporkova', *Chteniia Obshchestva Liubitelei drevnei pis'mennosti*, vol. II (1865), pp. 1–184.

Nikol'skii, Konstantin, *O sluzhbakh Russkoi tserkvi byvshikh v prezhnikh pechatnykh bogosluzhebnykh knigakh* (St Petersburg: Tipografiia Tovarishchestva 'Obshchestvennaia pol'za', 1885).

Nikon, Patriarch, *Patriarch Nikon on Church and State – Nikon's 'Refutation' (Vozrazhenie ili razorenie smirennogo Nikona, Bozhieiu milostiiu Patriarkha, protivo voprosov boiarina Simeona Streshneva)*, ed. Valerie A. Tumins and George Vernadsky (Berlin, New York, Amsterdam: Mouton, 1982).

Novgorodskaia pervaia letopis' starshego i mladshego izvodov, ed. A.N. Nasonov (Moscow and Leningrad: AN SSSR, 1950).

Novgorodskie letopisi (St Petersburg: Akademiia Nauk, 1879).

Novombergskii, N. I. (comp.), *Slovo i delo gosudarevy*, vol. I: *Protsessy do izdaniia Ulozheniia Alekseia Mikhailovicha 1649 g.* (Moscow: A. I. Snegireva, 1911; reprinted Moscow: Iazyki slavianskoi kul'tury, 2004).

Novosel'skii, A. A. (ed.), 'Rospis' krest'ianskikh dvorov, nakhodivshikhsia vo vladenii vyshego dukhovenstva, monastyrei i dumnykh liudei po perepisnym knigam 1678 g.', *Istoricheskii arkhiv* 4 (1949): 88–149.

Obolenskii, M. A. (ed.), *Sobornaia gramota dukhovenstva pravoslavnoi vostochnoi tserkvi, utverzhdaiushchaia san tsaria za velikim kniazem Ioannom IV Vasil'evichem, 1561 goda* (Moscow: Sinodal'naia tipografiia, 1850).

Olearius, Adam, *The Travels of Olearius in Seventeenth-Century Russia*, trans. and ed. Samuel H. Baron (Stanford, Calif.: Stanford University Press, 1967).

Ol'shevskaia, L. A. and Travnikov, S. N. (eds.), *Drevnerusskie pateriki* (Moscow: Nauka, 1999).

'Opis' domashnemu imushchestvu tsaria Ivana Vasil'evicha, po spiskam i knigam 90 i 91 godov', in *Vremennik Imperatorskogo moskovskogo obshchestva istorii i drevnostei rossiiskikh* 7 (Moscow: Universitetskaia tipografiia, 1850), Smes': 1–46.

Opis' Novgoroda 1617 goda, vyp.1–2 (Moscow: AN SSSR, 1984).

Ostromirovo Evangelie. Faksimil'noe vosproizvedenie (Leningrad: Aurora, 1988).

Ostrowski, Donald (ed.), *The Povest' vremennykh let: An Interlinear Collation and Paradosis* (Cambridge, Mass.: Harvard University Press, 2003).

Palitsyn, A., *Skazanie Avraamiia Palitsyna*, ed. L.V. Cherepnin (Moscow and Leningrad: AN SSSR, 1955).

Palmer, William, *The Patriarch and the Tsar*, 6 vols. (London: Trübner and Co., 1871–6).

Pamiatniki diplomaticheskikh snoshenii drevnei Rossii s derzhavami inostrannymi, 10 vols. (St Petersburg: Tipografiia II Otdeleniia Sobstvennoi E.I.V. Kantseliarii, 1851–71).

'Pamiatniki drevnei russkoi pis'mennosti, otnosiashchiesia k Smutnomu vremeni', *Russkaia istoricheskaia biblioteka*, vol. XIII (St Petersburg, 1891).

Pamiatniki literatury Drevnei Rusi. Konets XV – pervaia polovina XVI veka, comp. and ed. L. A. Dmitriev and D. S. Likhachev (Moscow: Khudozhestvennaia literatura, 1984).

Pamiatniki literatury Drevnei Rusi. Konets XVI–nachalo XVII vekov, comp. and ed. L. A. Dmitriev and D. S. Likhachev (Moscow: Khudozhestvennaia literatura, 1987).

Pavlov, A. S., 'Otryvki grecheskogo teksta kanonicheskikh otvetov russkogo mitropolita Ioanna II', *Zapiski Imperatorskoi Akademii nauk* 22 (1873), Appendix 5.

Perfecky, G. E. (trans.), *The Hypatian Codex, Part Two: The Galician-Volynian Chronicle* (Munich: Wilhelm Fink, 1973).

Petrei de Erlezund, P., *Istoriia o Velikom kniazhestve Moskovskom* (Moscow: Universitetskaia tipografiia, 1867).

Pistsovye knigi Moskovskogo gosudarstva, ed. N.V. Kalachov, vol. I, otdelenie 1 (St Petersburg, 1872); vol. I, otdelenie 2 (St Petersburg, 1877).

Pliguzov, A. I., and Tikhoniuk, I. A. (eds.), *Smuta v Moskovskom gosudarstve* (Moscow: Sovremennik, 1989).

Pokrovskii, N. N., *Sudnye spiski Maksima Greka i Isaka Sobaki* (Moscow: Glavnoe arkhivnoe upravlenie, 1971).

Polnoe sobranie zakonov Rossiiskoi imperii. Sobranie pervoe, 45 vols. (St Petersburg: Tipografiia II Otdeleniia S. I. V. Kantseliarii, 1830–43).

Polotskii, Simeon, *Simeon Polockij. Vertograd mnogocvetnyj*, ed. Anthony Hippisley and L. I. Sazonova, 3 vols. (Cologne: Böhlau, 1996–2000).

Popov, A. N., *Izbornik slavianskikh i russkikh sochinenii i statei, vnesennykh v khronografy russkoi redaktsii* (Moscow, 1869).

(ed.), 'Poslanie mnogoslovnoe, sochinenie inoka Zinoviia', *ChOIDR* (1880), no. 2: 1–305.

Possevino, Antonio, *The Moscovia of Antonio Possevino, S.J.*, intro. and trans. Hugh F. Graham, UCIS Series in Russian and East European Studies, no. 1 (Pittsburgh: University Center for International Studies, University of Pittsburgh, 1977).

Pouncy, Carolyn Johnston (trans. and ed.), *The Domostroi. Rules for Russian Households in the Time of Ivan the Terrible* (Ithaca, N.Y.: Cornell University Press, 1994).

Povest' vremennykh let, ed. V. P. Adrianova-Peretts and D. S. Likhachev with revisions by M. B. Sverdlov (St Petersburg: Nauka, 2nd edn. 1996; 1st edn, 2 vols., Moscow and Leningrad: AN SSSR, 1950).

Prodolzhenie drevnei rossiiskoi vivliofiki, 11 vols. (St Petersburg: Imperatorskaia Akademiia Nauk, 1786–1801); reprinted in Slavic printings and reprintings, 251, ed. C. H. van Schooneveld (The Hague and Paris: Mouton, 1970), vol. IX (1793).

PRP, 8 vols. (Moscow: Gosudarstvennoe izdatel'stvo iuridicheskoi literatury, 1952–63).

Pskovskie letopisi, ed. A. N. Nasonov, vol. I (Moscow and Leningrad: AN SSSR, 1941; reprinted Düsseldorf, The Hague: Brücken-Verlag GMBH, Europe Printing, 1967); vol. II (Moscow: AN SSSR, 1955; reprinted Moscow: Iazyki russkoi kul'tury, 2000).

PSRL, 43 vols. to date [2004], various locations, various publishers, various editions, 1841–.

Puteshestviia russkikh poslov XVI–XVII vv. Stateinye spiski (Moscow and Leningrad: AN SSSR, 1954).

Razriadnaia kniga 1475–1598 gg., ed. V. I. Buganov (Moscow: Nauka, 1966).

Razriadnaia kniga 1598–1605 gg., ed. V.I. Buganov (Moscow: AN SSSR, 1974).

Rossiia nachala XVII v. Zapiski kapitana Marzhereta, comp. Iu.A. Limonov (Moscow: AN SSSR, 1982).

Rozhdestvenskii, N. V., 'K istorii bor'by s tserkovnymi bezporiadkami, otgoloskami iazychestva i porokami v russkom bytu XVII v.', *ChOIDR* 201 (1902), kn.2: 1–31.

Russkaia Istoricheskaia Biblioteka, izdavaemaia Arkheograficheskoiu Kommissieiu, 39 vols. (St Petersburg: Arkheograficheskaia Kommissiia, 1872–1927).

Russkii feodal'nyi arkhiv. XIV–pervoi treti XVI veka, 5 vols. (Moscow: AN SSSR, Institut istorii SSSR, 1986–92).

RZ, ed. O. I. Chistiakov, 9 vols. (Moscow: Iuridicheskaia literatura, 1984–94), vols. i–iv (1984–6).

Rzhiga, V. F., 'Neizdannye sochineniia Maksima "Greka" ', *Byzantinoslavica* 6 (1935–6): 85–109.

Sbornik Imperatorskogo Russkogo istoricheskogo obshchestva, 148 vols. (St Petersburg: Obshchestvo, 1874–1916).

Schlichting, Albert, 'A Brief Account of the Character and Brutal Rule of Vasil'evich, Tyrant of Muscovy (Albert Schlichting on Ivan Groznyi)', trans. and ed. Hugh F. Graham, *CASS* 9 (1975): 204–72.

Serbina, K. N., *Kniga bol'shomu chertezhu* (Moscow and Leningrad: AN SSSR, 1950).

(ed.), *Ustiuzhskii letopisnyi svod* (Moscow and Leningrad: AN SSSR, 1950).

SGGD, 5 vols., Moscow, various publishers, 1813–94, vol. i (Moscow: Tipografiia N.S. Vsevolozhskogo, 1813); vol.ii (Moscow: Tipografiia Selivanskogo, 1819).

' "Slovo krata" v zashchitu monastyrskikh imushchestv', *ChOIDR* (1902), no. 2: 31–2.

Snosheniia Rossii s Kavkazom. Materialy izvlechennye iz Moskovskogo Ministerstva Inostrannykh del, 1578–1613, comp. S. L. Belokurov (Moscow: Universitetskaia Tipografiia, 1889).

Sobornoe ulozhenie 1649 goda: tekst, kommentarii, ed. L. I. Ivina, G. V. Abramovich et al. (Leningrad: Nauka, Leningradskoe otdelenie, 1987).

Staden, Heinrich von, *The Land and Government of Muscovy: A Sixteenth-Century Account*, trans. and ed. Thomas Esper (Stanford, Calif.: Stanford University Press, 1967).

Strukov, D., and Popov, I., *Risunki k izdaniiu 'Russkie starinnye znamena' Lukiana Iakovleva* (Moscow: Khromolitografiia V. Bakhman, 1865).

Sudebniki XV–XVI vekov, ed. B. D. Grekov (Moscow and Leningrad: AN SSSR, 1952).

Sudnye spiski Maksima Greka i Isaka Sobaki, ed. N. N. Pokrovskii (Moscow: Glavnoe arkhivnoe upravlenie pri Sovete ministrov SSSR, 1971).

The Testaments of the Grand Princes of Moscow, trans. and ed. with commentary by Robert Craig Howes (Ithaca, N.Y.: Cornell University Press, 1967).

Theophanes Continuatus, ed. I. Bekker (Corpus scriptorum historiae byzantinae) (Bonn: E. Weber, 1838).

Tikhoniuk, I. A., 'Chin postavleniia Dmitriia-vnuka', *Russkii feodal'nyi arkhiv* 3 (1987): 604–25.

Timofeev, Ivan, *Vremennik Ivana Timofeeva*, ed. and trans. O. L. Derzhavina (Moscow and Leningrad: AN SSSR, 1951).

Trakhaniot, George, 'Notes and Information about the Affairs and the Ruler of Russia', in Robert M. Croskey and E. C. Ronquist, 'George Trakhaniot's Description of Russia in 1486', *RH* 17 (1990): 55–64.

Troitskaia letopis': Rekonstruktsiia teksta, comp. M. D. Priselkov (Moscow and Leningrad: AN SSSR, 1950).

Tushinskii vor: lichnost', okruzhenie, vremia. Dokumenty i materialy. (Pamiatniki smutnogo vremeni), ed. and comp. V. I. Kuznetsov and I. P. Kulakova (Moscow: Izdatel'stvo Moskovskogo universiteta, 2001).

Tysiachnaia kniga 1550 g. i Dvorovaia tetrad' piatidesiatykh godov XVI veka, ed. A. A. Zimin (Moscow and Leningrad: AN SSSR, 1950).

Ul'fel'dt, Iakob, *Puteshestvie v Rossiiu*, ed. Dzh. Lind and A. L. Khoroshkevich (Moscow: Iazyki slavianskoi kul'tury, 2002).

Ustrialov, N. V., *Skazaniia sovremennikov o Dmitrii Samozvantse*, 1st edn, 5 parts (St Petersburg: Tipografiia Imperatorskoi Akademii Nauk, 1831–4; 3rd edn, St Petersburg: Tipografiia Imperatorskoi Akademii Nauk, 1859).

Veinberg, L. B., *Materialy po istorii Voronezhskoi i sosednikh gubernii. Drevnie akty XVII stoletiia*, vols. 1–16 (Voronezh, 1885–90).

and Poltoratskaia, A. A., *Materialy dlia istorii Voronezhskoi i sosednikh gubernii*, vol. II (Voronezh, 1891).

Viktorov, A. E., *Opisanie zapisnykh knig i bumag starinnykh dvortsovykh prikazov 1584–1725 g.*, 2 vols. (Moscow: S. P. Arkhipov, 1883).

Vladimirskaia, N. S. (ed.), *Orel i lev. Rossiia i Shvetsiia v XVII veke. Katalog vystavki. Gosudarstvennyi istoricheskii muzei, 4.04–1.07.2001* (Moscow: Gosudarstvennyi istoricheskii muzei, 2001).

Volotskii, Iosif, *Prosvetitel', ili oblichenie eresi zhidovstvuiushchikh*, 3rd edn, ed. A. Volkov (Kazan': Tipografiia Imperatorskogo universiteta, 1896); 4th edn (Kazan': Kazanskii universitet, 1904).

Vorms, A. E., et al. (eds.), *Pamiatniki istorii krest'ian XIV–XIX vv.* (Moscow: N. N. Klochkov, 1910).

Vossoedinenie Ukrainy s Rossiei. Dokumenty i materialy v trekh tomakh, 3 vols. (Moscow: AN SSSR, 1953).

Vosstanie I. Bolotnikova. Dokumenty i materialy, comp. A. I. Kopanev and A. G. Man'kov (Moscow: Izdatel'stvo sotsial'no-ekonomicheskoi literatury, 1959).

Vosstanie 1662 g. v Moskve. Sbornik dokumentov, comp. V. I. Buganov (Moscow: Nauka, 1964).

Vosstanie v Moskve 1682 goda. Sbornik dokumentov, comp. N. G. Savich (Moscow: Nauka, 1976).

Vysotskii, S. A., *Drevnerusskie nadpisi Sofii Kievskoi XI–XIV vv.*, vyp. I (Kiev: Naukova Dumka, 1966).

Srednevekovye nadpisi Sofii Kievskoi (po materialam XI–XVII vv.) (Kiev: Naukova Dumka, 1976).

Kievskie graffiti X–XVII vv. (Kiev: Naukova Dumka, 1985).

Zabelin, I. E., *Domashnii byt russkikh tsarei i tsarits v XVI i XVII stoletiiakh*, vol. III: *Materialy* (Moscow: Iazyki russkoi kul'tury, 2003).

Zakonodatel'nye akty Russkogo gosudarstva vtoroi poloviny XVI – pervoi poloviny XVII veka: Teksty (Leningrad: Nauka, 1986).

Zalizniak, A. A., *Drevnenovgorodskii dialekt* (Moscow: Iazyki russkoi kul'tury, 1995).

Zapiski inostrantsev o vosstanii Stepana Razina, ed. A. G. Man'kov (Leningrad: Nauka, 1968).

Zenkovsky, Serge A. (ed.), *Medieval Russia's Epics, Chronicles, and Tales* (New York: E. P. Dutton, 1974).

Zertsalov, A. N., comp., 'K istorii miatezha 1648 goda v Moskve i drugikh gorodakh', in his *Stat'i po russkoi istorii* (The Hague: Europe Printing, 1966).

Zhitie prepodobnogo Prokopiia ustiuzhskogo (St Petersburg: Sinodal'naia Tipografiia, 1893).

Zhmakin, V. I., 'Mitropolit Daniil i ego sochineniia', *ChOIDR* (1881), no. 2, app.: pp. 1–88.

Zimin, A. A., 'Kratkie letopisi XV–XVI vv.', *Istoricheskii arkhiv 5* (1950).

(ed.), *Gosudarstvennyi arkhiv Rossii XVI stoletiia. Opyt rekonstruktsii*, vol. III (Moscow: Institut istorii SSSR, 1978).

and Lur'e, Ia. S. (eds.), *Poslaniia Iosifa Volotskogo* (Moscow and Leningrad: AN SSSR, 1959).

Zolkiewski, Stanislas, *Expedition to Moscow*, ed. and trans. J. Giertych (London: Polonica, 1959).

II. SECONDARY SOURCES

1. Political history

(a) c.900–1462

Alef, Gustave, 'The Political Significance of the Inscriptions of Muscovite Coinage in the Reign of Vasili II', *Speculum* 34 (1959): 1–19; reprinted in his *Rulers and Nobles in Fifteenth-Century Muscovy* (London: Variorum Reprints, 1983).

'Muscovy and the Council of Florence', *SR* 20 (1961): 389–401; reprinted in his *Rulers and Nobles in Fifteenth-Century Muscovy* (London: Variorum Reprints, 1983).

'The Crisis of the Muscovite Aristocracy: A Factor in the Growth of Monarchical Power', *FOG* 15 (1970): 15–58; reprinted in his *Rulers and Nobles in Fifteenth-Century Muscovy* (London: Variorum Reprints, 1983).

'The Battle of Suzdal' in 1445. An Episode in the Muscovite War of Succession', *FOG* 25 (1978): 11–20; reprinted in his *Rulers and Nobles in Fifteenth-Century Muscovy* (London: Variorum Reprints, 1983).

Rulers and Nobles in Fifteenth-Century Muscovy (London: Variorum Reprints, 1983).

'The Origins of Muscovite Autocracy. The Age of Ivan III', *FOG* 39 (1986): 7–362.

Alekseev, L. V., *Polotskaia zemlia (Ocherki istorii severnoi Belorusii) v IX–XIII vv.* (Moscow: Nauka, 1966).

'Polotskaia zemlia', in L. G. Beskrovnyi (ed.), *Drevnerusskie kniazhestva X–XIII vv.* (Moscow: Nauka, 1975), pp. 202–39.

Smolenskaia zemlia v IX–XIII vv. Ocherki istorii Smolenshchiny i Vostochnoi Belorussii (Moscow: Nauka, 1980).

Allsen, Thomas T., 'Mongol Census Taking in Rus'', *HUS* 5 (1981): 32–53.

'Saray', *Encyclopedia of Islam*, 2nd edn, vol. IX (Leiden: E. J. Brill, 1996), pp. 41–4.

'Ever Closer Encounters: The Appropriation of Culture and the Apportionment of Peoples in the Mongol Empire', *Journal of Early Modern History* 1 (1997): 2–23.

Arakcheev, V. A., *Pskovskii krai v XV–XVII vekakh: Obshchestvo i gosudarstvo* (St Petersburg: Russko-Baltiiskii informatsionnyi tsentr BLITs, 2003).

Backus, Oswald P., *Motives of West Russian Nobles in Deserting Lithuania for Moscow, 1377–1514* (Lawrence: University of Kansas Press, 1957).

Bagalei, D. I., *Istoriia Severskoi zemli do poloviny XIV stoletiia* (Kiev, 1882).

Baumgarten, N. de, *Généalogies et mariages occidentaux des Rurikides russes du Xe au XIIIe siècle (Orientalia Christiana)* (Rome: Pont. Institutum Orientalium Studiorum, 1927), vol. 9, no. 35.

Généalogies des branches régnantes des Rurikides du XIIIe au XVIe siècle (Orientalia Christiana) (Rome: Pont. Institutum Orientalium Studiorum, 1934), vol. 35, no. 94.

Bernadskii, V. N., *Novgorod i Novgorodskaia zemlia* (Moscow and Leningrad: AN SSSR, 1961).

Beskrovnyi, L. G. (ed.), *Drevnerusskie kniazhestva X–XIII vv.* (Moscow: Nauka, 1975).

Birnbaum, Henrik, 'Iaroslav's Varangian Connection', *Scandoslavica* 24 (1978): 5–25.

Lord Novgorod the Great: Essays in the History and Culture of a Medieval City-State (Columbus, Oh.: Slavica, 1981).

Novgorod in Focus: Selected Essays (Columbus, Oh.: Slavica, 1996).

Bogatyrev, Sergei, *The Sovereign and his Counsellors. Ritualised Consultations in Muscovite Culture, 1350s–1570s* (Helsinski: Finnish Academy of Science and Letters, 2000).

Cherepnin, L. V., *Obrazovanie russkogo tsentralizovannogo gosudarstva v XIV–XV vekakh* (Moscow: Sotsial'no-ekonomicheskaia literatura, 1960).

Crummey, Robert O., *The Formation of Muscovy 1304–1613* (London and New York: Longman, 1987).

Danilevskii, I. N., *Drevniaia Rus' glazami sovremennikov i potomkov (IX–XII vv.)* (Moscow: Aspekt Press, 1998).

Davidson, H. R. Ellis, *The Viking Road to Byzantium* (London: George Allen and Unwin, 1976).

Dimnik, Martin, 'Principality of Galicia-Volynia', in *MERSH*, vol. xii (Gulf Breeze, Fla.: Academic International Press, 1979), pp. 66–9.

Mikhail, Prince of Chernigov and Grand Prince of Kiev, 1224–1246 (Toronto: Pontifical Institute of Mediaeval Studies, 1981).

'The Place of Ryurik Rostislavich's Death: Kiev or Chernigov?', *Mediaeval Studies* 44 (1982): 371–93.

'The "Testament" of Iaroslav "the Wise": A Re-Examination', *Canadian Slavonic Papers* 29 (1987): 369–86.

The Dynasty of Chernigov 1054–1146 (Toronto: Pontifical Institute of Mediaeval Studies, 1994).

'Succession and Inheritance in Rus' before 1054', *Mediaeval Studies* 58 (1996): 87–117.

'Igor's Defeat at the Kayala: The Chronicle Evidence', *Mediaeval Studies* 63 (2001): 245–82.

The Dynasty of Chernigov, 1146–1246 (Cambridge: Cambridge University Press, 2003).

Dolukhanov, P. M., *The Early Slavs. Eastern Europe from the Initial Settlement to the Kievan Rus* (London: Longman, 1996).

Dzhakson, T. N., *Austr í Görðum. Drevnerusskie toponimy v drevneskandinavskikh istochnikakh* (Moscow: Iazyki slavianskoi kul'tury, 2001).

(ed.), *Norna u istochnika Sud'by. Sbornik statei v chest' Eleny Aleksandrovny Mel'nikovoi* (Moscow: Indrik, 2001).

Ekzempliarskii, A. O., *Velikie i udel'nye kniaz'ia severnoi Rusi v Tatarskii period*, 2 vols. (St Petersburg: I. I. Tolstoi, 1889–91; reprinted The Hague: Europe Printing, 1966).

'Olga's Visit to Constantinople', *HUS* 14 (1990): 293–312.

Featherstone, J. M., 'Olga's Visit to Constantinople in *De cerimoniis*', *Revue des études byzantines* 61 (2003): 241–51.

Fennell, John, *The Emergence of Moscow 1304–1359* (Berkeley and Los Angeles: University of California Press, 1968).

The Crisis of Medieval Russia 1200–1304 (London and New York: Longman, 1983).

'The Last Years of Riurik Rostislavich', in D. C. Waugh (ed.), *Essays in Honor of A. Zimin* (Columbus, Oh.: Slavica, 1985), pp. 159–66.

Franklin, Simon, 'Pre-Mongol Rus': New Sources, New Perspectives?', *RR* 60 (2001): 465–73.

and Shepard, Jonathan, *The Emergence of Rus, 750–1200* (London and New York: Longman, 1996).

Golden, P. B., 'Rūs', in *The Encyclopaedia of Islam*, vol. VIII (Leiden: Brill, 1994), pp. 618–29.

Goldfrank, David, '*Muscovy and the Mongols*: What's What and What's Maybe', *Kritika* 1 (2000): 259–66.

Golovko, A. B., *Drevniaia Rus' i Pol'sha v politicheskikh vzaimootnosheniiakh X–pervoi treti XIII vv.* (Kiev: Naukova Dumka, 1988).

Golubovskii, P. V., *Istoriia Severskoi zemli do poloviny XIV stoletiia* (Kiev, 1881).

Gorskii, A. A. *Drevnerusskaia druzhina. K istorii genezisa klassovogo obshchestva i gosudarstva na Rusi* (Moscow: Prometei, 1989).

Moskva i Orda (Moscow: Nauka, 2000).

Grushevskii, A. S., *Ocherk istorii Turovo-Pinskogo kniazhestva XI–XIII vv.* (Kiev, 1901).

Gumilev, L. N., *Drevniaia Rus' i velikaia step'* (Moscow: Mysl', 1989).

Halbach, Uwe, *Der russische Fürstenhof vor dem 16. Jahrhundert: eine vergleichende Untersuchung zur politischen Lexikologie und Verfassungsgeschichte der alten Rus'* (Quellen und Studien zur Geschichte des östlichen Europa, 23) (Stuttgart: Steiner Verlag, 1985).

Halperin, Charles, 'The Russian Land and the Russian Tsar: The Emergence of Muscovite Ideology, 1380–1408', *FOG* 23 (1976): 7–103.

'Tverian Political Thought in the Fifteenth Century', *Cahiers du monde russe et soviétique* 18 (1977): 267–73.

Russia and the Golden Horde: The Mongol Impact on Medieval Russian History (Bloomington: Indiana University Press, 1985).

The Tatar Yoke (Columbus, Oh.: Slavica, 1986).

'Muscovite Political Institutions in the 14th Century', *Kritika* 1 (2000): 237–57.

Hrushevskii, M., *Ocherk istorii Kievskoi zemli ot smerti Iaroslava do kontsa XIV stoletiia* (Kiev, 1891).

Hurwitz, E. S., *Prince Andrej Bogoljubskij: The Man and the Myth* (Studia historica et philologica 12, sectio slavica 4) (Florence: Licosa Editrice, 1980).

Ianin, V. L., 'Bor'ba Novgoroda i Moskvy za Dvinskie zemli v 50-kh–70-kh gg. XV v.', *IZ* 108 (1982): 189–214.

'K khronologii i topografii ordynskogo pokhoda na Novgorod v 1238 g.', in *Issledovaniia po istorii i istoriografii feodalizma* (Moscow: Nauka, 1982), pp. 146–58.

Novgorodskie akty XII–XV vv. Khronologicheskii kommentarii (Moscow: Nauka, 1990).

Novgorod i Litva. Pogranichnye situatsii XIII–XV vekov (Moscow: Izdatel'stvo Moskovskogo universiteta, 1998).

'Kniaginia Ol'ga i problema stanovleniia Novgoroda', in *Drevnosti Pskova. Arkheologiia. Istoriia. Arkhitektura* (Pskov: Pskovskii gosudarstvennyi ob"edinennyi istoriko-arkhitekturnyi i khudozhestvennyi muzei-zapovednik, 2000).

U istokov novgorodskoi gosudarstvennosti (Novgorod: Novgorodskii gosudarstvennyi universitet, 2001).

Novgorodskie posadniki (Moscow: MGU, 1962; 2nd edn, Moscow: Iazyki slavianskoi kul'tury, 2003).

and Aleshkovskii, M.Kh., 'Proiskhozhdenie Novgoroda: K postanovke problemy', *Istoriia SSSR*, 1971, no. 2: 32–61.

Ianovskii, A. M., *Iurii Dolgorukii* (Moscow: Moskovskii rabochii, 1955).

Kämpfer, F., 'Eine Residenz für Anna Porphyrogenneta', *JGO* 41 (1993): 101–10.

Karamzin, N. M., *Istoriia gosudarstva Rossiiskogo*, 5th edn, 12 vols. and index (in 4 books) (St Petersburg: I. Dinerling, 1842–4; facsimile reprint Moscow: Kniga, 1988–9).

Karger, M. K., *Novgorod Velikii*, 4th edn (Leningrad: Iskusstvo, 1980).

Kazakova, N. A., *Russko-livonskie i russko-ganzeiskie otnosheniia* (Leningrad: Nauka, 1975).

Kazhdan, Alexander, 'Rus'-Byzantine Princely Marriages in the Eleventh and Twelfth Centuries', *HUS* 12/13 (1988/9 [pub. 1990]): 414–29.

Kleimola, A. M., and Lenhoff, G. D. (eds.), *Culture and Identity in Muscovy, 1359–1584* (UCLA Slavic Studies, new series, vol. III) (Moscow: ITZ-Garant, 1997).

Kollmann, Nancy Shields, *Kinship and Politics: The Making of the Muscovite Political System, 1345–1547* (Stanford, Calif.: Stanford University Press, 1987).

'Collateral Succession in Kievan Rus'', *HUS* 14 (1990): 377–87.

Kopanev, A. I., 'O "kupliakh" Ivana Kality', *IZ* 20 (1946): 24–37.

Korinnyi, N. N., *Pereiaslavskaia zemlia X–pervaia polovina XIII veka* (Kiev: Naukova Dumka, 1992).

Korpela, J., *Prince, Saint and Apostle: Prince Vladimir Svjatoslavic of Kiev, his Posthumous Life and the Religious Legitimization of the Russian Great Power* (Wiesbaden: Harrassowitz, 2001).

Kuchera, M. P., 'Pereiaslavskoe kniazhestvo', in L. G. Beskrovnyi (ed.), *Drevnerusskie kniazhestva X–XIII vv.* (Moscow: Nauka, 1975), pp. 118–43.

Kuchkin, V. A., *Formirovanie gosudarstvennoi territorii severo-vostochnoi Rusi v X–XIV vv.* (Moscow: Nauka, 1984).

'Dmitrii Donskoi', *VI*, 1995, nos. 5–6: 62–83.

Kuryuzawa, Takeo, 'The Debate on the Genesis of Russian Feudalism in Recent Soviet Historiography', in Takayuki Ito (ed.), *Facing up to the Past. Soviet Historiography under Perestroika* (Sapporo, Japan: Slavic Research Center, Hokkaido University, 1989), pp. 111–47.

Kuza, A. V., 'Novgorodskaia zemlia', in L. G. Beskrovnyi (ed.), *Drevnerusskie kniazhestva X–XIII vv.* (Moscow: Nauka, 1975), pp. 144–201.

Liaskoronskii, V. G., *Istoriia Pereiaslavskoi zemli s drevneishikh vremen do poloviny XIII stoletiia* (Kiev, 1897).

Limonov, Iu. A., *Vladimiro-Suzdal'skaia Rus': Ocherki sotsial'no-politicheskoi istorii*, ed. B. A. Rybakov (Leningrad: Nauka, 1987).

Lysenko, P. F., 'Kiev i Turovskaia zemlia', in L. D. Pobol' et al. (eds.), *Kiev i zapadnye zemli Rusi v IX–XIII vv.* (Minsk: Nauka i Tekhnika, 1982), pp. 81–108.

Martin, Janet, 'Muscovite Frontier Policy: The Case of the Khanate of Kasimov', *RH* 19 (1992): 169–79.

Medieval Russia 980–1584 (Cambridge: Cambridge University Press, 1995).

Mavrodina, R. M., *Kievskaia Rus' i kochevniki (pechenegi, torki, polovtsy). Istoriograficheskii ocherk* (Leningrad: Nauka, 1983).

Mel'nikova, E. A. (ed.), *Drevniaia Rus' v svete zarubezhnykh istochnikov* (Moscow: Logos, 1999).

Meyendorff, John, 'Alexis and Roman: A Study in Byzantino-Russian Relations (1352–1354)', *St. Vladimir's Theological Quarterly* 11 (1967): 139–48.

Byzantium and the Rise of Russia. A Study of Byzantino-Russian Relations in the Fourteenth Century (Cambridge: Cambridge University Press, 1981).

Miller, David B., 'The Kievan Principality in the Century before the Mongol Invasion: An Inquiry into Recent Research and Interpretation', *HUS* 10 (1986): 215–40.

Mongait, A. L., *Riazanskaia zemlia* (Moscow: AN SSSR, 1961).

Montgomery, J. E., 'Ibn Fadlān and the Rūsiyyah', *Journal of Arabic and Islamic Studies* 3 (2000): 1–25.

Morgan, David, *The Mongols* (Oxford and New York: Basil Blackwell, 1986).

Nasonov, A. N., *'Russkaia zemlia' i obrazovanie territorii drevnerusskogo gosudarstva* (Moscow: AN SSSR, 1951).

Mongoly i Rus' (Istoriia tatarskoi politiki na Rusi) (Moscow and Leningrad: AN SSSR, 1940; reprinted The Hague and Paris: Mouton, 1969).

Nazarenko, A. V., 'O russko-datskom soiuze v pervoi chetverti XI v.', in *Drevneishie gosudarstva na territorii SSSR. Materialy i issledovaniia. 1990 god* (Moscow: Nauka, 1991), pp. 167–90.

Drevniaia Rus' na mezhdunarodnykh putiakh. Mezhdistsiplinarnye ocherki kul'turnykh, torgovykh, politicheskikh sviazei IX–XII vekov (Moscow: Iazyki russkoi kul'tury, 2001).

Noonan, T. S., 'Why the Vikings First Came to Russia', *JGO* 34 (1986): 321–48; reprinted in his *The Islamic World, Russia and the Vikings, 750–900* (Aldershot: Ashgate, 1998), no. 1.

'Rus', Pechenegs and Polovtsy', *RH* 19 (1992): 300–26.

Obolensky, Dimitri, 'Byzantium, Kiev and Moscow: A Study in Ecclesiastical Relations', *Dumbarton Oaks Papers* 11 (Cambridge, Mass.: Harvard University Press, 1957), pp.23–78; reprinted in Dimitri Obolensky, *Byzantium and the Slavs: Collected Studies* (London: Variorum Reprints, 1971) [item] no. vi.

The Byzantine Commonwealth. Eastern Europe 500–1453 (London: Weidenfeld and Nicolson, 1971).

'Byzantium and Russia in the Late Middle Ages', in J. R. Hale, J. R. L. Highfield and B. Smalley (eds.), *Europe in the Late Middle Ages* (London: Faber and Faber, 1965), pp. 248–75; reprinted in Dimitri Obolensky, *Byzantium and the Slavs: Collected Studies* (London: Variorum Reprints, 1971).

Byzantium and the Slavs: Collected Studies (London: Variorum Reprints, 1971).

Byzantium and the Slavs (Crestwood, N.Y.: St Vladimir's Seminary Press, 1994).

Ostrowski, Donald, 'The Mongol Origins of Muscovite Political Institutions', *SR* 49 (1990): 525–42.

Muscovy and the Mongols: Cross-Cultural Influences on the Steppe Frontier, 1304–1589 (Cambridge: Cambridge University Press, 1998).

'Muscovite Adaptation of Steppe Political Institutions: a Reply to Halperin's Objections', *Kritika* 1 (2000): 267–304.

'Troop Mobilization by the Muscovite Grand Princes (1313–1533)', in Eric Lohr and Marshall Poe (eds.), *The Military and Society in Russia, 1450–1917* (Leiden, Boston and Köln: Brill, 2002), pp. 19–40.

Pashuto, V. T., *Ocherki po istorii Galitsko-Volynskoi Rusi* (Moscow: AN SSSR, 1950).

Vneshniaia politika Drevnei Rusi (Moscow: Nauka, 1968).

Pelenski, Jaroslaw, 'The Origins of the Official Muscovite Claims to the "Kievan Inheritance"', *HUS* 1 (1977): 29–52.

'The Contest between Lithuania-Rus' and the Golden Horde in the Fourteenth Century for Supremacy over Eastern Europe', *Archivum Eurasiae Medii Aevi* 2 (1982): 303–20.

'The Emergence of the Muscovite Claims to the Byzantine-Kievan "Imperial Inheritance"', *HUS* 7 (1983): 520–31.

'The Sack of Kiev in 1169: Its Significance for the Succession to Kievan Rus'', in his *The Contest for the Legacy of Kievan Rus'* (Boulder, Colo.: East European Monographs, 1998), pp. 45–60.

The Contest for the Legacy of Kievan Rus' (Boulder, Colo: East European Monographs, 1998).

Pletneva, S. A., 'Polovetskaia zemlia', in L. G. Beskrovnyi (ed.), *Drevnerusskie kniazhestva X–XIII vv.* (Moscow: Nauka, 1975), pp. 260–300.

Polovtsy (Moscow: Nauka, 1990).

Plugin, V. A., 'Sergei Radonezhskii – Dmitrii Donskoi – Andrei Rublev', *Istoriia SSSR*, 1989, no. 4: 71–88.

Poe, Marshall T., *The Russian Moment in World History* (Princeton: Princeton University Press, 2003).

Poppe, A., 'The Political Background to the Baptism of Rus'', *Dumbarton Oaks Papers* 30 (1976): 197–244; reprinted in his *The Rise of Christian Russia* (London: Variorum, 1982) no. 2.

Presniakov, A. E., *The Formation of the Great Russian State. A Study of Russian History in the Thirteenth to Fifteenth Centuries*, trans. A. E. Moorhouse (Chicago: Quadrangle Books, 1970).

Raba, Joel, 'The Authority of the Muscovite Ruler at the Dawn of the Modern Era', *JGO* 24 (1976): 321–44.

Roublev, Michel, 'The Mongol Tribute According to the Wills and Agreements of the Russian Princes', in Michael Cherniavsky (ed.), *The Structure of Russian History. Interpretive Essays* (New York: Random House, 1970), pp. 29–64. Originally published as 'Le Tribut aux Mongols d'après les Testaments et Accords des Princes Russes', *Cahiers du monde russe et soviétique* 7 (1966).

'The Periodicity of the Mongol Tribute as Paid by the Russian Princes during the Fourteenth and Fifteenth Centuries', *FOG* 15 (1970): 7–13.

Rybakov, B. A., *Kievskaia Rus' i russkie kniazhestva XII–XIII vv.* (Moscow: Nauka, 1982).

Kievan Rus (Moscow: Progress Publishers, 1984).

et al. (eds.), *Kulikovskaia bitva v istorii i kul'ture nashei Rodiny. (Materialy iubeleinoi nauchnoi konferentsii)* (Moscow: Moskovskii universitet, 1983).

Schramm, G., *Altrusslands Anfang. Historische Schlüsse aus Namen, Wörtern und Texten zum 9. und 10. Jahrhundert* (Freiburg im Breisgau: Rombach, 2002).

Sedov, V. V., 'Smolenskaia zemlia', in L. G. Beskrovnyi (ed.), *Drevnerusskie kniazhestva X–XIII vv.* (Moscow: Nauka, 1975), pp. 240–59.

Shtykhov, G. V., *Drevnii Polotsk, IX–XIII vv.* (Minsk: Nauka i Tekhnika, 1975).

Sofronenko, K. A., *Obshchestvenno-politicheskii stroi Galitsko-Volynskoi Rusi XI–XIII vv.* (Moscow: Gosiurizdat, 1955).

Solov'ev, S. M., *Istoriia Rossii s drevneishikh vremen*, 29 vols. in 15 books (Moscow: Izdatel'stvo sotsial'no-ekonomicheskoi literatury, 1959–66).

History of Russia from Earliest Times, ed. G. Edward Orchard, 50 vols. [projected] Gulf Breeze, Fla.: Academic International Press, 1978–).

Stokes, Anthony D., 'The System of Succession to the Thrones of Russia, 1054–1113', in R. Auty, L. R. Lewitter and A. P. Vlasto (eds.), *Gorski Vijenac: a Garland of Essays Offered to Professor E. M. Hill* (Cambridge: Modern Humanities Research Association, 1970), pp. 268–75.

Tatishchev, V. N., *Istoriia Rossiiskaia*, 7 vols. (Moscow and Leningrad: AN SSSR, 1962–8).

Tikhomirov, M. N., 'Moskovskie tretniki, tysiatskie, i namestniki', *Izvestiia AN SSSR*, seriia istorii i filosofii, 3 (1946): 309–20.

Tolochko, A. P., *Kniaz' v Drevnei Rusi: vlast', sobstvennost', ideologiia* (Kiev: Naukova Dumka, 1992).

Tolochko, O. P., 'Shche raz pro mistse smerti Riuryka Rostyslavycha', in V. P. Kovalenko et al. (eds.), *Sviatyi kniaz' Mykhailo Chernihivs'kyi ta ioho doba* (Chernihiv: Siverians'ka Dumka, 1996), pp. 75–6.

Tolochko, P. P., 'Kievskaia zemlia', in L. G. Beskrovnyi (ed.), *Drevnerusskie kniazhestva X–XIII vv.* (Moscow: Nauka, 1975), pp. 5–56.

Kiev i Kievskaia zemlia v epokhu feodal'noi razdroblennosti XII–XIII vekov (Kiev: Naukova Dumka, 1980).

Drevniaia Rus'. Ocherki sotsial'no-politicheskoi istorii (Kiev: Naukova Dumka, 1987).

Kyivs'ka Rus' (Kiev: Abrys, 1996).

Uspenskii, F. B., *Skandinavy. Variagi. Rus'. Istoriko-filologicheskie ocherki* (Moscow: Iazyki slavianskoi kul'tury, 2002).

Vernadsky, George, *Kievan Russia* (*A History of Russia*, vol. II), 7th printing (New Haven and London: Yale University Press, 1972; 1st edn, 1948).

The Mongols and Russia (*A History of Russia*, vol. III) (New Haven: Yale University Press and London: Oxford University Press, 1953).

Vodoff, Wladimir, 'A propos des "achats" (kupli) d'Ivan Ier de Moscou', *Journal des Savants* (1974): 95–127.

'Quand a pu être le Panégyrique du grand-prince Dmitrii Ivanovich, tsar' russe?', *CASS* 13 (1979): 82–101.

'La Place du grand-prince de Tver' dans les structures politiques russes de la fin du XIVe et du XVe siècle', *FOG* 27 (1980), 32–63.

Wörn, D., 'Studien zur Herrschaftsideologie des Grossfürsten Vsevolod III "Bol'shoe gnezdo" von Vladimir', *JGO* 27 (1979): 1–40.

Zaitsev, A. K., 'Chernigovskoe kniazhestvo', in L. G. Beskrovnyi (ed.), *Drevnerusskie kniazhestva X–XIII vv.* (Moscow: Nauka, 1975), pp. 57–117.

Zdan, Michael, 'The Dependence of Halych-Volyn' on the Golden Horde', *SEER* 35 (1957): 505–22.

Zimin, A. A., *Vitiaz' na rasput'e. Feodal'naia voina v Rossii XV v.* (Moscow: Mysl', 1991).

(b) 1462–1613

Alef, Gustave, 'The Adoption of the Muscovite Two-Headed Eagle: A Discordant View', *Speculum* 41 (1966): 1–21.

Babichenko, Denis, 'Kremlevskie tainy: 33-i element', *Itogi*, no. 37 (327), 17 September 2002: 36–9.

Backus, Oswald P., 'Treason as a Concept and Defections from Moscow to Lithuania in the Sixteenth Century', *FOG* 15 (1970): 119–44.

Bakhrushin, S. V., *Nauchnye trudy*, 4 vols. (in 5) (Moscow: AN SSSR, 1952–9).

'Ostiatskie i vogul'skie kniazhestva v XVI–XVII vv.', in his *Nauchnye trudy*, 4 vols. (Moscow: AN SSSR, 1952–9), vol. III, pt. 2 (1955), pp. 86–152.

Barbour, Philip L., *Dimitry, Called the Pretender, Tsar and Great Prince of All Russia, 1605–1606* (London: Macmillan, 1967).

Bazilevich, K. V., *Vneshnaia politika russkogo tsentralizovannogo gosudarstva. Vtoraia polovina XV veka* (Moscow: Izdatel'stvo Moskovskogo universiteta, 1952).

Berelowitch, André, *La Hiérarchie des égaux. La Noblesse russe d'Ancien Régime XVIe–XVIIe siècles* (Paris: Editions du Seuil, 2001).

Bogatyrev, Sergei, 'Groznyi tsar' ili groznoe vremia? Psikhologicheskii obraz Ivana Groznogo v istoriografii', *RH* 22 (1995): 285–308.

The Sovereign and his Counsellors. Ritualised Consultations in Muscovite Culture, 1350s–1570s (Helsinki: Finnish Academy of Science and Letters, 2000).

'Battle for Divine Wisdom. The Rhetoric of Ivan IV's Campaign against Polotsk', in Eric Lohr and Marshall Poe (eds.), *The Military and Society in Russia, 1450–1917* (Leiden: Brill, 2002), pp. 325–63.

'Localism and Integration in Muscovy', in Sergei Bogatyrev (ed.), *Russia Takes Shape. Patterns of Integration from the Middle Ages to the Present* (Helsinki: Finnish Academy of Science and Letters, 2004), pp. 59–127.

Bogdanov, A. P., 'Chiny venchaniia rossiiskikh tsarei', in B. A. Rybakov et al. (eds.), *Kul'tura srednevekovoi Moskvy XIV–XVII vv.* (Moscow: Nauka, 1995), pp. 211–24.

Brown, Peter B., 'Muscovite Government Bureaus', *RH* 10 (1983): 269–330.

Bulanin, D. M., 'Adashev Aleksei Fedorovich', in *Slovar' knizhnikov i knizhnosti Drevnei Rusi*, vyp. 2: *Vtoraia polovina XIV–XVI v.* (Leningrad: Nauka, Leningradskoe otdelenie, 1988), pt. 1, pp. 8–10.

Cherepnin, L.V., *Zemskie sobory Russkogo gosudarstva v XVI–XVII vv.* (Moscow: Nauka, 1978).

Croskey, Robert M., *Muscovite Diplomatic Practice in the Reign of Ivan III* (New York: Garland, 1987).

'Byzantine Greeks in Late Fifteenth- and Early Sixteenth-Century Russia', in Lowell Clucas (ed.), *The Byzantine Legacy in Eastern Europe* (Boulder, Colo.: East European Monographs, 1988), pp. 35–56.

and Ronquist, E.C., 'George Trakhaniot's Description of Russia in 1486', *RH* 17 (1990): 55–64.

Crummey, Robert O., *The Formation of Muscovy, 1304–1613* (London and New York: Longman, 1987).

'New Wine in Old Bottles? Ivan IV and Novgorod', *RH* 14 (1987): 61–76.

'The Latest from Muscovy', *RR* 60 (2001): 474–86.

Sundhaussen, Holm, and Vulpius, Ricarda (eds.), *Russische und Ukrainische Geschichte vom 16.–18.Jahrhundert = FOG* 58 (2001).

Czerska, D., *Borys Godunow* (Wrocław: Ossolineum, 1988).

Davies, Brian L., 'The Town Governors in the Reign of Ivan IV', *RH* 14 (1987): 77–143.

'The Politics of Give and Take: *Kormlenie* as Service Remuneration and Generalized Exchange, 1488–1726', in Ann M. Kleimola and Gail Lenhoff (eds.), *Culture and Identity in Muscovy, 1359–1584* (Moscow: ITZ-Garant, 1997), pp. 39-67.

'The Development of Russian Military Power, 1453–1815', in Jeremy Black (ed.), *European Warfare, 1453–1815* (Houndmills and New York: Macmillan, 1999), pp. 145–79.

Dewey, Horace W., 'The 1550 Sudebnik as an Instrument of Reform', *JGO* 10 (1962): 161–80.

and Kleimola, A. M., 'Promise and Perfidy in Old Russian Cross-Kissing', *Canadian Slavic Studies* 3 (1968): 327–41.

Donnelly, Alton S., *The Russian Conquest of Bashkiria, 1552–1740. A Case Study in Imperialism* (New Haven: Yale University Press, 1968).

Dunning, Chester S. L., *Russia's First Civil War: The Time of Troubles and the Founding of the Romanov Dynasty* (University Park, Pa.: Pennsylvania State University Press, 2001).

'Terror in the Time of Troubles', *Kritika* 4 (2003): 491–513.

Emerson, C., *Boris Godunov: Transpositions of a Russian Theme* (Bloomington and Indianapolis: Indiana University Press, 1986).

Fennell, J. L. I., *Ivan the Great of Moscow* (London: Macmillan, 1961).

Filiushkin, A. I., *Istoriia odnoi mistifikatsii. Ivan Groznyi i 'Izbrannaia Rada'* (Moscow: Voronezhskii gosudarstvennyi universitet, 1998).

'Diskursy Livonskoi voiny', *Ab Imperio* 4 (2001): 43–80.

'Post-Modernism and the Study of the Russian Middle Ages', *Kritika* 3 (2002): 89–109.

Flier, Michael S., 'Breaking the Code: The Image of the Tsar in the Muscovite Palm Sunday Ritual', in Michael S. Flier and Daniel Rowland (eds.), *Medieval Russian Culture*, vol. II (Berkeley: University of California Press, 1994), pp. 213–42.

Floria, B. N., *Russko-pol'skie otnosheniia i baltiiskii vopros v kontse XVI – nachale XVII v.* (Moscow: Nauka, 1973).

Russko-pol'skie otnosheniia i politicheskoe razvitie Vostochnoi Evropy (Moscow: Nauka, 1978).

Ivan Groznyi, 2nd edn (Moscow: Molodaia gvardiia, 2002).

Forsyth, James, *A History of the Peoples of Siberia* (Cambridge: Cambridge University Press, 1992).

Frost, Robert I., *The Northern Wars, 1558–1721* (London, New York: Longman, 2000).

Golubtsov, I. A., ' "Izmena" smolian pri Borise Godunove i "izvet Varlaama" ', *Uchenye zapiski instituta istorii RANION* 5 (1928): 218–51.

' "Izmena" Nagikh', *Uchenye zapiski instituta istorii RANION* 4 (1929): 55–70.

Gralia, I., *Ivan Mikhailov Viskovatyi: Kar'era gosudarstvennogo deiatelia v Rossii XVI v.* (Moscow: Radiks, 1994).

Grobovsky, A. N., *The 'Chosen Council' of Ivan IV. A Reinterpretation* (New York: Gaus, 1969).

Halperin, Charles J., 'Edward Keenan and the Kurbskii–Groznyi Correspondence in Hindsight', *JGO* 46 (1998): 376–403.

'Muscovy as a Hypertrophic State: A Critique', *Kritika* 3 (2002): 501–7.

Hellie, Richard, 'What Happened? How Did he Get away with it? Ivan Groznyi's Paranoia and the Problem of Institutional Restraints', *RH* 14 (1987): 199–224.

(ed.), *Ivan the Terrible: a Quarcentenary Celebration of his Death* = *RH* 14 (1987).

'Zemskii sobor', in *MERSH*, ed. Joseph L. Wieczynski, vol. XLV (Gulf Breeze, Fla.: Academic International Press, 1987), pp. 226–34.

'Thoughts on the Absence of Elite Resistance in Muscovy', *Kritika* 1 (2001): 5–20.

Hulbert, Ellerd, 'Sixteenth-Century Russian Assemblies of the Land: Their Composition, Organization, and Competence', unpublished Ph.D. dissertation, University of Chicago, 1970.

Hunt, Priscilla, 'Ivan IV's Personal Mythology of Kingship', *SR* 52 (1993): 769–809.

Ianov, Aleksandr, *Rossiia: U istokov tragedii 1462–1584* (Moscow: Progress, 2001).

Istoriia narodov Severnogo Kavkaza s drevneishikh vremen do kontsa XVIII v., ed. B. B. Piotrovskii (Moscow: Nauka, 1988).

Istoriia Sibiri, 5 vols. (Leningrad: Nauka, 1968).

Istoriia Urala s drevneishikh vremen do 1861 g. (Moscow: Nauka, 1989).

Iurganov, A. L., 'Staritskii miatezh', *VI*, 1985, no. 2: 100–10.

'Politicheskaia bor'ba v 30-e gg. XVI veka', *Istoriia SSSR*, 1988, no. 2: 101–12.

'Oprichnina i strashnyi sud', *Otechestvennaia istoriia*, 1997, no. 3: 52–75.

Iuzefovich, L. A., *'Kak v posol'skikh obychaiakh vedetsia . . .'* (Moscow: Mezhdunarodnye otnosheniia, 1988).

Kämpfer, Frank and Frötschner, Reinhard (eds.), *450 Jahre Sigismund von Herbersteins Rerum Moscoviticarum Commentarii 1549–1999* (Schriften zur Geistesgeschichte des östlichen Europa, vol. 24) (Wiesbaden: Harrassowitz Verlag, 2002).

Kappeler, Andreas, *The Russian Empire: A Multiethnic History*, trans. Alfred Clayton (Harlow: Longman, 2001).

Kashtanov, S. M., *Sotsial'no-politicheskaia istoriia Rossiia, kontsa XV–pervoi poloviny XVI veka* (Moscow: Nauka, 1967).

Kavel'makher, V. V., 'Gosudarev dvor v Aleksandrovskoi slobode. Opyt rekonstruktsii', in Iakob Ul'feldt, *Puteshestvie v Rossiiu*, ed. Dzh. Lind and A. L. Khoroshkevich (Moscow: Iazyki slavianskoi kul'tury, 2002), pp. 457–87.

Keenan, Edward L., 'Muscovy and Kazan, 1445–1552: A Study in Steppe Politics', unpublished Ph.D. dissertation, Harvard University, 1965.

'The *Jarlyk* of Axmed-Xan to Ivan III: A New Reading', *International Journal of Slavic Linguistics and Poetics* 12 (1969): 33–47.

The Kurbskii–Groznyi Apocrypha: The Seventeenth-Century Genesis of the 'Correspondence' Attributed to Prince A. M. Kurbskii and Tsar Ivan IV, with an appendix by Daniel C. Waugh (Cambridge, Mass.: Harvard University Press, 1971).

'Putting Kurbskii in his Place, or: Observations and Suggestions Concerning the Place of the *History of the Grand Prince of Muscovy* in the History of Muscovite Literary Culture', *FOG* 24 (1978): 131–61.

'Muscovite Political Folkways', *RR* 45 (1986): 115–81.

'Response to Halperin, "Edward Keenan and the Kurbskii–Groznyi Correspondence in Hindsight" ', *JGO* 46 (1998): 404–15.

Kennedy, Craig Gayen, 'The Juchids of Muscovy: A Study of Personal Ties between Émigré Tatar Dynasts and the Muscovite Grand Princes in the Fifteenth and Sixteenth Centuries', unpublished Ph.D. dissertation, Harvard University, 1994 (Ann Arbor: UMI, 1994, AAT 9520971).

Khodarkovsky, Michael, 'Of Christianity, Enlightenment, and Colonialism: Russia in the North Caucasus, 1500–1800', *Journal of Modern History* 71 (1999): 394–430.

Russia's Steppe Frontier: The Making of a Colonial Empire, 1500–1800 (Bloomington: Indiana University Press, 2002).

Khoroshkevich, A. L., 'Tsarskii titul Ivana IV i boiarskii "miatezh" 1553 goda', *Otechestvennaia istoriia*, 1994, no. 3: 23–42.

Rossiia v sisteme mezhdunarodnykh otnoshenii serediny XVI veka (Moscow: Drevlekhranil-ishche, 2003).

Khudiakov, M., *Ocherki po istorii Kazanskogo khanstva* (Kazan': Gosudarstvennoe izdatel'stvo, 1923; reprinted Kazan': Fond TIAK, 1990).

Kivelson, Valerie A., 'Muscovite "Citizenship": Rights without Freedom', *Journal of Modern History* 74 (2002): 465–89.

'On Words, Sources, and Historical Method: Which Truth about Muscovy?', *Kritika* 3 (2002), 487–99.

Kleimola, Ann M., 'Status, Place, and Politics: The Rise of mestnichestvo during the boiarskoe pravlenie', *FOG* 27 (1980): 195–214.

Kliuchevskii, V. O., 'Kurs russkoi istorii', in his *Sochineniia*, 8 vols. (Moscow, 1956–9), vol. III (Gosudarstvennoe Izdatel'stvo politicheskoi literatury, 1957).

'Sostav predstavitel'stva na zemskikh soborakh drevnei Rusi', in his *Sochineniia*, 8 vols. (Moscow, 1956–9), vol. VIII (Izdatel'stvo sotsial'no-ekonomicheskoi literatury, 1959), pp. 5–112.

Kollmann, Nancy Shields, 'Consensus Politics: The Dynastic Crisis of the 1490s Reconsid-ered', *RR* 45 (1986): 235–67.

'The Grand Prince in Muscovite Politics: The Problem of Genre in Sources on Ivan's Minority', *RH* 14 (1987): 293–313.

'Convergence, Expansion and Experimentation: Current Trends in Muscovite History-Writing', *Kritika* 2 (2001): 233–40.

Kosheleva, O., and Strucheva, M. A., *Gosudarev dvor v Rossii: konets XV–nachalo XVIII vv.: kata-log knizhnoi vystavki* (Moscow: Gosudarstvennaia publichnaia istoricheskaia biblioteka Rossii, 1997).

Kostomarov, N. I., 'Boris Godunov', in his *Russkaia istoriia v zhizneopisaniiakh ee glavneishikh deiatelei*, 3 vols. (St Petersburg: Tipografiia M. Stasiulevicha, 1873–88; reprinted Moscow: Kniga, 1990), vol. I, pp. 563–609.

Krom, M. M., 'Sud'ba regentskogo soveta pri maloletnem Ivane IV. Novye dannye o vnutripoliticheskoi bor'be kontsa 1533–1534 goda', *Otechestvennaia istoriia*, 1996, no. 5: 34–49.

'Politicheskii krizis 30–40kh godov XVI veka. Postanovka problemy', *Otechestvennaia istoriia* 1998, no. 5: 3–19.

Kusheva, E. I., 'Politika russkogo gosudarstva na Severnom Kavkaze v 1552–1572 gg.', *IZ* 34 (1950): 236–87.

Latkin, V. N., *Zemskie sobory drevnei Rusi* (St Petersburg: Izdatel'stvo L.F. Panteleeva, 1885).

Lenhoff, Gail, and Martin, Janet, 'Marfa Boretskaia, *posadnitsa* of Novgorod: A Reconsid-eration of her Legend and her Life', *SR* 59 (2000): 343–68.

Liubomirov, P.G., *Ocherk istorii Nizhegorodskogo opolcheniia 1611–1613 gg.*, rev. edn (Moscow: Gosudarstvennoe sotsial'no-ekonomicheskoe izdatel'stvo, 1939).

Loparev, Kh., 'O chine venchaniia russkikh tsarei', *Zhurnal Ministerstva Narodnogo Prosveshcheniia* (October 1887): 312–19.

Majeska, George P., 'The Moscow Coronation of 1498 Reconsidered', *JGO* 26 (1978): 353–61.

Markevich, A. I., *Istoriia mestnichestva v moskovskom gosudarstve v XV–XVII veke* (Odessa: Tipografiia Odesskogo Vestnika, 1888).

Martin, Janet, 'Muscovite Relations with the Khanate of Kazan' and the Crimea (1460s to 1521)', *CASS* 17 (1983): 435–53.

'Russian Expansion in the Far North', in Michael Rywkin (ed.), *Russian Colonial Expansion to 1917* (London: Mansell Publishing, 1988), pp. 35–48.

'The Novokshcheny of Novgorod: Assimilation in the Sixteenth Century', *Central Asian Survey* 9 (1990): 13–38.

'Muscovite Frontier Policy: The Case of the Khanate of Kasimov', *RH* 19 (1992): 169–79.

Medieval Russia, 980–1584 (Cambridge: Cambridge University Press, 1995).

'Tatars in the Muscovite Army during the Livonian War', in Eric Lohr and Marshall Poe (eds.), *The Military and Society in Russia, 1450–1917* (Leiden: Brill, 2002), pp. 365–87.

Martin, Russell E. 'Dynastic Marriage in Muscovy, 1500–1729', unpublished Ph.D. dissertation, Harvard University, 1996.

Miller, David B., 'The Coronation of Ivan IV of Moscow', *JGO* 15 (1967): 559–74.

'The Velikie Minei Chetii and the Stepennaia Kniga of Metropolitan Makarii and the Origins of Russian National Consciousness', *FOG* 26 (1979): 263–382.

'Creating Legitimacy: Ritual, Ideology, and Power in Sixteenth-Century Russia', *RH* 21 (1994): 289–315.

Mordovina, S.P., 'Kharakter dvorianskogo predstavitel'stva na zemskom sobore 1598 g.', *VI*, 1971, no.2: 55–63.

Morozova, L. E., 'Fedor Ivanovich', *VI*, 1997, no. 2: 49–71.

'Boris Fedorovich Godunov', *VI*, 1998, no. 1: 59–81.

Narody Sibiri, ed. M. G. Levina and L. P. Potapova (Moscow: AN SSSR, 1956).

Nosov, N. E., *Ocherki po istorii mestnogo upravleniia Russkogo gosudarstva pervoi poloviny XVI veka* (Moscow and Leningrad: AN SSSR, 1957).

Stanovlenie soslovno-predstavitel'nykh uchrezhdenii v Rossii. Izyskaniia o zemskoi reforme Ivana Groznogo (Leningrad: Nauka, Leningradskoe otdelenie, 1969).

Ocherki istorii SSSR. Period feodalizma. Konets XV v.–nachalo XVII v. (Moscow: AN SSSR, 1955).

Ostrowski, Donald, 'The Extraordinary Career of Tsarevich Kudai Kul/Peter in the Context of Relations between Muscovy and Kazan'', in Janusz Duzinkiewicz, Myroslav Popovych, Vladyslav Verstiuk and Natalia Yakovenko (eds.), *States, Societies, Cultures: East and West. Essays in Honor of Jaroslaw Pelenski* (New York: Ross Publishing, 2004), pp. 697–719.

Pashkova, T. I., *Mestnoe upravlenie v Russkom gosudarstve v pervoi polovine XVI v. Namestniki i volosteli* (Moscow: Drevlekhranilishche, 2000).

Pavlov, A.P., 'Sobornaia utverzhdennaia gramota ob izbranii Borisa Godunova na prestol', *Vspomogatel'nye istoricheskie distsipliny* 10 (1978): 206–25.

'Prikazy i prikaznaia biurokratiia (1584–1605 gg.)', *IZ* 116 (1988): 187–227.

Gosudarev dvor i politicheskaia bor'ba pri Borise Godunove (1584–1605 gg.) (St Petersburg: Nauka, 1992).

and Perrie, Maureen, *Ivan the Terrible* (Harlow: Longman, 2003).

Pelenski, Jaroslaw, *Russia and Kazan: Conquest and Imperial Ideology (1438–1560s)* (The Hague, Paris: Mouton, 1974).

'The Origins of the Official Muscovite Claims to the "Kievan Inheritance"', *HUS* 1 (1977): 29–52.

Perrie, Maureen, ' "Popular Socio-Utopian Legends" in the Time of Troubles', *SEER* 60 (1982): 223–43.

The Image of Ivan the Terrible in Russian Folklore (Cambridge: Cambridge University Press, 1987; paperback edn, 2002).

Pretenders and Popular Monarchism in Early Modern Russia: The False Tsars of the Time of Troubles (Cambridge: Cambridge University Press, 1995; paperback edn, 2002).

The Cult of Ivan the Terrible in Stalin's Russia (Houndmills: Palgrave, 2001).

Pipes, Richard, *Russia under the Old Regime* (Harmondsworth: Penguin Books, 1977).

Platonov, S. F., *Drevnerusskie skazaniia i povesti o Smutnom vremeni XVII v. kak istoricheskii istochnik* (St Petersburg: Tipografiia V. S. Balasheva, 1888; 2nd edn, St Petersburg: Tipografiia M.A. Aleksandrova, 1913).

Boris Godunov (Petrograd: Ogni, 1921).

The Time of Troubles, trans. J. T. Alexander (Lawrence: University of Kansas Press, 1970).

Boris Godunov, Tsar of Russia, trans. L. Rex Pyles, ed. J. T. Alexander (Gulf Breeze, Fla.: Academic International Press, 1972).

Ivan the Terrible, ed. and trans. Joseph L. Wieczynski, with 'In Search of Ivan the Terrible', by Richard Hellie (Gulf Breeze, Fla.: Academic International Press, 1974).

Ocherki po istorii Smuty v Moskovskom gosudarstve XVI–XVII vv., 5th edn (Moscow: Pamiatniki istoricheskoi mysli, 1995).

Pliukhanova, M.B., *Siuzhety i simvoly Moskovskogo tsarstva* (St Petersburg: Akropol', 1995).

Poe, Marshall, 'The Truth about Muscovy', *Kritika* 3 (2002): 473–86.

Polosin, I. I., *Sotsial'no-politicheskaia istoriia Rossii XVI–nachala XVII v.* (Moscow: AN SSSR, 1963).

'Uglichskoe sledstvennoe delo 1591 g.', in his *Sotsial'no-politicheskaia istoriia Rossii XVI–nachala XVII v.* (Moscow: AN SSSR, 1963), pp. 218–45.

Pouncy, Carolyn Johnston, ' "The blessed Sil'vestr" and the Politics of Invention in Muscovy, 1545–1700', *HUS* 19 (1995): 548–72.

Raba, Joel, 'The Moscow Kremlin: Mirror of the Newborn Muscovite State', *Slavic and Soviet* series 1, no. 2(1976): 3–49 plus map.

Rasmussen, Knud, 'On the Information Level of the Muscovite Posol'skij prikaz in the Sixteenth Century', *FOG* 24 (1978): 87–99.

Rowland, Daniel, 'The Problem of Advice in Muscovite Tales about the Time of Troubles', *RH* 6 (1979): 259–83.

'Did Muscovite Literary Ideology Place Limits on the Power of the Tsar, 1540s–1660s?', *RR* 49 (1990): 125–55.

'Ivan the Terrible as a Carolingian Renaissance Prince', *HUS* 19 (1995): 594–606.

'Moscow – the Third Rome or the New Israel?', *RR* 55 (1996): 591–614.

Sadikov, P. A., 'Pokhod tatar i turok na Astrakhan' v 1569 g.', *IZ* 22 (1947): 132–66.

Sanin, G. A. et al. (eds.), *Istoriia vneshnei politiki Rossii: Konets XV–XVII vek* (Moscow: Mezhdunarodnye otnosheniia, 1999).

Ševčenko, Ihor, 'A Neglected Byzantine Source of Muscovite Political Ideology', *Harvard Slavic Studies* 2 (1954): 141–79; reprinted in Michael Cherniavsky (ed.), *The Structure of Russian History. Interpretive Essays* (New York: Random House, 1970), pp. 80–107; and in Ihor Ševčenko, *Byzantium and the Slavs in Letters and Culture* (Cambridge, Mass.: Harvard Ukrainian Research Institute, 1991), pp. 49–87.

Shmidt, S. O., *U istokov rossiiskogo absoliutizma. Issledovanie sotsial'no-politicheskoi istorii vremeni Ivana Groznogo* (Moscow: Progress, 1996).

'Mitropolit Makarii i pravitel'stvennaia deiatel'nost' ego vremeni', in S. O. Shmidt, *Rossiia Ivana Groznogo* (Moscow: Nauka, 1999), pp. 239–45.

Rossiia Ivana Groznogo (Moscow: Nauka, 1999).

Skrynnikov, R. G., 'Zemskii sobor 1598 goda i izbranie Borisa Godunova na tron', *Istoriia SSSR*, 1977, no. 3: 141–57.

Ivan the Terrible, ed. and trans. Hugh F. Graham (Gulf Breeze, Fla.: Academic International Press, 1981).

Rossiia nakanune 'Smutnogo vremeni' (Moscow: Mysl', 1981).

Boris Godunov, ed. and trans. Hugh F. Graham (Gulf Breeze, Fla.: Academic International Press, 1982).

Boris Godunov (Moscow: Nauka, 1978; 3rd edn, 1983).

Sotsial'no-politicheskaia bor'ba v Russkom gosudarstve v nachale XVII veka (Leningrad: Izdatel'stvo Leningradskogo Universiteta, 1985).

Rossiia v nachale XVII v. Smuta (Moscow: Mysl', 1988).

Smuta v Rossii v nachale XVII v. Ivan Bolotnikov (Leningrad: Nauka, 1988).

The Time of Troubles. Russia in Crisis, 1604–1618, ed. and trans. Hugh F. Graham (Gulf Breeze, Fla: Academic International Press, 1988).

Samozvantsy v Rossii v nachale XVII veka: Grigorii Otrep'ev (Novosibirsk: Nauka, 1987; 2nd edn, Novosibirsk: Nauka, 1990).

Tsarstvo terrora (St Petersburg: Nauka, 1992).

'The Civil War in Russia at the Beginning of the Seventeenth Century (1603–1607): Its Character and Motive Forces', in Lindsey Hughes (ed.), *New Perspectives on Muscovite History* (London: Macmillan, 1993), pp. 61–79.

Tragediia Novgoroda (Moscow: Izdatel'stvo imeni Sabashnikovykh, 1994).

Smirnov, I. I., *Vosstanie Bolotnikova* (Leningrad: Gosudarstvennoe Izdatel'stvo politicheskoi literatury, 1951).

Ocherki politicheskoi istorii Russkogo gosudarstva 30–50kh godov XVI veka (Moscow and Leningrad: AN SSSR, 1958).

Stanislavskii, A. L., 'Opyt izucheniia boiarskikh spiskov kontsa XVI–nachala XVII v.', *Istoriia SSSR*, 1971, no. 4: 97–110.

Grazhdanskaia voina v Rossii XVII v. Kazachestvo na perelome istorii (Moscow: Mysl', 1990).

Stevens, Carol B., 'Banditry and Provincial Order in Sixteenth-Century Russia', in Ann M. Kleimola and Gail D. Lenhoff (eds.), *Culture and Identity in Muscovy, 1359–1584* (Moscow: ITZ-Garant, 1997), pp. 578–99.

Syroechkovskii, V. E., 'Puti i usloviia snoshenii Moskvy s Krymom na rubezhe XVI veka', *Izvestiia AN SSSR. Otdelenie obshchestvennykh nauk* 3 (1932): 193–237.

Szvák, Gyula (ed.), *Muscovy: Peculiarities of its Development* (Budapest: Magyar Ruszisztikai Intézet, 2003).

Tikhomirov, M. N., *Rossiia v XVI veke* (Moscow: AN SSSR, 1962).

Tiumentsev, I. O., *Smuta v Rossii v nachale XVII stoletiia: dvizhenie Lzhedmitriia II* (Volgograd: Volgogradskii Gosudarstvennyi Universitet, 1999).

Trepavlov, V. V., *Istoriia Nogaiskoi Ordy* (Moscow: Vostochnaia literatura, 2001).

Ul'ianovskii, V. I., *Rossiiskie samozvantsy: Lzhedmitrii I* (Kiev: Libid', 1993).

Uspenskii, B. A., 'Vospriiatie istorii v Drevnei Rusi i doktrina "Moskva – Tretii Rim"', in B. V. Raushenbakh (ed.), *Russkoe podvizhnichestvo* (Moscow: Nauka, 1996), pp. 464–501.

Vel'iaminov-Zernov, V. V., *Issledovanie o Kasimovskikh tsariakh i tsarevichakh*, 4 vols. (St Petersburg: Imperatorskaia Akademiia Nauk, 1863–87), vol. 1 (1863).

Vernadskii, V. N., *Novgorod i Novgorodskaia zemlia v XV veke* (Moscow and Leningrad: AN SSSR, 1961).

Vernadsky, George, *Russia at the Dawn of the Modern Age* (*A History of Russia*, vol. IV) (New Haven: Yale University Press, 1959).

Veselovskii, S. B., *D'iaki i pod'iachie XV–XVII vv.* (Moscow: Nauka, 1975).

Videkind, Iukhan [Johann Widekind], *Istoriia desiatiletnei shvedsko-moskovitskoi voiny* (Moscow: Pamiatniki istoricheskoi mysli, 2000).

Zharinov, G. V., 'O proiskhozhdenii tak nazyvaemoi "Opisi domashnemu imushchestvu tsaria Ivana Vasil'evicha . . ."', *Arkhiv russkoi istorii* 2 (Moscow: Roskomarkhiv, 1992): 179–85.

Zimin, A. A., 'O politicheskoi doktrine Iosifa Volotskogo', *TODRL* 9 (1953): 159–177.

'Nekotorye voprosy istorii krest'ianskoi voiny v Rossii v nachale XVII veka', *VI*, 1958, no. 3: 97–113.

Reformy Ivana Groznogo (Moscow: Izdatel'stvo sotsial'no-ekonomicheskoi literatury, 1960).

'Ivan Groznyi i Simeon Bekbulatovich v 1575 g.', *Uchenye zapiski Kazanskogo gosudarstvennogo pedagogicheskogo universiteta* 80: Iz istorii Tatari 4 (1970): 141–63.

Rossiia na poroge novogo vremeni (Ocherki politicheskoi istorii Rossii pervoi treti XVI v.) (Moscow: Mysl', 1972).

Rossiia na rubezhe XV–XVI stoletii (Ocherk sotsial'no-politicheskoi istorii) (Moscow: Mysl', 1982).

V kanun groznykh potriasenii. Predposylki pervoi krest'ianskoi voiny v Rossii (Moscow: Mysl', 1986).

Oprichnina (Moscow: Territoriia, 2001).

(c) 1613–89

Aleksandrov, V. A., and Pokrovskii, N. N., *Vlast' i obshchestvo: Sibir' v XVII v.* (Novosibirsk: Nauka, 1991).

Avrich, Paul, *Russian Rebels 1600–1800* (London: Allen Lane The Penguin Press, 1973).

Bakhrushin, S. V., 'Moskovskoe vosstanie 1648 g.', in his *Nauchnye trudy*, 4 vols. (Moscow: AN SSSR, 1952–9), vol. II (1954), pp. 46–91.

'Iasak v Sibiri v XVII v.', in his *Nauchnye trudy*, 4 vols. (Moscow: AN SSSR, 1952–9), vol. III, pt. 2 (1955), pp. 49–85.

'Ocherki po istorii krasnoiarskogo uezda v XVII v.', in his *Nauchnye trudy*, 4 vols. (Moscow: AN SSSR, 1952–9), vol. IV (1959), pp. 7–192.

Bogoiavlenskii, S. K., 'Prikaznye d'iaki XVII veka', *IZ* 1 (1937): 220–39.

Prikaznye sud'i XVII veka (Moscow and Leningrad: AN SSSR, 1946).

Bogoslovskii, M. M., *Zemskoe samoupravlenie na russkom severe v XVII veke*, ChOIDR, 1910, no. 232, kn. 1, pp. i–viii, 321 pp. and 105 pp. of addenda and 1912, no. 214, kn. 2, pp. i–iv, 311 pp.

Brown, Peter B., 'Early Modern Russian Bureaucracy: The Evolution of the Chancellery System from Ivan III to Peter the Great, 1478–1717', unpublished Ph.D. dissertation, University of Chicago, 1978.

'Muscovite Government Bureaus', RH 10 (1983): 269–330.

'The *Zemskii Sobor* in Recent Soviet Historiography', RH 10 (1983): 77–90.

'Bureaucratic Administration in Seventeenth-Century Russia', in J. Kotilaine and M. Poe (eds.), *Modernizing Muscovy: Reform and Social Change in Seventeenth-Century Russia* (London: RoutledgeCurzon, 2004), pp. 57–78.

Buganov, V. I., *Moskovskoe vosstanie 1662 g.* (Moscow: Nauka, 1964).

Moskovskie vosstaniia kontsa XVII veka (Moscow: Nauka, 1969).

Mir istorii. Rossiia v XVII stoletii (Moscow: Molodaia gvardiia, 1989).

Bushkovitch, Paul, *Peter the Great: the Struggle for Power, 1671–1725* (Cambridge and New York: Cambridge University Press, 2001).

Campbell, Ira L., 'The Composition, Character and Competence of the Assembly of the Land in Seventeenth-Century Russia', unpublished Ph.D. dissertation, University of Illinois, 1984.

Chernov, A. V., *Vooruzhennye sily Russkogo gosudarstva* (Moscow: Ministerstvo oborony SSSR, 1954).

Chicherin, B. N., *Oblastnye uchrezhdeniia Rossii v XVII veke* (Moscow: Tipografiia Aleksandra Semena, 1856).

Chistiakova, E.V., *Gorodskie vosstaniia v Rossii v pervoi polovine XVII veka (30–40-e gody)* (Voronezh: Izdatel'stvo Voronezhskogo universiteta, 1975).

and Solov'ev, V. M., *Stepan Razin i ego soratniki* (Moscow: Mysl', 1988).

Crummey, Robert O., 'The Origins of the Noble Official: The Boyar Elite, 1613–1689', in D. K. Rowney and W. M. Pintner (eds.), *Russian Officialdom: The Bureaucratization of Russian Society from the Seventeenth to the Twentieth Century* (Chapel Hill: University of North Carolina Press, 1980), pp. 46–75.

Aristocrats and Servitors: the Boyar Elite in Russia, 1613–1689 (Princeton: Princeton University Press, 1983).

'Court Spectacles in Seventeenth-Century Russia: Illusion and Reality', in Daniel C. Waugh (ed.), *Essays in Honor of A. A. Zimin* (Columbus, Oh.: Slavica Publishers, 1985), pp. 130–58.

'Muscovy and the "General Crisis of the Seventeenth Century" ', *Journal of Early Modern History* 2 (1998): 156–80.

'Seventeenth-Century Russia: Theories and Models', FOG 56 (2000): 113–31.

Holm Sundhaussen and Ricarda Vulpius (eds.), *Russische und Ukrainische Geschichte vom. 16. bis zum 18. Jahrhundert* = FOG 58 (2001).

Davies, Brian, 'The Role of the Town Governors in the Defense and Military Colonization of Muscovy's Southern Frontier: The Case of Kozlov, 1635–38' 2 vols., unpublished Ph.D. dissertation, University of Chicago, 1983.

'The Second Chigirin Campaign (1678): Late Muscovite Military Power in Transition', in Eric Lohr and Marshall Poe (eds.), *The Military and Society in Russia, 1450–1917* (Leiden: E. J. Brill, 2002), pp. 97–118.

State Power and Community in Early Modern Russia: The Case of Kozlov, 1635–1649 (Houndmills and New York: Palgrave Macmillan, 2004).

Demidova, N. F., 'Biurokratizatsiia gosudarstvennogo apparata absoliutizma v XVII–XVIII vv.', in N. M. Druzhinin (ed.), *Absoliutizm v Rossii (XVII–XVIII vv. Sbornik statei k semidesiatiletiiu so dnia rozhdeniia i sorokapiatiletiiu nauchnoi i pedagogicheskoi deiatel'nosti B. B. Kafengauza* (Moscow: Nauka, 1964), pp. 206–42.

'Prikaznye liudi XVII v. (Sotsial'nyi sostav i istochniki formirovaniia)', *IZ* 90 (1972): 332–54.

'Gosudarstvennyi apparat Rossii v XVII veke', *IZ* 108 (1982): 109–54.

Sluzhilaia biurokratiia v Rossii XVII v. i ee rol' v formirovanii absoliutizma (Moscow: Nauka, 1987).

Dukes, Paul, *The Making of Russian Absolutism, 1613–1801* (London and New York: Longman, 1982; 2nd edn 1990).

Epstein, Fritz T., 'Die Hof- und Zentralverwaltung im Moskauer Staat und die Bedeutung von G. K. Kotošichins zeitgenoessischem Werk "Über Russland unter der Herrschaft des Zaren Aleksej Michajlovic" für die russische Verwaltungsgeschichte', *Hamburger Historische Studien* 7 (1978): 1–228.

Eroshkin, N. P., *Ocherki istorii gosudarstvennykh uchrezhdenii dorevoliutsionnoi Rossii* (Moscow: Gosudarstvennoe Uchebno-Pedagogicheskoe izdatel'stvo Ministerstva prosveshcheniia RSFSR, 1960).

Flier, Michael S., 'Court Ceremony in an Age of Reform: Patriarch Nikon and the Palm Sunday Ritual', in Samuel H. Baron and Nancy Shields Kollmann (eds.), *Religion and Culture in Early Modern Russia and Ukraine* (DeKalb: Northern Illinois University Press, 1997), pp. 73–95.

Fuller, William C., Jr., *Strategy and Power in Russia, 1600–1914* (New York: Free Press, 1992).

Gorobets, V., 'Ukrainsko-rossiiskie otnosheniia v politiko-pravovoi status getmanshchiny', in A. I. Miller et al. (eds.), *Rossiia-Ukraina: istoriia vzaimootnoshenii* (Moscow: Iazyki mirovoi kul'tury, 1997), pp. 8–11.

Hatton, Ragnhild Marie, 'Russia and the Baltic', in Taras Hunczak (ed.), *Russian Imperialism from Ivan the Great to the Revolution* (New Brunswick, N. J.: Rutgers University Press, 1974), pp. 106–30.

Hellie, Richard, 'The Expanding Role of the State in Russia', in Jarmo T. Kotilaine and Marshall T. Poe (eds.), *Modernizing Muscovy: Reform and Social Change in Seventeenth-Century Russia* (London: Routledge, 2003), pp. 29–56.

Hosking, Geoffrey, *Russia: People and Empire 1552–1917* (London: HarperCollins, 1997).

Hrushevsky, Mykhailo, *History of Ukraine-Rus'*. Vol. VIII: *The Cossack Age, 1626–1650* (Edmonton: Canadian Institute of Ukrainian Studies, 2002).

Hughes, Lindsey, *Russia and the West, the Life of a Seventeenth-Century Westernizer, Prince V. V. Golitsyn (1643–1714)* (Newtonville, Mass.: ORP, 1984).

'Sophia, "Autocrat of All the Russias": Titles, Ritual and Eulogy in the Regency of Sophia Alekseevna (1682–89)', *Canadian Slavonic Papers* 28 (1986): 266–86.

Sophia, Regent of Russia, 1657–1704 (New Haven: Yale University Press, 1990).

Russia in the Age of Peter the Great (New Haven: Yale University Press, 1998).

'The Courts of Moscow and St Petersburg, c. 1547–1725', in John Adamson (ed.), *The Princely Courts of Europe 1500–1750* (London: Weidenfeld and Nicolson, 1999), pp. 294–313.

Peter the Great: A Biography (New Haven: Yale University Press, 2002).

Huttenbach, Henry, 'The Ukraine and Muscovite Expansion', in Taras Hunczak (ed.), *Russian Imperialism from Ivan the Great to the Revolution* (New Brunswick, N. J.: Rutgers University Press, 1974), pp. 167–97.

Ingerflom, C. S., 'Entre le mythe et la parole: l'action. Naissance de la conception politique du pouvoir en Russie', *Annales: histoire, sciences sociales* 51 (1996): 733–57.

Istoriia narodov Severnogo Kavkaza s drevneishikh vremen do kontsa XVIII v., ed. B. B. Piotrovskii (Moscow: Nauka, 1988).

Ivanov, P., *Opisanie gosudarstvennogo razriadnogo arkhiva* (Moscow: Tipografiia S. Silivanovskogo, 1842).

Kaminski, Andrzej Sulima, *Republic vs. Autocracy. Poland-Lithuania and Russia, 1686–1697* (Cambridge, Mass.: Harvard Ukrainian Research Institute, 1993).

Keep, J. L. H., *Soldiers of the Tsar: Army and Society in Russia, 1462–1874* (Oxford: Clarendon Press, 1985).

Khodarkovsky, Michael, *Where Two Worlds Met: The Russian State and the Kalmyk Nomads, 1600–1771* (Ithaca, N.Y.: Cornell University Press, 1992).

'The Stepan Razin Uprising: Was it a "Peasant War"?', *JGO* 42 (1994): 1–19.

Kivelson, Valerie A., 'The Devil Stole his Mind: The Tsar and the 1648 Moscow Uprising', *American Historical Review*, 98 (1993): 733–56.

Autocracy in the Provinces: The Muscovite Gentry and Political Culture in the Seventeenth Century (Stanford, Calif.: Stanford University Press, 1996).

Kliuchevskii, V. O., *A Course in Russian History: The Seventeenth Century* (Chicago: Quadrangle Books, 1968).

Boiarskaia duma drevnei Rusi. Opyt istorii pravitel'stvennogo uchrezhdeniia v sviazi s istoriei obshchestva, 3rd edn. (Moscow: Sinodal'naia tipografiia, 1902).

Kollmann, Nancy Shields, 'Ritual and Social Drama at the Muscovite Court', *SR* 45 (1986): 486–502.

Kostomarov, N. I., *Kazaki: istoricheskie monografii i issledovaniia* (Moscow: Charli, 1995).

Ruina. Mazepa. Mazepintsy (Moscow: Charli, 1995).

Kotilaine, Jarmo T., and Poe, Marshall T. (eds.), *Modernizing Muscovy: Reform and Social Change in Seventeenth-Century Russia* (London: RoutledgeCurzon, 2004).

Kozliakov, V. N., *Sluzhilyi gorod Moskovskogo gosudarstva XVII veka* (Iaroslavl': Iaroslavskii Gosudarstvennyi Pedagogicheskii Institut, 2000).

Krest'ianskie voiny v Rossii XVII–XVIII vekov: problemy, poiski, resheniia (Moscow: Nauka, 1974).

Kristensen [Christensen], Svend A., *Istoriia rossii XVII v. Obzor issledovanii i istochnikov* (Moscow: Progress, 1989).

Lantzeff, George V., *Siberia in the Seventeenth Century* (Berkeley: University of California Press, 1943).

and Pierce, Richard, *Eastward to Empire: Exploration and Conquest on the Russian Open Frontier, to 1750* (Montreal: McGill–Queen's University Press, 1973).

Lapman, Mark C., 'Political Denunciations in Muscovy, 1600 to 1649: The Sovereign's Word and Deed', unpublished Ph.D. dissertation, Harvard University, 1982.

Leont'ev, A. K., *Obrazovanie prikaznoi sistemy upravleniia v moskovskom gosudarstve* (Moscow: MGU, 1961).

Litavrin, G. G. (ed.), *Osmanskaia imperiia i strany Tsentral'noi, Vostochnoi i Iugo-Vostochnoi Evropy v XVII v.* (Moscow: Pamiatniki istoricheskoi mysli, 2001).

Longworth, Philip, *Alexis, Tsar of All the Russias* (London: Secker and Warburg, 1984).

Lukin, P. V., *Narodnye predstavleniia o gosudarstvennoi vlasti v Rossii XVII veka* (Moscow: Nauka, 2000).

Mal'tsev, A. N., *Rossiia i Belorussiia v seredine XVII veka* (Moscow: MGU, 1974).

Mousnier, Roland, *Peasant Uprisings in Seventeenth-Century France, Russia and China* (London: George Allen and Unwin, 1971).

Nazarov, V., 'The Peasant Wars in Russia and their Place in the History of the Class Struggle in Europe', in *The Comparative Historical Method in Soviet Mediaeval Studies* (Problems of the Contemporary World, no. 79) (Moscow: USSR Academy of Sciences, 1979), pp. 113–42.

Nikolaev, S. I., 'Poeziia i diplomatiia (iz literaturnoi deiatel'nosti Posol'skogo prikaza v 1670-kh gg.)', *TODRL* 42 (1989): 143–73.

Nikol'skii, V. K., 'Boiarskaia popytka 1681 g.', *Istoricheskie izvestiia izdavaemye Istoricheskim obshchestvom pri Moskovskom universitete* 2 (1917): 57–87.

Novosel'skii, A. A., *Bor'ba Moskovskogo gosudarstva s tatarami v pervoi polovine XVII veka* (Moscow: AN SSSR, 1948).

O'Brien, Bickford, 'Muscovite Prikaz Administration of the Seventeenth Century: The Quality of Leadership', *FOG* 24 (1978): 223–35.

Ocherki po istorii Bashkirskoi ASSR, vol. 1, pt. 1 (Ufa: Bashkirskoe izdatel'stvo, 1956).

Ogloblin, N. N., 'Provintsial'nye arkhivy v XVII veke', *Vestnik arkheologii i istorii, izdavaemyi Arkheologicheskim institutom* 6 (1886): 74–206.

'Obozrenie stolbtsov i knig Sibirskogo prikaza', 4 pts., *ChOIDR* 2 (1895): i–viii + 1–422; 1 (1898): 1–162; 3 (1900): i–iv + 1–394; 1 (1902): 1–288.

Ostrogorsky, G., 'Das Projekt einer Rangtabelle aus der Zeit des Tsaren Fedor Alekseevich', *Jahrbücher für Kultur und Geschichte der Slaven* 9 (1933): 86–138.

Ostrowski, Donald, 'The Assembly of the Land as a Representative Institution', in J. Kotilaine and M. Poe (eds.), *Modernizing Muscovy: Reform and Social Change in Seventeenth-Century Russia* (London: RoutledgeCurzon, 2004), pp. 117–42.

Pavlov, A.P., 'Gosudarev dvor v istorii Rossii XVII veka', *FOG* 56 (2000): 227–42.

Perrie, Maureen, 'Pretenders in the Name of the Tsar: Cossack "Tsareviches" in Seventeenth-Century Russia', *FOG* 56 (2000): 243–56.

[Perri, M.], 'V chem sostoiala "izmena" zhertv narodnykh vosstanii XVII veka?', in I.O. Tiumentsev (ed.), *Rossiia XV–XVIII stoletii. Sbornik nauchnykh statei* (Volgograd and St Petersburg: Volgogradskii Gosudarstvennyi Universitet, 2001), pp. 207–20.

'Indecent, Unseemly and Inappropriate Words: Popular Criticisms of the Tsar, 1648–50', *FOG* 58 (2001): 143–9.

'Popular Monarchism in Mid-17th-Century Russia: The Politics of the "Sovereign's *gramoty*"', in Gyula Szvák (ed.), *Muscovy: Peculiarities of its Development* (Budapest: Magyar Ruszisztikai Intézet, 2003), pp. 135–42.

Platonov, S. F., 'Boiarskaia duma – predshestvennitsa senata', in his *Stat'i po russkoi istorii (1883–1912)*, 2nd edn (St Petersburg: M. A. Aleksandrov, 1912), pp. 447–94.

Plavsic, B., 'Seventeenth-Century Chanceries and their Staffs', in D. K. Rowney and W. M. Pintner (eds.), *Russian Officialdom: The Bureaucratization of Russian Society from the Seventeenth to the Twentieth Century* (Chapel Hill: University of North Carolina Press, 1980), pp. 19–45.

Poe, Marshall T., 'The Consequences of the Military Revolution in Muscovy in Comparative Perspective', *Comparative Studies in Society and History* 38 (1996): 603–18.

'The Imaginary World of Semen Koltovskii: Genealogical Anxiety and Falsification in Seventeenth-Century Russia', *Cahiers du monde russe* 39 (1998): 375–88.

'The Military Revolution, Administrative Development, and Cultural Change in Early Modern Russia', *Journal of Early Modern History* 2 (1998): 247–73.

'What did Russians Mean When They Called Themselves "Slaves of the Tsar"?', *SR* 57 (1998): 585–608.

'Tsar Aleksei Mikhailovich and the Demise of the Romanov Political Settlement', *RR* 62 (2003): 537–64.

The Russian Elite in the Seventeenth Century, 2 vols. (Helsinki: Academia Scientiarum Fennica, 2003).

'Absolutism and the New Men of Seventeenth-Century Russia', in J. Kotilaine and M. T. Poe (eds.), *Modernizing Muscovy: Reform and Social Change in Seventeenth-Century Russia* (London: RoutledgeCurzon, 2004), pp. 97–116.

Pokrovskii, N. N., 'Sibirskie materialy XVII–XVIII vv. po "slovu i delu gosudarevu" kak istochnik po istorii obshchestvennogo soznaniia', in *Istochniki po istorii obshchestvennoi mysli i kul'tury epokhi pozdnego feodalizma* (Novosibirsk: Nauka, 1988), pp. 24–61.

Tomsk 1648–1649 gg.: Voevodskaia vlast' i zemskie miry (Novosibirsk: Nauka, 1989).

Popov, A. N., 'Turetskaia voina v tsarstvovanie Fedora Alekseevicha', *Russkii vestnik* 6 (1857): 145–80; and 7 (1857): 285–328.

Porfir'ev, S. I., *Neskol'ko dannykh o prikaznom upravlenii v Kazani v 1627 g.* (Kazan', 1911).

Porshnev, B. F., 'Sotsial'no-politicheskaia obstanovka v Rossii vo vremia Smolenskoi voiny', *Istoriia SSSR*, 1957, no. 5: 112–40.

'Razvitie "Balashovskogo" dvizheniia v fevrale-marte 1634 g.', in *Problemy obshchestvenno-politicheskoi istorii Rossii i slavianskikh stran. Sbornik statei k 70-letiiu akademika M.N. Tikhomirova* (Moscow: Izdatel'stvo vostochnoi literatury, 1963), pp. 225–35.

Muscovy and Sweden in the Thirty Years' War, 1630–1635, ed. Paul Dukes and trans. Brian Pearce (Cambridge: Cambridge University Press, 1995).

Riabov, S. I., *Voisko Donskoe i rossiiskoe samoderzhavie* (Volgograd: Peremena, 1993).

Samokvasov, D. Ia., *Russkie arkhivy i tsarskii kontrol' prikaznoi sluzhby v XVII veke* (Moscow, 1902).

Sedov, P. V., 'O boiarskoi popytke uchrezhdeniia namestnichestva v Rossii v 1681–82 gg.', *Vestnik LGU* 9 (1985): 25–9.

Smith, A., 'The Brilliant Career of Prince Golitsyn', *HUS* 19 (1995): 639–54.

Solov'ev, V. M., *Sovremenniki i potomki o vosstanii S. T. Razina* (Moscow: Izdatel'stvo Universiteta Druzhby Narodov, 1991).

Stashevskii, E. D., *Smolenskaia voina 1632–1634. Organizatsiia i sostoianie moskovskoi armii* (Kiev, 1919).

Stepanov, I. V., *Krest'ianskaia voina v Rossii v 1670–1671 gg. Vosstanie Stepana Razina*, 2 vols. (Leningrad: Izdatel'stvo Leningradskogo universiteta, 1966–72).

Stevens, Carol Belkin, *Soldiers on the Steppe: Army Reform and Social Change in Early Modern Russia* (De Kalb: Northern Illinois University Press, 1995).

Sysin, Frank E., *Between Poland and the Ukraine. The Dilemma of Adam Kysil, 1600–1653* (Cambridge, Mass.: Harvard University Press, 1985).

Tel'berg, G. G., *Ocherki politicheskogo suda i politicheskikh prestuplenii* (Moscow: Tipografiia Imperatorskogo Moskovskogo Universiteta, 1912).

Tikhomirov, M.N., *Klassovaia bor'ba v Rossii XVII v.* (Moscow: Nauka, 1969).

Torke, Hans-Joachim, *Die staatsbedingte Gesellschaft im Moskauer Reich: Zar und Zemlja in der altrussischen Herrschaftsverfassung 1613–1689* (Leiden: E. J. Brill, 1974).

  (ed.), *Von Moskau nach St. Petersburg. Das russische Reich im 17. Jahrhundert = FOG* 56 (2000).

Uroff, Benjamin P., 'Grigorii Karpovich Kotoshikhin, "On Russia in the Reign of Alexis Mikhailovich": An Annotated Translation', unpublished Ph.D. dissertation, University of Illinois, 1970.

Ustiugov, N. V., 'Evoliutsiia prikaznogo stroia russkogo gosudarstva v XVII v.', in *Absoliutizm v Rossii (XVII–XVIII vv.)* (Moscow: Nauka, 1964), pp. 134–67

Ustrialov, N., *Istoriia tsarstvovaniia Petra Velikogo*, 6 vols. (St Petersburg: Tipografiia II Otdeleniia S.I.V. Kantseliarii, 1858–63).

Verner, I. I., *O vremeni i prichinakh obrazovaniia moskovskikh prikazov*, 2 vols. (Moscow: Universitetskaia tipografiia, 1907–8).

Volkov, M. Ia., 'Ob otmene mestnichestva v Rossii', *Istoriia SSSR*, 1977, no. 2: 53–67.

Wortman, Richard, *Scenarios of Power. Myth and Ceremony in Russian Monarchy*, 2 vols. (Princeton: Princeton University Press, 1995–2000), vol. 1: *From Peter the Great to the Death of Nicholas I.*

Zaborovskii, L. V., *Rossiia, Rech' Pospolitaia, i Shvetsiia v seredine XVII v.* (Moscow: Nauka, 1981).

Zagorovskii, V. P., 'Sudostroenie na Donu i ispol'zovanie Rossieiu parusnogo-grebnogo flota v bor'be protiv Krymskogo khanstva i Turtsii', Kandidatskaia dissertatsiia, Voronezhskii Gosudarstvennyi Universitet, 1961.

Zaruba, V. N., *Ukrainskoe kazatskoe voisko v bor'be s turetskoi-tatarskoi agressiei* (Kharkov: Osnova, 1993).

2. Economic and social history

Agrarnaia istoriia Severo-Zapada Rossii XVI veka: Novgorodskie piatiny (Leningrad: Nauka, 1974).

Aleksandrov, V. A., 'Streletskoe naselenie iuzhnykh gorodov Rossii v XVIIv.', in *Novoe o proshlom nashei strany* (Moscow: Nauka, 1967), pp. 235–50.

et al., *Krest'ianstvo perioda pozdnego feodalizma (seredina XVII v.–1861 g.) (Istoriia krest'ianstva Rossii s drevneishikh vremen do 1917 g.*, vol. III) (Moscow: Nauka, 1993).

Alekseev, Iu. G., *Agrarnaia i sotsial'naia istoriia Severo-Vostochnoi Rusi XV–XVI vv. Pereiaslavskii uezd* (Moscow and Leningrad: Nauka, 1966).

and A. I. Kopanev, 'Razvitie pomestnoi sistemy v XVI v.', in N. I Pavlenko et al. (eds.), *Dvorianstvo i krepostnoi stroi Rossii XVI–XVIII vv. Sbornik statei, posviashchennyi pamiati Alekseia Andreevicha Novosel'skogo* (Moscow: Nauka, 1975), pp. 57–69.

Alexander, John T., *Bubonic Plague in Early Modern Russia: Public Health and Urban Disaster* (Baltimore: Johns Hopkins University Press, 1980).

Alferova, G. V., *Russkii gorod XVI–XVII vekov* (Moscow: Stroiizdat, 1989).

and Kharlamov, V. A., *Kiev vo vtoroi polovine XVII veke* (Kiev: Naukova Dumka, 1982).

The Archaeology of Novgorod, Russia. Recent Results from the Town and its Hinterland (Lincoln, Nebr.: Society for Medieval Archaeology, 1992).

Arkheologicheskoe izuchenie Novgoroda. Sbornik statei (Moscow: Nauka, 1978).

Attman, Artur, 'The Russian Market in World Trade, 1500–1800', *Scandinavian Economic History Review* 29 (1981): 177–202.

Avdusin, D. A. (ed.), *Smolensk i Gnezdovo (k istorii drevnerusskogo goroda)* (Moscow: Moskovskii Universitet, 1991).

and Pushkina, T. A., 'Three Chamber-Graves at Gnezdovo', *Fornvännen* 83 (1988): 20–33.

Bagalei, D. I., *Ocherki iz istorii kolonizatsii i byta stepnoi okrainy Moskovskogo gosudarstva* (Moscow, 1887).

Baranov, D. A., et al., *Russkaia izba. Illiustrirovannaia entsiklopediia. Vnutrennee prostranstvo izby. Mebel' i ubranstvo izby. Domashniaia i khoziaistvennaia utvar'* (St Petersburg: Iskusstvo, 1999).

Barashkov, Iu.A., *Arkhangel'sk: arkhitekturnaia biografiia* (Arkhangel'sk: Severo-Zapadnoe knizhnoe izdatel'stvo, 1984).

Baron, S. H., 'The Town in "Feudal" Russia', *SR* 28 (1969): 116–22.

'The Origins of Seventeenth-Century Moscow's Nemeckaja sloboda', *California Slavic Studies* 5 (1970): 1–17.

'The Weber Thesis and the Failure of Capitalist Development in "Early Modern" Russia', *JGO* 18 (1970): 320–36.

Bater, J. H., and French, R. A. (eds.), *Studies in Russian Historical Geography* (London: Academic Press, 1983).

Berelowitch, André, *La Hiérarchie des égaux. La Noblesse russe d'Ancien Régime XVIe–XVIIe siècles* (Paris: Editions du Seuil, 2001).

Berg, L. S., *Geograficheskie zony Sovetskogo Soiuza* (Moscow: OGIZ, 1947).

Bogoiavlenskii, S. K., 'Moskovskie slobody i sotni v XVII veke', in *Moskovskii krai v ego proshlom*, vol. II *(Trudy Obshchestva izucheniia Moskovskoi oblasti, vyp. 6)* (Moscow, 1930), pp. 117–31.

Boškovska, Nada, *Die russische Frau im 17. Jahrhundert* (Cologne, Weimar and Vienna: Böhlau Verlag, 1998).

'Muscovite Women during the Seventeenth Century: At the Peak of the Deprivation of their Rights or on the Road Towards New Freedom?', *FOG* 56 (2000): 47–62.

Brisbane, M., and Gaimster, D. R. M. (eds.), *Novgorod: The Archaeology of a Russian Medieval City and its Hinterland* (London: British Museum, 2001).

Brown, Peter B., 'Neither Fish nor Fowl: Administrative Legality in Mid- and Late-Seventeenth-Century Russia', *JGO* 50 (2002): 1–21.

Buchinskii, I. E., *O klimate proshlogo Russkoi ravniny* (Leningrad, 1958).

Bushkovitch, Paul, *The Merchants of Moscow, 1580–1650* (Cambridge: Cambridge University Press, 1980).

Bychkova, M. E., *Sostav klassa feodalov Rossii v XVI v.* (Moscow: Nauka, 1986).

Chechulin, N. D., *Goroda Moskovskogo gosudarstva v XVI veke* (St Petersburg: Tipografiia I. N. Skorokhodova, 1889; reprinted The Hague: Mouton, 1969).

Cherepnin, L. V., 'Obshchestvenno-politicheskie otnosheniia v drevnei Rusi i Russkaia pravda', in A. P. Novosel'tsev et al., *Drevnerusskoe gosudarstvo i ego mezhdunarodnoe znachenie* (Moscow: Nauka, 1965), pp. 128–278.

Novgorodskie berestyanye gramoty kak istoricheskii istochnik (Moscow: Nauka, 1969).

Chistiakova, E. U., 'Remeslo i torgovlia na Voronezhskom posade v seredine XVII v.', *Izvestiia Voronezhskogo Gosudarstvennogo universiteta* 25 (1954): 46–63.

Darkevich, V. P., 'K istorii torgovykh sviazei Drevnei Rusi', *Kratkie soobshcheniia o dokladakh i polevykh issledovaniiakh Instituta arkheologii* 138 (1974): 93–103.

and Edomakha, I. I., 'Pamiatnik zapadnoevropeiskoi torevtiki XII veka', *Sovetskaia arkheologiia* 3 (1964): 247–55.

Davies, Brian, 'Village into Garrison: The Militarized Peasant Communities of Southern Muscovy', *RR* 51 (1992): 481–501.

Degtiarev, A. Ia., 'O mobilizatsii pomestnykh zemel'' v XVI v.', in *Iz istorii feodal'noi Rossii. Stat'i i ocherki k 70-letiiu so dnia rozhdeniia prof. V. V. Mavrodina*, ed. A. Ia. Degtiarev et al. (Leningrad: Leningradskii universitet, 1978), pp. 85–91.

Russkaia derevnia v XV–XVII vekakh. Ocherki istorii sel'skogo rasseleniia (Leningrad: LGU, 1980).

Dewey, Horace W., 'The 1497 Sudebnik – Muscovite Russia's First National Law Code', *American Slavic and East European Review* 15 (1956): 325–38.

D'iakonov, M. A., *Ocherki iz istorii sel'skogo naseleniia v Moskovskom gosudarstve XVI–XVII vv.* (St Petersburg: Tipografiia I. N. Skorokhodova, 1898).

Dimnik, Martin, 'The Kuna and the Currency of Kievan Rus'', Julijan Dobrini (ed.), *Proceedings of the 3rd International Numismatic Congress in Croatia, 11–14 October, 2001, Pula, Croatia* (Pula: Dobrini and Dobrini, 2002), pp. 105–14.

Ditiatin, I. I., *Ustroistvo i upravlenie gorodov Rossii* (St Petersburg: Tipografiia Merkul'eva, 1875).

Dmitriev, F., *Istoriia sudebnykh instantsii i grazhdanskogo appelliatsionnogo sudoproizvodstva ot sudebnika do uchrezhdeniia o guberniiakh* (Moscow: Universitetskaia tipografiia, 1859).

Dobroklonskii, A. P., 'Solotchinskii monastyr', ego slugi i krest'iane v XVII veke', *ChOIDR* 1888, no. 144, kn. 1.

Dokuchaev, V. V., 'K ucheniiu o zonakh prirody', in his *Izbrannye trudy*, vol. III (Moscow: Gosudarstvennoe izdatel'stvo sel'skokhoziaistvennoi literatury, 1949), pp. 317–29.

Russkii chernozem (Moscow: Gosudarstvennoe izdatel'stvo sel'skokhoziaistvennoi literatury, 1952).

Dollinger, Phillippe, *The German Hansa*, trans. D. S. Ault and S. H. Steinberg (Stanford, Calif.: Stanford University Press, 1970).

Dulov, A.V., *Geograficheskaia sreda i istoriia Rossii* (Moscow: Nauka, 1983).

Eaton, Henry L., 'Decline and Recovery of the Russian Cities from 1500 to 1700', *CASS* 11 (1977): 220–52.

Fekhner, M. V., *Torgovlia russkogo gosudarstva so stranami Vostoka v XVI veke* (Moscow: Izdatel'stvo Gosudarstvennogo Istoricheskogo muzeia, 1952).

Floria, B. N., 'Torgovlia Rossii so stranami zapadnoi Evropy v Arkhangel'ske (konets XVI – nachalo XVII v.)', *Srednie veka* 36 (1973): 129–51.

French, R. A., 'The Early and Medieval Russian Town', in J. H. Bater and R.A. French (eds.), *Studies in Russian Historical Geography* (London: Academic Press, 1983), pp. 249–77.

   'The Urban Network of Later Medieval Russia', in *Geographical Studies on the Soviet Union: Essays in Honor of Chauncy D. Harris* (Chicago: University of Chicago, Department of Geography, Research Paper no. 211, 1984), pp. 29–51.

Froianov, I. Ia., *Kievskaia Rus'. Glavnye cherty sotsial'no-ekonomicheskogo stroia* (St Petersburg: Izdatel'stvo S.-Peterburgskogo universiteta, 1999).

Gaidukov, P. G., *Slavenskii konets srednevekovogo Novgoroda. Nutnyi raskop* (Moscow: Novgorodskii gosudarstvennyi ob"edinennyi muzei-zapovednik, 1992).

Gerasimov, M. M., 'Dokumental'nyi portret Ivana Groznogo', *Kratkie soobshcheniia Instituta arkheologii AN SSSR* 100 (1965): 139–42.

Gibson, James R., *Imperial Russia in Frontier America* (New York: Oxford University Press, 1976).

Glamann, Kristoff, 'The Changing Patterns of Trade', in *Cambridge Economic History of Europe*, vol. v (Cambridge: Cambridge University Press, 1977), pp. 185–289.

Glaz'ev, V. N., *Vlast' i obshchestvo na iuge Rossii v XVII veke: Protivodeistvie ugolovnoi prestupnosti* (Voronezh: Voronezhskii gosudarstvennyi universitet, 2001).

Golikova, N. B., *Ocherki po istorii gorodov Rossii kontsa XVII–nachala XVIII v.* (Moscow: Izdatel'stvo Moskovskogo universiteta, 1982).

Gol'tsberg, I. A. (ed.), *Agroklimaticheskii atlas mira* (Moscow and Leningrad: Gidrometeoizdat, 1972).

Gorod i gorozhane Rossii v XVII–pervoi polovine XIXv. Sbornik statei (Moscow: Institut Istorii AN SSSR, 1991).

Goroda feodal'noi Rossii: sbornik statei pamiati N.V. Ustiugova (Moscow: Nauka, 1966).

Gorskaia, N. A., *Monastyrskie krest'iane Tsentral'noi Rossii v XVII veke. O sushchnosti i formakh feodal'no-krepostnicheskikh otnoshenii* (Moscow: Nauka, 1977).

   et al., *Krest'ianstvo v periody rannego i razvitogo feodalizma* (*Istoriia krest'ianstva SSSR s drevneishikh vremen do velikoi oktiabr'skoi sotsialisticheskoi revoliutsii*, vol. ii) (Moscow: Nauka, 1990).

Gorskii, A. D., *Ocherki ekonomicheskogo polozheniia krest'ian Severo-Vostochnoi Rusi XIV–XV vv.* (Moscow: MGU, 1960).

   Bor'ba krest'ian za zemliu na Rusi v XV–nachale XVI veka (Moscow: MGU, 1974).

Got'e, Iu. V., *Zamoskovnyi krai v XVII veke* (Moscow: Gosudarstvennoe sotsial'no-ekonomicheskoe izdatel'stvo, 1937).

Grekov, B. D., 'Novgorodskii dom sviatoi Sofii. (Opyt izucheniia organizatsii i vnutrennikh otnoshenii krupnoi tserkovnoi votchiny)', (= his *Izbrannye trudy*, vol. IV) (Moscow: AN SSSR, 1960).

Gromyko, M. M., *Mir russkoi derevni* (Moscow : Molodaia Gvardiia, 1991).

Hamm, Michael (ed.), *The City in Russian History* (Lexington: University Press of Kentucky, 1976).

Hellie, Richard, 'Muscovite Law and Society. The *Ulozhenie* of 1649 as a Reflection of the Political and Social Development of Russia since the *Sudebnik* of 1589', unpublished Ph.D. dissertation, University of Chicago, 1965.

'Foundations of Russian Capitalism', *SR* 26 (1967): 148–54.

Enserfment and Military Change in Muscovy (Chicago: University of Chicago Press, 1971).

'The Stratification of Muscovite Society: The Townsmen', *RH* 5 (1978): 119–75.

Slavery in Russia 1450–1725 (Chicago: University of Chicago Press, 1982).

'*Sudebniki*', in *MERSH*, ed. Joseph L. Wieczynski, vol. XXXVIII (Gulf Breeze, Fla.: Academic International Press, 1984), pp. 15–22.

'The *Ulozhenie* of 1649', in *MERSH*, ed. Joseph L. Wieczynski, vol. XL (Gulf Breeze, Fla.: Academic International Press, 1985), pp. 192–8.

'Patterns of Instability in Russian and Soviet History', *Chicago Review of International Affairs* 1 (1989): 3–34 and 2 (1990): 3–16.

'Early Modern Russian Law: The *Ulozhenie* of 1649', and 'Ulozhenie Commentary: Preamble and Chapters 1–2', *RH* 15 (1988): 155–224; 'Commentary on Chapters 3 through 6', *RH* 17 (1990): 65–78; 'Commentary on Chapters 7–9', *RH* 17 (1990): 179–226; 'Commentary on Chapter 11 (The judicial process for peasants)', *RH* 17 (1990): 305–39.

'The Church and the Law in Late Muscovy: Chapters 12 and 13 of the *Ulozhenie* of 1649', *CASS* 25 (1991): 179–99.

'Russian Law From Oleg to Peter the Great', in Daniel H. Kaiser (ed. and trans.), *The Laws of Rus' – Tenth to Fifteenth Centuries* (Salt Lake City, Ut.: Charles Schlacks, 1992), pp. xi–xl.

The Economy and Material Culture of Russia, 1600–1725 (Chicago: University of Chicago Press, 1999).

'Russia, 1200–1815', in Richard Bonney (ed.), *The Rise of the Fiscal State in Europe, c.1200–1815* (Oxford: Oxford University Press, 1999), pp. 481–505.

'The Russian Smoky Hut and its Possible Health Consequences', *RH* 28 (2001): 171–84.

'The Costs of Muscovite Military Defense and Expansion', in Eric Lohr and Marshall Poe (eds.), *The Military and Society in Russia 1450–1917* (Leiden: Brill, 2002), pp. 41–66.

'Migration in Early Modern Russia, 1480s–1780s', in David Eltis (ed.), *Coerced and Free Migration. Global Perspectives* (Stanford, Calif.: Stanford University Press, 2002), pp. 292–323, 418–24.

'Le Commerce russe dans la deuxième moitié du XVIIIe siècle (1740–1810)', in *L'Influence française en Russie au XVIIIe siècle*, ed. Jean-Pierre Poussou et al. (Paris: Presses de l'Université de Paris-Sorbonne, 2004), pp. 73–82.

Hittle, J. Michael, *The Service City: State and Townsmen in Russia, 1600–1800* (Cambridge, Mass.: Harvard University Press, 1979).

Huttenbach, Henry R., 'Hydrography and the Origins of Russian Cartography', in *Five Hundred Years of Nautical Science* (London: National Maritime Museum, 1981), pp. 142–52.

Iakovlev, A. I., *Zasechnaia cherta Moskovskogo gosudarstva v XVII veke* (Moscow: Tipografiia G. Lissnera i D. Sobko, 1916).

Ianin, V. L., *Novgorodskaia feodal'naia votchina (Istoriko-genealogicheskoe issledovanie)* (Moscow: Nauka, 1981).

et al., *Problemy agrarnoi istorii (s drevneishikh vremen do XVIII v. vkliuchitel'no)* (Minsk: Nauka i tekhnika, 1978).

Iarushevich, Nikolai, hieromonach, *Tserkovnyi sud v Rossii do izdaniia sobornogo ulozheniia Alekseia Mikhailovicha (1649 g.) . . . Istoriko-kanonicheskoe issledovanie* (Petrograd: Sinodal'naia tipografiia, 1917).

Istoriia Moskvy, vol. 1: *Period feodalizma, XII–XVII vv.* (Moscow: AN SSSR, 1952).

Istoriia severnogo krest'ianstva, vol. 1: *Krest'ianstvo Evropeiskogo severa v period feodalizma* (Arkhangel'sk: Severo-Zapadnoe knizhnoe izdatel'stvo, 1984).

Iushkov, S. V., *Obshchestvenno-politicheskii stroi i pravo Kievskogo gosudarstva* (Moscow: Gosiurizdat, 1949).

Ivanov, Vladimir Ivanovich, *Monastyrskie krest'iane Pomor'ia v XVII v.* (Moscow: RAN, 1997).

Ivina, L. I., *Krupnaia votchina Severo-Vostochnoi Rusi kontsa XIV–pervoi poloviny XVI v.* (Leningrad: Nauka, 1979).

Kahan, A., *The Plow, the Hammer and the Knout: An Economic History of Eighteenth-Century Russia* (Chicago: Chicago University Press, 1985).

Kaiser, Daniel H., 'The Transformation of Legal Relations in Old Rus' (Thirteenth to Fifteenth Centuries)', unpublished Ph.D. dissertation, University of Chicago, 1977.

The Growth of the Law in Medieval Russia (Princeton: Princeton University Press, 1980).

'Death and Dying in Early Modern Russia', in Nancy Shields Kollmann (ed.), *Major Problems in Early Modern Russian History* (New York: Garland Publishers, 1992), pp. 217–57.

Karagodin, G.M., *Kniga o vodke i vinodelii* (Cheliabinsk: Ural LTD, 2000).

Kargalov, V. V., 'Posledstviia mongolo-tatarskogo nashestviia XIII v. dlia sel'skikh mestnostei Severo-Vostochnoi Rusi', *VI*, 1965, no. 3: 53–8.

Kashtanov, S. M., 'Feodal'nyi immunitet v gody boiarskogo pravleniia (1538–1548 gg.)', *IZ* 66 (1960): 239–68.

'K voprosu ob otmene tarkhanov v 1575/76 g.', *IZ* 77 (1965): 209–35.

'Finansovoe ustroistvo moskovskogo kniazhestva v seredine XIV v. po dannym dukhovnykh gramot', in V. T. Pashuto et al. (eds.), *Issledovaniia po istorii i istoriografii feodalizma. K 100-letiiu so dnia rozhdeniia akademika B. D. Grekova* (Moscow: Nauka, 1982), pp. 173–89.

Finansy srednevekovoi Rusi (Moscow: Nauka, 1988).

Kavelin, K., *Osnovnye nachala russkogo sudoustroistva i grazhdanskogo sudoproizvodstva* (Moscow: Tipografiia Avgusta Semena, 1844).

Kazanski, M., Nercessian, A., and Zuckerman, C. (eds.), *Les Centres proto-urbains russes entre Scandinavie, Byzance et Orient* (Réalités byzantines 7) (Paris: P. Lethielleux, 2000).

Khoroshkevich, A. L., 'Iz istorii ganzeiskoi torgovli (Vvoz v Novgorod blagorodnykh metallov v XIV–XV vv.)', in *Srednie veka. Sbornik*, no. 20 (Moscow: AN SSSR, 1961), pp. 98–120.

Torgovlia Velikogo Novgoroda s pribaltikoi i zapadnoi Evropoi v XIV–XV vekakh (Moscow: AN SSSR, 1963).

Kirchner, Walther, *Commercial Relations Between Russia and Europe, 1400–1800: Collected Essays* (Bloomington: Indiana University Press, 1966).

Kivelson, Valerie A., 'The Effects of Partible Inheritance: Gentry Families and the State in Muscovy', *RR* 53 (1994): 197–212.

'Male Witches and Gendered Categories in Seventeenth-Century Russia', *Comparative Studies in Society and History* 45 (2003): 606–31.

Kleimola, Ann M., *Justice in Medieval Russia : Muscovite Judgment Charters (pravye gramoty) of the Fifteenth and Sixteenth Centuries* (Philadelphia : American Philosophical Society, vol. 65, 1975).

Kobrin, V. B., 'Stanovlenie pomestnoi sistemy', *IZ* 105 (1980): 150–95.

Vlast' i sobstvennost' v srednevekovoi Rossii (XV–XVI vv.) (Moscow: Mysl', 1985).

Kobylianskii, V. D. (ed.), *Rozh'* (Leningrad: Agropromizdat, 1989).

Kochedatov, V. I., *Pervye russkie goroda Sibiri* (Moscow: Stroiizdat, 1978).

Kochin, G. E., *Sel'skoe khoziaistvo na Rusi v period obrazovaniia Russkogo tsentralizovannogo gosudarstva, konets XIII–nachalo XVI v.* (Moscow and Leningrad: Nauka, 1965).

Kolchin, B. A. and Makarova, T. I. (eds.), *Drevniaia Rus'. Byt i kul'tura* (Moscow: Nauka, 1997).

Kollmann, Nancy S., 'The Extremes of Patriarchy: Spousal Abuse and Murder in Early Modern Russia', *RH* 25 (1998): 133–40.

By Honor Bound: State and Society in Early Modern Russia (Ithaca, N. Y., and London: Cornell University Press, 1999).

'Lynchings and Legality in Early Modern Russia', *FOG* 58 (2001): 91–6.

'Russian Law in a Eurasian Setting: The Arzamas Region, Late Seventeenth–Early Eighteenth Century', in Gyula Szvák (ed.), *The Place of Russia in Eurasia* (Budapest: Magyar Ruszisztikai Intézet, 2001), pp. 200–6.

Kolycheva, E.I., *Agrarnyi stroi Rossii XVI veka* (Moscow: Nauka, 1987).

Kopanev, A. I., *Krest'ianstvo Russkogo Severa v XVI v.* (Leningrad: Nauka, 1978).

Kopanev, A. N., 'Naselenie russkogo gosudarstva v XVI veke', *IZ* 64 (1959): 233–54.

Koretskii, V. I., *Zakreposhchenie krest'ian i klassovaia bor'ba v Rossii vo vtoroi polovine XVI v.* (Moscow: Nauka, 1970).

Formirovanie krepostnogo prava i pervaia krest'ianskaia voina v Rossii (Moscow: Nauka, 1975).

Korobushkina, T. N., *Zemledelie na territorii Belorussii v X–XIII vv.* (Minsk: Nauka i Tekhnika, 1979).

Kostomarov, N., *Ocherki torgovli Moskovskogo gosudarstva v XVI i XVII stoletiiakh* (St Petersburg: N. Tiblen, 1862; reprinted The Hague: Europe Printing, 1966).

Kovalev, R. K., 'The Infrastructure of the Northern Part of the "Fur Road" between the Middle Volga and the East during the Middle Ages', *Archivum Eurasiae Medii Aevi* 11 (2000–01): 25–64.

Kratkii istoricheskii ocherk razvitiia vodianykh i sukhoputnykh soobshchenii i torgovykh portov v Rossii (St Petersburg: Kushnerev, 1900).

Kudriavtsev, A. S., *Ocherki istorii dorozhnogo stroitel'stva v SSSR* (Moscow, 1951).

Langer, Lawrence N., 'The Black Death in Russia: Its Effects upon Urban Labor', *RH* 2 (1975): 53–67.

'The Medieval Russian Town', in Michael Hamm (ed.), *The City in Russian History* (Lexington: University of Kentucky Press, 1976), pp. 11–33.

'Plague and the Russian Countryside: Monastic Estates in the Late Fourteenth and Fifteenth Centuries', *CASS* 10 (1976): 351–68.

Lappo-Danilevskii, A. S., *Organizatsiia priamogo oblozheniia v Moskovskom gosudarstve so vremen smuty do epokhi preobrazovanii* (St Petersburg: Tipografiia I. N. Skorokhodova, 1890; reprinted The Hague: Mouton, 1969).

Leont'ev, A. E., *Arkheologiia Meri. K predystorii severo-vostochnoi Rusi* (Moscow: Institut Arkheologii RAN, 1996).

Levin, Eve, *Sex and Society in the World of the Orthodox Slavs, 900–1700* (Ithaca, N. Y.: Cornell University Press, 1989).

Liebermann, V., 'Transcending East–West Dichotomies: State and Culture Formation in Six Ostensibly Different Areas', in V. Liebermann (ed.), *Beyond Binary Histories: Reimagining Eurasia to c. 1830* (Ann Arbor: University of Michigan Press, 1999), pp. 19–102.

Liubavskii, M. K., *Obzor istorii russkoi kolonizatsii*, reprint edn (Moscow: Izdatel'stvo Moskovskogo Universiteta, 1996).

Istoricheskaia geografiia Rossii v sviazi s kolonizatsiei (Moscow: I. I. Liubimov, 1909; reprinted St Petersburg: Lan', 2001).

Makarov, N. A. et al. (eds.), *Srednevekovoe rasselenie na Belom Ozere* (Moscow: Iazyki russkoi kul'tury, 2001).

Makovskii, D. P., *Razvitie tovarno-denezhnykh otnoshenii v sel'skom khoziaistve russkogo gosudarstva v XVI veke* (Smolensk: Smolenskii gosudarstvennyi pedagogicheskii institut, 1963).

Man'kov, A. G., *Ulozhenie 1649 goda – kodeks feodalnogo prava Rossii* (Leningrad: Nauka, 1980).

Zakonodatel'stvo i pravo Rossii vtoroi poloviny XVII v. (St Petersburg: Nauka, 1998).

Martin, Janet, 'Les uškujniki de Novgorod: Marchands ou Pirates?', *Cahiers du monde russe et soviétique* 16 (1975): 5–18.

'Muscovite Travelling Merchants: The Trade with the Muslim East (15th and 16th Centuries)', *Central Asian Survey* 4 (1985): 21–38.

Treasure of the Land of Darkness. The Fur Trade and its Significance for Medieval Russia (Cambridge: Cambridge University Press, 1986).

Mel'nikova, A. S., *Russkie monety ot Ivana Groznogo do Petra Velikogo. Istoriia russkoi denezhnoi sistemy s 1533 po 1682 god* (Moscow: Finansy i statistika, 1989).

Mel'nikova, E. A., *Skandinavskie runicheskie nadpisi. Novye nakhodki i interpretatsii* (Moscow: Vostochnaia Literatura, 2001).

Mertsalov, A. E., *Ocherki goroda Vologdy po pistsovoi knige 1627 goda* (Vologda, 1885).

Merzon, A. Ts. and Tikhonov, Iu. A., *Rynok Ustiuga Velikogo v period skladyvaniia vserossiiskogo rynka (XVII vek)* (Moscow: AN SSSR, 1960).

Mesiats, V. K. (ed.), *Sel'sko-khoziaistvennyi entsiklopedicheskii slovar'* (Moscow: Sovetskaia entsiklopediia, 1989).

Mezentsev, Volodymyr I., 'The Territorial and Demographic Development of Medieval Kiev and Other Major Cities of Rus': A Comparative Analysis Based on Recent Archaeological Research', *RR* 48 (1989): 145–70.

Mikhailov, K., 'Drevnerusskie kamernye pogrebeniia i Gnezdovo', *Arkheologicheskii Sbornik. Trudy Gosudarstvennogo Istoricheskogo Muzeia* 124 (2001): 159–75.

Mikhailov, M. M., *Russkoe grazhdanskoe sudoproizvodstvo v istoricheskom ego razvitii ot Ulozheniia 1649 goda do izdaniia svoda zakonov* (St Petersburg: Tipografiia II Otdeleniia S.I.V. Kantseliarii, 1856).

Miklashevskii, I. N., *K istorii khoziaistvennogo byta Moskovskogo gosudarstva*, vol. 1: *Zaselenie i sel'skoe khoziaistvo iuzhnoi okrainy v XVII veke* (Moscow: D. I. Inozemtsev, 1894).

Miliukov, P., *Ocherki po istorii russkoi kul'tury. Chast' pervaia: naselenie, ekonomicheskii, gosudarstvennyi i soslovnyi stroi* (St Petersburg: Mir Bozhii, 1896).

Miller, David B., 'Monumental Building as an Indicator of Economic Trends in Northern Rus' in the Late Kievan and Mongol Periods, 1138–1462', *American Historical Review* 94 (1989): 360–90.

'Monumental Building and Its Patrons as Indicators of Economic and Political Trends in Rus', 900–1262', *JGO* 38 (1990): 321–55.

Milner-Gulland, Robin, *The Russians* (Oxford: Blackwell, 1997).

Milov, L. V., *Velikorusskii pakhar' i osobennosti rossiiskogo istoricheskogo protsessa* (Moscow: Rosspen, 1998).

et al., *Tendentsii agrarnogo razvitiia Rossii pervoi poloviny XVII stoletiia. Istoriografiia, komp'iuter, metody issledovaniia* (Moscow: MGU, 1986).

Mironov, B. N., *Vnutrennii rynok Rossii vo vtoroi polovine XVIII–pervoi polovine XIX v.* (Leningrad: Nauka, 1981).

Moon, David, *The Russian Peasantry, 1600–1930. The World the Peasants Made* (London and New York: Longman, 1999).

Morgunov, I. I., 'O pogranichnom stroitel'stve Vladimira Sviatoslavicha na pereiaslavskom levoberezh'e', *Rossiiskaia Arkheologiia* 1999, no. 3: 69–78.

Mühle, E., *Die städtischen Handelszentren der nordwestlichen Ruś. Anfänge und frühe Entwicklung altrussischer Städte (bis gegen Ende des 12. Jahrhunderts)* (Stuttgart: Franz Steiner, 1991).

Murvar, V., 'Max Weber's Urban Typology and Russia', *Sociological Quarterly* 8 (1967): 481–94.

Nersesiants, V. S. (ed.), *Razvitie russkogo prava v XV–pervoi polovine XVII v.* (Moscow: Nauka, 1986).

Nevolin, K. A., 'O prostranstve tserkovnogo suda v Rossii do Petra Velikogo', in his *Polnoe sobranie sochinenii*, vol. VI (St Petersburg: Tipografiia Eduarda Pratsa, 1859).

'Obshchii spisok russkikh gorodov', in his *Polnoe sobranie sochinenii*, vol. VI (St Petersburg: Tipografiia Eduarda Pratsa, 1859), pp. 27–96.

Nikitin, A. V., 'Oboronitel'nye sooruzheniia zasechnoi cherty XVI–XVII vv.', in *Materialy i issledovaniia po arkheologii SSSR*, vol. 44 (1955), pp. 116–213.

Nikol'skaia, T. N., *Zemlia Viatichei. K istorii naseleniia basseina verkhnei i srednei Oki v IX–XIII vv.* (Moscow: Nauka, 1981).

Noonan, T. S., 'The Monetary History of Kiev in the Pre-Mongol Period', *HUS* 11 (1987): 384–443.

'The Flourishing of Kiev's International and Domestic Trade, ca. 1100–ca.1240', in I. S. Koropeckyj (ed.), *Ukrainian Economic History: Interpretive Essays* (Harvard: Harvard University Press, 1991), pp. 102–46.

'Forging a National Identity: Monetary Politics during the Reign of Vasilii I (1389–1425)', in A. M. Kleimola and G. D. Lenhoff (eds.), *Culture and Identity in Muscovy, 1359–1584* (Moscow: ITZ-Garant, 1997), pp. 495–529.

The Islamic World, Russia and the Vikings, 750–900. The Numismatic Evidence (Aldershot: Ashgate, 1998).

Nosov, E. N., *Novgorodskoe (Riurikovoe) Gorodishche* (Leningrad: Nauka, 1990).

Nosov, N. E., 'Russkii gorod i russkoe kupechestvo v XVI stoletii (k postanovke voprosa)', in *Issledovaniia po sotsial'no-politicheskoi istorii Rossii* (Leningrad: Nauka, 1971), pp. 152–77.

'Novgorod. Das mittelalterliche Zentrum und sein Umland im Norden Russlands', *Studien zur Siedlungsgeschichte und Archaeologie der Ostseegebiete*, Bd.1 (Wachholtz Verlag, 2001).

Novgorod: the Archaeology of a Russian Medieval City and its Hinterland, The British Museum Occasional Paper, No. 141 (London: British Museum, 2001).

Novgorodskii sbornik. 50 let raskopok Novgoroda (Moscow: Nauka, 1982).

Ogrizko, Z. A., *Iz istorii krest'ianstva na Severe feodal'noi Rossii XVII v. (Osobye formy krepostnoi zavisimosti)* (Moscow: Sovetskaia Rossiia, 1968).

Ostrowski, Donald, 'The Military Land Grant along the Muslim–Christian Frontier', *RH* 19 (1992): 327–59; and 'Errata', *RH* 21 (1994): 249–50.

'Early *pomest'e* Grants as a Historical Source', *Oxford Slavonic Papers* 33 (2000): 37–63.

Ovsiannikov, O. V., 'Kholmogorskii i Arkhangel'skii posady po pistsovym i perepisnym knigam XVII v.', in *Materialy po istorii Evropeiskogo Severa SSSR*, vol. 1 (Vologda, 1970), pp. 197–211.

'Oboronitel'nye sooruzheniia severorusskikh gorodov XVI–XVII vekov', in *Letopis' Severa*, VI (Moscow, 1972), pp. 211–23.

and Iasinskii, M. E., 'Gollandtsy. "Nemetskaia sloboda" v Arkhangel'ske XVII–XVIII vv.', in *Arkhangel'sk v XVIII veke* (St Petersburg: Russko-Baltiiskii informatsionnyi tsentr BLITs, 1997), pp. 108–80.

Pallot, J., and Shaw, D. J. B., *Landscape and Settlement in Romanov Russia, 1613–1917* (Oxford: Clarendon Press, 1990).

Paneiakh, V. M., 'Zakreposhchenie krest'ian v XVI v.: novye materialy, kontseptsii, perspektivy izucheniia (po povodu knigi V.I. Koretskogo)', *Istoriia SSSR*, 1972, no.1: 157–65.

Pashuk, A. I., *Sud i sudnichestvo na Livoberezhnii Ukraini v XVII–XVIII st.* (L'viv, 1967).

Pavlova, Elena, 'Private Land Ownership in Northeastern Russia during the Late Appanage Period (Last Quarter of the Fourteenth through the Middle of the Fifteenth Century)', unpublished Ph.D. dissertation, University of Chicago, 1998.

Pavlov-Sil'vanskii, N. P., *Gosudarevy sluzhilye liudi: liudi kabal'nye i dokladnye* (St Petersburg: Tipografiia M.M. Stasiulevicha, 1909).

Petrov, V. P., *Podsechnoe zemledelie* (Kiev: Naukova Dumka, 1968).

Pipes, Richard, 'Was there Private Property in Muscovite Russia?', *SR* 53 (1994): 524–30. [George G. Weickhardt, 'Response', *SR* 53 (1994): 531–8.]

Pletneva, S. A., *Ocherki khazarskoi arkheologii*, ed. V. I. Petrukhin (Moscow and Jerusalem: Mosty kul'tury-Gesharim, 1999).

Poe, Marshall, *'A People Born to Slavery': Russia in Early Modern Ethnography, 1476–1748* (Ithaca, N.Y., and London: Cornell University Press, 2000).

Pokrovskii, N. N., *Aktovye istochniki po istorii chernosochnogo zemlevladeniia v Rossii XIV-nachala XVI v.* (Novosibirsk: Nauka, 1973).

Postnikov, A. V., *Razvitie krupnomasshtabnoi kartografii v Rossii* (Moscow: Nauka, 1989).

Potin, V. M., *Drevniaia Rus' i evropeiskie gosudarstva v X–XIII vv. Istoriko-numizmaticheskii ocherk* (Leningrad: Sovetskii Khudozhnik, 1968).

Pushkareva, N. L., *Zhenshchiny drevnei Rusi* (Moscow: Mysl', 1989).

    Women in Russian History from the Tenth to the Twentieth Century, ed. Eve Levin (Armonk, N.Y.: M. E. Sharpe, 1997; and Stroud: Sutton, 1999).

    Zhenshchiny Rossii i Evropy na poroge novogo vremeni (Moscow: Institut etnologii i antropologii RAN, 1996).

Rabinovich, G. S., *Gorod soli: Staraia Russa v kontse XVI–seredine XVIII vekov* (Leningrad: Izdatel'stvo Leningradskogo universiteta, 1973).

Raeff, Marc, *The Well-Ordered Police State. Social and Institutional Change through Law in the Germanies and Russia, 1600–1800* (New Haven: Yale University Press, 1983).

Rapov, O. M., *Kniazheskie vladeniia na Rusi v X-pervoi polovine XIII v.* (Moscow: MGU, 1977).

Rozhkov, N., *Sel'skoe khoziaistvo Moskovskoi Rusi v XVI veke* (Moscow: Universitetskaia tipografiia, 1899).

Rozman, G., *Urban Networks in Russia, 1750–1800 and Pre-Modern Periodization* (Princeton: Princeton University Press, 1976).

Ryan, W. F., 'The Witchcraft Hysteria in Early Modern Europe: Was Russia an Exception?', *SEER* 76 (1998): 49–84.

Rybakov, B. A., 'Drevnosti Chernigova', in N. N. Voronin (ed.), *Materialy i issledovaniia po arkheologii drevnerusskikh gorodov*, vol. 1 (= *Materialy i issledovaniia po arkheologii SSSR*, no. 11, 1949), pp. 7–93.

Rybina, E. A., *Inozemnye dvory v Novgorode XII–XVII vv.* (Moscow: Izdatel'stvo Moskovskogo universiteta, 1986).

    Torgovlia srednevekovogo Novgoroda. Istoriko-arkheologicheskie ocherki (Velikii Novgorod: Novgorodskii gosudarstvennyi universitet, 2001).

Sakharov, A. N., *Russkaia derevnia XVII v. Po materialam Patriarshego khoziaistva* (Moscow: Nauka, 1966).

Sedov, P. V., 'Podnosheniia v moskovskikh prikazakh XVII veka', *Otechestvennaia istoriia*, 1996, no. 1: 139–50.

Serbina, K. N., *Ocherki iz sotsial'no-ekonomicheskoi istorii russkogo goroda: Tikhvinskii posad v XVI–XVII vv.* (Moscow and Leningrad: AN SSSR, 1951).

    'Iz istorii vozniknoveniia gorodov v Rossii XVI v.', in *Goroda feodal'noi Rossii* (Moscow: Nauka, 1966), pp. 135–43.

Sergeevich, V. I., *Russkie iuridicheskie drevnosti*, 3 vols. (St Petersburg: M. M. Stasiulevich, 1890–1903).

    Drevnosti russkogo prava (= 3rd edn of his *Russkie iuridicheskie drevnosti*), 3 vols. (St Petersburg: M. M. Stasiulevich, 1903–9): vol. II: *Veche i kniaz'. Sovetniki kniazia*, 3rd edn (1908; reprinted The Hague: Europe Printing, 1967).

Shapiro, A. L., *Russkoe krest'ianstvo pered zakreposhcheniem (XIV–XVI vv.)* (Leningrad: LGU, 1987).

et al., *Agrarnaia istoriia severo-zapada Rossii, vtoraia polovina XV–nachalo XVI v.* (Leningrad: Nauka, 1971).

et al., *Agrarnaia istoriia severo-zapada Rossii XVI veka. Sever. Pskov. Obshchie itogi razvitiia Severo-Zapada* (Leningrad: Nauka, 1978).

Shaw, D. J. B., 'Southern Frontiers of Muscovy, 1550–1700', in J. H. Bater and R. A. French (eds.), *Studies in Russian Historical Geography* (London: Academic Press, 1983), pp. 117–42.

Shennikov, A. A., *Dvor krest'ian Neudachki Petrova i Shestachki Andreeva. Kak byli ustroeny usad'by russkikh krest'ian v XVI veka* (St Petersburg: Russkoe geograficheskoe obshchestvo, 1993).

Shepard, J., 'A Cone-Seal from Shestovitsy', *Byzantion* 56 (1986): 252–74.

Shkvarikov, V. A., *Ocherk istorii planirovki i zastroiki russkikh gorodov* (Moscow: Gosudarstvennoe Izdatel'stvo Literatury po Stroitel'stvu i Arkhitekture, 1954).

Shmidt, Christoph, *Sozialkontrolle in Moskau: Justiz, Kriminalität und Leibeigenschaft, 1649–1785* (Stuttgart: F. Steiner Verlag, 1996).

Shtykhov, G. V., *Goroda Polotskoi zemli (IX–XIII vv.)* (Minsk: Nauka i Tekhnika, 1978).

Shunkov, V. I., *Ocherki po istorii kolonizatsii Sibiri v XVII–nachale XVIII vekov* (Moscow and Leningrad: AN SSSR, 1946).

Voprosy agrarnoi istorii Rossii (Moscow: Nauka, 1974).

Skripilev, E. A. (ed.), *Razvitie russkogo prava vtoroi poloviny XVII–XVIII vv.* (Moscow: Nauka, 1992).

Skrynnikov, R.G., 'Zapovednye i urochnye gody tsaria Fedora', *Istoriia SSSR*, 1973, no. 1: 99–129.

Smirnov, P. P., *Goroda Moskovskogo gosudarstva v pervoi polovine XVII veke*, vol. 1, pt. 2 (Kiev: A. I. Grossman, 1919).

Posadskie liudi i ikh klassovaia bor'ba do serediny XVII veka, 2 vols. (Moscow and Leningrad: AN SSSR, 1947–8).

Smith, R. E. F., *Peasant Farming in Muscovy* (Cambridge: Cambridge University Press, 1977).

and Christian, David, *Bread and Salt: A Social and Economic History of Food and Drink in Russia* (Cambridge: Cambridge University Press, 1984).

Snegirev, V., *Moskovskie slobody* (Moscow: Moskovskii rabochii, 1947).

Sorokin, A.N., *Blagoustroistvo drevnego Novgoroda* (Moscow: Obshchestvo istorikov arkhitektury, 1995).

Stalsberg, A., 'Scandinavian Viking-Age Boat Graves in Old Rus'', *RH* 28 (2001): 359–401.

Stashevskii, E. D., 'Sluzhiloe soslovie', in M. V. Dovnar-Zapol'skii (ed.), *Russkaia istoriia v ocherkakh i stat'iakh*, 3 vols. (Moscow: Moskovskoe uchebnoe knigoizdatel'stvo, 1909–12), vol. II, pp. 1–33.

Sverdlov, M. B., *Obshchestvennyi stroi Drevnei Rusi v russkoi istoricheskoi nauke XVIII–XX vv.* (St Petersburg: Dmitrii Bulanin, 1996).

Syroechkovskii, V. E., *Gosti-surozhane (Izvestiia gosudarstvennoi Akademii Istorii Material'noi Kul'tury, 127)* (Moscow and Leningrad: OGIZ, 1935).

Sytin, P. V., *Istoriia planirovki i zastroiki Moskvy. Materialy i issledovaniia*, vol. 1: 1147–1762 (Moscow: Trudy Muzeia Istorii i Rekonstruktsii Moskvy, vyp. 1, 1950).

Thompson, M. W., *Novgorod the Great: Excavations at the Medieval City Conducted by A.V. Artsikhovsky and B.A. Kolchin* (London: Evelyn, Adams and Mackay, 1967).

Tikhonov, Iu. A., *Pomeshchich'i krest'iane v Rossii. Feodal'naia renta v XVII–nachale XVIII v.* (Moscow: Nauka, 1974).

Tulupnikov, A. I. (ed.), *Atlas sel'skogo khoziaistva SSSR* (Moscow: GUGK, 1960).

Tverskoi, L.N., *Russkoe gradostroitel'stvo do kontsa XVII veka: planirovka i zastroika russkikh gorodov* (Moscow and Leningrad: AN SSSR, 1953).

Ustiugov, N.V., 'Remeslo i melkoe tovarnoe proizvodstvo v Russkom gosudarstve XVIIv.' *IZ* 34 (1950): 166–97.

Solevarennaia promyshlennost' Soli Kamskoi v XVII veke (Moscow: AN SSSR, 1957).

Veinberg, L. B., *Ocherk sel'skokhoziaistvennoi promyshlennosti Voronezhskoi gubernii* (Voronezh, 1891).

Veselovskii, S. B., *Selo i derevnia v Severo-Vostochnoi Rusi XIV–XVI vv.* (Moscow and Leningrad: OGIZ, 1936).

'Monastyrskoe zemlevladenie v moskovskoi Rusi vo vtoroi polovine XVI v.', *IZ* 10 (1941): 95–116.

Feodal'noe zemlevladenie v severo-vostochnoi Rusi (Moscow and Leningrad: AN SSSR, 1947).

Issledovaniia po istorii klassa sluzhilykh zemlevladel'tsev (Moscow: Nauka, 1969).

Vilkov, O. N., 'Tobol'sk – tsentr tamozhennoi sluzhby Sibiri XVII v.', in *Goroda Sibiri: ekonomika, upravlenie i kul'tura gorodov Sibiri v dosovetskii period* (Novosibirsk: Nauka, Sibirskoe otdelenie, 1974), pp. 131–69.

Vladimirskii-Budanov, M. F., *Obzor istorii russkogo prava*, 3rd edn (Kiev: N. Ia. Ogloblin, 1900).

Vlasova, I. V., *Traditsii krest'ianskogo zemlepol'zovaniia v Pomor'e i Zapadnoi Sibiri v XVII–XVIII vv.* (Moscow: Nauka, 1984).

Vodarskii, Ia. E., 'Chislennost' i razmeshchenie posadskogo naseleniia v Rossii vo vtoroi polovine XVII v.', in *Goroda feodal'noi Rossii* (Moscow: Nauka, 1966), pp. 271–97.

Naselenie Rossii za 400 let (Moscow: Prosveshchenie, 1973).

Naselenie Rossii v kontse XVII v. – nachale XVIII v. (Moscow: Nauka, 1977).

and Chistiakova, E.V., 'Spiski gorodov, posadov i ukreplennykh monastyrei v Rossii vo vtoroi polovine XVII v.', *Arkheograficheskii ezhegodnik* (Moscow, 1972), pp. 304–10.

Voronin, N. N., *K istorii sel'skogo poseleniia feodal'noi Rusi. Pogost, svoboda, selo, derevnia* (Leningrad: OGIZ, 1935).

Weickhardt, George G., 'Due Process and Equal Justice in the Muscovite Codes', *RR* 51 (1992): 463–80.

'The Pre-Petrine Law of Property', *SR* 52 (1993): 663–79.

'Pre-Petrine Law and Western Law: The Influence of Roman and Canon Law', *HUS* 19 (1995): 756–83.

'Legal Rights of Women in Russia, 1100–1750', *SR* 55 (1996): 1–23.

Willan, T. S., *The Early History of the Russia Company, 1553–1603* (Manchester: Manchester University Press, 1956).

Zabelin, I. E., *Domashnii byt russkikh tsarei v XVI i XVII stoletiiakh*, 4th edn, 2 pts (= *Domashnii byt russkogo naroda v XVI i XVII st.*, vol. 1) (Moscow: Iazyki russkoi kul'tury, 2000 (reprint of edition of 1915–18)).

Domashnii byt russkikh tsarits v XVI i XVII stoletiiakh, 3rd edn (= *Domashnii byt russkogo naroda v XVI i XVII st.*, vol. II) (Moscow: Iazyki russkoi kul'tury, 2001 (reprint of edition of 1901, with supplements)).

Zagorovskii, V. P., *Belgorodskaia cherta* (Voronezh: Izdatel'stvo Voronezhskogo Gosudarstvennogo Universiteta, 1969).

Iziumskaia cherta (Voronezh: Izdatel'stvo Voronezhskogo Gosudarstvennogo Universiteta, 1980).

Voronezh: istoricheskaia khronika (Voronezh: Tsentral'no-Chernozemnoe knizhnoe izdatel'stvo, 1989).

Zagoskin, N.P., *Russkie vodnye puti i sudovoe delo v do-petrovskoi Rossii* (Kazan', 1909).

Zakonodatel'nye akty Russkogo gosudarstva vtoroi poloviny XVI – pervoi poloviny XVII veka. Kommentarii (Leningrad: Nauka, Leningradskoe otdelenie, 1987).

Zaozerskaia, E. I., *U istokov krupnogo proizvodstva v russkoi promyshlennosti XVI–XVII vv.: k voprosu o genezise kapitalizma v Rossii* (Moscow: Nauka, 1970).

Zimin, A. A., 'Sostav russkikh gorodov XVI v.', *IZ* 52 (1955): 336–47.

Formirovanie boiarskoi aristokratii v Rossii v vtoroi polovine XV – pervoi tret'i XVI v. (Moscow: Nauka, 1988).

Zlotnik, Mark David, 'Immunity Charters and the Centralization of the Muscovite State', unpublished Ph.D. dissertation, University of Chicago, 1976.

3. The Orthodox Church

Anichkov, E. V., *Iazychestvo i Drevniaia Rus'* (St Petersburg: M. M. Stasiulevich, 1914).

Arrignon, J.-P., 'La Création des diocèses russes au milieu du XIIe siècle', in *Mille ans de christianisme russe, 988–1988. Actes du colloque international de l'Université Paris-Nanterre 20–23 janvier 1988* (Paris: YMCA, 1989), pp. 27–49.

Baron, Samuel H., and Nancy Shields Kollmann (eds.), *Religion and Culture in Early Modern Russia and Ukraine* (DeKalb: Northern Illinois University Press, 1997).

Belonenko, V. S. (ed.), *'Sikh zhe pamiat' prebyvaet vo veki' (Memorialnyi aspekt v kul'ture russkogo pravoslaviia)* (St Petersburg: Russkaia natsional'naia biblioteka, 1997).

Bogdanov, A. P., *Russkie patriarkhi, 1589–1700*, 2 vols. (Moscow: 'Terra', Izdatel'stvo 'Respublika', 1999).

Borisov, N. S., 'Moskovskie kniaz'ia i russkie mitropolity XIV veka', *VI*, 1986, no. 8: 30–43.

Russkaia tserkov' v politicheskoi bor'be XIV–XV vekov (Moscow: Moskovskii universitet, 1986).

Bosley, Richard D., 'The Changing Profile of the Liturgical Calendar in Muscovy's Formative Years', in A. M. Kleimola and G. D. Lenhoff (eds.), *Culture and Identity in Muscovy, 1359–1584* (Moscow: ITZ-Garant, 1997), pp. 26–38.

Bulavin, D. M., *Perevody i poslaniia Maksima Greka* (Leningrad: Nauka, 1984).

Bushkovitch, Paul, 'The Epiphany Ceremony of the Russian Court in the Sixteenth and Seventeenth Centuries,' *RR* 49 (1990): 1–18.

Religion and Society in Russia: The Sixteenth and Seventeenth Centuries (New York: Oxford University Press, 1992).

'The Life of Saint Filipp: Tsar and Metropolitan in the Late Sixteenth Century,' in Michael S. Flier and Daniel Rowland (eds.), *Medieval Russian Culture*, vol. II (Berkeley: University of California Press, 1994), pp. 29–46.

Challis, Natalie, and Dewey, Horace W., 'Basil the Blessed, Holy Fool of Moscow', *RH* 14 (1987): 47–59.

Cherniavsky, Michael, 'The Reception of the Council of Florence in Moscow', *Church History* 24 (1955): 347–59.

Crummey, Robert O., *The Old Believers & the World of Antichrist. The Vyg Community and the Russian State, 1694–1855* (Madison: University of Wisconsin Press, 1970).

DiMauro, Giorgio Giuseppe, 'The Furnace, the Crown, and the Serpent: Images of Babylon in Muscovite Rus'', unpublished Ph.D. dissertation, Harvard University, 2002.

Dmitriev, M. V., *Dissidents russes*, 2 vols. (vols. XIX, XX of André Séguenny (ed.), *Biblioteka Dissidentium*) (Baden-Baden: V. Koerner, 1997).

Emchenko, E. B., 'Zhenskie monastyri v Rossii', in N. V. Sinitsyna (ed.), *Monashestvo i monastyri v Rossii, XI–XX veka* (Moscow: Nauka, 2002), pp. 245–84.

Fedotov, G. P., *The Russian Religious Mind*, vol. I (Cambridge, Mass.: Harvard University Press, 1966).

Felmy, Karl Christian. *Die Deutung der Göttlichen Liturgie in der russischen Theologie : Wege und Wandlungen russischer Liturgie-Auslegung* (Arbeiten zur Kirchengeschichte, 54) (Berlin, New York: de Gruyter, 1984).

Fennell, John L. I., *A History of the Russian Church to 1448* (London and New York: Longman, 1995).

Flier, Michael S., 'The Iconology of Royal Ritual in Sixteenth-Century Muscovy', *Byzantine Studies: Essays on the Slavic World and the Eleventh Century*, ed. Speros Vryonis, Jr. (New York: Aristide D. Caratzas, 1992), pp. 53–76.

'Court Ceremony in an Age of Reform. Patriarch Nikon and the Palm Sunday Ritual', in Samuel H. Baron and Nancy Shields Kollmann (eds.), *Religion and Culture in Early Modern Russia and Ukraine* (DeKalb: Northern Illinois University Press, 1997), pp. 74–95.

'Till the End of Time: The Apocalypse in Russian Historical Experience before 1500', in Valerie A. Kivelson and Robert H. Greene (eds.), *Orthodox Russia: Belief and Practice under the Tsars* (University Park, Pa.: Pennsylvania State University Press, 2003), pp. 127–58.

Floria, B. N., *Otnosheniia gosudarstva i tserkvi u vostochnykh i zapadnykh slavian* (Moscow: Institut slavianovedeniia i balkanistiki RAN, 1992).

Fuhrmann, Joseph, 'Metropolitan Cyril II (1242–1281) and the Politics of Accommodation', *JGO* 24 (1976): 161–72.

Geanakoplos, Deno John, *Byzantine East & Latin West: Two Worlds of Christendom in Middle Ages and Renaissance, Studies in Ecclesiastical and Cultural History* (New York: Harper Torchbooks, 1966).

Golubinskii, Evgenii, *Istoriia russkoi tserkvi*, 2 vols. (in 4) (Moscow, 1900–10; reprinted The Hague: Mouton, 1969).

Gonneau, Pierre, *La Maison de Sainte Trinité: un grand monastère russe du Moyen-âge tardif (1354–1533)* (Paris: Klincksieck, 1992).

'The Trinity-Sergius Brotherhood in State and Society', in A. M. Kleimola and G. D. Lenhoff (eds.), *Culture and Identity in Muscovy, 1359–1584* (Moscow: ITZ-Garant, 1997), pp. 116–45.

Gorchakov, M. I., *Monastyrskii prikaz, 1649–1725 g. Opyt istoriko-iuridicheskogo issledovaniia* (St Petersburg: A. Transhel', 1868).

Gudziak, Borys A., *Crisis and Reform. The Kyivan Metropolitanate, the Patriarchate of Constantinople, and the Genesis of the Union of Brest* (Cambridge, Mass.: Harvard University Press, 1998).

Ianin, V. L., 'Monastyri srednevekovogo Novgoroda v strukture gosudarstvennykh institutov', *POLYTROPON: k 70-letiiu V.N. Toporova* (Moscow: Indrik, 1998), pp. 911–22.

Kaiser, Daniel H., 'Symbol and Ritual in the Marriages of Ivan IV', *RH* 14 (1987): 247–62.

' "Whose Wife Will She Be at the Resurrection?" Marriage and Remarriage in Early Modern Russia', *SR* 62 (2003): 302–23.

Kapterev, N. F., *Patriarkh Nikon i Tsar' Aleksei Mikhailovich*, 2 vols. (Sergiev Posad: Tipografiia Sviato-Troitskoi Sergievoi Lavry, 1909–12).

Kharakter otnoshenii Rossii k pravoslavnomu vostoku v XVI i XVII stoletiiakh (Sergiev Posad: Izdanie knizhnogo magazina M. S. Elova, 1914).

Kartashev, A. V., *Ocherki po istorii russkoi tserkvi*, 2 vols. (Moscow: Nauka, 1991).

Kazakova, N. A., and Lur'e, Ia. S. *Antifeodal'nye ereticheskie dvizheniia na Rusi XIV–nachala XVI veka* (Moscow and Leningrad: AN SSSR, 1955).

Keenan, Edward L., and Ostrowski, Donald G. (eds.), *The Council of 1503: Source Studies and Questions of Ecclesiastical Landowning in Sixteenth-Century Muscovy* (Cambridge, Mass.: Kritika, 1977).

Keep, J. L. H., 'The Régime of Filaret, 1619–1633', *SEER* 38 (1960): 334–60.

Kharlampovich, K. V., *Malorossiiskoe vliianie na velikorusskuiu tserkovnuiu zhizn'*, vol. 1 (Kazan': Izdanie knizhnogo magazina M. A. Golubeva, 1914; reprinted The Hague: Mouton, 1968).

Khoroshev, A.S., *Tserkov' v sotsial'no-politicheskoi sisteme Novgorodskoi feodal'noi respubliki* (Moscow: Izdatel'stvo Moskovskogo universiteta, 1980).

Politicheskaia istoriia russkoi kanonizatsii (XI–XVI vv.) (Moscow: Moskovskii universitet, 1986).

Klibanov, A. I., *Reformatsionnye dvizheniia v Rossii* (Moscow: AN SSSR, 1960).

Kliuchevskii, V. O., *Drevnerusskie zhitiia sviatykh kak istoricheskii istochnik* (Moscow: Tipografiia Gracheva, 1871).

Kollmann, Jack E., Jr., 'The Moscow *Stoglav* (Hundred Chapters) Church Council of 1551', unpublished Ph.D. dissertation, University of Michigan, 1978.

'The Stoglav Council and Parish Priests', *RH* 7 (1980): 65–91.

Kollmann, Nancy Shields, 'Pilgrimage, Procession and Symbolic Space in Sixteenth-Century Russian Politics', in Michael S. Flier and Daniel Rowland (eds.), *Medieval Russian Culture*, vol. II (Berkeley: University of California Press, 1994), pp. 163–81.

Kolycheva, E. I., 'Pravoslavnye monastyri vtoroi poloviny XV–XVI veka', in N. V. Sinitsyna (ed.), *Monashestvo i monastyri v Rossii, XI–XX veka* (Moscow: Nauka, 2002), pp. 81–115.

Kuchkin, V. A., 'O formirovanii Velikikh Minei Chetii mitropolita Makariia', in A. A. Sidorov (ed.), *Problemy rukopisnoi i pechatnoi knigi* (Moscow: Nauka, 1976), pp. 86–101.

'Sergei Radonezhskii', *VI*, 1992, no. 10: 75–92.

Lenhoff, Gail, 'Canonization and Princely Power in Northeast Rus': The Cult of Leontij Rostovskij', *Die Welt der Slaven*, N.F., 16 (1992): 359–80.

Early Russian Hagiography: The Lives of Prince Fedor the Black (Wiesbaden: Harrassowitz, 1997).

'Unofficial Veneration of the Daniilovichi in Muscovite Rus'', in A.M. Kleimola and G. D. Lenhoff (eds.), *Culture and Identity in Muscovy, 1359–1584* (Moscow: ITZ-Garant, 1997), pp. 391–416.

Levin, Eve, '*Dvoeverie* and Popular Religion', in Stephen K. Batalden (ed.), *Seeking God: The Recovery of Religious Identity in Orthodox Russia, Ukraine, and Georgia* (DeKalb: Northern Illinois University Press, 1993), pp. 29–52.

'Supplicatory Prayers as a Source for Popular Religious Culture in Muscovite Russia', in S. H. Baron and N. S. Kollmann (eds.), *Religion and Culture in Early Modern Russia and Ukraine* (DeKalb: Northern Illinois University Press, 1997), pp. 96–114.

Lidov, A. M. (ed.), *Ikonostas: proiskhozhdenie – razvitie – simvolika* (Moscow: Progress-Traditsiia, 2000).

Lilienfeld, Fairy von, *Nil Sorskij und seine Schriften: Die Krise der Tradition in Russland Ivans III* (Berlin: Evfangelische Verlagsanstalt, 1963).

Lobachev, S. V., *Patriarkh Nikon* (St Petersburg: Iskusstvo-SPB, 2003).

Lur'e, Ia. S., 'Kak ustanovilas' avtokefaliia russkoi tserkvi v XV v.', *Vspomogatel'nye istoricheskie distsipliny* 23 (1991): 181–98.

'Istochniki po istorii "novoiavivsheisia novgorodskoi eresi" ("zhidovstvuiushchikh")', *Jews and Slavs* 3 (1995): 199–223.

Makarii, Arkhimandrit (Veretennikov), *Zhizn' i trudy sviatitelia Makariia, mitropolita Moskovskogo i vseia Rusi* (Moscow: Izdatel'skii sovet Russkoi pravoslavnoi tserkvi, 2002).

Makarii, Metropolitan of Moscow, *Istoriia russkoi tserkvi*, 12 vols. (Düsseldorf: Brücken-Verlag, 1968–9).

Maloney, George A., *Russian Hesychasm: The Spirituality of Nil Sorskij* (The Hague: Mouton, 1973).

Meyendorff, Paul, *Russia, Ritual, and Reform: the Liturgical Reforms of Nikon in the 17th Century* (Crestwood, N.Y.: St Vladimir's Press, 1991).

Michels, Georg B., 'The Violent Old Belief: An Examination of Religious Dissent on the Karelian Frontier', *RH* 19 (1992): 203–29.

At War with the Church: Religious Dissent in Seventeenth-Century Russia (Stanford, Calif.: Stanford University Press, 1999).

'Ruling without Mercy: Seventeenth-Century Russian Bishops and their Officials', *Kritika* 4 (2003): 515–42.

Miller, David B., 'The Cult of Saint Sergius of Radonezh and Its Political Uses', *SR* 52 (1993): 680–99.

'Donors to the Trinity-Sergius Monastery as a Community of Venerators: Origins, 1360s–1462', in A. M. Kleimola and G. D. Lenhoff (eds.), *Culture and Identity in Muscovy, 1359–1584* (Moscow: ITZ-Garant, 1997), pp. 450–74.

'The Origin of Special Veneration of the Mother of God at the Trinity-Sergius Monastery: The Iconographic Evidence', *RH* 28 (2001): 303–14.

'Pogrebeniia riadom s Sergiem: Pogrebal'nye obychai v Troitse-Sergievom monastyre, 1392–1605', in T. N. Manushina and S. V. Nikolaeva (eds.), *Troitse-Sergieva Lavra v istorii, kul'ture i dukhovnoi zhizni Rossii* (Sergiev Posad: Ves' Sergiev Posad, 2002), pp. 74–89.

Motsia, A. P., 'Nekotorye svedeniia o rasprostranenii khristianstva na Rusi po dannym pogrebal'nogo obriada', in: *Obriady i verovaniia drevnego naseleniia Ukrainy. Sbornik nauchnykh trudov* (Kiev: Naukova Dumka, 1990), pp. 114–32.

Nikolaeva, S. V., 'Vklady i vkladchiki v Troitse-Sergiev Monastyr' v XVI–XVII vekakh. (Po vkladnym knigam XVII veka)', in *Tserkov' v istorii Rossii*, 3 vols. (Moscow: Institut rossiiskoi istorii Rossiiskoi akademii nauk, 1997–9): vol. II (1998), pp. 81–107.

Nikol'skii, N. M., *Istoriia russkoi tserkvi*, 4th edn (Moscow: Izdatel'stvo politicheskoi literatury, 1988).

Obolensky, Dimitri, 'Italy, Mount Athos, and Muscovy: The Three Worlds of Maximos the Greek (c. 1470–1556)', *Proceedings of the British Academy* 67 (1981): 143–61.

'Cherson and the Conversion of Rus': An Anti-revisionist View', *Byzantine and Modern Greek Studies* 13 (1989): 244–56.

'Byzantium, Kiev and Moscow: A Study in Ecclesiastical Relations', *Dumbarton Oaks Papers* 11 (Cambridge, Mass.: Harvard University Press, 1957); reprinted in his *Byzantium and the Slavs* (Crestwood, N.Y.: St Vladimir's Seminary Press, 1994), pp. 109–65.

Ostrowski, Donald, 'A "Fontological" Investigation of the Muscovite Church Council of 1503', unpublished Ph.D. dissertation, Pennsylvania State University, 1977 (Ann Arbor: UMI, 1977). AAT 7723262.

'Church Polemics and Monastic Land Acquisition in Sixteenth-Century Muscovy', *SEER* 64 (1986): 355–79.

'Why Did the Metropolitan Move from Kiev to Vladimir in the Thirteenth Century?', in Boris Gasparov and Olga Raevsky-Hughes (eds.), *Slavic Cultures in the Middle Ages (California Slavic Studies*, vol. 16) (Berkeley, Los Angeles, Oxford: University of California Press, 1993), pp. 83–101.

'500 let spustia. Tserkovnyi Sobor 1503 g.', *Palaeoslavica* 11 (2003): 214–39.

Pascal, Pierre, *Avvakum et les débuts du raskol*, 2nd edn (Paris and The Hague: Mouton, 1969).

Pelenski, Jaroslaw, 'The Origins of the Muscovite Ecclesiastical Claims to the Kievan Inheritance (Early Fourteenth Century to 1458/1461)', in Boris Gasparov and Olga Raevsky-Hughes (eds.), *Slavic Cultures in the Middle Ages (California Slavic Studies*, vol. 16) (Berkeley, Los Angeles and Oxford: University of California Press, 1993), pp. 102–15.

Pliguzov, Andrei, 'On the Title "Metropolitan of Kiev and All Rus'"', *HUS* 15 (1991): 340–53.

'Archbishop Gennadii and the Heresy of the "Judaizers"', *HUS* 16 (1992): 269–88.

' "Kniga na eretikov" Iosifa Volotskogo', in V. I. Buganov (ed.), *Istoriia i paleografiia: Sbornik statei*, 2 vols. (Moscow: Institut istorii AN, 1993), vol. I, pp. 90–139.

Polemika v russkoi tserkvi pervoi treti XVI stoletiia (Moscow: Indrik, 2002).

Podskalsky, Gerhard, *Christentum und theologische Literatur in der Kiever Rus' (988–1237)* (Munich: C. H. Beck, 1982).

Poppe, A., *The Rise of Christian Russia* (London: Variorum, 1982).

'Werdegang der Diözesanstruktur der Kiever Metropolitankirche in den ersten Jahrhunderten der Christianisierung der Ostslaven', in K. C. Felmy et al. (eds.), *Tausend Jahre Christentums in Russland. Zum Millennium der Taufe der Kiever Rus'* (Göttingen: Vandenhoeck and Ruprecht, 1988), pp. 251–90.

Rumiantseva, V. S., 'The Russian Church and State in the 17th Century', in *The Russian Orthodox Church. 10th to 20th Centuries* (Moscow: Progress, 1988), pp. 81–103.

Sedov, V. V., 'Rasprostranenie khristianstva v Drevnei Rusi', *Kratkie soobshcheniia Instituta arkheologii* 208 (1993): 3–11.

Senyk, Sophia, *A History of the Church in Ukraine*, vol. 1: *To the End of the Thirteenth Century* (Orientalia christiana analecta 243) (Rome: Pontificio Istituto Orientale, 1993).

Shchapov, Ia. N., *Kniazheskie ustavy i tserkov' v drevnei Rusi XI–XIV vv.* (Moscow: Nauka, 1972).

Gosudarstvo i tserkov' Drevnei Rusi X–XIII vv. (Moscow: Nauka, 1989).

State and Church in Early Russia 1 oth–13 th Centuries, trans. Vic Schneierson (New Rochelle, N.Y., Athens and Moscow: Aristide D. Caratzas, 1993).

Shepard, J., 'Some Remarks on the Sources for the Conversion of Rus'', in S. W. Swierkosz-Lenart (ed.), *Le origini e lo sviluppo della cristianità slavo-bixantina* (Nuovi studi storici 17) (Rome: Istituto storico italiano per il Medio Evo, 1992), pp. 59–95.

'The Coming of Christianity to Rus: Authorised and Unauthorised Versions', in C. Kendall et al. (eds.), *Conversion to Christianization* (forthcoming).

Shpakov, A. Ia., *Gosudarstvo i tserkov' v ikh vzaimnykh otnosheniiakh v Moskovskom gosudarstve* (Odessa: Tipografiia Aktsionernogo Iuzhno-russkogo Obshchestva pechatnogo dela, 1912).

Sinitsyna, N. V., *Maksim Grek v Rossii* (Moscow: Nauka, 1977).

'Tipy monastyrei i russkii asketicheskii ideal (XV–XVI vv.)', in N. V. Sinitsyna (ed.), *Monashestvo i monastyri v Rossii, XI–XX veka* (Moscow: Nauka, 2002), pp. 116–49.

Skrynnikov, R. G., *Sviatiteli i vlasti* (Leningrad: Lenizdat, 1990).

Gosudarstvo i tserkov' na Rusi XIV–XVI vv. (Novosibirsk: Nauka, 1991).

Krest i korona. Tserkov' i gosudarstvo na Rusi IX–XVII vv. (St Petersburg: Iskusstvo, 2000).

Smolitsch, Igor, *Russisches Mönchtum: Entstehung, Entwicklung und Wesen, 988–1917* (Das Östliche Christentum, n.F., Heft 10/11) (Würzburg: Augustinus-Verlag, 1953).

Spitsyn, A., 'Peshchnoe deistvo i khaldeiskaia peshch'', *Zapiski Imperatorskogo russkogo arkheologicheskogo obshchestva* 12 (1901): 95–136, 201–9.

Stefanovich, P. S., *Prikhod i prikhodskoe dukhovenstvo v Rossii v XVI–XVII vekakh* (Moscow: Indrik, 2002).

Steindorff, Ludwig, 'Klöster als Zentren der Tötensorge in Altrussland', *FOG* 50 (1995): 337–53.

'Sravnenie istochnikov ob organizatsii pominaniia usopshikh v Iosifo-Volokolamskom i Troitse-Sergievom monastyriakh v XVI veke', *Arkheograficheskii Ezhegodnik za 1996 g.* (Moscow: Nauka, 1998), pp. 65–78.

Stroev, P. M., *Spiski ierarkhov i nastoiatelei monastyrei rossiiskiia tserkvi* (St Petersburg: Tipografiia V. S. Balasheva, 1877).

Swoboda, Marina, '*The Furnace Play* and the Development of Liturgical Drama in Russia', *RR* 61 (2002): 220–34.

Taube, Moise, 'The Kievan Jew Zacharia and the Astronomical Works of the Judaizers', *Jews and Slavs* 3 (1995): 168–98.

'The "Poem of the Soul" in the *Laodicean Epistle* and the Literature of the Judaizers', *HUS* 19 (1995): 671–85.

'Posleslovie k "Logischeskim terminam" Maimonida i eres' zhidovstvuiushchikh', in *In Memoriam: Sbornik Pamiati Ia. S. Lur'e* (St Petersburg: Atheneum-Feniks, 1997), pp. 239–46.

Thomson, Francis J., 'The Slavonic Translation of the Old Testament', in J. Kras (ed.), *Interpretation of the Bible* (Ljubljana: Slovenska akademija znanosti in umetnosti, 1998), pp. 605–918.

Thyrêt, Isolde, *Between God and Tsar: Religious Symbolism and the Royal Women of Muscovite Russia* (DeKalb: Northern Illinois University Press, 2001).

Uspensky, Boris A., 'The Schism and Cultural Conflict in the Seventeenth Century', in Stephen K. Batalden (ed.), *Seeking God: the Recovery of Religious Identity in Orthodox Russia, Ukraine, and Georgia* (DeKalb: Northern Illinois University Press, 1993), pp.106–43.

Tsar' i patriarkh: Kharisma vlasti v Rossii. Vizantiiskaia model' i ee russkoe pereosmyslenie (Moscow: Iazyki russkoi kul'tury, 1998).

Velemirovič, Miloš, 'Liturgical drama in Byzantium and Russia', *Dumbarton Oaks Papers* 16 (1962): 351–85 + figures.

Vilinskii, S. G., *Poslaniia startsa Artemiia* (Odessa: Ekonomicheskaia tipografiia, 1906).

Vlasov, V. G., 'The Christianization of the Russian Peasants', in Marjorie Mandelstam Balzer (ed.), *Russian Traditional Culture: Religion, Gender, and Customary Law* (Armonk, N.Y.: M. E. Sharpe, 1992), pp. 16–33.

Vodarskii, Ia. E., 'Tserkovnye organizatsii i ikh krepostnye krest'iane vo vtoroi polovine XVII – nachale XVIII v.', in *Istoricheskaia geografiia Rossii. XII–nachalo XX v.* (Moscow: Nauka, 1975), pp. 70–96.

Zenkovsky, Serge A., *Russkoe staroobriadchestvo; dukhovnye dvizheniia semnadtsatogo veka* (Forum Slavicum, Bd. 21) (Munich: W. Fink, 1970).

Zhivov, V. M., and Uspenskii, B. A., 'Tsar' i Bog: Semioticheskie aspekty sakralizatsii monarkha v Rossii', in *Iazyki kul'tury i problemy perevodimosti* (Moscow: Nauka, 1978), pp. 47–153.

Zyzykin, M. V., *Patriarkh Nikon. Ego gosudarstvennye i kanonicheskie idei*, 3 vols. (Warsaw: Sinodal'naia Tipografiia, 1931–8).

4. Cultural and intellectual history

Alekseeva, M. A., 'Zhanr konkliuzii v russkom iskusstve kontsa XVII–nachala XVIII v.', in T. V. Alekseeva (ed.), *Russkoe iskusstvo barokko* (Moscow: Nauka, 1977), pp. 7–29.

Andreyev, N. E., 'Nikon and Avvakum on Icon-Painting', in his *Studies in Muscovy* (London: Variorum, 1970), essay XIII.

Baron, Samuel H., and Kollmann, Nancy Shields (eds.), *Religion and Culture in Early Modern Russia and Ukraine* (DeKalb: Northern Illinois University Press, 1997).

Batalov, A. L., 'K interpretatsii arkhitektury sobora Pokrova na rvu (o granitsakh ikonograficheskogo metoda)', in A. L. Batalov (ed.), *Ikonografiia arkhitektury: Sbornik nauchnykh trudov* (Moscow: Vsesoiuznyi nauchno-issledovatel'skii institut teorii arkhitektury i gradostroitel'stva, 1990), pp.15–37.

Moskovskoe kamennoe zodchestvo kontsa XVI veka: Problemy khudozhestvennogo myshleniia epokhi (Moscow: Rossiiskaia akademiia khudozhestv, 1996).

and Uspenskaia, L. S., *Sobor Pokrova na rvu (Khram Vasiliia Blazhennogo)* (Moscow: Severnyi Palomnik, 2002).

et al. (eds.), *Drevnerusskoe iskusstvo. Russkoe iskusstvo pozdnego srednevekov'ia, XVI vek* (St Petersburg: Dmitrii Bulanin, 2003).

and Viatchina, T. N., 'Ob ideinom znachenii i interpretatsii Ierusalimskogo obraztsa v russkoi arkhitekture XVI–XVII vv.', *Arkhitekturnoe nasledstvo* 36 (1988): 22–42.

Bekeneva, N. G., *Simon Ushakov 1626–1686* (Leningrad: Khudozhnik RSFSR, 1984).

Berezhkov, N. G., *Khronologiia russkogo letopisaniia* (Moscow: AN SSSR, 1963).

Billington, James, *The Icon and the Axe* (New York: Knopf, 1966).

Bocharov, G. N., 'Tsarskoe Mesto Ivana Groznogo v moskovskom Uspenskom sobore', in V. P. Vygolov (ed.), *Pamiatniki russkoi arkhitektury i monumental'nogo iskusstva: Goroda, ansambli, zodchie* (Moscow: Nauka, 1985), pp. 39–57.

Bogoiavlenskii, S. K., *Moskovskii teatr pri tsariakh Aleksee i Petre* (Moscow: Russkaia starina, 1914).

Briusova, V. G., *Gurii Nikitin* (Moscow: 'Izobrazitel'noe iskusstvo', 1982).

Russkaia zhivopis' XVII veka (Moscow: Iskusstvo, 1984).

Fedor Zubov (Moscow: 'Izobrazitel'noe iskusstvo', 1985).

'Kompozitsiia "Novozavetnoi Troitsy" v stenopisi Uspenskogo sobora', in E. S. Smirnova (ed.), *Uspenskii sobor Moskovskogo Kremlia* (Moscow: Nauka, 1985), pp. 87–99.

Brumfield, William Craft, *Gold in Azure: One Thousand Years of Russian Architecture* (Boston: David R. Godine, 1983).

A History of Russian Architecture (Cambridge: Cambridge University Press, 1993).

Brunov, N. I., *Khram Vasiliia Blazhennogo v Moskve: Pokrovskii sobor* (Moscow: Iskusstvo, 1988).

et al., *Istoriia russkoi arkhitektury*, 2nd edn, rev. and expanded (Moscow: Gosudarstvennoe Izdatel'stvo literatury po stroitel'stvu i arkhitekture, 1956).

Buseva-Davydova, I. L., *Khramy Moskovskogo Kremlia: Sviatyni i drevnosti* (Moscow: Nauka, 1997).

Bushkovitch, Paul, 'Cultural Change among the Russian Boyars 1650–1680. New Sources and Old Problems', *FOG* 56 (2000): 89–111.

Cherniavsky, Michael, *Tsar and People: A Historical Study of Russian National and Social Myths* (New Haven: Yale University Press, 1961).

'Ivan the Terrible and the Iconography of the Kremlin Cathedral of the Archangel Michael', *RH* 2 (1975): 3–28.

Chistov, K. V., *Russkie narodnye sotsial'no-utopicheskie legendy, XVII–XIX vv.* (Moscow: Nauka, 1967).

Russkaia narodnaia utopiia (genezis i funktsii sotsial'no-utopicheskikh legend) (St Petersburg: Dmitrii Bulanin, 2003).

Chrissides, N., 'Creating the New Educational Elite. Learning and Faith in Moscow's Slavo-Greco-Latin Academy, 1685–1694', unpublished Ph.D. thesis, Yale University, 2000.

Cracraft, James, *The Petrine Revolution in Russian Architecture* (Chicago: University of Chicago Press, 1988).

The Petrine Revolution in Russian Imagery (Chicago: University of Chicago Press, 1997).

Danilova, I. E., and Mneva, N. E., 'Zhivopis' XVII veka', in I. E. Grabar' (ed.), *Istoriia russkogo iskusstva*, 13 vols. (Moscow: AN SSSR, 1953–61), vol. IV (1959), pp. 354–466.

Dmitriev, L. A., 'Rol' i znachenie mitropolita Kipriana v istorii drevnerusskoi literatury', *TODRL* 19 (1963): 215–54.

Dolskaya, Olga, 'Vasilii Titov and the "Moscow Baroque" ', *Journal of the Royal Musical Association*, 118 (1993): 203–22.

'Choral Music in the Petrine Era', in A. G. Cross (ed.), *Russia in the Reign of Peter the Great: Old and New Perspectives* (Cambridge: Study Group on 18th-century Russia, 1998), pp. 173–86.

Evdokimov, G. S., Ruzaeva, E. I., and Iakovlev, D. E., 'Arkhitekturnaia keramika v dekore Moskovskogo velikokniazheskogo dvortsa v seredine XVI v.', in A. L. Batalov et al. (eds.), *Drevnerusskoe iskusstvo. Russkoe iskusstvo pozdnego srednevekov'ia, XVI vek* (St Petersburg: Dmitrii Bulanin, 2003), pp. 120–9.

Flier, Michael S., 'Filling in the Blanks: The Church of the Intercession and the Architectonics of Medieval Muscovite Ritual', *HUS* 19 (1995): 120–37.

'K semioticheskomu analizu Zolotoi palaty Moskovskogo Kremlia', in *Drevnerusskoe iskusstvo. Russkoe iskusstvo pozdnego srednevekov'ia: XVI vek* (St Petersburg: Dmitrii Bulanin, 2003), pp. 178–87.

'The Throne of Monomakh: Ivan the Terrible and the Architectonics of Destiny', in James Cracraft and Daniel Rowland (eds.), *Architectures of Russian Identity 1500 to the Present* (Ithaca, N.Y.: Cornell University Press, 2003), pp. 21–33.

and Daniel Rowland (eds.), *Medieval Russian Culture*, vol. II (Berkeley: University of California Press, 1994).

Floria, B. N., 'Nekotorye dannye o nachale svetskogo portreta v Rossii', *Arkhiv russkoi istorii*, vyp. I (1992): 133–41.

Franklin, Simon, *Writing, Society and Culture in Early Rus, c. 950–1300* (Cambridge: Cambridge University Press, 2002).

Freski Spasa-Nereditsy (Leningrad, 1925).

Gasparov, Boris, and Raevsky-Hughes, Olga (eds.), *Slavic Cultures in the Middle Ages* (*Christianity and the Eastern Slavs*, vol. 1) (*California Slavic Studies*, vol. 16) (Berkeley, Los Angeles and Oxford: University of California Press, 1993).

Gatova, T. A., 'Iz istorii dekorativnoi skul'ptury Moskvy nachala XVIII v.', in T. V. Alekseeva (ed.), *Russkoe iskusstvo XVIII veka* (Moscow: 'Iskusstvo', 1968), pp. 31–44.

Gippius, A. A., 'K attributsii novgorodskikh kratirov i ikony "Znamenie"', *Novgorod i Novgorodskaia zemlia. Istoriia i arkheologiia*, vyp. 13 (Novgorod: Novgorodskii gosudarstvennyi ob"edinennyi muzei-zapovednik, 1999), pp. 379–94.

Goggi, Gianluigi, 'The Philosophes and the Debate over Russian Civilization', in Maria Di Salvo and Lindsey Hughes (eds.), *A Window on Russia* (Rome: La Fenice Edizioni, 1996), pp. 299–305.

Golden, Peter B., 'Turkic Calques in Medieval Eastern Slavic', *Journal of Turkish Studies* 8 (1984): 103–11.

Gordeeva N., and Tarasenko, L., *Tserkov' Pokrova v Filiakh* (Moscow: 'Izobrazitel'noe iskusstvo', 1980).

Grabar', I. E., et al. (eds.), *Istoriia russkogo iskusstva*, 13 vols. (Moscow: AN SSSR, 1953–64), vol. III (1955), vol. IV (1959).

Howard, Jeremy, *The Scottish Kremlin Builder: Christopher Galloway* (Edinburgh : Manifesto, 1997).

Hughes, Lindsey, 'Byelorussian Craftsmen in Seventeenth-Century Russia and their Influence on Muscovite Architecture', *Journal of Byelorussian Studies* 3 (1976): 327–41.

'Western European Graphic Material as a Source for Moscow Baroque Architecture', *SEER* 55 (1977): 433–43.

'The Moscow Armoury and Innovations in 17th-Century Muscovite Art', *CASS* 13 (1979): 204–23.

'The 17th-Century "Renaissance" in Russia', *History Today* (February 1980), pp. 41–5.

'Moscow Baroque – a Controversial Style', *Transactions of the Association of Russian-American Scholars in USA* 15 (1982): 69–93.

'The Age of Transition: Seventeenth-Century Russian Icon-Painting', in Sarah Smyth and Stanford Kingston (eds.), *Icons 88* (Dublin: Veritas Publications, 1988), pp. 63–74.

'The West Comes to Russian Architecture', in Paul Dukes (ed.), *Russia and Europe* (London: Collins and Brown, 1991), pp. 24–47.

'Restoring Religion to Russian Art', in G. Hosking and R. Service (eds.), *Reinterpreting Russia* (London: Arnold, 1999), pp. 40–53.

'Attitudes towards Foreigners in Early Modern Russia', in Cathryn Brennan and Murray Frame (eds.), *Russia and the Wider World in Historical Perspective. Essays for Paul Dukes* (Basingstoke: Macmillan, 2000), pp. 1–23.

'Images of Greatness: Portraits of Peter I', in *Peter the Great and the West: New Perspectives*, ed. L. Hughes (Basingstoke: Palgrave, 2000), pp. 250–70.

'Images of the Elite: A Reconsideration of the Portrait in Seventeenth-Century Russia', *FOG* 56 (2000): 167–85.

'The Petrine Year: Anniversaries and Festivals in the Reign of Peter the Great (1682–1725)', in Karin Friedrich (ed.), *Festive Culture in Germany and Europe from the 16th to the 20th Century* (Lewiston, N.Y.: Mellen Press, 2000), pp. 148–68.

'Simon Ushakov's Icon "The Tree of the Muscovite State" Revisited', *FOG* 58 (2001): 223–34.

'Women and the Arts at the Russian Court from the 16th to the 18th Century', in J. Pomeroy and R. Gray (eds.), *An Imperial Collection. Women Artists from the State Hermitage* (Washington D. C.: National Museum of Women in the Arts, 2003), pp. 19–49.

Iakovlev, I. V., 'O date okonchaniia stroitel'stva Pokrovskogo sobora', *Ezhegodnik GIM. 1961* (Moscow: Gosudarstvennyi istoricheskii muzei, 1962), pp. 115–18.

Ianin, V. L., *Ia poslal tebe berestu . . .* , 3rd edn (Moscow: Iazyki russkoi kul'tury, 1998).

and Zalizniak, A.A., 'Novgorodskaia psaltyr' nachala XI veka – drevneishaia kniga Rusi', *Vestnik Rossiiskoi akademii nauk*, 71, 3 (2001): 202–9.

Ikonnikov, A. V., *Tysiachia let russkoi arkhitektury* (Moscow: Iskusstvo, 1990).

Iurganov, A. L., *Kategorii russkoi srednevekovoi kul'tury* (Moscow: MIROS, 1998).

Iz istorii russkoi kul'tury. T. I (Drevniaia Rus') (Moscow: Iazyki russkoi kul'tury, 2000).

Jensen, C. R. 'Music for the Tsar: A Preliminary Study of the Music of the Muscovite Court Theatre', *Musical Quarterly* 79 (1995): 368–401.

Kachalova, I. Ia., et al., *Blagoveshchenskii sobor Moskovskogo Kremlia* (Moscow: Iskusstvo, 1990).

Kalugin, V. V., *Andrei Kurbskii i Ivan Groznyi. Teoreticheskie vzgliady i literaturnaia tekhnika drevnerusskogo pisatelia* (Moscow: Iazyki russkoi kul'tury, 1998).

Kämpfer, Frank, ' "Rußland an der Schwelle zur Neuzeit": Kunst, Ideologie und historisches Bewußtsein unter Ivan Groznyj', *JGO* 23 (1975): 504–24.

'Über die theologische und architektonische Konzeption der Vasilij-Blažennyj-Kathedrale in Moskau', *JGO* 24 (1976): 481–98.

Das russische Herrscherbild von den Anfängen bis zu Peter dem Grossen. Studien zur Entwicklung politischer Ikonographie im byzantinischen Kulturkreis (Recklinghausen: A. Bongers, 1978).

Karlinsky, Simon, *Russian Drama from its Beginnings to the Age of Pushkin* (Berkeley: University of California Press, 1985).

Kazakova, N. A., *Vassian Patrikeev i ego sochineniia* (Moscow and Leningrad: AN SSSR, 1960).

Keenan, Edward L., *Josef Dobrovsky and the Origins of the Igor' Tale* (Cambridge, Mass.: Harvard University Press, 2004).

Kirichenko, E. I., *The Russian Style* (London: L. King, 1991).

Kliukanova, O. V., 'Novgorodskii amvon 1533 g.', in *Drevnerusskoe iskusstvo. Russkoe iskusstvo pozdnego srednevekov'ia: XVI vek* (St Petersburg: Dmitrii Bulanin, 2003), pp. 373–85.

Kolchin, B. A., Khoroshev, A. S. and Ianin, V. L., *Usad'ba novgorodskogo khudozhnika XII v.* (Moscow: Nauka, 1981).

Kol'tsova, T. M. (ed.), *Reznye ikonostasy i dereviannaia skul'ptura Russkogo Severa. Katalog vystavki* (Archangel and Moscow: MKRF, 1995).

Komech, A. I., and Podobedova, O. I. (eds.), *Drevnerusskoe iskusstvo. Khudozhestvennaia kul'tura X–pervoi poloviny XIII v.* (Moscow: Nauka, 1988).

Kostotchkina, Natalia, 'The Baroque in 17th-Century Russian Art: Icon-Painting, Painting, Decorative and Applied Art', unpublished MPhil. thesis, SSEES, University of London, 1994.

Kostsova, V., 'Tituliarnik sobraniia Gosudarstvennogo Ermitazha', *Trudy Gosudarstvennogo Ermitazha* 3 (1959): 16–40.

Lazarev, V. N., *Old Russian Murals and Mosaics* (London: Phaidon, 1966).

Lenhoff, Gail, *The Martyred Princes Boris and Gleb: a Socio-Cultural Study of the Cult and the Texts* (Columbus, Oh.: Slavica, 1989).

Likhachev, D. S., *Russkie letopisi i ikh kul'turno-istoricheskoe znachenie* (Moscow and Leningrad: AN SSSR, 1947).

'Barokko i ego russkii variant XVII veka', *Russkaia literatura*, 1969, no. 2: 18–45.

Razvitie russkoi literatury X–XVII vekov (Leningrad: Nauka, 1973).

'Slovo o polku Igoreve' i kul'tura ego vremeni* (Leningrad: Khudozhestvennaia Literatura, 1978).

Limonov, Iu. A., *Letopisanie Vladimiro-Suzdal'skoi Rusi* (Leningrad: Nauka, 1967).

Lopialo, K. K., 'K primernoi rekonstruktsii Zolotoi palaty Kremlevskogo dvortsa i ee monumental'noi zhivopisi', in O. I. Podobedova, *Moskovskaia shkola zhivopisi pri Ivane IV*, pp. 193–8 + figures.

Lotman, Ju. M. and Uspenskij, B. A., *The Semiotics of Russian Culture*, ed. Ann Shukman (Ann Arbor: Department of Slavic Languages and Literatures, University of Michigan, 1984).

'Binary Models in the Dynamics of Russian Culture to the End of the Eighteenth Century', in A. D. and A. S. Nakhimovsky (eds.), *The Semiotics of Russian Cultural History. Essays by Iurii M. Lotman, Lidiia Ia. Ginsburg, Boris A. Uspenskii* (Ithaca, N.Y., and London: Cornell University Press, 1985), pp. 30–66.

Luburkin, D. I., *Russkaia novolatinskaia poeziia: materialy k istorii XVII – pervaia polovina XVIII veka* (Moscow: RGGU, 2000).

Luppov, S. P., *Kniga v Rossii XVII veka* (Leningrad: Nauka, 1970).

Lur'e, Ia. S., *Ideologicheskaia bor'ba v russkoi publitsistike kontsa XV – nachala XVI veka* (Moscow and Leningrad: AN SSSR, 1960).

[Jakov S. Luria], 'Unresolved Issues in the History of the Ideological Movements of the Late Fifteenth Century', in Henrik Birnbaum and Michael S. Flier (eds.), *Medieval Russian Culture*, vol. 1 (Berkeley: University of California Press, 1984), pp. 150–171.

Dve istorii Rusi XV veka. Rannie i pozdnie, nezavisimye i ofitsial'nye letopisi ob obrazovanii Moskovskogo gosudarstva (St Petersburg: Dmitrii Bulanin, 1994).

Maiasova, N. A., *Arkhangel'skii sobor Moskovskogo Kremlia* (Moscow: Krasnaia ploshchad', 2002).

Medyntseva, A. A., *Gramotnost' v Drevnei Rusi. Po pamiatnikam epigrafiki X – pervoi poloviny XIII veka* (Moscow: Nauka, 2000).

Miller, David B., 'The Lübeckers Bartholomäus Ghotan and Nicolaus Bülow in Novgorod and Moscow and the Problem of Early Western Influences on Russian Culture', *Viator* 9 (1978): 395–412.

'The Viskovatyi Affair of 1553–1554: Official Art, the Emergence of Autocracy, and the Disintegration of Medieval Russian Culture', *RH* 8 (1981): 293–332.

Mishina, E. A., *Russkaia graviura na dereve XVII–XVIII vv.* (St Petersburg: Dmitrii Bulanin, 2000 [?]).

Morozov, V. V., and Chernetsov, A. V., 'Legenda o Monomakhovykh regaliiakh v iskusstve Moskvy XVI v.', in A. N. Sakharov (ed.), *Rim, Konstantinopol', Moskva: Sravnitel'no-istoricheskoe issledovanie tsentrov ideologii i kul'tury do XVII v.* (Moscow: Institut russkoi istorii RAN, 1997), pp. 367–72.

Morozova, L. E., *Sochineniia Zinoviia Otenskogo* (Moscow: Institut istorii AN SSSR, 1990).

Morris, Marcia A., *The Literature of Roguery in Seventeenth- and Eighteenth-Century Russia* (Evanston, Ill.: Northwestern University Press, 2000).

Nasibova, Aida, *The Faceted Chamber in the Moscow Kremlin*, trans. N. Johnstone (Leningrad: Aurora Publishers, 1978).

Nekrasov, A. I., (ed.), *Barokko v Rossii* (Moscow: GAKhN, 1926).

Odom, Anne, *Russian Enamels* (Baltimore: Walters Art Gallery, 1996).

Okenfuss, Max, *The Rise and Fall of Latin Humanism in Early-Modern Russia: Pagan Authors, Ukrainians, and the Resiliency of Muscovy* (Leiden and New York: Brill, 1995).

Ovchinnikova, E. S., *Portret v russkom iskusstve XVII veka* (Moscow: Iskusstvo, 1955).

Panchenko, A. M. (ed.), *Russkaia sillabicheskaia poeziia XVII–XVIII vv.* (Leningrad: Sovetskii pisatel', 1970).

Russkaia stikhotvornaia kul'tura XVII veka (Leningrad: Nauka, 1973).

Panova, T. D., 'Opyt izucheniia nekropolia Moskovskogo Kremlia', in V. F. Kozlov et al. (eds.), *Moskovskii nekropol'. Istoriia, arkheologiia, iskusstvo, okhrana* (Moscow: Nauchno-issledovatel'skii institut kul'tury, 1991), pp. 98–105.

Nekropoli Moskovskogo Kremlia (Moscow: Muzei-zapovednik 'Moskovskii Kreml'', 2003).

Pavlenko, A. A., 'Karp Zolotarev i Moskovskie zhivopistsy poslednei treti XVII v.', in *Pamiatniki kul'tury. Novye otkrytiia. 1982* (Leningrad: Nauka, 1984), pp. 310–16.

'Evoliutsiia russkoi ikonopisi i zhivopisnoe masterstvo kak iavlenie perekhodnogo perioda', in *Russkaia kul'tura v perekhodnyi period ot Srednevekov'ia k novomu vremeni* (Moscow: Institut rossiiskoi istorii RAN, 1992), pp. 103–8.

Petrukhin, V. J., 'The Early History of Old Russian Art: The Rhyton from Chernigov and Khazarian Tradition', *Tór* 27 (1995): 475–86.

Nachalo etnokul'turnoi istorii Rusi IX–XI vekov (Smolensk and Moscow: Rusich-Gnozis, 1995).

Drevniaia Rus': Narod. Kniaz'ia. Religiia, in *Iz istorii russkoi kul'tury, I (Drevniaia Rus')* (Moscow: Iazyki russkoi kul'tury, 2000).

Pod''iapol'skii, S. S., 'Moskovskii Kremlevskii dvorets XVI v. po dannym pis'mennykh istochnikov', in A.L. Batalov et al. (eds.), *Drevnerusskoe iskusstvo. Russkoe iskusstvo pozdnego srednevekov'ia, XVI vek* (St Petersburg: Dmitrii Bulanin, 2003), pp. 99–119.

Evdokimov, G. S., Ruzaeva, E. I., Iaganov, A.V., and Iakovlev, D. E., 'Novye dannye o Kremlevskom dvortse rubezha XV–XVI vv.', in A.L. Batalov et al. (eds.), *Drevnerusskoe iskusstvo. Russkoe iskusstvo pozdnego srednevekov'ia, XVI vek* (St Petersburg: Dmitrii Bulanin, 2003), pp. 51–98.

Podobedova, O. I., *Moskovskaia shkola zhivopisi pri Ivane IV: Raboty v Moskovskom Kremle 40-kh–70-kh godov XVI v.* (Moscow: Nauka, 1972).

Posokhin, M. V., et al., *Pamiatniki arkhitektury Moskvy. Kreml'. Kitai-gorod. Tsentral'nye ploshchadi* (Moscow: Iskusstvo, 1982).

Priselkov, M. D., *Istoriia russkogo letopisaniia XI–XV vv.* (Leningrad: LGU, 1940).

Prokhorov, G. M., *Povest' o Mitiae. Rus' i Vizantiia v epokhu kulikovskoi bitvy* (Leningrad: Nauka, 1978).

Rappoport, Pavel A., *Russkaia arkhitektura X–XIII vv.: katalog pamiatnikov* (Arkheologiia SSSR. Svod arkheologicheskikh istochnikov (E1–47)) (Leningrad: Nauka, 1982).

Drevnerusskaia arkhitektura (St Petersburg: Stroiizdat, 1993).

Building the Churches of Kievan Russia (Aldershot: Variorum, 1995).

Romodanovskaia, E. K., *Russkaia literatura na poroge novogo vremeni* (Novosibirsk: Nauka, 1994).

Rosovetskii, S. K., 'Ustnaia proza XVI–XVII vv. ob Ivane Groznom – pravitele', *Russkii fol'klor*, 20 (1981): 71–95.

Rovinskii, D. A., *Russkie gravery i ikh proizvedenie s 1564 do osnovaniia Akademii Khudozhestv* (Moscow: Izdatel'stvo grafa Uvarova, 1870).

Rowland, Daniel, 'Two Cultures, One Throneroom: Secular Courtiers and Orthodox Culture in the Golden Hall of the Moscow Kremlin', in Valerie A. Kivelson and Robert H. Greene (eds.), *Orthodox Russia: Belief and Practice under the Tsars* (University Park, Pa.: Pennsylvania State University Press, 2003), pp. 33–57.

Ryan, W. F., 'Aristotle and Pseudo-Aristotle in Kievan and Muscovite Russia', in J. Kraye et al. (eds.), *Pseudo-Aristotle in the Middle Ages* (London: Warburg Institute, 1986), pp. 97–109.

The Bathhouse at Midnight: An Historical Survey of Magic and Divination in Russia (Stroud: Sutton; and University Park, Pa.: Pennsylvania State University Press, 1999.

Rybakov, B. A., *Drevniaia Rus'. Skazaniia, byliny, letopisi* (Moscow: AN SSSR, 1963).
  'Slovo o polku Igoreve' i ego sovremenniki (Moscow: Nauka, 1971).
Rybakov, B. A., et al. (eds.), *Kul'tura srednevekovoi Moskvy XIV–XVII vv.* (Moscow: Nauka, 1995).
Sakharov, A., et al. (eds.), *Ocherki po istorii russkoi kul'tury XVII veka*, 2 vols. (Moscow: MGU, 1979).
Savarenskaia, T. F. (ed.), *Arkhitekturnye ansambli Moskvy XV–nachala XX vekov: Printsipy khudozhestvennogo edinstva* (Moscow: Stroiizdat, 1997).
Sazonova, L. I., *Poeziia russkogo barokko* (Moscow: Nauka, 1991).
Skrynnikov, R. G., 'Pervye tipografii v Rossii', *HUS* 19 (1995): 627–38.
Slovar' knizhnikov i knizhnosti Drevnei Rusi, 3 vols. (in 7) (St Petersburg: various publishers, 1987–2004).
Smirnova, E. S., 'Simon Ushakov – "Historicism" and "Byzantinism": On the Interpretation of Russian Painting from the Second Half of the Seventeenth Century', in Samuel H. Baron and Nancy Shields Kollmann (eds.), *Religion and Culture in Early Modern Russia and Ukraine* (DeKalb: Northern Illinois University Press, 1997), pp. 170–83.
  (ed.), *Uspenskii sobor Moskovskogo Kremlia* (Moscow: Nauka, 1985).
Sofronova, L. A., *Poetika slavianskogo teatra* (Moscow: Nauka, 1981).
Sokolova, I. M., *Monomakhov tron: Tsarskoe mesto Uspenskogo sobora Moskovskogo Kremlia, K 450-letiiu pamiatnika* (Moscow: Indrik, 2001).
Sterligova, I. A., 'Ierusalimy kak liturgicheskie sosudy v Drevnei Rusi', in Andrei Batalov and Aleksei Lidov (eds.), *Ierusalim v russkoi kul'ture* (Moscow: Nauka, 1994), pp. 46–62.
Tananaeva, L. I., 'Portretnye formy v Pol'she i v Rossii v XVII v. Nekotorye sviazi i paralleli', *Sovetskoe iskusstvoznanie '81* (1982): 85–125.
Thomson, Francis J., 'The Corpus of Slavonic Translations Available in Muscovy', in Boris Gasparov and Olga Raevsky-Hughes (eds.), *Slavic Cultures in the Middle Ages* (*Christianity and the Eastern Slavs*, vol. 1) (Berkeley: University of California Press, 1993), pp. 178–214.
  The Reception of Byzantine Culture in Mediaeval Russia (Aldershot: Ashgate, 1999).
Tolstaia, T. V., *Uspenskii sobor Moskovskogo Kremlia* (Moscow: Nauka, 1979).
Tserkva Bohoroytsi desiatynna v Kyevi (Kiev: ArtEk, 1996).
Voronin, N. N., *Zodchestvo severo-vostochnoi Rusi XII–XV vekov*, 2 vols. (Moscow: AN SSSR, 1961).
Vygolov, V. P., *Arkhitektura Moskovskoi Rusi serediny XV veka* (Moscow: Nauka, 1988).
Zabelin, I., 'Opis' stenopisnykh izobrazhenii pritchei v Zolotoi palate gosudareva dvortsa, sostavlennaia v 1676 g.', in *Materialy dlia istorii, arkheologii i statistiki g. Moskvy*, pt. 1 (Moscow: Moskovskaia gorodskaia tipografiia, 1884), pp.1238–55.
  and Shchepkin, V., 'Tron, ili Tsarskoe mesto Groznogo v Moskovskom Uspenskom sobore', in *Otchet imperatorskogo Rossiiskogo istoricheskogo muzeia imeni Imperatora Aleksandra III v Moskve* (Moscow: Sinodal'naia Tipografiia, 1908), pp. 66–80 + 20 tables.
Zalizniak, A. A., 'Novgorodskie berestianye gramoty s lingvisticheskoi tochki zreniia', in V. L. Ianin and A. A. Zalizniak (eds.), *Novgorodskie gramoty na bereste (iz raskopok 1977–1983 gg.)* (Moscow: Nauka, 1986), pp. 89–121.
  Drevnenovgorodskii dialekt (Moscow: Iazyki russkoi kul'tury, 1995).
Zarubin, N. N., *Biblioteka Ivana Groznogo. Rekonstruktsiia i bibliograficheskoe opisanie*, ed. A. A. Amosov (Leningrad: Nauka, Leningradskoe otdelenie, 1982).

Zemtsov, S. M., and Glazychev, V. L., *Aristotel' F'oravanti* (Moscow: Stroiizdat, 1985).

Zernova, A. S., *Knigi Kirillovskoi pechati, izdannye v Moskve v XVI–XVII vekakh. Svodnyi katalog* (Moscow: Gosudarstvennaia biblioteka SSSR, 1958).

Zguta, Russell, *Russian Minstrels: A History of the Skomorokhi* (Philadelphia: University of Pennsylvania Press, 1978).

Zhilina, N. V., *Shapka Monomakha: Istoriko-kul'turnoe i tekhnologicheskoe issledovanie* (Moscow: Nauka, 2001).

Zhivov, Viktor, 'Religious Reform and the Emergence of the Individual in Seventeenth-Century Russian Literature', in S. Baron and N. S. Kollmann (eds.), *Religion and Culture in Early Modern Russia and Ukraine* (DeKalb: Northern Illinois University Press, 1997), pp. 184–98.

Index

Konstantin Vasil'evich, prince of Suzdal' 154
Kopor'e 270, 426, 487
Kopystenskii (Kopystens'kyi), Zakhariia,
    Nomokanon of 627
Korela 270, 487
Korela, Don cossack ataman 412
Koren, Vasilii, wood block print carver 649
Koriak peoples 527
kormlenie (feeding) payments 225–6, 481–2
    to governors 308, 377, 473, 480–2
    to princes of Lithuania 202
Korovin, Il'ia ('Tsarevich Peter'), pretender
    417
Korsun', Articles of (1669) 509
Korsun', battle of (1648) 498
Kosagov, Grigorii, Muscovite commander 513
Kosoi, Feodosii, trial for heresy 356
Kosta, master-craftsman, Novgorod 198
Kostensk 579
Kostroma 422, 481, 649
    control of 143, 144, 167
    fortified by Iurii Dolgorukii 104
    population 302, 581
Kostroma Chancellery (*chetvert'*) (territorial),
    legal jurisdiction 566
Kotoshikhin, Grigorii 15, 445, 451, 460
Kovalevo, Novgorod, monastery church 209
Kozheozerskii monastery 629
Kozlov 494
    uprising (1648–9) 603
Krabbe, Evert, Danish envoy 604
Krapivna, near Tula 412
Kretnyi monastery 630
Kristler, Johann, engineer 643
Kriuk-Kolychev, I.F., conspiracy against Vasilii
    Shuiskii 422
Krivichi 189
    original inhabitants of Polotsk 47
Krizhanich, Iurii, political philosopher 436
Kromy 270
    defection of army to False Dmitrii at 284,
    412
Kseniia, Tsarevna, daughter of Boris
    Godunov 284
Kubenskii princes, court faction under Ivan
    IV 242
Kuchum, khan of Siberia 270, 328–9
Kudai Kul of Kazan' *see* Peter Ibraimov
Kudyr', khan of the Golden Horde 161
Kulikovo, battle of (1380) 162, 185, 202
Kumyks, North Daghestan 324, 537
    and Muscovy 332, 530
Kurakin princes 265, 266

Kurbskii, Prince Andrei Mikhailovich 15, 249
Kuritsyn, Fedor Vasil'evich, diplomat 375
    accused of heresy 349–50
Kuritsyn, Ivan-Volk, condemned as heretic 350
Kursk
    fortified town 270, 301, 497
    population 583
    surrender to False Dmitrii 411
    uprising (1648–9) 603

labour
    and land 382, 383, 552
    shortages 7, 296
labour law
    Muscovy 369n. 29
    Pskov 367
labour services 38, 283
Ladoga, Lake 51, 190
lakes 33, 51
land
    black lands 230
    court lands 230
    ecclesiastical 230, 238, 339, 351
    grants of 272, 414, 624
    heritable 231, 365, 574
    lack of market in 384, 541
    market in service tenure land 574
    and military service obligations 382–3
    monastic 95, 272, 355, 624
        bequests forbidden (1584) 272
    patrimonial 79, 383
    state control over 382
    votchiny (alienable) 230, 231, 383, 384
    see also inheritance law
landholding 286
    by Church 574, 624
    iqta (Muslim) 231
    land census (1580s–90s) 273
    laws on
        inheritance and ownership 565
        legal categories 230–1, 574
        Novgorod 372
        Pskov 365–6
        statutes of limitations 384
    see also pomest'e system
landowners
    boyars 207, 268, 283, 625
    clergy as 624
    and labour shortages 7, 296
    and obligations of service 7, 38
    and rights over peasants 273, 297, 562
    tarkhany tax privileges 272
    see also servitors (service classes)

Lightning Source UK Ltd.
Milton Keynes UK
UKHW010933080222
398351UK00007B/84

9 781107 639423